PENGUIN  CLASSICS

CAPITAL
VOLUME 3

KARL MARX was born at Trier in 1818 of a German-Jewish family converted to Christianity. As a student in Bonn and Berlin he was influenced by Hegel's dialectic, but he later reacted against idealist philosophy and began to develop his theory of historical materialism. He related the state of society to its economic foundations and mode of production, and recommended armed revolution on the part of the proletariat. In Paris in 1844 Marx met Friedrich Engels, with whom he formed a life-long partnership. Together they prepared the *Manifesto of the Communist Party* (1848) as a statement of the Communist League's policy. In 1848 Marx returned to Germany and took an active part in the unsuccessful democratic revolution. The following year he arrived in England as a refugee and lived in London until his death in 1883. Helped financially by Engels, Marx and his family nevertheless lived in great poverty. After years of research (mostly carried out in the British Museum), he published in 1867 the first volume of his great work, *Capital*. From 1864 to 1872 Marx played a leading role in the International Working Men's Association, and his last years saw the development of the first mass workers' parties founded on avowedly Marxist principles. Besides the two posthumous volumes of *Capital* compiled by Engels, Karl Marx's other writings include *The German Ideology*, *The Poverty of Philosophy*, *The 18th Brumaire of Louis Bonaparte*, *The Civil War in France*, *A Contribution to the Critique of Political Economy*, *Grundrisse: Foundations of the Critique of Political Economy* and *Theories of Surplus-Value*.

ERNEST MANDEL was born in 1923. He was educated at the Free University of Brussels, where he was later Professor for many years, and the École Pratique des Hautes Études in Paris. He gained his PhD from the Free University of Berlin. He was a Member of the Economic Studies Commission of FGTB (Belgian TUC) from 1954 to 1963 and was chosen for the annual Alfred Marshall Lectures by

Cambridge University in 1978. His many books include *The Formation of the Economic Thought of Karl Marx*, *Late Capitalism*, *The Long Waves of Capitalist Development*, *The Second Slump* and *The Marxist Theory of Bureaucracy*. His influential pamphlet, *An Introduction to Marxist Economics*, sold over half a million copies and was translated into thirty languages. Ernest Mandel died in July 1995. In its obituary the *Guardian* described him as 'one of the most creative and independent-minded revolutionary Marxist thinkers of the post-war world'.

KARL MARX

Capital

A Critique of
Political Economy

Volume Three

Introduced by
Ernest Mandel

Translated by
David Fernbach

Penguin Books
in association with New Left Review

PENGUIN BOOKS

Published by the Penguin Group
Penguin Books Ltd, 80 Strand, London WC2R 0RL, England
Penguin Putnam Inc., 375 Hudson Street, New York, New York 10014, USA
Penguin Books Australia Ltd, 250 Camberwell Road, Camberwell, Victoria 3124, Australia
Penguin Books Canada Ltd, 10 Alcorn Avenue, Toronto, Ontario, Canada M4V 3B2
Penguin Books India (P) Ltd, 11 Community Centre, Panchsheel Park, New Delhi – 110 017, India
Penguin Books (NZ) Ltd, Cnr Rosedale and Airborne Roads, Albany, Auckland, New Zealand
Penguin Books (South Africa) (Pty) Ltd, 24 Sturdee Avenue, Rosebank 2196, South Africa

Penguin Books Ltd, Registered Offices: 80 Strand, London WC2R 0RL, England

www.penguin.com

New Left Review, 7 Carlisle Street, London W1

This edition first published in Pelican Books 1981
Reprinted in Penguin Classics 1991
16

Edition and notes copyright © New Left Review, 1981
Introduction copyright © Ernest Mandel, 1981
Translation copyright © David Fernbach, 1981
All rights reserved

Printed in England by Clays Ltd, St Ives plc
Set in Monotype Times

ISBN-13: 978-0-14-044570-1

www.greenpenguin.co.uk

Contents

8 *Contents*

Introduction

If the first volume of *Capital* is the most famous and widely read, and if the second is the unknown one, the third is the most controversial. The disputes started before it was even published, as Frederick Engels indicates in his Preface. They continued after the latter brought it out in 1894, most notably in the form of a critique of Marx's economic doctrines by the Austrian economist Eugen von Böhm-Bawerk two years later.[1] They have been going on ever since. Hardly a year passes without some new attempt to refute one or other of Volume 3's main theses, or to indicate their alleged inconsistency with Volume 1.[2]

The reason for these insistent polemics is not hard to discover. Volume 1 concentrates on the factory, the *production* of surplus-value, and the capitalists' need constantly to increase this production. Volume 2 concentrates on the market-place and examines the reciprocal flows of commodities and money (purchasing power) which, as they realize their values, allow the economy to reproduce and grow (while requiring a proportional division both of commodities into different categories of specific use-value and of money flows into purchasing power for specific commodities[3]). While these volumes contain a tremendous amount of intellectual and moral dynamite aimed at bourgeois society and its prevailing

1. Eugen von Böhm-Bawerk, *Karl Marx and the End of his System*, New York, 1949.
2. Some recent examples: Ian Steedman, *Marx after Sraffa*, London, 1977; Anthony Cutler, Barry Hindess, Paul Hirst and Athar Hussein, *Marx's 'Capital' and Capitalism Today*, Vols. 1 and 2, London, 1977 and 1978; Leszek Kolakowski, *Main Currents of Marxism*, Volume 1, Oxford, 1978.
3. The term 'money flows' is adopted, since these include, in addition to 'revenues', money capital intended to reconstitute constant capital, to reconstitute variable capital (which is spent as revenue by workers, but must return in the form of money capital to the industrialists) and to expand both c and v.

ideology – with all that these entail for human beings, and above all for workers – they give no precise indication of the way in which the system's inner contradictions prepare the ground for its final and inevitable downfall.

Volume 1 shows us only that capitalism produces its own grave-digger in the form of the modern proletariat, and that social contradictions intensify inside the system. Volume 2 indicates that capitalism cannot achieve continuously enlarged reproduction; that its growth takes the form of the industrial cycle; that its equilibrium is only a product of constantly reappearing disequilibria; that periodic crises of overproduction are inevitable. But the precise way in which these contradictions (and many others) are interrelated, so that the basic laws of motion of the capitalist mode of production lead to explosive crises and its ultimate collapse, is not worked out in detail in these first volumes. They are initial stages in an analysis whose final aim is to explain how the system concretely operates – in 'essence' as in 'appearance'.

Such an explanation of the capitalist economy *in its totality* is precisely the object of Volume 3. However, it is not completed here. In the first place, Marx did not leave a finished manuscript of the volume, so that important sections are lacking. It is certain that the unfinished Part Seven, which ends with the barely initiated Chapter 52 on social classes, would have provided a vital link between the economic *content* of the class struggle between capital and labour, as developed at length in Volume 1, and its overall economic *outcome*, partially sketched in Chapters 11 and 15 of Volume 3.[4] In the second place, Volume 3 is subtitled 'The Process of Capitalist *Production* in its Totality'. But as we already know from Volume 2, the totality of the capitalist *system* includes circulation as well as production. In order to complete an examination of the capitalist system in its totality, *Capital* would have had to include supplementary volumes dealing, among other matters, with the world market, competition, the industrial cycle and the state. All this was contained in Marx's plan for *Capital*, and there is no indication that he abandoned it;[5] on the contrary, there are

4. See Marx's letter to Engels on 30 April 1868, in Marx/Engels, *Selected Correspondence*, Moscow, n.d., p. 250, where he indicates his plan for Volume 3: '. . . in conclusion, the class struggle, in which the movement and decomposition of the whole mess are resolved' (translation amended).

5. On Marx's initial plan for *Capital*, see Ernest Mandel, Introduction to Volume 1 of *Capital*, Pelican Marx Library, London, 1976, pp. 25–32.

passages here which confirm that he postponed detailed examination of these problems to later volumes, alas unwritten.[6] Volume 3 provides valuable indications of how Marx would have set about the integration of these questions into an overall view of the capitalist system. But it does not contain a fully developed theory of the world market, of (national and international) competition, or especially of industrial crisis. Many of the controversies centring around the third volume of *Capital* are precisely due to the incomplete nature – for the reasons just indicated – of some of the theories contained in it.

But the basic reason for the amplitude and duration of these polemics lies in the fact that Volume 3 aims to answer the question: 'Whither capitalism?' It seeks to show that the system is intrinsically ('immanently') crisis-ridden: that neither the efforts of individual capitalists nor those of public authorities can prevent crises from breaking out. It seeks to show that inherent mechanisms, which cannot be overcome without abolishing private property, competition, profit and commodity production (the market economy), must lead to a final collapse. That this judgement is unpalatable to capitalists and their hangers-on hardly needs emphasizing. That it is equally unwelcome to 'neutral' economists who, in spite of their claims to be value-free, in reality assume the permanence and preferability of commodity production and the market economy – as determined by human nature and corresponding to the interests of mankind – can also be taken for granted. Finally, that it poses formidable problems for philanthropists and social reformers who, though sharing Marx's indignation at the mass poverty and destitution provoked by the spontaneous workings of the system, believe that these can be overcome without getting rid of the system itself, has been confirmed repeatedly in theoretical discussions and political struggles within and around the labour movement since the end of the nineteenth century. So there are indeed compelling social reasons why Volume 3 should have created the furore it undoubtedly has.

THE PLAN OF VOLUME 3

Volume 3 is constructed with the same logical rigour as its predecessors. The substantive problem which Marx seeks to elucidate here is not that of the *origin* of the two basic categories of revenue:

6. See below, pp. 205, 298, 426, etc.

wages and profits. That problem was solved in Volume 1. What he wants to show here is how specific sectors of the ruling class participate in the distribution of the total mass of surplus-value produced by productive wage-labour, and how these specific economic categories are regulated. His inquiry deals fundamentally with four such ruling-class groups: industrial capitalists; commercial capitalists; bankers; capitalist landowners.[7] Five categories of revenue, therefore, appear in Volume 3: wages; industrial profits; commercial (and banking) profits; interest; land rent. These are further regrouped by Marx into three basic categories: wages, profits and land rent.

But in order to analyse the different parts into which the total mass of surplus-value is divided, a whole series of intermediate steps have to be taken. The *rate of profit* has to be distinguished – as a separate analytical category – from the rate of surplus-value, and the various factors which influence that rate of profit identified. The *tendency towards an equalization of the rate of profit* between all capitals, independently of the amount of surplus-value produced by their 'own' variable capital, i.e. by the productive wage-labourers whom they productively employ, has to be discovered. And from these two conceptual innovations is deduced the centre-piece of the entire volume: the *tendency of the average rate of profit to decline* – in the absence of countervailing tendencies. Having deduced profit in general from surplus-value in general, Marx goes on to show how profit itself becomes divided into entrepreneurial profit (be it in industry, transport or trade) and interest, i.e. that part of surplus-value which accrues to capitalists who own-money capital and limit themselves to lending it to entrepreneurs. Finally, the total mass of surplus-value which is divided among *all* entrepreneurs and money-lenders is reduced by introducing the category of surplus profit (surplus-value which does not participate in the general movement of equalization of the rate of profit). The reasons why such surplus profit can arise are studied in detail for one special case, that of land rent. But Marx makes it clear, especially in Chapters 10 and 14, that land rent is only a special case of a more general phenomenon. Therefore, we are justified in saying that what Part Six of Volume 3 is

7. Capitalist landowners, as distinct from feudal and semi-feudal ones: i.e. landowners who limit themselves to renting out land to capitalist or independent farmers for money income, without involving any form of feudal or semi-feudal bondage or service.

really all about is the more general problem of *monopoly* giving rise to surplus profit. In his theory of surplus profit, Marx anticipates the whole contemporary theory of monopoly prices and profits, while being much clearer as to their origins than are most of the academic economists who, throughout the twentieth century, have been trying to elucidate the mysteries of monopoly.[8]

The fundamental logic of Marx's *Capital* unfolds in all its majesty once we integrate the structure of Volume 3 into that of Volumes 1 and 2. The diagram on pages 14–15 gives a schematic representation of their overall contents and global cohesion.

THE EQUALIZATION OF THE RATE OF PROFIT

In Volume 1, Marx showed that surplus-value is only produced by living labour: from the capitalist's point of view, by that fraction of capital which is spent on purchasing labour-power, and not by that spent on buying buildings, machinery, raw materials, energy, etc. For this reason, Marx called the former fraction of capital *variable* and the latter *constant*. It would at first seem to follow that the greater the proportion of capital which each industrial branch spends on wages, the higher its rate of profit (the relation between the surplus-value produced and the total amount of capital invested, or spent in annual production). However, such a situation would contradict the basic logic of the capitalist mode of production, which consists of expansion, growth, enlarged reproduction, through a substitution of living by dead labour: through an increase in the organic composition of capital, with a growing part of total capital expenditure occurring in the form of expenditure for equipment, raw material and energy, as against expenditure for wages. This basic logic results both from capitalist competition (the reduction of cost price being, at least in the long run, a function of more and more efficient machinery, i.e. of technical progress which is essentially labour-saving) and from the class struggle (since again, in the long run, the only way in which the growth of capital accumulation can prevent labour shortage and hence a constant increase in the level of real wages, which

8. Among academic economists dealing with monopolies and oligopolies from the point of view of the search for surplus profits, see for example Joe Bain, *Barriers to New Competition*, Cambridge, Mass., 1956; Paolo Sylos-Labini, *Oligopolio e progresso tecnico*, Turin, 1964; Robert Dorfman, *Prices and Markets*, New York, 1967.

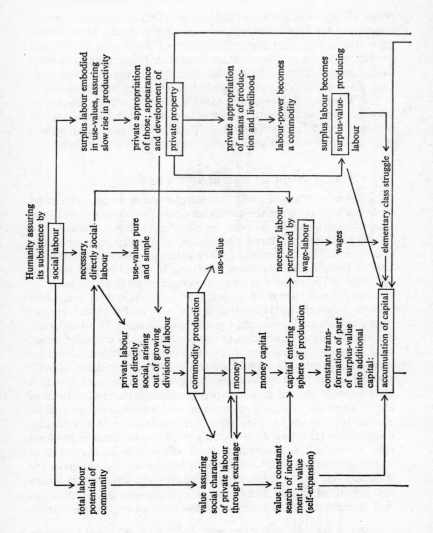

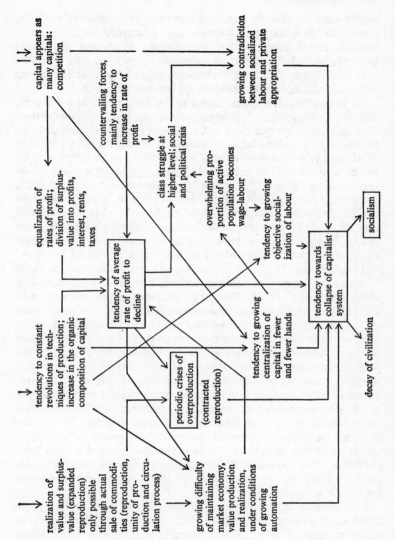

would end by sharply reducing the rate of surplus-value, is by accumulating a larger and larger part of capital in the form of fixed constant capital – i.e. substituting machinery for living labour). Moreover, empirical evidence overwhelmingly confirms that branches of production which are more labour-intensive than others do not normally realize a higher rate of profit.

So the conclusion Marx draws is the following: in a fully developed and normally functioning capitalist mode of production, each industrial branch does not receive directly the surplus-value produced by the wage-labour it employs. It only receives a fraction of all surplus-value produced, proportional to the fraction it represents of all capital expended. Surplus-value in a given bourgeois society (country) as a whole is *redistributed*. This results in an average rate of profit more or less applicable to each branch of capital. Branches of production which have an organic composition of capital *below* the social average (i.e. which employ more labour, spend more variable capital, in relation to total capital spent) do not realize part of the surplus-value produced by 'their' wage-labourers. This part of surplus-value is transferred to those branches of industry where the organic composition of capital is *above* the social average (i.e. which spend a larger proportion of total capital on equipment and raw material, a smaller proportion on wages, than the social average). Only those branches of industry whose individual organic composition of capital is identical to the social average realize all the surplus-value produced by the wage-labour they employ, without transferring any portion of it to other branches or receiving any fraction of surplus-value produced in other branches. As a result, each capital receives a part of the total surplus-value produced by productive labour which is proportional to its own part in total social capital. This is the material basis of the common interest of *all* owners of capital in the exploitation of labour – which thereby takes the form of a *collective class exploitation* (competition between many capitals only deciding the way in which this total mass is redistributed between the capitalists).

This *process* of equalization of the rate of profit raises three series of problems. What is its relation to the labour theory of value in general? What are the concrete mechanisms which allow equalization of the rate of profit to occur in real life? What is the 'technical' solution to the problem of transformation of values into prices of production (capital outlays, i.e. production costs, going into the output of each commodity + average profit multiplied by these outlays)? The first two problems have provoked relatively less controversy than the third, probably because of their more 'abstract' character. They are, however, of the highest importance for the inner cohesion of Marxist economic theory. Marx's treatment of them, moreover, shows his dialectical method at its most mature.

Briefly, with respect to the first, Marx argues that as value in the last analysis is a *social* not an individual category, those branches of industry which have an organic composition of capital below the social average objectively waste social labour from the point of view of capitalist society as a whole (i.e. from the point of view of 'equality' of commodity-owners).[9] Therefore, the market does not return to their owners all the value effectively created during the process of production in these branches. Inversely, those branches of industry which have an above-average organic composition of capital, i.e. an above-average social productivity of labour, objectively economize socially necessary labour. Their owners are rewarded for this by the market, which attributes to them a higher proportion of all surplus-value produced than that which is directly produced by the wage-labourers they employ.

Various objections have been raised to this solution. Is productivity of labour comparable in different branches of output, inasmuch as these do not produce goods that are interchangeable? This difficulty can be resolved dynamically, i.e. by comparing the different *rates of increase* in productivity of labour in different branches of output *over time*. More generally, the specific organic composition of capital in each branch of production, which constantly changes as a result of these different changes in the productivity of labour, can be considered as a general *index*, a means of measurement, of social productivity of labour.[10] In a *capitalist* market economy, with its constant revolutions in the techniques of production, its constant shifts in demand from one commodity to another, its constant flux of capital investment from one branch

9. See below, pp. 228–9, 893.

10. See below, p. 318: 'This progressive decline in the variable capital in relation to the constant capital, and hence in relation to the total capital as well, is identical with the progressively rising organic composition, on average, of the social capital as a whole. It is just another expression for the progressive development of the social productivity of labour . . .'

to another, this assumption is both theoretically tenable and empirically verifiable.

But is there not a basic contradiction between considering all labour effectively expended in the process of production of each branch of production as value-producing, and at the same time explaining the transfers of value (surplus-value) between different branches as a function of objective waste or economy of social labour?[11] I do not believe so. What we have here, on the contrary, is a demonstration of the unique way in which social labour and private labour are combined and interrelated under capitalism, i.e. under generalized commodity production.

For Marx, the problem of value as an embodiment of abstract human labour is not a problem of measurement, of *numéraire*, but a problem of essence.[12] Each community has at its disposal a given total labour capacity (a total number of producers effectively engaged in productive labour, multiplied by the socially accepted average of annual work-days and daily work-hours). This potential is an objective category, in a given country and for a given stretch of time (for purposes of simplification, we can take the work-year as the basic time-framework). From it flows the total value produced during a year (in so far as part of this labour potential has not been idle, for reasons independent of its will). Again, this is an objective social category: the total number of labour-hours effectively produced in the course of the process of production. The category of 'socially *necessary* labour', which treats some of these labour-hours as 'wasted' and hence not accounted for from a social point of view, only implies redistribution of value inside each branch of production, except in cases of monopoly.[13]

If we extend the same reasoning to the economy as a whole, nothing changes. All labour actually expended in the process of production has been value-producing. It cannot be made larger or smaller by anything which occurs outside the actual sphere of production. *The problem of compensation on the market for labour expenditure is one of distribution, not one of production.* Thus it is

11. See, for example, Joan Robinson, *An Essay on Marxian Economics*, London, 1966, pp. ix–x, 14–16.

12. Even Maurice Dobb, who should have known better, dealt with labour as a *numéraire* in *Storia del Marxismo*, Vol. 1, Turin, 1979, pp. 99–103.

13. Isaac Rubin, *Essays on Marx's Theory of Value*, Detroit, 1972, pp. 174–6.

perfectly possible that actually expended private labour in a given branch, at the average rate of productivity of that branch, is socially necessary labour and has really produced value, while at the same time the owners of the commodities in which it is embodied do not receive full compensation on the market for all that embodied value, or receive a counter-value higher than the amount of value embodied in their commodities.

This dialectical unity-and-contradiction between, on the one hand, private labour effectively expended in production and effectively value-producing and, on the other hand, socially compensated value is mediated through the understanding that total value is equal to total prices of production (i.e. represents an equal sum of labour-hours, or labour-weeks, or labour-years: an equal total labour potential). What is modified on the market, i.e. what the Volume 3 notions of 'objective waste' and 'objective economy' of social labour represent when different branches of production are compared (in contrast to the notions of 'waste' and 'economy' of quantities of social labour *inside* each separate branch of industry, studied in Volume 1), is exclusively a problem of (re)distribution of value, not one of production of value.

The second question regarding equalization of the rate of profit between different branches of industry is how this operates in practice. In order to understand this, we should start from the assumption that this equalization is always a *tendency*, never a permanent reality. If we start from the actual realization of the total mass of surplus-value produced in each branch of production by the capitalists operating in that branch, a much higher rate of profit will occur in those branches of production which have a lower organic composition of capital and spend a larger proportion of capital outlays on wages than in those which have a higher organic composition of capital and spend a larger proportion of total capital outlays on equipment and raw materials. All things remaining equal (which means, above all, not assuming for the moment any changes in the distribution of total demand for different use-values produced by different branches of output), such an above-average rate of profit will attract additional capital in these branches. This will increase production (supply) above social demand, which will precipitate a decline in prices, which will precipitate a decline in the rate of profit. Inversely, in those branches of production where the average organic composition of capital is above-average, hence the 'initial' rate of profit below average, capital will be withdrawn; production will decline, till it falls below social demand; prices will rise; profits will rise, until they reach the socially average rate of profit.

In other words, it is the flux and reflux of capital between different branches of production, from those with lower rates of profit to those with higher rates of profit, which is the driving force behind equalization of the rate of profit. This flux and reflux of capital between different branches of production is indeed the main way in which capital accumulation (growth) occurs in actual life, i.e. as an *uneven process*, all branches *never* growing at exactly the same rhythm and over the same span of time. Equalization of the rates of profit indeed presupposes their relative *inequality*. It is a process which constantly realizes itself by negating itself. Anybody who studies the real history of capitalist branches of industry, mining and transport may easily confirm this view.

This uneven process does not necessarily presuppose that it starts with great unevenness in the rates of profit between various branches, nor that higher rates of profit each time coincide with greater labour intensity in given branches of industry. Indeed, it would be sufficient to assume a single initial situation of that kind to make the process perfectly logical and coherent with the given analysis.[14] In fact, very early in the history of modern industrial capitalism, the average rate of profit is a *known* entity (bank credit and the stock exchange playing a not unimportant role in establishing this).[15] The *real* process is, therefore, not so much one of capital flowing from branches with below-average to branches with above-average rates of profit. *The real process is usually one of firms looking for surplus profits over and above the known average rate of profit*, essentially through revolutionary innovations (which might imply creating completely new branches of industry). The average rate of profit is constantly shaken and reestablished by the reactions which this constant revolution in the technique of production and the organization of labour provokes. Each firm trying to maximize its own rate of profit contributes, independently of its wishes and designs, to the tendential equalization of the rate of profit.

14. One could, for instance, make the case that the first capitalist firms engaged in canal-building, mining, etc. had a higher rate of profit than the initial textile mills, at the time of the industrial revolution, owing to their lower organic composition of capital.

15. See below, p. 311.

If we abandon the initial simplifying assumption of a stable structure of demand in a given time-span, we only have to introduce additional mediations; the result remains substantially the same. If, in regard to branches of industry with below-average organic composition of capital, there is additionally an above-average increase in social demand for their output, prices will decline less rapidly in spite of the influx of additional capital and the ensuing increase of production.[16] But this will only attract even more additional capital, until equalization of the rate of profit finally occurs. Inversely (and this occurs more often), if branches of industry with below-average organic composition are relatively 'older' branches suffering from relative decline of total demand, the influx of additional capital and the ensuing increase of output will lead more rapidly to a decline of prices and profits, and to the final equalization of the rate of profit. It is not necessary to repeat, for those branches which witness an outflow of capital because of initially lower rates of profit, the reasoning for the combination of fluctuations in final demand with the process of equalization of the rate of profit. It is an obvious counterpart of the analysis just developed.

It is the third category of problems raised by the equalization of the rates of profit between different branches of production which has provoked most argument: that concerning the 'technical' problem of the transformation of values into prices of production for each specific commodity (or group of commodities), i.e. the problem of how one can 'technically' prove the operation of the law of value under conditions of competition of capitals between different branches of output. This can be divided into two main bodies of argument, which I shall refer to as the feedback controversy and the monetary confusion.

TRANSFORMATION PROBLEM: THE FEEDBACK CONTROVERSY

The feedback controversy arises from the fact that, in the way in which Marx solves the transformation of values into prices of

16. Marx makes an additional point about the *relative weight* of firms operating at above-average, average and below-average levels of productivity in each branch of industry. This can lead to situations in which, temporarily, it is not the average level of productivity which determines the value of the commodity. But competition will rapidly do away with such situations, in the absence of structural scarcity or monopoly.

production in Chapter 9 of Volume 3, apparently only the values of currently produced commodities (outputs) are being 'transformed' and not the values of 'input-commodities'. Ever since the Prussian statistician Ladislaus von Bortkiewicz first raised this objection,[17] a constant stream of authors – some claiming to be Marxists, others obviously adhering to other economic doctrines or at any rate other theories of value – have repeated this assertion about a basic flaw in Marx's reasoning.[18]

This 'flaw' seems, at first sight, all the more evident in that Marx himself appeared to be aware of it. Again and again, the following passage from Chapter 9 has been quoted: 'The development given above also involves a modification in the determination of a commodity's cost price. It was originally assumed that the cost price of a commodity equalled the *value* of the commodities consumed in its production. But for the buyer of a commodity, it is the price of production that constitutes its cost price, and can thus enter into forming the price of another commodity. As the price of production of a commodity can diverge from its value, so the cost price of a commodity, in which the price of production of other commodities is involved, can also stand above or below the portion of its total value that is formed by the value of the means of production going into it. It is necessary to bear in mind this modified significance of the cost price, and therefore to bear in mind too that if the cost price of a commodity is equated with the value of the means of production used up in producing it, it is always possible to go wrong.'[19]

However, this quotation from Marx should not be made to say more than it does. It says only that *if one uses value calculations in inputs and prices-of-production calculations in outputs*, then one is likely to arrive at numerically erroneous conclusions. This is rather obvious, since the whole analysis precisely concerns the *deviation* of prices of production from values. But the extract

17. See Ladislaus von Bortkiewicz, 'Value and Price in the Marxian System', *International Economic Papers*, 1952.

18. It is impossible to give a full list of these authors. The most important sources are quoted in footnote 22 below. Three works less well known in the English-speaking world may be mentioned here: Gilbert Abraham-Frois and Edmond Berrebi, *Théorie de la valeur, des prix et de l'accumulation*, Paris, 1976; C. C. von Weiszäcker, 'Notizen zur Marx'schen Wertlehre', in Nutzinger and Wolfstetter, *Die Marx'sche Theorie und ihre Kritik*, Frankfurt, 1974; Gilles Dostaler, *Valeur et prix, histoire d'un débat*, Paris, 1978.

19. See below, pp. 264–5.

cited does not imply that prices of production of inputs should be calculated *within the same time-span* as prices of production of outputs. Such an interpretation is even explicitly rejected in a passage which immediately follows that quoted by von Bort-kiewicz and so many others: 'Our present investigation does not require us to go into further detail on this point. It still remains correct that the cost price of commodities is always smaller than their value. For even if a commodity's cost price may diverge from the value of the means of production consumed in it, this error in the past is a matter of indifference to the capitalist. *The cost price of the commodity is a given precondition, independent of his, the capitalist's, production*, while the result of his production is a commodity that contains surplus-value, and therefore an excess value over and above its cost price'[20] (my italics).

And even more clearly: 'For all the great changes that con-stantly occur in the actual rates of profit in particular spheres of production (as we shall later show), a genuine change in the general rate of profit, one not simply brought about by exceptional econ-omic events, is *the final outcome of a whole series of protracted oscillations*, which require a good deal of time before they are consolidated and balanced out to produce a change in the general rate. In all periods shorter than this, therefore, and even then leav-ing aside fluctuations in market prices, a change in prices of production is always to be explained *prima facie* by an actual change in commodity values, i.e. by a change in the total sum of labour-time needed to produce the commodities'[21] (my italics).

In other words, inputs in current cycles of production are *data*, which are given at the start of that cycle, and *do not have* a feed-back effect on the equalization of the rates of profit in various branches of production during that cycle. It is sufficient to assume that they are likewise calculated in prices of production and not in values, but that these prices of production result from equalization of rates of profit during the *previous* cycle of production, for any inconsistency to disappear.

Such an assumption eliminates the logical inconsistency of which von Bortkiewicz and his followers accuse Marx, between supposedly calculating inputs in the form of values and outputs in the form of prices of production. But is it compatible with what

20. See below, p. 265.
21. See below, p. 266.

we know about the actual operation of capital movements in a given time-span (a year, for example)? Could it not, for instance, be argued that raw-material prices fluctuate constantly, changing many times during one year: hence one may assume that, where this is the case, feedback effects do indeed occur; and that the final equalization of the rate of profit is not only a function of redistribution of surplus-value between branches of production whose commodities can be considered only as industrial outputs, but should include, at least with regard to raw materials, part of the inputs as participating in the current (annual) redistribution of surplus-value between various branches?

This objection, however, is not a valid one. I repeat, prices of production of raw materials, like all other inputs bought by capitalists currently occupied in production, are *unchangeable data*. They cannot vary through ups or downs of current production of surplus-value, or current changes in the organic composition of capital occurring during a given year. The capitalists have to pay a *given* price for them, which does not change *a posteriori* as a function of what is occurring during a given year in the field of final surplus-value redistribution. They are results of the equalization of the rate of profit which occurred during the previous period. Even if one were to assume that capitalists buy their raw materials currently and not only at the beginning of the year, and even if one were to eliminate all existing stocks of previously produced raw materials to explain the origin of these current purchases, the argument would still hold.

The formation of prices of production, i.e. the calculation of the average rate of profit, is not a constantly moving process. It is linked to the *overall* realization of surplus-value of *all* (most) of the commodities currently produced. That is why a minimum time-span must be assumed before one may speak of a new average rate of profit replacing a previous one. Even the assumption of such an annual change is probably an exaggeration, rather than an underestimate. Therefore, one has to assume that currently purchased raw materials on a quarterly or even monthly basis do not fundamentally change the prices of production (average rate of profit), as resulting from the capital movements which had occurred during the previous year. One should, of course, not confuse the formation of prices of production – which result from a redistribution of the total surplus-value produced for society as a whole – with current fluctuations of market prices, which Marx explicitly *excludes* from the study of prices of production, as is clearly stated in the passage cited above.

The reason for this relative rigidity of prices of production (of average rates of profit in a given country) is linked to the very nature of the processes of which the equalization of rates of profit is a result: the determination of the total mass of surplus-value (surplus labour) produced; and the fluxes and refluxes of capital (large-scale capital movements) between various branches of production, determining changes and differences in the organic composition of capital both of productive sectors as a whole and of each productive sector taken separately. It is clear that such *overall social movements* cannot vary from quarter to quarter, let alone from month to month. The relative indivisibility of fixed capital alone is a formidable obstacle to such broad movements under advanced capitalist conditions, except in the case of radical devalorization of capital under conditions of severe crisis. Therefore, not only is Marx theoretically consistent when he assumes prices of production of inputs resulting from equalization movements in different time-spans (during different years) from prices of production of outputs. This also corresponds much more closely to the real, empirically verifiable operation of the capitalist system as we know it than does the opposite assumption of von Bortkiewicz and his followers.

Numerous attempts have been made both to extend von Bortkiewicz's critique of Marx's solution to the transformation problem, and to provide an alternative solution to that proposed by von Bortkiewicz himself. J. Winternitz sought to formulate one in which total prices of production would still equal total value. More recently, Anwar Shaikh has proposed yet another solution, using the 'iterative method' rather than that of simultaneous equations.[22] However, mathematical models cannot, in and of

22. J. Winternitz, 'Values and Prices: A Solution of the So-Called "Transformation Problem" ', in *The Economic Journal*, June 1948; F. Seton, 'The "Transformation Problem" ', in *Review of Economic Studies*, Vol. 24, 1957; C. C. von Weiszäcker and Paul Samuelson, 'A New Labor Theory of Value for Rational Planning, through Use of the Bourgeois Profit Rate', in *Proceedings of the National Academy of Sciences*, *U.S.A.*, Vol. 68, No. 6, June 1971; A. Medio, 'Profit and Surplus-Value: Appearance and Reality in Capitalist Production', in E. K. Hunt and Jesse Schwartz (eds.), *A Critique of Economic Theory*, London, 1972; Elmar Wolfstetter, 'Surplus Labour, Synchronized Labour Costs and Marx's Labour Theory of Value', in *The Economic Journal*, Vol. 83, September 1973; Anwar Shaikh, 'Marx's Theory

themselves, 'solve' theoretical problems. They can only formalize interrelations previously understood as such, whose nature and implications have to be grasped before a meaningful formalization can take place. Unfortunately, many authors of such models operate by silently assuming correlations which have not been previously proved or empirically tested. Their equations lead to conclusions which are, of course, mathematically consistent, but may nevertheless be theoretically wrong: i.e. which do not correspond to a meaningful representation of the problem supposedly to be solved.

In the 'Okishio theorem', for instance, the author puts fixed capital between brackets altogether, in order to arrive at conclusions regarding the trend of the rate of profit. But if one postulates that precisely the growth of fixed capital is one of the main – if not the main – determinant of the tendency of the rate of profit to decline, then this theorem does not prove anything.[23] Similarly, in the von Bortkiewicz 'solution' of the transformation problem (accepted by Paul Sweezy, Piero Sraffa, F. Seton and many others), besides uniform profits for all products (not all branches of industry or even firms, which is quite another story), it is assumed that only those equations are needed for a solution which involve commodities entering into the production of other commodities. It is logical that, under these circumstances, the organic composition of department III (whose commodities do not enter the reproduction process) does not influence the average rate of profit.[24] But this tells us nothing either about department III in Marx's analysis, where such a distinction is explicitly excluded, or especially about what happens in the really functioning capitalist economy, i.e. in real life. To say that the organic com-

of Value and the "Transformation Problem" ', in Jesse Schwartz (ed.), *The Subtle Anatomy of Capitalism*, Santa Monica, 1977; Ira Gerstein, 'Production, Circulation and Value', in *Economy and Society*, Vol. 5, 1976; etc. A good summary of the bibliography on the subject is included in Carlo Benetti, Claude Berthomieu and Jean Cartelier, *Économie classique, économie vulgaire*, Paris, 1975.

23. N. Okishio, 'Technical Changes and the Rate of Profit', in *Kobe University Economic Review*, Vol. 7, 1961, pp. 85–90; N. Okishio, 'A Mathematical Note on Marxian Theorems', in *Weltwirtschaftliches Archiv*, Vol. 91 (1963 II), pp. 287–99.

24. I owe this observation to Emmanuel Farjoun, of the Hebrew University of Jerusalem.

position of the armaments industry, including its size, is immaterial to the real rate of profit of a real capitalist economy is quite untenable – especially if one takes a look at the size of that department in, say, 1943 in Germany or 1944 in the U.S.A.

TRANSFORMATION PROBLEM: THE MONETARY CONFUSION

A second line of attack on Marx's solution of the transformation problem has involved a confusion between prices of production and market prices, and more generally the introduction into the problem of questions concerning the expression of values as prices, i.e. money. Sweezy, in particular, has been guilty of such a confusion, in the way he has taken over von Bortkiewicz's critique.[25] Others, like Ian Steedman recently, have followed in his footsteps.[26]

Marx himself, however, makes crystal clear that prices of production *do not* concern market prices, i.e. values (or prices of production) expressed in money terms. The very title of Chapter 9 specifies this, referring as it does to the transformation of *values* of commodities into prices of production. Values are quantities of labour, and have nothing to do with money prices as such. The equalization of the rate of profit between different branches of production occurs through the transfer of *quantities of surplus-value* from one branch to another. Again, quantities of surplus-value are quantities of labour (surplus labour) and not quantities of money. At the end of the last passage cited from Volume 3, there follows a sentence which I deliberately omitted but will now quote – a sentence which again eliminates all doubt as to the non-inclusion of monetary questions in the transformation problem: 'We are not referring here, of course, to a mere change in the monetary expression of these values.'[27] If the problem does not concern changes in the monetary expression of values, it *ipso facto* does not concern changes in the monetary expression of prices of production either.

In Chapter 10, immediately following that in which he gives his solution to the transformation problem, Marx does indeed introduce market prices, and the influence of competition, etc. upon

25. Paul Sweezy, *The Theory of Capitalist Development*, New York, 1942, pp. 117–18.

26. Steedman, op. cit., pp. 45–7.

27. See below, p. 266.

them. But he there clearly and explicitly distinguishes fluctuations of market prices and of monetary expressions of value (prices of production) from fluctuations in the average rate of profit which determine fluctuations of prices of production.[28]

Behind this confusion, there lies an insufficient understanding of the nature of Marx's theory of money. Marx considers money (gold) as a *special commodity having its own 'intrinsic' value*. It is only for this reason that it can serve as a general equivalent for the exchange-value of all other commodities. It immediately follows that fluctuations of market prices (monetary prices, expressions of value in money) may always be the result of a *dual movement*: the changes in the value of a commodity and the changes in the value of the money-commodity, gold. But changes in the intrinsic value of the money-commodity have identical effects on the market prices of all other commodities, i.e. *cannot* change their mutual exchange relations (their mutual 'relative prices'). Paper money does not alter anything in this respect. Inflation of paper money only means that an increasing amount of paper dollars, paper pounds, etc. represents the same quantity (e.g. one ounce) of the money-commodity, gold. What is true for the money expression of value is likewise true for the money expression of prices of production, as they concern only a redistribution of quantities of surplus-value between different branches of production.

The 'inputs' in the reproduction tables could only be treated as inputs in really occurring capitalist production (i.e. in real life) if they were expressed in market prices, and not in prices of production: for capitalists obviously buy raw materials, machines, buildings, etc. at market prices. So the problem would be how to 'transform' values, not into prices of production, but into market prices; or, in two successive stages of transformation, values into prices of production and the latter into market prices. This final stage, of course, would have to involve real monetary problems: specifically, the interrelationship between the average value of commodities and the average value of gold. What is really involved in this controversy is whether the 'transformation problem' concerns the *immediate* move from essence to appearance, in other

---

28. Engels explicitly envisages the case where the total sum of money profits – resulting from market prices – is lower than the total sum of surplus-value produced, because in the meantime value has declined as a result of the rise in productivity of labour. See his letter to Conrad Schmidt of 12 March 1895, in *Selected Correspondence*, op. cit., pp. 564–5. ·

words to the process of production and circulation in day-to-day reality, or whether – as I would strongly maintain – it is only a *mediating link in the process of cognition*, which does not yet deal with immediately verifiable, empirical data, i.e. market prices.

The diagram on page 30 will help to elucidate the relations between Marx's various concepts of value, market value, price of production and market price, which are often rather confusing.

An excellent overall critique of the von Bortkiewicz/Sraffa 'corrections' of the way Marx deals with the relation between prices of production and values has been furnished by Pierre Salama.[29] It has, among other qualities, the merit of revealing a series of underlying theoretical assumptions of which the authors themselves are not always aware. It shows that a further disaggregation of the von Bortkiewicz system – in other words, the application to von Bortkiewicz of some of the criticisms he himself directs at Marx (for example, it is evident that in the aggregate of department I, those means of production which are exclusively used for the production of commodities in department III will have a different status) – leads unavoidably to the elimination of *all* value calculations and, therefore, of exploitation itself from the system. I do not want to imply that Salama, Farjoun and others have definitively resolved all the difficulties raised by the 'transformation problem': there is clearly still room for further discussion and research. But neither have von Bortkiewicz, Seton and Sraffa 'definitively' proved Marx wrong.

THE DECLINING RATE OF PROFIT CONTROVERSY

From his definition of the average rate of profit as the sum total of surplus-value produced during the process of production divided by the sum total of capital, Marx derives the central 'law of motion' of the capitalist mode of production. Since that part of capital which alone leads to the production of surplus-value (variable capital, used to buy labour-power) tends to become a smaller and smaller part of total capital, because of the fundamentally labour-saving tendency of technical progress – the gradual substitution of dead labour (machinery) for living labour – and because of the gradual increase of the value of raw materials in that of total output: since, in other words, the organic composition

29. Pierre Salama, *Sur la valeur*, Paris, 1975, pp. 164 ff.

specific commodity   money-commodity
(gold)

|

individual value
(quantity of labour contained in
it)

|

market value
(socially average – necessary –
quantity of labour contained in
it)

|

price of production
(socially necessary quantity of
labour modified by equalization
of rates of profit between different branches = average costs
of production in each branch +
average profit of all branches)

individual value
(quantity of labour contained in
the product of each specific gold
mine)

|

market value
(quantity of labour contained in
gold actually produced under
the lowest conditions of productivity)

|

price of production
(total costs of production in all
gold mines plus average profit,
divided by total output: there is
obviously no 'market price' of
gold, as this would mean the
value of gold expressed in gold)

'intrinsic' market prices of commodities
(prices of production of a given commodity expressed in
quantities of gold, of money)

|

'fluctuating' market prices of commodities
(prices of production of a given commodity expressed in
quantities of gold – of money – and modified under very
short-term fluctuations of supply and demand, i.e. fluctuating
around the 'axis' of 'intrinsic' market prices, i.e. of prices of
production, i.e. of values)

↑

operation of the law of value under capitalism
(fluctuations of 'intrinsic' market prices, other than very
short-term ones, are determined by relative value movements –
relative increases or decreases of productivity of labour – in
the output of a given commodity and in the output of gold,
mediated through deviations from the average rate of profit)

of capital in its value expression tends to increase, there is an inbuilt tendency for the average rate of profit to decline in the capitalist system.[30]

To be sure, Marx explicitly speaks about a *tendency*, not an uninterrupted linear development. He stresses that there are powerful countervailing forces at work under capitalism, to neutralize or even reverse the operation of the tendency of the average rate of profit to decline. Other forces tend, at least partially, to slow down the operation of this tendency.

The most important countervailing force is the possibility for the capitalist system to increase the rate of surplus-value. Indeed, from a purely 'technical' point of view, it might appear that the increase in the rate of surplus-value could indefinitely compensate for the increase in the organic composition of capital. If we change the determination of the rate of profit $\frac{s}{c + v}$ by dividing both the numerator and the denominator by v, we get the formula $pr' = \frac{\frac{s}{v}}{\frac{c}{v} + 1}$. In other words, the rate of profit is directly proportional to the rate of surplus-value $\frac{s}{v}$ and inversely proportional to the organic composition of capital $\frac{c}{v}$. If the rate of surplus-value increased in the same proportion as the organic composition of capital, the rate of profit would cease to decline.

However, a moment's reflection will show that such a proportional increase in the rate of surplus-value and the organic composition of capital is impossible in the long run. Theoretically, the organic composition of capital can rise to infinity. That is what it would be in fully automated production, from which living labour would be totally excluded.[31] But the rate of surplus-value

30. Georgios Stamatis has demonstrated exhaustively that in Chapter 13 of *Capital* Volume 3, Marx already develops the law of the tendency of the average rate of profit to decline under conditions of an *increase in the rate of surplus-value* – an increase caused by the same forces which lead to the increase in the organic composition of capital. The countervailing forces studied in Chapter 14 concern forms of increase in the rate of surplus-value which are *not* the result of an increase in the productivity of labour in department II, i.e. not a result of the declining value of wage-goods while real wages remain stable. See *Die 'spezifisch kapitalistischen' Produktionsmethoden und der tendenzielle Fall der allgemeinen Profitrate bei Karl Marx*, Berlin, 1977, pp. 116 ff.

31. Already today, labour costs have gone down to less than 0.1 per cent of total production costs in certain petro-chemical works: see Charles Levinson, *Capital, Inflation and the Multinationals*, London, 1971, pp. 228–9.

cannot rise to infinity. As long as living wage-labour is employed, no level of productivity (including that of fully automated factories) is imaginable in which workers reproduce the equivalent of all the consumer goods they need to reconstitute their labour-power in a couple of minutes' or even a couple of seconds' work. Indeed, the higher the existing level of productivity of labour and the higher the socially recognized average wage (real wage), the harder it becomes to increase the rate of surplus-value substantially, without seriously lowering real wages – which, besides provoking a sharp social and political crisis, would create a tremendous problem of overproduction (for the mass of use-values, including in the wage-goods department, increases even more quickly than productivity of labour and accumulation of capital).[32]

Furthermore, once we near complete automation, s – which is not a proportion but an absolute mass – starts to decline rapidly together with v, as the number of wage-earners and the total number of labour-hours diminish steeply. Indeed, in a fully automated economy, surplus-value would *disappear* altogether, as living-labour inputs in the process of production would have disappeared. So it would be absurd to consider formally a 'rate of surplus-value' $\frac{0}{0}$, when surplus-value itself would no longer exist.

Other countervailing forces enumerated by Marx include: the cheapening of elements of constant capital (both raw materials and machinery) which obviously, by slowing down the growth of $\frac{c}{v}$, simultaneously slows down the decline of the rate of profit; the quickened turnover of capital, since the annual mass of profit is a function of the number of production cycles which an identical circulating money capital can perform (this turnover is, in turn, a function both of a quickened circulation process – i.e. more rapid transport and sale of commodities – and of a shortened production process, a quicker pace of production, etc.); foreign trade, with the outflow of capital towards countries with a lower organic composition of capital; and, in general, the extension of capital investment into hitherto non-capitalistically organized branches of output, where initially the organic composition of capital is considerably lower than in traditional industry.[33] A lowering of real wages, by raising the rate of surplus-value over

32. See below, pp. 339–48, and Karl Marx, *Grundrisse*, Pelican Marx Library, London, 1973, pp. 244–6.
33. For example, many so-called 'service industries' under late capitalism.

and above the increase which normally results from a growth of productivity of labour in the wage-goods industry (which is – or can be – accompanied by stable and even rising real wages), will likewise put a brake upon the decline of the rate of profit.

Finally, Marx does not mention in Chapter 15 of Volume 3 what he had stressed in Chapter 14: that the decline in the *rate* of surplus-value can be (and normally is) accompanied by a rise in the *mass* of surplus-value – and, therefore, in the mass of profit. While this is not, in and of itself, a countervailing factor with respect to the tendency of the rate of profit to decline, it is clearly a countervailing factor with respect to some of the economic *consequences* of that tendency. It is obvious that the capitalist class will not significantly lower its investments (let alone close up shop altogether) when its profits rise from $100 to $200 billion, just because these $200 billion now represent 'only' a 5 instead of an 11 per cent return on total capital. It will look for many ways to redress this regrettable evolution, but it will definitely not be overtaken by panic or despair.

Traditionally, Marxists (and academic economists specializing in the theory of the industrial cycle) have considered Marx's theory of the tendency of the average rate of profit to decline within two specific – and very different – time-spans: inside the industrial (or business) cycle itself; and over the 'secular' time-span of the overall historical existence of the capitalist mode of production (for whose capacity or otherwise for indefinite survival it is a vital question). The 'theory of collapse' (*Zusammenbruchstheorie*), which relates to the latter time-span, will be dealt with at the end of this Introduction. As for the correlation between the ups and downs of the rate of profit and the business cycle, there is a wide consensus today between Marxists and academic economists specializing in business-cycle studies.[34] There remains, however, a third, intermediary, time-span to which hitherto too little attention has been paid: that of the 'long waves' of capitalist development, i.e. the successive periods of quicker and slower growth of the capitalist economy as a whole.

There is overwhelming evidence that on at least three occasions – after the revolutions of 1848; around 1893; and at the beginning of the Second World War in the United States, at the end of the forties in Western Europe and Japan – there was a significant

34. See, for example, W. C. Mitchell, *Business Cycles and their Causes*, Berkeley, 1941.

increase in the average rate of growth of capitalist production. Such an increase in the rate of growth is synonymous, from a Marxist point of view, with a stepped-up tempo of capital accumulation. And a long-term increase in the rate of capital accumulation is inconceivable, within the framework of Marxist economic theory, without a sudden and sustained upsurge instead of decline in the average rate of profit.

In order to make this real history of the capitalist mode of production comprehensible, against the background of Marx's tendency of the rate of profit to decline, we must examine the conditions which prevailed immediately prior to these three turning-points and at the start of the 'expansionary long waves'. In this way, we shall be able to ascertain to what extent the 'counteracting factors' enumerated by Marx *combined* in a particular way to neutralize, or even reverse, for a longer period than normally occurs at a certain stage of the industrial cycle, the tendency of the rate of profit to decline. I have sought elsewhere to demonstrate empirically that this was really the case.[35] It is not necessary to repeat that demonstration, but sufficient to state that such temporary neutralization of the law (which Marx also alludes to[36]) in no way contradicts its general validity. For the 'expansionary long waves' are regularly followed by 'depressive long waves', in which the tendency of the rate of profit to decline manifests itself in a yet stronger and more durable way than it does during the normal industrial cycle. Its actions can be delayed by countervailing factors, but only for it to reassert itself with a vengeance. That, at least, is the historical evidence to date, and it fully confirms Marx's analysis. The only additional conclusion to be drawn is that different time-spans have to be articulated with each other, if the concrete operation over time of the tendential law is to be fully grasped.

The very operation of the law (its truth content[37]) has been

35. See Ernest Mandel, *Late Capitalism*, London, 1975, Chapter 4; Ernest Mandel, *The Long Waves of Capitalist Development*, Cambridge, 1980.

36. See below, pp. 363 and 372.

37. This truth content cannot, of course, be defended by the absurd argument that the law manifests itself exclusively, or mainly, through its negation. This was the position adopted by several Soviet authors, before (unexpectedly for them) the 'second slump' broke out: e.g. S. L. Wygodski (*Der gegenwärtige Kapitalismus*, Cologne, 1972, p. 232), who saw the law as being confirmed by a tendency towards a rising rate of profit!

increasingly challenged during the last decades by a whole series of authors. This has partially been due to the fact that long-term stepped-up economic growth after the Second World War seemed somehow incompatible – in Marxist terms themselves – with a declining rate of profit. Hence the efforts of Gillman and others to discover new categories like 'realization expenses' (presumably to be deducted from surplus-value, which is thus reduced only to 'surplus-value appropriated by productive capital') or 'surplus', whose supposed growth would explain why the rate of profit as conceived by Marx stops falling, while it continues to fall if conceived otherwise.[38] In the meantime, however, events since 1974–5 have caught up with this type of argument, showing that the law more than ever retains its force.

More systematic have been the efforts of the neo-Ricardian school to challenge the law's validity, on both theoretical and empirical grounds. The main theoretical argument is the so-called Okishio theorem.[39] As every capitalist will introduce machinery only if this increases his rate of profit, how can increased profits for every capitalist lead to a decrease in the rate of profit for capitalists taken together?

There are, however, two flaws in this reasoning. In the first place, it is not true that every capitalist will introduce new machinery only if this increases his *rate* of profit. As Marx himself points out, this is certainly his *voluntary* inclination, but he may be *forced* to introduce new machinery, in order to keep his market share or even to save his firm from bankruptcy, i.e. in order to cut his cost price under the pressure of competition, in spite of the effect this decision has upon his rate of profit. In fact, it would be much more correct to say that capitalists will hesitate to introduce new machinery which cuts the *amount* of profit; but then, the amount (mass) of profit and the rate of profit are two quite different categories. The former may go up while the latter goes down.[40]

38. For example Joseph Gillman, *The Falling Rate of Profit*, London, 1957. Paul Baran and Paul Sweezy likewise counterpose a supposed tendency of the 'surplus' to rise, to the tendency of the rate of profit to decline, which according to these authors only applies in a 'competitive system': see *Monopoly Capital*, London, 1968, p. 80.

39. Okishio, 'Technical Changes', op. cit.

40. Georgios Stamatis has drawn attention to the decisive difference between an increase in unit *profit margins* (i.e. the difference between cost price and sale price per unit produced) and the Marxist concept of the *rate of*

In the second place, the argument shows an astonishing misunderstanding of the very nature of the capitalist 'laws of motion' of which the tendency for the average rate of profit to fall is so outstanding an example. These laws operate independently from, and in spite of, conscious decisions by individual capitalist firms. In fact, they can be said to be the objective and unforeseen *effects* of conscious decisions by these firms. No capitalist knows in advance what the real result of his decision to buy new machinery will be. Only when the commodities produced with the help of this new machinery have been sold, and several successive annual balance-sheets have been drawn up, will these results become known. It is, therefore, perfectly possible – indeed inevitable – that the purchase of more machinery by 'every capitalist' is *intended* to increase both his mass and his rate of profit, but that the final end-result of all these decisions will be a situation where the average rate of profit of all is actually reduced.[41]

As for the main empirical argument put forward by the neo-Ricardians, it states that the organic composition of capital is not rising at all over time but remaining more or less even. In other words, technical progress in the long run is neither essentially labour-saving nor essentially 'capital-saving', but neutral.[42] The index of this alleged stability of the organic composition of capital is an alleged stability of the capital/output ratio over time.

Now the capital/output ratio is definitely not identical (or

---

profit, in which the *total value of fixed capital* used to achieve this increase in profit margins has to be taken into account (op. cit., pp. 183 ff.). It is precisely the 'tragedy' for capital (expressed in the law of rising organic composition of capital) that the same capitalist methods of systematic mechanization, which lead to lower unit costs and rising unit profit margins, in the end result in an above-average increase in total fixed capital investment – which is one of the forces triggering off a rise in the organic composition of capital in a higher proportion than the rise in the rate of surplus-value, thereby causing the rate of profit to decline. Stamatis's book is amazingly schizophrenic. While the entire first part extols, in a painstaking and extremely detailed fashion, the relevance of Marx's theory of the tendency of the average rate of profit to fall, by a breathtaking *salto mortale*, the author then concludes that this very law no longer applies today, since capitalism no longer applies 'specific capitalist methods of production'!

41. Anwar Shaikh, 'Political Economy and Capitalism: Notes on Dobb's Theory of Crisis', *Cambridge Journal of Economics*, June 1978.

42. In fact, Roy Harrod is the main source for the notion of so-called 'neutral' technical progress.

parallel) to the organic composition of capital. Nor is the allegedly stable 'wage part' in the national income parallel (or identical) to a stable rate of surplus-value. In the case of the capital/output ratio, constant capital is mistakenly identified with fixed capital: i.e. the weight of the value of raw materials, which tends to become a growing part of the value of constant capital (and total capital), is completely eliminated from the reasoning. As for the 'wage bill', it mixes together variable capital, which is the payment of productive labour, with the payment of unproductive labour, which comes at least partially out of surplus-value.[43] Especially given the steady growth of unproductive labour in the history of late capitalism, the distinction is statistically decisive. In addition to this, Shaikh has demonstrated that the so-called stable capital/output ratio itself should be seriously challenged, from a statistical point of view, and that it corresponds to a large extent to an imprecise or wrong use of statistical categories by bourgeois statisticians.[44] Initial detailed studies have strikingly confirmed this judgement.[45]

There remains the fact that, as a result of the lack of transparency of real-value relations measured by current market prices, an empirical demonstration of the rising organic composition of capital is not easy to provide on a macro-economic basis, i.e. starting from national-income and gross-national-product statistics. But a close corollary of the organic composition of capital is the part of labour costs in total annual production costs.[46] Here we

43. See, on this subject, Anwar Shaikh, 'An Introduction to the History of Crisis Theories', in the U.R.P.E. anthology, *Capitalism in Crisis*, New York, 1977.

44. ibid., p. 235. Shaikh refers to an empirical study by Victor Perlo, 'Capital-Output Ratios in Manufacturing', *Quarterly Review of Economics and Business*, Vol. 8, No. 3, Autumn 1966.

45. See R. J. Gordon, 'A Rare Event', *Survey of Current Business*, July 1971, Vol. 51, No. 7, part 2; and the same author's articles in *American Economic Review*, June 1969, and *Review of Economics and Statistics*, November 1968. André Granou, Yves Baron and Bernard Billandot, in their *Croissance et Crises*, Paris, 1980 (pp. 102–4), defend the thesis that the capital/output ratio fell between the Great Depression and the immediate post-war period, rose between 1948 and 1958, declined again (or remained stable) between 1958 and 1968, but rose rapidly after 1968. The way in which they calculate this ratio, however, makes it to some extent the reciprocal of the rate of profit, since it incorporates the rate of surplus-value which rose strongly in the post-war period.

46. Corollary, but not identical. See the remarks by Engels on pp. 334–5 below.

are on much more solid statistical ground, since numerous monographs allow us to examine this relation for separate branches of production over time. One would have a hard time discovering a *single* branch of production in which labour costs constitute a larger part of total current (annual) production costs today than they did on the eve of the Second World War, or at the beginning of the twentieth century – let alone a century or century-and-a-half ago.[47] In spite of all the evident tendencies to cheapen the production of machinery and raw materials, which are as inherent in capitalism as is the tendency to cheapen the production of wage-goods, the *basic* trend of long-term capitalist growth and technical progress has indeed been a labour-saving one. What would the terms 'mechanization' and 'growing automation' express otherwise, if not precisely this basic trend? One of Marx's great theoretical achievements consisted in stressing this trend at a time when it was scarcely recognized as historically decisive for the capitalist mode of production.

MARXIST THEORIES OF CRISIS

As I said earlier, Marx did not leave us a completed, fully worked-out theory of crisis. His observations on the industrial cycle and capitalist crises of overproduction are dispersed among several of his major books and a whole number of articles and letters.[48] Yet it is tempting to see the tendency of the average rate of profit to fall as Marx's main contribution to an explanation of crises of overproduction, and several contemporary Marxist authors have indeed taken this view.[49] Is it correct?

47. See the numerous monographs on specific branches of industry which I cited in *Late Capitalism*, op. cit., pp. 199–204.
48. Apart from Volumes 2 and 3 of *Capital*, Marx's main contributions to crisis theory are to be found in *Theories of Surplus-Value*, London, 1969–72, and in his articles on current economic crises: see, for example, 'The State of Trade' (*Neue Rheinische Zeitung*, 7 March 1849), in Marx/Engels, *Collected Works*, Vol. 9, pp. 3–8; or various articles written in 1853 and 1856–7 for the *New York Daily Tribune* (*Collected Works*, Vols. 11, 12, 14, 15). Marx's correspondence with Engels also contains numerous comments on current crises.
49. See, for example, David Yaffe, 'The Marxian Theory of Crisis, Capital and the State', in *Economy and Society*, Vol. 2, No. 2, May 1973; Paul Mattick, 'Krisen und Krisentheorien', in a collection of articles by various authors with the same title, Frankfurt, 1974.

My answer would be: yes and no. There can be no doubt about the fact that, within the framework of the industrial cycle, the ups and downs of the rate of profit are closely correlated with the ups and downs of production. But this statement, in and of itself, is not sufficient to provide a *causal explanation* of the crisis. It can be (and has been) misunderstood in the mechanical sense that crises are 'caused' by insufficient surplus-value production[50] – which does not enable capital to become sufficiently valorized; which leads to a cut-down of current investment; which leads to a reduction of employment; which in turn leads to a new and cumulative reduction of income, sales, investment, employment, etc. This process continues till the fall in employment and de-valorization of capital have led to a sufficient increase in the rate of surplus-value, and sufficient decrease of the mass of capital, to enable the rate of profit to go up again – which then enables investment, employment, production, income, sales, etc. cumula-tively to grow again.

In this vulgar sense, explanation of overproduction crises by the decline in the rate of profit alone is both wrong and dangerous. It is wrong, because it confuses the impossibility of valorizing *additionally* accumulated capital with the impossibility of valor-izing all *previously invested* capital;[51] because it identifies fluctua-tions in the *investment decisions* of capitalist firms with the fluctua-tions of current surplus-value production. The former, however, may continue to grow when the latter is already declining, and vice versa. The explanation's main weakness is its concentration on the sphere of production alone, which, in the last analysis, is founded on a confusion about the very nature of the commodity

50. See Mattick, op. cit., p. 111: 'The accumulation of capital thus does not depend upon the realization of surplus-value, but the realization of surplus-value depends upon the accumulation of capital'; and ibid., p. 115: 'When surplus-value is not sufficient to continue the accumulation process in a profitable way, it can also not be realized through accumulation; it becomes unrealized surplus-value or over-production.' First over-accumulation is posited in an absolute way: there is not enough surplus-value to valorize all accumulated capital. Then the argument shifts to a relative one: there is still additional surplus-value, but it does not become accumulated, because it would give additional capital 0 per cent profit. But how is this to be seen independently from the market prices of the additionally produced com-modities? Does a fall of market prices leading to 0 per cent profit not reflect a previously existing glut, i.e. overproduction of commodities besides the over-accumulation of capital?

51. See below, pp. 360–61.

and of commodity production. In the same way as Jean-Baptiste Say's famous *loi des débouchés*, it assumes tacitly that there is no specific problem of value realization, only one of surplus-value production. This in turn assumes that what we have under capitalism is production for barter, not production for sale; and that somehow, at least at a macro-economic level, all value produced is automatically realized.

Marx himself explicitly refuted any such assumption. 'But this production of surplus-value is only the first act in the capitalist production process, and its completion only brings to an end the immediate production process itself. Capital has absorbed a given amount of unpaid labour. With the development of this process as expressed in the fall in the profit rate, the mass of surplus-value thus produced swells to monstrous proportions. Now comes the second act in the process. The total mass of commodities, the total product, must be sold, both that portion which replaces constant and variable capital, and that which represents surplus-value. If this does not happen, or happens only partly, or only at prices that are less than the price of production, then although the worker is certainly exploited, his exploitation is not realized as such for the capitalist, and may even not involve any realization of the surplus-value extracted, or only a partial realization; indeed, it may even mean a partial or complete loss of his capital. *The conditions for immediate exploitation and for the realization of that exploitation are not identical.* Not only are they separate in time and space, they are also separate in theory. *The former is restricted only by the society's productive forces, the latter by the proportionality between the different branches of production, and by the society's power of consumption.* And this is determined neither by the absolute power of production nor by the absolute power of consumption but rather by the power of consumption within a given framework of antagonistic conditions of distribution, which reduce the consumption of the vast majority of society to a minimum level, only capable of varying within more or less narrow limits. It is further restricted by the drive for accumulation, the drive to expand capital and produce surplus-value on a larger scale'[52] (my italics).

Furthermore, this vulgar theory of crises as caused by 'insufficient production of surplus-value' is obviously dangerous, from

52. See below, pp. 352–3.

the point of view of defending the working class against the capitalist onslaught which always coincides with a crisis of overproduction. For the conclusion which might be drawn from such an explanation is that the crisis could be overcome and employment rise again, if only real wages were to be cut and surplus-value (profits) thereby automatically increased.[53] The working class in general, and the trade unions in particular, are thereby confronted with an agonizing choice between defending real wages and fighting unemployment: i.e. they are made responsible for the loss of jobs. Needless to say, reformist proponents of class collaboration are only too ready to come forward with arguments of this kind, calling upon the workers to make the necessary sacrifices in order to 'save jobs' or 'restore full employment'. Experience, however, has shown time and again that this is not borne out empirically by the real course of the industrial cycle.[54] It represents an ideological weapon designed to impose the burden of the crisis on the working class and assist an increase in the rate of surplus-value, which is one of capital's main goals during and after a crisis. 'Profit squeeze' theories involve a similar danger of misuse by the capitalist side in the class struggle.[55]

Many extreme proponents of the decline-in-the-rate-of-profit explanation for capitalist crisis will answer indignantly that their

53. Arthur Pigou, the father of welfare economics, actually advocated a cut in wages to solve the great crisis of 1929–32. He forgot that, for the accumulation process to begin to rise again, it is not enough for profits (quantities of surplus-value) to be increased (this is evidently achieved by a cut in wages): capitalists must also expect the commodities produced by additional capital investment to be sold, which is unlikely when wage-cuts coincide with huge stocks of unsold commodities and huge unused capacities of existing equipment.

54. The great wage restraint imposed, for instance, on West German workers in 1976–7 and on Spanish workers in 1978–9 by their class-collaborationist trade-union leaderships did not lead to any significant decline of unemployment, although profits and investments rose. But investments were nearly exclusively rationalization investments, reducing rather than increasing employment.

55. See, for example, Andrew Glyn and Bob Sutcliffe, *British Capitalism and the Profit Squeeze*, London, 1972. In his *Political Economy and Capitalism*, London, 1938, Maurice Dobb postulates that capitalists introduce new machinery only when wages rise, i.e. that essentially the rise in the organic composition of capital is a function of a given level of wages. This is not the same as the 'profit squeeze' theory, but it is not far from it. Shaikh has correctly criticized these assumptions in 'Political Economy and Capitalism', op. cit.

analysis contains a built-in reply to employers' arguments: the decline of the rate of profit is a function of the rising organic composition of capital, which leads to over-accumulation, and not of a decline in the rate of surplus-value. Indeed, they often insist upon the fact that the rate of surplus-value continues to rise until the very eve of the crisis, but just cannot rise enough to offset the effects of the rising organic composition of capital.[56] They forget, however, that the rate of profit is a function both of the organic composition of capital and of the rate of surplus-value; that, except in the case of starvation wages, i.e. where any cut in real wages would bring them below the physiological minimum (a situation which no longer exists in any industrialized country), a cut in real wages *always* implies a rise in surplus-value produced, hence a higher rate of profit than existed before the cut.[57] We are thus back at square one: to argue that the crisis is *exclusively* caused by insufficient surplus-value production is to assist the employers' argument that it can, at least partially, be overcome by a cut in real wages.

This critique of the mechanical and one-sided explanation of crises of overproduction by the falling rate of profit alone can be extended, in a more general way, into a critique of *any* mono-causal explanation of crises. In the framework of Marxist economic theory, crises of overproduction are *simultaneously crises of over-accumulation of capital and crises of overproduction of commodities*. The former cannot be explained without pointing to the latter; the latter cannot be understood without referring to the former. This means that the crisis can be overcome only if there occurs simultaneously a rise in the rate of profit and an expansion of the market, a fact which disarms both the employers' and the reformists' arguments.

There are three main variants of mono-causal interpretation of Marx's theory of crisis:[58]

1. The pure *disproportionality* theory. This sees as the basic cause of the industrial cycle and the ensuing crisis, capitalist anarchy of

56. See, for example, Yaffe, op. cit.
57. See below, pp. 355–6.
58. The possible fourth variant of a mono-causal theory of crisis – the demographic one – is treated below as a sub-variant of the pure 'over-accumulation theory'.

production: the fact that, under conditions of capitalist market economy, capitalist investment decisions cannot spontaneously lead to 'equilibrium conditions' – the correct proportion of value fractions produced and money flows generated in department I and department II, which Marx defined in Volume 2 of *Capital*. Hence the unavoidable breakdown of equilibrium and the crisis.

The main proponents of this disproportionality theory of crisis were the Russian 'legal' Marxist Mikhail Tugan-Baranovsky and the Austro-Marxist Rudolf Hilferding. Nikolai Bukharin was strongly influenced by similar ideas.[59] The conclusions of the theory are obvious. If, through the growth of monopolies (a 'general cartel', as Hilferding called it), capitalists could 'organize' investment among themselves, there would be no crises of over-production. There would, indeed, be capitalism without crises.[60] As Roman Rosdolsky has pointed out, however, these theoreticians overlook the fact that the disproportion between production and consumption – the tendency of capitalism to develop productive forces in an unrestricted way, while it imposes strict limits upon consumption by the mass of people[61] – is inherent to capitalism, and independent from the disproportional development of department I and department II due to capitalist competition and anarchy of production (i.e. of investment decisions).[62]

The grotesque consequences to which mono-causal disproportionality explanations of capitalist crises may lead are best exemplified by Tugan-Baranovsky himself, who seriously argued – and demonstrated 'mathematically' – that department I could develop completely independently from department II, to the point where the output of consumer goods would tend to fall

59. Mikhail Tugan-Baranovsky, *Studien zur Geschichte und Theorie der Handelskrisen in England*, Jena, 1901; Rudolf Hilferding, *Das Finanzkapital*, Vienna, 1910; Nikolai Bukharin, *Imperialism and the Accumulation of Capital*, London, 1972. It is true that Bukharin is a bit more cautious than Hilferding, and takes into account the restricting force of limited mass consumption on capitalism's 'limitless' capacity for growth.

60. Tony Cliff, who shares this conviction, can easily imagine a capitalist economy without crises of overproduction – provided anarchy of production is overcome through planning. See *Russia: a Marxist Analysis*, London, 1970, p. 174.

61. See below, p. 615.

62. Roman Rosdolsky, *The Making of Marx's 'Capital'*, London, 1977, pp. 489–90, 496, etc.

towards zero, without such a development causing any crisis whatsoever.[63]

2. The pure *under-consumption by the masses* theory of crisis. This sees in the gap between output (or productive capacity) and mass consumption (workers' real wages or purchasing power) the essential cause of capitalist crises of overproduction, which essentially take the form of overproduction of commodities in department II. Over-accumulation (the decline of investment) and overproduction (or over-capacity) in department I appear as a result of this overproduction (over-capacity) in the consumer goods sector.

While this theory has many non-Marxist ancestors (Thomas Malthus, Sismonde de Sismondi, the Russian Narodniks), its main proponents among Marxists have been Karl Kautsky, Rosa Luxemburg, Nathalia Moszkowska, Fritz Sternberg and Paul Sweezy.[64] Its weakness lies in its basic assumption (not always clearly understood, but at least clearly expressed, by Sweezy) that somehow there is a *fixed proportion* between the development of department I and the development of the productive capacity of department II. Since, simultaneously, the growth in the organic composition of capital and in the rate of surplus-value increase the purchasing power for means of production more strongly than they do the purchasing power for consumer goods, the conclusion is obvious: there will be an unsaleable residue of consumer goods.

But not only is this assumption logically unproven. It is contrary to the very nature of capitalist growth, as characterized by growing mechanization or (to borrow a correct formula from the bourgeois economist von Böhm-Bawerk) 'roundaboutness' of production. Capitalist growth *does* imply that a larger proportion of total output takes the form of means of production, although this cannot be accompanied by an absolute decline in the produc-

63. Mikhail Tugan-Baranovsky, *Theoretische Grundlagen des Marxismus*, Leipzig, 1905.

64. Rosa Luxemburg, *The Accumulation of Capital*, London, 1963; Fritz Sternberg, *Der Imperialismus*, Berlin, 1926; Nathalia Moszkowska, *Das Marxsche System, ein Beitrag zu dessen Aufbau*, Berlin, 1929, and *Zur Kritik moderner Krisentheorien*, Prague, 1935; Léon Sartre, *Esquisse d'une théorie marxiste des crises périodiques*, Paris, 1937; Paul Sweezy, *The Theory of Capitalist Development*, op. cit.; as for Karl Kautsky, the reference is especially to his article in *Die Neue Zeit*, Vol. XX, No. 2, 1901–2, which is his longest contribution on the crisis problem.

tion of consumer goods or a stagnation in the productive capacity of department II. Once this is understood, neither the growth of $\frac{c}{v}$ nor the growth of $\frac{s}{v}$ need automatically lead to an overproduction of consumer goods. They will do so only if the fraction

$$\frac{\text{output I}}{\text{output II}}$$

grows *more slowly* than the fraction

$$\frac{\text{demand for means of production}}{\text{demand for consumer goods}}$$

But that such a development is inherent in the capitalist mode of production cannot be mathematically or logically demonstrated.

The danger in under-consumption theories (which, of course, Luxemburg completely avoided) is that they can lead to reformist conclusions, not dissimilar to the 'harmonicist' implications of disproportionality theories. The latter state that capitalism could avoid crisis if it 'organized' investment. The former tend to think that capitalism could avoid crisis if real wages were larger, or if the government distributed additional 'purchasing power' in the form of social security and unemployment disbursements – i.e. 'redistributed' national income in favour of the workers, 're-transformed' a part of surplus-value into additional indirect wages.[65]

What these 'solutions' overlook is the simple fact that capitalist production is not only a production of commodities which must be sold before surplus-value can be realized and capital accumulated. It is a production *for profit*. Any sizable redistribution of the national income in favour of workers' income, on the eve or in the early stages of a crisis, when the rate of profit has already been declining, means a further decline in that rate of profit through a reduction of the rate of surplus-value (this is, after all, what the 'redistribution of national income' is all about). Under these conditions, capitalists will not increase investment, even if sales of previously produced stocks of consumer goods go up. The depression will continue.

65. This is especially true for neo-Keynesian economists (some of them quite influential within the labour movement), in countries like Britain, France and West Germany. See, for example, *Alternative Wirtschaftspolitik* (Special issue of *Das Argument*), Berlin, 1979.

3. The pure *over-accumulation* theory, which sees the main reason for the crisis in the insufficient mass of surplus-value produced, compared to the total amount of accumulated capital. We have already dealt above with the weakness of this theory, and its dangerous implications from the point of view of the proletarian class struggle.

There is also, however, a specific demographic variant of the theory, which stresses the fact that, after long periods of capitalist prosperity, the reserve army of labour tends to disappear, and as a result real wages go up to a point where they cause a sharp decline in the rate of surplus-value and hence in the rate of profit.[66] While this eventuality, the border case of what Marx calls in Chapter 15 of Volume 3 'absolute over-accumulation of capital',[67] cannot be excluded from a general theoretical point of view, in the real history of capitalism – under conditions of extensive international mobility (migrations) of labour and of an even vaster potential for future migrations which exists in underdeveloped countries – any such 'population pressure' on capitalism seems centuries removed from us.[68] It likewise greatly underestimates capitalism's capacity rapidly to reconstruct a reserve army of labour, by concentrating on rationalization investments which are macroeconomically employment-reducing (i.e. by a medium-term increase in the average rate of growth of productivity of labour higher than the average rate of economic growth). This has been strikingly confirmed throughout the 1970s, when the total mass of unemployed in the imperialist (O.E.C.D.) countries, leaving firmly behind the 'near full-employment' conditions of the sixties, doubled from ten million in 1970 to twenty million in 1980,

66. See in particular Makatoh Itoh, 'Marxian Crisis Theories', in *Bulletin of the Conference of Socialist Economists*, Vol. IV, No. 1, February 1975. The first Marxist theoretician to attempt a demographic explanation of economic crisis was Otto Bauer, 'Die Akkumulation des Kapitals', in *Die Neue Zeit*, Vol. XXXI, No. 1, 1913.

67. See below, pp. 360–61.

68. Just to give an idea of such 'reserves', at present there are one million illegal immigrants a year from Mexico and Central America to the United States, a significant fraction of whom are promptly deported. But even at the present level of productivity of labour in Mexico and Central America (much lower than in the United States), the figure of unemployed in these two regions hovers around fifteen million: these represent a potential additional labour force for the United States. This is without even mentioning some fifty million housewives at present not gainfully employed!

while the total number of jobs destroyed in production through technical progress was far larger even than these ten million: millions of immigrant workers from the less industrialized countries had to return to their homelands; millions of women and young people 'dropped out of the labour market'; very many productive workers were transformed into unproductive ones.

A more sophisticated version of this theory has been proposed by the Hungarian Marxist Ferenc Janossy, who sees in the inability of capitalism to develop enough skilled (especially highly skilled) workers an unavoidable bottleneck which pushes up real wages at the end of 'prosperity'.[69] But here again the flexibility of capital, both in speeding up skill formation (including at factory level) and in reducing the need for highly skilled labour by technological change, is greatly underestimated.

Proponents of the pure over-accumulation theory of crisis often argue that, as long as accumulation of capital proceeds smoothly, consumption by the 'final consumers' automatically grows, as more wage-labour is being employed (generally at increasing wages) and unproductive consumption out of surplus-value also tends to grow. Hence no glut of consumer goods can appear, as long as the decline in the rate of profit has not significantly slowed down accumulation. The first part of the assertion is correct, as far as it goes. The conclusion, however, does not follow at all. The only thing this analysis proves is the fact that consumption (i.e. realization of surplus-value in department II) grows as long as accumulation grows. But it does not prove that consumption grows *in the same proportion* as does the productive capacity of department II. Indeed, the combined operation of the increasing organic composition of capital in department II and the increase in the rate of surplus-value in the overall economy makes it rather probable that (at least periodically) consumption, while growing, will grow less than productive capacity in department II. In which case, a glut of consumer goods can indeed occur before accumulation has slowed down in the economy taken as a whole.

Similarly, the assumption that a slow-down in current investment (in the last analysis determined by a decline in the average rate of profit) will trigger off the crisis before any overproduction of commodities actually manifests itself, is in the best of cases only one possible variant of the crisis scenario, and by no means

69. Ferenc Janossy, *Das Ende des Wirtschaftswunder*, Frankfurt, 1966.

the only one consistent either with Marx's analysis here in Volume 3 or with the empirical data of industrial cycles historically. Current investment decisions by capitalist firms are a function of two variables: *past* profit realizations (i.e. available surplus-value for accumulation) and *future* profit expectations. About the *current* rate of profit, which is a macro-economic end-result of many current changes, capitalist firms have no way of knowing anything precise, as long as their own and other capitalists' annual balance-sheets have not been drawn up. It is quite possible that past profit realization (e.g. in the previous year) does not yet reflect a decline in the rate of profit, but investment will still be cut precisely because there are growing signs of glut of the commodities which the firms produce (or already apparent phenomena of over-capacity). Conversely, it is equally possible that past profit realization already reflects the beginning of a decline in the rate of profit but investment decisions will still be expanding because, for whatever reason, the capitalist firm believes it can still significantly expand its sales. Profit expectations always include, besides the current trends of the rate of profit, estimates about expected market conditions and market shares. This is precisely one of the reasons why, under capitalism, there definitely exists a tendency for investment to 'overshoot' in certain circumstances, even after the rate of profit has started to decline. Many capitalist firms may believe that by continuing to expand investment and output, they can increase their own market share, profit from technological advantages vis-à-vis their competitors, etc. All these decisions cannot stop the rate of profit from declining. But they can produce growing overproduction of commodities before accumulation of capital actually slows down.

Elements of a correct theory of capitalist crisis are, of course, present in all three of the mono-causal explanations just outlined.[70] They have, precisely, to be integrated with each other to furnish such a theory. The easiest way to set about such an integration, in the light of Volume 3's basic insistence upon the tendency of the

70. While Lenin inclined towards a disproportionality explanation of capitalist crisis, he was prudent enough to write: 'The "consuming power of society" and "the proportional relation of the various branches of production" – are not conditions that are isolated, independent of and unconnected with each other. On the contrary, a certain level of consumption is one of the elements of proportionality.' *Collected Works*, Vol. 4, p. 58.

average rate of profit to fall, is by distinguishing a number of successive forms taken, over time, by the accumulation of capital.

In periods of strong upsurge of capitalist production – when business is brisk, current output is easily sold (indeed demand seems to be stronger than supply) and profits are high – there will be an 'investment boom' which will run rapidly into bottlenecks in both sub-sections of department I: that of machinery and equipment, and that of raw materials. Both these sub-sections of department I, by their very nature, are less flexible in adapting rapidly to demand than is department II. Hence additional investment, capital accumulation, will occur on a larger and larger scale in department I.[71] More means of production have to be produced to produce additional means of production for producing additional consumer goods. Good profit expectations in addition to high profit realizations are the motivation for this boom. Hence, there is a shift of investment towards department I. An uneven development (disproportion) between department I and department II is set into motion.

At a certain point in the boom, two parallel phenomena occur more or less simultaneously. On the one hand, the additional means of production produced come into the production process only after a certain time-lag. But when they enter into that process, they increase the productive capacity in both departments by leaps and bounds. But precisely the relatively high rates of profit and investment imply that real wages and consumer-goods demand from capitalists and their hangers-on could not have developed in the same proportion as this sudden increase in productive capacity in both departments (even if output grows less rapidly in department II than in department I, and even if real wages also grow). Hence a tendency to increasing overproduction (or overcapacity), in the first place in department II.

On the other hand, the massive introduction of new means of production in both departments does not occur with old techniques, but with new up-dated techniques characterized by a basically labour-saving bias, i.e. by an increased organic composition of

71. Marx even saw, in the massively bunched introduction of fixed capital at intervals of from seven to ten years, both one of the main reasons for the periodicity of the industrial cycle and the determining factor for its average duration. On the tendency of investment to 'overshoot', see J. R. Hicks, *A Contribution to the Theory of the Trade Cycle*, Oxford, 1951; Roy Harrod, *Economic Essays*, London, 1953; E. D. Domar, *Essays in the Theory of Economic Growth*, New York, 1957; etc.

capital. This presses down the rate of profit, especially since under boom conditions the rate of surplus-value cannot increase in the same proportion, or even does not increase at all.[72] Hence a tendency to over-accumulation: *part of newly accumulated capital* can no longer be invested at the average rate of profit, or is even not invested at all, pushed towards speculation, etc.[73]

Credit expansion, for a certain time, covers the gap. But it can only postpone the crash, not avoid it. Overproduction now tends to spread from department II to department I.[74] Growing overproduction of commodities (over-capacity in a growing number of branches of industry), combined with growing over-accumulation, must of necessity lead to sharp cut-backs in productive investment. Disproportionality between the two departments now jumps from an 'over-extension' of department I into an 'underdevelopment' of that department. Investment falls more quickly than current output.

As a result of the crash – which can, but does not necessarily, take the initial form of a credit and banking crash – there is a general collapse of commodity prices (expressed in gold), together with a decline in output and employment. There is a general devalorization of capital, as a result – simultaneously – of this collapse of prices (i.e. of commodity capital), of a large number of bankruptcies, and of a decline in the value of the fixed capital and raw-material stocks of surviving firms. But this general collapse of prices is nothing but the adaptation of market prices and prices of production (through a lower average rate of profit) to the general lowering in the value of the average commodity, which is the unavoidable outcome of the general increase of investment, organic composition of capital and average productivity of labour during the previous period. Capitalists try to postpone this hour of reckoning as long as possible – whence the over-extension of credit, speculation, over-trading, etc. on the eve of the crash. But they cannot postpone it indefinitely.

The effects of the crash, for the system as a whole, are healthy,

72. See below, pp. 359–60, 364–5.

73. See below, p. 359.

74. This, of course, is not an absolute rule. Overproduction *could start* in certain sub-sectors of department I. This has happened in some but not most concrete crises. The two latest crises – those of 1974–5 and 1979–80 – both started in automobiles and housing, i.e. durable consumer goods, subsectors of department II.

however nasty they may be for individual capitalists. General devalorization of capital is not accompanied by a proportional reduction in the mass of surplus-value produced. Or (which amounts to the same) an identical mass of surplus-value can now valorize a smaller total amount of capital. Hence the decline in the rate of profit can be stopped and even reversed. Large-scale reconstitution of the reserve army of labour, occurring during the crisis and the depression, makes possible a vigorous increase in the rate of surplus-value, not only through speed-ups but even through a cut in real wages, which in turn leads to a further rise in the rate of profit. Raw material prices generally fall more than the prices of finished goods, so part of constant capital becomes cheaper. The rise in the organic composition of capital is thereby slowed down, again pushing up the average rate of profit on industrial capital. A new cycle of stepped-up accumulation of capital, stepped-up productive investment, can now start, once stocks have become sufficiently depleted and current production sufficiently cut for demand again to outstrip supply, especially in department II.

It follows that the law of the tendency for the average rate of profit to decline is less a direct explanation for crises of over-production properly speaking, than a revelation of the basic mechanism of the industrial cycle as such: in other words, an uncovering of the specifically capitalist, i.e. uneven, disharmonious, mode of economic growth, which unavoidably leads to successive phases of declining rates of profit, and recuperation of the rate of profit as a result, precisely, of the consequences of the previous decline. This is true at least of the way in which this law operates over the seven–ten-year time-span – leaving aside, for the moment, the *memento mori* it implies for capitalism in a secular perspective.

There can be little doubt that this multi-causal explanation of capitalist crisis, rather than any of the mono-causal variants, corresponds to Marx's own conviction, at least as expressed here in Volume 3. In addition to the passage quoted on p. 40 above, three other passages can be cited which leave little room for alternative interpretations:

'Let us conceive the whole society as composed simply of industrial capitalists and wage-labourers. Let us also leave aside those changes in price which prevent large portions of the total capital from being replaced in their average proportions, and which, in the overall context of the reproduction process as a whole, particularly as developed by credit, must recurrently bring about a situation of general stagnation. Let us likewise ignore the fraudulent businesses and speculative dealings that the credit system fosters. In this case, a crisis would be explicable only in terms of a disproportion in production between different branches and a disproportion between the consumption of the capitalists themselves and their accumulation. But as things actually are, the replacement of the capitals invested in production depends to a large extent on the consumption capacity of the non-productive classes; while the consumption capacity of the workers is restricted partly by the laws governing wages, and partly by the fact that they are employed only as long as they can be employed at a profit for the capitalist class. *The ultimate reason for all real crises always remains the poverty and restricted consumption of the masses, in the face of the drive of capitalist production to develop the productive forces as if only the absolute consumption capacity of society set a limit to them.*'[75] (my italics)

'Periodically, however, too much is produced in the way of means of labour and means of subsistence, too much to function as means for exploiting the workers at a given rate of profit. *Too many commodities are produced for the value contained in them, and the surplus-value included in this value, to be realized under the conditions of distribution given by capitalist production, and to be transformed back into new capital,* i.e. it is impossible to accomplish this process without ever recurrent explosions.'[76] (my italics)

'The manufacturer may actually sell to the exporter, and the exporter to his foreign customer; the importer may sell his raw materials to the manufacturer, and the manufacturer sell his products to the wholesaler, etc. But at some particular imperceptible point *the commodity lies unsold;* or else the total stocks of producers and middlemen gradually become too high. It is precisely then that consumption is generally at flood tide, partly because one industrial capitalist sets a series of others in motion, partly because the workers these employ, being fully occupied, have more than usual to spend. The capitalists' expenditure increases with their revenue. And besides this, there is also, as we have already seen (Volume 2, Part Three), a constant circulation

75. See below, pp. 614–15.
76. See below, p. 367.

between one constant capital and another (even leaving aside the accelerated accumulation) which is initially independent of individual consumption in so far as it never goes into this *even though it is ultimately limited by it, for production of constant capital never takes place for its own sake, but simply because more of it is needed in those spheres of production* whose products do go into individual consumption. This can continue quite happily for a good while, stimulated by prospective demand, and in these branches of industry business proceeds very briskly, as far as both merchants and industrialists are concerned. The crisis occurs as soon as the returns of those merchants who sell far afield (or who have accumulated stocks at home) become so slow and sparse that the banks press for payment for commodities bought, or bills fall due before any resale takes place.'[77] (my italics)

CREDIT AND THE RATE OF INTEREST

In the same way as Volume 2 of *Capital* stressed the importance of previous accumulation (and presence) of money-capital, its periodic injection into circulation, and its periodic outflow from the operations of productive capital properly speaking, to make expanded reproduction (i.e. economic growth) possible for 'capital in general', Volume 3 stresses the key importance of credit for 'many capitals', i.e. for the fluctuations of the industrial cycle under conditions of competition.

The appearance of a generally known average rate of profit unavoidably leads to an equalization of the rate of interest too. Surplus-value is, first of all, split between profit for entrepreneurial capital (industrial profit, commercial profit, banking profit, and profit for agricultural entrepreneurs as distinct from passive landowners) on the one hand, and interest on the other. Through the capitalist banking system, all available money reserves (savings and non-invested surplus-value + idle money capital resulting from non-investment of part of surplus-value realized during previous cycles) are transformed into functioning capital, in other words lent to capitalist firms which are actually operating – i.e. employing wage-labour – be it in the sphere of production or in that of circulation. In this way, capitalists are able to operate with much more capital than they own personally. Capital accumulation can take place at a much quicker pace than would

77. See below, pp. 419–20.

be the case if each capitalist firm could practise enlarged reproduction only on the basis of the profits it had itself realized.

This constant expansion of credit, which has accompanied the
whole history of the capitalist mode of production, at first sight
seems to accentuate the tendency of the average rate of profit to
decline.[78] The total amount of profit distributed among the sum-
total of capitalist firms is now lower than the sum-total of surplus-
value produced, the difference being exactly the total amount of
interest paid out to the passive owners of money capital (which is
not to be confused with profits of banks, i.e. the average profits on
their own capital, not on their deposits). But this is, of course, a
false impression. The average rate of profit is the division of the
total amount of surplus-value produced by the total amount of
social capital. If, as a result of division of labour among capitalists or over-accumulation, part of that capital is not itself directly
productive, in other words, is not engaged in the direct production
of surplus-value, this does not change its nature as capital, i.e.
value constantly on the look-out for an accretion of value.

Hence, according to Marx here in Volume 3, the effects of credit
(like those of trade) on the tendency for the average rate of profit
to decline are opposite to what at first sight appears. They in
reality tend to put a brake upon that tendency, or even reverse it,
as a result of three simultaneous mechanisms which they unleash:

(1) Trade and credit allow capital to rotate more rapidly, thereby
increasing the number of productive cycles through which a
single sum of money capital can pass in, say, one year, thereby
increasing the mass of surplus-value and also the annual rate of
profit (since the same amount of surplus-value is produced during
each of these productive cycles, all other things remaining equal).[79]
This, by the way, is why industrialists are ready to allow commercial and banking capital to share in the general distribution of
entrepreneurial profit (total mass of surplus-value minus total

78. See below, pp. 735, 742–3.

79. Industrial capital can rotate more rapidly if wholesale and retail
merchants buy produced commodities immediately from industrial capitalists
and keep them in stock until the 'last customer' appears. This division of
labour inside the capitalist class, in which commercial capitalists buy commodities entering the sphere of circulation from industrial capitalists, explains
why the latter are ready to abandon part of surplus-value to the former, in the
form of commercial profits.

mass of interest), although neither commercial nor banking capital produces surplus-value. Such capital does not produce surplus-value itself, but it helps industrial capital and agricultural capital produce additional surplus-value.

(2) By enlarging the scope and tempo of accumulation of capital in the productive sphere, over and above profits directly owned by industrialists and capitalist farmers, commerce and trade accelerate the concentration of capital, thereby stimulating technical progress and the production of relative surplus-value, which again counteracts the tendency for the average rate of profit to decline.

(3) By the device of joint-stock companies (corporations), credit creates a situation in which a large part of capital, owned by stockholders, is not expected to receive the average rate of profit at all, but is content with the average rate of interest only. Hence, the average rate of entrepreneurial profit is much higher than it would be if all (or the largest part) of capital were directly entrepreneurial capital, i.e. had to receive the average rate of profit.[80]

The greater flexibility of money capital not tied to any specific firm or branch of industry is, in turn, one of the main reasons why the equalization of the rate of profit can so easily occur and be recognized under capitalism, i.e. why social capital remains relatively mobile in spite of growing capital investment in the form of fixed, relatively immobile capital. Parallel to the reserve army of labour, these huge reserves of money capital are the preconditions for sudden, rapid phases of feverish expansion, which characterize the industrial cycle and the very nature of capitalist growth, uneven and disharmonious. Indeed, the banking system in part plays the role of a social clearing-house, through which capital is constantly being transferred from branches which face stagnating or declining overall demand, to branches which face growing overall demand not satisfied by current production (or productive capacity). The deviations of distinct rates of profits from the average are the guiding mechanism for these transfers. In that sense, Marx stresses the key role of credit in expanding the accumulation of capital to its utmost limits, while at the same time

80. See below, pp. 347–8.

functioning as the main lever for over-speculation, over-trading and overproduction.

It follows that the credit cycle – and the ups and downs of the rate of interest – are partially desynchronized from the industrial cycle properly speaking. During the period of recovery and initial upsurge, money capital is relatively abundant; the level of self-financing of firms is high; the rate of interest is relatively low;[81] and the level of entrepreneurial profit is above average. Conversely, at the peak of the boom, during the phase of over-heating and during the crash, money capital becomes scarcer and scarcer; the level of self-financing declines precipitately; demand for money capital grows constantly; and the rate of interest grows by leaps and bounds, not in spite of but as a function of the decline in the average rate of profit. Firms now borrow not to expand business but to escape bankruptcy; not in order to gain additional entrepreneurial profits, but in order to save their capital. At this precise moment of the cycle, the rate of interest, therefore, can actually be above the rate of entrepreneurial profit (which cannot, of course, 'normally' be the case). But when, after the crash, the crisis and depression properly speaking set in, investment declines steeply; demand for credit collapses; and the rate of interest starts to slide rapidly, which helps the rate of entrepreneurial profit slowly to pick up again.

MARX'S THEORY OF SURPLUS PROFITS

The fact that Marx's theory of differential land rent in reality represents a special case of a more general theory of surplus profits has not hitherto been sufficiently appreciated. This is all the more strange in that Marx explicitly makes the point here in Volume 3, in several passages of Parts One and Two, and returns to the question at length in Parts Six and Seven.

The basic approach, once again, is a straightforward application of the labour theory of value. The question whether labour expended in the production of a given commodity is recognized as

81. Under conditions of permanent inflation of paper money, this applies, of course, to the 'real' and not to the 'nominal' rate of interest. The 'real' rate of interest is the 'nominal' rate minus the rate of inflation. The extent of credit inflation under late capitalism can be measured by the fact that we have known several lengthy periods of negative 'real' rates of interest in key capitalist countries.

average socially necessary labour or not is not a simple physical matter of an actual number of labour-hours expended – of a given fraction of society's total labour potential being used for producing a given commodity.[82] It is a function of the total amount of labour expended in all the units producing that given commodity, as compared to the total amount of labour which society wishes to devote to it.[83] It is a function of the relation between the productivity of labour in the given productive unit and the average productivity of labour in the branch of industry as a whole.

Marx distinguishes three basic situations of current production,

82. An important debate is occurring on this question among Marxists, with a number of non-Marxists also taking part. Isaac Rubin, while correctly denying a purely physiological (reified) definition of 'abstract labour', contends strongly that it is quantifiable, based upon labour-time and labour-intensity (op. cit., pp. 155–7). In my view, he is right and Catherine Colliot-Thélène in her Afterword to Rubin's *A History of Economic Thought* (London, 1979, pp. 405–15), is wrong when she asserts that there is a basic contradiction involved, when Marx defines 'socially necessary labour' both by the average productivity of labour in each industrial branch and by the relation between branch output and socially recognized *needs*. Where Colliot-Thélène sees a contradiction, there is in fact a difference – between *value production*, which is strictly limited to the sphere of production, and *value realization*, which occurs in the sphere of circulation and depends *inter alia* upon relations between the structure of production and the structure of demand. The law of value adapts the distribution of the labour force to social needs *post festum*, because under conditions of commodity production this cannot be done *a priori*. But this does not imply that labour expended in the production process has not been value-producing, i.e. that labourers (labour-time) engaged in 'unnecessary' production have been nonexistent. It just means that value produced has been redistributed: that the equivalent of some of it is not received by those who own the commodities thus produced.

83. This point, which I made in *Marxist Economic Theory* (London, 1962), is also highly controversial among Marxists. Marx himself, however, is quite clear on the subject (see below, p. 774): 'This is in fact the law of value as it makes itself felt, not in relation to the individual commodities or articles, but rather to the total products at a given time of particular spheres of social production autonomized by the division of labour; so that not only is no more labour-time devoted to each individual commodity than necessary, but out of the total social labour-time only the proportionate quantity needed is devoted to the various types of commodity. Use-value still remains a condition. But if in the case of the individual commodity this use-value depends on its satisfying in and of itself a social need, in the case of the mass social product it depends on its adequacy to the quantitatively specific social need for each particular kind of product, and therefore on the proportional division of the labour between these various spheres of production in accordance with these social needs, which are quantitatively circumscribed.' See too p. 786 below.

in relation to current social needs (not, of course, physical needs, but needs induced by commodity production and mediated through purchasing power as determined by capitalist norms of distribution – i.e. by the class structure of bourgeois society).

Case 1 concerns situations where there is a normal mobility of capital in relation to a given branch of output. Here, inflows and outflows of capital, regulated by oscillations of prices inducing oscillations of rates of profit, will normally balance out social supply and demand. In that case, equalization of the rate of profit will normally apply to the branch in question. Firms which operate at the average productivity of labour in the branch (which will be the general rule) will receive the average rate of profit. Firms which operate below the average productivity of labour will receive less than the average profit, and risk being crowded out of business in situations of crisis and depression. Firms which have made technological advances, which operate at a level of productivity of labour above the average, will enjoy a *temporary surplus profit*, i.e. a profit over and above the average profit resulting from the difference between their individual costs of production and the average costs of production in the branch. But this surplus profit will generally disappear in periods of crisis and depression, when the new technology will become generalized throughout the branch, and the average productivity of labour (the value of the commodity) adapted to that initially higher productivity.[84]

Case 2 concerns branches of production characterized by *structurally stagnant or declining demand*: i.e. 'outmoded' ones, with *structural* overproduction. Here, only firms operating at above-average productivity of labour will receive the average rate of profit. Firms operating at average productivity of labour will receive less than the average rate of profit. Firms operating at below-average levels of productivity of labour will sell at a loss and go out of business. In general, again, when there is normal mobility of capital, such branches of industry will become 'normalized' (i.e. revert to Case 1) even before a general crisis of overproduction occurs, through massive closures of productive units.

But then there is also Case 3, which we might characterize as one of *structurally (or institutionally) determined scarcity*: i.e. the

84. See below, pp. 279, 300 and 373–4.

case where an influx of capital is hampered (or prevented) by *natural or artificial monopolies*.[85] In such cases, there is a *long-term* preponderance of demand over supply. So the firms operating with the lowest productivity of labour in the branch still receive the average rate of profit (i.e. they determine the price of production, or the value, of the commodity produced in that branch).[86] Firms operating at a higher productivity of labour – at the average of the branch, or *a fortiori* at an above-average level – receive a *long-term surplus profit* protected by the very monopoly, i.e. by the powerful obstacle which hinders the influx of additional capital into the branch in question. This surplus profit does not even disappear in times of crisis and depression, although it will obviously be lowered in absolute terms, as a result of the fall in the average rate of profit.

These monopoly surplus profits are called differential rents. In *Capital* Volume 3, three such instances of differential rent are distinguished: land rent; mineral rents; and technological rents.[87] Land rent could be sub-divided into agricultural land rent and urban land rent.

Natural monopolies are determined by the fact that access to natural resources necessary for production (from a use-value point of view) is limited, and that these are not reproducible at will by capital. This applies to land as such, especially land of a given use-value (desired relative fertility, desired location); to mineral sources; to climatological preconditions for using land to produce certain specific use-values (e.g. cotton, natural rubber, tropical fruits, etc.).

Artificial monopolies are determined by limits in capital mobility related not to natural conditions but to conditions arising from the results of specific stages (forms) of accumulation of capital itself: concentration of capital (if, in order to start a new firm in a given branch of industry with minimum level of profitability, it is necessary to invest at least £500 million or $1,000 million, this is obviously an 'obstacle to entry' for most capitalists); monopoly rights in patents, inventions or research in certain new fields of production (or, which amounts to the same thing,

85. See below, pp. 301 and 1001.
86. See below, pp. 278–9.
87. I have used the formula 'technological rent' in extension of Marx's land rent, when conditions of 'artificial monopoly' are due to technological monopolies, similar to the monopoly in landownership.

qualitative advantages in the capacity to apply these); organized practices by a small number of firms dominating production in a given field, systematically resorted to in order to keep out potential competitors; and so on.

As clearly follows from this definition, natural and artificial monopolies, giving rise to surplus profits through putting a brake upon free entry of capital into branches of production where the rate of profit is higher than average, are always relative, never absolute. Land is not reproducible. But possibilities for capital investment on existing land can be vastly expanded. Furthermore, internationally, tremendous areas of potentially agricultural land are not yet exploited (in the nineteenth century, of course, these were many times greater than today). So *potential* agricultural land is still relatively abundant on a world scale. Capitalist technology, furthermore, can be pushed to the point where production becomes possible without the use of land. Mineral resources are finite. But synthetic production of originally natural raw materials (fibres, rubber, oil) is not finite, or at least not to anything like the same degree as natural raw materials properly speaking.

The bigger the initial capital outlays necessary for profitable production, the smaller the number of potential new competitors in a given branch of industry. But conversely, the higher the surplus profits enjoyed in these branches, the stronger the inducement for 'many capitals' to band together and risk the huge initial capital investments necessary to obtain a slice of the cake. The more that decisive advances in technology lead to stable surplus profits over longer periods, the stronger the pressure for potential competitors to leap ahead and bypass these advances by a new revolution in technology, etc.[88] One may conclude that all monopoly surplus profits are always limited in time and, in the long run, tend to disappear, and that commodities produced in initially monopolized branches tend to be exchanged at their prices of production. Whether this 'long run', at least for industrial products produced in monopolized branches under monopoly capitalism (i.e. since about 1890), is the 'long wave' – as I hypothe-

88. An impressive recent example is that of the increasing challenge to I.B.M.'s quasi-monopoly domination of the computer industry, as a result of the development of micro-processors and the attempt by Japanese trusts to bypass I.B.M. in the production of fifth-generation large computers.

sized in *Late Capitalism* – or not, remains a subject for further investigation.[89]

In order fully to grasp the relative (never absolute) nature of any monopoly, whether natural or artificial – and thus the limited nature in time of any form of surplus profits under capitalism – it is necessary to reintroduce into our analysis the phenomenon of structural scarcity which was its starting-point.[90] For it is only if obstructions to capital mobility, i.e. *obstacles to increases in output*, create conditions under which social demand for the goods produced in that given branch of output is for long periods higher than or equal to the total amount of commodities produced (including those produced under the lowest conditions of productivity of labour, or the lowest fertility of soil in agriculture) that units of production enjoying lower costs of production will be able to realize surplus profits in the form of *differential rents* (differential land rents, mineral rents, technological rents).

Once, however, social demand for the goods produced in the monopolized branch of industry recedes, or stagnates, or grows more slowly than does production even under conditions of relative monopoly, differential rent will tend to be reduced and surplus profits to decline. (This does not mean, of course, that they will disappear completely, where the monopoly is natural, as long as differences in fertility, etc. still subsist and determine different unit costs on different pieces of land, in different mines, etc.) The huge increases in average productivity of agricultural labour, which have been one of the main characteristics of the development of capitalism in the twentieth century, and have indeed exceeded the rate of growth of industrial productivity of labour, have completely altered the demand/supply relation for

89. See *Late Capitalism*, op. cit., pp. 545–6. The idea of an equalization of surplus profits side by side with the equalization of average profit, which implies the co-existence during a certain time-span of two average rates of profit, one in the monopolized and one in the non-monopolized sectors of production, was advanced in my *Marxist Economic Theory* (op. cit., Vol. 2, pp. 423–6) and defended in *Late Capitalism* (pp. 95, 538–49). It has been equally strongly challenged. Marx himself, however, explicitly proposes it here in *Capital* Volume 3 (see below, p. 1001).

90. Marx deals with this problem of structural scarcity on p. 279 below: 'If the demand is so strong, however, that it does not contract when price is determined by the value of commodities produced in the worst conditions, then it is these that determine the market value.'

basic foodstuffs in the advanced capitalist countries.[91] The situation of structural scarcity has been transformed into a situation of structural overproduction, co-determined by the decreasing place of food expenditure in total consumers' expenditure when real incomes rise (Engel's Law). Not only has differential rent, therefore, been strongly contracting in these countries, but large tracts of farm land have been reconverted into pastures, while in turn large tracts of pasture have been reconverted into forests or simply waste land. Massive closures of coal pits in the nineteen-fifties, sixties and early seventies, when oil was much cheaper than coal, are a parallel development in mining, with a co-related decline of differential coal-mining rents.

But the process can also be reversed. When social demand – mediated through an increase in market prices – suddenly surges beyond output for, say, ten or twenty years, i.e. when structural scarcity reappears, a massive reappearance of differential rents occurs. This is what has happened in gold production since the collapse of the Bretton Woods system, when it became impossible for the imperialist Central Banks to maintain the gold price at $35 or $42 (35 S. D. R.) an ounce.[92] The upsurge of the 'free market gold price', first to $100, then to $200, finally to more than $600 an ounce, has made many 'marginal' mines in South Africa (and elsewhere) profitable again, and led to a feverish development of capital investment in gold-mining. The more productive among the twenty main South African gold mines were producing gold at the end of 1979 at around $95 production costs per ounce (the single most productive mine at $64 an ounce). The less productive of these twenty mines had production costs of around $200 an ounce (with the highest single figure being $265). This situation gives a differential rent of more than $100 an ounce for the former

91. In the post-war period, agricultural productivity of labour has been rising faster than that of industry in most of the industrialized capitalist countries: in the United States, three times as fast during the 1950s. See Theodore Schultz, *Economic Crises in World Agriculture*, Ann Arbor, 1965, pp. 70–72.

92. S.D.R. (Special Drawing Rights, emitted by the International Monetary Fund and only used in inter-central-bank relations, not in relations with private capitalists, including private banks) are based on a common basket of currencies, and have thus been constantly re-appreciated against the dollar since 1971. Hence, the increase of the 'official' I.M.F. gold price (fixed at 35 S.D.R. per ounce), which rose from $35 to $42.

category of mines as against the latter, once gold is selling at more than \$200 + average profit: say, more than \$240 or \$250 an ounce.[93]

There is a more general reason why the capitalist mode of production produces both a tendency towards monopolization (e.g. as a result of increasing concentration and centralization of capital), and a tendency towards periodic decline of specific monopolies. This is the fact that surplus profits are deducted from the total amount of profit to be distributed among all those capitalists who participate in the equalization of the rate of profit: in other words, they tend to reduce the general cake distributed among all bourgeois except the monopolists. As there is a tendency for that average rate of profit to decline, monopolies of all kinds – including monopoly property in land – tend, therefore, to accentuate that decline. Hence, the pressure of capital to overcome natural or artificial barriers to the mobility of capital: to reduce the impact of monopolistic situations, or even try to eliminate them altogether. The outcome of this constant tug-of-war is a function of the relative strength of different layers of the ruling class. At least in the twentieth century, the pressure has been more successful with regard to absentee capitalist landlords (separate and apart from capitalist agricultural entrepreneurs) than with regard to industrial, transport or mining monopolies, although not a few cases of collapse of monopolistic surplus profits could be cited in these realms too.

This pressure remains, independently of whether one considers the surplus profits (additional surplus-value) of the monopolists to be actually produced inside the monopolized branches of output, or whether one considers them, at least in several cases, as resulting from transfers of value from non-monopolized to monopolized sectors of production. For, in both hypotheses, the mass of surplus-value to be shared out among all capitalists who do not enjoy rents is substantially lower than it would have been with a 'perfect' mobility of capital into all branches: in other words, their average rate of profit has been lowered. And when this accentuates a tendency which is already operating for deeper reasons, as has been indicated above, the counter-pressure will be all the more powerful.

93. Study by the Banque L. Dreyfus, reproduced in *Le Monde*, 29 January 1980.

THE SPECIFICITY OF CAPITALIST AGRICULTURE

In Volume 3 of *Capital*, Marx extends a notion which he had already stressed at the end of Volume 1: the key importance of private appropriation of land – the transformation of land into the private property of a given limited class of people – for the very birth, consolidation and expansion of the capitalist mode of production. This mode of production presupposes the appearance of a social class – the modern proletariat – which has no access to means of production and subsistence and is, therefore, under the economic compulsion to sell its labour-power. Means of subsistence are, in the first instance, food, which wherever access to land is free can be produced with minimal means of production. Hence, the creation of the modern proletariat hinges, to a large extent, on barring free access to land to people possessing no capital.

This process of private appropriation of land, which in Western Europe mainly took place between the fifteenth and eighteenth centuries and culminated in the sale of village 'free' land reserves (communal lands) unleashed by the French Revolution,[94] was repeated throughout the last part of the nineteenth and the whole of the twentieth century in Eastern Europe, North and South America, the Middle East, Africa, Japan and South-East Asia. The most repulsive form of forcible separation of the original population from its fertile land reserves occurred in Eastern and Southern Africa. It is going on to this very day in countries like Brazil, Iran, the Philippines and Mexico (despite the partial achievements of the 1910–17 Revolution).

However, the interrelation between consolidation of the capitalist mode of production, the process of capital accumulation and the struggle of capital against the tendency for the rate of profit to decline is much more complex than this compulsion to transform all land into private property.

For historical reasons, the generalization of private property in land, in Western, Central and a large part of Eastern Europe as well as in Japan, took the initial form of ownership by a social class separate and apart from 'functioning' capitalists (i.e. capitalist farmers, entrepreneurs) properly speaking. These

94. See (among others) Otto Bauer, *Der Kampf um Wald und Weide*, Vienna, 1925.

capitalist landowners (not to be confused with semi-feudal or feudal landlords) barred entry to their land by the capitalist class in general, unless they received a special 'unearned' income in the form of *absolute land rent* (the same rule applies, of course, to rentier-proprietors of urban land vis-à-vis capitalists engaged in the building industry). In other parts of the world, the phenomenon of private appropriation of 'surplus' land has involved other layers of the ruling class: sometimes foreign settlers appropriated it;[95] sometimes local landowners, merchants, usurers and other sectors of the ruling class operated in the same way. There are some cases, though rather rare, of combinations in one degree or another of both processes.

But in all cases where actual ownership of the land became separated from *capitalist* farming, absolute land rent appeared. And as is the case with differential land rent, absolute rent is a fraction of total surplus-value produced by the sum-total of commodity-producing labour, deducted from the residue to be divided between all capitalist entrepreneurs and owners of money capital. This deduction is all the more onerous in that, contrary to differential rent, it is not open to erosion or equalization through the laws of motion of the capitalist mode of production properly speaking (competition, technical progress, increase in the organic composition of capital, concentration and centralization of capital, etc.). It thus puts a brake upon capital accumulation in agriculture. Hence, the organic drive of capital to eliminate the separation of landownership and capitalist farming: by gradually transforming landowners into entrepreneurs, and land-renting farmers into a majority of wage-earners on the one hand and a minority of landowning farmers on the other. The transformation of a situation of structural scarcity of food into one of structural plenty (latent overproduction) in most of the industrialized countries powerfully assists this process.[96] It represents a *ten-*

95. In the second part of his remarkable study 'Value and Rent' (*Capital and Class*, Nos. 3 and 4), Robin Murray makes the point (pp. 13 ff.) that settlers overseas could generally expect a 'founder's rent' similar to Hilferding's founder's rent of large oligopolistic enterprises. I think he is right, at least with regard to overseas countries with above-average fertile land compared to West Europe. But he gives excessive weight to such 'rent' in explaining international migrations, capitalist expansionism and the origins of imperialism.

96. According to an O.E.C.D. note of February 1980, total wheat stocks in imperialist countries averaged more than fifty million tonnes in every single

dential disappearance of absolute rent in the imperialist countries.

Behind this process there lies an imperious long-term assertion of the law of value of a deeper kind. The *source* of absolute land rent is the lower organic composition of capital in agriculture as compared with industry, i.e. the higher mass of surplus-value produced by agricultural labourers as compared with industrial labourers employed by a same amount of total capital.[97] The barrier of landownership separated from capitalist enterprise makes it possible for landowners to prevent this supplementary amount of surplus-value from being sucked into the general process of equalization of profit between all capitalists. Thus rent is indeed an obstacle to the full flowering of capitalist agriculture: a source of relative backwardness of agriculture compared with industry, i.e. of agricultural productivity of labour compared with industrial productivity of labour. But Marx, who himself stressed this relative backwardness, noted that it was not a fixed and final characteristic of the capitalist mode of production, but could sooner or later be overcome. But when agriculture becomes more and more industrialized, when the substitution of human labour by dead labour (machinery, fertilizers, etc.) is applied on an ever-increasing scale in that branch of production, when contemporary *agro-business* arises, the difference in organic composition of agricultural as compared with industrial capital tends to disappear. Consequently, the material basis for absolute land rent disappears likewise. As Robin Murray has aptly expressed it: in the same way that the formal subordination of labour to capital is transformed into a real subordination in agriculture, formal subordination of land under capitalist agriculture is transformed into real subordination of land as a material element in capitalist agricultural production.[98]

The extent of this process of industrialization of agriculture can be measured by the following facts concerning the United States. Between 1915–19 and 1973–7, productivity of labour in wheat and soybean production increased tenfold, when measured by the labour-hours needed to produce 100 bushels. For maize,

---

year between 1970/71 and 1979/80. Total end-year stocks of butter and skimmed milk in the imperialist countries rose from 289,000 tonnes in 1970 to 1.4 million tonnes in 1979.

97. See below, pp. 894–6 and 906.
98. Murray, op. cit., p. 21.

the increase was actually thirtyfold! Production assets – including livestock and raw materials stocked on farms, thus roughly comparable to constant capital – per farm worker increased fivefold in current dollars between 1963 and 1978. Per capita disposable income per farm worker, however, only increased less than threefold, *half of which* originated from sources outside farming properly speaking. Wages for hired labour barely doubled during the same period. A good index of the increase in the organic composition of capital, if there ever was one! Simultaneously, the 'emancipation' of capitalist agriculture from the use of land has made giant strides in animal husbandry, as exemplified above all by hog-raising, cattle-raising and by the aptly termed 'broiler industry'. By 1972, 75 per cent of U.S. beef was raised on so-called feedlots, the largest accommodating as many as 125,000 cattle at a time.[99]

It should be noted that, while absolute land rent originating in the separation of landownership from capitalist farmers (differential land rent *does not* originate in ownership: ownership only determines who appropriates it) tends to disappear under conditions of 'industrialized' agriculture, it reappears in modified form as *generalized mortgaging of land* owned by small and medium-sized capitalist farmers – in other words, as the transfer of a significant part of surplus-value produced in agriculture to banks and finance capital.[100]

However, as I have already emphasized, real capital movements are guided not by the average rate of profit but by *deviations* from that average. So while capital tends to eliminate absolute rent in the older capitalist countries, it also constantly tends to reproduce it, essentially (but not exclusively) in countries where capitalism has penetrated belatedly. There thus operates, at the level of the

99. *US Department of Agriculture Statistics*, 1978, pp. 444, 426, 464; Murray, op. cit., p. 21.

100. See Karl Kautsky, *La Question agraire*, Paris, 1970, pp. 296–9. The growing role of big food-transforming firms (increasingly, multinationals themselves) and big cooperative societies controlled by rich farmers should also be mentioned: these tend more and more to cut farmers off from direct access to the market. According to the French economist Bernard Kayser, barely 25 per cent of France's agricultural production is sold by the farmers themselves to final consumers or self-consumed. All the rest passes through the hands of large capitalist intermediaries, which naturally take their own toll, similar to – and often parallel with – mortgage interest. (See *Économie et Statistiques*, No. 102, July–August 1978.)

world economy, a kind of process of internationalization of land appropriation and creation of absolute land rent.[101] Brazil offers some outstanding examples of this tendency.

Finally, since agricultural production is food production, and since food is an essential element of reproduction of labour-power – quantitatively its main element, at least in the earlier phases of development of the capitalist mode of production – there is another, contradictory, element in the relation between capitalism and agriculture. While for (real or potential) agricultural capitalists, the main problem is eliminating the dual structure of land-ownership and farming enterprise, for (national) capital as a whole, the main short-term problem is to ensure access to food on the cheapest possible conditions, be it through capitalist, semi-capitalist or pre-capitalist modes of production.

This means that capital as a whole has a vested interest, at least during early phases of capitalist development (which are being reproduced today in most semi-colonial countries, even those which are semi-industrialized), in maintaining a substantial part of the peasantry under conditions where it still has access to *some* land:[102] not enough to provide a minimum basis of livelihood, but sufficient to provide *part* of the annual food intake of the peasant family, forcing these peasants to look for employment during part of the year. Rising capitalism, therefore, both ruthlessly suppresses free access to land through generalization of private ownership of land, and skilfully defends *minifundia*, i.e. small-scale parcellized subsistence farms,[103] which enable wages to be pushed below the subsistence level since this semi-proletarian sub-section of the wage-earning class produces part of its own food. The political and social function of such deliberate policies by bourgeois governments has often been pointed out. They slow down the concentration and permanent urban settlement of

101. Murray, op. cit., pp. 24–5.
102. Migrant labour in South Africa and other settlers' colonies plays a similar role. See, for example, Harold Wolpe, 'Capitalism and Cheap Labour-Power in South Africa', *Economy and Society*, No. 14, 1972; R. T. Bell, 'Migrant Labour: Theory and Policy', *South African Journal of Economics*, Vol. 40, No. 4, December 1972; Francis Wilson, *Labour in the South African Gold Mines*, Cambridge, 1972; Giovanni Arrighi, 'Labour Supplies in Historical Perspective: A Study of the Proletarianization of the African Peasantry in Rhodesia', in G. Arrighi and John Saul, *Essays in the Political Economy of Africa*, New York, 1973.
103. See below, pp. 321, and 947–50.

the proletariat; they maintain an easily manipulated electoral base, that is less easy to unionize or organize in workers' parties; and so on. But the economic function of these policies must also be clearly acknowledged. They play an important role today in many semi-colonial countries, especially the more advanced ones. As for the *direct* exploitation of these miserable 'private owners' by capital, it takes the form not of extortion of land rent but of extortion of *usury interest*, the parcel owners being permanently and increasingly burdened by debt.

The *overall* evolution of agriculture under capitalism will be a resultant of the interaction of the five, often contradictory, tendencies just outlined. And this resultant becomes, in a certain sense, an index of the degree of maturity of capitalist development in the national economy as a whole. On a world scale, this culminates in a tragic end-result. The internationalization of absolute land rent means a growing gap between the average productivity of labour engaged in food production in the imperialist countries, on the one hand, and in the semi-colonial countries, on the other.[104] Both the growing penetration of capitalism into semi-colonial agriculture (with the accompanying phenomenon of increase in commercial as against food crops) and the attempts of bourgeois governments to 'stabilize' parcellized subsistence farming tend to increase that gap further. The consequence is that food surpluses on a world scale tend to become increasingly concentrated in fewer and fewer countries, most of them imperialist ones.[105] In other words, differential land rent on the world market is accessible only to a smaller and smaller number of capitalist large-scale farmers (agro-businesses).[106]

104. In wheat production, yield per hectare in 1977 varied between, on the one hand, 0.89 metric tons in Africa, 1.17 metric tons in South America, 1.36 metric tons in Asia and 1.45 metric tons in the U.S.S.R.; on the other, 3.86 metric tons in the E.E.C. countries, and over 4 metric tons in the richest agricultural states of the U.S. Mid-West.

105. In 1976, 90 per cent of world exports of wheat and wheat flour was made up by five countries: the United States, Canada, Australia, France and Argentina.

106. In the United States, less than 150,000 farms out of 1.7 million, i.e. those with sales of over $100,000, accounted for more than 50 per cent of the total value of all grain sold. This ratio of concentration is substantially higher in grain exports (*US Census of Agriculture: Summary and State Data*, 1977, pp. 1–25).

CAPITALISM AS A SYSTEM
AND THE BOURGEOISIE AS A CLASS

One of the outstanding features of *Capital* Volume 3 is the way in which Marx ties together economic analysis and social analysis at the level of the system in its totality – i.e. at a higher level than he did in Volume 1, inside the factory (the process of production properly speaking). In Chapters 48 and 51, here, he shows how the reproduction of a specific form of division of the 'national income' (annually produced new value) between wages on the one hand, and profits, interests and rents on the other, automatically reproduces capitalist relations of production – i.e. the basic class relations and class inequality which define the system.

It is the greatest theoretical weakness of reformism, under whatever form it appears, not to understand this basic truth. Whether wages are high or low, whether 'indirect' wages (social security payments) are inexistent or extensive,[107] they *cannot* upset the basic class relations and class inequality on which the capitalist mode of production is founded. Wages *cannot* rise to the point where they substantially lower surplus-value (profits), without setting into motion a massive 'investment strike' by capitalism (hence a steep decline of capital accumulation), coupled with a frantic attempt to step up the replacement of living labour by machinery – both processes acting to halt and reverse the rise in wages, through the effects of massive unemployment (and cuts in public 'social' expenditure). The one thing it is

---

107. Today, 'indirect' or 'socialized' wages (i.e. social security benefits, etc.) are quite a substantial part of the total reproduction costs of labour-power – according to certain authors, up to 50 per cent, at least in Britain and France (see Ian Gough, *The Political Economy of the Welfare State*, London, 1979, p. 109; A. Capian, 'Réflexions sur les déterminants de la socialisation du capital variable', in *Issues*, 4, 1979). This does not, however, represent any 'vertical' re-distribution of national income in favour of wages and at the expense of profits, for it is compensated by huge deductions from gross wages in the form of taxes and social security contributions – deductions which also amount to roughly 50 per cent. Instead, what is occurring is a 'horizontal' re-distribution, in favour of certain sectors of the wage-earning class and at the expense of others. Capian gives the example of France, where this system works in favour of higher salary-earning and at the expense of lower wage-earning categories, the former having only 18.2 per cent of their gross money incomes deducted for social security contributions, whereas the latter's deductions rise to 31.5 per cent.

impossible to do with capitalists is to force them to invest or produce at a loss!

In addition, the very trend towards increased organic composition of capital, towards increased concentration of capital, towards a strong rise in the minimum requirements for founding new productive units in all branches of production, constantly consolidates monopoly ownership of the means of production by the bourgeoisie as a class, making it physically impossible for even the best-paid workers to save enough out of their wages to embark seriously upon an industrial enterprise of their own.[108] While this is less true in small retail trade and small service business (or in small-scale farming, during times of acute unemployment[109]), the overall trend is very clear. Wages tend to be spent over the whole life-span of the wage-earner. They cannot lead to any serious accumulation of capital.[110] So wages do not just reproduce labour-power: they also reproduce a special class under permanent economic compulsion to sell its labour-power. Likewise, private appropriation of surplus-value does not just lead to accumulation of capital: it also reproduces a social class which can monopolize the means of production and, therefore, oblige the wage-earners continuously to sell their labour-power to the owners of capital; continuously to produce surplus labour, surplus-value and profits for the exclusive benefit of the latter.

To be sure, the two processes are not symmetrical. Even when real wages have a tendency to secular increase and 'workers' savings' become a large-scale phenomenon, these do not free the individual wage-earner from his proletarian condition; in other

108. Venture capital is generally small capital (as Marx himself observes here, on pp. 371–2 below) and generally condemned to bankruptcy or absorption before large businesses take over the innovations tried out by the adventurers. But even this venture capital is obviously out of range for normal wage-earners receiving the average wage (even that of a highly skilled worker).

109. In periods of large-scale unemployment, there is a small trickle of wage-earners again becoming subsistence farmers, especially in those advanced capitalist countries where there is abandoned agricultural land with more or less free access, on which, though it is impossible to produce the average rate of profit, it is possible to achieve production of use-values higher than the amount which could be purchased with unemployment compensation.

110. One has, of course, to include in the analysis the fact that, with the growth of mass production in more and more branches of industry, workers' 'induced needs' – and the number of goods and services which the average social wage is supposed to buy – tend to increase, as one of the by-products of capital accumulation itself.

words, they do not ensure him a high enough durable income (money reserve) to enable him to go into business for himself. They just represent 'deferred consumption', i.e. an additional insurance fund, over and above socialized 'indirect wages' (social security), to complement his reduced income in times of sickness, unemployment or retirement, or to defray such extra family expenditures as might be incurred for the better education or weddings of his children, etc. In addition, there exists under late capitalism a powerful incentive for the capitalist class to deprive workers of the right to dispose of these savings freely, or even to expropriate them *tout court* – inflation being only the mildest of the various forms of partial or total expropriation to which it resorts.[111]

On the other hand, the fact that all sectors of the bourgeois class have access to a fraction of the sum-total of socially produced surplus-value, even if their own capital is not directly used by themselves in surplus-value-producing endeavours, does not at all imply that this access is equal for every capitalist. Not only does the appearance of monopolies operate in the opposite direction. The law of concentration and centralization of capital acts even more powerfully to this effect. Stepped-up competition eliminates many more middle and large-scale capitalists (not to speak of petty ones) than upper layers of the wage-earning class succeed in breaking through the barrier to becoming small independent entrepreneurs in service industry, retail trade or agriculture.

The sum-total of the entire social evolution is a constant increase in that part of the population which is composed of wage-earners; a constant decline in that part which is composed of independent businessmen.[112] Not one of Marx's predictions has been more thoroughly confirmed by empirical evidence (repeated claims to the contrary notwithstanding[113]) than that which identified a long-term trend to class polarization under

111. In the case of the pension funds 'owned' by U.S. labour unions, but completely managed by the large banks, this *de facto* expropriation is already far advanced. It was completed in Nazi Germany.

112. In the United States, wage-earners as part of the total active population increased from 62 per cent in 1880 to 71 per cent in 1910, 78.2 per cent in 1940 and 89.9 per cent in 1970.

113. For example, Arnold Künzli, 'Für eine kopernikanische Wende des Sozialismus', in *Für Robert Havemann: ein Marxist in der DDR*, Munich, 1980.

capitalism. Marx was able to make that sweeping historical forecast, so strongly denied by almost all his contemporaries, because, basing himself on the laws of motion of capitalism, he understood that the division of 'net value' (value added) into wages and surplus-value *had* to lead, under the pressure of capitalist competition, to more and more wage-earners being unable to become capitalists and fewer and fewer capitalists being able to remain capitalists.

Capitalist relations of distribution, rooted in capitalist relations of production but by no means identical with them,[114] constantly reproduce these relations of production. But they also reproduce the basic material preconditions of class struggle and class solidarity, both in the sphere of distribution (i.e. on the market) and in the sphere of production (in the factory):

(1) The fact that the individual worker has no economic resources on which he can fall back, that he cannot 'wait' till its market price (the offered wage) goes up before selling his labour-power, makes collective organization of such sales by workers – i.e. unionization and collective bargaining – a powerful inbuilt tendency under capitalism, reproducing itself universally wherever wage-labour appears.

(2) The fact that the fluctuations of the reserve army of labour, in the last analysis, regulate the fluctuations of real wages creates a strong inbuilt interest for the mass of wage-earners as such to ensure high levels of employment, in other words to demand elementary economic policies *at the level of the economy as a whole* which tend to limit unemployment.[115]

(3) The fact that *surplus labour* is the very essence of surplus-value and profit (more exactly of RIP: Rents, Interests and Profits) creates an equally strong inbuilt tendency in the working class to challenge speed-ups, reorganizations and forms of control of the labour process which tend to increase the mass of surplus

114. Bourgeois norms of distribution remain operative in the transition period between capitalism and socialism, as well as in the first phase of communism (socialism). See Karl Marx, 'Critique of the Gotha Programme', in *The First International and After*, Pelican Marx Library, London, 1974, p. 346; Leon Trotsky, *The Revolution Betrayed*, New York, 1965, pp. 53–5.

115. This is at least the *long-term* interest of *all* wage-earners. Inasmuch as labour markets are partially fragmented, nationally and sectorally, i.e. since labour mobility is not unlimited, *short-term* interests of relatively privileged parts of the working class might conflict with long-term ones.

labour and its degrading, de-humanizing effects upon the individual worker as well as upon whole sections of the working
class.[116]

(4) Finally, the fact that capital *can and must* periodically challenge
all the partial conquests of the workers, both in the sphere of
distribution (increases in wages and social-security payments; free
collective bargaining, trade-union rights and the unrestricted right
to strike) and in the sphere of production (reduction of the working week and working day; forms of control over the rhythm of
work and the organization of the labour process; union rights
inside the work-place in general, etc.), especially through ruthless
revolutions in technology,[117] at least periodically teaches the most
intelligent, energetic and militant parts of the working class that
(to paraphrase Marx) it is not enough to fight for higher wages, it
is also necessary to fight for the abolition of the wage system.[118]

Conversely, the fact that, under the capitalist mode of production, ownership of any substantial quantity of money (the starting
level differing, of course, from period to period and from country
to country) automatically transforms that money into money
capital – which not only automatically partakes in the general
distribution of total socially produced surplus-value (through
acquiring the average rate of interest) but is also thus transformed
potentially into additional productive capital (money capital put
at the disposal of 'functioning' capitalists in the productive
sectors) – creates a powerful class solidarity among all owners of
capital in the common exploitation of all wage-earners as a class;
in other words, creates the material basis of bourgeois class
solidarity and class consciousness.[119]

In this sense, all capitalists have a common interest in opposing
'excessive' wage increases; in supporting all measures which
increase the mass of profits; in supporting speed-up practices and
'rationalization investments'; and in generalizing these through-

116. See, for example, Harry Braverman, *Labor and Monopoly Capital*,
New York, 1974, passim.

117. For instance, the long-term power of one of the most powerful and
militant craft unions capitalism has known in the industrialized countries, the
printers' union, has been severely undercut by the electronic composition
revolution in the printing trade.

118. Karl Marx, 'Wages, Price and Profit', in Marx/Engels, *Selected
Works in One Volume*, London, 1970, p. 226.

119. See below, pp. 270 and 300.

out industry and enterprises in general.[120] They have a common interest in trying to prevent the rise of militant unionism; or, when this becomes impossible, in trying to limit or curtail trade-union rights, to establish various forms of state control over trade unions, etc. – whatever their differences may be as to the tactics, forms, tempo or extent of such policies.

Likewise, the very nature of private ownership of capital and capitalist competition, through the mediation of each capitalist firm searching to maximize its own profit (i.e. striving for surplus profits over and above the average rate of profit), creates the mechanisms through which the general laws of motion of the system impose themselves. By this very fact, through elimination of the weakest capitalist firms, it ensures a temporary successful reversal of the tendency of the rate of profit to decline. Each capitalist working for his own individual interest thus, in so doing, ensures the long-term reproduction, consolidation and expansion of the capitalist system as a whole.

In the same way, the attempts of capitalists to increase the amount of surplus labour extracted from their own labour-force – by constantly striving to increase the productivity of labour, to organize mass production of an increasing number of commodities, and thereby to lower the value (expressed in gold prices) of all commodities – tend to create a collective interest of the bourgeois class in not limiting mass consumption (except in the initial stages of capitalist industrialization). This helps to counteract the difficulties of realizing the value (surplus-value) embodied in the constantly rising mountain of finished goods which inevitably accompanies enlarged reproduction and the accumulation of capital, in spite of the accompanying tendency towards increasing exploitation of productive wage-labour (towards a historically rising rate of surplus-value). This creates a basic class interest of the bourgeoisie in 'normal' rather than 'abnormal' conditions of

120. This is true not only for productive labour as such, but also for wage-labour employed by commercial and banking capital, etc. While this labour does not directly produce surplus-value, it enables capital invested in these spheres to appropriate part of surplus-value produced in the productive sectors. Industrialists accept this deduction, because it enables them to economize their own capital and increases the production of surplus-value as the result of a more rapid rotation of their capital. At the same time, however, they are interested in reducing to the utmost these 'circulation costs', which they understand to be precisely a deduction from their own profits. (See below, p. 413.)

exploitation, including whenever possible rising real wages and elementary social legislation, in order to defuse the explosive character of the class struggle. Direct repression designed to discipline the working class is used only under exceptional circumstances, in grave structural crises (whether economic, political or a combination of both).

Again, the two processes just outlined, whereby a self-conscious working class and a self-conscious bourgeois class are constituted as a direct product of the inner mechanisms of the capitalist mode of production, are not symmetrical. In spite of all the inherent segmentations of the working class – all the constantly recurring phenomena of division along craft, national, sex, generational, etc. lines – there are no inbuilt structural obstacles to the overall class solidarity of workers under capitalism. There are only different levels of consciousness, which make the conquest of that overall class solidarity more or less difficult, more or less uneven in time and space.

The same is not true of bourgeois class solidarity. In periods of prosperity, when their struggles are essentially for larger or smaller shares of an increasing mass of profits, class solidarity easily asserts itself among capitalists. In periods of crisis, however, competition has to take a much more savage form, since for each individual capitalist it is no longer a question of getting more or less profit, but one of his survival as a capitalist.[121] So there are instances of acute crisis of the system in which no economic or political solidarity *can* assert itself among the capitalist class; in which, even in the face of the gravest collective danger for the system as a whole, sectional or individual interests will prevail over collective, class ones.[122]

Of course, what I have just said applies to inter-capitalist competition, not to the class struggle between Capital and Labour as such, in which, by contrast, the graver the socio-political crisis, the more sharply ruling-class solidarity will assert itself. But the fundamental asymmetry of economic class solidarity within, respectively, the capital-owning and the wage-earning class has to be stressed. It is, in the last analysis, structurally connected with the basically different relations of capitalists and wage-earners

121. See below, p. 361.
122. This is true internationally even more than nationally. Imperialist wars are the extreme expression of this trend.

towards private property and competition. Private property and competition are built into the very nature of the capitalist class. Competition among wage-earners, however, is imposed upon them from outside, not structurally inherent in the very nature of the class. On the contrary, wage-earners normally and instinctively strive towards collective cooperation and solidarity.[123] Hence, to whatever extent competition among themselves is periodically reproduced, especially in times of economic crisis or after major social or political defeats, it can always be overcome by subsequent efforts to organize and to raise class consciousness assisted by the very advances of capital accumulation itself.

In Part Seven of Volume 3, Marx pays great attention to the mystifying appearance of revenues 'produced' by different 'factors of production': land, labour and capital. In our day, this mystification has been extended through the quest for growth rates or income accretions 'produced' by scientific progress or even by higher education.[124] In and of itself, 'science' produces neither value nor income. The results of scientific research, incorporated into new forms of machinery and new forms of labour organization, increase productivity of labour and thus undoubtedly contribute to the increase of material wealth. But this is something quite different from the production of value or income. What these formulas mystify is the fact that, under capitalism, private ownership of the means of production and the transformation of manual and intellectual labour – including scientifically creative labour – enable the capitalist (the capitalist firm) to incorporate into the total value produced in the course of the commodity-producing process the results of the cooperation, inventiveness and skill of all manpower employed. And this occurs essentially in the form of surplus-value, since the results in question do not directly change the reproduction costs of labour-power, which alone represent necessary labour (that part of value added which does not take the form of surplus-value). Qualities of labour thus appear as qualities separate and apart from labour:

123. This is rooted in the very process of production under large-scale industry, based upon cooperative labour organization.

124. See the two volumes of readings edited by Mark Blaug, *Economics of Education*, London, 1968 and 1969, which contain items with such expressive titles as 'Investment in Human Capital', 'Rates of Return to Investment in Schooling', 'Rate of Return on Investment in Education', 'The Productivity of Universities', and so on.

as either qualities of 'capital' (which is represented as a mass of things, instruments, machinery and other means of production) or qualities of 'science' (which is again separated from labour as some pure product of the brain).

For Marx, *scientific labour* is the very essence of 'general labour', i.e. creative labour developing new discoveries and inventions. But like collective (socialized) labour, it is indissociably related to the process of cooperation, of many manual and intellectual workers working together: 'These savings in the use of fixed capital, as we already said, are the result of the way the conditions of labour have been applied on a large scale. In short, the way in which they serve as conditions of directly social, socialized labour, of direct cooperation within the production process. This is firstly the only condition on which mechanical and chemical discoveries can be applied without increasing the price of commodities, and this is always the *sine qua non*. Next, it is only with production on a large scale that we can have the economy that arises from productive consumption in common. Finally, however, it is only the experience of the combined worker that discovers and demonstrates how inventions already made can most simply be developed, how to overcome the practical frictions that arise in putting the theory into practice – its application to the production process, and so on. We must distinguish here, incidentally, between universal labour and communal labour . . . Universal labour is all scientific work, all discovery and invention. It is brought about partly by the cooperation of men now living, but partly also by building on earlier work. Communal labour, however, simply involves the direct cooperation of individuals.'[125]

THE DESTINY OF CAPITALISM

Does *Capital* contain a theory of the final and inevitable downfall of the capitalist mode of production? Is the answer to this query to be found in Volume 3, and specifically in Marx's determination of the tendency for the average rate of profit to decline? Do the laws of motion of the capitalist mode of production imply that the system cannot forever survive its inner contradictions? These questions have been asked ever since *Capital* first appeared, by people supporting Marx's theories as well as by his opponents.

125. See below, pp. 198–9.

The so-called 'collapse controversy' has played a crucial role both in the history of Marxist theory after Marx and in the history of the international labour movement influenced by Marx's (or Marxist) ideas.

The initial position defended by 'orthodox' Marxists inside the Second International was cautious but nevertheless clear: the system would in the end collapse through a general sharpening of *all* its internal contradictions. Engels, by and large, supported this view.[126] It could undoubtedly base itself upon a number of passages from *Capital* (though, it is true, from Volume 1 rather than Volume 3).[127] Its main merit was to integrate the class struggle, the growth of the labour movement and of working-class consciousness, into overall perspectives regarding the final destiny of the capitalist system.

It should be stressed, however, that the question of whether capitalism can survive indefinitely or is doomed to collapse is not to be confused with the notion of its inevitable replacement by a *higher* form of social organization, i.e. with the inevitability of socialism. It is quite possible to postulate the inevitable collapse of capitalism without postulating the inevitable victory of socialism. Indeed, rather early in the history of revolutionary Marxism, the two were conceptually separated in a radical fashion, the destiny of capitalism being formulated in the form of a dilemma: the system cannot survive, but may give way either to socialism or to barbarism.[128]

While both Marx and Engels – and especially the older Engels, faced with the tremendous and apparently irresistible rise of the modern labour movement – exhibited a robust optimism as to the

126. See, for example, the Erfurt Programme of the German Social-Democratic Party, supervised by Engels. In August Bebel's famous Reichstag speech on 3 February 1893, highly praised by Engels, the collapse of capitalism was presented as resulting from the interaction of the decline of the middle classes, the growing concentration and centralization of capital, growing class polarization between capital and wage-labour, growing class contradictions, successive grave economic crises, growing dangers of war, growing threats against political democracy and growing class consciousness of the proletariat.

127. See Marx, *Capital* Volume 1, op. cit., pp. 929–30. Thus Lucio Colletti is wrong to reduce Marx's 'collapse theory' simply to the theory of the tendency of the average rate of profit to decline: see his Introduction to L. Colletti (ed.), *Il futuro del capitalismo, crollo o sviluppo?*, Bari, 1970, p. ci.

128. Rosa Luxemburg, 'What Does the Spartakusbund Want?', in R. Looker (ed.), *Rosa Luxemburg: Selected Political Writings*, London, 1972, p. 275.

future of socialism, they were always careful, when the question was posed at its most general, abstract, historical level, to reject any idea of historical inevitable sequences of social organization (modes of production). On a number of occasions, they pointed out that the passage from one mode of production to another depended upon the outcome of concrete class struggles, which might end either with the victory of the more progressive, revolutionary class, or in the mutual destruction of both the old ruling class and its revolutionary adversary and in a protracted decadence of society.

The initial position was challenged by the so-called revisionists around the German Eduard Bernstein, who denied that there was any inherent tendency for the inner contradictions of the capitalist mode of production to sharpen. They postulated, on the contrary, that these contradictions would decrease. They did not, however, conclude from this that capitalism would survive for ever, but rather believed that it would fade away gradually, so that there was no need to overthrow it by revolutionary means.[129] Most of the later variants of gradualism and reformism (including, in recent years, Euro-communism) have their common roots in Bernstein's writings, which are remarkable for the clear and consistent way in which they pose the problem[130] – the only trouble being that their predictions proved to be wrong.

Far from leading to permanent peace, capitalism has led to two world wars and risks a third one, suicidal for the whole of mankind. Far from its leading to an ever-smoother functioning of the international capitalist economy, we have witnessed the catastrophic crises of 1920–21, 1929–32 and 1938, followed, after the post-Second World War boom, by a new long slump starting in the late sixties or early seventies. And far from ever-increasing freedom and democracy, the twentieth century has seen much greater repression and far bloodier dictatorships than anything Marx, Engels or other nineteenth-century socialists ever witnessed or could have imagined in their day.

It is in this context that followers of Marx attempted to formulate in a more rigorous way the probable destiny of capitalism. Rosa Luxemburg was the first to try to elaborate, on a strictly

129. See, above all, Bernstein's own *Evolutionary Socialism*, New York, 1961.
130. See, as a typical example, Anthony Crosland, *The Future of Socialism*, London, 1956.

scientific basis, a theory of inevitable collapse of the capitalist mode of production. In her *The Accumulation of Capital*, she tried to show that enlarged reproduction, with full realization of surplus-value produced during the process of production properly speaking, was impossible under 'pure' capitalism. That mode of production, therefore, had an inherent tendency to expand into a non-capitalist milieu, i.e. to gobble up the large areas of petty commodity production still surviving inside the capitalist metropolis and to expand continuously towards the non-capitalist periphery, i.e. the colonial and semi-colonial countries. This expansion – including its most radical forms: contemporary colonialism and murderous colonial wars; imperialism and imperialist wars – was indispensable for the survival of the system. If and when that non-capitalist milieu disappeared, the system would collapse, since it would be unable fully to realize surplus-value. But Luxemburg made it clear that, long before that final moment, the simple consequences of these increasingly violent forms of expansion, as well as the consequences of the gradual shrinking of the non-capitalist milieu, would sharpen the inner contradictions of the system to the point of explosion, thereby preparing its revolutionary overthrow.[131]

I have already discussed, in the Introduction to Volume 2 of *Capital* (as well as in *Late Capitalism*), the strengths and weaknesses of Luxemburg's *The Accumulation of Capital*.[132] Here, I only wish to deal with a methodological objection which has been raised against Luxemburg's theory of collapse – and subsequently against a number of other such theories. Critics have alleged that, by basing the perspective of inevitable collapse of the capitalist mode of production exclusively on the system's laws of motion, its inner economic mechanism, Luxemburg was moving back towards 'economism'; that this was a regression from the way in which Marx and Engels themselves, and their first disciples, always integrated economic laws and movements with the class struggle, in order to arrive at overall historical projections and perspectives.[133]

131. Rosa Luxemburg, *The Accumulation of Capital*, London, 1963, passim.
132. Ernest Mandel, Introduction to *Capital* Volume 2, Pelican Marx Library, London, 1978, pp. 62 ff.
133. This argument was first directed against Luxemburg by Bukharin (see *Imperialism and the Accumulation of Capital*, op. cit., p. 115) and by Henryk

This objection, however, is unjustified. While it is true that the contemporary history of capitalism, indeed the history of any mode of production in any epoch, cannot be satisfactorily explained if the class struggle (and especially its outcome after certain decisive battles) is not treated as a partially autonomous factor, it is likewise true that the whole meaning of Marxism disappears if this partial autonomy is transformed into an absolute one. It is precisely the merit of Luxemburg, as well as of several of her subsequent antagonists in the 'collapse controversy', to have *related* the ups and downs of the class struggle to the inner laws of motion of the system. If one were to assume that either the infinite adaptability of the capitalist system, or the political astuteness of the bourgeoisie, or the inability of the proletariat to raise its consciousness to sufficient levels (not to speak of the alleged growing 'integration' of the working class into bourgeois society), could, in the long run and for an undefined length of time, neutralize or reverse that system's inner laws of motion and intrinsic contradictions, i.e. prevent them from asserting themselves, then the only scientifically correct conclusion would be that these laws of motion do not correspond to the system's essence: in other words, that Marx was basically mistaken when he thought he had discovered that essence. (This is something different, of course, from the possibility of *temporary* ups and downs in the sharpening of contradictions, which are not only possible but even inevitable, as Marx himself pointed out in his treatment of the tendency for the average rate of profit to decline.)

A second attempt to produce a scientifically rigorous 'collapse theory' (though in the event it was less rigorous, it should be said, than Luxemburg's) was made during and immediately after the First World War by certain leading radical Marxist economists who greatly influenced Lenin when he was drafting his *Imperialism, the Highest Stage of Capitalism*. The most prominent of these were the Russian Nikolai Bukharin and the Hungarian Eugen Varga.[134] While avoiding any 'mono-causal' reduction of the

Grossmann (*Das Akkumulations- und Zusammenbruchsgesetz des kapitalistischen Systems*, Frankfurt, 1967, p. 22), who both accused her of 'mechanical' economic determinism. Claudio Napoleoni formulates a similar reproach in Colletti (ed.), op. cit., pp. lii–liii.

134. Bukharin, op. cit., pp. 113–25; Eugen Varga, *Die Niedergangsperiode des Kapitalismus*, Hamburg, 1922, pp. 7–14.

problem to a single decisive factor, these authors formulated the hypothesis that capitalism had entered an irreversible period of historical decline, resulting from a combined manifestation of all its sharpened contradictions: reduction of markets; decline of. world trade; decline of the international division of labour; decline of money economy, and even a partial reversion to barter and pre-capitalist forms of production in capitalist countries; decline of material production; collapse of the credit system; absolute decline in the standard of living of the workers; recurrent wars and civil wars; recurrent revolutionary explosions and victorious socialist revolutions.

While this analysis may offer a relatively convincing description and explanation of what actually occurred in 1914 (or even 1912)– 1921 and again in 1930–40 (or even in certain parts of the world in 1945–8), it gets into serious trouble once confronted with post-Second World War developments in the international capitalist economy. Tending to theoretical eclecticism, it lacks the deeper rigour needed to tie all these various developments to the basic laws of motion of the system. In particular, it avoids any discussion of the reasons why the countervailing factors, enumerated by Marx as able temporarily to neutralize the tendency for the average rate of profit to fall, would definitely cease to be effective in the epoch of capitalist decline; why the huge devalorization and destruction of capital which occurred in the 1929–32 crisis and the Second World War, coupled with a huge upsurge in the rate of surplus-value (as a result both of catastrophic working-class defeats and of a powerful increase in the productivity of labour in department II, as a result of a new technological revolution), could not lead to a new upsurge in the productive forces – inevitably ending in a new reassertion of sharpened contradictions of the system.[135]

One offshoot of the Bukharin–Varga theory of the irreversible decline of the capitalist system since 1914 is the concept of 'general crisis of capitalism', in which the emphasis has become progressively shifted from the *inner* laws of motion of the system towards the *outside* challenges it is increasingly meeting as the

135. It is true that Varga took a more cautious attitude after the Second World War; however, this seems to represent a 'bridge' position on the way to the harmonicist conceptions of the theoreticians of 'state monopoly capitalism'. See *inter alia* his *Essais sur l'économie politique du capitalisme*, Moscow, 1967.

result of a chain of victorious socialist revolutions, which have led to a shrinking of the geographical area in which it can operate. In its initial form, the concept of a general crisis of capitalism – which originated from the victory of the October Revolution in Russia – still established an interrelation between that outside challenge and the ensuing sharpening of the system's inner contradictions.[136] But this has become less and less the case in later variants, especially the 'state monopoly capitalism' theory fully developed after the Second World War.

Here the 'basic' contradiction is clearly defined as that between the 'socialist camp' and the 'capitalist camp', and no longer as the increasingly explosive inner contradictions of the capitalist system itself. The paradox is even pushed to the point where Soviet authors seriously assert that, as a result of the 'competition between the two systems', capitalism is 'condemned' to continuous growth![137] In this way, the theory of collapse is 'dialectically' turned into its very opposite: the possibility for capitalism to survive for ever. The system's capacity to eliminate for an indefinite period the most serious effects of its inner contradictions is postulated – until such time as the economic, social and cultural superiority of the socialist camp finally asserts itself. It is hardly necessary to point out that this intellectual contortion is structurally related to the specific interests of the Soviet bureaucracy – both its attempts to maintain conditions of peaceful coexistence with international capitalism, and its concern to maintain the subordination of a large section of the international labour movement to its own diplomatic manoeuvres – and, as such, represents a typical phenomenon of ideological mystification.

A third – once again, more rigorous – attempt to theorize the inevitability of capitalism's collapse was offered in the late twenties by the Polish Marxist Henryk Grossmann. This was essentially a generalization – one could even say an extreme extrapolation – of Marx's law for the tendency of the average rate of profit to decline. Grossmann tried to prove that, in the long run, countervailing forces cannot prevent the law from asserting

136. See, for example, Eugen Varga, *Grundfragen der Ökonomik und Politik des Imperialismus nach dem zweiten Weltkrieg*, Berlin, 1955.

137. See, for example, N. Inosemzev, *Der heutige Kapitalismus*, Berlin, 1973, pp. 59, 94–5, 106–7. For a more general critique of the theory of 'state monopoly capitalism', see Ernest Mandel, *Late Capitalism*, op. cit., pp. 513–22; and Jacques Valier, *Le PCF et le capitalisme monopoliste d'état*, Paris, 1976.

itself *with increasing strength* – up to the point where *all* accumulated capital tends to be unable to become valorized, i.e. to the point where the total mass of surplus-value cannot ensure sufficient accumulation, even if the subsistence of the capitalist class itself falls to zero.[138] There are many weaknesses in this theory, which have been pointed out by a number of critics.[139] The main one is that Grossmann does not really *prove* that *all* the countervailing forces gradually lose their capacity to neutralize the declining rate of profit. He especially underestimates the effects of massive devalorization (and destruction) of capital, which has historically proven to be much larger in scope than he visualizes (his book was finished before the 1929–32 crisis unfolded to its full depth – and, of course, before the frightful destruction of the Second World War).

Therefore, Grossmann's somewhat arbitrary numerical starting-point – the reproduction schemas which Otto Bauer worked out in his reply to Luxemburg's *The Accumulation of Capital*[140] – leads to results which ignore the effects of devalorization cycles of capital. Such a hypothesis is untenable in the light of the real history of capitalism (which is a crisis-ridden history that has witnessed twenty-one crises of overproduction since the establishment of the world market for industrial goods). Marx explicitly points out this devalorization-of-capital function of capitalist crises in Chapter 15 of Volume 3 of *Capital*. Hence, one can only consider Grossmann's successive figures as representing not annual totals but averages for seven/ten-year cycles. Thus the final collapse of the system is postponed till the twenty-second century (after thirty-seven seven/ten-year cycles). If the initial proportions between department I and department II were more realistic – and they should have been, in the light of the real history of the capitalist mode of production which, in the 1920s, had nowhere even approached a situation in which two-thirds of current production occurred in department I – the postponement of the 'collapse' would be even more pronounced: it would occur only after fifty or sixty cycles, i.e. after 400 or 500 years. Inadvertently, Gross-

138. Grossmann, op. cit. (original edition Leipzig, 1929).

139. The most systematic critiques of Grossmann are to be found in Fritz Sternberg, *Eine Umwälzung der Wissenschaft?*, Berlin, 1930; and Nathalia Moszkowska, *Zur Kritik Moderner Krisentheorien*, Prague, 1935.

140. Otto Bauer, 'Die Akkumulation des Kapitals', in *Die Neue Zeit*, Vol. 31 (1913), part 1.

mann, obsessed by his mono-causal explanation for the inevitability of collapse, was led to demonstrate precisely the opposite of what he intended: the extreme longevity rather than the final collapse of the system, as a function of its inner laws of motion.

One might be tempted to treat the Baran/Sweezy theory of the growing difficulty of 'surplus realization' by monopoly capitalism as either a variant of Luxemburg's collapse theory or a fourth distinct collapse theory of its own.[141] This, however, is not the case, since Baran and Sweezy, while underlining the growing *difficulties* for 'surplus realization', at the same time stress the system's capacity to integrate the working class socially and thereby ensure its perpetuity – albeit under conditions of permanent quasi-stagnation – rather than its inevitable collapse. Like the more extreme proponents of the 'state monopoly capitalism' theory, these authors have to project the system's real enemies outside the system itself: third-world peasants; marginalized super-exploited layers; and so on. But they are nowhere able to demonstrate that these social forces anywhere have a potential social and economic strength comparable to that of the modern proletariat. Since such forces are not vital to the system's basic productive relations, they can be variously ignored, or integrated, or crushed, without making the system incapable of functioning.[142] So this is not really a 'collapse of capitalism' theory at all.

As in the case of the mono-causal theories of crisis, there are obviously correct elements in each of the three versions of collapse theory outlined above. These have to be tied together in order to furnish a coherent theory of the inevitable collapse of capitalism, consistent with all the inner laws of motion and contradictions of that mode of production, as unfolded by Marx's analysis in *Capital*.

One element in Grossmann's analysis is important, if not de-

141. Baran and Sweezy, op. cit., Chapters 3 and 4. There is a clear filiation between the Baran/Sweezy concept of capitalism tending towards economic stagnation, and the theories of neo-Keynesian (and sometimes semi-Marxist) authors like Michael Kalecki (*Studies in Economic Dynamics*, London, 1943; *Essays in the Theory of Economic Fluctuations*, London, 1939), J. Steindl (*Maturity and Stagnation in American Capitalism*, Oxford, 1952) or Joan Robinson.

142. It is no accident that most 'third-worldist' Marxists tend to exaggerate the ability of capitalism to 'restructure' itself on a world scale by purely economic processes, in order to overcome the current depression of the nineteen-seventies and eighties.

cisive, as the starting-point for such a synthesis: this is the point in time when, in addition to the tendency of the *rate* of surplus-value to decline, the *mass* of surplus-value ceases to grow and begins to decline – first gradually, then permanently. This would obviously be the most serious blow to a continuous process of capitalist accumulation. Grossmann, however, fails to point out the concrete content of such an incipient decline in surplus-value production, which I have tried to specify in *Late Capitalism*: a level of mechanization, of semi-automation – let us say, of spreading full automation – of a growing number of branches of output, in which the total input of productive labour-hours starts to decline, hence in which total value-production declines.

This does not automatically imply an *immediate* decline in the absolute mass of surplus-value, since the big increase in productivity of labour inherent in 'robotism' can reduce necessary labour-time proportionally to the reduction of absolute value production. In the long run, however, this is impossible without more and more severe reductions even in real wages. After a certain point, moreover, it becomes physically impossible. So the extension of automation beyond a given ceiling leads, inevitably, first to a reduction in the total volume of value produced, then to a reduction in the total volume of surplus-value produced. This in turn unleashes a fourfold combined 'collapse crisis': a huge crisis of decline in the rate of profit; a huge crisis of realization (the increase in the productivity of labour implied by robotism expands the mass of use-values produced in an even higher ratio than it reduces real wages, and a growing proportion of these use-values becomes unsaleable); a huge social crisis;[143] and a huge crisis of 'reconversion' (in other words, of capitalism's capacity to adapt) through devalorization – the *specific forms* of capital destruction threatening not only the survival of human civilization but even the physical survival of mankind or of life on our planet.[144]

143. See below, p. 372: 'A development in the productive forces that would reduce the absolute number of workers, and actually enable the country to accomplish its entire production in a shorter period of time, would produce a revolution, since it would put the majority of the population out of action.'

144. I cannot deal here with the problem of 'limits of growth', which some people have argued are inherent not in the capitalist mode of production as such but in large-scale industrial production itself, seen as inevitably depleting natural resources. Marx was very much aware of this problem (see below, pp. 949–50; and *Capital* Volume 1, op. cit., pp. 636–8). He saw it, however, as a

A way out is obviously possible, via the massive transformation of 'services' into commodity-producing branches (which add to total value production). Indeed, it is already starting in such key services as health, education, banking and public administration. This indicates how wrong it is to speak of late capitalism as a post-industrial society.[145] On the contrary, we are only now entering the age of full industrialization of a whole series of branches which have escaped that process up to now. But this only postpones the time of reckoning. For the industrialization of service sectors reproduces there, after a certain transition period, the very same processes of massive mechanization, semi-automation and full automation for which micro-processors have already provided the necessary technical tools (the same applies, incidentally, to the process of industrialization of underdeveloped countries as a way out of the structural crisis). So it is impossible to see how capitalism can escape its final fate: economic collapse.

In addition, with the development of semi-automation and automation, a new significant reversal occurs of the revolution constantly produced by capitalism in labour organization and the actual labour process. A massive reintroduction of intellectual labour into the process of production is inevitable, alongside an at least relative decline in the extreme parcellization of labour characteristic of Taylorism. The more wage-labour is employed for supervising functions and the maintenance of delicate and costly equipment, the more its own skill, level of culture and degree of involvement in the production process becomes an indispensable element of reproduction of capital. Hence, not only are the cooperative qualities of objectively socialized labour inside the factory developed to a higher degree. The consciousness of the workers that they are able to run factories instead of

---

by-product of the specific (and distorted) forms of technological development characteristic of capitalism, not as an inevitable product of the application of the natural sciences to production. This implies that the problem is soluble in a different social framework, without mankind having to forgo the advantages of freeing itself from uncreative mechanical labour. Some of the most acute non-Marxist critics of contemporary capitalist society from an ecological standpoint have come to similar conclusions: see, for example, Barry Commoner, *The Closing Circle*, London, 1972; Harry Rothman, *Murderous Providence*, London, 1972.

145. See, for instance, Daniel Bell, *The Coming of Post-Industrial Society*, New York, 1973.

capitalists or capitalist managers takes a giant leap forward. Thus the growing crisis of capitalist relations of production (both objectively and subjectively, i.e. in terms of their legitimacy in the eyes of the working class and of larger and larger sectors of the population as a whole), and the challenge which workers' struggles pose for these, become an integral part of the system's tendency towards collapse.

But it is evident that such a trend towards upgrading labour in productive sectors with the highest technological development must, of necessity, be accompanied by its very negation: a rise in mass unemployment, in the extent of marginalized sectors of the population, in the number of those who 'drop out' and of all those whom the 'final' development of capitalist technology expels from the process of production. This means only that the growing challenges to capitalist relations of production inside the factory are accompanied by growing challenges to all basic bourgeois relations and values in society as a whole, and these too constitute an important and periodically explosive element of the tendency of capitalism to final collapse.

As I said earlier, not necessarily of collapse in favour of a higher form of social organization or civilization. Precisely as a function of capitalism's very degeneration, phenomena of cultural decay, of retrogression in the fields of ideology and respect for human rights, multiply alongside the uninterrupted succession of multiform crises with which that degeneration will face us (has already faced us). Barbarism, as one possible result of the collapse of the system, is a much more concrete and precise perspective today than it was in the twenties and thirties. Even the horrors of Auschwitz and Hiroshima will appear mild compared to the horrors with which a continuous decay of the system will confront mankind. Under these circumstances, the struggle for a socialist outcome takes on the significance of a struggle for the very survival of human civilization and the human race. The proletariat, as Marx has shown, unites all the objective prerequisites for successfully conducting that struggle; today, that remains truer than ever. And it has at least the potential for acquiring the subjective prerequisites too, for a victory of world socialism. Whether that potential will actually be realized will depend, in the last analysis, upon the conscious efforts of organized revolutionary Marxists, integrating themselves with the spontaneous periodic striving of the proletariat to reorganize society along socialist lines, and leading it to precise goals: the conquest of state power and radical social revolution. I see no more reason to be pessimistic today as to the outcome of that endeavour than Marx was at the time he wrote *Capital*.

ERNEST MANDEL

NOTE

In this edition numbered footnotes are those of the original text. Those marked by asterisks, etc., are the translator's.

Preface

At long last I am able to make public this third volume of Marx's great work, which concludes the theoretical part. When I published the second volume in 1885, I believed that the third would most probably involve only technical difficulties, save perhaps for a few sections of particular importance. This was indeed the case, and yet I had no idea at that time of the difficulties that precisely these sections, the most important of all, had in store for me. Other unsuspected obstacles, too, contributed to the great delay in producing this volume.

First and foremost, I have been worried by persistent eye trouble, which has for years reduced the time I can spend working on written material to a minimum. Even now, I can only rarely take up my pen in artificial light. Then there were other tasks, which could not be pushed aside: new editions and translations of earlier works by Marx and myself, as well as revisions, prefaces and supplementary material, which often required further study, etc. Above all, here, I must mention the English edition of Volume 1, for whose text I bear ultimate responsibility and which therefore took a great deal of my time. Anyone who has at all followed the colossal increase in socialist literature over the last decade, and particularly the number of translations of earlier works by Marx and myself, will realize how fortunate I am that the number of languages in which I could be of use to translators, and thus could not refuse the task of revising their work, is very limited. But the growth of this literature was only a symptom of a corresponding expansion of the international working-class movement. And this, too, imposed new obligations on me. From the earliest days of our public activity, a sizable portion of the work of maintaining contact between the individual socialist and workers' movements in different lands has fallen to Marx and myself, and this work has grown in proportion to the strength of the movement as a whole. But while Marx took the main burden of this work, too, on himself, until his death, I have since had to deal with this ever mounting task alone. It is true that direct communication between the separate national parties has meanwhile become the norm, and is indeed becoming ever more so; yet my help is still required far more frequently than I would prefer, in the interests of my theoretical work. For someone like myself, however, who has been active in this movement for more than fifty years, the work arising therefrom is an inescapable duty and one that must immediately be fulfilled. Like the sixteenth century, our stirring age too sees pure theoreticians in the sphere of public affairs only on the side of reaction; and this very purity is the reason why these gentlemen are not genuine theorists at all but rather mere reactionary apologists.

The fact that I live in London means that in winter my party activity is largely limited to correspondence, but in summer it also requires a large number of personal meetings. And this circumstance, as well as the need to follow the progress of the movement in an ever growing number of countries and an even more rapidly growing number of journals, means that I can undertake the kind of work that brooks no interruption only in winter, particularly in the first three months of the year. After one is seventy, the Meynert fibres of association in the brain operate only with a certain annoying caution, and interruptions in difficult theoretical work can no longer be overcome as quickly or as easily as in the past. This has meant that the work of one winter, in so far as it was not fully completed, had for the most part to be started all over again the following winter, and this was the case in particular with Part Five, the most difficult part.

The reader will see from the information that follows that the editorial work for this volume was very different from that required for Volume 2. There was only one draft, and even this contained very major gaps. As a rule, the beginning of each section had been more or less carefully elaborated, and generally polished stylistically as well. But as the section in question went on, the draft would become ever more sketchy and fragmented, and contain ever more digressions on side issues that had emerged in the course of the investigation, the proper place for these being left to be settled later. The sentences, too, in which thoughts written down *in statu nascendi** found their expression, became ever

___
*Just as they arose.

longer and more intricate. At several points both handwriting and presentation betrayed only too clearly the onset and gradual progress of one of those bouts of illness, brought on by overwork, that made Marx's original work more and more difficult and eventually, at times, quite impossible. And no wonder! Between 1863 and 1867 Marx not only drafted the two last volumes of *Capital*,* as well as preparing the finished text of Volume 1 for publication, but he also undertook the gigantic work connected with the foundation and development of the International Working Men's Association. This is why we can already see in 1864 and 1865 the first signs of the illnesses that were responsible for Marx's failure to put the finishing touches to Volumes 2 and 3 himself.

My first job was to dictate the entire manuscript, which in its original form even I found it difficult to decipher, and have a readable copy made, something that already took a fair amount of time. Only when this was done could I embark on the actual editing. I confined this simply to what was most necessary, and wherever clarity permitted I retained the character of the original draft, not even deleting certain repetitions where these grasped the subject-matter from a different angle or expressed it in another way, as was Marx's custom. Wherever my alterations or additions are not simply editorial in character, or where I have had to take the factual material Marx provided and apply it to independent conclusions of my own, even if as far as possible in Marx's spirit, I have put the entire passage in pointed brackets and indicated it with my initials. Here and there my footnotes lack such brackets but wherever they are followed by my initials I bear responsibility for the whole note.†

As goes without saying in the case of a first draft, the manuscript contained several references to points that were to be developed later. These promises were not always kept. I have let the references

---

*Engels is evidently referring to Volumes 2 and 3 here, although in this same Preface he goes on to refer to *Theories of Surplus-Value* as Volume 4 of *Capital*, and Marx had always seen 'the history of the theory' as an integral concluding part of his *magnum opus*. The drafting of Volume 2, however, was rather more protracted than Engels presents it here; he himself gives the full details of this in his Preface to Volume 2 (Pelican edition, pp. 83 ff.).

†In the present edition, all Engels's substantial interpolations in the main body of the text are placed simply in parentheses and followed by his initials. This has not been done with his footnotes, but these too are always followed by his initials. Square brackets contain interpolations by the translator.

stand, as they show the author's intentions as far as future elaboration is concerned.

To come now to the details.

For Part One, the main manuscript could be used only with major limitations. The mathematical treatment of the relationship between rate of surplus-value and rate of profit (corresponding to our Chapter 3) was introduced in full right at the beginning, while the subject of our Chapter 1 appeared only later and in passing. Two attempted revisions came to the rescue here, each of eight folio sheets, though even these did not entirely fill the gap. The present Chapter 1 was put together from these drafts. Chapter 2 is from the main manuscript. For Chapter 3, there was not only a whole series of incomplete mathematical drafts but also an entire notebook from the 1870s, almost complete, which presented the relationship between the rate of surplus-value and the rate of profit in equations. My friend Samuel Moore, who also did the greater part of the English translation of Volume 1, took on the task of working up this notebook on my behalf, and as a former Cambridge mathematician he was far better equipped to do so. I prepared the present Chapter 3 from his *résumé*, occasionally also using the main manuscript. There was no more to Chapter 4 than the title. But since the point dealt with here is of decisive importance, i.e. the effect of the turnover on the profit rate, I elaborated it myself, which is why the entire chapter is placed here in brackets. It became apparent at this stage that the formula for the profit rate given in Chapter 3 needed a certain modification if it was to have general validity. From Chapter 5 onwards the main manuscript is the sole source for the remainder of this Part, even though here again a lot of transposition and supplementary material was necessary.

For the three following Parts I was able to keep almost completely to the original manuscript, apart from stylistic editing. Certain passages, generally to do with the effect of the turnover, had to be written in on the lines of the Chapter 4 I had introduced; these are also placed in brackets and bear my initials.

It was Part Five that presented the major difficulty, and this was also the most important subject in the entire book. Marx was engaged in elaborating precisely this Part, when he was attacked by one of the serious illnesses referred to above. Here, therefore, we did not have a finished draft, or even an outline plan to be filled in, but simply the beginning of an elaboration which petered out more than once in a disordered jumble of notes, comments and extract material. I sought at first to complete this Part by filling in the gaps and elaborating the fragments that were simply indicated, as I had more or less managed to do with Part One, so that it would at least contain, by and large, everything the author had intended to include. I made at least three attempts to do this, but failed on each occasion, and the time that was thereby lost is one of the main reasons for the delay in publication. I finally realized that this way was hopeless. I would have had to go through the whole of the literature in this field and would have produced something at the end of it that was not Marx's book. The only alternative was to make a fresh start, confine myself to arranging the material as best I could, and make only the most necessary alterations. In this way, the main work for this Part was finished early in 1893.

As far as the individual chapters are concerned, Chapters 21 to 24 were basically completed. For Chapters 25 and 26 the illustrative material had to be sorted out, and passages from other portions of the text had to be inserted. Chapters 27 and 29 could be reproduced almost directly from the manuscript, although Chapter 28 had to be partially rearranged. The real difficulty began with Chapter 30. From here on it was not only the illustrative material that needed correct arrangement, but also a train of thought that was interrupted continuously by digressions, asides, etc., and later pursued further in other places, often simply in passing. There then followed, in the manuscript, a long section headed 'The Confusion', consisting simply of extracts from the parliamentary reports on the crises of 1848 and 1857, in which the statements of some twenty-three businessmen and economic writers, particularly on the subjects of money and capital, the drain of gold, over-speculation, etc., were collected, with the occasional addition of brief humorous comments. Here, in one way or another, more or less all views then current on the relationship between money and capital were represented, and Marx intended to deal in a critical and satirical manner with the ensuing 'confusion' about what was money on the money market and what was capital. After several attempts, I came to the conclusion that it was impossible to produce this chapter; the material in question has been put in where the context provided the opportunity, especially the material with Marx's own comments.

What I have made into Chapter 32 then follows in more or less good order, but this is directly followed again by a new flood of extracts from the parliamentary reports, on all kinds of subjects relevant to this Part, mixed in with longer or shorter remarks by the author himself. Towards the end, the extracts and comments are focused more and more on the movement of the money metals and rates of exchange, and they close again with all kinds of supplementary remarks. The chapter on 'Pre-Capitalist Relations' (Chapter 36), however, was completed in full.

From all this material, including the 'Confusion' in so far as it had not already been utilized at earlier points, I compiled Chapters 33–35. This was only possible, of course, given substantial interpolations on my part, setting the passages in their context. In so far as these insertions are not simply formal in character, they are expressly indicated as my own. In this way I finally managed to introduce into the text *all* of the author's statements that were in any way pertinent to the matter in hand. All that remained was a small section of extracts that either simply repeated what had already been put forward elsewhere or dealt with points that the manuscript does not go into in any more detail.

The Part on ground-rent had been far more completely elaborated, even if not at all arranged, as is already apparent from the fact that Marx found it necessary in Chapter 43 (in the manuscript this is the last portion of the Part on rent) to recapitulate in brief the whole of this Part. This was extremely desirable as far as the editing of the text was concerned, in that in the manuscript Chapter 37 is followed by Chapters 45–47, before Chapters 38–44 eventually appear. Most work was required by the tables on the second form of differential rent, and by the discovery that the third case of this kind of rent that was to be treated in Chapter 43 was actually not analysed anywhere.

In the 1870s Marx embarked on entirely new and specific studies for this Part on ground-rent. For years he had been studying, in the original language, the statistical reports that the Russian 'reform' of 1861 had made unavoidable, as well as other publications on landed property which Russian friends put at his disposal as fully as anyone could desire. He made extracts from these and intended to make use of them in a new version of this section. Given the manifold diversity of forms of landed property and exploitation of the agricultural producers in Russia, this country was to play the same role in the Part on ground-rent as England had done for industrial wage-labour in Volume 1. Unfortunately Marx was never able to carry out this plan.

Part Seven, finally, was complete in the manuscript but only as a first draft, and its endlessly entangled sentences had first to be broken up before it was ready for publication. For the final chapter there is only the beginning. The intention here was to present the three great classes of developed capitalist society (landowners, capitalists and wage-labourers) that correspond to the three major forms of revenue (ground-rent, profit and wages), as well as the class struggle that is necessarily given with their very existence, as the actually present result of the capitalist period. Marx liked to leave conclusions of this kind for the final editing, shortly before printing, when the latest historical events would supply him, with unfailing regularity, with illustrations of his theoretical arguments, as topical as anyone could desire.

As also in Volume 2, quotations and illustrative material are significantly more sparse than in the first volume. Quotations from Volume 1 give the page numbers to the Second and Third Editions.* Where theoretical statements of earlier economists are referred to in the manuscript, it is generally only the name that is given, as the reference itself would be left to the final revision. I have naturally had to leave these as they were. As far as parliamentary reports are concerned, there are only four that are quoted,† though these are used quite substantially. They are:

(1) *Reports from Committees* (of the House of Commons), Vol. VIII, *Commercial Distress*, Vol. II, Part I, 1847–8, Minutes of Evidence. (Cited as *Commercial Distress, 1847–8*.)

(2) *Secret Committee of the House of Lords on Commercial Distress 1847, Report printed 1848, Evidence printed 1857* (because considered too compromising in 1848). (Cited as *C. D. 1848–57*).

(3) *Report: Bank Acts, 1857.* [(4)] Ditto, 1858. *Reports of the Committee of the House of Commons on the Effect of the Bank*

---

* As in our edition of Volume 2, all references to Volume 1 have been given simply the page numbers of the Pelican Marx Library edition, as well as the Chapter and Part divisions that are conventional to English editions of *Capital* Volume 1, and differ somewhat from the original (see p. 110, note, in Volume 1).

† This is not in fact correct, though these four are certainly the most frequently quoted.

Acts of 1844 and 1845. With evidence. (Cited as *B. A.* 1857 or 1858.)

I intend to start work on the fourth volume – the history of the surplus-value theory – as soon as I am at all able to do so.*

*

In the Preface to the second volume of *Capital* I had to settle accounts with certain gentlemen who were making a great to-do at that time about having allegedly discovered 'Marx's secret source in Rodbertus, as well as his superior predecessor'. I offered them the opportunity to show 'what Rodbertus's economics can accomplish' and asked them to explain, in particular, 'how an average rate of profit can and must come about, not only without violating the law of value, but precisely on the basis of this law' [Pelican edition, p. 102]. These same gentlemen, who were then proclaiming the brave Rodbertus to be an economic star of the first magnitude, for reasons either subjective or objective but generally quite other than scientific, have without exception failed to provide a single answer. Others, however, have taken the trouble to concern themselves with the problem.

In his critical review of Volume 2, Professor W. Lexis takes up the question, even if he does not try to give a direct solution (*Conrads Jahrbücher* [new series], Vol. 11, 5, 1885, pp. 452–65).†

'The solution of this contradiction' (between the Ricardo/Marx law of value and the equal average rate of profit), he says, 'is impossible if the various types of commodity are considered *separately* and their values are to be equal to their exchange-values and these in turn equal or proportionate to their prices.'

According to him, the solution is possible only if 'the measurement of value in terms of labour is abandoned so far as the individual commodities are concerned, and we focus merely on commodity production *as a whole* and its distribution between the entire classes of capitalists and workers ... The working class receives only a certain portion of the total product ... the other part, which accrues to the capitalists, forms what Marx calls the

---

*In fact, Engels did not live to commence this task, which was begun only after his death by Karl Kautsky. *Theories of Surplus-Value* was first published, in a rather unsatisfactory edition, in 1905.

† The *Jahrbücher für Nationalökonomie und Statistik* was a fortnightly magazine produced in Jena from 1863 to 1897. It was edited by Joseph Conrad from 1872 to 1890 and subsequently by Wilhelm Lexis.

surplus product and accordingly also ... the surplus-value. The members of the capitalist class now distribute this total surplus-value among themselves, *not* according to the number of workers that they each employ, but rather in proportion to the volume of capital applied by each, with the land and soil also being taken into account as a capital value.' Marx's ideal values, determined by the units of labour embodied in commodities, do not correspond to prices, but can 'be considered as the starting-point of a shift which leads to the actual prices. These latter are governed by the fact that capitals of equal size demand equal profits.' This means that some capitalists receive higher prices for their commodities than their ideal value, while others receive lower prices. 'But since the losses and gains in surplus-value cancel one another out within the capitalist class, the overall amount of surplus-value is the same as if all prices were proportionate to the commodities' ideal values.'

It is clear that the question is very far from being solved here. Yet it is correctly *posed*, by and large, even if in a loose and superficial way. And this is indeed more than we might expect from someone who, like this writer, takes a certain pride in representing himself as a 'vulgar economist'. It is even surprising, if we compare it with the achievements of other vulgar economists, which we shall go on to consider. This writer's vulgar economics, in fact, falls in a class of its own. Profit on capital *can* be derived in Marx's way, he agrees, but nothing *forces* us to this conception. On the contrary. Vulgar economics has an explanation of its own, which is allegedly at least more plausible:

'The capitalist sellers, i.e. the raw material producer, the manufacturer, the wholesale trader and the retailer, make a profit in their businesses by each selling dearer than he buys, i.e. by increasing the price that his commodities cost him by a certain percentage. Only the worker is unable to obtain an additional value of this kind, for his unfortunate position vis-à-vis the capitalist compels him to sell his labour for the same price that it costs him himself, i.e. for the means of subsistence that he needs ... these price additions thus retain their full significance vis-à-vis the workers as purchasers, and act so as to transfer a portion of the value of the total product towards the capitalist class.'

Now it does not need a great effort of thought to realize that this 'vulgar economic' explanation of profit on capital leads to the same result in practice as Marx's theory of surplus-value; that the workers, for Lexis, find themselves in exactly the same 'unfortunate position' vis-à-vis the capitalist as they do for Marx; that they are equally swindled, since every non-worker can sell above price, whereas the worker cannot do so; and that on the basis of this theory a vulgar socialism can be constructed which is similarly at least plausible, like that constructed in England on the basis of the Jevons–Menger theory of use-value and marginal utility. I would even suppose that if Mr George Bernard Shaw were acquainted with this theory of profit he would grasp hold of it with both hands, say farewell to Jevons and Karl Menger, and build the Fabian church of the future anew on this rock.*

In reality, however, this theory is simply a paraphrase of Marx's. What pays for all these price additions? Answer: the workers' 'overall product'. And this is because the commodity 'labour', or, as Marx would say, 'labour-power', has to be sold below its price. For if it is the common property of all commodities to be sold for more than their costs of production, with labour alone being the exception and being always sold at its cost of production, then in fact labour is sold below the price that is the rule in this vulgar-economic universe. The excess profit that accrues as a consequence to the capitalist or the capitalist class consists in, and can ultimately only come into being from, the fact that the worker, after reproducing the replacement for the price of his labour, has still to produce a further product for which he is not paid – surplus product, the product of unpaid labour, surplus-value. Lexis is extremely prudent in his choice of expression. He does not say outright that he shares this above conception. But if this is how he sees it, it is as clear as day that what we have here is not one of the usual run of vulgar economists, of whom Lexis himself says that every one is, in Marx's eyes, 'in the best of cases merely a hopeless dimwit', but a Marxist disguised as a vulgar economist. Whether this disguise is deliberate or not is a psychological question with no interest for us here. Anyone who might care to explore this question will perhaps also investigate how it was possible for a man as shrewd as Lexis undoubtedly is to have ever

*The Englishman William Stanley Jevons (1835–82) and the Austrian Carl Menger (1840–1921) are of course still honoured today in academic economics as co-founders of the 'marginalist' school. Shaw, as a leading member of the Fabian Society, was very much a part of the embryonic socialist movement in London in Engels's last years. Engels's verdict on Shaw: 'very talented and witty as a belletrist but absolutely useless as an economist and politician, although honest and not a careerist' (Engels to Kautsky, 4 September 1892; *Selected Correspondence*, London, 1965, p. 446).

defended, even if only once, such utter nonsense as bimetallism.

The first person who genuinely tried to answer the question was Dr Conrad Schmidt, in *Die Durchschnittsprofitrate auf Grundlage des Marx'schen Werthgesetzes* (Dietz, Stuttgart, 1889). Schmidt attempts to bring the details of market price formation into harmony both with the law of value and with the average rate of profit. What the industrial capitalist receives in his product is, firstly, the replacement for the capital he has advanced, and secondly, a surplus product which he has not paid for. In order to obtain this surplus product, however, he must advance his capital in production; i.e. he must apply a certain definite quantity of objectified labour in order to appropriate this surplus product. The capital he advances is therefore, for the capitalist, the quantity of objectified labour that is socially necessary to procure this surplus product. The same applies to every other industrial capitalist. Now, since according to the law of value products are exchanged in proportion to the labour socially necessary for their production, and since for the capitalist the labour necessary for the creation of his surplus product is precisely the stored-up, past labour in his capital, it therefore follows that surplus products are exchanged in proportion to the capitals required for their production and not according to the labour *actually* embodied in them. The share that falls to each unit of capital is therefore equal to the sum of all surplus-value produced, divided by the sum of the capitals to which this is related. In this conception, equal capitals yield equal profits in the same period of time, and this is achieved by adding the cost price of the surplus product calculated in this way, i.e. the average profit, to the cost price of the paid part of the product, and by selling both parts, paid and unpaid product, at this increased price. The average rate of profit is established even though the average prices of the various commodities are determined, as Schmidt holds, by the law of value.

Schmidt's construction is extremely ingenious, quite on Hegelian lines, but in common with the majority of Hegel's constructions, it is not correct. Whether the product is surplus or paid makes no difference; if the law of value is to hold *directly* for the average prices, both parts must be sold in proportion to the socially necessary labour required for their production and expended in it. Right from the outset, the law of value is directed against the notion derived from the capitalist mode of thought that the stored-up past labour of which capital consists is not only a definite sum of ready-made value but also, as a factor of production and profit formation, itself a source of further value on top of that which it already has; it maintains that this property is possessed only by living labour. It is well enough known that capitalists expect equal profits in proportion to the size of their capitals, and view their capital advance, therefore, as a kind of cost price for their profit. But if Schmidt uses this conception in order to bring the prices calculated in terms of the average profit rate into harmony with the law of value, he abandons the law of value itself, by making a conception totally at variance with this law into one of its co-determinant factors.

Either stored-up labour forms value alongside living labour. In which case the law of value does not hold.

Or it does not form value. In which case Schmidt's demonstration is incompatible with the law of value.

Schmidt was led astray in this way when he was already very close to the solution, because he believed he needed a mathematical formula, if possible, which would show the agreement between the average price of each commodity and the law of value. But even if here, so close to his goal, he took the wrong track, the remainder of his booklet shows the understanding with which he drew further conclusions from the first two volumes of *Capital*. He has the honour of having independently found the correct solution to the formerly unexplained tendency for the rate of profit to fall, which Marx provides in Part Three of Volume 3, as well as deriving commercial profit from industrial surplus-value and making a whole series of observations about interest and ground-rent in which points are anticipated which Marx develops in Parts Four and Five of this volume.

In a later work (*Neue Zeit*, 1892–3, nos. 3 and 4), Schmidt tries to solve the problem in another way. Here he argues that it is competition that establishes the average rate of profit, by making capital migrate from branches of production with below-average profit into branches in which above-average profit can be made. That competition is the great leveller of profits is no new discovery. But Schmidt now attempts to prove that this levelling of profits is identical with the reduction of the sale price of the excess commodities produced to the value which society can pay for them according to the law of value. Why this could not bring about the intended result is sufficiently clear from Marx's own discussions in this volume.

After Schmidt, Peter Fireman applied himself to the problem (*Conrads Jahrbücher*, 3rd series, Vol. 3 [1892], p. 793). I do not intend to go into his remarks about other aspects of Marx's presentation. They rest on the misunderstanding to the effect that Marx seeks to define where he only explains, and that one can generally look in Marx for fixed, cut-and-dried definitions that are valid for all time. It should go without saying that where things and their mutual relations are conceived not as fixed but rather as changing, their mental images, too, i.e. concepts, are also subject to change and reformulation; that they are not to be encapsulated in rigid definitions, but rather developed in their process of historical or logical formation. It will be clear, then, why at the beginning of Volume 1, where Marx takes simple commodity production as his historical presupposition, only later, proceeding from this basis, to come on to capital – why he proceeds precisely there from the simple commodity and not from a conceptually and historically secondary form, the commodity as already modified by capitalism. Fireman of course cannot see this at all. But we shall leave this aside here, as well as other secondary matters which might give equal cause for all kinds of objection, and pass immediately to the heart of the matter. While theory teaches the writer that, at a given rate of surplus-value, the mass of surplus-value is proportionate to the amount of labour-power employed, experience shows him that, at a given rate of profit, the mass of profit is proportionate in magnitude to the total capital invested. Fireman explains this by the fact that profit is only a conventional phenomenon (by which he means a phenomenon specific to the social formation in question, standing and falling together with it); its existence is simply bound up with capital. And capital, when it is strong enough to extract a profit for itself, is required by competition to extract an equal rate of profit for all capitals concerned. Without an equal rate of profit, no capitalist production is possible; but once this form of production is pre-supposed, the mass of profit received by each individual capitalist can only depend, with a given rate of profit, on the size of his capital. Profit, on the other hand, consists of surplus-value, of unpaid labour. How, then, does there take place the transformation of surplus-value, whose magnitude is governed by the exploitation of labour, into profit, whose magnitude is governed by the amount of capital required?

'Simply through this, that in all those branches of production where the ratio of ... constant capital to variable is greatest, commodities are sold above their value, which also means that in those branches where the ratio of constant capital to variable, $c:v$, is lowest, commodities are sold below their value, and that only where $c:v$ is a certain average are commodities parted with at their true value ... Is this incongruence between particular prices and their respective values a refutation of the value principle? By no means. Owing to the fact that the prices of some commodities rise above their values in the same degree as the prices of others fall below theirs, the total sum of prices equals the total sum of values ... "In the last instance" the incongruence disappears.'

This incongruence is a 'disturbance': 'but in the exact sciences a calculable disturbance is never treated as refuting a law.'

If we compare this with the corresponding passages in Chapter 9, we shall find that Fireman put his finger on the decisive point. Yet the number of intermediate links which would still have been needed, even after this discovery, to enable Fireman to arrive at a complete and concrete solution to the problem is shown by the undeservedly cool reception met with by his very important article. Even though many people were interested in the problem, they were all still afraid of getting their fingers burned. And this is explained not only by the incomplete form in which Fireman left his findings, but also by his undeniably inadequate conception of Marx's presentation and his general criticism of it based on this conception.

Wherever the opportunity presents itself, in the shape of a knotty problem, Professor Julius Wolf of Zürich never fails to make a fool of himself. The whole problem, he informs us (*Conrads Jahrbücher*, 3rd series, Vol. 2 [1891], pp. 352 ff.), is solved by relative surplus-value. The production of relative surplus-value depends on the increase of constant capital in relation to variable:

'An increase in constant capital presupposes an increase in the productivity of the workers. But since this increased productivity leads to an increase in surplus-value (by lowering the cost of the workers' means of subsistence), there is a direct connection between an increase in surplus-value and an increased share of constant capital in the total capital. With variable capital remaining the same and constant capital growing, therefore, surplus-value must rise, according to Marx's theory. This was the question put to us.'

True, Marx does say the exact opposite at a hundred places in the first volume. The contention, too, that according to Marx relative surplus-value rises in proportion with constant capital, given a fall in variable capital, is astonishing enough to put even parliamentary language to shame. Mr Julius Wolf shows in these lines only that he has understood neither relatively nor absolutely the slightest thing about absolute or relative surplus-value. He even says himself: 'We seem to find ourselves here, at first sight, in a tangle of inconsistencies', which is incidentally the only true thing he says in his entire article. But what does that matter? Mr Julius Wolf is so proud of his brilliant discovery that he is unable to refrain from praising Marx for it posthumously and lauding his own unfathomable nonsense as a 'recent indication of the keen and far-sighted way in which his' (Marx's) 'critical theory of the capitalist economy is set out'!

Still better things are to come. Mr Wolf says:

'Ricardo maintained both: equal expenditure of capital, equal surplus-value (profit), and: equal expenditure of labour, equal surplus-value (in absolute amount). The question was then how the one principle fitted in with the other. But Marx did not accept the question in this form. *He has undoubtedly shown (in the third volume)* that the second contention is not an unconditional consequence of the law of value, that it even contradicts his law of value, and must therefore be immediately discarded.'

He goes on to investigate who has gone wrong, himself or Marx. He does not think for a moment, of course, that the error is on his side.

It would only offend my readers, and misconstrue completely the comic character of the situation, if I were to waste any further words on this prize gem. I would only add that, with the same boldness which enabled him to say in advance what Marx had 'undoubtedly shown in the third volume', he takes the opportunity to report on an alleged item of gossip among his fellow professors, according to which Conrad Schmidt's above-mentioned book 'was directly inspired by Engels'. Mr Julius Wolf! It may well be the custom in your milieu for a man who publicly sets others a problem to make known the solution quietly to his personal friends. I am quite prepared to believe that you are capable of this. But the present Preface should make clear to you that, in the world in which I operate, it is simply unnecessary to resort to meanness of this kind.

Marx had only just died when Mr Achille Loria rushed to

publish an article on him in the *Nuova Antologia* (April 1883), a biography swarming with false statements followed by a criticism of his public activity, both political and literary. In this article Loria twisted and distorted Marx's materialist conception of history with a confidence that indicated the existence of a broader purpose. And this purpose was achieved: in 1886 the same Mr Loria published a book, *La teoria economica della costituzióne politica*, in which he proclaimed to his astonished contemporaries that Marx's theory of history, which he had so completely and deliberately misrepresented in 1883, was actually his own discovery. Marx's theory, moreover, was reduced here to a quite philistine level; and the historical evidence and examples are full of blunders which would not be tolerated from a fourth-former. But what does this matter? The discovery that political conditions and events have their explanation in the corresponding economic conditions has now been shown to have been made not by Marx in 1845 but by Mr Loria in 1886. At least he has impressed this on his compatriots and, now that his book has appeared in French, on some Frenchmen as well. He can now run round Italy posing as the author of a new and epoch-making theory of history, until the Italian socialists find time to strip the illustrious Loria of his stolen peacock feathers.

But this is just to give a taste of Loria's style. He assures us that all Marx's theories rest on deliberate sophistry (*un consaputo sofisma*); that Marx does not flinch from paralogisms, even when he recognizes them as such (*sapendoli tali*), etc. And after giving his readers a whole series of these vulgar fairy-tales, so that they have all that is needed to see Marx as a careerist *à la* Loria, staging his little effects with the same repulsive and petty humbug as our Padua professor, he can now reveal to them an important secret. With this, he takes us back to the rate of profit.

According to Marx, Mr Loria says, the mass of surplus-value produced in a capitalist industrial firm (and Mr Loria identifies this mass with the profit) is governed by the variable capital applied, since constant capital does not yield any profit. But this is in conflict with the real state of affairs. For, in practice, profit is governed not by the variable capital but by the total capital. Marx sees this himself (Volume 1, Chapter 11) and concedes that the facts seem at least to contradict his theory. How then does he solve the contradiction? He refers his readers to a later volume that has not yet appeared. Loria had already told *his* readers earlier on that he didn't believe Marx intended for a moment to write this volume, and he now exclaims in triumph:

'I was not wrong, therefore, in maintaining that this second volume, with which Marx constantly threatened his opponents, though it never appeared, might very well have been a sly expedient which he resorted to when scientific arguments failed him (*un ingegnoso spediente ideato dal Marx a sostituzione degli argomenti scientifici*).'

And if anyone is still not convinced that Marx stands on the same level of scientific fraud as the illustrious Loria – well, we can just give him up as a dead loss!

We had thus learned, according to Mr Loria, that Marx's theory of surplus-value was absolutely incompatible with the fact of a general and uniform rate of profit. Then Volume 2 appeared, and with it the question that I publicly set on this very point.* Had Mr Loria been a timid German, he might have experienced a certain degree of embarrassment. But he is a cocky Southerner and comes from a hot climate where, as he can testify, brazenness [*Unverfrorenheit*] is a natural condition.† The problem of the rate of profit had been publicly raised. Mr Loria publicly declared it to be insoluble. And for this very reason, he is now going to outdo himself by publicly solving it.

This miracle was performed in *Conrads Jahrbücher*, new series, Vol. 20 [1890], pp. 272 ff., in an article on Conrad Schmidt's above-mentioned book. Once Loria had learned from Schmidt how commercial profit comes into existence, everything became immediately clear to him.

'Now since the determination of value by labour-time gives those capitalists who deploy a greater part of their capital in wages an advantage, unproductive' (i.e. commercial) 'capital can extract a higher interest' (i.e. profit) 'from these advantaged capitalists, and bring about equality between the various industrial capitalists ... If, for example, industrial capitalists A, B and C each spend 100 working days on production, but use 0, 100 and 200 units of constant capital respectively, and if the wage for 100 working days represents 50 working days, then each capitalist receives a surplus-value of 50 working days, and the rate of profit is 100 per cent for the first capitalist, 33.3 per cent for the second

*See above, p. 98.
†This is a play on words. *Unverfrorenheit*, taken literally, means 'un-frozen-ness' – hence 'a natural condition in a hot climate'.

and 20 per cent for the third. If however a fourth capitalist D accumulates an unproductive capital of 300, which demands an interest' (profit) 'to the value of 40 working days from A, and an interest of 20 working days from B, then the rate of profit for capitalists A and B falls in each case to 20 per cent, as is already the case with C, while D, with a capital of 300, receives a profit of 60, i.e. a rate of profit of 20 per cent, just like the other capitalists.'

With this astounding dexterity, Loria solves by sleight of hand the same question that he had declared insoluble ten years before. Unfortunately he did not disclose to us the secret of what it is that gives this 'unproductive capital' the power not only to pinch from the industrialists this extra profit above the average, but also to hang on to it for themselves, in the same way as the landowner confiscates the surplus profit of the farmer as ground-rent. If this actually were the case, the merchant would in fact extract a tribute from the industrialist completely analogous to ground-rent and thereby establish the average rate of profit. Commercial capital is of course a very important factor in the formation of the general profit rate, as almost everyone knows. But only a literary adventurer, who at the bottom of his heart simply thumbs his nose at all economics, can permit himself to maintain that this commercial capital has the magic power to absorb all excess surplus-value over and above the general rate of profit, and moreover, even before such a rate is established, to transform it into a ground-rent for itself, and all this without needing anything like landed property. No less astonishing is the contention that commercial capital manages to discover those very industrialists whose surplus-value just covers the average rate of profit, and is pleased to ease the burden of these wretched victims of Marx's law of value by selling their products for them gratis, without even asking a commission. What a trickster one must be to imagine that Marx needed any such miserable subterfuge.

But it is only when we compare him with his northern competitors, such as Mr Julius Wolf, that our illustrious Loria shines forth in all his glory, even though Wolf, too, was not born yesterday. What a yelping cub Wolf seems, even in his thick tome on *Socialism and the Capitalist Social Order*, compared with this Italian! How awkwardly – I am almost tempted to say 'modestly' – he stands beside the noble audacity with which our maestro takes it for granted that Marx, no more and no less than all others, was just as much a conscious sophist, paralogist, braggart and charlatan as Mr Loria himself, and that, whenever he got stuck, Marx hoodwinked his public with the promise of a conclusion to his theory in an ensuing volume, which, as he himself well knew, he neither could nor intended to deliver! Unlimited impudence, combined with an eel-like flair for slipping out of impossible situations; heroic contempt for kicks received, hasty appropriation of other people's achievements, importunate charlatanry and self-advertisement, and orchestration of his fame by a coterie of his friends – who could equal Loria in all this?

Italy is the land of classicism. Since the great age when it saw the dawn of the modern world, it has produced magnificent characters unequalled in their classical perfection, from Dante down to Garibaldi. But the period of subjugation and foreign rule also left its classical character masks, including the two especially finely carved types of Sganarella and Dulcamara.* Our illustrious Loria embodies the classical unity of these two.

To conclude, I must take my readers across the ocean. In New York, Dr (med.) George C. Stiebeling also found a solution to the problem, and an extremely simple one at that. So simple, indeed, that no one anywhere would acknowledge it. Seized with anger, Stiebeling complained most bitterly, on both sides of the great water, in an unending series of pamphlets and newspaper articles. He was told in *Neue Zeit*† that his entire solution rested on a mistake in calculation. But this failed to move him; Marx, too, had made similar mistakes, and was right for all that about many things. Let us take a look, then, at Stiebeling's solution.

'I take two factories, working for the same time with equal capitals, but with different ratios of constant and variable capital. The total capital $(c + v)$ I take as y, and the difference in the ratio of constant to variable capital I take as x. In factory I, $y = c + v$; in factory II, $y = (c - x) + (v + x)$. The rate of surplus-value in factory I is then $\frac{s}{v}$, and in factory II $\frac{s}{v + x}$. By profit (p) I mean the total surplus-value (s) by which the total capital y or $c + v$ is expanded in the given time, therefore $p = s$. The rate of profit is accordingly $\frac{p}{y}$ or $\frac{s}{c + v}$ in factory I, and $\frac{p}{y}$ or $\frac{s}{(c - x) + (v + x)}$ in

---

*Characters from the Italian *Commedia dell'Arte*.

†By the time Engels wrote this in 1894, the magazine *Neue Zeit*, under the editorship of Karl Kautsky, had already established its reputation as the leading theoretical organ of German Social-Democracy and hence of Marxism in general. The article Engels refers to here was contained in issue no. 3 for 1887.

factory II, i.e. also $\frac{s}{c+v}$. The . . . problem is thus resolved on the basis of the law of value, in such a way that with equal capitals and equal time, but unequal quantities of living labour, a change in the rate of surplus-value still gives an equal average rate of profit' (G. C. Stiebeling, *Das Werthgesetz und die Profitrate*, John Heinrich, New York [1890]).

Fine and illuminating as the above calculation is, we must still ask our Dr Stiebeling *one* question. How does he know that the sum of surplus-value that factory I produces is exactly equal to the sum of surplus-value produced in factory II? As far as c, v, y and x are concerned, i.e. all the other factors in his calculation, he tells us expressly that they have the same value for both factories, but he does not say a single word about s. This however in no way follows from the mere fact that he denotes the two quantities of surplus-value involved here with the same algebraic symbol s. It is rather just what has to be proved, since Dr Stiebeling also identifies the profit p with the surplus-value, without more ado. Only two things are possible. Either the two s's are both equal, in which case each factory produces an equal amount of surplus-value, and also equal profit, and then Dr Stiebeling has assumed in advance what he is supposed to have proved. Or else the one factory produces a bigger sum of surplus-value than the other, and then his whole calculation breaks down.

Dr Stiebeling spared neither time nor money to construct whole castles of calculation on this basic error and put them on show to the public. I can give him the comforting assurance that they are almost all equally false, and that in those exceptional cases where this is not so, they prove something quite different from what he intends. Thus Stiebeling demonstrates the empirical fall in the rate of profit by comparing the U.S. census reports of 1870 and 1880, but explains this in a completely false way and holds that Marx's theory of a constant and stable rate of profit has to be corrected on the basis of practical experience. It follows however from Part Three of this third volume that Marx's 'stable rate of profit' is a pure figment of Stiebeling's imagination, and that the tendency for the rate of profit to fall rests on causes that run diametrically counter to those given by Dr Stiebeling. I am sure Dr Stiebeling has the best of intentions, but if people want to concern themselves with scientific questions, the first thing they must do is learn to read the texts they wish to use as their author wrote them, and above all not read into them things they do not contain.

The overall result of our investigation, so far as the question at hand is concerned, is again that it is only the Marxian school that has achieved anything. Fireman and Conrad Schmidt, if they read this third volume, may each be well satisfied with his own work.

London, 4 October 1894.   Frederick Engels

Capital

Volume Three

The Transformation
of Surplus-Value
into Profit, and of the
Rate of Surplus-Value
into the Rate of Profit

Chapter 1: Cost Price and Profit

In Volume 1 we investigated the phenomena exhibited by the *process of capitalist production*, taken by itself, i.e. the immediate production process, in which connection all secondary influences external to this process were left out of account. But this immediate production process does not exhaust the life cycle of capital. In the world as it actually is, it is supplemented by the *process of circulation*, and this formed our object of investigation in the second volume. Here we showed, particularly in Part Three, where we considered the circulation process as it mediates the process of social reproduction, that the capitalist production process, taken as a whole, is a unity of the production and circulation processes. It cannot be the purpose of the present, third volume simply to make general reflections on this unity. Our concern is rather to discover and present the concrete forms which grow out of the *process of capital's movement considered as a whole*. In their actual movement, capitals confront one another in certain concrete forms, and, in relation to these, both the shape capital assumes in the immediate production process and its shape in the process of circulation appear merely as particular moments. The configurations of capital, as developed in this volume, thus approach step by step the form in which they appear on the surface of society, in the action of different capitals on one another, i.e. in competition, and in the everyday consciousness of the agents of production themselves.

*

The value of any commodity C produced in the capitalist manner can be depicted by the formula: $C = c + v + s$. If we subtract from the value of this product the surplus-value s, there remains a mere equivalent or replacement value in commodities for the capital value $c + v$ laid out on the elements of production.

Let us say that the production of a certain article requires a capital expenditure of £500: £20 for wear and tear of the instruments of labour, £380 for raw materials and £100 for labour-power. If we take the rate of surplus-value as 100 per cent, the value of the product is $400_c + 100_v + 100_s = £600$.

After deducting the surplus-value of £100, there remains a commodity value of £500, and this simply replaces the capital expenditure of £500. This part of the value of the commodity, which replaces the price of the means of production consumed and the labour-power employed, simply replaces what the commodity cost the capitalist himself and is therefore the cost price of the commodity, as far as he is concerned.

What the commodity costs the capitalist, and what it actually does cost to produce it, are two completely different quantities. The portion of the commodity's value that consists of surplus-value costs the capitalist nothing, for the very reason that it costs the worker his unpaid labour. But since the worker, in the situation of capitalist production, is himself an ingredient of the functioning productive capital that belongs to the capitalist, and the capitalist is therefore the actual commodity producer, the cost price of the commodity necessarily appears to him as the actual cost of the commodity itself. If we call the cost price k, the formula $C = c + v + s$ is transformed into the formula $C = k + s$, or commodity value = cost price + surplus-value.

When we combine the various portions of commodity value that simply replace the capital value spent in the commodity's production, under the heading of cost price, we express on the one hand the specific character of capitalist production. The capitalist cost of the commodity is measured by the expenditure of *capital*, whereas the actual cost of the commodity is measured by the expenditure of *labour*. The capitalist cost price of the commodity is thus quantitatively distinct from its value or its actual cost price; it is smaller than the commodity's value, for since $C = k + s$, $k = C - s$. On the other hand, however, the cost price of the commodity is by no means simply a category that exists only in capitalist book-keeping. The independence that this portion of value acquires makes itself constantly felt in practice in the actual production of the commodity, as it must constantly be transformed back again into the form of productive capital by way of the circulation process, i.e. the cost price of the commodity must continuously buy back the elements of production consumed in its production.

Yet the category of cost price has nothing to do with the formation of commodity value or the process of capital's valorization. If I know that five-sixths of a commodity value of £600, i.e. £500, is simply an equivalent, a replacement value, for the capital of £500 that has been spent, and that this is therefore just sufficient to buy back the material elements of this capital, I still neither know how this five-sixths of the commodity's value which forms its cost price was produced, nor can I explain the origin of the last sixth that forms its surplus-value. Our investigation will show, however, that cost price does none the less, in the economy of capital, present the false semblance of an actual category of value production.

To return to our example. If we suppose that the value produced by one worker in an average social working day is expressed in a sum of money to the value of 6 shillings, then the capital advanced, $£500 = 400_c + 100_v$, is the value product of $1,666\frac{2}{3}$ of such 10-hour working days, of which $1,333\frac{1}{3}$ working days are crystallized in the value of the means of production, $= 400_c$, and $333\frac{1}{3}$ in the value of the labour-power, $= 100_v$. Given the rate of surplus-value of 100 which we assumed, the actual production of the new commodity costs for its part an expenditure of labour-power of $100_v + 100_s$, or $666\frac{2}{3}$ 10-hour working days.

We know from Volume 1 (Chapter 9, p. 320) that the value of the product newly formed, in this case £600, is composed of (1) the reappearing value of the constant capital of £400 spent on means of production, and (2) a newly produced value of £200. The cost price of the commodity, £500, comprises the reappearing 400_c plus a half of the newly produced value of £200 (100_v), two elements of commodity value that are completely different as far as their origins are concerned.

By the purposive character of the labour spent during these $666\frac{2}{3}$ 10-hour working days, the value of the means of production consumed, a total of £400, is transferred from these means of production to the product. This old value reappears therefore as a component of the product's value, though it does not originate in the production process of *this* commodity. It exists only as a component of the commodity's value because it existed previously as a component of the capital advanced. The constant capital that was spent is thus replaced by the portion of commodity value that it itself adds to this commodity value. This element of the cost price has therefore a dual significance. On the one hand it enters into the cost price of the commodity because it is a component of commodity value, and replaces the capital used up; on the other hand it forms a component of this commodity value only because it is the value of capital that has been used up, or because the means of production cost such and such an amount.

It is quite the reverse with the other component of cost price. The $666\frac{2}{3}$ days' labour expended during the production of the commodity forms a new value of £200. Out of this new value, one part simply replaces the variable capital of £100 that was advanced, or the price of the labour-power employed. But this advance of capital value does not go in any way into the formation of the new value. Within the capital that is advanced, labour-power counts as a *value*, but in the production process it counts as the *creator of value*. In place of the value of the labour-power, which is what figures in the capital advance, we have the living, value-creating labour-power that actually *functions* as productive capital.

The distinction between these various components of commodity value, which together form the cost price, leaps to the eye as soon as there is a change in the value of either the constant or the variable portion of the capital spent. Say that the price of the same means of production, or the constant portion of capital, rises from £400 to £600, or falls conversely to £200. In the first case, it is not only the cost price of the commodity that rises from £500 to $600_c + 100_v = £700$ but the commodity value itself also rises from £600 to $600_c + 100_v + 100_s = £800$. In the second case, not only does the cost price fall from £500 to $200_c + 100_v = £300$ but the commodity value itself falls from £600 to $200_c + 100_v + 100_s = £400$. Because the constant capital that is used up transfers its own value to the product, the value of the product rises or falls, other circumstances remaining the same, just as that capital value does. But let us now assume instead that, with other circumstances still remaining the same, the price of the same amount of labour-power rises from £100 to £150, or falls to £50. In the first case, the cost price of £500 certainly rises to $400_c + 150_v = £550$, and falls in the second case from £500 to $400_c + 50_v = £450$. But in both of these cases the commodity value remains unchanged at £600; the first time as $400_c + 150_v + 50_s$ and the second time as $400_c + 50_v + 150_s$. The variable capital advanced does not add its own value to the product. In place of its value, it is the new value created by labour that enters the product. Therefore a change in the absolute size of the variable capital, in so far as this expresses simply a change in the price of labour-power, does not change in the least the absolute size of the commodity value, because it does not affect that absolute size of the new value which active labour-power creates. A change of this kind affects only the ratio between the two components of this new value, one of which forms a surplus-value, while the other simply replaces the variable capital and thus enters into the cost price of the commodity.

All that the two portions of the cost price have in common, in our case the 400_c and 100_v, is that they are both portions of commodity value which replace capital that was advanced.

From the standpoint of capitalist production, however, this actual state of affairs necessarily appears upside down.

Among other things, the capitalist mode of production is distinguished from the mode of production founded on slavery by the fact that the value or price of labour-power is expressed as the value or price of labour itself, i.e. as wages (Volume 1, Chapter 19). The variable component of the capital value advanced thus appears as capital spent on wages, as a capital value which pays the value or price of all labour spent in production. If we assume for example that an average social working day of 10 hours is embodied in a sum of money of 6 shillings, the variable capital of £100 that is advanced is the monetary expression of a value produced in $333\frac{1}{3}$ 10-hour working days. But the value of the labour-power purchased, which figures here in the capital advance, does not form any part of the actually functioning capital. In the production process, it is living labour-power itself that appears in its place. If the rate of exploitation of this labour-power is 100 per cent, as in our example, it is used for $666\frac{2}{3}$ 10-hour working days and hence adds to the product a new value of £200. In the capital advance, however, the variable capital of £100 figures as capital laid out on wages, or as the price of the labour performed in these $666\frac{2}{3}$ 10-hour working days. £100 divided by $666\frac{2}{3}$ gives us the price of one 10-hour working day as 3 shillings, the value product of 5 hours' labour.

If we now compare capital advance on the one hand and commodity value on the other, we have:

I. Capital advance of £500 = £400 in capital spent on means of production (price of the means of production) + £100 in capital spent on labour (price of 666⅔ working days, i.e. wages for the same).

II. Commodity value of £600 = cost price of £500 (£400 price of the means of production + £100 price of the 666⅔ working days) + £100 surplus-value.

In this formula, the portion of capital laid out on labour is distinguished from that laid out on means of production such as cotton or coal only by the fact that it serves as payment for a materially different element of production and in no way by the fact that it plays a functionally different role in the process of forming commodity value, and therefore also in the valorization process of capital. In the cost price of the commodity there appears once again the price of the means of production, in the shape in which this figured already in the capital advance, and indeed precisely because these means of production were used in a way appropriate to the purpose. In exactly the same way, there appears again in the cost price of the commodity the price or wages for the 666⅔ working days spent on its production, as this already figured in the capital advance, and again because this amount of labour was used in an appropriate way. What we see here are only finished and existing values – the value portions of the capital advanced which enter the formation of the product's value – and not an element that creates new value. The distinction between constant and variable capital has disappeared. The entire cost price of £500 now has the dual significance that it is firstly the component of the commodity value of £600 that replaces the capital of £500 consumed in the commodity's production; and that secondly this component of commodity value itself exists only because it existed formerly as the cost price of the elements of production employed, means of production and labour, i.e. as a capital advance. The capital value returns as the commodity's cost price, because and in so far as it was spent as a capital value.

The circumstance that the various value components of the capital advanced are laid out on materially distinct elements of production, on means of labour, raw and ancillary materials, and on labour itself, only means that the cost price of the commodity must buy back again these materially distinct elements of production. With respect to the formation of the cost price itself, on the other hand, the only distinction that matters is the distinction between fixed and circulating capital. In our example, the depreciation of the means of labour was reckoned at £20 ($400_c = £20$ for depreciation of the means of labour + £380 for materials). If the value of these means of labour was formerly £1,200, before the production of the commodity in question, it exists after this production in two forms, £20 as part of the value of the commodity, and $1,200 - 20 = £1,180$ as the remaining value of the means of labour, which is to be found now as before in the capitalist's possession, not as a value element of his commodity capital but as an element of his productive capital. In contrast to the means of labour, production materials and wages are used up completely in the production of the commodity, so that their entire value enters the value of the commodity produced. We have already seen in connection with the turnover how these different components of the capital advanced assume the forms of fixed and circulating capital.

The capital advanced is therefore £1,680, a fixed capital of £1,200 plus a circulating capital of £480 (= £380 in production materials and £100 in wages).

The cost price of the commodity, on the other hand, is £500 (£20 for depreciation of fixed capital, £480 for circulating capital).

This difference between the cost price of the commodity and the advance of capital is however merely a confirmation that the cost price is formed exclusively by the capital actually used up on the commodity's production.

In the production of the commodity, means of labour to a value of £1,200 are applied, but out of this capital value that is advanced only £20 is lost in production. The fixed capital applied thus enters into the commodity's cost price only partially, as it is only partially used up in its production. The circulating capital applied enters the cost price of the commodity completely, because it is completely used up in its production. What does this demonstrate, if not that the fixed and circulating portions of capital that are consumed equally enter the cost price of their commodity in proportion to the magnitude of their value, and that this component of commodity value always derives simply from the capital used up in its production? If this were not the case, there would be no reason why the fixed capital of £1,200 that is advanced should not also add to the value of the product the £1,180 that it does not lose in the production process, instead of just the £20 that it actually does lose.

This difference between fixed and circulating capital, in connection with the calculation of the cost price, thus only confirms the apparent origin of the cost price in the capital value expended, or the price that the expended elements of production, labour included, cost the capitalist himself. As far as value formation is concerned, however, the variable portion of capital, that laid out on labour-power, is expressly identified here with constant capital (the portion of capital consisting of production materials), under the heading of circulating capital, and thus the valorization process of capital is completely mystified.[1]

So far we have considered only one element of commodity value, the cost price. We must now take a look at the other component, the excess over the cost price or the surplus-value. Surplus-value is at first, therefore, an excess commodity value over and above the cost price. But since the cost price is equal to the value of the capital expended and is also continuously transformed back into the material elements of this capital, this additional value is a value accruing to the capital expended in the production of the commodity and returning from its circulation.

We have already seen how although s, the surplus-value, derives only from a change in the value of v, the variable capital, and is therefore originally simply an increment to the variable capital, it can also, once the production process is completed, form a value increment to $c + v$, the total capital expended. The formula $c + (v + s)$, which indicates that s is produced by transforming the determinate capital value v advanced in labour-power into a variable magnitude, can also be represented as $(c + v) + s$. Before production began we had a capital of £500. After production is over, we have the capital of £500 plus a value increment of £100.[2]

1. The confusion to which this can give rise in the minds of the economists is shown in Volume 1, Chapter 9, 3, pp. 333–8, with the example of N. W. Senior.*

* Nassau W. Senior (1790–1864) was one of the principal exponents of 'vulgar economics' in England and particularly notorious for his opposition to the legal restriction of working hours, on the basis of his theory of the 'last hour' (ibid).

2. 'From what has gone before we know that surplus-value is purely the result of an alteration in the value of v, of that part of the capital which was converted into labour-power; consequently, $v + s = v + \Delta v$ (v plus an increment of v). But the fact that it is v alone that varies, and the conditions of that variation, are obscured by the circumstance that in consequence of the increase in the variable component of the capital, there is also an increase in the sum total of the capital advanced. It was originally £500 and becomes £590' (Volume 1, Chapter 9, p. 322).

Yet the surplus-value forms an addition not only to the part of the capital advanced that enters the process of valorization, but also to the part that does not enter this process; i.e. a value addition not only to the capital expended that is replaced out of the cost price of the commodity, but also to the capital applied to production in general. Before the production process we had a capital value of £1,680: £1,200 in fixed capital laid out on means of labour, of which only £20 enters the value of the commodity as depreciation, plus £480 circulating capital in production materials and wages. After the production process we have £1,180 as the value component of the productive capital, plus a commodity capital of £600. If we add these two sums of value together, the capitalist now possesses a value of £1,780. If he deducts from this the total capital of £1,680 that he advanced, there remains an additional value of £100. Thus the £100 surplus-value forms as much an addition to the total capital applied of £1,680 as to the fraction of this, £500, that is used up in the course of production.

It is clear enough to the capitalist that this additional value derives from the productive activities which he undertakes with his capital, i.e. that it derives from the capital itself. For after the production process he has it, and before the production process he did not. As far as the capital actually used up in the course of production is concerned, in the first place the surplus-value appears to derive equally from the different value elements of this capital, both means of production and labour. For these elements are both equally involved in the formation of the cost price. They both add their values, present as capital advances, to the value of the product and are not distinguished as constant and variable magnitudes. This becomes evident if we suppose for a moment that all the capital expended would consist either exclusively of wages or exclusively of the value of means of production. In the first case we would then have, instead of the commodity value $400_c + 100_v + 100_s$, a commodity value $500_v + 100_s$. The capital of £500 laid out on wages is the value of all the labour applied in the production of the commodity value of £600 and forms for this reason the cost price of the entire product. The formation of this cost price, through which the value of the capital expended reappears as a value component of the product, is however the only process in the formation of this commodity value that we know of. We know nothing of where its surplus-value component of £100 comes from. Exactly the same happens in the second case, where we take the commodity value as $500_c + 100_s$. We know in both cases that the surplus-value derives from a given value because this value was advanced in the form of productive capital, leaving aside the question whether this took the form of labour or that of means of production. Yet the capital value advanced cannot form surplus-value simply by virtue of its having been used up and forming therefore the cost price of the commodity. For to the precise extent that it forms the cost price of the commodity, it does not form any surplus-value, but simply an equivalent, a replacement value, for the capital used up. To the extent that it does form surplus-value, therefore, it forms this not in its specific capacity as capital that has been used up, but rather as advanced and therefore applied capital in general. Surplus-value thus derives as much from the part of the capital advanced that does not enter the cost price of the commodity as from the part of it that does enter the cost price; in short, it derives equally from the fixed and circulating components of the capital applied. In its material capacity, the entire capital serves to form the product, the means of labour as much as the production materials and labour itself. The entire capital is materially involved in the labour process, even if only a part of it is involved in the process of valorization. This is perhaps the very reason why it contributes only in part towards the formation of the cost price, but in full towards the formation of surplus-value. However this might be, the upshot is that the surplus-value springs simultaneously from all parts of the capital applied. The deduction may be substantially abbreviated, as in the clear and simple words of Malthus: 'The capitalist ... *expects* an equal profit upon all the parts of the capital which he advances.'[3]

As this supposed derivative of the total capital advanced, the surplus-value takes on the transformed form of *profit*. A sum of value is therefore capital if it is invested in order to produce a profit,[4] or alternatively profit arises because a sum of value is

3. Malthus, *Principles of Political Economy*, 2nd edition, London, 1836, p. 268. [Marx's emphasis.]*

* Marx treated the Rev. Thomas Robert Malthus (1766–1834) as a serious if minor economist, despite the reactionary ideology in which his theoretical contributions were buried. See *Theories of Surplus-Value*, Part III, Chapter 19. A comprehensive collection of Marx and Engels's references to Malthus, chiefly in his capacity as ideologist, can be found in *Marx and Engels on Malthus*, London, 1953, edited by Ronald Meek.

4. 'Capital: that which is expended with a view to profit.' Malthus, *Definitions in Political Economy*, London, 1827, p. 86.

employed as capital. If we call profit p, the formula $C = c + v + s = k + s$ is converted into the formula $C = k + p$, or *commodity value = cost price + profit*.

Profit, as we are originally faced with it, is thus the same thing as surplus-value, save in a mystified form, though one that necessarily arises from the capitalist mode of production. Because no distinction between constant and variable capital can be recognized in the apparent formation of the cost price, the origin of the change in value that occurs in the course of the production process is shifted from the variable capital to the capital as a whole. Because the price of labour-power appears at one pole in the transformed form of wages, surplus-value appears at the other pole in the transformed form of profit.

We have already seen that the cost price of a commodity is less than its value. Since $C = k + s, k = C - s$. The formula $C = k + s$ can be reduced to $C = k$, commodity value = cost price, only if $s = 0$, a case that never arises in conditions of capitalist production, even if certain special market conditions may cause the sale price of commodities to fall to their cost price or even below.

If the commodity is sold at its value, a profit is realized that is equal to the excess of its value over its cost price, i.e. equal to the entire surplus-value contained in the commodity value. But the capitalist can sell the commodity at a profit even if he sells it at less than its value. As long as its sale price is above its cost price, even if below its value, a part of the surplus-value contained in it is always realized, i.e. a profit is made. In our example the commodity value is £600, the cost price £500. If the commodity is sold at £510, £520, £530, £560 or £590, it is sold respectively at £90, £80, £70, £40 or £10 below its value, and yet a profit of £10, £20, £30, £60 or £90 is made for all that. An indefinite series of sale prices is evidently possible between the value of a commodity and its cost price. The greater the element of commodity value consisting of surplus-value, the greater the practical room for these intermediate prices.

This not only enables us to explain such everyday phenomena of competition as, for instance, certain cases of under-selling, an abnormally low level of commodity prices in certain branches of industry,[5] etc. The basic law of capitalist competition, which political economy has so far failed to grasp, the law that governs

5. Cf. Volume 1, Chapter 20, pp. 686 ff.

the general rate of profit and the so-called prices of production determined by it, depends, as we shall see, on this difference between the value and the cost price of commodities, and the possibility deriving from this of selling commodities below their value at a profit.

The minimum limit to the sale price of a commodity is imposed by its cost price. If it is sold beneath this cost price, the components of productive capital that were expended cannot be fully replaced from the price of sale. If this process continues long enough, the capital value advanced will disappear completely. From this standpoint alone, the capitalist is inclined to treat the cost price as the real *inner* value of the commodity, as it is the price he needs merely to preserve his capital. Added to this, however, is the fact that the cost price of the commodity is the purchase price which the capitalist has himself paid for its production, i.e. the purchase price determined by the production process itself. The excess value or surplus-value realized with the sale of the commodity thus appears to the capitalist as an excess of its sale price over its value, instead of an excess of its value over its cost price, so that the surplus-value concealed in the commodity is not simply realized by its sale, but actually derives from the sale itself. We have already dealt with this illusion in detail in Volume 1, Chapter 5 ('Contradictions in the General Formula') and will simply return for a moment here to the form in which it was given new currency by Torrens and others, as an alleged advance in political economy beyond Ricardo.*

'The natural price, consisting of the cost of production, or, in other words, of the capital expended in raising or fabricating commodities, cannot include the profit ... The farmer, we will suppose, expends one hundred quarters of corn in cultivating his fields, and obtains in return one hundred and twenty quarters. In this case, twenty quarters, being the excess of produce above

---

* Throughout Marx's mature economic writings, he treats David Ricardo (1772–1823), whose main work *On the Principles of Political Economy and Taxation* appeared in 1817, as representing the high point of classical political economy; after 1830, the growth of working-class struggle led bourgeois economics to retreat from its own previous scientific discoveries, and to the rise of vulgar economics (see Marx's Postface to the Second Edition of *Capital* Volume 1, pp. 96–7). Like that of Adam Smith, Ricardo's work forms a constant reference point throughout *Capital*, and Marx devotes several chapters of *Theories of Surplus-Value* (Part II in the standard edition) to a critique of Ricardo's ideas.

expenditure, constitute the farmer's profit; but it would be absurd to call this excess, or profit, a part of the expenditure ... The master manufacturer expends a certain quantity of raw material, of tools and implements of trade, and of subsistence for labour, and obtains in return a quantity of finished work. This finished work must possess a higher exchangeable value than the materials, tools, and subsistence, by the advance of which it was obtained.'

Torrens concludes from this that the excess of the sale price over the cost price, or the profit, derives from the fact that the consumers 'either by immediate or circuitous barter give some greater portion of all the ingredients of capital than their production costs'.[6]

In actual fact, the excess over a given magnitude can in no way form part of that magnitude, and so profit, the excess of a commodity's value over the capitalist's outlays, cannot form any part of these outlays. Thus if commodity value is formed without any other element besides the capitalist's advance of value, there is no way of seeing how any more value is to come out of production than went into it, unless something is to come out of nothing. Torrens manages to evade this creation from nothing only by shifting it from the sphere of commodity production to the sphere of commodity circulation. Profit cannot derive from production, says Torrens, for if it did it would already be included in the costs of production and would not be an excess over and above these costs. Profit cannot derive from commodity exchange, Ramsay answers him, unless it is already present before this exchange takes place.* The sum of values of the products exchanged is evidently not affected by the exchange of the products whose value sum this is. It should also be noted here that Malthus appeals expressly to Torrens's authority,[7] even though he himself explains the sale

6. R. Torrens, *An Essay on the Production of Wealth*, London, 1821, pp. 51–3 and 349.

7. Malthus, *Definitions in Political Economy*, London, 1853, pp. 70, 71. [See also *Theories of Surplus-Value*, Part III, p. 24.]

* Marx has already alluded to Ramsay's criticism of Torrens in Volume 1 of *Capital*, p. 264 and note. Sir George Ramsay (1800–1871) was considered by Marx to be one of the last representatives of classical (bourgeois) political economy. His *An Essay on the Distribution of Wealth* was published in Edinburgh in 1836, and Marx devotes Chapter XXII of *Theories of Surplus-Value* (Part III) to Ramsay's views. Colonel Robert Torrens (1780–1864) is discussed more briefly in Chapter XX of *Theories of Surplus-Value* (Part III), 'The Disintegration of the Ricardian School'; he was also a supporter of the 'Currency Principle', on which see below, Chapter 34.

of commodities above their value in a different way – or rather does not explain it, as all arguments of this kind are unfailingly reducible, in effect, to the same thing as the negative weight of phlogiston, which was so renowned in its time.*

In a social order dominated by capitalist production, even the non-capitalist producer is dominated by capitalist ways of thinking. Balzac, a novelist who is in general distinguished by his profound grasp of real conditions, accurately portrays in his last novel, *Les Paysans*, how the small peasant eager to retain the good-will of the money-lender performs all kinds of services for him unpaid, yet does not see himself as giving something for nothing, as his own labour does not cost him any cash expenditure. The money-lender for his part kills two birds with one stone. He spares cash expenditure on wages and, as the peasant is gradually ruined by depriving his own fields of labour, he enmeshes him ever deeper in the web of usury.

The unthinking notion that the cost price of the commodity is its real price and that surplus-value springs from selling the commodity above its value, i.e. that commodities are sold at their values when their sale price is equal to their cost price – i.e. equal to the price of the means of production consumed in them, plus wages – has been trumpeted forth by Proudhon with his customary pseudo-scientific quackery as a newly discovered secret of socialism. In fact this reduction of the values of commodities to their cost prices forms the foundation for his People's Bank.† We have already shown how the various components of commodity value can be represented by proportionate parts of the product itself. (See Volume 1, Chapter 9, 2, pp. 329–30.) If for example the value of 20 lb. of yarn is 30 shillings, made up of 24s. means of production, 3s. labour-power and 3s. surplus-value, this surplus-value can be represented as one-tenth of the product, or 2 lb. of yarn.

* For Engels's explicit analogy between Marx's theory of value and the refutation of the phlogiston theory, see his Preface to Volume 2 of *Capital*, pp. 97–8.

† Marx criticized the theoretical basis of Proudhon's 'People's Bank' in *The Poverty of Philosophy* (1847). In January 1849, Proudhon established his bank in Paris, and in line with his doctrine its practice included the extension of interest-free credit (*crédit gratuit*). After two months the bank went into forced liquidation. See also below, p. 743. From the 1840s through to his death in 1864, Pierre-Joseph Proudhon, a worker in origin, was the most influential French socialist theorist, and as such the object of frequent criticism by Marx. Cf. *Grundrisse*, pp. 137, 248, 264–6, 424–6, 488, 640–41, 754–8, and 843–5.

If these 20 lb. of yarn are now sold at their cost price, for 27s., the buyer receives 2 lb. of yarn for nothing, or the commodity is sold at one-tenth below its value. The worker has still performed his surplus labour, but now for the buyer of the yarn instead of for the capitalist yarn producer. It would be quite wrong to suppose that, if all commodities were sold at their cost prices, the result would in fact be the same as if they were all sold above their cost prices but at their values. For even if the value of labour-power, the length of the working day and the rate of exploitation are taken as everywhere the same, yet the amounts of surplus-value that the values of the various different kinds of commodities contain are completely unequal, according to the differing organic compositions of the capitals advanced for their production.[8]

8. 'The masses of value and of surplus-value produced by different capitals – the value of labour-power being given and its degree of exploitation being equal – vary directly as the amounts of the variable components of these capitals, i.e. the parts which have been turned into living labour-power' (Volume 1, Chapter 11, p. 421).

Chapter 2: The Rate of Profit

The general formula for capital is $M - C - M'$, i.e. a sum of value is cast into circulation in order to extract a greater sum. The process that creates this greater sum of value is capitalist production; the process that realizes it is the circulation of capital. The capitalist does not produce commodities for their own sake, neither for their use-value nor for his own personal consumption. The product in which the capitalist is really interested is not the palpable product itself, but rather the excess in the value of the product over and above the value of the capital consumed in it. The capitalist advances the capital as a whole without considering the different roles that its components will play in the production of surplus-value. He advances all these components equally, not only so as to reproduce the capital he has advanced but also to produce an excess value over and above this. He can convert the value he advances into a higher value only by exchanging it with living labour, by the exploitation of living labour. But he can exploit labour only in so far as he advances at the same time the conditions for the realization of this labour, i.e. means and object of labour, machinery and raw materials, that is by transforming a certain sum of value that he has in his possession into the form of the conditions of production. Similarly, he is only a capitalist at all, and can only undertake the process of exploiting labour, because he confronts, as proprietor of the conditions of labour, the worker as the mere owner of labour-power. We have already shown in Volume 1 how it is precisely the possession of these means of production by the non-workers that turns the workers into wage-labourers and the non-workers into capitalists.*

It makes no difference to the capitalist whether we see him as advancing the constant capital to make a profit out of his variable

* See in particular pp. 270–74 and 874–6.

capital, or advancing the variable capital in order to valorize the constant; whether he lays out money on wages in order to give machines and raw material a higher value, or advances money in machinery and raw material in order to exploit labour. Even though it is only the variable part of capital that creates surplus-value, it does so only under the condition that the other parts are advanced as well, i.e. the conditions of production for labour. Since the capitalist can exploit labour only by advancing constant capital, and since he can valorize the constant capital only by advancing the variable, these are both one and the same in his eyes, and this is all the more so in that the actual degree of his profit is determined in relation not to his variable capital but to his total capital; not by the rate of surplus-value but by the rate of profit, which, as we shall see, may remain the same while expressing different rates of surplus-value.

The costs of the product include all the components of its value which the capitalist has paid for, or for which he has cast an equivalent into the production process. These costs must be replaced even if his capital is to do no more than maintain itself, reproduce its original magnitude.

The value contained in a commodity is equal to the labour-time taken in making it, and this consists of both paid and unpaid labour. The costs of the commodity for the capitalist, on the other hand, include only the part of the labour objectified in it for which he has actually paid. The surplus labour contained in the commodity costs the capitalist nothing, even though it costs the worker labour, every bit as much as the paid labour does, and even though both paid and unpaid labour create value and enter the commodity as elements of value formation. The capitalist's profit, therefore, comes from the fact that he has something to sell for which he has not paid. The surplus-value or profit consists precisely in the excess of commodity value over its cost price, i.e. in the excess of the total sum of labour contained in the commodity over the sum of labour that is actually paid for. The surplus-value, from wherever it may derive, is consequently an excess over and above the total capital advanced. This excess then stands in a certain ratio to the total capital, as expressed by the fraction $\frac{s}{C}$, where C stands for the total capital. We thus obtain the *rate of profit* $\frac{s}{C} = \frac{s}{c + v}$, as distinct from the rate of surplus-value $\frac{s}{v}$.

The rate of surplus-value, as measured against the variable capital, is known as the rate of surplus-value; the rate of surplus-value, as measured against the total capital, is known as the rate of profit. These are two different standards for measuring the same quantity, and as a result are able to express the different relations in which the same quantity may stand.

It is the transformation of surplus-value into profit that is derived from the transformation of the rate of surplus-value into the profit rate, not the other way round. In actual fact, the rate of profit is the historical starting-point. Surplus-value and the rate of surplus-value are, relative to this, the invisible essence to be investigated, whereas the rate of profit and hence the form of surplus-value as profit are visible surface phenomena.

As far as the individual capitalist is concerned, it is evident enough that the only thing that interests him is the ratio of the surplus-value, the excess value which he receives from selling his commodities, to the total capital advanced for the production of these commodities, whereas not only do the specific ratios of this excess value to the particular components of his capital, and its inner connections with them, not interest him, but it is actually in his interest to disguise these particular ratios and inner connections.

Even though the excess value of the commodity over its cost price arises in the immediate process of production, it is only in the circulation process that it is realized, and it appears all the more readily to derive from the circulation process in as much as in the world as it actually is, the world of competition, i.e. on the market, it depends on market conditions whether or not this excess is realized and to what extent. It needs no further elaboration here that, if a commodity is sold above or below its value, there is simply a different distribution of the surplus-value, and that this distribution, the altered ratio in which various individuals partake of the surplus-value, in no way affects either the magnitude or the character of the surplus-value itself. Not only is the circulation process, for its part, the scene of those transformations that were considered in Volume 2, but these also coincide with actual competition, the purchase and sale of commodities above or below their value, so that, as far as the individual capitalist is concerned, the surplus-value that he realizes depends just as much on this mutual cheating as on the direct exploitation of labour.

The circulation process is affected by the circulation time as well as by the working time, the time of circulation restricting the surplus-value that can be realized in a certain period. Other aspects deriving from circulation also react with decisive effect on the immediate process of production itself. Both these processes, the immediate process of production and the circulation process, constantly run into one another and intertwine, and in this way their distinguishing features are continuously blurred. In the circulation process, as we have already shown, the production of surplus-value, and of value in general, assumes new characteristics. Capital runs through the cycle of its transformations, and finally it steps as it were from its inner organic life into its external relations, relations where it is not capital and labour that confront one another, but on the one hand capital and capital, and on the other hand individuals as simple buyers and sellers once again. Circulation time and working time cut across each other's paths, and both appear to determine surplus-value in the same way. The original form in which capital and wage-labour confront one another is disguised by the intervention of relations that seem to be independent of this; surplus-value itself does not appear as having been produced by the appropriation of labour-time, but as the excess of the sale price of commodities over their cost price, this latter readily presenting itself therefore as their proper value (*valeur intrinsèque*), so that profit appears as an excess of the sale price of commodities over their immanent value.

It is true that the nature of surplus-value persistently impresses itself on the capitalist's consciousness in the course of the immediate production process, as we were shown by his greed for the labour-time of others, etc., when we were simply considering surplus-value as such. However:

(1) The immediate process of production is itself simply an evanescent moment, which is constantly passing over into the process of circulation, and vice versa, so that any inkling of the source of his profit, i.e. of the nature of surplus-value, which dawns more or less clearly on the capitalist in the production process itself, appears at the most as an equally valid moment alongside the notion that the excess that is realized stems from a movement that is independent of the production process itself and derives from the sphere of circulation, a movement therefore that capital possesses independently of its relation to labour. These phenomena of circulation are even adduced by modern economists such as Ramsay, Malthus, Senior, Torrens, etc. as direct proofs that capital in its mere material existence, independently of its social relation to labour (which is precisely how it comes to be

capital), is an autonomous source of surplus-value alongside labour and independent of it.

(2) Under the heading of costs, which include not only wages but also the price of raw material, the depreciation of the machinery, etc., the extortion of unpaid labour appears simply as an economy in the payment for one of the articles that comprise these costs, simply as a lesser payment for a certain quantity of labour, an economy similar to that made when raw material is bought more cheaply or the wear and tear of machinery is reduced. The extortion of surplus labour then loses its specific character. Its specific relationship to surplus-value is obscured, and this is greatly furthered and facilitated by the representation of the value of labour-power in the form of wages, as we showed in Volume 1, Part Six [Chapter 19].

Since all sections of capital equally appear as sources of the excess value (profit), the capital relation is mystified.

Yet the way that surplus-value is transformed into the form of profit, by way of the rate of profit; is only a further extension of that inversion of subject and object which already occurs in the course of the production process itself. We saw in that case how all the subjective productive forces of labour present themselves as productive forces of capital.* On the one hand, value, i.e. the past labour that dominates living labour, is personified into the capitalist; on the other hand, the worker conversely appears as mere objectified labour-power, as a commodity. This inverted relationship necessarily gives rise, even in the simple relation of production itself, to a correspondingly inverted conception of the situation, a transposed consciousness, which is further developed by the transformations and modifications of the circulation process proper.

As can be studied in the case of the Ricardian school, it is completely wrong-headed to seek directly to present the laws of the profit rate as laws of the rate of surplus-value, or vice versa. In the mind of the capitalist these things are of course not distinguished. The expression $\frac{s}{C}$ measures surplus-value against the value of the total capital advanced for its production, of which one part is completely consumed in this production, while another part is simply applied. In fact, the ratio $\frac{s}{C}$ expresses the degree of valorization of the whole capital advanced; i.e. viewed in accord-

---

* Volume 1, pp. 450–53.

ance with the conceptual, inner connection and the actual nature of surplus-value, it shows how the variation of the variable capital is related in magnitude to the total capital advanced.

In itself, the value of the total capital stands in no inner relationship to the amount of surplus-value, at least not directly. As far as its material elements are concerned, the total capital minus the variable capital, i.e. the constant capital, consists of the material conditions for the realization of labour – its materials and means. In order that a definite quantity of labour may be realized in commodities, and therefore form value, a definite quantity of materials and means of labour is required. There is a definite technical proportion between the amount of labour and the mass of means of production to which this living labour is to be added, a proportion that depends on the particular character of the labour. There is also therefore a definite proportion between the amount of surplus-value or surplus labour, and the mass of means of production. If the labour needed for the production of the worker's wage amounts to 6 hours per day, for example, the worker has to work for 12 hours in order to perform 6 hours of surplus labour and create a surplus-value of 100 per cent. In 12 hours he consumes twice as much in the way of means of production as he does in 6 hours. But this does not mean that the surplus-value he adds in 6 hours stands in any direct relationship to the value of the means of production that are used in these 6 or 12 hours. Their value is completely immaterial here; what matters is the amount technically needed. It is quite unimportant whether the raw material or means of labour are cheap or dear, as long as they possess the use-value required and are present in the technically prescribed proportions for the labour they are to absorb. But if I know that x lb. of cotton are spun in an hour, and they cost y shillings, I also know that in 12 hours $12x$ lb. of cotton, $= 12y$ shillings, are spun, and I can then calculate the ratio of the surplus-value to the value spun in 12 hours as well as to the value spun in 6. However, the ratio of living labour to the *value* of these means of production comes into question here only in as much as y shillings serves as the name for x lb. of cotton; because a certain specific quantity of cotton has a definite price, and conversely, therefore, a specific price can serve as an index for a definite quantity of cotton, as long as the price of cotton does not change. If I know that in order to appropriate 6 hours' surplus labour I have to have the workers perform 12 hours' labour, I must have enough cotton ready for 12 hours, and if I know the price of this quantity of cotton, there exists in this roundabout way a certain relationship between the price of cotton (as index of the quantity needed) and the surplus-value. But I can never argue conversely from the price of the raw material to the quantity of raw material that can be spun in one hour but will not do for six. There is thus no inner and necessary relationship between the value of the constant capital and the surplus-value, nor, hence, is there one between the value of the total capital ($= c + v$) and the surplus-value.

If the rate of surplus-value and its absolute magnitude are both given, the rate of profit expresses no more than what it in fact is, i.e. an alternative measurement of surplus-value, its measurement in terms of the value of the total capital, instead of in terms of the value of that part of capital from which it directly derives by way of its exchange against labour. In actuality, however, i.e. in the world of phenomena, things are the other way round. Surplus-value is given, but given as an excess of the sale price of the commodity over its cost price; and it therefore remains a mystery how this excess arises – from the exploitation of labour in the production process, from the mutual cheating of the dealers in the circulation process, or from both. What is also given is the relationship of this excess to the value of the total capital, i.e. the rate of profit. The calculation of this excess of the sale price over the cost price in terms of the total capital advanced is very important, and naturally so, since this is in fact the way that we find the ratio in which the total capital has been valorized or its degree of valorization. But if we start from this rate of profit, we can never establish any specific relationship between the excess and the part of capital laid out on wages. We shall see in a later chapter the amusing capers Malthus cuts when he tries in this way to penetrate the secret of surplus-value and its specific relationship to the variable part of capital.* What the rate of profit as such shows is rather a uniform relationship of the excess to equally important parts of the capital, which from this point of view exhibits no internal distinctions apart from that between fixed and circulating. Even this distinction arises only in so far as the excess is calculated in two ways. Firstly, as a simple quantity: the excess over and above the cost price. In this first form the circulating capital enters the cost price in full, while the fixed capital enters only to the

* See *Theories of Surplus-Value*, Part III, pp. 31–4.

extent of its depreciation. Secondly, there is the relationship of this excess value to the total value of the capital advanced. Here the value of the entire fixed capital comes into the calculation as much as the value of the circulating capital. The circulating capital thus comes into the calculation in the same way each time, while the fixed capital is involved in the first case in a different way from the circulating capital, in the second case in the same way. Thus the distinction between circulating and fixed capital suggests itself here to us as the only one.

We might say in the Hegelian fashion that the excess is reflected back into itself from the rate of profit, or else that the excess, which is characterized more specifically by the rate of profit, appears as an excess which the capital produces over and above its own value, either annually or in some definite period of circulation.

Thus even if the rate of profit is numerically different from the rate of surplus-value, while surplus-value and profit are in fact the same and even numerically identical, profit is still for all that a transformed form of surplus-value, a form in which its origin and the secret of its existence are veiled and obliterated. In point of fact, profit is the form of appearance of surplus-value, and the latter can be sifted out from the former only by analysis. In surplus-value, the relationship between capital and labour is laid bare. In the relationship between capital and profit, i.e. between capital and surplus-value as it appears on the one hand as an excess over the cost price of the commodity realized in the circulation process and on the other hand as an excess determined more precisely by its relationship to the total capital, *capital appears as a relationship to itself*, a relationship in which it is distinguished, as an original sum of value, from another new value that it posits. It appears to consciousness as if capital creates this new value in the course of its movement through the production and circulation processes. But how this happens is now mystified, and appears to derive from hidden qualities that are inherent in capital itself.

The further we trace out the valorization process of capital, the more is the capital relationship mystified and the less are the secrets of its internal organization laid bare.

In this Part, the rate of profit is taken as numerically different from the rate of surplus-value; profit and surplus-value on the other hand are treated as numerically identical magnitudes, different only in form. In the following Part we shall observe the further development of the externalization by which profit presents itself as a magnitude distinct from surplus-value in a numerical respect as well.

Chapter 3: The Relationship between Rate of Profit and Rate of Surplus-Value

As was indicated at the close of the previous chapter, we assume here, as throughout this Part, that the sum of profit that accrues to a given capital is the same as the total sum of surplus-value which this capital produces in a given period of circulation. We therefore ignore for the time being the division of this surplus-value into various subordinate forms: interest, ground-rent, taxes, etc., as also the fact that surplus-value by no means coincides in the majority of cases with profit, as the latter is appropriated by way of the prevailing rate of profit, which we shall return to in Part Two.

In so far as profit is taken as quantitatively equal to surplus-value, its magnitude, and the magnitude of the rate of profit, are determined by simple numerical ratios, the numbers involved being given or definable in each individual case. Our investigation is firstly, therefore, a purely mathematical one.

We shall keep the symbols that were used in the first and second volumes. The total capital C is divided into constant capital c and variable capital v, and produces a surplus-value s. The ratio between this surplus-value and the variable capital advanced, i.e. $\frac{s}{v}$, we call the rate of surplus-value, and we denote it by s'. Since $\frac{s}{v} = s'$, $s = s'v$. If this surplus-value is related to the total capital instead of just the variable capital, it is called profit (p), and the ratio between the surplus-value and the total capital C, i.e. $\frac{s}{C}$, is known as the rate of profit, p'. We therefore have:

$$p' = \frac{s}{C} = \frac{s}{c + v}$$

and if we substitute for s the value $s'v$, as above, we have

$$p' = \frac{s'v}{C} = \frac{s'v}{c + v},$$

an equation which can also be expressed as the proportionality:

$$p' : s' = v : C;$$

rate of profit is to rate of surplus-value as variable capital is to total capital.

It follows from this proportionality that p', the rate of profit, is always smaller than s', the rate of surplus-value, since v, the variable capital, is always smaller than C, the sum of $v + s$, variable and constant capital. The only exception is the case, impossible in practice, where $v = C$, and where the capitalist thus advances no constant capital, no means of production, but simply wages.

But a further series of factors have also to be taken into account in our analysis, factors which affect the sizes of c, v and s in a decisive way, and which must therefore be briefly mentioned.

Firstly, the *value of money*. This we can take as constant throughout.

Secondly, the *turnover*. We shall ignore this factor completely, for the time being, since its influence on the profit rate will be dealt with in a later chapter. (Here we shall simply anticipate the point that the formula $p' = \frac{s'v}{C}$ is strictly correct only for a single turnover period of the variable capital, while for the annual turnover the simple rate of surplus-value s' has to be replaced by $s'n$, the annual rate of surplus-value, n standing for the number of turnovers that the variable capital makes in the course of a year; see Volume 2, Chapter 16, 1 – F.E.)

The third factor involved is the *productivity of labour*, whose influence on the rate of surplus-value we have already gone into in some detail in Volume 1, Part Four. This can however also exert a direct influence on the rate of profit, at least that of an individual capital, if, as explained in Volume 1, Chapter 12, pp. 433ff., this individual capital operates with a productivity higher than the social average, produces its products at a lower value than the average social value of the same commodity, and in this way realizes an extra profit. But we shall also leave this case out of consideration here, as in this Part we also proceed from the assumption that commodities are produced under normal social conditions and are sold at their values. We therefore assume in each individual case that the productivity of labour remains constant. In actual fact, the value composition of the capital applied in a particular branch of industry, i.e. a specific ratio between variable and constant capital, expresses in each case a definite level of labour productivity. Thus as soon as this ratio experiences any change that is not simply due either to a change in value of the material components of the constant capital, or to a change in wages, the productivity of labour must also have undergone a change, and we shall therefore find often enough that the changes in the factors c, v and s also involve changes in labour productivity.

The same applies to the remaining three factors: *length of working day, intensity of labour, and wages*. Their influence on the mass and rate of surplus-value was developed in detail in Volume 1 [Chapter 17]. We can well understand, therefore, how, even if we proceed for the sake of simplicity from the assumption that these three factors remain constant, the changes that v and s undergo nevertheless also involve changes in the size of these determining moments of theirs. And we may briefly remind ourselves here that wages affect the size and the rate of surplus-value in the opposite direction to the length of the working day and the intensity of labour; a rise in wages reduces surplus-value, while an extension of the working day and a greater intensity of labour both increase it.

Let us take for example a capital of 100, producing a surplus-value of 20 with 20 workers in a 10-hour working day, and a total weekly wage bill of 20. We then have:

$$80_c + 20_v + 20_s; \quad s' = 100 \text{ per cent}, \quad p' = 20 \text{ per cent}.$$

If the working day is now extended to 15 hours, without an increase in wages, the total value produced by the 20 workers is increased from 40 to 60 ($10:15 = 40:60$). Since v, the wages paid, remains the same, the surplus-value rises from 20 to 40, and we have:

$$80_c + 20_v + 40_s; \quad s' = 200 \text{ per cent}, \quad p' = 40 \text{ per cent}.$$

If the wage for the same 10 hours' labour falls from 20 to 12, we then have the same total value product of 40 as before, but differently distributed; v falls to 12 and thus leaves a remainder o 28 for s. We then have:

$$80_c + 12_v + 28_s; \quad s' = 233\tfrac{1}{3} \text{ per cent}, \quad p' = \frac{28}{92} = 30\frac{10}{23} \text{ per cent}.$$

We see therefore how an extension of the working day (or, alternatively, an increase in the intensity of labour) and a fall in wages both raise the mass and with it the rate of surplus-value; conversely, a rise in wages, with other circumstances remaining the same, would reduce the rate of surplus-value. If v grows owing to a rise in wages, this does not express an increased quantity of labour but simply its dearer payment; s' and p' do not rise but fall.

It is already evident here that changes in the working day, the intensity of labour and wages cannot take place without a simultaneous change in v and s and their relationship, and thus also in p', the ratio between s and $c + v$, the total capital; and it is also evident that changes in the ratio of s to v also involve changes in at least one of the three conditions of labour that have been mentioned.

Here we see precisely the special organic connection that the variable capital has with the movement of the capital as a whole and its valorization, as well as its distinction from the constant capital. The constant capital, in so far as the formation of value is concerned, is important only on account of the value that it has. It is quite immaterial here, as far as value formation is concerned, whether a constant capital of £1,500 represents 1,500 tons of iron at £1 a ton or 500 tons at £3. The quantity of actual material in which its value is expressed is completely unimportant for the formation of value and for the rate of profit, which varies in the opposite direction to the value of the constant capital, irrespective of what relationship the increase or decrease in this value has to the mass of material use-values that it represents.

The case of the variable capital is completely different. What matters above all here is not the value that it actually has, the amount of labour objectified in it, but rather this value as a mere index of the total labour that it sets in motion, which is not expressed in it. The difference between this total labour and the labour expressed and therefore paid for in the variable capital, i.e. the portion that forms surplus-value, is greater in proportion as the labour contained in the variable capital gets smaller. Say that a working day of 10 hours $=$ 10 shillings. If the necessary labour, the labour that replaces wages, i.e. replaces the variable capital, is 5 hours, then the surplus-value is 5 shillings; if the necessary labour is 4 hours $=$ 4 shillings, the surplus labour is 6 hours and the surplus-value 6 shillings.

Hence as soon as the value of the variable capital ceases to be an index of the mass of labour that it sets in motion, and the basis of this index itself changes, the rate of surplus-value changes in the opposite direction and in inverse proportion.

We can now move on to apply the above equation for the profit rate, $p' = \frac{s'v}{C}$, to the various possible cases. We shall let the individual factors of $\frac{s'v}{C}$ vary successively in value, and establish the effect of these changes on the rate of profit. We thus obtain various sets of cases which we can consider either as successive changes in circumstances for the action of one and the same capital, or, indeed, as different capitals, existing simultaneously alongside one another, and brought in for purposes of comparison, e.g. from different branches of industry or from different countries. If it therefore appears forced or practically impossible to interpret some of our examples as chronologically successive states of one and the same capital, this objection disappears as soon as they are viewed as the result of a comparison between separate capitals.

We shall therefore divide the product $\frac{s'v}{C}$ into its two factors s' and $\frac{v}{C}$. First we shall take s' as constant and investigate the effect of possible variations in $\frac{v}{C}$, then take the fraction $\frac{v}{C}$ as constant and put s' through its possible variations. Finally we shall take all the factors as variable, and in this way exhaust all the cases from which the laws governing the profit rate may be derived.

I. s' constant, $\frac{v}{C}$ variable

This case, which comprises a number of subordinate ones, can be covered by a general formula. If we have two capitals C and C_1, with their variable components v and v_1 respectively, a common rate of surplus-value s' and rates of profit p' and p'_1, then:

$$p' = \frac{s'v}{C}; p'_1 = \frac{s'v_1}{C_1}.$$

C and C_1, as well as v and v_1, will then stand in certain definite ratios, and if $\frac{C_1}{C} = E$, and $\frac{v_1}{v} = e$, then $C_1 = EC$ and $v_1 = ev$. By substituting these values into the above equation for p'_1, we obtain:

$$p'_1 = s' \frac{ev}{EC}.$$

We can also obtain a second formula from the above two equations, if we transform them into the following proportionality:

$$p':p'_1 = s'\,\frac{v}{C}:s'\,\frac{v_1}{C_1} = \frac{v}{C}:\frac{v_1}{C_1}.$$

Since the value of a fraction remains the same if numerator and denominator are both multiplied or divided by the same number, we can reduce $\frac{v}{C}$ and $\frac{v_1}{C_1}$ to percentages by taking both C and C_1 as 100. We then have $\frac{v}{C} = \frac{v}{100}$ and $\frac{v_1}{C_1} = \frac{v_1}{100}$. Multiplying the above proportionality by 100 to remove these denominators of 100, we get:

$$p' : p'_1 = v : v_1.$$

In other words, given any two capitals functioning with the same rate of surplus-value, the rates of profit stand in the same proportion as the variable components of the capitals, each calculated as a percentage of its total capital.

These two forms cover all cases of variation in $\frac{v}{C}$.

Before we investigate each of these particular cases, one further remark. Since C is the sum of c and v, the constant and the variable capital, and since the rate of surplus-value as well as the profit rate is customarily expressed as a percentage, it is generally convenient to take the sum $c + v$ as also $= 100$, i.e. to express c and v in percentages too. It is not immaterial for determining the mass of profit, but it is so far as the rate of profit is concerned, whether we say that a capital of 15,000, of which 12,000 is constant capital and 3,000 variable, produces a surplus-value of 3,000 or whether we reduce the capital to percentages:

$$15,000\ C = 12,000_c + 3,000_v\ (+\ 3,000_s)$$
$$100\ C = \quad 80_c + \quad 20_v\ (+\quad 20_s).$$

In both cases the rate of surplus-value $s' = 100$ per cent and the rate of profit $p' = 20$ per cent.

It is the same if we compare two capitals with one another, for example comparing the above capital with a second one:

$$12,000\ C = 10,800_c + 1,200_v\ (+\ 1,200_s)$$
$$100\ C = \quad 90_c + \quad 10_v\ (+\quad 10_s).$$

Here $s' = 100$ per cent and $p' = 10$ per cent, and the comparison with the previous capital is far easier to make in the percentage form.

If on the other hand we are dealing with changes taking place in one and the same capital, the percentage form can be used only rarely, as it almost always obliterates these changes. If a capital passes from the percentage form:

$$80_c + 20_v + 20_s$$

to the percentage form:

$$90_c + 10_v + 10_s$$

we cannot tell whether the new percentage composition $90_c + 10_v$ has come about by an absolute decline in v, or an absolute rise in c, or both. The absolute magnitudes must also be known here. And in our analysis of the following particular cases of variation, it is precisely how this change has come about that matters; whether the $80_c + 20_v$ became $90_c + 10_v$ because $12,000_c + 3,000_v$ underwent a transformation, say, into $27,000_c + 3,000_v$ ($90_c + 10_v$ in percentage terms), i.e. through an increase in the constant capital, the variable capital remaining the same; or whether it assumed this new shape through a reduction in the variable capital, the constant capital remaining the same, i.e. because it changed into $12,000_c + 1,333\frac{1}{3}_v$ (also $90_c + 10_v$ in percentage terms); or finally through a change in both these quantities, resulting in $13,500_c + 1,500_v$ (again $90_c + 10_v$ in percentage terms). But we shall have to analyse all these cases in succession, thereby dispensing with the convenience of the percentage form, or only applying it as a supplement to the main argument.

1. s' and C constant, v variable

If there is a change in the magnitude of v, C can remain unaltered only if its other component, the constant capital c, changes by the same amount as v, but in the opposite direction. If C was originally $80_c + 20_v = 100$ and v is then reduced to 10, C can remain at 100 only if c rises to 90; $90_c + 10_v = 100$. In general, if v is changed to $v \pm d$, to v increased or decreased by d, then c must be transformed to $c \mp d$, varying by the same amount in the opposite direction, in order that the conditions of the present case may be satisfied.

In the same way, given an unaltered rate of surplus-value s' but a changing variable capital, the mass of surplus-value must change, since $s = s'v$, and one of the factors of $s'v$, namely v, has been given another value.

The assumptions of the case at hand, together with the original equation

$$p' = s' \frac{v}{C},$$

give us the second equation:

$$p'_1 = s' \frac{v_1}{C},$$

by variation of v. v has now been changed to v_1, and we have to find p'_1, the ensuing new rate of profit.

This is found by the appropriate proportionality:

$$p' : p'_1 = s' \frac{v}{C} : s' \frac{v_1}{C} = v : v_1.$$

Or, with the rate of surplus-value and the total capital both remaining the same, the original profit rate is related to the new profit rate arrived at by a change in the variable capital, as the original variable capital is to the new variable capital.

If the capital was originally, as above,

I. $15,000 \, C = 12,000_c + 3,000_v \, (+ \, 3,000_s)$; and it is now

II. $15,000 \, C = 13,000_c + 2,000_v \, (+ \, 2,000_s)$; then $C = 15,000$ and $s' = 100$ per cent in both cases, and the rate of profit in case I, 20 per cent, is related to that in case II, $13\frac{1}{3}$ per cent, as the variable capital in case I, 3,000, is related to that in case II, 2,000; i.e. 20 per cent : $13\frac{1}{3}$ per cent = 3,000 : 2,000.

The variable capital can either rise or fall. Let us first take an example in which it rises. Say that a capital is originally constituted, and functions, as follows:

I. $100_c + 20_v + 10_s$; $C = 120$, $s' = 50$ per cent, $p' = 8\frac{1}{3}$ per cent.

The variable capital now rises to 30. According to our assumption, the constant capital must fall from 100 to 90, so that the total capital remains the same at 120. The surplus-value produced must rise by 15, given the same rate of surplus-value of 50 per cent. We then have:

II. $90_c + 30_v + 15_s$; $C = 120$, $s' = 50$ per cent, $p' = 12\frac{1}{2}$ per cent.

Let us proceed first of all on the assumption that wages are unchanged. In that case the other factors involved in the rate of surplus-value, i.e. the working day and the intensity of labour, must also have remained the same. The increase·in v (from 20 to 30) can only mean therefore that half as many workers again as before are employed. This means that the total value produced also rises by a half, from 30 to 45, while it is divided just as before, with two-thirds going to wages and a third to surplus-value. At the same time, however, as the increase in the number of workers, the constant capital, the value of the means of production, has fallen from 100 to 90. We have therefore a case of a decline in labour productivity combined with a simultaneous decline in constant capital. Is this case economicaily possible?

In agriculture and the extractive industries, where a decline in labour productivity and a consequent increase in the number of workers employed is easy to comprehend, this process – within the confines of capitalist production, and on its basis – is linked not with a decline in constant capital but with an increase. Even if the above decline in c were occasioned simply by a fall in price, an individual capital would be able to make the transition from I to II only under quite exceptional conditions. With two independent capitals, however, invested in different countries, or in different branches of agriculture or extractive industry, it would be by no means unusual if in one case more workers (hence a bigger variable capital) were employed and worked with less expensive or less plentiful means of production than in the other case.

Let us now drop the assumption that wages remain the same and explain the rise in variable capital from 20 to 30 in terms of an increase of a half in wages. We then have a completely different picture. The same number of workers – let us say 20 – carry on working with the same or only insignificantly reduced means of production. If the working day remains unaltered – at 10 hours for example – the total value produced remains similarly unaffected; it is still 30, just as before. But this 30 would now be fully employed in replacing the variable capital of 30 that was advanced; the surplus-value would have completely disappeared. We presupposed, however, that the rate of surplus-value remained constant at 50 per cent, as in I. This is possible only if the working day is also extended by half and increased to 15 hours. 20 workers would then produce in 15 hours a total value of 45, and all the conditions would be fulfilled:

II. $90_c + 30_v + 15_s$; $C = 120$, $s' = 50$ per cent,
  $p' = 12\frac{1}{2}$ per cent.

In this case, the 20 workers need no more means of labour, tools, machinery, etc. than in I. It is only the raw or ancillary materials that would have to be increased by half. If these materials fall in price, the transition from I to II would be much more possible as an economic phenomenon, given our assumptions, even for one and the same capital. And the capitalist would be compensated at least partially, by a bigger profit, for the loss that the devaluation of his constant capital would have caused him.

Let us now assume that the variable capital falls instead of rising. Then we need only reverse our above example, taking II as the original capital and moving from II to I.

II. $90_c + 30_v + 15_s$ is then transformed into

I. $100_c + 20_v + 10_s$; and it is readily apparent that by this reversal, the rates of profit in the two cases and the conditions governing their mutual relationship are not changed in the slightest.

If v falls from 30 to 20, because one-third less labour is engaged with an increased constant capital, this is simply the normal case in modern industry: rising productivity of labour, the operation of greater quantities of means of production by fewer workers. And in Part Three of this volume we shall see how this movement is necessarily bound up with a simultaneous fall in the rate of profit.

But if the reason for the fall in v from 30 to 20 is that the same number of workers are employed at a lower wage rate, then, so long as the working day is unchanged, the total value product remains unaltered at $30_v + 15_s = 45$. Since v has fallen to 20, the surplus-value has risen to 25 and the rate of surplus-value from 50 per cent to 125 per cent, which would be against our assumption. In order to remain within the limits of our example, the surplus-value, at a rate of 50 per cent, must fall instead to 10, and thus the total value produced from 45 to 30, and this is possible only if the working day is cut by one-third. We then have, as above:

$100_c + 20_v + 10_s$; $s' = 50$ per cent, $p' = 8\frac{1}{3}$ per cent.

We need hardly point out that a reduction in working hours of this kind combined with a fall in wages would not occur in practice. But this is beside the point. The rate of profit is a function of several variables, and if we want to know how these variables act on the profit rate we must investigate in turn the individual effect of each, irrespective of whether an isolated effect of this kind is economically possible or not in the case of one and the same capital.

2. *s' constant, v variable, C altered by the variation of v*

This case is different from the previous one only in degree. Instead of decreasing or increasing by the same amount as *v* increases or decreases, *c* now remains constant. But under today's conditions of large-scale industry and agriculture, variable capital is only a relatively small portion of the total capital and hence any reduction or growth in the total capital that is brought about by a change in the variable capital is also relatively slight. If we start once again with a capital such as:

I. $100_c + 20_v + 10_s$; $C = 120$, $s' = 50$ per cent,
$p' = 8\frac{1}{3}$ per cent,

this might perhaps be changed to something like:

II. $100_c + 30_v + 15_s$; $C = 130$, $s' = 50$ per cent,
$p' = 11\frac{7}{13}$ per cent.

The opposite case of a decline in the variable capital would again be illustrated by the reverse transition from II to I.

Economic conditions here would be essentially the same as in the previous case, and hence need no further explanation. The transition from I to II involves a decline of a third* in the productivity of labour, or the operation of 100_c requires half as much labour again in II as it does in I. This case is possible in agriculture.[9]

Whereas in the previous case the total capital was held constant

---

* Marx says 'a half', a slip arising from measuring the decline against the resulting figure rather than the original one.
9. The manuscript has here: 'For later investigation, how this case is related to ground-rent.' – F.E.

by the conversion of constant capital into variable or vice versa, now the increase in the variable portion means that extra capital is tied up, while a decrease involves the release of capital that had previously been needed.

3. *s'* and *v* constant, *c* and therefore also *C* variable

In this case the equation:

$$p' = s' \frac{v}{C}$$

is changed to:

$$p'_1 = s' \frac{v}{C_1},$$

and by cancelling out on both sides, we get the proportionality·

$$p'_1 : p' = C : C_1;$$

with the same rate of surplus-value and the same variable capital, the profit rate stands in inverse proportion to the total capital.

Say that we have three capitals or three different states of the same capital:

  I. $80_c + 20_v + 20_s$; $C = 100$, $s' = 100$ per cent,
       $p' = 20$ per cent;
  II. $100_c + 20_v + 20_s$; $C = 120$, $s' = 100$ per cent,
       $p' = 16\frac{2}{3}$ per cent;
  III. $60_c + 20_v + 20_s$; $C = 80$, $s' = 100$ per cent,
       $p' = 25$ per cent;

then 20 per cent : $16\frac{2}{3}$ per cent = 120 : 100; and 20 per cent : 25 per cent = 80 : 100.

The general formula given above for variations in $\frac{v}{C}$, where s' was constant, was:

$$p'_1 = s' \frac{ev}{EC}; \text{ it now becomes: } p'_1 = s' \frac{v}{EC},$$

since *v* does not undergo any alteration, and the factor $e = \frac{v_1}{v}$ is therefore 1.

Since $s'v = s$, the mass of surplus-value, and since s' and v both remain constant, s is also unaffected by any variation in C; the mass of surplus-value remains the same as before the change.

If c were to fall to zero, we would have $p' = s'$, the rate of profit equal to the rate of surplus-value.

The alteration in c can come about either from a change merely in the value of the material elements of the constant capital, or from a changed technical composition of the total capital, i.e. a change in the productivity of labour in the branch of production in question. In the latter case, the productivity of social labour, which rises with the development of large-scale industry and agriculture, would successively move from III to I and from I to II in the above example. A quantity of labour that is paid 20 and produces a value of 40 would start by being used to operate a mass of means of labour to the value of 60; if its productivity rose, the means of labour put into operation would grow first to 80, and then to 100, if their value remained the same. The reverse sequence would indicate a decline in productivity; the same quantity of labour would set less means of production in motion, and the business would be cut back, as can well happen in agriculture, mining, etc.

A saving in constant capital both increases the rate of profit and releases capital as well, and this is important for the capitalist. We shall return to this point later, as well as investigating the effect of changes in the prices of the elements of constant capital, raw materials in particular.*

We see here again how a variation in constant capital has the same effect on the rate of profit, irrespective of whether this variation is brought about by an increase or decrease in the material components of c, or simply by a change in their value.

4. *s' constant, v, c and C all variable*

In this case, the above general formula for changes in the profit rate, $p'_1 = s' \frac{ev}{EC}$, still applies. It results from this that, with the rate of surplus-value remaining the same:

(a) The rate of profit falls if E is greater than e, i.e. if the constant capital is increased in such a way that the total capital increases more sharply than the variable capital. If a capital of $80_c + 20_v + 20_s$ is changed to a composition of $170_c + 30_v + 30_s$, then s' remains at 100 per cent, but $\frac{v}{C}$ falls from $\frac{20}{100}$ to $\frac{30}{200}$, despite the fact that v has increased as well as C, and the rate of profit accordingly falls from 20 per cent to 15 per cent.

---

* All this forms the subject-matter of Chapters 5 and 6.

(b) The rate of profit remains unchanged only if $e = E$, i.e. if the fraction $\frac{v}{C}$ retains the same value despite the apparent change, thus if both numerator and denominator are multiplied or divided by the same figure. $80_c + 20_v + 20_s$ and $160_c + 40_v + 40_s$ evidently have the same profit rate of 20 per cent, because s' remains at 100 per cent and $\frac{v}{C} = \frac{20}{100} = \frac{40}{200}$ exhibits the same value in both examples.

(c) The rate of profit rises if e is greater than E, i.e. if the variable capital rises more sharply than the total capital. If $80_c + 20_v + 20_s$ becomes $120_c + 40_v + 40_s$, then the rate of profit of 20 per cent rises to 25 per cent, because with s' unaltered, $\frac{v}{C} = \frac{20}{100}$ has risen to $\frac{40}{160}$, from $\frac{1}{5}$ to $\frac{1}{4}$.

Where v and C both change in the same direction, we can conceive this change in their magnitudes as if both vary to a certain extent in the same ratio, so that up to this point $\frac{v}{C}$ remains unaltered. Beyond this point, then, only one of them varies, and we can thereby reduce this more complicated case to one or other of the previous simpler ones.

If $80_c + 20_v + 20_s$ changes to $100_c + 30_v + 30_s$, the ratio between v and c, and therefore also between v and C, remains unaltered up to the point $100_c + 25_v + 25_s$. The rate of profit, therefore, is so far unaffected. We can now take this $100_c + 25_v + 25_s$ as our starting-point; we find that v rises by 5, to 30_v, and C thereby rises from 125 to 130, and we are thus faced with case 2, that of a variation simply in v and the variation in C that this occasions. The rate of profit, which was originally 20 per cent, is increased by this addition of 5_v, to $23\frac{1}{13}$ per cent, given the same rate of surplus-value.

The same reduction to a simpler case can also take place even if v and C move in opposite directions. Let us proceed again from $80_c + 20_v + 20_s$, and let this change to the form $110_c + 10_v + 10_s$. A change to $40_c + 10_v + 10_s$ would have kept the profit rate the same as it was originally, i.e. 20 per cent. The addition of 70_c to this intermediate form makes it fall to $8\frac{1}{3}$ per cent. We have again reduced the example to a variation in only one of the variables, i.e. c.

Thus the simultaneous variation of v, c and C does not offer any new aspects, and always leads back in the last analysis to a case in which only one factor is variable.

Even the sole case that still remains has really been dispensed with already, i.e. the case in which v and c remain numerically the same, but their material elements undergo a change in value – v represents a different quantity of labour set in motion, and c a different quantity of means of production.

In the capital of $80_c + 20_v + 20_s$, the 20_v might originally represent the wages of 20 workers for a 10-hour working day. Say that the wage of each worker now rises from 1 to $1\frac{1}{4}$. In this case, 20_v only suffices to pay 16 workers instead of 20. But if the 20 workers produced a value of 40 in their 200 hours' work, then the 16, in a 10-hour day that amounts to 160 hours' work in all, will produce a value of only 32. After subtracting 20_v for wages, only 12 of the 32 is left for surplus-value; the rate of surplus-value would then have fallen from 100 per cent to 60 per cent. But since, according to our assumption, the rate of surplus-value has to remain constant, the working day must be extended by a quarter, from 10 hours to $12\frac{1}{2}$. If 20 workers produce a value of 80 in a working day of 10 hours, i.e. 200 hours' work in all, 16 workers produce the same value in $12\frac{1}{2}$ hours per day, which also comes to 200 hours, so that the capital of $80_c + 20_v$ still produces the same surplus-value of 20 as it did before.

Conversely, if wages fall in such a way that 20_v covers the wages of 30 workers, s' can remain constant only if the working day is reduced from 10 hours to $6\frac{2}{3}$. $20 \times 10 = 30 \times 6\frac{2}{3} = 200$ working hours.

We have already explained in essentials how c can retain the same value expression in money throughout all these conflicting assumptions, while representing the differing quantities of means of production which correspond to the changed conditions. This case would however be very exceptional in its pure form.

As far as a change in value of the elements of c is concerned, a change that increases or decreases certain elements while leaving their value sum c unaltered, this disturbs neither the rate of profit nor the rate of surplus-value, as long as it does not bring with it any alteration in the magnitude of v.

In this way we have dealt with all possible cases of variation of v, c and C in our equation. We have seen how the profit rate can fall, rise or remain the same, with the rate of surplus-value constant throughout, in so far as the slightest alteration in the ratio between v and c or C is sufficient to alter the profit rate as well.

It has also become evident that there is always a limit to the variation of v beyond which it is economically impossible for s' to remain constant. Since any unilateral variation of c must similarly reach a limit at which v can no longer remain constant, it is clear that limits are placed on all possible variations of $\frac{v}{C}$ beyond which s' must also vary. In the case of these variations in s', which we shall now turn to investigate, the mutual interaction of the various different variables in our equation appears even more clearly.

II. s' variable

We can obtain a general formula for the rates of profit corresponding to different rates of surplus-value, irrespective of whether $\frac{v}{C}$ remains constant or also varies, if we convert the equation: $p' = s' \frac{v}{C}$ into the equation: $p'_1 = s'_1 \frac{v_1}{C_1}$, in which p'_1, s'_1, v_1 and C_1 stand for the new values of p', s', v and C.

We then get: $p' : p'_1 = s' \frac{v}{C} : s'_1 \frac{v_1}{C_1}$, and therefore:

$$p'_1 = \frac{s'_1}{s'} \times \frac{v_1}{v} \times \frac{C}{C_1} \times p'.$$

1. s' variable, $\frac{v}{C}$ constant

In this case we have equations:

$$p' = s' \frac{v}{C} \text{ and } p'_1 = s'_1 \frac{v}{C},$$

such that $\frac{v}{C}$ has the same value in both cases. It follows therefore that $p' : p'_1 = s' : s'_1$.

The rates of profit for two capitals of the same composition are in direct proportion to their respective rates of surplus-value. Since the absolute magnitudes of v and C do not come into play in the fraction $\frac{v}{C}$, but simply the ratio between the two, this holds for all capitals of the same composition, whatever their absolute magnitude may be.

$80_c + 20_v + 20_s$; $C = 100$, $s' = 100$ per cent, $p' = 20$ per cent
$160_c + 40_v + 40_s$; $C = 200$, $s' = 50$ per cent, $p' = 10$ per cent
100 per cent : 50 per cent = 20 per cent : 10 per cent.

If the absolute magnitudes of v and C are the same in both cases, the profit rates also stand in the same ratio as the masses of surplus-value:

$$p' : p'_1 = s'v : s'_1 v = s : s_1.$$

For example:

$$80_c + 20_v + 20_s; s' = 100 \text{ per cent}, p' = 20 \text{ per cent}$$
$$80_c + 20_v + 10_s; s' = 50 \text{ per cent}, p' = 10 \text{ per cent}$$
$$20 \text{ per cent} : 10 \text{ per cent} = 100 \times 20 : 50 \times 20 = 20_s : 10_s.$$

It is evident now that given capitals of the same composition either absolutely or relatively, the rate of surplus-value can vary only if either wages, or the length of the working day, or again the intensity of labour, also vary. In the following three cases:

I. $80_c + 20_v + 10_s; s' = 50$ per cent, $p' = 10$ per cent
II. $80_c + 20_v + 20_s; s' = 100$ per cent, $p' = 20$ per cent
III. $80_c + 20_v + 40_s; s' = 200$ per cent, $p' = 40$ per cent,

the total value produced is 30 in I ($20_v + 10_s$), 40 in II and 60 in III. This can happen in three different ways.

Firstly, if wages vary, so that 20_v represents a different number of workers in each individual case. Let us assume that, in case I, 15 workers are employed for 10 hours at a wage of £1⅓, to produce the value of £30, of which £20 replaces wages and £10 remains for surplus-value. If wages fall to £1, then 20 workers are employed for 10 hours and produce a value of £40, of which £20 is wages and £20 surplus-value. If wages fall yet further to £⅔, then 30 workers are employed for 10 hours and produce a value of £60, of which £40 remains for surplus-value after subtracting the £20 for wages.

This case, that of a constant percentage composition of capital, constant working day, constant intensity of labour, with changes in the rate of surplus-value brought about by changes in wages, is the only one that meets Ricardo's assumption:

'Profits would be high or low, *exactly in proportion* as wages would be low or high' (*Principles*, Chapter I, section iii, p. 18 in the *Works of D. Ricardo*, ed. MacCulloch, 1852).*

Secondly, it can happen if the intensity of labour varies. In this case, for example, 20 workers might make 30 items of a certain commodity in case I, 40 in case II and 60 in case III, working with the same means of labour for 10 hours a day, with each item representing a new value of £1 over and above the value of the

---

* Pelican edition of Ricardo's *Principles of Political Economy, and Taxation*, p. 69. The emphasis in this quotation is Marx's own.

means of production consumed in it. Since 20 items, = £20, are always needed to replace wages, there remains for surplus-value in case I 10 items, = £10, in case II 20 items, = £20, and in case III 40 items, = £40.

The third possibility is that the working day varies in length. If 20 workers work with the same intensity for 9 hours in case I, 12 hours in case II, and 18 hours in case III, their total products will stand in the ratio of 9 : 12 : 18, i.e. 30 : 40 : 60, and since wages are 20 each time, there again remains 10, 20 or 40 left over for surplus-value.

A rise or fall in wages thus effects an opposite change in the rate of surplus-value, while a rise or fall in the intensity of labour, or an extension or reduction of the working day, both effect a change in the same direction, and with $\frac{v}{C}$ constant, the rate of profit is therefore similarly affected.

2. s' and v variable, C constant

In this case, we have the proportionality:

$$p' : p'_1 = s' \frac{v}{C} : s'_1 \frac{v_1}{C} = s'v : s'_1 v_1 = s : s_1.$$

The rates of profit stand in the same ratio as the respective masses of surplus-value.

Variation in the rate of surplus-value, with variable capital remaining the same, means a change in the size and distribution of the value product. Simultaneous variation in v and s' similarly entails a different distribution, but not always a change in the magnitude of the value product. Three cases are possible:

(a) The variations in v and s' take place in opposite directions, but by the same amount.* For example,

* It is readily apparent here that v and s' in no sense vary 'by the same amount' in this example, or even in the same proportion. If it is really v and s that are to vary 'in opposite directions, but by the same amount', then if we call the values of v, s, and s' after this variation v_1, s_1, and s'_1, we can derive the following formula for the effect on s' of changes in v.

Given that $v + s = v_1 + s_1$, then substituting vs' for s, we get:

$$v + vs' = v_1 + vs'_1, \text{ or:}$$

$$s'_1 = \frac{v}{v_1} (1 + s') - 1$$

On the basis of this formula, case (b) below can similarly be reduced to an inequality.

$80_c + 20_v + 10_s$; $s' = 50$ per cent, $p' = 10$ per cent
$90_c + 10_v + 20_s$; $s' = 200$ per cent, $p' = 20$ per cent.

Here the value product is the same in both cases, and so too, therefore, is the quantity of labour that is performed. $20_v + 10_s = 10_v + 20_s = 30$. The distinction is simply that in the first case 20 is paid for wages and 10 for surplus-value, while in the second case wages amount only to 10, and surplus-value is therefore 20. This is the only case in which a simultaneous variation in v and s' leaves the number of workers, the labour intensity and the length of the working day unaffected.

(b) The variations in s' and v still occur in opposite directions, but not to the same extent in each case. Either the variation in v must predominate, or that in s'.

I. $80_c + 20_v + 20_s$; $s' = 100$ per cent, $p' = 20$ per cent
II. $72_c + 28_v + 20_s$; $s' = 71\frac{3}{7}$ per cent, $p' = 20$ per cent
III. $84_c + 16_v + 20_s$; $s' = 125$ per cent, $p' = 20$ per cent.

In case I a value product of 40 involves a payment of 20_v, in case II a product of 48 a payment of 28_v, and in case III one of 36 a payment of 16_v. Both the value product and the wages have altered; but an alteration in the value product means an alteration in the quantity of labour performed, and therefore either in the number of workers, the duration of labour, or its intensity, if not more than one of these three.

(c) s' and v both vary in the same direction; in this case the effect of one reinforces that of the other.

$90_c + 10_v + 10_s$; $s' = 100$ per cent, $p' = 10$ per cent
$80_c + 20_v + 30_s$; $s' = 150$ per cent, $p' = 30$ per cent
$92_c + 8_v + 6_s$; $s' = 75$ per cent, $p' = 6$ per cent.

Here, too, the three value products are different, i.e. 20, 50 and 14; and this difference in the quantity of labour in each case can again be reduced to a difference in the number of workers, the duration or intensity of labour, or any combination of these factors.

3. s', v and C all variable
This case offers no new aspects and is settled by the general formula given under heading *II*, *s' variable* [p. 156].

*

The impact of a change in the rate of surplus-value on the profit rate can thus be covered by the following cases:

1. p' is increased or diminished in the same ratio as s', if $\frac{v}{C}$ remains constant.

$$80_c + 20_v + 20_s; s' = 100 \text{ per cent}, p' = 20 \text{ per cent}$$
$$80_c + 20_v + 10_s; s' = 50 \text{ per cent}, p' = 10 \text{ per cent}$$
100 per cent : 50 per cent = 20 per cent : 10 per cent.

2. p' rises or falls in a higher ratio than s', if $\frac{v}{C}$ moves in the same direction as s', i.e. increases or decreases according to whether s' increases or decreases.

$$80_c + 20_v + 10_s; s' = 50 \text{ per cent}, p' = 10 \text{ per cent}$$
$$70_c + 30_v + 20_s; s' = 66\tfrac{2}{3} \text{ per cent}, p' = 20 \text{ per cent}$$
50 per cent : 66$\tfrac{2}{3}$ per cent < 10 per cent : 20 per cent.

3. p' rises or falls in a lower ratio than s', if $\frac{v}{C}$ changes in the opposite direction to s', but in a lower ratio.

$$80_c + 20_v + 10_s; s' = 50 \text{ per cent}, p' = 10 \text{ per cent}$$
$$90_c + 10_v + 15_s; s' = 150 \text{ per cent}, p' = 15 \text{ per cent}$$
50 per cent : 150 per cent > 10 per cent : 15 per cent.

4. p' rises, even though s' falls, or falls, even though s' rises, if $\frac{v}{C}$ changes in the opposite direction to s', and in a higher ratio.

$$80_c + 20_v + 20_s; s' = 100 \text{ per cent}, p' = 20 \text{ per cent}$$
$$90_c + 10_v + 15_s; s' = 150 \text{ per cent}, p' = 15 \text{ per cent}.$$

Here s' has risen from 100 per cent to 150 per cent, while p' has fallen from 20 per cent to 15 per cent.

5. Finally, p' remains constant even though s' rises or falls, if $\frac{v}{C}$ changes in the opposite direction to s', but in exactly the same ratio.

It is only this last case that still requires some further discussion. We saw above, with the variations in $\frac{v}{C}$, how one and the same rate of surplus-value can be expressed in the most varied rates of profit. Here we see that one and the same rate of profit can be based on very different rates of surplus-value. But while with s' constant, any change whatsoever in the ratio of v to C is sufficient to induce a variation in the rate of profit, a change in s' must involve an exactly corresponding, but opposite, change in $\frac{v}{C}$, if the profit rate is to remain the same. This is possible only very exceptionally in the case of one and the same capital, or with two capitals in the same country.

Let us take for example a capital

$$80_c + 20_v + 20_s; C = 100, s' = 100 \text{ per cent}, p' = 20 \text{ per cent},$$

and assume that wages fall in such a way that the same number of workers can be had for 16_v as previously with 20_v. With conditions remaining otherwise unchanged, we would then have 4_v set free, giving

$$80_c + 16_v + 24_s; C = 96, s' = 150 \text{ per cent}, p' = 25 \text{ per cent}.$$

If p' is still to be 20 per cent, as before, the total capital has to increase to 120, and the constant capital therefore to 104:

$$104_c + 16_v + 24_s; C = 120, s' = 150 \text{ per cent}, p' = 20 \text{ per cent}.$$

This would be possible only if a change in the productivity of labour took place simultaneously with the fall in wages, and required this changed composition of capital; or alternatively, if the money value of the constant capital rose from 80 to 104 – in other words, a chance combination of conditions that only comes about in exceptional circumstances. In actual fact a change in s' which is not simultaneously a change in v, thus also giving rise to a change in $\frac{v}{c}$, is conceivable only under quite special conditions, i.e. in those branches of industry in which only fixed capital and labour are applied, and the object of labour is provided by nature.

The position is different when comparing rates of profit in two countries. Here the same rate of profit expresses in most cases different rates of surplus-value.

It results from all these five cases, therefore, that a rising profit rate can correspond to a falling or a rising rate of surplus-value, a falling profit rate can correspond to a rising or a falling rate of surplus-value, and a rate of profit that remains the same can also correspond to a rising or a falling rate of surplus-value. We have already shown under heading *I* [s' constant, $\frac{v}{c}$ variable] that a rising, falling or unchanged rate of profit can also correspond to a rate of surplus-value that remains the same.

*

The rate of profit is thus determined by two major factors: the rate of surplus-value and the value composition of the capital.

The effects of these two factors can be briefly summarized as follows, and we are able now to express the composition in percentages, since it is immaterial here in which of the two portions of capital the change originates.

The rates of profit of two different capitals, or of one and the same capital in two successive and different states,

are equal:

(1) given the same percentage composition and the same rate of surplus-value;

(2) given unequal percentage compositions and unequal rates of surplus-value, if the [mathematical] product of the rate of surplus-value and the percentage of the variable part of capital (s' and v) is the same in each case, i.e. the *mass* of surplus-value reckoned as a percentage of the total capital ($s = s'v$); in other words, when the factors s' and v stand in inverse proportion to one another in the two cases.

They are unequal:

(1) given the same percentage composition, if the rates of surplus-value are unequal, in which case they stand in the same ratio as these rates of surplus-value;

(2) given the same rate of surplus-value and different percentage compositions, in which case they stand in the same ratio as the variable portions of the capitals;

(3) given different rates of surplus-value and different percentage compositions, in which case they stand in the same proportion as the products $s'v$, i.e. as the masses of surplus-value reckoned as a percentage of the total capital.[10]

10. The manuscript also contains further and very detailed calculations on the mathematical difference between rate of surplus-value and rate of profit ($s' - p'$), a difference which has all kinds of interesting properties, and whose movement presents cases in which the two rates draw apart and cases in which they converge. These movements can also be represented by curves. I have refrained from reproducing this material, since it is of little importance for the immediate aim of this book, and all that is required here is to draw attention to this point for those readers who might wish to pursue it further. – F.E.

Chapter 4: The Effect of the Turnover
on the Rate of Profit*

(The effect of the turnover on the production of surplus-value, and consequently also of profit, has already been discussed in Volume 2. To summarize it in brief, the time required for the turnover has the effect that the whole capital cannot be simultaneously employed in production. One part of this capital therefore always lies fallow, whether in the form of money capital, stocks of raw materials, finished but still unsold commodity capital, or outstanding debts that are not yet due for payment. The capital that is in active production, active in the production and appropriation of surplus-value, is always reduced by this amount, and the surplus-value that is produced and appropriated is reduced in the same proportion. The shorter the turnover time, the smaller is this idle portion of capital compared with the whole; the greater therefore is the surplus-value appropriated, other conditions being equal.

We explained in detail in the second volume how a reduction in the turnover time or in one of its two component sections, production time and circulation time, raises the mass of surplus-value produced.† But since the rate of profit simply expresses the ratio of the mass of surplus-value produced to the total capital engaged in producing it, it is evident that any reduction of this kind raises the rate of profit as well. The points made in Part Two of the second volume with respect to surplus-value apply equally here to profit and the rate of profit, and do not need to be repeated. There are simply a few key aspects we would like to emphasize.

The main means whereby production time is reduced is an increase in the productivity of labour, which is commonly known as industrial progress. If this does not also involve a major increase in the total capital investment, due to the installation of expensive

* As he explains in the Preface, the whole of this chapter was written by Engels. It is therefore placed in parentheses.
† Chapter 16, pp. 369 ff.

machinery etc., and therefore a fall in the rate of profit as reckoned on the total capital, then this profit rate must rise. And this is decidedly the case with many of the most recent advances in the metallurgical and chemical industries. The newly discovered methods of iron and steel preparation associated with Bessemer, Siemens, Gilchrist-Thomas and others shorten what were previously very protracted processes to a minimum. The preparation of alizarin dye from coal-tar gives the same result in a few weeks, and using apparatus that is already in use for coal-tar dyes, as previously took several years. The madder from which the dye was previously prepared needed a year to grow, and the roots were left to mature for several years after that before they were used.

The main means of cutting circulation time has been improved communications. And the last fifty years have brought a revolution in this respect that is comparable only with the industrial revolution of the second half of the last century. On land the Macadamized road has been replaced by the railway, while at sea the slow and irregular sailing ship has been driven into the background by the rapid and regular steamer line; the whole earth has been girded by telegraph cables. It was the Suez canal that really opened the Far East and Australia to the steamer. The circulation time for a shipment of goods to the Far East, which in 1847 was at least twelve months (see Volume 2, p. 329), has now been more or less reduced to as many weeks. The two major foci of crisis between 1825 and 1857, America and India, have been brought 70 to 90 per cent closer to the industrial countries of Europe by this revolution in the means of commerce, and have lost in this way a good deal of their explosive potential. The turnover time of world trade as a whole has been reduced to the same extent, and the efficacy of the capital involved in it has been increased two or three times and more. It is evident that this cannot but have had its effect on the profit rate.

In order to present the effect of the turnover of the total capital on the profit rate in its pure form, we must assume that all other circumstances are equal for the two capitals we are comparing. The percentage composition in particular must be taken as the same, as well as the rate of surplus-value and the length of the working day. Let us take a capital A with a composition of $80_c + 20_v = 100C$, a rate of surplus-value of 100 per cent, and a twice-yearly turnover. Its annual product is then $160_c + 40_v + $

40_s. But for the purposes of the profit rate we calculate this 40_s not on the capital value of 200 turned over, but rather on the capital value of 100 that was advanced, and we thus get $p' = 40$ per cent.

Let us compare this with a capital $B = 160_c + 40_v = 200C$, with the same rate of surplus-value, but turning over only once in the year. Its annual product is then $160_c + 40_v + 40_s$, the same as above. This time however the 40_s has to be calculated on a capital advance of 200, which results in a profit rate of 20 per cent, i.e. only half the rate for A.

The result is therefore that for capitals of the same percentage composition, with the same rate of surplus-value and the same working day, the profit rates of two capitals vary inversely as their turnover times. If either the composition or the rate of surplus-value or the working day or the wage of labour is not the same in the two cases to be compared, further differences in the rate of profit are also brought about, but these are independent of the turnover, and do not concern us here; they have already been discussed in Chapter 3.

The direct effect of the abbreviated turnover time on the production of surplus-value, and therefore also on profit, consists in the increased effectiveness which this gives to the variable portion of capital, as discussed in Volume 2, Chapter 16: 'The Turnover of Variable Capital'. There it was seen how a variable capital of 500 which turns over ten times in the year appropriates just as much surplus-value in this period as a variable capital of 5,000, with the same rate of surplus-value and the same wages, which turns over only once in the year.

Let us take a capital I, consisting of 10,000 fixed capital, its annual depreciation being 10 per cent = 1,000, 500 circulating constant capital, and 500 variable capital. With a rate of surplus-value of 100 per cent, the variable capital turns over ten times in the year. For the sake of simplicity we shall assume in all the following examples that the circulating constant capital turns over in the same period as the variable, which will generally be the case in practice. The product of such a turnover period will then be:

$$100_c \text{ (depreciation)} + 500_c + 500_v + 500_s = 1,600,$$

and the product of the whole year, with ten turnovers:

$$1,000_c \text{ (depreciation)} + 5,000_c + 5,000_v + 5,000_s = 16,000;$$

$$C = 11,000, \; s = 5,000, \; p' = \frac{5,000}{11,000} = 45\frac{5}{11} \text{ per cent.}$$

Let us now take a capital II: fixed capital 9,000 with annual depreciation 1,000, circulating constant capital 1,000, variable capital 1,000, rate of surplus-value 100 per cent, turnovers of variable capital five per year. The product of one of these turnover periods of the variable capital will then be:

$$200_c \text{ (depreciation)} + 1,000_c + 1,000_v + 1,000_s = 3,200,$$

and the total annual product over five turnovers:

$$1,000_c \text{ (depreciation)} + 5,000_c + 5,000_v + 5,000_s = 16,000;$$
$$C = 11,000, \; s = 5,000, \; p' = \frac{5,000}{11,000} = 45\frac{5}{11} \text{ per cent.}$$

We may also take a capital III in which there is no fixed capital, but simply 6,000 circulating constant capital and 5,000 variable capital. It turns over once a year, say, with a rate of surplus-value of 100 per cent. The total annual product is then:

$$6,000_c + 5,000_v + 5,000_s = 16,000;$$
$$C = 11,000, \; s = 5,000, \; p' = 45\frac{5}{11} \text{ per cent.}$$

In all three cases, therefore, we have the same annual mass of surplus-value = 5,000, and since the total capital is the same in all these cases, i.e. 11,000, we have the same profit rate of $45\frac{5}{11}$ per cent.

If in the case of the above capital I there took place not ten but only five turnovers of its variable portion, the matter would be different. The product of one turnover would then be:

$$200_c \text{ (depreciation)} + 500_c + 500_v + 500_s = 1,700;$$

or the annual product:

$$1,000_c \text{ (depreciation)} + 2,500_c + 2,500_v + 2,500_s = 8,500;$$
$$C = 11,000, \; s = 2,500, \; p' = \frac{2,500}{11,000} = 22\frac{8}{11} \text{ per cent.}$$

The profit rate has now fallen by half, as the turnover time has doubled.

The mass of surplus-value appropriated in the course of a year is therefore equal to the mass of surplus-value appropriated in one turnover period of the *variable* capital, multiplied by the number of such turnovers in a year. If we call the surplus-value or profit annually appropriated S, the surplus-value appropriated in one turnover period s, and the number of turnovers made by the variable capital in a year n, then $S = sn$ and the annual rate of surplus-value $S' = s'n$, as already set out in Volume 2, Chapter 16, 1.

It goes without saying that the formula for the profit rate $p' = s'\frac{v}{C} = s'\frac{v}{c+v}$ is correct only if the v in the numerator is the same as that in the denominator. The v in the denominator is the entire part of the total capital that is spent on average as variable capital, on wages. The v in the numerator is initially determined simply by the fact that a certain quantity of surplus-value $= s$ has been produced and appropriated by it, related to it by the rate of surplus-value s', which equals $\frac{s}{v}$. It is only in this way that the equation $p' = \frac{s}{c+v}$ was transformed into the equation $p' = s'\frac{v}{c+v}$. The v in the numerator can now be more accurately defined by the condition that it must be equal to the v in the denominator, i.e. to the entire variable part of the capital C. In other words, the equation $p' = \frac{s}{C}$ can be transformed into $p' = s'\frac{v}{c+v}$ without risk of error only if s stands for the surplus-value produced in a *single* turnover period of the variable capital. If s comprises only a part of this surplus-value, $s = s'v$ is still correct, but this v is now smaller than the v in $C = c + v$, as it is smaller than the whole of the variable capital that is laid out on wages. But if s comprises more than the surplus-value of one turnover of v, a part of this v or even the whole of it functions twice, firstly in the first turnover, then in the second or further turnovers; the v that produces surplus-value and is the sum of all wages paid is thus greater than the v in $c + v$, and the calculation is false.

In order that the formula for the annual rate of profit may be completely correct, we must replace the simple rate of surplus-value with the annual rate, S' or $s'n$ in place of s'. In other words, we must multiply s', the rate of surplus-value – or else multiply the v, the variable capital v contained in C – by n, the number of turnovers that this variable capital makes in a year, and we then obtain $p' = s'n\frac{v}{C}$, the formula for calculating the annual rate of profit.

The capitalist himself does not know in most cases how much variable capital he employs in his business. We have already seen in Chapter 8 of Volume 2, and we shall now see further, that the only distinction within his capital that impresses itself on the capitalist as fundamental is the distinction between fixed and circulating capital. From the same till that contains the part of his circulating capital that exists in his hands in the money form, in so far as this is not placed in the bank, he fetches both money for wages and money for raw and ancillary materials, and enters both of these in the same cash account. Even if he were to keep a separate record for wages paid, this would simply indicate the total sum paid at the end of the year, i.e. vn, and not the variable capital v itself. In order to arrive at this sum he would have to make a special calculation, such as is given in the following example.

Let us take the spinning mill described in Volume 1 [Chapter 9, 1, pp. 327–8], with its 10,000 spindles, and assume that the data given for one week in April 1871 are the same for the whole year. The fixed capital in the form of machinery was £10,000. The circulating capital was not given; we shall take it to be £2,500, a fairly high figure, but one that is justified by the assumption we must constantly make at this stage, that there are no credit operations, i.e. no permanent or temporary use of other people's capital. The week's product was composed, as far as its value was concerned, of £20 for depreciation of machinery, £358 advance of circulating constant capital (rent £6, cotton £342, coal, gas and oil £10), £52 laid out as variable capital on wages, and £80 surplus-value, i.e. 20_c (depreciation) $+ 358_c + 52_v + 80_s = 510$.

The weekly advance of circulating capital was therefore $358_c + 52_v = 410$, and its percentage composition $87.3_c + 12.7_v$.* Calculated on the whole circulating capital of £2,500, this gives a constant capital of £2,182 and a variable capital of £318. Since the total outlay on wages for the whole year comes to 52 times £52, i.e. £2,704, the upshot is that the variable capital of £318 has turned over almost exactly $8\frac{1}{2}$ times in the course of the year. The rate of surplus-value is $\frac{80}{52} = 153\frac{11}{13}$ per cent. From these elements we can calculate the rate of profit by using the formula $p' = s'n\frac{v}{C}$, with $s' = 153\frac{11}{13}$, $n = 8\frac{1}{2}$, $v = 318$, $C = 12,500$. The result is that $p' = 153\frac{11}{13} \times 8\frac{1}{2} \times \frac{318}{12,500} = 33.27$ per cent.

We can test this by using the simple formula $p'\frac{s}{C}$. The total surplus-value or profit over the whole year amounts to £80 $\times$ 52 $=$ £4,160, and this divided by the total capital of £12,500 gives 33.28 per cent, pretty well the same figure as above. This is an

* Engels has rounded off all these calculations.

abnormally high rate of profit, which can only be explained by extremely favourable temporary conditions (very cheap cotton prices combined with very high prices for yarn) and would certainly not have prevailed for a whole year in actual fact.

In the formula $p' = s'n \frac{v}{C}$, $s'n$, as already stated, is what was designated in Volume 2 as the annual rate of surplus-value. In the above case it amounts to $153\frac{11}{13}$ per cent $\times 8\frac{1}{2}$, which is $1,307\frac{9}{13}$ per cent. If a certain worthy was shocked by the enormous size of the annual rate of surplus-value of 1,000 per cent given in one of the examples in Volume 2, he can perhaps console himself with the actual fact of an annual rate of surplus-value of more than 1,300 per cent taken from a practical example in Manchester. In periods of greatest prosperity, such as we have of course not seen now for a long while, a rate of this level is by no means rare.

We have here incidentally an example of the actual composition of capital in modern large-scale industry. The total capital is divided into £12,182 constant and £318 variable, making £12,500 altogether. In percentages, $97\frac{1}{2}_c + 2\frac{1}{2}_v = 100C$. Only a fortieth part of the total is needed for the payment of wages, though this serves more than eight times in the course of a year.

Since there are certainly only a few capitalists who make calculations of such a kind about their businesses, statistical material is almost completely absent on the ratio of the constant part o the total social capital to the variable part. Only the U.S. Census gives what is possible under present-day conditions, the sum of the wages paid in each branch of business and the profits made. Dubious as these data are, owing to the way they rely on the unchecked information of the industrialists themselves, they are none the less extremely valuable and the only data that we have on the subject. In Europe we are far too kind-hearted to expect such revelations on the part of our great industrialists. – F.E.)

Chapter 5: Economy in the Use of Constant Capital

I. GENERAL CONSIDERATIONS

An increase in absolute surplus-value or an extension of surplus labour and hence the working day, with variable capital remaining the same and thus the same number of workers being employed at the same nominal wage, causes a relative fall in the value of constant capital compared with the total capital and the variable capital, and thus raises the rate of profit, quite apart from the growth in the mass of surplus-value and a possibly rising rate of surplus-value. (It is immaterial here whether overtime is paid or not.) The volume of fixed capital (factory buildings, machinery, etc.) remains the same, whether work continues for 16 hours or for 12. The extension of the working day requires no new expenditure on this, the most expensive portion of the constant capital. The value of the fixed capital, moreover, is now reproduced in a shorter series of turnover periods, and the time for which it has to be advanced in order to make a certain profit is reduced. The lengthening of the working day thus raises profits even if overtime is paid, and up to a certain point this is true even if overtime is paid at a higher rate than normal working hours. The ever-growing need to increase fixed capital in the modern industrial system was therefore a major stimulus for profit-mad capitalists to prolong the working day.[11]

The situation is different when the working day remains constant. Here, one solution is to increase the number of workers and with them also, to a certain degree, the amount of fixed capital – buildings, machinery, etc. – so as to exploit a greater mass of labour (for we ignore here any deductions from wages,

11. 'Since in all factories there is a very large amount of fixed capital in buildings and machinery, the greater the number of hours that machinery can be kept at work the greater will be the return' (*Reports of the Inspectors of Factories ... 31 October 1858*, p. 8).

or depression of wages below their normal level). Alternatively, if the intensity of labour is to be increased, labour productivity raised, or more relative surplus-value produced in any way, then the mass of the circulating part of constant capital will have to grow in those branches of industry that use raw materials, since more raw materials, etc. are worked up in the given space of time. Secondly, the amount of machinery set in motion by the same number of workers will have to grow, and this too is a part of constant capital. A growth in surplus-value is therefore accompanied by a growth in constant capital, and the growing exploitation of labour by an increase in the price paid for the conditions of production by means of which labour is exploited, i.e. by greater outlays of capital. The rate of profit is thereby reduced on the one hand, even if increased on the other.

A whole series of current expenses remains almost if not completely the same whether the working day is shorter or longer. The costs of supervision are less for 500 workers over 18 hours than for 750 workers over 12. 'The expense of working a factory 10 hours almost equals that of working it 12' (*Reports of the Inspectors of Factories . . . 31 October 1848*, p. 37).

Local and state taxes, fire insurance, the wages of various permanent staff, the depreciation of machinery and various other factory expenses continue unchanged whether working hours are long or short. They rise relative to profit, in so far as production declines. (*Reports of the Inspectors of Factories . . . 31 October 1862*, p. 19.)

The time which the value of machinery and other components of fixed capital takes for its reproduction is determined in practice not by their own effective duration, but by the duration of the labour process in which they function and are used. If the workers have to drudge for 18 hours instead of 12, this adds three extra days to the week, one week becomes one and a half, two years become three. If overtime is not paid, then besides their normal surplus labour-time the workers give a third week or year gratis for every two. In this way the reproduction of the machinery's value is speeded up by 50 per cent, and accomplished in two-thirds of the time previously needed.

In our present investigation, as in that of fluctuations in the price of raw materials (Chapter 6), we proceed from the assumption that the rate and mass of surplus-value are given – in order to avoid needless complications.

As already emphasized in the analysis of cooperation,* the division of labour and machinery, the economy in the conditions of production which characterizes production on a large scale arises in essentials from the way that these conditions function as conditions of social and socially combined labour, i.e. as social conditions of labour. They are consumed in common in the production process, consumed by the collective worker instead of being consumed in fragmented form by a mass of unconnected workers or workers directly cooperating only to a small degree. In a large factory with one or two central motors, the costs of these motors do not grow in the same proportion as the number of machines to which they impart motion; even the working machine itself does not increase in cost in proportion to the rising number of tools, as it were its organs, with which it functions. The concentration of the means of production also saves on all manner of buildings, not only workshops proper, but also stores, etc. The same is true of expenses for heating and lighting, and so on. Other conditions of production also remain the same, whether they are used by many or by few.

But all these economies, arising from the concentration of means of production and their employment on a massive scale, presuppose as an essential condition the concentration of the workers in one place, and their cooperation, i.e. the social combination of labour. They thus arise as much from the social character of labour as surplus-value does from the surplus labour of each individual worker taken in isolation. Even the constant improvements that are possible and necessary arise solely from the social experiences and observations that are made possible and promoted by the large-scale production of the combined collective worker.

The same applies also to the second major aspect of the economical use of the conditions of production. By this we mean the transformation of the refuse of production, its so-called waste products, back into new elements of production, either in the same branch of industry or in others; the processes by which this so-called refuse is sent back into the cycle of production, and thus consumption – productive or individual. This branch of savings, too, which we shall deal with somewhat more closely later on,† is the result of social labour on a large scale. It is the resulting

* Volume 1, Chapter 13, pp. 441–3.
† See below, pp. 195–8.

massive scale of these waste products that makes them into new objects of trade and therefore new elements of production. It is only as the waste products of production in common, and hence of production on a large scale, that they acquire this importance for the production process and remain bearers of exchange-value. The waste products, quite apart from the service that they perform as new elements of production, reduce the cost of raw material, to the extent that they can be resold, for this cost always includes the normal wastage, i.e. the average quantity that is lost in the course of processing. To the extent that the costs of this portion of constant capital are reduced, the rate of profit is correspondingly increased, with a given magnitude of variable capital and a given rate of surplus-value.

If surplus-value is a given factor, the profit rate can be increased only by reducing the value of the constant capital required for the production of the commodities in question. In so far as the constant capital is involved in production, all that matters is its use-value, not its exchange-value. The amount of labour that the flax in a spinning mill can absorb depends not on its value but on its quantity, once the level of labour productivity, i.e. the level of technical development, is given. In the same way, the assistance that a machine gives to three workers, say, depends not on its value but rather on its use-value as a machine. At one stage of technical development a bad machine may be expensive, at another stage a good machine may be cheap.

The increased profit that a capitalist obtains through a fall in the cost of cotton and spinning machinery, for example, is the result of an increase in labour productivity, and indeed not in the spinning mill, but rather in the production of machines and cotton. A smaller amount of expenditure on the conditions of labour is needed in order to objectify a given quantity of labour and thus appropriate a given quantity of surplus labour. The costs of appropriating a certain quantity of surplus labour therefore fall.

We have already discussed the saving brought about because the collective worker – the socially combined worker – employs the means of production in common in the production process. A further saving, that arising from the reduction of the circulation time (the development of the means of communication being the decisive material aspect here), will be considered again below. Here, however, we must firstly dwell on the economies that arise from the continuous improvement of machinery, namely (1) in its material, e.g. iron instead of wood; (2) in the cheapening of machinery through the improvement of machine-building in general, so that even if the value of the fixed part of constant capital constantly grows with the development of labour on a large scale, it in no way grows to the same degree;[12] (3) the special improvements that enable machinery that is already installed to operate more cheaply and efficiently, e.g. improvements to steam boilers, etc., which we shall also discuss later on in more detail; (4) the reduction of wastage by better machinery.

Everything that reduces the depreciation of machinery, and of the fixed capital in general, for a given period of production, not only cheapens the individual commodity, since each individual commodity reproduces its aliquot share of the depreciation in its price, but also reduces the aliquot capital expenditure for this period. Repair work and the like, to the extent that it is needed, counts as part of the original costs of the machinery. Its reduction, as a consequence of the machinery's greater durability, reduces the price of the machinery proportionately.

For all economies of this kind it is largely true once again that this is possible only for the combined worker and can often be realized only by work on a still larger scale. It demands a still greater direct combination of workers in the actual process of production.

On the other hand, however, the development of the productive power of labour in *one* branch of production, e.g. of iron, coal, machines, construction, etc., which may in turn be partly connected with advances in the area of intellectual production, i.e. the natural sciences and their application, appears as the condition for a reduction in the value and hence the costs of means of production in *other* branches of industry, e.g. textiles or agriculture. This is evident enough, for the commodity that emerges from one branch of industry as a product enters another branch as means of production. Its cheapness or otherwise depends on the productivity of labour in the branch of production from which it emerges as a product, and is at the same time a condition not only for the cheapening of the commodities into the production of which it enters as means of production, but also for the reduction in value of the constant capital whose element it now becomes, and therefore for an increase in the rate of profit.

12. See Ure on advances in factory construction. [See below, p. 199.]

The characteristic feature of this kind of economy in the constant capital, which proceeds from the progressive development of industry, is that here the rise in the profit rate for *one* branch of industry depends on the development of labour productivity in *another*. The benefit that accrues here to the capitalist is once more an advantage produced by social labour, even though not by the workers whom he directly exploits. This development in productivity can always be reduced in the last analysis to the social character of the labour that is set to work, to the division of labour in society, and to the development of intellectual labour, in particular of the natural sciences. What the capitalist makes use of here are the benefits of the entire system of the social division of labour. Here it is the development of labour productivity in its external department, the department that provides him with means of production, which causes the value of the constant capital applied by the capitalist to fall relatively and the profit rate therefore to rise.

A different form of increase in the profit rate arises not from economy in the labour by which the constant capital is produced, but rather from economy in the employment of the constant capital itself. By the concentration of workers and their cooperation on a large scale, constant capital is spared. The same buildings, heating and lighting equipment, etc. cost relatively less for production on a large scale than on a small scale. The same holds for power and working machinery. Even if its value rises absolutely, it falls relatively, in relation to the increasing extension of production and to the size of the variable capital or the mass of labour-power that is set in motion. The economy that a capital makes in its own branch of production consists firstly and most directly in economizing on labour, i.e. in reducing the paid labour of its own workers; the economy previously mentioned, however, consists in the greatest possible appropriation of unpaid alien labour in the most economical fashion; i.e. in operating at the given scale of production with the lowest possible costs. In so far as this kind of economy is not dependent on the already mentioned exploitation of the productivity of the social labour applied in the production of constant capital, but is economy in the use of the constant capital itself, it arises either directly from cooperation and the social form of labour within the actual branch of production in question, or else from the production of machinery, etc. on a scale at which its value does not increase to the same extent as its use-value.

Two points must be borne in mind here. In the first place, if the value of c were 0, we would have $p' = s'$, and the rate of profit would be at its maximum. Secondly, however, what is important for the direct exploitation of labour itself is by no means the value of the means of exploitation applied, whether that of the fixed capital or that of the raw and ancillary materials. In so far as they serve to absorb labour, as media in or through which the labour and therefore also the surplus labour is objectified, the exchange-value of these machines, buildings, raw materials, etc. is completely irrelevant. The only thing that matters here is on the one hand the quantity of these means of exploitation technically required for combination with a certain quantity of labour, and on the other hand their appropriateness to their purpose, i.e. not only good machines are required, but also good raw and ancillary material. The rate of profit depends in part on the quality of the raw material. Good material makes little waste, and thus a smaller amount of raw material is needed to absorb the same quantity of labour. The resistance the working machine meets with is also reduced to some extent. In part this even affects surplus-value and its rate. With bad raw material the worker needs more time to work up the same quantity; if wages remain the same, this results in a deduction from the surplus-value. There is also a very significant effect on the reproduction and accumulation of capital, which, as explained in Volume 1, pp. 752 ff., depends still more on the productivity of the labour applied than on its amount.

The fanaticism that the capitalist shows for economizing on means of production is now comprehensible. If nothing is to be lost or wasted, if the means of production are to be used only in the manner required by production itself, then this depends partly on the workers' training and skill and partly on the discipline that the capitalist exerts over the combined workers, which would become superfluous in a state of society where the workers worked on their own account, just as it is already almost superfluous in the case of piece-work. The same fanaticism is also expressed inversely in the form of skimping on elements of production, which is a major way of lowering the value of the constant capital in relation to the variable and thus of increasing the rate of profit. In this connection we have the sale of these elements of production above their value, in so far as this value reappears in the product, which is an important aspect of fraud. This aspect plays a decisive role in German industry, in particular, whose very motto is: People cannot fail to appreciate it if we send them first good samples, and then bad goods. However, these phenomena pertain to competition and do not concern us here.

It must be noted how this rise in the rate of profit brought about by a reduction in the value of the constant capital, and thus in its expense, is completely independent of whether the branch of industry in which it takes place produces luxury products, means of subsistence that enter the consumption of the workers, or means of production. This would be important only in as much as it affected the rate of surplus-value, which depends essentially on the value of labour-power, i.e. on the value of the worker's customary means of subsistence. Here, on the contrary, surplus-value and its rate are taken as given. How the surplus-value is related to the total capital – and this is what determines the profit rate – depends under these circumstances exclusively on the value of the constant capital and in no way on the use-value of the elements of which this consists.

Of course the relative cheapening of the means of production does not exclude a growth in their absolute value; for the absolute scale on which they are applied increases extraordinarily with the development of labour productivity and the growing scale of production that accompanies it. Economy in the use of constant capital, from whatever aspect it is viewed, is firstly the result of nothing more than the fact that the means of production function in common and are used as the common means of production of the combined worker, so that this economy itself appears as a product of the social character of directly productive labour; secondly, however, it is also the result of the development of labour productivity in those spheres that provide capital with its means of production, so that even if labour as a whole is considered vis-à-vis capital as a whole, and not merely the workers employed by capitalist X vis-à-vis this capitalist X, this economy again presents itself as the product of the development of the productive forces of social labour, and the distinction is simply that capitalist X benefits not only from the productivity of labour in his own firm, but also from that of other firms as well. Yet the economical use of constant capital still appears to the capitalist as a requirement completely alien to the worker and absolutely independent of him, a requirement which does not concern the worker in the least. Nevertheless, it always remains very clear to the capitalist that the worker certainly does have something to do with whether the capitalist buys more or less labour for the same amount of money (for this is how the transaction between capitalist and worker appears in his consciousness). To a still higher level than is the case with other powers intrinsic to labour, this economy in the use of means of production, this method of attaining a certain result with the least possible expense, appears as a power inherent in capital and a method specific to and characteristic of the capitalist mode of production.

This way of conceiving things is all the less surprising in that it corresponds to the semblance of the matter and that the capital relation actually does conceal the inner connection in the state of complete indifference, externality and alienation in which it places the worker vis-à-vis the conditions of realization of his own labour.

Firstly, the means of production which comprise the constant capital simply represent the capitalist's money (as the body of the Roman debtor represented the money of his creditor, according to Linguet),* and are connected to him alone, while the worker, in so far as he comes into contact with them in the actual process of production, deals with them only as use-values for production, means and materials of labour. The decrease or increase in this value is therefore a question that affects his relationship to the capitalist as little as whether he works with copper or with iron. But the capitalist likes to conceive things differently, as we shall see later, as soon as there is an increase in the value of the means of production and hence a decline in the rate of profit.

Secondly, in so far as these means of production are at the same time a means for exploiting labour in the capitalist production process, the relative cheapness or otherwise of these means of exploitation concerns the worker as little as a horse is concerned with the expense of its bit and bridle.

Finally, as we have already seen,† the worker actually treats the social character of his work, its combination with the work of others for a common goal, as a power that is alien to him; the

---

* In his book *Théorie des lois civiles, ou principes fondamentaux de la société*, London, 1767, Simon-Nicolas-Henri Linguet (1736–94), a leading figure of the French Enlightenment, held that the Roman creditors literally 'cut shares' in their debtors' bodies, and ate these (Vol. 2, Bk 5, Ch. 20). Cf. *Capital* Volume 1, p. 400, n. 19. For Marx's comments on Linguet's criticism of the situation of the modern working class from a reactionary point of view, see *Theories of Surplus-Value*, Part I, Chapter VII.

† See Volume 1, pp. 447 ff.

conditions in which this combination is realized are for him the property of another, and he would be completely indifferent to the wastage of this property if he were not himself constrained to economize on it. It is quite different with factories that belong to the workers themselves, as at Rochdale.*

It need hardly be mentioned that, in as much as the productivity of labour in one branch of industry has the effect of cheapening and improving the means of production in another, and thus serves to increase the rate of profit, this general connection of social labour presents itself as something completely alien to the workers, something that simply concerns the capitalist, in as much as he alone buys these means of production and appropriates them. Though he buys the product of the workers in a different branch of industry with the product of the workers in his own branch, and thus disposes of the product of other workers only in so far as he has appropriated the product of his own workers without payment, this is a relationship that is concealed by the circulation process, etc.

A further aspect, moreover, is that, since production on a large scale developed first in the capitalist form, the profit-mania and competition which compel commodities to be produced as cheaply as possible give economy in the use of constant capital the appearance of something peculiar to the capitalist mode of production and therefore make it seem a function of the capitalist.

Just as the capitalist mode of production promotes on the one hand the development of the productive forces of social labour, so on the other hand does it promote economy in the use of constant capital.

Yet there is more to this than the alienation and indifference that the worker, as the bearer of living labour, has towards the economical, i.e. rational and frugal use of his conditions of labour. The contradictory and antithetical character of the capitalist mode of production leads it to count the squandering of the life and health of the worker, and the depression of his conditions of existence, as itself an economy in the use of constant capital, and hence a means for raising the rate of profit.

Since the worker spends the greater part of his life in the production process, the conditions of this process are to a great extent

* These factories were offshoots of the Society of Equitable Pioneers established in 1844, and today remembered more as the starting-point of consumer cooperatives.

conditions of his active life process itself, his conditions of life, and economy in these conditions of life is a method of increasing the profit rate. In just the same way, we previously saw how overwork, the transformation of the worker into a beast of burden, is a method of accelerating the self-valorization of capital, the production of surplus-value.* This economy extends to crowding workers into confined and unhealthy premises, a practice which in capitalist parlance is called saving on buildings; squeezing dangerous machines into the same premises and dispensing with means of protection against these dangers; neglect of precautionary measures in those production processes whose very nature is harmful to health or involves risk, as in mining, etc. Not to speak of the absence of all provisions that would make the production process humane, comfortable or simply bearable for the worker. From the standpoint of the capitalist this would be a senseless and purposeless waste. Yet for all its stinginess, capitalist production is thoroughly wasteful with human material, just as its way of distributing its products through trade, and its manner of competition, make it very wasteful of material resources, so that it loses for society what it gains for the individual capitalist.

As capital has the tendency to reduce the direct employment of living labour to the necessary minimum and constantly shorten the labour needed for the creation of a product by exploiting the social productivity of labour, i.e. economizing as much as possible on directly applied living labour, so it also has the tendency to apply this labour, which has already been reduced to its necessary amount, under the most economical circumstances, i.e. to reduce the value of the constant capital applied to the absolute minimum. If the value of commodities is determined by the necessary labour-time contained in them and not simply by labour-time as such, it is capital that first makes a reality of this mode of determination and immediately goes on to reduce continually the labour socially necessary for the production of a commodity. The price of the commodity is therefore reduced to a minimum through reducing to a minimum each part of the labour required to produce it.

We have to make a certain distinction, in connection with this economy in the use of constant capital. If the mass of the capital applied grows, and with it also the sum of capital value, this first involves simply the concentration of more capital in a single hand.

* See Volume 1, Chapter 10.

However, it is precisely this greater mass employed by one capital (which generally corresponds also to an absolutely greater, if relatively smaller number of workers) that permits economies in constant capital. If we take the individual capitalist, we see a growth in the size of his necessary capital outlay, and particularly in the fixed capital; but in relation to the mass of material to be worked up and the labour to be exploited, its value relatively declines.

We shall now elaborate this with some brief illustrations. We begin with what is really the end, economies in the conditions of production, in so far as these present themselves at the same time as the conditions of existence and life of the worker himself.

2. SAVINGS ON THE CONDITIONS OF WORK AT THE WORKERS' EXPENSE

Coal Mining. Neglect of the Most Necessary Outlays

'Under the competition which exists among the coal-owners and coal-proprietors . . . no more outlay is incurred than is sufficient to overcome the most obvious physical difficulties; and under that which prevails among the labouring colliers, who are ordinarily more numerous than the work to be done requires, a large amount of danger and exposure to the most noxious influences will gladly be encountered for wages a little in advance of the agricultural population round them, in an occupation, in which they can moreover make a profitable use of their children. This double competition is quite sufficient . . . to cause a large proportion of the pits to be worked with the most imperfect drainage and ventilation; often with ill-constructed shafts, bad gearing, incompetent engineers; and ill-constructed and ill-prepared bays and roadways; causing a destruction of life, and limb, and health, the statistics of which would present an appalling picture' (*First Report on Children's Employment in Mines and Collieries, etc.,* 21 April 1829, p. 102).

Around 1860, an average of some fifteen men were killed each week in the English coal mines. According to the report on *Coal Mine Accidents* (6 February 1862), a total of 8,466 had been killed in the ten years 1852–61. But this number is far too small, as the report itself admits, since in the first few years, when the inspectors had only just been appointed and their districts were far too large, a great number of accidents and deaths were not reported at all. The very fact that, despite the great butchery that still goes on and the insufficient number and restricted powers of the inspectors, the number of accidents has dropped sharply since the inspection system was established indicates the natural tendency of capitalist exploitation. These human sacrifices are due for the most part to the filthy avarice of the coal-owners, who for instance often have only one shaft sunk, so that not only is no effective ventilation possible, but also there is no escape if this shaft gets blocked.

If we consider capitalist production in the narrow sense and ignore the process of circulation and the excesses of competition, it is extremely sparing with the realized labour that is objectified in commodities. Yet it squanders human beings, living labour, more readily than does any other mode of production, squandering not only flesh and blood, but nerves and brain as well. In fact it is only through the most tremendous waste of individual development that the development of humanity in general is secured and pursued, in that epoch of history that directly precedes the conscious reconstruction of human society. Since the whole of the economizing we are discussing here arises from the social character of labour, it is in fact precisely this directly social character of labour that produces this waste of the workers' life and health. The question raised by factory inspector R. Baker is very pertinent here:

'The whole question is one for serious consideration, in what way this *sacrifice of infant life occasioned by congregational labour** can be best averted?' (*Reports of the Inspectors of Factories . . . 31 October 1863*, p. 157 [Marx's emphasis].)

Factories

Under this heading belong the suppression of all precautionary measures as to the safety, comfort and health of the workers, even in factories proper. A great part of the casualty lists that tot up the injured and the dead of the industrial army (see the annual Factory Reports) stem from this. Also insufficient space, ventilation, etc.

* 'Congregational labour' means here labour carried on by large masses of people working in association.

In October 1855 Leonard Horner* was already complaining about the resistance that a very large number of factory-owners were placing to the legal provisions for safety devices on horizontal shafts, even though the danger was continually being demonstrated by accidents, often fatal ones, and this safety appliance is neither expensive nor in any way disturbs the work. (*Reports of the Inspectors of Factories . . . October 1855*, p. 6.) The factory-owners were given open support in resisting these and other legal provisions by the unpaid Justices of the Peace who had to decide on the cases, and were generally factory-owners themselves, or friends of factory-owners. The kind of verdict that these gentlemen gave was revealed by Lord Campbell, who said with regard to one of them, in dealing with an appeal against it, 'It is not an interpretation of the Act of Parliament, it is a repeal of the Act of Parliament' (ibid., p. 11). In the same report, Horner relates how in many factories the machines are switched on without the workers being given advance warning. Since there is always something to be done on the machines when they are standing still, some hands and fingers are always busy with this, and accidents constantly arise simply from failing to give a signal (ibid., p. 44). The factory-owners of the time formed a 'trade union' to resist the factory legislation, the so-called 'National Association for the Amendment of the Factory Laws', based in Manchester, which collected a sum of more than £50,000 in March 1855 from contributions on the basis of 2 shillings per horse-power, to meet the legal costs of members prosecuted by the factory inspectors and conduct their cases on behalf of the Association. The object was to prove 'killing no murder'† if done for the sake of profit. The factory inspector for Scotland, Sir John Kincaid, tells of a firm in Glasgow which surrounded all its machines with safety-guards for the price of £9 1s. 0d. If that firm had joined the Association, it would have had to pay a contribution of £11 for its 110 horse-power, i.e. more than the total cost of its safety-guards. But the National Association was expressly founded in 1854 to defy the Act that prescribed safety-guards of this kind. During the entire

* Leonard Horner (1785–1864) has already appeared frequently in *Capital* Volume 1. As head of the Factory Inspectorate, he demonstrated a firm commitment to improving working-class conditions. See in particular Marx's eulogy to him in Volume 1, p. 334, note 10.

† Marx is alluding to the pamphlet *Killing No Murder* published in 1657 by the Leveller Sexby, calling with appropriate moral and religious justification for the assassination of Cromwell.

period from 1844 to 1854 the factory-owners had not taken the least bit of notice of this Act. The factory inspectors then informed the factory-owners that the Act was now to be taken seriously, at Palmerston's instigation. The factory-owners promptly formed their Association, its most prominent members including many who were themselves J.P.s, and in this capacity had actually to apply the Act. When the new Home Secretary, Sir George Grey, proposed a compromise solution in April 1855, by which the government would be content with safety-guards that were scarcely more than nominal, the Association indignantly rejected even this. In the course of various legal cases, the celebrated engineer William Fairbairn used his reputation as an expert in defence of economy and the violated freedom of capital. The head of the Factory Inspectorate, Leonard Horner, was persecuted and slandered by the factory-owners in every conceivable way.

The factory-owners did not rest until they had obtained a judgement from the Queen's Bench Division to the effect that the Act of 1844 did not prescribe any safety-guards for horizontal shafts if these were more than seven feet above ground level, and they finally managed in 1856, with the help of the hypocrite Wilson-Patten – one of those pious persons whose prominently displayed religion makes them always ready to do dirty work for the knights of the money-bag – to put through a new Act of Parliament which was sufficiently to their satisfaction. This Act actually withdrew from the workers all special protection and referred them to the ordinary courts if they wished to seek compensation for injuries caused by machine accidents – sheer mockery, given English legal costs. It also made it almost impossible for the factory-owners to lose a case, by a very neatly worded clause providing for expert testimony. The upshot was a rapid increase in the accident rate. In the six months from May to October 1858, inspector Baker alone reported an increase of 21 per cent against the previous half-year. In his opinion, 36.7 per cent of all the accidents could have been avoided. Yet in 1858 and 1859 the number of accidents was significantly lower than it had been around 1845 and 1846, some 29 per cent lower in fact, even though the number of workers in the branches of industry covered by the Inspectorate had increased by 20 per cent. What was the cause of this? In as much as the question has been settled at this date (1865), it was principally due to the introduction of new machines which were already provided with safety-guards, which the factory-owners could leave in existence as they did not cost them any extra. A few workers also managed to extract heavy legal compensation for lost arms, and have these judgements upheld even by the highest courts. (*Reports of the Inspectors of Factories . . . 30 April 1861*, p. 31, and April 1862, p. 17.)

So much for economy in the means for protecting the lives and limbs of the workers – including many children – from dangers that directly arise from their use of machinery.

Work in Enclosed Spaces in General

It is well enough known how much economy on space, and therefore on buildings, crowds workers together in cramped conditions. A further factor is economy on means of ventilation. These two things, together with long working hours, produce a great increase in respiratory diseases and consequently increased mortality. The following illustrations are taken from the *Reports on Public Health*, Sixth Report, 1863. This report was compiled by Dr John Simon, already well-known to us from Volume 1.

Just as the combination of workers and their cooperation is what permits the use of machines on a large scale, concentration of means of production and economy in their use, so this working together *en masse* in enclosed spaces and under conditions where the decisive factor is not the health of the worker, but the ease with which the product may be constructed – this massive concentration in the same workshop – which is on the one hand a source of growing profit for the capitalist, is on the other hand the cause of a squandering of the worker's life and health, if it is not compensated for both by shorter working hours and by special precautionary measures.

Dr Simon puts forward the following rule, which he backs up with a mass of statistics: 'In proportion as the people of a district are attracted to any collective indoor occupation, in such proportion, other things being equal, the district death-rate by lung diseases will be increased' (p. 23). The cause is bad ventilation. 'And probably in all England there is no exception to the rule, that, in every district which has a large indoor industry, the increased mortality of the workpeople is such as to colour the death-return of the whole district with a marked excess of lung disease' (p. 23).

The mortality figures for industries carried on in confined

spaces, which were investigated by the Board of Health in 1860 and 1861, show that, out of a given number of men aged between 15 and 55, where we find 100 cases of death from consumption and other lung diseases in the agricultural districts of England, the rate for the same male population is 166 in Coventry, 167 in Blackburn and Skipton, 168 in Congleton and Bradford, 171 in Leicester, 182 in Leek, 184 in Macclesfield, 190 in Bolton, 192 in Nottingham, 193 in Rochdale, 198 in Derby, 203 in Salford and Ashton-under-Lyne, 218 in Leeds, 220 in Preston and 263 in Manchester (p. 24). The following table gives a still more striking illustration, taking the deaths from pulmonary diseases for each sex separately for the age group between 15 and 25, calculated on

District	Chief industry	Deaths from pulmonary diseases between the ages of 15 and 25, per 100,000 population	
		Men	Women
Berkhampstead Leighton	Straw plaiting (women)	219	578
Buzzard	Straw plaiting (women)	309	554
Newport Pagnell	Lace manufacture (women)	301	617
Towcester	Lace manufacture (women)	239	577
Yeovil	Manufacture of gloves (mainly women)	280	409
Leek	Silk industry (predominantly women)	437	856
Congleton	Silk industry (predominantly women)	566	790
Macclesfield	Silk industry (predominantly women)	593	890
Healthy country district	Agriculture	331	333

a base of 100,000. The districts selected are those in which women alone are engaged in those industries carried on in confined spaces, while men work in all different branches of industry.

In the silk industry districts, where male participation in factory work is greater, their mortality is also more significant. The death rate from consumption, etc. for both sexes here reveals, as it says in this report, 'the atrocious circumstances under which much of our silk industry is conducted'. And this is the same silk industry in which the factory-owners, appealing to the exceptionally favourable health conditions in their business, demanded exceptionally long working hours from children under 13 years of age, and in part obtained these too (Volume 1, Chapter 10, 6, pp. 405–7).

'Probably no industry which has yet been investigated has afforded a worse picture than that which Dr Smith gives of tailoring: – "Shops vary much in their sanitary conditions, but almost universally are overcrowded and ill-ventilated, and in a high degree unfavourable to health ... Such rooms are necessarily warm; but when the gas is lit, as during the day-time on foggy days, and at night during the winter, the heat increases to 80° and even to upwards of 90°, causing profuse perspiration, and condensation of vapour upon the panes of glass, so that it runs down in streams or drops from the roof, and the operatives are compelled to keep some windows open, at whatever risk to themselves of taking cold." And he gives the following account of what he found in 16 of the most important West End shops – "The largest cubic space in these ill-ventilated rooms allowed to each operative is 270 feet, and the least 105 feet, and in the whole average only 156 feet per man. In one room, with a gallery running round it, and lighted only from the roof, from 92 to upwards of 100 men are employed, where a large number of gas-lights burn, and where the urinals are in the closest proximity, the cubic space does not exceed 150 feet per man. In another room, which can only be called a kennel in a yard, lighted from the roof, and ventilated by a small skylight opening, five to six men work in a space of 112 cubic feet per man" ... Tailors, in those atrocious workshops which Dr Smith describes, work generally for about 12 or 13 hours a day, and at some times the work will be continued for 15 or 16 hours' (pp. 25, 26, 28).

It should be noted, and indeed it was noted by Dr John Simon, Chief Medical Officer of the Privy Council and author of this report, that in the age-group 25–35 the mortality of both tailors and typesetters and printers in London was under-reported, as in these two lines of business the London employers take on a large number of young people (probably up to 30 years of age) as apprentices and 'improvers', i.e. for further training. These increase the number of employees on which the industrial death rates for London are calculated, but they do not share to the same

Number of persons employed	Branches of industry and locality	Death rate per 100,000 between the ages of		
		25 and 35	35 and 45	45 and 55
958,265	Agriculture, England and Wales	743	805	1,145
22,301 men and⎱ 12,377 women ⎰	Tailoring, London	958	1,262	2,093
13,803	Typesetters and printers, London	894	1,747	2,367

proportion in the number of deaths in London, as their stay there is only temporary. If they become ill during this time, they go back home to the country, and it is there that their death is registered if they die. This state of affairs affects the younger age-groups even more and renders the London mortality rates for these groups completely valueless as measurements of industrial disease (p. 30).

What is true of tailoring is true also of the typesetters, among whom lack of ventilation, foul air, etc. is supplemented by night work. Their customary working day lasts for 12 or 13 hours, and sometimes 15 or 16. 'Great heat and foulness which begin when the gas-jets are lit . . . It not infrequently happens that fumes from a foundry, or foul odours from machinery or sinks, rise from the lower room, and aggravate the evils of the upper one. The heated air of the lower rooms always tends to heat the upper by warming the floor, and when the rooms are low, and the consumption of gas great, this is a serious evil, and one only surpassed in the case where the steam-boilers are placed in the lower room, and supply unwished-for heat to the whole house . . . As a general expression, it may be stated that universally the ventilation is defective, and quite insufficient to remove the heat and the products of the combustion of gas in the evening and during the night, and that in many offices, and particularly in those made from dwelling-houses, the condition is most deplorable . . . And in some offices (especially those of weekly newspapers) there will be work – work too, in which boys between 12 and 16 years of age take equal part – for almost uninterrupted periods of two days and a night at a time; while, in other printing-offices which lay themselves out for the doing of "urgent" business, Sunday gives no relaxation to the workman, and his working-days become seven instead of six in every week' (pp. 26, 28).

We met with the milliners and dressmakers already in Volume 1, Chapter 10, 3, pp. 364–5, in relation to overwork. In the report we are citing at present, their places of work are described by Dr Ord. Even where they are better during the day, they are over-heated, foul and unhealthy during the hours that gas is burned. In thirty-four workshops of the better sort Dr Ord found that the average amount of room for each female worker was as follows (in cubic feet): '. . . In four cases more than 500, in four other cases from 400 to 500, . . . in seven others from 200 to 250, in four others from 150 to 200, and in nine others only from 100 to 150. The largest of these allowances would but be scanty for continuous work, unless the space were thoroughly well ventilated; and, except with extra-ordinary ventilation, its atmosphere could not be tolerably whole-some during gas-light.'

Here is Dr Ord's observation on a workshop of the inferior class that he visited, one conducted on behalf of a middleman: 'One room area in cubical feet, 1,280; persons present, 14; area to each, in cubical feet, 91.5. The women here were weary-looking and squalid; their earnings were stated to be 7s. to 15s. a week, and their tea . . . Hours 8 a.m. to 8 p.m. The small room into which these 14 persons were crowded was ill-ventilated. There were two movable windows and a fire-place, but the latter was blocked up and there was no special ventilation of any kind' (p. 27).

The same report remarks with regard to overwork among milliners and dressmakers: '. . . The overwork of the young women in fashionable dressmaking establishments does not, for more than about four months of the year, prevail in that mon-strous degree which has on many occasions excited momentary public surprise and indignation; but for the indoor hands during these months it will, as a rule, be of full 14 hours a day, and will, when there is pressure, be, for days together, of 17 or even 18 hours. At other times of the year the work of the indoor hands ranges probably from 10 to 14 hours; and uniformly the hours for out-door hands are 12 or 13. For mantle-makers, collar-makers, shirt-makers, and various other classes of needleworkers (including persons who work at the sewing-machine) the hours spent in the common workroom are fewer – generally not more than 10 to 12 hours; but, says Dr Ord, the regular hours of work are subject to considerable extension in certain houses at certain times, by the practice of working extra hours for extra pay, and in other houses by the practice of taking work away from houses of business, to be done after hours at home, both practices being, it may be added, often compulsory' (p. 28).

In a note to this page, Dr John Simon writes: 'Mr Radcliffe . . . the Honorary Secretary of the Epidemiological Society . . . happening to have unusual opportunities for questioning the young women employed in first-class houses of business . . . has found that in only one out of twenty girls examined who called themselves "quite well" could the state of health be pronounced good; the rest exhibiting in various degrees evidences of depressed physical power, nervous exhaustion, and numerous functional disorders thereupon dependent. He attributes these conditions in the first place to the length of the hours of work – the minimum of which he estimates at 12 hours a day out of the season; and secondarily to . . . crowding and bad ventilation of workrooms, gas-vapours, insufficiency or bad quality of food, and inattention to domestic comfort.'

The conclusion that the Chief Medical Officer comes to is that 'it is practically impossible for workpeople to insist upon that which in theory is their first sanitary right – the right that whatever work their employer assembles them to do, shall, so far as depends upon him, be, at his cost, divested of all needlessly unwholesome circumstances; . . . while workpeople are practically unable to exact that sanitary justice for themselves, they also (notwithstanding the presumed intentions of the law) cannot expect any effectual assistance from the appointed administrators of the Nuisances Removal Acts' (p. 29). 'Doubtless there may be some small technical difficulty in defining the exact line at which employers shall become subject to regulation. But . . . in principle, the sanitary claim is universal. And in the interest of myriads of labouring men and women, whose lives are now needlessly afflicted and shortened by the infinite physical suffering which their mere employment engenders, I would venture to express my hope, that universally the sanitary circumstances of labour may, at least so far, be brought within appropriate provisions of law, that the effective ventilation of all indoor workplaces may be ensured, and that in every naturally insalubrious occupation the specific health-endangering influence may as far as practicable be reduced' (p. 31).

3. ECONOMY IN THE GENERATION AND TRANSMISSION OF POWER, AND ON BUILDINGS

In his report for October 1852, Leonard Horner quotes a letter from the famous engineer James Nasmyth of Patricroft, the inventor of the steam-hammer, which says among other things:
'... The public are little aware of the vast increase in driving power which has been obtained by such changes of system and improvements' (of steam-engines) 'as I allude to. The engine power of this district' (Lancashire) 'lay under the incubus of timid and prejudiced traditions for nearly forty years, but now we are happily emancipated. During the last fifteen years, but more especially in the course of the last four years' (since 1848) 'some very important changes have taken place in the system of working condensing steam-engines ... The result ... has been to realize a much greater amount of duty or work performed by the identical engines, and that again at a very considerable reduction of the expenditure of fuel ... For a great many years after the introduction of steam-power into the mills and manufactories of the above-named districts, the velocity of which it was considered proper to work condensing steam-engines was about 220 feet per minute of the piston; that is to say, an engine with a 5-feet stroke was restricted by "rule" to make 22 revolutions of the crankshaft per minute. Beyond this speed it was not considered prudent or desirable to work the engine; and as all the mill gearing ... were made suitable to this 220 feet per minute speed of piston, this slow and absurdly restricted velocity ruled the working of such engines for many years. However, at length, either through fortunate ignorance of the "rule", or by better reasons on the part of some bold innovator, a greater speed was tried, and as the result was highly favourable, others followed the example, by, as it is termed, "letting the engine away", namely, by so modifying the proportions of the first motion wheels of the mill gearing as to permit the engine to run at 300 feet and upwards per minute, while the mill gearing generally was kept at its former speed ... This "letting the engine away" ... has led to the almost universal "speeding" of engines, because it was proved that not only was there available power gained from the identical engines, but also as the higher velocity of the engine yielded a greater momentum in the fly-wheel the motion was found to be much more regular ... We ... obtain more power from a steam-engine by simply permitting its piston to

move at a higher velocity (pressure of steam and vacuum in the condenser remaining the same) ... Thus, for example, suppose any given engine yields 40 horse-power when its piston is travelling at 200 feet per minute, if by suitable arrangement or modification we can permit this same engine to run at such a speed as that its piston will travel through space at 400 feet per minute (pressure of steam and vacuum, as before said, remaining the same), we shall then have just double the power ... and as the pressure by steam and vacuum is the same in both cases, the strain upon the parts of this engine will be no greater at 400 than at 200 feet speed of piston, so that the risk of "break-down" does not materially increase with the increase of speed. All the difference is, that we shall in such case consume steam at a rate proportional to the speed of piston, or nearly so; and there will be some small increase in the wear and tear of "the brasses" or rubbing-parts, but so slight as to be scarcely worth notice ... But in order to obtain increase of power from the same engine by permitting its piston to travel at a higher velocity it is requisite ... to burn more coal per hour under the same boiler, or employ boilers of greater evaporating capabilities, i.e., greater steam-generating powers. This accordingly was done, and boilers of greater steam-generating or water-evaporating powers were supplied to the old "speeded" engines, and in many cases near 100 per cent more work was got out of the identical engines by means of such changes as above named. About ten years ago the extraordinary economical production of power as realized by the engines employed in the mining operations of Cornwall began to attract attention; and as competition in the spinning trade forced manufacturers to look to "savings" as the chief source of profits, the remarkable difference in the consumption of coal per horse-power per hour, as indicated by the performance of the Cornish engines, as also the extraordinary economical performance of Woolf's double-cylinder engines, began to attract increased attention to the subject of economy of fuel in this district, and as the Cornish and double-cylinder engines gave a horse-power for every 3½ to 4 pounds of coal per hour, while the generality of cotton-mill engines were consuming 8 or 12 pounds per horse per hour, so remarkable a difference induced mill-owners and engine-makers in this district to endeavour to realize, by the adoption of similar means, such extraordinary economical results as were proved to be common in Cornwall and France, where the high price of coal had compelled manufacturers to look more sharply to such costly departments of their establishments. The result of this increased attention to economy of fuel has been most important in many respects. In the first place, many boilers, the half of whose surface had been in the good old times of high profits left exposed quite naked to the cold air, began to get covered with thick blankets of felt, and brick and plaster, and other modes and means whereby to prevent the escape of that heat from their exposed surface which had cost so much fuel to maintain. Steam-pipes began to be "protected" in the same manner, and the outside of the cylinder of the engine felted and cased in with wood in like manner. Next came the use of "high steam," namely, instead of having the safety-valve loaded so as to blow off at 4, 6, or 8 lbs. to the square inch, it was found that by raising the pressure to 14 or 20 lbs. . . . a very decided economy of fuel resulted; in other words, the work of the mill was performed by a very notably reduced consumption of coals, . . . and those who had the means and the boldness carried the increased pressure and "expansion system" of working to the full extent, by employing properly constructed boilers to supply steam of 30, 40, 50, 60, and 70 lbs. to the square inch; pressures which would have frightened an engineer of the old school out of his wits. But as the economic results of so increasing the pressure of steam . . . soon appeared in most unmistakable £ s. d. forms, the use of high-pressure steam-boilers for working condensing engines became almost general. And those who desired to go to the full extent . . . soon adopted the employment of the Woolf engine in its full integrity, and most of our mills lately built are worked by the Woolf engines, namely, those on which there are two cylinders to each engine, in one of which the high-pressure steam from the boiler exerts or yields power by its excess of pressure over that of the atmosphere, which, instead of the said high-pressure steam being let pass off at the end of each stroke free into the atmosphere, is caused to pass into a low-pressure cylinder of about four times the area of the former, and after due expansion passes to the condenser; the economic result obtained from engines of this class is such that the consumption of fuel is at the rate of from $3\frac{1}{2}$ to 4 lbs. of coal per horse per hour; while in the engines of the old system the consumption used to be on the average from 12 to 14 lbs. per horse per hour. By an ingenious arrangement, the Woolf system of double cylinder or combined low and high pressure engine has been introduced extensively to already existing engines, whereby their performance has been

increased both as to power and economy of fuel. The same result
... has been in use these eight or ten years, by having a high-
pressure engine so connected with a condensing engine as to
enable the waste steam of the former to pass on to and work the
latter. This system is in many cases very convenient.

'It would not be very easy to get an exact return as to the increase
of performance or work done by the identical engines to which
some or all of these improvements have been applied; I am confi-
dent, however, ... that from the same weight of steam-engine
machinery we are now obtaining at least 50 per cent more duty or
work performed on the average, and that in many cases, the identical steam-engines which in the days of the restricted speed of 220
feet per minute yielded 50 horse-power, are now yielding upwards
of 100. The very economical results derived from the employment
of high-pressure steam in working condensing steam-engines,
together with the much higher power required by mill extensions
from the same engines, has within the last three years led to the
adoption of tubular boilers, yielding a much more economical
result than those formerly employed in generating steam for mill
engines' (*Reports of the Inspectors of Factories ... October 1852*,
pp. 23–7).

What is true for power generation holds also for the mechanisms that transmit power, as well as for the actual working machines themselves:

'The rapid strides with which improvement in machinery has
advanced within these few years have enabled manufacturers to
increase production without additional moving power. The more
economical application of labour has been rendered necessary by
the diminished length of the working-day, and in most well-
regulated mills an intelligent mind is always considering in what
manner production can be increased with decreased expenditure.
I have before me a statement, kindly prepared by a very intelligent
gentleman in my district, showing the number of hands employed,
their ages, the machines at work, and the wages paid from 1840
to the present time. In October 1840, his firm employed 600 hands,
of whom 200 were under 13 years of age. In October last, 350
hands were employed, of whom 60 only were under 13; the same
number of machines, within very few, were at work, and the same
sum in wages was paid at both periods' (Redgrave's Report in
Reports of the Inspectors of Factories ... October 1852, pp. 58–9).

These improvements in machinery show their full effect only

when they are installed in new and purpose-built factory buildings.

'As regards the improvement made in machinery, I may say in the first place that a great advance has been made in the construction of mills adapted to receive improved machinery ... In the bottom room I double all my yarn, and upon that single floor I shall put 29,000 doubling spindles. I effect a saving of labour in the room and shed of at least 10 per cent, not so much from any improvement in the principle of doubling yarn, but from a concentration of machinery under a single management; and I am enabled to drive the said number of spindles by one single shaft, a saving in shafting, compared with what other firms have to use to work the same number of spindles, of 60 per cent, in some cases 80 per cent. There is a large saving in oil, and shafting, and in grease ... With superior mill arrangements and improved machinery, at the lowest estimate I have effected a saving in labour of 10 per cent, a great saving in power, coal, oil, tallow, shafting and strapping' (Evidence of a cotton spinner, *Reports of the Inspectors of Factories ... October 1863*, pp. 109, 110).

4. UTILIZATION OF THE REFUSE OF PRODUCTION

As the capitalist mode of production extends, so also does the utilization of the refuse left behind by production and consumption. Under the heading of production we have the waste products of industry and agriculture, under that of consumption we have both the excrement produced by man's natural metabolism and the form in which useful articles survive after use has been made of them. Refuse of production is, therefore, in the chemical industry, the by-product which gets lost if production is only on a small scale; in the production of machinery, the heap of iron filings that appears to be waste but is then used again as raw material for iron production, etc. The natural human waste products, remains of clothing in the form of rags, etc. are the refuse of consumption. The latter are of the greatest importance for agriculture. But there is a colossal wastage in the capitalist economy in proportion to their actual use. In London, for example, they can do nothing better with the excrement produced by $4\frac{1}{2}$ million people than pollute the Thames with it, at monstrous expense.

The increase in the cost of raw materials, of course, provides the incentive to make use of waste products.

The general conditions for this re-utilization are: the massive presence of this refuse, a thing which results only when labour is carried on on a large scale; the improvement of machines, so that materials that were previously unusable in their given form are converted into a form suitable for new production; and finally, scientific progress – especially in chemistry, which discovers the useful properties of such waste products. Of course, great economies of this kind can also be found in the small-scale, almost horticultural agriculture carried on in Lombardy, southern China and Japan. In general, however, agricultural productivity is obtained in this system only at the cost of a great prodigality in human labour-power withdrawn from other spheres of production.

So-called waste products play an important role in almost every industry. In the Factory Report of October 1863, for example, one reason why farmers in England, as well as in many parts of Ireland, are unwilling to grow flax, and only rarely do so, was given as follows: 'The great waste . . . which has taken place at the little water scutch mills . . . the waste in cotton is comparatively small, but in flax very large. The efficiency of water steeping and of good machine scutching will reduce this disadvantage very considerably . . . Flax [is] scutched in Ireland in a most shameful way, and a large percentage [is] actually lost by it, equal to 28 or 30 per cent' (*Reports of the Inspectors of Factories . . . 31 October 1863*, pp. 139, 142). All of this could be avoided by the use of better machines. There was such a wastage of oakum that the factory inspector says: 'I have been informed with regard to some of the scutch mills in Ireland, that the waste made at them has often been used by the scutchers to burn on their fires at home, and yet it is very valuable' (p. 140 of the above report). As for cotton waste, we shall come back to this below in dealing with fluctuations in the prices of raw materials.

The wool industry was rather cleverer than the linen: 'It was once the common practice to decry the preparation of waste and woollen rags for re-manufacture, but the prejudice has entirely subsided as regards the shoddy trade, which has become an important branch of the woollen trade of Yorkshire, and doubtless the cotton waste trade will be recognized in the same manner as supplying an admitted want. Thirty years since, woollen rags, i.e., pieces of cloth, old clothes, etc., of nothing but wool, would average about £4 4s. per ton in price: within the last few years they have become worth £44 per ton, and the demand for them has so increased that means have been found for utilizing the rags of fabrics of cotton and wool mixed by destroying the cotton and leaving the wool intact, and now thousands of operatives are engaged in the manufacture of shoddy, from which the consumer has greatly benefited in being able to purchase cloth of a fair and average quality at a very moderate price' (*Reports of the Inspectors of Factories . . . 31 October 1863*, p. 107).

By the end of 1862, rejuvenated shoddy already accounted for a third of all wool used by English industry (*Reports of the Inspectors of Factories . . . 31 October 1862*, p. 81). The 'great benefit' for the 'consumer' was that his woollen clothes took only a third of the previous time to wear out and a sixth of the time to become threadbare.

The English silk industry followed the same downward path. Between 1839 and 1862 the use of genuine raw silk declined somewhat, while that of silk waste doubled. Improved machinery made it possible to manufacture silk that could be used for many purposes out of what had previously been a quite valueless material.

The most striking example of the use of waste products is provided by the chemical industry. Not only does this make use of its own waste products by finding new applications for them, but it also employs those of a great range of other industries and converts coal-tar, for example, which was previously almost useless, into aniline dyes, alizarin and most recently also into medicines.

This economy in the refuse of production, achieved by re-use, should be distinguished from economy in the creation of waste, i.e. reduction of the refuse of production to its minimum and the maximum direct use of all raw and ancillary materials engaged in production.

Reduction in waste is partly brought about by the quality of the machinery used. Oil, soap, etc. are saved in proportion to the more precise working and better polishing of the machine components. This concerns the ancillary materials. The most important thing, however, is that it depends on the quality of the machines and tools that are used whether a greater or lesser part of the raw material is transformed into waste by the production process. Finally, this depends on the quality of the raw material itself. This in turn depends partly on the development of the extractive industries and of agriculture, by which these raw materials are produced (thus it depends on the advance of civilization in general), partly on the development of the processing which the raw material undergoes before its entry into manufacture.

'Parmentier has shown that in a relatively short space of time, i.e. since the age of Louis XIV, the art of milling corn has been very much improved in France, so that the new mills can supply up to half as much again in the way of bread. The annual consumption of corn in Paris was calculated originally at 4 *setiers* per capita, later at 3, then 2, while today it is only $1\frac{1}{3}$ *setiers* or approximately 342 lbs. . . . In the Perche, where I have lived for a long while, the crudely constructed mills with their millstones of granite and trap rock have generally been rebuilt according to the laws of mechanics, which has advanced so much in the last thirty years. Good millstones from La Ferté have been installed, corn has been milled twice over, the milling sack has been made to move in a circle, and the amount of flour produced is a sixth greater from the same quantity of corn. I find it easy to explain, therefore, the enormous disproportion in the daily consumption of corn between the Romans and ourselves. The entire reason is simply the inadequate procedures in milling and bread preparation. I can also explain in this way the remarkable state of affairs that Pliny reports (XVIII, c. 20) . . . Flour was sold in Rome at 40, 48 or 96 *as* per *modius*, depending on quality. These prices, so high in proportion to the corn prices of today, are to be explained by the mills of the time, which were still imperfect and in a state of infancy, and the substantial milling costs to which this gave rise' (Dureau de la Malle, *Économie politique des Romains*, Paris, 1840, I, pp. 280–81).

5. ECONOMY THROUGH INVENTIONS

These savings in the use of fixed capital, as we said earlier, are the result of the way the conditions of labour have been applied on a large scale. In short, the way in which they serve as conditions of directly social, socialized labour, of direct cooperation within the production process. This is firstly the only condition on which mechanical and chemical discoveries can be applied without increasing the price of commodities, and this is always the *sine qua non*. Next, it is only with production on a large scale that we can have the economy that arises from productive consumption in common. Finally, however, it is only the experience of the combined worker that discovers and demonstrates how inventions already made can most simply be developed, how to overcome the practical frictions that arise in putting the theory into practice – its application to the production process, and so on.

We must distinguish here, incidentally, between universal labour and communal labour. They both play their part in the production process, and merge into one another, but they are each different as well. Universal labour is all scientific work, all discovery and invention. It is brought about partly by the cooperation of men now living, but partly also by building on earlier work. Communal labour, however, simply involves the direct cooperation of individuals.

All this receives fresh confirmation from certain facts that have frequently been observed:

(1) The great difference in costs between the first construction of a new machine and its reproduction. See Ure and Babbage.*

(2) The much greater costs that are always involved in an enterprise based on new inventions, compared with later establishments that rise up on its ruins, *ex suis ossibus*.† The extent of this is so great that the pioneering entrepreneurs generally go bankrupt, and it is only their successors who flourish, thanks to their possession of cheaper buildings, machinery etc. Thus it is generally the most worthless and wretched kind of money-capitalists that draw the greatest profit from all new developments of the universal labour of the human spirit and their social application by combined labour.

---

* This is Charles Babbage (1792–1871), best remembered as the inventor of the first calculating machine. Marx refers to his book *On the Economy of Machinery and Manufactures*, London, 1832. The work on the same subject by Andrew Ure (1778–1857), *The Philosophy of Manufactures*, published in 1835, Marx considered the best work of its time on large-scale industry, and he makes frequent use of it in Volume 1 of *Capital*.

† from its bones.

Chapter 6: The Effect of Changes in Price

I. FLUCTUATIONS IN THE PRICE OF RAW MATERIAL; THEIR DIRECT EFFECTS ON THE RATE OF PROFIT

Here, as before, we assume there is no change in the rate of surplus-value. This is a necessary assumption, if we are to investigate the situation in its pure form. It would certainly be possible, however, at a constant rate of surplus-value, for a certain capital to employ a greater or lesser number of workers as the result of a contraction or expansion which the fluctuations in raw material prices we are about to consider might bring about. In this case the mass of surplus-value could change, even though the rate was constant. This is however a side-effect, which we shall not consider here. If an improvement in machinery and a change in the price of raw material simultaneously affect the number of the workers employed by a given capital, or else the level of wages, we simply have to combine (1) the effect that the variation in constant capital has on the profit rate, and (2) the effect that the variation in wages has on the profit rate. The result is then immediately given.

Here too, as in the previous case, it should be noted that, like those variations which result from economy in the use of constant capital, variations resulting from fluctuations in the price of raw material also always affect the rate of profit, even if they leave wages, and thus the rate and mass of surplus-value, completely undisturbed. In $s' \frac{v}{C}$, they alter the value of C and therefore the value of the fraction as a whole. It is therefore completely immaterial here – as distinct from what we found in considering surplus-value – in what spheres of production these variations take place; whether the branches of industry that they affect produce means of subsistence for the workers or constant capital for the production of these means of subsistence, or whether they do not. The argument developed here is equally valid when these variations occur in luxury production, and by luxury production here we mean all production that is not required by the reproduction of labour-power.

Under raw material we also include the ancillary materials such as indigo, coal, gas, etc. Moreover, in so far as machinery is considered under this heading, it has its own raw material consisting of iron, wood, leather, etc. Its price is therefore also affected by fluctuations in the price of the raw material involved in its construction. In as much as its price is raised by fluctuations in the price of the raw material of which it consists, or of the ancillary material that it needs in the course of its operation, the rate of profit falls in proportion to this, and vice versa.

In the investigations which follow we shall confine ourselves to fluctuations in price of that raw material which actually goes into the process of production of the commodity, and not consider the raw material of machines that function as means of labour or the ancillary materials required in their use. The only point we want to note here is that natural riches in the shape of iron, coal, wood, etc., the main elements in the construction and use of machines, appear now as a natural fruit borne by capital and form an element in the determination of the rate of profit that is independent of the high or low level of wages.

Since the rate of profit is $\frac{s}{c}$ or $\frac{s}{c+v}$, it is clear that everything that gives rise to a change in the magnitude of c, and therefore of C, also brings about a change in the profit rate, even if s, v and their reciprocal relationship remain constant. Raw material, however, forms a major component of constant capital. Even in branches of industry that do not use any specific raw material of their own, there is still raw material in the form of ancillary material or the components of the machinery, etc., and so its fluctuations in price still influence the rate of profit accordingly. If the price of raw material falls by a sum we shall call d, then $\frac{s}{c}$ or $\frac{s}{c+v}$ is changed to $\frac{s}{c-d}$ or $\frac{s}{(c-d)+v}$, and the rate of profit falls. As long as other circumstances are equal, the rate of profit falls or rises in the opposite direction to the price of the raw material. This shows among other things how important low raw material prices are for industrial countries, even if variations in raw material prices were not accompanied by fluctuations in the product's orbit of sale, i.e. quite apart from the relationship between demand and supply. It also explains how foreign trade influences the rate of profit, irrespective of any effect that it has on wages by cheapening the necessary means of subsistence. Foreign

trade particularly affects the prices of the raw or ancillary materials used in industry and agriculture. The fact that any understanding of the rate of profit and its specific difference from the
rate of surplus-value has been so completely lacking is responsible
for a situation in which on the one hand those economists who
emphasize the important influence of raw material prices on the
rate of profit, as established by practical experience, give this a
quite false theoretical explanation (Torrens), while on the other
hand those economists who hold firmly to the general principles,
such as Ricardo, fail to recognize the influence of such things as
world trade on the profit rate.*

We can thus understand how important for industry is the
abolition or reduction of import duties on raw materials. To let
in raw materials as freely as possible was already a principal
doctrine of the system of protection in its more rational presenta-
tions. This was, alongside the repeal of the Corn Laws, the main
preoccupation of the English Free-Traders, when they took care
to abolish the duty on cotton as well.

To give one example of how important low prices are for an
ancillary material and not just for raw materials proper, we may
take an ancillary material that is also a major foodstuff: flour,
which is used in the cotton industry. As long ago as 1837, R. H.
Greg[13] calculated that the 100,000 power-looms and 250,000 hand-
looms that were then used for cotton-weaving in Britain annually
consumed some 41 million pounds of flour for smoothing the
warp. In addition, a further third of this amount was used in
bleaching and other processes. Greg calculates that the total value
of the flour consumed in this way was £342,000 per year for the
preceding ten years. Comparison with flour prices on the Continent
showed that the higher price for flour forced on the factory-
owners by the duties on corn amounted to some £170,000 a year
alone. For 1837, Greg estimates it as at least £200,000, and speaks
of one single firm for which this excess price amounted to £1,000
a year. As a result, 'great manufacturers, thoughtful, calculating
men of business, have said that ten hours' labour would be quite

* Marx is referring here to pp. 28 ff. of Torrens's *An Essay on the Production
of Wealth*, London, 1821, and to Chapter VI of Ricardo's *Principles of
Political Economy, and Taxation*, 'On Profits'. On Torrens, see also *Theories
of Surplus-Value*, Part III, Chapter XX, 1, b, pp. 71–9.

13. *The Factory Question and the Ten Hours Bill* by R. H. Greg, London,
1837, p. 115.

sufficient, if the Corn Laws were repealed' (*Reports of the Inspectors of Factories ... 31 October 1848*, p. 98).

The Corn Laws were repealed, and the duties on cotton and other raw materials abolished as well. But scarcely had this been achieved when the factory-owners' opposition to the Ten Hours Bill became more violent than ever. When despite this the Ten Hours Bill did become law soon afterwards, its first effect was an attempt at a general reduction of wages.*

The value of the raw and ancillary materials goes at a single stroke into the value of the product for which they are used, while the value of the elements of fixed capital goes in only to the extent of their depreciation, and thus only gradually. It follows from this that the price of the product is affected to a much higher degree by the price of raw material than by that of fixed capital, even though the rate of profit is determined by the total value of the capital applied, irrespective of how much of this is consumed or not. It is evident however – even if this is mentioned only in passing, as we are still assuming here that commodities are sold at their values and are not yet concerned with the fluctuations in price that are brought about by competition – that the expansion or contraction of the market depends on the price of the individual commodity and stands in an inverse relationship to the rise or fall in this price. It happens in fact, therefore, that a rise in the price of raw material does not lead the price of the manufactured product to rise in the same proportion, or to fall in the same proportion when the price of the raw material falls. The rate of profit thus falls more sharply in the one case, and rises more sharply in the other, than would be the case if commodities were sold at their values.

Moreover, the size and value of the machines employed grows as the productivity of labour develops, but not in the same proportion as this productivity itself, i.e. the proportion to which these machines supply an increased product. Thus in any branch of industry that uses raw materials, i.e. wherever the object of labour is already the product of earlier labour, the increasing productivity of labour is expressed precisely in the proportion in which a greater quantity of raw material absorbs a certain amount of labour, i.e. in the increasing mass of raw material that is transformed into products, worked up into commodities, in an hour, for example. In proportion therefore as the productivity of labour

* See Volume 1, pp. 395 ff.

develops, the value of the raw material forms an ever-growing component of the value of the commodity produced, not only because it enters into it as a whole, but because in each aliquot part of the total product, the part formed by the depreciation of the machines and the part formed by newly added labour both constantly decline. As a result of this falling movement, a relative growth takes place in the other component of value, that formed by the raw material, provided that this growth is not cancelled out by a corresponding decline in the raw material's value arising from the increasing productivity of the labour applied in its own creation.

Moreover, since the raw and ancillary materials, just like wages, form components of the circulating capital and must therefore be constantly replaced out of each sale of the product, whereas as far as the machine is concerned it is only the depreciation that has to be replaced and at first only in the form of a reserve fund (in this connection it is in no way so essential that each individual sale should contribute its part to this reserve fund, as long as we assume that the year's sale as a whole provides its annual share), we see here again how a rise in the price of raw material can cut back or inhibit the entire reproduction process, since the price obtained by the commodity's sale no longer suffices to replace all of its elements; or it makes it impossible to continue the process on a scale that corresponds with its technical basis, so that either only a section of the machinery is being used, or the whole machinery cannot work for the full customary time.

The costs resulting from waste, finally, vary in direct proportion to the fluctuations in the price of the raw material, rising when this rises and falling when it falls. Here too, however, there is a limit. In 1850 it could still be said: 'One source of considerable loss arising from an advance in the price of the raw material would hardly occur to any one but a practical spinner, viz., that from waste. I am informed that when cotton advances, the cost to the spinner, of the lower qualities especially, is increased in a ratio beyond the advance actually paid, because the waste made in spinning coarse yarns is fully 15 per cent; and this rate, while it causes a loss of $\frac{1}{2}$d. per lb. on cotton at $3\frac{1}{2}$d. per lb., brings up the loss to 1d. per lb. when cotton advances to 7d.' (*Reports of the Inspectors of Factories ... 30 April 1850*, p. 17). But when the American Civil War caused cotton to rise to prices almost unheard of in a hundred years, the report sang quite a different tune:

'The price now given for waste, and its re-introduction in the factory in the shape of cotton waste, go some way to compensate for the difference in the loss by waste, between Surat cotton and American cotton, about 12½ per cent.

'The waste in working Surat cotton being 25 per cent, the cost of the cotton to the spinner is enhanced one-fourth before he has manufactured it. The loss by waste used not to be of much moment when American cotton was 5d. or 6d. per lb., for it did not exceed ¾d. per lb., but it is now of great importance when upon every lb. of cotton which costs 2s. there is a loss by waste equal to 6d.'[14] (*Reports of the Inspectors of Factories . . . October 1863*, p. 106.)

2. REVALUATION AND DEVALUATION OF CAPITAL; RELEASE AND TYING-UP OF CAPITAL

The phenomena under investigation in this chapter assume for their full development the credit system and competition on the world market, the latter being the very basis and living atmosphere of the capitalist mode of production. These concrete forms of capitalist production, however, can be comprehensively depicted only after the general nature of capital is understood; it is therefore outside the scope of this work to present them – they belong to a possible continuation.* Yet the phenomena listed in the title to this section can still be discussed here in broad lines. They are both inter-related and related to the rate and mass of profit. And this reason alone justifies a brief account of them, because they make it appear as if it is not only the rate of profit but also its mass (which is in fact identical with the mass of surplus-value) that can increase and decrease independently of movements of surplus-value, whether of its mass or its rate.

Should the release and tying-up of capital on the one hand, and its rise and fall in value on the other, be treated as separate phenomena?

14. The final sentence from the report is in error. The loss due to waste should be 3d. instead of 6d. This loss is 25 per cent in the case of Surat, but only 12½ to 15 per cent in the case of American cotton, and it is this that is meant here, the same percentage having been correctly calculated on the price of 5–6d. per lb. It is true, none the less, that the proportion of waste was often significantly higher than before on American cotton shipped to Europe during the latter years of the Civil War. – F.E.

* See below, p. 426.

The first question that arises is what it is that we understand by the release and tying-up of capital. Revaluation and devaluation, for their part, are self-explanatory. We simply mean that the capital present increases or decreases in value as the result of certain general economic conditions (since what is involved here is not the particular fate of one single private capital), i.e. that the value of the capital advanced to production rises or falls independently of its valorization by the surplus labour it employs.

By the tying-up of capital we mean that, out of the total value of the product, a certain additional proportion must be transformed back into the elements of constant or variable capital, if production is to continue on its old scale. By the release of capital we mean that a part of the product's total value which previously had to be transformed back into either constant or variable capital becomes superfluous for the continuation of production on the old scale and is now available for other purposes. The release or tying-up of capital is different from the release or tying-up of revenue. If the annual surplus-value on a capital $C = x$, for example, the cheapening of those commodities that go into the consumption of the capitalist may bring it about that $x - a$ is sufficient to procure the same mass of satisfactions, etc. as before. A portion of the capitalist's revenue $= a$ is thus set free and can now serve either to expand his consumption or be transformed back into capital (accumulation). Conversely, if $x + a$ is required in order to continue with the same mode of life, either this expenditure must be restricted or else a portion of income $= a$ that was previously accumulated must now be spent as revenue.

The revaluation or devaluation of capital value may affect either constant or variable capital or both, and in the case of constant capital it can again relate to either the fixed or the constant portion or both.

In the case of constant capital we have to consider both raw materials, which we take as including also ancillary materials and semi-finished products, and also machinery and other fixed capital.

Previously, we considered variation in the price or value of the raw material with particular respect to the influence of this on the rate of profit, and put forward the general law that, with other things being equal, the rate of profit varies inversely as the value of the raw material. This law is unconditionally correct for capital that is newly engaged in a certain business and where the investment of capital, the transformation of money into productive capital, takes place for the first time.

But apart from this newly invested capital, a large part of the already functioning capital is located in the circulation sphere, only one portion being in the sphere of production. One part exists as a commodity on the market and has to be transformed into money; another part exists as money in some form or other and has to be transformed back into the conditions of production; a third part, finally, exists within the sphere of production, partly in the original form of means of production, raw material, ancillary material, semi-finished articles, machinery and other fixed capital purchased on the market, partly again as products still in the course of completion. The effect of a rise or fall in capital value depends here very largely on the respective proportions of these components. Let us firstly leave all fixed capital out of account for the sake of simplification and simply consider the part of the constant capital that consists of raw and ancillary materials, and commodities in the course of preparation and in finished form on the market.

If the price of a raw material rises – cotton for example – the price of cotton goods rises as well: both semi-finished goods such as yarn, and finished products such as cloth, etc. which are produced with this more expensive cotton. And cotton that has not yet been worked up, but is still in the warehouse, rises just as much in value as cotton that is in the course of manufacture. As the retrospective expression of more labour-time, this cotton adds a higher value to the product which it goes into as a component than it possessed originally and the capitalist paid for it.

Thus if an increase in the price of raw material takes place with a significant amount of finished goods already present on the market, at whatever stage of completion, then the value of these commodities rises and there is a corresponding increase in the value of the capital involved. The same applies to stocks of raw material, etc. in the hands of the producers. This revaluation can compensate the individual capitalist, or a whole particular sphere of capitalist production – even more than compensate, perhaps – for the fall in the rate of profit that follows from the raw material's rise in price. Without going into the detailed effects of competition here, we may remark for the sake of completeness that (1) if there are substantial stocks of raw material in the warehouse, they counteract the price increase arising from the conditions of their production; (2) if the semi-finished or finished goods on the market press heavily on the supply, they may prevent the price of these goods from rising in proportion to the price of their raw material.

The reverse is the case with a fall in the price of raw material which would otherwise increase the rate of profit, if all other circumstances were the same. The commodities on the market, articles still in preparation and stocks of raw material are all devalued, and this counteracts the simultaneous rise in the rate of profit.

The smaller the amount of stock to be found in the production sphere and on the market at the end of the business year, at the time when raw materials are supplied afresh on a massive scale (or, in the case of agricultural production, after the harvest), the more visible the effect of a change in raw material prices.

Our whole investigation has proceeded from the assumption that any rise or fall in prices is an expression of real fluctuations in value. But since we are dealing here with the effect that these price fluctuations have on the profit rate, it is actually a matter of indifference what their basis might be. The present argument is just as valid if prices rise or fall not as a result of fluctuations in value, but rather as a result of the intervention of the credit system, competition, etc.

Since the rate of profit is equal to the proportionate excess in the value of the product over the value of the total capital advanced, an increase in the rate of profit that arose from a devaluation of the capital advanced would involve a loss in capital value, while a decline in the profit rate that arose from a rise in value of the capital advanced could well involve a gain.

As far as the other portion of constant capital is concerned, machinery and fixed capital in general, the revaluation that takes place here and particularly affects buildings, land, etc. cannot be explained without the theory of ground-rent and thus does not belong here. The following points, however, are of general importance for devaluation:

(1) The constant improvements which rob existing machinery, factories, etc. of a part of their use-value, and therefore also their exchange-value. This process is particularly significant at times when new machinery is first introduced, before it has reached a certain degree of maturity, and where it thus constantly becomes outmoded before it has had time to reproduce its value. This is

one of the reasons for the unlimited extension of working hours that is usual in periods of this kind, work based on alternating day and night shifts, so that the value of the machines is reproduced without too great costs having to be borne for wear and tear. If the short working life of the machines (their short life-expectancy vis-à-vis prospective improvements) were not counter-balanced in this way, they would transfer too great a portion of their value to the product in the way of moral depreciation* and would not even be able to compete with handicraft production.[15]

Once machines, factory buildings or any other kind of fixed capital have reached a certain degree of maturity, so that they remain unchanged for a long while at least in their basic construction, a further devaluation takes place as a result of improvements in the methods of reproduction of this fixed capital. The value of machines, etc. now falls not because they are quickly supplanted or partially devalued by newer, more productive machines, etc., but because they can now be reproduced more cheaply. This is one of the reasons why large enterprises often flourish only under their second owners, after the first have gone bankrupt. The second owner, by buying them cheaply, starts production with a smaller outlay of capital.

It is particularly apparent in the case of agriculture how the same causes that raise or lower the price of the product also raise or lower the value of the capital, since this consists to a large extent of that product itself, e.g. corn or cattle. (Ricardo.)‡

*

The variable capital has still to be mentioned.

In as much as the value of labour-power rises because the value

---

* On 'moral depreciation' (*moralischer Verschleiss*) see also *Capital* Volume 2, pp. 250, 264. The reason for this rather awkward term is that *Verschleiss* as such means depreciation in the sense of wear and tear, which is what Marx is discussing in Volume 2. In the present volume, however, he generally describes this phenomenon as a form of devaluation (*Entwertung*).

15. Babbage, among others, gives examples [op. cit.]. The customary expedient – reduction of wages – was applied here too, and so this constant devaluation has a completely different effect from the one Mr Carey dreams of in his harmonious head.†

† Henry Charles Carey (1793–1879) was an American 'vulgar economist' and champion of the 'harmony of interests' between opposing classes.

‡ *Principles*, Chapter II, 'On Rent'.

of the means of subsistence required for its reproduction rises, or conversely falls because the value of these means of subsistence falls (and a revaluation or devaluation of the variable capital can mean nothing more than these two cases), and assuming that the working day remains constant, a revaluation of this kind means a fall in surplus-value and a devaluation means a rise. However, other circumstances can also be linked with this, such as the release and tying-up of capital, which we have not yet investigated and should now indicate in brief.

If wages fall, owing to a fall in the value of labour-power (though this may even be associated with a rise in the actual price of labour), a portion of the capital previously laid out on wages is set free. There is a release of variable capital. For capital that is newly invested, this has simply the effect of enabling it to function at an increased rate of surplus-value. The same quantity of labour is set in motion with less money than before, and in this way the unpaid portion of labour is increased at the cost of the paid portion. But for capital that was already invested earlier, not only does the rate of surplus-value increase, but on top of this a portion of the capital previously laid out on wages is set free. This was formerly tied up and formed a portion constantly deducted from the proceeds of production, a portion which was laid out on wages and had to function as variable capital if the business was to proceed on the old scale. This portion now becomes available and can be used for new capital investment, whether to extend the same business or to function in another sphere of production.

Let us assume for example that £500 was originally required to set 500 workers in motion for a week, and that now only £400 is required for this. If the mass of value produced is £1,000 in each case, the mass of surplus-value was in the first case £500 per week, and the rate of surplus-value 100 per cent; after the fall in wages, however, the mass of surplus-value is £1,000 − £400 = £600, and its rate $\frac{600}{400}$ = 150 per cent. And this increase in the rate of surplus-value is the only effect for someone opening a new business in that sphere of production with a variable capital of £400 and a corresponding constant capital. In a business that is already functioning, however, not only has the mass of surplus-value risen from £500 to £600 and the rate of surplus-value from 100 to 150 per cent, as a result of the devaluation of the variable capital; apart from this, £100 of variable capital has been set free, and this is now available to exploit more labour. Not only is the same amount of labour exploited more profitably, but the release of £100 enables the same variable capital of £500 to exploit more workers than before at the higher rate.

Now the other way round. If we take it that the original division of the product, with 500 workers employed, is $400_v + 600_s = 1,000$, the rate of surplus-value = 150 per cent. The worker thus receives a weekly wage of £$\frac{4}{5}$ = 16 shillings. If these 500 workers now cost £500 per week, as the result of a rise in the value of variable capital, the weekly wage of each rises to £1, and £400 can only set 400 workers in motion. If the same number of workers are set in motion as before, we have $500_v + 500_s = 1,000$; the rate of surplus-value would have fallen from 150 to 100 per cent, i.e. by a third. For a capital that is invested here for the first time, the only effect of this would be that the rate of surplus-value was lower. With conditions remaining otherwise the same, the rate of profit would accordingly have fallen, if not to the same degree. If for example $c = 2,000$, we have in the first case $2,000_c + 400_v + 600_s = 3,000$; $s' = 150$ per cent, $p' = \frac{600}{2,400} = 25$ per cent; in the second case, $2,000_c + 500_v + 500_s = 3,000$; $s' = 100$ per cent, $p' = \frac{500}{2,500} = 20$ per cent. For the capital already operating, on the other hand, the effect is a dual one. With £400 variable capital, only 400 workers can now be employed, and this is at a surplus-value rate of 100 per cent. The total surplus-value they produce is only £400. Moreover, since a constant capital of £2,000 now requires 500 workers to set it in motion, 400 workers only set in motion a constant capital of £1,600. Thus if production is to be continued on its former scale and a fifth of the machinery is not to come to a halt, the variable capital must be increased by £100, so that it can employ the same 500 workers as before. And this is possible only because capital that was formerly available is now tied up, in that part of the accumulation fund designed to expand the business now serves simply to fill the gap, or, alternatively, a portion designed to be spent as revenue is added to the original capital. With a £100 increase in the outlay of variable capital, £100 less surplus-value is then produced. More capital is needed to set the same number of workers in motion, and at the same time the surplus-value that each of these individual workers supplies is reduced.

The advantages that arise from the release of variable capital, and the disadvantages that arise from its being tied up, both exist only for capital that is already in operation and thus reproduces itself in given conditions. For capital that is to be newly invested, the advantage or disadvantage is in each case confined to this: there will occur a rise or fall in the rate of surplus-value and a corresponding if not proportionate change in the rate of profit.

*

The release and tying-up of variable capital that has just been investigated is the result of the devaluation and revaluation of the elements of variable capital, i.e. the costs of reproduction of labour-power. Variable capital can also be set free if the development of productivity leads to a reduction in the number of workers required to set the same amount of constant capital in motion, with the rate of wages remaining the same. In the reverse sense, additional variable capital may be tied up if more workers are required for the same amount of constant capital, owing to a decline in the productivity of labour. If a portion of the capital earlier applied as variable capital is now applied in the form of constant capital, however, i.e. if there is only a different distribution of the component elements of the same capital, then although this certainly has an influence on the rate of surplus-value and the rate of profit, it does not come under the heading of the tying-up and release of capital that we are considering here.

As we already saw, constant capital can also be tied up or released as the result of a rise or fall in the value of its material elements. Apart from this, constant capital can be tied up (without a part of the variable capital being transformed into constant) only if the productivity of labour increases, i.e. if the same amount of labour produces a larger product and therefore sets more constant capital in motion. The same thing can happen in certain circumstances if productivity declines, as in agriculture for example, so that the same amount of labour needs more means of production to produce the same product, e.g. a greater amount of seed, fertilizer, drainage, etc. Constant capital can be released without any devaluation if improvements, the harnessing of natural forces, etc. place a constant capital of lesser value in a position technically to perform the same service as one of higher value did earlier.

We saw in Volume 2 how, after commodities are transformed into money, are sold, a definite portion of this money must be transformed back into the material elements of constant capital, and moreover in the proportions that are required by the specific technical character of the sphere of production in question. Ignoring wages, i.e. variable capital, the most important element in all branches of production is raw material, including the ancillary materials that are particularly important in branches of production which do not involve any raw material proper, as with mining and the extractive industries in general. The portion of the price which must replace the wear-and-tear of the machinery enters the account more in an ideal sense, as long as the machinery is still at all serviceable; it does not very much matter whether it is paid for and converted into money today or tomorrow, or at any particular point in the capital's turnover time. It is different with the raw material. If its price rises, it may be impossible to replace it completely after deducting wages from the value of the commodity. Violent fluctuations in price thus lead to interruptions, major upsets and even catastrophes in the reproduction process. It is particularly agricultural products, whose raw materials derive from organic nature, that are most subject to these fluctuations in value, as a result of variations in the harvest, etc. (Quite apart from the impact of the credit system.) The same quantity of labour may here be expressed in very diverse amounts of use-values, depending on uncontrollable natural conditions, the seasons of the year, etc., and a particular quantity of these use-values will accordingly have very different prices. If a value x is expressed in 100 lb. of a commodity a, the price of 1 lb. of a is $\frac{x}{100}$; if it is expressed in 1,000 lb. of a, the price of 1 lb. is $\frac{x}{1,000}$; and so on. This is one element in the price fluctuations of raw materials. A second element is this – and we mention it here only for the sake of completeness, since competition and the credit system both still lie outside the orbit of our discussion. In the nature of the case, plant and animal products, whose growth and production are subject to certain organic laws involving naturally determined periods of time, cannot suddenly be increased in the same degree as, say, machines and other fixed capital, coal, ore, etc., which, assuming the requisite natural conditions, can be significantly increased in a very short period in an industrially developed country. It is possible, therefore, and indeed unavoidable when capitalist production is fully developed, that the production and increase of the portion of constant capital that consists of fixed capital, machinery, etc. may run significantly ahead of the portion consisting of organic raw materials, so that the demand for these raw materials grows more rapidly than their supply, and their price therefore rises. This rise in price leads to the following changes: (1) these raw materials are supplied from a greater distance, since the rise in their price can meet greater costs of transport; (2) their production is expanded, though by the nature of things the volume of products can only increase a year later; and (3) all kinds of surrogates are now employed that were previously unused, and more economical use is made of waste products. When the price rise begins to have a marked effect on the expansion of production and supply, the turning-point has generally been already reached, at which demand falls as a consequence of the continuing increase in the price of the raw material and of all commodities it enters into as an element, bringing about a reaction in its turn on the raw material's price. Apart from the convulsions that achieve this effect by devaluing capital in various ways, still other circumstances come into play, which we must now go on to mention.

First of all, however, one thing should be clear from what has already been said. The more capitalist production is developed, bringing with it greater means for a sudden and uninterrupted increase in the portion of the constant capital that consists of machinery, etc., and the more rapid the accumulation (particularly in times of prosperity), the greater is the relative overproduction of machinery and other fixed capital, the more frequent the relative overproduction of plant and animal raw materials, and the more marked the previously described rise in their price and the corresponding reaction. The more frequent, therefore, are those revulsions which have their basis in this violent price fluctuation, and are a major element in the reproduction process.

When these high prices collapse, because their rise has provoked a decline in demand as well as an expansion of production, a supply from distant regions that were previously drawn on far less, if at all, and consequently a situation in which the supply of raw materials overtakes the demand, then the result can be considered from different aspects. The sudden collapse in the price of raw materials places shackles on their reproduction, and in this way the monopoly of the original supplying countries, which produce in favourable conditions, is re-established – perhaps with certain limitations, but re-established anyhow. The impulse that was given may indeed cause the reproduction of the raw materials to proceed on an expanded scale, particularly in those countries that more or less possess a monopoly in this production. But the basis on which production proceeds as a result of the expanded machinery, etc. and which must now prevail as the new normal basis, after a few fluctuations, has been very much expanded by the events of the previous turnover cycle. Among some of the secondary sources of supply, however, the reproduction that has at first increased will have again experienced a significant restriction. The export tables readily show how during the last thirty years (up to 1865) Indian cotton production has risen whenever there has been a shortfall in American production and then suddenly contracted more or less seriously. In periods when raw materials become dearer, the industrial capitalists get together and form associations to regulate production. This was the case for instance in 1848, in Manchester, after the rise in cotton prices, and similarly for the production of flax in Ireland. As soon as the immediate impulse has gone by and the general principle of competition ('buying in the cheapest market') reigns sovereign once more, instead of promoting productive capacity in suitable countries of origin, which these associations set out to do, irrespective of the immediate momentary price at which these countries can supply the product, it is left once more to 'prices' to regulate supply. All ideas of a common, all-embracing and far-sighted control over the production of raw materials – a control that is in fact incompatible, by and large, with the laws of capitalist production, and hence remains forever a pious wish, or is at most confined to exceptional common steps in moments of great and pressing danger and perplexity – all such ideas give way to the belief that supply and demand will mutually regulate one another.[16] The capitalists'

16. Since the above was written (1865), competition on the world market has increased significantly owing to the rapid development of industry in all civilized countries, particularly America and Germany. The fact that the modern productive forces, rapidly and gigantically surging forward, are daily and increasingly outgrowing the laws of capitalist commodity exchange within which they are supposed to move – this fact impresses itself more and more today even on the consciousness of the capitalists. There are two particular symptoms of this. Firstly, the new mania for general protective tariffs, differing from the old protectionism because they are precisely designed to protect exportable articles. Secondly, the cartels (trusts) formed by manufacturers in whole branches of production for the regulation of production and therewith prices and profits too. It is readily apparent that these experiments can be pursued only in a relatively favourable economic climate. The first storm is bound to bowl them over and show how, much as production does need regulating, it is certainly not the capitalist class that is called to this task. In the meantime, the only purpose these cartels serve to promote is the swallowing of the little fish by the big fish even more rapidly than before. – F.E.

superstition on this matter is so crude that even the factory inspectors pass astonished remarks on it time and again in their reports. The alternation of good and bad years, of course, does bring cheaper raw materials round again. Apart from the immediate effect that this has on extending demand, the effect on the profit rate that we have already mentioned also serves as a stimulus. And the process depicted above, with the production of raw materials being gradually overtaken again by the production of machines, etc., is then repeated once more on a larger scale. Any actual improvement in the raw material, so that not only the required quantity was supplied, but also the required quality, for instance American-quality cotton from India, would necessitate a regular and steady rise in European demand over a long period (quite apart from the economic conditions to which Indian production is subject in its own country). The production of raw materials is thus expanded only in sudden jerks, before being violently contracted once more. This can all be studied very well, as indeed can the spirit of capitalist production in general, from the cotton famine of 1861–5, a situation in which a raw material that is one of the most essential elements of reproduction was quite lacking for a time. Prices can also rise in a situation of full supply, if this is full only under difficult conditions. Alternatively there may be a genuine lack of raw material. In the cotton crisis, we had originally the latter case.

The more we look back at the history of production in the most recent period, the more regularly we find, particularly in the key branches of industry, a constantly repeated alternation between relative price increase and a subsequent depreciation of raw materials supplied by organic nature that arises from this. The above arguments are illustrated by the following example taken from the reports of the Factory Inspectorate.

The moral of the tale, which can also be extracted from other discussions of agriculture, is that the capitalist system runs counter to a rational agriculture, or that a rational agriculture is incompatible with the capitalist system (even if the latter promotes technical development in agriculture) and needs either small farmers working for themselves or the control of the associated producers.

*

We now give the illustrations from the English factory reports promised above.

'The state of trade is better; but the cycle of good and bad times diminishes as machinery increases, and the changes from the one to the other happen oftener, as the demand for raw materials increases with it ... At present, confidence is not only restored after the panic of 1857, but the panic itself seems to be almost forgotten. Whether this improvement will continue or not depends greatly upon the price of raw materials. There appear to me evidences already, that in some instances the maximum has been reached, beyond which their manufacture becomes gradually less and less profitable, till it ceases to be so altogether. If we take, for instance, the lucrative years in the worsted trade of 1849 and 1850, we see that the price of English combing wool stood at 1s. 1d., and of Australian at between 1s. 2d. and 1s. 5d. per lb., and that on the average of the ten years from 1841 to 1850, both inclusive, the average price of English wool never exceeded 1s. 2d. and of Australian wool 1s. 5d. per lb. But that in the commencement of the disastrous year of 1857, the price of Australian wool began with 1s. 11d., falling to 1s. 6d. in December, when the panic was at its height, but has gradually risen again to 1s. 9d. through 1858, at which it now stands; whilst that of English wool, commencing with 1s. 8d., and rising in April and September 1857 to 1s. 9d., falling in January 1858 to 1s. 2d., has since risen to 1s. 5d., which is 3d. per lb. higher than the average of the ten years to which I have referred ... This shows, I think, one of three things, – either that the bankruptcies which similar prices occasioned in 1857 are forgotten; or that there is barely the wool grown which the existing spindles are capable of consuming; or else, that the prices of manufactured articles are about to be permanently higher ... And as in past experience I have seen spindles and looms multiply both in numbers and speed in an incredibly short space of time, and our exports of wool to France increase in an almost equal ratio, and as both at home and abroad the age of sheep seems to be getting less and less, owing to increasing populations and to what the agriculturalists call "a quick return on stock", so I have often felt anxious for persons whom, without this knowledge, I have seen embarking skill and capital in undertakings, wholly reliant for their success on a product which can only be increased according to organic laws ... The same state of supply and demand of all raw materials ... seems to account for many of the fluctuations in the cotton trade during past periods, as well as for the condition of the English wool market in the autumn of 1857, with its overwhelming consequences' (R. Baker in *Reports of the Inspectors of Factories . . . 31 October 1858*, pp. 56–61).[17]

The high point of the worsted industry in the West Riding of Yorkshire was 1849–50. The number of persons employed in it was 29,246 in 1838, 37,060 in 1843, 48,097 in 1845, and 74,891 in 1850. In the same region there were 2,768 power-looms in 1838, with 11,458 in 1841, 16,870 in 1843, 19,121 in 1845 and 29,539 in 1850. (*Reports of the Inspectors of Factories . . . 31 October 1850*, p. 60.) This burgeoning prosperity was already beginning to wear thin in October 1850. In his report for April 1851, sub-inspector Baker says of Leeds and Bradford: 'The state of trade is, and has been for some time, very unsatisfactory. The worsted spinners are fast losing the profits of 1850, and, in the majority of cases, the manufacturers are not doing much good. I believe, at this moment, there is more woollen machinery standing than I have almost ever known at one time, and the flax spinners are also turning off hands and stopping frames. The cycles of trade, in fact, in the textile fabrics, are now extremely uncertain, and I think we shall shortly find to be true . . . that there is no comparison made between the producing power of the spindles, the quantity of raw material, and the growth of the population' (*Reports of the Inspectors of Factories . . . 30 April 1851*, p. 52).

The same applies to the cotton industry. In the report for October 1858 that has already been quoted, we read: 'Since the hours of labour in factories have been fixed, the amounts of consumption, produce, and wages in all textile fabrics have been reduced to a rule of three . . . I quote from a recent lecture delivered by . . . the present Mayor of Blackburn, Mr Baynes, on the cotton trade, who by such means has reduced the cotton statistics of his own neighbourhood to the closest approximation:

' "Each real and mechanical horse-power will drive 450 self-acting mule spindles with preparation, or 200 throstle spindles, or 15 looms for 40 inches cloth, with winding, warping, and sizing. Each horse-power in spinning will give employment to $2\frac{1}{2}$ operatives, but in weaving to 10 persons, at wages averaging full 10s. 6d. a week to each person . . . The average counts of yarn spun and woven are from 30s. to 32s. twist, and 34s. to 36s. weft yarns; and

17. It goes without saying that, unlike Mr Baker, we do not seek to *explain* the wool crisis of 1857 in terms of the disproportion in price between raw material and manufactured item. This was simply a symptom, while the crisis was a general one. – F.E.

taking the spinning production at 13 ounces per spindle per week, will give 824,700 lbs. yarn spun per week, requiring 970,000 lbs. or 2,300 bales of cotton, at a cost of £28,300 . . . The total cotton consumed in this district (within a five-mile radius round Blackburn) per week is 1,530,000 lbs., or 3,650 bales, at a cost of £44,625 . . . This is one-eighteenth of the whole cotton spinning of the United Kingdom, and one-sixth of the whole power-loom weaving."

'Thus we see that, according to Mr Baynes's calculations, the total number of cotton spindles in the United Kingdom is 28,800,000, and supposing these to be always working full time, that the annual consumption of cotton ought to be 1,432,080,000 lbs. But as the import of cotton, less the export in 1856 and 1857, was only 1,022,576,832 lbs., there must necessarily be a deficiency of supply equal to 409,503,168 lbs. Mr Baynes, however, who has been good enough to communicate with me on this subject, thinks that an annual consumption of cotton based upon the quantity used in the Blackburn district would be liable to be overcharged, owing to the difference, not only in the counts spun, but in the excellence of the machinery. He estimates the total annual consumption of cotton in the United Kingdom at 1,000,000,000 lbs. But if he is right, and there really is an excess of supply equal to 22,576,832 lbs., supply and demand seem to be nearly balanced already, without taking into consideration those additional spindles and looms which Mr Baynes speaks of as getting ready for work in his own district, and, by parity of reasoning, probably in other districts also' (pp. 59, 60).

3. GENERAL ILLUSTRATION: THE COTTON CRISIS 1861–5

Prehistory: 1845–60

1845. High tide of the cotton industry. Cotton prices very low. Leonard Horner says on this subject: 'For the last eight years I have not known so active a state of trade as has prevailed during the last summer and autumn, particularly in cotton spinning. Throughout the half-year I have been receiving notices every week of new investments of capital in factories, either in the form of new mills being built, of the few that were untenanted finding occupiers, of enlargements of existing mills, of new engines of increased power, and of manufacturing machinery' (*Reports of the Inspectors of Factories . . . 31 October 1845*, p. 13).

1846. Complaints begin. 'For a considerable time past I have heard from the occupiers of cotton-mills very general complaints of the depressed state of their trade ... for within the last six weeks several mills have begun to work short time, usually eight hours a day instead of twelve; this appears to be on the increase ... There has been a great advance in the price of the raw material, ... there has been not only no advance in the manufactured articles, but ... prices are lower than they were before the rise in cotton began. From the great increase in the number of cotton mills within the last four years, there must have been, on the one hand, a greatly increased demand for the raw material, and, on the other, a greatly increased supply in the market of the manufactured articles; causes that must concurrently have operated against profits, supposing the supply of the raw material and the consumption of the manufactured article to have remained unaltered; but, of course, in the greater ratio by the late short supply of cotton, and the falling off in the demand for the manufactured articles in several markets, both home and foreign' (*Reports of the Inspectors of Factories ... 31 October 1846*, p. 10).

A rising demand for raw material naturally goes hand in hand with an excess supply of finished goods on the market. The expansion of industry at that time, incidentally, and the subsequent stagnation, were not confined to the cotton districts. In the worsted centre of Bradford, there were 490 mills in 1846, as against only 318 in 1836. These figures do not nearly begin to express the actual rise in production, as existing mills were also significantly expanded at the same time. This is true above all of flax-spinning. 'All have contributed more or less, during the last ten years, to the overstocking of the market, to which a great part of the present stagnation of trade must be attributed ... The depression ... naturally results from such rapid increase of mills and machinery' (*Reports of the Inspectors of Factories ... 31 October 1846*, p. 30).

1847. Monetary crisis in October. Bank rate at 8 per cent. There had already occurred the collapse of the railway bubble, and the speculation in East Indian bills. However:

'Mr Baker enters into very interesting details, respecting the increased demand, in the last few years, for cotton, wool, and flax, owing to the great extension of these trades. He considers the increased demand for these raw materials, occurring, as it has, at a period when the produce has fallen much below an average supply, as almost sufficient, even without reference to the monetary derangement, to account for the present state of these branches. This opinion is fully confirmed, by my own observations and conversation with persons well acquainted with trade. Those several branches were all in a very depressed state, while discounts were readily obtained at and under 5 per cent. The supply of raw silk has, on the contrary, been abundant, the prices moderate, and the trade, consequently, very active, till ... the last two or three weeks, when there is no doubt the monetary derangement has affected not only the persons actually engaged in the manufacture, but more extensively still, the manufacturers of fancy goods, who were great customers to the throwster. A reference to published returns shows that the cotton trade had increased nearly 27 per cent in the last three years. Cotton has consequently increased, in round numbers, from 4d. to 6d. per lb., while twist, in consequence of the increased supply, is yet only a fraction above its former price. The woollen trade began its increase in 1836, since which Yorkshire has increased its manufacture of this article 40 per cent, but Scotland exhibits a yet greater increase. The increase of the worsted trade[18] is still larger. Calculations give a result of upwards of 74 per cent increase within the same period. The consumption of raw wool has therefore been immense. Flax has increased since 1839 about 25 per cent in England, 22 per cent in Scotland, and nearly 90 per cent in Ireland;[19] the consequence of this, in connexion with bad crops, has been that the raw material has gone up £10 per ton, while the price of yarn has fallen 6d. a bundle' (*Reports of the Inspectors of Factories ... 31 October 1847*, pp. 30–31).

1849. Business was picking up again from the last months of 1848 onwards. 'The price of flax, which has been so low as to almost guarantee a reasonable profit under any future circumstances, has induced the manufacturers to carry on their work very steadily ... The woollen manufacturers were exceedingly busy for a while in the early part of the year ... I fear that consignments

18. A sharp distinction is made in England between woollen manufacture proper, which spins and weaves carded yarn from short wool (main centre Leeds), and worsted manufacture, which spins and weaves worsted yarn from long wool (main centre Bradford). – F.E.

19. The rapid expansion of machine-spinning for linen in Ireland dealt a death-blow to the export of handwoven German linen from Silesia, Lusatia and Westphalia. – F.E.

of woollen goods often take the place of real demand, and that periods of apparent prosperity, i.e., of full work, are not always periods of legitimate demand. In some months the worsted has been exceedingly good, in fact flourishing ... At the commencement of the period referred to, wool was exceedingly low; what was bought by the spinners was well bought, and no doubt in considerable quantities. When the price of wool rose with the spring wool sales, the spinner had the advantage, and the demand for manufactured goods becoming considerable and imperative, they kept it' (*Reports of the Inspectors of Factories ... 30 April 1849*, p. 42).

'If we look at the variations in the state of trade, which have occurred in the manufacturing districts of the kingdom for a period now of between three and four years, I think we must admit the existence of a great disturbing cause somewhere ... but may not the immensely productive power of increased machinery have added another element to the same cause?' (*Reports of the Inspectors of Factories ... 30 April 1849*, pp. 42, 43).

In November 1848, May 1849 and during the summer through to October, business became ever more lively. 'The worsted stuff of trade, of which Bradford and Halifax are the great hives of industry, has been the one most active; this trade has never before reached anything like the extent, to which it has now attained ... Speculation, and uncertainty as to the probable supply of cotton wool, have ever had the effect of causing greater excitement, and more frequent alterations in the state of that branch of manufacture, than any other. There is ... at present an accumulation in stock of the coarser kinds of cotton goods, which creates anxiety on the part of the smaller spinners, and is already acting to their detriment, having caused several of them to work their mills short time' (*Reports of the Inspectors of Factories ... 31 October 1849*, pp. 64–5).

1850. April. Brisk trade continues. The exception: 'The great depression in a part of the cotton trade ... attributable to the scarcity in the supply of the raw material more especially adapted to the branch engaged in spinning low numbers of cotton yarns, or manufacturing heavy cotton goods. A fear is entertained that the increased machinery built recently for the worsted trade, may be followed with a similar reaction. Mr Baker computes that in the year 1849 alone the worsted looms have increased their produce 40 per cent, and the spindles 25 or 30 per cent, and they are still increasing at the same rate' (*Reports of the Inspectors of Factories . . . 30 April 1850*, p. 54).

1850. October. 'The high price of raw cotton continues . . . to cause a considerable depression in this branch of manufacture, especially in those descriptions of goods in which the raw material constitutes a considerable part of the cost of production . . . The great advance in the price of raw silk has likewise caused a depression in many branches of that manufacture' (*Reports of the Inspectors of Factories . . . 31 October 1850*, p. 14).

According to the report of the committee of the Royal Society for the Promotion and Improvement of the Growth of Flax in Ireland, as quoted here, the high price of flax, combined with a low price level for other agricultural products, ensured a significant increase in flax production for the following year (p. 33).

1853. April. Extreme prosperity. L. Horner says in his report: 'At no period during the last seventeen years that I have been officially acquainted with the manufacturing districts in Lancashire have I known such general prosperity; the activity in every branch is extraordinary' (*Reports of the Inspectors of Factories . . . 30 April 1853*, p. 19).

1853. October. Depression in the cotton industry. 'Overproduction' (*Reports of the Inspectors of Factories . . . 31 October 1853*, p. 15).

1854. April. 'The woollen trade, although not brisk, has given full employment to all the factories engaged upon that fabric, and a similar remark applies to the cotton factories. The worsted trade generally has been in an uncertain and unsatisfactory condition during the whole of the last half-year . . . The manufacture of flax and hemp are more likely to be seriously impeded, by reason of the diminished supplies of the raw materials from Russia due to the Crimean war' (*Reports of the Inspectors of Factories . . . 30 April 1854*, p. 37).

1859. 'The trade in the Scottish flax districts still continues depressed – the raw material being scarce, as well as high in price; and the inferior quality of the last year's crop in the Baltic, from whence come our principal supplies, will have an injurious effect on the trade of the district; jute, however, which is gradually superseding flax in many of the coarser fabrics, is neither unusually high in price, nor scarce in quantity . . . about one half of the machinery in Dundee is now employed in jute spinning' (*Reports of the Inspectors of Factories . . . 30 April 1859*, p. 19). 'Owing to the high price of the raw material, flax spinning is still far from remunerating, and while all the other mills are going full time, there are several instances of the stoppage of flax machinery ... Jute spinning is ... in a rather more satisfactory state, owing to the recent decline in the price of material, which has now fallen to a very moderate point' (*Reports of the Inspectors of Factories ... 31 October 1859*, p. 20).

1861–4. American Civil War. Cotton Famine. The Biggest Example of an Interruption in the Production Process Caused by a Lack of Raw Material and an Increase in its Price.

1860. April. 'With respect to the state of trade, I am happy to be able to inform you that, notwithstanding the high price of raw material, all the textile manufactures, with the exception of silk, have been fairly busy during the past half-year ... In some of the cotton districts hands have been advertised for, and have migrated thither from Norfolk and other rural counties ... There appears to be, in every branch of trade, a great scarcity of raw material. It is ... the want of it alone, which keeps us within bounds. In the cotton trade, the erection of new mills, the formation of new systems of extension, and the demand for hands, can scarcely, I think, have been at any time exceeded. Everywhere there are new movements in search of raw material' (*Reports of the Inspectors of Factories ... 30 April 1860*, p. 57).

1860. October. 'The state of trade in the cotton, woollen, and flax districts has been good; indeed in Ireland, it is stated to have been "very good" for now more than a year; and that it would have been still better, but for the high price of raw material. The flax spinners appear to be looking with more anxiety than ever to the opening out of India by railways, and to the development of its agriculture, for a supply of flax which may be commensurate with their wants' (*Reports of the Inspectors of Factories ... 31 October 1860*, p. 37).

1861. April. 'The state of trade is at present depressed ... A few cotton mills are running short time, and many silk mills are only partially employed. Raw material is high. In almost every branch of textile manufacture it is above the price at which it can be manufactured for the masses of the consumers' (*Reports of the Inspectors of Factories ... 30 April 1861*, p. 33).

It had become evident that 1860 was a year of overproduction in the cotton industry; the effect of this was still making itself felt in subsequent years. 'It has taken between two and three years to absorb the overproduction of 1860 in the markets of the world' (*Reports of the Inspectors of Factories . . . 31 October 1863*, p. 127). 'The depressed state of the markets for cotton manufactures in the East, early in 1860, had a corresponding effect upon the trade of Blackburn, in which 30,000 power-looms are usually employed almost exclusively in the production of cloth to be consumed in the East. There was consequently but a limited demand for labour for many months prior to the effects of the cotton blockade being felt . . . Fortunately this preserved many of the spinners and manufacturers from being involved in the common ruin. Stocks increased in value so long as they were held, and there had been consequently nothing like that alarming depreciation in the value of property which might not unreasonably have been looked for in such a crisis' (*Reports of the Inspectors of Factories . . . 31 October 1862*, pp. 29, 31).

1861. October. 'Trade has been for some time in a very depressed state . . . It is not improbable indeed that during the winter months many establishments will be found to work very short time. This might, however, have been anticipated . . . irrespective of the causes which have interrupted our usual supplies of cotton from America and our exports, short time must have been kept during the ensuing winter in consequence of the great increase of production during the last three years, and the unsettled state of the Indian and Chinese markets' (*Reports of the Inspectors of Factories . . . 31 October 1861*, p. 19).

Cotton Waste. East Indian Cotton (Surat). Influence on Wages. Improvements in Machinery. Replacement of Cotton by Starch Flour and Minerals. Effect of this Starch Flour Sizing on the Workers. Manufacturers of Finer Grades of Yarn. Factory-Owners' Fraud

'A manufacturer writes to me thus: "As to estimates of consumption per spindle, I doubt if you take sufficiently into calculation the fact that when cotton is high in price, every spinner of ordinary yarns (say up to 40s.) (principally 12s. to 32s.) will raise his counts as much as he can, that is, will spin 16s. where he used to spin 12s., or 22s. in the place of 16s., and so on; and the manufacturer using these fine yarns will make his cloth the usual weight by the addition of so much more size. The trade is availing itself of this resource at present to an extent which is even discreditable. I have heard on good authority of ordinary export shirting weighing 8 lbs. which was made of $5\frac{1}{4}$ lbs. cotton and $2\frac{3}{4}$ lbs. size ... In cloths of other descriptions as much as 50 per cent size is sometimes added; so that a manufacturer may and does truly boast that he is getting rich by selling cloth for less money per pound than he paid for the mere yarn of which they are composed " ' (*Reports of the Inspectors of Factories ... 30 April 1864*, p. 27).

'I have also received statements that the weavers attribute increased sickness to the size which is used in dressing the warps of Surat cotton, and which is not made of the same material as formerly, viz., flour. This substitute for flour is said, however, to have the very important advantage of increasing greatly the weight of the cloth manufactured, making 15 lbs. of the raw material to weigh 20 lbs. when woven into cloth' (*Reports of the Inspectors of Factories ... 31 October 1863*, p. 63. This substitute was ground talcum, called China clay, or gypsum, called French chalk). 'The earnings of the weavers' (meaning the operatives) 'are much reduced from the employment of substitutes for flour as sizing for warps. This sizing, which gives weight to the yarn, renders it hard and brittle. Each thread of the warp in the loom passes through a part of the loom called "a heald", which consists of strong threads to keep the warp in its proper place, and the hard state of the warp causes the threads of the heald to break frequently; and it is said to take a weaver five minutes to tie up the threads every time they break; and a weaver has to piece these ends at least ten times as often as formerly, thus reducing the productive powers of the loom in the working-hours' (ibid., pp. 42–3).

'In Ashton, Stalybridge, Mossley, Oldham, etc., the reduction of the time has been fully one-third, and the hours are lessening every week ... Simultaneously with this diminution of time there is also a reduction of wages in many departments' (*Reports of the Inspectors of Factories ... 31 October 1861*, pp. 12–13).

At the beginning of 1861 there was a strike of power-loom weavers in certain parts of Lancashire. Various factory-owners had announced a reduction in wages of from 5 to $7\frac{1}{2}$ per cent. The operatives insisted that wage-rates should be kept the same and working hours cut instead. This was not conceded, and the strike began. After a month, the workers had to admit defeat. They then suffered both things: 'In addition to the reduction of wages to which the operatives at last consented, many mills are now running short time' (*Reports of the Inspectors of Factories ... 30 April 1861*, p. 23).

1862. April. 'The sufferings of the operatives since the date of my last report have greatly increased; but at no period of the history of manufactures, have sufferings so sudden and so severe been borne with so much silent resignation and so much patient self-respect' (*Reports of the Inspectors of Factories ... 30 April 1862*, p. 10). 'The proportionate number of operatives wholly out of employment at this date appears not to be much larger than it was in 1848, when there was an ordinary panic of sufficient consequences to excite alarm amongst the manufacturers, so much as to warrant the collection of similar statistics of the state of the cotton trade as are now issued weekly ... In May 1848, the proportion of cotton operatives out of work in Manchester out of the whole number usually employed was 15 per cent, on short time 12 per cent, while 70 per cent were in full work. On the 28th of May of the present year, of the whole number of persons usually employed 15 per cent were out of work, 35 per cent were on short time, and 49 per cent were working full time ... In some other places, Stockport for example, the averages of short time and of non-employment are higher, whilst those of full time are less,' because coarser grades are spun there than in Manchester (p. 16).

1862. October. 'I find by the last return to Parliament that there were 2,887 cotton factories in the United Kingdom in 1861, 2,109 of them being in my district (Lancashire and Cheshire). I was aware that a very large proportion of the 2,109 factories in my district were small establishments, giving employment to few persons, but I have been surprised to find how large that proportion is. In 392, or 19 per cent, the steam-engine or water-wheel is under 10 horse-power; in 345, or 16 per cent, the horse-power is above 10 and under 20; and in 1,372 the power is 20 horses and more ... A very large proportion of these small manufacturers – being more than a third of the whole number – were operatives themselves at no distant period; they are men without command of capital ... The brunt of the burden then would have to be borne by the remaining two-thirds' (*Reports of the Inspectors of Factories ... 31 October 1862*, pp. 18, 19).

According to the same report, only 40,146 cotton workers in Lancashire and Cheshire were at that time fully employed, or 11.3 per cent of the total; 134,767 or 38 per cent were working short-time, and 179,721 or 50.7 per cent were unemployed. If we sub-tract the figures for Manchester and Bolton, where it is princi-pally finer grades of yarn that are spun, the situation was even worse, i.e. fully employed 8.5 per cent, on short-time 38 per cent, unemployed 53.5 per cent (pp. 19, 20).

'Working up good or bad cotton makes a material difference to the operative. In the earlier part of the year, when manufacturers were endeavouring to keep their mills at work by using up all the moderately priced cotton they could obtain, much bad cotton was brought into mills in which good cotton was ordinarily used, and the difference to the operatives in wages was so great that many strikes took place on the ground that they could not make a fair day's wages at the old rates ... In some cases, although working full time, the difference in wages from working bad cotton was as much as one half' (p. 27).

1863. April. 'During the present year there will not be full em-ployment for much more than one half of the cotton operatives in the country' (*Reports of the Inspectors of Factories ... 30 April 1863*, p. 14).

'A very serious objection to the use of Surat cotton, as manu-facturers are now compelled to use it, is that the speed of the machinery must be greatly reduced in the processes of manufac-ture. For some years past every effort has been made to increase the speed of machinery, in order to make the same machinery produce more work; and the reduction of the speed becomes therefore a question which affects the operative as well as the manufacturer; for the chief part of the operatives are paid by the work done; for instance, spinners are paid per lb. for the yarn spun, weavers per piece for the number of pieces woven; and even with the other classes of operatives paid by the week there would be a diminution of wages in consideration of the less amount of goods produced. From inquiries I have made, and statements placed in my hands, of the earnings of cotton operatives during the present year, I find there is a diminution averaging 20 per cent upon their former earnings, in some instances the diminution has been as much as 50 per cent, calculated upon the same rate of wages as prevailed in 1861' (p. 13). '... The sum earned depends upon ... the nature of the material operated upon ... The position of the operatives in regard to the amount of their earnings is very much better now' (October 1863) 'than it was this time last year. Machinery has improved, the material is better understood, and the operatives are able better to overcome the difficulties they had to contend with at first. I remember being in a sewing school' (a charity institution for unemployed) 'at Preston last spring, when two young women, who had been sent to work at a weaving shed the day before, upon the representation of the manufacturer that they could earn 4s. per week, returned to the school to be readmitted, complaining that they could not have earned 1s. per week. I have been informed of "self-acting minders" . . . men who manage a pair of self-acting mules, earning at the end of a fortnight's full work 8s. 11d., and that from this sum was deducted the rent of the house, the manufacturer, however, returning half the rent as a gift.' (How generous!) 'The minders took away the sum of 6s. 11d. In many places the self-acting minders ranged from 5s. to 9s. per week, and the weavers from 2s. to 6s. per week in the last months of 1862 . . . At the present time a much more healthy state of things exists, although there is still a great decrease in the earnings in most districts . . . There are several causes which have tended to the reduction of earnings, besides the shorter staple of the Surat cotton and its dirty condition; for instance, it is now the practice to mix "waste" largely with Surat, which consequently increases the difficulties of the spinner or minder. The threads, from their shortness of fibre, are more liable to break in the drawing out of the mule and in the twisting of the yarn, and the mule cannot be kept so continuously in motion . . . Then, from the great attention required in watching the threads in weaving, many weavers can only mind one loom, and very few can mind more than two looms . . . There has been a direct reduction of 5, $7\frac{1}{2}$ and 10 per cent upon the wages of the operatives . . . In the majority of cases the operative has to make the best of his material, and to earn the best wages he can at the ordinary rates . . . Another difficulty the weavers have sometimes to contend with is, that they are expected to produce well-finished cloth from inferior materials, and are subject to fine for the flaws in their work' (*Reports of the Inspectors of Factories . . . 31 October 1863*, pp. 41–3).

Wages were wretched enough even with full-time working. The cotton workers willingly volunteered for all the public works they could be employed in, such as drainage, road-building, stone-breaking and street-paving, so as to get relief (which was in effect a form of relief to the factory-owners; see Volume 1, pp. 720–21) from the local authorities. The entire bourgeoisie stood guard over the workers. If starvation wages were offered and a worker was unwilling to accept them, the Relief Committee struck him off the relief list. This was a real golden age for the factory-owning gentlemen, in as much as the workers either starved or had to work at the price most profitable for the bourgeoisie, while the Relief Committees acted as their guard-dogs. The factory-owners also placed obstacles to emigration, as far as they could, in secret agreement with the government, partly so as to keep their capital in constant readiness (in the form of the workers' flesh and blood), partly to make sure of the rent they extorted from the workers for their dwellings.

'The Relief Committees acted with great strictness upon this point. If work was offered, the operatives to whom it was proposed were struck off the lists, and thus compelled to accept the offer. When they objected to accept work . . . the cause has been that their earnings would have been merely nominal, and the work exceedingly severe' (*Reports of the Inspectors of Factories . . . 31 October 1863*, p. 97).

The workers were prepared to do any kind of work they were put to under the Public Works Act. 'The principle upon which industrial employments were organized varied considerably in different towns, but in those places even in which the outdoor work was not absolutely a labour test the manner in which labour was remunerated by its being paid for either at the exact rate of relief, or closely approximating the rate, it became in fact a labour test' (p. 69). 'The Public Works Act of 1863 was intended to remedy this inconvenience, and to enable the operative to earn his day's wages as an independent labourer. The purpose of this Act was three-fold: firstly, to enable local authorities to borrow money of the Exchequer Loan Commissioners' (with consent of the President of the Central Relief Committee); 'secondly, to facilitate the improvement of the towns of the cotton districts; thirdly, to provide work and remunerative wages to the unemployed operatives.'

By the end of October 1863, loans to the sum of £883,700 had been granted under this Act (p. 70). The works undertaken were chiefly the digging of canals, road-building, street-paving, construction of reservoirs, etc.

Mr Henderson, President of the Blackburn Relief Committee, writes on this subject to factory inspector Redgrave: 'Nothing in my experience, during the present period of suffering and distress, has struck me more forcibly or given me more satisfaction, than the cheerful alacrity with which the unemployed operatives of this district have accepted of the work offered to them through the adoption of the Public Works Act, by the Corporation of Blackburn. A greater contrast than that presented between the cotton spinner as a skilled workman in a factory, and as a labourer in a sewer 14 or 18 feet deep, can scarcely be conceived.' (Depending on the size of their families, the workers were entitled to a sum of from 4 to 12 shillings per week, the latter figure, a truly colossal amount, often having to suffice for a family of eight persons. The municipal philistines profited from this in two ways. Firstly, they received money for improving their smoky and neglected towns at exceptionally low rates of interest; secondly, they paid the workers far below the regular wage-rates.) 'Accustomed as he had been to a temperature all but tropical, to work at which agility and delicacy of manipulation availed him infinitely more than muscular strength, and to double and sometimes treble the remuneration which it is possible for him now to obtain, his ready acceptance of the proffered employment involved an amount of self-denial and consideration the exercise of which is most creditable. In Blackburn the men have been tested at almost every variety of outdoor work; in excavating a stiff heavy clay soil to a considerable depth, in draining, in stone-breaking, in road-making, and in excavating for street sewers to a depth of 14, 16, and sometimes 20 feet. In many cases while thus employed they are standing in mud and water to the depth of 10 or 12 inches, and in all they are exposed to a climate which, for chilly humidity, is not surpassed I suppose, even if it is equalled, by that of any district in England' (pp. 91–2). 'The conduct of the operatives has been almost blameless, and their readiness to accept and make the best of outdoor labour' (p. 69).

1864. April. 'Complaints are occasionally made in different districts of the scarcity of hands, but this deficiency is chiefly felt in particular departments, as, for instance, of weavers ... These complaints have their origin as much from the low rate of wages which the hands can earn owing to the inferior qualities of yarn used, as from any positive scarcity of workpeople even in that particular department. Numerous differences have taken place during the past month between the masters of particular mills and their operatives in respect to the wages. Strikes, I am sorry to say, are but too frequently resorted to ... the effect of the Public Works Act is felt as a competition by the mill-owners. The local committee at Bacup has suspended operations, for although all the mills are not running, yet a scarcity of hands has been experienced' (*Reports of the Inspectors of Factories . . . 30 April 1864*, pp. 9, 10).

Indeed, the factory-owners' idyll was now over. As a result of the Public Works Act, the demand for labour grew so steeply that many factory workers were now earning 4 to 5 shillings a day in the Bacup quarries. The public works were therefore gradually closed down – this new edition of the *Ateliers nationaux* of 1848, but this time set up for the advantage of the bourgeoisie.*

Experiments 'in corpore vili'†

'Although I have given the actual earnings of the operatives' (fully employed) 'in several mills, it does not follow that they earn the same amount week by week. The operatives are subject to great fluctuation, from the constant experimentalizing of the manufacturers upon different kinds and proportions of cotton and waste in the same mill, the "mixings" as it is called being frequently changed; and the earnings of the operatives rise and fall with the quality of the cotton mixings; sometimes they have been within 15 per cent of former earnings, and then in a week or two, they have fallen from 50 to 60 per cent.'

Inspector Redgrave, who is talking here, goes on to give details of wages taken from practical experience; the following will serve here as example.

A, weaver, family of six, employed for four days a week, 6s. 8½d.; B, twister, four and a half days a week, 6s.; C, weaver, family of four, five days a week, 5s. 1d.; D, slubber, family of six, four days a week, 7s. 10d.; E, weaver, family of seven, three days, 5s., and so on. Redgrave continues: 'The above returns are deserving of consideration, for they show that work would become a misfortune in many a family, as it not merely reduces the income, but brings it so low as to be utterly insufficient to provide more than a small portion of the absolute wants, were it not that supplemental relief is granted to operatives when the wages of the family do not reach the sum that would be given to them as

* The original National Workshops set up in France after the February revolution of 1848 were ostensibly the satisfaction of a working-class demand. See Marx's pamphlet 'The Class Struggles in France' in *The Revolutions of 1848*, Pelican Marx Library, pp. 53–4.

† on a worthless body.

relief, if they were all unemployed' (*Reports of the Inspectors of Factories . . . 31 October 1863*, pp. 50–53).

'In no week since the 5th of June last was there more than two days seven hours and a few minutes employment for all the workers' (ibid., p. 121).

From the time the crisis began, up until 25 March 1863, almost £3 million was dispensed by the Poor Law authorities, the Central Relief Committee and the Mansion House Committee in London (p. 13).

'In a district in which the finest yarn is spun . . . the spinners suffer an indirect reduction of 15 per cent in consequence of the change from South Sea Island to Egyptian cotton . . . In an extensive district, in many parts of which waste is largely used as a mixture with Surat . . . the spinners have had a reduction of 5 per cent, and have lost from 20 to 30 per cent in addition, through working Surat and waste. The weavers are reduced from 4 looms to 2 looms. In 1860, they averaged 5s. 7d. per loom, in 1863, only 3s. 4d. The fines, which formerly varied from 3d. to 6d.' (for the spinner) 'on American, now run up to from 1s. to 3s. 6d.'

In one district where Egyptian cotton was used, mixed with East Indian: 'the average of the mule spinners, which was in 1860 18s. to 25s., now averages from 10s. to 18s. per week, caused, in addition to inferior cotton, by the reduction of the speed of the mule to put an extra amount of twist in the yarn, which in ordinary times would be paid for according to list' (pp. 43, 44). 'Although the Indian cotton may have been worked to profit by the manufacturer, it will be seen' (see the wage list on p. 53) 'that the operatives are sufferers compared with 1861, and if the use of Surat be confirmed, the operatives will want to earn the wages of 1861, which would seriously affect the profits of the manufacturer, unless he obtain compensation either in the price of the raw cotton or of his products' (p. 105).

Rent of Houses. 'The rent is frequently deducted from the wages of operatives, even when working short time, by the manufacturers whose cottages they may be occupying. Nevertheless the value of this class of property has diminished, and houses may be obtained at a reduction of from 25 to 50 per cent upon the rent of the houses in ordinary times; for instance, a cottage which would have cost 3s. 6d. per week can now be had for 2s. 4d. per week, and sometimes even for less' (p. 57).

Emigration. The factory-owners were of course against workers emigrating, firstly because, 'looking forward to the recovery of the cotton trade from its present depression, they keep within their reach the means whereby their mills can be worked in the most advantageous manner'. On the other hand, 'many manufacturers are owners of the houses in which operatives employed in their mills reside, and some unquestionably expect to obtain a portion of the back rent owing' (p. 96).

Mr Bernal Osborne said in a speech to his parliamentary electors on 22 October 1864 that the workers of Lancashire had behaved like the ancient philosophers (Stoics). Not like sheep?

Chapter 7: Supplementary Remarks

We continue to assume, as throughout this Part, that the mass of profit appropriated in each particular sphere of production is equal to the sum of the surplus-value produced in this sphere by the total capital applied. The bourgeois, however, will still not conceive profit as identical with surplus-value, i.e. with unpaid surplus labour, and this for the following reasons:

(1) In the process of circulation, he forgets the production process. The realization of commodity value – including the realization of surplus-value – he takes as the making of this surplus-value. (A blank in the manuscript here indicates that Marx intended to develop this point in more detail. – F.E.)

(2) We have shown that, even assuming the same degree of exploitation of labour, and ignoring all modifications introduced by the credit system, all mutual swindling and cheating among the capitalists themselves and all favourable selections of the market, rates of profit can be very different according to whether raw materials are purchased cheaply or less cheaply, with more or less specialist knowledge; according to whether the machinery employed is productive, suitable and cheap; according to whether the overall arrangement of the production process in its various stages is more or less satisfactory, with wastage of material avoided, management and supervision simple and effective, etc. In short, given the surplus-value that accrues to a certain variable capital, it still depends very much on the business acumen of the individual, either the capitalist himself or his managers and salespeople, whether this same surplus-value is expressed in a higher or lower rate of profit and therefore whether it delivers a greater or lesser amount of profit. The same surplus-value of £1,000, the product of £1,000 in wages, may involve £9,000 of constant capital in business A, and £11,000 in business B. In case A we have $p' = \frac{1,000}{10,000} = 10$ per cent; in case B, $p' = \frac{1,000}{12,000} = 8\frac{1}{3}$ per cent. In the

first case the total capital produces relatively more profit than in the second, i.e. the rate of profit is higher there, even though the variable capital advanced (£1,000) and the surplus-value that is extracted from it (£1,000) are the same in both cases, and there is thus in each case an equal exploitation of the same number of workers. This variation in the way the same mass of surplus-value is expressed, or the variation in the rate of profit and therefore in the profit itself, with the same exploitation of labour, may also stem from other sources; it can even arise purely and simply from the variation in the business skill with which the two enterprises are conducted. And this circumstance misleads the capitalist by convincing him that his profit is due not to the exploitation of labour, but at least in part also to other circumstances independent of this, and in particular his own individual action.

*

The arguments developed in this first Part show the errors of that view (Rodbertus)* according to which (in distinction from ground-rent, where the land area can remain the same, for example, while the rent rises), even a large variation in the capital can remain without effect on the proportion between capital and profit, i.e. on the profit rate, because if the mass of profit grows, so does the mass of the capital on which it must be calculated, and vice versa.

This is true in only two cases. Firstly, if, other things being equal, and in particular the rate of surplus-value, there is a change in the value of the money commodity. (This is so even with a purely nominal change in value, the rise and fall of tokens of value, as long as other factors remain the same.) Let the total capital be £100 and the profit £20, so that the rate of profit is 20 per cent. If the price of gold is now halved or doubled, in the first case the same capital that was previously worth £100 is now worth £200, and the profit has a value of £40 instead of £20 (i.e. it is expressed in this new amount of money). In the second case, the capital falls to a value of £50, and the profit is now expressed in a product valued at £10. In both cases, however, $200:40 = 50:10$

* Johann Karl Rodbertus-Jagetzow (1805–75) was a Prussian landowner, and in his writings a 'state socialist', i.e. in fact a representative of agrarian capitalism who supported Bismarck's active intervention in economic management. See Volume 1 of *Capital*, p. 669, Volume 2, pp. 88–102, and *Theories of Surplus-Value*, Part II, Chapter VIII, pp. 15–114, and Chapter IX, pp. 127–61.

$= 100{:}20 = 20$ per cent. There would be no real change in the capital value in any case such as this, but simply a change in the monetary expression of the same value and surplus-value. The rate of profit, $\frac{s}{C}$, could not be affected.

The other case is when there is a real change in capital value, but this change is not accompanied by a change in the ratio $v{:}c$, i.e. when the rate of surplus-value is constant and the ratio of the capital invested in labour-power (the variable capital, taken as an index of the labour-power set in motion) to the capital invested in means of production remains the same. Under these conditions, if we take C or nC or $\frac{C}{n}$, e.g. 1,000 or 2,000 or 500, the total profit will be in the first case 200, in the second case 400 and in the third case 100, but $\frac{200}{1{,}000} = \frac{400}{2{,}000} = \frac{100}{500} = 20$ per cent; i.e. the rate of profit remains unchanged here because the composition of the capital remains the same and is not affected by its change in magnitude. Hence the increase or decrease in the mass of profit simply indicates an increase or decrease in the size of the capital applied.

In the first case, therefore, there is simply an apparent change in magnitude of the capital applied; in the second case there is a real change in magnitude, but no change in the capital's organic composition, in the proportion between its variable and its constant parts. Leaving aside these two cases, however, a change in the magnitude of capital applied is either the *result* of a change in the value of one of its components, and thus a change in their relative magnitude (as long as the surplus-value does not itself change with the variable capital); or else this change in magnitude is the *cause* of a change in the relative magnitude of its two organic components (as with large-scale operations, the introduction of new machinery, etc.). In all these cases, therefore, a change in the magnitude of the capital applied must be accompanied by a simultaneous change in the rate of profit, as long as other things remain equal.

*

An increase in the rate of profit always stems from a relative or absolute increase in the surplus-value in relation to its costs of production, i.e. to the total capital advanced, or from a reduction in the difference between the rate of profit and the rate of surplus-value.

Fluctuations in the rate of profit that are independent of changes in either the capital's organic components or its absolute magnitude are possible only if the value of the capital advanced, whatever might be the form – fixed or circulating – in which it exists, rises or falls as a result of an increase or decrease in the labour-time necessary for its reproduction, an increase or decrease that is independent of the capital already in existence. The value of any commodity – and thus also of the commodities which capital consists of – is determined not by the necessary labour-time that it itself contains, but by the *socially* necessary labour-time required for its reproduction. This reproduction may differ from the conditions of its original production by taking place under easier or more difficult circumstances. If the changed circumstances mean that twice as much time, or alternatively only half as much, is required for the same physical capital to be reproduced, then given an unchanged value of money, this capital, if it was previously worth £100, would now be worth £200, or alternatively £50. If this increase or decrease in value affects all components of the capital equally, the profit is also expressed accordingly in twice or only half the monetary sum. But if it involves a change in the organic composition of the capital, the ratio between the variable and the constant portions of the capital, then, if other circumstances remain the same, the profit rate will rise with a relatively rising share of variable capital and fall with a relatively falling share. If it is only the money value that rises or falls (as a result of a change in the value of money), the monetary expression of the surplus-value rises or falls in the same proportion. The profit rate then remains unchanged.

Part Two

The Transformation
of Profit
into Average Profit

Chapter 8: Different Compositions of Capital in Different Branches of Production, and the Resulting Variation in Rates of Profit

In the previous Part we showed, among other things, how the rate of profit may vary, either rising or falling, even with the same rate of surplus-value. In this chapter we now assume that the degree of exploitation of labour, i.e. the rate of surplus-value, and the length of the working day, is the same in all the spheres of production among which social labour is divided in the country in question. As far as the many variations in the exploitation of labour between different spheres of production are concerned, Adam Smith has already shown fully enough how they cancel one another out through all kinds of compensations, either real or accepted by prejudice, and how therefore they need not be taken into account in investigating the general conditions, as they are only apparent and evanescent.* Other distinctions, for instance in the level of wages, depend to a large measure on the distinction between simple and complex labour that was mentioned already in the first chapter of Volume 1, p. 135, and although they make the lot of the workers in different spheres of production very unequal, they in no way affect the degree of exploitation of labour in these various spheres. If the work of a goldsmith is paid at a higher rate than that of a day-labourer, for example, the former's surplus labour also produces a correspondingly greater surplus-value than does that of the latter. And even though the equalization of wages and working hours between one sphere of production and another,

* *The Wealth of Nations*, Book One, Chapter X; pp. 201–47 in the Pelican edition. In this classic work, published in 1776, Adam Smith (1732–90) gave bourgeois political economy its developed form, his book being not just scientifically important, but also a major ideological weapon for the developing industrial capitalist class. For both these reasons, Smith's work forms a constant reference point for Marx throughout *Capital*. In *Theories of Surplus-Value*, in particular (Part I, Chapter III), Marx develops his fullest criticism of Smith's fundamental theoretical conceptions. See also Volume 2, Chapters 10 and 19.

or between different capitals invested in the same sphere of production, comes up against all kinds of local obstacles, the advance of capitalist production and the progressive subordination of all economic relations to this mode of production tends nevertheless to bring this process to fruition. Important as the study of frictions of this kind is for any specialist work on wages, they are still accidental and inessential as far as the general investigation of capitalist production is concerned and can therefore be ignored. In a general analysis of the present kind, it is assumed throughout that actual conditions correspond to their concept, or, and this amounts to the same thing, actual conditions are depicted only in so far as they express their own general type.

The distinctions between rates of surplus-value in different countries and hence between the different national levels of exploitation of labour are completely outside the scope of our present investigation. The object of this Part is simply to present the way in which a general rate of profit is arrived at within one particular country. It is clear for all, however, that in comparing different national rates of profit one need only combine what has been developed earlier with the arguments to be developed here. One would first consider the variation between national rates of surplus-value and then compare, on the basis of these given rates of surplus-value, how national rates of profit differ. In so far as their variation is not the result of variation in the national rates of surplus-value, it must be due to circumstances in which, as in this chapter, surplus-value is assumed to be everywhere the same, to be constant.

We showed in the previous chapter that, if the rate of surplus-value is taken as constant, the rate of profit yielded by a particular capital can rise or fall as a result of circumstances that increase or decrease the value of one or other portion of the constant capital, and thereby affect the ratio between the constant and variable components of the capital as a whole. We also noted that circumstances which lengthen or shorten a capital's turnover time may affect the rate of profit in a similar way. Since the amount of profit is identical with the amount of surplus-value, with surplus-value itself, it was also apparent that the *amount* of profit – as distinct from the *rate* of profit – was not affected by the fluctuations in value just mentioned. These only modified the rate in which a given surplus-value and hence also a profit of given magnitude was expressed, i.e. its relative magnitude, its magnitude compared with the magnitude of the capital advanced. In so far as these fluctuations in value led to the tying-up or the release of capital, both the rate of profit and profit itself could be affected by this indirect route. However, this was true only of capital already invested, not of new capital investments; and moreover the expansion or contraction of profit itself was always dependent on the extent to which more or less labour could be set in motion with the same capital, as a result of these price fluctuations, i.e. the extent to which a greater or lesser amount of surplus-value could be produced with the same capital, at the same rate of surplus-value. Far from contradicting the general law or forming an exception to it, this apparent exception was in actual fact only a special case of the general law's application.

It was shown in the previous Part that, with a constant level of exploitation of labour, the profit rate alters with changes in the value of the constituent elements of the constant capital, as well as with changes in the capital's turnover time. From this it follows naturally that the rates of profit in different spheres of production that exist simultaneously alongside one another will differ if, other things remaining equal, either the turnover times of the capitals invested differ, or the value relations between the organic components of these capitals in different branches of production. What we previously viewed as changes that the same capital underwent in succession, we now consider as simultaneous distinctions between capital investments that exist alongside one another in different spheres of production.

We have now to investigate: (1) differences in the *organic composition* of capitals, (2) differences in their turnover time.

For this whole investigation, when we speak of the composition or the turnover of capital in a specific branch of production, it should be clear enough that we always mean the normal, average situation for capital invested in this branch of production, and refer always to the average of the total capital in the sphere in question, not to chance differences between individual capitals invested there.

Since we also assume that the rate of surplus-value and the working day are constant and since this assumption also involves constancy of wages, a certain quantity of variable capital means a certain quantity of labour-power set in motion and hence a certain quantity of labour objectifying itself. Thus if £100 expresses the weekly wage of 100 workers, thus indicating 100 units of labour-power, then $n \times £100$ expresses the wages of $n \times 100$ workers, and £ $\frac{100}{n}$ the wages of $\frac{100}{n}$ workers. The variable capital serves here, as always when wages are taken as constant, as an index of the mass of labour set in motion by a certain total capital; variations in the magnitude of the variable capital applied serve as indices of variations in the mass of labour-power applied. If £100 represents 100 workers per week, and thus 6,000 hours' labour if the workers work a 60-hour week, then £200 represents 12,000 hours' labour, and £50 only 3,000.

By the composition of capital we mean, as already stated in Volume 1, the ratio between its active and its passive component, between variable and constant capital. Two relationships are involved here which are not of equal importance, even though they may in certain circumstances produce the same effect.

The first relationship depends on technical conditions and is to be taken as given, at any particular stage of development of productivity. A certain quantity of labour-power, represented by a certain number of workers, is required to produce a certain volume of products in a day, for example, and this involves putting a certain definite mass of means of production in motion and consuming them productively – machines, raw materials etc. A definite number of workers corresponds to a definite quantity of means of production, and thus a definite amount of living labour to a definite amount of labour already objectified in means of production. This proportion can vary greatly between different spheres of production and often even between different branches of one and the same industry, although it may also happen to be the same in branches of industry that are very far apart.

This proportion constitutes the technical composition of capital, and is the actual basis of its organic composition.

But it is possible for the proportion to be the same in different branches of industry only in so far as variable capital serves simply as an index of labour-power, and constant capital as an index of the volume of means of production that labour-power sets in motion. Certain operations in copper or iron, for example, may involve the same proportion between labour-power and means of production. But because copper is dearer than iron, the value relationship between variable and constant capital will be different in each case, and so therefore will be the value composition of the two capitals taken as a whole. The distinction between technical composition and value composition shows itself in every branch of industry by the way the value ratio between the two portions of capital may change while the technical composition remains constant, whereas, with a changed technical composition, the value ratio may remain the same; the latter, of course, happens only if the change in the proportionate quantities of means of production and labour-power applied is cancelled out by an opposite change in their values.

The *organic* composition of capital is the name we give to its value composition, in so far as this is determined by its technical composition and reflects it.[20]

The variable capital, therefore, is assumed to be an index of a definite amount of labour-power, a definite number of workers or definite masses of living labour set in motion. We saw in the previous Part how changes in the magnitude of the variable capital may represent nothing but a higher or lower price for the same amount of labour. Here, however, this does not apply, as both the rate of surplus-value and the working day are taken as constant, and the wage for a certain labour-time is also given. A difference in the magnitude of the constant capital, on the other hand, may well be the index of a change in the volume of means of production set in motion by a certain quantity of labour-power; though it can also arise from a difference in the value that the means of production set in motion in one sphere of production have as compared with those in other spheres. Here, therefore, these two aspects both come into consideration.

The following fundamental point should also be noted:

Assume that £100 is the weekly wage for 100 workers, the working week is 60 hours, and the rate of surplus-value is 100 per cent. In this case, the workers work 30 of these 60 hours for themselves and 30 gratis for the capitalist. The £100 in wages actually embodies only 30 working hours of these 100 workers, or a total of 3,000 hours, while the other 3,000 hours that they work are embodied in the £100 surplus-value or profit that the capitalist tucks away. Even though the wage of £100 does not express the value in which the week's work of 100 workers is objectified, it still indicates, since the length of the working day and the rate of surplus-value are given, that 100 workers are set in motion for a

20. The above point has already been developed in brief in the third edition of Volume 1 [Pelican edition, p. 762, at the beginning of Chapter 25]. But since the two earlier editions do not contain this passage, it was all the more necessary to repeat it here. – F.E.

total of 6,000 hours. The capital of £100 indicates this for two reasons. Firstly, because it indicates the number of workers set in motion, since £1 = 1 worker per week, i.e. £100 = 100 workers; the second reason is this: owing to the fact that each worker, set in motion at the given rate of surplus-value of 100 per cent, performs as much labour again as is contained in his wage, i.e. £1, this wage, which is the expression of half a week's labour, sets a whole week's labour in motion, and similarly £100, though it contains only 50 weeks' labour, sets in motion 100 weeks'. There is therefore a very fundamental distinction to be made between the variable capital laid out on wages to the extent that its value, the sum of wages paid, represents a definite quantity of objectified labour, and the variable capital to the extent that its value is simply an index of the mass of living labour that it sets in motion. This last is always greater than the labour contained in the variable capital and is thus also expressed in a higher value than that of the variable capital; in a value that is determined on the one hand by the number of workers that this variable capital sets in motion and on the other hand by the quantity of surplus labour they perform.

Considering the variable capital in this way, we arrive at two conclusions:

If a capital invested in sphere of production A spends only 100 in variable capital against 600 in constant, for each 700 overall, while in sphere of production B 600 is spent in variable capital and only 100 in constant, then that total capital A of 700 sets in motion a labour-power of only 100, thus under our above assumptions only 100 working weeks or 6,000 hours of living labour, while the equally large total capital B sets in motion 600 working weeks and therefore 36,000 hours of living labour. The capital in sphere A would therefore appropriate only 50 working weeks' or 3,000 hours' surplus labour, while the capital of equal size in sphere B would appropriate 300 working weeks or 18,000 hours. The variable capital is not only an index of the labour it itself contains, but also, at a given rate of surplus-value, of the excess or surplus labour that it sets in motion over and above this amount. At the same level of exploitation of labour, the profit would be $\frac{100}{700} = \frac{1}{7} = 14\frac{2}{7}$ per cent in the first case, and $\frac{600}{700} = 85\frac{5}{7}$ per cent in the second case, six times as much. Not only that, but the actual profit in this case would itself be six times greater, 600 for B as against 100 for A, as six times as much living labour has been set in motion with the same capital, and so six times as much surplus-value, and thus six times as much profit, has been made with the same degree of exploitation of labour.

If in sphere A it was not £700 but £7,000 that had been invested, as against a capital of only £700 in sphere B, then capital A, with the organic composition remaining the same, would use £1,000 of this £7,000 as variable capital and thus employ 1,000 workers for a week = 60,000 hours' living labour, of which 30,000 hours would be surplus labour. But A would still, as before, set in motion only a sixth as much living labour for each £700 as would B and would therefore produce only a sixth as much profit. If we consider the rate of profit, then $\frac{1,000}{7,000} = \frac{100}{700} = 14\frac{2}{7}$ per cent, against $\frac{600}{700}$ or $85\frac{5}{7}$ per cent for capital B. With equal amounts of capital, the rates of profit here are different, since at equal rates of surplus-value the masses of surplus-value and therefore profit that are produced differ as a result of the different masses of living labour set in motion.

The same result follows in fact if the technical conditions in the one sphere of production are the same as in the other, but the value of the constant capital element is greater or less. Let us assume that both capitals employ £100 as variable capital and thus use 100 workers for a week to set the same quantity of machinery and raw material in motion, but that this quantity is dearer in case B than in case A. In this case, £100 variable capital would be combined with, say, £200 constant capital in case A and £400 in case B. At a rate of surplus-value of 100 per cent, then, the surplus-value produced is in both cases £100, and the profit in both cases similarly £100. But in A, $\frac{100}{200c + 100v} = \frac{1}{3} = 33\frac{1}{3}$ per cent, while in B, $\frac{100}{400c + 100v} = \frac{1}{5} = 20$ per cent. In actual fact, if we take a definite aliquot part of the total capital in both cases, then in case B only £20 of each £100, or a fifth, forms the variable capital, while in case A £33$\frac{1}{3}$ of each £100, or a third, is variable capital. B produces less profit for each £100 than does A, because it sets less living labour in motion [for each £100]. The difference in the rate of profit is thus reduced here again to a difference in the mass of profit – because mass of surplus-value – produced for each 100 units of capital invested.

The distinction between this second example and the one before is simply this: the equalization of A and B in the second case would require no more than a change in the value of the constant capital, either in A or B, with the technical basis remaining the same; in the first case, on the other hand, the technical composition itself differs between the two spheres of production and would have to be transformed in order for such an equalization to occur.

Differing organic compositions of capitals are thus independent of their absolute magnitudes. The only question is always how much of each 100 units is variable capital and how much is constant.

Capitals of the same size, or capitals of different magnitudes reduced to percentages, operating with the same working day and the same degree of exploitation of labour, thus produce very different amounts of surplus-value and therefore profit, and this is because their variable portions differ according to the differing organic composition of capital in different spheres of production, which means that different quantities of living labour are set in motion, and hence also different quantities of surplus labour, of the substance of surplus-value and therefore of profit, are appropriated. Equal-sized portions of the total capital in different spheres of production include sources of surplus-value of unequal size, and the only source of surplus-value is living labour. At any given level of exploitation of labour, the mass of labour set in motion by a capital of 100, and thus also the surplus labour it appropriates, depends on the size of its variable component. If a capital whose percentage composition is $90_c + 10_v$ were to produce just as much surplus-value or profit, at the same level of exploitation of labour, as a capital of $10_c + 90_v$, it would be as clear as day that surplus-value and hence value in general had a completely different source from labour, and in this way any rational basis for political economy would fall away. If we continue to take £1 as the weekly wage of one worker for 60 hours' work and the rate of surplus-value as 100 per cent, it is readily apparent that the total value product that a worker can supply in a week is £2. Therefore, 10 workers cannot supply more than £20, and as £10 of this £20 has to replace the wages, these workers cannot create a surplus-value greater than £10. However, 90 workers whose total product was £180 and whose wages £90 would create a surplus-value of £90. The rate of profit here would be in the one case 10 per cent and in the other case 90 per cent. If it should be otherwise, value and surplus-value would have to be something other than objectified labour. Since capitals of equal size in different spheres of production, capitals of different size considered by percentage, are unequally divided into a constant and a variable element, set in motion unequal amounts of living labour and hence produce unequal amounts of surplus-value or profit, the rate of profit, which consists precisely of the surplus-value calculated as a percentage of the total capital, is different in each case.

But if capitals of equal size in different spheres of production, and thus capitals of different size, taken by percentage, produce unequal profits as a result of their differing organic composition, it follows that the profits of unequal capitals in different spheres of production cannot stand in proportion to their respective sizes, and that profits in different spheres of production are not proportionate to the magnitudes of the capitals that are respectively employed. For if profits did increase in proportion to the size of the capital applied, this would imply that the percentage of profit was always the same and that capitals of equal size had the same rate of profit in different spheres of production, despite their varying organic composition. It is only within the same sphere of production, where the organic composition of capital is therefore given, or between different spheres of production with the same organic composition of capital, that the mass of profit stands in exact proportion to the mass of capital employed. If the profits of unequal capitals were in proportion to their size, this would mean that equal capitals yielded equal profits, or that the rate of profit was the same for all capitals irrespective of their magnitude and their organic composition.

The above argument assumes that commodities are sold at their values. The value of a commodity is equal to the value of the constant capital contained in it, plus the value of the variable capital reproduced in it, plus the increment on this variable capital, the surplus-value produced. Given a certain rate of surplus-value, its mass evidently depends on the mass of the variable capital. The value produced by a capital of 100 would be in the one case $90_c + 10_v + 10_s = 110$; in the other case $10_c + 90_v + 90_s = 190$. If commodities are sold at their values, the first product is sold at 110, of which 10 represents surplus-value or unpaid labour; the second product is sold at 190, of which 90 is surplus-value or unpaid labour.

This is particularly important when the rates of profit in different countries are compared with one another. In a European country the rate of surplus-value might be 100 per cent, i.e. the worker might work half the day for himself and half the day for his employer; in an Asian country it might be 25 per cent, i.e. the worker might work four-fifths of the day for himself and one-fifth of the day for his employer. In the European country, however, the composition of the national capital might be $84_c + 16_v$, and in the Asian country, where little machinery, etc. is used and relatively little raw material productively consumed in a given period of time, the composition might be $16_c + 84_v$. We then have the following calculation:

In the European country, the value of the product $= 84_c + 16_v + 16_s = 116$; rate of profit $= \frac{16}{100} = 16$ per cent.

In the Asian country, the value of the product $= 16_c + 84_v + 21_s = 121$; rate of profit $= \frac{21}{100} = 21$ per cent.

The rate of profit in the Asian country would thus be some 25 per cent higher than in the European country, even though the rate of surplus-value was only a fourth as great. Carey, Bastiat* and their like would draw precisely the opposite conclusion.

We may remark in passing that different national rates of profit generally depend on different national rates of surplus-value; but in this chapter we are comparing unequal rates of profit that spring from one and the same rate of surplus-value.

Besides the differing organic composition of capital, i.e. besides the different masses of labour, and therefore, other things being equal, of surplus labour as well, set in motion by capitals of the same size in different spheres of production, there is a further source of inequality between rates of profit: the variation in the length of capital turnover in the different spheres of production. We have already seen in Chapter 4 that with the same composition of capital, other things being equal, rates of profit vary in inverse proportion to the turnover time, and similarly that the same variable capital, taking different periods of time to turn over, brings in unequal masses of surplus-value in the course of the year. Variation in the turnover time is thus a further reason why capitals of equal size do not produce equally large profits in equal periods of time, and why rates of profit thus vary between the different spheres.

As far as concerns the proportion in which the capital is composed of fixed and circulating elements, this does not in any way affect the profit rate, taken by itself. It can only affect it either if this differing composition coincides with a differing ratio between

* Marx regarded Frédéric Bastiat (1801–50) as 'the most superficial and thus successful representative of apologetic vulgar economics' (Postface to the Second German Edition of *Capital* Volume 1, p. 98).

the variable and constant portions, in which case the variation in the rate of profit is due to this difference and not to the different ratio between circulating and fixed; or alternatively if the varying ratio between fixed and circulating components involves a variation in the turnover time that it takes to realize a certain profit. If capitals exhibit different proportions of fixed and circulating capital, this always has an influence on their turnover time and gives rise to differences in it; but it does not follow from this that the turnover time in which the same capitals realize a certain profit necessarily differs. Though A might always have to convert a greater portion of its product into raw material, etc., while B uses the same machines for a longer time with less raw material, both have regularly committed a portion of their capital, to the extent of their production; the one in raw material, i.e. circulating capital, the other in machines, etc., i.e. in fixed capital. A is constantly transforming a portion of its capital from the commodity form into the money form, and from this back into the form of raw material; while B uses part of its capital as an instrument of labour for a longer period of time without such a change. If both of them employ the same amount of labour, they will certainly sell products of unequal value in the course of a year, but in each case the mass of products will contain the same amount of surplus-value, and their rates of profit will be the same, calculated on the total capital advanced, despite the differences in their composition in terms of fixed and circulating capital, and similarly their turnover time. The two capitals realize equal profits in equal times, even though they take different times to turn over.[21] Variation in the turnover time is significant in and of itself only in so far as it affects the mass of surplus-value that the same capital can appropriate and realize in a given time. Thus if unequal compositions

21. It follows from Chapter 4 that the above argument is correct only when capitals A and B have a different value composition, but nevertheless their variable components in percentage terms are directly proportionate to their turnover times, or in inverse proportion to their number of turnovers. Capital A is composed, say, of 20_c fixed and 70_c circulating, i.e. $90_c + 10_v = 100$. Given a rate of surplus-value of 100 per cent, the 10_v produces 10_s in one turnover; rate of profit for the turnover 10 per cent. Capital B, on the other hand, is 60_c fixed $+ 20_c$ circulating, i.e. $80_c + 20_v = 100$. The 20_v, for one turnover at the above rate of surplus-value, produces a surplus of 20_s; rate of profit for the turnover 20 per cent, i.e. double that of A. But if A turns over twice a year and B only once, then A too produces $2 \times 10 = 20_s$ in the year, and the annual rate of profit is the same in both cases, i.e. 20 per cent. – F.E.

of circulating and fixed capital do not necessarily go together with unequal turnover times, which in turn mean unequal rates of profit, it is evident that, in so far as the latter does occur, this does not arise from the unequal composition of circulating and fixed capital as such, but rather from the way that this latter simply indicates an inequality in turnover times that affects the rate of profit.

Thus the differing proportions of circulating and fixed capital, of which constant capital is composed, in the different branches of industry, do not have any bearing in themselves on the rate of profit; what is decisive is the ratio between the variable capital and the constant, while the value of the constant capital, and thus its relative magnitude in relation to the variable, is quite independent of the fixed or circulating character of its components. We do find, however – and this can lead to incorrect conclusions – that where fixed capital is strongly developed, this is simply an expression of the fact that production is pursued on a large scale and that constant capital is very much predominant over variable, i.e. that the living labour-power applied is small in comparison with the volume of means of production that it sets in motion.

We have shown, therefore, that in different branches of industry unequal profit rates prevail, corresponding to the different organic composition of capitals, and, within the indicated limits, corresponding also to their different turnover times; so that at a given rate of surplus-value it is only for capitals of the same organic composition – assuming equal turnover times – that the law holds good, as a general tendency, that profits stand in direct proportion to the amount of capital, and that capitals of equal size yield equal profits in the same period of time. The above argument is true on the same basis as our whole investigation so far: that commodities are sold at their values. There is no doubt, however, that in actual fact, ignoring inessential, accidental circumstances that cancel each other out, no such variation in the average rate of profit exists between different branches of industry, and it could not exist without abolishing the entire system of capitalist production. The theory of value thus appears incompatible with the actual movement, incompatible with the actual phenomena of production, and it might seem that we must abandon all hope of understanding these phenomena.

It has emerged from Part One of this volume that cost prices are the same for the products of different spheres of production if equal portions of capital are advanced in their production, no matter how different the organic composition of these capitals might be. In the cost price, the distinction between variable and constant capital is abolished, as far as the capitalist is concerned. For him, a commodity which he must lay out £100 to produce costs the same whether he lays out $90_c + 10_v$ or $10_c + 90_v$. In each case it costs him £100, neither more nor less. Cost prices are the same for equal capital investments in different spheres, however much the values and surplus-values produced may differ. This equality in the cost prices forms the basis for the competition between capital investments by means of which an average profit is produced.

Chapter 9: Formation of a General Rate of Profit (Average Rate of Profit), and Transformation of Commodity Values into Prices of Production

At any one given time, the organic composition of capital depends on two factors: firstly, on the technical proportion between the labour-power and the means of production applied, and secondly, on the price of those means of production. As we have seen, this must be considered in percentage terms. We express the organic composition of a capital that consists of four-fifths constant and one-fifth variable capital by using the formula $80_c + 20_v$. We also assume for the sake of comparison an unchanged rate of surplus-value, say 100 per cent; any rate will do. The capital of $80_c + 20_v$ then yields a surplus-value of 20_s, which makes a rate of profit of 20 per cent on the total capital. The actual value of the product depends on how large the fixed part of the constant capital is and on how much of it goes into the product as depreciation, how much does not. But since this fact is completely immaterial as far as the rate of profit is concerned, and thus also for the present investigation, we shall assume for the sake of simplicity that in all cases the constant capital enters as a whole into the annual product of these capitals. We shall also assume that capitals in different spheres of production annually realize the same amount of surplus-value in proportion to the size of their variable components; and we shall ignore for the time being the differences that may be produced here by variation in the turnover times. This point will be dealt with later.

Let us take five different spheres of production, each with a different organic composition for the capital invested in it, as on the following page.

We now have very different rates of profit in different spheres of production with a uniform exploitation of labour, rates which correspond to the differing organic composition of the capitals involved.

The total sum of the capitals applied in the five spheres is 500;

Capitals	Rate of surplus-value	Surplus-value	Value of product	Rate of profit
I. $80_c + 20_v$	100%	20	120	20%
II. $70_c + 30_v$	100%	30	130	30%
III. $60_c + 40_v$	100%	40	140	40%
IV. $85_c + 15_v$	100%	15	115	15%
V. $95_c + 5_v$	100%	5	105	5%

the total sum of the surplus-value they produce 110; the total value of the commodities they produce 610. If we treat the 500 as one single capital, with I–V simply forming different portions of it (as for instance a cotton mill will have different proportions between variable and constant capital in its various departments, e.g. the carding, combing, spinning and weaving shops, and the average proportion has to be calculated for the entire factory), then the average composition of the capital of 500 would be 500 = $390_c + 110_v$, or in percentages $78_c + 22_v$. Treating the capitals of 100 as each simply a fifth of the total capital, its composition would be this average one of $78_c + 22_v$; in the same way the average surplus-value of 22 would accrue to each of these capitals of 100, the average rate of profit would thus be 22 per cent, and the price of each fifth of the total product produced by this capital of 500 would be 122. The product of each fifth of the total capital advanced would thus have to be sold at 122.

Yet in order not to arrive at totally incorrect conclusions, we must not take all the cost prices as 100.

With $80_c + 20_v$, and a rate of surplus-value of 100 per cent, the total value of the commodities produced by capital I would be $80_c + 20_v + 20_s = 120$, assuming the entire constant capital were to enter into the annual product. This may well be the case in some spheres of production, in certain conditions, but hardly with a ratio between c and v of 4:1. In considering the values of the commodities produced by each different capital of 100, therefore, we must take into account the fact that they differ according to the different composition of c in terms of its fixed and circulating components, and that the fixed components of different capitals may themselves depreciate either faster or more slowly and thus add unequal quantities of value to the product in the same period. This is immaterial, however, as far as the profit rate is concerned. Whether the 80_c gives up its value of 80 to the annual product, or

50, or 5, and whether the annual product is accordingly $80_c + 20_v + 20_s = 120$, or $50_c + 20_v + 20_s = 90$, or $5_c + 20_v + 20_s = 45$, in all these cases the excess of the value of the product over its cost price is 20, and in all these cases this 20 has to be calculated on a basis of 100 to arrive at the rate of profit; the profit rate of capital I is thus always 20 per cent. In order to make this still clearer, we can let different parts of the constant capital enter the value of the product, taking the same five capitals as above:

Capitals	Rate of surplus-value	Surplus-value	Rate of profit	Used up c	Value of commodities	Cost price	
I. $80_c + 20_v$	100%	20	20%	50	90	70	
II. $70_c + 30_v$	100%	30	30%	51	111	81	
III. $60_c + 40_v$	100%	40	40%	51	131	91	
IV. $85_c + 15_v$	100%	15	15%	40	70	55	
V. $95_c + 5_v$	100%	5	5%	10	20	15	
$390_c + 110_v$	—	110	110%	—	—	—	Total
$78_c + 22_v$	—	22	22%	—	—	—	Average

If we again treat capitals I–V as a single total capital, we see that in this case, too, the sum of the five capitals, $500 = 390_c + 110_v$, remains the same in composition, and thus their average composition is still $78_c + 22_v$; the average surplus-value is therefore 22. If this surplus-value were evenly distributed among capitals I–V, we would arrive at the following commodity prices:

Capitals	Surplus-value	Value of commodities	Cost-price of commodities	Price of commodities	Rate of profit	Divergence of price from value
I. $80_c + 20_v$	20	90	70	92	22%	+ 2
II. $70_c + 30_v$	30	111	81	103	22%	− 8
III. $60_c + 40_v$	40	131	91	113	22%	− 18
IV. $85_c + 15_v$	15	70	55	77	22%	+ 7
V. $95_c + 5_v$	5	20	15	37	22%	+ 17

Taken together, commodities are sold at $2 + 7 + 17 = 26$ above their value, and $8 + 18 = 26$ below their value, so that the divergences of price from value indicated above cancel each other out when surplus-value is distributed evenly, i.e. through adding the average profit of 22 on the capital advance of 100 to the respective cost prices of commodities I–V. To the same extent that one section of commodities is sold above its value, another is sold below it. And it is only because they are sold at these prices that the rates of profit for capitals I–V are equal at 22 per cent, irrespective of their different ˙organic compositions. The prices that arise when the average of the different rates of profit is drawn from the different spheres of production, and this average is added to the cost prices of these different spheres of production, are the *prices of production*. Their prerequisite is the existence of a general rate of profit, and this presupposes in turn that the profit rates in each particular sphere of production, taken by itself, are already reduced to their average rates. These particular rates are $_c$ in each sphere of production and are to be developed from the value of the commodity as shown in the first Part of this volume. In the absence of such a development, the general rate of profit (and hence also the production price of the commodity) remains a meaningless and irrational conception. Thus the production price of a commodity equals its cost price plus the percentage profit added to it in accordance with the general rate of profit, its cost price plus the average profit.

As a result of the differing organic composition of capitals applied in different branches of production, as a result therefore of the circumstance that according to the different percentage that the variable part forms in a total capital of a given size, very different amounts of labour are set in motion by capitals of equal size, so too very different amounts of surplus labour are appropriated by these capitals, or very different amounts of surplus-value are produced by them. The rates of profit prevailing in the different branches of production are accordingly originally very different. These different rates of profit are balanced out by competition to give a general rate of profit which is the average of all these different rates. The profit that falls to a capital of given size according to this general rate of profit, whatever its organic composition might be, we call the average profit. That price of a commodity which is equal to its cost price, plus the part of the annual average profit on the capital applied in its production (not simply the capital consumed in its production) that falls to its share according to its conditions of turnover, is its price of production. Let us take for example a capital of 500, of which 100 is fixed capital, 10 per cent of this being the depreciation of a circulating capital of 400 during one turnover period. Let the average profit for the duration of this turnover period be 10 per cent. The cost price of the product produced during this turnover is then 10_c for depreciation plus 400 $(c + v)$ circulating capital = 410, and its price of production 410 cost price plus 50 (10 per cent profit on 500) = 460.

Thus although the capitalists in the different spheres of production get back on the sale of their commodities the capital values consumed to produce them, they do not secure the surplus-value and hence profit that is produced in their own sphere in connection with the production of these commodities. What they secure is only the surplus-value and hence profit that falls to the share of each aliquot part of the total social capital, when evenly distributed, from the total social surplus-value or profit produced in a given time by the social capital in all spheres of production. For each 100 units, every capital advanced, whatever may be its composition, draws in each year, or in any other period of time, the profit that accrues to 100 units in this period of time as an nth part of the total capital. The various different capitals here are in the position of shareholders in a joint-stock company, in which the dividends are evenly distributed for each 100 units, and hence are distinguished, as far as the individual capitalists are concerned, only according to the size of the capital that each of them has put into the common enterprise, according to his relative participation in this common enterprise, according to the number of his shares. While the portion of this commodity price that replaces the parts of the capital that are consumed in the production of the commodities, and with which these capital values must be bought back again – while this portion, the cost price, is completely governed by the outlay within each respective sphere of production, the other component of commodity price, the profit that is added to this cost price, is governed not by the mass of profit that is produced by this specific capital in its specific sphere of production, but by the mass of profit that falls on average to each capital invested, as an aliquot part of the total social capital invested in the total production, during a given period of time.[22]

22. Cherbuliez.*

If a capitalist sells his commodities at their price of production, he withdraws money according to the value of the capital that he consumed in their production and adds a profit to this in proportion to the capital he advanced as a mere aliquot part of the total social capital. His cost prices are specific [to his sphere of production]. But the profit on top of this cost price is independent of his particular sphere of production, it is a simple average per 100 units of capital advanced.

Let us suppose that the five different capital investments in the above example, I–V, belong to one and the same person. The variable and constant capital consumed in the production of the commodities in each particular investment I–V would be given, and this share in the value of commodities I–V would obviously form a portion of their price, since this is the least price required to replace the portion of capital that is advanced and consumed. These cost prices would thus be different for each kind of commodity I–V and would be fixed differently by the proprietor. As far as the different masses of surplus-value or profit produced in I–V were concerned, however, the capitalist might very well count them all as profit on the total capital he advanced, so that a definite aliquot part would fall to each capital of 100. The cost prices would therefore be different for each of the commodities produced in the individual investments I–V; but the share of the sale price that arose from the profit added per 100 units of capital would be the same. The total price of commodities I–V would thus be the same as their total value, i.e. the sum of the cost prices I–V plus the sum of the surplus-value or profit produced; in point of fact, therefore, the monetary expression for the total quantity of labour, both past and newly added, contained in commodities I–V. And in the same manner, the sum of prices of production for the commodities produced in society as a whole – taking the totality of all branches of production – is equal to the sum of their values.

This seems contradicted by the fact that the elements of productive capital are generally bought on the market in capitalist production, so that their prices include an already realized profit

---

* Antoine-Élisée Cherbuliez (1797–1869) was a Swiss economist whose theories combined elements from Sismondi and Ricardo. Marx is referring here to his book *Richesse ou pauvreté*, Paris, 1841, pp. 70–72. See also *Theories of Surplus-Value*, Part III, Chapter XXIII, 'Cherbuliez'.

and accordingly include the production price of one branch of industry together with the profit contained in it, so that the profit in one branch of industry goes into the cost price of another. But if the sum of the cost prices of all commodities in a country is put on one side and the sum of the profits or surplus-values on the other, we can see that the calculation comes out right. Take for example a commodity A; its cost price may contain the profits of B, C, D, just as the profits of A may in turn go into B, C, D, etc. If we make this calculation, the profit of A will be absent from its own cost price, and the profits of B, C, D, etc. will be absent from theirs. None of them includes his own profit in his cost price. And so if there are n spheres of production, and in each of them a profit of p is made [and the symbol for the cost price of a single commodity is k], then the cost price in all together is $k - np$. Considering the calculation as a whole, to the same extent that the profits of one sphere of production go into the cost price of another, to that extent these profits have already been taken into account for the overall price of the final end-product and cannot appear on the profit side twice. They appear on this side only because the commodity in question was itself an end-product, so that its price of production does not go into the cost price of another commodity.

If a certain sum p goes into the cost price of a commodity for the profit of the producers of the means of production and on this cost price a profit of p_1 is added, the total profit $P = p + p_1$. The total cost price of the commodity, discounting all portions of the price that count towards profit, is then its own cost price minus P. Using the symbol k again for this cost price, it is evident that $k + P = k + p + p_1$. In dealing with surplus-value in Volume 1, Chapter 9, 2, pp. 331–2, we have already seen that the product of any capital can be treated as if one part simply replaces capital, while the other only represents surplus-value. To apply this method of reckoning to the total social product, we have to make certain rectifications, since, considering the whole society, the profit contained in the price of flax, for instance, cannot figure twice, not as both part of the price of the linen and as the profit of the flax producers.

There is no distinction between profit and surplus-value when the surplus-value of A, for instance, goes into the constant capital of B. As far as the value of commodities is concerned, it is completely immaterial whether the labour contained in them is paid or unpaid. This shows only that B pays the surplus-value of A. In the total account, A's surplus-value cannot figure twice.

The distinction is rather this. Apart from the fact that the price of the product of capital B, for example, diverges from its value, because the surplus-value realized in B is greater or less than the profit added in the price of the products of B, the same situation also holds for the commodities that form the constant part of capital B, and indirectly, also, its variable capital, as means of subsistence for the workers. As far as the constant portion of capital is concerned, it is itself equal to cost price plus surplus-value, i.e. now equal to cost price plus profit, and this profit can again be greater or less than the surplus-value whose place it has taken. As for the variable capital, the average daily wage is certainly always equal to the value product of the number of hours that the worker must work in order to produce his necessary means of subsistence; but this number of hours is itself distorted by the fact that the production prices of the necessary means of subsistence diverge from their values. However, this is always reducible to the situation that whenever too much surplus-value goes into one commodity, too little goes into another, and that the divergences from value that obtain in the production prices of commodities therefore cancel each other out. With the whole of capitalist production, it is always only in a very intricate and approximate way, as an average of perpetual fluctuations which can never be firmly fixed, that the general law prevails as the dominant tendency.

Since the general rate of profit is formed by the average of the various different rates of profit on each 100 units of capital advanced over a definite period of time, say a year, the distinction made between the different capitals by the distinction in turnover times is also obliterated. But this distinction plays a decisive role for the various different rates of profit in the various spheres of production, by means of whose average the general rate of profit is formed.

In our previous illustration of the formation of the general rate of profit, every capital in every sphere of production was taken as 100, and we did this in order to make clear the percentage differences in the rates of profit and hence also the differences in the values of the commodities that are produced by capitals of equal size. It should be understood, however, that the actual masses of surplus-value that are produced in each particular sphere of production depend on the magnitude of the capitals applied, since the composition of capital is given in each of these given spheres of production. Yet the particular *rate* of profit of an individual sphere of production is not affected by whether a capital of 100, $m \times 100$ or $xm \times 100$ is applied. The profit rate remains 10 per cent, whether the total profit is 10 on 100 or 1,000 on 10,000.

However, since the rates of profit in the various spheres of production differ, in that very different masses of surplus-value and therefore profit are produced according to the proportion that variable capital forms in the total, it is evident that the average profit per 100 units of social capital, and hence the average or general rate of profit, will vary greatly according to the respective magnitudes of the capitals invested in the various spheres. Let us take four capitals A, B, C, D. Say that the rate of surplus-value for all of them is 100 per cent. Let the variable capital for each 100 units of the total capital be 25 for A, 40 for B, 15 for C and 10 for D. Each 100 units of the total capital then yields a surplus-value or profit of 25 for A, 40 for B, 15 for C and 10 for D; a total of 90, and thus, if the four capitals are equal in size, an average rate of profit of $\frac{90}{4} = 22\frac{1}{2}$ per cent.

If the total capitals were instead A = 200, B = 300, C = 1,000 and D = 4,000, the profits produced would then be 50, 120, 150 and 400 respectively. Altogether a profit of 720 on a capital of 5,500, or an average rate of profit of $13\frac{1}{11}$ per cent.

The masses of total value produced vary according to the different sizes of the total capitals respectively advanced in A, B, C and D. For the formation of the general rate of profit, therefore, it is not only a question of the difference in *rates* of profit between the various spheres of production, from which a simple average is to be taken, but also of the relative weight which these different rates of profit assume in the formation of this average. This depends however either on the relative size of the capital invested in each particular sphere, or on which particular aliquot part of the total social capital is invested in each particular sphere of production. It must naturally make a great deal of difference whether it is a greater or lesser part of the total capital that yields a higher or lower profit rate. And this depends in turn upon how much capital is invested in those spheres where the variable capital is relatively large or small compared with the total capital. It is the same as in the case of the average rate of interest that a money-lender makes if he lends different capitals at different rates of interest, e.g. at 4, 5, 6, 7 per cent, etc. The average rate is completely dependent on how much of his capital he had lent out at each of these different interest rates.

The general rate of profit is determined therefore by two factors:

(1) the organic composition of the capitals in the various spheres of production, i.e. the different rates of profit in the particular spheres;

(2) the distribution of the total social capital between these different spheres, i.e. the relative magnitudes of the capitals invested in each particular sphere, and hence at a particular rate of profit; i.e. the relative share of the total social capital swallowed up by each particular sphere of production.

In Volumes 1 and 2 we were only concerned with the *values* of commodities. Now a part of this value has split away as the *cost price*, on the one hand, while on the other, the *production price* of the commodity has also developed, as a transformed form of value.

If we take it that the composition of the average social capital is $80_c + 20_v$ and the annual rate of surplus-value $s' = 100$ per cent, the average annual profit for a capital of 100 is 20 and the average annual rate of profit is 20 per cent. For any cost price k of the commodities annually produced by a capital of 100, their price of production will be $k + 20$. In those spheres of production where the composition of capital is $(80 - x)_c + (20 + x)_v$, the surplus-value actually created within this sphere, or the annual profit produced, is $20 + x$, i.e. more than 20, and the commodity value produced is $k + 20 + x$, more than $k + 20$, or more than the price of production. In those spheres where the composition of capital is $(80 + x)_c + (20 - x)_v$, the surplus-value or profit annually created is $20 - x$, i.e. less than 20, and the commodity value therefore $k + 20 - x$, i.e. less than the price of production, which is $k + 20$. Leaving aside any variation in turnover time, the production prices of commodities would be equal to their values only in cases where the composition of capital was by chance precisely $80_c + 20_v$.

The specific degree of development of the social productivity of labour differs from one particular sphere of production to another, being higher or lower according to the quantity of means of production set in motion by a certain specific amount of labour, and thus by a specific number of workers once the working day is given. Hence its degree of development depends on how small a quantity of labour is required for a certain quantity of means of production.

We therefore call capitals that contain a greater percentage of constant capital than the social average, and thus a lesser percentage of variable capital, capitals of *higher* composition. Conversely, those marked by a relatively smaller share of constant capital, and a relatively greater share of variable, we call capitals of *lower* composition. By capitals of average composition, finally, we mean those whose composition coincides with that of the average social capital. If this average social capital is composed of $80_c + 20_v$, in percentages, then a capital of $90_c + 10_v$ is *above* the social average and one of $70_c + 30_v$ is *below* this average. In general, for an average social capital composed of $m_c + n_v$, where m and n are constant magnitudes and $m + n = 100$, $(m + x)_c + (n - x)_v$ represents an individual capital or group of capitals of higher composition, and $(m - x)_c + (n + x)_v$ one of lower composition. How these capitals function after the average rate of profit is established, on the assumption of one turnover in the year, is shown by the following table, in which capital I represents the average composition, with an average rate of profit of 20 per cent.

I. $80_c + 20_v + 20_s$. Rate of profit = 20 per cent.
    Price of the product = 120. Value = 120.
II. $90_c + 10_v + 10_s$. Rate of profit = 20 per cent.
    Price of the product = 120. Value = 110.
III. $70_c + 30_v + 30_s$. Rate of profit = 20 per cent.
    Price of the product = 120. Value = 130.

Commodities produced by capital II thus have a value less than their price of production, and those produced by capital III have a price of production less than their value. Only for capitals such as I, in branches of production whose composition chanced to coincide with the social average, would the value and the price of production be the same. In applying these terms to specific cases, of course, we must bear in mind that the ratio between c and v may depart from the general average not just as a result of a difference in the technical composition, but also simply because of a change in value of the elements of constant capital.

The development given above also involves a modification in the determination of a commodity's cost price. It was originally assumed that the cost price of a commodity equalled the *value* of the commodities consumed in its production. But for the buyer of a commodity, it is the price of production that constitutes its cost price and can thus enter into forming the price of another commodity. As the price of production of a commodity can diverge from its value, so the cost price of a commodity, in which the price of production of other commodities is involved, can also stand above or below the portion of its total value that is formed by the value of the means of production going into it. It is necessary to bear in mind this modified significance of the cost price, and therefore to bear in mind too that if the cost price of a commodity is equated with the value of the means of production used up in producing it, it is always possible to go wrong. Our present investigation does not require us to go into further detail on this point. It still remains correct that the cost price of commodities is always smaller than their value. For even if a commodity's cost price may diverge from the value of the means of production consumed in it, this error in the past is a matter of indifference to the capitalist. The cost price of the commodity is a given precondition, independent of his, the capitalist's, production, while the result of his production is a commodity that contains surplus-value, and therefore an excess value over and above its cost price. As a general rule, the principle that the cost price of a commodity is less than its value has been transformed in practice into the principle that its cost price is less than its price of production. For the total social capital, where price of production equals value, this assertion is identical with the earlier one that the cost price is less than the value. Even though it has a different meaning for the particular spheres of production, the basic fact remains that, taking the social capital as a whole, the cost price of the commodities that this produces is less than their value, or than the price of production which is identical with this value for the total mass of commodities produced. The cost price of a commodity simply depends on the quantity of paid labour it contains, while the value depends on the total quantity of labour it contains, whether paid or unpaid; the price of production depends on the sum of paid labour plus a certain quantity of unpaid labour that is independent of its own particular sphere of production.

The formula that the price of production of a commodity = $k + p$, cost price plus profit, can now be stated more exactly; since $p = kp'$ (where p' is the general rate of profit), the price of production = $k + kp'$. If $k = 300$ and $p' = 15$ per cent, the price of production $k + kp' = 300 + 300 \times \frac{15}{100} = 345$.

The price of production of commodities in a particular sphere of production may undergo changes of magnitude:

(1) while the value of the commodities remains the same (so that the same quantity of dead and living labour goes into their production afterwards as before), as the result of a change in the general rate of profit that is independent of the particular sphere in question;

(2) while the general rate of profit remains the same, by a change in value either in the particular sphere of production itself, as the result of a technical change or as the result of a change in the value of the commodities that go into its constant capital as formative elements;

(3) finally, by the common action of these two circumstances.

For all the great changes that constantly occur in the actual rates of profit in particular spheres of production (as we shall later show), a genuine change in the general rate of profit, one not simply brought about by exceptional economic events, is the final outcome of a whole series of protracted oscillations, which require a good deal of time before they are consolidated and balanced out to produce a change in the general rate. In all periods shorter than this, therefore, and even then leaving aside fluctuations in market prices, a change in prices of production is always to be explained *prima facie* by an actual change in commodity values, i.e. by a change in the total sum of labour-time needed to produce the commodities. We are not referring here, of course, to a mere change in the monetary expression of these values.[23]

It is clear on the other hand that, taking the total social capital as a whole, the sum of values of the commodities produced by it (or, expressed in money, their price) = value of constant capital + value of variable capital + surplus-value. Assuming a constant level of exploitation of labour, the profit rate can only change here, with the mass of surplus-value remaining the same, in three cases: if the value of the constant capital changes, if the value of the variable capital changes, or if both change. All these result in a change in C, thereby changing $\frac{s}{C}$, the general rate of profit. In each case, therefore, a change in the general rate of profit assumes a change in the value of the commodities which enter as formative elements into the constant capital, the variable capital, or both simultaneously.

Alternatively, the general rate of profit can change, with the

23. Corbet [*An Inquiry into the Causes and Modes of the Wealth of Individuals*, London, 1841], p. 174.

value of commodities remaining constant, if the level of exploitation of labour changes.

Or again, the level of exploitation of labour remaining the same, the general rate of profit can change if the sum of labour applied changes in relation to the constant capital, as a result of technical changes in the labour process. But technical changes of this kind must always show themselves in, and thus be accompanied by, a change in value of the commodities whose production now requires either more or less labour than it did before.

We saw in the first Part how surplus-value and profit were identical, seen from the point of view of their mass. But the rate of profit is from the very beginning different from the rate of surplus-value, though at first this appears simply as a different way of calculating the same thing. Given however that the rate of profit can rise or fall, with the rate of surplus-value remaining the same, and that all that interests the capitalist in practice is his rate of profit, this circumstance also completely obscures and mystifies the real origin of surplus-value from the very beginning. The difference in magnitude, however, was simply between rate of surplus-value and rate of profit and not between surplus-value and profit themselves. Because the rate of profit measures surplus-value against the total capital and the latter is its standard, surplus-value itself appears in this way as having arisen from the total capital, and uniformly from all parts of it at that, so that the organic distinction between constant and variable capital is obliterated in the concept of profit. In actual fact, therefore, surplus-value denies its own origin in this, its transformed form, which is profit; it loses its character and becomes unrecognizable. And yet, up to this point, the distinction between profit and surplus-value simply involved a qualitative change, a change of form, while any actual difference in magnitude at this initial stage of the transformation lay simply between the rate of profit and the rate of surplus-value and not yet between profit and surplus-value as such.

It is quite a different matter as soon as a general rate of profit is established, and with this an average profit corresponding to the amount of capital invested in the various spheres of production.

It is now purely accidental if the surplus-value actually produced in a particular sphere of production, and therefore the profit, coincides with the profit contained in the commodity's sale price. In the case now under consideration, profit and surplus-value themselves, and not just their rates, will as a rule be genuinely different magnitudes. At a given level of exploitation of labour, the mass of surplus-value that is created in a particular sphere of production is now more important for the overall average profit of the social capital, and thus for the capitalist class in general, than it is directly for the capitalist within each particular branch of production. It is important for him only in so far as the quantity of surplus-value created in his own branch intervenes as a co-determinant in regulating the average profit.[24] But this process takes place behind his back. He does not see it, he does not understand it, and it does not in fact interest him. The actual difference in magnitude between profit and surplus-value in the various spheres of production (and not merely between rate of profit and rate of surplus-value) now completely conceals the true nature and origin of profit, not only for the capitalist, who has here a particular interest in deceiving himself, but also for the worker. With the transformation of values into prices of production, the very basis for determining value is now removed from view. The upshot is this: in the case of a simple transformation from surplus-value into profit, the portion of commodity value that forms this profit confronts the other portion of value as the commodity's cost price, and the concept of value thus already goes by the board as far as the capitalist is concerned, because he does not have to deal with the total labour that the production of the commodity cost, but only the part of the total labour that he has paid for in the form of means of production, living or dead, so that profit appears to him as something standing outside the immanent value of the commodity. But what happens now [with the establishment of a general rate of profit] is that this idea is completely confirmed, reinforced and hardened by the fact that the profit added to the cost price is not actually determined, if the particular spheres of production are taken separately, by the value formation that proceeds within these branches, but on the contrary established quite externally to them.

This inner connection is here revealed for the first time. But as we shall see from what follows, and also from Volume 4,* all economics up till now has either violently made abstraction from the distinctions between surplus-value and profit, between rate of

---

24. This is obviously leaving aside the possibility of extracting a temporary super-profit by means of depressing wages, monopoly pricing, etc. – F.E.

* Marx refers to *Theories of Surplus-Value*.

surplus-value and rate of profit, so that it could retain the determination of value as its basis, or else it has abandoned, along with this determination of value, any kind of solid foundation for a scientific approach, so as to be able to retain those distinctions which obtrude themselves on the phenomenal level. This confusion on the part of the theorists shows better than anything else how the practical capitalist, imprisoned in the competitive struggle and in no way penetrating the phenomena it exhibits, cannot but be completely incapable of recognizing, behind the semblance, the inner essence and the inner form of this process.

All the laws governing rises and falls in the profit rate, developed in the first Part, have in fact the following double significance:

(1) On the one hand they are laws of the general rate of profit. Given the many different causes that lead the profit rate to rise or fall, according to our arguments developed above, one might believe that the general rate of profit would have to change every single day. But as the movement of one sphere of production will cancel out the movement of another, the forces mutually counteract and paralyse each other. We shall see later on in what direction such fluctuations tend in the last analysis. But this process is slow, and the suddenness, multilateral character and differential duration of fluctuations in the particular spheres of production lead to a situation in which they partly compensate for one another in their temporal succession, so that a fall in price succeeds a rise, and vice versa, and they therefore remain local, i.e. confined to the particular sphere of production concerned. The various local fluctuations, in other words, reciprocally neutralize one another. Changes take place within each particular sphere of production, departures from the general profit rate, which on the one hand balance each other out over a certain period of time and hence do not react back on the general rate, while on the other hand they do not react back on it because they are cancelled out by other simultaneous local fluctuations. Since the general rate of profit is determined not only by the average rate of profit in each sphere, but also by the distribution of the total capital between the various particular spheres, and since this distribution is constantly changing, we have again a constant source of change in the general rate of profit – but a source of change that also becomes paralysed, for the most part, given the uninterrupted and all-round character of this movement.

(2) Within each sphere there is room for shorter or longer

periods in which the profit rate in this sphere fluctuates, before this fluctuation, a rise or a fall, is consolidated for a sufficient time to affect the general rate of profit and thus to have more than a local significance. Within these spatial and temporal limits, therefore, the laws of the profit rate developed in the first Part of this volume similarly continue to apply.

The theoretical opinion regarding the first transformation of surplus-value into profit, i.e. that each portion of capital yields profit in a uniform way,[25] expresses a practical state of affairs. However an industrial capital may be composed, whether a quarter is dead labour and three-quarters living labour, or whether three-quarters is dead labour and only a quarter sets living labour in motion, so that in the one case three times as much surplus labour is sucked out, or surplus-value produced, as in the other – with the same level of exploitation of labour and ignoring individual differences, which disappear anyway, since in both cases we are concerned only with the average composition of the sphere of production as a whole – in both cases it yields the same profit. The individual capitalist (or alternatively the sum total of capitalists in a particular sphere of production), whose vision is a restricted one, is right in believing that his profit does not derive just from the labour employed by him or employed in his own branch. This is quite correct as far as his average profit goes. How much this profit is mediated by the overall exploitation of labour by capital as a whole, i.e. by all his fellow-capitalists, this interconnection is a complete mystery to him, and the more so in that even the bourgeois theorists, the political economists, have not yet revealed it. Saving of labour – not only the labour necessary to produce a specific product, but also the number of workers employed – and a greater use of dead labour (constant capital), appears a quite correct economic operation, and seems from the very beginning not to affect the general rate of profit and the average profit in any manner. How therefore can living labour be the exclusive source of profit, since a reduction in the quantity of labour needed for production not only seems not to affect the profit, but rather to be the immediate source of increasing profit, in certain circumstances, at least for the individual capitalist?

If the portion of the cost price which represents constant capital

25. Malthus. [*Principles of Political Economy*, 2nd edn, London, 1836, p. 268.]

rises or falls in a given sphere of production, this is the portion that comes out of the circulation sphere and goes into the commodity's production process from the outset either enlarged or reduced. But say that the workers employed produce more or less in the same period of time, i.e. with the number of workers remaining the same, the quantity of labour required for the production of a certain amount of commodities changes. In this case, the part of the cost price that represents the value of the variable capital may remain the same and thus go into the cost price of the total product with the same magnitude. But each of the individual commodities whose sum comprises the total product now contains more or less labour (paid and therefore also unpaid), i.e. also more or less of the outlay for this labour, a greater or smaller portion of the wages. The total paid by the capitalist in wages remains the same, but this is different when calculated on each item of the individual commodity. There is thus a change in this part of the commodity's cost price. Now it does not matter whether the cost price of the individual commodity rises or falls as a result of such changes in value, either its own or the value of its commodity elements (or alternatively the cost price of the sum of commodities produced by a capital of given size) – if the average profit is 10 per cent, for example, it remains 10 per cent, even though this 10 per cent, taken for the individual commodity, may represent a very different magnitude as a result of the change in the individual cost price brought about by the change in value we have just presupposed.[26]

As far as the variable capital is concerned – and this is the most important thing, since it is the source of surplus-value and since everything that conceals its position in the capitalist's enrichment mystifies the entire system – the situation looks cruder, or at least this is the way it appears to the capitalist. A variable capital of £100, say, represents the wages of 100 workers. If these 100 workers, with a given working day, produce a weekly product of 200 items of a commodity, $= 200C$, then $1C$ – ignoring the portion of the cost price that the constant capital adds – costs $£\frac{100}{200}$ = 10 shillings, since £100 $= 200C$. Let us now assume a change in the productivity of labour; if this doubles, the same number of workers produce twice this $200C$ in the same space of time as they formerly took to produce $200C$. In this case, as far as the cost

2 . Corbet [op. cit., p. 20].

price consists simply of labour, £100 now equals $400C$, and so $1C$ = £$\frac{100}{400}$ = 5 shillings. If productivity had been reduced by a half, the same labour would only produce $\frac{200C}{2}$, and since $\frac{200C}{2}$ = £100, $1C$ would now equal £$\frac{200}{200}$ = £1. The changes in the labour-time required for the production of the commodities, and therefore in their value, now appear in connection with the cost price, and therefore also with the price of production, as a different distribution of the same wages over more or fewer commodities, according to whether more or fewer commodities are produced in the same labour-time for the same wages. What the capitalist sees, and therefore the political economist as well, is that the part of the paid labour that falls to each item of the commodity changes with the productivity of labour, and so too therefore does the value of each individual article; he does not see that this is also the case with the unpaid labour contained in each article, and the less so, as the average profit is in fact only accidentally determined by the unpaid labour absorbed in his own sphere. The fact that the value of commodities is determined by the labour they contain now continues to percolate through only in this crudified and naive form.

Chapter 10: The Equalization of the General Rate of Profit through Competition. Market Prices and Market Values. Surplus Profit

In some branches of production the capital employed has a composition we may describe as 'mean' or 'average', i.e. a composition exactly or approximately the same as the average of the total social capital.

In these spheres, the production prices of the commodities produced coincide exactly or approximately with their values as expressed in money. If there were no other way of arriving at a mathematical limit, it could be done as follows. Competition distributes the social capital between the various spheres of production in such a way that the prices of production in each of these spheres are formed after the model of the prices of production in the spheres of mean composition, i.e. $k + kp'$ (cost price plus the product of the average rate of profit and the cost price). This average rate of profit, however, is nothing more than the percentage profit in spheres of mean composition, where the profit therefore coincides with the surplus-value. The rate of profit is thus the same in all spheres of production, because it is adjusted to that of these average spheres, where the average composition of capital prevails. The sum of the profits for all the different spheres of production must accordingly be equal to the sum of surplus-values, and the sum of prices of production for the total social product must be equal to the sum of its values. It is evident, however, that the equalization between spheres of production of different composition must always seek to adjust these to the spheres of mean composition, whether these correspond exactly to the social average or just approximately. Between these spheres that approximate more or less to the social average, there is again a tendency to equalization, which seeks the 'ideal' mean position, i.e. a mean position which does not exist in reality. In other words, it tends to shape itself around this ideal as a norm. In this way there prevails, and necessarily so, a tendency to make production prices into mere transformed forms of value, or to transform profits into mere portions of surplus-value that are distributed not in proportion to the surplus-value that is created in each particular sphere of production, but rather in proportion to the amount of capital applied in each of these spheres, so that equal amounts of capital, no matter how they are composed, receive equal shares (aliquot parts) of the totality of surplus-value produced by the total social capital.

For capitals of mean or approximately mean composition, the price of production thus coincides exactly or approximately with the value, and the profit with the surplus-value they produce. All other capitals, whatever might be their composition, progressively tend to conform with the capitals of mean composition under the pressure of competition. But since the capitals of mean composition are equal or approximately equal to the average social capital, it follows that all capitals, whatever the surplus-value they themselves produce, tend to realize in the prices of their commodities not this surplus-value, but rather the average profit, i.e. they tend to realize the prices of production.

It can also be added here, firstly, that wherever an average profit is established, i.e. a general rate of profit, and however this result may have been brought about, this average profit can be nothing other than the profit on the average social capital, the total sum of profit being equal to the total sum of surplus-value, and secondly that the prices produced by adding this average profit onto the cost prices can be nothing other than the values which have been transformed into prices of production. It would change nothing if, for whatever reason, capitals in certain spheres of production were not subjected to the process of equalization. The average profit would then be calculated on the portion of the social capital that was involved in the equalization process. It is clear enough that the average profit can be nothing other than the total mass of surplus-value, distributed between the masses of capital in each sphere of production in proportion to their size. It is the sum total of the realized unpaid labour, and this grand total is represented, just like the paid labour, dead and living, in the total mass of commodities and money that accrues to the capitalists.

The really difficult question here is this: how does this equalization lead to a general rate of profit, since this is evidently a result and cannot be a point of departure?

It is clear first of all that an assessment of commodity values in money, for example, can only be a result of exchanging them, and that, if we presuppose an assessment of this kind, we have to view it as a result of real exchanges of one commodity value against another. How therefore is this exchange of commodities at their actual values supposed to have come about?

Let us assume to start with that all commodities in the various spheres of production were sold at their actual values. What would happen then? According to our above arguments, very different rates of profit would prevail in the various spheres of production. It is, *prima facie*, a very different matter whether commodities are sold at their values (i.e. whether they are exchanged with one another in proportion to the value contained in them, at their value prices) or whether they are sold at prices which make their sale yield equal profits on equal amounts of the capitals advanced for their respective production.

If capitals that set in motion unequal quantities of living labour produce unequal amounts of surplus-value, this assumes that the level of exploitation of labour, or the rate of surplus-value, is the same, at least to a certain extent, or that the distinctions that exist here are balanced out by real or imaginary (conventional) grounds of compensation. This assumes competition among the workers, and an equalization that takes place by their constant migration between one sphere of production and another. We assume a general rate of surplus-value of this kind, as a tendency, like all economic laws, and as a theoretical simplification; but in any case this is in practice an actual presupposition of the capitalist mode of production, even if inhibited to a greater or lesser extent by practical frictions that produce more or less significant local differences, such as the settlement laws for agricultural labourers in England, for example. In theory, we assume that the laws of the capitalist mode of production develop in their pure form. In reality, this is only an approximation; but the approximation is all the more exact, the more the capitalist mode of production is developed and the less it is adulterated by survivals of earlier economic conditions with which it is amalgamated.

The whole difficulty arises from the fact that commodities are not exchanged simply as *commodities*, but as the *products of capitals*, which claim shares in the total mass of surplus-value according to their size, equal shares for equal size. And the total price of the commodities that a given capital produces in a given period of time has to satisfy this demand. The total price of these commodities, however, is simply the sum of the prices of the individual commodities that form the product of the capital in question.

The salient point will best emerge if we consider the matter as follows. Let us suppose the workers are themselves in possession of their respective means of production and exchange their commodities with one another. These commodities would not be products of capital. According to the technical nature of their work, the value of the means and material of labour applied in the different branches of production would vary; similarly, even ignoring the unequal value of the means of production applied, different masses of these means of production would be required for a given amount of labour, since a certain commodity can be prepared in one hour, while another takes a day, etc. Let us further assume that these workers work on the average for the same length of time, taking into account the adjustments that arise from the varying intensity, etc. of the work. Firstly, then, two workers would both have replaced their outlays, the cost prices of the means of production they had consumed, in the commodities that formed the products of their respective day's labour. These outlays would vary according to the technical nature of the branch of labour. Next, they would both have created an equal quantity of new value, i.e. the working day added to the means of production. This would comprise their wages plus surplus-value, the surplus labour over and above their necessary requirements, though the result of this would belong to themselves. If we express ourselves in capitalist terms, they would both receive the same wages plus the same profit, which would be equal to the value expressed in the product, say, of a 10-hour working day. Commodity I, for example, might contain a greater share of value in relation to the means of production applied to produce it than commodity II; and in order to introduce all possible distinctions, commodity I might also absorb more living labour than commodity II and require more labour-time for its production. The values of these commodities I and II would therefore be very different. So, too, the sums of commodity value that are the respective products of the work performed by workers I and II in a given time. Profit rates would also be very different for I and II, if we give this name here to the ratio of the surplus-value to the total value laid out on means of production. The means of subsistence which I and II consume every day in the course of production, and which represent wages, here form the portion of the means of production advanced which we would elsewhere call variable capital. But the surplus-values would be the same for both I and II, given the same working time, or, more precisely, since I and II each receive the value of the product of one working day, they therefore receive equal values, after deducting the value of the 'constant' elements advanced, and one part of these values can be viewed as a replacement for the means of subsistence consumed in the course of production, the other as the additional surplus-value on top of this. If worker I has higher outlays, these are replaced by the greater portion of value of his commodities that replaces this 'constant' part, and he therefore again has a greater part of his product's total value to transform back into the material elements of this constant part, while II, if he receives less for this, has also that much less to transform back. Under these conditions, the difference in the profit rate would be a matter of indifference, just as for a present-day wage-labourer it is a matter of indifference in what profit rate the surplus-value extorted from him is expressed, and just as in international trade the differences in profit rates between different nations are completely immaterial as far as the exchange of their commodities is concerned.

The exchange of commodities at their values, or at approximately these values, thus corresponds to a much lower stage of development than the exchange at prices of production, for which a definite degree of capitalist development is needed.

Whatever may be the ways in which the prices of different commodities are first established or fixed in relation to one another, the law of value governs their movement. When the labour-time required for their production falls, prices fall; and where it rises, prices rise, as long as other circumstances remain equal.

Apart from the way in which the law of value governs prices and their movement, it is also quite apposite to view the values of commodities not only as theoretically prior to the prices of production, but also as historically prior to them. This applies to those conditions in which the means of production belong to the worker, and this condition is to be found, in both the ancient and the modern world, among peasant proprietors and handicraftsmen who work for themselves. This agrees, moreover, with the opinion we expressed previously,[27] viz. that the development of products into commodities arises from exchange between different communities, and not between the members of one and the same community.† This is true not only for the original condition, but also for later social conditions based on slavery and serfdom, and for the guild organization of handicraft production, as long as the means of production involved in each branch of production can be transferred from one sphere to another only with difficulty, and the different spheres of production therefore relate to one another, within certain limits, like foreign countries or communistic communities.

If the prices at which commodities exchange for one another are to correspond approximately to their values, nothing more is needed than (1) that the exchange of different commodities ceases to be purely accidental or merely occasional; (2) that, in so far as we are dealing with the direct exchange of commodities, these commodities are produced on both sides in relative quantities that approximately correspond to mutual need, something that is learned from the reciprocal experience of trading and which therefore arises precisely as a result of continuing exchange; and (3) that, as far as selling is concerned, no natural or artificial monopolies enable one of the contracting parties to sell above

27. At that time, in 1865, this was still simply Marx's 'opinion'. Today, after the comprehensive investigations of the primitive community by writers from Maurer to Morgan, it is an established fact scarcely anywhere contested. – F.E.*

* Georg Ludwig von Maurer (1790–1872), historian and student of early German society. His work is frequently referred to in the Marx–Engels correspondence, from 1868 onwards ('He shows in detail how private property in land is a subsequent development', Marx to Engels, 14 March 1868), and his work later served as the basis for Engels's essay 'The Mark' (1882). Still greater is the importance Marx and Engels attached to the work of the American Lewis Henry Morgan (1818–81), author of *Ancient Society* (1877). Though it was Engels who was to use this as the main source for his own *The Origin of the Family, Private Property and the State* (1884), it was in fact Marx who 'discovered' Morgan's book and first made annotated extracts of it, partly used by Engels in his own work. 'Morgan discovered the Marxian materialist conception of history independently within the limits prescribed by his subject' (Engels to Kautsky, 16 February 1884; *Selected Correspondence*, London, 1965, p. 368).

† See Volume 1, p. 182, and *A Contribution to the Critique of Political Economy*, London, 1971, pp. 50, 149, 208.

value, or force them to sell cheap, below value. By accidental monopoly, we mean the monopoly that accrues to buyer or seller as a result of the accidental state of supply and demand.

The assumption that commodities from different spheres of production are sold at their values naturally means no more than that this value is the centre of gravity around which price turns and at which its constant rise and fall is balanced out. Besides this, however, there is always a *market value* (of which more later), as distinct from the individual value of particular commodities produced by the different producers. The individual value of some of these commodities will stand below the market value (i.e. less labour-time has been required for their production than the market value expresses), the value of others above it. Market value is to be viewed on the one hand as the average value of the commodities produced in a particular sphere, and on the other hand as the individual value of commodities produced under average conditions in the sphere in question, and forming the great mass of its commodities. Only in extraordinary situations do commodities produced under the worst conditions, or alternatively the most advantageous ones, govern the market value, which forms in turn the centre around which market prices fluctuate – these being the same for all commodities of the same species. If the supply of commodities at the average value, i.e. the mean value of the mass that lies between the two extremes, satisfies the customary demand, the commodities whose individual value stands below the market price will realize an extra surplus-value or surplus profit, while those whose individual value stands above the market price will be unable to realize a part of the surplus-value which they contain.

It is of no assistance to say that the sale of commodities produced under the worst conditions shows that these are required to meet the demand. If the price were higher than the mean market value in the case assumed, the demand would be less. At a given price, a species of commodity can only take up a certain area of the market; this area remains the same through changes in price only if the higher price coincides with a smaller quantity of commodities and a lower price with a greater quantity. If the demand is so strong, however, that it does not contract when price is determined by the value of commodities produced in the worst conditions, then it is these that determine the market value. This is possible only if demand rises above the usual level, or supply falls below this. Finally, if the mass of commodities produced is too great to find a complete outlet at the mean market value, market value is determined by the commodities produced under the best conditions. These commodities may be sold completely or approximately at their individual value, for instance, in which connection it may happen that the commodities produced under the worst conditions may fail even to realize their cost prices, while those produced under average conditions realize only a part of the surplus-value they contain. What we have said here of market value holds also for the price of production, as soon as this takes the place of market value. The price of production is regulated in each sphere, and regulated too according to particular circumstances. But it is again the centre around which the daily market prices revolve, and at which they are balanced out in definite periods. (Cf. Ricardo on the determination of price of production by producers working under the worst conditions.)*

In whatever way prices are determined, the following is the result:

(1) The law of value governs their movement in so far as reduction or increase in the labour-time needed for their production makes the price of production rise or fall. It is in this sense that Ricardo, who certainly feels that his prices of production depart from the values of commodities, says that 'the inquiry to which I wish to draw the reader's attention relates to the effect of the variations in the relative value of commodities, and not in their absolute value'.†

(2) The average profit, which determines the prices of production, must always be approximately equal to the amount of surplus-value that accrues to a given capital as an aliquot part of the total social capital. Suppose that the general rate of profit and hence the average profit itself is expressed in a money value that is higher than that of the actual average surplus-value. As far as the capitalists are concerned, it is all the same whether they charge one another 10 per cent profit or 15 per cent. The one percentage covers no more actual commodity value than the other does, since the inflation of the monetary expression is mutual. For the workers, however (we assume that they receive their normal wages, so that the rise in the average profit is not an actual

---

* *On the Principles of Political Economy and Taxation*, Ch. II.
  ibid., p. 64.

deduction from the wage, expressing something completely different from the capitalist's normal surplus-value), the increase in commodity prices resulting from this rise in the average profit must correspond to an increase in the monetary expression of the variable capital. In actual fact, a general nominal increase of this kind in the profit rate, and hence in average profit, over and above the level given by the proportion of the actual surplus-value to the total capital advanced, is not possible unless it brings with it an increase in wages and similarly an increase in the price of those commodities which form the constant capital. The same is true the other way round with a decrease. Since it is the total value of the commodities that governs the total surplus-value, while this in turn governs the level of average profit and hence the general rate of profit – as a general law or as governing the fluctuations – it follows that the law of value regulates the prices of production.

What competition brings about, first of all in one sphere, is the establishment of a uniform market value and market price out of the various individual values of commodities. But it is only the competition of capitals in *different* spheres that brings forth the production price that equalizes the rates of profit between those spheres. The latter process requires a higher development of the capitalist mode of production than the former.

In order that commodities from the same sphere of production, of the same type and approximately the same quality, may be sold at their value, two things are necessary:

(1) First, the different individual values must be equalized to give a *single* social value, the market value presented above, and this requires competition among producers of the same type of commodity, as well as the presence of a market on which they all offer their commodities. Looking at the market price for identical commodities, commodities which are identical but each produced under circumstances of a character which varies slightly according to the individual, we may say that if this market price is to correspond to the market value, and not diverge from it, either by rising above or falling below, then the pressures that the various sellers exert on one another must be strong enough to put on the market the quantity of commodities that is required to fulfil the social need, i.e. the quantity for which the society is able to pay the market value. If the mass of products oversteps this need, commodities have to be sold below their market value, and conversely they are sold above the market value if the mass of

products is not large enough, or, what comes to the same thing, if the pressure of competition among the sellers is not strong enough to compel them to bring this mass of commodities to the market. If the market value changes, the conditions at which the whole mass of commodities can be sold will also change. If the market value falls, the social need is on average expanded (this always means here the need which has money to back it up), and within certain limits the society can absorb larger quantities of commodities. If the market value rises, the social need for the commodities contracts and smaller quantities are absorbed. Thus if supply and demand regulate market price, or rather the departures of market price from market value, the market value in turn regulates the relationship between demand and supply, or the centre around which fluctuations of demand and supply make the market price oscillate.

If we consider the matter more closely, we see that the same conditions that obtain for the value of the individual commodity reproduce themselves here as conditions for the value of the total amount of any one type; we see how capitalist production is, right from the start, mass production, and how even what is produced in smaller amounts by many petty producers in other, less developed modes of production is concentrated on the market as a common product in great quantities in the hands of a relatively few merchants, at least as far as the major commodities are concerned, and accumulated and brought to sale in the same way: as the common product of a whole branch of production, or of a bigger or smaller contingent of such a branch.

Let us note here, but merely in passing, that the 'social need' which governs the principle of demand is basically conditioned by the relationship of the different classes and their respective economic positions; in the first place, therefore, particularly by the proportion between the total surplus-value and wages, and secondly, by the proportion between the various parts into which surplus-value itself is divided (profit, interest, ground-rent, taxes, etc.). Here again we can see how absolutely nothing can be explained by the relationship of demand and supply, before explaining the basis on which this relationship functions.

Even though both commodities and money are unities of exchange-value and use-value, we have already seen (Volume 1, Chapter 1, 3) how, in the course of buying and selling, the two determinations are distributed in a polarized way at the two extremes, so that the commodity (seller) represents use-value and money (buyer) represents exchange-value. It was one precondition for the sale that the commodity should have use-value, and thus satisfy a social need. The other precondition was that the quantity of labour contained in the commodity should represent socially necessary labour, that the individual value of the commodity (and what is the same thing under this assumption, the sale price) should therefore coincide with its social value.[28]

Let us now apply this to the mass of commodities present on the market and forming the product of an entire sphere.

The matter will be represented most easily if we conceive the entire mass of commodities, to start with that of *one* branch of production, as a *single* commodity, and add together the sum of the prices of many identical commodities to arrive at *one* price. What we said of the individual commodity now applies word for word to the mass of commodities of a certain branch of production which are to be found on the market. The fact that the individual value of a commodity agrees with its social value is now realized in, or subsequently determines, the fact that the total quantity contains the socially necessary labour involved in its production and that the value of this mass equals its market value.

Let us now assume that great quantities of these commodities are produced in something like the same normal social conditions, so that this value is also the individual value of the individual commodities making up this mass. If only a relatively small proportion are produced in worse conditions, and another portion in better conditions, so that the individual value of the one part is greater than the mean value of the great bulk of the commodities, and that of the other part lower than this mean, then these two extremes will cancel one another out, so that the average value of the commodities at the extremes is the same as the value of the mass of average commodities, and the market value is determined by the value of the commodities produced under average conditions.[29] The value of the overall mass of commodities is equal to the actual sum of values of all individual commodities taken together, both those produced in average conditions, and those produced in better or worse ones. In this case, the market value or social value of the mass of commodities – the necessary labour-

28. K. Marx, *A Contribution to the Critique of Political Economy* [pp. 27–52].
29. K. Marx, *A Contribution* . . . [ibid.].

time they contain – is determined by the value of the great middling mass.

Now assume on the contrary that the total quantity of the commodities in question brought to market remains the same, but the value of those produced under worse conditions is not balanced out by the value of those produced under better conditions, so that the part of the total produced under worse conditions forms a relatively significant quantity, both vis-à-vis the average mass and vis-à-vis the opposite extreme. In this case it is the mass produced under the worse conditions that governs the market, or social, value.

Let us finally assume that the mass of commodities produced under better-than-average conditions significantly exceeds that produced under worse conditions and is itself of significant magnitude in relation to that produced under average conditions. In that case the market value would be regulated by the part produced under the most favourable conditions. We leave aside here the situation where the market is over-supplied, in which case it is always the portion produced under the most favourable conditions that governs the market price; here we are not dealing with market price in so far as this differs from market value, but simply with the various determinations of this market value itself.[30]

Strictly speaking (though this is of course only approximately

30. The controversy between Storch and Ricardo in connection with ground-rent (a controversy only as far as the subject is concerned, as neither party paid any attention to the other), over the question whether market value (in their terms market price or price of production) is governed by commodities produced under the least favourable conditions (Ricardo) or the most favourable (Storch), is thus resolved in this way, that both are right and both are wrong, and also that both have entirely omitted to consider the average case.* Compare Corbet on those cases where price is governed by the commodities produced under the best conditions.† And compare this: 'It is not meant to be asserted by him' (Ricardo) 'that two particular lots of two different articles, as a hat and a pair of shoes, exchange with one another when those two particular lots were produced by equal quantities of labour. By "commodity" we must here understand the "description of commodity", not a particular individual hat, pair of shoes, etc. The whole labour which produces all the hats in England is to be considered, to this purpose, as divided among all the hats. This seems to me not to have been expressed at first, and in the general statements of this doctrine.' (*Observations on Certain Verbal Disputes in Political Economy, etc.*, London, 1821, pp. 53–4.)

* Henri Storch (1766–1835) was a Russian vulgarizer of classical political economy, though he wrote in French. The work Marx is referring to here is his

true in actual practice and is modified there in a thousand ways), in case I the market value of the entire mass, as governed by the average values, is equal to the sum of its individual values; even though for the commodities produced at the two extremes this value is expressed as an average value which is imposed on them. Those producing at the worst extreme then have to sell their commodities below their individual value, while those at the best extreme sell theirs above it.

In case II, the individual amounts of commodities produced at the two extremes do not balance one another, but it is rather those produced under the worst conditions that decide the issue. Strictly speaking, the average price or market value of each individual commodity or each aliquot part of the total mass is now determined by the total value of this mass, which is arrived at by adding together the values of the commodities produced under various different conditions, and by the aliquot part of this total value that falls to the share of the individual commodity. The market value obtained in this way is not only above the individual value of the favourable extreme, but also above that of the middle stratum of commodities; but it would always remain less than the individual value of the commodities produced at the unfavourable extreme. How close it would be to this, or whether it would ultimately even coincide with it, depends completely on the volume of the commodities produced at the unfavourable extreme in the sphere of commodities in question. If demand is only marginally predominant, it is the individual value of the unfavourably produced commodities that governs the market price.

Finally, if, as in case III, the commodities produced at the favourable extreme are greater in quantity, not only compared with the other extreme, but also with the middle conditions, then the market value falls below the average value. The average value, calculated by adding the sums of value at the two extremes and in the middle, here stands below the middle value and is nearer or further from it according to the relative place taken by the favourable extreme. If demand is weak in relation to supply, the favour-

---

Cours d'économie politique, vol. 2, St Petersburg, 1815, pp. 78–9. (See *Theories of Surplus-Value*, Part II, p. 99.)

† A reference to T. Corbet, *An Inquiry into the Causes and Modes of the Wealth of Individuals; or the Principles of Trade and Speculation Explained*, London, 1841, pp. 42–4.

ably situated part, however big it might be, forcibly makes room for itself by drawing the price towards its individual value. The market value can never coincide with this individual value of the commodities produced under the most favourable conditions, except in cases where supply sharply outweighs demand.

This establishment of the market price, which we have depicted here only *abstractly*, is brought about on the actual market itself by competition among the buyers, assuming that demand is strong enough to absorb the whole mass of commodities at the values established in this way. And here we come to the other point.

(2) To say that a commodity has use-value is simply to assert that it satisfies some kind of social need. As long as we were dealing only with an individual commodity, we could take the need for this specific commodity as already given, without having to go in any further detail into the quantitative extent of the need which had to be satisfied. The quantity was already implied by its price. But this quantity is a factor of fundamental importance as soon as we have on the one hand the product of a whole branch of production and on the other the social need. It now becomes necessary to consider the volume of the social need, i.e. its quantity.

In the above determinations of market value, we assumed that the mass of commodities produced remains the same, is given; that the only change taking place is in the proportion between the components of this mass which are produced under different conditions, and therefore that the market value of the same mass of commodities is regulated differently. Let us take this mass to be the customary quantity supplied and ignore here the possibility that one part of the commodities produced may be temporarily withdrawn from the market. If the demand for this commodity now also remains that customary, the commodity is sold at its market value, which may be governed by any one of the three cases investigated above. The mass of commodities not only satisfies a need, but it satisfies this need on its social scale. If however the quantity supplied is less than the demand, or alternatively more, this market price deviates from the market value. In the first case, if the quantity is too small, it is always the commodities produced under the worst conditions that govern the market value, while if it is too large, it is those produced under the best conditions; i.e. it is one of the two extremes that determines the market value, despite the fact that the proportions produced under the different conditions, taken by themselves, would lead to a different result. If the difference between the demand for the product and the quantity produced is more significant, the market price will diverge more sharply from the market value, either upwards or downwards. This difference between the quantity of commodities produced and the quantity of these commodities which would be sold at their market value can arise for two reasons. Either the former quantity itself changes, becoming either too little or too much, so that reproduction would take place on a scale different from that which regulated the given market value. In this case it is the supply that has changed, even though the demand remains the same, and in this way we have relative overproduction or underproduction. Alternatively, however, the reproduction, i.e. the supply, remains the same, but demand rises or falls, something which can happen for various reasons. Even though the absolute size of the supply remains the same here, its relative magnitude has changed, i.e. its magnitude compared with or measured against the need. The effect is the same as in the first case, but in the opposite direction. Finally, if changes occur on both sides, but either in the opposite direction, or else in the same direction but not to the same degree, if in other words changes occur in both directions, which nevertheless affect the earlier proportion between the two sides, the end result must still amount to one of the two cases considered above.

The real difficulty in pinning down the general concepts of demand and supply is that we seem to end up with a tautology. Let us first take supply, the product which is actually on sale in the market or can be delivered to it. So as not to get entangled in useless details, we refer here to the mass of the annual reproduction in each particular branch of industry and ignore therefore the greater or lesser capacity that various commodities possess for being withdrawn from the market and stored up for consumption next year, say. This annual reproduction is firstly expressed as a definite quantity, in measure or number, according to whether the commodity is measured continuously or discretely; it is not just mere use-values that satisfy human needs, but these use-values are available on the market on a given scale. Secondly, however, this quantity of commodities has a definite market value, which can be expressed as a multiple of the market value of the individual commodity, or the measure that serves as a unit. There is no necessary connection between the quantitative volume of commodities existing on the market and their market value, since some commodities, for example, have a generically high value, others a generically low one, so that a given sum of value may be expressed in a very small quantity of the one and a very large quantity of the other. Between the quantity of the article on the market and the market value of this article there is only this one connection: on a given basis of labour productivity in the sphere of production in question, the production of a particular quantity of this article requires a particular quantity of social labour-time, even though this proportion may be completely different from one sphere of production to another and has no intrinsic connection with the usefulness of the article or the particular character of its use-value. All other things being equal, if quantity a of a certain species of commodity costs labour-time b, then quantity na costs labour-time nb. Moreover, in so far as society wants to satisfy its needs, and have an article produced for this purpose, it has to pay for it. In actual fact, since commodity production presupposes the division of labour, if the society buys these articles, then in so far as it spends a portion of its available labour-time on their production, it buys them with a certain quantity of the labour-time that it has at its disposal. The section of society whose responsibility it is under the division of labour to spend its labour on the production of these particular articles must receive an equivalent in social labour represented in those articles that satisfy its needs. There is no necessary connection, however, but simply a fortuitous one, between on the one hand the total quantity of social labour that is spent on a social article, i.e. the aliquot part of its total labour-power which the society spends on the production of this article, and therefore the proportion that the production of this article assumes in the total production, and on the other hand the proportion in which the society demands satisfaction of the need appeased by that particular article. Even if an individual article, or a definite quantity of one kind of commodity, may contain simply the social labour required to produce it, and as far as this aspect is concerned the market value of this commodity represents no more than the necessary labour, yet, if the commodity in question is produced on a scale that exceeds the social need at the time, a part of the society's labour-time is wasted, and the mass of commodities in question then represents on the market a much smaller quantity of social labour than it actually contains. (Only when production is subjected to the genuine, prior control of society will society establish the connection between the amount of social labour-time applied to the production of particular articles, and the scale of the social need to be satisfied by these.) These commodities must therefore be got rid of at less than their market value, and a portion of them may even be completely unsaleable. (The converse is the case if the amount of social labour spent on a particular kind of commodity is too small for the specific social need which the product is to satisfy.) But if the volume of social labour spent on the production of a certain article corresponds in scale to the social need to be satisfied, so that the amount produced corresponds to the customary measure of reproduction, given an unchanged demand, then the commodity will be sold at its market value. The exchange or sale of commodities at their value is the rational, natural law of the equilibrium between them; this is the basis on which divergences have to be explained, and not the converse, i.e. the law of equilibrium should not be derived from contemplating the divergences.

Let us now examine the other aspect, demand.

Commodities are bought as means of production or as means of subsistence (it makes no difference that many kinds of commodity may serve both these ends), they are bought to go into either productive or individual consumption. There is therefore both demand from producers (here capitalists, as we assume that the means of production are transformed into capital) and demand from consumers. Both of these at first appear to assume a given volume of social needs on the demand side, to which definite quantities of social production in the various branches are to correspond. If the cotton industry is to carry on its annual reproduction at a given level, it requires the usual amount of cotton, and as far as the annual expansion of production is concerned, other things being equal, capital accumulation will require an additional quantity. The same is the case as regards means of subsistence. The working class must find at least the same amount of necessary provisions available, even if perhaps somewhat differently distributed among various kinds of provision, if it is to go on living on the average in its customary manner; and taking the annual growth in population into account, it also needs an additional quantity. The same is also true for the other classes, with varying degrees of modification.

It appears, therefore, that there is a certain quantitatively defined social need on the demand side, which requires for its fulfilment a definite quantity of an article on the market. In fact, however, the quantitative determination of this need is completely elastic and fluctuating. Its fixed character is mere illusion. If means of subsistence were cheaper or money wages higher, the workers would buy more of them, and a greater 'social need' for these kinds of commodity would appear, not to mention those paupers, etc. whose 'demand' is still below the narrowest limits of their physical need. If cotton, on the other hand, became cheaper, the capitalists' demand for cotton would grow, more excess capital would be put into the cotton industry, and so on. It must never be forgotten in this connection that the demand for productive consumption, on our assumptions, is the capitalist's demand, and that his true purpose is the production of surplus-value, so that it is only with this in mind that he produces a particular kind of commodity. This does not prevent the capitalist, in so far as he is present on the market as buyer of cotton, for example, from being the representative of the need for cotton, since it is completely unimportant for the seller of cotton whether the buyer transforms it into shirting or gun-cotton, or whether he uses it to stop up his own and the world's ears. And yet the capitalist's purpose exerts a great influence on the kind of buyer he is. His need for cotton is modified fundamentally by the fact that all it really clothes is his need to make a profit. The extent to which the need for commodities as represented on the *market*, i.e. demand, is different in quantity from the *genuine social need* is of course very different for different commodities; what I mean here is the difference between the quantity of commodities that is demanded and the quantity that would be demanded at other money prices, or with the buyers being in different financial and living conditions.

Nothing is easier to understand than the disproportions between demand and supply, and the consequent divergences of market prices from market values. The real difficulty lies in determining what is involved when demand and supply are said to coincide.

Demand and supply coincide if they stand in such a relationship that the mass of commodities produced by a certain branch of production can be sold at its market value, neither above it nor below. This is the first thing we are told.

The second is that when commodities can be sold at their market value, demand and supply coincide.

If demand and supply coincide, they cease to have any effect, and it is for this very reason that commodities are sold at their market value. If two forces act in opposing directions and cancel one another out, they have no external impact whatsoever, and phenomena that appear under these conditions must be explained otherwise than by the operation of these two forces. If demand and supply cancel one another out, they cease to explain anything, have no effect on market value and leave us completely in the dark as to why this market value is expressed in precisely such a sum of money and no other. The real inner laws of capitalist production clearly cannot be explained in terms of the interaction of demand and supply (not to mention the deeper analysis of these two social driving forces which we do not intend to give here), since these laws are realized in their pure form only when demand and supply cease to operate, i.e. when they coincide. In actual fact, demand and supply never coincide, or, if they do so, it is only by chance and not to be taken into account for scientific purposes; it should be considered as not having happened. Why then does political economy assume that they do coincide? In order to treat the phenomena it deals with in their law-like form, the form that corresponds to their concept, i.e. to consider them independently of the appearance produced by the movement of demand and supply. And, in addition, in order to discover the real tendency of their movement and to define it to a certain extent. For the disproportions are contrary in character and, since they constantly follow one another, they balance each other out in their movement in contrary directions, their contradiction. Thus if there is no single individual case in which demand and supply actually do coincide, their disproportions still work out in the following way – and the result of a divergence in one direction is to call forth a divergence in the opposite direction – that supply and demand always coincide if a greater or lesser period of time is taken as a whole; but they coincide only as the average of the movement that has taken place and through the constant movement of their contradiction. Market prices that diverge from market values balance out on average to become market values, since the departures from these values balance each other as pluses and minuses, when their average is taken. And this average figure is by no means of merely theoretical significance. It is, rather, practically important for capital whose investment is calculated over the fluctuations and compensations of a more or less fixed period of time.

The relationship between demand and supply thus explains on the one hand simply the divergences of market price from market value, while on the other hand it explains the tendency for these divergences to be removed, i.e. for the effect of the demand and supply relationship to be cancelled. (The exceptional cases of those commodities which have prices without having any value will not be considered here.) Demand and supply can cancel the effect that their disproportion produces in various different ways. If demand falls, for example, and with it the market price, this can lead to a withdrawal of capital and thus a reduction in the supply. But it can also lead to a fall in the market value itself as a result of inventions which reduce the necessary labour-time; this would also be a way of bringing the market value into line with the market price. Conversely, if demand rises, so that the market price rises above the market value, this can lead to the investment of too much capital in this branch of production and a consequent rise in production so great as to make the market price actually fall below the market value; alternatively it may lead to a rise in price that depresses demand. It may also lead, in this or that branch of production, to a rise in the market value itself for a shorter or longer period, because part of the products demanded have to be produced during this time under worse conditions.

If demand and supply determine the market price, then market price in turn, and at a further remove market value, also determine demand and supply. As far as demand is concerned, this is self-evident, since this moves in the opposite direction to price, expanding when it falls and vice versa. But the same is true of supply. For the prices of means of production that go into the commodities supplied determine the demand for these means of production, and hence also the supply of the commodities whose supply brings with it a demand for those means of production. Cotton prices determine the supply of cotton goods.

On top of this confusion – the determination of price by demand and supply, and the determination of demand and supply by price – demand also determines supply and conversely supply determines demand, production determines the market and the market determines production.[31]

31. The following 'subtlety' is sheer stupidity: 'Where the quantity of wages, capital, and land, required to produce an article, are become different from what they were, that which Adam Smith calls the natural price of it, is also different, and that price, which was previously its natural price, becomes,

Even the ordinary economist (see footnote) understands that without a change in supply or demand brought about by extraneous circumstances, the relationship between the two can still change as the result of a change in the commodity's market value. Even he has to concede that, whatever the market value may be, demand and supply must balance out in order for this market value to emerge. In other words, the relationship between demand and supply does not explain market value, but it is the latter, rather, that explains fluctuations in demand and supply. The author of the *Observations* continues, after the passage quoted in the above footnote: 'This proportion' (between demand and supply) 'however, if we still mean by "demand" and "natural price", what we meant just now, when referring to Adam Smith, must always be a proportion of equality; for it is only when the supply is equal to the effectual demand, that is, to that demand which will neither more nor less than pay the natural price, that the natural price is in fact paid; consequently, there may be two very different natural prices, at different times, for the same commodity, and yet the proportion, which the supply bears to the

with reference to this alteration, its market-price; because, though neither the supply, nor the quantity wanted, may have been changed' – both of these change here, precisely because the market value, or, as Adam Smith has it, the price of production, changes as a result of the change in value – 'that supply is not now exactly enough for those persons who are able and willing to pay what is now the cost of production, but is either greater or less than that; so that the proportion between the supply and what is with reference to the new cost of production the effectual demand, is different from what it was. An alteration in the rate of supply will then take place, if there is no obstacle in the way of it, and at last bring the commodity to its new natural price. It may then seem good to some persons to say that, as the commodity gets to its natural price by an alteration in its supply, the natural price is as much owing to one proportion between the demand and supply, as the market-price is to another; and consequently, that the natural price, just as much as the market-price, depends on the proportion that demand and supply bear to each other . . . The great principle of demand and supply is called into action to determine what A. Smith calls natural prices as well as market-prices' (Malthus, *Observations on Certain Verbal Disputes, etc.*, London, 1821, pp. 60–61). This clever man does not understand that in the case in question it is precisely the change in cost of production, and also therefore in value, that has brought about the change in demand, i.e. in the relationship of demand and supply, and that this change in demand can induce a change in supply. This would however prove completely the opposite of what our theorist wants to prove, which is that the change in cost of production is in no way governed by the relationship of demand and supply, but on the contrary is what governs this relationship.

demand, be in both cases the same, namely, the proportion of equality.'

It is conceded, then, that in the case where we have two different 'natural prices' for the same commodity at different times, demand and supply can and must coincide each time, if the commodity is to be sold at its 'natural price' in both cases. But since there is no difference in the relationship between demand and supply from one occasion to the other, but rather a difference in the magnitude of the 'natural price' itself, the latter is evidently determined independently of demand and supply and can certainly not be determined by them.

If a commodity is to be sold at its market value, i.e. in proportion to the socially necessary labour contained in it, the total quantity of social labour which is applied to produce the overall amount of this kind of commodity must correspond to the quantity of the social need for it, i.e. to the social need with money to back it up. Competition, and the fluctuations in market price which correspond to fluctuations in the relationship of demand and supply, constantly seek to reduce the total quantity of labour applied to each kind of commodity to this level.

In the relationship of demand and supply for commodities we have firstly a repetition of the relationship between use-value and exchange-value, commodity and money, buyer and seller; secondly, we have the relationship of producer and consumer, even though both may be represented by third parties, in the shape of merchants. As far as the buyer and seller are concerned, the relationship can be created simply by putting the two face to face with one another as individuals. Three persons are enough for the complete metamorphosis of a commodity, and hence for the whole process of sale and purchase. A transforms his commodity into B's money by selling B the commodity and he then transforms his money back into commodities which he buys with this money from C; the entire process takes place between these three parties. Moreover, in dealing with money we assumed that commodities were sold at their values; there was no reason at all to consider prices that diverged from values, as we were concerned simply with the changes of form which commodities undergo when they are turned into money and then transformed back from money into commodities again. As soon as a commodity is in any way sold, and a new commodity bought with the proceeds, we have the entire metamorphosis before us, and it is completely immaterial here whether the commodity's price is above or below its value. The commodity's value remains important as the basis, since any rational understanding of money has to start from this foundation, and price, in its general concept, is simply value in the money form. In treating money as means of circulation, moreover, we did not assume simply one metamorphosis by a single commodity. We considered rather the way these metamorphoses were socially intertwined. Only in this way did we come to the circulation of money and the development of its function as means of circulation. But however important this framework was for money's transition into its function as means of circulation and for the altered form that it assumes as a result, it is immaterial as far as the transaction between individual buyers and sellers is considered.

When we consider supply and demand, on the other hand, the supply is equal to the sum of commodities provided by all the sellers or producers of a particular kind of commodity, and the demand is equal to the sum of all buyers or consumers (individual or productive) of that same kind of commodity. These totals, moreover, act on one another as unities, as aggregate forces. Here the individual has an effect only as part of a social power, as an atom in the mass, and it is in this form that competition brings into play the *social* character of production and consumption.

The side that is temporarily weaker in competition is also that in which the individual operates independently of the mass of his competitors, and often directly against them, illustrating precisely in this way the dependence of one on the other, whereas the stronger side always acts towards its opponent as a more or less united whole. If demand is greater than supply for this particular kind of commodity, one buyer outbids the others – within certain limits – and thus raises the commodity's price above its market value for everyone, while on the other hand the sellers all seek to sell at a high market price. If, inversely, the supply is greater than the demand, one seller begins to unload his goods more cheaply and the others have to follow, while the buyers all work to depress the market price as far as possible below the market value. Each is only concerned with the common interest as long as he obtains more with it than he would against it. And this unity of action ceases as soon as one entire side or other weakens, when each individual independently tries to extract what he can. If one seller produces more cheaply and can more easily undercut the others, carving out a bigger share of the market by selling below the current market price or market value, then he does so, and the action once begun, it gradually forces the others to introduce the cheaper form of production and thereby reduces the socially necessary labour to a new and lower level. If one side has the upper hand, each of its members profits; it is as if they had a common monopoly to exert. As for the weaker side, each member can try for his own part to be stronger (e.g. he may try to be the one operating with lower production costs), or at least he may endeavour to come out as well as possible, and here it is a case of devil take the hindmost, even if this action ultimately affects all his associates.[32]

Demand and supply imply the transformation of value into market value, and in as much as they act on a capitalist basis, and commodities are the products of capital, they imply capitalist processes of production, i.e. conditions that are much more intricate than the mere purchase and sale of commodities. Here it is not simply a question of the formal conversion of commodity value into price, i.e. a mere change of form; what is involved are specific quantitative divergences of market prices from market values and, at a further remove, from prices of production. For simply buying and selling, it is enough that commodity producers confront one another. Demand and supply, on further analysis, imply the existence of various different classes and segments of classes which distribute the total social revenue among themselves and consume it as such, thus making up a demand created out of revenue; while it is also necessary to understand the overall configuration of the capitalist production process if one is to comprehend the demand and supply generated among the producers as such.

In capitalist production it is not simply a matter of extracting, in return for the mass of value thrown into circulation in the

32. 'If each man of a class could never have more than a given share, or aliquot part, of the gains and possessions of the whole, he would readily combine to raise the gain;' (he does so whenever the relationship of demand and supply permits) 'this is monopoly. But where each man thinks that he may anyway increase the absolute amount of his own share, though by a process which lessens the whole amount, he will often do it; this is competition' (*An Inquiry into those Principles Respecting the Nature of Demand, etc.*, London, 1821, p. 105).

commodity form, an equal mass of value in a different form – whether money or another commodity – but rather of extracting for the capital advanced in production the same surplus-value or profit as any other capital of the same size, or a profit proportionate to its size, no matter in what branch of production it may be applied. The problem therefore is to sell commodities, and this is a minimum requirement, at prices which deliver the average profit, i.e. at prices of production. This is the form in which capital becomes conscious of itself as a *social power*, in which every capitalist participates in proportion to his share in the total social capital.

Firstly, capitalist production as such is indifferent to the particular use-values it produces, and in fact to the specific character of its commodities in general. All that matters in any sphere of production is to produce surplus-value, to appropriate a definite quantity of unpaid labour in labour's product. And it is similarly in the very nature of wage-labour subjected to capital that it is indifferent to the specific character of its work; it must be prepared to change according to the needs of capital and let itself be flung from one sphere of production to another.

Secondly, one sphere of production really is as good and as bad as any other; each yields the same profit and each would be pointless if the commodity it produced did not satisfy some kind of social need.

If commodities were sold at their values, however, this would mean very different rates of profit in the different spheres of production, as we have already explained, according to the differing organic composition of the masses of capital applied. Capital withdraws from a sphere with a low rate of profit and wends its way to others that yield higher profit. This constant migration, the distribution of capital between the different spheres according to where the profit rate is rising and where it is falling, is what produces a relationship between supply and demand such that the average profit is the same in the various different spheres, and values are therefore transformed into prices of production. Capital arrives at this equalization to a greater or lesser extent, according to how advanced capitalist development is in a given national society: i.e. the more the conditions in the country in question are adapted to the capitalist mode of production. As capitalist production advances, so also do its requirements become more extensive, and it subjects all the social preconditions that frame the production process to its specific character and immanent laws.

This constant equalization of ever-renewed inequalities is accomplished more quickly, (1) the more mobile capital is, i.e. the more easily it can be transferred from one sphere and one place to others; (2) the more rapidly labour-power can be moved from one sphere to another and from one local point of production to another.

The first of these conditions implies completely free trade within the society in question and the abolition of all monopolies other than natural ones, i.e. those arising from the capitalist mode of production itself. It also presupposes the development of the credit system, which concentrates together the inorganic mass of available social capital vis-à-vis the individual capitalist. It further implies that the various spheres of production have been subordinated to capitalists. This last is already contained in the assumption that we are dealing with the transformation of values into prices of production for all spheres of production that are exploited in the capitalist manner; and yet this equalization comes up against major obstacles if several substantial spheres of production are pursued non-capitalistically (e.g. agriculture by small peasant farmers), these spheres being interposed between the capitalist enterprises and linked with them. A final precondition is a high population density.

The second condition presupposes the abolition of all laws that prevent workers from moving from one sphere of production to another or from one local seat of production to any other. Indifference of the worker to the content of his work. Greatest possible reduction of work in all spheres of production to simple labour. Disappearance of all prejudices of trade and craft among the workers. Finally and especially, the subjection of the worker to the capitalist mode of production. Further details on this belong in the special study of competition.*

From what has been said so far, we can see that each individual capitalist, just like the totality of all capitalists in each particular sphere of production, participates in the exploitation of the entire working class by capital as a whole, and in the level of this exploitation; not just in terms of general class sympathy, but in a

* See below, p. 426.

direct economic sense, since, taking all other circumstances as given, including the value of the total constant capital advanced, the average rate of profit depends on the level of exploitation of labour as a whole by capital as a whole.

The average rate of profit coincides with the average surplus-value that capital produces for each 100 units, and as far as surplus-value is concerned, what has been said above is evident enough from the very start. As far as the average profit goes, the only additional aspect determining the profit rate is the value of the capital advanced. In actual fact, the particular interest that one capitalist or capital in a particular sphere of production has in exploiting the workers he directly employs is confined to the possibility of taking an extra cut, making an excess profit over and above the average, either by exceptional overwork, by reducing wages below the average, or by exceptional productivity in the labour applied. Apart from this, a capitalist who employed no variable capital at all in his sphere of production, hence not a single worker (in fact an exaggerated assumption), would have just as much an interest in the exploitation of the working class by capital and would just as much derive his profit from unpaid surplus labour as would a capitalist who employed only variable capital (again an exaggerated assumption) and therefore laid out his entire capital on wages. With a given working day, the level of exploitation of labour depends on its average intensity, and, conversely, given the intensity, on the length of the working day. The rate of surplus-value depends on the level of exploitation of labour, and thus, for a given mass of variable capital, the size of the surplus-value and the amount of profit also depend on this. The special interest possessed by the capital in one sphere, as distinct from the total capital, in the exploitation of the workers directly employed by it, is paralleled by the interest of the individual capitalist, as distinct from his sphere, in the exploitation of the workers exploited personally by him.

Each particular sphere of capital, however, and each individual capitalist, has the same interest in the productivity of the social labour applied by the total capital. For two things are dependent on this. Firstly, the mass of use-values in which the average profit is expressed; and this is important for two reasons, as it serves both as the accumulation fund for new capital and as the revenue fund for consumption. Secondly, the value level of the total capital advanced (both constant and variable), which, with a given size of surplus-value or profit for the entire capitalist class, determines the profit rate, or the profit on a particular quantity of capital. The specific productivity of labour in one particular sphere, or in one individual business in this sphere, concerns the capitalists directly involved in it only in so far as it enables this particular sphere to make an extra profit in relation to the total capital, or the individual capitalist in relation to his sphere.

We thus have a mathematically exact demonstration of why the capitalists, no matter how little love is lost among them in their mutual competition, are nevertheless united by a real freemasonry vis-à-vis the working class as a whole.

The price of production includes the average profit. And what we call price of production is in fact the same thing that Adam Smith calls 'natural price', Ricardo 'price of production' or 'cost of production', and the Physiocrats '*prix nécessaire*', though none of these people explained the difference between price of production and value. We call it the price of production because in the long term it is the condition of supply, the condition for the reproduction of commodities, in each particular sphere of production.[33] We can also understand why those very economists who oppose the determination of commodity value by labour-time, by the quantity of labour contained in the commodity, always speak of the prices of production as the centres around which market prices fluctuate. They can allow themselves this because the price of production is already a completely external-ized and *prima facie* irrational form of commodity value, a form that appears in competition and is therefore present in the con-sciousness of the vulgar capitalist and consequently also in that of the vulgar economist.

*

We saw in the course of our argument how market value (and everything that was said about this applies with the necessary limitations also to price of production) involves a surplus profit for those producing under the best conditions in any particular sphere of production. Excluding all cases of crisis and over-production, this holds good for all market prices, no matter how they might diverge from market values or market prices of production. The concept of market price means that the same price

33. Malthus [*Principles of Political Economy*, loc. cit., pp. 77–8].

is paid for all commodities of the same kind, even if these are produced under very different individual conditions and may therefore have very different cost prices. (We say nothing here about surplus profits that result from monopolies in the customary sense of the term, whether artificial or natural.)

But a surplus profit can also arise if certain spheres of production are in a position to opt out of the transformation of their commodity values into prices of production, and the consequent reduction of their profits to the average profit. In the Part on ground-rent, we shall have to consider the further configuration of these two forms of surplus profit.

Chapter 11: The Effects of General Fluctuations in Wages on the Prices of Production

Let the average composition of the social capital be $80_c + 20_v$, and profit 20 per cent. In this case the rate of surplus-value is 100 per cent. A general rise in wages, everything else being equal, means a fall in the rate of surplus-value. For the average capital, profit and surplus-value coincide. Say that wages rise by 25 per cent. The same amount of labour which previously cost 20 to set in motion now costs 25. We then have a turnover value of $80_c + 25_v + 15_s$, instead of $80_c + 20_v + 20_s$. The labour set in motion by the variable capital still produces a value sum of 40, as before. But if v rises from 20 to 25, the excess s or p is now only 15. A profit of 15 on 105 is $14\frac{2}{7}$ per cent, and this would be the new average rate of profit. Since the production price of commodities produced by the average capital coincides with their value, the production price of these commodities would not have changed. The increase in wages would therefore involve a decline in profit, but no change in the value of commodities or their price of production.

Previously, when the average rate of profit was 20 per cent, the production price of the commodities produced in one turnover period was equal to their cost price plus a profit of 20 per cent on this, i.e. $k + kp' = k + \frac{20k}{100}$; here k is a variable magnitude differing according to the value of the means of production that go into the commodities and according to the amount of depreciation that the fixed capital employed in their production surrenders to the product. After the rise in wages, the production price would now come to $k + \frac{14\ 2/7\ k}{100}$.

Let us first take a capital whose composition is lower than the original composition of the average social capital $80_c + 20_v$ (which has now been changed to $76\frac{4}{21}{}_c + 23\frac{17}{21}{}_v$);* for example,

* i.e. $80_c + 25_v$ reduced to a percentage.

$50_c + 50_v$. If we assume for the sake of simplification that the entire fixed capital goes into the annual product as depreciation and that the turnover time is the same as in case I, the production price of the annual product would have amounted, before the rise in wages, to $50_c + 50_v + 20_p = 120$. A wage rise of 25 per cent means a rise in variable capital from 50 to $62\frac{1}{2}$, for the same amount of labour set in motion. If the annual product were sold at the former production price of 120, this would give us $50_c + 62\frac{1}{2}_v + 7\frac{1}{2}_p$, i.e. a profit rate of $6\frac{2}{3}$ per cent. The new average rate of profit, however, is $14\frac{2}{7}$ per cent, and since we take all other circumstances as remaining the same, our capital of $50_c + 62\frac{1}{2}_v$ must also make this profit. A capital of $112\frac{1}{2}$, at a profit rate of $14\frac{2}{7}$ per cent, makes a profit of $16\frac{1}{14}$. The production price of the commodities it produces is therefore now $50_c + 62\frac{1}{2}_v + 16\frac{1}{14}_p = 128\frac{8}{14}$. As a result of the wage rise of 25 per cent, the price of production of the same quantity of the same commodity has risen from 120 to $128\frac{8}{14}$, or by more than 7 per cent.

Let us now take a sphere of production with a higher composition than the average capital, e.g. $92_c + 8_v$. The original average profit here is also 20, and if we again assume that the entire fixed capital goes into the annual product, and that the turnover time is the same as in the first two cases, the production price of the commodities is also 120.

As a result of the 25 per cent wage rise, the variable capital grows from 8 to 10, for the same amount of labour, and the cost price of the commodities therefore grows from 100 to 102, while the average profit rate of 20 per cent falls to $14\frac{2}{7}$ per cent. But $100 : 14\frac{2}{7} = 102 : 14\frac{4}{7}$. The profit that now accrues to 102 is therefore $14\frac{4}{7}$, and the total product is therefore sold at $k + kp' = 102 + 14\frac{4}{7} = 116\frac{4}{7}$. The production price has thus fallen from 120 to $116\frac{4}{7}$, or by $3\frac{3}{7}$.

The result of the wage rise of 25 per cent is thus as follows:

(I) for capital of an average social composition, the commodity's price of production remains unchanged;

(II) for capital of a lower composition, the production price rises, though not in the same ratio as the profit has fallen;

(III) for capital of a higher composition, the production price falls, though again not in the same ratio as the profit.

Since the production price of commodities produced by the average capital has remained the same, namely equal to the value of the product, the sum of production prices for the products of all capitals has also remained the same, namely equal to the sum of values produced by the total capital; the rises on the one hand and the falls on the other balance out at the level of the socially average capital, taking this over the entire capital of the society.

If the production price for commodities in example II rises, while it falls in example III, this opposite effect which is produced by the fall in the rate of surplus-value or the general rise in wages already shows how there can be no corresponding compensation in prices for the rise in wages, since in example III the fall in the price of production can in no way compensate the capitalists for the fall in their profit, while in example II the rise in price still does not prevent a fall in profit. In each case, rather, both where the price rises and where it falls, profit is the same as for the average capital, whose prices remain unaffected. It is the same for both II and III, a fall in the average profit of $5\frac{5}{7}$ per cent, or somewhat over 25 per cent [of the original rate]. It follows from this that, if the price did not rise in example II and fall in example III, II would be sold at less than the new, lower, average profit, and III at more than this. It is immediately clear that according to whether 50, 25 or 10 out of every 100 units of capital are laid out on labour, a rise in wages will necessarily have very different effects on a capitalist who lays out a tenth of his capital on wages, one who lays out a quarter, and one who lays out a half. The rise in the price of production on the one hand and its fall on the other, according to whether the capital involved has a lower or higher composition than the social average, is accomplished only by the process of equalization at the new, lower, average rate of profit.

How then would the prices of production of commodities produced by capitals that diverge in contrary directions from the social average composition be affected by a general fall in wages, with a corresponding general rise in the rate of profit, and hence in average profits? We have simply to turn the above example round to obtain the result (a result which Ricardo does not investigate).

I. Average capital $80_c + 20_v = 100$; rate of surplus-value 100 per cent; production price = commodity value = $80_c + 20_v + 20_p = 120$; rate of profit 20 per cent. If wages fall by a quarter, the same constant capital will be set in motion by 15_v instead of by 20_v. We then have a commodity value of $80_c + 15_v + 25_p = 120$. The quantity of labour produced by v remains unaffected, except that the new value it creates is differently distributed between capitalist and worker. The surplus-value has risen from 20 to 25, and the rate of surplus-value from $\frac{20}{20}$ to $\frac{25}{15}$, i.e. from 100 per cent to $166\frac{2}{3}$ per cent. The profit is now 25 on 95, and the profit rate therefore $26\frac{6}{19}$ per cent. The new percentage composition of capital is now $84\frac{4}{19}c + 15\frac{15}{19}v = 100$.

II. Below average composition. Originally $50_c + 50_v$ as above. The wage cut of a quarter reduces v to $37\frac{1}{2}$, and the total capital advanced therefore to $50_c + 37\frac{1}{2}v = 87\frac{1}{2}$. If we apply to this the new rate of profit of $26\frac{6}{19}$ per cent, we get $100:26\frac{6}{19} = 87\frac{1}{2}:23\frac{1}{8}$. The same mass of commodities that previously cost 120 now costs $87\frac{1}{2} + 23\frac{1}{8} = 110\frac{10}{19}$; a fall in price of almost 10.

III. Above average composition. Originally $92_c + 8_v = 100$. The wage cut of a quarter reduces 8_v to 6_v, and the total capital to 98. $100:26\frac{6}{19} = 98:25\frac{15}{19}$. The production price of the commodities, which was previously $100 + 20 = 120$, is now, after the fall in wages, $98 + 25\frac{15}{19} = 123\frac{15}{19}$; i.e. a rise of almost 4.

We can thus see how it is only necessary to pursue the same development as before in the reverse direction and make the requisite changes; the conclusion is that a general fall in wages leads to a general rise in surplus-value, in the rate of surplus-value, and with other things remaining equal, also in the profit rate, even if in a different proportion; it leads to a fall in production prices for the commodity products of capitals of lower than average composition and a rise in production prices for the commodity products of capitals of higher than average composition. Exactly the opposite result as that which arose from a general rise in wages.[34] In both cases, that of a rise in wages and that of a fall, the working day is assumed to remain the same, and so are the prices of all necessary means of subsistence. A fall in wages is thus only possible here either if wages previously stood above the normal price of labour, or if they are now to be pushed below it.

34. It is quite characteristic of Ricardo, whose mode of procedure here is of course different from ours, as he did not understand the adjustment of values to production prices, that he did not once consider this possibility, but only the first case, a rise in wages and its influence on the production prices of commodities.* And the *servum pecus imitatorum*† did not even succeed in making this quite self-evident and in fact tautological practical application.

* *Principles*, Chapter I, vii.

† 'slavish breed of imitators' – i.e. in this case Ricardo's followers. A paraphrase of a passage in Horace's letters, Book 1, letter 19: '*O imitatores, servum pecus*' ('oh imitators, you slavish breed').

How the matter is affected if the rise or fall in wages derives from a change in the values and hence in the production prices of commodities that customarily go into the workers' consumption will in part be further investigated below, in the section on ground-rent. The following points, however, have to be made here once and for all:

If the rise or fall in wages results from a change in the value of the necessary means of subsistence, the only modification of the process analysed above occurs when the commodities whose price-changes serve to increase or lessen the variable capital also enter as constituent elements into the constant capital and hence do not simply affect wages. But in so far as they do only affect wages, the above argument contains all that has to be said.

In this entire chapter, we have assumed that the establishment of a general rate of profit, an average profit, and thus also the transformation of values into production prices, is a given fact. All that has been asked is how a general rise or fall in wages affects the prices of production of commodities, prices we have assumed to be given in advance. This is a very secondary question compared with the other important points which have been dealt with in this Part. Yet it is the only question Ricardo deals with which is relevant here, and as we shall see he deals with it only in a one-sided and inadequate way.*

* See *Theories of Surplus-Value*, Part II, pp. 189–203.

Chapter 12: Supplementary Remarks

I. THE CAUSES OF A CHANGE IN THE PRICE OF PRODUCTION

The price of production of a commodity can vary for only two reasons:

(1) A change in the general rate of profit. This is possible only if the average rate of surplus-value itself alters, or, given an average rate of surplus-value, the ratio between the sum of surplus-value appropriated and the total social capital advanced.

In so far as the change in the rate of surplus-value does not rest on the depression of wages below their normal level, or a rise above this – and movements of this kind are never more than oscillations – it can occur only because the value of labour-power has either fallen or risen; both of these are impossible without a change in the productivity of that labour which produces the means of subsistence, i.e. without a change in value of the commodities that are consumed by the worker.

Alternatively, there may be a change in the ratio between the sum of surplus-value appropriated and the total social capital advanced. Since this change does not arise from the rate of surplus-value, it must proceed from the total capital, and moreover from its constant part. The mass of this, in its technical aspect, is increased or reduced in proportion to the labour-power bought by the variable capital, and the sum of its value then rises or falls with the growth or decline in the mass itself; thus the mass of constant capital rises or falls similarly in proportion to the sum of value of the variable capital. If the same labour sets more constant capital in motion, it has become more productive, and vice versa. Thus a change has taken place in the productivity of labour and a change must have occurred in the value of certain commodities.

Both of these cases are therefore covered by the following law: if the production price of a commodity changes as the result of a change in the general rate of profit, its own value may well remain unaffected. However, there must have been a change in its value relative to other commodities.

(2) The general rate of profit remains unaltered. In this case the production price of a commodity can change only because its value has altered; because more or less labour is required for its actual reproduction, whether because of a change in the productivity of the labour that produces the commodity in its final form, or in that of the labour producing those commodities that go towards producing it. The price of production of cotton yarn may fall either because raw cotton is produced more cheaply, or because the work of spinning has become more productive as a result of better machinery.

Price of production, as we have already shown, is $k + p$, cost price plus profit. But this $= k + kp'$, where k, the cost price, is a magnitude which varies according to the different spheres of production and is everywhere equal to the value of the constant and variable capital used up to produce the commodity, while p' is the average rate of profit calculated as a percentage. If $k = 200$ and $p' = 20$ per cent, the price of production $k + kp' = 200 + 200 \times \frac{20}{100} = 200 + 40 = 240$. It is evident that this price of production may remain the same even though the value of the commodity changes.

All changes in the price of production of a commodity can be ultimately reduced to a change in value, but not all changes in the value of a commodity need find expression in a change in the price of production, since this is not determined simply by the value of the particular commodity in question, but rather by the total value of all commodities. A change in commodity A, therefore, may be balanced by an opposite change in commodity B, so that the general proportion remains the same.

2. THE PRODUCTION PRICE OF COMMODITIES OF AVERAGE COMPOSITION

We have already seen that the divergence of price of production from value arises for the following reasons:

(1) because the average profit is added to the cost price of a commodity, rather than the surplus-value contained in it;

(2) because the price of production of a commodity that diverges in this way from its value enters as an element into the cost price of other commodities, which means that a divergence from the value of the means of production consumed may already be contained in the cost price, quite apart from the divergence that may arise for the commodity itself from the difference between average profit and surplus-value.

It is quite possible, accordingly, for the cost price to diverge from the value sum of the elements of which this component of the price of production is composed, even in the case of commodities that are produced by capitals of average composition. Let us assume that the average composition is $80_c + 20_v$. It is possible now that, for the actual individual capitals that are composed in this way, the 80_c may be greater or less than the value of c, the constant capital, since this c is composed of commodities whose prices of production are different from their values. The 20_v can similarly diverge from its value, if the spending of wages on consumption involves commodities whose prices of production are different from their values. The workers must work for a greater or lesser amount of time in order to buy back these commodities (to replace them) and must therefore perform more or less necessary labour than would be needed if the prices of production of their necessary means of subsistence did coincide with their values.

Yet this possibility in no way affects the correctness of the principles put forward for commodities of average composition. The quantity of profit that falls to the share of these commodities is equal to the quantity of surplus-value contained in them. For the above capital, with its composition of $80_c + 20_v$, for example, the important thing as far as the determination of surplus-value is concerned is not whether these figures are the expression of actual values, but rather what their mutual relationship is; i.e. that v is one-fifth of the total capital and c is four-fifths. As soon as this is the case, as assumed above, the surplus-value v produces is equal to the average profit. On the other hand, because it is equal to the average profit, the price of production = cost price + profit = $k + p = k + s$, which is equal in practice to the commodity's value. In other words, an increase or decrease in wages in this case leaves $k + p$ unaffected, just as it would leave the commodity's value unaffected, and simply brings about a corresponding converse movement, a decrease or increase, on the side of the profit rate. If an increase or decrease in wages did affect the price of commodities in this case, the profit rate in these spheres of average composition would come to stand below or above its level in the other spheres. It is only in so far as their prices remain unaltered that the spheres of average composition maintain the same level of profit as the others. The same thing thus takes place in practice as if the products of these spheres were sold at their actual values. For if commodities are sold at their actual values, it is clear that with other circumstances remaining the same, a rise or fall in wages provokes a corresponding fall or rise in profit but no change in the commodity's value, and that in no circumstances can a rise or fall in wages ever affect the value of commodities, but only the size of the surplus-value.

3. THE CAPITALIST'S GROUNDS FOR COMPENSATION

It has been said that competition equalizes profit rates between the different spheres of production to produce an average rate of profit, and that this is precisely the way in which the values of products from these various spheres are transformed into prices of production. This happens, moreover, by the continual transfer of capital from one sphere to another, where profit stands above the average for the time being. Something that must also be considered here, however, is the cycle of fat and lean years that follow one another in a given branch of industry over a particular period of time, and the fluctuations in profit that these involve. This uninterrupted emigration and immigration of capitals that takes place between various spheres of production produces rising and falling movements in the profit rate which more or less balance one another out and thus tend to reduce the profit rate everywhere to the same common and general level.

This movement of capitals is always brought about in the first place by the state of market prices, which raise profits above the general average level in one place, and reduce it below the average in another. We are still leaving commercial capital out of consideration for the time being, as we have yet to introduce it, but as is shown by the paroxysms of speculation in certain favoured articles that suddenly break out, this can withdraw masses of capital from one line of business with extraordinary rapidity and fling them just as suddenly into another. In every sphere of actual production, however, industry, agriculture, mining, etc., the transfer of capital from one sector to another presents significant difficulties, particularly on account of the fixed capital involved. Experience shows, moreover, that if one branch of industry, e.g. cotton, yields extraordinarily high profits at one time, it may bring in very low profits at another, or even run a loss, so that in a particular cycle of years the average profit is more or less the same as in other branches. Capital soon learns to reckon with this experience.

What competition does *not* show, however, is the determination of values that governs the movement of production; that it is values that stand behind the prices of production and ultimately determine them. Competition exhibits rather the following phenomena: (1) average profits that are independent of the organic composition of capital in the various spheres of production, i.e. independent of the mass of living labour appropriated in a given sphere of exploitation; (2) rises and falls in the prices of production as a result of changes in the wage level – a phenomenon which at first sight seems completely to contradict the value relationship of commodities; (3) fluctuations in market prices that reduce the average market price of a commodity over a given period of time, not to its market *value* but rather to a market price of production that diverges from this market value and is something very different. All these phenomena *seem* to contradict both the determination of value by labour-time and the nature of surplus-value as consisting of unpaid surplus labour. *In competition, therefore, everything appears upside down.* The finished configuration of economic relations, as these are visible on the surface, in their actual existence, and therefore also in the notions with which the bearers and agents of these relations seek to gain an understanding of them, is very different from the configuration of their inner core, which is essential but concealed, and the concept corresponding to it. It is in fact the very reverse and antithesis of this.

Moreover, as soon as capitalist production has reached a certain level of development, the equalization between the various rates of profit in individual spheres which produces the general rate of profit does not just take place through the interplay of attraction and repulsion in which market prices attract or repel capital. Once average prices and the market prices corresponding to them have been established for a certain length of time, the various individual capitalists become *conscious* that *certain differences* are balanced out in this equalization, and so they take these into account in their calculations among themselves. These differences are actively present in the capitalists' view of things and are taken into account by them as grounds for compensation.

The basic notion in this connection is that of average profit itself, the idea that capitals of equal size must yield equal profits in the same period of time. This is based in turn on the idea that capital in each sphere of production has to participate according to its size in the total surplus-value extorted from the workers by the total social capital; or that each particular capital should be viewed simply as a fragment of the total capital and each capitalist in fact as a shareholder in the whole social enterprise, partaking in the overall profit in proportion to the size of his share of capital.

This idea is then the basis of the capitalist's calculation, for example, that a capital that turns over more slowly, either because the commodity in question remains in the production process for a longer period or because it has to be sold on distant markets, still charges the profit it would otherwise lose by raising its price and compensates itself in this way. Another example is how capital investments that are exposed to greater risk, as in shipping, for instance, receive compensation through increased prices. Once capitalist production is properly developed, and with it the insurance system, the risk is in fact the same for all spheres of production (see Corbet); * those more endangered simply pay higher insurance premiums and receive these back in the price of their commodities. In practice this always boils down to the situation that any circumstance that makes one capital investment less profitable and another one more so (and all these investments are taken as equally necessary, within certain limits) is invariably taken into account as a valid reason for compensation, without there being any need for the constant repetition of the activities of competition in order to demonstrate the justification for including such motives or factors in the capitalist's calculations. He simply forgets (or rather he no longer sees it, since competition does not show it to him) that all these grounds for compensation that make themselves mutually felt in the reciprocal calculation of commodity prices by the capitalists in different branches of production

* *An Inquiry into the Causes and Modes of the Wealth of Individuals*, London, 1841, pp. 100–102.

are simply related to the fact that they all have an equal claim on the common booty, the total surplus-value, in proportion to their capital. It *appears* to them, rather, that the profit which they pocket is something different from the surplus-value they extort; that the grounds for compensation do not simply equalize their participation in the total surplus-value, but that they actually *create profit itself*, since profit seems to derive simply from the addition to the cost price made with one justification or another.

Finally, what was said in Chapter 7, p. 236, about the capitalist's ideas as to the source of surplus-value applies also to the average profit. The only way in which the situation looks different in this second case is that for a given market price and a given level of exploitation of labour, savings on the cost price depend on individual talent, attention, etc.

Part Three

The Law of the Tendential Fall in the Rate of Profit

Chapter 13: The Law Itself

Once wages and the working day are given, a variable capital, which we can take as 100, represents a definite number of workers set in motion; it is an index of this number. Say that £100 provides the wages of 100 workers for one week. If these 100 workers perform as much surplus labour as necessary labour, they work as much time for the capitalist each day, for the production of surplus-value, as they do for themselves, for the reproduction of their wages, and their total value product would then be £200, the surplus-value they produce amounting to £100. The rate of surplus-value $\frac{s}{v}$ would be 100 per cent. Yet, as we have seen, this rate of surplus-value will be expressed in very different rates of profit, according to the differing scale of the constant capital c and hence the total capital C, since the rate of profit is $\frac{s}{C}$. If the rate of surplus-value is 100 per cent, we have:

if $c = 50$ and $v = 100$, then $p' = \frac{100}{150} = 66\frac{2}{3}$ per cent;

if $c = 100$ and $v = 100$, then $p' = \frac{100}{200} = 50$ per cent;

if $c = 200$ and $v = 100$, then $p' = \frac{100}{300} = 33\frac{1}{3}$ per cent;

if $c = 300$ and $v = 100$, then $p' = \frac{100}{400} = 25$ per cent;

if $c = 400$ and $v = 100$, then $p' = \frac{100}{500} = 20$ per cent.

The same rate of surplus-value, therefore, and an unchanged level of exploitation of labour, is expressed in a falling rate of profit, as the value of the constant capital and hence the total capital grows with the constant capital's material volume.

If we further assume now that this gradual change in the composition of capital does not just characterize certain individual spheres of production, but occurs in more or less all spheres, or at least the decisive ones, and that it therefore involves changes in the average organic composition of the total capital belonging to a given society, then this gradual growth in the constant capital, in relation to the variable, must necessarily result in a *gradual fall in the general rate of profit*, given that the rate of surplus-value, or the level of exploitation of labour by capital, remains the same. Moreover, it has been shown to be a law of the capitalist mode of production that its development does in fact involve a relative decline in the relation of variable capital to constant, and hence also to the total capital set in motion.* This simply means that the same number of workers or the same quantity of labour-power that is made available by a variable capital of a given value, as a result of the specific methods of production that develop within capitalist production, sets in motion, works up, and productively consumes, within the same period, an ever-growing mass of means of labour, machinery and fixed capital of all kinds, and raw and ancillary materials – in other words, the same number of workers operate with a constant capital of ever-growing scale. This progressive decline in the variable capital in relation to the constant capital, and hence in relation to the total capital as well, is identical with the progressively rising organic composition, on average, of the social capital as a whole. It is just another expression for the progressive development of the social productivity of labour, which is shown by the way that the growing use of machinery and fixed capital generally enables more raw and ancillary materials to be transformed into products in the same time by the same number of workers, i.e. with less labour. There corresponds to this growing volume of constant capital – although this expresses only at a certain remove the growth in the actual mass of use-values which the constant capital consists of in material terms – a continual cheapening of the product. Each individual product, taken by itself, contains a smaller sum of labour than at a lower stage of development of production, where the capital laid out on labour stands in a far higher ratio to that laid out on means of production. The hypothetical series we constructed at the opening of this chapter therefore expresses the actual tendency of capitalist production. With the progressive decline in the variable capital in relation to the constant capital, this tendency leads to a rising organic composition of the total capital, and the direct result of

* See Volume 1, Chapter 25, 2, pp. 772–81.

this is that the rate of surplus-value, with the level of exploitation of labour remaining the same or even rising, is expressed in a steadily falling general rate of profit. (We shall show later on why this fall does not present itself in such an absolute form, but rather more in the tendency to a progressive fall.) * The progressive tendency for the general rate of profit to fall is thus simply *the expression, peculiar to the capitalist mode of production*, of the progressive development of the social productivity of labour. This does not mean that the rate of profit may not fall temporarily for other reasons as well, but it does prove that it is a self-evident necessity, deriving from the nature of the capitalist mode of production itself, that as it advances the general average rate of surplus-value must be expressed in a falling general rate of profit. Since the mass of living labour applied continuously declines in relation to the mass of objectified labour that it sets in motion, i.e. the productively consumed means of production, the part of this living labour that is unpaid and objectified in surplus-value must also stand in an ever-decreasing ratio to the value of the total capital applied. But this ratio between the mass of surplus-value and the total capital applied in fact constitutes the rate of profit, which must therefore steadily fall.

Simple as the law appears from the above arguments, not one of the previous writers on economics succeeded in discovering it, as we shall see later on.† These economists perceived the phenomenon, but tortured themselves with their contradictory attempts to explain it. And given the great importance that this law has for capitalist production, one might well say that it forms the mystery around whose solution the whole of political economy since Adam Smith revolves and that the difference between the various schools since Adam Smith consists in the different attempts made to solve it. If we consider, on the other hand, how previous political economy has fumbled around with the distinction between constant and variable capital, but has never managed to formulate this in any definite way; how it has never presented surplus-value as something separate from profit, nor profit in general, in its pure form, as distinct from the various constituents of profit which have attained an autonomous position towards each other (such as industrial profit, commercial profit, interest, ground-rent); how it has essentially never analysed the differences

* See below, Chapter 14.
† See *Theories of Surplus-Value*, Part II, pp. 438–69 and 542–6.

in the organic composition of capital, and hence has not analysed the formation of the general rate of profit either – then it ceases to be a puzzle that political economy has never found this puzzle's solution.

We are deliberately putting forward this law before depicting the decomposition of profit into various categories which have become mutually autonomous. The independence of this presentation from the division of profit into various portions, which accrue to different categories of persons, shows from the start how the law in its generality is independent of that division and of the mutual relationships of the categories of profit deriving from it. Profit, as we speak of it here, is simply another name for surplus-value itself, only now depicted in relation to the total capital, instead of to the variable capital from which it derives. The fall in the rate of profit thus expresses the falling ratio between surplus-value itself and the total capital advanced; it is therefore independent of any distribution of this surplus-value we may care to make among the various categories.

We have seen that at one stage of capitalist development, when the composition of capital $c:v$ is $50:100$ for example, a rate of surplus-value of 100 per cent is expressed in a rate of profit of $66\frac{2}{3}$ per cent, while at a higher stage of development, where $c:v$ is $400:100$ say, the same rate of surplus-value is expressed in a rate of profit of only 20 per cent. What applies to different successive stages of development in one country applies also to different countries that find themselves in differing stages of development at the same point in time. In the undeveloped country, where the composition of capital is on the average as first mentioned, the general rate of profit would be $66\frac{2}{3}$ per cent, while in the country at a much higher level of development it would be 20 per cent.

The distinction between the two national rates of profit could disappear, or even be reversed, if in the less developed country labour was less productive, i.e. a greater quantity of labour was expressed in a smaller quantity of the same commodity and a greater exchange-value in less use-value, so that the worker would have to spend a greater portion of his time in reproducing his own means of subsistence or their value, leaving a smaller portion for producing surplus-value, thus providing less surplus labour, so that the rate of surplus-value would be lower. If the worker in the less advanced country worked two-thirds of the day for himself, for instance, and one-third for the capitalist, then, on the assumptions of the above example, the same labour-power would be paid $133\frac{1}{3}$ and would provide a surplus of only $66\frac{2}{3}$. To the variable capital of $133\frac{1}{3}$ there would correspond a constant capital of 50. The rate of surplus-value would now come to $133\frac{1}{3}:66\frac{2}{3} = 50$ per cent, and the rate of profit to $183\frac{1}{3}:66\frac{2}{3}$ or approximately $36\frac{1}{2}$ per cent.

Since we have not investigated up till now the various components into which profit is divided, so that these do not exist for us as yet, the following point is anticipated here simply for the sake of avoiding any misunderstandings. When comparison is made between countries at different levels of development, and particularly between countries of developed capitalist production and those where labour is not yet formally subsumed * by capital although in reality the worker is already exploited by the capitalist (in India, for example, where the ryot operates as an independent peasant farmer, and his production is not yet subsumed under capital, although the money-lender may well extort from him in the form of interest not only his entire surplus labour, but even – to put it in capitalist terms – a part of his wages), it would be quite wrong to seek to measure the national rate of profit by the level of the national rate of interest. Interest here includes both the entire profit and more than the profit, whereas in countries where capitalist production is developed it simply expresses an aliquot part of the surplus-value or profit produced. Moreover, in the former case the rate of interest is predominantly determined by factors such as the level of advances by money-lenders to the big landowners who are the recipients of ground-rent, which have nothing at all to do with profit but rather express the extent to which the money-lender himself appropriates this ground-rent.

In countries where capitalist production stands at different levels of development and between which the organic composition of capital consequently varies, the rate of surplus-value (as one factor that determines the rate of profit) may be higher in a country where the normal working day is shorter than in one where it is longer. Firstly, if the English working day of 10 hours is equal to an Austrian working day of 14 hours, on account of its higher intensity, then, given the same division of the working day, 5 hours' surplus labour in the one country may represent a higher

* On the concepts of 'formal' and 'real subsumption', see 'Results of the Immediate Process of Production', published as an Appendix to the Pelican Marx Library edition of *Capital* Volume 1, pp. 1019–38.

value on the world market than 7 hours' in the other. Secondly, a greater part of the working day in England may form surplus labour than in Austria.

The law of the falling rate of profit, as expressing the same or even a rising rate of surplus-value, means in other words: taking any particular quantity of average social capital, e.g. a capital of 100, an ever greater portion of this is represented by means of labour and an ever lesser portion by living labour. Since the total mass of living labour added to the means of production falls in relation to the value of these means of production, so too does the unpaid labour, and the portion of value in which it is represented, in relation to the value of the total capital advanced. Alternatively, an ever smaller aliquot part of the total capital laid out is converted into living labour, and hence the total capital absorbs ever less surplus labour in relation to its size, even though the ratio between the unpaid and paid parts of the labour applied may at the same time be growing. The relative decline in the variable capital and increase in the constant capital, even while both portions grow in absolute terms, is, as we have said, simply another expression for the increased productivity of labour.

Say that a capital of 100 consists of $80_c + 20_v$, and the latter represents 20 workers. Let the rate of surplus-value be 100 per cent, so that the workers work half the day for themselves and half the day for the capitalist. In a less developed country, the capital might be $20_c + 80_v$, with the latter portion representing 80 workers. But these workers might need two-thirds of the working day for themselves and work only one-third of the day for the capitalist. Taking everything else as equal, the workers in the first case produce a value of 40, in the second case a value of 120. The first capital produces $80_c + 20_v + 20_s = 120$, rate of profit 20 per cent; the second capital produces $20_c + 80_v + 40_s = 140$, rate of profit 40 per cent. This rate is thus as large again as in the first case, even though the rate of surplus-value here was 100 per cent, twice that in the second case, where it is only 50 per cent. The reason for this is that a capital of the same size appropriates in the first case the surplus labour of only 20 workers, as against that of 80 workers in the second case.

The law of a progressive fall in the rate of profit, or the relative decline in the surplus labour appropriated in comparison with the mass of objectified labour that the living labour sets in motion, in no way prevents the absolute mass of labour set in motion and exploited by the social capital from growing, and with it the absolute mass of surplus labour it appropriates; any more than it prevents the capitals under the control of individual capitalists from controlling a growing mass of labour and hence of surplus labour, this latter even if there is no increase in the number of workers under their command.

If we take a given working population, of 2 million for example, and further assume that the length and intensity of the average working day is given, as well as wages, and hence also the relationship between necessary and surplus labour, then the total labour of these 2 million workers always produces the same magnitude of value, and the same thing is true of their surplus labour, as expressed in surplus-value. But as the mass of constant (fixed and circulating) capital set in motion by this labour grows, so there is a fall in the ratio between this magnitude and the value of the constant capital, which grows with its mass, even if not in the same proportion. This ratio falls, and with it the profit rate, even though capital still commands the same mass of living labour as before and absorbs the same mass of surplus labour. If the ratio changes, this is not because the mass of living labour falls but rather because the mass of already objectified labour that it sets in motion rises. The decline is relative, not absolute, and it has in fact nothing whatsoever to do with the absolute amount of the labour and surplus labour set in motion. The fall in the rate of profit does not arise from an absolute decline in the variable component of the total capital but simply from a relative decline, from its decrease in comparison with the constant component.

What holds when the amount of labour and surplus labour is at a constant level holds also when the number of workers is growing, and when, accordingly, under the given assumptions, the mass of labour under capital's command is growing in general, and its unpaid portion, surplus labour, is growing in particular. If the working population rises from 2 to 3 millions and the amount of variable capital laid out on wages similarly becomes 3 million instead of 2, while the constant capital rises from 4 million to 15 million, then under the given assumptions (working day and rate of surplus-value constant) the mass of surplus labour and surplus-value still rises by a half, by 50 per cent, from 2 to 3 million. It is none the less the case, however, that despite this growth of 50 per cent in the absolute mass of surplus labour and hence surplus-value, the ratio of variable capital to constant would fall from

2:4 to 3:15, and the relationship between the surplus-value and the total capital would stand as follows (in millions):

I. $4_c + 2_v + 2_s$; $C = 6$, $p' = 33\frac{1}{3}$ per cent.
II. $15_c + 3_v + 3_s$; $C = 18$, $p' = 16\frac{2}{3}$ per cent.

While the mass of surplus-value has risen by a half, the rate of profit has fallen to half its previous level. But profit is nothing more than the surplus-value reckoned in terms of the social capital, and the mass of profit, therefore, its absolute magnitude, is the same as the absolute magnitude of surplus-value, considering it on a social scale. The absolute magnitude of profit, its total mass, would thus have grown by 50 per cent, despite the enormous decline in the ratio between this mass of profit and the total capital advanced, i.e. despite the enormous decline in the general rate of profit. The number of workers employed by capital, i.e. the absolute mass of labour it sets in motion, and hence the absolute mass of surplus labour it absorbs, the mass of surplus-value it produces, and the absolute mass of profit it produces, *can* therefore grow, and progressively so, despite the progressive fall in the rate of profit. This not only *can* but *must* be the case – discounting transient fluctuations – on the basis of capitalist production.

The capitalist production process is essentially, and at the same time, a process of accumulation. We have shown how, with the progress of capitalist production, the mass of value that must simply be reproduced and maintained rises and grows with the rising productivity of labour, even if the labour-power applied remains constant. But as the social productivity of labour develops, so the mass of use-values produced grows still more, and the means of production form a portion of these. The additional labour, moreover, which has to be appropriated in order for this additional wealth to be transformed back into capital does not depend on the value of these means of production (including means of subsistence), since the worker is not concerned in the labour process with the value of the means of production but rather with their use-value. Accumulation itself, however, and the concentration of capital it involves, is simply a material means for increasing productivity. And this growth in the means of production entails a growth in the working population, the creation of a surplus population that corresponds to the surplus capital or even exceeds its overall requirements, thus leading to an over-population of workers. A momentary excess of surplus capital over the working population it commands has a double effect. On the one hand it will gradually increase the working population by raising wages, hence attenuating the destructive influences that decimate the offspring of the workers and making marriage easier, while on the other hand, by using methods that create relative surplus-value (introduction and improvement of machinery), it produces far more quickly an artificial and relative over-population, which in turn is the forcing house for a really rapid increase in the number of people – since, under capitalist production, misery produces population. It thus follows from the very nature of the capitalist accumulation process, and this process is simply one aspect of the capitalist process of production, that the increased mass of means of production designed to be turned into capital finds a correspondingly increased and even excessive working population available for exploitation. As the process of production and accumulation advances, therefore, the mass of surplus labour that can be and is appropriated *must* grow, and with it too the absolute mass of profit appropriated by the social capital. But the same laws of production and accumulation mean that the value of the constant capital increases along with its mass, and progressively more quickly than that of the variable portion of capital which is converted into living labour. The same laws, therefore, produce both a growing absolute mass of profit for the social capital, and a falling rate of profit.

We entirely leave aside here the fact that the same amount of value represents a progressively rising mass of use-values and satisfactions, with the progress of capitalist production and with the corresponding development of the productivity of social labour and multiplication of branches of production and hence products.

The course of the development of capitalist production and accumulation requires increasingly large-scale labour processes and hence increasingly large dimensions and increasingly large advances of capital for each individual establishment. The growing concentration of capitals (accompanied at the same time, though in lesser degree, by a growing number of capitalists) is therefore both one of its material conditions and one of the results that it itself produces. Hand in hand with this, in a relationship of reciprocity, goes progressive expropriation of the more or less immediate producers. In this way a situation comes about in which the individual capitalists have command of increasingly large armies of workers (no matter how much the variable capital may fall in relation to the constant capital), so that the mass of surplus-value and hence profit which they appropriate grows, along with and despite the fall in the rate of profit. The reasons that concentrate massive armies of workers under the command of individual capitalists are precisely the same reasons as also swell the amount of fixed capital employed, as well as the raw and ancillary materials, in a growing proportion as compared with the mass of living labour applied.

The only other thing that needs to be mentioned here is that with a given working population, if the rate of surplus-value grows, whether by prolongation or intensification of the working day or by reductions in the value of wages as a result of the developing productivity of labour, then the mass of surplus-value and hence the absolute mass of profit must also grow, despite the relative lessening of variable capital in relation to constant.

The same development of the productivity of social labour, the same laws that are evident in the relative fall in variable capital as a proportion of the total capital, and the accelerated accumulation that follows from this – while on the other hand this accumulation also reacts back to become the starting-point for a further development of productivity and a further relative decline in the variable capital – this same development is expressed, leaving aside temporary fluctuations, in the progressive increase in the total labour-power applied and in the progressive growth in the absolute mass of surplus-value and therefore in profit.

How, then, should we present this double-edged law of a decline in the profit *rate* coupled with a simultaneous increase in the absolute *mass* of profit, arising from the same reasons? A law based on the fact that, under the given conditions, the mass of surplus labour and hence surplus-value that is appropriated grows, and that, viewing the total capital as a whole, or the individual capital as simply a piece of the total capital, profit and surplus-value are identical quantities?

Let us take an aliquot part of the capital as a basis for reckoning the profit rate, say 100. This 100 represents the average composition of the total capital, say $80_c + 20_v$. We saw in Part Two of this volume how the average rate of profit in the various branches of production is determined not by any one particular composition of capital but rather by its average social composition.

With the relative decline in the variable portion as compared with the constant, and hence also as a fraction of the total capital of 100, the profit rate falls if the level of exploitation of labour remains constant, or even if it rises; hence the relative magnitude of surplus-value falls, i.e. its relationship to the value of the total capital of 100 that is advanced. But it is not only this relative magnitude that falls. The amount of surplus-value or profit absorbed by the total capital of 100 also falls in absolute terms. At a rate of surplus-value of 100 per cent, a capital of $60_c + 40_v$ produces a mass of surplus-value and hence profit of 40; a capital of $70_c + 30_v$ produces a mass of profit of 30; with a capital of $80_c + 20_v$, the profit falls to 20. This fall bears on the mass of surplus-value and hence of profit, and it follows from the fact that because the total capital of 100 sets in motion less living labour in general, it also sets in motion less surplus labour and hence produces less surplus-value, with the level of exploitation remaining the same. Whatever aliquot part of the social capital we take as the standard for measuring surplus-value, i.e. whatever part of the capital of average social composition – and this is the case with any calculation of profit – a relative fall in surplus-value is always identical with an absolute fall. The rate of profit falls from 40 per cent to 30 per cent and 20 per cent in the above cases, because the mass of surplus-value and hence profit produced by the same capital itself falls from 40 to 30 and 20 in absolute terms. Since the size of the capital against which we measure the surplus-value is given as 100, a fall in the ratio of surplus-value to this magnitude, which itself remains constant, can only be another expression for the decline in the absolute magnitude of surplus-value and profit. This is in fact a tautology. But the reason for this decline, as has been shown, lies in the nature of development of the capitalist process of production.

On the other hand, however, the same reasons that produce an absolute decline in surplus-value and hence profit on a given capital, thus also in the rate of profit as reckoned as a percentage, bring about a growth in the absolute mass of the surplus-value and profit appropriated by the social capital (i.e. by the totality of capitalists). How are we to explain this, what is it dependent on, or what conditions are involved in this apparent contradiction?

If any aliquot part of the social capital, say 100, and hence any capital of 100 of average social composition, is a given magnitude, so that as far as it is concerned the decline in the rate of profit coincides with a decline in the absolute amount of profit, precisely because the capital on which this is measured is a constant magnitude, then the magnitude of the total social capital, on the other hand, just like that of the capital to be found in the hands of any individual capitalist, is a variable magnitude, and it must vary in inverse proportion to the decline in its variable portion if it is to fulfil the conditions we have presupposed.

When the percentage composition in the previous example was $60_c + 40_v$, the surplus-value or profit on it was 40 and the rate of profit therefore 40 per cent. Let us assume that at this level of composition the total capital was 1 million. The total surplus-value and total profit would then amount to 400,000. If the composition were later to become $80_c + 20_v$, the surplus-value or profit on each 100 would be 20, with the level of exploitation remaining the same. But the surplus-value or profit grows in its absolute mass, as we have shown, despite this decline in the rate of profit or the decline in the production of surplus-value by each capital of 100, and this growth might be from 400,000 to 440,000, say. This is possible only if the total capital that corresponds to this new composition has grown to 2,220,000. The mass of the total capital set in motion has risen to 220 per cent of its initial value, whereas the rate of profit has fallen by 50 per cent. If the capital had simply doubled, then at a rate of profit of 20 per cent it could only have produced the same amount of surplus-value and profit as the old capital of 1,000,000 did at 40 per cent. Had it grown by less than this, it would have produced less surplus-value or profit than the capital of 1,000,000 did previously, although at its earlier composition this would only have had to grow from 1,000,000 to 1,100,000 in order for its surplus-value to rise from 400,000 to 440,000.

Here we can see asserting itself the law we developed earlier,* according to which the relative decline in the variable capital, and thus the development of the social productivity of labour, means that an ever greater amount of total capital is required in order to set the same quantity of labour-power in motion and to absorb the same amount of surplus labour. In the same proportion as capitalist production develops, therefore, there also develops the possibility of a relative surplus working population, not because the productivity of social labour *declines* but rather because it *increases*, i.e. not from an absolute disproportion between labour and means of subsistence, or the means of producing these means

* See Volume 1, Chapter 25, 2, pp. 772–81.

of subsistence, but rather from a disproportion arising from the capitalist exploitation of labour, the disproportion between the progressive growth of capital and the relative decline in its need for a growing population.

A fall of 50 per cent in the rate of profit is a fall of a half. If the mass of profit is to remain the same, therefore, the capital must double. In general, if the mass of profit is to remain the same with a declining rate of profit, the multiplier that indicates the growth in the total capital must be the same as the divisor that indicates the fall in the profit rate. If the rate of profit falls from 40 per cent to 20 per cent, the total capital must rise in the ratio of 20:40 if the result is to remain the same. If the profit rate had fallen from 40 per cent to 8 per cent, the capital would have to grow in the ratio 8:40, i.e. by five times. A capital of 1,000,000 at 40 per cent produces 400,000, and a capital of 5,000,000 at 8 per cent also produces 400,000. This is necessary if the resultant is to remain the same. If it is to grow, on the other hand, the capital must grow in a higher ratio than that in which the profit rate falls. In other words, if the variable component of the total capital is not just to remain the same in absolute terms, but rather to grow, even though its percentage falls as a proportion of the total capital, then the total capital must grow in a higher ratio than that at which the percentage of variable capital falls. It must grow so much that in its new composition it requires not only the former amount of variable capital, but still more than this, for the purchase of labour-power. If the variable part of a capital of 100 falls from 40 to 20, the total capital must rise to more than 200 if it is to deploy a variable capital of more than 40.

Even if the exploited mass of the working population remains constant and it is only the length and intensity of the working day that increases, the mass of capital applied must still rise, since it must rise even if the same mass of labour is to be deployed under the former conditions of exploitation, with an altered composition of capital.

Thus the same development in the social productivity of labour is expressed, with the advance of the capitalist mode of production, on the one hand in a progressive tendency for the rate of profit to fall and on the other in a constant growth in the absolute mass of the surplus-value or profit appropriated; so that, by and large, the relative decline in the variable capital and profit goes together with an absolute increase in both. This two-fold effect, as explained, can be expressed only in a growth in the total capital that takes place more rapidly than the fall in the rate of profit. In order to apply an absolutely greater variable capital at a higher composition, or with a relatively steeper increase in the constant capital, the total capital must grow not only in the same proportion as this higher composition, but still faster than it. It follows from this that the more the capitalist mode of production is developed, the more an ever greater amount of capital is needed to employ the same amount of labour-power (and this is still more the case if the amount of labour-power is growing). The rising productivity of labour thus necessarily gives rise, on the capitalist basis, to a permanent apparent surplus working population. If the variable capital forms only a sixth of the total capital instead of a half, as formerly, then in order to employ the same amount of labour-power, the total capital must be tripled; but if it is to employ double the labour-power, this capital must be increased six-fold.

Previous economists, not knowing how to explain the law of the falling rate of profit, invoked the rising mass of profit, the growth in its absolute amount, whether for the individual capitalist or for the social capital as a whole, as a kind of consolation, but this was also based on mere commonplaces and imagined possibilities.

It is no more than a tautology to say that the mass of profit is determined by two factors, firstly by the rate of profit and secondly by the mass of capital applied at this rate. The fact that the mass of profit may possibly grow, therefore, despite a simultaneous fall in the rate of profit, is only an expression of this tautology and does not get us a single step further, since it is equally possible for the capital to grow without the mass of profit growing, and, indeed, the capital might even grow while the mass of profit falls. 25 per cent on 100 gives 25, 5 per cent on 400 gives only 20.[35]

35. 'We should also expect that, however the rate of the profits of stock might diminish in consequence of the accumulation of capital on the land and the rise of wages, yet the aggregate amount of profits would increase. Thus supposing that, with repeated accumulations of £100,000, the rate of profit should fall from 20 to 19, to 18, to 17 per cent, a constantly diminishing rate, we should expect that the whole amount of profits received by those successive owners of capital would be always progressive; that it would be greater when the capital was £200,000, than when £100,000; still greater when £300,000; and so on, increasing, though at a diminishing rate, with every increase of capital. This progression, however, is only true for a certain time, thus 19 per cent on £200,000 is more than 20 per cent on £100,000; again 18 per cent on £300,000 is more than 19 per cent on £200,000; but after capital has accumulated to a

But if the same reasons that make the profit rate fall also promote accumulation, i.e. the formation of additional capital, and if all additional capital also sets additional labour in motion and produces additional surplus-value; if on the other hand the very fact of the fall in the rate of profit means that the constant capital and with it the total amount of the former capital has grown, then the entire process ceases to be a mystery. We shall see later on † how resort was made to deliberate miscalculation, in an attempt to swindle away the possibility of an increase in the mass of profit together with a decline in the profit rate.

We have seen how it is that the same reasons that produce a tendential fall in the general rate of profit also bring about an accelerated accumulation of capital and hence a growth in the absolute magnitude or total mass of the surplus labour (surplus-value, profit) appropriated by it. Just as everything is expressed upside down in competition, and hence in the consciousness of its agents, so too is this law – I mean this inner and necessary connection between two apparently contradictory phenomena. It is evident that, on the figures given above, a capitalist controlling a large capital will make more profit in absolute terms than a smaller capitalist making apparently high profits. The most superficial examination of competition also shows that, under certain conditions, if the bigger capitalist wants to make more room for himself on the market and expel the smaller capitalists, as in times of crisis, he makes practical use of this advantage and deliberately lowers his profit rate in order to drive the smaller ones from the field. Commercial capital in particular, which we shall discuss in more detail later, also exhibits phenomena that

---

large amount, and profits have fallen, the further accumulation diminishes the aggregate of profits. Thus, suppose the accumulation should be £1,000,000, and the profits 7 per cent, the whole amount of profits will be £70,000; now if an addition of £100,000 capital be made to the million, and profits should fall to 6 per cent, £66,000 or a diminution of £4,000 will be received by the owners of the stock, although the whole amount of stock will be increased from £1,000,000 to £1,100,000.' Ricardo, *Political Economy*, Chapter VI, [Pelican edition, pp., 142–3]. In point of fact, what is assumed here is that the capital grows from 1,000,000 to 1,1000,000, i.e. by 10 per cent, while the rate of profit falls from 7 per cent to 6 per cent, i.e. by 14$\frac{2}{7}$ per cent. *Hinc illae lacrimae!* *

* 'Hence those tears!' Terence, *The Maid of Andros*, Act 1, Scene 1.

† See *Theories of Surplus-Value*, Part II, pp. 438–66 and 542–6.

allow the fall in profit to be seen as a result of the expansion of business and hence of the capital concerned. We shall give the proper scientific expression for this false conception later on. Similar superficial considerations arise from comparing the rates of profit that are made in particular branches of business, according to whether these are subject to the regime of free competition or to monopoly. The entire shallow conception that thrives in the heads of the agents of competition can be found in our Roscher, namely his assertion that this reduction in the rate of profit is 'more clever and more humane'.* Here the decline in the rate of profit appears as a *result* of the increase of capital and the capitalists' consequent calculation that a lower rate of profit will enable them to tuck away a greater mass of profit. All this (with the exception of Adam Smith, on whom more later)† is based on a complete misconception of what the general rate of profit actually is and on the crude idea that prices are determined by adding a more or less arbitrary quota of profit onto the commodity's actual value. Crude as these notions are, they are a necessary product of the upside-down way that the immanent laws of capitalist production present themselves within competition.

*

The law that the fall in the rate of profit occasioned by the development of productivity is accompanied by an increase in the mass of profit is also expressed in this way: the fall in the price of commodities produced by capital is accompanied by a relative rise in the amount of profit contained in them and realized by their sale.

Since the development of productivity and the higher composition of capital corresponding to it leads to an ever greater amount of means of production being set in motion by an ever smaller amount of labour, each aliquot part of the total product, each individual commodity or each specific group of commodities absorbs less living labour and also contains less objectified labour, both in terms of the depreciation of the fixed capital applied and in terms of the raw and ancillary materials that are consumed. Each individual commodity therefore contains a smaller sum of

* W. Roscher, *Die Grundlagen der Nationalökonomie*, 3rd edn, Stuttgart and Augsburg, 1858, p. 192. Wilhelm Roscher (1817–94) was a German vulgar economist and founder of the 'historical school' of economics.

† See *Theories of Surplus-Value*, Part II, pp. 222–35.

labour objectified in means of production and labour newly added in the course of production. The price of the individual commodity therefore falls. The profit contained in the individual commodity may still increase for all that, if the rate of absolute or relative surplus-value rises. It contains less newly added labour, but the unpaid portion of this labour grows in proportion to the paid part. Yet this is only true within certain definite limits. With the enormous decrease, in the course of the advance of production, of the absolute amount of living labour newly added to the individual commodity, the unpaid labour it contains also undergoes an absolute decline, no matter how much it may have grown in relation to the paid portion. The profit on each individual commodity becomes very much reduced as labour productivity develops, despite the rise in the rate of surplus-value; and this reduction, just like the fall in the rate of profit, is slowed down only by the cheapening of the elements of constant capital and the other circumstances adduced in Part One of this volume, which increase the rate of profit with a given or even falling rate of surplus-value.

If there is a fall in the price of the individual commodities whose sum makes up capital's total product, this means nothing more than that a given quantity of labour is realized in a greater mass of commodities, so that each individual commodity contains less labour than before. This is the case even if one part of the constant capital, e.g. raw material, rises in price. With the exception of isolated cases (e.g. when the productivity of labour cheapens all the elements of both constant and variable capital to the same extent), the rate of profit will fall, despite the higher rate of surplus-value: (1) because even a greater unpaid portion of the smaller total sum of newly added labour is less than a smaller aliquot unpaid portion of the greater total sum was, and (2) because the higher composition of capital is expressed, in the case of the individual commodity, in the fact that the whole portion of this commodity's value that represents newly added labour falls in comparison with the portion of value that represents raw materials, ancillary materials, and wear and tear of the fixed capital. This change in the proportion between the various components of the individual commodity's price, the decline in the portion of price that represents newly added living labour, and the increase in the portions of price that represent previously objectified labour – this is the form the decline of the variable capital as against the constant takes in the price of the individual commodity. Just as this decline is absolute for a given amount of capital, e.g. 100, so it is also absolute for each individual commodity as an aliquot part of the capital reproduced. Even so, the rate of profit, if calculated simply on the price elements of the individual commodity, would be expressed differently from how it actually is. And this is for the following reason.

(The rate of profit is calculated on the total capital applied, but for a specific period of time, in practice a year. The proportion between the surplus-value or profit made and realized in a year and the total capital, calculated as a percentage, is the rate of profit. And so this is not necessarily identical with a rate of profit in which it is not the year but rather the turnover period of the capital in question that is taken as the basis of calculation; it is only if this capital turns over precisely once in the year that the two things coincide.

To put it another way, the profit made in the course of a year is simply the sum of the profits on the commodities produced and sold in the course of that year. If we calculate the profit on the cost price of the commodities, we obtain a rate of profit $\frac{p}{k}$, where p is the profit realized in the course of the year and k is the sum of the cost prices of the commodities produced and sold in the same period. It is readily apparent that this profit rate $\frac{p}{k}$ can only coincide with the actual profit rate $\frac{p}{C}$, mass of profit divided by the total capital, when $k = C$, i.e. when the capital turns over just once in the year.

Let us take three possible situations for an industrial capital.

I. A capital of £8,000 produces and sells 5,000 items of a certain commodity each year, at 30 shillings per item, so that its annual turnover is £7,500. On each item it makes a profit of 10 shillings, a total of £2,500 per year. Each item therefore contains a capital advance of 20 shillings and a profit of 10 shillings, so that the profit rate on each item is $\frac{10}{20} = 50$ per cent. In the sum of £7,500 turned over, £5,000 is capital advance and £2,500 is profit; the rate of profit on the turnover, $\frac{p}{k}$, is similarly 50 per cent. Reckoned on the basis of the total capital, however, the rate of profit $\frac{p}{C}$ is $\frac{2,500}{8,000} = 31\frac{1}{4}$ per cent.

II. Say that the capital now increases to £10,000. As a result of increased labour productivity, it is able to produce 10,000 items of the commodity each year at a cost price of 20 shillings. Say that it sells these with 4 shillings profit on each, i.e. at 24 shillings per item. The price of the annual product is then £12,000, of which £10,000 is capital advance and £2,000 is profit. $\frac{p}{k}$ is $\frac{4}{20}$ reckoned per item, or $\frac{2,000}{10,000}$ reckoned on the annual turnover, i.e. in both cases 20 per cent, and since the total capital is equal to the sum of the cost prices, i.e. £10,000, the actual profit rate, $\frac{p}{C}$, is this time also 20 per cent.

III. Say that the capital grows to £15,000 and the productivity of labour continues to rise, so that it now produces annually some 30,000 items of the commodity at a cost price of 13 shillings each, selling these with 2 shillings profit, i.e. at 15 shillings. The annual turnover is therefore $30,000 \times 15$ shillings $= £22,500$, of which £19,500 is capital advance and £3,000 is profit. $\frac{p}{k}$ is thus $\frac{2}{13} = \frac{3,000}{19,500} = 15\frac{5}{13}$ per cent. $\frac{p}{C}$, on the other hand, is $\frac{3,000}{15,000} = 20$ per cent.

We see, therefore, that only in case II, where the capital value turned over is the same as the total capital, is the rate of profit on each item of the commodity or on the sum turned over the same as the profit rate calculated on the total capital. In case I, where the sum turned over is less than the total capital, the profit rate calculated on the cost price of the commodity is higher; in case III, where the total capital is less than the sum turned over, this profit rate is less than the actual rate of profit, calculated on the total capital. This is a general rule.

In commercial practice, the turnover is generally worked out only roughly. It is assumed that the capital has turned over once as soon as the sum of commodity prices realized reaches the sum of the total capital applied. But the *capital* can have completed a whole cycle only if the sum of the *cost prices* of the commodities realized equals the sum of the total capital. – F.E.)

We see here once again how important it is in capitalist production not to view the individual commodity or the commodity product of some particular period of time in isolation, as a simple commodity; it must rather be viewed as the product of the capital advanced, and in relation to the total capital that produces this commodity.

Even though the *rate* of profit cannot just be calculated by measuring the mass of surplus-value produced and realized against the portion of capital consumed which reappears in the commodity, but one must rather measure it against this portion plus the portion of capital which is admittedly not consumed, but is still applied in production and continues to serve there, the *mass* of profit can nevertheless only be equal to the mass of profit or surplus-value actually contained in the commodities and destined to be realized by their sale.

If industrial productivity increases, the price of the individual commodity falls. Less labour is contained in it, both paid and unpaid. The same labour may produce three times the product, for instance, in which case two-thirds less labour is needed for each individual item. Since profit can only be a portion of the labour contained in the individual commodity, the profit on each individual commodity must decrease, and this is true within certain limits even if the rate of surplus-value rises. In all cases, however, the profit on the total product does not fall below the original mass of profit as long as the capital continues to employ the same mass of workers as before at the same level of exploitation. (This can even be the case if fewer workers are employed at a higher level of exploitation.) For in the same ratio as the profit on the individual commodity falls, the number of products rises. The mass of profit remains the same, even though it is differently distributed over the sum of commodities; and this in no way changes the distribution between worker and capitalist of the quantity of value created by the newly added labour. The mass of profit can rise, employing the same amount of labour, only if the unpaid surplus labour grows, or, with the level of exploitation of labour remaining the same, if the number of workers increases. Both of these factors may operate simultaneously. In all these cases – and on the basis of our assumptions they imply a growth in the constant capital in relation to the variable, and an increase in the total capital applied – the individual commodity contains a smaller amount of profit, and the profit rate falls, even when calculated on the individual commodity; a given quantity of additional labour is expressed in a greater quantity of commodities, and the price of the individual commodity falls. Viewed abstractly, the rate of profit might remain the same despite a fall in the price of the individual commodity as a result of increased productivity, and hence despite a simultaneous increase in the number of these cheaper commodities – for example if the increase in productivity affected all the ingredients of the commodity uniformly and simultaneously, so that their total price fell in the same proportion as the productivity of labour increased, while the ratio between the various ingredients of the commodity's price remained the same. The rate of profit could even rise, if a rise in the rate of surplus-value was coupled with a significant reduction in the value of the elements of constant capital, and fixed capital in particular. In practice, however, the rate of profit will fall in the long run, as we have already seen. In no case does the fall in the price of the individual commodity, taken by itself, permit any conclusion as to the rate of profit. It all depends on the size of the total capital involved in its production. Say that the price of one yard of material falls from 3 shillings to $1\frac{2}{3}$ shillings; if we know that before the fall in price, $1\frac{2}{3}$ shillings went on constant capital, $\frac{2}{3}$ shillings on wages and $\frac{2}{3}$ was profit, while after the fall in price 1 shilling went on constant capital, $\frac{1}{3}$ shilling on wages and $\frac{1}{3}$ shilling was profit, we still do not know whether the rate of profit has remained the same or not. This will depend on whether and by how much the total capital advanced has grown and how many yards more it produces in a given time.

The phenomenon arising from the nature of the capitalist mode of production, that the price of an individual commodity or a given portion of commodities falls with the growing productivity of labour, while the number of commodities rises; that the amount of profit on the individual commodity and the rate of profit on the sum of commodities falls, but the mass of profit on the total sum of commodities rises – this phenomenon simply appears on the surface as a fall in the amount of profit on the individual commodity, a fall in its price, and a growth in the mass of profit on the increased total number of commodities produced by the total social capital or the total capital of the individual capitalist. The matter is then conceived as if the capitalist voluntarily made less profit on the individual commodity, but compensated himself by the greater number of commodities which he now produces. This conception rests on the notion of *profit upon alienation* * which is derived from the viewpoint of commercial capital.

We have already seen, in Parts Four and Seven of Volume 1, how the growing mass of commodities, and the cheapening of the individual commodity that accompanies the rising productivity of labour, does not in itself affect the proportion of paid and unpaid labour in the individual commodity (in so far as these

* A notion of Sir James Steuart, which Marx criticizes in *Theories of Surplus-Value*, Part I, pp. 41–3.

commodities do not go towards determining the price of labour-power), despite the falling price.

Since everything presents a false appearance in competition, in fact an upside-down one, it is possible for the individual capitalist to imagine: (1) that he reduces his profit on the individual commodity by cutting its price, but makes a bigger profit on account of the greater quantity of commodities that he sells; (2) that he fixes the price of the individual commodity and then determines the price of the total product by multiplication, whereas the original process is one of division (see Volume 1, Chapter 12, pp. 433–4), and this multiplication comes in only at second hand and is correct only on the premise of that division. In point of fact, the vulgar economist does nothing more than translate the peculiar notions of the competition-enslaved capitalist into an ostensibly more theoretical and generalized language, and attempt to demonstrate the validity of these notions.

In actual fact, the fall in commodity prices and the rise in the mass of profit on the increased mass of cheapened commodities is simply another expression of the law of the falling profit rate in the context of a simultaneously rising mass of profit.

An investigation of how far a falling rate of profit can coincide with rising prices would be no more pertinent here than the earlier point elaborated in Volume 1, pp. 433–4, in connection with relative surplus-value. The capitalist who employs improved but not yet universally used methods of production sells below the market price, but above his individual price of production; his profit rate thus rises, until competition cancels this out; in the course of this period of adjustment, the second requirement is fulfilled, i.e. growth in the capital laid out; and according to the level of this growth, the capitalist will then be in a position to employ a portion of the workers employed earlier, perhaps all of them or even a greater number, under the new conditions, and thus to produce the same amount of profit or even a larger amount.

Chapter 14: Counteracting Factors

If we consider the enormous development in the productive powers of social labour over the last thirty years * alone, compared with all earlier periods, and particularly if we consider the enormous mass of fixed capital involved in the overall process of social production quite apart from machinery proper, then instead of the problem that occupied previous economists, the problem of explaining the fall in the profit rate, we have the opposite problem of explaining why this fall is not greater or faster. Counteracting influences must be at work, checking and cancelling the effect of the general law and giving it simply the character of a tendency, which is why we have described the fall in the general rate of profit as a tendential fall. The most general of these factors are as follows.

I. MORE INTENSE EXPLOITATION OF LABOUR

The level of exploitation of labour, the appropriation of surplus labour and surplus-value, can be increased by prolonging the working day and making work more intense. These points have been developed in detail in Volume 1, in connection with the production of absolute and relative surplus-value. There are many aspects to the intensification of labour that involve a growth in the constant capital as against the variable, i.e. a fall in the rate of profit, such as when a single worker has to supervise a larger amount of machinery. In this case, as also with most procedures that serve to produce relative surplus-value, the same reasons that bring about a rise in the rate of surplus-value can also involve a fall in its mass, taking given magnitudes of total capital applied. There are also other factors in this intensification, as for example the accelerated speed of the machines, which will use up more raw

* i.e. 1835–65.

material in the same space of time, but, as far as the fixed capital is concerned, the fact that this wears out the machines that much faster does not in any way affect the ratio of their value to the price of the labour that sets them in motion. In particular, however, it is the prolongation of the working day, this discovery of modern industry, which increases the amount of surplus labour appropriated without basically altering the ratio of the labour-power applied to the constant capital that this sets in motion, and which in point of fact rather reduces the constant capital in relative terms. It has already been shown, moreover, and this forms the real secret of the tendential fall in the rate of profit, that the procedures for producing relative surplus-value are based, by and large, either on transforming as much as possible of a given amount of labour into surplus-value or on spending as little as possible labour in general in relation to the capital advanced; so that the same reasons that permit the level of exploitation of labour to increase make it impossible to exploit as much labour as before with the same total capital. These are the counter-acting tendencies which, while they act to bring about a rise in the rate of surplus-value, simultaneously lead to a fall in the mass of surplus-value produced by a given capital, hence a fall in the rate of profit. The introduction of female and child labour on a mass scale should be mentioned here too, in so far as the family as a whole has now to supply capital with a greater quantity of surplus labour than before, even if the sum of their wages increases, which is by no means always the case.

Everything that promotes the production of relative surplus-value by the simple improvement of methods, without a change in the magnitude of capital applied, has the same effect – in agriculture for example. Even though the constant capital applied does not grow here in proportion to the variable, there is still a rise in the volume of the product in relation to the labour-power applied. The same thing takes place if the productivity of labour (irrespective of whether its product goes into the consumption of the workers or into the elements of constant capital) is freed from restraints on commerce, arbitrary restrictions, or limitations which have become irksome in the course of time, and generally from fetters of any kind, without any initial impact on the proportion of variable to constant capital.

It might be asked whether these factors that inhibit the fall in the profit rate, though in the final instance they always accelerate it further, include the temporary but ever repeated increases in surplus-value that appear now in this branch of production, now in that, and raise it above the general level for the capitalist who makes use of inventions, etc. before they are universally applied. This question must be answered in the affirmative.

The mass of surplus-value that a capital of given size produces is the product of two factors, the rate of surplus-value and the number of workers employed at this rate. With a given rate of surplus-value, therefore, it depends on the number of workers, and with a given number of workers it depends on the rate – in general, therefore, it depends on the product of the absolute size of the variable capital and the rate of surplus-value. Now we have seen that the same factors that increase the rate of relative surplus-value lower the amount of labour-power applied on average. It is evident, however, that this effect can be greater or less, depending on the specific proportions in which this antithetical movement takes place, and that the tendency for the profit rate to be reduced, in particular, is attenuated by the increase in the rate of absolute surplus-value that stems from the prolongation of the working day.

In connection with the profit rate, we have found that to a fall in the rate, resulting from a rise in the mass of total capital applied, there corresponds in general an increase in the amount of profit. Taking the total variable capital of the society as a whole, the surplus-value it produces is the same as the profit. Besides the absolute amount of surplus-value, the rate of surplus-value has also risen; the former because the amount of labour-power applied by the society has grown and the latter because the level of exploitation of this labour has increased. But with respect to a capital of given magnitude, e.g. 100, the rate of surplus-value can grow while the average mass of surplus-value falls, since the rate is determined by the ratio in which the variable portion of the capital is valorized, while the mass is determined by the proportion that the variable capital forms in the total.

The rise in the rate of surplus-value – particularly since it takes place under circumstances in which, as mentioned above, there is no increase in the constant capital as against the variable, or no relative increase – is a factor which contributes to the determination of the mass of surplus-value and hence also the rate of profit. It does not annul the general law. But it has the effect that this law operates more as a tendency, i.e. as a law whose absolute realization is held up, delayed and weakened by counteracting factors. However, as the same factors that increase the rate of surplus-value (and the extension of the working day is itself a result of large-scale industry) tend to reduce the amount of labour-power employed by a given capital, the same factors tend both to reduce the rate of profit and to slow down the movement in this direction. If one worker is compelled to do work that it would really be rational for two to perform, and if this happens under circumstances in which this one worker can replace three, then one worker can now provide as much surplus labour as two did before, and to this extent the rate of surplus-value rises. But this one will not supply as much surplus labour as three did before, and this makes the mass of surplus-value fall. Its fall is compensated for or limited by the rise in the rate of surplus-value. If the entire population is set to work at the increased rate of surplus-value, the mass of surplus-value rises, even though the population remains the same. Still more is this the case with a growing population; and even though this growth is linked with a relative fall in the number of workers employed, compared with the size of the total capital, the fall is still moderated or halted by the higher rate of surplus-value.

Before we leave this point, it should be stressed once again that the *rate* of surplus-value can rise, with a constant amount of capital, even though the *mass* of surplus-value falls – and vice versa. The mass of surplus-value is equal to the rate multiplied by the number of workers; but the rate is never calculated on the total capital, but only on the variable capital, in actual fact on each working day individually. Once the size of the capital value is given, however, the *rate of profit* can never rise or fall without a similar rise or fall in the *mass of surplus-value*.

2. REDUCTION OF WAGES BELOW THEIR VALUE

We simply make an empirical reference to this point here, as, like many other things that might be brought in, it has nothing to do with the general analysis of capital, but has its place in an account of competition, which is not dealt with in this work. It is none the less one of the most important factors in stemming the tendency for the rate of profit to fall.

3. CHEAPENING OF THE ELEMENTS OF CONSTANT CAPITAL

Everything is relevant here that has been said in Part One of this volume about the causes that raise the rate of profit while the rate of surplus-value remains constant, or at least raise it independently of the latter. In particular, therefore, the fact that, viewing the total capital as a whole, the value of the constant capital does not increase in the same proportion as its material volume. For example, the quantity of cotton that a single European spinning operative works up in a modern factory has grown to a most colossal extent in comparison with that which a European spinner used to process with the spinning wheel. But the value of the cotton processed has not grown in the same proportion as its mass. It is the same with machines and other fixed capital. In other words, the same development that raises the mass of constant capital in comparison with variable reduces the value of its elements, as a result of the higher productivity of labour, and hence prevents the value of the constant capital, even though this grows steadily, from growing in the same degree as its material volume, i.e. the material volume of the means of production that are set in motion by the same amount of labour-power. In certain cases, the mass of the constant capital elements may increase while their total value remains the same or even falls.

Also related to what has been said is the devaluation of existing capital (i.e. of its material elements) that goes hand in hand with the development of industry. This too is a factor that steadily operates to stay the fall in the rate of profit, even though in certain circumstances it may reduce the mass of profit by detracting from the mass of capital that produces profit. We see here once again how the same factors that produce the tendency for the rate of profit to fall also moderate the realization of this tendency.

4. THE RELATIVE SURPLUS POPULATION

The creation of such a surplus population is inseparable from the development of labour productivity and is accelerated by it, the same development as is expressed in the decline in the profit rate. The more the capitalist mode of production is developed in a country, the more strikingly does the relative surplus population obtrude there. It is in turn a reason why the more or less incomplete subordination of labour to capital persists in several branches of production, and longer indeed than would seem to correspond at first sight to the general level of development; this is a result of the cheapness and quantity of available or dismissed wage-labourers and of the greater resistance that many branches of production, by their nature, oppose to the transformation of manual work into machine production. Furthermore, new branches of production open up, particularly in the field of luxury consumption, which precisely take this relative surplus population as their basis, a population often made available owing to the preponderance of constant capital in other branches of production; these base themselves in turn on a preponderance of the element of living labour, and only gradually pass through the same trajectory as other branches. In both cases variable capital forms a significant proportion of the total and wages are below the average, so that both the rate and mass of surplus-value in these branches of production are unusually high. Now since the general rate of profit is formed by the equalization of the rates of profit in the various particular branches of production, here again the same reasons that produce the tendential fall in the rate of profit also produce a counterweight to this tendency, which paralyses its effect to a greater or lesser extent.

5. FOREIGN TRADE

In so far as foreign trade cheapens on the one hand the elements of constant capital and on the other the necessary means of subsistence into which variable capital is converted, it acts to raise the rate of profit by raising the rate of surplus-value and reducing the value of constant capital. It has a general effect in this direction in as much as it permits the scale of production to be expanded. In this way it accelerates accumulation, while it also accelerates the fall in the variable capital as against the constant, and hence the fall in the rate of profit. And whereas the expansion of foreign trade was the basis of capitalist production in its infancy, it becomes the specific product of the capitalist mode of production as this progresses, through the inner necessity of this mode of production and its need for an ever extended market. Here again we can see the same duality of effect. (Ricardo completely overlooked this aspect of foreign trade.) *

There is a further question, whose specific analysis lies beyond the limits of our investigation: is the general rate of profit raised by the higher profit rate made by capital invested in foreign trade, and colonial trade in particular?

Capital invested in foreign trade can yield a higher rate of

* Cf. Chapter VII of Ricardo's *Principles*.

profit, firstly, because it competes with commodities produced by other countries with less developed production facilities, so that the more advanced country sells its goods above their value, even though still more cheaply than its competitors. In so far as the labour of the more advanced country is valorized here as labour of a higher specific weight, the profit rate rises, since labour that is not paid as qualitatively higher is nevertheless sold as such. The same relationship may hold towards the country to which goods are exported and from which goods are imported: i.e. such a country gives more objectified labour in kind than it receives, even though it still receives the goods in question more cheaply than it could produce them itself. In the same way, a manufacturer who makes use of a new discovery before this has become general sells more cheaply than his competitors and yet still sells above the individual value of his commodity, valorizing the specifically higher productivity of the labour he employs as surplus labour. He thus realizes a surplus profit. As far as capital invested in the colonies, etc. is concerned, however, the reason why this can yield higher rates of profit is that the profit rate is generally higher there on account of the lower degree of development, and so too is the exploitation of labour, through the use of slaves and coolies, etc. Now there is no reason why the higher rates of profit that capital invested in certain branches yields in this way, and brings home to its country of origin, should not enter into the equalization of the general rate of profit and hence raise this in due proportion, unless monopolies stand in the way.[36] There is in particular no reason why this should not be so when the branches of capital investment in question are subject to the laws of free competition. What Ricardo has in mind, on the other hand, is this: higher prices are obtained abroad; commodities are bought there and sent home in exchange; these commodities are therefore sold on the domestic market, so that the favoured spheres of production can have at most a temporary advantage over others. As soon as we take our leave of the money form, however, this semblance vanishes. The privileged country receives more labour in exchange for less, even though this difference, the excess, is pocketed by a particular class, just as in the exchange

36. Adam Smith is right here, as against Ricardo, who says: 'They contend, that the equality of profits will be brought about by the general rise of profits; and I am of the opinion, that the profits of the favoured trade will speedily subside to the general level.' [Pelican edition, p. 148.]

between labour and capital in general. Thus in as much as the profit rate is higher because it is generally higher in the colonial country, favourable natural conditions there may enable it to go hand in hand with lower commodity prices. An equalization still takes place, but not an equalization at the old level, as Ricardo believes.

But this same foreign trade develops the capitalist mode of production at home, and hence promotes a decline in variable capital as against constant, though it also produces overproduction in relation to the foreign country, so that it again has the opposite effect in the further course of development.

We have shown in general, therefore, how the same causes that bring about a fall in the general rate of profit provoke counter-effects that inhibit this fall, delay it and in part even paralyse it. These do not annul the law, but they weaken its effect. If this were not the case, it would not be the fall in the general rate of profit that was incomprehensible, but rather the relative slowness of this fall. The law operates therefore simply as a tendency, whose effect is decisive only under certain particular circumstances and over long periods.

Before we proceed any further, we should like to repeat again two points that have already been developed several times, in order to avoid any misunderstanding.

Firstly, the same process that leads to the cheapening of commodities as the capitalist mode of production develops leads to a change in the organic composition of the social capital applied in commodity production, and leads as a result to a fall in the profit rate. Thus the reduction in the relative cost of the individual commodity, or even in the part of this cost that represents the wear and tear of the machinery, should not be confused with the rising value of the constant capital compared with the variable, even though, conversely, any reduction in the relative cost of the constant capital, with the volume of its material elements remaining the same or increasing, acts to increase the rate of profit, i.e. acts to reduce proportionately the value of the constant capital, compared with the variable capital that is applied on a scale which declines progressively.

Secondly, the fact that the additional living labour contained in the individual commodities which together compose the product of capital stands in a declining ratio to the materials of labour these contain and the means of labour consumed in them; the fact, therefore, that an ever smaller quantity of additional living labour is objectified in them, because less labour is required for their production as social productivity develops – this fact does not affect the proportion in which the living labour contained in the commodity is divided between paid and unpaid. On the contrary. Even though the total amount of the additional living labour contained in it falls, the unpaid part still grows in proportion to the paid part, either by an absolute or a proportionate fall in this paid part; for the same mode of production that reduces the total mass of additional living labour in a commodity is accompanied by a rise in absolute and relative surplus-value. The tendential fall in the rate of profit is linked with a tendential rise in the rate of surplus-value, i.e. in the level of exploitation of labour. Nothing is more absurd, then, than to explain the fall in the rate of profit in terms of a rise in wage rates, even though this too may be an exceptional case. Only when the relationships that form the rate of profit have been understood will statistics be able to put forward genuine analyses of wage-rates in different periods. The profit rate does not fall because labour becomes less productive but rather because it becomes more productive. The rise in the rate of surplus-value and the fall in the rate of profit are simply particular forms that express the growing productivity of labour in capitalist terms.

6. THE INCREASE IN SHARE CAPITAL

The above five points can also be supplemented by the following one, though we cannot go any deeper into it at this point. As capitalist production advances, and with it accelerated accumulation, one portion of capital is considered simply to be interest-bearing capital and is invested as such. This is not in the sense in which any capitalist who loans out capital is content to take the interest, while the industrial capitalist pockets the entrepreneurial profit. Nor does it affect the level of the general rate of profit, for as far as this is concerned, profit = interest + profit of all kinds + ground-rent, its distribution between these particular categories being a matter of indifference. It is rather in the sense that these capitals, although invested in large productive enterprises, simply yield an interest, great or small, after all costs are deducted – so-called 'dividends'. This is the case with railways, for example. These do not therefore enter into the equalization of the general rate of profit, since they yield a profit rate less than the average. If they did go in, the average rate would fall much lower. From a theoretical point of view, it is possible to include them, and we should then obtain a profit rate lower than that which apparently exists and is really decisive for the capitalists, since it is precisely in these undertakings that the proportion of constant capital to variable is at its greatest.

Chapter 15: Development of the Law's Internal Contradictions

1. GENERAL CONSIDERATIONS

We saw in Part One of this volume how the profit rate always expresses the rate of surplus-value lower than it actually is. We have now seen how even a rising rate of surplus-value tends to be expressed in a falling rate of profit. The profit rate would only be equal to the rate of surplus-value if $c = 0$, i.e. if the total capital were laid out on wages. A falling rate of profit, then, expresses a falling rate of surplus-value only if the ratio between the value of the constant capital and the amount of labour-power that this sets in motion remains unchanged, or if this latter amount has risen in relation to the value of the constant capital.

Ricardo, while claiming to be dealing with the rate of profit, actually deals only with the rate of surplus-value, and this only on the assumption that the working day is a constant magnitude, both intensively and extensively.

A fall in the profit rate, and accelerated accumulation, are simply different expressions of the same process, in so far as both express the development of productivity. Accumulation in turn accelerates the fall in the profit rate, in so far as it involves the concentration of workers on a large scale and hence a higher composition of capital. On the other hand the fall in the profit rate again accelerates the concentration of capital, and its centralization, by dispossessing the smaller capitalists and expropriating the final residue of direct producers who still have something left to expropriate. In this way there is an acceleration of accumulation as far as its mass is concerned, even though the rate of this accumulation falls together with the rate of profit.

On the other hand, however, in view of the fact that the rate at which the total capital is valorized, i.e. the rate of profit, is the spur to capitalist production (in the same way as the valorization of capital is its sole purpose), a fall in this rate slows down the formation of new, independent capitals and thus appears as a threat to the development of the capitalist production process; it promotes overproduction, speculation and crises, and leads to the existence of excess capital alongside a surplus population. Thus economists like Ricardo, who take the capitalist mode of production as an absolute, feel here that this mode of production creates a barrier for itself and seek the source of this barrier not in production but rather in nature (in the theory of rent). The important thing in their horror at the falling rate of profit is the feeling that the capitalist mode of production comes up against a barrier to the development of the productive forces which has nothing to do with the production of wealth as such; but this characteristic barrier in fact testifies to the restrictiveness and the solely historical and transitory character of the capitalist mode of production; it bears witness that this is not an absolute mode of production for the production of wealth but actually comes into conflict at a certain stage with the latter's further development.

Of course, Ricardo and his school were considering only industrial profit, within which they included interest. Yet the rate of ground-rent also has a tendency to fall, even though its absolute mass grows and it may even grow in relation to industrial profit. (See Edward West, who put forward the law of ground-rent *before* Ricardo.)* If we take the total social capital C, and call the industrial profit that remains after deducting interest and ground-rent p_1, interest i and ground-rent r, then $\frac{s}{C} = \frac{p}{C} = \frac{p_1 + i + r}{C} = \frac{p_1}{C} + \frac{i}{C} + \frac{r}{C}$. We have already seen that while s, the total sum of surplus-value, grows steadily as capitalist production develops, $\frac{s}{C}$ steadily declines, since C grows more quickly than s. It is no contradiction, therefore, that p_1, i and r may each increase even though $\frac{s}{C} = \frac{p}{C}$ and its component parts $\frac{p_1}{C}$, $\frac{i}{C}$ and $\frac{r}{C}$ become ever smaller, or that p_1 may grow in relation to i, or r in relation to p_1, or even in relation to both p_1 and i. Given that the total surplus-value or profit ($s = p$) rises, while the rate of profit $\frac{s}{C} = \frac{p}{C}$ simultaneously falls, the ratios between the component parts p_1, i and r into which $s = p$ breaks down may alter in any way possible within the limits given by the total sum s, without thereby affecting the magnitude of either s or $\frac{s}{C}$.

* *Essay on the Application of Capital to Land* . . ., By a Fellow of University College, Oxford, London, 1815.

The reciprocal variation of p_1, i and r is simply a varying distribution of s under various headings. Thus either $\frac{p}{c}$, $\frac{i}{c}$ or $\frac{r}{c}$ – the rate of individual industrial profit, the rate of interest or the ratio of rent to the total capital – may rise in relation to the other fractions, even though $\frac{s}{c}$, the general rate of profit, falls; the only requirement is that the sum of all three $= \frac{s}{c}$. If the rate of profit falls from 50 per cent to 25, because the composition of capital, given a rate of surplus-value of 100 per cent for example, alters from $50_c + 50_v$ to $75_c + 25_v$, then in the first case a capital of 1,000 will give a profit of 500, while in the second case a capital of 4,000 will give a profit of 1,000. s or p will have doubled, while p' has fallen by half. Now if, out of the original 50 per cent, 20 was industrial profit proper, 10 interest and 20 rent, we would have $\frac{p_1}{c} = 20$ per cent, $\frac{i}{c} = 10$ per cent and $\frac{r}{c} = 20$ per cent. So if the proportions remain the same after the rate has fallen to 25 per cent, we will have $\frac{p_1}{c} = 10$ per cent, $\frac{i}{c} = 5$ per cent and $\frac{r}{c} = 10$ per cent. If on the other hand $\frac{p_1}{c}$ now falls to 8 per cent and $\frac{i}{c}$ to 4 per cent, then $\frac{r}{c}$ will rise to 13 per cent. The proportionate size of r would have risen against p_1 and i, but p' would still have remained unchanged. On both assumptions the sum total of p_1, i and r would have risen, since this is now the product of a capital four times larger than before. Furthermore, Ricardo's assumption that industrial profit (plus interest) originally accounted for the entire surplus-value is both historically and theoretically false. It is only the progress of capitalist production, rather, which (1) gives industrial and commercial capitalists the entire profit, in the first instance, for later redistribution, and (2) reduces rent to the surplus over and above profit. On this capitalist basis, rent then grows once more, as a portion of profit (i.e. of the surplus-value considered as product of the total capital), but not the specific portion of the product pocketed by the capitalist.

Assuming the necessary means of production, i.e. a sufficient accumulation of capital, the creation of surplus-value faces no other barrier than the working population, if the rate of surplus-value, i.e. the level of exploitation of labour, is given; and no other barrier than this level of exploitation, if the working population is given. And the capitalist production process essentially consists of this production of surplus-value, represented in the surplus product or the aliquot portion of commodities produced in which unpaid labour is objectified. It should never be forgotten that the production of this surplus-value – and the transformation of a portion of it back into capital, or accumulation, forms an integral part of surplus-value production – is the immediate purpose and the determining motive of capitalist production. Capitalist production, therefore, should never be depicted as something that it is not, i.e. as production whose immediate purpose is consumption, or the production of means of enjoyment for the capitalist. This would be to ignore completely its specific character, as this is expressed in its basic inner pattern.

It is the extraction of this surplus-value that forms the immediate process of production, and this faces no other barriers than those just mentioned. As soon as the amount of surplus labour it has proved possible to extort has been objectified in commodities, the surplus-value has been produced. But this production of surplus-value is only the first act in the capitalist production process, and its completion only brings to an end the immediate production process itself. Capital has absorbed a given amount of unpaid labour. With the development of this process as expressed in the fall in the profit rate, the mass of surplus-value thus produced swells to monstrous proportions. Now comes the second act in the process. The total mass of commodities, the total product, must be sold, both that portion which replaces constant and variable capital and that which represents surplus-value. If this does not happen, or happens only partly, or only at prices that are less than the price of production, then although the worker is certainly exploited, his exploitation is not realized as such for the capitalist and may even not involve any realization of the surplus-value extracted, or only a partial realization; indeed, it may even mean a partial or complete loss of his capital. The conditions for immediate exploitation and for the realization of that exploitation are not identical. Not only are they separate in time and space, they are also separate in theory. The former is restricted only by the society's productive forces, the latter by the proportionality between the different branches of production and by the society's power of consumption. And this is determined neither by the absolute power of production nor by the absolute power of consumption but rather by the power of consumption within a given framework of antagonistic conditions of distribution, which reduce the consumption of the vast majority of society to a minimum level, only capable of varying within more or less narrow limits. It is further restricted by the drive for accumulation, the drive to expand capital and produce surplus-value on a larger scale. This is the law governing capitalist production, arising from the constant revolutions in methods of production themselves, from the devaluation of the existing capital which is always associated with this, and from the general competitive struggle and the need to improve production and extend its scale, merely as a means of self-preservation, and on pain of going under. The market, therefore, must be continually extended, so that its relationships and the conditions governing them assume ever more the form of a natural law independent of the producers and become ever more uncontrollable. The internal contradiction seeks resolution by extending the external field of production. But the more productivity develops, the more it comes into conflict with the narrow basis on which the relations of consumption rest. It is in no way a contradiction, on this contradictory basis, that excess capital coexists with a growing surplus population; for although the mass of surplus-value produced would rise if these were brought together, yet this would equally heighten the contradiction between the conditions in which this surplus-value was produced and the conditions in which it was realized.

Once a certain rate of profit is given, the mass of profit always depends on the magnitude of the capital advanced. But accumulation is then determined by the part of this mass that is transformed back into capital. This part, since it is equal to profit minus the revenue consumed by the capitalists, will depend not only on the value of the total profit but also on the cheapness of the commodities which the capitalist can buy with it; commodities which go partly into his own consumption, his revenue, and partly into his constant capital. (Wages here are taken as given.)

The mass of capital that the worker sets in motion, and whose value he maintains by his labour and makes reappear in the product, is completely different from the value that he adds. If the mass of capital is 1,000 and the labour added is 100, the capital reproduced is 1,100. If the mass is 100 and the labour added is 20, the capital reproduced is 120. The rate of profit is 10 per cent in the one case, and 20 per cent in the other. Nevertheless, more can be accumulated out of 100 than out of 20. Thus the stream of capital (leaving aside its devaluation as the result of a rise in productivity), or its accumulation, flows on in proportion to the impetus that it already possesses and not in proportion to the rate of profit. It is possible to have a high rate of profit even if labour is unproductive, if this is based on a high rate of surplus-value and the working day is very long; this is possible where the workers' needs are very slight and the average wage very low, even though labour is unproductive. The low level of wages corresponds to a lack of energy on the workers' part. Capital therefore accumulates slowly, despite the high profit rate. The population is stagnant, and the product requires a great deal of labour-time, even though the wages that the workers are paid are so small.

The rate of profit does not fall because the worker is less exploited, but rather because less labour is generally applied in relation to the capital invested.

If a falling rate of profit coincides with a rise in the mass of profit, as we have shown, then a greater part of the annual product of labour is appropriated by the capitalist under the heading of capital (as replacement for the capital used up) and a relatively smaller part is appropriated under the heading of profit. Hence the fantasy of Reverend Chalmers to the effect that the smaller the mass of the annual product the capitalists spend as capital, the greater the profits they pocket.* The Established Church, of course, is a great help to them here, in making sure that a large portion of the surplus product is consumed instead of being capitalized. The reverend gentleman confuses cause and effect. The mass of profit certainly does grow, even at a smaller rate of profit, as the capital laid out increases. But this brings about a simultaneous concentration of capital, since the conditions of production now require the use of capital on a massive scale. It also leads to the centralization of this capital, i.e. the swallowing-up of small capitalists by big, and their decapitalization. This is simply the divorce of the conditions of labour from the producers raised to a higher power, these smaller capitalists still counting among the producers, since their own labour still plays a role. The work done by the capitalist, in general, stands in inverse proportion to the size of his capital, i.e. to the degree in which he is a capitalist. It is in fact this divorce between the conditions of labour on the one hand and the producers on the other that forms the concept of capital, as this arises with primitive accumulation (Volume 1,

* Cf. Thomas Chalmers, *On Political Economy in Connexion with the Moral State and Moral Prospects of Society*, 2nd edn, Glasgow, 1832, p. 88. In *Theories of Surplus-Value*, Part I, p. 290, Marx describes Chalmers as 'one of the most fanatic Malthusians'. Like Malthus he was himself a cleric, in fact Professor of Divinity at Glasgow University.

Part Eight), subsequently appearing as a constant process in the accumulation and concentration of capital, before it is finally expressed here as the centralization of capitals already existing in a few hands, and the decapitalization of many. This process would entail the rapid breakdown of capitalist production, if counteracting tendencies were not constantly at work alongside this centripetal force, in the direction of decentralization.

2. THE CONFLICT BETWEEN THE EXTENSION OF PRODUCTION AND VALORIZATION

The development of the social productivity of labour is reflected in two ways – firstly, in the size of the productive forces already produced, the scale of the conditions of production in both value and mass, in so far as these are the conditions for new production to take place, and in the absolute magnitude of the productive capital already accumulated; secondly, in the relatively low proportion of capital, out of the total, that is laid out on wages, i.e. in the relatively small amount of living labour that is required to reproduce and valorize a given capital, and for mass production. This presupposes at the same time the concentration of capital.

As far as the labour-power applied is concerned, the development of productivity again takes a double form – firstly, there is an increase in surplus labour, i.e. a shortening of necessary labour-time, the time required for the reproduction of labour-power; secondly, there is a decline in the total amount of labour-power (number of workers) applied to set a given capital in motion.

These two movements not only go hand in hand; they mutually condition one another, and are phenomena that express the same law. But they affect the profit rate in opposite directions. The total mass of profit is the same as the total mass of surplus-value, and the rate of profit $\frac{s}{c} = \frac{\text{surplus-value}}{\text{total capital advanced}}$. But surplus-value, in its total amount, is determined firstly by its rate and secondly by the mass of labour that is applied at this rate at any one time or, which comes to the same thing, by the magnitude of the variable capital. One of these factors, the rate of surplus-value, is rising; the other factor, the number of workers, is falling (relatively or absolutely). In so far as the development of productivity reduces the paid portion of the labour applied, it increases surplus-value by lifting its rate; but in so far as it reduces the total quantity of labour applied by a given capital, it reduces the number by which the rate of surplus-value has to be multiplied in order to arrive at its mass. Two workers working for 12 hours a day could not supply the same surplus-value as 24 workers each working 2 hours, even if they were able to live on air and hence scarcely needed to work at all for themselves. In this connection, therefore, the compensation for the reduced number of workers provided by a rise in the level of exploitation of labour has certain limits that cannot be overstepped; this can certainly check the fall in the profit rate, but it cannot cancel it out.

As the capitalist mode of production develops, so the rate of profit falls, while the mass of profit rises together with the increasing mass of capital applied. Once the rate is given, the absolute amount by which capital grows depends on its existing magnitude. But if this magnitude is given, the proportion in which it grows, i.e. its rate of growth, depends on the profit rate. A rise in productivity (which moreover always goes hand in hand with devaluation of the existing capital, as already mentioned) can increase the magnitude of the capital only if it increases the part of the annual profit that is transformed back into capital, by raising the rate of profit. In so far as labour productivity is concerned, this [the possible increase in the magnitude of the capital] can come about (since this productivity is not directly relevant to the *value* of the existing capital) only in so far as it either involves a rise in the relative surplus-value or else reduces the value of the constant capital, in other words cheapens either the commodities that go into the reproduction of labour-power or the elements of constant capital. Both of these, however, involve a devaluation of the existing capital, and both go hand in hand with a reduction in the variable capital as against the constant. Both processes condition the fall in the profit rate, and both delay it. In so far, moreover, as the higher rate of profit gives rise to an increased demand for labour, it leads to an increase in the working population and hence in the exploitable material which is precisely what makes capital capital.

Indirectly, however, the development of labour productivity contributes to an increase in the existing capital value, since it increases the mass and diversity of use-values in which the same exchange-value is represented, and which form the material substratum, the objective elements of this capital, the substantial objects of which constant capital consists directly and variable capital at least indirectly. The same capital and the same labour produce more things that can be transformed into capital, quite apart from exchange-value. These things can serve to absorb additional labour, and thus additional surplus labour also, and can in this way form additional capital. The mass of labour that capital can command does not depend on its value but rather on the mass of raw and ancillary materials, of machinery and elements of fixed capital, and of means of subsistence, out of which it is composed, whatever their value may be. Since the mass of labour applied thus grows, and the mass of surplus labour with it, the value of the capital reproduced and the surplus-value newly added to it grow as well.

Yet these two aspects involved in the accumulation process cannot just be considered as existing quietly side by side, which is how Ricardo treats them; they contain a contradiction, and this is announced by the appearance of contradictory tendencies and phenomena. The contending agencies function simultaneously in opposition to one another.

Simultaneously with impulses towards a genuine increase in the working population, which stem from the increase in the portion of the total social product that functions as capital, we have those agencies that create a relative surplus population.

Simultaneously with the fall in the profit rate, the mass of capital grows, and this is associated with a devaluation of the existing capital, which puts a stop to this fall and gives an accelerating impulse to the accumulation of capital value.

Simultaneously with the development of productivity, the composition of capital becomes higher, there is a relative decline in the variable portion as against the constant.

These various influences sometimes tend to exhibit themselves side by side, spatially; at other times one after the other, temporally; and at certain points the conflict of contending agencies breaks through in crises. Crises are never more than momentary, violent solutions for the existing contradictions, violent eruptions that re-establish the disturbed balance for the time being.

To express this contradiction in the most general terms, it consists in the fact that the capitalist mode of production tends towards an absolute development of the productive forces irrespective of value and the surplus-value this contains, and even irrespective of the social relations within which capitalist production takes place; while on the other hand its purpose is to maintain the existing capital value and to valorize it to the utmost extent possible (i.e. an ever accelerated increase in this value). In its specific character it is directed towards using the existing capital value as a means for the greatest possible valorization of this value. The methods through which it attains this end involve a decline in the profit rate, the devaluation of the existing capital and the development of the productive forces of labour at the cost of the productive forces already produced.

The periodical devaluation of the existing capital, which is a means, immanent to the capitalist mode of production, for delaying the fall in the profit rate and accelerating the accumulation of capital value by the formation of new capital, disturbs the given conditions in which the circulation and reproduction process of capital takes place, and is therefore accompanied by sudden stoppages and crises in the production process.

The relative decline in the variable capital as against the constant, which goes hand in hand with the development of the productive forces, gives a spur to the growth of the working population, while it continuously creates an artificial surplus population as well. The accumulation of capital, from the point of view of value, is slowed down by the falling rate of profit, which then serves yet again to accelerate the accumulation of use-value, while this in turn accelerates the course of accumulation in terms of value.

Capitalist production constantly strives to overcome these immanent barriers, but it overcomes them only by means that set up the barriers afresh and on a more powerful scale.

The *true barrier* to capitalist production is *capital itself*. It is that capital and its self-valorization appear as the starting and finishing point, as the motive and purpose of production; production is production only for *capital*, and not the reverse, i.e. the means of production are not simply means for a steadily expanding pattern of life for the *society* of the producers. The barriers within which the maintenance and valorization of the capital-value has necessarily to move – and this in turn depends on the dispossession and impoverishment of the great mass of the producers – therefore come constantly into contradiction with the methods of production that capital must apply to its purpose and which set its course towards an unlimited expansion of production, to production as an end in itself, to an unrestricted development of the social productive powers of labour. The means – the unrestricted development of the forces of social production – comes into persistent conflict with the restricted end, the valorization of the existing capital. If the capitalist mode of production is therefore a historical means for developing the material powers of production and for creating a corresponding world market, it is at the same time the constant contradiction between this historical task and the social relations of production corresponding to it.

3. SURPLUS CAPITAL ALONGSIDE SURPLUS POPULATION

As the profit rate falls, so there is a growth in the minimum capital that the individual capitalist needs in order to make productive use of labour; he needs this minimum capital both to exploit labour in general and to ensure that the labour-time spent on the production of commodities is necessary labour-time and does not overstep the average labour-time that is socially necessary for the production of these commodities. Concentration grows at the same time, since beyond certain limits a large capital with a lower rate of profit accumulates more quickly than a small capital with a higher rate of profit. This growing concentration leads in turn, at a certain level, to a new fall in the rate of profit. The mass of small fragmented capitals are thereby forced onto adventurous paths: speculation, credit swindles, share swindles, crises. The so-called plethora of capital is always basically reducible to a plethora of that capital for which the fall in the profit rate is not outweighed by its mass – and this is always the case with fresh off-shoots of capital that are newly formed – or to the plethora in which these capitals, which are incapable of acting by themselves, are available to the leaders of great branches of business in the form of credit. This plethora of capital arises from the same causes that produce a relative surplus population and is therefore a phenomenon that complements this latter, even though the two things stand at opposite poles – unoccupied capital on the one hand and an unemployed working population on the other.

Overproduction of capital and not of individual commodities – though this overproduction of capital always involves over-production of commodities – is nothing more than over-accumulation of capital. To understand what this over-accumulation is (we shall study it in more detail below), we have only to take it as an absolute. When would the overproduction of capital be absolute? And indeed we refer here to an overproduction which does not just extend to this or that or a few major areas of production, but is rather itself absolute in scope, so that it involves all fields of production.

There would be an absolute overproduction of capital as soon as no further additional capital could be employed for the purpose of capitalist production. But the purpose of capitalist production is the valorization of capital, i.e. appropriation of surplus labour, production of surplus-value, of profit. Thus as soon as capital has grown in such proportion to the working population that neither the absolute labour-time that this working population supplies nor its relative surplus labour-time can be extended (the latter would not be possible in any case in a situation where the demand for labour was so strong, and there was thus a tendency for wages to rise); where, therefore, the expanded capital produces only the same mass of surplus-value as before, there will be an absolute overproduction of capital; i.e. the expanded $C + \Delta C$ will not produce any more profit, or will even produce less profit, than the capital C did before its increase by ΔC. In both cases there would even be a sharper and more sudden fall in the general rate of profit, but this time on account of a change in the composition of capital which would not be due to a development in productivity, but rather to a rise in the money value of the variable capital on account of higher wages and to a corresponding decline in the proportion of surplus labour to necessary labour.

In actual fact, the situation would take the form that one portion of the capital would lie completely or partially idle (since it would first have to expel the capital already functioning from its position, to be valorized at all), while the other portion would be valorized at a lower rate of profit, owing to the pressure of the unoccupied or semi-occupied capital. The fact that a portion of the additional capital might take the place of the old, and that the old capital might thus take up a position within the additional capital, would be a matter of indifference here, as the old capital sum would be on one side of the account, the additional capital on the other. The fall in the profit rate would be accompanied this time by an absolute decline in the mass of profit, since on our assumptions the mass of labour-power applied has not increased and the rate of surplus-value not risen, so that the mass of surplus-value, too, could not be increased. And the reduced mass of profit would have to be calculated on an enlarged total capital. But even if we assume that the occupied capital continued to be valorized at the old rate of profit, so that the profit rate remained unchanged, then the mass of profit would still be calculated on the basis of an enlarged total capital, and this also would imply a fall in the rate of profit. If a total capital of 1,000 yields a profit of 100 and after being increased to 1,500 it still yields a profit of only 100, then in the second case 1,000 yields only $66\frac{2}{3}$. The valorization of the old capital would have experienced an absolute decline. The capital of 1,000, under the new conditions, would not yield more than a capital of $666\frac{2}{3}$ did earlier.

It is clear however that this kind of actual devaluation of the old capital would not take place without a struggle, and that the additional capital ΔC could not function as capital without a struggle. That competition which results from the overproduction of capital would not cause a fall in the rate of profit. Rather the reverse. Since the reduced rate of profit and the overproduction of capital spring from the same situation, a competitive struggle would now be unleashed. The capitalists already functioning would let the portion of ΔC that was already in their hands lie more or less idle, so as not to devalue their own original capital themselves and not constrict its place in the field of production, or else they would apply it so as to shift the idleness of the additional capital onto the more recent interlopers and onto their competitors in general, even at a temporary loss.

The part of ΔC that was in new hands would attempt to find a place for itself at the cost of the old capital, and would partly succeed in this, forcing a portion of the old capital to lie idle. It would compel this to evacuate its former place and would itself take the place of the additional capital that was employed only partially or not at all.

Whatever the circumstances, one part of the old capital would have to lie idle as far as its property as capital was concerned, i.e. the property of functioning as capital and being valorized. As to which section is particularly to be affected by this idling, this is decided in the course of the competitive struggle. As long as everything goes well, competition acts, as is always the case when the general rate of profit is settled, as a practical freemasonry of the capitalist class, so that they all share in the common booty in proportion to the size of the portion that each puts in. But as soon as it is no longer a question of division of profit, but rather of loss, each seeks as far as he can to restrict his own share of this loss and pass it on to someone else. For the class as a whole, the loss is unavoidable. But how much each individual member has to bear, the extent to which he has to participate in it, now becomes a question of strength and cunning, and competition now becomes a struggle of enemy brothers. The opposition between the interest of each individual capitalist and that of the capitalist class as a whole now comes into its own, in the same way as competition was previously the instrument through which the identity of the capitalists' interests was asserted.

How then is this conflict to be resolved? How are the relations corresponding to a 'healthy' movement of capitalist production to be restored? The method of resolution is already implicit in the way in which the conflict is stated. It involves this, that capital should lie idle, or even, in part, be destroyed, either to the entire value of the additional capital ΔC or at least to one part of this; although this loss is by no means uniformly distributed amongst all the particular individual capitalists, as our depiction of the conflict has shown, the distribution being decided instead by a competitive struggle in which the loss is divided very unevenly and in very different forms according to the particular advantages or positions that have already been won, in such a way that one capital lies idle, another is destroyed, a third experiences only a relative loss or simply a temporary devaluation, and so on.

Under all circumstances, however, the balance will be restored by capital's lying idle or even by its destruction, to a greater or lesser extent. This will also extend in part to the material substance of capital; i.e. part of the means of production, fixed and circulating capital, will not function and operate as capital, and a part of the productive effort that was begun will come to a halt. Even though, as far as this aspect goes, time affects and damages all means of production (except the land), what we have here is a far more intense actual destruction of means of production as the result of a stagnation in their function. The major effect here, however, is simply that these means of production cease to be active as means of production; a shorter or longer disruption occurs in their function as means of production.

The chief disruption, and the one possessing the sharpest character, would occur in connection with capital in so far as it possesses the property of value, i.e. in connection with capital *values*. The portion of capital value that exists simply in the form of future claims on surplus-value and profit, in other words promissory notes on production in their various forms, is devalued simultaneously with the fall in the revenues on which it is reckoned.

A portion of ready gold and silver lies idle and does not function as capital. Part of the commodities on the market can complete their process of circulation and reproduction only by an immense reduction in their prices, i.e. by a devaluation in the capital they represent. The elements of fixed capital are more or less devalued in the same way. Added to this is the fact that since certain price relationships are assumed in the reproduction process, and govern it, this process is thrown into stagnation and confusion by the general fall in prices. This disturbance and stagnation paralyses the function of money as a means of payment, which is given along with the development of capital and depends on those pre-supposed price relationships. The chain of payment obligations at specific dates is broken in a hundred places, and this is still further intensified by an accompanying breakdown of the credit system, which had developed alongside capital. All this therefore leads to violent and acute crises, sudden forcible devaluations, an actual stagnation and disruption in the reproduction process, and hence to an actual decline in reproduction.

But other agencies come into play at the same time. Stagnation in production makes part of the working class idle and hence places the employed workers in conditions where they have to accept a fall in wages, even beneath the average; an operation that has exactly the same effect for capital as if relative or absolute surplus-value had been increased while wages remained at the average. Periods of prosperity facilitate marriage among the workers and reduce the decimation of their offspring, factors which, however much they might involve a real increase in popul-ation, do not involve any increase in the population actually working, but do have the same effect on the relationship between the workers and capital as if the number of workers actually active had increased. The fall in prices and the competitive struggle, on the other hand, impel each capitalist to reduce the individual value of his total product below its general value by employing new machinery, new and improved methods of labour and new forms of combination. That is, they impel him to raise the productivity of a given quantity of labour, to reduce the proportion of variable capital to constant and thereby to dismiss workers, in short to create an artificial surplus population. The devaluation of the elements of constant capital, moreover, itself involves a rise in the profit rate. The mass of constant capital applied grows as against the variable, but the value of this mass may have fallen. The stagnation in production that has intervened prepares the ground for a later expansion of production – within the capitalist limits.

And so we go round the whole circle once again. One part of the capital that was devalued by the cessation of its function now regains its old value. And apart from that, with expanded conditions of production, a wider market and increased productivity, the same cycle of errors is pursued once more.

Even under the most extreme assumption that might be made, absolute overproduction of capital is not absolute overproduction in general, not absolute overproduction of the means of production. It is an overproduction of means of production only in so far as *these function as capital*, and hence have to produce an additional value in proportion to their value that has expanded together with their mass, i.e. have to valorize their value.

It is still overproduction, for all that, since the capital is unable to exploit labour at the level of exploitation that is required by the 'healthy' and 'normal' development of the capitalist production process, at a level of exploitation that at least increases the mass of profit along with the growing mass of capital applied; that therefore excludes a situation in which the rate of profit falls to the same degree as capital grows, or even falls more quickly than this.

Overproduction of capital never means anything other than overproduction of means of production – means of labour and means of subsistence – that can function as capital, i.e. can be applied to exploiting labour at a given level of exploitation; a given level, because a fall in the level of exploitation below a certain point produces disruption and stagnation in the capitalist production process, crisis, and the destruction of capital. It is no contradiction that this overproduction of capital is accompanied by a greater or smaller relative surplus population. The same causes that have raised the productivity of labour, increased the mass of commodity products, extended markets, accelerated the accumulation of capital, in terms of both mass and value, and lowered the rate of profit, these same causes have produced, and continue constantly to produce, a relative surplus population, a surplus population of workers who are not employed by this excess capital on account of the low level of exploitation of labour at which they would have to be employed, or at least on account of the low rate of profit they would yield at the given rate of exploitation.

If capital is sent abroad, this is not because it absolutely could not be employed at home. It is rather because it can be employed abroad at a higher rate of profit. But this capital is absolutely surplus capital for the employed working population and for the country in question. It exists as such alongside the relative surplus population, and this is an example of how the two things exist side by side and reciprocally condition one another.

On the other hand, the fall in the profit rate that is bound up with accumulation necessarily gives rise to a competitive struggle. Compensation for the fall in the profit rate by an increase in the mass of profit is possible only for the total social capital and for the big capitalists who are already established. New and independently operating additional capital finds no compensatory conditions of this kind ready made; it must first acquire them, and so it is the fall in the profit rate that provokes the competitive struggle between capitals, and not the reverse. This competitive struggle, moreover, is accompanied by a temporary rise in wages and a further temporary fall in the profit rate, deriving from this. The same thing is evident in the overproduction of commodities and the over-supply of markets. Since capital's purpose is not the satisfaction of needs but the production of profit, and since it attains this purpose only by methods that determine the mass of production by reference exclusively to the yardstick of production, and not the reverse, there must be a constant tension between the restricted dimensions of consumption on the capitalist basis, and a production that is constantly striving to overcome these immanent barriers. Moreover, capital consists of commodities, and hence overproduction of capital involves overproduction of commodities. Thus we have the singular phenomenon that the same economists who deny overproduction of commodities admit overproduction of capital. If it is said that there is no general overproduction, but simply a disproportion between the various branches of production, this again means nothing more than that, within capitalist production, the proportionality of the particular branches of production presents itself as a process of passing constantly out of and into disproportionality, since the interconnection of production as a whole here forces itself on the agents of production as a blind law, and not as a law which, being grasped and therefore mastered by their combined reason, brings the productive process under their common control. Countries where the capitalist mode of production is not developed are also required to consume and produce on a level that suits the countries of the capitalist mode of production. If it is said that overproduction is only relative, this is completely correct; but the whole capitalist mode of production is precisely such a relative mode of production, whose barriers are not absolute, but only absolute for it, on its basis. How else could there be a lack of demand for those very goods that the mass of the people are short of, and how could it be that this demand has to be sought abroad, in distant markets, in order to pay the workers back home the average measure of the necessary means of subsistence? It is because it is only in this specific, capitalist context that the surplus product receives a form in which its proprietor can make it available for consumption as soon as it has been transformed back into capital for himself. If it is said, finally, that the capitalists have only to exchange their commodities among themselves and consume them, then the whole character of capitalist production is forgotten, and it is forgotten that what is involved is the valorization of capital, not its consumption. In short, all the objections raised against the obvious phenomena of overproduction (phenomena that remain quite impervious to these objections) amount to saying that the barriers to *capitalist* production are not barriers to *production in general* and are therefore also not barriers to this specific, capitalist mode of production. But the contradiction in this capitalist mode of production consists precisely in its tendency towards the absolute development of productive *forces* that come into continuous conflict with the specific *conditions* of production in which capital moves, and can alone move.

It is not that too many means of subsistence are produced in relation to the existing population. On the contrary. Too little is produced to satisfy the mass of the population in an adequate and humane way.

Nor are too many means of production produced to employ the potential working population. On the contrary. What is produced is firstly too great a section of the population which is in fact incapable of work, which owing to its situation is dependent on the exploitation of the labour of others or on kinds of work that can only count as such within a miserable mode of production.* Secondly, not enough means of production are produced to allow the whole potential working population to work under the most productive conditions, so that their absolute labour-time is cur-

---

* Marx is most probably referring here to petty commodity production, in particular the production of smallholding peasants.

tailed by the mass and effectiveness of the constant capital applied during this labour-time.

Periodically, however, too much is produced in the way of means of labour and means of subsistence, too much to function as means for exploiting the workers at a given rate of profit. Too many commodities are produced for the value contained in them, and the surplus-value included in this value, to be realized under the conditions of distribution given by capitalist production, and to be transformed back into new capital, i.e. it is impossible to accomplish this process without ever-recurrent explosions.

It is not that too much wealth is produced. But from time to time, too much wealth is produced in its capitalist, antagonistic forms.

The barriers to the capitalist mode of production show themselves as follows:

(1) in the way that the development of labour productivity involves a law, in the form of the falling rate of profit, that at a certain point confronts this development itself in a most hostile way and has constantly to be overcome by way of crises;

(2) in the way that it is the appropriation of unpaid labour, and the proportion between this unpaid labour and objectified labour in general – to put it in capitalist terms, profit and the proportion between this profit and the capital applied, i.e. a certain rate of profit – it is this that determines the expansion or contraction of production, instead of the proportion between production and social needs, the needs of socially developed human beings. Barriers to production, therefore, arise already at a level of expansion which appears completely inadequate from the other standpoint. Production comes to a standstill not at the point where needs are satisfied, but rather where the production and realization of profit impose this.

If the rate of profit falls, on the one hand we see exertions by capital, in that the individual capitalist drives down the individual value of his own particular commodities below their average social value, by using better methods, etc., and thus makes a surplus profit at the given market price; on the other hand we have swindling and general promotion of swindling, through desperate attempts in the way of new methods of production, new capital investments and new adventures, to secure some kind of extra profit, which will be independent of the general average and superior to it.

The rate of profit, i.e. the relative growth in capital, is particularly important for all new off-shoots of capital that organize themselves independently. And if capital formation were to fall exclusively into the hands of a few existing big capitals, for whom the mass of profit outweighs the rate, the animating fire of production would be totally extinguished. It would die out. It is the rate of profit that is the driving force in capitalist production, and nothing is produced save what can be produced at a profit. Hence the concern of the English economists over the decline in the profit rate. If Ricardo is disquieted even by the very possibility of this, that precisely shows his deep understanding of the conditions of capitalist production. What other people reproach him for, i.e. that he is unconcerned with 'human beings' and concentrates exclusively on the development of the productive forces when considering capitalist production – whatever sacrifices of human beings and capital *values* this is bought with – is precisely his significant contribution. The development of the productive forces of social labour is capital's historic mission and justification. For that very reason, it unwittingly creates the material conditions for a higher form of production. What disturbs Ricardo is the way that the rate of profit, which is the stimulus of capitalist production and both the condition for and the driving force in accumulation, is endangered by the development of production itself. And the quantitative relation is everything here. In actual fact, the underlying reason is something deeper, about which he has no more than a suspicion. What is visible here in a purely economic manner, i.e. from the bourgeois standpoint, within the limits of capitalist understanding, from the standpoint of capitalist production itself, are its barriers, its relativity, the fact that it is not an absolute but only a historical mode of production, corresponding to a specific and limited epoch in the development of the material conditions of production.

4. SUPPLEMENTARY REMARKS

Since the development of labour productivity is far from uniform in the various branches of industry and, besides being uneven in degree, often takes place in opposite directions, it so happens that the mass of average profit (= surplus-value) is necessarily very far below the level one would expect simply from the development of productivity in the most advanced branches. And if the development of productivity in different branches of industry does not just proceed in very different proportions, but often also in opposite directions, this does not arise simply from the anarchy of competition and the specific features of the bourgeois mode of production. The productivity of labour is also tied up with natural conditions, which are often less favourable as productivity rises – as far as that depends on social conditions. We thus have a contrary movement in these different spheres: progress here, regression there. We need only consider the influence of the seasons, for example, on which the greater part of raw materials depend for their quantity, as well as the exhaustion of forests, coal and iron mines, and so on.

If the circulating part of the constant capital (raw material, etc.) steadily grows in mass together with the productivity of labour, this is not the case for the fixed capital – buildings, machinery, lighting and heating installations, and so on. Even though these become dearer in absolute terms as the physical mass of the machinery grows, they become relatively cheaper. If five workers produce ten times as many commodities as before, this does not mean that the outlay on fixed capital increases ten-fold. Even though the value of this portion of constant capital grows with the development of productivity, it is far from growing in the same ratio. We have already emphasized several times the distinction between the relationship of constant capital to variable as this is expressed in the fall in the profit rate, and the same relationship as presented – with the development of labour productivity – with respect to the individual commodity and its price.

(The value of a commodity is determined by the total labour-time contained in it, both past and living. The rise in labour productivity consists precisely in the fact that the share of living labour is reduced and that of past labour increased, but in such a way that the total sum of labour contained in the commodity declines; in other words the living labour declines by more than the past labour increases. The past labour embodied in the value of a commodity – the constant portion of capital – consists partly of the wear and tear of the fixed capital and partly of the circulating constant capital that goes completely into the commodity: raw and ancillary materials. The portion of value deriving from raw and ancillary materials must fall with the [rising] productivity of labour, since, as far as these materials go, this productivity is precisely expressed in the fact that their value has fallen. And yet it is precisely a characteristic of rising labour productivity that the fixed portion of the constant capital should experience a very sharp increase, and with this also the portion of value that it transfers to the commodities as wear and tear. For a new method of production to prove itself as a genuine advance in productivity, it must transfer a smaller additional share of value to the individual commodity for depreciation of the fixed capital than the portion of value that is deducted because less living labour is spared; it must in other words reduce the value of the commodity. And this necessity is self-evident, even if, as does happen in individual cases, an additional portion of value goes into the formation of the commodity for more or dearer raw or ancillary materials, besides the additional portion for depreciation of the fixed capital. All this additional value must be more than outweighed by the reduction in value that arises from the decrease in living labour.

This reduction in the total quantity of labour going into the commodity appears accordingly as the fundamental characteristic of a rise in labour productivity, irrespective of the social conditions under which production is carried on. In a society where the producers govern their production by a plan drawn up in advance, or even in simple commodity production, the productivity of labour is in fact invariably measured by such a standard. But what is the situation in capitalist production?

Assume that a certain branch of capitalist production produces a normal item of its commodity under the following conditions: the depreciation of the fixed capital comes to $\frac{1}{2}$ shilling per item; $17\frac{1}{2}$ shillings go on raw and ancillary materials; 2 shillings on wages; and the rate of surplus-value is 100 per cent, so that surplus-value amounts to 2 shillings. The total value is then 22 shillings. We assume for the sake of simplicity that capital in this branch of production has the average social composition, so that the production price of the commodity coincides with its value and the capitalist's profit coincides with the surplus-value he makes. The cost price of the commodity is then $\frac{1}{2} + 17\frac{1}{2} + 2 = 20$ shillings, and the average profit rate $\frac{2}{20} = 10$ per cent, with the production price of the article the same as its value of 22 shillings.

Now let us assume a machine is invented that cuts the living labour required for each item by half, while it produces a threefold increase in the share of value attributable to the depreciation of fixed capital. The matter then stands as follows: depreciation $1\frac{1}{2}$ shillings, raw and ancillary materials $17\frac{1}{2}$ shillings, wages

1 shilling and surplus-value 1 shilling, making a total of 21 shillings. The value of the commodity has now fallen by 1 shilling; the new machine has definitely raised the productivity of labour. But as far as the capitalist is concerned, the situation is thus: his cost price is now $1\frac{1}{2}$ shillings depreciation, $17\frac{1}{2}$ shillings raw and ancillary materials, and 1 shilling labour, making 20 shillings altogether, the same as before. Since the profit rate is not altered simply by the introduction of this new machine, he keeps 10 per cent on top of his cost price for himself, making 2 shillings. The price of production is therefore unchanged at 22 shillings, though this is now 1 shilling above the value. For a society producing under capitalist conditions, the commodity has *not* become cheaper and the new machine is *not* an improvement. The capitalist, therefore, has no interest in introducing the new machine. And since introducing it would also make his old machinery simply worthless, when it has not yet worn out, transforming it into nothing more than scrap-iron, so that he would actually suffer a positive loss, he refrains from what would be, for him, a piece of utopian stupidity.

For capital, therefore, the law of increased productivity of labour is not unconditionally valid. For capital, this productivity is not raised simply because more living labour in general is spared than is added in past labour, but only if more of the *paid* part of living labour is spared, as we have already indicated in brief in Volume 1, Chapter 15, pp. 515 ff. At this point the capitalist mode of production falls into a new contradiction. Its historical mission is ruthlessly to expand the productivity of human labour, to drive it onwards in geometrical progression. It is untrue to its mission as soon as it starts to inhibit the development of productivity, as it does here. It thereby simply shows once more that it is becoming senile and has further and further outlived its epoch.)[37]

In competition, the rising minimum amount of capital needed for the successful pursuit of an independent industrial business takes the following form, as productivity increases. Once the new and more expensive equipment has been generally introduced, smaller capitals are in future excluded from this line of business. Only when mechanical inventions in the various spheres of production are in their infancy can smaller capitals function indepen-

37. I have put the above in parentheses because, although it is re-edited from a note in the original manuscript, it goes beyond the original material in certain particulars. – F.E.

dently. Very large undertakings, on the other hand, where the proportion of constant capital is extraordinarily high, such as railways, do not yield the average profit rate, but only a portion of this, an interest. If this were not so the general rate of profit would fall still lower. And yet a great accumulation of capital in the form of shares finds a direct field of employment here.

Growth of capital, i.e. accumulation of capital, involves a reduction in the rate of profit only in so far as this growth brings with it those changes in the ratio between the organic components of capital that were considered above. Yet despite the constant and daily transformations in the mode of production, a greater or smaller part of this total capital, now this, now that, continues to accumulate for a certain period of time on the basis of a given average ratio of these components, so that its growth does not involve any organic change and is thus no cause for a fall in the rate of profit. This constant enlargement of the capital, and therefore also an expansion in production on the basis of the old methods which goes smoothly forward while new methods are already introduced alongside, is a further reason why the rate of profit does not decline in the same measure as the total social capital grows.

The increase in the absolute number of workers, despite the relative decline in the variable capital laid out on wages, does not take place in all branches of production and does not take place evenly in the branches where it does. In agriculture, the decline in the element of living labour may be absolute.

It is simply the needs of the capitalist mode of production, moreover, that lead the number of wage-labourers to increase absolutely, despite this relative decline. As far as this mode of production is concerned, labour-power is superfluous the moment it is no longer necessary to occupy it for 12 to 15 hours per day. A development in the productive forces that would reduce the absolute number of workers, and actually enable the whole nation to accomplish its entire production in a shorter period of time, would produce a revolution, since it would put the majority of the population out of action. Here we have once again the characteristic barrier to capitalist production, and we see how this is in no way an absolute form for the development of the productive forces and the creation of wealth, but rather comes into conflict with this at a certain point in its development. One aspect of this conflict is presented by the periodic crises that arise when one or another section of the working population is made superfluous in its old employment. The barrier to capitalist production is the surplus time of the workers. The absolute spare time that the society gains is immaterial to capitalist production. The development of productivity is only important to it in so far as it increases the surplus labour-time of the working class and does not just reduce the labour-time needed for material production in general; in this way it moves in a contradiction.

We have seen how the growing accumulation of capital involves its growing concentration. Thus the power of capital grows, in other words the autonomy of the social conditions of production, as personified by the capitalist, is asserted more and more as against the actual producers. Capital shows itself more and more to be a social power, with the capitalist as its functionary – a power that no longer stands in any possible kind of relationship to what the work of one particular individual can create, but an alienated social power which has gained an autonomous position and confronts society as a thing, and as the power that the capitalist has through this thing. The contradiction between the general social power into which capital has developed and the private power of the individual capitalists over these social conditions of production develops ever more blatantly, while this development also contains the solution to this situation, in that it simultaneously raises the conditions of production into general, communal, social conditions. This transformation is brought about by the development of the productive forces under capitalist production and by the manner and form in which this development is accomplished.

*

No capitalist voluntarily applies a new method of production, no matter how much more productive it may be or how much it might raise the rate of surplus-value, if it reduces the rate of profit. But every new method of production of this kind makes commodities cheaper. At first, therefore, he can sell them above their price of production, perhaps above their value. He pockets the difference between their costs of production and the market price of the other commodities, which are produced at higher production costs. This is possible because the average socially necessary labour-time required to produce these latter commodities is greater than the labour-time required with the new method of production. His production procedure is ahead of the social average. But competition makes the new procedure universal and subjects it to the general law. A fall in the profit rate then ensues – firstly perhaps in this sphere of production, and subsequently equalized with the others – a fall that is completely independent of the capitalists' will.

It should also be noted at this point that the same law prevails even in those spheres of production whose products do not enter either directly or indirectly into the workers' consumption, or into the conditions of production of their means of subsistence; i.e. it prevails even in those spheres of production in which no cheapening of commodities can increase relative surplus-value and make labour-power cheaper. (In fact, a cheapening of constant capital in any of these branches may increase the profit rate, if the level of exploitation of labour remains the same.) As soon as the new mode of production begins to spread, giving actual proof that these commodities can be produced more cheaply, then those capitalists who operate under the old conditions of production must sell their product below its full price of production; the value of this commodity has fallen, so that they need more labour-time to produce it than is socially necessary. In short, and this appears as the effect of competition, they must also introduce the new mode of production which reduces the ratio of variable capital to constant.

The application of machinery reduces the price of the commodities produced with that machinery owing to various factors, which can always be reduced to the decline in the quantity of labour absorbed by each individual commodity; but in addition to this there is the decline in the portion of value that goes into the individual commodity as the depreciation element of the machinery. The slower the machinery's depreciation, the more commodities it is distributed over, the more living labour it replaces before the day when its reproduction falls due. In both cases the quantity and value of the fixed constant capital are increased as against the variable.

'All other things being equal, the power of a nation to save from its profits varies with the rate of profits, is great when they are high, less, when low; but as the rate of profit declines, all other things do not remain equal . . . A low rate of profit is ordinarily accompanied by a rapid rate of accumulation, relatively to the numbers of the people, as in England . . . a high rate of profit by a lower rate of accumulation, relatively to the numbers of the people.' Examples: Poland, Russia, India, etc. (Richard Jones, *An*

Introductory Lecture on Political Economy, London, 1833, pp. 50 ff.)*

Jones is right to stress that, despite the falling rate of profit, the 'inducements and faculties to accumulate' increase. Firstly, on account of the growing relative surplus population. Secondly, because as the productivity of labour grows, so does the mass of use-values represented by the same exchange-value, i.e. the material elements of capital. Thirdly, because of the increasing diversity of branches of production. Fourthly, through the development of the credit system, joint-stock companies, etc., and the ease with which the possessor of money can now transform it into capital without having to become an industrial capitalist. Fifthly, the growth in needs and the desire for enrichment. Sixthly, the growing mass of investment of fixed capital, and so on.

*

Three cardinal facts about capitalist production:

(1) The concentration of the means of production in a few hands, which means that they cease to appear as the property of the immediate workers and are transformed on the contrary into social powers of production. Even if this is at first as the private property of capitalists. The latter are trustees of bourgeois society, though they pocket all the fruits of this trusteeship.

(2) The organization of labour itself as social labour: through cooperation, division of labour and the association of labour with natural science.

On both these counts the capitalist mode of production abolishes private property and private labour, even if in antithetical forms.

(3) Establishment of the world market.

The tremendous productive power, in proportion to the population, which is developed within the capitalist mode of production, and – even if not to the same degree – the growth in capital values (not only in their material substratum), these growing far more quickly than the population, contradicts the basis on behalf of which this immense productive power operates, since this basis becomes ever narrower in relation to the growth of wealth; and it also contradicts the conditions of valorization of this swelling capital. Hence crises.

* The Rev. Richard Jones (1790–1855), the third (with Malthus and Chalmers) in a trinity of economist parsons, though Marx ranks him somewhat higher than he does his two colleagues. See *Theories of Surplus-Value*, Part III, Chapter XXIV.

Part Four

The Transformation of Commodity Capital and Money Capital into Commercial Capital and Money-Dealing Capital (Merchant's Capital)*

* It is clear from the first paragraph of Part Four that the expression 'merchant's capital' is intended to cover both 'commercial capital' and 'money-dealing capital'.

Chapter 16: Commercial Capital

Merchant's or trading capital is divided into two forms or sub-species, commercial capital and money-dealing capital, which we shall go on to distinguish in such detail as is needed in order to analyse capital in its basic inner structure. And this is all the more necessary in so far as modern economics, and even its best representatives, lump trading capital and industrial capital directly together and in fact completely overlook trading capital's characteristic peculiarities.

*

The movement of commodity capital has been analysed in Volume 2 [Chapter 3]. Taking the social capital as a whole, one part of this is always on the market as a commodity, waiting to pass over into money, even though this part is always composed of different elements, as well as changing in magnitude; another part is on the market as money, waiting to pass over into commodities. Capital is always involved in this movement of transition, this metamorphosis of form. In as much as this function acquires independent life as a special function of a special capital and is fixed by the division of labour as a function that falls to a particular species of capitalists, commodity capital becomes commodity-dealing capital or commercial capital.

We have already explained (Volume 2, Chapter 6, 'The Costs of Circulation', 2 and 3) the extent to which the transport industry, storage and the dispersal of goods in a distributable form should be viewed as production processes that continue within the process of circulation. These incidents in the circulation of the commodity capital are sometimes confused with the functions peculiar to commercial capital; they are sometimes linked in practice with the specific functions peculiar to this capital, although as the social division of labour develops, so the function of commercial capital also evolves in a pure form, i.e. separately from these real functions and independent of them. For our purpose, where what matters is to define the specific difference of this special form of capital, we can therefore ignore these functions. In so far as capital that functions exclusively in the circulation process, and especially commercial capital, sometimes combines part of these functions with its own, it does not appear in its pure form. We only have this pure form once those functions are discarded and removed.

We have seen how the existence of capital as commodity capital, and the metamorphosis that it undergoes as commodity capital within the sphere of circulation, on the market – a metamorphosis that breaks down into buying and selling, the transformation of commodity capital into money capital and of money capital into commodity capital – forms a phase in industrial capital's reproduction process and thus in its production process as a whole; but that at the same time, in this function as circulation capital, it is distinguished from its own existence as productive capital. These are two separate and distinct forms of existence of the same capital. One part of the overall social capital is always to be found in this form as circulation capital on the market, in the course of this metamorphosis, although for any individual capital its existence as commodity capital and its metamorphosis as such forms only a point of transition, ever vanishing and ever repeated, a transition stage in the continuity of its production process; although, accordingly, the elements of commodity capital to be found on the market are constantly changing, since they are constantly being withdrawn from the commodity market and just as constantly returned to it as the new product of the production process.

Commercial capital, then, is nothing but the transformed form of a portion of this circulation capital which is always to be found on the market, in the course of its metamorphosis, and perpetually confined to the circulation sphere. We refer here to a portion only, because another part of the buying and selling of commodities always takes place directly between the industrial capitalists themselves. We shall ignore this other portion of the circulation capital completely in the present investigation, since it contributes nothing to the theoretical definition, to our understanding of the specific nature of commercial capital, and has moreover been exhaustively dealt with, for our purposes, in Volume 2.

The dealer in commodities, like any other capitalist, first appears on the market as the representative of a certain sum of money that he advances as a capitalist, i.e. which he seeks to transform from x (the original value) into $x + \Delta x$ (this sum plus the profit on it). As he is not just a capitalist, but a commodity dealer at that, it goes without saying that his capital has to appear on the market originally in the form of money capital, since he does not produce any commodities himself but simply deals in them, facilitating their movement; and in order to deal in them, he must first buy them, and be therefore the possessor of money capital.

Let us assume that a commodity dealer has £3,000 that he valorizes as trading capital. Say that he uses this £3,000 to buy, for example, 30,000 yards of linen from a linen manufacturer, at 2 shillings per yard. He later sells this 30,000 yards again. If the average rate of profit is 10 per cent and after deducting all his incidental expenses he makes an annual profit of 10 per cent, by the end of the year he has transformed his £3,000 into £3,300. How he makes this profit is a question we shall go into only later. Here we want first of all to consider just the form of his capital's movement. He keeps buying linen for £3,000 and keeps selling it again; and he constantly repeats this operation of buying in order to sell, $M-C-M'$, the simple form of capital, when it is completely restricted to the circulation process and not interrupted by the interval of the production process that lies outside its own movement and function.

What then is the relationship between this commodity-dealing capital and commodity capital as a mere form of existence of industrial capital? As far as the linen manufacturer is concerned, he has realized the value of his linen with the merchant's money, thus completing the first phase in the metamorphosis of his commodity capital, its transformation into money; and if other circumstances remain the same he can now transform this money back into yarn, coal, wages and so on, as well as into means of subsistence, etc., in consuming his revenue. Leaving his expenditure of revenue aside, therefore, he can now continue the reproduction process.

But although the metamorphosis of the linen into money, its sale, has already taken place as far as its producer is concerned, this has not yet happened for the linen itself. This is still on the market as commodity capital as before, with the allotted role of completing its first metamorphosis and being sold. Nothing has happened to the linen except a change in the person of its owner.

As far as its own function is concerned, its position in the process, it is still commodity capital as before, a saleable commodity; but now it is in the hands of the merchant instead of in those of the producer. The function of selling the linen, of facilitating the first phase in its metamorphosis, has been taken over from the producer by the merchant and transformed into his special business, whereas it was formerly a function that remained for the producer himself to perform, after he had completed the function of producing it.

Let us assume that the merchant does not succeed in selling his 30,000 yards in the interval that the linen producer takes before putting a further 30,000 yards on the market, at a value of £3,000 as before. The merchant cannot buy this again, since he still has the 30,000 unsold yards in stock and has not yet transformed that back into money capital. There is now a hold-up, an interruption in the reproduction. The linen producer may well have additional money capital at his disposal, which he could transform into productive capital and thus continue the process, independently of the sale of this 30,000 yards. But to make this assumption would not alter things at all. As far as the capital advanced in the 30,000 yards is concerned, its reproduction process is and remains interrupted. Here we thus have palpable evidence that the operations of the merchant are nothing more than those operations that must always be performed to transform the producer's commodity capital into money, operations which accomplish the functions of commodity capital in the circulation and reproduction process. If selling were the exclusive business of a mere agent of the producer, instead of being performed by an independent merchant, and purchase likewise, this connection would not be obscured for one moment.

Commercial capital, therefore, is absolutely nothing more than the commodity capital of the producer which has to go through the process of transformation into money, to perform its function as commodity capital on the market; only instead of being an incidental operation carried out by the producer himself, this function now appears as the exclusive operation of a particular species of capitalist, the merchant, and acquires independence as the business of a particular capital investment.

This is evident even in the specific form of circulation of this commercial capital. The merchant buys a commodity and later sells it: $M-C-M'$. In simple commodity circulation, or even in commodity circulation as this appears as a circulation process of industrial capital, $C'-M-C$, the circulation is effected in such a way that each piece of money changes hands twice. The linen producer sells his commodity, the linen, transforming it into money; the buyer's money passes into his hands. With this same money he buys yarn, coal, labour, etc., parting with this money once again in order to transform the value of the linen back into the commodities that form its elements of production. The commodity he buys is not the same as the commodity he sells, it is not a commodity of the same kind. He has sold products and bought means of production. But it is a different matter with the movement of commercial capital. With his £3,000 the linen dealer buys 30,000 yards of linen; he sells the same 30,000 yards in order to recover his money capital from the circulation sphere (£3,000 plus profit). Here it is not the same pieces of money that change place twice, but rather the same commodity; it passes from the hands of the seller into those of the buyer, and from the hands of this buyer, who has now become a seller, into those of another buyer. It is sold twice and can still be sold several more times, given the interposition of a series of further merchants; and it is precisely through this repeated sale, the double change of place of the same commodity, that the money advanced by the first buyer for the purchase of the commodity effects its return to him. In the case $C'-M-C$, the same money's double change of place makes it possible for the commodity to be alienated in one shape and appropriated again in another. In the case $M-C-M'$, the double change of place of the same commodity makes it possible for the money advanced to be withdrawn from circulation again. All this shows precisely that the commodity has not yet been definitively sold when it passes from the hands of the producer into those of the merchant, and that the latter is only continuing the operation of sale – or the facilitation of the commodity capital's function. It also shows at the same time how what was for the productive capitalist $C-M$, simply a function of his capital in its transient shape of commodity capital, is for the merchant $M-C-M'$, a particular valorization of the money capital he has advanced. One phase of the commodity's metamorphosis now exhibits itself, with respect to the merchant, as $M-C-M'$, i.e. as the evolution of a specific kind of capital.

The merchant definitively sells the commodity, i.e. the linen, to the consumer, whether this is a productive consumer (e.g. a bleacher) or an individual who uses the linen for his own private purpose. In this way the capital he has advanced returns to him (with a profit), and he can begin the operation afresh. If his money had functioned merely as means of payment when he bought the linen, he would only have needed to pay six weeks later, and if he had sold before this time, he could have paid the linen producer without himself having to advance any money capital. If he had not sold the linen, he would have had to advance the £3,000 when it fell due instead of immediately the linen was delivered to him; and if he had sold the linen below the price he bought it at, because of a fall in its market price, he would have had to replace the missing amount from his own capital.

What then gives commercial capital the character of an independently functioning capital, whereas in the hands of the producer who makes his own sales it obviously appears as no more than a particular form of his capital at a particular phase in its reproduction process, during its stay in the circulation sphere?

Firstly, the fact that the commodity capital achieves its definitive transformation into money, and thus its first metamorphosis, its function on the market that falls to it as commodity capital, in the hands of an agent distinct from the producer, and that this function of commodity capital is facilitated by the operation of the merchant, by his buying and selling, this operation thereby taking the form of a specific business of its own, separate from the other functions of industrial capital and hence autonomous. It is a particular form of the social division of labour, such that one part of the function which has to be performed in a particular phase of the capital's reproduction process, here the phase of circulation, appears as the exclusive function of a specific agent of circulation distinct from the producer. But this does not mean that this special business necessarily appears as the function of a special capital, different from industrial capital which is going through its reproduction process and independent of it; it does not appear like this in practice when trading is pursued simply by travelling salesmen or other direct agents of the industrial capitalist. A second aspect must also be involved.

The second aspect enters the scene in this way. The independent circulation agent, the merchant, advances money capital (whether his own or borrowed) in this position. What is simply C–M as far as an industrial capital involved in its reproduction process is concerned, the transformation of commodity capital into

money capital or a simple sale, presents itself for the merchant as
$M-C-M'$, as the purchase and sale of the same commodity, so
that the money capital that he parts with on the purchase returns
to him through the sale.

It continues to be $C-M$, the transformation of commodity
capital into money capital, that presents itself for the merchant as
$M-C-M$, in so far as he advances capital for purchasing the
commodity from the producers; it continues to be the first
metamorphosis of the commodity capital, even though the same
act may present itself for a producer or for the industrial capital in
the course of its reproduction process as $M-C$, the transformation
of money back into commodity (the means of production), i.e.
as the second phase in the metamorphosis. For the linen producer,
$C-M$ was the first metamorphosis, the transformation of his commodity capital into money capital. For the merchant, however,
this act takes the form $M-C$, the transformation of his money
capital into commodity capital. If he now sells the linen to the
bleacher, this in turn represents $M-C$ for the bleacher, the transformation of money capital into productive capital, or the second
metamorphosis of his commodity capital; but for the merchant
it is $C-M$, the sale of the linen that he had bought. In point of
fact, it is only now that the commodity capital that the linen
manufacturer has produced is finally sold; the merchant's
$M-C-M$, in other words, simply represents a mediatory process
for the $C-M$ between two producers. Let us assume, alternatively,
that the linen manufacturer buys yarn from a yarn dealer with
part of the value of the linen he sold. For him, therefore, this is
$M-C$. But for the merchant who sells the yarn, it is $C-M$, the
resale of the yarn; and with regard to the yarn itself as commodity
capital, it is simply its definitive sale, with which it passes from
the circulation sphere into that of consumption, $C-M$, the decisive
conclusion of its first metamorphosis. Thus whether the merchant
buys from the industrial capitalist or sells to him, his $M-C-M$, the
circuit of commercial capital, only ever expresses what with
respect to the commodity capital itself, as a transitional form of
the industrial capital being reproduced, is simply $C-M$, simply the
completion of its first metamorphosis. The $M-C$ of the commercial
capital is for the industrial capitalist simply $C-M$, but it is not so
for the commodity capital he produced. It is only a transition of
the commodity capital from the hands of the industrialist into
those of the agent of circulation; and it is only the commercial

capital's $C-M$ that is the decisive $C-M$ for the functioning commodity capital. $M-C-M$ is only two $C-M$'s performed by the same commodity capital, it consists simply of two successive sales, which between them simply make possible its final and definitive sale.

Thus the way that commodity capital assumes in commercial capital the form of an independent variety of capital is by the merchant advancing money capital that is valorized as capital, and functions as capital, only because it is exclusively engaged in facilitating the metamorphosis of commodity capital, in making it fulfil its function as commodity capital, i.e. its transformation into money. Money capital does this through perpetually buying and selling commodities. This is its exclusive operation; this activity that facilitates the circulation process of industrial capital is the exclusive function of the money capital with which the merchant operates. By way of this function he transforms his money into money capital, puts his M forward as $M-C-M'$, and by this same process he transforms commodity capital into commercial, commodity-dealing capital.

Commercial capital, in so far and as long as it exists in the form of commodity capital – and what we are considering here is the reproduction process of the entire social capital – is evidently nothing more than the part of industrial capital that is still on the market and engaged in its process of metamorphosis. This now exists and functions as commodity capital. Thus it is only the *money* capital advanced by the merchant, the money capital exclusively designed for buying and selling, which never assumes any other form than that of commodity capital and money capital, never assumes that of productive capital, and remains for ever penned into capital's circulation sphere – it is only this money capital that has now to be considered with regard to the overall reproduction process of capital.

Once the producer, the linen manufacturer, has sold his 30,000 yards to the merchant for £3,000, he uses the money thus released to buy the means of production he needs, and his capital goes back again into the production process. His production process continues, it goes forward without a break. As far as he is concerned, the transformation of his commodity into money has already taken place. But this transformation has not taken place for the linen itself, as we have seen already. It has not yet been decisively transformed back into money, not yet gone into either

productive or individual consumption as a use-value. The linen
dealer now represents the same commodity capital on the market
as the linen producer originally represented there. For the latter,
the process of metamorphosis has been shortened, but only to
continue on its way in the hands of the merchant.

If the linen producer had to wait until his linen really had
ceased to be a commodity, until it had passed to its final buyer,
the productive or individual consumer, then his reproduction
process would be interrupted. Or, in order not to interrupt it, he
would have to restrict his operations, transform a smaller part of
his linen into yarn, coal, labour, etc., in short into the elements of
productive capital, and retain a greater part of this as a monetary
reserve. This would make it possible for one part of his capital to
be present on the market as a commodity, while another part
carried on the production process, so that when this latter part
entered the market as a commodity, the other part would flow
back in the money form. This division of his capital is not abolished
by the intervention of the merchant. But without the latter, the
part of the circulation capital that exists in the form of a money
reserve would always have to be greater in proportion to the part
employed in the form of productive capital, and the scale of
reproduction would be accordingly restricted. Instead of this, the
producer can now regularly apply a greater part of his capital in
the actual production process, leaving a smaller part as a money
reserve.

This is why another part of the social capital, in the form of
commercial capital, is always to be found in the circulation sphere.
It is regularly applied simply to buying and selling commodities.
There thus seems to be only a change in the persons that have this
capital in their hands.

If, instead of buying linen for £3,000 with the intention of
selling it again, the merchant were himself to apply this £3,000
productively, the society's productive capital would be that much
greater. However, the linen producer would then have to keep a
larger part of his capital as a money reserve, and so would the
merchant now turned industrial capitalist. If the merchant
remains a merchant, on the other hand, the producer saves time
in selling which he can apply to supervising the production process,
while the merchant has to spend his entire time selling.

Given that commercial capital does not overstep its necessary
proportions, we can assume the following.

(1) As a result of the division of labour, the capital that is exclusively concerned with buying and selling is smaller than it would be if the industrial capitalist had to conduct the entire commercial part of his business himself. (And besides the money that has to be laid out on the purchase of commodities, this capital also includes the money laid out for the labour needed to pursue the merchant's business, as well as for the merchant's constant capital, warehouses, transport, etc.)

(2) Because the merchant is exclusively concerned with this business, not only is the producer's commodity converted into money sooner, but the commodity capital itself goes through its metamorphosis more quickly than it would in the hands of the producer.

(3) Taking commercial capital as a whole in relation to industrial capital, a single turnover of commercial capital can correspond not only to the turnovers of several capitals in one sphere of production, but also to the turnovers of a number of capitals in different spheres. The former is the case if the linen dealer, for example, after he has used his £3,000 to buy the product of a linen producer and sold this again before the producer in question puts the same quantity of goods on the market once more, buys the product of another linen producer, or several other linen producers, and sells this also, thus facilitating the turnovers of various capitals in the same sphere of production. The latter is the case if the merchant, after selling the linen, now buys silk, for example, and thus facilitates the turnover of a capital in another sphere.

The following general point should be noted. The turnover of industrial capital is restricted not just by the circulation time, but also by the production time. The turnover of commercial capital, in so far as it deals with just one particular kind of commodity, is not restricted by the turnover of a single industrial capital but rather by the turnover of all industrial capitals in the same branch of production. After the merchant has bought and sold one producer's linen, he can buy and sell that of another, before the first puts his commodity on the market again. The same commercial capital can thus successively facilitate the different turnovers of various capitals invested in a branch of production, so that its turnover is not identical with the turnovers of one individual industrial capital and hence does not replace only the monetary reserve that this particular industrial capitalist had to keep to himself. Naturally, the turnover of commercial capital in one sphere of production is restricted by the overall production in this sphere. But it is not restricted by the limits of production or the turnover time of an individual capital in this sphere, in as much as this turnover time is determined by the production time. Let us assume that A supplies a commodity that takes three months to produce. After the merchant has bought and sold it, say in one month, he can buy and sell the same product as supplied by another producer. Or after he has sold one farmer's corn, for example, he can buy and sell a second farmer's with the same money, and so on. The turnover of his capital is limited by the amount of corn that he can successively buy and sell in a given time, e.g. a year, but the turnover of the farmer's capital, quite apart from its circulation time, is restricted also by its production time, which covers a whole year.

The turnover of the same commercial capital can just as easily mediate the turnovers of capitals in various branches of production.

To the extent that the same commercial capital serves in different turnovers to transform various commodity capitals successively into money, and thus buys and sells them in a series, it performs the same function, as money capital in relation to commodity capital, that money does in general vis-à-vis commodities as a result of the number of times it circulates in a given period.

The turnover of commercial capital is not identical with the turnover or the reproduction, once only, of an equally large industrial capital; it is equal, rather, to the sum of the turnovers of a number of such capitals, whether in the same sphere of production or in different ones. The more quickly the commercial capital turns over, the smaller is the part of the total money capital that figures as commercial capital, and vice versa. The less developed production is, the greater is the sum of commercial capital in proportion to the amount of commodities put into circulation in general; the smaller, however, it is in absolute terms or compared with more developed conditions. And conversely. In undeveloped conditions of this kind, therefore, the greater part of money capital proper is in the hands of merchants, so that their wealth constitutes monetary wealth as far as others are concerned.

The velocity of circulation of the money capital advanced by the merchant depends (1) on the speed with which the production process is repeated and the various production processes are linked together; (2) on the speed of consumption.

The turnover described above does not require the entire commercial capital to be used to its full extent in buying commodities and then re-selling them. The merchant rather performs both movements at the same time. His capital is then divided into two parts, the first consisting of commodity capital and the second of money capital. He buys in one place, and transforms his money into commodities. He sells somewhere else, and transforms another part of the commodity capital into money. On the one hand his capital flows back to him as money capital, while on the other hand he receives back commodity capital. The greater the part existing in one form, the smaller that existing in the other. This fluctuates and is balanced out. If the use of money as means of circulation is combined with its use as means of payment and the credit system that grows up on this basis, there is still a further reduction in the money capital portion of the commercial capital in relation to the volume of transactions that this commercial capital performs. If I buy £1,000 worth of wine on three months' credit and I sell this wine for cash before the three-month period expires, not a single penny has to be advanced for the transaction. In this case, moreover, it is as clear as day that the money capital that figures here as commercial capital is nothing more than industrial capital itself in its form of money capital, in its own reflux in the money form. (If the producer who has sold commodities on three months' credit for £1,000 can get his promissory note discounted at the bank, this in no way alters the matter and has nothing to do with commercial capital.) If the market price of the commodity were to fall in the meantime by a tenth, say, not only would the merchant not receive any profit, but he would get only £2,700 back instead of £3,000. He would have to put up a further £300 in order to pay. This £300 functions simply as a reserve for settling the difference in price. But the same thing holds for the producer. If he had himself sold while prices were falling, he would also have lost £300 and could not begin production again on the same scale without a reserve capital.

The linen dealer buys linen from the manufacturer for £3,000; the latter spends, say, £2,000 out of this £3,000 on buying yarn; he buys this yarn from the yarn dealer. The money with which the manufacturer pays the yarn dealer is not the linen dealer's money, for the latter has received commodities to this amount in exchange.

It is the money form of his own capital. In the hands of the yarn dealer, this £2,000 seems to be money capital on its reflux; but how far is it really money capital, as distinct from simply £2,000 as the money form shed by the linen and assumed by the yarn? If the yarn dealer has bought on credit and sells for cash before his payment period expires, this £2,000 does not contain a single penny of commercial capital as distinct from the money form that industrial capital itself assumes in the course of its cycle. Commercial capital, therefore, in so far as it is not simply a form of industrial capital that happens to be found, in the shape of commodity capital or money capital, in the hands of the merchant, is nothing but the portion of money capital that belongs to the merchant himself, and is circulated in the purchase and sale of commodities. This portion represents, on a reduced scale, the portion of the capital advanced for production that always had to exist as a money reserve, a means of purchase, in the hands of the industrialist, and circulate as his money capital. This portion is now to be found, reduced, in the hands of merchant capitalists; and as such it functions exclusively in the circulation process. It is a part of the total capital which, leaving aside the expenditure of revenue, has to keep circulating on the market as a means of purchase, in order to keep the continuity of the reproduction process going. It is all the smaller in relation to the total capital, the quicker the reproduction process and the more developed the function of money as means of payment, i.e. the credit system.[38]

38. So that he can classify commercial capital as production capital, Ramsay confuses it with the transport industry and calls commerce 'the transport of commodities from one place to another' (*An Essay on the Distribution of Wealth*, p. 19). The same confusion can already be found in Verri (*Meditazioni sulla economia politica*, § 4, p. 32) and Say (*Traité d'économie politique*, I, pp. 14, 15).* S. P. Newman says in his *Elements of Political Economy* (Andover and New York, 1835): 'In the existing economical arrangements of society, the very act, which is performed by the merchant, of standing between the producer and the consumer, advancing to the former capital and receiving products in return, and then handing over these products to the latter, receiving back capital in return, is a transaction which both facilitates the economical processes of the community, and adds value to the products in relation to which it is performed' (p. 174). Thus producer and consumer each save time and money by the intervention of the merchant. This service requires an advance of capital and labour and has to be paid for, 'since it adds value to products, for the same products in the hands of consumers are worth more than in the hands of producers'. And in this way commerce appears to him, just as to Mr Say, as 'strictly an act of production' (p. 175). Newman's view

Commercial capital is nothing more than capital functioning within the circulation sphere. The circulation process is one phase in the reproduction process as a whole. But in the process of circulation, no value is produced, and thus also no surplus-value. The same value simply undergoes changes of form. Nothing at all happens except the metamorphosis of commodities, which by its very nature has nothing to do with the creation or alteration of value. If a surplus-value is realized on the sale of the commodity produced, this is because it already existed in the commodity. Nor does the buyer realize any surplus-value with the second act, the exchange of the money capital back into commodities (elements of production). What happens here is rather that the production of surplus-value is begun, by the exchange of money for means of production and labour-power. In fact, in as much as these metamorphoses cost circulation time – a time during which capital produces nothing at all, and therefore certainly does not produce any surplus-value – there is a restriction on the creation of value, and the surplus-value, as expressed in the profit rate, will actually vary inversely with the length of the circulation time. Commercial capital thus creates neither value nor surplus-value, at least not directly. In so far as it contributes towards shortening the circulation time, it can indirectly help the industrial capitalist to increase the surplus-value he produces. In so far as it helps to extend the market and facilitates the division of labour between

---

is fundamentally false. The *use-value* of a commodity is greater in the hands of the consumer than it is in those of the producer, because it is only here that it is at all realized. For the use-value of a commodity is realized, and begins to function, only when the commodity passes into the sphere of consumption. In the hands of the producer, it exists only in potential form. But a commodity is not paid for twice over, first for its exchange-value and then for its use-value as something extra. By paying its exchange-value, I appropriate its use-value. And the exchange-value does not increase in the slightest by the fact that the commodity passes from the hands of the producer or the middleman into those of the consumer.

* Pietro Verri (1728–97), an Italian, was one of the first economists to advance beyond the Physiocratic conception that agriculture alone was truly productive. (See *Theories of Surplus-Value* Part I, Chapter II, pp. 67–8.) Jean-Baptiste Say (1767–1832), whose *Traité d'économie politique* first appeared in 1817, is far more important in the history of economic thought. He took advantage of the confusion in Adam Smith's theory of the revenues of the three major classes to found the vulgar-economic doctrine of the 'factors of production'. See below, Chapter 48, pp. 953–70.

capitals, thus enabling capital to operate on a bigger scale, its functioning promotes the productivity of industrial capital and its accumulation. In so far as it cuts down the turnover time, it increases the ratio of surplus-value to the capital advanced, i.e. the rate of profit. And in so far as a smaller part of capital is confined to the circulation sphere as money capital, it increases the portion of capital directly applied in production.

Chapter 17: Commercial Profit

We saw in Volume 2 that the pure functions of capital in the circulation sphere create neither value nor surplus-value.* These 'pure functions' are the operations which the industrial capitalist has to undertake firstly to realize the value of his commodities, and secondly to transform this value back into the commodities' elements of production, the operations for effecting the metamorphoses of commodity capital, $C'-M-C$, i.e. the acts of sale and purchase. On the contrary, it was shown that the time these operations require sets limits to the formation of value and surplus-value, objectively as far as the commodities are concerned and subjectively as regards the capitalist. What applies to the metamorphosis of commodity capital as such is naturally not changed in any way when a part of this capital assumes the form of commercial, commodity-dealing capital, and the operations which effect the metamorphosis of commodity capital come to appear as the special business of a special section of capitalists, or as the exclusive function of one portion of the money capital. The metamorphosis of commodity capital $C'-M-C$ consists of the sale and purchase of commodities, and if these operations are not such as to create any value or surplus-value for the industrial capitalists themselves, they cannot possibly do so when they are performed by other persons instead. Moreover, if we consider the portion of the total social capital that must always be in existence as money capital if the reproduction process is not to be interrupted by the process of circulation but rather to be continuous, then if this money capital creates neither value nor surplus-value, it cannot acquire such properties if, instead of being put into circulation by the industrial capitalist, it is always put into

* See Volume 2, Chapter 5.

circulation by a special division of capitalists, to perform the same functions. The manner in which commercial capital can be indirectly productive, and the extent of this, have already been indicated, and we shall go into this in more detail later.

Commercial capital, therefore, stripped of all the heterogeneous functions that may be linked to it, such as storage, dispatch, transport, distribution and retailing, and confined to its true function of buying in order to sell, creates neither value nor surplus-value, but simply facilitates their realization, and with this also the actual exchange of the commodities, their transfer from one hand to another, society's metabolic process. And yet, since the circulation phase of industrial capital forms just as much a phase in the reproduction process as production does, the capital that functions independently in the circulation process must yield the average profit just as much as the capital that functions in the various branches of production. If commercial capital were to yield a higher average profit than industrial capital, a part of industrial capital would change into commercial capital. If it yielded a lower average profit, the opposite process would take place. No species of capital finds it easier than commercial capital to change its function and designation.

Since commercial capital does not itself produce any surplus-value, it is clear that the surplus-value that accrues to it in the form of the average profit forms a portion of the surplus-value produced by the productive capital as a whole. The question now is this. How does commercial capital attract the part of the surplus-value or profit produced by productive capital that falls to its share?

It is a mere semblance that commercial profit is just a supplement, a nominal increase in the price of commodities above their value.

It is clear that the merchant can obtain his profit only from the price of the commodities he sells, and also that this profit which he makes on the sale of his commodities must be equal to the difference between his purchase price and his sale price; it must be equal to the excess of the latter over the former.

It may well happen that additional costs (costs of circulation) go into the commodity after its purchase and before its sale, though it is equally possible for this not to be the case. If such costs are involved, it is clear that the excess of the sale price over the purchase price does not just represent pure profit. To simplify the investigation, however, we assume to start with that no costs of this nature are involved.

For the industrial capitalist, the difference between the sale price and the purchase price of his commodities is the difference between their price of production and their cost price, or, if we consider the social capital as a whole, the difference between the value of these commodities and their cost price for the capitalists, which is further resolved into the difference between the total quantity of labour objectified in them and the quantity of paid labour objectified in them. Before the commodities that the industrial capitalist buys are put back on the market again as commodities for sale, they pass through the production process, and it is here alone that the component of their price that will later be realized as profit is produced. The situation with the commodity dealer is somewhat different. He has commodities in his possession only as long as they are in their circulation process. He simply continues the sale of them begun by the productive capitalist, the realization of their price, and so he does not make them undergo any intervening process in which they might absorb new surplus-value. All the industrial capitalist does in circulation is realize a surplus-value or profit that has already been produced; the merchant, on the other hand, does not merely realize his profit in and through circulation, he also makes it there. This appears to be possible only because he sells commodities which were sold to him by the industrial capitalist at their prices of production – or, if we take the commodity capital as a whole, at their values, i.e. at more than these prices of production, making a nominal addition to their prices; looking at this again from the point of view of the total commodity capital, because he sells them at more than their value and pockets the difference between their nominal value and their real value, i.e. sells them dearer than they are.

The form of this addition is very simple to understand. Say for instance that a yard of linen costs 2 shillings. If I am to make 10 per cent profit on re-selling it, I must add one-tenth to its price and so I sell the yard at 2s. $2\frac{2}{5}$d. The difference between its actual price of production and its sale price is then $2\frac{2}{5}$d., and this is a profit of 10 per cent on 2 shillings. In point of fact I sell the yard of linen to its buyer at a price that is really the price of $1\frac{1}{10}$ yards. Or, what comes to the same thing, it is just as if I sold the buyer only $\frac{10}{11}$ yards for 2 shillings and kept $\frac{1}{11}$ for myself. In fact I can buy back $\frac{1}{11}$ of a yard with the 2⅔d., taking the price per yard at 2s. 2⅔d. This would simply be a roundabout way of sharing in the surplus-value and surplus product by making a nominal increase in the prices of commodities.

This is the realization of commercial profit by an addition to the price of commodities, as it presents itself at first sight. And in fact the whole idea that profit is derived from a nominal increase in commodity prices, or by selling them above their value, arises from the viewpoint of commercial capital.

When we look more closely, however, we soon see that this is just an illusion. And, assuming the predominance of the capitalist mode of production, this is not the way commercial profit is realized. (What we are dealing with here is always the average, and not individual cases.) Why do we assume that the merchant can only realize a profit of say 10 per cent on his commodities by selling them at 10 per cent above their prices of production? Because we have assumed that the producer of these commodities, the industrial capitalist (and it is he, as the personification of industrial capital, who always faces the outside world as 'the producer'), has sold them to the merchant at their price of production. If the purchase prices that the merchant pays for commodities are equal to their prices of production, and in the last analysis therefore to their values, so that the production price, and in the last instance the value of commodities, expresses the cost price to the merchant, then in fact the excess of his sale price over his purchase price – and this difference forms the only source of his profit – must be an excess of its commercial price over its production price, and in the last analysis the merchant sells all commodities above their values. But why did we assume that the industrial capitalist sold commodities to the merchant at their prices of production? Or rather, what was involved in this assumption? That merchant's capital (and here we are still dealing with this only as commercial, commodity-dealing capital) does not enter into the formation of the general rate of profit. In explaining the general rate of profit, we necessarily proceeded from this assumption, firstly because merchant's capital as such did not yet exist for us and secondly because the average profit, and therefore the general rate of profit, had necessarily to be developed as an equalization of the profits or surplus-values that are actually produced by industrial capitals in different spheres of production. In connection with commercial capital, on the other hand, we are

dealing with a capital that takes a share in profit without participating in production. It is now necessary, therefore, to supplement
the earlier presentation.

Let us assume that the total industrial capital advanced during
the year is $720_c + 180_v = 900$ (say in millions of pounds sterling),
and that $s' = 100$ per cent. The product is then $720_c + 180_v +
180_s$. If we call this product or the commodity capital produced C,
then its value or price of production (since the two coincide when
we take the totality of commodities) $= 1,080$ and the rate of
profit on the total capital of 900 is 20 per cent. This 20 per cent, as
explained already, is the average rate of profit, since here we are
reckoning surplus-value not on this or that capital of particular
composition, but rather on the total industrial capital with its
average composition. So $C = 1,080$ and the rate of profit is 20 per
cent. But we are now going to assume that besides this industrial
capital of 900 there is also a commercial capital of 100, taking the
same proportionate share in profit according to its size. According to our assumptions, this is one-tenth of a total capital of 1,000.
It thus takes a one-tenth share in the total surplus-value of 180
and gets a profit rate of 18 per cent. The profit to be divided
among the remaining nine-tenths of the total capital is now only
162, or similarly 18 per cent on the capital of 900. Thus the price
at which C is sold to the merchants by the holders of this industrial capital of 900 is $720_c + 180_v + 162_s = 1,062$. If the merchant
adds to his capital of 100 the average profit of 18 per cent, he sells
the commodities at $1,062 + 18 = 1,080$, i.e. at their price of
production, or, taking the commodity capital as a whole, at their
value, even though he only makes his profit in and through
circulation and only by the excess of his sale price over and above
his purchase price. If he still does not sell the commodities above
their value or price of production, this is precisely because he
bought them from the industrial capitalists below their value or
price of production.

Commercial capital thus contributes to the formation of the
general rate of profit according to the proportion it forms in the
total capital. If the average rate of profit is 18 per cent in the case
we are considering here, it would be 20 per cent if one-tenth of the
total capital were not commercial capital and the general rate of
profit were not consequently reduced by one-tenth. We thus
obtain a stricter and more accurate definition of the production
price. By price of production we still understand, as before, the

price of the commodity as equal to its cost (i.e. the value of the constant and variable capital it contains) plus the average profit on this. But this average profit is now determined differently. It is determined by the total profit that the total productive capital produces; but it is not calculated just on this total productive capital alone, so that, if this is 900, as above, and the profit is 180, the average rate of profit would be $\frac{180}{900} = 20$ per cent; it is calculated, rather, on the total productive and commercial capital together, so that if 900 is productive and 100 commercial capital, the average rate of profit is $\frac{180}{1,000} = 18$ per cent. The price of production is therefore k (the cost) + 18 per cent, instead of k + 20 per cent. The average rate of profit already takes into account the part of the total profit that accrues to commercial capital. The real value or production price of the total commodity capital is therefore $k + p + m$ (where m is commercial profit). The price of production, i.e. the price at which the industrial capitalist sells as such, is therefore less than the real production price of the commodity; or, if we consider all commodities together, the price at which the industrial capitalist class sells them is less than their value. In the above case, therefore, 900 (cost) + 18 per cent of 900, or 900 + 162, = 1,062. Now since the merchant sells at 118 commodities that cost him 100, he still adds 18 per cent; but because the commodities that he bought at 100 are worth 118, he does not sell them above their value. In future we shall keep the expression 'price of production' for the more exact sense just developed.* It is clear then that the industrial capitalist's profit is equal to the excess of the production price of his commodity over its cost price and that, as distinct from this industrial profit, commercial profit is equal to the excess of the sale price over the commodity's production price, which is its purchase price for the merchant; but the real price of the commodity = its production price + the commercial profit. Just as industrial capital only realizes profit that is already contained in the value of the commodity as surplus-value, so commercial capital does so only because the whole of the surplus-value or

---

* i.e. the price at which the industrial capitalist sells to the merchant, and not as Marx originally developed the concept, the price at which the industrial capitalist sells when there is no independent commercial capital intervening. It is rather confusing that Marx still refers to this latter as the 'real price of production', but this is presumably because it is at that price that the commodity is finally sold.

profit is not yet realized in the price of the commodity as realized by industrial capital.[39] The merchant's sale price is higher than his purchase price not because it is above the total value, but rather because his purchase price is below this total value.

Commercial capital is involved in the equalization of surplus-value that forms average profit, therefore, even though it is not involved in the production of this surplus-value. The general rate of profit thus already takes account of the deduction from the surplus-value which falls to commercial capital, i.e. a deduction from the profit of industrial capital.

It follows from the preceding:

(1) The bigger commercial capital is in comparison with industrial capital, the smaller the rate of industrial profit, and vice versa.

(2) It was shown in Part One that the rate of profit is always expressed in a lower figure than the rate of actual surplus-value, i.e. it always underestimates the exploitation of labour. In the above case, for example, we have $720_c + 180_v + 180_s$, a rate of surplus-value of 100 per cent expressed in a profit rate of only 20 per cent. This difference is still greater in so far as the average profit itself, taking into account the share that accrues to commercial capital, is that much smaller, here 18 per cent instead of 20 per cent. The average rate of profit for the directly exploiting capitalist thus makes the rate of profit appear smaller than it actually is.

Assuming that all other circumstances are the same, the relative size of commercial capital (though retail traders, a hybrid species, form an exception) will be in inverse proportion to the speed of its turnover, i.e. in inverse proportion to the overall vigour of the reproduction process. In the course of scientific analysis, the formation of the general rate of profit appears to proceed from industrial capitals and the competition between them, being only later rectified, supplemented and modified by the intervention of commercial capital. In the course of historical development, the situation is exactly the reverse. It is commercial capital which first fixes the prices of commodities more or less according to their values, and it is the sphere of circulation that mediates the reproduction process in which a general rate of profit is first formed.

39. John Bellers [*Essays about the Poor, Manufactures, Trade, Plantations, and Immorality*, London, 1699, p. 10].

Commercial profit originally determines industrial profit. It is only when the capitalist mode of production has come to prevail, and the producer has himself become a merchant, that commercial profit is reduced to the aliquot share of the total surplus-value that accrues to commercial capital as an aliquot part of the total capital concerned in the process of social reproduction.

In the supplementary equalization of profits brought about by the intervention of commercial capital, we saw that no additional element goes into the value of the commodity for the money capital that the merchant advances, and that the addition to the price, whereby the merchant makes his profit, is simply the portion of commodity value that productive capital has not included in the production price of the commodity, and has in fact left out. The case of this money capital is similar to that of the industrial capitalist's fixed capital. In so far as it is not consumed, its value does not constitute an element of the commodity's value. In the price the merchant pays for the commodity capital, he replaces its production price, $= M$, in money. His sale price, as analysed above, $= M + \Delta M$, this ΔM representing the addition to commodity price determined by the general rate of profit. When he sells the commodity, he receives back the original money capital he advanced for its purchase and this ΔM as well. We can see here again how his money capital is nothing more than the commodity capital of the industrial capitalist turned into money capital, which can no more affect the value of this commodity capital than if the latter were sold directly to the final consumer instead of to the merchant. All that actually happens is that the final consumer's payment is anticipated. But this is correct only if, as we have so far assumed, the merchant has no expenses, i.e. if he does not have to advance any other capital, circulating or fixed, in the process of commodity metamorphosis, buying and selling, besides the money capital he advanced to buy the commodity from its producer. This is not the case, however, as we saw in discussing the costs of circulation (Volume 2, Chapter 6). And these costs of circulation represent in part costs that the merchant has to reclaim from other agents of circulation and in part costs that arise directly from his specific business.

Whatever kind of circulation costs these may be, whether they arise from the business of the merchant pure and simple and belong therefore to the merchant's specific circulation costs, or whether they represent charges arising from belated production processes that are inserted within the circulation process, such as dispatch, transport, storage, etc., they always require on the part of the merchant, besides the money capital advanced in commodity purchase, an additional capital that is advanced in purchase and payment for these means of circulation. In so far as this cost element consists of circulating capital, it goes completely into the sale price of the commodities as an additional element, while in so far as it consists of fixed capital, it goes in according to the degree of its depreciation; but in so far as these are purely commercial costs of circulation, this element forms only a nominal value and not a real addition to commodity value. Whether circulating or fixed, however, this entire additional capital goes into the formation of the general rate of profit.

The purely commercial costs of circulation (i.e. excluding the costs of dispatch, transport, storage, etc.) are the costs that are necessary to realize the value of the commodity, whether transforming it from commodity into money or from money into commodity – to effect its exchange. In this connection we ignore completely any eventual production processes that continue during the act of circulation and can exist quite separately from commerce as such; as for instance the transport industry proper and the dispatch of goods can be completely separate from trade, as branches of industry, and actually are so. Goods for purchase and sale may also be kept in docks and other public storage areas, with the costs arising from this being charged to the merchant by third parties, in so far as he has to advance them. All this is to be found in the wholesale trade proper, where commercial capital appears in its purest form, hardly mixed up at all with other functions. The haulier, the railway director and the shipowner are not 'merchants'. The costs we are considering here are those of buying and selling. We have already noted earlier that these break down into accounting, book-keeping, marketing, correspondence, etc. The constant capital required for this consists of offices, paper, postage, etc. The other costs are reducible to variable capital that is advanced for commercial employees. (Dispatch charges, transport costs, advances of customs duties, etc. may partly be considered as advanced by the merchant in the purchase of commodities, and hence going into his purchase price.)

All these costs are incurred not in the production of the commodities' use-value, but rather in the realization of their value;

they are pure costs of circulation. They do not come into the immediate production process, but they do come into the circulation process and hence into the overall process of reproduction.

The only part of these costs that concerns us at this point is that laid out as variable capital. (Also to be investigated are, firstly, how the law that only necessary labour goes into commodity value applies in the circulation process. Secondly, how accumulation appears in the case of commercial capital. Thirdly, how commercial capital functions in the actual overall process of social reproduction.)

These costs arise from the economic form of the product as a commodity.

If the labour-time that the industrial capitalists themselves lose in selling their commodities directly to one another – i.e. in objective terms the commodities' circulation time – does not add any value to these commodities, it is clear that this labour-time does not change its character by devolving on the merchant instead of the industrial capitalist. The transformation of commodities (products) into money and of money into commodities (means of production) is a necessary function of industrial capital and hence a necessary operation for the capitalist, who is in fact simply personified capital, capital endowed with its own consciousness and will. But these functions neither increase value nor create surplus-value. The merchant, by performing these operations and carrying on the functions of capital in the circulation sphere after the productive capitalist has ceased to do this, simply takes the place of the industrial capitalist. The labour-time that these operations cost is being employed on necessary operations in the reproduction process of capital, but it does not add any extra value. If the merchant did not perform these operations (and so did not spend the labour-time they require), he would not be using his capital as a circulation agent of industrial capital; he would not be continuing the function that the industrial capitalist has abandoned, and hence would not share as a capitalist, and in proportion to the capital he advanced, in the mass of profit produced by the industrial capitalist class. Thus the merchant capitalist does not need to employ any wage-labourers in order to take a share in this mass of surplus-value, to valorize his advance as capital. If his business and his capital are small, he may himself be the only worker employed. He is paid by the part of the profit that accrues to him from the difference between the purchase price of the commodities and their real price of production.*

On the other hand, in this case, if the capital advanced by the merchant is small, the profit he realizes may not be any greater than the wage of a better-paid skilled worker; it may even be less than this. And in point of fact, functioning alongside him are the direct commercial agents of productive capitalists – buyers, salesmen, commercial travellers – receiving the same income or higher, whether in the form of a wage or a share in the profit made on each sale (commission, percentage). In the one case the merchant pockets the commercial profit as an independent capitalist; in the other case the direct employee of the industrial capitalist is paid a part of the profit in the form of either a wage or a proportionate share in the profit of the industrial capitalist whose agent he is, and in this case his principal pockets both the industrial and the commercial profit. But in all these cases, even though the income the circulation agent receives may appear to him as a simple wage, as payment for the work he has performed, and even though, where it does not take this form, the size of his profit may still be only equivalent to the wage of a better-paid worker, this income still derives solely from the commercial profit. This results from the fact that his labour is not value-creating labour.

The fact that the circulation operation is prolonged means for the industrial capitalist, (1) a personal loss of time, in so far as he is prevented from performing his own function as director of the production process; (2) an extended stay of his product, in its money or commodity form, in the circulation process, a process in which it is not valorized and in which the immediate process of production is interrupted. If this is not to be interrupted, either production must be cut back or additional money capital must be advanced so that the production process can continue on the same scale. In each case, what this amounts to is that either a smaller profit is made with the former capital or additional money capital has to be advanced in order to make the previous profit. This is just the same if the merchant replaces the industrial capitalist. Instead of the industrial capitalist spending more time on the circulation process, the merchant now spends this time; instead of his being forced to advance additional capital for circulation, the merchant advances it; or, what comes to the same

* See above, p. 399, note.

thing, whereas previously a substantial portion of the industrial capital was constantly entering and leaving the circulation process, now the merchant's capital is cooped up there permanently. And whereas previously the industrial capitalist made a smaller profit, now he has to abandon a part of his profit completely to the merchant. In so far as commercial capital remains confined to the limits within which it is necessary, the distinction is simply that this division of capital's function enables less time to be devoted exclusively to the circulation process, and less additional capital advanced for it, so that the reduction in the total profit which now takes the form of commercial profit is less than it would be otherwise. If, in the above example, $720_c + 180_v + 180_s$, together with a commercial capital of 100, leaves the industrial capitalist a profit of 162 or 18 per cent, thus bringing about a deduction of 18, then the additional capital needed to do without the independent operations of commercial capital might perhaps be 200, and we would then have a total advance of 1,100 by the industrial capitalist instead of 900, so that the surplus-value of 180 would represent a profit rate of only $16\frac{4}{11}$ per cent.

If the industrial capitalist who is his own merchant has advanced – besides the additional capital with which he buys new commodities before his product, which is still in circulation, has been transformed into money – still further capital in order to realize the value of his commodity capital, i.e. for the circulation process (office expenses and wages for commercial employees), then, although this certainly forms additional capital, it does not form any more surplus-value. It must be replaced out of the commodities' value, for a portion of this value must be reconverted back into these circulation costs, even if no additional surplus-value is formed in this way. As far as the total social capital is concerned, what this amounts to is that a part of this capital is required for secondary operations that are not a part of the valorization process, and that this part of the social capital has to be constantly reproduced for this purpose. In this way, the profit rate for both individual capitalists and the industrial capitalist class as a whole is reduced, a result that follows from every injection of additional capital in so far as this is required to set the same amount of variable capital in motion.

If these additional costs that are bound up with the circulation business as such are taken over from the industrial capitalist by the merchant, there is still this reduction in the profit rate, but to a lesser extent and in a different manner. What happens now is that the merchant advances more capital than would be necessary if these costs did not exist, and that the profit on this additional capital raises the total commercial profit, so that commercial capital enters together with industrial capital into the equalization of the average rate of profit on a greater scale, and the average profit falls. If, in our above example, a further additional capital of 50 was advanced for the costs in question, besides the commercial capital of 100, the total surplus-value of 180 would now be distributed between a productive capital of 900 and a commercial capital of 150, making a total of 1,050. The average rate of profit would thus fall to $17\frac{1}{7}$ per cent. The industrial capitalist sells the commodities to the merchant at $900 + 154\frac{2}{7} = 1,054\frac{2}{7}$, and the merchant sells them for 1,130 (1,080 + 50 for expenses that he has to recover). It must be assumed that the division between commercial and industrial capital involves a centralization of trading costs and a consequent reduction in them.

The question now arises as to the position of the commercial wage-labourers employed by the merchant capitalist, in this case the dealer in commodities.

From one point of view, a commercial employee of this kind is a wage-labourer like any other. Firstly, in so far as his labour is bought with the merchant's variable capital, not with money that he spends as revenue; it is bought, in other words, not for a personal service but for the purpose of valorizing the capital advanced in it. Secondly, in so far as the value of his labour-power, and therefore his wage, is determined, like that of all other wage-labourers, by the production and reproduction costs of this particular labour-power and not by the product of his labour.

But there is necessarily the same difference between him and the workers directly employed by industrial capital as there is between industrial capital and commercial capital, and consequently between the industrial capitalist and the merchant. Since the merchant, being simply an agent of circulation, produces neither value nor surplus-value (for the additional value that he adds to commodities by his expenses is reducible to the addition of previously existing value, even though the question still arises here as to how he maintains and conserves the value of this constant capital), the commercial workers whom he employs in these same functions cannot possibly create surplus-value for him directly. Here, just as with the productive workers, we assume that wages are determined by the value of labour-power, i.e. the merchant does not enrich himself by a deduction from wages, so that in reckoning his costs he does not put down an advance for labour that he only pays in part. In other words, he does not enrich himself by cheating his clerks, etc.

The problem that arises in connection with these commercial workers is by no means that of explaining how they directly produce profit for their employers, even though they do not directly produce surplus-value (of which profit is simply a trans-formed form). This question has in fact already been resolved by the general analysis of commercial profit. Just as industrial capital makes its profit by selling labour that is already contained and realized in the commodity, labour for which it has not paid an equivalent, so commercial capital makes a profit by not paying productive capital in full for the unpaid labour contained in the commodity (in so far as the capital laid out in order to produce the commodity functions as an aliquot part of the total industrial capital), and, as against this, itself receiving the additional portion which it has not paid for once the commodity has been sold. Commercial capital's relationship to surplus-value is different from that of industrial capital. The latter produces surplus-value by directly appropriating the unpaid labour of others. The former appropriates a portion of this surplus-value by getting it trans-ferred from industrial capital to itself.

It is only by way of its function in the realization of values that commercial capital functions as capital in the reproduction process, and therefore draws, as functioning capital, on the surplus-value that the total capital produces. For the individual merchant, the amount of his profit depends on the amount of capital that he can employ in this process, and he can employ all the more capital in buying and selling, the greater the unpaid labour of his clerks. The very function by virtue of which the commercial capitalist's money is capital is performed in large measure by his employees, on his instructions. Their unpaid labour, even though it does not create surplus-value, does create his ability to appropriate surplus-value, which, as far as this capital is concerned, gives exactly the same result; i.e. it is its source of profit. Otherwise the business of commerce could never be conducted in the capitalist manner, or on a large scale.

Just as the unpaid labour of the worker creates surplus-value for productive capital directly, so also does the unpaid labour of the commercial employee create a share in that surplus-value for commercial capital.

The difficulty is rather as follows. Since the labour-time and labour of the merchant himself is not value-creating labour, even though it procures him a share in the surplus-value already produced, what is the situation with the variable capital that he lays out on the purchase of commercial labour-power? Should this variable capital be included as part of the cost of the outlay of the commercial capital the merchant has advanced? If not, this would seem to contradict the law of the equalization of the profit rate; what capitalist would advance 150, if he could reckon only 100 of it as capital advanced? If it is included, however, this would seem to contradict the very nature of commercial capital, since this kind of capital does not function as capital by setting the labour of others in motion, in the manner of industrial capital, but rather by itself working, i.e. itself performing the functions of buying and selling, and it is precisely in this way that it transfers to itself a part of the surplus-value the industrial capital has created.

(The following points have therefore to be investigated: the merchant's variable capital; the law of necessary labour in the circulation sphere; how the work of the merchant maintains the value of his constant capital; the role of commercial capital in the overall reproduction process; and finally the division into commodity capital and money capital on the one hand and into commercial capital and money-dealing capital on the other.)

If each merchant possessed only the amount of capital that he was personally able to turn over by his own work, there would be an infinite fragmentation of commercial capital, a fragmentation which would necessarily increase with the progress of the capitalist mode of production and in the same measure, since the productive capital would produce on a larger and larger scale and would operate with larger and larger quantities. This would mean a growing disproportion between the two forms of capital. To the same extent as capital was centralized in the sphere of production, it would be decentralized in the sphere of circulation. In this way, the purely commercial business of the industrial capitalist and his purely commercial tasks would be infinitely expanded, in as much as he would have to deal with 100 or even 1,000 different merchants. The result would be the loss of a large part of the advantage that derives from the autonomous position of commercial capital;

and besides the purely commercial costs, the other costs of circulation – those of grading, dispatch, etc. – would also grow. This is how industrial capital would be affected. Let us now consider the commercial capital; in the first place, how commercial work proper would be affected. It takes no more time to reckon with large figures than with small. It takes ten times longer to make ten purchases of £100 than *one* purchase of £1,000. It takes ten times as much correspondence work, paper and postage to write to ten small merchants as to *one* big one. A well-defined division of labour in the commercial office, where one person keeps the books, another the cash-box, a third writes letters, this one buys, another sells, that one travels, etc., spares a tremendous amount of labour-time, so that the number of workers involved in wholesale trade is in no way proportionate to the comparative scale of the transactions. In commerce, in fact, far more than in industry, the same function takes the same amount of labour-time whether it is performed on a large or small scale. Thus concentration historically appears in commerce earlier than in the industrial workshop. There are also the expenses for constant capital. A hundred small offices cost infinitely more than one big one, a hundred small warehouses more than a big warehouse, etc. Transport costs, which commerce is concerned with at least as costs to be advanced, also grow with this fragmentation.

The industrial capitalist would have to spend more labour and incur greater circulation costs on the commercial side of his business. The same commercial capital, if divided between many small merchants, would require many more workers to carry out its functions, on account of this fragmentation, and besides this a larger commercial capital would be required to turn over the same commodity capital.

Let us call the total commercial capital directly invested in the buying and selling of commodities B, and the corresponding variable capital laid out for payment of the commercial assistants b. $B + b$ will necessarily be less than the total commercial capital B would be if each merchant struggled by without assistance, i.e. if one portion was not invested as b. But we have still not finished with this problem.

The price at which the commodities are sold must be sufficient (1) to pay the average profit on $B + b$. This is already explained by the fact that $B + b$ is always a reduction on the original B and represents a smaller commercial capital than would be needed without the b. But this sale price must also be sufficient (2) to replace, besides the seemingly additional profit on b, also the wages paid, the merchant's actual variable capital $= b$. It is this latter that creates the difficulty. Does b form a new component of the price, or is it simply a part of the profit made with $B + b$ that appears as wages as far as the commercial employees are concerned and appears to the merchant himself as simply the replacement of his variable capital? In the latter case, the profit which the merchant makes on the capital $B + b$ that he advances would be equal simply to the profit that accrues to B, according to the general rate of profit, b being paid in the form of wages, but without this yielding any profit.

It all boils down to finding the limits of b (in the mathematical sense). We must first define the problem more precisely. Let us call the capital directly laid out on buying and selling commodities B, the constant capital utilized for this function K (the material expenses involved) and the variable capital that the merchant lays out b.

The replacement of B presents no difficulty at all. For the merchant it is simply the realized purchase price, or the price of production for the manufacturer. The merchant pays this price, and on resale he receives back B as a portion of his sale price; and besides this B, the profit on B, as already explained. Say that the commodity costs £100, and the profit on it is 10 per cent. The commodity is then sold at 110. The commodity still costs 100, as before, so that the commercial capital of 100 only adds 10 to it.

If we now take K, this is at most as large as, though in actual fact it is smaller than, the portion of constant capital that the producer would need for selling and buying; this would of course be in addition to the constant capital he uses directly in production. None the less, this part must always be recovered in the price of the commodity, or, what comes to the same thing, a corresponding part of the commodity must always be spent and reproduced in this form – taking the total social capital as a whole. This part of the constant capital advanced would have the same constricting effect on the profit rate as does all constant capital directly invested in production. In as much as the industrial capitalist hands over the commercial side of his business to the merchant, he does not need to advance this portion of capital. Instead of him, it is the merchant who advances it. Yet this is really only an advance in name, in as much as the merchant neither produces nor reproduces the constant capital that he uses (his material expenses). The production of these appears therefore as a separate business of certain industrial capitalists, or at least a part of their business, so that these play the same role as those supplying constant capital to the producers of means of subsistence. The merchant thus receives firstly the replacement for this constant capital, and secondly the profit on it. On both counts, the profit of the industrial capitalist is reduced. But because of the concentration and economy that results from the division of labour, this reduction is less than it would be if he had to advance this capital himself. The reduction in the profit rate is less, because the capital advanced in this way is less.

Formerly, the sale price amounted to $B + K +$ the profit on $(B + K)$. After what was said before, this part of the sale price presents no difficulty. But now we have also b, or the variable capital advanced by the merchant.

The sale price now becomes $B + K + b +$ the profit on $(B + K) +$ the profit on b.

B only replaces the purchase price, and it does not add anything to this price besides the profit on B. K not only adds the profit on K, but also K itself; but $K +$ the profit on K, the part of the circulation costs advanced in the form of constant capital $+$ the corresponding average profit, would be greater in the hands of the industrial capitalist than in the hands of the commercial capitalist. The reduction in the average profit takes this form, that the full average profit is calculated after the deduction of $B + K$ from the industrial capital advanced. However, this deduction from the average profit for $B + K$ is paid to the merchant, so that it appears as the profit of a special capital, commercial capital.

But the situation is different with ($b +$ the profit on b), or, in the case given here, since we have assumed a profit rate of 10 per cent, $b + \frac{1}{10}b$. And this is where the real difficulty lies.

What the merchant buys with b, according to our assumptions, is merely commercial labour, i.e. labour needed for the functions of capital circulation, $C-M$ and $M-C$. But commercial labour is the labour that is always necessary for a capital to function as commercial capital, for it to mediate the transformation of commodities into money and money into commodities. It is labour that realizes values but does not create any. And only in so far as a capital performs these functions – i.e. in so far as a capitalist performs these operations and this labour with his capital – does this capital function as commercial capital and take part in settling the general rate of profit, by drawing its dividends from the total profit. In (b + the profit on b), however, it seems that first the labour is paid (since it comes to the same thing whether the industrial capitalist pays the merchant for his own labour or for that of his employees), and secondly the profit on the payment for this labour that the merchant himself would have had to perform. Commercial capital seems to receive firstly the repayment of b and secondly the profit on it; this arises because it firstly gets paid for the labour by way of which it functions as *commercial* capital, and secondly gets paid the profit because it functions as *capital*, i.e. in its capacity as a functioning capital it performs labour that is paid for in profit. This is the question which we have to resolve.

Let us take $B = 100$, $b = 10$ and the rate of profit = 10 per cent. We put $K = 0$, so as to avoid unnecessarily reintroducing an element of the purchase price that does not belong here and has already been dealt with. The purchase price would then be (B + profit on B) + (b + profit on b) = $B + Bp' + b + bp'$ (where p' is the rate of profit), = $100 + 10 + 10 + 1 = 121$.

But if the merchant did not lay out this b on wages – since b is paid simply for commercial labour, i.e. for labour needed to realize the value of the commodity capital which industrial capital puts on the market – the matter would stand as follows. To buy or sell $B = 100$, the merchant gives up his time, and we shall assume that this is the only time available to him. The commercial labour represented by $b = 10$, if it were not paid as wages but rather by way of profit, would presuppose another commercial capital of 100, since 10 per cent of this gives $b = 10$. This second $B = 100$ would not go additionally into the price of the commodity, but the 10 per cent certainly would. There would therefore be two operations at 100, giving 200, buying commodities for 200 + 20 = 220.

Since commercial capital is nothing at all but the form in which a part of the industrial capital functioning in the circulation process has become autonomous, all questions relating to it must be resolved in this way: the problem must at the outset be put in the form in which the phenomena peculiar to commercial capital do not yet appear independently but are still in direct connection with industrial capital, of which commercial capital is a branch. Commercial capital, with an office instead of a workshop, functions continuously in the circulation process. And so the *b* that is at issue here must firstly be investigated on the spot, in the commercial office of the industrial capitalist himself.

Right from the beginning, this office is always infinitesimally small in relation to the industrial workshop. Yet it is evident none the less that, as the scale of production is expanded, the commercial operations that the circulation of industrial capital requires are increased, both those required to sell the product in the form of commodity capital and those required to transform the money thus obtained back into means of production, as well as to keep the accounts for the whole process. Price calculation, bookkeeping, fund management and correspondence are all part of this. The more the scale of production grows, the greater are industrial capital's commercial operations, although the increase is by no means in the same proportion, and the greater also the labour and other circulation costs involved in the realization of value and surplus-value. It is necessary therefore to employ commercial workers who make up a proper commercial office. The expenditure on this, even though incurred in the form of wages, is distinct from the variable capital laid out on the purchase of productive labour. It increases the outlays of the industrial capitalist, the mass of capital he has to advance, without directly increasing the surplus-value. For this is an outlay for labour employed simply in realizing values already created. Just like other outlays of the same kind, this too reduces the rate of profit, because the capital advanced grows, but not the surplus-value. The surplus-value *s* remains constant, but the capital advanced *C* still grows from C to ΔC, so that the profit rate $\frac{s}{C}$ is replaced by the smaller profit rate $\frac{s}{C + \Delta C}$. The industrial capitalist therefore attempts to keep these circulation costs to a minimum, just as he does his outlay on constant capital. Industrial capital therefore does not behave towards its commercial employees as it does to its productive wage-labourers. The more of the latter are employed, with other circumstances remaining the same, the more massive is production and the greater the surplus-value or profit. Conversely, however, the greater the scale of production and the greater the value and surplus-value to be realized, the greater therefore the commodity capital produced, the more, accordingly, do office expenses grow in absolute terms, even if not relatively, and provide the occasion for a particular kind of division of labour. The extent to which profit is the prerequisite for these outlays is shown among other things by the way that, as commercial salaries increase, a part of these is often paid as a percentage of the profit. It lies in the nature of the thing that a labour that consists simply in intermediary operations, involving partly the calculation of values, partly their realization, and partly again the transformation of the money realized back into means of production, a labour whose scope thus depends on the magnitude of values produced and to be realized – that a labour of this kind functions not as the cause of the respective magnitudes and amounts of these values, as does directly productive labour, but is rather a consequence of them. It is similar with the other costs of circulation. If there is much to be weighed, measured, packed and transported, there must be plenty there in the first place. The amount of packing and transport work, etc. depends on the mass of the commodities that are objects of this activity and not the other way round.

The commercial worker does not produce surplus-value directly. But the price of his labour is determined by the value of his labour-power, i.e. its cost of production, although the exercise of this labour-power, the exertion, expenditure of energy and wear and tear it involves, is no more limited by the value of his labour-power than it is in the case of any other wage-labourer. His wage therefore does not stand in any necessary relationship to the amount of profit that he helps the capitalist to realize. What he costs the capitalist and what he brings in for him are different quantities. What he brings in is a function not of any direct creation of surplus-value but of his assistance in reducing the cost of realizing surplus-value, in so far as he performs labour (part of it unpaid). The commercial worker proper belongs to the better-paid class of wage-labourer; he is one of those whose labour is skilled labour, above-average labour. His wage, however, has a tendency to fall, as the capitalist mode of production advances, even in relation to average labour. Firstly, because the division of labour within the commercial office means that only a one-sided development of ability need be produced and that much of the cost of producing this ability to work is free for the capitalist, since the worker's skill is rather developed by the function itself, and indeed is developed all the more quickly, the more one-sided the function becomes with the division of labour. Secondly, because basic skills, knowledge of commerce and languages, etc., are reproduced ever more quickly, easily, generally and cheaply, the more the capitalist mode of production adapts teaching methods, etc. to practical purposes. The general extension of popular education permits this variety of labour to be recruited from classes which were formerly excluded from it and were accustomed to a lower standard of living. This also increases supply, and with it competition. With a few exceptions, therefore, the labour-power of these people is devalued with the advance of capitalist production; their wages fall, whereas their working ability increases. The capitalist increases the number of these workers, if he has more value and profit to realize. The increase in this labour is always an effect of the increase in surplus-value, and never a cause of it.[39] [a]

*

A certain duplication consequently takes place. On the one hand the functions of commodity capital and money capital (and consequently also of commercial capital) are general formal determinations of industrial capital. On the other hand, special capitals, and consequently also a special set of capitalists, are exclusively engaged in these functions; and these functions develop into special spheres for the valorization of capital.

It is only with commercial capital that the commercial functions and circulation costs acquire autonomy. The aspect of industrial capital that pertains to circulation consists not only in its regular forms of commodity capital and money capital, but also in the commercial office alongside the workshop. But with commercial capital this acquires autonomy. For the latter, the commercial office forms its only workshop. The part of capital applied in the form of the circulation costs appears much greater with the wholesale merchant than with the industrialist, because besides the business office that goes together with every industrial workshop, the part of capital that has to be employed in this way by the overall class of industrial capitalists as a whole is now

---

39 [a] We can give an example of this prognosis, written in 1865, of the fate of the commercial proletariat since this time, in the form of the hundreds of German clerks skilled in all commercial operations and in three or four languages, who are offering their services in vain in the City of London for a weekly wage of 25 shillings – well below the wage of a skilled mechanic. A gap of two pages in the manuscript here indicates that this point was to be further developed. Reference should also be made to Volume 2, Chapter 6 ('The Costs of Circulation'), pp. 207–14, which already touches on various points pertinent here. – F.E.

concentrated in the hands of individual merchants By taking charge of the circulation function, they also take over the circulation costs that arise from it.

To industrial capital, the costs of circulation appear as expenses, which they are. To the merchant, they appear as the source of his profit, which – on the assumption of a general rate of profit – stands in proportion to the size of these costs. The outlay that has to be made on these circulation costs is therefore a productive investment as far as commercial capital is concerned. For it, therefore, the commercial labour that it buys is also directly productive.

Chapter 18: The Turnover of Commercial Capital. Prices

The turnover of industrial capital is the unity of its production and circulation times and consequently embraces the entire production process. The turnover of commercial capital, on the other hand, since it is nothing but the movement of commodity capital that has become autonomous, represents only the first phase in the commodity metamorphosis, C–M, as the reflux movement of a special capital; M–C, C–M, from the merchant's point of view, is the turnover of commercial capital. The merchant buys, transforming his money into commodities, then sells, transforming the same commodities again into money, and so on in constant repetition. Within the circulation sphere, the metamorphosis of industrial capital always presents itself as C_1–M–C_2; the money obtained from the sale of C_1, the commodity produced, is used to buy C_2, new means of production; this is in fact an exchange of C_1 and C_2, and the same money therefore changes hands twice. Its movement mediates the exchange of two different kinds of commodities, C_1 and C_2. In the merchant's case, however, it is the same commodity that changes hands twice in M–C–M′; it simply mediates the reflux to him of his money.

If the merchant's capital is £100, for example, and he uses it to buy commodities for £100, later selling these commodities for £110, this has made his capital of £100 turn over once, and the number of turnovers per year depends upon how often this movement of M–C–M′ is repeated.

We are completely leaving aside here the costs that may be involved in the difference between the purchase price and the sale price, since these costs in no way affect the form we are initially concerned to analyse.

The number of turnovers of a given commercial capital is thus completely analogous here with the repeated circuits of money as a simple means of circulation. Just as the same shilling circulating

ten times buys ten times its value in commodities, so the same
money capital belonging to the merchant, £100 for example, buys
ten times its value in commodities, or realizes a total commodity
capital of ten times its value, £1,000. But there is a difference, and
it is this: with the circulation of money as means of circulation,
the same piece of money passes through different hands, and this
is how it repeatedly performs the same function and how the
velocity of the circulation substitutes for the quantity of money in
circulation. In the merchant's case, however, the same money
capital, irrespective of the pieces of money of which it is composed,
repeatedly buys and sells commodity capital to the amount of its
value and hence repeatedly returns to the same owner as $M + \Delta M$,
flowing back to its starting-point as value plus surplus-value.
This is what characterizes its turnover as a turnover of capital. It
always withdraws more money from circulation than it puts in. It
goes without saying, of course, that as the turnover of commercial
capital accelerates (and this is also where the function of money
as means of payment predominates, with the development of the
credit system), the same quantity of money also circulates more
quickly.

The repeated turnover of commercial capital, however, is never
anything more than a repetition of buying and selling; whereas the
repeated turnover of industrial capital expresses the periodicity
and renewal of the entire reproduction process (including the
process of consumption). For commercial capital, on the contrary,
this is simply an external condition. Industrial capital must
constantly put commodities on the market and withdraw them
from it again, if the rapid turnover of commercial capital is to
remain possible. If the reproduction process is generally slow,
so is the turnover of commercial capital. Now commercial capital
certainly facilitates the turnover of productive capital; but it only
does this in so far as it cuts down the latter's circulation time. It
has no direct effect on the production time, which also forms a
barrier to the turnover time of industrial capital. This is the first
limit to the turnover of commercial capital. Secondly, however,
quite apart from the barrier formed by reproductive consumption,
this turnover is decisively restricted by the speed and volume of
the total individual consumption, since the overall part of the
commodity capital that goes into the consumption fund depends
on this.

Now, leaving aside completely the turnovers within the world of commerce, where one merchant after the other sells the same commodity, a kind of circulation which may present a very flourishing appearance in periods of speculation, commercial capital first of all abbreviates the phase C–M for productive capital. Secondly, given the modern credit system, it has a large part of the society's total money capital at its disposal, so that it can repeat its purchases before it has definitively sold what it has already bought; and in this connection it is immaterial whether our merchant has sold directly to the final consumer or whether there are twelve other merchants between the two. Given the tremendous elasticity of the reproduction process, which can always be driven beyond any given barrier, he finds no barrier in production itself, or only a very elastic one. Besides the separation of C–M and M–C, which follows from the nature of the commodity, an active demand is now therefore created. Despite the autonomy it has acquired, the movement of commercial capital is never anything more than the movement of industrial capital within the circulation sphere. But by virtue of this autonomy, its movement is within certain limits independent of the reproduction process and its barriers, and hence it also drives this process beyond its own barriers. This inner dependence in combination with external autonomy drives commercial capital to a point where the inner connection is forcibly re-established by way of a crisis.

This explains the phenomenon that crises do not first break out and are not first apparent in the retail trade, which bears on immediate consumption, but rather in the sphere of wholesale trade, as well as banking, which places the money capital of the entire society at the wholesalers' disposal.

The manufacturer may actually sell to the exporter, and the exporter to his foreign customer; the importer may sell his raw materials to the manufacturer, and the manufacturer sell his products to the wholesaler, etc. But at some particular imperceptible point the commodity lies unsold; or else the total stocks of producers and middlemen gradually become too high. It is precisely then that consumption is generally at flood tide, partly because one industrial capitalist sets a series of others in motion, partly because the workers these employ, being fully occupied, have more than usual to spend. The capitalists' expenditure increases with their revenue. And besides this, there is also, as we have already seen (Volume 2, Part Three),* a constant circulation between one constant capital and another (even leaving aside the accelerated accumulation) which is initially independent of individual consumption in so far as it never goes into this even though it is ultimately limited by it, for production of constant capital takes place never for its own sake but simply because more of it is needed in those spheres of production whose products do go into individual consumption. This can continue quite happily for a good while, stimulated by prospective demand, and in these branches of industry business proceeds very briskly, as far as both merchants and industrialists are concerned. The crisis occurs as soon as the returns of these merchants who sell far afield (or who have accumulated stocks at home) become so slow and sparse that the banks press for payment for commodities bought, or bills fall due before any resale takes place. And then we have the crash, putting a sudden end to the apparent prosperity.

The superficial and irrational character of commercial capital's turnover is still greater in so far as the turnover of the same commercial capital can mediate the turnovers of very different productive capitals at the same time or in succession.

But not only can the turnover of commercial capital mediate the turnovers of various different industrial capitals; it can also mediate the opposing phases of commodity capital's metamorphosis. The merchant may for instance buy linen from the manufacturer and sell it to the bleacher. Here, therefore, the turnover of the same merchant's capital – in actual fact the same $C–M$, the realization of the linen – represents two opposite phases for two different industrial capitals. If the merchant sells for productive consumption, his $C–M$ represents the $M–C$ of one industrial capital and his $M–C$ the $C–M$ of another.

If, as in this present chapter, we leave aside K, the costs of circulation, i.e. the portion of capital that the merchant advances besides the sum laid out on the purchase of commodities, of course we must also leave aside ΔK, the additional profit that he makes on this additional capital. This is the strictly logical and mathematically correct way of looking at things, if it is a question of seeing how profit and turnover of commercial capital affect prices.

If the production price of 1 lb. of sugar is £1, with £100 the

* See in particular pp. 498–501 and 505–9.

merchant can buy 100 lb. of sugar. If this is the amount he buys and sells in the course of a year, and the average annual rate of profit is 15 per cent, he will add £15 to this £100, and 3 shillings to each £1, the production price of 1 lb. He will thus sell the sugar at £1 3s. a lb. If the production price of 1 lb. of sugar falls to 1 shilling, then with his £100 the merchant will now buy 2,000 lb., and sell each 1 lb. at 1s. 1¼d. The annual profit on the capital of £100 laid out in his sugar business will still be £15, as before. It is simply that he has to sell 100 lb. in one case and 2,000 lb. in the other. The level of the price of production, whether high or low, has nothing to do with the profit rate; but it has a decisive effect on the aliquot part of the sale price of each 1 lb. of sugar that goes to form commercial profit; i.e. the addition to the price that the merchant makes on a certain quantity of commodity (product).*
If the production price of a commodity is low, so is the sum that the merchant advances in its purchase price, i.e. for a given quantity, and so too, at a given rate of profit, is the amount of profit he makes on a given quantity of this cheaper commodity. Alternatively, and this comes to the same thing, he can buy a larger amount of this cheaper commodity with a given capital, of e.g. £100, and the overall profit of £15 which he makes on his £100 is then distributed in small fractions over the individual portions of this mass of commodities. And vice versa. This depends completely on the higher or lower productivity of the industrial capital whose commodities he trades in. If we ignore those cases where the merchant is a monopolist and also monopolizes production, as was the case with the Dutch East India Company in its day, nothing could be more ridiculous than the prevailing conception that it depends on the merchant whether he wants to sell many commodities at a low profit on the individual commodity, or a few commodities at a high profit. The two limits to his sale price are, on the one hand, the production price of the commodity, which he has no control over; and on the other hand the average rate of profit, which he has no control over either. The only thing on which he can make a decision, though the size of his available capital and other circumstances play a part here too, is whether he wants to deal in expensive commodities or in cheap ones. The attitude of the merchant therefore depends entirely on the degree of development of the capitalist mode of

* Here Marx evidently means the absolute profit per lb., and not the relative profit.

production and not on his own will. The old Dutch East India Company, as a purely commercial company having a monopoly of production, imagined it could still pursue, under completely changed conditions, a method that corresponded at most to the beginnings of capitalist production.[40]

The following circumstances foster the popular prejudice mentioned above, which, moreover, like all wrong ideas about profit, etc., arises from taking the viewpoint of trade alone and from commercial preconceptions.

Firstly, phenomena of competition, which pertain simply to the division of commercial profit among the individual merchants, the shareholders in the total commercial capital; e.g. when one merchant sells more cheaply than another, so as to drive his competitor from the field.

Secondly, an economist of Professor Roscher's calibre can still imagine, in Leipzig, that it was reasons of 'good sense and humanity' that produced the change in sale prices, and that this was not the result of a revolution in the actual mode of production.*

Thirdly, if production prices fall as a result of increases in the productivity of labour, and if sale prices therefore fall as well, then demand often rises still more quickly than supply, and with it market prices, so that the sale prices yield more than the average profit.

Fourthly, a merchant may reduce the sale price (and this means nothing but a reduction in the standard profit that he adds to the price), in order to turn over a larger capital more quickly in his business.

All these are matters that pertain simply to competition among the merchants themselves.

40. 'Profit, on the general principle, is always the same, whatever be price; keeping its place like an incumbent body on the swelling or sinking tide. As, therefore, prices rise, a tradesman raises price; as prices fall, a tradesman lowers price' (Corbet, *An Inquiry into the Causes, etc. of the Wealth of Individuals*, London, 1841, p. 20). Here, as throughout the text, attention is paid only to ordinary trade, not to speculation, the examination of which lies outside the ambit of our discussion, together with everything that pertains to the division of commercial capital. 'The profit of trade is a value added to capital which is independent of price, the second' (speculation) 'is founded on the variation in the value of capital or in price itself' (ibid., p. 128).

* Wilhelm Roscher, *Die Grundlagen der Nationalökonomie*, 3rd edn, Stuttgart and Augsburg, 1858, p. 192.

We have already shown in Volume 1 * how a high or low level of commodity prices determines neither the mass of surplus-value that a given capital produces nor the rate of surplus-value; even though according to the relative quantity of commodities that a given amount of labour produces, the price of the individual commodity will be higher or lower, and therefore also the surplus-value component of this price. The unit prices of commodities are determined, in so far as they correspond to values, by the total quantity of labour objectified in these units. If only a little labour is objectified in many commodities, the price of the individual commodity will be low and so will be the surplus-value contained in it. But how the labour embodied in a commodity is divided into paid and unpaid labour, and what proportion of this price thus represents surplus-value, has nothing to do with this total amount of labour, i.e. with the price of the commodity. The rate of surplus-value does not depend on the absolute size of the surplus-value, but rather on its relative size, its relationship to the wages that went into the commodity in question. Hence the rate can be high even though the absolute amount of surplus-value in each individual commodity is small. This absolute amount of surplus-value in each individual commodity depends in the first place on the productivity of labour and only secondly on its division between paid and unpaid.

As far as the commercial sale price is concerned, the production price is a given external assumption.

The high level of commercial commodity prices at an earlier period was due (1) to the high level of production prices, i.e. the low productivity of labour; (2) to the absence of a general rate of profit, since commercial capital drew a far higher proportion of the surplus-value than would accrue to it in conditions of general mobility of capital. The cessation of this situation, therefore, is in both respects the result of the development of the capitalist mode of production.

Turnovers of commercial capital are longer or shorter in various branches of trade, and the number of turnovers in the year thus more or less. Within the same branch of trade, the turnover is quicker or slower in different phases of the economic cycle. There is however an average number of turnovers, which is discovered by experience.

* Chapter 17.

We have already seen how the turnover of commercial capital differs from that of industrial capital. This follows from its very nature; one individual phase in the turnover of industrial capital appears as the complete turnover for an independently functioning commercial capital or even for a part of it. It stands also in a different relationship to the determination of profit and price.

As far as industrial capital is concerned, its turnover expresses on the one hand the periodicity of reproduction and depends therefore on the amount of commodities that are put on the market in a certain period of time. On the other hand, the circulation time also forms a limit, even if an extendable one, which may have a more or less constricting effect on the formation of value and surplus-value through its effect on the scale of the production process. Thus the turnover exerts its determining function on the mass of surplus-value annually produced, and hence on the formation of the general rate of profit, not as a positive factor but rather as a constricting one. The average rate of profit, on the other hand, is a given magnitude as far as commercial capital is concerned. Commercial capital does not have a direct effect on the creation of profit or surplus-value and it enters as a determining element into the formation of the general rate of profit only in so far as it draws its dividends from the mass of profit that industrial capital produces, according to the proportion that it forms in the total capital.

The greater the number of turnovers made by an industrial capital, under the conditions developed in Volume 2, Part Two, the greater is the mass of profit that it forms. Now it is true that the establishment of a general rate of profit means that this total profit is divided among the various capitals not according to the ratio in which they directly participate in its production, but rather according to the aliquot parts that they form in the total capital, i.e. in proportion to their size. But this does not alter the essence of the question. If the number of turnovers of an industrial capital is greater, so is the mass of profit, the mass of surplus-value annually produced, and hence, with other circumstances remaining the same, also the rate of profit. It is different with commercial capital. Here the rate of profit is a given magnitude, determined on the one hand by the mass of profit that industrial capital produces and on the other by the relative size of the overall commercial capital, by its quantitative proportion in the total capital advanced in the production and circulation process. The number of its turnovers, however, has a determining effect on its relationship to the total capital, or the relative size of the commercial capital needed for circulation, in that it is evident that the absolute size of the commercial capital required stands in inverse proportion to the speed of its turnover; its relative magnitude, however, or the share that it forms in the total capital, is given by its absolute magnitude, all other circumstances remaining the same. Say that the total capital is £10,000; then, if the commercial capital is one-tenth of this, it is £1,000; if the total capital is £1,000, then one-tenth of this is £100. In this respect its absolute magnitude varies although its relative magnitude remains the same, varying with the magnitude of the total capital. Here, however, we take its relative magnitude as given, say one-tenth of the total capital. And this relative magnitude is itself determined in turn by the turnover. Given a rapid turnover, its absolute size may be £1,000, for example, in the first case, £100 in the second case, so that its relative size is one-tenth. With a slower turnover, its absolute size may be £2,000 in the first case and £200 in the second. Its relative magnitude would have grown from one-tenth of the total capital to one-fifth. Circumstances that shorten the average turnover of commercial capital, such as the development of means of transport, for example, reduce in the same proportion the absolute magnitude of this commercial capital and hence raise the general rate of profit. And vice versa. The developed capitalist mode of production, compared with earlier conditions, has a double effect on commercial capital; the same amount of commodities are turned over with a smaller amount of actually functioning commodity capital; while on account of the more rapid turnover of this commercial capital and the greater speed of the reproduction process on which it depends, the ratio of commercial capital to industrial capital is reduced. On the other hand, with the development of the capitalist mode of production all production becomes commodity production, and hence the whole of the product comes into the hands of agents of circulation, in which connection it may also be added that in an earlier mode of production, under which production was carried out on a smaller scale, quite apart from the mass of products that were directly consumed in kind by the producers themselves and the mass of services that were performed in kind too, a very large proportion of the producers sold their commodities directly to their consumers or worked to their personal orders. Thus even though commercial capital is larger in earlier modes of production in proportion to the commodity capital it turns over:

(1) It is smaller in absolute terms, because an incomparably smaller part of the entire product is produced as a commodity, has to go into circulation as commodity capital, and comes into the hands of merchants; it is smaller, because the commodity capital is smaller. But it is at the same time relatively greater, and not only on account of the slower rate of its turnover and in proportion to the mass of commodities that it turns over. It is also greater because the price of this mass of commodities, and also therefore the commercial capital that has to be advanced for it, is greater as a result of the lower productivity of labour compared with capitalist production, so that the same value is expressed in a smaller amount of commodities.

(2) Not only is a greater mass of commodities produced on the basis of the capitalist mode of production (in which connection the reduced value of this mass of commodities must be taken into account), but the same mass of products, e.g. of corn, forms a greater mass of commodities; i.e. more and more of it comes into commerce. The result of this, moreover, is that not only does the mass of commercial capital grow, but so too does that of all the capital invested in circulation, e.g. in shipping, railways, telegraphs, etc.

(3) However, and this is an aspect to be discussed when we come to 'Competition among Capitals', * non-functioning or only semi-functioning commercial capital also grows with the progress of the capitalist mode of production, with the increased ease of entry into the retail trade, with speculation and a surplus of unoccupied capital.

However, taking the magnitude of the commercial capital in relation to the total capital as given, the variations in turnover between various branches of commerce do not affect the total profit that accrues to the commercial capital, nor do they affect the general rate of profit. The merchant's profit is determined not by the mass of commodity capital he turns over, but rather by the amount of money capital he advances in order to mediate this turnover. If the general annual rate of profit is 15 per cent and the

---

* In 1865, when the manuscript of Volume 3 was written, Marx evidently still intended to devote a special study to the phenomena of competition. See above, pp. 10–11, and the Introduction to the Pelican Marx Library edition of *Capital* Volume 1, pp. 27–8.

merchant advances £100, then, if his capital turns over once a year, he will sell his commodities at £115. If his capital turns over five times a year, he will sell a commodity capital with a purchase price of £100 five times a year at a price of £103, and in the whole year therefore a commodity capital of £500 at £515. This gives him, as before, an annual profit of £15 on the capital of £100 he has advanced. If this were not the case, commercial capital would yield a far higher profit than industrial capital in relation to the number of its turnovers, and this would contradict the law of the general rate of profit.

The number of turnovers of commercial capital in various branches of commerce thus has a direct effect on the commercial prices of commodities. The level of the commercial price supplement, that is to say the aliquot part of the commercial profit on a given capital that is added to the production price of the individual commodity, stands in inverse proportion to the number of turnovers or the speed of turnover of the commercial capital in the particular line of business in question. If a commercial capital turns over five times a year, it adds to the same value of commodity capital only a fifth the increase that another commercial capital, able to turn over only once a year, adds to a commodity capital of equal value.

The way that sale prices are affected by the average turnover time of capitals in various branches of commerce can be reduced to the principle that, according to the velocity of this turnover, the same mass of profit that is determined by the general annual profit rate for a given amount of commercial capital – determined independently, that is, of the particular character of this capital's commercial operations – is differently distributed over commodity masses of the same value, adding for example $\frac{15}{5} = 3$ per cent when it turns over five times a year, as against 15 per cent when it turns over only once.

Thus the same percentage of commercial profit in different lines of business raises the sale prices of the commodities in question by quite different percentages, calculated on the values of these commodities, in direct proportion to the differences in the turnover times.

As far as industrial capital is concerned, on the other hand, its turnover time has no effect on the value of the individual commodities produced, even though it does affect the mass of the values and surplus-values that a given capital produces in a given time, via the mass of labour exploited. This is concealed and appears as something different when we look at production prices, but that is simply because the production prices of various commodities diverge from their values, according to the laws already developed. Taking the production process as a whole, and the total mass of commodities produced by industrial capital, the general law is immediately confirmed.

Thus, while a closer consideration of the influence of turnover time on value formation in the case of the individual capital leads back to the general law and the basis of political economy, viz. that commodity values are determined by the labour-time they contain, the influence of the turnover of commercial capital on commercial prices exhibits phenomena which, in the absence of a very far-reaching analysis of the intermediate stages of the process, seem to presuppose a purely arbitrary determination of prices, i.e. a determination simply by the fact that capital happens to have made up its mind to make a certain amount of profit per year. It seems in particular, through this influence of the turnover, as if the circulation process as such determines the prices of commodities, and that this is within certain limits independent of the process of production. All superficial and distorted views of the overall reproduction process are derived from consideration of commercial capital and from the notions that its specific movements give rise to in the heads of the agents of circulation.

As the reader will have recognized in dismay, the analysis of the real, inner connections of the capitalist production process is a very intricate thing and a work of great detail; it is one of the tasks of science to reduce the visible and merely apparent movement to the actual inner movement. Accordingly, it will be completely self-evident that, in the heads of the agents of capitalist production and circulation, ideas must necessarily form about the laws of production that diverge completely from these laws and are merely the expression in consciousness of the apparent movement. The ideas of a merchant, a stock-jobber or a banker are necessarily quite upside-down. The ideas of the manufacturers are vitiated by the acts of circulation to which their capital is subjected and by the equalization of the general rate of profit.[41]

41. The following observation, if very naïve, is at the same time quite correct. 'Thus the fact that one and the same commodity is to be obtained from different sellers at essentially different prices also has its basis very frequently in an incorrect calculation' (Feller and Odermann, *Das Ganze der*

Competition, too, necessarily plays in their minds a completely upside-down role. If the limits of value and surplus-value are given, it is easy to perceive how the competition between capitals transforms values into prices of production and still further into commercial prices, transforming surplus-value into average profit. But without these limits, there is absolutely no way of seeing why competition should reduce the general rate of profit to one limit rather than to another, to 15 per cent instead of 1,500 per cent. It can at most reduce it to *one* level. But there is absolutely no element in it that can determine this level itself.

From the standpoint of commercial capital, therefore, turnover itself seems to determine price. On the other hand, while the speed of industrial capital's turnover, in so far as it enables a given capital to exploit more or less labour, has a determining and delimiting effect on the mass of profit, and hence on the general rate of profit as well, commercial capital is faced with the rate of profit as something external to it, and this rate's inner connection with the formation of surplus-value is completely obliterated. If the same industrial capital, with other circumstances remaining the same, and particularly with the same organic composition, turns over four times a year instead of twice, it produces twice as much surplus-value and thus profit; and this is palpably evident whenever the industrial capital in question possesses the monopoly of an improved mode of production, which permits it this accelerated turnover for as long as this monopoly lasts. The differing turnover time in different branches of commerce, however, does manifest itself inversely, in this way: the profit made on the turnover of a certain commodity capital stands in inverse proportion to the number of turnovers of the money capital that turns over this commodity capital. 'Small profits and quick returns', in other words, appears to the shopkeeper as a principle that he follows on principle.

It is readily apparent, of course, that this law applies only to the turnovers of commercial capital in a particular line of business, and, leaving aside the mutually compensatory alternation of quicker and slower turnovers, holds only for the average turnover made by the whole commercial capital applied in this branch. The

---

kaufmännischen Arithmetik, 7th edn, [Leipzig] 1859, [p. 451].) This shows how the determination of price becomes purely theoretical, i.e. abstract.

capital of A, involved in the same branch as B, may make more or less than the average number of turnovers. In this case, the others conversely make less or more. This in no way affects the turnover of the total mass of commodity capital invested in this branch. But it is of decisive importance for the individual merchant or retailer. In such a case he may make a surplus profit, just as industrial capitalists make surplus profits if they produce under more favourable conditions than the average. If competition compels it, he can sell more cheaply than his fellows without reducing his profit below the average. If the conditions that enable him to have a quicker turnover can themselves be purchased, e.g. the location of his sales outlet, he may pay extra rent for this; i.e. a part of his surplus profit is transformed into ground-rent.

Chapter 19: Money-Dealing Capital

The purely technical movements that money undergoes in the circulation process of industrial capital, and, we can now add, also that of commodity-dealing, commercial capital (since this takes over part of the circulation movement of industrial capital as its own specific movement) – these movements, having acquired autonomy as the function of a special capital which practises them, and them alone, as its specific operations, transform this capital into money-dealing capital. A part of the industrial capital, and more directly also of the commercial capital, exists throughout not only in the money form, as money capital in general, but as money capital in the process of these technical functions. A definite part of the total capital now separates off and becomes autonomous in the form of money capital, its capitalist function consisting exclusively in that it performs these operations for the entire class of industrial and commercial capitalists. Just as, in the case of commercial capital, a part of the industrial capital present in the circulation process in the form of money capital separates off and performs these operations of the reproduction process for the whole of the remaining capital. The movements of this money capital are thus again simply movements of a now independent part of the industrial capital in the course of its reproduction process.

It is only where capital is newly invested – which is also the case with accumulation – that capital in its money form appears as the starting-point and finishing-point of the movement. For any capital that is already in its process, both starting-point and finishing-point appear as simply points of transition. In as much as industrial capital, between its emergence from the production sphere and its re-entry into it, has to undergo the metamorphosis $C'-M-C$, M is in fact, as was already shown in connection with simple commodity circulation, simply the end result of one phase in this metamorphosis, only to be the starting-point of its opposite, complementary phase. And even though, as far as commercial capital is concerned, the industrial capital's *C–M* always presents itself as *M–C–M*, yet for it too, as soon as it is actually in operation, the actual process is also a continuous one of *C–M–C*. Commercial capital, however, goes through the acts *C–M* and *M–C* simultaneously. That is, it is not just that *one* capital is in the *C–M* stage while the other is in the stage *M–C*, but rather that the same capital is always buying and selling at the same time on account of the continuity of the production process; it is always in both stages simultaneously. While one part of the capital is being transformed into money, so as later to be transformed back into commodities, the other part is simultaneously being transformed into commodities, so as later to be transformed back into money.

Whether the money functions here as means of circulation or means of payment depends on the form of the commodity exchange. In both cases, the capitalist always has to make payments to many people and receive money in payment from many people. This merely technical operation of monetary payment and receipt itself constitutes work, and, in so far as the money functions as means of payment, it makes it necessary for accounts to be drawn up and balanced. This work is a cost of circulation and not value-creating labour. It is cut down by being undertaken for the capitalist class as a whole by a special department of agents or capitalists.

A certain section of capital must always exist as a hoard, as potential money capital: a reserve of means of purchase and payment, of unoccupied capital in the money form, waiting to be utilized; part of the capital constantly returns in this form. On top of the taking-in and paying-out of money, and book-keeping, the hoard itself has to be looked after, which is again a special operation. In point of fact, the hoard is constantly dissolved into means of circulation and payment, and reformed from money received from sales and from payments falling due; and it is this constant movement of the section of capital that exists as money dissociated from the capital function itself, this purely technical operation, that gives rise to special work and costs – costs of circulation.

The division of labour brings it about that these technical operations required by the functions of capital are performed as far as possible for the capitalist class as a whole by a particular division of agents or capitalists, as their exclusive functions, or are concentrated in their hands. There is here a double division of labour, just as with commercial capital. It becomes a special business, and because it is performed as a special business for the monetary mechanism of the entire class, it is concentrated and undertaken on a large scale; so that we find a further division of labour within this special business, both a division into various branches independent of one another, and the development of the workplace within these branches (large offices, numerous book-keepers and cashiers, highly developed division of labour). The payment and receipt of money, settlement of balances, keeping of current accounts, storage of money, etc., in separation from the acts that make these technical operations necessary, make the capital advanced in these functions into money-dealing capital.

The various operations whose achievement of an autonomous position as special businesses gives rise to the money trade arise out of the various characteristics of money itself and its functions, which capital therefore also has to perform in the form of money capital.

I have already indicated earlier how money in general developed originally in the exchange of products between different communities.[42]

Dealing in money, therefore, i.e. trade in the money commodity, first develops out of international trade. As soon as various national coinages exist, merchants who buy abroad have to convert their own national coin into the local coinage and vice versa, or else convert coins of various kinds into uncoined pure silver or gold as world money. Hence the exchange business, which should be viewed as one of the spontaneous bases of the modern money trade.[43] From this there developed exchange banks, in which silver

42. *A Contribution to the Critique of Political Economy* [p. 50]. [See also *Capital* Volume 1, Chapter 2.]

43. 'The great differences among coins as regards their weight and standard, and the imprints stamped on them by the many princes and cities that had minting rights, made it always necessary, in businesses where settlement in one particular form of coin was needed, to make use of the local currency. In order to make cash payments, merchants who travelled to a foreign market provided themselves with uncoined pure silver, or even gold. They similarly exchanged the local coins they received for uncoined silver or gold when they set out to return home. Exchange dealing, the conversion of uncoined precious metal into local coin and vice versa, consequently became a very widespread and profitable business' (Hüllmann, *Städtewesen des Mittelalters*, Bonn 1826–9,

(or gold) functions as world money – known as bank or commercial money – as distinct from currency. Exchange transactions, if only involving notes for payment to travellers from a money-changer in one country to one in another, were already developed in Rome and Greece out of the actual business of money-changing.

Trade in gold and silver as commodities (raw materials for the production of luxury goods) forms the spontaneous basis of the bullion trade, the trade that mediates the functions of money as world money. These functions, as previously explained (Volume 1, Chapter 3, 3, c), are of two kinds: circulation back and forth between the various national spheres of circulation, for the settlement of international payments, as well as the movement of capital lent at interest; and the movement from the sources of precious metal production across the world market, and distribution of this supply between the various national spheres of circulation. In England, goldsmiths still functioned as bankers for the greater part of the seventeenth century. We shall completely ignore for the moment the way that the settlement of international payments develops further in the exchange business, etc., together with everything related to dealings in securities, in short, all the specific forms of the credit system, which we are not yet concerned with here.

As world money, national money discards its local character; one national money is expressed in another, and in this way they

---

I, pp. 437–8). 'Exchange banks do not owe their name . . . to exchange in the sense of bills of exchange, but rather to the exchange of different kinds of money. Long before the establishment of the Amsterdam Exchange Bank in 1609, there were already money-changers and exchange businesses in the trading cities of the Netherlands, and even exchange banks . . . The business of a money-changer was to exchange the many different kinds of coin that were brought into the country by foreign traders for the current legal tender . . . The orbit of their activity gradually widened . . . They became the cashiers and bankers of their day. But the Amsterdam government saw a danger in the combination of cashier activity with exchange activity, and so as to combat this danger, it took the decision to establish a big institution which was to undertake both exchange and cashier business on behalf of the public authority. This was the celebrated Amsterdam Exchange Bank of 1609. The exchange banks of Venice, Genoa, Stockholm and Hamburg similarly owe their foundation to the continuous need for converting different varieties of money. Out of all these, the Hamburg bank is the only one still in existence today, since the need for an institution of this kind is still felt in this trading city, having as it does no coinage of its own . . .' (S. Vissering, *Handboek van Praktische Staathuishoudkunde*, Amsterdam, 1860, I, pp. 247–8).

are all reduced to their gold or silver content. Since both these commodities circulate as world money, they have to be reduced in turn to their mutual value ratio, which is constantly changing. The money-dealer makes it his own special business to carry on this intermediary function. Money-changing and the bullion trade are thus the original forms of the money business and arise from the double function of money: as national coin and as world money.

The capitalist production process, and trade in general, even on the basis of pre-capitalist modes of production, lead to the following results.

Firstly, the accumulation of money as a hoard, in this case as the section of capital that must always exist in the money form, as a reserve fund of means of purchase and payment. This is the first form of the hoard, as it reappears in the capitalist mode of production and generally comes into being with the development of commercial capital, at least for the use of this capital. In both cases this applies as much to international circulation as to domestic. This hoard is in constant flux, constantly spilling out into circulation and returning from it. The second form of the hoard is that of idle capital temporarily unoccupied in the money form, together with newly accumulated money capital that has not yet been invested. The functions that this hoard formation itself makes necessary start with its storage, book-keeping, etc.

Secondly, however, and linked with this, is the expenditure of money in buying, and its receipt from selling, paying and the receipt of payments, settlement of payments, etc. To start with, the money-dealer does all this as a simple *cashier* for merchants and industrial capitalists.[44]

44. 'The institution of cashier has perhaps nowhere kept its original and independent character in so pure a form as in the trading cities of the Netherlands' (on the origin of the cashier business in Amsterdam see E. Luzac, *Hollands Rijkdom*, Part III). 'Its functions overlap to a certain extent with those of the old Amsterdam Exchange Bank. The cashier receives a certain sum of money from the merchants who make use of his services, opening a "credit" for them in his accounts; they also send him their claims for payment, which he collects for them and credits them with; on the other hand he makes payments against their drafts (*kassiers briefjes*) and debits the sums involved to their current account. For these entries and payments he makes a small charge, gaining an appropriate wage for his labour, simply on the strength of the size of turnover between the parties involved. If there are payments to be settled between two merchants, both of whom use the same

Money-dealing is fully developed, even if still in its first beginnings, as soon as the functions of lending and borrowing, and trade on credit, are combined with its other functions. We shall deal with this in the next Part, on interest-bearing capital.

The bullion trade itself, the transfer of gold or silver from one country to another, is simply the result of commodity trade, determined by the rate of exchange, which expresses the state of international payments and the rate of interest in various markets. The bullion dealer as such only transmits the results.

In considering money and how its movements and formal characteristics develop out of simple commodity circulation, we saw (Volume 1, Chapter 3) that the movement of the quantities of money circulating as means of purchase and payment is determined by the volume and speed of the metamorphosis of commodities; and this metamorphosis, as we know now, is itself simply an aspect of the reproduction process as a whole. As far as obtaining the money material (gold and silver) from its source of production is concerned, this is reducible to direct commodity exchange, exchange of gold or silver as a commodity against other commodities, and is thus just as much an aspect of commodity exchange as obtaining iron or other metals. As far as the movement of precious metals on the world market is concerned, however (we ignore here such movements as express the transfer of loan capital, a transfer which also takes place in the form of commodity capital), this is as completely determined by inter-

---

cashier, then these are adjusted very simply by entries on both accounts, while the cashiers settle their mutual claims among themselves each day. The cashier business as such thus consists in this making of payments; it excludes industrial undertakings, speculation and the opening of overdrafts; for the rule here must be that the cashier does not permit any payment by his clients over and above their credit' (Vissering, op. cit., pp. 243–4). On the cashiers' associations in Venice: 'Because of Venice's needs, and its peculiar geography, which made it more troublesome to carry cash around than in other places, the merchants of this city set up cashiers' associations with appropriate safeguards, supervision and management. The members of such an association subscribed certain sums on which they drew drafts for their creditors, whereupon the sum paid was deducted from the debtor's account on the page of the book set aside for that purpose, and the sum with which the creditor was credited was added to his account. Such were the first beginnings of the so-called giro banks. These associations are certainly old. But to relate them to the twelfth century is to confuse them with the State Loan Institution set up in 1171' (Hüllmann, op. cit., pp. 453–4).

national commodity exchange as the movement of money as a means of domestic purchase and payment is determined by domestic commodity exchange. The export and import of precious metals from one national sphere of circulation to another, in as much as this is caused simply by the devaluation of a national currency, or by bi-metallism, lies outside monetary circulation proper and is merely a correction of aberrations brought about by arbitrary state decrees. As far as the formation of hoards is concerned, finally, in so far as this represents a reserve fund of means of purchase and payment, whether for domestic or for foreign trade, and is also merely a form of temporarily idle capital, in both cases this formation is simply a necessary precipitate of the circulation process.

Monetary circulation as a whole is a mere resultant of commodity circulation, in its volume, its forms and its movements, and from the capitalist standpoint commodity circulation itself represents simply the circulation process of capital (including the exchange of capital for revenue and of revenue for revenue, in so far as the expenditure of revenue is realized in retail trade). In the same way, it is completely self-evident that money-dealing does not just mediate the mere result and form of appearance of commodity circulation, i.e. the circulation of money. This monetary circulation itself, as a moment of commodity circulation, is given in advance for money-dealing. The latter's mediatory role is rather confined to the technical operations of monetary circulation, which it concentrates, reduces and simplifies. Money-dealing does not form hoards, but it supplies the technical means for hoard formation, in so far as this is voluntary (and not the expression of unoccupied capital or of a disturbance in the reproduction process), thus reducing it to its economic minimum; for the reserve fund of means of purchase and payment, if managed on behalf of the capitalist class as a whole, does not need to be so great as if each capitalist had to keep his fund separately. The money trade does not buy precious metals, but only mediates their distribution after the commodity trade has bought them. Money-dealing mediates the settlement of accounts, in so far as money functions as means of payment, and by the mechanism it creates for these settlements it reduces the quantity of money these require; but it determines neither the relationship nor the volume of these mutual payments. The bills and cheques, for example, which are exchanged for one another in banks and clearing houses derive from completely independent businesses and are the results of already given operations, so that all that is involved here is a better technical settlement of these results. In so far as money circulates as means of purchase, the volume and number of purchases and sales is completely independent of money-dealing. This can only abbreviate the technical operations that accompany these transactions and thereby also reduce the quantity of ready cash needed for their turnover.

Money-dealing in the pure form in which we are considering it here, i.e. separate from the credit system, thus only bears on the technical side of one aspect of commodity circulation, i.e. monetary circulation and the various functions of money that arise from it.

This distinguishes money-dealing quite fundamentally from dealing in commodities, which mediates the metamorphosis of commodities and commodity exchange, even though it allows this process of commodity capital to appear as the process of a special capital separate from industrial capital. If therefore commodity-dealing commercial capital displays a special form of circulation, $M–C–M$, where it is the commodity that changes place twice and brings about the reflux of money, as opposed to $C–M–C$, where it is money that changes hands twice and mediates commodity exchange, no such special form can be seen in the case of money-dealing capital.

Where money capital is advanced by a special section of capitalists in this technical mediation of monetary circulation – this capital representing on a diminished scale the additional capital which the merchants and industrial capitalists would otherwise have to advance for this purpose themselves – there we also have the general form of capital $M–M'$. The advance of M means that the person advancing it receives $M + \Delta M$. But the mediation between M and M' involves only the technical aspects of the metamorphosis, and not its material aspects.

It is clear enough that the mass of money capital which the money dealers operate with is the circulating money capital of the merchants and industrialists, and that the operations the money dealers perform are simply the operations of the merchants and industrialists, mediated by the former.

It is equally clear that their profit is simply a deduction from surplus-value, since they are dealing only with values already realized (even if realized only in the form of claims for payment).

Just as with commodity trade, here too we find a duplication of functions. For one section of the technical operations connected with money circulation must be performed by the commodity dealers and producers themselves.

Chapter 20: Historical Material on Merchant's Capital

The special form in which money is accumulated by commercial and money-dealing capital will be considered only in the next Part.

From what has already been developed, it should be clear enough that nothing could be more absurd than to treat merchant's capital, whether in the form of commercial capital or of money-dealing capital, as a special kind of industrial capital, in the way that mining, agriculture, stock-raising, manufacture, transport, etc. are branches resulting from the social division of labour and as such form particular spheres of investment for industrial capital. Even the simple observation that every industrial capital, when it is in the circulation phase of its reproduction process, performs exactly the same functions as commodity capital and money capital, which appear as the exclusive functions of merchant's capital in its two forms, would make this crude conception quite impossible. In commercial and money-dealing capital, rather, the distinctions between industrial capital as productive capital and the same capital in the sphere of circulation attain autonomy in the following way: the specific forms and functions that capital temporarily assumes in the latter case come to appear as independent forms and functions of a part of the capital that has separated off and become completely confined to this sphere. The transformed form of industrial capital, and the material distinctions between productive capitals applied in different ways as a result of the nature of the different branches of industry, are poles apart.

Besides the off-hand way in which economists always treat distinctions of form, since they are in actual fact interested only in the substantive side, there are in the case of the vulgar economist two further reasons for this confusion. Firstly, his inability to explain commercial profit and its characteristic features; secondly, his apologetic endeavour to derive the forms of commodity capital and money capital, and consequently commodity-dealing and money-dealing capital, forms which arise from the specific form of the capitalist mode of production (which presupposes as its initial basis the circulation of commodities, and hence of money), as forms which necessarily arise from the production process as such.

If commercial and money-dealing capital were distinct from cereal cultivation only in the same way as this is distinct from stock-raising and manufacture, it would be as clear as day that production in general and capitalist production in particular were completely the same, and in particular that the distribution of the social product among the members of society, whether for productive or for individual consumption, has to be effected just as eternally by merchants and bankers as the consumption of meat must be by stock-raising and that of articles of clothing by their manufacture.[45]

The great economists such as Smith, Ricardo, etc. focused their attention on the basic form of capital, capital as industrial capital, and in fact treated circulation capital (money and commodity capital) only in so far as it is itself a phase in that capital's reproduction process. They were therefore perplexed by commercial capital as a special variety of its own. The principles about value formation, profit, etc. derived straight from the examination of industrial capital cannot be applied directly to commercial capital. They therefore entirely ignored the latter. They only refer to it as a

45. Our wise Roscher has cleverly worked out that if certain features characterize trade as a 'mediation' between producers and consumers, 'one' must equally well be able to characterize production itself as a 'mediation' of consumption (between whom?). From this it naturally follows that commercial capital is a part of productive capital, just like agricultural and industrial capital. Thus because one can say that man can only mediate his consumption by production (and he has to do this even without a Leipzig education), or that labour is necessary for the appropriation of nature (which you can if you like call 'mediation'), it follows as a matter of course that a social 'mediation' that arises from a specific social form of production – precisely *because* it is a mediation – has the same absolute and necessary character, the same status. The term mediation settles everything. Besides, merchants are not mediators between producers and consumers (we ignore here for the time being those consumers who do not produce), but rather mediate the exchange of products between these producers; they are simply intermediaries in an exchange that would still go on in thousands of cases even without them.

kind of industrial capital. Where they deal with it specifically, as Ricardo does in connection with foreign trade, they seek to demonstrate that it creates no value (and consequently also no surplus-value). But what holds for foreign trade holds also for commerce within a country.

*

Up to now we have considered merchant's capital from the standpoint of the capitalist mode of production and within its limits. And yet not only trade, but also trading capital, is older than the capitalist mode of production, and is in fact the oldest historical mode in which capital has an independent existence.

Since we have already seen that money-dealing and the capital advanced in it needs nothing more for its development than the existence of large-scale trade in general, and subsequently of commercial, commodity-dealing capital, it is only this latter which we have to deal with now.

Because commercial capital is confined to the circulation sphere, and its sole function is to mediate the exchange of commodities, no further conditions are needed for its existence – leaving aside undeveloped forms that arise from barter – than are necessary for the simple circulation of commodities and money. Or, one might say that precisely the latter is *its* condition of existence. Whatever mode of production is the basis on which the products circulating are produced – whether the primitive community, slave production, small peasant and petty-bourgeois production, or capitalist production – this in no way alters their character as commodities, and as commodities they have to go through the exchange process and the changes of form that accompany it. The extremes between which commercial capital mediates are given, as far as it is concerned, just as they are given for money and its movement. The only thing necessary is that these extremes should be present as commodities, whether production is over its whole range commodity production or whether it is merely the surplus from producers who work to satisfy their own direct needs that is put on the market. Commercial capital simply mediates the movement of these extremes, the commodities, as preconditions already given to it.

The extent to which production goes into trade and passes through the hands of merchants depends on the mode of production, reaching a maximum with the full development of capitalist production, where the product is produced simply as a commodity and not at all as a direct means of subsistence. On the other hand, whatever mode of production is the basis, trade promotes the generation of a surplus product designed to go into exchange, so as to increase the consumption or the hoards of the producers (which we take here to mean the owners of the products). It thus gives production a character oriented more and more towards exchange-value.

The metamorphosis of commodities, their movement, consists (1) materially, in the exchange of different commodities for one another, (2) formally, in the transformation of commodities into money, selling, and the transformation of money into commodities, buying. And the function of commercial capital is reducible to these functions, the exchange of commodities through buying and selling. Commercial capital thus simply mediates the exchange of commodities, though it should be understood right from the start that this is not just an exchange between the immediate producers. In the case of the slave relationship, the serf relationship, and the relationship of tribute (where the primitive community is under consideration), it is the slaveowner, the feudal lord or the state receiving tribute that is the owner of the product and therefore its seller. The merchant buys and sells for many people. Sales and purchases are concentrated in his hands, and in this way buying and selling cease to be linked with the direct need of the buyer (as merchant).

But whatever the social organization of the spheres of production whose commodity exchange the merchant mediates, his wealth always exists as money wealth and his money always functions as capital. Its form is always $M-C-M'$; money, the independent form of exchange-value, is the starting-point, and the increase of exchange-value the independent purpose. Commodity exchange itself, and the operations that mediate it – separated from production and performed by non-producers – becomes simply a means of increasing wealth, and not just wealth, but wealth in its general social form as exchange-value. The driving motive and determining purpose here is the transformation of M into $M + \Delta M$; the acts $M-C$ and $C-M'$ that mediate the act $M-M'$ appear simply as transitional moments in this transformation of M into $M + \Delta M$. This $M-C-M'$, as the characteristic movement of commercial capital, is distinguished from $C-M-C$, commodity trade between the producers themselves, with the exchange of use-values as its ultimate purpose.

The less developed production is, the more monetary wealth is concentrated in the hands of merchants and appears in the specific form of mercantile wealth.

Within the capitalist mode of production – i.e. once capital takes command of production itself and gives it a completely altered and specific form – commercial capital appears simply as capital in a *particular* function. In all earlier modes of production, however, commercial capital rather appears as the function of capital *par excellence*, and the more so, the more production is directly the production of the producer's means of subsistence.

Thus there is no problem at all in understanding why commercial capital appears as the historic form of capital long before capital has subjected production itself to its sway. Its existence, and its development to a certain level, is itself a historical precondition for the development of the capitalist mode of production (1) as precondition for the concentration of monetary wealth, and (2) because the capitalist mode of production presupposes production for trade, wholesale outlet rather than supply to the individual client, so that a merchant does not buy simply to satisfy his own personal needs, but rather concentrates in his act of purchase the purchase acts of many. On the other hand, every development in commercial capital gives production a character oriented ever more to exchange-value, transforming products more and more into commodities. Even so, this development, taken by itself, is insufficient to explain the transition from one mode of production to the other, as we shall soon see in more detail.

In the context of capitalist production, commercial capital is demoted from its earlier separate existence, to become a particular moment of capital investment in general, and the equalization of profits reduces its profit rate to the general average. It now functions simply as the agent of productive capital. The particular social conditions that form with the development of commercial capital no longer play a determining part here; on the contrary, where commercial capital predominates, obsolete conditions obtain. This is true even within the same country, where for example purely trading cities exhibit a far greater analogy with past conditions than do manufacturing towns.[46]

46. W. Kiesselbach (*Der Gang des Welthandels in Mittelalter*, [Stuttgart] 1860) is still living in a mental world where commercial capital is the general form of capital. He has not the slightest suspicion of the modern meaning of capital, as little as Herr Mommsen when he speaks of 'capital' and the rule

The independent and preponderant development of capital in the form of commercial capital is synonymous with the non-subjection of production to capital, i.e. with the development of capital on the basis of a social form of production that is foreign to it and independent of it. The independent development of commercial capital thus stands in inverse proportion to the general economic development of society.

If independent mercantile wealth is the prevailing form of capital, this means that the circulation process has attained independence vis-à-vis its extremes, and these are the exchanging producers themselves. These extremes remain separate from the circulation process, and this process from them. Here the product becomes a commodity through trade. It is trade that shapes the products into commodities; not the produced commodities whose movement constitutes trade. Capital as capital, therefore, appears first of all in the circulation process. In this circulation process, money develops into capital. It is in circulation that the product first develops as an exchange-value, as commodity and money. Capital can be formed in the circulation process, and must be formed there, before it learns to master its extremes, the various spheres of production between which circulation mediates. The circulation of money and commodities can mediate spheres of production with the most diverse organization, which in their internal structure are still oriented principally to the production of use-values. When the circulation process becomes independent in this way, as a process in which the spheres of production are linked together by a third party, this expresses a double situation. On the one hand, that circulation has still not mastered production, but is related to it simply as its given precondition. On the other hand, that the production process has not yet absorbed circulation into it as a mere moment. In capitalist production, on the contrary, both these things are the case. The production process is completely based on circulation, and circulation is a mere moment and

---

of capital in his *Römische Geschichte*. In modern English history, the actual merchant estate and the trading cities also appear to be politically reactionary and in league with the landed and financial aristocracies against industrial capital. Compare for example the political role of Liverpool as against Manchester and Birmingham. The complete domination of industrial capital has been acknowledged by English commercial capital and by the 'moneyed interest' (financial aristocracy) only since the abolition of the corn duties.

a transition phase of production, simply the realization of a product produced as a commodity and the replacement of its elements of production produced as commodities. The form of capital that stems directly from circulation – commercial capital – now appears simply as one of the forms of capital in its movement of reproduction.

The law that the independent development of commodity capital stands in inverse proportion to the level of development of capitalist production appears particularly clearly in the history of the carrying trade, as conducted by the Venetians, Genoans, Dutch, etc., where the major profit was made not by supplying a specific national product, but rather by mediating the exchange of products between commercially – and generally economically – undeveloped communities and by exploiting both the producing countries.[47] Here we have commercial capital in its pure form, quite separate from the extremes, the spheres of production, between which it mediates. This is one of the main sources from which it is formed. But this monopoly of the carrying trade, and the trade itself, declines with the progress of the economic development of the peoples originally exploited by it from both sides, and whose lack of development was the basis of its existence. In connection with the carrying trade, this appears not only as a decline in one particular branch of trade, but also as a decline in the supremacy of the exclusively trading peoples and in their commercial wealth in general, which rested on the basis of this carrying trade. This is simply a particular form which the subordination of commercial capital to industrial capital takes with the progressive development of capitalist production. As for the manner and form in which commercial capital operates where it dominates production directly, a striking example is given not only by colonial trade in general (the so-called colonial system),

47. 'The inhabitants of trading cities, by importing the improved manufactures and expensive luxuries of richer countries, afforded some food to the vanity of the great proprietors, who eagerly purchased them with great quantities of the rude produce of their own lands. The commerce of a great part of Europe in those times, accordingly, consisted chiefly in the exchange of their own rude for the manufactured produce of more civilized nations . . . But when this taste became so general as to occasion a considerable demand, the merchants, in order to save the expense of carriage, naturally endeavoured to establish some manufactures of the same kind in their own country' (Adam Smith, [*The Wealth of Nations*,] Book Three, Chapter III [pp. 503–4]).

but quite particularly by the operations of the former Dutch East India Company.

Since the movement of commercial capital is $C-M-C'$, the merchant's profit is firstly made by acts simply within the process of circulation, i.e. the two acts of purchase and sale. Secondly, it is realized in the final act, the sale. It is thus 'profit upon alienation'.* At first appearance, pure and independent commercial profit seems impossible so long as products are sold at their values. 'Buy cheap and sell dear' is the law of commerce, not the exchange of equivalents. The concept of value is involved here in so far as the various commodities are all values and therefore money; from the qualitative point of view, they are equally expressions of social labour. But they are not equal values. The quantitative relationship in which products exchange is at first completely accidental. They assume the commodity form in so far as they are in some way exchangeable, i.e. are expressions of some third thing. Continued exchange, and regular reproduction for exchange, gradually abolishes this accidental character. At the outset, however, this does not occur for the producers and consumers but rather for the mediator between the two, the merchant, who compares money prices and pockets the difference. It is through his movement that the equivalence is established.

Commercial capital, in the first instance, is simply the mediating movement between extremes it does not dominate and preconditions it does not create.

Just as money arises from the simple form of commodity circulation, $C-M-C$, and not only as a measure of value and means of circulation, but also as an absolute form of the commodity and therefore of wealth, as a hoard, and makes its conservation and accumulation into an end in itself, so also, from the mere circulation form of commodity capital, $M-C-M'$, do money and the hoard develop into something that is maintained and increased simply by alienation.

The trading peoples of old existed like the gods of Epicurus in the *intermundia*, or like the Jews in the pores of Polish society.† The

* See above, p. 337.

† According to the Greek philosopher Epicurus (*c.* 341–*c.* 270 B.C.), the gods existed only in the *intermundia*, or spaces between different worlds, and had no influence on the course of human affairs. Marx had studied Epicurus's conception for his doctoral dissertation (*Collected Works*, Vol. 1, London, 1975, p. 51), and in Volume 1 of *Capital* he makes the identical double analogy that he does here (Pelican edition, p. 172).

trade of the first independent and highly developed trading cities and peoples, as a pure carrying trade, rested on the barbarism of the producing peoples between whom they acted as intermediaries.

In the stages that preceded capitalist society, it was trade that prevailed over industry; in modern society it is the reverse. Trade naturally reacts back to a greater or lesser extent on the communities between which it is pursued; it subjects production more and more to exchange-value, by making consumption and existence more dependent on sale than on the direct use of the product. In this way it dissolves the old relationships. It increases monetary circulation. It no longer just takes hold of surplus production, but gradually gobbles up production itself and makes entire branches of production dependent on it. This solvent effect, however, depends very much on the nature of the community of producers.

When commercial capital exchanges the products of undeveloped communities, commercial profit not only appears as defrauding and cheating but to a large extent does derive precisely from this. Apart from the fact that it exploits the difference between production prices in various countries (and in this connection it acts to equalize and establish commodity values), these modes of production enable commercial capital to appropriate for itself a preponderant part of the surplus product: partly by acting as middleman between communities whose production is still basically oriented to use-value, so that the sale of that part of their product that in some way or other steps into circulation, and thus the sale of products at their value in general, is of subordinate importance for their economic organization; and partly because in those earlier modes of production the principal proprietors of the surplus product whom the merchant trades with, i.e. the slave-owner, the feudal lord and the state (e.g. the oriental despot), represent the consumption wealth which the merchant sets out to trap, as Adam Smith correctly perceived in the passage quoted with regard to the feudal period.* Commercial capital, when it holds a dominant position, is thus in all cases a system of plunder,[48]

* See above, p. 446, note 47.

48. 'Now there is a great complaint among the merchants about the nobles, or robbers, because they have to trade with great danger, and are liable to be imprisoned, beaten, taken hostage or robbed. If they were to suffer such things for the sake of justice, the merchants would be saints . . . But since the same great injustice and unchristian thieving and robbing are committed by

just as its development in the trading peoples of both ancient and modern times is directly bound up with violent plunder, piracy, the taking of slaves and subjugation of colonies; as in Carthage and Rome, and later with the Venetians, Portuguese, Dutch, etc.

The development of trade and commercial capital always gives production a growing orientation towards exchange-value, expands its scope, diversifies it and renders it cosmopolitan, developing money into world money. Trade always has, to a greater or lesser degree, a solvent effect on the pre-existing organizations of production, which in all their various forms are principally oriented to use-value. But how far it leads to the dissolution of the old mode of production depends first and foremost on the solidity and inner articulation of this mode of production itself. And what comes out of this process of dissolution, i.e. what new mode of production arises in place of the old, does not depend on trade, but rather on the character of the old mode of production itself. In the ancient world, the influence of trade and the development of commercial capital always produced the result of a slave economy; or, given a different point of departure, it also meant the transformation of a patriarchal slave system oriented towards the production of the direct means of

---

merchants the whole world over, even against one another, is it any wonder that God has arranged things so that such great wealth unjustly made should again be lost or robbed, and the merchants themselves beaten about the head or imprisoned? . . . And the princes should see to it that such unjust dealing is punished with due penalty, and take care that their subjects should not be so shamefully abused by merchants. Because they fail to do so, God uses knights and robbers as his devils to punish the injustice of the merchants, just as he plagued Egypt and plagues the whole world with devils, or destroys it through enemies. He thus sets one rogue against the other, without in this way implying that knights are lesser robbers than are merchants, although merchants daily rob the whole world, while a knight may rob one or two people once or twice a year . . . Heed the words of Isaiah: your very rulers are confederate with thieves. For they hang the thieves who have stolen a guilder or half a guilder, but they mingle with those who rob the whole world and steal more surely than any others, so confirming the proverb that big thieves hang little thieves. Or as the Roman senator Cato said, "Mean thieves lie in dungeons and in the stocks, while public thieves go about in gold and silk." What will God's final word be? He will do as he said to Ezekiel; he will amalgamate princes and merchants, one thief with another, like lead and iron, as when a city burns down, leaving neither princes nor merchants' (Martin Luther, *Bücher vom Kaufhandel und Wucher. Vom Jahr 1527*).*

* *Von Kaufshandlung und Wucher*, Wittenberg, 1524.

subsistence into one oriented towards the production of surplus-value. In the modern world, on the other hand, its outcome is the capitalist mode of production. It follows that this result is itself conditioned by quite other circumstances than the development of commercial capital.

It lies in the nature of the case that as soon as specifically urban industry separates off from agriculture, its products are commodities from the start, so that their sale requires the mediation of trade. The dependence of trade on urban development is to this extent self-evident, as is the conditioning of the latter by trade. However, the degree to which industrial development goes hand in hand with these processes is dependent on entirely different circumstances. Ancient Rome, in the late republican era, saw the development of commercial capital to a higher level than ever before in the ancient world, without any kind of progress in the development of crafts; whereas in Corinth and other Greek cities of Europe and Asia Minor, a high level of craft development accompanied the development of trade. On the other hand, in diametrical opposition to urban development and its conditions, the commercial spirit and the development of commercial capital are often characteristic of non-settled, nomadic peoples.

There can be no doubt – and this very fact has led to false conceptions – that the great revolutions that took place in trade in the sixteenth and seventeenth centuries, along with the geographical discoveries of that epoch, and which rapidly advanced the development of commercial capital, were a major moment in promoting the transition from the feudal to the capitalist mode of production. The sudden expansion of the world market, the multiplication of commodities in circulation, the competition among the European nations for the seizure of Asiatic products and American treasures, the colonial system, all made a fundamental contribution towards shattering the feudal barriers to production. And yet the modern mode of production in its first period, that of manufacture, developed only where the conditions for it had been created in the Middle Ages. Compare Holland with Portugal, for example.[49] And whereas in the sixteenth century,

49. The predominant role of the basis laid by fishing, manufacture and agriculture for Holland's development, quite apart from other circumstances, was already being discussed by writers of the eighteenth century. See Massie, for example.* As against the earlier conception that underestimated the scope and significance of Asiatic, ancient and medieval trade, it has now become the

and partly still in the seventeenth, the sudden expansion of trade
and the creation of a new world market had an overwhelming
influence on the defeat of the old mode of production and the rise
of the capitalist mode, this happened in reverse on the basis of
the capitalist mode of production, once it had been created. The
world market itself forms the basis for this mode of production.
On the other hand, the immanent need that this has to produce on
an ever greater scale drives it to the constant expansion of the
world market, so that now it is not trade that revolutionizes
industry, but rather industry that constantly revolutionizes trade.
Moreover, commercial supremacy is now linked with the greater
or lesser prevalence of the conditions for large-scale industry.
Compare England and Holland, for example. The history of
Holland's decline as the dominant trading nation is the history of
the subordination of commercial capital to industrial capital. The
obstacles that the internal solidity and articulation of pre-capitalist
national modes of production oppose to the solvent effect of trade
are strikingly apparent in the English commerce with India and
China. There the broad basis of the mode of production is formed
by the union between small-scale agriculture and domestic
industry, on top of which we have in the Indian case the form of
village communities based on common property in the soil, which
was also the original form in China. In India, moreover, the
English applied their direct political and economic power, as
masters and landlords, to destroying these small economic
communities.[50] In so far as English trade has had a revolutionary

fashion to overestimate this to an extraordinary extent. The best antidote to
this view is to consider and contrast English exports and imports today with
those of the beginning of the eighteenth century. And yet these were already
incomparably greater than those of any earlier trading people. (See [Adam]
Anderson, *History of Commerce* [pp. 261 ff.].)

* Joseph Massie, *An Essay on the Governing Causes of the Natural Rate of
Interest, etc.*, London, 1750 (published anonymously). In *Capital* Volume 1,
Marx called this an 'epoch-making anonymous work' (p. 650) for its pioneer-
ing conception of the relationship between interest and profit. See also
Theories of Surplus-Value, Part I, pp. 373–7.

50. More than that of any other nation, the history of English economic
management in India is a history of futile and actually stupid (in practice,
infamous) economic experiments. In Bengal they created a caricature of
English large-scale landed property; in the south-east they created a caricature
of peasant smallholdings. In the north-west they did all they could to transform the Indian economic community with common property in the soil into a
caricature of itself.

effect on the mode of production in India, this is simply to the extent that it has destroyed spinning and weaving, which form an age-old and integral part of this unity of industrial and agricultural production, through the low price of English commodities. In this way it has torn the community to pieces. Even here, their work of dissolution is succeeding only very gradually. These effects are felt still less in China, where no assistance is provided by direct political force. The great economy and saving of time that results from the direct connection of agriculture and manufacture presents a very stubborn resistance here to the products of large-scale industry, whose prices include the *faux frais* [overhead expenses] of the circulation process with which they are everywhere perforated. In contrast to English trade, Russian trade leaves the economic basis of Asiatic production quite untouched.[51]

The transition from the feudal mode of production takes place in two different ways. The producer may become a merchant and capitalist, in contrast to the agricultural natural economy and the guild-bound handicraft of medieval urban industry. This is the really revolutionary way. Alternatively, however, the merchant may take direct control of production himself. But however frequently this occurs as a historical transition – for example the English clothier of the seventeenth century, who brought weavers who were formerly independent under his control, selling them their wool and buying up their cloth – it cannot bring about the overthrow of the old mode of production by itself, but rather preserves and retains it as its own precondition. Right up to the middle of this century, for example, the manufacturer in the French silk industry, and the English hosiery and lace industries too, was a manufacturer only in name. In reality he was simply a merchant, who kept the weavers working in their old fragmented manner and exercised only control as a merchant; it was a merchant they were really working for.[52] This method always stands in the way of the genuine capitalist mode of production and

51. Since Russia has been making the most frantic attempts to develop a capitalist production of its own, one that is exclusively directed towards its home market and the adjacent Asiatic one, this is beginning to change. – F.E.

52. The same applies to the ribbon and braid makers of the Rhineland, and also the silk-weavers there. At Krefeld a special railway was built for the commerce between these rural hand-weavers and the urban 'manufacturer', but subsequently all the hand-weavers were made redundant by mechanization. – F.E.

disappears with its development. Without revolutionizing the mode of production, it simply worsens the conditions of the direct producers, transforms them into mere wage-labourers and proletarians under worse conditions than those directly subsumed by capital, appropriating their surplus labour on the basis of the old mode of production. Somewhat modified, the same relationships are to be found in the manufacture of furniture in London, which is partly carried out on a handicraft basis. This is particularly the case in Tower Hamlets. The whole of furniture production is divided into very many separate branches. One firm just makes chairs, another tables, a third chests and so on. But these firms themselves are conducted more or less on a handicraft basis, by one master with a few journeymen. Despite this, production is on too large a scale to work directly for private clients. The buyers are the proprietors of furniture stores. On Saturday the master goes to these stores and sells his products, with as much haggling over the price as there is in the pawnshop over an advance on some item or other. These masters need their weekly sale simply to buy more raw material for the coming week and to pay wages. Under these conditions they are really only middlemen between the merchant and their own workers. The merchant is the real capitalist and pockets the greater part of the surplus-value.[53] Things are similar in the transition to manufacture from branches that were formerly pursued as handicrafts or as sidelines to rural industry. The transition to large-scale industry depends on the technical development of the small owner-operated establishment, whether it already employs machines that admit of a handicraft-like operation. Instead of by hand, the machine is now driven by steam, as has been happening recently in the English hosiery trade, for example.

The transition can thus take three forms.* First, the merchant becomes an industrialist directly; this is the case with crafts that are founded on trade, such as those in the luxury industries, where the merchants import both raw materials and workers from

53. Since 1865 this system has been put on a much wider basis. Details of it are given in the *First Report of the Select Committee of the House of Lords on the Sweating System*, London, 1888. – F.E.

* If the 'two forms' of transition referred to on p. 452 above have now become three, this is because Marx has now added, as the first case, the rather exceptional one in which the mode of production is transformed to a genuinely capitalist one at the merchant's initiative.

abroad, as they were imported into Italy from Constantinople in the fifteenth century. Second, the merchant makes the small masters into his middlemen, or even buys directly from the independent producer; he leaves him nominally independent and leaves his mode of production unchanged. Third, the industrialist becomes a merchant and produces directly on a large scale for the market.

In the Middle Ages, the merchant was simply someone who 'transferred' commodities, as Poppe correctly put it,* whether these were produced by guilds or by peasants. The merchant becomes an industrialist, or at least has craftsmen in his employment, and particularly small rural producers. Alternatively, the producer becomes a merchant. Whereas before the master-weaver gradually received his wool from the merchant in small portions and worked along with his journeymen for the merchant, now the weaver buys wool or yarn himself, and sells the merchant his cloth. The elements of production go into the production process as commodities that he has himself bought. And instead of producing for the individual merchant or for particular customers, the weaver now produces for the entire world of commerce. The producer is his own merchant. Commercial capital now simply performs the circulation process. At first, trade is the precondition for the transformation of guild and rural domestic crafts into capitalist businesses, not to mention feudal agriculture. It develops the product into a commodity, partly by creating a market for it, partly by supplying new commodity equivalents and new raw and ancillary materials for production, and thereby opening new branches of production that are based on trade from the very beginning – both on production for the market and world market, and on conditions of production that derive from the world market. As soon as manufacture becomes somewhat stronger, and still more so large-scale industry, it creates a market for itself and uses its commodities to conquer it. Trade now becomes the servant of industrial production, for which the constant expansion of the market is a condition of existence. An ever-increasing mass production swamps the existing market and thus works steadily towards its expansion, breaking through its barriers. What restricts this mass production is not trade (in as much as this only

* Johann Poppe, *Geschichte der Technologie seit der Wiederherstellung der Wissenschaften bis an das Ende des achtzehnten Jahrhunderts*, Vol. 1, Göttingen, 1807, p. 70.

expresses existing demand), but rather the scale of the capital functioning and the productivity of labour so far developed. The industrial capitalist is constantly faced with the world market; he compares and must compare his own cost prices not only with domestic market prices, but with those of the whole world. Previously, this comparison was almost exclusively the task of merchants and ensured commercial capital its mastery over industrial.

The first theoretical treatment of the modern mode of production – mercantilism – necessarily proceeded from the superficial phenomena of the circulation process, as these acquire autonomy in the movement of commercial capital. Hence it only grasped the semblance of things. This was partly because commercial capital is the first independent mode of existence of capital in general. And partly on account of the overwhelming influence that commercial capital exercised in the period when feudal production was first overthrown, the period of the rise of modern production. The genuine science of modern economics begins only when theoretical discussion moves from the circulation process to the production process. Interest-bearing capital, too, is an age-old form of capital. But we shall see later why mercantilism did not take this as its basis, but rather engaged in polemics with it.

Part Five

The Division of Profit into Interest and Profit of Enterprise

Chapter 21: Interest-Bearing Capital

On our first consideration of the general or average rate of profit (Part Two of this volume), we did not yet have this rate before us in its finished form, since the equalization that produced it still appeared simply as an equalization of the industrial capitals applied in different spheres. This was supplemented in Part Four, where we discussed the participation of commercial capital in this equalization, and commercial profit. The general rate of profit and the average profit were then presented within more closely defined limits than before. In the further course of our analysis it should be borne in mind that when we speak of the general rate of profit or the average profit from now on, this is in the latter sense, i.e. always with respect to the finished form of the average rate. Since this is now the same for industrial and commercial capital, it is also no longer necessary to make a distinction between industrial and commercial profit, once it is a question of this average rate of profit. Whether capital is invested industrially in the sphere of production, or commercially in that of circulation, it yields the same annual average profit in proportion to its size.

On the basis of capitalist production, money – taken here as the independent expression of a sum of value, whether this actually exists in money or in commodities – can be transformed into capital, and through this transformation it is turned from a given, fixed value into a self-valorizing value capable of increasing itself. It produces profit, i.e. it enables the capitalist to extract and appropriate for himself a certain quantity of unpaid labour, surplus product and surplus-value. In this way the money receives, besides the use-value which it possesses as money, an additional use-value, namely the ability to function as capital. Its use-value here consists precisely in the profit that it produces when transformed into capital. In this capacity of potential capital, as a means to the production of profit, it becomes a commodity, but a commodity of a special kind. Or what comes to the same thing, capital becomes a commodity.[54]

Let us take the average annual rate of profit as 20 per cent. Under average conditions, then, and with the average level of intelligence and activity appropriate to the intended purpose, a machine with a value of £100 that is applied as capital yields a profit of £20. Thus a man who has £100 at his disposal holds in his hands the power of making this £100 into £120, and thus producing a profit of £20. What he possesses is a potential capital of £100. If this man makes over his £100 for a year to someone else, who actually does use it as capital, he gives him the power to produce £20 profit, a surplus-value that costs him nothing and for which he does not pay any equivalent. If the second man pays the proprietor of the £100 a sum of £5, say, at the end of the year, i.e. a portion of the profit produced, what he pays for with this is the use-value of the £100, the use-value of its capital function, the function of producing a £20 profit. The part of the profit paid in this way is called interest, which is thus nothing but a particular name, a special title, for a part of the profit which the actually functioning capitalist has to pay to the capital's proprietor, instead of pocketing it himself.

It is clear that the possession of this £100 gives its owner the power of drawing an interest, a certain part of the profit that his capital produces. If he did not give the other person the £100, the latter would be unable to produce the profit or to function at all as a capitalist with respect to this £100.[55]

It is nonsense for Gilbart to speak of natural justice in this connection (see note). The justice of transactions between agents of production consists in the fact that these transactions arise from the relations of production as their natural consequence. The legal forms in which these economic transactions appear as voluntary actions of the participants, as the expressions of their common will and as contracts that can be enforced on the parties concerned

54. A few passages could be quoted here in which economists, too, see the matter in this way. – 'You' (the Bank of England) 'are very large dealers in the *commodity of capital*?' [Marx's italics], a director of that Bank was asked when appearing as a witness for the *Report on Bank Acts*, H. of C. 1857 [p. 104].

55. 'That a man who borrows money with a view of making a profit by it, should give some portion of this profit to the lender, is a self-evident principle of natural justice' (James Gilbart, *The History and Principles of Banking*, London, 1834, p. 163).

by the power of the state, are mere forms that cannot themselves determine this content. They simply express it. The content is just so long as it corresponds to the mode of production and is adequate to it. It is unjust as soon as it contradicts it. Slavery, on the basis of the capitalist mode of production, is unjust; so is cheating on the quality of commodities.

The £100 produces a profit of £20 by functioning as capital, whether industrial or commercial. But the *sine qua non* of this capital function is that it is actually spent as capital, that the money is laid out on the purchase of means of production (in the case of industrial capital) or of commodities (in the case of commercial capital). If it is to be spent, however, it must first be available. If A, the proprietor of the £100, either spent it for his private consumption or treated it as a hoard, it could not be spent as capital by B, the functioning capitalist. B does not spend his own capital, but that of A; yet he cannot spend A's capital unless A wills it. In point of fact, therefore, it is A who originally spends the £100 as capital, even though his function as a capitalist is entirely restricted to this act of expenditure. As far as the £100 is concerned, B functions as a capitalist only because A turns the £100 over to him and hence spends it as capital.

Let us firstly consider the characteristic circulation of interest-bearing capital. The second thing to investigate then is the specific way it is sold as a commodity, i.e. lent instead of being relinquished once and for all.

The starting-point is the money that A advances to B. This can occur either with or without security. The first form is however of greater antiquity, with the exception of advances on commodities or papers such as bills, stocks, etc. These particular forms do not concern us here. What we have to deal with is interest-bearing capital in its ordinary form.

In B's hands, the money really is transformed into capital, going through the movement $M-C-M'$ and then returning to A as M', as $M + \Delta M$, where ΔM represents the interest. For the sake of simplification, we leave aside for the time being the case where the capital remains in B's hands for a protracted period and the interest is paid at regular intervals.

The movement is thus: $M-M-C-M'-M'$.

What appears in duplicate here is, (1) the expenditure of the money as capital, and (2) its reflux as realized capital, as M' or $M + \Delta M$.

In the movement of commercial capital $M-C-M'$, the same commodity changes hands twice, or, if merchant sells to merchant, several times; but each time the same commodity changes place in this way it displays a metamorphosis, a purchase or sale, no matter how often this process might be repeated before its definitive fall into consumption.

In $C-M-C$, on the other hand, we have a double change of place by the same money, but one which displays the complete metamorphosis of the commodity, this being first transformed into money, and then out of money again into another commodity.

With interest-bearing capital, as against this, M's first change of place is neither a moment of commodity metamorphosis nor of the reproduction of capital. This begins only the second time it is spent, in the hands of the functioning capitalist, who uses it to pursue trade or transforms it into productive capital. M's first change of place here expresses nothing more than its transfer or making over from A to B; a transfer which customarily takes place under certain legal forms and provisions.

This double expenditure of the money as capital, the first time as a simple transfer from A to B, is matched by its double reflux. As M' or $M + \Delta M$, it flows back from the movement cycle to the functioning capitalist B. B then transfers it again to A, but with a part of the profit as well, as realized capital, $M + \Delta M$, where ΔM does not amount to the whole profit, but simply the part of the profit that is interest. It flows back to B as he has paid it out, as functioning capital, but as the property of A. For its reflux movement to be complete, B has to transfer it again to A. Besides the capital sum, however, B has also to surrender to A a part of the profit he has made on this capital sum, under the heading of interest, since A has given the money to him only as capital, i.e. as value that is not just maintained in the course of its movement, but creates a surplus-value for its owner. It remains in B's hands only as long as it is functioning capital. And on its reflux – after the prescribed interval has elapsed – it ceases to function as capital. As capital that is no longer functioning, it must be transferred back again to A, who has not ceased to be its legal owner.

The form of lending which is characteristic of this commodity capital as a commodity can incidentally also be found in other transactions, in place of the form of sale. The form of lending results from capital's characteristic here of emerging as a commodity, or, in other words, it results from the fact that money as capital becomes a commodity.

We have already seen (Volume 2, Chapter 1), and recall here only briefly, that capital functions in the circulation process as commodity capital and money capital. In neither of these two forms, however, does capital as capital become a commodity.

Once productive capital has been transformed into commodity capital, it must be put on the market and sold as a commodity. Here it functions simply as a commodity. The capitalist appears simply as the seller of a commodity and the buyer as the buyer of a commodity. As a commodity, the product must realize its value in the circulation process, by its sale, and must assume its transformed form as money. It is quite immaterial here whether this commodity is bought by a consumer as means of subsistence or by a capitalist as means of production, as a component of capital. In the act of circulation the commodity capital functions simply as a commodity, not as capital. It is commodity *capital* as distinct from a simple commodity (1) because it is already pregnant with surplus-value, so that the realization of its value is at the same time the realization of surplus-value; though this does not alter its simple existence as a commodity, as a product with a definite price; (2) because this function that it has as a commodity is a moment of its reproduction process as capital, and hence its movement as a commodity, because this is simply a partial movement in its process, is also its movement as capital; it does not become so by the mere act of selling, but only because this act is connected with the total movement of this particular sum of value as capital.

As money capital, likewise, it actually operates simply as money, i.e. as means of purchase for commodities (the elements of production). If this money is also money capital, a form of capital, this is not the result of the act of purchase, the actual function that it performs here as money, but rather of the way in which this act is connected with the overall movement of capital, in that this act, which it performs as money, introduces the capitalist production process.

In so far as it actually functions, however, and actually plays its role in the process, commodity capital is active here only as commodity, and money capital only as money. In no individual moment of the metamorphosis, taken by itself, does the capitalist sell the commodity to the buyer *as capital*, even though it represents capital for him, nor does the buyer alienate his money as capital to the seller. In both cases the commodity is alienated simply as commodity and the money simply as money, as the means for purchasing commodities.

It is only in the context of the whole process, at the moment where the point of departure appears as simultaneously the point of return, in $M–M'$ or $C–C'$, that capital emerges in the circulation process as capital (whereas it emerges in the production process as capital by the subordination of the worker to the capitalist and the production of surplus-value). At the moment of return, however, the mediation has disappeared. What does exist is M' or $M + \Delta M$ (whether this value sum increased by ΔM exists in the form of money, commodities or elements of production), a sum of money equal to that originally advanced plus an excess over this, the realized surplus-value. And precisely at this point of return, where the capital exists as realized capital, as valorized value, in this form – in so far as it is taken as a point of repose, imaginary or real – the capital does not enter circulation but rather appears as withdrawn from circulation, as the result of the entire process. In so far as it is spent again, it is never alienated to a third party *as capital* but rather sold to him as a simple commodity or given to him in return for a commodity as simply money. It never appears in its circulation process as capital but only as commodity or money, and here this is its only existence *for others*. Commodity and money are capital here not because commodities are turned into money and money into commodities, not in their actual relationships to buyers or sellers, but simply in their ideal relationships, either to the capitalist himself (considered subjectively) or as moments of the reproduction process (considering it objectively). It is not in the process of circulation that capital exists as capital in its real movement but only in the process of production, the process of exploiting labour-power.

With interest-bearing capital the situation is different, and this is precisely what constitutes its specific character. The owner of money who wants to valorize this as interest-bearing capital parts with it to someone else, puts it into circulation, makes it into a commodity *as capital*; as capital not only for himself but also for others. It is not simply capital for the person who alienates it, but it is made over to the other person as capital right from the start, as value that possesses the use-value of creating surplus-value or profit; as a value that continues its movement after it has functioned and returns to the person who originally spent it, in this case the money's owner. That is, it is removed from him only for a certain interval, only temporarily stepping from the possession of its proprietor into the possession of the functioning capitalist. It is neither paid out nor sold, but simply lent; alienated only on condition that it is, first, returned to its starting-point after a definite period of time, and second, is returned as realized capital, so that it has realized its use-value of producing surplus-value.

A commodity that is lent out as capital is lent either as fixed or as circulating capital, according to its specific properties. Money can be lent in both forms; it is lent as fixed capital, for example, if it is repaid in the form of an annuity, so that a portion of the capital always returns together with the interest. Certain commodities, by the nature of their use-value, can be lent only as fixed capital, such as houses, boats, machines, etc. But all loan capital, whatever form it might have and no matter how its repayment might be modified by the nature of its use-value, is always simply a special form of money capital. For what is lent here is always a definite sum of money, and it is on this sum that the interest is reckoned. If what is lent is neither money nor circulating capital, it is also paid back in the way that fixed capital returns. The lender receives both a periodic interest and a part of the used-up value of the fixed capital itself, an equivalent for the depreciation over this period. And at the end of the loan's term, the unused portion of the fixed capital is returned in kind. If the loaned capital is circulating capital, it similarly returns to the lender in the general mode of reflux of circulating capital.

The *manner* of the reflux is thus determined in each case by the actual cyclical movement of capital as it reproduces itself and its specific varieties. But for loan capital, the reflux takes the *form* of repayment, because the advance, the alienation of the loan capital, has the form of a loan.

In this chapter we shall be dealing only with money capital proper, from which the other forms of loan capital are derived.

The capital lent out flows back in a double sense. In the reproduction process it returns to the functioning capitalist, and then its return is repeated once again as a transfer to the lender, the money capitalist, as a repayment to its real proprietor, a return to its legal starting-point.

In the actual process of circulation, capital always appears as commodity or money, and its movement is reducible to a series of purchases and sales. In short, the circulation process is reducible to the metamorphosis of commodities. It is different when we consider the reproduction process as a whole. If we proceed from money (and it is the same thing if we proceed from the commodity, for we are then proceeding from its value, and thus viewing it too in the guise of money), a certain sum of money is given out and it returns after a given period with an increment. What returns is the replacement for the sum of money advanced, plus a surplus-value. It has been maintained and increased in the course of a certain cyclical movement. But money that is lent as capital is hired out precisely as a sum of money that is maintained and increased, a sum which returns with an addition after a certain period and can go through the same process once again. It is not given out as money or as a commodity, i.e. neither exchanged for a commodity when it is advanced as money nor sold for money when it is advanced as a commodity. It is rather given out as capital. The reflexive relationship in which capital presents itself when we view the capitalist production process as a whole and a unity, and in which capital appears as money breeding money, is here simply embodied in it as its character, its capacity, without the intervening mediating movement. And it is in this capacity that it is alienated, when it is lent out as money capital.

Proudhon's bizarre conception of the role of money capital is put forward in his *Gratuité du crédit. Discussion entre M. F. Bastiat et M. Proudhon*, Paris, 1850. Lending appears to Proudhon as an evil because it is not selling. A loan made on interest 'is the ability to sell the same object over and over again, always receiving the price afresh without ever abandoning ownership over the thing sold' (p. 9).*

The object – money, house, etc. – does not change its owner, as it does in buying and selling. But Proudhon does not see that when money is given out in the form of interest-bearing capital, no equivalent for it is received in return. It is true that in any act of buying and selling, in fact whenever an exchange process takes place, the object is given away. But the value is never given away. What is given away on sale is the commodity and not its value, which is returned in the form of money, or, what is here just another form of this, a bill or entitlement to payment. On purchase, money is given away, but not its value, which is replaced in the

* These are not Proudhon's own words, but those of Charles-François Chevé, editor of *La Voix du Peuple*, whose letter opens the discussion volume in question. He is however paraphrasing Proudhon's idea.

form of commodities. The industrial capitalist keeps the same value in his hands throughout the reproduction process (leaving aside the surplus-value), simply in different forms.

In so far as exchange takes place, i.e. exchange of objects, there is no change in value. The capitalist in question always keeps the same value in his hands. While the capitalist is producing surplus-value, there is no exchange; by the time exchange takes place, the surplus-value is already contained in the commodities. As soon as we consider not the isolated acts of exchange but rather the overall circuit of capital, M–C–M', what happens is that a definite sum of value is constantly advanced, and this sum of value plus the surplus-value or profit is withdrawn from the circulation sphere. The mediation of this process, however, is not to be seen in the simple acts of exchange alone. And it is precisely this process of M as capital which the interest of the lending money-capitalist is based on and from which it derives.

'In point of fact,' says Proudhon, 'the hat-maker who sells hats . . . retains their value, neither more nor less. But the lending capitalist . . . not only receives his capital back without deduction; he receives more than this capital, more than he puts into the exchange. On top of the capital, he receives an interest' (p. 69).

Here the hat-maker represents the productive capitalist in contrast to the lending capitalist. Proudhon has evidently not managed to penetrate the secret of how the productive capitalist can sell commodities at their values (the adjustment to prices of production is in his version a matter of indifference), and by that very act receive a profit over and above the capital he puts into the exchange. Let us assume that the price of production of 100 hats is £115 and that this production price happens to be equal to the value of the hats; i.e. the capital that produces the hats is of average social composition. If the profit is 15 per cent, the hat-maker realizes a profit of £15 by selling the commodities at their value of £115. To him, they cost only £100. If he has produced them with his own capital, he pockets the entire excess of £15; if with borrowed capital, he has possibly to give up £5 of this as interest. This in no way affects the value of the hats, but simply the distribution of the surplus-value already contained in the hats among different people. And since the value of the hats is not affected by the payment of interest, it is nonsense for Proudhon to say:

'Since in trade, the interest on capital is added to the worker's wages to make up the price of the commodity, it is impossible for the worker to buy back the product of his own labour. *Vivre en travaillant** is a principle that involves a contradiction, under the rule of interest' (p. 105).[56]

How little Proudhon has understood the nature of capital is shown by the following sentence, in which he describes the movement of capital in general in terms of the characteristic movement of interest-bearing capital:

'Since, through exchange, money capital always returns to its source with an accumulation of interest, reinvestment enables the same individual to draw a continual profit' [p. 154].

What still remains a puzzle to him in the specific movement of interest-bearing capital? The categories: buying, price, alienation of goods, and the immediate form in which surplus-value appears here; in brief the phenomenon that here capital has become a commodity as capital, that buying has therefore been transformed into lending, and price into a share in the profit.

The return of capital to its point of departure is always the characteristic movement of capital in its overall circuit. This is in no way something exclusively distinctive of interest-bearing capital. What distinguishes interest-bearing capital is the superficial form of the return, separated off from the mediating circuit. The lending capitalist parts with his capital, transfers it to the industrial capitalist, without receiving an equivalent. But this is in no way an act of the actual cyclical process of capital; it simply introduces this circuit, which is to be effected by the industrial capitalist. This first change of place on the part of the money does not express any act of metamorphosis, neither purchase nor sale. Ownership is not surrendered, since no exchange takes place and

* *Vivre en travaillant, mourir en combattant* (Live working, die fighting) was a traditional slogan of the French working class, particularly associated with the Lyons insurrection of 1834.

56. As Proudhon would have it, then, 'a house', 'money', etc. should not be lent as 'capital', but rather as 'commodities ... at cost price' (pp. 43, 44). Luther stands somewhat above Proudhon. He already knew that profit-making is independent of the form of lending or buying: 'They turn buying also into usury. But this is too much to tackle at once. We must confine ourselves for the time being to dealing with usury in lending, and after setting this right (after the day of judgement), we shall go on to give *usury in buying* its lesson too' [Marx's italics]. (M. Luther, *An die Pfarrherrn wider den Wucher zu predigen* [To the Clergy, to Preach against Usury, etc.], Wittenberg, 1540.)

no equivalent is received. The return of the money from the industrial capitalist to the lending capitalist simply supplements the first act in which the capital is given out. Advanced in the money form, the capital returns to the industrial capitalist again in the money form by way of the cyclical process. But since the capital did not belong to him when he gave it out, it cannot belong to him on its return. Its progress through the reproduction process cannot possibly transform the capital into his property. He therefore has to give it back to the lender. The initial act which transfers the capital from the lender to the borrower is a legal transaction which has nothing to do with the actual reproduction process of capital, but simply introduces it. The repayment which transfers the capital that has flowed back from the borrower to the lender again is a second legal transaction, the complement of the first; the one introduces the real process, the other is a subsequent act after that is completed. The point of departure and point of return, the lending-out of the capital and its recovery, thus appear as arbitrary movements mediated by legal transactions, which take place before and after the real movement of capital and have nothing to do with it as such. It would make no difference to this real movement if the capital belonged to the industrial capitalist from the start and returned to him alone therefore as his own property.

In the first introductory act, the lender hands over his capital to the borrower. In a second, subsequent and concluding act, the borrower gives this capital back to the lender. In so far as the transaction between these two is concerned (we leave aside for the time being the interest), in so far as we are dealing therefore simply with the movement of the capital lent between lender and borrower, these two acts (separated by a longer or shorter interval, during which the real reproduction movement of the capital takes place) encompass the whole of this movement. And this movement, namely the act of giving out money on condition of repayment, is the general movement of lending and borrowing, this specific form of a merely conditional alienation of money or commodities.

The characteristic movement of capital in general, the return of money to the capitalist, the return of capital to its point of departure, receives in the case of interest-bearing capital a completely superficial form, separated from the real movement whose form it is. A hands over his money not as money but rather as capital.

There is no change here in the capital itself. It simply changes hands. Its actual transformation into capital is accomplished only in the hands of B. But for A, it has become capital simply by having been given to B. The actual reflux of the capital from the production and circulation process only takes place for B. For A, the reflux takes place in the same form as the alienation. The giving-out or lending of money for a certain time, and the repayment of this with interest (surplus-value), is the entire form of the movement attributable to interest-bearing capital as such. The real movement of the money lent out as capital is an operation lying beyond the transactions between lenders and borrowers. In these transactions, taken by themselves, this mediation is obliterated, invisible and not directly involved. Capital as a special kind of commodity also has a kind of alienation peculiar to it. Here therefore the return does not appear as a consequence and result of a definite series of economic processes, but rather as a consequence of a special legal contract between buyer and seller. The period of the reflux depends on the course of the reproduction process; in the case of interest-bearing capital, its return as capital *seems* to depend simply on the contract between lender and borrower. And so the reflux of the capital, in connection with this transaction, no longer appears as a result determined by the production process, but rather as if the capital lent out had never lost the form of money. Of course, these transactions are actually determined by the real refluxes. But this is not apparent in the transaction itself. It is also in no way always the case in practice. If the real reflux does not take place at the right time, the borrower must look to see what other sources of help he can draw on to fulfil his obligations to the lender. The mere *form* of capital – money that is given out as a sum A and returns as a sum $A + \frac{1}{x} A$, after a certain period of time, but without any other mediation besides this temporal interval – is simply the irrational form of the real capital movement

In the real movement of capital, the return is a moment in the circulation process. Money is first transformed into means of production; the production process transforms it into a commodity; by the sale of the commodity it is transformed back into money, and in this form it returns to the hands of the capitalist who first advanced the capital in its money form. But in the case of interest-bearing capital the return, like the giving out, is simply the result of a legal transaction between the owner of the capital and a second person. All that we see is the giving-out and the repayment. Everything that happens in between is obliterated.

But because money advanced as capital has the property of returning to the person advancing it, to whoever spends it as capital, because $M-C-M'$ is the immanent form of the capital movement, for this very reason the owner of money can lend it as capital, as something which possesses the property of returning to its point of departure and of maintaining and increasing itself in the movement it undergoes. He gives it out as capital because, after being applied as capital, it flows back to its starting-point; the borrower can repay it after a given period of time precisely because it flows back to himself.

The assumption behind the lending of money as capital, therefore, giving it out on condition of its repayment after a certain time, is that the money really is applied as capital and really does flow back to its point of departure. In other words, the real cyclical movement of money as capital is the assumption behind the legal transaction by which the borrower of the money has to return it to the lender. If the borrower does not apply it as capital, that is his affair. The lender lends it as capital, and as capital it has to pass through the functions of capital, which include the circuit of money capital right through to its return to its starting-point in the money form.

The acts of circulation $M-C$ and $C-M'$ in which the sum of value functions as money or as commodity are simply intermediary processes, particular moments of its total movement. As capital, it undergoes the total movement $M-M'$. It is advanced as money or a sum of value in some form or other, and returns as this sum of value. The lender of money does not spend this on purchasing a commodity, or if the sum of value exists in commodities he does not sell these in exchange for money; he rather advances it as capital, as $M-M'$, as value which returns again to its point of departure at a definite date. Instead of buying or selling, he lends. This lending is thus the appropriate form for its alienation *as capital*, instead of as money or commodity. This in no way implies that lending cannot also be a form for transactions that have nothing to do with the capitalist reproduction process at all.

*

Up to now we have only considered the movement of the *capital* lent between its owner and the industrial capitalist. We must now turn to investigate *interest*.

The lender puts his money out as capital; the value sum that he alienates to someone else is capital, and this is why it flows back to him. But this return alone would not be the reflux of a value sum lent *as capital*, as opposed to the simple repayment of a sum of value previously loaned. In order to flow back as capital, the sum of value advanced must not only have maintained itself in the movement, but valorized itself, it must have increased its value, so as to return with a surplus-value as $M + \Delta M$, where this ΔM is interest, or that part of the average profit which does not remain in the hands of the functioning capitalist, but falls rather to the money capitalist.

To say that it is alienated by him as capital means that it has to be returned to him as $M + \Delta M$. But we still have to consider the form in which interest flows back at regular intervals in the meantime, without the capital, whose repayment only follows at the end of an extended period.

What does the money capitalist give the borrower, the industrial capitalist? What actually does he alienate to him? For it is only the act of alienation that makes the lending of money into the alienation of money as capital, i.e. the alienation of capital as a commodity.

It is only by way of this alienation that the money-lender's capital is given out as a commodity, or that the commodity in his possession is given to someone else as capital.

What is alienated in the case of ordinary sale? Not the value of the commodity sold, for this only changes its form. It exists ideally in the commodity as its price, before it is really transferred to the hands of the seller in the form of money. The same value and the same magnitude of value here undergo only a change of form. At one point they exist in the commodity form, at another point they exist in the money form. What is really alienated by the seller, and thus transferred to the individual or productive consumption of the buyer, is the use-value of the commodity, the commodity as a use-value.

What then is the use-value that the money capitalist alienates for the duration of the loan and makes over to the productive capitalist, the borrower? It is the use-value that money receives through the fact that it can be transformed into capital, that it can function as capital so as to produce in its movement a definite surplus-value, the average profit (anything more or less than this quantity appears here as merely accidental), besides conserving its original value. With other commodities, the use-value is ultimately consumed, and in this way the substance of the commodity disappears, and with it its value. The commodity of capital, on the other hand, has the peculiar property that the consumption of its use-value not only maintains its value and use-value but in fact increases it.

It is this use-value that money has as capital – the capacity to produce the average profit – that the money capitalist alienates to the industrial capitalist for the period during which he gives him control of the capital loaned.

The money loaned in this way is to a certain extent analogous in this respect to labour-power, in its position vis-à-vis the industrial capitalist. The difference is this: the industrial capitalist pays the value of the labour-power, whereas he simply repays the value of the loaned capital. The use-value of labour-power for the industrial capitalist is that of producing more value (profit) in its use than it possesses and costs itself. This excess value is its use-value for the industrial capitalist. And the use-value of the loaned money capital similarly appears as a capacity to represent and increase value.

The money capitalist in actual fact alienates a use-value, and for this reason what he gives out is given out as a commodity. To this extent the analogy with any other commodity is complete. Firstly it is a value transferred from one hand to another. In the case of the simple commodity, the commodity as such, both buyer and seller retain in their hands the same value, only in a different form; both of these still keep the same value that they alienated, the one in the commodity form, the other in the money form. The difference in the case of the loan is that in this transaction the money capitalist is now the only one who gives out value; but he preserves this by the subsequent repayment. In the loan, only one party receives value, since only one party gives value out. Secondly, one party alienates a real use-value, and the other party receives and uses it. As distinct from an ordinary commodity, however, this use-value is itself a value, i.e. the excess of the value that results from the use of the money as capital over its original magnitude. The profit is this use-value.

The use-value of money lent out is its capacity to function as capital and as such to produce the average profit under average conditions.[57]

What then does the industrial capitalist pay, i.e. what is the price of the capital lent out?

'That which men pay as interest for the use of what they borrow,' according to Massie, 'is a part of the profit it is capable of producing.'[58]

What the buyer of an ordinary commodity buys is its use-value, what he pays is its value. What the borrower of the money buys is likewise its use-value as capital; but what does he pay for this? Certainly not its price or value, as with other commodities. The value does not change its form between lender and borrower, as it does between buyer and seller, so that this value exists at one point in the form of money, and at another in the form of a commodity. The identity between the value given out and that received back is displayed here in a completely different way. The sum of value, the money, is given out without an equivalent and returned after a certain period of time. The lender remains the owner of this value throughout, even after it has been transferred from him to the borrower. With simple commodity exchange, the money is always on the side of the buyer; but with lending, the money is on the side of the seller. It is he who gives the money away for a certain time, and it is the buyer of the capital who receives it as a commodity. But this is possible only in so far as the money functions as capital and is therefore advanced. The borrower borrows the money as capital, as self-valorizing value. But it does not become capital in itself, just like any capital at its starting-point, until the moment of its advance. It is only by its use that it is valorized and realized as capital. But it is as *realized* capital that the borrower has to pay it back, i.e. as value plus surplus-value (interest); and the latter can only be a part of the profit he has realized. Only a part, and not the whole. For the use-value for the

57. 'The equitableness of taking interest depends not upon a man's making or not making profit, but upon its' (i.e. the sum borrowed's) 'being capable of producing profit if rightly employed' (*An Essay on the Governing Causes of the Natural Rate of Interest, wherein the Sentiments of Sir W. Petty and Mr Locke, on that Head, are Considered*, London, 1750, p. 49. The author of this anonymous work is J. Massie).

58. 'Rich people, instead of employing their money themselves . . . let it out to other people for them to make profit of, reserving for the owners a proportion of the profits so made' (op. cit., pp. 23–4).

borrower is that it produces him a profit. Otherwise the lender would not have been able to alienate the use-value. On the other hand, the whole profit cannot fall to the borrower. Otherwise, he would pay nothing for the alienation of the use-value. He would only repay the money advanced to the lender as simple money, not as capital, as realized capital, for it is realized capital only as $M + \Delta M$.

Both lender and borrower put out the same sum of money as capital. But it is only in the hands of the borrower that it functions as such. Profit is not doubled by the double existence of the same sum of money as capital for two persons. It can only function for both of them as capital by a division of the profit. The part accruing to the lender is called interest.

The entire transaction takes place, according to our assumptions, between two kinds of capitalist, the money capitalist and the industrial or commercial capitalist.

It must never be forgotten that capital as capital is a commodity here, and that the commodity we are dealing with is capital. All the relationships that appear here, therefore, would be irrational from the standpoint of the simple commodity, or even from the standpoint of capital in so far as it functions as commodity capital in its reproduction process. Lending and borrowing, instead of selling and buying, is here a distinction proceeding from the specific nature of the commodity of capital. Similarly the fact that what is paid here is interest instead of the price of the commodity. If interest is spoken of as the price of money capital, this is an irrational form of price, in complete contradiction with the concept of the price of a commodity.[59] Here, price is reduced to its purely abstract form, completely lacking in content, as simply a particular sum of money that is paid for something which somehow or other figures as a use-value; whereas in its concept, price is the value of this use-value expressed in money.

Interest as the price of capital is a completely irrational expression right from the start. Here a commodity has a double value,

59. 'The term "value", when applied to currency, has three several meanings ... (2) currency, actually in hand ... compared with the same amount of currency to be received upon a future day. In this case the value of currency is measured by the rate of interest, and the rate of interest being determined by the ratio between the amount of liable capital and the demand for it' (Colonel R. Torrens, *On the Operation of the Bank Charter Act of 1844, etc.*, 2nd edn, 1847 [pp. 5, 6]).

firstly a value, and then a price that is different from this value, although price is the money expression of value. Money capital is at first nothing more than a sum of money, or the value of a certain quantity of commodities assessed as a sum of money. If a commodity is lent as capital, this is only the disguised form of a sum of money. For what is lent as capital is not a certain number of pounds of cotton, but rather a certain amount of money that exists in the form of cotton as the cotton's value. The price of capital therefore relates to it as a sum of money, even if not as currency, as Mr Torrens believes (see note 59 above). How then is a sum of value to have a price besides its own price, besides the price that is expressed in its own money form? Price, after all, is the value of the commodity as distinct from its use-value (and this is also the case with market price, whose distinction from value is not qualitative, but merely quantitative, bearing exclusively on the magnitude of value). A price that is qualitatively distinct from value is an absurd contradiction.[60]

Capital manifests itself as capital by its valorization; the extent of this valorization expresses the quantitative extent to which it is realized as capital. The surplus-value or profit produced by it – the rate or level of this – is measurable only in comparison with the value of the capital advanced. And so the greater or lesser valorization of interest-bearing capital is also measurable only by comparing the amount of interest, the part of the total profit falling to this capital, with the value of the capital advanced. If price thus expresses the value of a commodity, interest expresses the valorization of money capital and appears therefore as the price that the lender is paid for it. We see from this how completely absurd it is to try to apply directly the simple relationships of exchange mediated by money, buying and selling, to this phenomenon, as Proudhon does. The basic assumption is precisely that money

60. 'The ambiguity of the term "value of money" or "of the currency", when employed indiscriminately as it is, to signify both value in exchange for commodities and value in use of capital, is a constant source of confusion' (Tooke, *Inquiry into the Currency Principle*, p. 77). The major confusion here (which in fact lies in the thing itself), i.e. that value as such (interest) comes to be the use-value of capital, is something that Tooke does not see.*

* Thomas Tooke (1774–1859), critic of Ricardo's theory of money, and author of a multi-volume *History of Prices*. Marx described him as 'the last English economist of any value'. Cf. *A Contribution to the Critique of Political Economy*, pp. 185–7.

functions as capital and hence can be made over to someone else as potential capital.

Capital itself appears here as a commodity in so far as it is offered on the market and the use-value of money as capital really is alienated. Its use-value however is to produce a profit. The value of money or commodities as capital is not determined by their value as money or commodities but rather by the quantity of surplus-value that they produce for their possessor. The product of capital is profit. On the basis of capitalist production, the difference between money spent as money and money advanced as capital is simply a difference of application. Money or a commodity is already potential capital in itself, just as labour-power is potential capital. For (1) money can be turned into elements of production, and is already, just as it is, simply an abstract expression of these elements, their existence as value; (2) the material elements of wealth possess the property of being already potential capital, because their complementary antithesis, the thing that makes them capital – namely wage-labour – is present as soon as capitalist production is assumed.

The antithetical social determination of material wealth – its antithesis to labour as wage-labour – is already expressed in capital ownership as such, quite apart from the production process. This one moment, then, separated from the capitalist production process itself, whose constant result it is, and as whose constant result it is also its constant presupposition, is expressed in this way: that money, and likewise commodities, are in themselves latent, potential capital, i.e. can be sold as capital; in this form they give control of the labour of others, give a claim to the appropriation of others' labour, and are therefore self-valorizing value. It also emerges very clearly here how this relationship is the title to, and the means to the appropriation of, the labour of others, and not any kind of labour that the capitalist is supposed to offer as an equivalent.

Capital further appears as a commodity in so far as the division of profit into interest and profit proper is governed by supply and demand, i.e. by competition, just like the market prices of commodities. But here the distinction is just as striking as the analogy. If supply and demand coincide, the market price of the commodity corresponds to its price of production, i.e. its price is then governed by the inner laws of capitalist production, independent of competition, since fluctuations in supply and demand explain nothing but divergences between market prices and prices of production – divergences which are mutually compensatory, so that over certain longer periods the average market prices are equal to the prices of production. As soon as they coincide, these forces cease to have any effect, they cancel each other out, and the general law of price determination then emerges as the law of the individual case as well; market price then corresponds to price of production in its immediate existence and not only as an average of all price movements, and the price of production, for its part, is governed by the immanent laws of the mode of production. Similarly with wages. If supply and demand coincide, their effect ceases, and wages are equal to the value of labour-power. It is different, though, with interest on money capital. Here competition does not determine divergences from the law, for there *is* no law of distribution other than that dictated by competition; as we shall go on to see, there is no 'natural' rate of interest. What is called the natural rate of interest simply means the rate established by free competition. There are no 'natural' limits to the interest rate. Where competition does not just determine divergences and fluctuations, so that in a situation where its reciprocally acting forces balance, all determination ceases, what is to be determined is something inherently lawless and arbitrary. More about this in the next chapter.

In the case of interest-bearing capital, everything appears in a superficial manner: the advance of capital as a mere transfer from lender to borrower; the reflux of the realized capital as a mere transfer back, a repayment with interest from the borrower to the lender. So, too, does the property inherent to the capitalist mode of production, that the rate of profit is determined not simply by the ratio of the profit made in one individual turnover to the capital value advanced, but also by the length of this turnover time itself, i.e. as the profit that industrial capital yields in particular periods of time. This too takes a completely superficial form in the case of interest-bearing capital, i.e. it appears that a certain interest is paid to the lender for a certain interval of time.

With his customary insight into the inner connections of things, the romantic Adam Müller (*Elemente der Staatskunst* [Elements of Statecraft], Berlin, 1809 [part iii], p. 138) says:

'In determining the price of things, time is unimportant; in determining interest, time is the principal thing involved.'

He does not see how production time and circulation time come into play in determining the prices of commodities, and how it is precisely in this way that the rate of profit is determined for a given period of turnover of capital, while interest is determined precisely by this determination of profit for a given period. His wisdom here, as always, lies in the way that he sees clouds of dust on the surface and pretentiously proclaims this dust to be something mysterious and significant.

Chapter 22: Division of Profit.
Rate of Interest.
'Natural' Rate of Interest

The object of this chapter, like the various phenomena of credit that we shall be dealing with later, cannot be investigated in detail. Competition between lenders and borrowers, and the resulting short-term fluctuations in the money market, fall outside the scope of our discussion. The circuit which the rate of interest describes during the industrial cycle can only be dealt with after the cycle itself. Nor can we go into the latter here. The same applies for the approximate equalization of the rate of interest, more or less, on the world market. All that we are concerned with here is the independent form of interest-bearing capital and the way that interest acquires autonomy vis-à-vis profit.

Since interest is simply a part of profit, a part which we have assumed the industrial capitalist has to pay to the money capitalist, the maximum limit of interest would seem to be the profit itself, in which case the share that accrues to the functioning capitalist would be zero. Leaving aside those special cases where interest is actually greater than profit, so that it cannot all be paid out of the profit, we might perhaps consider the maximum limit of interest as the whole profit minus the part of it reducible to 'wages of superintendence', to be developed later. The minimum limit of interest is completely indeterminate. It could fall to any level, however low. But countervailing circumstances constantly enter to raise it above this relative minimum.

'The relation between the sum paid for the use of capital and the capital expresses the rate of interest as measured in money.' 'The rate of interest depends (1) on the rate of profit; (2) on the proportion in which the entire profit is divided between the lender and borrower' (*The Economist*, 22 January 1853). 'If that which men pay as interest for the use of what they borrow, be a part of the profits it is capable of producing, this interest must always be governed by those profits' (Massie, op. cit., p. 49).

We shall start by assuming a fixed ratio between the total profit and the part of it paid to the money capitalist as interest. Then it is clear that the interest will rise or fall with the total profit, and the latter is determined by the general rate of profit and its fluctuations. If the average profit rate is 20 per cent, for example, and interest a quarter of the profit, the interest rate will be 5 per cent; if profit is 16 per cent, interest will be 4 per cent. Given a rate of profit of 20 per cent, interest could rise to 8 per cent and the industrial capitalist would still make the same profit as with a profit rate of 16 per cent and an interest rate of 4 per cent; i.e. 12 per cent. If interest were to rise to 6 or 7 per cent, he would in fact retain a greater part of the profit. But if interest is a constant proportion of the average profit, it will follow that the higher the general rate of profit, the greater is the absolute difference between total profit and interest, and the greater therefore the total profit that accrues to the functioning capitalist, and vice versa. Let us assume that interest is one-fifth of the average profit. $\frac{1}{5}$ of 10 is 2; the difference between the total profit and the interest is 8. $\frac{1}{5}$ of 20 is 4. The difference $= 20 - 4 = 16$; $\frac{1}{5}$ of 25 is 5; difference $= 25 - 5 = 20$; $\frac{1}{5}$ of 30 is 6; difference $= 30 - 6 = 24$; $\frac{1}{5}$ of 35 is 7; difference $= 35 - 7 = 28$. The various interest rates of 4, 5, 6 and 7 per cent would here always be one-fifth or 20 per cent of the total profit. As the rate of profit varies, so different rates of interest can express the same aliquot part of the total profit or the same percentage share in it. With interest such a constant proportion, the industrial profit (the difference between the total profit and the interest) would be greater, the higher the general rate of profit, and vice versa.

All other circumstances taken as equal, i.e. taking the ratio between interest and total profit as more or less constant, the functioning capitalist will be able and willing to pay a higher or lower interest in direct proportion to the level of his profit rate.[61] Since we have seen that the level of the profit rate stands in inverse proportion to the development of capitalist production, it follows that the higher or lower rate of interest in a country stands in the same inverse proportion to the level of industrial development, particularly in so far as the variation in the rate of interest expresses an actual variation in the profit rate. We shall see later on that this need by no means always be the case. In this sense one

61. 'The natural rate of interest is governed by the profits of trade to particulars' (Massie, op. cit., p. 51).

can say that interest is governed by profit, and more precisely by the general rate of profit. And this kind of regulation applies even to its average.

At all events, the average rate of profit should be considered as ultimately determining the maximum limit of the interest.

We shall immediately go on to consider more closely this circumstance that interest is to be related to the average profit. Where a given whole such as profit is to be divided in two, the first thing that matters is of course the size of the whole to be divided, and this, the magnitude of profit, is determined by the average rate of profit. Once the general rate of profit is given, i.e. the amount of profit on a capital of given size, which we can take as 100, then interest evidently varies in inverse proportion to the part of profit that remains to the functioning capitalist who operates with borrowed capital. And the circumstances that determine the magnitude of the profit to be divided, the value product of unpaid labour, are very different from those that determine its distribution among these two kinds of capitalist, and often operate in completely opposite directions.[62]

If we consider the turnover cycles in which modern industry moves – inactivity, growing animation, prosperity, overproduction, crash, stagnation, inactivity, etc., cycles which it falls outside the scope of our argument to analyse further – we find that a low level of interest generally corresponds to periods of prosperity or especially high profit, a rise in interest comes between prosperity and its collapse, while maximum interest up to extreme usury corresponds to a period of crisis.[63] From summer 1843 onwards there was a period of marked prosperity. The rate of interest, which in spring 1842 was still $4\frac{1}{2}$ per cent, fell in spring and summer

62. The following note occurs at this point in the manuscript: 'The course of this chapter suggests it is better, before the laws of distribution of profit are investigated, to develop first of all the way in which the quantitative division becomes a qualitative one. No more is needed to make the transition from the previous chapter to this point, than to take interest as a portion of profit that is not yet determined more specifically.' – F.E

63. 'In the first period, immediately after pressure, money is abundant without speculation; in the second period, money is abundant and speculations abound; in the third period, speculation begins to decline and money is in demand; in the fourth period, money is scarce and a pressure arrives' (Gilbart, *A Practical Treatise on Banking*, 5th edn, Vol. I, London, 1849, p. 149).

1843 to 2 per cent;[64] in September it even fell to $1\frac{1}{2}$ per cent (Gilbert [op. cit.], I, p. 166). During the crisis of 1847, it rose to 8 per cent and more.

Yet low interest can also be accompanied by stagnation, and a moderate rise in interest by growing animation.

The rate of interest reaches its highest level during crises, when people have to borrow in order to pay, no matter what the cost. And since a rise in interest corresponds to a fall in the price of securities, this is at the same time a very suitable opportunity for people with available money capital to buy up such interest-bearing securities at ridiculously low prices, and in the regular course of events these securities are bound to reach at least their average price again as soon as the interest rate falls.[65]

But there is also a tendency for the rate of interest to fall, quite independently of fluctuations in the rate of profit. And there are two major reasons for this.

(1) 'Were we even to suppose that capital was never borrowed with any view but to productive employment, I think it very possible that interest might vary without any change in the rate of gross profits. For as a nation advances in the career of wealth, a class of men springs up and increases more and more, who by the labours of their ancestors find themselves in the possession of funds sufficiently ample to afford a handsome maintenance from the interest alone. Very many also who during youth and middle age were actively engaged in business, retire in their latter days to live quietly on the interest of the sums they have themselves accumulated. This class, as well as the former, has a tendency to increase with the increasing riches of the country, for those who begin with a tolerable stock are likely to make an independence sooner than they who commence with little. Thus it comes to pass, that in old and rich countries, the amount of national capital belonging to those who are unwilling to take the trouble of employ-

64. Tooke explains this 'by the accumulation of surplus-capital necessarily accompanying the scarcity of profitable employment for it in previous years, by the release of hoards, and by the revival of confidence in commercial prospects' (*History of Prices from 1839 till 1847*, London, 1848, p. 54).

65. 'An old customer of a banker was refused a loan upon a £200,000 bond; when about to leave to make known his suspension of payment, he was told there was no necessity for the step, under the circumstances the banker would buy the bond at £150,000' ([H. Roy] *The Theory of the Exchanges. The Bank Charter Act of 1844, etc.*, London, 1869, p. 80).

ing it themselves, bears a larger proportion to the whole productive stock of the society, than in newly settled and poorer districts. How much more numerous in proportion to the population is the class of *rentiers* . . . in England! As the class of *rentiers* increases, so also does that of lenders of capital, for they are one and the same' (Ramsay, *An Essay on the Distribution of Wealth*, pp. 201–2).

(2) The development of the credit system, the ever growing control this gives industrialists and merchants over the monetary savings of all classes of society through the mediation of the bankers, as well as the progressive concentration of these savings on a mass scale, so that they can function as money capital, must also press down the rate of interest. More on this later.

As far as the determination of the rate of interest is concerned, Ramsay says it 'depends partly upon the rate of gross profits, partly on the proportion in which these are separated into profits of capital and those of enterprise. This proportion again depends upon the competition between the lenders of capital and the borrowers; which competition is influenced, though by no means entirely regulated, by the rate of gross profit expected to be realized.[66] And the reason why competition is not exclusively regulated by this cause, is, because on the one hand many borrow without any view to productive employment; and, on the other, because the proportion of the whole capital to be lent, varies with the riches of the country independently of any change in gross profits' (Ramsay, op. cit., pp. 206–7).

In order to find the average rate of interest, we have to calculate (1) the average interest rate as it varies over the major industrial cycles; (2) the rate of interest in those investments where capital is lent for longer periods.

The prevailing average rate of interest in a country, as distinct from the constantly fluctuating market rate, cannot be determined by any law. There is no natural rate of interest, therefore, in the sense that economists speak of a natural rate of profit and a natural rate of wages. Massie was already completely correct when he noted (op. cit., p. 49):

'The only thing which any man can be in doubt about on this occasion, is, what proportion of these profits do of right belong to

66. Since the rate of interest is determined by and large by the average profit rate, extraordinary swindling can very often go together with a low rate of interest. For example the railway swindle of summer 1844. The Bank of England's interest rate was only raised to 3 per cent on 16 October 1844.

the borrower, and what to the lender; and this there is no other method of determining than by the opinions of borrowers and lenders in general; for right and wrong, in this respect, are only what common consent makes so.'

The coincidence of demand and supply means nothing at all here, even taking the average rate of profit as given. Where this formula is resorted to in other cases (and this is then correct for practical purposes), it serves as a formula for finding basic rules which are independent of competition and, instead, determine it (regulating limits or limiting quantities); i.e. it is a formula for those caught up in the practice of competition, in its manifestations and in the ideas that develop out of these. With it they can arrive at some idea, even if still a superficial one, of the inner connection of economic relations that presents itself within competition. It is a method of getting from the variations that accompany competition to the limits of these variations. This is not the case with the average rate of interest. There is no reason at all why the average conditions of competition, of equilibrium between lender and borrower, should give the lender an interest of 3, 4, 5 per cent, etc. on his capital, or alternatively a certain percentage, 20 per cent or 50 per cent, of the gross profit. Where, as here, it is competition as such that decides, the determination is inherently accidental, purely empirical, and only pedantry or fantasy can seek to present this accident as something necessary.[67] Nothing is more amusing in the parliamentary reports of 1857 and 1858

67. J. G. Opdyke, for example, in his *Treatise on Political Economy* (New York, 1851) makes a most unsuccessful attempt to explain the general phenomenon of a 5 per cent rate of interest in terms of eternal laws. But incomparably more naïve is Herr Karl Arnd in *Die naturgemässe Volkswirthschaft gegenüber dem Monopoliengeist und dem Kommunismus, etc.* [Natural Economics Opposed to the Spirit of Monopoly and Communism], Hanau, 1845. Here we may read: 'In the natural course of the production of goods, there is only *one* phenomenon which seems to regulate to some extent the rate of interest, at least in fully developed countries; this is the ratio by which the volume of timber in European forests increases through its annual growth. This growth takes place, quite independently of its exchange-value' (how curious of the trees to arrange their growth independently of their exchange-value!) 'in the ratio of 3 or 4 to 100. Accordingly, therefore' (since the growth of trees is quite independent of their exchange-value, however much their exchange-value may depend on their growth) 'we should not expect a reduction below the level which it' (the rate of interest) 'has at present in the richest countries' (pp. 124–5). This deserves to be known as the 'primordial forest rate of interest', and its discoverer makes a further praiseworthy contribution to 'our science' in this work as the 'philosopher of the dog tax' [pp. 420–21].

concerning bank legislation and the commercial crisis than when directors of the Bank of England, London and country bankers and professional theorists chatter back and forth about the 'real rate produced', without getting any further than such commonplaces as, for example, that 'the price paid for the use of loanable capital should vary with the supply of such capital', that 'a high rate and a low profit cannot permanently exist', and other platitudes of the same kind.[68] Custom, legal tradition, etc. are just as much involved in the determination of the average rate of interest as is competition itself, in so far as this average rate exists not only as an average number but as an actual magnitude. An average interest must be assumed in many legal contexts where interest has to be reckoned. If we go on to ask why the limits of the average interest rate cannot be derived from general laws, the answer simply lies in the nature of interest. It is merely a part of the average profit. The same capital appears in a double capacity, as capital for loan in the hands of the lender, and as industrial or commercial capital in the hands of the functioning capitalist. But it functions only once, and produces profit only once. In the production process itself, the character of capital as loan capital does not play any role. How the two parties who have claims on this profit actually share it between them is as it stands a purely empirical fact, pertaining to the realm of chance, just as the respective shares in the common profit of a business partnership are distributed among its various members. With the division between surplus-value and wages, on which the determination of the profit rate essentially depends, two quite different elements are involved, labour-power and capital. It is the functions of two independent variables which set limits to one another, and the *quantitative division* of the value produced emerges from their *qualitative distinction*. We shall see later on that the same thing takes place with the division of surplus-value between rent and profit. With interest, there is nothing of the kind. Here, on the contrary, the *qualitative distinction* proceeds from the *purely quantitative division* of the same piece of surplus-value, as we shall immediately go on to see.

68. The Bank of England raises and lowers its discount rate according to the inflow and outflow of gold, though always of course with regard to the rate prevailing in the open market. 'By which gambling in discounts, by anticipation of the alterations in the bank-rate, has now become half the trade of the great heads of the money centre' – i.e. the London money market ([H. Roy] *The Theory of the Exchanges, etc.*, p. 113).

From what has already been developed, it follows that there is no 'natural' rate of interest. But if on the one hand the average or middling rate of interest, as distinct from the constantly fluctuating market rate, cannot be given limits by a general law, since what is involved is simply a distribution of the gross profit between two persons who possess capital under different titles, the rate of interest, conversely, whether it is the average rate or the market rate of the time, appears as something quite different from the general rate of profit, as a uniform, definite and palpable magnitude.[69]

The rate of interest is related to the profit rate in a similar way as the market price of a commodity is to its value. In so far as the rate of interest is determined by the profit rate, this is always through the general rate of profit and not through the specific profit rates that may prevail in particular branches of industry, still less by the extra profit that the individual capitalist might make in a particular sphere of business.[70] The general rate of profit, in fact, reappears in the average rate of interest as an empirical, given fact, even though the latter is not a pure or reliable expression of the former.

It is certainly true that the interest rate itself is always different according to the class of security provided by the borrowers, and

69. 'The price of commodities fluctuates continually; they are all made for different uses; the money serves for all purposes. The commodities, even those of the same kind, differ according to quality; cash money is always of the same value, or at least is assumed to be so. Thus it is that the price of money, which we designate by the term interest, has a greater stability and uniformity than that of any other thing' (J. Steuart, *Principles of Political Economy*, French translation, 1789, IV, p. 27).

70. 'This rule of dividing profits is not, however, to be applied particularly to every lender and borrower, but to lenders and borrowers in general ... remarkably great and small gains are the reward of skill and the want of understanding, which lenders have nothing at all to do with; for as they will not suffer by the one, they ought not to benefit by the other. What has been said of particular men in the same business is applicable to particular sorts of business; if the merchants and tradesmen employed in any one branch of trade get more by what they borrow than the common profits made by other merchants and tradesmen of the same country, the extraordinary gain is theirs, though it required only common skills and understanding to get it; and not the lenders', who supplied them with money ... for the lenders would not have lent their money to carry on any branch of trade upon lower terms than would admit of paying so much as the common rate of interest; and therefore they ought not to receive more than that, whatever advantages may be made by their money' (Massie, op. cit., pp. 50, 51).

according to the duration of the loan as well; but for each of these categories, it is uniform at a given moment of time. This distinction, therefore, does not militate against the fixed and uniform character of the rate of interest.[71]

In any given country, the average rate of interest is constant over long periods, because the general rate of profit changes only in the long run – despite constant change in the particular rates of profit, a change in one sphere being offset by an opposite change in another. And the relative constancy of the profit rate is precisely reflected in this more or less constant character of the average or common rate of interest.

As far as the permanently fluctuating market rate of interest is concerned, this is a fixed magnitude at any given moment, just like the market price of commodities, because on the money market all capital for loan confronts the functioning capital as an overall mass; i.e. the relationship between the supply of loan capital on the one hand, and the demand for it on the other, is what determines the market level of interest at any given time. This is all the more true, the more the development and associated concentration of the credit system gives loan capital a general social character, and puts it on the money market all at once, simultaneously. The general rate of profit, on the other hand, only ever exists as a tendency, as a movement of equalization between particular rates of profit. The competition between capitalists – which is itself this movement of equalization – consists here in their withdrawing capital bit by bit from those spheres where profit is below the average for a long period, and similarly injecting it bit by bit into spheres where it is above this; or, alternatively, in their dividing additional capital between these spheres in varying proportions.

71. Bank-rate	5%
Market rate of discount, 60 days' drafts	$3\frac{5}{8}\%$
Ditto, 3 months'	$3\frac{1}{2}\%$
Ditto, 6 months'	$3\frac{5}{16}\%$
Loans to bill-brokers, day to day	1 to 2%
Ditto, for one week	3%
Last rate for fortnight, loans to stockbrokers	$4\frac{3}{4}$ to 5%
Deposit allowance (banks)	$3\frac{1}{2}\%$
Ditto (discount houses)	3 to $3\frac{1}{4}\%$

The above figures for interest rates on the London money market on 9 December 1889, taken from the financial page of the *Daily News* of 10 December, show how large this variation may be on one and the same day. The minimum here is 1 per cent and the maximum 5 per cent. – F. E.

There is a constant variation in the injection and withdrawal of capital vis-à-vis these various spheres, never a simultaneous effect on a mass scale as with the determination of the interest rate.

We have seen that although it is a category absolutely different from the commodity, interest-bearing capital becomes a commodity *sui generis* with interest as its price, and this price, just like the market price of an ordinary commodity, is fixed at any given time by demand and supply. The market rate of interest, though in constant flux, thus appears at any given moment as every bit as fixed and uniform as the momentary market price of any commodity. The money capitalists supply this commodity, and the functioning capitalists buy it; they constitute the demand for it. This process of fixing the rate by supply and demand does not apply to the equalization that produces the general rate of profit. If the prices of commodities in one sphere are below or above their price of production (and in this connection we ignore the fluctuations connected with the industrial cycle, or those that simply bear on the individual business), an equalization takes place by the expansion or contraction of production, i.e. an increase or decrease in the quantity of commodities that these industrial capitals put on the market, mediated by the immigration or emigration of capital with respect to these particular spheres of production. It is the equalization brought about in this way, whereby the average market prices of commodities are reduced to their prices of production, that corrects divergences between the particular rates of profit and the general or average profit rate. This process never appears and never can appear as if industrial or commercial capital *as such* were a commodity vis-à-vis a buyer, in the way that interest-bearing capital is. It appears only in the fluctuations and equalizations that reduce the market prices of commodities to their production prices; not as the direct establishment of an average profit. The general rate of profit is determined in fact (1) by the surplus-value that the total capital produces; (2) by the ratio of this surplus-value to the value of the total capital; and (3) by competition, but only in so far as this is the movement through which the capitals invested in particular spheres of production seek to draw equal dividends from this surplus-value in proportion to their relative size. The general rate of profit, in other words, obtains its determination in quite different and far more complicated ways than does the market rate of interest, which is directly and immediately determined by the relation of supply and demand, and it is therefore not a palpable and given fact in the way that the interest rate is. The particular profit rates in the various spheres of production are themselves more or less uncertain; but in so far as they do show themselves, it is not their uniformity that is apparent but rather their variation. The general rate of profit itself simply appears as the minimum limit of profit, not as an empirical and directly visible form of the actual profit rate.

In stressing this distinction between the interest rate and the profit rate, we have so far left aside the following two factors, which favour the consolidation of the interest rate: (1) the historical pre-existence of interest-bearing capital and the existence of a general rate of interest handed down by tradition; (2) the far stronger direct influence that the world market exerts on the establishment of the interest rate, independently of the conditions of production in a country, as compared with its influence on the profit rate.

Average profit does not appear as a directly given fact, but rather as the end-product of an equalization of opposing tendencies that can only be established by investigation. With the interest rate it is different. Where it is a universal governing rule, which occurs at least locally, it is a fact fixed every day, a fact that even serves industrial and commercial capital as a presupposition and postulate in their operating calculations. It becomes a general property of any sum of £100 that it will yield 2, 3, 4, 5 per cent. Meteorological reports do not show more precisely the level of the barometer and thermometer than do stock-market reports the level of the interest rate, not for this capital or that, but rather for the generality of loan capital to be found on the money market.

On the money market it is only lenders and borrowers who face one another. The commodity has the same form, money. All particular forms of capital, arising from its investment in particular spheres of production or circulation, are obliterated here. It exists in the undifferentiated, self-identical form of independent value, of money. Competition between particular spheres now ceases; they are all thrown together as borrowers of money, and capital confronts them all in a form still indifferent to the specific manner and mode of its application. Here capital really does emerge, in the pressure of its demand and supply, as *the common capital of the class*, whereas industrial capital appears like this only in the movement and competition between the particular spheres. Money capital on the money market, moreover, really does possess the form in which it is distributed as a common element among these various spheres, among the capitalist class, quite irrespective of its particular application, according to the production requirements of each particular sphere. On top of this, with the development of large-scale industry money capital emerges more and more, in so far as it appears on the market, as not represented by the individual capitalist, the proprietor of this or that fraction of the mass of capital on the market, but rather as a concentrated and organized mass, placed under the control of the bankers as representatives of the social capital in a quite different manner to real production. The result is that, as far as the form of demand goes, capital for loan is faced with the entire weight of a class, while, as far as supply goes, it itself appears *en masse* as loan capital.

These are some of the reasons why the general rate of profit presents a blurred and hazy picture compared with the sharply defined rate of interest, which although its level fluctuates always confronts the borrowers as fixed and given, because it fluctuates in the same way for them all. In the same way, changes in the value of money do not prevent it from having the same value in relation to every commodity, and market prices of commodities fluctuate daily, although this does not prevent them from being noted every day in the reports. It is just the same with the rate of interest, which is noted just as regularly as the 'price of money'. This is because capital itself is offered here as a commodity in the money form. The establishment of its price is therefore the establishment of its market price, just as with all other commodities; and so the rate of interest presents itself always as a general rate of interest, as so much for so much money, as quantitatively determined. The rate of profit, on the other hand, can vary even within the same sphere, given the same market price, according to the different conditions in which individual capitals produce the same commodity; for the profit rate on an individual capital is not determined simply by the market price of the commodity, but rather by the difference between market price and cost price. And these various rates of profit, firstly within the same sphere and then within the various different spheres, can be equalized only through constant fluctuations.

*

(Note for later elaboration.) A particular form of credit. We know that when money functions as means of payment instead of means of purchase, the commodity is alienated first and its value realized only later. If payment takes place only after the commodity has been re-sold, this sale does not appear as a consequence of the purchase, but rather it is by the sale that the purchase is realized. Sale, in other words, becomes a means of purchase. – Secondly, certificates of debt, bills, etc. become means of payment for the creditor. – Thirdly, money is replaced by the settlement of outstanding debt certificates.

Chapter 23: Interest and Profit of Enterprise

Interest, as we have seen in the two preceding chapters, originally appears, originally is, and remains in reality nothing but a part of the profit, i.e. the surplus-value, which the functioning capitalist, whether industrialist or merchant, must pay to the owner and lender of capital in so far as the capital he uses is not his own but borrowed. If he simply uses his own capital, there is no such division of the profit; it belongs to him completely. In fact, in so far as the owners of capital use it themselves in the reproduction process, they do not compete together to determine the interest rate, and it is clear here already how the category of interest – which is impossible without the establishment of a rate of interest – lies outside the movement of industrial capital itself.

'The rate of interest may be defined to be that proportional sum which the lender is content to receive, and the borrower to pay, annually, or for any longer or shorter period, for the use of a certain amount of moneyed capital ... When the owner of a capital employs it actively in reproduction, he does not come under the head of those capitalists, the proportion of whom, to the number of borrowers, determines the rate of interest' (Th. Tooke, *History of Prices*, London, 1838, II, pp. 355–6).

It is in fact only the division of capitalists into money capitalists and industrial capitalists that transforms a part of the profit into interest and creates the category of interest at all; and it is only the competition between these two kinds of capitalist that creates the rate of interest.

As long as a capital is functioning in the reproduction process – even assuming that it belongs to the industrial capitalist himself, so that he does not have to pay it back to a lender – what he has at his disposal as a private person is not this capital itself but simply the profit, which he can spend as revenue. As long as his capital functions as capital, it belongs to the reproduction process and is tied down in it. Certainly he is its owner, but this ownership does not enable him, as long as he uses it as capital for the exploitation of labour, to dispose of it in any other way. It is just the same with the money capitalist. As long as his capital is lent out and operates as money capital, bringing him interest, a part of the profit, he cannot dispose of the principal. This is apparent as soon as he lends it for a year or more, say, and receives interest at certain dates without the repayment of his capital. But even the repayment makes no difference here. If he receives it back, he must always lend it out afresh if it is to operate as capital for him, in this case money capital. As long as it is in his hands, it does not bear any interest and does not operate as capital; and once it does bear interest and operate as capital, it is no longer in his hands. Hence the possibility of lending capital in perpetuity. The following points made by Tooke against Bosanquet are therefore completely false. He quotes Bosanquet (*Metallic, Paper, and Credit Currency*, London, 1842, p. 73): 'Were the rate of interest reduced as low as 1 per cent, capital borrowed would be placed nearly on a par with capital possessed.'

Tooke then makes the following comment: 'That a capital borrowed at that, or even a lower rate, should be considered nearly on a par with capital possessed, is a proposition so strange as hardly to warrant serious notice were it not advanced by a writer so intelligent, and, on some points of the subject, so well informed. Has he overlooked the circumstance, or does he consider it of little consequence, that there must, by the supposition, be a condition of repayment?' (Th. Tooke, *An Inquiry into the Currency Principle*, 2nd edn, London, 1844, p. 80).

If interest were zero, the industrial capitalist who had borrowed capital would be in the same position as the one working with his own capital. Both would pocket the same average profit, and their capital, whether it was borrowed or their own, would operate as capital only by producing a profit. The repayment requirement would make no difference here. The closer the rate of interest is to zero, if it falls to 1 per cent, for instance, the more borrowed capital stands on the same level as capital actually owned. If money capital is to continue to exist as money capital, it must always be lent out afresh, and moreover at the prevailing rate of interest, say 1 per cent, and to the same class of industrial and commercial capitalists. As long as these function as capitalists, the distinction between the one who operates with borrowed

capital and the one who operates with his own is simply that one
has to pay interest and the other does not; one pockets the whole
profit p, the other $p - i$, profit minus interest; the closer i is to
zero, the closer $p - i$ is to p, i.e. the more the two capitals stand on
the same footing. One has to pay back his capital and borrow
anew; but the other, as long as his capital is to function, must
similarly advance it afresh each time to the production process,
and has no control over it that is independent of this process.
The sole distinction that still remains is the obvious distinction
that one is the proprietor of his capital and the other is not.

The question that now arises is this. How does this purely
quantitative division of profit into net profit and interest turn
into a qualitative distinction? In other words, how does it
happen that even the capitalist who simply uses his own capital,
and no borrowed capital, classes part of his gross profit under the
special category of interest and takes particular account of it as
such? And how does it subsequently happen that all capital,
whether borrowed or not, is distinguished as interest-bearing
capital from itself in its function as capital bringing a net profit?

We must realize that not just any chance quantitative division
of profit turns into a qualitative one in this way. For example,
some industrial capitalists enter into association to pursue a
particular business and divide the profit among themselves on the
basis of legally established provisions. Others carry on their
business without associates, each on his own account. These latter
do not reckon their profit under two categories, one part as
individual profit, the other as company profit for their non-
existent associates. Here, therefore, the quantitative division does
not become a qualitative one. There is a quantitative division when
the owner happens to consist of several legal persons; there is
no such division when this is not the case.

In order to answer this question, we must pause a bit longer to
consider the real starting-point of interest formation; i.e. we must
proceed from the assumption that the money capitalist and productive capitalist actually do come face to face, not just as legally
separate persons but as persons who play quite different roles in
the reproduction process, or in whose hands the same capital
really does go through a double and completely different movement. The one simply lends the capital, the other applies it
productively.

For the productive capitalist working with borrowed capital, the gross profit breaks down into two parts, the interest that he has to pay to the lender, and the excess over and above this interest, which forms his own share in the profit. If the general rate of profit is given, this latter part is determined by the rate of interest; if the rate of interest is given, it is determined by the profit rate. Besides, however much the gross profit, the actual value magnitude of the total profit, may diverge from the average profit in any individual case, the part that belongs to the functioning capitalist is determined by the interest, since interest is fixed by the general rate of interest (leaving aside any special legal stipulations), and presupposed in advance before the production process begins – i.e. before its result, the gross profit, is obtained. We have seen how the specific and characteristic product of capital is surplus-value, and at a further remove profit. But for the capitalist working with borrowed capital, the part of the profit that remains for him after interest is paid is not profit, but profit minus interest. It is this part of the profit, therefore, that ne-cessarily appears to him as the product of capital in its actual func-tioning; and this really is the case for him, since he represents capital only as functioning capital. He is its personification in so far as it functions, and it functions in so far as it is profitably invested in industry or trade and he performs through his use of it the operations prescribed by the line of business in question. In opposition to the interest which he has to pay to the lender out of the gross profit, the remaining part of the profit which accrues to him necessarily assumes the form of industrial or commercial profit, or, to describe it with a German expression which embraces both these things, the form of profit of enterprise [*Unternehmerge-winn*]. If the gross profit is equal to the average profit, the size of this profit of enterprise is determined exclusively by the rate of interest. If the gross profit diverges from the average profit, the difference between it and the average profit (after interest is deducted on both sides) is determined by all the conjunctures that give rise to such a temporary divergence, whether in the profit rate in one particular sphere of production as opposed to the general profit rate, or in the profit made by an individual capitalist in a certain sphere as opposed to the average profit in this sphere. We have seen of course that the profit rate, even within the production process itself, does not depend only on the surplus-value but on many other factors besides: on the purchase prices of the means of production, on methods that are more than averagely productive, on economizing on constant capital, etc. And, leaving aside the price of production, it depends on the state of the trade cycle, and with each individual business deal on the greater or lesser cunning and perseverance of the capitalist, whether and how far he buys or sells below or above the production price and thereby appropriates a greater or lesser share of the total surplus-value in the circulation process. In each case, however, the quantitative division of the gross profit is transformed here into a qualitative one, and this is all the more so in that the quantitative division itself depends on *what* is to be divided, *how* the active capitalist looks after his capital and what gross profit it yields him as functioning capital, i.e. as the result of his functioning as an active capitalist. We assume here that the functioning capitalist is not the capital's owner. Property in capital is represented in relation to him by the lender, the money capitalist. The interest that he pays to the lender appears therefore as a part of the gross profit that accrues to property in capital as such. In contrast to this, the part of the profit that falls to the active capitalist, now as profit of enterprise, appears to derive exclusively from the operations or functions that he performs with the capital in the reproduction process, especially therefore the functions that he performs as an entrepreneur in industry or trade. In relation to him, in other words, interest appears as the mere fruit of property in capital, of capital in itself, abstracted from the reproduction process of capital in so far as it does not 'work', i.e. function; whereas profit of enterprise appears to him as the exclusive fruit of the functions he performs with the capital, as the fruit of capital's movement and process, a process that appears to him now as his own activity, in contrast to the non-activity and non-participation of the money capitalist in the production process. This qualitative separation between the two parts of gross profit, so that interest is the fruit of capital in itself, of property in capital without reference to the production process, while profit of enterprise is the fruit of capital actually in process, operating in the production process, and hence of the active role that the person who uses capital plays in the reproduction process – this qualitative separation is in no way merely the subjective conception of the money capitalist on the one hand and the industrial capitalist on the other. It rests on objective fact, for interest accrues to the money capitalist, the lender, who is simply the owner of the capital and thus does represent mere property in capital before the production process and outside it; while profit of enterprise accrues to the merely functioning capitalist, who is not the owner of capital.

Both for the industrial capitalist in so far as he works with borrowed capital, and for the money capitalist in so far as he does not apply his capital himself, the merely quantitative division of gross profit between two different persons, with different legal titles to the same capital and hence to the profit it produces, turns into a qualitative distinction. One part of the profit now appears in and of itself as the fruit that accrues to capital in *one* capacity, as interest; the other part appears as a specific fruit of capital in an opposite capacity, and hence as profit of enterprise: one as the simple fruit of property in capital, the other as the fruit of merely functioning with capital, as the fruit of capital as capital in process, or of the functions that the active capitalist exercises. And this mutual ossification and autonomization of the two parts of the gross profit, as if they derived from two essentially separate sources, must now be fixed for the entire capitalist class and the total capital. Furthermore, this is true irrespective of whether the capital applied by the active capitalist is borrowed or not, or whether or not the money capitalist who owns the capital uses it himself. The profit on any capital, and thus also the average profit based on the equalization of capitals among themselves, breaks down or is divided into two qualitatively different, mutually autonomous and independent parts, interest and profit of enterprise, which are both determined by particular laws. The capitalist who works with his own capital, as well as the one working with borrowed capital, divides his gross profit into interest that accrues to him as owner, as lender of his own capital to himself, and profit of enterprise, which accrues to him as an active, functioning capitalist. It becomes a matter of indifference, as far as this division is concerned, whether the capitalist really does have to share with another or not. The person who applies the capital, even if he works with his own capital, breaks down into two persons, the mere owner of capital and its user; his capital itself, with respect to the categories of profit that it yields, breaks down into *owned* capital, capital *outside* the production process, which yields an interest, and capital *in* the production process, which yields profit of enterprise as capital in process.

Interest is now established in such a way that it does not appear as a division of the gross profit that is irrespective of production, taking place only incidentally when the industrialist operates with the capital of others. Even when he operates with his own capital, his profit is divided into interest and profit of enterprise. In this way the merely quantitative division becomes a qualitative one; it takes place independently of the accidental circumstance whether the industrialist is the owner of his capital or not. It is not simply various quotas of the profit distributed to different persons, but two different categories of profit, which stand in different relationships to capital, i.e. in a relationship to different capacities of capital.

It is now very easy to see why this division of the gross profit into interest and profit of enterprise, once it becomes a qualitative one, receives this character of a qualitative division for the total capital and the capitalist class as a whole.

Firstly, this results from the simple empirical circumstance that the majority of industrial capitalists operate both with their own and with borrowed capital, even if in different ratios, and that the ratio between their own and the borrowed capital changes from one period to another.

Secondly, the transformation of a part of the gross profit into the form of interest transforms its other part into profit of enterprise. This latter is in point of fact only the antithetical form that the excess of gross profit over interest assumes as soon as the latter exists as a category of its own. The general question of how gross profit is differentiated into interest and profit of enterprise comes down simply to the question of how a part of the gross profit is invariably ossified and autonomized as interest. Historically, however, interest-bearing capital exists as a ready-made form handed down, and hence interest as a ready-made subordinate form of the surplus-value produced by capital, long before the capitalist mode of production and the conceptions of capital and profit corresponding to it come into existence. In the popular mind, therefore, money capital or interest-bearing capital is still seen as capital as such, capital *par excellence*. Hence we have on the other hand, and prevailing down to Massie's time, the notion that it is money as such that is paid interest. The circumstance that loan capital yields interest whether it is actually applied as capital or not – even if borrowed only for consumption – confirms the conception that this kind of capital is quite independent. The best proof of the independent form that interest assumes as against profit, and interest-bearing capital against industrial capital, in the earliest periods of the capitalist mode of production, is that it was discovered only in the middle of the eighteenth century (by Massie* and subsequently by Hume †) that interest is just one part of the gross profit, and that it actually needed any such discovery.

Thirdly, whether the industrial capitalist operates with his own capital or with borrowed capital in no way alters the fact that the class of money capitalists confronts him as a special kind of capitalist, money capital as an autonomous kind of capital, and interest as the separate form of surplus-value that corresponds to this specific capital.

From the *qualitative* point of view, interest is the surplus-value supplied by capital as simple ownership, which capital yields in itself, even if its owner remains outside the reproduction process; surplus-value therefore yielded in separation from its process.

From the *quantitative* point of view, the part of the profit that forms interest seems to be related not to industrial and commercial capital as such but rather to money capital, and the rate of this part of the surplus-value, the interest rate, confirms this relationship. This is firstly because the rate of interest – despite its dependence on the general rate of profit – is separately determined, and secondly because it appears, just like the market price of commodities, as something hard and fast, for all its changes: a palpable and always given relationship as opposed to the intangible rate of profit. If all capital were to be found in the hands of industrial capitalists, there would be no interest and no rate of interest. The independent form that the quantitative division of the gross profit assumes produces this qualitative distinction. If we compare the industrial capitalist with the money capitalist, he is distinguished simply by profit of enterprise, that is, the surplus of gross profit over average interest, which the rate of interest causes to appear as an empirically given quantity. If we compare him on the other hand with the industrial capitalist who operates with his own instead of borrowed capital, the latter is distinguished from him as a money capitalist simply in so far as he pockets the interest him-

* Joseph Massie, *An Essay on the Governing Causes of the Natural Rate of Interest*, London, 1750.

† David Hume (1711–76), the empiricist philosopher, doubled as economist, as indeed his friend and fellow-Scot Adam Smith did as philosopher. Here Marx refers to Hume's essay 'On Interest', published in 1764. (See also *Theories of Surplus-Value*, Part I, Addendum 7, 'Hume and Massie'.)

self instead of paying it out. From both sides, the part of the gross profit which is distinct from interest appears to him as profit of enterprise, and interest itself appears as a surplus-value that capital yields in and of itself and which it would therefore yield even without productive application.

For the individual capitalist, this is in practice correct. He has the choice between lending his capital out as interest-bearing capital or valorizing it himself as productive capital, no matter whether it exists as money capital right at the start or has first to be transformed into money capital. Taken generally, i.e. when we apply it to the whole social capital, as is done by some vulgar economists and even given out as the basis of profit, this is of course quite absurd. It is utter nonsense to suggest that all capital could be transformed into money capital without the presence of people to buy and valorize the means of production, i.e. the form in which the entire capital exists, apart from the relatively small part existing in money. Concealed in this idea, moreover, is the still greater nonsense that capital could yield interest on the basis of the capitalist mode of production without functioning as productive capital, i.e. without creating surplus-value, of which interest is simply one part; that the capitalist mode of production could proceed on its course without capitalist production. If an inappropriately large number of capitalists sought to transform their capital into money capital, the result would be a tremendous devaluation of money capital and a tremendous fall in the rate of interest; many people would immediately find themselves in the position of being unable to live on their interest and thus compelled to turn themselves back into industrial capitalists. But, as we have said above, for the individual capitalist this is in fact how it is. Even if he operates with his own capital, therefore, he necessarily considers the part of his average profit which is equal to the average interest as the fruit of his capital as such, leaving aside the production process; and in contrast to this part that is given a separate existence as interest, he considers the excess of the gross profit over and above this as simply profit of enterprise.

Fourthly (a gap in the manuscript).

We have seen, therefore, that the part of the profit which the functioning capitalist has to pay to the mere owner of the capital borrowed is transformed into the separate form for a part of the profit that all capital yields as such, whether borrowed or not, under the name of interest. How large this part is depends on the average rate of interest. Its origin is evident only in the way that the functioning capitalist, in so far as he is the owner of his own capital, does not compete – at least not actively – in determining the rate of interest. The purely quantitative division of profit between two persons with different legal titles to it has been transformed into a qualitative distinction that seems to arise from the very nature of capital and profit. For, as we have seen, as soon as a part of the profit generally assumes the form of interest, the difference between the average profit and the interest, or the part of profit over and above the interest, is transformed into a form antithetical to interest, that of profit of enterprise. These two forms, interest and profit of enterprise, exist only in their antithesis. Thus they are neither of them related to the surplus-value, of which they are simply parts, under different categories, titles or names, but rather related to each other. It is because one part of profit has been turned into interest that the other part accordingly appears as profit of enterprise.

By profit here we always mean the average profit, since the divergences therefrom of either individual profit or profit in different spheres of production – i.e. the variations in the division of the average profit or surplus-value that swing back and forth with the competitive struggle – are quite immaterial to us here. This applies throughout the present investigation.

Interest, then, is the net profit, as Ramsay describes it, yielded by property in capital as such, whether to the mere lender who remains outside the reproduction process or to the owner who employs his capital productively himself. Yet it does not yield him this net profit in so far as he is a functioning capitalist but rather as a money capitalist, the lender of his own capital as interest-bearing capital to himself as functioning capitalist. Just as the transformation of money and value in general into capital is the constant result of the capitalist production process, so its existence as capital is in the same way the constant presupposition of this process. Through its capacity to be transformed into means of production, it always commands unpaid labour and hence transforms the production and circulation process of commodities into the production of surplus-value for its possessor. Interest therefore simply expresses the fact that value in general – objectified labour in its general social form – value that assumes the form of means of production in the actual production process, confronts living labour-power as an autonomous power and is the means of appropriating unpaid labour; and that it is this power in so far as it confronts the worker as the property of another. On the other hand, however, this antithesis to wage-labour is obliterated in the form of interest; for interest-bearing capital as such does not have wage-labour as its opposite but rather functioning capital; it is the capitalist actually functioning in the reproduction process whom the lending capitalist directly confronts, and not the wage-labourer who is expropriated from the means of production precisely on the basis of capitalist production. Interest-bearing capital is capital *as property* as against capital *as function*. But if capital does not function, it does not exploit workers and does not come into opposition with labour.

On the other hand, profit of enterprise does not form an antithesis with wage-labour but rather with interest.

Firstly, taking the average profit as given, the rate of profit of enterprise is determined not by wages but rather by the rate of interest. It is either high or low in inverse proportion to the latter.[72]

Secondly, the functioning capitalist derives his claim to profit of enterprise, and thus profit of enterprise itself, not from his ownership of capital but rather from the function of capital as opposed to the capacity in which it exists only as inert property. This antithesis directly emerges as soon as he operates with borrowed capital, where interest and profit of enterprise accrue to two different persons. Profit of enterprise arises from the function of capital in the reproduction process, i.e. as a result of the operations and activity by which the functioning capitalist mediates these functions of industrial and commercial capital. But it is no sinecure to be a representative of functioning capital, unlike the case with interest-bearing capital. On the basis of capitalist production, the capitalist directs both the production process and the circulation process. The exploitation of productive labour takes effort, whether he does this himself or has it done in his name by others. In opposition to interest, therefore, his profit on enterprise presents itself to him as independent of his property in capital and rather as the result of his functions as non-owner, as a *worker*.

He inevitably gets the idea into his head, therefore, that his profit of enterprise – very far from forming any antithesis with wage-labour and being only the unpaid labour of others – is

72. 'The profits of enterprise depend upon the net profits of capital, not the latter upon the former' (Ramsay, *Essay on the Distribution of Wealth*, p. 214). For Ramsay, net profits always means interest.

rather itself a *wage*, 'wages of superintendence of labour', a higher wage than that of the ordinary wage-labourer, (1) because it is complex labour, and (2) because he himself pays the wages. That his function as a capitalist consists in producing surplus-value, i.e. unpaid labour, and in the most economical conditions at that, is completely forgotten in the face of the antithesis that interest accrues to the capitalist even if he does not perform any function as capitalist, but is simply the owner of capital; while profit of enterprise, on the other hand, accrues to the functioning capitalist even if he is not the owner of the capital with which he functions. In the face of the antithetical form of the two parts into which profit and thus surplus-value divides, it is forgotten that both are simply parts of surplus-value and that such a division can in no way change its nature, its origin and its conditions of existence.

In the reproduction process, the functioning capitalist represents capital against the wage-labourers as the property of others, and the money capitalist participates in the exploitation of labour as represented by the functioning capitalist. If it is only as representative of the means of production vis-à-vis the workers that the active capitalist can exercise his function, have the workers work for him or have the means of production function as capital, this is forgotten in the face of the opposition between the function of capital in the reproduction process and mere ownership of capital outside the reproduction process.

In point of fact, the form that the two parts of profit or surplus-value assume as interest and profit of enterprise does not express any relationship with labour, because this relationship exists only between labour and profit, or rather surplus-value, as the sum of these two parts, their whole and their unity. The ratio in which profit is divided, and the different legal titles by which this division takes place, already assume that profit is ready-made and presuppose its existence. If the capitalist is the actual owner of the capital with which he functions, he pockets the entire profit or surplus-value; it is all the same for the worker whether this is what he does or whether he has to pay one part to a third party as the legal proprietor. The basis for the division of the profit between two kinds of capitalist is thus transformed imperceptibly into the basis of existence of the profit or surplus-value to be divided, which capital derives as such from the reproduction process quite apart from any later division. From the fact that interest confronts profit of enterprise, and vice versa, but neither confronts labour, it seems to follow that profit of enterprise plus interest, i.e. profit and consequently surplus-value, is derived – from what? From the antithetical form of its two parts! But profit is produced before this division takes place, and before there can be any talk of it.

Interest-bearing capital proves itself as such only in so far as the money lent really is transformed into capital and produces a surplus, of which interest is one part. This does not by itself rule out that interest-bearing might be its inherent property, independent of the production process. Labour-power, for instance, proves its value-creating property only if it is activated and realized in the labour process; but this does not exclude it being potentially in itself already value-creating activity as a capacity, and as such it does not just arise from the process but is rather presupposed by it. It is bought as the ability to create value. It can be bought by someone without their having it work productively; i.e. for purely personal purposes, services, etc. The same with capital. It is the thing of its borrower, whether or not he uses it as capital, and thus really does set in motion its inherent property of producing surplus-value. What he pays for in both cases is the surplus-value inherently contained in the commodity of capital as a potentiality.

*

Let us now take a closer look at profit of enterprise.

Since the aspect of capital's specific social determination in the capitalist mode of production – capital ownership which possesses the capacity of command over the labour of others – becomes fixed, with interest appearing as the part of surplus-value that capital produces in this connection, so the other part of surplus-value, profit of enterprise, necessarily appears as if it does not derive from capital as capital, but rather from the production process independently of its specific social determination, which indeed has already obtained its particular mode of existence in the form of interest on capital. However, the production process, when separated from capital, is simply the labour process in general. The industrial capitalist, as distinct from the owner of capital, appears therefore not as functioning capital but rather as a functionary independent of capital, as a simple bearer of the labour process in general; as a worker, and a wage-worker at that.

Interest in itself expresses precisely the existence of the conditions of labour as capital, in their social antithesis to labour and their transformation into personal powers vis-à-vis labour and over labour. Interest represents mere ownership of capital as a means of appropriating the product of other people's labour. But it represents this character of capital as something that falls to it outside the production process and is in no way the result of the specifically capitalist character of this production process itself. It presents it not in direct antithesis to labour, but, on the contrary, with no relationship to labour at all, merely as a relationship between one capitalist and another. Thus as a capacity that is external and indifferent to the actual relationship between capital and labour. In interest, therefore, the particular form of profit in which the antithetical character of capital acquires an autonomous expression, it does so in such a way that this antithesis is completely obliterated in this expression and completely abstracted from it. Interest is a relationship between two capitalists, not between capitalist and worker.

On the other hand, this form of interest gives the other part of profit the qualitative form of profit of enterprise, and subsequently of wages of superintendence. The particular functions which the capitalist has to perform as such, and which fall to his part precisely as distinct from the workers and in opposition to them, are presented as simply functions of labour. He obtains surplus-value not because he works as a *capitalist* but rather because, leaving aside his capacity as a capitalist, he *also* works. This part of surplus-value is therefore no longer surplus-value at all, but rather its opposite, the equivalent for labour performed. Since the estranged character of capital, its antithesis to labour, is shifted outside the actual process of exploitation, i.e. into interest-bearing capital, this process of exploitation itself appears as simply a labour process, in which the functioning capitalist simply performs different work from that of the workers. The labour of exploiting and the labour exploited are identical, both being labour. The labour of exploiting is just as much labour as the labour that is exploited. The social form of capital devolves on interest, but expressed in a neutral and indifferent form; the economic function of capital devolves on profit of enterprise, but with the specifically capitalist character of this function removed.

Exactly the same thing takes place here in the consciousness of the capitalist, as with the grounds of compensation discussed in Part Two of this volume with respect to the equalization of the average profit. These grounds of compensation which go to determine the division of surplus-value are turned, in the capitalist's way of conceiving things, into grounds for the existence and (subjective) justification of profit as such.

The idea of profit of enterprise as a wage for supervising labour, an idea arising from the antithesis between this profit and interest, finds further support in that one part of the profit actually can be separated off as wages, and really does separate off; or rather, a part of wages, conversely, on the basis of the capitalist mode of production, appears as an integral component of profit. As Adam Smith already rightly realized, this part presents itself in its pure form as independent and completely separate both from profit in general (as the sum of interest and profit of enterprise), and also from the part of profit that remains after deduction of interest as the so-called profit of enterprise, in the payment of a manager in those branches of business where the scale, etc. permits sufficient division of labour for a special salary to be paid to such a person.

The work of supervision and management necessarily arises where the direct production process takes the form of a socially combined process, and does not appear simply as the isolated labour of separate producers.[73] But it takes two different forms.

On the one hand, in all labour where many individuals cooperate, the interconnection and unity of the process is necessarily represented in a governing will, and in functions that concern not the detailed work but rather the workplace and its activity as a whole, as with the conductor of an orchestra. This is productive labour that has to be performed in any combined mode of production.

On the other hand – and quite apart from the commercial department – this work of supervision necessarily arises in all modes of production that are based on opposition between the worker as direct producer and the proprietor of the means of production. The greater this opposition, the greater the role that this work of supervision plays. It reaches its high point in the

73. 'Superintendence is here' (in the case of the peasant proprietor) 'completely dispensed with' (J. E. Cairnes, *The Slave Power*, London, 1862, pp. 48–9).*

* John Elliot Cairnes (1823–75), an English writer active in opposing slavery in the United States, was evidently held in high regard by Marx, who quotes him several times in *Capital* Volume 1 and elsewhere.

slave system.[74] But it is also indispensable in the capitalist mode of production, since here too the production process is at the same time a process of consumption of labour-power by the capitalist. In despotic states, too, the work of supervision and all-round intervention of the government involves both aspects: the performance of those common tasks that arise from the nature of all communities, and the specific functions that arise from the opposition between the government and the mass of the people.

With the writers of antiquity, who had the slave system in mind, we find in their theory (and this was also the case in practice) that the two aspects of supervisory work coincide as inseparably as they do with the modern economists who view the capitalist mode of production as the absolute mode. On the other hand, as I shall show right away with an example, the apologists of the modern slave system know just as well how to use supervisory work as a justificatory ground for slavery as other economists do for the wage-labour system.

The *villicus* of Cato's time: 'At the head of the slave-worked estate (*familia rustica*) stood the manager (*villicus*, from *villa*), whose job it was to take and spend, buy and sell; he received his instructions from the master, and gave both orders and punishment in his absence . . . The manager of course had more freedom than the other slaves. The Magonian books* advise that he should be permitted to marry and raise children, as well as keeping his own money; Cato said he should be married to the female manager. He alone had any prospect of obtaining his freedom, as a reward from the master for good behaviour. The other slaves all formed a common household . . . Every slave, including the manager himself, received his necessities at the master's expense at definite intervals and in fixed amounts, and had to make do with this . . . The quantity depended on the work, so that the manager, for instance, whose work was lighter than the other slaves, received a smaller ration' (Mommsen, *Römische Geschichte*, 2nd edn, 1856, I, pp. 809–10).

74. 'If the nature of the work requires that the workmen' (i.e. the slaves) 'should be dispersed over an extended area, the number of overseers, and, therefore, the cost of the labour which requires this supervision, will be proportionately increased' (Cairnes, op. cit., p. 44).

* The books of Mago, a Carthaginian writer of unknown date, were translated into Latin at the order of the Roman senate. They served as the official model for the rational organization of agriculture on a slave basis.

Aristotle: 'Ὁ γὰρ δεσπότης οὐκ ἐν τῷ κτᾶσθαι τοὺς δούλους, ἀλλ' ἐν τῷ χρῆσθαι δούλοις.' ('For the master' – the capitalist – 'proves himself such not by obtaining slaves' – ownership of capital, which gives him the power to buy labour – 'but by employing slaves' – using labourers, nowadays wage-labourers, in the production process.) ''Εστι δ'αὕτη ἡ ἐπιστήμη οὐδὲν μέγα ἔχουσα οὐδὲ σεμνόν' ('There is nothing great or sublime about this science') 'ἃ γὰρ τὸν δοῦλον ἐπίστασθαι δεῖ ποιεῖν, ἐκεῖνον δεῖ ταῦτα ἐπίστασθαι ἐπιτάττειν.' ('but whatever the slave is to perform, the master must be able to order.') 'Διὸ ὅσοις ἐξουσία μὴ αὐτοὺς κακοπαθεῖν, ἐπίτροπος λαμβάνει ταύτην τὴν τιμήν, αὐτοὶ δὲ πολιτεύονται ἢ φιλοσοφοῦσιν.' ('Whenever the masters are not compelled to plague themselves with supervision, the overseer assumes *this honour*, while the masters pursue public affairs or philosophy'.) (Aristotle, *De republica*, Bekker edn, Book I, 7).

What Aristotle is saying, in very blunt terms, is that domination, in the economic domain as well as in the political, imposes on those in power the functions of dominating, so that, in the economic domain, they must know how to consume labour-power. And he adds that this supervisory work is not a matter of very great moment, which is why the master leaves the 'honour' of this drudgery to an overseer as soon as he is wealthy enough.

This work of management and supervision, in so far as it is not simply a particular function arising from the nature of all combined social labour, but arises rather from the opposition between the owner of the means of production and the owner of mere labour-power – whether labour-power is bought with the worker himself, as in the slave system, or alternatively the worker sells his own labour-power, so that the production process appears at the same time as a process of consumption of labour by capital – this function arising from the servitude of the direct producer is made often enough into a justification of that relationship itself, and the exploitation and appropriation of the unpaid labour of others is just as often presented as the wage due to the owner of capital. This has never been done better than by a defender of slavery in the United States, the lawyer O'Conor, at a meeting in New York on 19 December 1859, under the slogan of 'Justice for the South':

'Now, gentlemen,' he said amid thunderous applause, 'to that condition of bondage the Negro is assigned by Nature . . . He has strength, and has the power to labour; but the Nature which created the power denied to him either the intellect to govern, or willingness to work.' (Applause.) 'Both were denied to him. And that Nature which deprived him of the will to labour, gave him a master to coerce that will, and to make him a useful . . . servant in the clime in which he was capable of living, useful for himself and for the master who governs him . . . I maintain that it is not injustice to leave the Negro in the condition in which Nature placed him, to give him a master to govern him . . . nor is it depriving him of any of his rights to compel him to labour in return. and afford to that master just compensation for the labour and talent employed in governing him and rendering him useful to himself and to the society'.*

Now the wage-labourer, just like the slave, must have a master, to make him work and govern him. And once this relationship of domination and servitude is assumed, it is quite in order for the wage-labourer to be compelled to produce, besides his own wages, also the wages of supervision, a compensation for the work of dominating and supervising him, or 'just compensation for the labour and talent employed in governing him and rendering him useful to himself and to the society'.

The work of supervision and management, in so far as it arises from the antithetical character, the domination of capital over labour, and is therefore common to all modes of production which, like the capitalist one, are based on class opposition, is also directly and inseparably fused, under the capitalist system, with the productive functions that all combined social labour assigns to particular individuals as their special work. The wages of an *epitropos*, or *régisseur* as he was known in feudal France, become completely separated from profit and even take the form of wages for skilled labour, as soon as the business is conducted on a sufficiently large scale for such a manager to be paid, even though our industrial capitalists are still a long way from 'pursuing public affairs or philosophy'.

Mr Ure has already noted how it is not the industrial capitalists but rather the industrial managers who are 'the soul of our industrial system'.[75] As far as the commercial side of the business goes,

* *New York Daily Tribune*, 20 December 1859. From 1852 to 1862, Marx was himself a regular contributor to this paper, which then adopted a strongly democratic and anti-slavery position.

75. A. Ure, *Philosophy of Manufactures*, French translation, 1836, I, p. 67. Here this Pindar of the manufacturers also testifies that most of the latter have not the slightest understanding of the machinery they use.

all that is necessary has already been said in the previous Part.*

Capitalist production has itself brought it about that the work of supervision is readily available, quite independent of the ownership of capital. It has therefore become superfluous for this work of supervision to be performed by the capitalist. A musical conductor need in no way be the owner of the instruments in his orchestra, nor does it form part of his function as a conductor that he should have any part in paying the 'wages' of the other musicians. Cooperative factories provide the proof that the capitalist has become just as superfluous as a functionary in production as he himself, from his superior vantage-point, finds the large landlord. In so far as the work of the capitalist does not arise from the production process simply as a capitalist process, i.e. does not come to an end with capital itself; in so far as it is not confined to the function of exploiting the labour of others; in so far therefore as it arises from the form of labour as social labour, from the combination and cooperation of many to a common result, it is just as independent of capital as is this form itself, once it has burst its capitalist shell. To say that this labour, as capitalist labour, is necessarily the function of the capitalist means nothing more than that the *vulgus* cannot conceive that forms developed in the womb of the capitalist mode of production may be separated and liberated from their antithetical capitalist character. Vis-à-vis the money capitalist, the industrial capitalist is a worker, but his work is that of a capitalist, i.e. an exploiter of the labour of others. The wage that he claims and draws for this work is precisely the quantity of others' labour that is appropriated, and depends directly upon the rate of exploitation of this labour, as long as he makes the effort required for this exploitation. It does not depend on the amount of effort this exploitation costs him, which can be devolved on a manager against moderate payment. After every crisis one can see many ex-manufacturers in the English factory districts who are now supervising their own former factories as managers for the new owners, often their creditors, in return for a modest wage.[76]

* pp. 403–4 above.

76. In one case of which I have personal knowledge, a manufacturer whose business failed in the crisis of 1868 subsequently became the paid employee of his own former workers. After it went bankrupt, the factory had been taken over by a workers' cooperative and the former owner employed as a manager. – F. E.

The wages of management, both commercial and industrial, appear as completely separate from profit of enterprise both in the workers' cooperative factories and in capitalist joint-stock companies. The separation of managerial wages from profit of enterprise, which in other cases appears accidental, is here a constant factor. In the case of the cooperative factory, the antithetical character of the supervisory work disappears, since the manager is paid by the workers instead of representing capital in opposition to them. Joint-stock companies in general (developed with the credit system) have the tendency to separate this function of managerial work more and more from the possession of capital, whether one's own or borrowed; just as with the development of bourgeois society the judicial and administrative functions became separate from landed property, which they were attributes of in the feudal period. But since on the one hand the functioning capitalist confronts the mere owner of capital, the money capitalist, and with the development of credit this money capital itself assumes a social character, being concentrated in banks and loaned out by these, no longer by its direct proprietors; and since on the other hand the mere manager, who does not possess capital under any title, neither by loan nor in any other way, takes care of all real functions that fall to the functioning capitalist as such, there remains only the functionary, and the capitalist vanishes from the production process as someone superfluous.

From the published accounts[77] of the cooperative factories in England, we can see that—after deducting the wages of the manager, which form a part of the variable capital laid out, just like the wages of the other workers – their profit was greater than the average, even though they sometimes paid a much higher interest than private factories did. The reason for this higher profit was in all these cases a greater economy in the use of constant capital. What is important for us in this connection is that here the average profit (= interest + profit of enterprise) presents itself palpably and in actual fact as a magnitude completely separate from the wages of management. Since profit here was higher than average, so profit of enterprise was also higher than elsewhere.

The same fact is apparent in certain capitalist joint-stock undertakings, e.g. the joint-stock banks. The London and Westminster

77. The accounts referred to here only go up to 1864, since the above was written in 1865. – F. E.

Bank paid an annual dividend of 30 per cent in 1863, the Union Bank of London and others paid 15 per cent. In addition to the managers' salaries, the interest paid on deposits is deducted from gross profit. The high profit is explained here by the small proportion of the paid-up capital in relation to deposits. For example, in the case of the London and Westminster Bank for 1863: paid-up capital £1,000,000; deposits £14,540,275. In that of the Union Bank of London for 1863: paid-up capital £600,000, deposits £12,384,173.

The confusion between profit of enterprise and the wages of supervision or management originally arose from the antithetical form that the surplus of profit over interest assumes in opposition to this interest. It was subsequently developed with the apologetic intention of presenting profit not as surplus-value, i.e. as unpaid labour, but rather as the wage that the capitalist himself receives for the work he performs. The socialists then raised the demand that profit should be reduced in practice to what it claimed to be in theory, i.e. simply to the wages of supervision. And this demand came up against the theoretical embellishment still more uncomfortably, the more the wages of superintendence on the one hand found their particular level and market price, just like every other wage, with the formation of a numerous class of industrial and commercial managers;[78] and the more they fell on the other hand, just like wages for skilled labour in general, with the general development that reduces the costs of production of labour-power with special training.[79] With the development of cooperatives on

78. 'Masters are labourers as well as their journeymen. In this character their interest is precisely the same as that of their men. But they are also either capitalists, or the agents of the capitalists, and in this respect their interest is decidedly opposed to the interests of the workmen' (p. 27). 'The wide spread of education among the journeymen mechanics of this country diminishes daily the value of the labour and skill of almost all masters and employers by increasing the number of persons who possess their peculiar knowledge' (p. 30; Thomas Hodgskin, *Labour Defended against the Claims of Capital, etc.*, London, 1825).*

* Thomas Hodgskin (1787–1869), one of the 'Ricardian socialists' much admired by Marx, who sought to use Ricardo's economics to show the exploitation of the working class. See *Theories of Surplus-Value*, Part III, Chapter XXI, 3.

79. 'The general relaxation of conventional barriers, the increased facilities of education tend to bring down the wages of skilled labour instead of raising those of the unskilled' (J. S. Mill, *Principles of Political Economy*, 2nd edn, London, 1849, I, p. 479).

the workers' part, and joint-stock companies on the part of the bourgeoisie, the last pretext for confusing profit of enterprise with the wages of management was removed, and profit came to appear in practice as what it undeniably was in theory, mere surplus-value, value for which no equivalent was paid, realized unpaid labour; so that the functioning capitalist really exploits labour, and the fruits of his exploitation, if he operates with borrowed capital, are divided into interest and profit of enterprise, the surplus of the profit over the interest.

On the basis of capitalist production, a new swindle with the wages of management develops in connection with joint-stock companies, in that, over and above the actual managing director, a number of governing and supervisory boards arise, for which management and supervision are in fact a mere pretext for the robbery of shareholders and their own enrichment. Very nice details of this are to be found in *The City or the Physiology of London Business; with Sketches on 'Change, and the Coffee Houses*, London, 1845. 'What bankers and merchants gain by the direction of eight or nine different companies, may be seen from the following illustration: The private balance sheet of Mr Timothy Abraham Curtis, presented to the Court of Bankruptcy when that gentleman failed, exhibited a sample of the income netted from directorship . . . between £800 and £900 a year. Mr Curtis having been associated with the Courts of the Bank of England, and the East India House, it was considered quite a plum for a public company to acquire his services in the board-room' (pp. 81, 82).

The remuneration of these company directors is at least one guinea (21 shillings) for each weekly meeting. Hearings before the bankruptcy court show that the wages of supervision are in inverse proportion, as a rule, to the actual supervision exercised by these nominal directors.

Chapter 24: Interest-Bearing Capital as the Superficial Form of the Capital Relation

In interest-bearing capital, the capital relationship reaches its most superficial and fetishized form. Here we have $M-M'$, money that produces more money, self-valorizing value, without the process that mediates the two extremes. In commercial capital, $M-C-M'$, at least the general form of the capitalist movement is present, even though this takes place only in the circulation sphere, so that profit appears as merely profit upon alienation; but for all that, it presents itself as the product of a social *relation*, not the product of a mere *thing*. The form of commercial capital still exhibits a process, the unity of opposing phases, a movement that breaks down into two opposite procedures, the purchase and sale of commodities. This is obliterated in $M-M'$, the form of interest-bearing capital. If £1,000 is lent out by a capitalist, for example, and the interest rate is 5 per cent, the value of the £1,000 as capital for one year is $C + Ci'$, where C is the capital and i' the rate of interest. In this case we have 5 per cent $= \frac{5}{100} = \frac{1}{20}$; $1,000 + (1,000 \times \frac{1}{20}) =$ £1,050. The value of £1,000 as capital is £1,050. In other words, capital is not a simple quantity. It is a *relation* of quantities, a ratio between the principal as a given value, and itself as self-valorizing value, as a principal that has produced a surplus-value. And as we have seen, capital presents itself in this way, as this directly self-valorizing value, for all active capitalists, whether they function with their own capital or with borrowed capital.

$M-M'$. Here we have the original starting-point of capital, money in the formula $M-C-M'$, reduced to the two extremes $M-M'$, where $M' = M + \Delta M$, money that creates more money. This is the original and general formula for capital reduced to a meaningless abbreviation. It is capital in its finished form, the unity of the production and circulation processes, and hence capital yielding a definite surplus-value in a specific period of time. In the form of interest-bearing capital, capital appears immediately in this form, unmediated by the production and circulation processes. Capital appears as a mysterious and self-creating source of interest, of its own increase. The *thing* (money, commodity, value) is now already capital simply as a thing; the result of the overall reproduction process appears as a property devolving on a thing in itself; it is up to the possessor of money, i.e. of commodities in their ever-exchangeable form, whether he wants to spend this money as money or hire it out as capital. In interest-bearing capital, therefore, this automatic fetish is elaborated into its pure form, self-valorizing value, money breeding money, and in this form it no longer bears any marks of its origin. The social relation is consummated in the relationship of a thing, money, to itself. Instead of the actual transformation of money into capital, we have here only the form of this devoid of content. As in the case of labour-power, here the use-value of money is that of creating value, a greater value than is contained in itself. Money as such is already potentially self-valorizing value, and it is as such that it is lent, this being the form of sale for this particular commodity. Thus it becomes as completely the property of money to create value, to yield interest, as it is the property of a pear tree to bear pears. And it is as this interest-bearing thing that the money-lender sells his money. Nor is that all. The actually functioning capital, as we have seen, presents itself in such a way that it yields interest not as functioning capital, but rather as capital in itself, as money capital.

There is still a further distortion. While interest is simply one part of the profit, i.e. the surplus-value, extorted from the worker by the functioning capitalist, it now appears conversely as if interest is the specific fruit of capital, the original thing, while profit, now transformed into the form of profit of enterprise, appears as a mere accessory and trimming added in the reproduction process. The fetish character of capital and the representation of this capital fetish is now complete. In $M-M'$ we have the irrational form of capital, the misrepresentation and objectification of the relations of production, in its highest power: the interest-bearing form, the simple form of capital, in which it is taken as logically anterior to its own reproduction process; the ability of money or a commodity to valorize its own value independent of reproduction – the capital mystification in the most flagrant form.

For vulgar economics, which seeks to present capital as an independent source of wealth, of value creation, this form is of course a godsend, a form in which the source of profit is no longer recognizable and in which the result of the capitalist production process – separate from the process itself – obtains an autonomous existence.

It is only in money capital that capital becomes a commodity, whose self-valorizing quality has a fixed price as expressed in the prevailing rate of interest.

As interest-bearing capital, and moreover in its immediate form of interest-bearing money capital (the other forms of interest-bearing capital, which do not concern us here, are derived from this form and presuppose it), capital obtains its pure fetish form, $M-M'$ being the subject, a thing for sale. Firstly, by way of its continuing existence as money, a form in which all capital's determinations are dissolved and its real elements are invisible. Money is in fact the very form in which the distinctions between commodities as different use-values are obliterated, and hence also the distinctions between industrial capitals, which consist of these commodities and the conditions of their production; it is the form in which value – and here capital – exists as autonomous exchange-value. In the reproduction process of capital, the money form is an evanescent moment, a moment of mere transition. On the money market, on the contrary, capital always exists in this form. Secondly, the surplus-value it creates, here again in the form of money, appears to accrue to it as such. Like the growth of trees, so the generation of money (τόκος)* seems a property of capital in this form of money capital.

In interest-bearing capital, the movement of capital is abbreviated. The mediating process is omitted, and a capital of 1,000 is characterized as a thing that in itself is 1,000 and in a certain period is transformed into 1,100, just as wine in the cellar improves its use-value after a given period of time. Capital is now a thing, but the thing is capital. The money's body is now by love possessed.†
As soon as it is lent, or else applied in the reproduction process (in so far as it yields interest to the functioning capitalist as its owner, separate from profit of enterprise), interest accrues to it no matter whether it is asleep or awake, at home or abroad, by day

---

* The Greek word for interest means literally 'what has been born'.

† Goethe, *Faust*, Part I, Auerbach's Cellar in Leipzig, line 2141 ('*als hätt' es Lieb' im Leibe*').

and by night. In interest-bearing capital, therefore (and all capital is money capital in its value expression, or is now taken as the expression of money capital), the hoarder's most fervent wish is realized.

It is this ingrown existence of interest in money capital as a thing (which is how the production of surplus-value by capital appears here) that Luther was so concerned with in his naïve polemic against usury. After he explains that interest may be demanded if the failure to repay a loan at the specified date causes the lender certain expenses that he has to pay, or if he missed the opportunity for a profitable bargain (he gives the example of the purchase of a garden), he continues:

'Now that I have loaned you this (100 guilders), you have caused me to suffer two-fold damage, since I cannot pay on the one hand and cannot buy on the other, but must suffer a loss on both counts, and this is called *duplex interesse, damni emergentis et lucri cessantis* [a double damage, both from the loss caused and from the profit missed] ... On hearing that Hans has suffered a loss with the 100 guilders he lent, and demands just compensation for this, they rush in and charge double on each 100 guilders, a double reimbursement, i.e. for the cost of the payment, and the inability to buy the garden, just as if the 100 guilders *had had these two losses grown on to it naturally* [Marx's emphasis], so that wherever they have 100 guilders, they put it out and count two losses of this kind on top of it, even though they have not suffered them ... This is why you are a usurer, taking damages from your neighbour's money for a supposed loss which in fact no one caused you, and which you can neither prove nor reckon. Damages of this kind the lawyers call *non verum sed phantasticum interesse* [not actual damages, but imagined damages]. A loss which each conjures up for himself ... it is no good to say that the losses might have been incurred, because I was not able to pay or buy. That would be a case of *ex contingente necessarium*, making something out of a thing that is not, and making what is uncertain into something completely sure. Surely usury of this kind would devour the whole world in a few years ... If the lender meets with an unhappy accident, and he needs to recover from it, then he may demand damages, but in trade it is different, and just the opposite. There they scheme to profit at the cost of their needy neighbours, seeking to accumulate wealth and get rich, to be lazy and idle and live in luxury on the labour of other people, without care, danger or loss. To sit by my stove and let my 100 guilders gather wealth for me in the country, and yet keep it in my pocket because it is only a loan, without any danger or risk – my dear friend, who would not like that?' (Martin Luther, *An die Pfarrherrn wider den Wucher zu predigen, etc.*, Wittenberg, 1540.)

The conception of capital as value that reproduces itself and increases in reproduction, by virtue of its innate property as ever persisting and growing value – i.e. by virtue of the scholastics' 'hidden quality' – is behind Dr Price's amazing fancies, which leave far behind the fantasies of the alchemists; fancies which Pitt took quite seriously, and which he made the basis of his financial policy in his bills setting up the sinking fund.*

'Money bearing compound interest increases at first slowly. But, the rate of increase being continually accelerated, it becomes in some time so rapid, as to mock all the powers of the imagination. One penny, put out at our Saviour's birth to 5 per cent compound interest, would, before this time, have increased to a greater sum, than would be contained in a hundred and fifty millions of earths, all solid gold. But if put out to simple interest, it would, in the same time, have amounted to no more than seven shillings and four pence half-penny. Our government has hitherto chosen to improve money in the last, rather than the first of these ways.' [80]

---

* Marx discussed this 'sinking fund' and its political implications in one of his articles for the *New York Daily Tribune*, 'Mr Disraeli's Budget', published on 7 May 1858.

80. Richard Price, *An Appeal to the Public on the Subject of the National Debt*, London, 1772 [p. 19]. He makes the naïve wisecrack: 'It is borrowing money at simple interest, in order to improve it at compound interest' (R. Hamilton, *An Inquiry into the Rise and Progress of the National Debt of Great Britain*, 2nd edn, Edinburgh, 1814 [p. 133]). According to this, borrowing would be the most secure means of enrichment for private persons too. But if I borrow £100 at an annual interest of 5 per cent, for example, and assuming that this advance is for 100 million years, in the meantime I still have only £100 to lend out each year, and similarly £5 to pay. This process never enables me to lend out £105 simply by having borrowed £100. How would I then be able to pay the 5 per cent? By a new loan, or, if I am the state, by taxation. If the industrial capitalist borrows money and has to pay 5 per cent as interest out of a profit of say 15 per cent, he might consume 5 per cent (although his appetite grows with his income) and capitalize 5 per cent. In other words, 15 per cent profit is already presupposed, if 5 per cent interest is to be regularly paid. If the process continues, the profit rate will fall for the reasons already developed, say from 15 per cent to 10 per cent. But Price forgets completely that the interest of 5 per cent presupposed a rate of profit of 15 per cent, and he lets this rate continue with the accumulation of capital. He does not have

He flies still higher in his *Observations on Reversionary Payments, etc.*, London, 1772: 'A shilling put out to 6 per cent compound interest at our Saviour's birth' (presumably in the Temple of Jerusalem) 'would . . . have increased to a greater sum than the whole solar system could hold, supposing it a sphere equal in diameter to the diameter of Saturn's orbit.' 'A state need never therefore be under any difficulties; for with the smallest savings it may in as little time as its interest can require pay off the largest debts' (pp. xiii, xiv).

What a charming theoretical introduction for the English national debt!

Price was simply dazzled by the incredible figures that arise from geometric progression. Since he viewed capital as a self-acting automaton, without regard to the conditions of reproduction and labour, as a mere number that increases by itself (just as Malthus saw people in his own geometric progression), he could imagine he had found the law of its growth in the formula $s = c(1 + i)^n$, where s = sum of capital + compound interest, c = the capital advanced, i = the rate of interest (expressed in aliquot parts of 100), and n = the number of years for which the process continues.

Pitt took Dr Price's mystification quite seriously. In 1786 the House of Commons resolved that £1,000,000 should be raised for public purposes. According to Price, whom Pitt believed, nothing could be better than to tax the people with a view to 'accumulating' the sum raised, and thus spiriting away the national debt by the mystery of compound interest. That resolution of the House of Commons was soon followed by a bill drawn up by Pitt, which provided for the accumulation of £250,000, 'until, with the expired annuities, the fund should have grown to £4,000,000 annually' (Act 26, George III, Chapter XXXI).

In a speech of 1792, in which Pitt proposed to increase the sum devoted to the sinking fund, he adduced machines, credit, etc., among the reasons for England's commercial supremacy, but as 'the most widespread and enduring cause, that of accumulation'. This principle, he said, was completely developed in the work of

---

to bother with the real process of accumulation at all, but only to lend money out, for it to return to him with interest. How it accomplishes this is quite immaterial to him, since this is in fact the innate quality of interest-bearing capital.

Adam Smith, that genius . . . and this accumulation, he continued, was accomplished by laying aside at least a portion of the annual profit for the purpose of increasing the principal, which was to be employed in the same manner the following year, and which thus yielded a continual profit. By way of Dr Price, therefore, Pitt transformed Adam Smith's theory of accumulation into the enrichment of a nation by accumulation of debts, and thus arrived at the comforting progress towards an infinity of loans – loans to pay loans with.

Already with Josiah Child, the father of modern banking, we find that '£100 put out at 10 per cent for seventy years, at compound interest would produce £102,400' (*Traité sur le commerce, etc.*, par J. Child, French translation, Amsterdam and Berlin, 1754, p. 115. Written in 1669).

How far Dr Price's conception has unwittingly been taken over by modern economics is shown by the following quotation from *The Economist*: 'Capital, with compound interest on every portion of capital saved, is so all-engrossing that all the wealth in the world from which income is derived, has long ago become the interest of capital . . . All rent is now the payment of interest on capital previously invested in the land' (*The Economist*, 19 July 1851).

All wealth that can ever be produced belongs to capital in its capacity as interest-bearing capital, and everything that it has received up till now is only a first instalment for its 'all-engrossing' appetite. By its own inherent laws, all surplus labour that the human race can supply belongs to it. Moloch.

Finally, the following hodge-podge by the 'Romantic' Müller: 'Dr Price's tremendous growth of compound interest, or of the self-accelerating forces of human beings, presupposes an undivided or uninterrupted and uniform arrangement for several centuries, if it is to produce these tremendous effects. As soon as capital is broken up into individual branches, which start to grow independently, the entire accumulation of forces begins afresh. Nature has distributed over a career of some twenty to twenty-five years the progression of force that is the average lot of each individual worker (!). After this period has elapsed, the worker abandons his career and must now transfer the capital obtained through compound interest on labour to a new worker, in most cases dividing it among several workers or children. The latter must first learn to activate and apply the capital that falls to them before they can actually draw compound interest from it. Moreover, a tremendous amount of the capital bourgeois society obtains, even in the most energetic communities, is accumulated only gradually over long years, and not directly applied to the expansion of labour. Rather, once a certain sum has been collected, it is transferred to another individual, a worker, a bank or the state, in the form of a loan. The recipient of this, then, in so far as it is he who actually puts the capital in motion, draws compound interest from it, and can easily require the lender to content himself with simple interest. Finally, the law of consumption, greed and waste reacts against that tremendous progression in which the forces of men and their products might increase, if the law of production or thrift alone prevailed' (A. Müller, op. cit., III, pp. 147–9).

It would be impossible to drivel out a more hair-raising absurdity than this in so few lines. Not to mention the comic confusion of worker with capitalist, the value of labour-power with interest on capital, etc. – the receipt of compound interest is simply explained by saying that capital is lent out and then brings in compound interest. Our Müller's procedure is characteristic of the Romantics in every detail. Its content is formed out of everyday prejudices, skimmed from the most superficial appearance of things. This false and trivial content is then supposedly 'elevated' and rendered poetic by a mystifying mode of expression.

The accumulation process of capital may be conceived as an accumulation of compound interest, in so far as the part of profit (surplus-value) that is transformed back into capital, i.e. which serves to absorb new labour, may be called interest. However:

1. Apart from all the accidental circumstances, a large part of the existing capital is always being more or less devalued in the course of the reproduction process, since the value of commodities is determined not by the labour-time originally taken by their production, but rather by the labour-time that their reproduction takes, and this steadily decreases as the social productivity of labour develops. At a higher level of development of social productivity, therefore, all existing capital, instead of appearing as the result of a long process of capital accumulation, appears as the result of a relatively short reproduction period.[81]

81. See Mill and Carey, and Roscher's uncomprehending commentary on them.*
* Marx's references here are to John Stuart Mill, *Principles of Political*

2. As was shown in Part Three of this volume, the profit rate decreases in proportion to the growing accumulation of capital and the accompanying rise in the productivity of social labour, this being expressed precisely in the relative decrease of variable capital vis-à-vis constant. In order to produce the same rate of profit, therefore, if the constant capital set in motion by a worker increases ten-fold, the surplus labour-time would have to increase ten-fold as well, and very soon the total labour-time, or even the full twenty-four hours of the day, would not be sufficient, even if it were entirely appropriated by capital. Price's progression depends on the idea that the rate of profit does not decline, as does every idea of this 'all-engrossing capital at compound interest'.[82]

The identity of surplus-value and surplus labour sets a qualitative limit to the accumulation of capital: the *total working day*, the present development of the productive forces and population, which limits the number of working days that can be simultaneously exploited. But if surplus-value is conceived in the irrational form of interest, the limit is only quantitative, and beggars all fantasy.

Interest-bearing capital, however, displays the conception of the capital fetish in its consummate form, the idea that ascribes to the accumulated product of labour, in the fixed form of money at that, the power of producing surplus-value in geometric progression by way of an inherent secret quality, as a pure automaton, so that this accumulated product of labour, as *The Economist* believes, has long since discounted the whole world's wealth for all time,

---

Economy, Vol. 1, 2nd edn, London, 1848, pp. 91–2; H. C. Carey, *Principles of Social Science*, Vol. 3, Philadelphia, 1859, pp. 71–3; and W. Roscher, *Die Grundlagen der Nationalökonomie*, 3rd edn, Stuttgart, 1858, § 45.

Marx's attitude towards Mill deserves careful attention, Mill being the fountainhead of economic theory for the British Labour movement. As distinct from the mere apologetics of 'vulgar economics', Mill 'tried to harmonize the political economy of capital with the claims, no longer to be ignored, of the proletariat' (*Capital*, Volume 1, Postface to the Second Edition, p. 98). Chapter 51 of the present volume, 'Relations of Distribution and Relations of Production', is primarily devoted to criticizing Mill's basic position.

82. 'It is clear, that no labour, no productive power, no ingenuity, and no art, can answer the overwhelming demands of compound interest. But all saving is made from the revenue of the capitalist, so that actually these demands are constantly made and as constantly the productive power of labour refuses to satisfy them. A sort of balance is, therefore, constantly struck' (*Labour Defended Against the Claims of Capital*, p. 23. By Hodgskin).

as belonging to it by right and rightfully coming its way. The product of past labour, and past labour itself, is seen as pregnant in and of itself with a portion of present or future living surplus labour. We know however that in actual fact the preservation and thus also the reproduction of the value of products of past labour is *only* the result of their contact with living labour; and secondly, that the command that the products of past labour exercise over living surplus labour lasts only as long as the capital relation, the specific social relation in which past labour confronts living labour as independent and superior.

Chapter 25: Credit and Fictitious Capital

It lies outside the scope of our plan to give a detailed analysis of the credit system and the instruments this creates (credit money, etc.). Only a few points will be emphasized here, which are necessary to characterize the capitalist mode of production in general. In this connection, we shall simply be dealing with commercial and bank credit. The connection between the development of this and the development of state credit remains outside our discussion.

I have already shown (in Volume 1, Chapter 3, 3, b) how the function of money as means of payment develops out of simple commodity circulation, so that a relationship of creditor and debtor is formed. With the development of trade and the capitalist mode of production, which produces only for circulation, this spontaneous basis for the credit system is expanded, generalized and elaborated. By and large, money now functions only as means of payment, i.e. commodities are not sold for money, but for a written promise to pay at a certain date. For the sake of brevity, we can refer to all these promises to pay as bills of exchange. Until they expire and are due for payment, these bills themselves circulate as means of payment; and they form the actual commercial money. To the extent that they ultimately cancel each other out, by the balancing of debts and claims, they function absolutely as money, even though there is no final transformation into money proper. As these mutual advances by producers and merchants form the real basis of credit, so their instrument of circulation, the bill of exchange, forms the basis of credit money proper, banknotes, etc. These are not based on monetary circulation, that of metallic or government paper money, but rather on the circulation of bills of exchange.

W. Leatham (banker in Yorkshire) writes in his *Letters on the Currency*, 2nd edn, London, 1840: 'I find, then, the amount for the whole of the year of 1839 . . . to be £528,493,842' (he assumes that foreign bills of exchange make up about a fifth of the total) 'and the amount of bills out at one time in the above year, to be £132,123,460' (p. 56). The bills of exchange make up 'one component part greater in amount than all the rest put together' (p. 3). 'This enormous superstructure of bills of exchange rests (!) upon the base formed by the amount of banknotes and gold, and when, by events, this base becomes too much narrowed, its solidity and very existence is endangered' (p. 8). 'If I estimate the whole currency' (he means of the banknotes) 'and the amount of the liabilities of the Bank and country bankers, payable on demand, I find a sum of 153 million, which, by law, can be converted into gold . . . and the amount of gold to meet this demand' only 14 million (p. 11). 'The bills of exchange are not . . . placed under any control, except by preventing the abundance of money, excessive and low rates of interest or discount, which create a part of them, and encourage their great and dangerous expansion. It is impossible to decide what part arises out of real *bona fide* transactions, such as actual bargain and sale, or what part is fictitious and mere accommodation paper, that is, where one bill of exchange is drawn to take up another running, in order to raise a fictitious capital, by creating so much currency. In times of abundance and cheap money this I know reaches an enormous amount' (pp. 43–4). J. W. Bosanquet, *Metallic, Paper and Credit Currency*, London, 1842: 'An average amount of payments to the extent of upwards of £3,000,000 is settled through the Clearing House' (where the London bankers exchange due bills and filed cheques) 'every day of business in the year, and the daily amount of money required for the purpose is little more than £200,000' (p. 86). (In 1889, the total turnover of the Clearing House amounted to £7,618¾ million, which, in roughly 300 business days, averages £25½ million daily. – F. E.) 'Bills of exchange act undoubtedly as currency, independent of money,' in as much as they transfer property from hand to hand by endorsement (p. 92). It may be assumed that 'upon an average there are two endorsements upon every bill in circulation, and . . . each bill performs two payments before it becomes due. Upon this assumption it would appear, that by endorsement alone property changed hands, by means of bills of exchange, to the value of twice five hundred and twenty-eight million, or £1,056,000,000, being at the rate of more than £3,000,000 per day, in the course of the year 1839. We may safely therefore conclude, that deposits and bills of exchange together, perform the functions of money, by transferring property from hand to hand without the aid of money, to an extent daily of not less than £18,000,000' (p. 93).

Tooke has the following to say about credit in general: 'Credit, in its most simple expression, is the confidence which, well, or ill-founded, leads a person to entrust another with a certain amount of capital, in money, or in goods computed at a value in money agreed upon, and in each case payable at the expiration of a fixed term. In the case where the capital is lent in money, that is whether in banknotes, or in a cash credit, or in an order upon a correspondent, an addition for the use of the capital of so much upon every £100 is made to the amount to be repaid. In the case of goods the value of which is agreed in terms of money, constituting a sale, the sum stipulated to be repaid includes a consideration for the use of the capital and for the risk, till the expiration of the period fixed for payment. Written obligations of payment at fixed dates mostly accompany these credits, and the obligations or promissory notes after date being transferable, form the means by which the lenders, if they have occasion for the use of their capital, in the shape whether of money or goods, before the expiration of the term of the bills they hold, are mostly enabled to borrow or to buy on lower terms, by having their own credit strengthened by the names on the bills in addition to their own' (*Inquiry into the Currency Principle*, p. 87).

Charles Coquelin, 'Du crédit et des banques dans l'industrie', *Revue des Deux Mondes*, 1842, Vol. 31: 'In every country, the greater part of credit transactions take place within the orbit of industry . . . the raw material producer advances his product to the manufacturer who processes it, and receives from him a promise to pay on a certain date. The manufacturer, after completing his share in the work, advances his product in turn to another manufacturer who is to process it further, on similar conditions, and in this way credit extends ever further, from one person to another, right through to the consumer. The wholesaler makes advances of commodities to the retailer, while he himself receives these from the manufacturer or an agent. Everyone borrows with one hand and lends with the other, sometimes money, but far more frequently products. There is thus an incessant exchange of advances in industry, which combine and intersect each other in all directions. The development of credit is nothing more than the multiplication and growth of these mutual advances, and this is the true seat of its power' [p. 797].

The other aspect of the credit system involves the development of the money trade, which in capitalist production naturally keeps step with the development of trade in commodities. We have seen in the previous Part (Chapter 19) how the maintenance of a reserve fund for businessmen, the technical operations of receiving and paying out money, international payments, and hence the bullion trade as well, are concentrated in the hands of money-dealers. Alongside this money-dealing, the other side of the credit system also develops, the management of interest-bearing capital or money capital as the special function of the money-dealers. The borrowing and lending of money becomes their special business. They appear as middlemen between the real lender of money capital and its borrower. To put it in general terms, the business of banking consists from this aspect in concentrating money capital for loan in large masses in the bank's hands, so that, instead of the individual lender of money, it is the bankers as representatives of all lenders of money who confront the industrial and commercial capitalists. They become the general managers of money capital. On the other hand, they concentrate the borrowers vis-à-vis all the lenders, in so far as they borrow for the entire world of trade. A bank represents on the one hand the centralization of money capital, of the lenders, and on the other hand the centralization of the borrowers. It makes its profit in general by borrowing at lower rates than those at which it lends.

The loan capital which the banks have at their disposal accrues to them in several ways. What is firstly concentrated in their hands, as the cashiers of the industrial capitalists, is the money capital which every producer and merchant keeps as a reserve fund or which flows to him as payment. These funds are thus transformed into money capital for loan. In this way the reserve fund of the business community is restricted to the necessary minimum, by being concentrated as a social fund, and one part of the money capital, which would otherwise be dormant in reserve, is loaned out and functions as interest-bearing capital. Secondly, their loan capital is formed from the deposits made by money capitalists, who hand over to them the job of loaning it out. With the development of the banking system, and particularly once they pay interest on deposits, the money savings and the temporarily unoccupied money of all social classes are also deposited with them. Small sums which are incapable of functioning as money capital by themselves are combined into great masses and thus form a monetary power. This collection of small amounts, as a particular function of the banking system, must be distinguished from the banks' function as middlemen between actual money capitalists and borrowers. Finally, revenues that are to be consumed only gradually are also deposited with the banks.

Lending is effected (we are dealing here only with commercial credit proper) by discounting bills – transforming them into money before their due date – and by advances of various kinds: direct advances on personal credit; loans against securities, such as interest-bearing paper, government paper and stocks of all sorts; and notably also advances against bills of lading, dock warrants and other certified titles to ownership of goods, as well as overdrafts on deposits, etc.

Now the credit that the banker gives can be provided in various forms, e.g. in bills and cheques on other banks, credit facilities of a similar kind, and finally, if the bank is authorized to issue notes, in its own banknotes. A banknote is nothing more than a bill on the banker, payable at any time to its possessor and given by the banker in place of private drafts. This last form of credit seems especially striking and important to the layman, firstly because this kind of credit money emerges from commercial circulation into general circulation and functions here as money; also because in most countries the major banks that issue notes are a peculiar mishmash between national banks and private banks and actually have the government's credit behind them, their notes being more or less legal tender; and because it is evident here that what the banker is dealing in is credit itself, since the banknote merely represents a circulating token of credit. But the banker also deals in credit in every other form, even if he advances money deposited with him in cash. In actual fact, banknotes are simply the small change of wholesale trade, and the deposit is always the main thing as far as the banks are concerned. The Scottish banks provide the best proof of this.

Special credit institutions, like special forms of banks, need not be considered in any more detail for our present purpose.

'The business of bankers . . . may be divided into two branches . . . One branch of the bankers' business is to *collect* capital from those who have not immediate employment for it, and to distribute or transfer it to those who have. The other branch is to receive deposits of the *incomes* of their customers, and to pay out the amount, as it is wanted for expenditure by the latter in the objects of their consumption . . . The former being a circulation of *capital*, the latter of *currency* . . .' One 'relates to the concentration of capital on the one hand and the distribution of it on the other', the other 'is employed in administering the circulation for local purposes of the district' (Tooke, *Inquiry into the Currency Principle*, pp. 36, 37).*

We shall return to this passage in Chapter 28.

Reports of Committees, Vol. VIII. *Commercial Distress*, Vol. II, part I, 1847–8. Minutes of Evidence. (Quoted from now on as *Commercial Distress*, 1847–8.) In the 1840s, twenty-one-day drafts of one bank on another were often accepted in lieu of banknotes when discounting bills of exchange in London. (Evidence of J. Pease, country banker, nos. 4636 and 4645.) According to the same report, it was customary for bankers to give their customers bills of this kind in payment quite regularly, whenever money was tight. If the recipients wanted banknotes, they had to have these bills discounted again. For the banks, this amounted to a privilege of coining money. Messrs Jones Loyd and Co. had made payments in this way 'from time immemorial', whenever money was scarce and the interest rate above 5 per cent. The customer was eager to get these banker's bills, as it was easier for him to get a bill on Jones Loyd and Co. discounted than his own; they often changed hands twenty or thirty times (ibid., nos. 901 to 905, 992).

All these forms are ways of making claims for payment transferable. 'There is scarcely any shape into which credit can be cast, in which it will not at times be called to perform the functions of money; and whether that shape be a banknote, or a bill of exchange, or a banker's cheque, the process is in every essential particular the same, and the result is the same' (Fullarton, *On the Regulation of Currencies*, 2nd edn, London, 1845, p. 38†) – 'Banknotes are the small change of credit' (p. 51).

The following passages are from J. W. Gilbart's *The History and Principles of Banking*, London, 1834. 'The trading capital of a bank may be divided into two parts: the invested capital, and

* From here to the end of Chapter 34, emphases in quotations have all been added by Marx, unless indicated to the contrary.

† John Fullarton (1780–1849), mentioned here for the first time in this volume, was a notable opponent of the quantity theory of money; his ideas are dealt with in detail in Chapter 28.

the borrowed banking capital' (p. 117). 'There are three ways of raising a banking or borrowed capital. First, by receiving deposits; secondly, by the issuing of notes; thirdly, by the drawing of bills. If a person will lend me £100 for nothing, and I lend that £100 to another person at 4 per cent interest, then, in the course of a year, I shall gain £4 by the transaction. Again, if a person will take my "promise to pay",' ('I promise to pay' is the usual formula for English banknotes) 'and bring it back to me at the end of the year, and pay me 4 per cent for it, just the same as though I had lent him 100 sovereigns, then I shall gain £4 by that transaction: and again, if a person in a country town brings me £100 on condition that, twenty-one days afterwards, I shall pay the same amount to a person in London, then whatever interest I can make of the money during the twenty-one days, will be my profit. This is a fair representation of the operations of banking, and of the way in which a banking capital is created by means of deposits, notes, and bills' (p. 117). 'The profits of a banker are generally in proportion to the amount of his banking or borrowed capital ... To ascertain the real profit of a bank, the interest upon the invested capital should be deducted from the gross profit, and what remains is the banking profit' (p. 118). '*The advances of bankers to their customers are made with other people's money*' (p. 146). 'Precisely those bankers who do not issue notes, create a banking capital by the discounting of bills. They render their discounts subservient to the increase of their deposits. The London bankers will not discount except for those houses who have deposit accounts with them' (p. 119). 'A party who has had bills discounted, and has paid interest on the whole amount, must leave some portion of that amount in the hands of the banker without interest. By this means the banker obtains more than the current rate of interest on the money actually advanced, and raises a banking capital to the amount of the balance left in his hands' (pp. 119–20).

Economizing on reserve funds, deposits, cheques: 'Banks of deposit serve to economize the use of the circulating medium. This is done upon the principle of transfer of titles ... Thus it is that banks of deposit ... are enabled to settle a large amount of transactions with a small amount of money. The money thus liberated, is employed by the banker in making advances, by discount or otherwise, to his customers. Hence the principle of transfer gives additional efficiency to the deposit system ...' (p. 123). 'It matters not whether the two parties, who have dealings with each other, keep their accounts with the same banker or with different bankers; for, as the bankers exchange their cheques with each other at the clearing house ... The deposit system might thus, by means of transfers, be carried to such an extent as wholly to supersede the use of a metallic currency. Were every man to keep a deposit account at a bank, and make all his payments by cheques, money might be superseded, and cheques become the sole circulating medium. In this case, however, it must be supposed that the banker has the money in his hands, or the cheques would have no value' (p. 124).

The centralization of local commerce in the hands of the banks is effected: (1) by branch banks; the country banks have branch establishments in the smaller towns of their area; the London banks in the different districts of London; (2) by agencies: 'Each country banker employs a London agent to pay his notes or bills ... and to receive sums that may be lodged by parties residing in London for the use of parties residing in the country' (p. 127). 'Each banker accepts the notes of others, but does not reissue them. In all larger cities they come together once or twice a week and exchange their notes. The balance is paid by a draft on London' (p. 134). 'It is the object of banking to give facilities to trade, and whatever gives facilities to trade gives facilities to speculation. Trade and speculation are in some cases so nearly allied, that it is impossible to say at what precise point trade ends and speculation begins ... Wherever there are banks, capital is more readily obtained, and at a cheaper rate. The cheapness of capital gives facilities to speculation, just in the same way as the cheapness of beef and of beer gives facilities to gluttony and drunkenness' (pp. 137, 138). 'As banks of circulation always issue their own notes, it would seem that their discounting business was carried on exclusively with this last description of capital, but it is not so. It is very possible for a banker to issue his own notes for all the bills he discounts, and yet nine-tenths of the bills in his possession shall represent real capital. For, although in the first instance, the banker's notes are given for the bill, yet these notes may not stay in circulation until the bill becomes due – the bill may have three months to run, the notes may return in three days' (p. 172). 'The overdrawing of a cash credit account is a regular matter of business; it is, in fact, the purpose for which the cash credit has been granted ... Cash credits are granted not only upon personal security, but also upon the security of the Public Funds' (pp. 174,

175). 'Capital advanced, by way of loan, on the securities of merchandise, would produce the same effects as if advanced in the discounting of bills. If a party borrows £100 on the security of his merchandise, it is the same as though he had sold his merchandise for a £100 bill, and got it discounted with the banker. By obtaining this advance he is enabled to hold over this merchandise for a better market, and avoids a sacrifice which, otherwise, he might be induced to make, in order to raise the money for urgent purposes' (pp. 180–81).

The Currency Theory Reviewed, etc., pp. 62, 63: 'It is unquestionably true that the £1,000 which you deposit at A today may be reissued tomorrow, and form a deposit at B. The day after that, reissued from B, it may form a deposit at C ... and so on to infinitude; and that the same £1,000 in money may thus, by a succession of transfers, multiply itself into a sum of deposits absolutely indefinite. It is possible, therefore, that *nine-tenths of all the deposits in the United Kingdom may have no existence beyond their record in the books of the bankers* who are respectively accountable for them ... Thus in Scotland, for instance, currency' (mostly paper money at that) 'has never exceeded £3 million, the deposits in the banks are estimated at £27 million ... Unless a run on the banks be made, the same £1,000 would, if sent back upon its travels, cancel with the same facility a sum equally indefinite. As the same £1,000 with which you cancel your debt to a tradesman today, may cancel his debt to the merchant tomorrow, the merchant's debt to the bank the day following, and so on without end; so the same £1,000 may pass from hand to hand, and bank to bank, and cancel any conceivable sum of deposits.'

(We have seen how Gilbart was already aware in 1834 that 'whatever gives facilities to trade gives facilities to speculation. Trade and speculation are in some cases so nearly allied, that it is impossible to say at what precise point trade ends and speculation begins.' The easier it is to obtain advances on unsold commodities, the more these advances are taken up and the greater is the temptation to manufacture commodities or dump those already manufactured on distant markets, simply to receive advances of money on them. As to how the entire business community in a country can be caught up in swindling of this kind, and where it ends up, we have a striking example in the history of English commerce between 1845 and 1847.

At the end of 1842 the depression which English industry had been suffering almost uninterruptedly since 1837 began to ease. In the two following years the export demand for English industrial products rose even more; 1845–6 marked the period of greatest prosperity. In 1843 the Opium War had opened up China to English trade. The new market offered a new pretext for an expansion that was already in full swing, particularly in the cotton industry. 'How can we ever produce too much? We have 300 million people to clothe,' I was told at the time by a Manchester manufacturer. But all the newly erected factory buildings, new steam engines and spinning and weaving machines were not sufficient to absorb Lancashire's streaming surplus-value. The same passion which increased production went into the building of railways. The thirst of the manufacturers and merchants for speculation found initial satisfaction, from summer 1844 onwards. Stock was underwritten to the limits of possibility, i.e. as far as there was money to cover the initial payments. As for the rest, a way would be found! When the further payments did fall due – and according to Question 1059, *Commercial Distress*, 1848–57, the capital invested in railways in 1846–7 amounted to £75 million – recourse to credit was necessary, and the main business of the firm generally had to suffer.

This business was already under strain in the majority of cases. The enticingly high profits had led to operations more extensive than the liquid resources available could justify. But the credit was there, easy to obtain and cheap at that. The bank rate was low: $1\frac{3}{4}$ to $2\frac{3}{4}$ per cent in 1844, below 3 per cent until October 1845, then rising for a short period to 5 per cent (February 1846) before falling again to $3\frac{1}{4}$ per cent in December 1846. In its vaults, the Bank had a gold reserve of unheard-of dimensions. All domestic share prices stood higher than ever before. Why let the splendid opportunity pass? Why not get into the swing of it? Why not send all that could be manufactured to foreign markets which were crying out for English goods? And why should the manufacturer himself not pocket the double profit from selling his yarn and cloth in the Far East and selling the return cargo in England?

This was the origin of the system of mass consignments to India and China against advances, which developed very soon into a system of consignments simply for the sake of the advances, as is described in more detail in the following notes, and which could lead only to a massive flooding of the markets and a crash.

The crash was precipitated by the harvest failure of 1846. England, and Ireland especially, needed an enormous import of provisions, particularly corn and potatoes. But the countries that supplied these could be paid only to an exceedingly small extent in English industrial products. Precious metal had to be given in payment; at least £9 million in gold went abroad. A full £7½ million of this came from the Bank of England's reserves, substantially impairing its freedom of action on the money market. The other banks, whose reserves were with the Bank of England and in practice identical with its own, now had likewise to restrict their accommodation of money. The rapid and easy flow of payments came to a halt, at first here and there and then generally. The Bank rate, which in January 1847 was still 3 to 3½ per cent, rose in April, when the first panic broke out, to 7 per cent; in summer there was a small and temporary respite (6½ per cent, 6 per cent), but when the new harvest was also bad, panic broke out afresh and more violently. The Bank's official minimum lending rate rose to 7 per cent in October, and in November to 10 per cent, so that the great majority of bills could be discounted only at colossal and usurious rates of interest, if at all. The general stagnation of payments caused the bankruptcy of a few leading firms and very many medium and small ones; the Bank itself was in danger of collapse, as a result of the clever Bank Act of 1844 and the restrictions this imposed.* The government suspended the Bank Act on 25 October, bowing to a universal demand, and thereby released the Bank from the absurd legal fetters imposed on it. It was now able to put its supply of banknotes into circulation without any obstacle; and since the credit of these banknotes was actually guaranteed by the credit of the nation, and thus unimpaired, the monetary tightness was decisively eased. Of course a great number of firms still collapsed, both small and large, those that were hopelessly ensnared, but the peak of the crisis was over, and the Bank rate fell again to 5 per cent in December. During 1848 a new revival of business activity began to develop, breaking the edge of the revolutionary movements on the Continent in 1849 and leading in the 1850s to a previously unheard-of industrial prosperity, only to be followed by the crash of 1857. – F. E.)

(1) A document issued by the House of Lords in 1848 deals with the colossal devaluation of government bonds and other stocks

* See below, Chapter 34.

during the crisis of 1847. According to this, the fall in value by 23 October 1847, compared with the level in February the same year, was:

On English government bonds	£93,824,217
On dock and canal stock	£ 1,358,288
On railway stock	£19,579,820
Total	£114,762,325

(2) As for swindling in the East India trade, where bills were no longer drawn because commodities had been sold, but rather commodities sold in order to draw bills which could be discounted and converted into money, the *Manchester Guardian* has a report on 24 November 1847.

Mr A in London instructs a Mr B to buy from the manufacturer C in Manchester commodities for shipment to D in East India. B pays C in six months' drafts to be made out by C on B. B secures himself by six months' drafts on A. As soon as the goods are shipped, A makes out six months' drafts on D against the mailed bill of lading. 'The shipper and the co-signee were thus both put in possession of funds – months before they actually paid for the goods; and, very commonly, these bills were renewed at maturity, on pretence of affording time for the returns in a "long trade." Unfortunately losses by such a trade, instead of leading to its contraction, led directly to its increase. The poorer men became, the greater need they had to purchase, in order to make up, by new advances, the capital they had lost on the past adventures. Purchases thus became, not a question of supply and demand, but the most important part of the finance operations of a firm labouring under difficulties. But this is only one side of the picture. What took place in reference to the export of goods at home, was taking place in the purchase and shipment of produce abroad. Houses in India, who had credit to pass their bills, were purchasers of sugar, indigo, silk, or cotton, – not because the prices advised from London by the last overland mail promised a profit on the prices current in India, but because former drafts upon the London house would soon fall due, and must be provided for. What way so simple as to purchase a cargo of sugar, pay for it in bills upon the London house at ten months' date, transmit the shipping documents by the overland mail; and, in less than two months, the goods on the high seas, or perhaps not yet passed the mouth of the Hoogly, were pawned in Lombard Street – putting the London house in funds eight months before the drafts against those goods fell due. And all this went on without interruption or difficulty, as long as bill-brokers had abundance of money "at call", to advance on bills of lading and dock warrants, and to discount, without limit, the bills of India houses drawn upon the eminent firms in Mincing Lane.'

(This fraudulent procedure remained in vogue as long as goods had to sail to and from India round the Cape. Now that they pass through the Suez canal, and in steamships at that, this method of creating fictitious capital has lost its foundation: the long journey time. In fact, now that the telegraph makes the state of the Indian market known to the English businessman the same day, and the state of the English market to the Indian dealer, such a method has become completely impossible. – F. E.)

(3) The following passage is taken from the report on *Commercial Distress*, 1847–8, already quoted: 'In the last week of April, 1847, the Bank of England advised the Royal Bank of Liverpool that it would thereafter reduce its discount business with the latter bank by one half. The announcement operated with peculiar hardship on this account, that the payments into Liverpool had latterly been much more in bills than in cash; and the merchants who generally brought to the Bank a large proportion of cash with which to pay their acceptances, had latterly been able to bring only bills which they had received for their cotton and other produce, and that increased very rapidly as the difficulties increased ... The acceptances ... which the Bank had to pay for the merchants, were acceptances drawn chiefly upon them from abroad, and they have been accustomed to meet those acceptances by whatever payment they received for their produce ... The bills that the merchants brought ... in lieu of cash, which they usually brought ... were of various dates, and of various descriptions; a considerable number of them were bankers' bills, of three months' date, the large bulk being cotton bills. These bills of exchange, when bankers' bills, were accepted by London bankers, and by merchants in every trade that we could mention – the Brazilian, the American, the Canadian, the West Indian ... The merchants did not draw upon each other; but the parties in the interior, who had purchased produce from the merchants, remitted to the merchants bills on London bankers, or bills on various parties in London, or bills upon anybody. The announcement of the Bank of England

caused a reduction of the maturity terms of bills drawn against sales of foreign products, frequently extending to over three months' (pp. 26, 27).

As described above, the period of prosperity of 1844–7 was linked in England with the first great railway swindle. The report quoted has the following to say as to the effect of this on business in general. In April 1847 'almost all mercantile houses had begun to starve their business more or less ... by taking part of their commercial capital for railways' (p. 42). 'Loans were made on railway shares at a high rate of interest, say, 8 per cent, by private individuals, by bankers and by fire-offices' (p. 66). 'Loans to so great an extent by commercial houses to railways induced them to lean too much upon banks by the discount of paper, whereby to carry on their commercial operations' (p. 67). (Question:) 'Should you say that the railway calls had had a great effect in producing the pressure which there was' (on the money-market) 'in April and October' (1847)? – (Answer:) 'I should say that they had had hardly any effect at all in producing the pressure in April; I should imagine that up to April, and up, perhaps, to the summer, they had increased the power of bankers in some respects rather than diminished it; for the expenditure had not been nearly so rapid as the calls; the consequence was, that most of the banks had rather a large amount of railway money in their hands in the beginning of the year.' (This is corroborated in numerous statements made by bankers in *C. D.* 1848–57). 'In the summer that melted gradually away, and on the 31st of December it was materially less. One cause ... of the pressure in October was the gradual diminution of the railway money in the bankers' hands; between the 22nd of April and the 31st of December the railway balances in our hands were reduced one-third; and the railway calls have also had this effect ... throughout the Kingdom; they have been gradually draining the deposits of bankers' (pp. 43, 44).

The same was said by Samuel Gurney (head of the notorious firm of Overend, Gurney and Co.). 'During the year 1846 ... there had been a considerable demand for capital, for the establishment of railways ... but it did not increase the value of money ... There was a condensation of small sums into large masses, and those large masses were used in our market; so that, upon the whole, the effect was to throw more money into the money-market of the City than to take it out' [p.159].

A. Hodgson, director of the Liverpool Joint-Stock Bank, shows how far the bankers' reserves may consist of bills of exchange: 'It has been our habit to keep at least nine-tenths of all our deposits, and all money we have of other persons, in our bill case, in bills that are falling due from day to day ... so much so, that during the time of the run, the bills falling due were almost equal to the amount of the run upon us day by day' (p. 53).

Speculative bills. – '5092. Who were those bills (against sold cotton) generally accepted by?' – (R. Gardner, the cotton manufacturer repeatedly mentioned in this work:) 'Produce brokers: a person buys cotton, and places it in the hands of a broker, and draws upon that broker, and gets the bills discounted.' – '5094. And they are taken to the banks at Liverpool, and discounted? – Yes, and in other parts besides ... I believe if it had not been for the accommodation thus granted, and principally by the Liverpool banks, cotton would never have been so high last year as it was by 1½d. or 2d. a pound.' – '600. You have stated that a vast amount of bills were put in circulation, drawn by speculators upon cotton brokers in Liverpool; does that system extend to your advance on acceptances upon colonial and foreign produce as well as on cotton?' (A. Hodgson, a Liverpool banker:) 'It refers to all kinds of colonial produce, but to cotton most especially.' – '601. Do you, as a banker, discourage as far as you can that description of paper? – We do not; we consider it a very legitimate description of paper, when kept in moderation. This description of paper is frequently renewed.'

Swindling in the East Indian and Chinese market in 1847. Charles Turner (head of one of the leading East India houses in Liverpool): 'We are all aware of the events which have taken place as regards the Mauritius trade, and other trades of that kind. The brokers have been in the habit ... not only of advancing upon goods after their arrival to meet the bills drawn against those goods, which is perfectly legitimate, and upon the bills of lading ... but ... they have advanced upon the produce before it was shipped, and in some cases before it was manufactured. Now, to speak of my own individual instance: I have bought bills in Calcutta to the extent of six or seven thousand pounds in one particular instance; the proceeds of the bills went down to the Mauritius, to help in the growth of sugar; those bills came to England, and above half of them were protested; for when the shipments of sugar came forward, instead of being held to pay those bills, it had been mortgaged to third parties ... before it was shipped, in fact almost before it was boiled' (p. 78). 'Now manufacturers are insisting upon cash, but it does not amount to much, because if a buyer has any credit in London, he can draw upon the house, and get the bill discounted; he goes to London, where discounts now are cheap; he gets the bill discounted, and pays cash to the manufacturer . . . It takes twelve months, at least, for the shipper of goods to get his return from India . . . a man with ten or fifteen thousand pounds would go into the Indian trade; he would open a credit with a house in London, to a considerable extent, giving that house one per cent; he, drawing upon the house in London, on the understanding that the proceeds of the goods that go out are to be returned to the house in London, but it being perfectly understood by both parties that the man in London is to be kept out of a cash advance; that is to say, in other words, the bills are to be renewed till the proceeds come home. The bills were discounted at Liverpool, Manchester . . . or in London . . . many of them lie in the Scotch banks' (p. 79). – '786. There is one house which failed in London the other day, and in examining their affairs, a transaction of this sort was proved to have taken place; there is a house of business at Manchester, and another at Calcutta; they opened a credit account with a house in London to the extent of £200,000; that is to say, the friends of this house in Manchester, who consigned goods to the East India House from Glasgow and from Manchester, had the power of drawing upon the house in London to the extent of £200,000; at the same time, there was an understanding that the corresponding house in Calcutta were to draw upon the London house to the extent of £200,000; with the proceeds of those bills sold in Calcutta, they were to buy other bills, and remit them to the house in London, to take up the first bills drawn from Glasgow . . . There would have been £600,000 of bills created upon that transaction.' – '971. At present, if a house in Calcutta purchase a cargo' (for England) 'and give their own bills upon their correspondent in London in payment, and they send the bills of lading home to this country, those bills of lading . . . immediately become available to them in Lombard Street for advances, and they have eight months' use of the money before their correspondents are called upon to pay.'

(4) In 1848, a secret committee of the House of Lords sat to investigate the causes of the crisis of 1847. The evidence taken by this committee was not published until 1857 (*Minutes of Evidence, taken before the Secret Committee of the H. of L. appoin-*

ted to inquire into the Causes of Distress, etc., 1857; quoted as *C. D.* 1848–57). In this, Mr Lister, director of the Union Bank of Liverpool, said among other things:

'2444. In the spring of 1847 there was an undue extension of credit . . . because a man transferred property from business into railways and was still anxious to carry on the same extent of business. He probably first thought that he could sell the railway shares at a profit and replace the money in his business. Perhaps he found that could not be done, and he then got credit in his business where formerly he paid in cash. There was an extension of credit from that circumstance.'

'2500. Were those bills . . . upon which the banks had sustained a loss by holding them, principally bills upon corn or bills upon cotton? – They were bills upon all kinds of produce, corn and cotton and sugar, all foreign produce of all descriptions. There was scarcely any thing perhaps with the exception of oil, that did not go down.' – '2506. A broker who accepts a bill will not accept it without a good margin as to the value.'

'2512. There are two kinds of bills drawn against produce; the first is the original bill drawn abroad upon the merchant, who imports it . . . The bills which are drawn against produce frequently fall due before the produce arrives. The merchant, therefore, when it arrives, if he has not sufficient capital, has to pledge that produce with the broker till he has time to sell that produce. Then a new species of bill is immediately drawn by the merchant in Liverpool upon the broker, on the security of that produce . . . Then it is the business of the banker to ascertain from the broker whether he has the produce, and to what extent he has advanced upon it. It is his business to see that the broker has property to protect himself if he makes a loss.'

'2516. We also receive bills from abroad . . . A man buys a bill abroad on England, and sends it to a house in England; we cannot tell whether that bill is drawn prudently or imprudently, whether it is drawn for produce or for wind.'

'2533. You said that almost every kind of foreign produce was sold at a great loss. Do you think that that was in consequence of undue speculation in that produce? – It arose from a very large import, and there not being an equal consumption to take it off. It appears that consumption fell off a great deal.' – '2534. In October produce was almost unsaleable.'

How the height of the crash sees a general *sauve-qui-peut* is testified to in the same report by an expert of the highest rank, the worthy and wily Samuel Gurney of Overend, Gurney and Co. '1262 . . . When a panic exists a man does not ask himself what he can get for his bank-notes, or whether he shall lose 1 or 2 per cent by selling his exchequer bills, or 3 per cent. If he is under the influence of alarm he does not care for the profit or loss, but makes himself safe and allows the rest of the world to do as they please.'

(5) On the mutual satiation of the two markets, Mr Alexander, a merchant in the East India trade, said before the House of Commons committee on the Bank Act of 1857 (quoted as *B. A.* 1857): '4330. At the present moment, if I lay out 6s. in Manchester, I get 5s. back in India; if I lay out 6s. in India, I get 5s. back in London.' So that the Indian market was satiated by England and the English market similarly by India. And this was the case in 1857, scarcely ten years after the bitter experience of 1847!

Chapter 26: Accumulation of Money Capital, and its Influence on the Rate of Interest

'In England there takes place a steady accumulation of additional wealth, which has a tendency ultimately to assume the form of money. Now, next in urgency, perhaps, to the desire to acquire money, is the wish to part with it again for some species of investment that shall yield either interest or profit; for money itself, as money, yields neither. Unless, therefore, concurrently with this ceaseless influx of surplus capital, there is a gradual and sufficient extension of the field for its employment, we must be subject to periodical accumulations of money seeking investment, of more or less volume, according to the movement of events. For a long series of years, the grand absorbent of the surplus wealth of England was our public debt ... As soon as in 1816 the debt reached its maximum, and operated no longer as an absorbent, a sum of at least seven-and-twenty million per annum was necessarily driven to seek other channels of investment. What was more, various return payments of capital were made ... Enterprises which entail a large capital and create an opening from time to time for the excess of unemployed capital ... are absolutely necessary, at least in our country, so as to take care of the periodical accumulations of the superfluous wealth of society, which is unable to find room in the usual fields of application' (*The Currency Theory Reviewed*, London, 1845, pp. 32–4).

Of 1845, the same author says: 'Within a very recent period prices have sprung upwards from the lowest point of depression ... Consols touch par ... The bullion in the vaults of the Bank of England has ... exceeded in amount the treasure held by that establishment since its institution. Shares of every description range at prices on the average wholly unprecedented, and interest has declined to rates which are all but nominal. If these be not evidences that another heavy accumulation of unemployed wealth exists at this hour in England, that another period of speculative excitement is at hand' (ibid., p. 36).

'Although . . . the import of bullion is no sure sign of gain upon the foreign trade, yet, in the absence of any explanatory cause, it does *prima facie* represent a portion of it' (J. G. Hubbard, *The Currency and the Country*, London, 1843, pp. 40–41). 'Suppose . . . that at a period of steady trade, fair prices . . . and full, but not redundant circulation, a deficient harvest should give occasion for an import of corn, and an export of gold to the value of five million. The circulation' (meaning, as we shall presently see, idle money-capital rather than means of circulation – F. E.) 'would of course be reduced by the same amount. An equal quantity of the circulation might still be held by individuals, but the deposits of merchants at their bankers, the balances of bankers with their money-broker, and the reserve in their till, will all be diminished, and the immediate result of this reduction in the amount of unemployed capital will be a rise in the rate of interest. I will assume from 4 per cent to 6. Trade being in a sound state, confidence will not be shaken, but credit will be more highly valued' (ibid., p. 42). 'But imagine . . . that all prices fall . . . The superfluous currency returns to the bankers in increased deposits – the abundance of unemployed capital lowers the rate of interest to a minimum, and this state of things lasts until either a return of higher prices or a more active trade call the dormant currency into service, or until it is absorbed by investments in foreign stocks or foreign goods' (p. 68).

The following extracts are again taken from the parliamentary report on *Commercial Distress* 1847–8. The harvest failure and famine of 1846–7 made a major import of foodstuffs necessary. 'These circumstances caused the imports of the country to be very largely in excess over . . . exports . . . a considerable drain upon the banks, and an increased application to the discount brokers . . . for the discount of bills . . . They began to scrutinize the bills . . . The facilities of houses then began to be very seriously curtailed, and the weak houses began to fail. Those houses which . . . relied upon their credit . . . went down. This increased the alarm that had been previously felt; and the bankers and others finding that they would not rely with the same degree of confidence that they had previously done upon turning their bills and other money securities into bank-notes, for the purpose of meeting their engagements, still further curtailed their facilities, and in many cases refused them altogether; they locked up their bank-notes, in many instances to meet their own engagements; they were afraid of parting with them . . . The alarm and confusion were increased daily; and unless Lord John Russell . . . had issued the letter to the Bank . . . universal bankruptcy would have been the issue' (pp. 74–5).

Russell's letter suspended the Bank Act. The above-mentioned Charles Turner testified: 'Some houses had large means, but not available. The whole of their capital was locked up in estates in the Mauritius, or indigo factories, or sugar factories. Having incurred liabilities to the extent of £500,000 or £600,000 they had no available assets to pay their bills, and eventually it proved that to pay their bills they were entirely dependent upon their credit' (p. 81).

And Samuel Gurney, as already mentioned: 'At present (1848) there is a limitation of transaction and a great super-abundance of money.' – '1763. I do not think it was owing to the want of capital; it was owing to the alarm that existed that the rate of interest got so high.'

In 1847 England paid at least £9 million abroad in gold for the import of foodstuffs. £7½ million of this came from the Bank of England and £1½ million from other sources (p. 301). Morris, Governor of the Bank of England: 'The public stocks in the country and canal and railway shares had already by the 23rd of October 1847 been depreciated in the aggregate to the amount of £114,752,225' (p. 312). Again Morris, when questioned by Lord G. Bentinck: 'Are you not aware that all property invested in stocks and produce of every description was depreciated in the same way; that raw cotton, raw silk and unmanufactured wool were sent to the continent at the same depreciated price . . . and that sugar, coffee and tea were sacrificed as at forced sales? – It was . . . inevitable that the country should make a considerable sacrifice for the purpose of meeting the efflux of bullion which had taken place in consequence of the large importation of food.' – 'Do not you think it would have been better to trench upon the £8,000,000 lying in the coffers of the Bank than to have endeavoured to get the gold back again at such a sacrifice? – *No, I do not.*'

Now for the commentary on this heroism. Disraeli examines Mr W. Cotton, a director of the Bank of England and former Governor: 'What was the rate of dividend paid to the Bank proprietors in 1844? – It was 7 per cent for the year.' – 'What is the dividend . . . for 1847? – 9 per cent.' – 'Does the Bank pay the income tax for its proprietors in this year? – It does.' – 'Did it do so in 1844? – It did not.' [83] – 'Then this Bank Act (of 1844) has worked very well for the proprietors? . . . The result is, that since the passing of the Act, the dividend to the proprietors has been raised from 7 per cent to 9 per cent, and the income tax, that previously to the Act was paid by the proprietors, is now paid by the Bank? – *It is so*' (Nos. 4356–61).

On the question of hoarding by the banks during the crisis of 1847, Mr Pease, a country banker, had this to say: '4605. As the Bank was obliged still to raise its rate of interest, every one seemed apprehensive; country bankers increased the amount of bullion in their hands, and increased their reserve of notes, and many of us who were in the habit of keeping, perhaps, a few hundred pounds of gold and bank-notes, immediately laid up thousands in our desks and drawers, as there was an uncertainty about discounts, and about our bills being current in the market, a general hoarding ensued.'

A committee member remarked: '4691. Then, whatever may have been the cause during the last 12 years, the result has been rather in favour of the Jew and money-dealer, than the productive classes generally.'

Tooke also explains how much the money-dealer exploits a period of crisis: 'In the hardware districts of Warwickshire and Staffordshire, a great many orders for goods were declined to be accepted in 1847, because the rate of interest which the manufacturer had to pay for discounting his bills more than absorbed all his profit' (No. 5451).

Let us now take another parliamentary report which has already been quoted: *Report of Select Committee on Bank Acts, communicated from the Commons to the Lords, 1857* (quoted from now on as *B. A.* 1857). In this, Mr Norman, a director of the Bank of England and a leading spokesman for the Currency Principle,* is questioned as follows:

'3635. You stated, that you consider that the rate of interest depends, not upon the amount of notes, but upon the supply and

---

83. In other words, they previously used first to fix the dividend, and then deduct the income tax as the dividend was paid to the individual shareholders. After 1844, however, the Bank first paid income tax on its total profit, and the dividend was then paid 'free of income tax'. The same nominal percentages, therefore, are higher in the latter case by the amount of tax paid. – F. E.

* See Chapter 34 below.

demand of capital. Will you state what you include in "capital", besides notes and coin? – I believe that the ordinary definition of "capital" is commodities or services used in production.' – '3636. Do you mean to include all commodities in the word "capital" when you speak of the rate of interest? – All commodities used in production.' – '3637. You include all that in the word "capital", when you speak of what regulates the rate of interest? – Yes. Supposing a cotton manufacturer to want cotton for his factory, the way in which he goes to work to obtain it is, probably, by getting an advance from his banker, and with the notes so obtained he goes to Liverpool, and makes a purchase. What he really wants is the cotton; he does not want the notes or the gold, except as a means of getting the cotton. Or he may want the means of paying his workmen; then again, he borrows the notes, and he pays the wages of the workmen with the notes; and the workmen, again, require food and lodging, and the money is the means of paying for those.' – '3638. But interest is paid for the money? – It is, in the first instance; but take another case. Supposing he buys the cotton on credit, without going to the bank for an advance, then the difference between the ready-money price and the credit price at the time at which he is to pay for it is the measure of the interest. Interest would exist if there was no money at all.'

This complacent rubbish is entirely worthy of this pillar of the Currency Principle. First the discovery, worthy of a genius, that banknotes or gold are means of buying something, and that people do not borrow them for their own sake. And what is the interest rate supposed to be governed by on this assumption? By the demand and supply of commodities, which is what we have always been told governs the market price of commodities. But quite different rates of interest are compatible with the same market prices. Now the cunning emerges. He is faced with the correct remark, 'But interest is paid for the money', which of course implies the question: What has the interest that the banker receives without in any way dealing in commodities got to do with these commodities? And do not manufacturers receive the same rate of interest for money they put out in completely different markets, i.e. in markets where there is a quite different relationship between the demand and supply of the commodities needed for production? – To this question, our celebrated genius replies that, if the manufacturer buys cotton on credit, then 'the difference between the ready-money price and the credit price at the time at which he is to pay for it is the measure of the interest'. Quite the opposite. The prevailing rate of interest, the regulation of which it is the task of our genius Norman to explain, is the measure of the difference between the cash price and the price on credit. First of all, the cotton is for sale at its cash price. This is determined by the market price, which is itself governed by the state of demand and supply. Say that the price is £1,000. This concludes the transaction between the manufacturer and the cotton broker, as far as buying and selling is concerned. But now there is a second transaction as well. This is one between lender and borrower. The value of £1,000 is advanced to the manufacturer in cotton, and he has to pay it back in money, say in three months' time. The interest on £1,000 for three months, as determined by the market rate of interest, then forms the extra charge over and above the cash price. The price of cotton is determined by supply and demand. But the price for the advance of the cotton's value for three months, for the £1,000, is determined by the rate of interest. And this circumstance, i.e. that the cotton itself is transformed in this way into money capital, proves to Mr Norman that interest would exist even if money did not. If there was no money at all, there would certainly not be a general rate of interest.

The first thing to note is a vulgar conception of capital as 'commodities used in production'. In so far as these commodities figure as capital, they express their value as *capital*, as distinct from their value as *commodities*, in the profit that is made from their productive or commercial use. And the rate of profit necessarily has always something to do with the market price of the commodities bought and the demand and supply for them, even if it is determined by quite different factors. There is no doubt at all that the rate of profit forms a general limit to the rate of interest. But what Mr Norman is supposed to tell us is just how this limit is determined. And it is determined by the demand and supply for money capital *as distinct* from other forms of capital. It could now be asked further: how is the demand and supply for money capital determined? There is beyond doubt a tacit connection between the supply of material capital and the supply of money capital, and it is equally clear that the industrial capitalists' demand for money is determined by the circumstances of actual production. Instead of enlightening us on this subject, Norman offers us the wisdom that the demand for money capital is not identical with the demand for money as such; and this only because Overstone, he, and the other currency prophets always have at the back of their minds a bad conscience about the way they are seeking by way of artificial legislative intervention to make the means of circulation into capital as such, and to raise the rate of interest.

Now to Lord Overstone, alias Samuel Jones Loyd, when he has to explain why he takes 10 per cent for his 'money' because 'capital' is so scarce.

'3653. The fluctuations in the rate of interest arise from one of two causes: an alteration in the value of capital' (Superb! The value of capital, generally speaking is precisely the rate of interest! A change in the rate of interest, therefore, is derived here from a change in the rate of interest. 'The value of capital', as we have already shown, never means anything else in theory. Or else, if Lord Overstone understands by value of capital the rate of profit, then this penetrating thinker comes back to the fact that the interest rate is governed by the profit rate!) 'or an alteration in the amount of money in the country. All great fluctuations of interest, great either in their duration or in the extent of the fluctuation, may be distinctly traced to alterations in the value of capital. Two more striking practical illustrations of that fact cannot be furnished than the rise in the rate of interest in 1847 and during the last two years (1855–6); the minor fluctuations in the rate of interest, which arise from an alteration in the quantity of money, are small both in extent and in duration. They are frequent, and the more rapid and frequent they are, the more effectual they are for accomplishing their destined purpose,' i.e. to enrich bankers like Overstone. Friend Samuel Gurney expresses himself very naïvely on this before the House of Lords committee, *C. D.* 1848[–57]: '1324. Do you think that the great fluctuations in the rate of interest which have taken place in the last year are advantageous or not to bankers or dealers in money? – I think they are advantageous to dealers in money. All fluctuations in trade are advantageous to the knowing man.' – '1325. May not the banker suffer eventually from the high rates of interest, by impoverishing his best customers? – No; I do not think it has that effect perceptibly.'

Voilà ce que parler veut dire [That's what I call talking].

We shall return to the question of how the rate of interest is influenced by the sum of money available. But it must be noted at this point already that Overstone is guilty here again of a *quid pro quo*. In 1847, the demand for money capital decreased for various reasons. (Before October there was no worry about monetary tightness, or the 'quantity of money' as he called it above.) Dearer corn, rising cotton prices, the unsaleability of sugar on account of overproduction, railway speculation and crash, the flooding of foreign markets with cotton goods, the forcible export and import trade with India described above, for the purpose of speculation in bills of exchange. All these things, overproduction in industry as well as underproduction in agriculture, i.e. quite different reasons, led to a rise in the demand for money capital, i.e. for credit and money. The increased demand for money capital had its origins in the course of the production process itself. But whatever the cause, it was the demand for *money* capital that made the rate of interest, the value of money capital, rise. If Overstone is trying to say that the value of money capital rose because it rose, this is a tautology. But if by 'value of capital' what he means here is a rise in the profit rate as a cause of the rise in the rate of interest, this immediately proves to be false. The demand for money capital, and thus the 'value of capital', can rise even though profit is falling; as soon as the relative supply of money capital falls, its 'value' rises. What Overstone is trying to prove is that the crisis of 1847, and the high rate of interest that accompanied it, had nothing to do with the 'quantity of money' present, i.e. with the provisions of the 1844 Bank Act which he had inspired; although it actually did have something to do with it, as soon as fear of exhaustion of the Bank's reserve (and this was a creation of Overstone's) added monetary panic to the 1847–8 crisis. But this is not the point here. There was a dearth of money capital brought about by the excessive size of operations, in comparison with the means available, and brought to a head by a disturbance in the reproduction process that resulted from the harvest failure, the over-investment in railways, overproduction particularly in cotton goods, swindling in the Indian and Chinese trade, speculation, excessive imports of sugar, and so on. What people who had bought corn at 120 shillings per quarter lacked, when the price fell to 60 shillings, was the 60 shillings too much which they had paid, and the corresponding credit for this in loans with the corn as security. It was in no way a lack of banknotes that prevented them from converting their corn into money at the former price of 120 shillings. The same with those who had imported too much sugar, which became unsaleable. The same with the gentlemen who had tied up their floating capital in railways and had found a replacement by conducting their 'legitimate' business on credit. All this, for Overstone, is expressed in 'a moral sense of the enhanced value of money'. But this enhanced value of money capital corresponded directly to the fallen monetary value of real capital (commodity capital and productive capital). The value of capital in the one form rose, because the value of capital in the other form fell. Overstone, however, tries to identify these two values of two different kinds of capital in a single unique value of capital, and moreover by opposing both of them to a lack of means of circulation, of ready money. The same amount of money capital, however, can be loaned with very different quantities of the circulation medium.

Let us take his own example of 1847. The official Bank rate was as follows. January, $3-3\frac{1}{2}$ per cent; February, $4-4\frac{1}{2}$ per cent; March, generally 4 per cent; April (panic), $4-7\frac{1}{2}$ per cent; May, $5-5\frac{1}{2}$ per cent; June, mostly $5\frac{1}{2}$ per cent; July, 5 per cent; August, $5-5\frac{1}{2}$ per cent; September, 5 per cent, with minor variations of $5\frac{1}{4}$, $5\frac{1}{2}$ and 6 per cent; October, 5, $5\frac{1}{2}$, 7 per cent; November, 7–10 per cent; December, 7–5 per cent. – In this case interest rose because profits declined and the money values of commodities fell enormously. So if Overstone says on this that the rate of interest rose in 1847 because the value of capital rose, he can only mean by the value of capital the value of money capital, and the value of money capital is precisely the rate of interest and nothing else. But later on he gives the game away and identifies the value of capital with the rate of profit.

As far as the high interest rate paid in 1856 is concerned, Overstone was in fact unaware that this was in part a symptom that the kind of credit-jobbers were coming to the fore who paid interest not out of their profits, but out of other people's capital; he contended only a few months before the crisis of 1857 that 'business is perfectly sound'.

He went on to testify: '3722. That idea of the profits of trade being destroyed by a rise in the rate of interest is most erroneous. In the first place, a rise in the rate of interest is seldom of any long duration; in the second place, if it is of long duration, and of great extent, it is really a rise in the value of capital, and why does value of capital rise? Because the rate of profit is increased.'

Here, then, we finally learn what the 'value of capital' means. Besides, the rate of profit can remain high for a long period, even though profit of enterprise falls and the interest rate rises, so that interest comes to absorb the greater part of profits.

'3724. The rise in the rate of interest has been in consequence of the great increase in the trade of the country, and the great rise in the rate of profits; and to complain of the rise in the rate of interest as being destructive of the two things, which have been its own cause, is a sort of logical absurdity, which one does not know how to deal with.'

This is about as logical as if he had said: The increased profit rate has been in consequence of a rise in commodity prices brought about by speculation, and to complain that the rise in prices destroys its own cause, i.e. speculation, is a logical absurdity, etc. Only for a usurer enamoured of his high rate of interest is it a logical absurdity that a thing can ultimately destroy its own cause. The greatness of the Romans was the cause of their conquests, and it was their conquests that destroyed their greatness. Wealth is the cause of luxury, and luxury has a destructive effect on wealth. The artful dodger! There is no better sign of the idiocy of the present bourgeois world than the respect that the 'logic' of this millionaire, this 'dung-hill aristocrat', enjoyed throughout England. Moreover, if a high rate of profit and the expansion of business can be the cause of a high interest rate, this in no way means that a high interest rate is the cause of high profits. And the question is precisely whether this high interest persisted (as was actually discovered in the crisis) or even reached its climax after the high rate of profit had gone the way of all flesh.

'3718. With regard to a great rise in the rate of discount, that is a circumstance entirely arising from the increased value of capital, and the cause of that increased value of capital I think any person may discover with perfect clearness. I have already alluded to the fact that during the thirteen years this Act has been in operation, the trade of this country has increased from £45,000,000 to £120,000,000. Let any person reflect upon all the events which are involved in that short statement; let him consider the enormous demand upon capital for the purpose of carrying on such a gigantic increase of trade, and let him consider at the same time that the natural source from which that great demand should be supplied, namely, the annual savings of this country, has for the last three or four years been consumed in the unprofitable expenditure of war. I confess that my surprise is, that the rate of interest is not much higher than it is; or, in other words, my surprise is, that the pressure for capital to carry on these gigantic operations, is not far more stringent than you have found it to be.'

What an amazing jumble of words from our usurer logician! Here he is again with his increased value of capital! He seems to imagine that on the one hand there was this enormous expansion of the reproduction process, i.e. an accumulation of real capital, and that on the other hand there was a 'capital' for which an 'enormous demand' developed, in order to bring about this gigantic increase of trade! But wasn't this gigantic increase in production itself the increase in capital, and if it created a demand, did it not create at the same time the supply, and at the same time also an increased supply of money capital? If the rate of interest rose to a very high level, this was simply because the demand for money capital grew still more quickly than the supply, which means that, as industrial production expanded, it was conducted to a greater extent on the basis of credit. In other words, the real industrial expansion gave rise to an increased demand for 'accommodation', and this latter demand is evidently what our banker understands by the 'enormous demand upon capital'. But it was certainly not just the expansion of *demand* for capital that raised the export trade from £45 million to £120 million. And what does Overstone mean, moreover, when he says that the annual savings of the country consumed by the Crimean war form the natural source from which this great demand should have been supplied? Firstly, how then did England accumulate in 1792–1815, which was a war of a quite different order from the little Crimean war? Secondly, if the natural source dried up, from what source did capital flow? As is well known, England did not take out any loans from foreign countries. If there was an artificial source as well as this natural one, it would certainly be the method most favoured by a nation to use the natural source in war and the artificial source in business. But if there was only the old money capital, could its effectiveness be doubled by a high rate of interest? Mr Overstone evidently believes that the country's annual savings (which in this case were allegedly consumed) are simply transformed into money capital. But if there was no real accumulation, i.e. a rise in production and an increase in the means of production, what would be the good of an accumulation of claims on this production in the money form?

The rise in the 'value of capital' which follows from the high rate of profit is lumped together by Overstone with the rise that follows from an increased demand for money capital. This demand may arise from causes completely independent of the rate of profit. He himself adduces as an example that in 1847 it rose as a result of the devaluation of real capital. According to whether it suits him, he relates the value of capital either to real capital or to money capital.

A further sign of our banking lord's dishonesty, as well as his restricted banker's point of view, is given in the following passage: (3728. Question:) 'You have stated that the rate of discount is of no material moment you think to the merchant; will you be kind enough to state what you consider the ordinary rate of profit?' – Lord Overstone declares it 'impossible' to give an answer. '3729. Supposing the average rate of profit to be, say, from 7 to 10 per cent, a variation of from 2 to 7 or 8 per cent in the rate of discount must materially affect the rate of profit, must it not?'

(The question itself confuses the rate of profit of enterprise with the rate of profit, and overlooks the fact that the profit rate is the common source of both interest and profit of enterprise. The interest rate can leave the rate of profit unaffected, but not profit of enterprise. Overstone's response:)

'In the first place parties will not pay a rate of discount which seriously interrupts their profits; they will discontinue their business rather than do that.'

(Certainly, if they could do so without being ruined. As long as their profits are high, they pay the discount rate because they wish to, and when it is low, they pay it because they have to.)

'What is the meaning of discount? Why does a person discount a bill? . . . Because he wants to obtain the command of a greater quantity of capital.'

(*Halte-là* [hold it]! Because he wants to anticipate the return in money of his tied-up capital, and prevent his business coming to a standstill. Because he has to meet payments that are due. He requires more capital only if the business is going well, or if he is speculating with someone else's capital, even when business is bad. Discounting is in no way simply a means for expanding his business.)

'And why does he want to obtain the command of a greater quantity of capital? Because he wants to employ that capital; and why does he want to employ that capital? Because it is profitable to him to do so; it would not be profitable to him to do so if the discount destroyed his profit.'

Our self-satisfied logician assumes that bills are discounted only in order to expand a business, and that the business is expanded because it is profitable. The first assumption is false. The ordinary businessman discounts his bills to anticipate the money form of his capital and in this way keep the reproduction process going; not to expand his business or spend additional capital, but rather to balance the credit he gives with the credit he takes. If he does want to expand his business on credit, it is little use to him to get bills of exchange discounted, as this simply converts money capital that he already has from one form to another; he would rather take out a fixed loan for a longer period. The credit swindler, however, gets his accommodation bills discounted to expand his business and to cover one squalid deal with another; not to make profit, but to get his hands on other people's capital.

After Lord Overstone has identified discounting in this way with borrowing extra capital (instead of with converting bills of exchange that represent capital into cash), he immediately retracts as soon as the screws are applied. (3730. Question:) 'Merchants being engaged in business, must they not for a certain period carry on their operations in despite of any temporary increase in the rate of discount?' – (Overstone:) 'There is no doubt that in any particular transaction, if a person can get his command of capital at a low rate of interest rather than at a high rate of interest, taken in that limited view of the matter, that is convenient to him.'

But it is not at all a limited view of the matter when Lord Overstone suddenly comes to understand by 'capital' simply his banking capital, and to see the man who discounts a bill of exchange with him as a man without capital, since his capital exists in the commodity form, or the money form of his capital is a bill which Lord Overstone converts into another money form.

3732. 'With reference to the Act of 1844, can you state what has been about the average rate of interest in proportion to the amount of bullion in the Bank; would it be a fact that when the amount of bullion has been about £9,000,000 or £10,000,000 the rate of interest has been 6 or 7 per cent, and that when it has been £16,000,000, the rate of interest has been, say, from 3 to 4 per cent?' (The questioner is trying to compel him to explain the rate of interest, as influenced by the amount of bullion in the Bank, on the basis of the rate of interest influenced by the value of capital.) 'I do not apprehend that that is so . . . but if it is, then I think we must take still more stringent measures than those adopted by the Act of 1844, because if it be true that the greater the store of bullion, the lower the rate of interest, we ought to set to work, according to that view of the matter, to increase the store of bullion to an indefinite amount, and then we should get the interest down to nothing.'

The questioner, Cayley, undisturbed by this bad joke, continues: '3733. If that be so, supposing that £5,000,000 of bullion was to be restored to the Bank, in the course of the next six months the bullion then would amount, say, to £16,000,000, and supposing that the rate of interest was thus to fall to 3 or 4 per cent, how could it be stated that that fall in the rate of interest arose from a great decrease of the trade of the country? – I said that the recent rise in the rate of interest, not that the fall in the rate of interest, was closely connected with the great increase in the trade of the country.'

But what Cayley said was this. If a rise in the rate of interest, together with a contraction in the gold reserve, is a sign of an expansion of business, then a fall in the rate of interest, together with an expansion in the gold reserve, must be a sign of a contraction of business. Overstone has no answer to this.

(3736. Question:) 'I observed you' (in the original text always 'your Lordship') 'to say that money was the instrument for obtaining capital.' (This is precisely the confusion, to see it as an instrument; it is a *form* of capital.) 'Under a drain of bullion (of the Bank of England) is not the great strain, on the contrary, for *capitalists* to obtain money?' – (Overstone:) 'No, it is not the capitalists, it is those who are not capitalists, who want to obtain money and why do they want to obtain money? ... Because through the money they obtain the command of the capital of the capitalist to carry on the business of the persons who are not capitalists.'

He now explains in so many words that manufacturers and merchants are not capitalists, and that the capitalist's only capital is simply his money capital. '3737. Are not the parties who draw bills of exchange capitalists? – The parties who draw bills of exchange may be, and may not be, capitalists.' Now he is stuck.

The question is then asked whether the merchants' bills of exchange do not represent commodities that they have sold or shipped. He denies that these bills represent the value of commodities in the same way as banknotes represent gold. (3740, 3741.) This is a little insolent.

'3742. Is it not the merchant's object to get money? – No;

getting money is not the object in drawing the bill; getting money is the object in discounting the bill.'

Drawing bills of exchange is transforming commodities into a form of credit money, just as discounting bills is transforming this credit money into a different money, i.e. banknotes. Overstone at least concedes that the purpose of discounting is to receive money. Previously he had claimed that discounting was not to transform capital from one form into the other, but simply to obtain additional capital.

'3743. What is the great desire of the mercantile community under pressure of panic, such as you state to have occurred in 1825, 1837 and 1839; is their object to get possession of capital or the legal tender? – Their object is to get the command of capital to support their business.'

Their object is to obtain means of payment for bills on themselves that fall due, on account of the shortage of credit that has set in, and not to have to unload their commodities below their proper price. If they do not have any capital at all themselves, of course they obtain capital with these means of payment, since they obtain value without an equivalent. The demand for money as such always consists simply in the desire to convert value from the form of commodities or creditor's claims into the form of money. Hence, even aside from crises, the great distinction between borrowing capital and discounting, the latter being simply the transformation of monetary claims from one form into another, or into actual money itself.

(As editor, I permit myself an interpolation here.

For both Norman and Loyd-Overstone, the banker is always someone who 'advances capital', and his client the person who demands 'capital' from him. Thus Overstone says that someone has a bill of exchange discounted with him 'because he wants to obtain *capital*' (3729), and that it is convenient for this person if he 'can get his *command over capital* at a low rate of interest' (3730). 'Money is the instrument for obtaining *capital*' (3736), and in time of panic the great desire of the entire business community is 'to get the command of *capital*' (3742). [All emphases are Engels's.] For all Loyd-Overstone's confusion as to what capital is, it emerges clearly enough that what he describes as capital is what the banker gives his client, a capital that the client did not possess previously and which is advanced to him, being in addition to what the client previously disposed of.

The banker has grown so accustomed to figuring as distributor of the available social capital in the money form (distributing it in loans) that any function in which he hands out money appears to him as a loan. All money that he pays out appears to him as an advance. If the money is directly given out as a loan, this is literally correct. If it is used to discount bills of exchange, it is in fact an advance for him until the bill falls due. Thus the idea is reinforced in his mind that he can make no payments that are not advances. And, moreover, advances not just in the sense that any investment of money with the object of making interest or profit is considered in economics as an advance which the owner of the money makes in his capacity as private person, to himself in his capacity as entrepreneur. But rather advances in the specific sense that the banker transfers a sum to his client as a loan, which increases by that much the capital at the latter's disposal.

It is this idea, transferred from the banker's office to political economy, that has led to the confusing controversy as to whether what the banker makes available to his clients in cash is capital or mere money, means of circulation, 'currency'. In order to decide this basically simple question, we have to put ourselves in the position of the bank's client. The question is what he requires and obtains.

If the bank grants the client a loan simply on his personal credit, without any security on his part, the matter is clear. He receives without condition an advance of a certain value in addition to the capital that he previously applied. He receives it in the money form; not just money, but money *capital*.

But if the advance is made against securities, etc., which have to be deposited with the bank, it is an advance in the sense that money is paid to him under condition of its repayment, but it is not an advance of capital. For these securities also represent capital, and moreover a higher amount than the advance. The recipient thus receives less capital value than he deposits; and this is in no way an acquisition of extra capital for him. He does not undertake the transaction because he needs capital, but rather because he needs money. Thus there is an advance of *money* here, but not an advance of capital.

If the advance is made by discounting bills of exchange, the *form* of an advance also disappears. There is just a simple sale and purchase. The bill becomes by endorsement the property of the bank, the money becoming the property of the client. There is no question now of repayment. If the client uses a bill of exchange or a similar instrument of credit to buy cash, this is no more an advance than if he had bought the cash with some commodity or other, cotton, iron or corn. And still less can there be any question here of an advance of *capital*. Every purchase and sale between one dealer and another is a transfer of capital. But there is only an advance when the transfer of capital is not reciprocal, but is rather one-sided and for a certain period of time. Thus there can only be a capital advance with the discount of a bill if the bill is an accommodation bill, not representing any commodities sold, and this no banker will accept if he recognizes it for what it is. In the regular discount business, therefore, the bank's client does not receive any advance, either in capital or in money, but he receives money for the commodity he has sold.

The cases where the client seeks and obtains capital from the bank are thus quite clearly distinct from those where he simply obtains an advance of money, or buys something from the bank. And as Loyd-Overstone in particular is accustomed only in the rarest of cases to advance his funds without collateral (he was my firm's banker in Manchester), it is equally clear that his pretty description of the masses of capital that the generous bankers advance to manufacturers in need is sheer invention.

In Chapter 32 Marx says essentially the same thing: 'The demand for means of payment is simply a demand for convertibility into *money*, in so far as the merchants and producers are able to offer good security; it is a demand for *money capital*, in so far as this is not the case, i.e. in so far as an advance of means of payment gives them not only the *money form*, but also the equivalent that they lack for payments, in whatever form this might be' [p. 648]. And in Chapter 33: 'When the credit system is developed, so that money is concentrated in the hands of the banks, it is they who advance it, *at least nominally*. This advance is only related to the money in circulation. It is an advance of *circulation*, not an advance of the capitals it circulates' [p. 664, Engels's emphasis]. Mr Chapman, too, who ought to know, confirms the above interpretation of the discount business (*B. A.* 1857): 'The banker has the bill, the banker has *bought the bill*' (Evidence. Question 5139) [Engels's emphasis].

We shall come back to this theme again in Chapter 28. – F. E.)

'3744. Will you be good enough to describe what you actually mean by the term "capital"?' – (Overstone:) 'Capital consists of various commodities, by means of which trade is carried on; there is fixed capital and there is circulating capital. Your ships, your docks, your wharves . . . are fixed capital; your provisions, your clothes, etc., are circulating capital.'

'3745. Is the country oppressed under a drain of bullion? – Not in the rational sense of the word.' (Then comes the old Ricardian theory of money.) . . . 'In the natural state of things the money of the world is distributed amongst the different countries of the world in certain proportions, those proportions being such that under that distribution (of money) the intercourse between any one country and all the other countries of the world jointly will be an intercourse of barter; but disturbing circumstances will arise to affect that distribution, and when those arise, a certain portion of the money of any given country passes to other countries.' – '3746. Your Lordship now uses the term "money". I understood you before to say that it was a loss of capital. – That what was a loss of capital?' – '3747. The export of bullion? – No, I did not say so. If you treat bullion as capital, no doubt it is a loss of capital; it is parting with a certain proportion of those precious metals which constitute the money of the world.' – '3748. I understood Your Lordship to say that an alteration in the rate of discount was a mere sign of an alteration in the value of capital? – I did.' – '3749. And that the rate of discount generally alters with the state of the store of bullion in the Bank of England? – Yes, but I have already stated that the fluctuations in the rate of interest, which arise from an alteration in the quantity of money' (what he therefore means here is the quantity of actually existing gold) 'in a country, are very small.'

'3750. Then, does Your Lordship mean that there is a less capital than there was, when there is a more continuous yet temporary increase in the rate of discount than usual? – Less, in one sense of the word. The proportion between capital and the demand for it is altered; it may be by an increased demand, not by a diminution of the quantity of capital.'

(But it was this very capital that was just now money or gold, and a little earlier on the rise in the rate of interest was explained by a high rate of profit that arose from the expansion of the business or capital, not from its contraction.)

'3751. What is the capital which you particularly allude to? – That depends entirely upon what the capital is which each person wants. It is the capital which the country has at its command for conducting its business, and when that business is doubled, there must be a great increase in the demand for the capital with which it is to be carried on.'

(This artful banker first doubles business activity, and then the demand for capital with which this is to be doubled. All he ever sees is his client, who asks Mr Loyd for a bigger capital to double his business with.)

'Capital is like any other commodity' (but according to Mr Loyd capital is nothing but the totality of commodities), 'it will vary in its price' (hence commodities change their price twice, once as commodities and the other time as capital) 'according to the supply and demand.'

'3752. The changes in the rate of discount are generally connected with the changes in the amount of gold which there is in the coffers of the Bank. Is it that capital to which Your Lordship refers? – No.' – '3753. Can Your Lordship point to any instance in which there has been a large store of capital in the Bank of England connected with a high rate of discount? – The Bank of England is not a place for the deposit of capital, it is a place for the deposit of money.' – '3754. Your Lordship has stated that the rate of interest depends upon the amount of capital; will you be kind enough to state what capital you mean, and whether you can point to any instance in which there has been a large store of bullion in the Bank and at the same time a high rate of interest? – It is very probable' (aha!) 'that the accumulation of bullion in the Bank may be coincident with a low rate of interest, because a period in which there is a diminished demand for capital' (namely, money-capital; the period to which reference is made here, 1844 and 1845, was a period of prosperity) 'is a period, during which, of course, the means or instrument through which you command capital may accumulate.' – '3755. Then you think that there is no connection between the rate of discount and the amount of bullion in the coffers of the Bank? – There may be a connection, but it is not a connection of principle' (his Bank Act of 1844, however, made it a principle of the Bank of England to regulate the interest rate by the quantity of bullion in its possession), 'there may be a coincidence of time.' – '3758. Do I rightly understand you to say, that the difficulty of merchants in this country, under a state of pressure, in consequence of a high rate of discount, is in getting capital, and not in getting money? – You are putting two things together which I do not join in that form; their difficulty is in getting capital, and their difficulty also is in getting money . . . The difficulty of getting money and the difficulty of getting capital is the same difficulty taken in two successive stages of its progress.'

Now the fish is caught again. The first difficulty is to discount a bill or obtain an advance by depositing commodities as security. It is the difficulty of transforming capital or a commercial token of value for capital into money. And this difficulty is expressed, among other things, in a high rate of interest. But once the money is received, where then is the second difficulty? If it is only a question of paying, does anyone ever have difficulty in getting rid of his money? And if it is a question of buying, when has anyone ever found difficulty in buying in times of crisis? And even assuming that this refers to a particular case, with an increase in the price of corn, cotton, etc., the difficulty could still not present itself in the value of the money capital, i.e. the rate of interest, but would rather do so in the price of the commodity; and this difficulty is already solved in that our man now has the money that he needs to buy it with.

'3760. But a higher rate of discount is an increased difficulty of getting money? – It is an increased difficulty of getting money, but it is not because you want to have the money; it is only the form' (and this form brings profit into the banker's pocket) 'in which the increased difficulty of getting capital presents itself according to the complicated relations of a civilized state.'

3763. (Overstone's reply:) 'The banker is the go-between who receives deposits on the one side, and on the other applies those deposits, entrusting them, *in the form of capital*, to the hands of persons who, etc.'

Here we finally have what *he* means by capital. He transforms money into capital by 'entrusting' it, as he puts it rather euphemistically, i.e. lending it out at interest.

After Lord Overstone had previously said that a change in the discount rate was not essentially connected with a change in the amount of the bank's gold reserve, or the amount of money present, but was at most connected by coincidence in time, he repeats:

'3805. When the money in the country is diminished by a drain, its value increases, and the Bank of England must conform to that alteration in the value of money' (i.e. in the value of money *as capital*, or in other words, in the rate of interest, for the value of money *as money*, compared with commodities, remains the same), 'which is meant by the technical term of raising the rate of interest.'

'(3819.) I never confound those two.' – Meaning money and capital, for the simple reason that he never distinguished between them.

'(3834.) The very large sum, which had to be paid' (for corn in 1847), 'which was *in point of fact capital*, for the supply of the necessary provisions of the country.'

'(3841.) The variations in the rate of discount have no doubt a very close relation to the state of the reserve' (of the Bank of England), 'because the state of the reserve is the indicator of the increase or the decrease of the quantity of money in the country; and in proportion as the money in the country increases or decreases, the value of that money will increase or decrease, and the bank-rate of discount will conform to that change.'

Here, therefore, he concedes what he denied categorically in no. 3755.

'3842. There is an intimate connection between them.' Namely, a connection between the amount of gold in the Issue Department and the reserve of notes in the Banking Department. Here he explains the changes in the rate of interest in terms of the changes in the quantity of money. What he says about this is false. The reserve can decline because the money in circulation in the country increases. This is the case if the public accept more notes and there is no decline in the metal reserve. But then the interest rate rises, because the banking capital of the Bank of England is limited by the Act of 1844. Overstone, however, cannot speak of this, since according to this Act the two departments of the Bank have nothing to do with one another.

'3859. A high rate of profit will always create a great demand for capital; a great demand for capital will raise the value of it.'

Here at last we have the connection between the high profit rate and the demand for capital, as Overstone conceives it. Now in 1844–5, for example, there was a high rate of profit in the cotton industry, since raw cotton was cheap and remained so despite a strong demand for cotton goods. The value of capital (and from an earlier passage, Overstone means by capital that which every person needs in his business), i.e. in this case the value of the raw cotton, was not increased for the manufacturers. Now the high rate of profit may have caused many cotton manufacturers to expand their businesses. In this way their demand for *money* capital would rise, but not for anything else.

'3889. Bullion may or may not be money, just as paper may or may not be a bank-note.'

'3896. Do I correctly understand Your Lordship that you give up the argument, which you used in 1840, that the fluctuations in the notes out of the Bank of England ought to conform to the fluctuations in the amount of bullion? – I give it up so far as this ... that now with the means of information which we possess, the notes out of the Bank of England must have added to them the notes which are in the banking reserve of the Bank of England.'

This is superlative. The arbitrary stipulation that the Bank prints as many paper notes as it has gold in its reserve, plus £14 million more, naturally means that its note issue fluctuates with the fluctuations in the gold reserve. But since the present 'means of information which we possess' show clearly that the mass of notes that the Bank may manufacture (and which the Issue Department transfers to the Banking Department) – that this circulation between the two departments of the Bank of England, which fluctuates with the fluctuations in its money reserve, does not determine the fluctuations in the circulation of banknotes outside the walls of the Bank of England, it follows that the latter, the real circulation, now becomes completely immaterial for the Bank's management, and the circulation between the two departments of the Bank, whose difference from the real circulation is shown by the reserve, becomes the sole decisive factor. For the world outside, this is important only in so far as the reserve indicates how close the Bank is to the legal maximum of its note issue, and how much its clients can still obtain from the Banking Department.

The following is a brilliant example of Overstone's *mala fides*.*

'4243. Does the quantity of capital, do you think, oscillate from month to month to such a degree as to alter its value in the way exhibited of late years in the oscillations in the rate of discount? – The relation between the demand and the supply of capital may undoubtedly fluctuate, even within short periods ... If France tomorrow put out a notice that she wishes to borrow a very large loan, there is no doubt that it would immediately cause a great alteration *in the value of money*, that is to say, *in the value of capital*, in this country.'

'4245. If France announces, that she wants suddenly, for any purpose, 30 millions' worth of commodities there will be a great demand for *capital*, to use the more scientific and the simpler term.'

* bad faith.

'4246. The *capital*, which France would wish to buy with her loan, is *one* thing, and the *money* with which she buys it is *another*, is it the *money*, which alters in value, or not? – We seem to be reviving the old question, which I think is more fit for the chamber of a student than for this committee room.'

And with this he retires, though not into the chamber of a student.[84]

84. More on Overstone's confusion of concepts where capital is concerned is to be found at the end of Chapter 32. – F. E.

Chapter 27: The Role of Credit
in Capitalist Production

The general observations we have so far made on the credit system are as follows:

I. Its necessary formation to bring about the equalization of the profit rate or the movement of this equalization, on which the whole of capitalist production depends.

II. The reduction of circulation costs.

1. A major cost of circulation is money itself, in so far as it is itself value. And this is economized on in three ways by credit.

A. In that money is completely dispensed with in a large portion of transactions.

B. In that the circulation of the circulating medium is accelerated.[85] This partly coincides with what is said under 2 below. On the one hand the acceleration is technical; i.e. with the volume and number of real turnovers of commodities for consumption remaining the same, a smaller quantity of money or money tokens performs the same service. This is connected with the technique of

85. 'The average of notes in circulation during the year was, in 1812, 106,538,000 francs; in 1818, 101,205,000 francs; whereas the movement of the currency, or the annual aggregate of disbursements and receipts upon all accounts, was, in 1812, 2,837,712,000 francs; in 1818, 9,665,030,000 francs. The activity of the currency in France, therefore, during the year 1818, as compared with its activity in 1812, was in the proportion of three to one. The great regulator of the velocity of circulation is credit . . . This explains, why a severe pressure upon the money-market is generally coincident with a full circulation' (*The Currency Theory Reviewed, etc.*, p. 65). – 'Between September 1833 and September 1843 nearly 300 banks were added to the various issuers of notes throughout the United Kingdom; the result was a reduction in the circulation to the extent of two million and a half; it was £36,035,244 at the close of September 1833, and £33,518,554 at the close of September 1843' (ibid., p. 53). – 'The prodigious activity of Scottish circulation enables it, with £100, to effect the same quantity of monetary transactions, which in England it requires £420 to accomplish' (ibid., p. 55. This last refers only to the technical side of the operation).

banking. On the other hand, credit accelerates the velocity of the metamorphosis of commodities, and with this the velocity of monetary circulation.

C. The replacement of gold money by paper.

2. Acceleration, through credit, of the individual phases of circulation or commodity metamorphosis, then an acceleration of the metamorphosis of capital and hence an acceleration of the reproduction process in general. (On the other hand, credit also enables the acts of buying and selling to take a longer time, and hence serves as a basis for speculation.) Contraction of the reserve fund, which can be viewed in two ways: on the one hand as a reduction in the circulating medium, on the other hand as a restriction of the part of capital that must always be in existence in the money form.[86]

III. Formation of joint-stock companies. This involves:

1. Tremendous expansion in the scale of production, and enterprises which would be impossible for individual capitals. At the same time, enterprises that were previously government ones become social.*

2. Capital, which is inherently based on a social mode of production and presupposes a social concentration of means of production and labour-power, now receives the form of social capital (capital of directly associated individuals) in contrast to private capital, and its enterprises appear as social enterprises as opposed to private ones. This is the abolition of capital as private property within the confines of the capitalist mode of production itself.

3. Transformation of the actual functioning capitalist into a mere manager, in charge of other people's capital, and of the capital owner into a mere owner, a mere money capitalist. Even if the dividends that they draw include both interest and profit of enterprise, i.e. the total profit (for the manager's salary is or should be simply the wage for a certain kind of skilled labour, its price being regulated in the labour market like that of any other labour), this total profit is still drawn only in the form of interest, i.e. as a mere reward for capital ownership, which is now as

86. 'Before the establishment of the banks . . . the amount of capital withdrawn for the purposes of currency was greater, at all times, than the actual circulation of commodities required' (*The Economist*, 1845, p. 238).

* The word '*gesellschaftlich*' used here has the double sense of 'social' (as opposed to individual) and 'joint-stock' (as opposed to government).

completely separated from its function in the actual production process as this function, in the person of the manager, is from capital ownership. Profit thus appears (and no longer just the part of it, interest, that obtains its justification from the profit of the borrower) as simply the appropriation of other people's surplus labour, arising from the transformation of means of production into capital; i.e. from their estrangement vis-à-vis the actual producer; from their opposition, as the property of another, vis-à-vis all individuals really active in production from the manager down to the lowest day-labourer. In joint-stock companies, the function is separated from capital ownership, so labour is also completely separated from ownership of the means of production and of surplus labour. This result of capitalist production in its highest development is a necessary point of transition towards the transformation of capital back into the property of the producers, though no longer as the private property of individual producers, but rather as their property as associated producers, as directly social property. It is furthermore a point of transition towards the transformation of all functions formerly bound up with capital ownership in the reproduction process into simple functions of the associated producers, into social functions.

Before we go on, the following economically important fact must be noted. Since profit here simply assumes the form of interest, enterprises that merely yield an interest are possible, and this is one of the reasons that hold up the fall in the general rate of profit, since these enterprises, where the constant capital stands in such a tremendous ratio to the variable, do not necessarily go into the equalization of the general rate of profit.

(Since Marx wrote the above passage, new forms of industrial organization have been developed, as is well-known, representing the second and third degree of joint-stock company. The speed with which production can nowadays be increased in all fields of large-scale industry, which is greater every day, is confronted by the ever increasing slowness in expanding the market for this increased volume of products. What production produces in months the market can absorb only in years. On top of this there are the protectionist policies by which each industrial country puts up a barrier against others, particularly against England, and artificially boosts domestic productive capacity still further. The results are general and chronic overproduction, depressed prices, falling profits, even their complete cessation; in brief, the ancient and celebrated freedom of competition is at the end of its road and must itself confess its evident and scandalous bankruptcy. A further reason is that in each country the big industrialists in a particular branch of industry come together to form a cartel to regulate production. A committee fixes the quantity each establishment is to produce, and has the last word in dividing up the incoming orders. In a few cases it came to the formation of temporary international cartels, for instance between the English and the German iron producers. But even this form of socialization of production did not suffice. The conflict of interests between the individual businesses broke through too often and restored competition. The next stage, therefore, in certain branches where the scale of production permitted, was to concentrate the entire production of the branch of industry in question into *one* big joint-stock company with a unified management. In America this has already been achieved in several cases, while in Europe the biggest example up till now is the United Alkali Trust, which has brought the entire British production of alkali into the hands of a single firm. The former owners of more than thirty individual plants received the assessed value of their entire establishments in shares, to a total of some £5 million, which represents the fixed capital of the trust. The technical management remains in the same hands as before, but financial control is concentrated in the hands of the general management. The floating capital, amounting to some £1 million, was offered to public subscription. The total capital is thus £6 million. In this branch, therefore, which forms the basis of the entire chemical industry, competition has been replaced in England by monopoly, thus preparing in the most pleasing fashion its future expropriation by society as a whole, by the nation. – F. E.)

This is the abolition of the capitalist mode of production within the capitalist mode of production itself, and hence a self-abolishing contradiction, which presents itself *prima facie* as a mere point of transition to a new form of production. It presents itself as such a contradiction even in appearance. It gives rise to monopoly in certain spheres and hence provokes state intervention. It reproduces a new financial aristocracy, a new kind of parasite in the guise of company promoters, speculators and merely nominal directors; an entire system of swindling and cheating with respect to the promotion of companies, issue of shares and share dealings. It is private production unchecked by private ownership.

IV. Apart from the joint-stock system – which is an abolition of capitalist private industry on the basis of the capitalist system itself, and which destroys private industry to the same degree that it spreads and takes over new spheres of production – credit offers the individual capitalist, or the person who can pass as a capitalist, an absolute command over the capital and property of others, within certain limits, and, through this, command over other people's labour.[87] It is disposal over social capital, rather than his own, that gives him command over social labour. The actual capital that someone possesses, or is taken to possess by public opinion, now becomes simply the basis for a superstructure of credit. This is especially the case in wholesale trade, and the greater part of the social product passes through this. All standards of measurement, all explanatory reasons that were still more or less justified within the capitalist mode of production, now vanish. What the speculating trader risks is social property, not his own. Equally absurd now is the saying that the origin of capital is saving, since what this speculator demands is precisely that *others* should save for him. (As recently the whole of France saved up one and a half thousand million francs for the Panama swindlers. The whole Panama swindle is exactly described here, a full twenty years before it took place. – F. E.) The other saying about abstention is diametrically refuted by his luxury, which also becomes a means of credit. Conceptions that still had a certain meaning at a less developed state of capitalist production now become completely meaningless. Success and failure lead in both cases to the centralization of capitals and hence to expropriation on the most enormous scale.

87. See for example the list of bankruptcies for a crisis year like 1857 in *The Times*, and compare the actual assets of those declared bankrupt with the amount of their debts. 'The truth is that the power of purchase by persons having capital and credit is much beyond anything that those who are unacquainted practically with speculative markets have any idea of' (Tooke, *Inquiry into the Currency Principle*, p. 79). 'A person having the reputation of capital enough for his regular business, and enjoying good credit in his trade, if he takes a sanguine view of the prospect of a rise of price of the article in which he deals, and is favoured by circumstances in the outset and progress of his speculation, may effect purchases to an extent perfectly enormous compared with his capital' (ibid., p. 136). 'Merchants, manufacturers, etc., carry on operations much beyond those which the use of their own capital alone would enable them to do ... Capital is rather the foundation upon which a good credit is built than the limit of the transactions of any commercial establishment' (*The Economist*, 1847, p. 1333).

Expropriation now extends from the immediate producers to the small and medium capitalists themselves. Expropriation is the starting-point of the capitalist mode of production, whose goal is to carry it through to completion, and even in the last instance to expropriate all individuals from the means of production – which, with the development of social production, cease to be means and products of private production, and can only remain means of production in the hands of the associated producers, as their social property, just as they are their social product. But within the capitalist system itself, this expropriation takes the antithetical form of the appropriation of social property by a few; and credit gives these few ever more the character of simple adventurers. Since ownership now exists in the form of shares, its movement and transfer become simply the result of stock-exchange dealings, where little fishes are gobbled up by the sharks, and sheep by the stock-exchange wolves. In the joint-stock system, there is already a conflict with the old form, in which the means of social production appear as individual property. But the transformation into the form of shares still remains trapped within the capitalist barriers; instead of overcoming the opposition between the character of wealth as something social, and private wealth, this transformation only develops this opposition in a new form.

The cooperative factories run by workers themselves are, within the old form, the first examples of the emergence of a new form, even though they naturally reproduce in all cases, in their present organization, all the defects of the existing system, and must reproduce them. But the opposition between capital and labour is abolished here, even if at first only in the form that the workers in association become their own capitalist, i.e. they use the means of production to valorize their own labour. These factories show how, at a certain stage of development of the material forces of production, and of the social forms of production corresponding to them, a new mode of production develops and is formed naturally out of the old. Without the factory system that arises from the capitalist mode of production, cooperative factories could not develop. Nor could they do so without the credit system that develops from the same mode of production. This credit system, since it forms the principal basis for the gradual transformation of capitalist private enterprises into capitalist joint-stock companies, presents in the same way the means for the gradual extension of cooperative enterprises on a more or less national scale. Capitalist joint-stock companies as much as cooperative factories should be viewed as transition forms from the capitalist mode of production to the associated one, simply that in the one case the opposition is abolished in a negative way, and in the other in a positive way.

Up till now, we have considered the development of credit – and the latent abolition of capital ownership contained within it – principally in relation to industrial capital. In the following chapters we discuss credit in relation to interest-bearing capital as such, both its effect on this and the form that it assumes in this connection. With respect to this, in general, a few more specifically economic points remain to be made.

But first of all this:

If the credit system appears as the principal lever of overproduction and excessive speculation in commerce, this is simply because the reproduction process, which is elastic by nature, is now forced to its most extreme limit; and this is because a great part of the social capital is applied by those who are not its owners, and who therefore proceed quite unlike owners who, when they function themselves, anxiously weigh the limits of their private capital. This only goes to show how the valorization of capital founded on the antithetical character of capitalist production permits actual free development only up to a certain point, which is constantly broken through by the credit system.[88] The credit system hence accelerates the material development of the productive forces and the creation of the world market, which it is the historical task of the capitalist mode of production to bring to a certain level of development, as material foundations for the new form of production. At the same time, credit accelerates the violent outbreaks of this contradiction, crises, and with these the elements of dissolution of the old mode of production.

The credit system has a dual character immanent in it: on the one hand it develops the motive of capitalist production, enrichment by the exploitation of others' labour, into the purest and most colossal system of gambling and swindling, and restricts ever more the already small number of the exploiters of social wealth; on the other hand however it constitutes the form of transition towards a new mode of production. It is this dual

88. Thomas Chalmers.

character that gives the principal spokesmen for credit, from Law through to Isaac Péreire,* their nicely mixed character of swindler and prophet.

* On John Law (1671–1729), see below, p. 739. Isaac Péreire (1806–80), a Bonapartist supporter and deputy, founded the Crédit Mobilier with his brother Jacob-Émile Péreire. See below, pp. 741–3.

Chapter 28: Means of Circulation and Capital.
The Views of Tooke and Fullarton

The distinction between currency and capital, as made by Tooke,[89] Wilson* and others (and in this connection the distinctions between means of circulation as money, as money capital in

89. We reproduce here the pertinent passage from Tooke, already quoted on pp. 529–30, in his original words. [Earlier Marx had quoted this passage in German translation.] 'The business of bankers, setting aside the issue of promissory notes payable on demand, may be divided into two branches, corresponding with the distinction pointed out by Dr (Adam) Smith of the transactions between dealers and dealers, and between dealers and consumers. One branch of the bankers' business is to collect *capital* from those who have not immediate employment for it, and to distribute or transfer it to those who have. The other branch is to receive deposits of the *incomes* of their customers, and to pay out the amount, as it is wanted for expenditure by the latter in the objects of their consumption . . . the former being a circulation of *capital*, the latter of *currency*' (Tooke, *Inquiry into the Currency Principle*, London, p. 36). The first is 'the concentration of capital on the one hand and the distribution of it on the other'; the latter is 'administering the circulation for local purposes of the district' (ibid., p. 37).

Kinnear comes much closer to the correct conception, in the following passage: 'Money . . . is employed to perform two operations essentially distinct . . . As a medium of exchange between dealers and dealers, it is the instrument by which transfers of capital are effected; that is, the exchange of a certain amount of capital in money for an equal amount of capital in commodities. But money employed in the payment of wages and in purchase and sale between dealers and consumers is not capital, but income; that portion of the incomes of the community, which is devoted to daily expenditure. It circulates in constant daily use, and is that alone which can, with strict propriety, be termed currency. Advances of capital depend entirely on the will of the Bank and other possessors of capital, for borrowers are always to be found; but the amount of the currency depends on the wants of the community, among whom the money circulates, for the purposes of daily expenditure' (J. G. Kinnear, *The Crisis and the Currency*, London, 1847).

* James Wilson (1805–60), after being the founder (1843) and first editor of *The Economist*, distinguished at this time as a leading exponent of free trade, became Financial Secretary to the Treasury from 1853 to 1858. He opposed the quantity theory of money and the 1844 Bank Act based on this.

general, and as interest-bearing or *monied capital* as the English put it, are simply lumped together haphazardly), comes down to two things.

The means of circulation circulates on the one hand as *coin* (money), in so far as it mediates the *expenditure of revenue*, i.e. commerce between individual consumers and retail traders; and in this category we count all merchants who sell to the consumer direct – to individual consumers as distinct from productive consumers or producers. Here money circulates in the function of coin, even though it constantly *replaces capital*. A certain part of the money of a country is always devoted to this function, even though the particular pieces of which this part consists are constantly changing. On the other hand, however, in so far as money mediates the *transfer of capital*, whether as means of purchase (means of circulation) or means of payment, it is *capital*. Thus it is neither the function of means of purchase nor that of means of payment that distinguishes it from coin; for money can function as means of purchase between one dealer and another, if the one buys from the other with cash, and it can even function between dealer and consumer as means of payment if credit is given, the revenue being consumed first and paid for only afterwards. The difference is rather that in the second case this money does not just replace capital for one party, the seller, but is also spent and advanced as capital by the other party, the buyer. The distinction is in fact one between the *money form of revenue* and the *money form of capital*, not between currency and capital, for a certain definite quantity of money *circulates* in the transactions between dealers as well as in the transactions between dealers and consumers, so that it is equally *circulation* in both functions. Tooke's conception, therefore, introduces confusion into the question in various ways:

(1) By confusing the functional characteristics;

(2) By bringing in the question of the overall quantity of money circulating, in both functions taken together;

(3) By bringing in the question of the relative proportions of the circulating medium in the two functions, and hence in the two spheres of the reproduction process.

(1) The confusion of the functional characteristics, i.e. the fact that money is currency in the one form and capital in the other. In so far as money serves for one or the other of these functions, for realizing revenue or for transferring capital, it functions either

in buying and selling or in payment, as means of purchase or payment, and in the broader sense of the terms as means of circulation. The further characteristic that it may have in the accounts of its spender or receiver, that it represents either capital or revenue for him, alters absolutely nothing here, and this too can be shown in two ways. Although the kinds of money circulating in the two spheres are different, yet the same piece of money, for instance a £5 note, moves from one sphere to the other and performs both functions in turn; this is unavoidable simply because the retail trader can give his capital its money form only in the form of the coin that he receives from his buyers. We can assume that small change proper has the centre of gravity of its circulation in the realm of retail trade. The retailer is constantly using it to give change and receiving it back again from his customers in payment. But he also receives money, i.e. coin, in the metal that is a measure of value, e.g. sovereigns in England, and even banknotes, particularly notes of lower denominations, £5 and £10. These gold coins and notes, as well as some surplus small change, he deposits each day or each week in the bank, and he pays for his purchases with cheques on his bank deposit. But the same gold coins and notes are just as constantly withdrawn from the bank by the public as a whole in their capacity as consumers, as the money form of their revenue, either directly or indirectly (e.g. smaller coins by the manufacturers for payment of wages); they are constantly flowing back to the retail traders, for whom they thus realize a part of their capital afresh and at the same time part of their revenue. This last fact is important and is completely overlooked by Tooke. Only in so far as money is laid out as money capital, at the beginning of the reproduction process (Volume 2, Part One), does capital value exist in its pure form. For the commodity produced contains not only capital but also surplus-value; it is not just inherently capital but capital that has already become such, capital together with the source of revenue incorporated in it. What the retail trader parts with in exchange for the money that flows back to him, i.e. his commodity, is thus for him capital plus profit, capital plus revenue.

Moreover, since the circulating money flows back to the retailer, it restores the money form of his capital.

It is completely mistaken, therefore, to transform the distinction between circulation as circulation of revenue and as circulation of capital into a distinction between currency and capital. In Tooke's case, this mode of expression arises through his simply taking the point of view of the banker issuing his own banknotes. The amount of his notes that are continuously in the hands of the public (even if this always consists of different particular notes) and function as means of circulation cost him nothing besides paper and printing costs. The notes are circulating certificates of indebtedness (bills of exchange) made out in his own name, even if they bring him in money and thus serve as a means of valorizing his capital. But they are different from capital, whether his own or borrowed. And this is the origin of a special distinction for him between currency and capital, which has nothing to do with defining the concepts as such, let alone Tooke's suggested definitions.

The particular character of money – whether it functions as the money form of revenue or of capital – does not at first affect its character as a means of circulation. It retains this character whether it performs one function or the other. If the money appears as the money form of revenue, however, it functions more as a means of circulation in the strict sense (coin, means of purchase), on account of the fragmentation of these purchases and sales, and because the majority of revenue spenders, the workers, can buy relatively little on credit; while in the world of trade and commerce, where the circulating medium is the money form of capital, money functions principally as means of payment, partly on account of concentration and partly on account of the prevailing credit system. But the distinction between money as means of payment and money as means of purchase (circulating medium) is a distinction within money itself, not a distinction between money and capital. If more copper and silver circulates in the retail trade, and in the wholesale trade more gold, this does not make the distinction between silver and copper on the one hand and gold on the other into a distinction between currency and capital.

(2) Bringing in the question of the quantity of money circulating in the two functions together. In as much as money circulates, whether as means of purchase or means of payment – irrespective of in which of the two spheres and independently of its function of realizing revenue or capital – the laws developed earlier in considering simple commodity circulation (Volume 1, Chapter 3, 2, b) still apply for the quantity of money circulating. In both cases the amount of money in circulation, the amount of

currency, is determined by the same factors: viz. the velocity of circulation, i.e. the number of times the same function of means of purchase and payment is repeated by the same piece of money in a given period of time; the mass of simultaneous sales and purchases, or payments; the sum of the prices of the commodities circulating; and finally the balances of payments that have to be settled at the same time. Whether the money functioning in this way represents capital or revenue for those who pay it and receive it is absolutely without any bearing on the matter. Its quantity is determined simply by its function as means of purchase and payment.

(3) On the question of the relative quantities of the circulating medium in the two functions, and hence in the two spheres of the reproduction process. The two spheres of circulation have an inner connection, since on the one hand the amount of revenue to be spent expresses the scale of consumption, while on the other the amount of capital circulating in production and trade expresses the scale and speed of the reproduction process. Nevertheless, the same factors have different effects, and even work in opposite directions, on the quantity of money circulating in the two functions or spheres, or on the amount of currency, as the English banking term has it. And this gives a new occasion for Tooke's absurd distinction between currency and capital. The fact that the Currency Principle gentlemen confuse two disparate things is in no way a reason for presenting this as a conceptual distinction.

In times of prosperity, of great expansion, when the reproduction process exhibits a great acceleration and energy, the workers are fully employed. In most cases there is even a rise in wages, which to some extent balances the fall in wages below the average level in the other phases of the commercial cycle. At the same time, the capitalists' revenues grow significantly. Consumption generally rises. Commodity prices rise just as regularly, at least in certain decisive branches of business. The result of this is that the quantity of money in circulation grows, at least within certain limits, since the greater velocity of circulation places its own barriers on the growth in the quantity of the circulating medium. Since the part of the social revenue that consists of wages is originally advanced by the industrial capitalist in the form of variable capital, and always in the money form, he needs more money for this circulation in times of prosperity. We must not however count this twice: once as money needed to circulate the variable capital, and then again as money needed to circulate the workers' revenue. The money paid to the workers as wages is spent in the retail trade and returns with the same weekly regularity to the banks in the deposits of the retail trader, after it has mediated all kinds of intermediate transactions in smaller circuits. In times of prosperity the reflux of money proceeds smoothly for the industrial capitalists, and so their need for monetary accommodation is not increased by their having to pay more in wages, more money for the circulation of their variable capital.

The overall result is that in periods of prosperity the mass of the circulating medium that serves for the expenditure of revenue experiences a decisive growth.

As far as concerns the means of circulation needed for transfers of capital, i.e. transfers simply between the capitalists themselves, this period of brisk business is at the same time a period of elastic and easy credit. The velocity of circulation between capitalist and capitalist is regulated directly by credit, and the amount of the circulating medium required to settle payments and make cash purchases undergoes a relative decline. It may expand in absolute terms, but it always decreases relatively, compared with the expansion of the reproduction process. A larger mass of payments, on the one hand, is settled without any intervention of money; on the other hand, given the vigour of the process, there is a quicker movement of the same quantities of money, as both means of purchase and payment. The same amount of money mediates the reflux of a greater number of individual capitals.

On the whole, the monetary circulation appears 'full' in such periods, although its division II (transfer of capital) is at least relatively contracted, while division I (expenditure of revenue) undergoes an absolute expansion.

The refluxes express the transformation of commodity capital back into money, $M–C–M'$, as we have seen in considering the reproduction process (Volume 2, Part One). Credit makes the reflux in the money form independent of the point in time of the actual reflux, whether we are dealing with the industrial capitalist or the merchant. Each of these sells on credit; his commodity is alienated before it is transformed back into money for him, i.e. flows back to him in the money form. On the other hand he buys on credit, and thus the value of his commodity has been transformed back for him either into productive capital or into commodity capital even before this value is actually transformed into money, before the commodity's price falls due and is paid. In such times of prosperity, the reflux takes place smoothly and easily. The retail trader is certain to pay the wholesaler, the latter the manufacturer, and he the importer of raw material, etc. The appearance of rapid and assured refluxes always persists for a certain time after these are really at an end, by virtue of the credit that has already been given, since the credit refluxes stand in for real ones. The banks begin to scent danger as soon as their clients deposit more bills of exchange with them than money. See the evidence of the Liverpool bank director quoted above, p. 541.

To repeat here what I have already noted earlier: 'In periods of expanding credit the velocity of currency increases faster than the prices of commodities, whereas in periods of contracting credit the velocity of currency declines faster than the prices of commodities' (*A Contribution to the Critique of Political Economy*, p. 105).

In periods of crisis, the opposite is the case. Circulation no. I contracts, prices fall, and so do wages; the number of workers employed is restricted, the amount turned over declines. In circulation no. II, on the other hand, the need for monetary accommodation grows with the decline in credit, a point which we shall immediately go into in more detail.

There can be no doubt at all that with the decline in credit, which goes together with a stagnation in the reproduction process, the amount of currency required for no. I, the expenditure of revenue, declines, whereas that for no. II, the transfer of capital, increases. It remains to be investigated, however, how far this is identical with the assertions of Fullarton and others:

'A demand for capital on loan and a demand for additional circulation are quite distinct things, and not often found associated' (Fullarton, op. cit., p. 82; title of Chapter 5).[90]

90. 'It is a great error, indeed, to imagine that the demand for pecuniary accommodation' (that is, for the loan of capital) 'is identical with a demand for additional means of circulation, or even that the two are frequently associated. Each demand originates in circumstances peculiarly affecting itself, and very distinct from each other. It is when everything looks prosperous, when wages are high, prices on the rise, and factories busy, that an additional supply of *currency* is usually required to perform the additional functions inseparable from the necessity of making larger and more numerous payments; whereas it is chiefly in a more advanced stage of the commercial cycle, when difficulties begin to present themselves, when markets are overstocked, and returns delayed, that interest rises, and a pressure comes upon the Bank for advances of *capital*. It is true that there is no medium through which the Bank is accustomed to advance capital except that of its promissory notes; and that

It is clear in the first place that in the former of the two above cases, the period of prosperity, when the quantity of the circulating medium must grow, there is a growing demand for it. But it is just as clear that, if a manufacturer draws more out of his bank

---

to refuse the notes, therefore, is to refuse the accommodation. But the accommodation once granted, everything adjusts itself in conformity with the necessities of the market; the loan remains, and the currency, if not wanted, finds its way back to the issuer. Accordingly, a very slight examination of the Parliamentary Returns may convince any one, that the securities in the hands of the Bank of England fluctuate more frequently in an opposite direction to its circulation than in concert with it, and that the example, therefore, of that great establishment furnishes no exception to the doctrine so strongly pressed by the country bankers, to the effect that no bank can enlarge its circulation, if that circulation be already adequate to the purposes to which a banknote currency is commonly applied; but that every addition to its advances, after that limit is passed, must be made from its capital, and supplied by the sale of some of its securities in reserve, or by abstinence from further investment in such securities. The table compiled from the Parliamentary Returns for the interval between 1833 and 1840, to which I have referred in a preceding page, furnishes continued examples of this truth; but two of these are so remarkable that it will be quite unnecessary for me to go beyond them. On the 3rd of January, 1837, when the resources of the Bank were strained to the uttermost to sustain credit and meet the difficulties of the money-market, we find its advances on loan and discount carried to the enormous sum of £17,022,000, an amount scarcely known since the war, and almost equal to the entire aggregate issues which, in the meanwhile, remain unmoved at so low a point as £17,076,000! On the other hand, we have on the 4th of June, 1833, a circulation of £18,892,000, with a return of private securities in hand, nearly, if not the very lowest on record for the last half-century, amounting to no more than £972,000!' (Fullarton, op. cit., pp. 97, 98).

We can see from the following evidence of Mr Weguelin, Governor of the Bank of England, that a 'demand for pecuniary accommodation' need in no way be identical with a 'demand for gold' (what Wilson, Tooke and the others call capital): 'The discounting of bills to that extent' (one million daily for three successive days) 'would not reduce the reserve' (of banknotes), 'unless the public demanded a greater amount of active circulation. The notes issued on the discount of bills would be returned through the medium of the bankers and through deposits. Unless these transactions were for the purpose of exporting bullion, and unless there were an amount of internal panic which induced people to lock up their notes, and not to pay them into the hands of the bankers ... the reserve would not be affected by the magnitude of the transactions.' – 'The Bank may discount a million and a half a day, and that is done constantly, without its reserve being in the slightest degree affected, the notes coming back again as deposits, and no other alteration taking place than the mere transfer from one account to another' (*Report on Bank Acts*, 1857, Evidence, nos. 241, 500). The notes therefore serve here merely as means of transferring credits.

deposit in gold or banknotes because he has to spend more capital in the money form, it is not his demand for capital that grows on this account but only his demand for this particular form of expending his capital. The demand relates only to the technical form in which he puts his capital into circulation. This is just as, according to the differential development of the credit system, for example, the same variable capital, the same amount of wages, requires a greater quantity of circulating medium in one country than in another; in England, for example, more than in Scotland, in Germany more than in England. In agriculture, too, the same capital active in the reproduction process requires different amounts of money in different seasons to perform its function.

But the opposition that Fullarton makes is incorrect. It is in no way, as he claims, the strong demand for loans that distinguishes the period of stagnation from that of prosperity, but rather the ease with which this demand is satisfied in the time of prosperity and the difficulty of satisfying it once stagnation has set in. It is in fact precisely the tremendous development of the credit system during the period of prosperity, and also therefore the enormous rise in the demand for loan capital and the readiness with which this is made available in such periods, that leads to the shortage of credit in the period of stagnation. Thus it is not a difference in the demand for loans that distinguishes the two periods.

As we have noted before, the two periods are distinguished in the first place by the fact that in the period of prosperity it is the demand for means of circulation between consumers and dealers that is dominant, while in the period of depression it is the demand for means of circulation between capitalists. In the period of stagnation the first declines while the second increases.

What strikes Fullarton and others as decisively important is the phenomenon that, at such times, while securities in the hands of the Bank of England increase, its note circulation declines, and vice versa. The volume of securities, however, expresses the volume of monetary accommodation, of discounted bills of exchange, and of advances against marketable securities. Thus Fullarton says in the passage quoted above (p. 580, note 90) that securities in the hands of the Bank of England generally fluctuate in an opposite direction to its note circulation, and that this confirms the old-established principle of the private banks that no bank can increase its note issue beyond a certain definite amount, determined by the needs of its clientele. If it wants to make further advances above this amount, it must make these out of its own capital, i.e. either realize on securities or utilize deposits which it would otherwise have invested in securities.

We see now what Fullarton means by capital. In his view, capital is involved when the bank can no longer make advances with its own banknotes, its own promises to pay, which of course cost it nothing. But with what does it make these advances? With the proceeds from the sale of 'securities in reserve', i.e. government paper, stocks and other interest-bearing paper. And what does it sell these securities for? For money, gold or banknotes, in so far as the latter are legal tender, as those of the Bank of England are. What it advances, therefore, is in all circumstances money. If it advances gold, this is obvious. If notes, then these notes now represent capital, since the bank has parted with a real value in exchange, i.e. interest-bearing securities. In the case of the private banks, the notes that accrue to them by the sale of securities can only be, in the main, either notes of the Bank of England or its own notes, since others are only accepted with reticence in payment for securities. But if it is the Bank of England itself, then those of its own notes that it retains cost it capital, i.e. interest-bearing securities. Besides, it thereby withdraws its own notes from circulation. If it reissues these notes again or issues new notes to the same amount instead, these now represent capital. Moreover, they represent capital just as much when they are used for advances to capitalists as when they are used later, when the demand for this monetary accommodation subsides, for new investments in securities. In all these circumstances, the term capital is used here simply in the banking sense, where it means that the banker is forced to lend more than just his credit.

As is well known, the Bank of England makes all its advances in its own notes. If despite this, then, the Bank's note circulation normally decreases as the discounted bills and securities in its possession – i.e. the advances it has made – increase, what then becomes of the notes put into circulation, and how do they flow back to the Bank?

To start with, if the demand for monetary accommodation arises from an unfavourable national balance of payments and hence mediates a drain of gold, the matter is very simple. The banknotes are exchanged against gold at the Bank itself, in the Issue Department, and the gold is exported. It is the same as if the Bank paid gold directly, without the mediation of notes, as it does

in discounting bills of exchange. A rising demand of this kind –
and in certain cases it reaches £7 to £10 million – naturally adds
not a single £5 note to the country's domestic circulation. If it is
now said that the Bank advances capital in this case and not
currency, this has a double meaning. Firstly, that it does not
advance credit but real value, a part of its own capital or the capital
deposited with it. Secondly, that it advances money not for
domestic circulation but rather for international circulation,
world money. And for this purpose the money must always exist
in its hoard form, its metallic embodiment; in the form in which
it is not only the form of value but itself equal to the value whose
money form it is. Even though this gold now represents capital
both for the Bank and for the exporting gold dealer, banking
capital or commercial capital, the demand does not arise for it as
capital but rather as the absolute form of money capital. It arises
in the very same moment as the foreign markets are flooded with
unrealizable English commodity capital. What is demanded is not
capital as *capital* but rather capital as *money*, in the form in which
money is a commodity on the general world market; and this is
its original form as precious metal. The drain of gold is not, as
Fullarton, Tooke, etc. say, 'simply a question of capital'. It is
rather a 'question of money', even if in a specific function. The
fact that it is not a question of *domestic* circulation, as the Currency
Theory people maintain, in no way proves, as Fullarton and
others believe, that it is just a 'question of capital'. It is 'a question
of money', in the form in which money is an international means
of payment.

'Whether that capital' (the purchase price for the millions of
quarters of foreign wheat imported into the home country after a
harvest failure) 'is transmitted in merchandise or in specie, is a
point which in no way affects the nature of the transaction'
(Fullarton, op. cit., p. 131).

But it has a very definite effect on whether there is a drain of
gold or not. Capital is converted into the form of precious metal
because it cannot be converted at all into the form of commodities,
or not without a very major loss. The anxiety that the modern
banking system has when faced with a drain of gold goes beyond
anything that the Monetary System ever dreamed of, even though
for it precious metal was the only true wealth. Let us take for
example the following statement of the Governor of the Bank of

England, Morris, before the parliamentary committee investigating the crisis of 1847–8.

(3846. Question:) 'When I spoke of the depreciation of stocks and fixed capital, are you not aware that all property invested in stocks and produce of every description was depreciated in the same way; that raw cotton, raw silk, and unmanufactured wool were sent to the continent at the same depreciated price, and that sugar, coffee and tea were sacrificed as at forced sales? – It was inevitable that the country should make *a considerable sacrifice* for the purpose of meeting the *efflux of bullion* which had taken place in consequence of the large importation of food.' – '3848. Do not you think it would have been better to trench upon the £8 million lying in the coffers of the Bank, than to have endeavoured to get the gold back again at such a sacrifice? – *No, I do not.*'

Here gold is taken as the only true wealth.

Tooke's discovery as quoted by Fullarton, that 'with only one or two exceptions, and those admitting of satisfactory explanation, every remarkable fall of exchange, followed by a drain of gold, that has occurred during the last half-century, has been coincident throughout with a comparatively low state of the circulating medium, and vice versa' (Fullarton, p. 121), shows that these drains of gold take place in most cases after a period of excitement and speculation, as 'the signal of a collapse already commenced . . . an indication of overstocked markets, of a cessation of the foreign demand for our productions, of delayed returns, and, as the necessary sequel of all these, of commercial discredit, manufactories shut up, artisans starving, and a general stagnation of industry and enterprise' (p. 129).

This is also of course the best refutation of the Currency people's contention that 'a full circulation drives out bullion and a low circulation attracts it'.

On the other hand, however, although it is generally in periods of prosperity that the Bank of England has a strong gold reserve, this is always formed in the slack and stagnant period that follows the storm.

All this wisdom about the drain of gold, then, amounts to saying that the demand for *international* means of circulation and payment is different from the demand for *domestic* means of circulation and payment (which is why it goes without saying that 'the existence of a drain does not necessarily imply any diminution of the internal demand for circulation', as Fullarton says on p. 112); and that the export of precious metals abroad is not the same as putting notes or coin into circulation domestically. Moreover, I have already shown earlier that the movement of the hoard that is set aside as a reserve fund for international payments has in and of itself nothing to do with the movement of money as means of circulation.* However, there is a certain complication involved here, in so far as the different functions of the hoard which I developed from the nature of money – its function as a reserve fund of means of payment, for payments that fall due at home; as a reserve fund of circulating medium; finally as a reserve fund for world money – are all imposed upon a single reserve fund. From which it follows that in certain circumstances a drain of gold from the Bank domestically may be combined with a drain abroad. A still further complication arises from the additional function that is quite arbitrarily laid on this hoard, namely to serve as a guarantee for the convertibility of banknotes, in countries where the credit system and credit money are developed. On top of all this, finally, we have (1) the concentration of the national reserve fund in a single principal bank, and (2) its reduction to the minimum possible. Hence Fullarton's complaint (p. 143):

'One cannot contemplate the perfect silence and facility with which variations of the exchange usually pass off in continental countries, compared with the state of feverish disquiet and alarm always produced in England whenever the treasure at the Bank seems to be at all approaching to exhaustion, without being struck with the great advantage in this respect which a metallic currency possesses.'

But if we leave aside for now the drain of gold, how then can a bank that issues banknotes, such as the Bank of England, increase the amount of monetary accommodation it provides without increasing its note issue?

All notes outside the walls of the bank, whether they are actually circulating or are dormant in private hoards, are in circulation as far as the bank itself is concerned, i.e. outside its possession. Thus if the bank expands its discounting and money-lending business, its advances against securities, then the banknotes issued must flow back to it again or otherwise the sum in circulation would increase, which is precisely not supposed to be the case. This reflux can take place in two ways.

* See Volume 1, pp. 242–4.

Firstly, the bank pays notes to A against securities; A uses these to pay B for a bill of exchange that falls due; and B deposits the notes again with the bank. The circulation of these notes is at an end, but the loan remains.

('The loan remains, and the currency, if not wanted, finds its way back to the issuer': Fullarton, p. 97.)

The notes that the bank advanced to A have now returned to it; on the other hand the bank is a creditor to A or whoever has drawn the bill of exchange that A had discounted, while it is a debtor to B for the sum of value expressed in these notes, and B thereby has at his disposal a corresponding part of the bank's capital.

Secondly, A pays to B, and either B himself or C, the person to whom he again pays these notes, uses the notes to pay bills due to the bank, directly or indirectly. In this case the bank is paid with its own notes. And in this way the transaction is completed (until A's repayment to the bank).

How far, then, should the bank's advance to A be considered as an advance of capital, and how far as simply an advance of means of payment?[91]

(This depends on the nature of the advance itself. There are three cases to be considered.

First case. A obtains the sum advanced by the bank on his personal credit, without giving any security for it. In this case he has received not only an advance of means of payment, but unquestionably also a new capital, which he can use as additional capital in his business, and valorize, until it has to be repaid.

Second case. A has given the bank securities as collateral, whether government bonds or stocks, and received on them, say, a cash advance of up to two-thirds their present value. In this case he has received means of payment that he needed, but no additional capital, for he has given into the bank's possession a greater capital value than he received from it. But this greater capital value was on the one hand of no use for his immediate need, as means of payment, since it was invested at interest in a specific form; while on the other hand A had his reasons for not trans-

91. The passage now following was incomprehensible in the original manuscript and has been newly drafted by the editor, up to the end of the parentheses. This point has already been dealt with in a different context in Chapter 26 [pp. 557–9] – F. E.

forming it directly into means of payment by selling it. His securities had among other things the property of functioning as reserve capital, and he let them continue to function as such. There has therefore been a temporary mutual transfer of capital between A and the bank, so that A has not received any extra capital (on the contrary!), though he has received the means of payment he needed. For the bank, on the other hand, the transaction involves the temporary tying-up of money capital in a loan, a transformation of money capital from one form to another, and this transformation is precisely the basic function of banking.

Third case. A has a bill of exchange discounted at the bank and receives the amount due for it in cash, after deduction of the discount. In this case, he has sold a non-liquid form of money capital to the bank in exchange for the sum of value in liquid form; the bill of exchange that had not yet expired in return for ready cash. The bill is now the bank's property. It makes no difference at all that A, as the last endorser of the bill, is responsible for it to the bank in default of payment. He shares this responsibility with the other endorsers and with the drawer of the bill, all of whom are duly responsible to him. In this case, therefore, there is no advance at all, but simply an ordinary purchase and sale. A, therefore, has nothing to repay to the bank. The bank reimburses itself by cashing the bill when it falls due. Here, too, there has been a reciprocal transfer of capital between A and the bank, and this, moreover, is just like the purchase and sale of any other commodity; for this reason A does not receive any additional capital. What he needed and received was means of payment, and he receives this in that the bank transforms the one form of his money capital – the bill of exchange – into the other – money.

It is only in the first case, therefore, that there can be any talk of a genuine capital advance. In the second and third cases, it occurs at most in the sense that every investment of capital implies an 'advance'. In this sense, the bank advances A money capital; but for A this is money *capital* at most in the sense that it is a part of his capital in general. And he requires and uses it not especially as capital, but rather especially as means of payment. Otherwise every ordinary sale of commodities, by which means of payment are also obtained, would have to be seen as obtaining an advance of capital. – F. E.)

In the case of private banks with rights of note issue, the distinction is that, if their notes neither remain in local circulation nor return to the banks in the form of deposits or for payment of bills falling due, these notes then fall into the possession of people to whom they must pay gold or Bank of England notes in exchange for them. In this case the advance of their notes actually represents an advance of Bank of England notes, or, what is the same thing for them, of gold, i.e. a part of their banking capital. The same applies when the Bank of England itself, or any other bank which is subject to a legal maximum in its note issue, has to sell securities in order to withdraw its own notes from circulation and to issue them again in advances; here its own notes represent a part of its mobilizable banking capital.

Even if circulation were purely metallic, there could be at the same time (1) a drain of gold (what is meant here is evidently a drain of gold in which at least one part goes abroad – F. E.) that empties the vaults, while, (2) since the bank's principal requirement for gold is simply to make payments (to settle past transactions), its advances on securities could greatly increase, but return to it in the form of deposits or in repayment of bills falling due. So that on the one hand its overall reserves would decrease with an increase in securities in the bank's portfolio, while on the other hand the same sum that it formerly had as an owner would now be a sum for which it was in debt to its depositors, and finally the total quantity of circulating medium would decline.

It has so far been assumed that the advances are made in notes and involve at least a temporary increase in the note issue, even if this immediately vanishes again. But this is not necessary. Instead of paper notes, the bank can open a credit account for A, so that A, as its debtor, becomes an imaginary depositor. He pays his creditors with cheques on the bank, and the recipient of these cheques pays them again to his banker, who exchanges them in the clearing house against the cheques drawn on him. In this case there is no intervention of notes, and the entire transaction is confined to one in which the bank settles its own debt with a cheque drawn on itself, its actual compensation consisting in its claim against A. In this case the bank has advanced to A a part of its banking capital, in the form of a part of its own claim as a creditor.

In so far as this demand for monetary accommodation is a demand for capital, it is simply a demand for money capital, capital from the standpoint of the banker; i.e. a demand for gold (in the case of a drain of gold abroad) or for notes on the national bank, which a private bank can obtain only by buying them with an

equivalent, so that they represent capital for it. Or finally it might
be a question of interest-bearing securities, government bonds,
stocks, etc. that have to be sold if gold or notes are to be obtained.
These securities, however, if they are in government bonds, are
capital only for the person who has bought them, to whom they
represent his purchase price, the capital he has invested in them.
They are not capital in themselves, but simply creditor's claims;
if they are in mortgages, they are simply claims on future payments of ground-rent; and if they are stocks of some other kind,
they are simply property titles which give the holder a claim to
future surplus-value. None of these things are genuine capital,
they do not constitute any component of capital and are also in
themselves not values. By similar transactions, money that belongs
to the bank can be transformed into deposits, so that the bank
becomes a claimant for this money instead of its owner, and holds
it under a different title. Important as this is for the bank itself, it
in no way affects the amount of capital stored in the country, or
even the money capital. Capital figures here simply as money
capital and, if it is not present in the actual money form, as a mere
title to capital. This is very important, since the scarcity of, and
pressing demand for, *banking* capital is confused with a restriction
of *actual* capital, which in such cases, on the contrary, is present in
excess in the form of means of production and products, and
stifles the markets.

It is very simple to explain, therefore, how the amount of
securities held by the bank as collateral increases, and the growing
demand for monetary accommodation can be satisfied by the
bank, at the same time as the total quantity of means of circulation
remains the same or declines. In periods of tight money such as
these, moreover, this total quantity is kept in check in two ways:
(1) by a drain of gold; (2) by the demand for money simply as
means of payment, where the notes issued flow back immediately
or where the transaction takes place by way of book credit, without
any mediation of notes. In the latter case, payments are effected
simply by a credit transaction, the settlement of these payments
being the sole object of the exercise. It is money's peculiar property
that where it functions simply in settlement of payments (and in
times of crisis an advance is obtained in order to pay, not to buy;
to settle past transactions, not to start new ones), its actual
circulation is simply a vanishing magnitude, even when this
settlement does not take place entirely by credit operations, with-

out any intervention of money; i.e. that when there is a great demand for monetary accommodation, a tremendous mass of these transactions can take place without any expansion in the circulation. The simple fact that the Bank of England's circulation remains stable or even declines, at the same time as it performs a great deal of monetary accommodation, is in no way *prima facie* proof, as Fullarton, Tooke and others assume (in consequence of their error in seeing monetary accommodation as identical with the receipt of capital on loan, of additional capital), that the circulation of money (banknotes) in its function as means of payment does not increase and expand. Since the circulation of notes as means of purchase declines in times of business stagnation, where such a great deal of accommodation is required, their circulation as means of payment can increase while the total sum in circulation, the sum of notes functioning as means of purchase and of payment, still remains stable or even declines. Circulation of banknotes as means of payment, these notes immediately flowing back to the bank that issued them, is precisely not circulation in the eyes of these economists.

If circulation as means of payment increases to a higher degree than circulation as means of purchase declines, the total circulation will grow, even though the quantity of money functioning as means of purchase experiences a significant decline. And this actually does happen at certain points in the crisis, i.e. when there is a complete breakdown of credit, when not only are commodities and securities unsaleable, but it has also become impossible to get bills of exchange discounted, and nothing counts any more except money payment, or as the merchant says: cash. Since Fullarton and the others do not understand that the circulation of notes as means of payment is a characteristic of these times of monetary shortage, they treat this phenomenon as accidental.

'With respect again to those examples of eager competition for the possession of banknotes, which characterize seasons of panic and which may sometimes, as at the close of 1825, lead to a sudden, though only temporary, enlargement of the issues, even while the efflux of bullion is still going on, these, I apprehend, are not to be regarded as among the natural or necessary concomitants of a low exchange; the demand in such cases is not for circulation' (read circulation as a means of purchase), 'but for hoarding, a demand on the part of alarmed bankers and capitalists which arises generally in the last act of the crisis' (hence, for a reserve of means of payment), 'after a long continuation of the drain, and is the precursor of its termination' (Fullarton, p. 130).

We have already discussed in connection with our treatment of money as means of payment (Volume 1, Chapter 3, 3, b) how, in the case of a violent interruption in the chain of payments, money reverts from its merely ideal form into the material and also absolute form of value vis-à-vis commodities. A few examples of this were given there, in notes [51 and 52]. This interruption itself is in part the effect, in part the cause, of the collapse of credit and the circumstances that accompany it: flooding of markets, devaluation of commodities, interruption of production, etc.

It is clear, however, that Fullarton transforms the distinction between money as means of purchase and money as means of payment into a false distinction between currency and capital. And at the bottom of this again lies the narrow-minded banker's conception of circulation.

It might still be asked what is lacking in such difficult times, capital, or money in its capacity as means of payment? And this is a well-known controversy.

At first, in so far as the embarrassment is demonstrated by a drain of gold, it is clear that what is demanded is the international means of payment. But money in its capacity as international means of payment is gold in its metallic reality, as itself a valuable substance, an amount of value. It is also capital, but capital not as commodity capital but rather as money capital, capital not in the form of commodity but rather in the form of money (and moreover of money in the pre-eminent sense of the term, in which it exists on the general world commodity market). There is no opposition here between the demand for money as means of payment and the demand for capital. The opposition is rather between capital in its money form and in its commodity form; and the form in which it is required here, and can alone function, is its money form.

Apart from this demand for gold (or silver), it cannot be said that in such periods of crisis there is in any sense a lack of capital. Under extraordinary circumstances, such as a rise in grain prices, a cotton famine, etc., this can be the case; but these are in no way necessary or regular accompaniments of such periods; and the existence of such a lack of capital, therefore, cannot be immediately inferred from a demand for monetary accommodation. On the contrary. Markets are glutted, swamped with commodity capital. Hence it is in any case not a lack of *commodity* capital that gives rise to the difficulty. We shall return to this question later.

Chapter 29: Banking Capital's
Component Parts

We must now take a closer look at what banking capital consists of.

We have just seen how Fullarton and others transform the distinction between money as means of circulation and money as means of payment (also as world money, in so far as a drain of gold is involved) into a distinction between circulation ('currency') and capital.

The special role that capital plays here means that the amount of attention enlightened economics devoted to insisting that money was not capital is paralleled by this banker's economics, which tries just as assiduously to insist that money is actually capital *par excellence*.

In the further course of our investigations we shall show how money capital is confused in this context with 'moneyed capital' in the sense of interest-bearing capital, although money capital in the former sense is never more than a transitional form of capital as distinct from its other forms, i.e. commodity capital and productive capital.

Banking capital consists of (1) cash, in the form of gold or notes; (2) securities. These latter may again be divided into two parts: commercial paper, current bills of exchange that fall due on specified dates, their discounting being the specific business of the banker; and public securities such as government bonds, treasury bills and stocks of all kinds, in short interest-bearing paper, which is essentially different from bills of exchange. Mortgages, too, can be included in this category. The capital which has these as its tangible component parts can also be broken down into the banker's own invested capital, and the deposits that form his banking or borrowed capital. Notes must also be added here, in the case of banks which have the right to issue them. We shall leave these deposits and notes aside to start with. It is clear enough that the actual components of banker's capital – money, bills of exchange and interest-bearing paper – are not affected by whether these various elements represent his own capital, or deposits, the capital of other people. The subdivisions remain the same whether he pursues his business simply with his own capital or whether he conducts it entirely with capital which has been deposited with him.

The form of interest-bearing capital makes any definite and regular monetary revenue appear as the interest on a capital, whether it actually derives from a capital or not. The money income is first transformed into interest, and with the interest we then have the capital from which it derives. Likewise, with interest-bearing capital, any sum of value appears as capital as soon as it is not spent as revenue; i.e. as a 'principal' in contrast to the possible or actual interest it can bear.

The matter is simple. Say that the average rate of interest is 5 per cent per year. A sum of £500, then, if transformed into interest-bearing capital, would bring in a yearly £25. Hence every fixed annual income of £25 is seen as the interest on a capital of £500. Yet this is and remains a purely illusory notion, except in the case where the source of the £25, whether this is a mere title of ownership or claim, or whether it is an actual element of production, such as a piece of land for example, is directly transferable, or assumes a form in which it is transferable. Let us take the national debt and wages as examples.

The state has to pay its creditors a certain sum of interest each year for the capital it borrows. In this case the creditor cannot recall his capital from the debtor but can only sell the claim, his title of ownership. The capital itself has been consumed, spent by the state. It no longer exists. What the state's creditor possesses is (1) the state's promissory note for, say, £100; while (2) this note gives him a claim on the state's annual revenue, i.e. the proceeds of the year's taxation, to a certain amount, say £5 or 5 per cent; (3) he is free to sell this promissory note to anyone he likes. If the rate of interest is 5 per cent, and assuming the state's security is good, owner A can generally sell the note for £100 to B: since it is the same thing for B whether he lends out £100 at 5 per cent per year or assures himself of an annual tribute of £5 from the state by paying out £100. But in all these cases, the capital from which the state's payment is taken as deriving, as interest, is illusory and fictitious. It is not only that the sum that was lent to the state no longer has any kind of existence. It was never designed to be spent as capital, to be invested, and yet only by being invested as capital could it have been made into a self-maintaining value. As far as the original creditor A is concerned, the share of the annual taxation he receives represents interest on his capital, just as does the share of the wealth of the spendthrift that accrues to the money-lender, but in neither case has the sum of money lent been laid out as capital. The possibility of selling the state's promissory note represents for A the potential return of his principal. As far as B is concerned, from his own private standpoint his capital is then invested as interest-bearing capital. In actual fact, he has simply taken the place of A, and bought A's claim on the state. No matter how these transactions are multiplied, the capital of the national debt remains purely fictitious, and the moment these promissory notes become unsaleable, the illusion of this capital disappears. Yet this fictitious capital has its characteristic movement for all that, as we shall see soon.

Moving from the capital of the national debt, where a negative quantity appears as capital – interest-bearing capital always being the mother of every insane form, so that debts, for example, can appear as commodities in the mind of the banker – we shall now consider labour-power. Here wages are conceived as interest, and hence labour-power as capital that yields this interest. If the wage for a year comes to £50, say, and the rate of interest is 5 per cent, one annual labour-power is taken as equal to a capital of £1,000. Here the absurdity of the capitalist's way of conceiving things reaches its climax, in so far as instead of deriving the valorization of capital from the exploitation of labour-power, they explain the productivity of labour-power by declaring that labour-power itself is this mystical thing, interest-bearing capital. In the second half of the seventeenth century (with Petty, for example) this was a favourite notion, but it is still used today, in all seriousness, by vulgar economists and especially by German statisticians.[1] Unfortunately, however, two inconvenient circumstances militate

---

1. 'The worker has a capital value which is found by considering the monetary value of his annual service as a payment of interest ... If the average daily wage is capitalized at a rate of 4 per cent, we make the average value for an agricultural worker of the male sex to be 1,500 thalers in German Austria, 1,500 thalers in Prussia, 3,750 thalers in England, 2,000 thalers in France, and 750 thalers in Russia proper' (Von Reden, *Vergleichende Kulturstatistik* [Comparative Cultivation Statistics], Berlin, 1848, p. 434).

against this unthinking notion: first, the worker has to work in order to receive this interest, and second, he cannot turn the capital value of his labour-power into money by transferring it to someone else. Rather, the annual value of his labour-power is his average annual wage, and his labour has to replace its buyer with this value itself plus the surplus-value that is its valorization. Under the slave system the worker does have a capital value, namely his purchase price. And if he is hired out, the hirer must first pay the interest on this purchase price and on top of this replace the capital's annual depreciation.

The formation of fictitious capital is known as capitalization. Any regular periodic income can be capitalized by reckoning it up, on the basis of the average rate of interest, as the sum that a capital lent out at this interest rate would yield. For example, if the annual income in question is £100 and the rate of interest 5 per cent, then £100 is the annual interest on £2,000, and this £2,000 is then taken as the capital value of the legal ownership title to this annual £100. For the person who buys this ownership title, the annual £100 does actually represent the conversion of the capital he has invested into interest. In this way, all connection with the actual process of capital's valorization is lost, right down to the last trace, confirming the notion that capital is automatically valorized by its own powers.

Even when the promissory note – the security – does not represent a purely illusory capital, as it does in the case of national debts, the capital value of this security is still pure illusion. We have already seen how the credit system produces joint-stock capital. Securities purport to be ownership titles representing this capital. The shares in railway, mining, shipping companies, etc. represent real capital, i.e. capital invested and functioning in these enterprises, or the sum of money that was advanced by the shareholders to be spent in these enterprises as capital. It is in no way ruled out here that these shares may be simply a fraud. But the capital does not exist twice over, once as the capital value of the ownership titles, the shares, and then again as the capital actually invested or to be invested in the enterprises in question. It exists only in the latter form, and the share is nothing but an ownership title, *pro rata*, to the surplus-value which this capital is to realize. A may sell this title to B, and B to C. These transactions have no essential effect on the matter. A or B has then transformed his title into capital, but C has transformed his capital into a mere ownership title to the surplus-value expected from this share capital.

The independent movement of these ownership titles' values, not only those of government bonds, but also of shares, strengthens the illusion that they constitute real capital besides the capital or claim to which they may give title. They become commodities, their prices having a specific movement and being specifically set. Their market values receive a determination differing from their nominal values, without any change in the value of the actual capital (even if its valorization does change). On the one hand their market values fluctuate with the level and security of the receipts to which they give a legal title. If the nominal value of a share, i.e. the sum advanced which the share originally represents, is £100, and the enterprise yields 10 per cent instead of 5 per cent, its market value rises, other circumstances being equal, since, when capitalized at 5 per cent, it now represents a fictitious capital of £200. Someone who buys it for £200 gets a revenue of 5 per cent on his capital investment. The opposite is the case when the revenue from the enterprise declines. The market value of these securities is partly speculative, since it is determined not just by the actual revenue but rather by the anticipated revenue as reckoned in advance. But if we take the valorization of the actual capital to be constant, or, where no such capital exists, as in the case of national debts, if we take the annual yield to be fixed by law as well as sufficiently guaranteed, the prices of these securities rise and fall in inverse proportion to the rate of interest. If the interest rate rises from 5 per cent to 10 per cent, a security that ensures a yield of £5 now represents a capital of only £50. If the interest rate falls to $2\frac{1}{2}$ per cent, the same security represents a capital of £200. Its value is always simply the capitalized yield, i.e. the yield as reckoned on an illusory capital at the existing rate of interest. In times of pressure on the money market, therefore, these securities fall in price for two reasons: first, because the interest rate rises, and second, because they are put up for sale in massive quantities, to be converted into money. This fall in price occurs irrespective of whether the yield these securities ensure for their owner is constant, as in the case of government bonds, or whether the valorization of the real capital that they represent may be affected by the disturbance in the reproduction process, as in the case of industrial undertakings. In the latter case, we simply have a further devaluation besides that already mentioned. Once the storm is over, these securities rise again to their former level, in so far as the undertakings they represent have not come to grief and are not fraudulent. Their depreciation in a crisis is a powerful means of centralizing money wealth.[2]

In so far as the rise or fall in value of these securities is independent of the movement in the value of the real capital that they represent, the wealth of a nation is just as great afterwards as before.

'The public stocks and canal and railway shares had already by the 23rd of October, 1847, been depreciated in the aggregate to the amount of £114,752,225' (Morris, Governor of the Bank of England, evidence in the *Report on Commercial Distress*, 1847–8).

As long as their depreciation was not the expression of any standstill in production and in railway and canal traffic, or an abandonment of undertakings already begun, or a squandering of capital in positively worthless enterprises, the nation was not a penny poorer by the bursting of these soap bubbles of nominal money capital.

All these securities actually represent nothing but accumulated claims, legal titles, to future production. Their money or capital value either does not represent capital at all, as in the case of national debts, or is determined independently of the real capital value they represent.

In all countries of capitalist production, there is a tremendous amount of so-called interest-bearing capital or 'moneyed capital' in this form. And an accumulation of money capital means for the most part nothing more than an accumulation of these claims to production, and an accumulation of the market price of these claims, of their illusory capital value.

One portion of banker's capital is invested in these so-called interest-bearing securities. This is actually part of the reserve capital and does not function in the banking business proper. The most important portion consists of bills of exchange, i.e.

2. Directly after the February revolution [of 1848], when commodities and securities in Paris were extremely devalued and totally unsaleable, a Swiss merchant in Liverpool, Mr E. Zwilchenbart (who related this to my father), sold whatever he could for cash, travelled to Paris, and went to Rothschild with the proposal to do a joint deal. Rothschild stared at him fixedly and then rushed up to him and said, grasping him by both shoulders: '*Avez-vous de l'argent sur vous?*' – '*Oui, M. le baron.*' – '*Alors vous êtes mon homme!*' [Do you have money in your pocket?' – 'Yes, Baron'. – 'Then you're the man for me!' – And they both made a handsome profit. – F. E.

promises to pay issued by industrial capitalists or merchants. For the money-lender, these bills are interest-bearing paper; i.e. when he buys them, he deducts interest for the period that they still have to run. This is called discounting. The deduction from the face value of the bill thus depends on the rate of interest at the time.

The final portion of the banker's capital consists of his money reserve in gold or notes. Deposits, unless tied up for a longer period by contract, are always at the depositors' disposal. They are in a state of perpetual flux. But if some depositors withdraw their deposits, others replace them, so that the overall average fluctuates only a little in times of normal business.

The banks' reserve funds, in countries of developed capitalist production, always express the average amount of money existing as a hoard, and a part of this hoard itself consists of paper, mere drafts on gold, which have no value of their own. The greater part of banker's capital is therefore purely fictitious and consists of claims (bills of exchange) and shares (drafts on future revenues). It should not be forgotten here that this capital's money value, as represented by these papers in the banker's safe, is completely fictitious even in so far as they are drafts on certain assured revenues (as with government securities) or ownership titles to real capital (as with shares), their money value being determined differently from the value of the actual capital that they at least partially represent; or, where they represent only a claim to revenue and not capital at all, the claim to the same revenue is expressed in a constantly changing fictitious money capital. Added to this is the fact that this fictitious capital of the banker represents to a large extent not his own capital but rather that of the public who deposit with him, whether with interest or without.

Deposits are always made in money, gold or notes, or else in drafts on money. Except for the reserve fund, which contracts or expands according to the needs of actual circulation, these deposits are in fact always either in the hands of industrial capitalists and merchants, serving to discount their bills of exchange and make them advances; or else they are in the hands of dealers in securities (stockbrokers), private persons who have sold securities, or the government (in the case of treasury bills and new loans). The deposits themselves play a double role. On the one hand, as already mentioned, they are lent out as interest-bearing capital and are thus not to be found in the banks' safes, figuring instead in their books as credits held by the depositors. On the other hand, they function as mere book entries of this kind in so far as the reciprocal credits of the depositors are settled by cheques on their deposits and mutually cancelled; and it is completely immaterial in this connection whether the deposits are with the same banker, so that they can cancel the various accounts against one another, or whether they are with different banks, which exchange their cheques on one another and simply pay the balances.

With the development of interest-bearing capital and the credit system, all capital seems to be duplicated, and at some points triplicated, by the various ways in which the same capital, or even the same claim, appears in various hands in different guises.[3] The greater part of this 'money capital' is purely fictitious. With the exception of the reserve fund, deposits are never more than credits with the banker, and never exist as real deposits. In so far as they are used in clearing-house transactions, they function as capital for the bankers, after these latter have lent them out. The bankers pay one another reciprocal drafts on these non-existent deposits by balancing these credits against each other.

Adam Smith says of the role that capital plays in the lending of money: 'Even in the monied interest, however, the money is, as it were, but the deed of assignment, which conveys from one hand to another those capitals which the owners do not care to employ

3. This duplication and triplication of capital has been taken very much further in recent years, e.g. through the financial trusts, which already require a column of their own in the London stock-market reports. A company is formed for the purpose of purchasing a certain class of interest-bearing paper, for instance securities issued by foreign governments, English municipal loans, American public bonds, railway stocks, etc. The capital involved, say £2 million, is obtained by a share issue; the directors of the company buy up the values in question, or speculate in them more or less actively, and they distribute the annual interest received among the shareholders as dividends, after deducting expenses. In certain joint-stock companies, moreover, the custom has developed of dividing ordinary shares into two classes, 'preferred' and 'deferred'. Preferred shares receive a fixed interest payment, say 5 per cent, on condition that the overall profit permits this; if something remains over, this goes to the holders of the deferred shares. In this way, the more 'solid' capital investment in preferred shares is more or less separated from actual speculation, in deferred. Since certain large undertakings do not want to avail themselves of this new method, companies have come to be formed which invest a million pounds, say, or even a few million, in the shares of these firms, subsequently issuing new shares for the nominal value of the shares bought, but with one half preferred and the other deferred. In these cases the original shares are duplicated, by serving as the basis for a new share issue. – F. E.

themselves. Those capitals may be greater in almost any proportion than the amount of the money which serves as the instrument of their conveyance; the same pieces of money successively serving for many different loans, as well as for many different purchases. A, for example, lends to W a thousand pounds, with which W immediately purchases of B a thousand pounds' worth of goods. B, having no occasion for the money himself, lends the identical pieces to X, with which X immediately purchases of C another thousand pounds' worth of goods. C, in the same manner, and for the same reason, lends them to Y, who again purchases goods with them of D. In this manner the same pieces, either of coin or of paper, may, in the course of a few days, serve as the instrument of three different loans, and of three different purchases, each of which is, in value, equal to the whole amount of those pieces. What the three men, A, B and C, assign to the three borrowers, W, X and Y, is the power of making those purchases. In this power consist both the value and the use of the loans. The stock lent by the three monied men is equal to the value of the goods which can be purchased with it, and is three times greater than that of the money with which the purchases are made. Those loans, however, may be all perfectly well secured, the goods purchased by the different debtors being so employed, as, in due time, to bring back, with a profit, an equal value either of coin or of paper. And as the same pieces of money can thus serve as the instrument of different loans to three, or for the same reason, to thirty times their value, so they may likewise successively serve as the instrument of repayment' (Book II, Chapter IV [Pelican edition, p. 452]).

Since the same piece of money can make several different purchases, depending on the velocity of its circulation, it can equally be used for various different loans, for purchases move it from one hand to another, and a loan is simply a transfer from one hand to another that is not mediated by any sale. For each seller, the money represents the transformed form of his commodity; nowadays, when every commodity is expressed as a capital value, the money in its various loans successively represents different capitals, which is simply a different way of putting the previous statement that it can successively realize different commodity values. Money also serves, as a means of circulation, to transfer material capitals from one hand to another. In a loan, it is not transferred from one hand to another as a means of circulation. As long as it remains in the lender's possession, it is not a means of circulation in his hands but the value-existence of his capital. And it is in this form that he transfers it to someone else in a loan. If A had lent money to B, and B to C, without any purchases intervening, the same money would not represent three capitals but only one, just *one* capital value. How many capitals it actually does represent depends on how often it functions as the value form of various different commodity capitals.

What Adam Smith says about loans in general applies equally to deposits, this being simply a particular name for loans that the public make to the bankers. The same pieces of money can serve as instrument for any number of deposits.

'It is unquestionably true that the £1,000 which you deposit at A today may be reissued tomorrow, and form a deposit at B. The day after that, reissued from B, it may form a deposit at C . . . and so on to infinitude; and that the same £1,000 in money may, thus, by a succession of transfers, multiply itself into a sum of deposits absolutely indefinite. It is possible, therefore, that nine-tenths of all the deposits in the United Kingdom may have no existence beyond their record in the books of the bankers who are respectively accountable for them . . . Thus in Scotland, for instance, currency has never exceeded £3 million, the deposits in the banks are estimated at £27 million. Unless a run on the banks be made, the same £1,000 would, if sent back upon its travels, cancel with the same facility a sum equally indefinite. As the same £1,000, with which you cancel your debt to a tradesman today, may cancel his debt to the merchant tomorrow, the merchant's debt to the bank the day following, and so on without end; so the same £1,000 may pass from hand to hand, and bank to bank, and cancel any conceivable sum of deposits' (*The Currency Theory Reviewed*, pp. 62–3).

Just as everything in this credit system appears in duplicate and triplicate, and is transformed into a mere phantom of the mind, so this also happens to the 'reserve fund', where one might finally expect to lay hold of something solid.

Let us listen once more to Mr Morris, Governor of the Bank of England: 'The reserves of the private bankers are in the hands of the Bank of England in the shape of deposits . . . An export of gold acts exclusively, in the first instance, upon the reserve of the Bank of England; but it would also be acting upon the reserves of the bankers, in as much as it is a withdrawal of a portion of the reserves which they have in the Bank of England. It would be

acting upon the reserves of all the bankers throughout the country'
(*Commercial Distress*, 1847–8 [Nos. 3639, 3642]).

Ultimately, therefore, what these reserve funds actually boil
down to is the reserve fund of the Bank of England.[4] But this
reserve fund, too, has a double existence. The reserve fund of the
Banking Department is equal to the excess of notes that the Bank
is authorized to issue over the notes that are actually in circulation.
The legal maximum note issue is £14 million (the amount for
which no metal reserve is required, this being the approximate
sum of the government's debt to the Bank), plus the Bank's total
reserve of precious metal. So if this reserve is also £14 million, the
Bank can issue £28 million in notes, and if £20 million of these are

4. The extent to which this tendency has grown since Marx wrote is shown
by the following official tabulation of the reserves of the fifteen largest London
banks for November 1892, taken from the *Daily News* of 15 December:

Name of bank	Liabilities	Cash reserves	Percentages
City	£9,317,629	£746,551	8.01
Capital and Counties	11,392,744	1,307,483	11.47
Imperial	3,987,400	447,157	11.22
Lloyds	23,800,937	2,966,806	12.46
London and Westminster	24,671,559	3,818,885	15.50
London and S. Western	5,570,268	812,353	14.58
London Joint Stock	12,127,993	1,288,977	10.62
London and Midland	8,814,499	1,127,280	12.79
London and County	37,111,035	3,600,374	9.70
National	11,163,829	1,426,225	12.77
National Provincial	41,907,384	4,614,780	11.01
Parrs and the Alliance	12,794,489	1,532,707	11.98
Prescott and Co.	4,041,058	538,517	13.07
Union of London	15,502,618	2,300,084	14.84
Williams, Deacon and Manchester and Co.	10,452,381	1,317,628	12.60
Total	£232,655,823	£27,845,807	11.97

Of these reserves of almost £28 million, £25 million at the very least is
deposited with the Bank of England, leaving at most £3 million in the safes
of the fifteen banks themselves. But the bullion reserve of the Bank of England's
Banking Department, in the same month of November 1892, was never as
much as £16 million! – F. E.

already in circulation, the reserve fund of the Banking Department is £8 million. This £8 million in notes is then the legal banking capital that the Bank has at its disposal and at the same time the reserve fund for its deposits. Should a drain of gold take place, reducing the metal reserve by £6 million – for which an equal sum in notes has to be destroyed – the Banking Department's reserve falls from £8 million to £2 million. On the one hand, the Bank increases its interest rate very sharply; on the other hand, the banks which have deposited with it, as well as its other depositors, see the reserve fund for their own credits with the Bank take a sharp drop. In 1857, London's four largest joint-stock banks threatened that if the Bank of England did not obtain a 'government letter' suspending the Bank Act of 1844,[5] they would call in their deposits and bankrupt the Banking Department. Thus the Banking Department can fail to meet obligations, as in 1847, while there are still several millions in the Issue Department (e.g. £8 million in 1847), as guarantee for the convertibility of notes in circulation. Though this is in turn an illusion.

'That large portion (of deposits) for which the bankers themselves have no immediate demand passes into the hands of the billbrokers, who give to the banker in return commercial bills already discounted by them for persons in London and in different parts of the country as a security for the sum advanced by the banker. The billbroker is responsible to the banker for payment of this money at call; and such is the magnitude of these transactions, that Mr Neave, the present Governor of the Bank [of England], stated in evidence, "We know that one broker had 5 million, and we were led to believe that another had between 8 and 10 million; there was one with 4, another with $3\frac{1}{2}$, and a third with above 8. I speak of deposits with the brokers"' (*Report of Committee on Bank Acts*, 1857–8, p. 5, Section 8).

'The London billbrokers carried on their enormous transactions without any cash reserve, relying on the run off of their bills falling due, or in extremity, on the power of obtaining advances from the Bank of England on the security of bills under discount. Two billbroking houses in London suspended payment in 1847; both

5. The suspension of the 1844 Bank Act enables the Bank to issue an unlimited sum of banknotes, irrespective of the extent to which these are covered by its gold reserve; i.e. to create an unlimited amount of fictitious, paper money capital and use this to make advances to the banks and billbrokers, and through them to the world of commerce. – F.E.

afterwards resumed business. In 1857, both suspended again. The liabilities of one house in 1847 were, in round numbers, £2,683,000, with a capital of £180,000; the liabilities of the same house, in 1857, were £5,300,000, the capital probably not more than one-fourth of what it was in 1847. The liabilities of the other firm were between £3,000,000 and £4,000,000 at each period of stoppage, with a capital not exceeding £45,000' (ibid., p. xxi, section 52).

Chapter 30: Money Capital and Real Capital: I

The only difficult questions which we are now coming on to in connection with the credit system are as follows.

Firstly, the accumulation of money capital as such. How far is it, and how far is it not, an index of genuine capital accumulation, i.e. of reproduction on an expanded scale? Is the phenomenon of a 'plethora' of capital, an expression used only of interest-bearing capital, i.e. money capital, simply a particular expression of industrial overproduction, or does it form a separate phenomenon alongside this? Does such a plethora, an over-supply of money capital, coincide with the presence of stagnant sums of money (bullion, gold coin and banknotes), so that this excess of actual money is an expression and form of appearance of this plethora of loan capital?

And *secondly*, to what extent does monetary scarcity, i.e. a shortage of loan capital, express a lack of real capital (commodity capital and productive capital)? To what extent, on the other hand, does it coincide with a lack of money as such, a lack of means of circulation?

In as much as we have so far considered the specific form of accumulation of money capital, and of money wealth in general, this reduces itself to the accumulation of proprietary claims to labour. Accumulation of capital in the form of the national debt, as we have shown, means nothing more than the growth of a class of state creditors with a preferential claim to certain sums from the overall proceeds of taxation.[6] In the way that even an accumu-

6. 'Government bonds are no more than imaginary capital, representing the portion of annual revenue destined for the payment of debts. A capital of equal size has been frittered away; this gives the loan its denomination, but it is not what the government bond represents, for the capital no longer exists in any form. In the meantime, new wealth must arise from the labour of industry; an annual part of this wealth is assigned in advance to those who

lation of debts can appear as an accumulation of capital, we see the distortion involved in the credit system reach its culmination. These promissory notes which were issued for a capital originally borrowed but long since spent, these paper duplicates of annihilated capital, function for their owners as capital in so far as they are saleable commodities and can therefore be transformed back into capital.

As we have seen, the ownership titles to joint-stock companies, railways, mines, etc. are genuinely titles to real capital. Yet they give no control over this capital. The capital cannot be withdrawn. They give only a legal claim to a share of the surplus-value that this capital is to produce. But these titles similarly become paper duplicates of the real capital, as if a bill of lading simultaneously acquired a value alongside the cargo it refers to. They become nominal representatives of non-existent capitals. For the actual capital exists as well, and in no way changes hands when these duplicates are bought and sold. They become forms of interest-bearing capital because not only do they assure certain revenues but the capital values invested in them can also be repaid by their sale. In so far as the accumulation of these securities expresses an accumulation of railways, mines, steamships, etc., it expresses an expansion of the actual reproduction process, just as the expansion of a tax list on personal property, for example, indicates an expansion of this property itself. But as duplicates that can themselves be exchanged as commodities, and hence circulate as capital values, they are illusory, and their values can rise and fall quite independently of the movement in value of the actual capital to which they are titles. Their values, i.e. their listings on the stock exchange, have a necessary tendency to rise with the fall in the rate of interest, in so far as this is a simple result of the tendential

---

lent the wealth that was squandered. This part is taken in taxes from those who produce wealth, and given to the state's creditors, while the customary ratio in the country between capital and interest forms the basis for assuming an imaginary capital, of sufficient size to yield the annual interest that the creditors have to receive' (Sismondi, *Nouveaux Principes*, II, pp. 229, 230).*

* J.-C.-L. Simonde de Sismondi (1773–1842) was a Swiss economist and historian. Contemporary with the utopian socialists, he also criticized certain of the contradictions of the developing capitalist society, but this was from the restricted standpoint of the petty bourgeoisie; Sismondi idealized petty commodity production. See Marx's Postface to the Second German Edition of *Capital* Volume 1, p. 96.

fall in the rate of profit, independent of the specific movements of money capital, so that this imaginary wealth, which according to its value expression gives each person his aliquot share of a definite original nominal value, already expands for this reason as capitalist production develops.[7]

Profits and losses that result from fluctuations in the price of these ownership titles, and also their centralization in the hands of railway magnates etc., are by the nature of the case more and more the result of gambling, which now appears in place of labour as the original source of capital ownership, as well as taking the place of brute force. This kind of imaginary money wealth makes up a very considerable part not only of the money wealth of private individuals but also of banking capital, as already mentioned.

One point which we mention here only to get it quickly out of the way is that the accumulation of money capital might also be taken to mean the accumulation of wealth in the hands of bankers (money-lenders by profession), as intermediaries between the private money capitalists on the one hand, and the state, local authorities and borrowers engaged in the process of reproduction on the other; for the entire immense extension of the credit system, and credit as a whole, is exploited by the bankers as their private capital. These fellows have their capital and revenue permanently in the money form or in the form of direct claims to money. The accumulation of wealth by this class may proceed in a very different way from that of actual accumulation, but it proves in any case that they put away a good proportion of the latter.

To reduce the question at issue here to narrower limits. Government bonds, shares and other securities of all kinds are all spheres of investment for loanable capital, for capital that is designed to be interest-bearing. They are forms for lending it out. But they are not themselves the loanable capital that is invested in them. On the other hand, in so far as credit plays a direct role in the reproduction process, what the industrialist or merchant needs when he wants to have bills discounted or take out a loan is neither shares

7. One part of the accumulated money capital for loan is in actual fact simply the expression of industrial capital. If England invested, say, £80 million in American railways and other undertakings in 1857, this investment was effected almost entirely through the supply of English goods for which the Americans did not have to make any return payment. The English exporter drew bills on America against the goods, and these bills were purchased by English subscribers who sent them to America in payment for their shares.

nor government stock. What he needs is money. That is why he pledges or sells these securities if he cannot obtain money in any other way. It is *this* accumulation of loan capital that we have to deal with here, and, moreover, the accumulation of loanable money capital in particular. What is involved here is not the lending of houses, machines or other fixed capital. Nor is it the advances that industrialists and merchants make to one another in commodities within the ambit of the reproduction process, although we shall also have to investigate that point in more detail. What we are concerned with here is exclusively the monetary loans that the bankers, as intermediaries, make to the industrialists and merchants.

*

We shall therefore start by analysing commercial credit, i.e. the credit that capitalists involved in the reproduction process give one another. This forms the basis of the credit system. Its representative is the bill of exchange, a promissory note with a fixed date of payment, a 'document of deferred payment'. Each person gives credit in one direction and receives credit from another. We shall start by completely ignoring banker's credit, which is an entirely separate and essentially different element. In so far as these bills of exchange continue to circulate among the merchants themselves as means of payment, by endorsement from one to another, but without the intervention of any discounting, all that happens is a transfer of the claim from A to B, and absolutely nothing in the relationship is changed. One person simply takes the place of another. Say that spinner A has to pay a bill to cotton-broker B, and the latter to importer C. If C also exports yarn, which happens frequently enough, he can buy yarn from A against a bill of exchange, and spinner A can settle with broker B with the latter's own bill of exchange, which C received in payment. In this case it is at most a balance that remains to be paid in the form of money. The entire transaction then simply mediates the exchange of cotton and yarn. The exporter simply represents the spinner and the cotton-broker the cotton planter.

Two things should be noted about this circuit of purely commercial credit.

Firstly, the settlement of these reciprocal claims depends on the reflux of the capital; i.e. *C–M*, which is simply delayed. If the spinner has received a bill from a manufacturer of cotton goods, the manufacturer is able to pay when the goods he has on the market have meanwhile been sold. If the speculator in corn has given a bill of exchange on his factor, the factor is able to pay the money after the corn has been sold at the expected price. These payments thus depend on the fluidity of reproduction, i.e. of the production and consumption process. But since the credits are reciprocal, the ability of each person to pay depends at the same time on the ability of another to pay; for, when drawing a bill, the drawee can have counted either on the return of capital in his own business or on a return in the business of a third party who has to pay him a bill in the intervening period. Apart from the prospective return, payment is possible only by means of reserve capital which the person drawing the bill has at his disposal, in order to meet his obligations in case returns are delayed.

Secondly, this credit system does not obviate the need for cash payments. For a start, a large proportion of expenses must always be paid in cash – wages, taxes, etc. But if for example B, who accepts a bill from C in lieu of immediate payment, has himself to pay a bill that falls due to D before the former bill falls due to him, he must also have cash for this. A complete circuit of reproduction such as was assumed above, from the cotton planter to the cotton spinner and vice versa, can only be an exception, and must always be broken in several places. We have seen in connection with the reproduction process (Volume 2, Part Three [pp. 498–501]) how the producers of constant capital exchange part of their constant capital with one another. In this case, the bills may more or less balance. The same thing happens when production is on an ascending curve, and the cotton broker draws on the spinner, the spinner on the cotton-goods manufacturer, the latter on the exporter, and he on the importer (perhaps again an importer of cotton). But the circuit of transactions and consequent doubling back of the series of claims are not one and the same thing. The spinner's claim on the weaver, for example, is not settled by the claim of the coal supplier on the machine-builder; the spinner never makes counter-claims on the machine-builder in the course of his business, since his product, yarn, never becomes an element in the machine-builder's reproduction process. Claims of this kind must therefore be settled in money.

The limits of this commercial credit, considered by itself, are (1) the wealth of the industrialists and merchants, i.e. the reserve capital at their disposal in case of a delay in returns; (2) these returns themselves. They may be delayed in time, or commodity prices may fall in the meantime, or again the commodities may temporarily become unsaleable as a result of a glut on the market. The longer bills run for, the greater the reserve capital needed and the greater the possibility that returns may be diminished or delayed as a result of a fall in price or an excess of supply on the market. Returns are that much less certain, moreover, the more the original transaction was inspired by speculation on a rise or fall in commodity prices. It is clear, however, that with the development of labour productivity and hence of production on a large scale, (1) markets expand and become further removed from the point of production, (2) credit must consequently be prolonged, and (3) as a result, the speculative element must come more and more to dominate transactions. Large-scale production for distant markets casts the entire product into the arms of commerce; but it is impossible for the nation's capital to double, so that commerce would purchase the entire national product with its own capital before selling it again. Credit is thus indispensable here, a credit that grows in volume with the growing value of production and grows in duration with the increasing distance of the markets. A reciprocal effect takes place here. The development of the production process expands credit, while credit in turn leads to an expansion of industrial and commercial operations.

If we consider this credit in separation from banker's credit, it is evident that it grows with the scale of industrial capital itself. Loan capital and industrial capital are identical here; the capitals loaned are commodity capitals designed either for final individual consumption or to replace constant elements of productive capital. So what appears here as loaned capital is always capital that exists in a certain phase of the reproduction process, but is transferred from one hand to another by purchase and sale while the equivalent for it is paid by the buyer only later, after the stipulated interval. Cotton, for instance, is transferred to the spinner against a bill of exchange, yarn to the merchant against a bill of exchange, from the merchant to the exporter against a bill of exchange, from the exporter to a merchant in India, again against a bill of exchange, the merchant selling it and buying indigo, and so on. During this transfer from one hand to another, the cotton is undergoing its transformation into finished goods, and these goods are ultimately shipped to India and exchanged for indigo, which is shipped to Europe and goes into the reproduction process once again. The different phases of reproduction are mediated here by credit. The spinner has not paid for the cotton, nor the cotton-goods manufacturer for the yarn, nor the merchant for the cotton goods, etc. In the first acts of the process, the commodity, cotton, goes through its various phases of production, and its transfer is mediated by credit. But once the cotton has received its final form as a commodity in the course of production, the same commodity capital still has to go through the hands of various merchants, who effect its transport to a distant market and buy other commodities in exchange, these going either into consumption or into the reproduction process. There are thus two sections to be distinguished here: in the first section credit mediates the actual successive phases in the production of the article in question; in the second, it simply mediates the transfer from the hands of one merchant to those of another, which includes transport – the act *C–M*. But here, too, at least the commodity is permanently engaged in the act of circulation, i.e. in a phase of the reproduction process.

What is loaned here, therefore, is never unoccupied capital but rather capital that must change its form in the hands of its owner, that exists in a form in which it is simply commodity capital for him, i.e. capital that must be transformed back and in the first instance at least converted into money. Thus it is the metamorphosis of the commodity that is mediated here by way of credit; not only *C–M*, but also *M–C* and the actual production process. A great deal of credit in the reproduction circuit – leaving aside banker's credit – does not mean a great deal of unoccupied capital which is offered for loan and seeks profitable investment, but rather a high level of employment of capital in the reproduction process. What credit mediates here is therefore (1) as far as the industrial capitalists are concerned, the transition of industrial capital from one phase to another, the connection of spheres of production that belong together and mesh into one another; (2) as far as the merchants are concerned, the transport and transfer of commodities from one hand to another until their definitive sale for money or their exchange with another commodity.

The maximum of credit is the same thing here as the fullest employment of industrial capital, i.e. the utmost taxing of its reproductive power irrespective of the limits of consumption. These limits to consumption are extended by the stretching of the reproduction process itself; on the one hand this increases the consumption of revenue by workers and capitalists, while on the other it is itself identical with the stretching of productive consumption.

As long as the reproduction process is fluid, so that returns remain assured, this credit persists and extends, and its extension is based on the extension of the reproduction process itself. As soon as any stagnation occurs, as a result of delayed returns, overstocked markets or fallen prices, there is a surplus of industrial capital, but in a form in which it cannot accomplish its function. A great deal of commodity capital; but unsaleable. A great deal of fixed capital; but in large measure unemployed as a result of the stagnation in reproduction. Credit contracts, (1) because this capital is unoccupied, i.e. congealed in one of its phases of reproduction, because it cannot complete its metamorphosis; (2) because confidence in the fluidity of the reproduction process is broken; (3) because the demand for this commercial credit declines. The spinner who restricts his production and has a lot of unsold yarn in store does not need to buy cotton on credit; the merchant does not need to buy any goods on credit, as he already has more than enough.

So if there is a disturbance in this expansion, or even in the normal exertion of the reproduction process, there is also a lack of credit; it is more difficult to obtain goods on credit. The demand for cash payment and distrust of credit selling is especially characteristic of the phase in the industrial cycle that follows the crash. In the crisis itself, since everyone has goods to sell and cannot sell, even though they have to sell in order to pay, the quantity of capital blocked in its reproduction process, though not of unoccupied capital to be invested, is precisely at its greatest, even if the lack of credit is also most acute (and hence, as far as bank credit goes, the discount rate at its highest). Capital already invested is in fact massively unemployed, since the reproduction process is stagnant. Factories stand idle, raw materials pile up, finished products flood the market as commodities. Nothing could be more wrong, therefore, than to ascribe such a situation to a lack of productive capital. It is precisely then that there is a surplus of productive capital, partly in relation to the normal though temporarily contracted scale of reproduction and partly in relation to the crippled consumption.

Let us conceive the whole society as composed simply of industrial capitalists and wage-labourers. Let us also leave aside those changes in price which prevent large portions of the total capital from being replaced in their average proportions, and which, in the overall context of the reproduction process as a whole, particularly as developed by credit, must recurrently bring about a situation of general stagnation. Let us likewise ignore the fraudulent businesses and speculative dealings that the credit system fosters. In this case, a crisis would be explicable only in terms of a disproportion in production between different branches and a disproportion between the consumption of the capitalists themselves and their accumulation. But as things actually are, the replacement of the capitals invested in production depends to a large extent on the consumption capacity of the non-productive classes; while the consumption capacity of the workers is restricted partly by the laws governing wages and partly by the fact that they are employed only as long as they can be employed at a profit for the capitalist class. The ultimate reason for all real crises always remains the poverty and restricted consumption of the masses, in the face of the drive of capitalist production to develop the productive forces as if only the absolute consumption capacity of society set a limit to them.

The only case in which we can speak of a genuine lack of productive capital, at least in the case of developed capitalist countries, is that of a general harvest failure, affecting either the staple foodstuffs or the principal raw materials for industry.

But on top of this commercial credit we also have monetary credit proper. Advances between industrialists and merchants fuse together with the advancing of money to them by bankers and money-lenders. In the discounting of bills of exchange, the advance is purely nominal. A manufacturer sells his product for a bill of exchange and discounts this bill with a billbroker. But in actual fact the latter only advances his banker's credit, and the banker in turn advances the money capital of his depositors, who consist of the industrialists and merchants themselves, though also including workers (by means of savings banks) as well as landlords and other unproductive classes. As far as each individual manufacturer or merchant is concerned, then, both the need for a strong reserve capital and dependence on actual returns are dispensed with. On the other hand, however, this is so much complicated by simple bill-jobbing, and by dealing in commodities with no other purpose than that of fabricating bills of exchange, that the appearance of very solid business with brisk returns can merrily persist even when returns have in actual fact long since been made only at the cost of swindled money-lenders and swindled producers. This is why business always seems almost exaggeratedly healthy immediately before a collapse. The best proof of this is provided by the *Reports on Bank Acts* of 1857 and 1858, for example, in which bank directors, merchants, in short a whole series of experts summoned to give evidence, with Lord Overstone at their head, all congratulated one another on the blooming and healthy state of business – just one month before the crisis broke out in August 1857. It is particularly striking how Tooke, as the historian of all these crises, falls victim to the illusion once again in his *History of Prices*. Business is always thoroughly sound, and the campaign in fullest swing, until the sudden intervention of the collapse.

*

We return now to the accumulation of money capital.

Not every increase in money capital for loan is an index of genuine capital accumulation or an expansion of the reproduction process. This is shown most clearly in the phase of the industrial cycle immediately after the crisis, when loan capital lies idle on a massive scale. At these moments, when the production process has undergone a contraction (and after the crisis of 1847, production in the English industrial districts was cut by a third), when commodity prices stand at their lowest point, and when the entrepreneurial spirit is crippled, there is a low rate of interest, which in this case simply indicates an increase in loanable capital precisely as a result of the contraction and paralysis of industrial capital. It is obvious enough that less means of circulation are required with lower commodity prices, fewer dealings and a contraction in the capital laid out on wages; that after the settlement of debts abroad, partly by a drain of gold and partly by bankruptcies, no additional money is required to carry out the function of world money; and finally that the scale of the discount business also declines with the number and amount of bills of exchange to be discounted. The demand for loanable money capital therefore declines, both for means of circulation and for means of payment (there is no question yet of new capital investment), so that this capital becomes relatively abundant. But the supply of loanable money capital also undergoes a positive increase in conditions such as these, as we shall show later on.

After the crisis of 1847, for example, there was 'a limitation of transactions and a great superabundance of money' (*Commercial*

Distress, 1847–8, Evidence, no. 1664). The rate of interest was very low on account of the 'almost perfect destruction of commerce and the almost total want of means of employing money' (ibid., p. 45, evidence of Hodgson, Director of the Royal Bank of Liverpool). The nonsense that these gentlemen concocted to explain the situation (and Hodgson, moreover, is one of the best of them) can be seen from the following sentence: 'The pressure' (1847) 'arose from the real diminution of the moneyed capital of the country, caused partly by the necessity of paying in gold for imports from all parts of the world, and partly by the absorption of floating into fixed capital.'

We are not told how the absorption of floating capital into fixed is supposed to reduce the money capital in a country. In the case of railways, for example, which were the principal sphere of investment for capital at that time, no gold or paper is used to make viaducts and rails, and the money for railway shares, in so far as it is deposited simply for payments, functions just like all other money deposited with the banks, and even temporarily increases the loanable money capital, as we have already shown; to the extent that it is actually spent on construction, it circulates in the country as means of purchase and payment. It is only in so far as fixed capital is not exportable, i.e. in so far as its export is actually impossible, so that no capital is obtained by way of returns for articles exported, including returns in cash or bullion, that the money capital can be affected. But English export goods, too, were at that time stockpiled and unsaleable on a massive scale in foreign markets. For the merchants and manufacturers in Manchester, etc. who had tied up a part of their normal working capital in railway shares and were therefore dependent on borrowed capital to conduct their business, their floating capital really had been fixed, and they had to bear the consequences of this. But it would have been the same thing if they had invested the capital that rightly belonged to their business, but had been withdrawn, in mines, for example, instead of in railways, even though the products of mining are floating capital again themselves – iron, coal, copper, etc. The real reduction in available money capital as a result of harvest failure, the import of corn and export of gold, was of course an occurrence that had nothing to do with the railway swindle.

'Almost all mercantile houses had begun to starve their business more or less ... by taking part of their commercial capital for railways.' – 'Loans to so great an extent by commercial houses to railways induced them to lean too much upon . . . banks by the discount of paper, whereby to carry on their commercial operations' (the same Hodgson, op. cit., p. 67). 'In Manchester there have been immense losses in consequence of the speculation in railways' (R. Gardner, the man quoted previously in Volume 1, Chapter 15, 3, c [pp. 535–6], and in several other places; Evidence, no. 4884, op. cit.).

One major cause of the 1847 crisis was the colossal saturation of the market and the boundless fraud in the East Indian trade. Other factors, too, however, contributed to the downfall of very wealthy firms in this sector. 'They had large means, but not available. The whole of their capital was locked up in estates in the Mauritius, or indigo factories, or sugar factories. Having incurred liabilities to the extent of £500,000–600,000, they had no available assets to pay their bills, and eventually it proved that to pay their bills they were entirely dependent upon their credit' (Charles Turner, big East India merchant in Liverpool, no. 730, op. cit.).

Gardner, too (no. 4872, op. cit.): 'Immediately after the China treaty, so great a prospect was held out to the country of a great extension of our commerce with China, that there were many large mills built with a view to that trade exclusively, in order to manufacture that class of cloth which is principally taken for the China market, and our previous manufactures had the addition of all those.' – '4874. How has that trade turned out? – Most ruinous, almost beyond description; I do not believe, that of the whole of the shipments that were made in 1844 and 1845 to China, above two-thirds of the amount have ever been returned; in consequence of tea being the principal article of repayment and of the expectation that was held out, we, as manufacturers, fully calculated upon a great reduction in the duty on tea.'

Then we have the characteristic credo of the English manufacturer, in a naïve version: 'Our commerce with no foreign market is limited by their power to purchase the commodity, but it is limited in this country by our capability of consuming that which we receive in return for our manufactures.'

(The relatively poor countries with which England trades can of course pay for and consume any amount of English manufactures, but unfortunately rich England cannot assimilate the products sent in return.)

'4876. I sent out some goods in the first instance, and the goods sold at about 15 per cent loss, from the full conviction that the price, at which my agents could purchase tea, would leave so great a profit in this country as to make up the deficiency ... but instead of profit, I lost in some instances 25 and up to 50 per cent.' – '4877. Did the manufacturers generally export on their own account? – Principally; the merchants, I think, very soon saw that the thing would not answer, and they rather encouraged the manufacturers to consign than take a direct interest themselves.'

In 1857, on the other hand, the losses and bankruptcies fell principally on the merchants, as this time the manufacturers left them with the task of flooding the foreign markets 'on their own account'.

*

An expansion of money capital arising from the fact that, as a result of the spread of banking (see the example of the Ipswich bank, below, where, in the few years immediately prior to 1857, the farmers' deposits rose four times over), what was formerly a private hoard or a reserve of coin is now always transformed for a certain period into loanable capital, no more expresses a growth in productive capital than did the growing deposits in the London joint-stock banks once these began to pay interest on deposits. As long as the scale of production remains the same, this expansion simply gives rise to an abundance of loanable money capital as compared with productive capital. Hence a low rate of interest.

If the reproduction process has reached the flourishing stage that precedes that of over-exertion, commercial credit undergoes a very great expansion, this in turn actually forming the 'healthy' basis for a ready flow of returns and an expansion of production. In this situation, the rate of interest is still low, even if it has risen above its minimum. This is actually the *only* point in time at which it may be said that a low rate of interest, and hence a relative abundance of loanable capital, coincides with an actual expansion of industrial capital. The ease and regularity of returns, combined with an expanded commercial credit, ensures the supply of loan capital despite the increased demand and prevents the interest level from rising. This is also the point when jobbers first enter the picture on a notable scale, operating without reserve capital or even without capital at all, i.e. completely on money credit. Added to this too is a great expansion of fixed capital in all forms and the opening of large numbers of new and far-reaching undertakings. Interest now rises to its average level. It reaches its maximum again as soon as the new crisis breaks out, credit suddenly dries up, payments congeal, the reproduction process is paralysed and, save for the exceptions mentioned earlier, there is an almost absolute lack of loan capital alongside a surplus of unoccupied industrial capital.

By and large, therefore, the movement of loan capital, as expressed in the rate of interest, runs in the opposite direction to that of industrial capital. The phase in which the low but above minimum rate of interest coincides with the 'improvement' and growing confidence after the crisis, and particularly the phase in which it reaches its average level, the mid-point equidistant between its minimum and maximum – only these two phases show a combination of abundant loan capital and a big expansion in industrial capital. At the beginning of the industrial cycle, however, a low rate of interest coincides with a contraction of industrial capital, and at the end of the cycle a high rate of interest coincides with an over-abundance of industrial capital. The low rate of interest that accompanies the 'improvement' phase expresses the fact that commercial credit only needs a small amount of bank credit, since it still stands on its own two feet.

This industrial cycle is such that the same circuit must periodically reproduce itself, once the first impulse has been given.[8] In

8. As I have already noted elsewhere,* the last great general crisis represented a turning-point. The acute form of the periodic process with its former ten-year cycle seems to have given way to a more chronic and drawn-out alternation, affecting the various industrial countries at different times, between a relatively short and weak improvement in trade and a relatively long and indecisive depression. Perhaps what is involved is simply an extension of the cycle's duration. When world trade was in its infancy, 1815–47, cycles of approximately five years could be discerned; between 1847 and 1867 the cycle was definitely a ten-year one; might we now be in the preparatory phase of a new world crash of unheard-of severity? Many things seem to point this way. Since the last general crisis of 1867, great changes have occurred. The colossal expansion of means of communication – ocean-going steamships, railways, electric telegraphs, the Suez canal – has genuinely established the world market for the first time. Alongside England, which formerly had a monopoly of industry, we have a whole series of competing industrial countries; the investment of surplus European capital in all parts of the globe is infinitely greater and more widespread, so that this is far more broadly distributed and local over-speculation is more easily overcome. All these things mean that most of the former breeding-grounds of crises and occasions for crisis formation have been abolished or severely weakened. Competition in the home market is

the slack phase, production falls below the level it attained in the previous cycle and for which the technical basis is now laid. In the phase of prosperity – the middle period – it develops further on this basis. In the period of overproduction and swindling, the productive forces are stretched to their limit, even beyond the capitalist barriers to the production process.

The reason for the lack of means of payment in the crisis period is self-evident. The convertibility of bills of exchange has replaced the metamorphosis of the actual commodities, and all the more so at such a time in so far as one group of firms is operating purely on credit. Ignorant and confused banking laws, such as those of 1844–5, may intensify the monetary crisis. But no bank legislation can abolish crises themselves.

In a system of production where the entire interconnection of the reproduction process rests on credit, a crisis must evidently break out if credit is suddenly withdrawn and only cash payment is accepted, in the form of a violent scramble for means of payment. At first glance, therefore, the entire crisis presents itself as simply a credit and monetary crisis. And in fact all it does involve is simply the convertibility of bills of exchange into money. The majority of these bills represent actual purchases and sales, the ultimate basis of the entire crisis being the expansion of these far beyond the social need. On top of this, however, a tremendous number of these bills represent purely fraudulent deals, which now come to light and explode; as well as unsuccessful speculations conducted with borrowed capital, and finally commodity capitals that are either devalued or unsaleable, or returns that are never going to come in. It is clear that this entire artificial system of forced expansion of the reproduction process cannot be cured by now allowing one bank, e.g. the Bank of England, to give all the swindlers the capital they lack in paper money and to buy all the depreciated commodities at their old nominal values. Moreover,

---

also retreating in the face of the cartels and trusts, while on the foreign market it is restricted by the customs tariffs with which all major industrial countries except England surround themselves. But these tariffs themselves are nothing less than the weapons for the final general industrial campaign to decide supremacy on the world market. And so each of the elements that counteracts a repetition of the old crises, conceals within it the nucleus of a far more violent future crisis. – F. E.

* *Capital* Volume 1, Preface to the English edition, Pelican edition, p. 113.

everything here appears upside down, since in this paper world the real price and its real elements are nowhere to be seen, but simply bullion, metal coin, notes, bills and securities. This distortion is particularly evident in centres such as London, where the monetary business of an entire country is concentrated; here the whole process becomes incomprehensible. It is somewhat less so in the centres of production.

It should also be remarked in passing, in connection with the over-abundance of industrial capital that appears during crises, that commodity capital is inherently already money capital, i.e. a certain sum of value expressed in the commodity's price. As a use-value it is a certain quantity of particular useful objects, and these are present in excess at the moment of crisis. But as inherently money capital, potential money capital, it is subject to constant expansion and contraction. On the eve of the crisis, and during it, the commodity capital is contracted in its capacity as potential money capital. It represents less money capital for its owner and his creditors (also as security for bills of exchange and loans) than at the time it was bought and when the discounts and loans made with it as security were concluded. If this is the supposed sense of the contention that the money capital of a country is reduced in times of pressure, it is identical with saying that commodity prices have fallen. Such a collapse in prices, incidentally, only balances their earlier inflation.

The incomes of the unproductive classes, and of those who live on fixed incomes, remain for the most part stationary during the price inflation that goes hand in hand with overproduction and over-speculation. Their consumption power thus undergoes a relative decline, and with this also their ability to replace the portion of the total reproduction that would normally go into their consumption. Even if their demand remains nominally the same, it still declines in real terms.

As regards the question of imports and exports, it should be noted that all countries are successively caught up in the crisis, and that it is then apparent that they have all, with few exceptions, both exported and imported too much; i.e. the *balance of payments is against them all*, so that the root of the problem is actually not the balance of payments at all. England, for example, suffers from a drain of gold. It has imported too much. But at the same time every other country is overburdened with English goods. They too have imported too much, or been made to import too much.

(There is a distinction, however, between the country that exports on credit, and those that do not, or only a little. The latter then import on credit; and this is only not the case if the goods in question are sent out on consignment.) The crisis may break out first of all in England, the country that gives the most credit and takes the least, because the balance of payments, i.e. the balance of payments due, which must be settled immediately, is *against it*, even though the overall balance of trade is *in its favour*. This fact is partly to be explained in terms of the credit given by England and partly in terms of the amount of loaned capital sent abroad, which means that a large quantity of returns flows back to England in commodities, in addition to trading returns in the strict sense. (Sometimes the crisis breaks out first of all in America, the country that takes the most credit for trade and capital from England.) The crash in England, introduced and accompanied by a drain of gold, settles England's balance of payments, partly by bankrupting its importers (on which more below), partly by driving part of its commodity capital abroad at low prices, and partly by the sale of foreign securities, the purchase of English ones, etc. The sequence now reaches another country. The balance of payments was temporarily in its favour; but now the normal interval between the balancing of payments and the balancing of trade is abolished or at least cut short by the crisis; all payments have to be settled at once. The same situation then repeats itself here. England now has a reflux of gold, the other country a drain. What appears in one country as excessive importing appears in the other as excessive exporting, and vice versa. But excessive importing and exporting has taken place in every country (here we are not referring to harvest failures, etc., but rather to a general crisis); i.e. overproduction, fostered by credit and the accompanying general inflation in prices.

In 1857 the crisis broke out in the United States. This led to a drain of gold from England to America. But as soon as the American bubble burst, the crisis reached England, with a drain of gold from America to England. Similarly between England and the Continent. In times of general crisis the balance of payments is against every country, at least against every commercially developed country, but always against each of these in succession – like volley firing – as soon as the sequence of payments reaches it; and once the crisis has broken out in England, for example, this sequence of dates is condensed into a fairly short period. It is then evident that all these countries have simultaneously over-exported (i.e. over-produced) and over-imported (i.e. over-traded) and that in all of them prices were inflated and credit overstretched. In every case the same collapse follows. The phenomenon of a drain of gold then affects each of them in turn, and shows by its very universality: (1) that the drain of gold is simply a phenomenon of the crisis, and not its basis; (2) that the sequence in which this drain of gold affects the different countries simply indicates when the series reaches them, for a final settlement of accounts; when their own day of crisis comes and its latent elements in turn emerge in their own case.

It is characteristic of the English economic writers – and the economic literature worth mentioning since 1830 principally boils down to writing on currency, credit and crises – that they consider the export of precious metal that occurs in times of crisis, despite the turn in the exchange rates, simply from the English standpoint, as a purely national phenomenon, and resolutely close their eyes to the fact that, if their bank raises the interest rate in times of crisis, all other European banks do the same thing, and that, if they raise a cry of distress about the drain of gold today, this is echoed tomorrow in America and the day after that in Germany and France.

In 1847, 'the engagements running upon this country had to be met' (mostly for corn). 'Unfortunately, they were met to a great extent by failures' (wealthy England obtained a breathing space for itself by defaulting on its obligations vis-à-vis the Continent and America), 'but to the extent to which they were not met by failures, they were met by the exportation of bullion' (*Report of Committee on Bank Acts*, 1857).

Thus in so far as a crisis in England is intensified by the banking legislation, this legislation is also a means of cheating the corn-exporting countries in times of famine, first of their corn and then of the money for their corn. A ban on the export of corn in times such as these, in the case of countries that are themselves suffering to a greater or lesser extent from rising prices, is thus a very rational defence against this plan by the Bank of England, 'to meet engagements' for corn imports 'by failures'. Far better that the corn producers and speculators should lose a part of their profits for the good of their own country than their capital for the good of England.

We conclude from what has been said here that commodity

capital largely loses its capacity to represent potential money capital in time of crisis, and generally when business stagnates. The same is true of fictitious capital, interest-bearing paper, in as much as this itself circulates as money capital on the stock exchange. As the interest rate rises, its price falls. It falls further, owing to the general lack of credit, which compels the owners of this paper to unload it onto the market on a massive scale in order to obtain money. In the case of shares, finally, their price falls partly as a result of a decline in the revenues on which they are claims and partly as a result of the fraudulent character of the enterprises which they very often represent. This fictitious money capital is enormously reduced during crises, and with it the power of its owners to use it to borrow money in the market. The reduction in the money value of these securities on the stock-exchange list, however, has nothing to do with the real capital that they represent. As against this, it has a lot to do with the solvency of their owners.

Chapter 31: Money Capital and Real Capital: II (Continuation)

We have still not finished with the question of how far the accumulation of capital in the form of money capital for loan coincides with genuine accumulation, the expansion of the reproduction process.

The transformation of money into money capital for loan is a far simpler matter than the transformation of money into productive capital. But we must distinguish here between two different things:

(1) the mere transformation of money into loan capital;

(2) the transformation of capital or revenue into money that is transformed into loan capital.

It is only the latter point which is related to the genuine accumulation of industrial capital, and only this can involve a positive accumulation of capital for loan.

I. TRANSFORMATION OF MONEY INTO LOAN CAPITAL

We have already seen how a pile-up or over-abundance of loan capital, which is related to productive accumulation only by standing in inverse proportion to it, can arise. This is the case in two phases of the industrial cycle, firstly at the time when industrial capital in the two forms of productive capital and commodity capital has contracted, i.e. at the beginning of the cycle after the crisis; and secondly at the time when improvement sets in but commercial credit still has little need for bank credit. In the first case the money capital that was formerly applied to production and trade appears as unoccupied loan capital; in the second case it is applied on an increasing scale but at a very low rate of interest, since it is now the industrial and commercial capitalists who set terms to the money capitalist. The surplus of loan capital expresses in the first case the stagnation of industrial capital, and in the second case the relative independence of commercial credit from bank credit, resting on the fluidity of returns, short terms of credit and operations predominantly conducted with one's own capital. The speculators who rely on the credit capital of others have not yet appeared on the scene; while people who operate with their own capital are still far removed from anything like pure credit operations. In the first phase, the surplus of loan capital expresses the exact opposite of genuine accumulation. In the second phase it coincides with the renewed expansion of the reproduction process: it accompanies it without causing it. The surplus of loan capital is already on the decline and is still only relative to the demand. In both cases the expansion of the accumulation process proper is promoted, because the low rate of interest, which coincides in the first case with low prices, and in the second case with slowly rising prices, increases the portion of the profit that is transformed into profit of enterprise. This is all the more so when interest rises to its average level during the height of the prosperity period; although it has risen, it has not done so in relation to profit.

We have seen on the other hand how an accumulation of loan capital may take place without any genuine accumulation, by purely technical means such as the expansion and concentration of the banking system, saving on the circulation reserve or even on private individuals' reserve funds or means of payment, which are in this way transformed into loan capital for short periods. Although this loan capital, which is therefore known also as floating capital, only ever receives the form of loan capital for short periods (and thus should only be used for short-term discounting), it is constantly flowing back and forth. If one person withdraws it, someone else puts it in. The amount of money capital for loan (and here we are not referring at all to loans for several years, but simply to short-term loans against bills of exchange and deposits) thus actually grows quite independently of genuine accumulation.

Bank Committee, 1857. Question 501. 'What do you mean by "floating capital"?' – (Answer of Mr Weguelin, Governor of the Bank of England:) 'It is capital applicable to loans of money for short periods ... (502) The Bank of England notes ... the country banks circulation, and the amount of coin which is in the country.' – (Question:) 'It does not appear from the returns before the Committee, if by floating capital you mean the active circulation' (of the notes of the Bank of England), 'that there is any very great variation in the active circulation?' (Though it is a very major distinction as to who it is that advances the active circulation, the money-lender or the reproductive capitalist himself. Weguelin's answer:) 'I include in floating capital the reserves of the bankers, in which there is a considerable fluctuation.'

This means, therefore, that a major fluctuation takes place in the portion of deposits which the bankers have not lent out again but which figures rather as their reserves, though a lot of it also figures as the reserve of the Bank of England, with which their reserves are deposited. The same gentleman finally says that floating capital may be bullion, including metal money (503). It is truly amazing how all the categories of political economy take on a new meaning and form in this credit gibberish of the money market. Floating capital here is the expression for circulating capital, which is of course something completely different, and money is capital, and bullion is capital, and banknotes are circulation, and capital is a commodity, and debts are commodities, and fixed capital is money invested in paper that is hard to sell!

'The joint-stock banks of London ... have increased their deposits from £8,850,774 in 1847 to £43,100,724 in 1857 ... The evidence given to your Committee leads to the inference that of this vast amount, a large part has been derived from sources not heretofore made available for this purpose; and that the practice of opening accounts and depositing money with bankers has extended to numerous classes who did not formerly employ their capital(!) in that way. It is stated by Mr Rodwell, the Chairman of the Association of the Private Country Bankers' (distinguished from joint-stock banks), 'and delegated by them to give evidence to your Committee, that in the neighbourhood of Ipswich this practice has lately increased four-fold among the farmers and shopkeepers of that district; that almost every farmer, even those paying only £50 per annum rent, now keeps deposits with bankers. The aggregate of these deposits of course finds its way to the employments of trade, and especially gravitates to London, the centre of commercial activity, where it is employed first in the discount of bills, or in other advances to the customers of the London bankers. That large portion, however, for which the bankers themselves have no immediate demand passes into the hands of the billbrokers, who give to the banker in return commercial bills already discounted by them for persons in London and in different parts of the country, as a security for the sum advanced by the banker' (*Bank Committee*, 1858, p. [v, para.] 8).

Since the banker makes advances to the billbroker on the bill that the broker has already once discounted, he actually rediscounts it; but in actual fact very many of these bills have already been rediscounted by the billbroker, and with the same money that the banker uses to rediscount the bills presented by the billbroker, the broker rediscounts new bills. This leads to the following situation: 'Extensive fictitious credits have been created by means of accommodation bills, and open credits, great facilities for which have been afforded by the practice of joint-stock country banks discounting such bills, and rediscounting them with the billbrokers in the London market, upon the credit of the bank alone, without reference to the quality of the bills otherwise' (ibid. [p. xxi, para. 54]).

The following passage from *The Economist* sheds an interesting light on this rediscounting, and on the assistance that this purely technical increase in the money capital for loan provides for credit swindles:

'For some years past capital' (namely, loanable money-capital) 'has accumulated in some districts of the country more rapidly than it could be used, while, in others, the means of employing capital have increased more rapidly than the capital itself. While the bankers in the purely agricultural districts throughout the kingdom found no sufficient means of profitably and safely employing their deposits in their own districts, those in the large mercantile towns, and in the manufacturing and mining districts, have found a larger demand for capital than their own means could supply. The effect of this relative state of different districts has led, of late years, to the establishment and rapid extension of a new class of houses in the distribution of capital, who, though usually called billbrokers, are in reality bankers upon an immense scale. The business of these houses has been to receive, for such periods, and at such rates of interest as were agreed upon, the surplus-capital of bankers in those districts where it could not be employed, as well as the temporary unemployed moneys of public companies and extensive mercantile establishments, and advance them at higher rates of interest to bankers in those districts where capital was more in demand, generally by rediscounting the bills taken from their customers . . . and in this way Lombard Street has become the great centre in which the transfer of spare capital has been made from one part of the country, where it could not be profitably employed, to another, where a demand existed for it, as well as between individuals similarly circumstanced. At first these transactions were confined almost exclusively to borrowing and lending on banking securities. But as the capital of the country rapidly accumulated, and became more economized by the establishment of banks, the funds at the disposal of these "discount houses" became so large that they were induced to make advances first on dock warrants of merchandise' (storage bills on commodities in docks), 'and next on bills of lading, representing produce not even arrived in this country, though sometimes, if not generally, secured by bills drawn by the merchant upon his broker. This practice rapidly changed the whole character of English commerce. The facilities thus afforded in Lombard Street gave extensive powers to the brokers in Mincing Lane. who on their part . . . offered the full advantage of them to the importing merchant; who so far took advantage of them, that, whereas twenty-five years ago, the fact that a merchant received advances on his bills of lading, or even his dock warrants, would have been fatal to his credit, the practice has become so common of late years that it may be said to be now the general rule, and not the rare exception, as it was twenty-five years ago. Nay, so much further has this system been carried, that large sums have been raised in Lombard Street on bills drawn against the *forthcoming* crops of distant colonies. The consequence of such facilities being thus granted to the importing merchants led them to extend their transactions abroad, and to invest their floating capital with which their business has hitherto been conducted, in the most objectionable of all fixed securities – foreign plantations – over which they could exercise little or no control. And thus we see the direct change of credit through which the capital of the country, collected in our rural districts, and in small amounts in the shape of deposits in country banks, and centres in Lombard Street for employment, has been, first, made available for the extending operations in our mining and manufacturing districts, by the rediscount of bills to banks in those localities; next, for granting greater facilities for the importation of foreign produce by advances upon dock warrants and bills of lading, and thus liberating the "legitimate" mercantile capital of houses engaged in foreign and colonial trade, and inducing to its most objectionable advances on foreign plantations' (*The Economist*, 1847, p. 1334).

That is the 'nice' way to devour credits. The rural depositor imagines he is simply depositing with his banker, and also imagines that when the banker makes loans it is to private individuals whom he knows. He does not have the remotest suspicion that the banker puts his deposit at the disposal of a London billbroker, over whose operations neither of them have the slightest control.

We have already seen how major public undertakings, such as railway construction, can temporarily increase loan capital, in that the sums paid up always remain for a certain while in the hands of the banks and are at their disposal until they are actually spent.

*

The volume of loan capital, moreover, is completely different from the quantity of circulation. By quantity of circulation, here, we mean the sum of all banknotes in circulation in a particular country, together with all metal money, including precious metal in the form of bullion. A part of this quantity forms the banks' reserve and is constantly fluctuating in size.

'On November 12, 1857' (the date of the suspension of the Bank Act of 1844), 'the entire reserve of the Bank of England was only £580,751 (including London and all its branches); their deposits at the same time amounting to £22,500,000; of which near six and a half million belonged to London bankers' (*Bank Acts*, 1858, p. lvii).

Variations in the rate of interest (setting aside those taking place over longer periods, or the differences between interest rates in different countries; the first kind being conditioned by variations in the general rate of profit, and the second by differences in profit rates and in the development of credit) depend on the supply of loan capital (all other factors, the state of confidence, etc., taken as equal), i.e. of capital lent in the form of money, in metal or notes; as distinct from industrial capital that is lent as such, in the commodity form, by commercial credit among the reproductive agents themselves.

But the volume of this loanable money capital is still different from and independent of the quantity of money in circulation.

If £20 is lent five times in the course of a day, a money capital of £100 is lent altogether, and this would equally mean that this £20 had functioned at least four times as means of purchase or payment; for if it were without the mediation of purchase and payment, so that it had not represented the transformed form of capital (commodities, including labour-power) at least four times, it would not constitute a capital of £100 but simply five claims of £20 each.

In countries where credit is highly developed, we may assume that all money capital available for loan exists in the form of deposits with banks and money-lenders. This at least holds good for business as a whole. On top of this, in times of good business, before speculation properly so called gets going, the greater part of the circulatory functions will be performed, with credit easy and confidence growing, simply through a credit transfer, without the intervention of metal or paper money.

The very possibility that large sums will be deposited while the amount of means of circulation is relatively small depends entirely on:

(1) the number of purchases and payments that the same piece of money performs;

(2) the number of return migrations in which it comes back to the banks as a deposit, so that its repeated function as means of purchase and payment is mediated by its renewed transformation into a deposit. A retail trader, for instance, may deposit £100 a week with his banker in money; the banker uses this to pay out a part of the manufacturer's deposit; the latter pays this to his workers, and they use it to pay the retailer, who deposits it again with the bank. The £100 deposited by the retailer has thus to serve firstly to pay out a deposit of the manufacturer's, secondly to pay the workers, thirdly to pay the retailer himself and fourthly to deposit a further part of the same retailer's money capital; for at the end of twenty weeks, if he did not have to draw on this money himself, he would have deposited £2,000 in the bank, using the same £100.

The extent to which this money capital is unoccupied is shown only in the ebb and flow of the banks' reserve funds. This is why Mr Weguelin, Governor of the Bank of England in 1857, concludes that the gold in the Bank of England is the 'only' reserve capital:

'1258. Practically, I think, the rate of discount is governed by the amount of unemployed capital which there is in the country.

The amount of unemployed capital is represented by the reserve of the Bank of England, which is practically a reserve of bullion. When, therefore, the bullion is drawn upon, it diminishes the amount of unemployed capital in the country, and consequently raises the value of that which remains.' – '1364. The reserve of bullion in the Bank of England is, in truth, the central reserve, or hoard of treasure, upon which the whole trade of the country is carried on . . . And it is upon that hoard or reservoir that the action of the foreign exchanges always falls' (*Report on Bank Acts*, 1857).

*

One measure for the accumulation of genuine capital, i.e. productive and commodity capital, is provided by the statistics of exports and imports. And there it is constantly apparent that for the period over which English industry moved in ten-year cycles (1815–70), the maximum for the final period of prosperity *before* the crisis reappeared as the minimum for the period of prosperity that followed next, only to rise then to a new and much higher maximum.

The real or declared value of products exported from Great Britain and Ireland in the prosperous year of 1824 was £40,396,300. With the crisis of 1825, the volume of exports fell below this sum, and fluctuated between an annual total of £35 and £39 million. With the return of prosperity in 1834, it rose above the earlier peak to £41,649,191, and in 1836 reached a new maximum of £53,368,571. In 1837 it fell again to £42 million, so that the new minimum was already higher than the maximum of the previous cycle, and it subsequently fluctuated between £50 and £53 million. The return of prosperity raised the 1844 export total to £58½ million, already exceeding the 1836 maximum by far. In 1845 the total for the year reached £60,111,082; it then fell back to somewhat over £57 million in 1846, almost £59 million in 1847, and almost £53 million in 1848, rising in 1849 to £65½ million, in 1853 to almost £99 million, 1854 £97 million, 1855 £94½ million, 1856 almost £116 million, and reaching a maximum in 1857 of £122 million. In 1858 it fell to £116 million, but had already risen in 1859 to £130 million, in 1860 to almost £136 million, in 1861 to only £125 million (here again the new minimum is higher than the previous cycle's maximum), and in 1863 to £146½ million.

The same thing can of course also be shown for imports, which indicate the expansion of the market. Here we are concerned only with the scale of production. (This is of course true for England only for the period of its effective industrial monopoly; but it is true in general for the totality of countries with modern large-scale industry, as long as the world market is still expanding. – F. E.)

2. TRANSFORMATION OF CAPITAL OR REVENUE INTO MONEY THAT IS TRANSFORMED INTO LOAN CAPITAL

Here we are considering the accumulation of money capital in so far as this does not express a stagnation in the flow of commercial credit, or saving either on the actual circulating medium or on the reserve capital of the agents engaged in reproduction.

Leaving aside these two cases, accumulation of money capital may arise through an exceptional influx of gold, as happened in 1852 and 1853 as a result of the new gold mines in Australia and California. This gold was deposited in the Bank of England. The depositors accepted notes in return, which they did not directly deposit again with bankers. In this way, the circulating medium underwent an extraordinary increase. (Evidence of Weguelin, *B. A.* 1857, no. 1329.) The Bank tried to valorize these deposits by reducing its discount rate to 2 per cent. In the course of six months in 1853, the quantity of gold piled up in the Bank grew to some £22–£23 million.

All money-lending capitalists obviously accumulate directly in the money form, while we have seen that real accumulation by industrial capitalists occurs as a rule through an increase in the elements of reproductive capital itself. The development of the credit system and the tremendous concentration of the money-lending business in the hands of big banks must therefore already accelerate in and of itself the accumulation of loanable capital, as a form separate from genuine accumulation. This rapid development of loan capital is therefore a result of the genuine accumulation, as an effect of the development of the reproduction process, and the profit that forms the source of accumulation for these money capitalists is simply a deduction from the surplus-value that the reproductive agents extract (as well as an appropriation of part of the interest on the savings of *others*). Loan capital accumulates at the expense of both the industrial and commercial capitalists. We have seen how, in the bad phases of the industrial cycle, the rate of interest may rise so high that it temporarily swallows up profits entirely for some branches of business, particularly those unfavourably located. At the same time, the prices of government paper and other securities fall. This is the moment when money capitalists buy up this devalued paper on a massive scale, as it will soon go up again in the later phases, and even rise above its normal level. They will then sell it off, thereby appropriating a part of the public's money capital. Those securities that are not sold off yield a higher interest, since they were bought below their price. But all the profit which the money capitalists make, and which they turn back into capital, they transform first of all into money capital for loan. Thus we already have an accumulation of this money capital as distinct from the genuine accumulation – even if the accumulation of its off-shoot – when we simply consider the money capitalists, bankers, etc. themselves, as the accumulation of this particular class of capitalists. And this must grow with each extension of the credit system, as it accompanies the genuine expansion of the reproduction process.

If the rate of interest is low, this devaluation of money capital falls principally on the depositors and not on the banks. Before the development of joint-stock banking, three-quarters of all bank deposits in England did not receive any interest. And where interest is now paid, this is at least 1 per cent less than the market rate.

As far as the monetary accumulation of the remaining classes of capitalist is concerned, we ignore here the part that is invested in interest-bearing paper and accumulates in this form. We shall simply consider the portion that is placed on the market as money capital for loan.

Here we have firstly the section of profit that is not spent as revenue, being rather designed for accumulation, but which the industrial capitalists concerned do not have any immediate employment for in their own businesses. This profit exists first of all in commodity capital, making up a portion of its value, and is realized in money together with it. If it is not then transformed back into the commodity capital's elements of production (we leave aside here for the time being the merchant, whom we shall deal with later more specifically), it must persist for a certain period in the money form. Its amount rises with the volume of the capital itself, even given a declining rate of profit. The part to be spent as revenue is gradually consumed, but in the meantime it constitutes loan capital as a deposit with the banker. And so even the growth of the part of the profit spent as revenue is expressed in a gradual and constantly repeated accumulation of loan capital. Similarly, too, the other part, which is designed for accumulation. With the development of the credit system and its organization, the rise in revenue, i.e. in the consumption of the industrial and commercial capitalists, is thus itself expressed as an accumulation of loan capital. And this holds good of all revenues, in so far as they are only gradually consumed – i.e. ground-rent, the higher forms of salary, the incomes of the unproductive classes, etc. All of these assume for a time the form of money revenue and can hence be converted into deposits and thereby into loan capital. It is true of all revenue, whether designed for consumption or for accumulation, that as soon as it exists in any kind of monetary form it is a portion of value of the commodity capital that is transformed into money, and is therefore the expression and result of genuine accumulation, though not productive capital itself. If a spinner has exchanged his yarn for cotton, save for the part that forms revenue and is exchanged for money, the actual existence of his industrial capital is the yarn that has passed into possession of the weaver, or perhaps even into that of the private consumer; and this yarn, moreover, whether it serves for reproduction or for consumption, is the existence of both capital value and of the surplus-value contained in it. The amount of surplus-value transformed into money depends on the amount of surplus-value contained in the yarn. But as soon as it is transformed into money, this money is simply the value existence of that surplus-value. And as such it becomes an element of loan capital. No more is needed for this than that it should be transformed into a deposit, if it has not already been lent out by its owner. To be transformed back into productive capital, on the other hand, it must already have reached a certain minimum limit.

Chapter 32: Money Capital and Real Capital: III (Conclusion)

The massive nature of the sum of money which has to be transformed back into capital in this way is the result of the massive scale of the reproduction process; but considered for itself, as money capital for loan, it is not itself a sum of reproductive capital.

The most important thing in our presentation so far is the point that the expansion of that portion of revenue that is destined for consumption (and in this connection we ignore the worker, since his revenue = the variable capital) presents itself first of all as an accumulation of money capital. There is thus an element in the accumulation of money capital that is essentially separate from the genuine accumulation of industrial capital; for the portion of the annual product designed for consumption is in no way capital. A part of it *replaces* capital, i.e. the constant capital of the producers of means of consumption, but in so far as it really is transformed into capital, it exists in kind as the natural form of the revenue of this constant capital's producers. The same money that represents revenue, that serves simply to mediate consumption, is regularly transformed for a certain period into loanable money capital. In as much as this money represents wages, it is at the same time the money form of variable capital; and in as much as it replaces the constant capital of the producers of means of consumption, it is the money form that their constant capital temporarily assumes, and serves to purchase the elements of their constant capital that are to be replaced in kind. Neither in one form nor the other does it in itself represent accumulation, even though its volume grows with the scale of the reproduction process. But it temporarily performs the function of money for loan, i.e. of money capital. In this respect, therefore, the accumulation of money capital must always reflect a greater accumulation of capital than is actually taking place, in so far as the expansion of individual consumption, because mediated by money, appears as an accumulation of money capital, since it supplies the money form for genuine accumulation, for money that initiates new capital investments.

The accumulation of money capital for loan thus partly represents nothing more than the fact that all money into which industrial capital is transformed in the course of its circuit assumes the form, not of money that the reproductive agents *advance* but of money that they *borrow*; so that in actual fact the advance of money that must occur in the reproduction process appears as an advance of borrowed money. Here, on the basis of commercial credit, one party lends another the money that he needs in the reproduction process. But this takes the form that the banker to whom one section of reproductive agents lend money lends this in turn to the other section of reproductive agents, which makes the banker appear as the benefactor; while at the same time disposal over this capital passes entirely to the bankers as intermediaries.

There are still some special forms of the accumulation of money capital to be explained. Capital may be set free, for example, by a fall in the price of the elements of production, raw materials, etc. If the industrialist cannot directly expand his reproduction process, one part of his money capital is ejected from the circuit as superfluous and is transformed into money capital for loan. Secondly, however, capital is released in the money form, particularly in the case of the merchant, as soon as there are any interruptions to business. If the merchant has settled a whole series of deals and these interruptions mean that he can only begin a new series later, the money that is realized represents for him simply a hoard, superfluous capital. But at the same time it directly represents an accumulation of money capital for loan. In the first case, the accumulation of money capital expresses the repetition of the reproduction process under more favourable conditions, the genuine release of a portion of capital previously tied up, enabling the reproduction process to be expanded with the same monetary means. In the second case, on the other hand, there is simply an interruption in the flow of transactions. But in both cases, money is transformed into loanable money capital, representing an accumulation of it, and has the same effect on the money market and the rate of interest, even though in the one case the genuine accumulation process is promoted, while in the other case it is inhibited. Finally, accumulation of money capital is effected by various people who have feathered their nests and withdrawn from the reproduction process. The greater the profits made in the course of the industrial cycle, the more of these people there are. In this case the accumulation of capital for loan expresses on the one hand a genuine accumulation (in its relative volume); on the other hand simply the degree to which industrial capitalists are transformed into simple money capitalists.

As far as the other portion of the profit is concerned, that not destined to be consumed as revenue, this is transformed into money capital only if it cannot be directly used to expand business in the sphere of production in which the profit was made. This can happen for two reasons: either because this sphere is saturated with capital; or else because in order to function as capital, the accumulation must first have attained a certain volume, according to the due proportions for investment of new capital in this particular business. It is then firstly transformed into money capital for loan and serves to expand production in other spheres. Taking all other circumstances as equal, the amount of profit destined for transformation back into capital will depend on the amount of profit made and hence on the expansion of the reproduction process itself. But if this new accumulation comes up against difficulties of application, against a lack of spheres of investment, i.e. if branches of production are saturated and loan capital is over-supplied, this plethora of loanable money capital proves nothing more than the barriers of *capitalist* production. The resulting credit swindling demonstrates that there is no positive obstacle to the use of this excess capital. But there is an obstacle set up by its own laws of valorization, by the barriers within which capital can valorize itself as capital. A plethora of money capital as such does not necessarily signify overproduction, or even a lack of spheres of employment for capital.

The accumulation of loan capital simply means that money is precipitated as loanable money. This process is very different from a genuine transformation into capital; it is simply the accumulation of money in a form in which it can be transformed into capital. As we have shown, however, this accumulation can express elements that are very different from genuine accumulation. With genuine accumulation constantly expanding, this expanded accumulation of money capital can be in part its result, in part the result of elements that accompany it but are quite different from it, and in part also the result even of blockages in genuine accumulation. The very fact that the accumulation of loan capital is augmented by these elements that are independent of genuine accumulation, even if they accompany it, must lead to a regular plethora of money capital at certain phases of the cycle, and this plethora develops as the credit system improves. At the same time as this, there develops the need to pursue the production process beyond its capitalist barriers: too much trade, too much production, too much credit. This must also happen always in forms that bring about a reaction.

As far as the accumulation of money capital from ground-rent, wages, etc. goes, it is unnecessary to go into this here. The only element to be stressed is that as capitalist production and its division of labour progress, the job of genuine saving and abstinence (by hoarders), in so far as this supplies elements of accumulation, is left to those who receive the minimum of such elements, and often enough lose what they have saved, as workers do when banks collapse. For the industrial capitalist does not 'save' his capital but rather disposes of the savings of others in proportion to the size of this capital; while the money capitalist makes the savings of other people into his capital, and the credit that the reproductive capitalists give one another, and that the public give them, he makes into his own source of private enrichment. The final illusion of the capitalist system, that capital is the offspring of a person's own work and savings, is thereby demolished. Not only does profit consist in the appropriation of other people's labour, but the capital with which this labour of others is set in motion and exploited consists of other people's property, which the money capitalist puts at the disposal of the industrial capitalist and for which he in turn exploits him.

We still need to say something about credit capital.

How often the same piece of money can serve as loan capital depends entirely, as we have already developed above, on:

(1) How often it realizes commodity values in sale or in payment, i.e. transfers capital, as well as how often it realizes revenue. How often it comes into someone else's hands as realized value, whether that of capital or of revenue, hence depends evidently on the scale and volume of real transactions.

(2) This depends on economy in payments and the development and organization of the credit system.

(3) It depends finally on the linkage and speed of action of credits, so that if the money is precipitated at one point as a deposit, it is immediately sent out again as a loan.

Even on the assumption that the form in which the loan capital exists is simply that of actual money, gold or silver – the commodity whose material serves as a measure of value – a large portion of this money capital is still necessarily always merely fictitious, i.e. a title to value, just like value tokens. In as much as money functions in the circuit of capital, it certainly forms money capital at one point, but it is not transformed into loanable money capital; it is rather exchanged for the elements of productive capital, or paid out as a means of circulation when revenue is realized, so that it cannot be transformed into loan capital for its possessor. In so far as it is transformed into loan capital and the same money repeatedly represents loan capital, it is still clear that it only exists at *one* point as metal money; at all other points it exists simply in the form of a claim to capital. The accumulation of these claims, on our assumptions, arises from a genuine accumulation, i.e. from the transformation of the value of commodity capital, etc. into money; and yet the accumulation of these claims or titles as such is still different both from the genuine accumulation from which it arises and from the future accumulation (the new production process) which is mediated by the lending of money.

Prima facie, loan capital always exists in the form of money,[9]

9. *B. A.* 1857, evidence of Twells, banker: '4516. As a banker, do you deal in capital or in money? – We deal in money.' – '4517. How are the deposits paid into your bank? – In money.' – '4518. How are they paid out? – In money.' – '4519. Then can they be called anything else but money? – No.'

Overstone shows persistent confusion between 'capital' and 'money' (see Chapter 26). 'Value of money', for him, also means interest, in so far as this is determined by the quantity of money; but interest is supposed to be the 'value of capital', in so far as it is determined by the demand for productive capital and by the profit that this yields. He says (4140): 'The use of the word "capital" is very dangerous.' – (4148) 'The export of bullion from this country is a diminution of the quantity of money in this country, and a diminution of the quantity of money in this country must of course create a pressure upon the money-market generally' (but not in the capital market, according to him). – (4112) 'As the money goes out of the country, the quantity in the country is diminished. That diminution of the quantity remaining in the country produces an increased value of that money.' (What this originally means in his theory is a rise in the value of money as money in comparison to commodity values, brought about by a contraction in circulation; i.e. where this rise in the value of money = a fall in the value of commodities. But since in the meantime it has been incontrovertibly demonstrated even for him that the quantity of money in circulation does *not* determine prices, it is now the reduction in money as means of circulation that is supposed to raise its value as interest-bearing capital, and hence the later as a claim to money, since the money in which it originally existed is now in the hands of the borrower in the actual money form. For the lender, it has been transformed into a claim to money, into an ownership title. The same quantity of actual money can therefore represent very different quantities of money capital. Mere money, whether it represents realized capital or realized revenue, becomes loan capital by the simple act of lending it out, by its transformation into a deposit, if we consider the general form in the developed credit system. The deposit is money capital for the depositor. But in the hands of the banker it may only be potential money capital, lying idle in his safe instead of in that of its owner.[10]

As material wealth increases, the class of money capitalists

---

rate of interest.) 'And that increased value of what remains stops the exit of money, and is kept up until it has brought back that quantity of money which is necessary to restore the equilibrium.' We shall continue with Overstone's contradictions later on.

10. This is the point where there enters the confused notion that both things are 'money', the deposit as a claim to payment from the banker, and the deposited money in the banker's possession. Banker Twells, before the Bank Acts Committee of 1857, takes the following example: 'If I begin business with £10,000, I buy with £5,000 commodities and put them into warehouse. I deposit the other £5,000 with a banker, to draw upon it and use it as I require. I consider it still £10,000 capital to me, though £5,000 is in the shape of deposits or money' (4528). – The following peculiar debate then unfolds. – (4531) 'You have parted with your £5,000 of notes to somebody else? – Yes.' (4532) 'Then he has £5,000 of deposits? – Yes.' – (4533) 'And you have £5,000 of deposits left? – Exactly.' – (4534) 'He has £5,000 in money, and you have £5,000 in money? – Yes.' – (4535) 'But it is nothing but money at last? – No.' The confusion arises in part from this: A, who has deposited the £5,000, can draw on it, and disposes of it just as well as if he still had it. To this extent, it functions for him as potential money. But whenever he draws on it, he destroys his deposit *pro tanto*. If he withdraws actual money and his money has already been lent again, he is paid not with his own money, but rather with the money someone else has deposited. If he pays a debt to B with a cheque on his banker, B deposits this cheque with his banker, and if A's banker has likewise a cheque on B's banker, so that the two bankers simply exchange cheques, the money that A deposited has performed money functions twice: firstly, in the hands of the person who received the money that A had deposited; secondly, in the hands of A himself. In the second function, there is an adjustment of claims (the claim of A on his banker and the claim of the latter on B's banker) without the intervention of money. Here the deposit has a double effect as money, i.e. first as actual money and subsequently as a claim to money. Mere claims to money can only take the place of money in the balancing of claims.

grows. On the one hand there is an increase in the number and wealth of the retired capitalists, the rentiers; and secondly the credit system must be further developed, which means an increase in the number of bankers, money-lenders, financiers, etc. With the expansion of available money capital, the volume of interest-bearing paper, government paper, shares, etc. also expands, as explained already. At the same time, however, so does the demand for available money capital, since the jobbers who speculate in this paper play a major role in the money market. If all purchases and sales of this paper were simply the expression of genuine capital investment, it would be right to say that they could have no effect on the demand for loan capital, since if A sells his paper, he withdraws just as much money as B puts into paper. Even then, however, in view of the fact that the paper certainly exists, while the capital that it originally represented does not (at least not as money capital), a new demand for money capital of this kind is always created to that extent. But at all events it is then money capital, which was previously at B's disposition, and is now at A's.

B. A. 1857, no. 4886. 'Do you consider that it is a correct description of the causes which determined the rate of discount, to say that it is fixed by the quantity of capital on the market, which is applicable to the discount of mercantile bills, as distinguished from other classes of securities?' – (Chapman:) 'No, I think that the question of interest is affected by all convertible securities of a current character; it would be wrong to limit it simply to the discount of bills, because it would be absurd to say that when there is a great demand for money upon' (the deposit of) 'Consols, or even upon Exchequer bills, as has ruled very much of late, at a rate much higher than the commercial rate, our commercial world is not affected by it; it is very materially affected by it.' – '4890. When sound and current securities, such as bankers acknowledge to be so, are on the market, and people want to borrow money upon them, it certainly has its effect upon commercial bills; for instance, I can hardly expect a man to let me have money at 5 per cent upon commercial bills, if he can lend his money at the same moment at 6 per cent upon Consols, or whatever it may be; it affects us in the same manner; a man can hardly expect me to discount bills at $5\frac{1}{2}$ per cent, if I can lend my money at 6 per cent.' – '4892. We do not talk of investors who buy their £2,000, or £5,000, or £10,000, as affecting the money-market materially. If you ask me as to the rate of interest upon' (a deposit of) 'Consols, I allude to people, who deal in hundreds of thousands of pounds, who are what are called jobbers, who take large portions of loans, or make purchases on the market, and have to hold that stock till the public take it off their hands at a profit; these men, therefore, want money.'

With the development of the credit system, large and concentrated money markets are created, as in London, which are at the same time the major seats of dealings in these securities. The bankers put the public's money capital at the disposal of this gang of dealers on a massive scale, and so the brood of gamblers multiplies.

'Money upon the Stock Exchange is, generally speaking, cheaper than it is elsewhere,' said the then Governor of the Bank of England before the House of Lords Secret Committee (*C. D.* 1848, printed 1857, no. 219).

We have already shown in dealing with interest-bearing capital that the average interest over a period of several years is determined, other things being equal, by the average rate of profit, and not by profit of enterprise, which is no more than profit minus interest.*

Also mentioned already, and to be investigated further below, is the fact that the variations in commercial interest – the interest charged by money-lenders for discounting and loans within the world of trade – also show a phase in the course of the industrial cycle in which the rate of interest rises above its minimum and reaches the average medium level (which it then later exceeds), this movement being the result of a rise in profits.

Two things however should be noted here.

Firstly, if the interest rate remains high for a long period of time (and here we are speaking of the interest rate in a particular country, such as England, where the average rate of interest is given for a relatively long period and is also expressed in the interest paid for long-term loans – what we might call private interest), this is *prima facie* evidence that the rate of profit during this period is also high, but it does not necessarily prove that the rate of profit of enterprise is high. This latter distinction more or less disappears for capitalists working predominantly with their own capital; they realize the high rate of profit, since they pay their interest to themselves. The possibility of a high rate of interest of

* See Chapter 22.

longer duration – we are not referring here to the specific phase of pressure on the money market – is given by the high rate of profit. It is possible however that this high rate of profit, after deducting the high rate of interest, leaves only a low rate of profit of enterprise. The latter may contract, while the high rate of profit continues. This is possible because enterprises once embarked upon must be continued. In this phase, operations are conducted largely with credit capital (other people's); and the high rate of profit may in places be speculative and prospective. It is possible to pay interest at a high rate with a high rate of profit but a declining profit of enterprise. It can be paid – and this is partly the case in periods of speculation – not out of profits but out of the borrowed capital itself, and this situation can last a good while.

Secondly, to say that the demand for money capital and hence the interest rate rises because the profit rate is high is not the same as saying that the demand for industrial capital rises and that this is why the interest rate is high.

In times of crisis the demand for loan capital, and with it the interest rate, reaches its maximum; the rate of profit as good as disappears, and with it the demand for industrial capital. In times such as these everyone borrows simply to pay, to settle commitments already entered into. In the period when business revives after the crisis, on the other hand, loan capital is demanded in order to buy, and to transform the money capital into productive or commercial capital. And then it is demanded either by the industrial capitalist or by the merchant. The industrial capitalist invests it in means of production and labour-power.

The rising demand for labour-power can never be in itself a reason for a rising rate of interest, in so far as this is determined by the profit rate. Higher wages are never a cause of higher profit, even though, taking particular phases of the industrial cycle, they may be one of its results.

The demand for labour-power may increase because the exploitation of labour is proceeding under particularly favourable conditions, but the rising demand for labour-power and hence for variable capital does not in and of itself increase profits but rather reduces them in proportion. Yet the demand for variable capital may increase, and thus also the demand for money capital, while this in turn increases the rate of interest. The market price of labour-power then rises above its average, a more than average number of workers come to be employed, while at the same time the rate of interest rises, because the demand for money capital rises in these conditions. An increased demand for labour-power raises the price of this commodity just like any other, without raising profits, which depend principally on the relative cheapness of this particular commodity. At the same time, however, under the conditions we have assumed, this demand raises the rate of interest, by increasing the demand for money capital. If the money capitalist, instead of lending out money, should transform himself into an industrialist, the fact that he has to pay more for labour would not in and of itself increase his profit but would rather lead to a proportionate reduction in it. The combination of circumstances may still be such that his profit rises, but this is never because he pays more for labour. The latter circumstance, however, in as much as it increases the demand for money capital, is sufficient to raise the interest rate. If wages rise for whatever reason, in otherwise unfavourable conjunctures, the rise in wages causes the profit rate to fall, although the rate of interest rises to the extent that the wage rise increases the demand for money capital.

Apart from labour, what Overstone calls the 'demand for capital' consists simply of the demand for commodities. The demand for commodities raises their price, whether this demand rises above the average, or the supply falls below its average. If the industrial capitalist or merchant now has to pay £150, for example, for the same quantity of commodities for which he formerly paid £100, he would have to borrow £150 instead of £100 and would therefore have to pay £7$\frac{1}{2}$, at a 5 per cent rate of interest, instead of £5. The amount of interest he has to pay rises, because of the rise in the amount of capital borrowed.

Mr Overstone's entire aim is to present the interests of loan capital and industrial capital as identical, while his Bank Act is precisely calculated to exploit the difference between these interests for the benefit of money capital.

It is possible that the demand for commodities, in the case where their supply has fallen below the average, absorbs no more money capital than before. The same sum, and perhaps a smaller one, has to be paid for their overall value, but a smaller quantity of use-values is received for this sum. In this case, the demand for loanable money capital remains the same, i.e. the interest rate will not rise, even though the demand for commodities has risen in relation to their supply and the commodities' price has therefore risen as well. The rate of interest can only be affected when the total demand for loan capital grows, and under the above assumptions this is not the case.

The supply of an article, however, may fall below its average, as is the case with a harvest failure in corn, cotton, etc., while the demand for loan capital grows on the speculation that prices will rise still higher, the most immediate means to make them rise being to withdraw a part of the supply temporarily from the market. In order to pay for the commodities bought without selling them, gold is obtained by way of commercial 'bill of exchange operations'. In this case the demand for loan capital grows, and the rate of interest may rise as a result of this attempt to block the supply of commodities to the market artificially. The higher rate of interest then expresses an artificial reduction in the supply of commodity capital.

On the other hand the demand for an article may increase because its supply has increased and the article stands below its average price.

In this case, the demand for loan capital may remain the same or even fall, because more commodities are to be had with the same sum of money. There could also be a speculative formation of stocks, partly for use at a favourable moment for the purpose of production, partly in expectation of a later rise in price. In this case, the demand for loan capital could grow, so that the higher rate of interest would be an expression of capital investment in the formation of excessive stocks of the elements of productive capital. All we are considering here is the demand for loan capital as it is influenced by the demand and supply for commodity capital. We have already explained earlier how the changing condition of the reproduction process in the various phases of the industrial cycle affects the supply of loan capital. The trivial statement that the market rate of interest is determined by the supply and demand for (loan) capital is cunningly conflated by Overstone with his own assumption in which loan capital is identical with capital in general, and he seeks in this way to transform the money-lender into the only capitalist and his capital into the only capital.

In times of pressure, the demand for loan capital is a demand for means of payment and nothing more than this; in no way is it a demand for money as means of purchase. The interest rate can then rise very high, irrespective of whether real capital – productive and commodity capital – is abundant or scarce. The demand for means of payment is simply a demand for convertibility into *money*, in so far as the merchants and producers are able to offer good security; it is a demand for *money capital*, in so far as this is not the case, i.e. in so far as an advance of means of payment gives them not only the *money form*, but also the *equivalent* that they lack for payments, in whatever form this might be. This is the point at which both sides in the present controversy in the theory of crises are simultaneously right and wrong. Those who say there is simply a lack of means of payment either have in mind the owners of *bona fide* securities or else they are fools who believe it the duty of a bank, and within its power, to transform every bankrupt swindler into a solvent capitalist by means of paper tokens. Those who say there is simply a lack of capital are either merely splitting hairs, since in times such as these *inconvertible* capital is present on a massive scale as a result of over-importing and overproduction, or else they are just referring to those credit-jobbers who actually are put in a position where they can no longer obtain other people's capital to operate with and then demand that the bank should not only help them pay for the capital lost but also enable them to continue their swindling.

It is the foundation of capitalist production that money confronts commodities as an autonomous form of value, or that exchange-value must obtain an autonomous form in money, and this is possible only if one particular commodity becomes the material in whose value all other commodities are measured, this thereby becoming the universal commodity, the commodity *par excellence*, in contrast to all other commodities. This must show itself in two ways, particularly in developed capitalist countries, which replace money to a large extent either by credit operations or by credit money. In times of pressure, when credit contracts or dries up altogether, money suddenly confronts commodities absolutely as the only means of payment and the true existence of value. Hence the general devaluation of commodities and the difficulty or even impossibility of transforming them into money, i.e. into their own purely fantastic form. Secondly, however, credit money is itself only money in so far as it absolutely represents real money to the sum of its nominal value. With the drain of gold, its convertibility into money becomes problematic, i.e. its identity with actual gold. Hence we get forcible measures, putting up the rate of interest, etc. in order to guarantee the conditions of this convertibility. This can be more or less intensified by erroneous legislation based on incorrect theories of money and enforced on the nation in the interest of money-dealers such as Overstone and company. But the basis for it is provided by the basis of the mode of production itself. A devaluation of credit money (not to speak of a complete loss of its monetary character, which is in any case purely imaginary) would destroy all the existing relationships. The value of commodities is thus sacrificed in order to ensure the fantastic and autonomous existence of this value in money. In any event, a money value is only guaranteed as long as money itself is guaranteed. This is why many millions' worth of commodities have to be sacrificed for a few millions in money. This is unavoidable in capitalist production, and forms one of its particular charms. In former modes of production, this does not happen, because given the narrow basis on which these move, neither credit nor credit money is able to develop. As long as the *social* character of labour appears as the *monetary existence* of the commodity and hence as a *thing* outside actual production, monetary crises, independent of real crises or as an intensification of them, are unavoidable. It is evident on the other hand that, as long as a bank's credit is not undermined, it can alleviate the panic in such cases by increasing its credit money, whereas it increases this panic by contracting credit. The entire history of modern industry shows that metal would be required only to settle international trade and its temporary imbalances, if production at home were organized. The suspension of cash payments by the so-called national banks, which is resorted to as the sole expedient in all extreme cases, shows that even now no metal money is needed at home.

It would be ridiculous to say of two individuals that they both have an unfavourable balance of payments in their dealings with one another. If they are each mutually debtor and creditor, it is clear that when their claims do not balance, one of them must be debtor to the other for the remainder. With nations, this is in no way the case. And this fact is recognized by all economists in the statement that the balance of payments may be favourable or unfavourable for a country, even though the balance of trade must ultimately balance out. The balance of payments is distinct from the balance of trade in that it is that balance of trade which must be settled at a particular date. The effect of crises, then, is to compress the difference between the balance of payments and the balance of trade into a short period of time; and the specific conditions that develop in nations affected by a crisis, and hence by the arrival of this date of payment, already involve a contraction of this kind in the settlement period. Firstly, the shipment of precious metals abroad; then the forced selling of goods sent on consignment; the export of commodities in order to sell them off cheaply or obtain money advances on them at home; the recall of credit, the fall in security values, the forced selling of foreign securities, the attraction of foreign capital to invest in these devalued securities, and finally bankruptcy, which settles a whole series of claims. In this connection, metal is often still sent to the country where the crisis has broken out, because drafts on it are uncertain and payment in metal more secure. Added to this is the fact that, in relation to Asia, all capitalist countries are generally debtors simultaneously, either directly or indirectly. Once these various factors exert their full effect on the other countries involved, these too experience an export of gold or silver, i.e. their payments fall due, and the same phenomenon is repeated.

In the case of commercial credit, interest, as the difference between the credit price and the cash price, is involved in the price of a commodity only in so far as bills of exchange have a longer term than usual. In other cases not. And this is explained by the fact that each person takes this credit from one direction and extends it in another. (This does not tally with my own experience. – F. E.) But in so far as discounting is involved here in this way, it is not governed by this commercial credit, but rather by the money market.

If the demand and supply of money capital, which determines the rate of interest, were identical with the demand and supply of real capital, as Overstone maintains, then according to whether we considered various different commodities or the same commodity at different stages (raw material, semi-finished goods, finished product), interest would have to be both low and high at the same time. In 1844 the Bank of England's interest rate fluctuated between 4 per cent (from January to September) and $2\frac{1}{2}$–3 per cent (from November to the end of the year). In 1845 it was $2\frac{1}{2}$, $2\frac{3}{4}$ and 3 per cent from January to October, and between 3 and 5 per cent during the remaining months. The average price of fair Orleans cotton was $6\frac{1}{4}$d. in 1844 and $4\frac{7}{8}$d. in 1845. On 3 March 1844, the Liverpool cotton stock was 627,042 bales, and on 3 March 1845, 773,800 bales. To judge from the low price of cotton, the rate of interest should have been low in 1845, which was in fact the case for the greater part of the year. But to judge from the yarn, it should still have been high, for prices were relatively high and profits absolutely so. From cotton at 4d. a lb. in 1845, yarn could be spun at a cost of 4d. (good secunda mule twist no. 40), which thus cost the spinner a total of 8d.; but he could sell this in September and October 1845 at 10½d. or 11d. per lb. (See evidence of Wylie, below.)

The whole question can be resolved in the following way.

The demand and supply for loan capital would be identical with the demand and supply for capital in general (although this last phrase is absurd; for the industrialist or merchant, commodities are a form of his capital, but he never demands capital as such, but always a particular commodity, buying and paying for it as a commodity, corn or cotton, irrespective of the role it has to fulfil in the circuit of his capital), if there were no money-lenders and instead of them the lending capitalist owned machines, raw material, etc. and lent these out or hired them, as houses are rented now, to industrial capitalists who were themselves the owners of a section of these objects. In conditions such as these, the supply of loan capital would be identical with the supply of elements of production for the industrial capitalist, and of commodities for the merchant. It is evident however that the division of profit between lender and borrower would then be completely dependent, in the first place, on the ratio in which this capital is borrowed and in which it is the property of the person using it.

According to Mr Weguelin (*B. A.* 1857), the rate of interest is determined by 'the amount of unemployed capital' (252); it is 'but an indication of a large amount of capital seeking employment' (271). Later this unemployed capital is called 'floating capital' (485), and by this he understands 'the Bank of England notes and other kinds of circulation in the country, for instance, the country banks circulation and the amount of coin which is in the country ... I include in floating capital the reserves of the bankers' (502, 503) and later also gold bullion (503). Thus the same Mr Weguelin says that the Bank of England exerts great influence upon the rate of interest in times when 'we' (the Bank of England) 'are holders of the greater portion of the unemployed capital' (1198), whereas according to the above evidence of Mr Overstone, the Bank of England 'is no place for capital'. Mr Weguelin further says: 'I think the rate of discount is governed by the amount of unemployed capital which there is in the country. The amount of unemployed capital is represented by the reserve of the Bank of England, which is practically a reserve of bullion. When, therefore, the bullion is drawn upon, it diminishes the amount of unemployed capital in the country and consequently raises the value of that which remains' (1258).

John Stuart Mill says (2102): 'The Bank is obliged to depend for the solvency of its Banking Department upon what it can do to replenish the reserve in that department; and therefore as soon as it finds that there is any drain in progress, it is obliged to look to the safety of its reserve, and to commence contracting its discounts or selling securities.'

Taking the Banking Department by itself, the reserve is a reserve for deposits only. According to the Overstones, the Banking Department should simply act as a banker, without regard to the 'automatic' note issue. But in times of real pressure, the Bank of England keeps a very sharp eye on the metal reserve, independently of the reserve of the Banking Department, which consists simply of notes; and it must do so, if it does not want to go broke. For to the same extent that the metal reserve disappears, so too does the reserve of banknotes, and no one should know this better than Mr Overstone, who so wisely established this very device in his 1844 Bank Act.

Chapter 33: The Means of Circulation
under the Credit System

'The great regulator of the velocity of the currency is credit. This explains why a severe pressure upon the money-market is generally coincident with a full circulation' (*The Currency Theory Reviewed*, p. 65).

This should be taken in a double sense. On the one hand, all methods that save means of circulation are founded on credit. Secondly, however, let us take a £500 note. Say that A gives this to B today in payment for a bill of exchange; B deposits it the same day with his banker; the latter uses it still the same day to discount a bill for C; C pays it into his bank, this bank gives it to the billbroker as an advance, etc. The speed with which the note circulates here, serving to make purchases or payments, is mediated by the speed with which it returns time after time to someone or other in the form of a deposit and is transferred to someone else in the form of a loan. Pure economizing on means of circulation appears in its most highly developed form in the clearing house, the simple exchange of bills falling due, where the principal function of money as means of payment is simply to settle the balances. But the existence of these bills of exchange itself depends on the credit that the industrialists and merchants give one another. If this credit declines, so does the number of bills, particularly the long-term ones, and so too therefore does the effectiveness of this method of settlement. And this economy that consists in the removal of money from transactions and depends entirely on the function of money as means of payment, depending in turn on credit, must be one of two kinds (apart from the greater or lesser development of technique in the concentration of these payments): reciprocal claims, represented by bills of exchange or cheques, are balanced by the same banker, who simply transfers the claim from one person's account to the other's; or else the various bankers settle them among themselves.[11] The concentration of £8–£10 million in bills of exchange in the hands of a bill-broker, such as the firm of Overend, Gurney & Co., was one of the principal means for expanding the scope of this settlement at the local level. By this kind of economizing, the effectiveness of the means of circulation is increased, in so far as a smaller quantity is required simply to settle the balance. The velocity of the money circulating as means of circulation, on the other hand (which can also be economized on), depends entirely on the flow of purchases and sales, or else on the interlinking of payments, in so far as these follow successively in money. But in this way credit mediates and increases the velocity of circulation. The individual piece of money may effect only five transactions, for instance, remaining for longer in each individual hand – as a mere means of circulation without the intervention of credit – if A, its original owner, buys from B, B from C, C from D, D from E, and E from F, i.e. if its transition from one hand to the other is mediated simply by actual purchases and sales. But if B deposits the money received in payment from A with his banker, who passes it to C in discounting a bill of exchange, C buying from D, D depositing it with his banker and the latter lending it to E, who buys from F, then even its velocity as a mere means of circulation (means of purchase) is mediated by several credit operations: B's depositing with his banker and the latter's discounting for C, D's depositing with his banker and the latter's discounting for E; four credit operations in all. Without these credit operations, the same piece of money would not have performed five purchases successively in a given period of time. The fact that it changed hands without the mediation of actual purchase and sale – as a deposit and by dis-

11. Average number of days for which a banknote remains in circulation:

Year	£5 note	£10 note	£20–100	£200–500	£1,000
1792	—	236	209	31	22
1818	148	137	121	18	13
1846	79	71	34	12	8
1856	70	58	27	9	7

(Table compiled by Marshall, the Bank of England cashier; in *Report on Bank Acts*. 1857, II, Appendix, pp. 300, 301.)*

* Marx has in fact condensed the tables that he cites here. And for the years 1792 and 1818, the figures he gives under the headings £20–£100 and £200–£500 are in fact the respective figures for £20 and £200 notes only.

counting – means that its change of hands in the series of real transactions is accelerated.

We have already shown how one and the same banknote can form deposits with different bankers. In the same way, it can form different deposits with the same banker. He discounts B's bill of exchange with the note that A has deposited, B pays to C, and C deposits the note with the same banker who gave it out.

*

In considering simple monetary circulation (Volume 1, Chapter 3, 2), we already showed how the quantity of money actually circulating, taking the velocity of circulation and economy of payment as given, is determined by the price of commodities and the number of transactions. The same law prevails in the case of note circulation.

The following table shows the yearly average of Bank of England notes in the hands of the public, subdivided into the totals for £5 and £10 notes, notes of £20 to £100, and of £200 to £1,000; also the percentage of the total circulation that was supplied by each of these categories. The totals are in thousands, the last three figures having been deleted.

Year	£5–10 notes	%	£20–100 notes	%	£200–1,000 notes	%	Totals in £
1844	9,263	45.7	5,735	28.3	5,253	26.0	20,241
1845	9,698	46.9	6,082	29.3	4,942	23.8	20,722
1846	9,918	48.9	5,778	28.5	4,590	22.6	20,286
1847	9,591	50.1	5,498	28.7	4,066	21.2	19,155
1848	8,732	48.3	5,046	27.9	4,307	23.8	18,085
1849	8,692	47.2	5,234	28.5	4,477	24.3	18,403
1850	9,164	47.2	5,587	28.8	4,646	24.0	19,398
1851	9,362	48.1	5,554	28.5	4,557	23.4	19,473
1852	9,839	45.0	6,161	28.2	5,856	26.8	21,856
1853	10,699	47.3	6,393	28.2	5,541	24.5	22,653
1854	10,565	51.0	5,910	28.5	4,234	20.5	20,709
1855	10,628	53.6	5,706	28.9	3,459	17.5	19,793
1856	10,680	54.4	5,645	28.7	3,323	16.9	19,648
1857	10,659	54.7	5,567	28.6	3,241	16.7	19,467

(*B A*. 1858, p. xxvi.)

The total sum of banknotes in circulation thus underwent a

positive decline between 1844 and 1857, even though trade more than doubled, as is shown by the export and import figures. Low denomination notes of £5 and £10 increased, as the table shows, from £9,263,000 in 1844 to £10,659,000 in 1857. And this went parallel with the increase in gold circulation which was so marked at this very time. Notes of higher denominations (£200 to £1,000), on the other hand, declined from £5,856,000 in 1852 to £3,241,000 in 1857, a decline of more than £2½ million. This has been explained as follows: 'On the 8th June 1854, the private bankers of London admitted the joint-stock banks to the arrangements of the clearing house, and shortly afterwards the final clearing was adjusted in the Bank of England. The daily clearances are now effected by transfers in the accounts which the several banks keep in that establishment. In consequence of the adoption of this system, the large notes which the bankers formerly employed for the purpose of adjusting their accounts are no longer necessary' (*B. A.* 1858, p. v).

The low minimum to which the use of money in wholesale trade has been reduced can be seen by comparing the table reproduced in Volume 1, Chapter 3, p. 238, note 54, which was submitted to the Bank Acts Committee by Morrison, Dillon & Co., one of the largest of those London wholesalers where a retail trader can purchase his entire stock of commodities of all kinds.

According to the evidence of W. Newmarch (*B. A.* 1857, no. 1741), other factors also contributed to the saving on means of circulation: the penny post, railways, telegraphs, in short the improved means of communication; so that England can do approximately five or six times the amount of business with the same note circulation. This however is said to be essentially due to the withdrawal of notes of more than £10 from circulation. This seems to him a natural explanation for the fact that in Scotland and Ireland, where £1 notes also circulate, the note circulation has risen by approximately 31 per cent (1747). The total circulation of banknotes in the United Kingdom, including these £1 notes, is £39 million (1749). The gold circulation is £70 million (1750). In Scotland the note circulation in 1834 was £3,120,000; in 1844, £3,020,000; in 1854, £4.050,000 (1752).

It already emerges from this that it is in no way in the power of the note-issuing banks to increase the number of notes in circulation, as long as these notes are exchangeable at any time against metal money. (Marx is not referring at all here to inconvertible paper money; inconvertible banknotes can become general means of circulation only where they are in actual fact supported by the state's credit, as is the case today in Russia, for example. These therefore fall under the laws of inconvertible state paper money, as already developed: Volume 1, Chapter 3, 2, c: 'Coin. The Symbol of Value'. – F. E.)

The amount of notes in circulation is governed by the needs of commerce, and each superfluous note immediately finds its way back to its issuer. Since in England it is only the notes of the Bank of England that enjoy general circulation as legal tender, we can ignore here the insignificant and simply local note circulation of the provincial banks.

Before the Bank Acts Committee of 1858, Mr Neave, Governor of the Bank of England, gave the following evidence: '947. (Question:) Whatever measures you resort to, the amount of notes with the public, you say, remains the same; that is somewhere about £20,000,000? – In ordinary times, the uses of the public seem to want about £20,000,000. There are special periodical moments when, through the year, they rise to another £1,000,000 or £1,500,000. I stated that, if the public wanted more, they could always take it from the Bank of England.' – '948. You stated that during the panic the public would not allow you to diminish the amount of notes; I want you to account for that. – In moments of panic, the public have, as I believe, the full power of helping themselves as to notes; and of course, as long as the Bank has a liability, they may use that liability to take the notes from the Bank.' – '949. Then there seems to be required, at all times, somewhere about £20,000,000 of legal tender? – £20,000,000 of notes with the public; it varies. It is £18,500,000, £19,000,000, £20,000,000, and so on; but taking the average, you may call it from £19,000,000 to £20,000,000.'

Evidence of Thomas Tooke to the House of Lords Committee on Commercial Distress (*C. D.* 1848–57), no. 3094: 'It has no power of its own volition to extend the amount of its circulation in the hands of the public; but the Bank has the power of reducing the amount of the notes in the hands of the public, not however without a very violent operation.'

J. C. Wright, banker in Nottingham for thirty years, says this of the Bank of England notes, after explaining in detail how it is impossible for the provincial banks to keep in circulation more notes than the public need and want at the time (*C. D.* 1848–57, no. 2844): 'I am not aware that there is any check upon the Bank of England' (in respect of note issue) 'but any excess of circulation will go into the deposits and thus assume a different name.'

The same holds true for Scotland, where there is almost nothing but paper in circulation, since there as in Ireland £1 notes are also permitted, and 'the Scotch hate gold'. Kennedy, director of a Scottish bank, declares that the banks could never reduce their note circulation and 'conceives that so long as there are internal transactions requiring notes or gold to perform them, bankers must, either through the demands of their depositors or in one shape or another, furnish as much currency as those transactions require ... The Scottish banks can restrict their transactions, but they cannot control their currency' (ibid., nos. 3446, 3448).

Likewise Anderson, director of the Union Bank of Scotland, ibid., no. 3578: 'The system of exchanges between yourselves' (among the Scottish banks) 'prevents any over-issue on the part of any one bank? – Yes; there is a more powerful preventive than the system of exchanges' (which has really nothing to do with this, but does indeed guarantee the ability of the notes of each bank to circulate throughout Scotland), 'the universal practice in Scotland of keeping a bank account; everybody who has any money at all has a bank account and puts in every day the money which he does not immediately want, so that at the close of the business of the day there is no money scarcely out of the banks except what people have in their pockets.'

The same also applies to Ireland, viz. the evidence of the Governor of the Bank of Ireland, MacDonnell, and the director of the Provincial Bank of Ireland, Murray, before the same committee.

The note circulation is not only independent of the will of the Bank of England, it is equally independent of the state of the gold reserve in the Bank's vaults, which is what ensures the convertibility of these notes.

'On September 18, 1846, the circulation of the Bank of England was £20,900,000 and the bullion in the Bank £16,273,000; and on April 5, 1847, the notes in circulation were £20,815,000 and the bullion £10,246,000 ... It is evident that £6 million of gold were exported, without any contraction of the currency of the country' (J. G. Kinnear, *The Crisis and the Currency*, London, 1847, p. 5).

Naturally this holds good only under the conditions prevailing in England today, and even then only in so far as legislation does not enforce a different ratio between note issue and metal reserve.

So it is simply the needs of business itself that exert an influence on the quantity of money in circulation – notes and gold. The first thing to be considered here are the periodic fluctuations that repeat themselves each year, whatever the general state of business might be, so that for twenty years past, 'the circulation is high in one month, and it is low in another month, and in a certain other month occurs a medium point' (Newmarch, *B. A.* 1857, no. 1650).

Thus in August of each year a few £ millions, mostly in gold, pass from the Bank of England into domestic circulation, to pay for the costs of the harvest; since what this involves is principally the payment of wages, banknotes are used but little in England. This money then flows back to the Bank again, up to the end of the year. In Scotland, £1 notes are given almost invariably in place of sovereigns; here, therefore, it is the note circulation that expands in the corresponding case, in fact twice a year, in May and November, by some £3 to £4 million; fourteen days later the reflux has already set in, and within a month it is almost complete. (Anderson, op. cit. [*C. D.* 1848–57], nos. 3595–3600.)

The Bank of England's note circulation also undergoes a temporary fluctuation each quarter as a result of the quarterly payment of 'dividends', i.e. interest on the national debt, banknotes firstly being withdrawn from circulation and then distributed amongst the public; but these flow back very quickly. Weguelin (*B. A.* 1857, no. 38) puts the total fluctuation to which this gives rise at £2½ million. Mr Chapman, on the other hand, of the notorious firm of Overend, Gurney and Co., reckons the disturbance produced in the money market to be much higher. 'When you abstract from the circulation £6,000,000 or £7,000,000 of revenue in anticipation of dividends, somebody must be the medium of supplying that in the intermediate times' (*B. A.* 1857, no. 5196).

Far more important and persistent are the fluctuations in the total circulating medium that correspond to the various phases of the industrial cycle. Let us hear on this subject another partner in the same firm, the worthy Quaker Samuel Gurney (*C. D.* 1848–57, no. 2645): 'At the end of October' (1847) 'the amount of banknotes in the hands of the public was £20,800,000. At that period there was great difficulty in getting possession of banknotes in the money-market. This arose from the alarm of not being able to get them in consequence of the restriction of the Act of 1844. At present' (March 1848) 'the amount of banknotes in the hands of the public is ... £17,700,000, but there being now no commercial alarm whatsoever, it is much beyond what is required. There is no banking house or money-dealer in London, but what has a larger amount of banknotes than they can use.' – '2650. The amount of banknotes ... out of the custody of the Bank of England affords a totally insufficient exponent of the active state of the circulation, without taking into consideration likewise ... the state of the commercial world and the state of credit.' – '2651. The feeling of surplus that we have under the present amount of circulation in the hands of the public arises in a large degree from our present state of great stagnation. In a state of high prices and excitement of transaction £17,700,000 would give us a feeling of restriction.'

(As long as the state of business is such that the returns on advances made come in regularly, so that credit remains unimpaired, the expansion and contraction of circulation is governed simply by the needs of the industrialists and merchants. Since in England at least gold does not come into the picture for wholesale trade, and the gold circulation, apart from the seasonal fluctuations, can be seen as a magnitude that is fairly constant over a longish period of time, the Bank of England's note circulation provides a sufficiently exact measurement of these changes. In the quiet period after the crisis, transactions are at their lowest; with the revival of demand there is also a greater requirement for means of circulation, which rises with increasing prosperity; the quantity of means of circulation reaches its high point in the period of over-exertion and over-speculation – then the crisis breaks out, and overnight the banknotes that were still so abundant the day before have vanished from the market, and with them the discounter of bills, the advancer on securities, the buyer of commodities. The Bank of England is supposed to help; but even its powers are soon exhausted, and the Bank Act of 1844 compels it to contract its note circulation at the very moment when the entire world is crying out for banknotes, when the owners of commodities cannot sell and yet are supposed to pay, and are ready to make any sacrifice, so long as they can obtain banknotes.

'During an alarm,' says banker Wright, whom we met above (op. cit., no. 2930), 'the country requires twice as much circulation as in ordinary times, because the circulation is hoarded by bankers and others.'

In so far as a crisis breaks out, it is then simply a question of means of payment. But since each person is dependent on someone else for the arrival of these means of payment, and no one knows whether the other will be in a position to pay on the due date, a real steeplechase breaks out for those means of payment that are to be found in the market, i.e. for banknotes. Each person hoards as many as he can get his hands on, so that the notes vanish from circulation the very day they are most needed. Samuel Gurney (*C. D.* 1848–57, no. 1116) estimates a figure of £4–£5 million for the banknotes put under lock and key at the moment of panic in October 1847. – F. E.)

In this connection the evidence to the 1857 Bank Acts Committee of Gurney's partner, the afore-mentioned Chapman, is highly interesting. I give here the principal content of this in its original context, although some points that it covers we shall investigate only later. Mr Chapman expresses the matter as follows:

'4963. I have also no hesitation in saying that I do not think it is a proper condition of things that the money-market should be under the power of any individual capitalist (such as does exist in London), to create a tremendous scarcity and pressure, when we have a very low state of circulation out. That is possible . . . there is more than one capitalist, who can withdraw from the circulating medium £1,000,000 or £2,000,000 of notes, if they have an object to attain by it.'

4965. A big speculator can sell £1 or £2 millions worth of Consols, and thus take money out of the market. Something of this kind happened quite recently, 'it creates a very violent pressure'.

4967. The notes, besides, are then quite unproductive. 'But that is nothing, if it effects his great object; his great object is to knock down the funds, to create a scarcity, and he has it perfectly in his power to do so.'

To give one example. One morning there was a great demand for money from the stock exchange. No one knew the cause. Someone asked Chapman to lend him £50,000 at 7 per cent. Chapman was greatly surprised, as his rate of interest was much lower; he agreed. Very soon the man returned and took a further £50,000 at $7\frac{1}{2}$ per cent, then £100,000 at 8 per cent, and wanted still more at $8\frac{1}{2}$ per cent. Chapman then got worried himself. It subsequently emerged that a major sum of money had suddenly been withdrawn from the market. However, said Chapman, 'I did lend a large sum at 8 per cent; I was afraid to go beyond; I did not know what was coming.'

It should never be forgotten that although a fairly constant sum of £19–£20 million in notes is ostensibly in the hands of the public, yet the portion of these notes that is actually circulating, on the one hand, and the portion that lies unoccupied in the banks as a reserve, on the other, are both constantly and substantially changing. If the reserve is large, i.e. the actual circulation low, it is said from the standpoint of the money market that the circulation is full, or money is plentiful; if the reserve is small, i.e. the actual circulation full, the money market call it low and say money is scarce, i.e. only a small amount represents unoccupied loan capital. A genuine expansion or contraction of circulation independent of the phases of the industrial cycle – one in which the amount that the public needs remains the same – is only to be found for technical reasons, e.g. at the payment date of taxes or of interest on the national debt. With tax payment, notes and gold flow into the Bank of England in more than their customary measure, and in fact circulation contracts, irrespective of the need for it. Conversely, when dividends are paid out on the national debt. In the first case, loans are taken out from the Bank in order to obtain means of circulation. In the latter case the rate of interest charged by the private banks falls on account of the temporary growth in their reserves. This has nothing to do with the absolute total of means of circulation, but simply with the banking house that puts these means of circulation into circulation, for which this process appears as an alienation of loan capital and which therefore pockets the profit on it.

In the one case there is simply a temporary displacement of the circulating medium, which the Bank of England adjusts by making short-term advances at low interest shortly before the due date of the quarterly taxes and the likewise quarterly dividends; the additional notes paid out in this way then first of all fill the gaps that the payment of taxes gives rise to, while their repayment to the Bank immediately afterwards brings back the surplus notes which the paying out of dividends has placed with the public.

In the other case, a low or full circulation is never more than a different distribution of the same mass of means of circulation between active circulation and deposits, i.e. as an instrument for loans.

On the other hand, if for example an influx of gold leads to an increase in the number of notes given out by the Bank of England in return, these help the business of discounting outside the Bank and flow back in the repayment of loans, so that the absolute volume of notes in circulation is only temporarily increased.

If the circulation is full, on account of an expansion of business (which is only possible given relatively low prices), the rate of interest may be relatively high on account of the demand for loan capital that results from rising profits and increased new investments. If it is low, on account of a contraction of business or possibly a greater ease of credit, the rate of interest may be low even if prices are high. (See Hubbard.) *

The absolute quantity of circulation has a determining effect on the rate of interest only in periods of pressure. In this case, either the demand for a full circulation is merely a demand for means of hoarding (apart from the reduced velocity with which the money circulates, and with which the same identical pieces of money are constantly converted into loan capital), on account of the lack of credit, as in 1847, when the suspension of the Bank Act did not lead to any expansion in the circulation but was sufficient to bring hoarded notes to light again and make them circulate actively. Or else more means of circulation may really be required under these circumstances, in the way that the circulation really did grow for some time in 1857 after the suspension of the Bank Act.

In other cases the absolute quantity of circulation has no effect on the rate of interest, since firstly, taking the economy and velocity of circulation as constant, it is determined by the price of commodities and the volume of transactions (in which case one element generally counteracts the effect of the other) and ultimately by the state of credit, whereas it in no way conversely determines the latter; and since, secondly, commodity prices and interest do not stand in any necessary relationship.

Under the Bank Restriction Act (1797–1820)† there was a surplus of 'currency', with the rate of interest always far higher than since the resumption of cash payment. It later fell sharply with the restriction of note issue and rising bill quotations. In

* See below, pp. 683–5.

† The Bank Restriction Act, designed to cope with the needs of the British government in the wars with France, freed the Bank of England from the obligation of exchanging its notes for gold.

1822, 1823 and 1832, the total circulation was low and the rate of interest similarly so. In 1824, 1825 and 1836 the circulation was high and the rate of interest rose. In summer 1830 the circulation was high, the rate of interest low. Since the gold discoveries, monetary circulation has expanded throughout Europe, and the interest rate has risen. The interest rate thus does not depend on the amount of money in circulation.

The distinction between the issue of means of circulation and the lending of capital is best shown in connection with the actual reproduction process. In Volume 2, Part Three, we saw how the various components of production are exchanged one for another. For example, variable capital consists materially of the means of subsistence of the workers, a portion of their own product. But it is paid out to them bit by bit in money. This the capitalist has to advance, and it depends very much on the organization of the credit system whether he can pay out the new variable capital again the next week with the old money that he paid out the week before. It is similar in the acts of exchange between the various components of a total social capital, e.g. between means of consumption and the means of production of these. The money for their circulation, as we have seen, must be advanced by one or both of the exchanging parties. It then remains in circulation, but returns time and again, after completing its exchange, to the person who advanced it, since it was advanced by him over and above the industrial capital he actually employed. (See Volume 2, Chapter 20.) When the credit system is developed, so that money is concentrated in the hands of the banks, it is they who advance it, at least nominally. This advance is only related to the money in circulation. It is an advance of circulation, not an advance of the capitals it circulates.

Chapman: '5062. There may be times, when the notes in the hands of the public, though they may be large, are not to be had.' There is money, even during a panic; but everyone takes good care not to transform it into loanable capital, loanable money; each holds on to it for actual needs of payment.

'5099. The country bankers in rural districts send up their unemployed balances to yourselves and other houses? – Yes.' – '5100. On the other hand, the Lancashire and Yorkshire districts require discounts from you for the use of their trades? – Yes.' – '5101. Then by that means the surplus money of one part of the country is made available for the demands of another part of the country? – Precisely so.'

Chapman says that the banks' custom of investing their surplus money capital for a short term in the purchase of Consols and treasury bills has greatly increased in recent times, since it became the custom to lend out this 'money at call' (i.e. money whose repayment may be demanded at any time, from one day to the next). He himself sees the purchase of this kind of paper as most unsuitable for his business. He therefore invests it in good bills of exchange, with one portion falling due each day, so that he always knows how much ready money he can count on. (5101–5105.)

The very growth of exports, for more or less every country, but particularly for the country that gives credit, presents itself as a growing demand on the domestic money market, which however is felt as such only in times of pressure. In periods when exports are increasing, long-term bills of exchange are generally drawn by manufacturers on the export merchant, against consignments of British manufacturers. (5126.)

'5127. Is it not frequently the case that an understanding exists that those bills are to be redrawn from time to time? – (Chapman:) That is a thing which they keep from us; we should not admit any bill of that sort ... I dare say it is done, but I cannot speak to a thing of the kind.' (The innocent Chapman.) '5129. If there is a large increase of the exports of the country, as there was last year, of £20 million, will not that naturally lead to a great demand for capital for the discount of bills representing those exports? – No doubt.' – '5130. Inasmuch as this country gives credit, as a general rule, to foreign countries for all exports, it would be an absorption of a corresponding increase of capital for the time being? – This country gives an immense credit; but then it takes credit for its raw material. We are drawn upon from America always at 60 days, and from other parts at 90 days. On the other hand we give credit; if we send goods to Germany, we give two or three months.'

Wilson asks Chapman (5131) whether bills are not already drawn on England against these imported raw materials and colonial goods at the same time as they are loaded, and whether the goods do not themselves already arrive simultaneously with the bills of lading. Chapman believes that this is the case, but knows nothing of this 'commercial' business; better informed people should be asked. In the export trade to America, Chapman says, 'the goods are symbolized in transit' [5133]; this gibberish is supposed to mean that the English export merchant draws a four-month bill against the commodities on one of the major American banking houses in London, and the banking house receives collateral from America.

'5136. As a general rule, are not the more remote transactions conducted by the merchant, who waits for his capital until the goods are sold? – There may be houses of great private wealth, who can afford to lay out their own capital and not take any advance upon the goods; but the most part are converted into advances by the acceptances of some well-known established houses.' – '5137. Those houses are resident in . . . London, or Liverpool, or elsewhere.' – '5138. Therefore, it makes no difference, whether the manufacturer lays out his money, or whether he gets a merchant in London or Liverpool to advance it; it is still an advance in this country? – Precisely. The manufacturer in few cases has anything to do with it' (but in 1847 in almost every case). 'A man dealing in manufactured goods, for instance, at Manchester, will buy his goods and ship them through a house of respectability in London; when the London house is satisfied that they are all packed according to the understanding, he draws upon this London house for six months against these goods to India or China, or wherever they are going; then the banking world comes in and discounts that bill for him; so that, by the time he has to pay for those goods, he has the money all ready by the discount of that bill.' – '5139. Although he has the money, the banker is laying out of his money? – *The banker has the bill; the banker has bought the bill*; he uses his banking capital in that form, namely, in discounting commercial bills.'

(Thus Chapman, too, sees the discounting of bills not as an advance, but rather as a purchase of commodities. – F. E.)

'5140. Still that forms part of the demand upon the money-market in London? – No doubt; it is the substantial occupation of the money-market and of the Bank of England. The Bank of England are as glad to get these bills as we are, because they know them to be good property.' – '5141. In that way, as the export trade increases, the demand upon the money-market increases also? – As the prosperity of the country increases, we' (the Chapmans) 'partake of it.' – '5142. Then when these various fields for the employment of capital increase suddenly, of course, the natural consequence is that the rate of interest is higher? – No doubt about it.'

In 5143 Chapman cannot 'quite understand, that under our large exports we have had such occasion for bullion'.

In 5144 the worthy Wilson asks: 'May it not be that we give larger credits upon our exports than we take credits upon our imports? – I rather doubt that point myself. If a man accepts against his Manchester goods sent to India, you cannot accept for less than ten months. We have had to pay America for her cotton' (that is perfectly true) 'some time before India pays us; but still it is rather refined in its operation.' – '5145. If we have had an increase, as we had last year, of £20 million in our exports of manufactures we must have had a very large increase of imports of raw material previously to that' (and in this way over-exports are already identified with over-imports, and overproduction with over-trading), 'in order to make up that increased quantity of goods? – No doubt.' – '5146. We should have to pay a very considerable balance, that is to say, the balance, no doubt, would run against us during that time, but in the long run, with America . . . the exchanges are in our favour, and we have been receiving for some time past large supplies of bullion from America.'

In 5148 Wilson asks the arch-usurer Chapman whether he does not consider his high interest rate as a token of great prosperity and high profits. Chapman, evidently astonished by the naïveté of this sycophant, naturally confirms this, but is honest enough to make the following qualification: 'There are some, who cannot help themselves; they have engagements to meet, and they must fulfil them, whether it is profitable or not; but, for a continuance' (of the high rate of interest), 'it would indicate prosperity.'

Both men forget that a high rate of interest can also indicate, as was the case in 1857, that the knights errant of credit are making the country unsafe. In this case, they can pay high rates of interest because they pay out of other people's pockets (though in this way they help to determine the interest rate for everyone), meanwhile living in style on anticipated profits. At the same time, incidentally, precisely this can be a very profitable business for manufacturers, etc. The system of advances makes returns absolutely deceptive. This also explains the following, which needs no explanation as far as the Bank of England is concerned, since when interest rates are high it discounts at a lower rate than the others.

'5156. I should say,' says Chapman, 'that our discounts, taking the present moment, when we have had for so long a high rate of interest, are at their maximum.' (Chapman said this on 21 July 1857, a few months before the crash.) '5157. In 1852' (when the interest rate was low) 'they were not nearly so large.' Because at that time business was still much healthier.

A particularly amusing aspect of Chapman's evidence is how these people actually view the public's money as their own property and believe they have a right to it, to ensure the permanent convertibility of the bills they discount. The questions and answers show great naïveté. It turns out to be the duty of legislation to ensure the permanent convertibility of the bills of exchange accepted by the major firms and to make sure that the Bank of England will rediscount them for the billbrokers under all circumstances. 1857, incidentally, saw the bankruptcy of three such billbrokers, to the tune of some £8 million, their own capital being infinitesimal in comparison with these debts.

'5177. Do you mean by that that you think that they' (that is bills accepted by Barings or Loyds) 'ought to be discountable on compulsion, in the same way that a Bank of England note is now exchangeable against gold by compulsion? – I think it would be a very lamentable thing, that they should not be discountable; a most extraordinary position, that a man should stop payment, who had the acceptances of Smith, Payne & Co., or Jones, Loyd & Co. in his hands, because he could not get them discounted.' – '5178. Is not the engagement of Messrs Baring an engagement to pay a certain sum of money when the bill is due? – That is perfectly true; but Messrs Baring, when they contract that engagement, and every other merchant who contracts an engagement, never dream that they are going to pay it in sovereigns; they expect that they are going to pay it at the Clearing House.' – '5180. Do you think that there should be any machinery contrived by which the public would have a right to claim money before that bill was due by calling upon somebody to discount it? – No, not from the acceptor; but if you mean by that that we are not to have the possibility of getting commercial bills discounted, we must alter the whole constitution of things.' – '5182. Then you think that it' (commercial bill) 'ought to be convertible into money, exactly in the same way that a Bank of England note ought to be convertible into gold? – Most decidedly so, under certain circumstances.' – '5184. Then you think that the provisions of the currency should be so shaped that a bill of exchange of undoubted character ought at all times to be as readily exchangeable against money as a bank-note? – I do.' – '5185. You do not mean to say that either the Bank of England or any individual should, by law, be compelled to exchange it? – I mean to say this, that in framing a bill for the currency, we should make provision to prevent the possibility of an inconvertibility of the bills of exchange of the country arising, assuming them to be undoubtedly solid and legitimate.'

This is the convertibility of the commercial bill of exchange against the convertibility of the banknote.

'5190. The money-dealers of the country only, in point of fact, represent the public' – as Mr Chapman did later at the Assizes in the Davidson case. See the *Great City Frauds.**

'5196. During the quarters' (when the dividends are paid) 'it is ... absolutely necessary that we should go to the Bank of England. When you abstract from the circulation £6,000,000 or £7,000,000 of revenue in anticipation of the dividends, somebody must be the medium of supplying that in the intermediate time.' (In this case the question at issue is the supply of money, not of capital or loan capital.)

'5169. Everybody acquainted with our commercial circle must know that when we are in such a state that we find it impossible to sell Exchequer bills, when India bonds are perfectly useless, when you cannot discount the first commercial bills, there must be great anxiety on the part of those whose business renders them liable to pay the circulating medium of the realm on demand, which is the case with all bankers. Then the effect of that is to make every man double his reserve. Just see what the result of that is throughout the country, that every country banker, of whom there are about 500, has to send up to his London correspondent to remit him £5,000 in banknotes. Taking such a limited sum as that as the average, which is quite absurd, you come to £2,500,000 taken out of the circulation. How is that to be supplied?'

Those private capitalists, etc. who have money, on the other hand, do not want to let go of it whatever the interest, for, as Chapman puts it, they say: '5195. We would rather have no interest at all, than have a doubt about our getting the money in case we require it.'

'5173. Our system is this: That we have £300,000,000 of liabili-

* Seton Laing, *New Series of the Great City Frauds of Cole, Davidson and Gordon*, 5th edn, London [1869].

ties which may be called for at a single moment to be paid in the coin of the realm, and that coin of the realm, if the whole of it is substituted, amounts to £23,000,000, or whatever it may be; is not that a state which may throw us into convulsions at any moment?' Hence the sudden collapse of the credit system into the monetary system in times of crisis.

Apart from the domestic panic during crises, we can speak of the quantity of money only in so far as metal world money is involved. And it is precisely this that Chapman excludes, speaking only of £23 million in *banknotes*.

The same Chapman: '5218. The primary cause of the derangement of the money-market' (in April and later in October 1847) 'no doubt was in the quantity of money which was required to regulate our exchanges, in consequence of the extraordinary importations of the year.'

Firstly, this reserve of world-market money was at that time reduced to its minimum. Secondly, it served at the same time as security for the convertibility of credit money, banknotes. It thus combined two completely different functions, although both of these arise from the nature of money, since real money is always world-market money, and credit money always depends on this world-market money.

In 1847, without the suspension of the 1844 Bank Act, 'the clearing houses could not have been settled' (5221).

Yet Chapman did have some inkling of the impending crisis: '5236. There are certain conditions of the money-market (and the present is not very far from it), where money is exceedingly difficult, and recourse must be had to the Bank.'

'5239. With reference to the sums which we took from the Bank on the Friday, Saturday and Monday, the 19th, 20th, and 22nd of October, 1847, we should only have been too thankful to have got the bills back on the Wednesday following; the money reflowed to us directly the panic was over.' On Tuesday, 23 October, the Bank Act was suspended, and the crisis thereby curbed.

Chapman believes (5274) that the bills of exchange running on London amount at any one time to some £100–£200 million. This does not include local bills on provincial centres.

'5287. Whereas in October 1856, the amount of the notes in the hands of the public ran up to £21,155,000, there was an extraordinary difficulty in obtaining money; notwithstanding that the public held so much, we could not touch it.' This was due to the anxiety produced by the straits in which the Eastern Bank had found itself for a while (March 1856).

5290. As soon as the panic is over, 'all bankers deriving their profit from interest begin to employ the money immediately'.

5302. Chapman explains the disquiet at the decline in the bank reserve not from fear for the deposits, but rather because all those who might suddenly have to pay large sums of money knew very well that they could be driven to the Bank as the last resort in time of pressure on the money market; and 'if the banks have a very small reserve, they are not glad to receive us; but on the contrary'.

It is very pleasant, incidentally, to observe how the reserve dwindles away as an actual magnitude. The banks keep a minimum for their current business, partly with themselves and partly with the Bank of England. The billbrokers hold the 'loose bank money of the country' without a reserve. And all the Bank of England has to set against its liabilities for deposits is simply the reserves of the bankers and others, besides 'public deposits', etc. It allows this reserve to fall to the lowest possible point, e.g. some £2 million. Apart from this £2 million in paper, therefore, the entire swindle has absolutely no other reserve than the metal reserve in times of pressure (and these periods reduce the reserve, because notes that come in against the metal that leaves the Bank must be destroyed). Hence any reduction of the metal reserve adds to the crisis with a drain of gold.

'5306. If there should not be currency to settle the transactions at the clearing house, the only next alternative which I can see is to meet together, and to make our payments in first-class bills, bills upon the Treasury, and Messrs Smith, Payne, and so forth.' – '5307. Then, if the government failed to supply you with a circulating medium, you would create one for yourselves? – What can we do? The public come in, and take the circulating medium out of our hands; it does not exist.' – '5308. You would only then do in London what they do in Manchester every day of the week? – Yes.'

Chapman has a very good answer to the question put to him by Cayley (a Birmingham man of the Attwood school) * concerning Overstone's conception of capital: '5315. It has been stated before this Committee, that in a pressure like that of 1847, men are not looking for money, but are looking for capital; what is your

---

* The Birmingham school of 'little shilling men', represented in particular by Thomas Attwood, saw money as simply an ideal measure, and advocated reducing the gold content of the coinage. Cf. *A Contribution* . . ., p. 82.

opinion in that respect? – I do not understand it; we only deal in money; I do not understand what you mean by it.' – '5316. If you mean thereby' (commercial capital) 'the quantity of money which a man has of his own in his business, if you call that capital, it forms, in most cases, a very small proportion of the money which he wields in his affairs through the credit which is given him by the public' – through the mediation of the Chapmans.

'5339. Is it the want of property that makes us give up our specie payments? – Not at all . . . It is not that we want property, but it is that we are moving under a highly artificial system; and if we have an immense superincumbent demand upon our currency, circumstances may arise to prevent our obtaining that currency. Is the whole commercial industry of the country to be paralysed? Shall we shut up all the avenues of employment?' – '5338. If the question should arise whether we should maintain specie payments, or whether we should maintain the industry of the country, I have no hesitation in saying which I should drop.'

As to the hoarding of banknotes 'with a view to aggravate the pressure and to take advantage of the consequences' (5358), he says that this can happen very easily. Three major banks would suffice. '5383. Must it not be within your knowledge, as a man conversant with the great transactions of this metropolis, that capitalists do avail themselves of these crises to make enormous profit out of the ruin of the people who fall victims to them? – There can be no doubt about it.'

And we may well believe Mr Chapman here, even though he finally broke his own neck, commercially speaking, in an attempt to make 'enormous profit out of the ruin of the victims'. For if his partner Gurney says that any change in business is advantageous for someone who is well informed, Chapman says: 'The one section of the community knows nothing of the other; one is the manufacturer, for instance, who exports to the Continent, or imports his raw commodity; he knows nothing of the man who deals in bullion' (5046). And this is how it happened that one day Gurney and Chapman were themselves not 'well informed', and fell into a notorious bankruptcy.

We have already seen how the issue of notes does not mean in all cases an advance of capital. The evidence of Tooke before the House of Lords Committee of 1848 on Commercial Distress, which now follows, only goes to show that an advance of capital, even if brought about by the Bank through the issue of new notes, does not by itself mean an increase in the amount of notes in circulation.

'3099. Do you think that the Bank of England for instance might enlarge its advances greatly, and yet lead to no additional issue of notes? – There are facts in abundance to prove it; one of the most striking instances was in 1835, when the Bank made use of the West India deposits and of the loan from the East India Company in extended advances to the public. At that time the amount of notes in the hands of the public was actually rather diminished. And something like the same discrepancy is observable in 1846 at the time of the payment of the railway deposits into the Bank; the securities' (in discount and deposits) 'were increased to about thirty million, while there was no perceptible effect upon the amount of notes in the hands of the public.'

But, in addition to banknotes, wholesale trade has a second and far more important means of circulation: bills of exchange. Mr Chapman has shown us how essential it is for the regular course of business that good bills are always taken in payment under all circumstances. '*Gilt nicht mehr der Tausves Jontof, was soll gelten, Zeter, Zeter!*' * How then are these two means of circulation related?

Gilbart says on this score: '. . . The reduction of the amount of the note circulation uniformly increases the amount of the bill circulation. These bills are of two classes – commercial bills and bankers' bills . . . when money becomes scarce, the money-lenders say, "draw upon us and we will accept". And when a country banker discounts a bill for his customer, instead of giving him the cash, he will give him his own draft at twenty-one days upon his London agent. These bills serve the purpose of a currency' (J. W. Gilbart, *An Inquiry into the Causes of the Pressure*, etc., p. 31).

In somewhat modified form, this is confirmed by Newmarch, *B. A.* 1857, no. 1426:

'There is no connection between the variations in the amount of bill circulation and the variations in the banknote circulation . . . the only pretty uniform result is . . . that whenever there is any pressure upon the money-market, as indicated by a rise in the rate of discount, then the volume of the bill circulation is very much increased, and vice versa.'

---

* 'If the Tausves-Jontof's worthless,
  What is any worth? God save us!' (Heine, *Disputation*).
Tausves-Jontof was a medieval commentary on the Hebrew Talmud.

The bills drawn in a time such as this, however, are in no way the short-term bank bills that Gilbart mentions. On the contrary, they are to a large extent bills of accommodation, which do not represent any real transactions at all, or only such as are embarked upon simply so as to draw bills on them; we have already given sufficient examples of both kinds. *The Economist* (Wilson) therefore says on the security of such bills in comparison with banknotes:

'Notes payable on demand can never be kept out in excess, because the excess would always return to the bank for payment, while bills at two months may be issued in great excess, there being no means of checking the issue till they have arrived at maturity, when they may have been replaced by others. For a people to admit the safety of the circulation of bills payable only on a distant day, and to object to the safety of a circulation of paper payable on demand, is, to us, perfectly unaccountable' (*The Economist*, 1847, p. 575).

The amount of bills in circulation, therefore, just like the amount of banknotes, is determined solely by the needs of commerce; in the 1850s, the U.K. circulation in ordinary times, besides £39 million in banknotes, came to some £300 million in bills of exchange, of which £100–£120 million were on London alone. The scale on which these bills circulate has no influence on the volume of note circulation and is influenced by the latter solely in times of tight money, when the quantity of bills increases and their quality deteriorates. Finally, at the moment of crisis, the bill circulation completely collapses; no one has any use for promises to pay, each wanting only to accept cash payment; only the banknote still keeps its ability to circulate, at least up till now in England, since the Bank of England is backed by the entire wealth of the nation.

*

We have seen how even Mr Chapman, though in 1857 he was still himself a magnate on the money market, complained bitterly that there were several large money capitalists in London who were strong enough to bring the entire money market into disorder at a given moment and in this way fleece the smaller money-dealers most shamelessly. There were supposedly several great sharks of this kind who could significantly intensify a difficult situation by selling £1 or £2 millions worth of Consols and in this way taking an equivalent sum of banknotes (and thereby available loan capital) out of the market. The collaboration of three big banks in such a manoeuvre would suffice to turn a pressure into a panic.

The biggest capital power in London is of course the Bank of England, but its position as a semi-state institution makes it impossible for it to assert its domination in so brutal a fashion. None the less, it too is sufficiently capable of looking after itself – particularly since the 1844 Bank Act.

The Bank of England has a capital of £14,553,000, and besides this disposes of a 'balance' of some £3 million, i.e. undistributed profits, as well as all monies that the government receives in taxes, etc., which have to be deposited with it until they are used. If we add to this the sum of other deposits (in ordinary times some £30 million) and the banknotes issued without reserve backing, then Newmarch seems quite moderate in his assessment when he says (*B. A.* 1857, no. 1889): 'I satisfied myself that the amount of funds constantly employed in the' (London) 'money-market may be described as something like £120,000,000; and of that £120 000,000 a very considerable proportion, something like 15 or 20 per cent, is wielded by the Bank of England.'

In as much as the Bank issues notes that are not backed by the metal reserve in its vaults, it creates tokens of value that are not only means of circulation, but also form additional – even if fictitious – capital for it, to the nominal value of these fiduciary notes. And this extra capital yields it an extra profit. – In *B. A.* 1857, Wilson asks Newmarch: '1563. The circulation of a banker, so far as it is kept out upon the average, is an addition to the effective capital of that banker, is it not? – Certainly.' – '1564. Then whatever profit he derives from that circulation is a profit derived from credit, and not from a capital which he actually possesses? – Certainly.'

The same holds true of course for note-issuing private banks. In his answers nos. 1866–1868, Newmarch considers two-thirds of all these issued notes (for the last third, these banks must have metal reserves) as 'the creation of so much capital', because this amount of metal money is saved. The banker's profit on this may not be greater than the profit of other capitalists. The fact remains that he draws his profit from this national saving on metal money. But the fact that a national saving appears as a private profit is in no way shocking to the bourgeois economist, since profit in general is the appropriation of the nation's labour. Is there anything more crazy than that between 1797 and 1817, for example, the Bank of England, whose notes only had credit thanks to the state, then got paid by the state, i.e. by the public, in the form of interest on government loans, for the power that the state gave it to transform these very notes from paper into money and lend them to the state?

The banks, moreover, have still other ways of creating capital. According to the same Newmarch, the provincial banks, as already mentioned above, are obliged to send their surplus funds (i.e. Bank of England notes) to London billbrokers, who send them in exchange discounted bills. It is these bills which the provincial banks use to serve their customers, since their general rule is not to re-issue bills of exchange received from local clients, so that their business operations do not become known in their own locality. These bills of exchange received from London can be issued not only to clients who have direct payments to make in London, in case these do not prefer to get the bank's own draft on London; they also serve to settle payments in the provinces, for the banker's endorsement secures them local credit. In Lancashire, for example, they have driven out of circulation all the notes of the local banks and a great part of the Bank of England's notes (ibid., nos. 1568–1574).

We see here, therefore, how the banks create credit and capital, (1) by issuing their own banknotes; (2) by writing drafts on London running for up to twenty-one days, which will however be paid to them in cash immediately they are written; (3) by re-issuing bills of exchange, whose creditworthiness is created first and foremost by the endorsement of the bank, at least for the district in question.

The power of the Bank of England is shown by its regulation of the market rate of interest. In times when business runs its normal course, it may happen that the Bank of England cannot check a moderate drain of gold from its metal reserve by raising its discount rate,[12] since the demand for means of payment is satisfied

12. At the general stockholders' meeting of the Union Bank of London, on 17 January 1894, the chairman, Mr Ritchie, recalled how the Bank of England had put up its discount rate from $2\frac{1}{2}$ per cent (July) to 3 per cent and 4 per cent in August, and since despite this fully £$4\frac{1}{2}$ million in gold had been lost, to 5 per cent, on which gold flowed back and the Bank rate was reduced to 4 per cent in September and 3 per cent in October. This Bank rate, however, was not recognized in the market. 'When the bank-rate was 5 per cent, the dis-

by the private and joint-stock banks, and by billbrokers, who have acquired a great deal of capital power in the last thirty years. It then has to employ other means. But for critical moments, what banker Glyn (of Glyn, Mills, Currie & Co.) testified to the Committee on Commercial Distress (1848–57) still holds true: '1709. Under circumstances of great pressure upon the country the Bank of England commands the rate of interest.' – '1710. In times of extraordinary pressure . . . whenever the discounts of the private bankers or brokers become comparatively limited, they fall upon the Bank of England, and then it is that the Bank of England has the power of commanding the market rate.'

As a public institution under state protection, however, and endowed with state privileges, it cannot exploit its power relentlessly, as a private firm can allow itself to do. And this is why Hubbard stated to the Bank Acts Committee of 1857: '2844. (Question:) Is not it the case that when the rate of discount is highest, the Bank is the cheapest place to go, and that, when it is the lowest, the billbrokers are the cheapest parties? – (Hubbard:) That will always be the case, because the Bank of England never goes quite so low as its competitors, and when the rate is highest, it is never quite as high.'

It is still a serious event in business life when the Bank puts the screw on, as the customary expression goes, i.e. puts up an interest rate that is already above the average. 'As soon as the Bank puts on the screw, all purchases for foreign exportation immediately cease . . . the exporters wait until prices have reached the lowest point of depression, and then, and not till then, they make their purchases. But when this point has arrived, the exchanges have been rectified – gold ceases to be exported before the lowest point of depression has arrived. Purchases of goods for exportation may have the effect of bringing back some of the gold which has been sent abroad, but they come too late to prevent the drain' (J. W. Gilbart, *An Inquiry into the Causes of the Pressure on the Money-Market*, London, 1840, p. 35). – 'Another effect of regulating the currency by the foreign exchanges is that it leads in seasons

---

count rate was $3\frac{1}{2}$ per cent, and the rate for money $2\frac{1}{4}$ per cent; when the bank-rate fell to 4 per cent, the discount rate was $2\frac{5}{8}$ per cent and the money rate $1\frac{3}{4}$ per cent; when the bank-rate was 3 per cent, the discount rate fell to $1\frac{1}{2}$ per cent and the money rate to something below that' (*Daily News*, 18 January 1894). – F. E.

of pressure to an enormous rate of interest' (ibid., p. 40). – 'The cost of rectifying the exchanges falls upon the productive industry of the country, while during the process the profits of the Bank of England are actually augmented in consequence of carrying on her business with a less amount of treasure' (ibid., p. 52).

However, friend Samuel Gurney says, 'The great fluctuations in the rate of interest are advantageous to bankers and dealers in money – all fluctuations in trade are advantageous to the knowing man.'

And even if the Gurneys skim off the cream by a ruthless exploitation of the commercial distress, while the Bank of England cannot do this with the same freedom, quite handsome profits fall its way too – not to speak of the private profits that come the way of the gentlemen directors as a result of their exceptional opportunity for knowing the overall state of business. According to data presented to the Lords Committee of 1817 on the resumption of cash payment, the Bank of England's total profits for the period 1797–1817 were as follows:

Bonuses and increased dividends	7,451,136
New stock divided among proprietors	7,276,500
Increased value of capital	14,553,000
Total	29,280,636

this being for nineteen years on a capital of £11,642,400 (D. Hardcastle, *Banks and Bankers*, 2nd edn, London, 1843, p. 120). If we calculate the total profits of the Bank of Ireland, which also suspended cash payment in 1797, according to the same principle, we arrive at the following result:

Dividends as by returns due 1821	4,736,085
Declared bonus	1,225,000
Increased assets	1,214,800
Increased value of capital	4,185,000
Total	11,360,885

on a capital of £3 million (ibid., pp. 363–4).

Talk about centralization! The credit system, which has its focal point in the allegedly national banks and the big money-lenders and usurers that surround them, is one enormous centralization and gives this class of parasites a fabulous power not only to decimate the industrial capitalists periodically but also to interfere in actual production in the most dangerous manner – and this crew know nothing of production and have nothing at all to do with it. The Acts of 1844 and 1845 are proof of the growing power of these bandits, added to whom are the financiers and stock-jobbers.

If anyone should still doubt that these honourable bandits exploit national and international production simply in the interest of production and the exploited themselves, he will certainly learn better from the following homily on the high moral dignity of the banker:

'Banking establishments are ... moral and religious institutions ... How often has the fear of being seen by the watchful and reproving eye of his banker deterred the young tradesman from joining the company of riotous and extravagant friends? ... What has been his anxiety to stand well in the estimation of his banker? ... Has not the frown of his banker been of more influence with him than the jeers and discouragements of his friends? Has he not trembled to be supposed guilty of deceit or the slightest mis-statement, lest it should give rise to suspicion, and his accommodation be in consequence restricted or discontinued? ... And has not that friendly advice been of more value to him than that of priest?' (G. M. Bell, a Scottish bank director, in *The Philosophy of Joint-Stock Banking*, London, 1840, pp. 46, 47).

Chapter 34: The Currency Principle
and the English Bank Legislation
of 1844

(In an earlier work,[13] we investigated Ricardo's theory of the value of money in relation to commodity prices; we can confine ourselves here, therefore, to what is most essential. According to Ricardo, the value of (metal) money is determined by the labour-time objectified in it, but only as long as the quantity of money stands in the right proportion to the quantity and price of the commodities to be exchanged. If the quantity of money rises above this proportion, its value falls and commodity prices rise; if it falls below the right proportion, its value rises and commodity prices fall – as long as other factors remain the same. In the first case, the country which has this surplus of gold will export the gold that has fallen below its value and import commodities; in the second case gold will flow into the countries where it is priced above its value, while the under-valued commodities from there will flow to other markets, where they can obtain normal prices. Since on these assumptions 'even gold in the form of coin or bullion can become a value-token representing a larger or smaller value than its own, it is obvious that any convertible banknotes that are in circulation must share the same fate. Although banknotes are convertible and their real value accordingly corresponds to their nominal value, "the aggregate currency consisting of metal and of convertible notes" may appreciate or depreciate if, for reasons described earlier, the total quantity either rises above or falls below the level which is determined by the exchange-value of the commodities in circulation and the metallic value of gold. This depreciation, not of notes in relation to gold, but of gold and notes taken together, i.e., of the aggregate means of circulation of a country, is one of Ricardo's main discoveries, which Lord Overstone and Co. pressed into their service and turned into a funda-

13. See *A Contribution to the Critique of Political Economy*, pp. 169 ff.

mental principle of Sir Robert Peel's bank legislation of 1844 and 1845' (op. cit., pp. 173–4).

We do not need to repeat here the demonstration of the absurdity of this theory of Ricardo's that is given in that text. All that concerns us now is the form and manner in which Ricardo's doctrines were taken up and elaborated by the school of banking theorists who dictated Peel's Bank Acts.

'The commercial crises of the nineteenth century, and in particular the great crises of 1825 and 1836, did not lead to any further development of Ricardo's currency theory, but rather to new practical applications of it. It was no longer a matter of single economic phenomena – such as the depreciation of precious metals in the sixteenth and seventeenth centuries confronting Hume, or the depreciation of paper currency during the eighteenth century and the beginning of the nineteenth confronting Ricardo – but of big storms on the world market, in which the antagonism of all elements in the bourgeois process of production explodes; the origin of these storms and the means of defence against them were sought within the sphere of currency, the most superficial and abstract sphere of this process. The theoretical assumption which actually serves the school of economic weather experts as their point of departure is the dogma that Ricardo had discovered the laws governing purely metallic currency. It was thus left to them to subsume the circulation of credit money or banknotes under these laws.

'The most common and conspicuous phenomenon accompanying commercial crises is a sudden fall in the general level of commodity prices occurring after a prolonged general rise of prices. A general fall of commodity prices may be expressed as a rise in the value of money relative to all other commodities, and, on the other hand, a general rise of prices may be defined as a fall in the relative value of money. Either of these statements describes the phenomenon but does not explain it . . . The different terminology has just as little effect on the task itself as a translation of the terms from German into English would have. Ricardo's monetary theory proved to be singularly apposite since it gave to a tautology the semblance of a causal relation. What is the cause of the general fall in commodity prices which occurs periodically? It is the periodically occurring rise in the relative value of money. What on the other hand is the cause of the recurrent general rise in commodity prices? It is the recurrent fall in the relative value of money. It would be just as correct to say that the recurrent rise and fall of prices is brought about by their recurrent rise and fall ... Once the transformation of the tautology into a causal relationship is taken for granted, everything else follows easily. The rise in commodity prices is due to a fall in the value of money, the fall in the value of money, however, as we know from Ricardo, is due to excessive currency, that is to say, to the fact that the amount of money in circulation rises above the level determined by its own intrinsic value and the intrinsic value of commodities. Similarly in the opposite case, the general fall of commodity prices is due to the value of money rising above its intrinsic value as a result of an insufficient amount of currency. Prices therefore rise and fall periodically, because periodically there is too much or too little money in circulation. If it is proved, for instance, that the rise of prices coincided with a decreased amount of money in circulation, and the fall of prices with an increased amount, then it is nevertheless possible to assert that, in consequence of some reduction or increase – which can in no way be ascertained statistically – of commodities in circulation, the amount of money in circulation has relatively, though not absolutely, increased or decreased. We have seen that, according to Ricardo, even when a purely metallic currency is employed, these variations in the level of prices must take place, but, because they occur alternately, they neutralize one another. For example, an insufficient amount of currency brings about a fall in commodity prices, the fall of commodity prices stimulates an export of commodities to other countries, but this export leads to an influx of money into the country, the influx of money causes again a rise in commodity prices. When there is an excessive amount of currency the reverse occurs: commodities are imported and money exported. Since notwithstanding these general price movements, which arise from the very nature of Ricardo's metallic currency, their severe and vehement form, the form of crisis, belongs to periods with developed credit systems, it is clear that the issue of banknotes is not exactly governed by the laws of metallic currency. The remedy applicable to metallic currency is the import and export of precious metals, which are immediately thrown into circulation as coin, their inflow or outflow thus causing commodity prices to fall or to rise. The banks must now artificially exert the same influence on commodity prices by imitating the laws of metallic currency. If gold is flowing in from abroad, it is a proof that there is an insufficient amount of currency, that the value of money is too high and commodity prices too low, and banknotes must therefore be thrown into circulation in accordance with the newly imported gold. On the other hand, banknotes must be taken out of circulation in accordance with an outflow of gold from the country. In other words the issue of banknotes must be regulated according to the import and export of the precious metals or according to the rate of exchange. Ricardo's wrong assumption that gold is simply specie and that consequently the whole of the imported gold is used to augment the money in circulation thus causing prices to rise, and that the whole of the gold exported represents a decrease in the amount of specie and thus causes prices to fall – this theoretical assumption is now turned *into a practical experiment by making the amount of specie in circulation correspond always to the quantity of gold in the country.* Lord Overstone (Jones Loyd, the banker), Colonel Torrens, Norman, Clay, Arbuthnot and numerous other writers known in England as the "currency school" have not only preached this doctrine, but have made it the basis of the present English and Scottish banking legislation by means of Sir Robert Peel's Bank Acts of 1844 and 1845. The analysis of the ignominious fiasco they suffered both in theory and practice, after experiments on the largest national scale, can only be made in the section dealing with the theory of credit' (ibid., pp. 182–5).

This school met criticism from Thomas Tooke, James Wilson (in *The Economist* of 1844–7) and John Fullarton. We have already seen several times, particularly in Chapter 28 of this volume, how inadequately these critics penetrated the nature of gold and how unclear they were as to the relationship between money and capital. We quote here simply a few instances in connection with the proceedings of the House of Commons Committee of 1857 on the Peel Bank Acts (*B. A.* 1857) – F. E.)

J. G. Hubbard, former Governor of the Bank of England, testifies: '2400. The effect of the export of bullion ... has no reference whatever to the prices of commodities. It has an effect, and a very important one, upon the price of interest-bearing securities, because, as the rate of interest varies, the value of commodities which embodied that interest is necessarily powerfully affected.'

He produces two tables for the years 1834–43 and 1845–56, which show how the price movements for fifteen of the most important items of commerce were quite independent of the inflow and outflow of gold, and of the rate of interest. They do show, however, a close connection between the inflow and outflow of gold, on the one hand, which is in fact the 'representative of our uninvested capital', and the rate of interest on the other.

'In 1847, a very large amount of American securities were retransferred to America, and Russian securities to Russia, and other continental securities were transferred to those places from which we drew our supplies of grain.'

The fifteen items on which the following tables of Hubbard's are based are: raw cotton, cotton yarn, cotton fabrics, wool, woollen cloth, flax, linen, indigo, pig-iron, tin, copper, tallow, sugar, coffee and silk.

I. 1834–43

Date	Bullion reserve of Bank	Market rate of discount	Of fifteen major articles		
			Price increase	Price decrease	Un-changed
1834, 1 March	£9,104,000	2¾%	—	—	·
1835, 1 March	6,274,000	3¾%	7	7	1
1836, 1 March	7,918,000	3½%	11	3	1
1837, 1 March	4,077,000	5%	5	9	1
1838, 1 March	10,471,000	2¾%	4	11	—
1839, 1 Sept.	2,684,000	6%	8	5	2
1840, 1 June	4,571,000	4¾%	5	9	1
1840, 1 Dec.	3,642,000	5¾%	7	6	2
1841, 1 Dec.	4,873,000	5%	3	12	—
1842, 1 Dec.	10,603,000	2½%	2	13	—
1843, 1 June	11,566,000	2¼%	1	14	—

II. 1844–53

Date	Bullion reserve of Bank	Market rate of discount	Of fifteen major articles		
			Price increase	Price decrease	Un-changed
1844, 1 March	£16,162,000	2¼%	—	—	—
1845, 1 Dec.	13,237,000	4½%	11	4	—
1846, 1 Sept.	16,366,000	3%	7	8	—
1847, 1 Sept.	9,140,000	6%	6	6	3
1850, 1 March	17,126,000	2½%	5	9	1
1851, 1 June	13,705,000	3%	2	11	2
1852, 1 Sept.	21,853,000	1¾%	9	5	1
1853, 1 Dec.	15,093,000	5%	14	—	1

Hubbard makes the following comment on these: 'As in the years 1834–43, so in the period 1844–53, the upward and downward movements in the bullion of the Bank have invariably been accompanied with a decrease or increase in the loanable value of money advanced on discount; and, as in the earlier period, so in this, the variations in the prices of commodities in this country exhibit an entire independence of the amount of circulation as shown in the fluctuations in bullion of the Bank of England' (*Bank Acts Report*, 1857, II, pp. 290–91).

Since the demand and supply of commodities regulates their market price, it is evident here how false is Overstone's identification of the demand for loanable money capital (or rather the gap between its demand and supply), as expressed in the discount rate, with the demand for real 'capital'. The contention that commodity prices are governed by fluctuations in the total amount of 'currency' is now concealed beneath the phrase that the fluctuations in the discount rate express fluctuations in the demand for actual material capital, as distinct from money capital. We have already seen how both Norman and Overstone actually maintained this before the Committee in question and to what weak subterfuges they were forced to resort, particularly the latter until he was finally cornered (Chapter 26). This is in actual fact the old humbug that changes in the quantity of gold, since they increase or decrease the amount of means of circulation in a country, must necessarily raise or lower commodity prices there. If gold is exported, then according to this currency theory commodity prices in the country where the gold goes must rise, and with them also the value of the exports of the gold-exporting country on the market of the gold-importing one; the value of the latter's exports on the former market, on the other hand, would fall, since their value would rise in their country of origin, where the gold finds its way. In actual fact, a decline in the amount of gold simply raises the rate of interest, while an increase lowers it; and if these fluctuations in the interest rate did not come into account in establishing the cost price, or determining demand and supply, commodity prices would be completely unaffected.

In the same report, N. Alexander, head of a big firm in the India trade, expresses himself as follows on the sharp drain of silver to India and China in the mid-1850s, partly as a result of the Chinese civil war, which put a stop to the supply of English fabrics to China, and partly as a result of the silkworm disease in Europe, which sharply reduced silk production in Italy and France.

'4337. Is the drain for China or for India? – You send the silver to India, and you buy opium with a great deal of it, all which goes on to China to lay down funds for the purchase of the silk; and the state of the markets in India (in spite of the accumulation of silver there) makes it a more profitable investment for the merchant to lay down silver than to send piece-goods or English manufactures.' – '4338. In order to obtain the silver, has there not been a great drain from France? – Yes, very large.' – '4344. Instead of bringing in silk from France and Italy, we are sending it there in large quantities, both from Bengal and from China.'

Thus silver was sent to Asia, where it is the money metal, instead of commodities, not because the price of these commodities had risen in the country that produced them (England), but because it had fallen – owing to excessive imports – in the country which imported them; even though England had to obtain this silver from France, and to pay for it partly with gold. According to the currency theory, prices should have fallen in England and risen in India and China as a result of such imports.

A further example. In his evidence to the House of Lords Committee (*C. D.* 1848–57), Wylie, one of the leading Liverpool merchants, said: '1994. At the close of 1845 there was no trade that was more remunerating, and in which there were such large profits' (than cotton spinning). 'The stock of cotton was large and good, useful cotton could be bought at 4d. per pound, and from such cotton good secunda mule twist no. 40 was made at an expense not exceeding a like amount, say at a cost of 8d. per pound·in all to the spinner. This yarn was largely sold and contracted for in September and October 1845 at $10\frac{1}{2}$ and $11\frac{1}{4}$d. per pound, and in some instances the spinners realized a profit equal to the first cost of the cotton.' – '1996. The trade continued to be remunerative until the beginning of 1846.' – '2000. On 3 March 1844, the stock of cotton' (627,042 bales) 'was more than double what it is this day' (on 7 March 1848, when it was 301,070 bales) and yet the price then was $1\frac{1}{4}$d. per pound dearer.' ($6\frac{1}{4}$d. as against 5d.) – At the same time yarn, good secunda mule twist no. 40, had fallen from $11\frac{1}{2}$–12d. to $9\frac{1}{2}$d. per lb. in October, and to $7\frac{3}{4}$d. at the end of December 1847; yarn was sold at the purchase price of the cotton from which it had been spun (ibid., nos. 2021 and 2022).

This exposes the self-interest in Overstone's wisdom that money is 'dear' because capital is 'scarce'. On 3 March 1844 the Bank rate stood at 3 per cent; in October and November 1847 it went up to 8 and 9 per cent, and on 7 March 1848 was down to 4 per cent again. Owing to the complete stagnation in sales and the panic, with its correspondingly high rate of interest, cotton prices had been driven far below the level corresponding to the supply. The result of this was on the one hand a tremendous decline in imports in 1848 and on the other hand a decline in production in America; hence a new rise in cotton prices in 1849. According to Overstone, the reason why commodities were too dear was that there was too much money in the country.

'2002. The late decline in the condition of the cotton manufactories is not to be ascribed to the want of the raw material, as the price seems to have been lower, though the stock of the raw material is very much diminished.'

But Overstone conveniently confuses the price or value of a commodity with the value of money, i.e. the rate of interest. In answer to question 2026, Wylie delivers his overall verdict on the currency theory, on the basis of which Cardwell and Sir Charles Wood,* in May 1847, 'asserted the necessity of carrying out the Bank Act of 1844 in its full and entire integrity'. 'These principles seemed to me to be of a nature that would give an artificial high value to money and an artificial and ruinously low value to all commodities and produce.' He goes on to say of the effects of this Bank Act on the general state of business: 'As bills at four months, which is the regular course of drafts, from manufacturing towns on merchants and bankers for the purchase of goods going to the United States, could not be discounted except at great sacrifices, the execution of orders was checked to a great extent, until after the Government Letter of 25 October' (suspension of the Bank Act), 'when those four months' bills became discountable' (2097).

The suspension of the Bank Act brought salvation for the provinces, too. '2102. Last October [1847] there was scarcely an American buyer purchasing goods here who did not at once curtail his orders as much as he possibly could; and when our advices of the dearness of money reached America, all fresh orders

---

* Sir Charles Wood (1800–1885), later Viscount Halifax, a Whig politician, was at that time Chancellor of the Exchequer. Edward, Viscount Cardwell (1813–86), a Peelite who later held several ministerial posts for the Liberal party, is remembered in particular for the reforms he introduced as Secretary for War (1868–74).

ceased.' – '2134. Corn and sugar were special. The corn market was affected by the prospects of the harvest, and sugar was affected by the immense stocks and imports.' – '2163. Of our indebtedness to America . . . much was liquidated by forced sales of consigned goods, and I fear that much was cancelled by the failures here.' – '2196. If I recollect rightly, *70 per cent was paid on our Stock Exchange in October 1847.*'

(The crisis of 1837 with its long aftermath, added to which was a further regular crisis in 1842, and the self-interested blindness of the industrialists and merchants, who were resolved not to notice any overproduction – this was all nonsense and an impossibility, said the vulgar economists! – all this finally brought about the mental confusion that allowed the currency school to translate their dogma into practice on a national scale. And thus the Bank legislation of 1844–5 went through.

The 1844 Bank Act divides the Bank of England into an Issue Department and a Banking Department. The former receives securities – for the most part government stock – for £14 million, as well as the entire metal reserve, of which no more than one quarter may consist of silver, and issues a sum of notes corresponding to this total amount. In so far as these are not in the hands of the public, they remain in the Banking Department and form its ever ready reserve, together with the small amount of coin needed for everyday use (about £1 million). The Issue Department gives the public gold for notes and notes for gold; all other dealings with the public are the concern of the Banking Department. Those private banks in England and Wales that were entitled in 1844 to issue their own notes retain this right, but their note issue is fixed. If one of these banks ceases to issue its own notes, the Bank of England can increase its own fiduciary note issue by two-thirds of the quota thus made available; in this way its issue has been increased, by 1892, from £14 million to £16½ million (£16,450,000 to be precise).

Thus, for every £5 that leaves the Bank's reserve in gold, a £5 note comes back to the Issue Department and is destroyed; for every five sovereigns that come into the reserve, a new £5 note is put into circulation. This is how Overstone's ideal paper circulation, governed precisely by the laws of metal circulation, is carried out in practice, and in this way, according to the currency people's contention, crises are made impossible once and for all.

In reality, however, the separation of the Bank into two independent departments withdrew the directors' power of free disposal of their entire available means at decisive moments, so that situations could come about in which the Banking Department was faced with bankruptcy while the Issue Department still had several millions in gold, and besides this its £14 million intact in securities. And this could happen all the more easily in so far as every crisis has a point marked by a sharp drain of gold abroad, which has principally to be covered by the Bank's metal reserve. But for every £5 that flows abroad in this way, a £5 note is withdrawn from circulation at home, so that the amount of means of circulation is reduced at the very moment when most is required, and with the greatest urgency at that. The Bank Act of 1844 thus directly provokes the entire world of commerce into meeting the outbreak of a crisis by putting aside a reserve stock of banknotes, thereby accelerating and intensifying the crisis. And by this artificial intensification of the demand for monetary accommodation, i.e. for means of payment, at the same time as the supply of these is declining, a demand which takes effect at the decisive moment, it drives the interest rate in crisis times up to a previously unheard-of level. Thus instead of abolishing crises, it rather intensifies them to a point at which either the entire world of industry has to collapse, or else the Bank Act. On two occasions, 25 October 1847 and 12 November 1857, the crisis reached such a height; the government then freed the Bank from the restriction on its note issue, by suspending the Act of 1844, and this was sufficient on both occasions to curb the crisis. In 1847 the certainty that banknotes could now once more be had in exchange for first-class securities was sufficient to bring £4–£5 million in notes back to the light of day and into active circulation; in 1857 rather less than £1 million in notes were issued above the legal quota, but only for a very short time.

Also to be mentioned here is that some parts of the legislation of 1844 reflected the memory of the first twenty years of the century, the time when the Bank suspended cash payment and banknotes depreciated in value. The fear that banknotes might lose their credit is still very much apparent here; a very excessive fear, since as early as 1825 the issue of a rediscovered supply of old £1 notes, which had been taken out of circulation, curbed the crisis and thereby showed that even at that period the credit of these banknotes remained unimpaired, even at a time of most general and pronounced lack of confidence. And this is quite comprehensible, for in fact the entire nation and its credit stands behind these tokens. – F. E.)

Let us listen now to a few witnesses on the effect of the Bank Act. John Stuart Mill believed that the Bank Act of 1844 had kept down over-speculation. This wise man had the good fortune to give his evidence on 12 June 1857. Four months later, the crisis broke out. He literally congratulated the 'bank directors and the commercial public generally' on the fact that they 'understand much better than they did the nature of a commercial crisis, and the extreme mischief which they do both to themselves and to the public by upholding over-speculation' (*B. A.* 1857, no. 2031).

The wise Mill believed that if £1 notes were issued 'as advances to manufacturers and others, who pay wages ... the notes may get into the hands of others who expend them for consumption, and in that case the notes do constitute in themselves a demand for commodities and may for some time tend to promote a rise of prices' [no. 2066].

Does Mr Mill thus assume that the manufacturers would pay higher wages if they paid them in paper instead of in gold? Or does he believe that if the manufacturer obtained his advance in £100 notes and exchanged these for gold, these wages would then form less demand than if paid in £1 notes? Does he not know that in certain mining districts, for example, wages actually are paid in notes from local banks, so that several workers receive a £5 note together? Does this increase their demand? Or are bankers easier with manufacturers in small notes, advancing more money than in larger denominations?

(This peculiar fear that Mill had of £1 notes would be inexplicable if his entire work on political economy did not exhibit an eclecticism which never flinches from any contradictions. On the one hand, he supports Tooke on many points against Overstone, while on the other hand he believes commodity prices are determined by the amount of money present. He is thus in no way convinced that for each £1 issued – all other things remaining the same – a sovereign finds its way into the Bank's reserve; he fears that the quantity of means of circulation might be increased and thereby devalued, so that commodity prices would rise. It is this and nothing else that is hidden behind his above caution. – F. E.)

On the division of the Bank into two departments and the excessive precautions taken to safeguard the cashing of notes, Tooke makes the following statement to the *C. D.* 1848–57:

The greater fluctuations of the interest rate in 1847, as compared with 1837 and 1839, are due solely to the separation of the Bank into two departments (3010). – The safety of banknotes was affected neither in 1825 nor in 1837 and 1839 (3015). – The demand for gold in 1825 was aimed only at filling the vacuum created by the complete discredit of the £1 notes of the country banks; this vacuum could be filled only by gold, until such time as the Bank of England also issued £1 notes (3022). – In November and December 1825 not the slightest demand existed for gold for export purposes (3023).

'In point of discredit at home as well as abroad. A failure in paying the dividends and the deposits would be of far greater consequence than the suspending of the payment of banknotes' (3028).

'3035. Would you not say that any circumstance, which had the effect of ultimately endangering the convertibility of the note, would be one likely to add serious difficulty in a moment of commercial pressure? – Not at all.'

'In the course of 1847 . . . an increased issue from the circulating department might have contributed to replenish the coffers of the Bank, as it did in 1825' (3058).

Before the Committee on *B. A.* 1857, Newmarch states: '1357. The first mischievous effect . . . of that separation of departments' (of the Bank) 'and . . . a necessary consequence from the cutting in two of the reserve of bullion has been that the banking business of the Bank of England, that is to say, the whole of that part of the operation of the Bank of England which brings it more immediately into contact with the commerce of the country, has been carried on upon a moiety only of its former amounts of reserve. Out of that division of the reserve has arisen, therefore, this state of things, that whenever the reserve of the Banking Department has been diminished, even to a small extent, it has rendered necessary an action by the Bank upon its rate of discount. That diminished reserve, therefore, has produced a frequent succession of changes and jerks in the rate of discount.' – '1358. The alterations since 1844' (until June 1857) 'have been some sixty in number, whereas the alterations prior to 1844 in the same space of time certainly did not amount to a dozen.'

Palmer's evidence to the Lords Committee (*C. D.* 1848–57) is also of particular interest, since he had been a director of the Bank of England since 1811 and Governor for a period.

'828. In December 1825, there was about £1,100,000 of bullion remaining in the Bank. At that period it must undoubtedly have failed *in toto*, if this Act had been in existence' (meaning the Act of 1844). 'The issue in December, I think, was 5 or 6 millions of notes in a week, which relieved the panic that existed at that period.'

'825. The first period' (since 1 July 1825) 'when the present Act would have failed, if the Bank had attempted to carry out the transactions then undertaken, was on the 28th of February 1837; at that period there were £3,900,000 to £4,000,000 of bullion in the possession of the Bank, and then the Bank would have been left with £650,000 only in the reserve. Another period is in the year 1839, which continued from the 9th of July to the 5th of December.' – '826. What was the amount of the reserve in that case? – The reserve was minus altogether £200,000 upon the 5th of September. On the 5th of November it rose to about a million or a million and a half.' – '830. The Act of 1844 would have prevented the Bank giving assistance to the American trade in 1837.' – '831. There were three of the principal American houses that failed ... Almost every house connected with America was in a state of discredit, and unless the Bank had come forward at that period, I do not believe that there would have been more than one or two houses that could have sustained themselves.' – '836. The pressure in 1837 is not to be compared with that of 1847. The pressure in the former year was chiefly confined to the American trade.' – 838. (Early in June 1837 the management of the Bank discussed the question of overcoming the pressure.) 'Some gentlemen advocated the opinion ... that the correct principle was to raise the rate of interest, by which the price of commodities would be lowered; in short, to make money dear and commodities cheap, by which the foreign payment would be accomplished.' – '906. The establishment of an artificial limitation of the powers of the Bank under the Act of 1844, instead of the ancient and natural limitation of the Bank's powers, namely, the actual amount of its specie, tends to create artificial difficulty, and therefore an operation upon the prices of merchandise that would have been unnecessary but for the provisions of the Act.' – '968. You cannot, by the working of the Act of 1844, materially reduce the bullion, under ordinary circumstances, below nine million and a half. It would then cause a pressure upon prices and credit which would occasion such an advance in the exchange with foreign countries as to increase the import of bullion, and to that extent add to the amount in the Issue Department.' – '996. Under the limitation that you '(the Bank)' are now subject to, you have not the command of silver to an extent that you require at a time when silver would be required for an action upon the foreign exchanges.' – '999. What was the object of the regulation restricting the Bank as to the amount of silver to one-fifth? – I cannot answer that question.'

The intention was to make money dear; similarly, the currency theory apart, with the separation of the Bank's two departments and the compulsion for the Scottish and Irish banks to keep gold in their reserve for any issue of notes above a certain amount. This led to a decentralization of the nation's metal reserve, which made it less capable of correcting unfavourable exchange rates. All the following stipulations lead to raising the rate of interest: that the Bank of England may not issue more than £14 million in notes aside from those issued against its gold reserve; that the Banking Department is to be administered as an ordinary bank, forcing the interest rate down when there is excess money and driving it up when there is a shortage; the restriction of the silver reserve, the principal means of rectifying exchange rates with the Continent and with Asia; the regulations for the Scottish and Irish banks, which never need gold for export but must now keep it under the pretext of a convertibility of their notes which is in fact pure illusion. The fact is that the Act of 1845 produced the first run on the Scottish banks for gold, in 1857. The new banking legislation also makes no distinction between a drain of gold abroad and a domestic drain, even though the effects of these two things are self-evidently quite different. Hence the constant and violent fluctuations in the market rate of interest. As regards silver, Palmer says twice (992 and 994) that the Bank can buy silver in exchange for notes only if the exchange rate is in England's favour, so that there is an excess of silver; for: '1003. The only object in holding a considerable amount of bullion in silver is to facilitate making the foreign payment so long as the exchanges are against the country.' – '1004. Silver is ... a commodity which, being money in every other part of the world, is therefore the most direct commodity ... for the purpose' (payments abroad). 'The United States latterly have taken gold alone.'

In his opinion, the Bank did not need to raise the interest rate above its old level of 5 per cent in times of pressure, as long as gold was not drawn abroad by an unfavourable rate of exchange. Were it not for the Act of 1844, all first-class bills could still be discounted without difficulty at the old rate (1018 to 1020). But with the 1844 Bank Act and the situation in which the Bank found itself in October 1847, 'there was no rate of interest which the Bank could have charged to houses of credit, which they would not have been willing to pay to carry on their payments.'

And this high rate of interest was precisely the aim of the Act. In 1029 he refers to a 'great distinction which I wish to draw between the action of the rate of interest upon a foreign demand' (for precious metal) 'and an advance in the rate for the object of checking a demand upon the Bank during a period of internal discredit.' – '1023. Previously to the Act of 1844 ... when the exchanges were in favour of the country, and positive panic and alarm existed through the country, there was no limit put upon the issue, by which alone that state of distress could be relieved.'

These are the words of a man who was a director of the Bank of England for thirty-nine years. Let us now listen to a private banker, Twells, a partner in Spooner, Attwood and Co. since 1801. He is the only one out of all these witnesses before the *B. A.* 1857 who provides us with any insight into the actual state of affairs in the country, and sees the crisis impending. In other respects, however, he is a kind of Birmingham 'little shilling man', like his partners, the Attwood brothers, who are the founders of this school. (See *Contribution to the Critique of Political Economy*, p. 82.) He states: '4488. How do you think that the Act of 1844 has operated? – If I were to answer you as a banker, I should say that it has operated exceedingly well, for it has afforded a rich harvest to bankers and' (money-) 'capitalists of all kinds. But it has operated very badly to the honest industrious tradesman who requires steadiness in the rate of discount, that he may be enabled to make his arrangements with confidence ... It has made money-lending a most profitable pursuit.' – '4489. It' (the Bank Act) 'enables the London joint-stock banks to return from 20 to 22 per cent to their proprietors? – The other day one of them was paying 18 per cent and I think another 20 per cent; they ought to support the Act of 1844 very strongly.' – '4490. The little tradesmen and respectable merchants, who have not a large capital ... it pinches them very much indeed ... The only means that I have of knowing is that I observe such an amazing quantity of their acceptances unpaid. They are always small, perhaps ranging from £20 to £100, a great many of them are unpaid and go back unpaid to all parts

of the country, which is always an indication of suffering amongst
... little shopkeepers.'

In 4494 he explains that business is presently unprofitable. His
following remarks are important, since he saw the latent presence
of the crisis when none of the others suspected it.

'4494. Things keep their prices in Mincing Lane, but we sell
nothing, we cannot sell upon any terms; we keep the nominal
price.'

4495. He relates a particular case. A Frenchman sends a broker in
Mincing Lane commodities for £3,000 to sell at a given price. The
broker cannot obtain this price, and the Frenchman cannot sell
below the price. The commodities are still around, but the
Frenchman needs money. The broker therefore advances him
£1,000, the Frenchman drawing a three-month bill of exchange on
the broker for £1,000, with the goods as security. Three months
later the bill falls due, but the commodities are still unsaleable.
The broker then has to pay the bill, and although he has security
for £3,000, he cannot cash this and gets into difficulties. Thus one
person drags another down with him.

'4496. With regard to the large exports ... where there is a
depressed state of trade at home, it necessarily forces large exportation.' – '4497. Do you think that the home consumption has been
diminished? – *Very much indeed ... immensely ...* the shopkeepers are the best authorities.' – '4498. Still the importations are
very large, does not that indicate a large consumption? – It does,
if you can sell; but many of the warehouses are full of these things;
in this very instance which I have been relating, there is £3,000
worth imported, which cannot be sold.'

'4514. When money is dear, would you say that capital would be
cheap? – Yes.'

This fellow thus in no way shares Overstone's opinion that
high interest is the same thing as dear capital.

How business is now conducted: '4616. Others are going to a
very great extent, carrying on a prodigious trade in exports and
imports, to an extent far beyond what their capital justifies them
in doing; there can be no doubt of all of that. These men may
succeed; they may by some lucky venture get large fortunes, and
put themselves right. That is very much the system in which a great
deal of trade is now carried on. Persons will consent to lose 20, 30,
and 40 per cent upon a shipment; the next venture may bring it
back to them. If they fail in one after another, then they are

broken up; and that is just the case which we have often seen recently; mercantile houses have broken up, without one shilling of property being left.'

'4791. The low rate of interest' (during the previous ten years) 'operates against bankers, it is true, but I should have very great difficulty in explaining to you, unless I could show you the books, how much higher the profits' (his own) 'are now than they used to be formerly. When interest is low, from excessive issues, we have large deposits; when interest is high, we get the advantage in that way.' – '4794. When money is at a moderate rate, we have more demand for it; we lend more; it operates in that way' (for us, the bankers). 'When it gets higher, we get more than a fair proportion for it; we get more than we ought to do.'

We have seen how all the experts consider the credit of Bank of England notes as unshakeable. Nevertheless, the Bank Act ties up absolutely some £9 to £10 million in gold, for the convertibility of these notes. The sanctity and inviolability of the reserve is thereby carried much farther than among the hoarders of old. W. Brown (Liverpool) testifies (*C. D.* 1848–57, no. 2311): 'This money' (the metal reserve in the Issue Department) 'might as well have been thrown into the sea from any use that it was of at that time, there being no power to employ any of it without violating the Act of Parliament.'

The building contractor E. Capps, whom we already met with earlier, and from whose evidence we took the description of the modern building system in London (Volume 2, Chapter 12), gives his opinion of the 1844 Bank Act in the following words: '5508. Then upon the whole . . . you think that the present system' (of bank legislation) 'is a somewhat adroit scheme for bringing the profits of industry periodically into the usurer's bag? – I think so. I know that it has operated so in the building trade.'

As already mentioned, the 1845 Bank Act forced the Scottish banks into a system that was closer to the English. They were now obliged to hold gold in reserve for any note issue beyond a limit fixed for each bank. The effect this had is shown by some of the witnesses before the *B. A.* 1857.

Kennedy, director of a Scottish bank: '3375. Was there anything that you can call a circulation of gold in Scotland previously to the passing of the Act of 1845? – None whatever.' – '3376. Has there been any additional circulation of gold since? – None whatever; the people dislike gold.' – 3450. The sum of about £900,000 in gold, which the Scottish banks are compelled to keep since 1845, can only be injurious in his opinion and 'absorbs unprofitably so much of the capital of Scotland'.

Anderson, director of the Union Bank of Scotland: '3588. The only pressure upon the Bank of England by the banks in Scotland for gold was for foreign exchanges? – It was; and that is not to be relieved by holding gold in Edinburgh.' – '3590. Having the same amount of securities in the Bank of England' (or in the private banks of England), 'we have the same power that we had before of making a drain upon the Bank of England.'

Finally, a further article from *The Economist* (Wilson): 'The Scotch banks keep unemployed amounts of cash with their London agents; these keep them in the Bank of England. This gives to the Scotch banks, within the limits of these amounts, command over the metal reserve of the Bank, and here it is always in the place where it is needed, when foreign payments are to be made.'

This system was upset by the 1845 Act. In consequence of the Act of 1845 for Scotland 'of late a large drain of the coin of the Bank has taken place, to supply a mere contingent demand in Scotland, which may never occur ... Since that period there has been a large sum uniformly locked up in Scotland, and another considerable sum constantly travelling back and forward between London and Scotland. If a period arrives when a Scotch bank expects an increased demand for its notes, a box of gold is brought down from London; when this period is past, the same box, generally unopened, is sent back to London' (*The Economist*, 23 October 1847).

(And what does the father of the Bank Act, banker Samuel Jones Loyd, alias Lord Overstone, have to say to all this?

He already repeated before the Lords Committee of 1848 on Commercial Distress that 'pressure, and a high rate of interest, caused by the want of sufficient capital, cannot be relieved by an extra issue of banknotes' (1514), even though the mere *permission* for an increased note issue in the government letter of 25 October 1847 had sufficed to blunt the edge of the crisis.

He still maintains that 'the high rate of interest and the depression of the manufacturing interests was the necessary result of the diminution of the *material* capital applicable to manufacturing and trading purposes' (1604).

And yet the depressed condition of manufacturing industry for months back meant that material commodity capital overflowed the warehouses and was actually unsaleable, while for that very reason material productive capital lay either completely or partially idle, so as not to produce still more unsaleable commodity capital.

And before the Bank Acts Committee of 1857 he says: 'By strict and prompt adherence to the principles of the Act of 1844, everything has passed off with regularity and ease, the monetary system is safe and unshaken, the prosperity of the country is undisputed, the public confidence in the wisdom of the Act of 1844 is daily gaining strength, and if the Committee wish for further practical illustration of the soundness of the principles on which it rests, or of the beneficial results which it has ensured, the true and sufficient answer to the Committee is, look around you, look at the present state of the trade of this country, . . . look at the contentment of the people, look at the wealth and prosperity which pervades every class of the community, and then having done so, the Committee may be fairly called upon to decide whether they will interfere with the continuance of an Act under which those results have been developed' (*B. A.* 1857, no. 4189).

The antistrophe to this dithyramb that Overstone sang to the Committee on 14 July came on 12 November the same year, in the form of the letter to the Bank directors in which the government suspended the miracle-working act of 1844, in order to save what could still be saved. – F. E.)

Chapter 35: Precious Metal
and Rate of Exchange

I. THE MOVEMENT OF THE GOLD RESERVE

With respect to the stockpiling of notes in times of pressure, we should note that the hoarding of precious metals repeated here is the same as marked times of disturbance in the most primitive social conditions. The Act of 1844 is interesting in its effects in so far as it seeks to transform all the country's precious metal into means of circulation; it seeks to compensate for a drain of gold by a contraction of the means of circulation and for an influx of gold by an expansion of the means of circulation. When put to the test, the opposite was proved. With a single exception, which we shall mention immediately, the quantity of Bank of England notes in circulation since 1844 has never reached the maximum that the Bank was authorized to issue. The crisis of 1857 showed on the other hand that in certain circumstances this maximum is not sufficient. Between 13 and 30 November 1857, a daily average of £488,830 above the maximum was in circulation (*B. A.* 1858, p. xi). The legal maximum at that time was £14,475,000 plus the metal reserve in the Bank's vaults.

As far as the inflow and outflow of precious metal goes, the following points are to be noted.

(1) The ebb and flow of metal within a region that does not produce gold or silver should be distinguished from the flow of gold and silver from their sources of production to the various other countries, and the distribution of this additional metal among the latter.

Before the opening of the gold mines in Russia, California and Australia, the supply since the beginning of the century had only been sufficient for the replacement of worn-down coins, for the traditional use as a luxury material and for the export of silver to Asia.

Since that time, however, the export of silver to Asia has grown extraordinarily, with the Asian trade of America and Europe. The silver exported from Europe was largely replaced by the additional gold. Further, a portion of the gold newly imported was absorbed by the domestic money circulation. It was estimated that up to 1857 approximately £30 million worth of gold had been added to England's domestic circulation.[14] Moreover, the average level of metal reserves has increased since 1844 for all the central banks of Europe and North America. The growth of the domestic money circulation immediately meant that after a panic, in the subsequent period of stagnation, bank reserves grew much more quickly as a result of the greater quantity of gold coin thrust out of domestic circulation and immobilized. Finally, the consumption of precious metal for luxury articles has risen since the new gold discoveries, as a result of increasing wealth.

(2) Precious metal is constantly moving back and forth between the countries that do not produce gold and silver; the same country is both constantly importing and constantly exporting. It is only a preponderant movement in one direction or the other that determines an ultimate outflow or inflow, since these movements, which tend simply to oscillate and often do so in parallel, to a large extent neutralize one another. But for this very reason, the fact that the two movements are constant and their courses run parallel with each other on the whole, as far as their result is concerned, is overlooked. The matter is always conceived as if an excess import or export of precious metal were simply the effect

14. How this affected the money market is shown by the following testimony of W. Newmarch [*B. A.* 1857]. '1509. At the close of 1853, there was a considerable apprehension in the public mind, and in September of that year the Bank of England raised its discount on three occasions . . . In the early part of October there was a considerable degree of apprehension and alarm in the public mind. That apprehension and alarm was relieved to a very great extent before the end of November, and was almost wholly removed, in consequence of the arrival of nearly £5,000,000 of treasure from Australia . . . The same thing happened in the autumn of 1854, by the arrival in the months of October and November of nearly £6,000,000 of treasure. The same thing happened again in the autumn of 1855, which we know was a period of excitement and alarm, by the arrivals, in the three months of September, October and November, of nearly £8,000,000 of treasure, and then at the close of last year, 1856, we find exactly the same occurrence. In truth, I might appeal to the observation almost of any member of the Committee, whether the natural and complete solvent to which we have got into the habit of looking for any financial pressure, is not the arrival of a gold ship.'

and expression of the import and export relationship for commodities, whereas it also expresses a relationship between the import and export of precious metal that is independent of commodity trade.

(3) The preponderance of imports over exports, or vice versa, can be broadly measured by the increase or decrease in the metal reserves of the central banks. The preciseness of this measurement depends of course first and foremost on how much the banking system is centralized. For on this depends the extent to which the precious metal stockpiled in the so-called national bank represents the whole of the nation's metal reserve. But even on the assumption that this is in fact the case, the measurement is still not exact, since in certain circumstances an additional import of precious metal may be absorbed by domestic circulation and the growing luxury use of gold and silver, and, moreover, since a withdrawal of gold coin for domestic circulation might take place without any additional import, so that the metal reserve could decline even without a simultaneous increase in exports.

(4) An export of metal takes the form of a 'drain' if the movement of decline persists for a long period, so that the decline presents itself as a general tendency and the national bank's metal reserve is significantly depressed below its average level, until something like its average minimum is reached. This latter is fixed more or less arbitrarily, since it is determined differently in each particular case by legislation governing the backing for cash payment of notes, etc. As to the quantitative limits that such a drain of gold could attain in England, Newmarch states before the Bank Acts Committee of 1857, Evidence, no. 1494: 'Judging from experience, it is very unlikely that the efflux of treasure arising from any oscillation in the foreign trade will proceed beyond £3,000,000 or £4,000,000.' In 1847, the Bank of England's gold reserve saw its lowest level on 23 October, a drop of £5,198,156 from 26 December 1846, and of £6,453,748 from the highest point in that year (29 August).

(5) The function of the metal reserve held by a so-called national bank, a function that is far from being the only thing governing the size of the metal reserve, since this can grow simply through the crippling of domestic and foreign business, is threefold: (i) a reserve fund for international payments, i.e. a reserve fund of world money; (ii) a reserve fund for the alternately expanding and contracting domestic metal circulation; (iii) (and this is connected

with the banking function and has nothing to do with the function of money as simple money) a reserve fund for the payment of deposits and the convertibility of notes. It can therefore also be affected by conditions that bear on only one of these three functions. Thus as an international fund, it may be affected by the balance of payments, whatever the reasons determining this and whatever their relationship to the balance of trade. As a reserve fund for domestic metal circulation, it may be affected by the expansion or contraction of the latter. The third function, as a guarantee fund, while it does not determine the autonomous movement of the metal reserve, still has a double effect. If notes are issued to replace metal money in domestic circulation (and also therefore silver coin in countries where silver is the measure of value), the second function of the reserve fund disappears. And a part of the precious metal that has served for this purpose will now permanently find its way abroad. In this case, there is no withdrawal of metal coin from domestic circulation, nor, therefore, is there any temporary strengthening of the metal reserve by the immobilization of a portion of the coined metal in circulation. Moreover, if a minimum metal reserve must be maintained under all circumstances for the payment of deposits and the convertibility of notes, this affects the workings of a drain or influx of gold in a particular way; it affects the portion of the reserve which the bank is bound to maintain under all circumstances, or else the part which it might seek to get rid of at another time as useless. With a purely metallic circulation and a centralized banking system, the bank would similarly have to treat its metal reserve as a guarantee for the payment of its deposits, and a drain of metal could lead to the same panic as in Hamburg in 1857.

(6) With the possible exception of 1837, the real crisis has always broken out only after the exchange rates have moved, i.e. once the import of precious metal has the upper hand again over the export.

In 1825 the actual crash occurred after the drain of gold had ceased. In 1839 a drain of gold took place without leading to a crash. In 1847 the drain of gold ceased in April and the crash came in October. In 1857 the drain of gold abroad had ceased by the beginning of November and the crash came only later in the month.

This tendency was particularly clear in the crisis of 1847, when the drain of gold had already ceased in April, after causing a relatively mild preliminary crisis, while the commercial crisis proper broke out only in October.

The following statements were made before the Secret Committee of the House of Lords on Commercial Distress, 1848, the evidence only being printed in 1857 (cited as *C. D.* 1848–57).

Evidence of Tooke: 'In April 1847, a stringency arose, which, strictly speaking, equalled a panic, but was of relatively short duration and not accompanied by any commercial failures of importance. In October the stringency was far more intensive than at any time during April, an almost unheard-of number of commercial failures taking place (2996). – In April the rates of exchange, particularly with America, compelled us to export a considerable amount of gold in payment for unusually large imports; only by an extreme effort did the Bank stop the drain and drive the rates higher (2997). – In October the rates of exchange favoured England (2998). – The change in the rates of exchange had begun in the third week of April (3000). – They fluctuated in July and August; since the beginning of August they always favoured England (3001). – The drain on gold in August arose from a demand for internal circulation' [3003].

J. Morris, Governor of the Bank of England. Although the exchange rate after August 1847 was in England's favour, and an influx of gold thus took place, the metal reserve in the Bank still declined. '£2,200,000 went out into the country in consequence of the internal demand' (137). – This is explained on the one hand by an increased employment of labourers in railway construction, and on the other by the 'circumstance of the bankers wishing to provide themselves with gold in times of distress' (147).

Palmer, ex-Governor of the Bank of England and a director since 1811: '684. During the whole period from the middle of April 1847 to the day of withdrawing the restrictive clause in the Act of 1844 the foreign exchanges were in favour of this country.'

The drain of metal, which gave rise to a specifically monetary panic in April 1847, is thus here as always simply a precursor of the crisis, and had already turned before this broke out. In 1839, at a time of severe business depression, a very pronounced drain of metal took place – for corn, etc. – but without a crisis or monetary panic.

(7) As soon as the general crisis has burned itself out, and we again have a state of equilibrium, the gold and silver (leaving aside the influx of fresh precious metal from the producing countries) is

again distributed in the proportions in which it previously existed as hoards in the various countries. With circumstances remaining otherwise the same, the relative size of the hoard in each country is determined by this country's role in the world market. It flows out of a country that has a greater share than normal, and into another; these movements of ebb and flow simply bring about its original distribution among the various national reserves. This redistribution is nevertheless mediated by the effect of various different circumstances that will be mentioned in dealing with the exchange rates. As soon as the normal distribution is re-established – from this moment on – there is first of all a growth and then again a drain. (This last sentence is evidently applicable only to England, as the focal point of the world money market. – F. E.)

(8) A drain of metal is generally the symptom of a change in the state of foreign trade, and this change is in turn an advance warning that conditions are again approaching a crisis.[15]

(9) The balance of payments may be in favour of Asia and against Europe and America.[16]

*

Imports of precious metal take place principally at two moments.

(1) In the first phase of low interest rates which follows the crisis and is marked by a contraction of production; as well as the subsequent phase in which the interest rate rises but has not yet reached its average level. This is the phase in which returns are brisk and commercial credit high, so that the demand for loan capital does not grow in proportion to the expansion of production. In both of these phases, where loan capital is relatively abundant, the superfluous influx of capital in the form of gold and

15. According to Newmarch, a drain of gold abroad can arise for one of three reasons, in particular: (1) for a purely commercial reason, i.e. if imports have become greater than exports, as was the case between 1836 and 1844, and again in 1847, with particularly steep imports of corn; (2) to procure the means for investing English capital abroad, as for railways in India in 1857; and (3) for final expenditure abroad, as for war purposes in the East in 1853 and 1854.

16. (1918) Newmarch: 'When you combine India and China, when you bring into account the transactions between India and Australia, and the still more important transactions between China and the United States, the trade being a triangular one, and the adjustment taking place through us . . . then it is true that the balance of trade was not merely against this country, but against France, and against the United States' (*B. A.* 1857).

silver, i.e. a form in which it can function at first only as loan capital, has an important effect on the rate of interest and hence on the entire business climate.

(2) A drain, i.e. a continued heavy export, of precious metal appears as soon as returns are no longer easy, markets are over-stocked and the apparent prosperity is maintained only by credit; i.e. when a very pronounced demand for loan capital already exists, so that the rate of interest has reached at least its average level. Under these circumstances, which are precisely reflected in the drain of precious metal, the effect of a continued withdrawal of capital, in a form in which it exists directly as loan capital, is significantly intensified. This must have a direct effect on the rate of interest. But instead of the rise in the interest rate restricting credit transactions, it expands them and leads to an excessive strain on all their resources. This period therefore precedes the crash.

Newmarch was asked (*B. A.* 1857): '1520. But then the volume of bills in circulation increases with the rate of discount? – It seems to do so.' – '1522. In quiet ordinary times the ledger is the real instrument of exchange; but when any difficulty arises; when, for example, under such circumstances as I have suggested, there is a rise in the bank-rate of discount . . . then the transactions naturally resolve themselves into drawing bills of exchange, those bills of exchange being not only more convenient as regards legal proof of the transaction which has taken place, but also being more convenient in order to effect purchases elsewhere, and being pre-eminently convenient as a means of credit by which capital can be raised.'

Added to this is the fact that as soon as somewhat threatening circumstances lead the Bank to raise its discount rate – which at the same time makes it probable that the Bank will restrict the term of the bills of exchange it is prepared to discount – a general fear sets in that this will mount to a crescendo. Everyone, there-fore, and the credit-jobber above all, seeks to discount the future and have as many means of credit as possible at his disposal at the given moment. The reasons just adduced mean that it is not the mere quantity of precious metal imported or exported that operates as such, but that this firstly has its effect by way of the specific character of precious metal as capital in the money form, while secondly it acts as the feather which, added to the weight already on the scales, is enough to tip the balance decisively to one side; it has this effect because it intervenes in circumstances where anything extra on one side or the other is sufficient to tip the scales. Were it not for these reasons, it would be completely impossible to understand how a drain of gold of £5–£8 million, say, and this is the limit of our experience up till now, could exert any significant effect. This small increase or decrease in capital, which appears insignificant even against the £70 million in gold that is the average circulation in England, is infinitesimal against the total volume of English production.[17] But it is precisely the development of the credit and banking system which on the one hand seeks to press all money capital into the service of production (or what comes to the same thing, to transform all money income into capital), while on the other hand it reduces the metal reserve in a given phase of the cycle to a minimum, at which it can no longer perform the functions ascribed to it – it is this elaborate credit and banking system that makes the entire organism over-sensitive. At a less developed level of production, a contraction or expansion of the reserve in comparison with its average magnitude is a matter of relative indifference. Similarly, on the other hand, even a very severe drain of gold is relatively without effect, unless it takes place during the critical period of the industrial cycle.

The explanation we have given has ignored those cases in which the drain of metal arises as a result of harvest failures, etc. Here, a major and sudden disturbance in the balance of production, as expressed in the drain of gold, obviates the need for any further explanation. The effect is all the greater, the more this disturbance arises at a period when production is working at high pressure.

We have also ignored the function of the metal reserve as the guarantee for the convertibility of banknotes and as the pivot of the entire credit system. The central bank is the pivot of the credit system. And the metal reserve is in turn the pivot of the bank.[18]

17. See for example Weguelin's ridiculous response when he says that an outflow of £5 million in money is that much capital less, and seeks to use this to explain phenomena that do *not* occur even with infinitely greater rises in price, or with devaluations, expansions and contractions of the actual industrial capital. On the other hand, no less ridiculous is the attempt to explain these phenomena as direct symptoms of an expansion or contraction in the mass of real capital (looked at from the point of view of its material elements).

18. Newmarch (*B. A.* 1857): '1364. The reserve of bullion in the Bank of England is, in truth, the central reserve or hoard of treasure upon which the whole trade of the country is made to turn; all the other banks in the country

It is inevitable that the credit system should collapse into the monetary system, as I have already shown in Volume 1, Chapter 3, in connection with means of payment. Both Tooke and Loyd-Overstone concede that the utmost sacrifice of real wealth is necessary at the critical moment in order to maintain the metal basis. The dispute simply turns on a plus or minus and on the more or less rational way to cope with something unavoidable.[19] A certain quantity of metal that is insignificant in comparison with production as a whole is the acknowledged pivot of the system. Hence, on top of the terrifying illustration of this pivotal character in crises, the beautiful theoretical dualism. As long as it claims to treat 'of capital', enlightened economics looks down on gold and silver with the utmost disdain, as the most indifferent and useless form of capital. As soon as it deals with banking, however, this is completely reversed, and gold and silver become capital *par excellence*, for whose preservation every other form of capital and labour have to be sacrificed. But in what way are gold and silver distinguished from other forms of wealth? Not by magnitude, for this is determined by the amount of labour embodied in them. But rather as autonomous embodiments and expressions of the *social* character of wealth. (The wealth of society consists simply of the wealth of those individuals who are its private proprietors. It only proves itself to be social by the fact that these individuals exchange qualitatively different use-values with one another in order to satisfy their needs. In capitalist production, they can do this only by way of money. Thus it is only by way of money that the individual's wealth is realized as social wealth; the social nature of that wealth is embodied in money, in this thing. – F. E.) This social existence that it has thus appears as something beyond, as a thing, object or commodity outside and alongside the real elements of social wealth. Credit, being similarly a social form of wealth, displaces money and usurps its position. It is confidence in the social character of production that makes the money form of products

look to the Bank of England as the central hoard or reservoir from which they are to draw their reserve of coin; and it is upon that hoard or reservoir that the action of the foreign exchanges always falls.'

19. 'Practically, then, both Mr Tooke and Mr Loyd would meet an additional demand for gold . . . by an early . . . contraction of credit by raising the rate of interest, and restricting advances of capital . . . But the principles of Mr Loyd lead to certain' (legal) 'restrictions and regulations which . . . produce the most serious inconvenience' (*The Economist*, 1847, p. 1418).

appear as something merely evanescent and ideal, as a mere notion. But as soon as credit is shaken, and this is a regular and necessary phase in the cycle of modern industry, all real wealth is supposed to be actually and suddenly transformed into money, into gold and silver – a crazy demand, but one that necessarily grows out of the system itself. And the gold and silver that is supposed to satisfy these immense claims amounts in all to a few millions in the vaults of the bank.[20] A drain of gold, therefore, shows strikingly by its effects that production is not really subjected to social control, as social production, and that the social form of wealth exists alongside wealth itself as a *thing*. The capitalist system does have this in common with earlier systems of production in so far as these are based on commodity trade and private exchange. But it is only with this system that the most striking and grotesque form of this absurd contradiction and paradox arises, because (1) in the capitalist system production for direct use-value, for the producer's own use, is most completely abolished, so that wealth exists only as a social process expressed as the entwinement of production and circulation; and (2) because with the development of the credit system, capitalist production constantly strives to overcome this metallic barrier, which is both a material and an imaginary barrier to wealth and its movement, while time and again breaking its head on it.

In the crisis we get the demand that all bills of exchange, securities and commodities should be simultaneously convertible into bank money all at once, and this bank money again into gold.

2. THE EXCHANGE RATE

(The barometer for the international movement of the money metals is of course the rate of exchange. If England has to make more payments to Germany than Germany to England, in London the price of the mark as expressed in sterling rises, while in Hamburg and Berlin the price of sterling expressed in marks falls. If this surplus of English payment obligations towards Germany does not balance out again, for instance through a predominance

20. 'You quite agree that there is no mode by which you can modify the demand for bullion except by raising the rate of interest?' – Chapman (associate member of the great billbroking firm of Overend, Gurney & Co.): 'I should say so . . . When our bullion falls to a certain point, we had better sound the tocsin at once and say we are drooping, and every man sending money abroad must do it at his own peril' (*B. A.* 1857, Evidence, no. 5057).

of German purchases from England, the sterling price for bills of exchange in marks on Germany must rise to a point at which it pays to send metal from England to Germany in payment – gold coin or bullion – instead of bills of exchange. This is the typical course of events.

If this export of precious metal becomes more large-scale and persists for a longer time, the English bank reserves are affected, and the English money market – in the first place, the Bank of England – must take protective measures. Essentially these consist, as we have already seen, in putting up the rate of interest. With a major drain of gold, the money market usually becomes tight, i.e. the demand for loan capital in the money form significantly outweighs the supply, and a higher rate of interest then arises quite spontaneously; the discount rate decreed by the Bank of England corresponds to the actual situation and prevails in the market. But there are also cases where the drain of metal arises from out of the ordinary business transactions (e.g. from loans to foreign countries, capital investment abroad, etc.), so that the state of the London money market as such in no way justifies an effective raising of interest rates; the Bank of England then first has to 'make money scarce' by large-scale borrowing 'on the open market', as the expression goes, thus artificially producing the situation that justifies raising interest rates, or makes this necessary; a manoeuvre that becomes harder every year. – F. E.)

How this raising of the interest rate affects the rates of exchange is shown by the following evidence before the 1857 House of Commons Committee on Bank Legislation (cited as *B. A.* 1857).

John Stuart Mill: '2176. When there is a state of commercial difficulty there is always . . . a considerable fall in the price of securities . . . foreigners send over to buy railway shares in this country, or English holders of foreign railway shares sell their foreign railway shares abroad . . . there is so much transfer of bullion prevented.' – '2182. A large and rich class of bankers and dealers in securities, through whom the equalization of the rate of interest and the equalization of commercial pressure between different countries usually takes place . . . are always on the look out to buy securities which are likely to rise . . . The place for them to buy securities will be the country which is sending bullion away.' – '2184. These investments of capital took place to a very considerable extent in 1847, to a sufficient extent to have relieved the drain considerably.'

J. G. Hubbard, ex-Governor of the Bank of England, and a director since 1838: '2545. There are great quantities of European securities ... which have a European currency in all the different money-markets, and those bonds, as soon as their value is ... reduced by 1 or 2 per cent in one market, are immediately purchased for transmission to those markets where their value is still unimpaired.' – '2565. Are not foreign countries considerably in debt to the merchants of this country? – Very largely.' – '2566. Therefore, the cashment of those debts might be sufficient to account for a very large accumulation of capital in this country? – In 1847, the ultimate restoration of our position was effected by our striking off so many millions previously due by America. and so many millions due by Russia to this country.'

(England was in debt to those very countries for corn, to the tune of 'so many millions', and also did not fail to 'strike off' the greater part by the bankruptcy of English debtors. See the 1857 *Report on the Bank Acts*, as quoted in Chapter 30 above, p. 624 – F. E.)

'2572. In 1847, the exchange between this country and St Petersburg was very high. When the Government Letter came out authorizing the Bank to issue irrespectively of the limitation of £14,000,000' (above and beyond the gold reserve – F. E.), 'the stipulation was that the rate of discount should be 8 per cent. At that moment, with the then rate of discount, it was a profitable operation to order gold to be shipped from St Petersburg to London and on its arrival to lend it at 8 per cent up to the maturity of the three months' bills drawn against the purchase of gold.' – '2573. In all bullion operations there are many points to be taken into consideration; there is the rate of exchange and the rate of interest, which is available for the investment during the period of the maturity of the bill' (drawn against it – F. E.).

Rate of Exchange with Asia

The following points are important, firstly, because they show how England, when its rate of exchange with Asia is unfavourable, manages to recoup its losses from other countries whose imports from Asia are paid for through English middlemen. Secondly, however, because here again Mr Wilson makes the stupid attempt to identify the impact of an export of precious metal on the rate of exchange with the impact of an export of capital in general on the rate; the export in question being in both cases not a means of purchase or payment but an export for capital investment. It is self-evident, to start with, that if so and so many million pounds are sent to India, to be invested there in railways, then whether they are sent in precious metal or in iron rails is simply a difference in form, the same amount of capital being transferred in each case from one country to the other; this transfer, moreover, does not go into the ordinary commercial account, and the exporting country does not expect any other return for it than the subsequent annual revenue from the earnings of these railways. If this export takes place in the form of precious metal, then, because precious metal as such is directly loanable money capital and the basis of the entire money system, it will not necessarily always have a direct effect on the money market and thereby on the rate of interest in the country exporting this precious metal, though it does have this effect in the cases so far developed. It has a similarly direct effect on the rate of exchange. In particular, precious metal is sent in payment only in so far as the bills of exchange that are offered on the London money market, on India for example, are insufficient to make these extra remittances. The demand for bills of exchange on India thus outweighs the supply, and so the rate of exchange turns temporarily against England; not because England is in debt to India but rather because it has to send extraordinary sums to India. In the long run, such an export of precious metal to India must have the effect of increasing the Indian demand for English commodities, because it indirectly raises India's power to consume European goods. If however the capital is dispatched in the form of rails, etc., it cannot have any influence on the rate of exchange, since India does not have to make any return payment for these. For this very reason, it also need not have any effect on the money market. Wilson seeks to elicit an effect of this kind from the fact that extra outlays such as these lead to an extra demand for monetary accommodation, and thus affect the rate of interest. This may well be the case; but to contend that it has to take place under any circumstances is totally mistaken. Wherever the rails may be sent and laid, whether on English soil or on Indian, they represent nothing but a certain expansion of English production in a particular sphere. To maintain that an increase in production, even a very substantial one, cannot take place without driving up the rate of interest is sheer foolishness. Monetary accommodation may grow, i.e. the sum of dealings in which credit operations are involved; but these operations can increase while the given rate of interest remains the same. This was in fact the case in England during the railway mania of the 1840s. The interest rate did not rise. And it is obvious that in so far as real capital comes into consideration, in this case commodities, the effect on the money market is exactly the same whether these commodities are designed for export abroad or for domestic use. There could only be a distinction if England's capital investment abroad had a limiting effect on its commercial exports – on exports that have to be paid for and thus bring a return – or in so far as these capital investments in general were already a symptom of an over-taxing of credit and the beginning of fraudulent operations.

In the following extract, Wilson is the questioner and Newmarch replies.

'1786. On a former day you stated, with reference to the demand for silver for the East, that you believed that the exchanges with India were in favour of this country, notwithstanding the large amount of bullion that is continually transmitted to the East; have you any ground for supposing the exchanges to be in favour of this country? – Yes, I have . . . I find that the real value of the exports from the United Kingdom to India in 1851 was £7,420,000; to that is to be added the amount of India House drafts, that is, the funds drawn from India by the East India Company for the purpose of their own expenditure. Those drafts in that year amounted to £3,200,000, making, therefore, the total export from the United Kingdom to India £10,620,000. In 1855 . . . the actual value of the export of goods from the United Kingdom had risen to £10,350,000 and the India House drafts were £3,700,000, making, therefore, the total export from this country £14,050,000. Now as regards 1851, I believe there are no means of stating what was the real value of the import of goods from India to this country, but in 1854 and 1855 we have a statement of the real value; in 1855, the total real value of the imports of goods from India to this country was £12,670,000 and that sum, compared with the £14,050,000 I have mentioned, left a balance in favour of the United Kingdom, as regards the direct trade between the two countries, of £1,380,000.'

Wilson comments on this that the exchange rates are also affected by indirect trade. Thus exports from India to Australia and North America are covered by drafts on London and have exactly the same effect on the exchange rate as if the commodities went directly from India to England. If India and China are taken together, moreover, the balance would be against England, since China always has sizeable payments to make to India for opium, and England has payments to make to China, the sums involved going on to India by this detour. (1787, 1788.)

In 1791 Wilson then asks whether the effect on the exchange rates would not be the same irrespective of whether the capital 'went in the form of iron rails and locomotives, or whether it went in the form of coin'. Newmarch's response to this is quite correct: the £12 million that was sent to India in recent years for railway construction has served to purchase an annuity which India has to pay to England at regular intervals. 'But as far as regards the immediate operation on the bullion market, the investments of the £12 million would only be operative as far as bullion was required to be sent out for actual money disbursements.'

1797. (Weguelin asks:) 'If no return is made for this iron' (rails), 'how can it be said to affect the exchanges? – I do not think that that part of the expenditure which is sent out in the form of commodities affects the computation of the exchange . . . The computation of the exchange between two countries is affected, one might say, solely by the quantity of obligations or bills offering in one country, as compared with the quantity offering in the other country against it; that is the rationale of the exchange. Now, as regards the transmission of those £12,000,000, the money in the first place is subscribed in this country . . . now, if the nature of the transaction was such that the whole of that £12,000,000 was required to be laid down in Calcutta, Bombay, and Madras in treasure . . . a sudden demand would very violently operate upon the price of silver, and upon the exchange, just the same as if the India Company were to give notice tomorrow that their drafts were to be raised from £3,000,000 to £12,000,000. But half of those £12,000,000 is spent . . . in buying commodities in this country . . . iron rails and timber, and other materials . . . it is an expenditure in this country of the capital of this country for a particular kind of commodity to be sent out to India, and there is an end of it.' – 1798. (Weguelin:) 'But the production of those articles of iron and timber necessary for the railways produces a large consumption of foreign articles, which might affect the exchange? – Certainly.'

Wilson then offers the opinion that iron largely represents labour, while the wages paid for this labour largely represent imported goods (1799). He goes on to ask:

'1801. But speaking quite generally, it would have the effect of turning the exchanges against this country if you sent abroad the articles which were produced by the consumption of the imported articles without receiving any remittance for them either in the shape of produce or otherwise? – That principle is exactly what took place in this country during the time of the great railway expenditure' (1845). 'For three or four or five years, you spent upon railways £30,000,000, nearly the whole of which went in the payment of wages. You sustained in three years a larger population employed in constructing railways, and locomotives, and carriages, and stations than you employed in the whole of the factory districts. The people . . . spent those wages in buying tea and sugar and spirits and other foreign commodities; those commodities were imported; but it was a fact, that during the time this great expenditure was going on the foreign exchanges between this country and other countries were not materially deranged. There was no efflux of bullion, on the contrary, there was rather an influx.'

1802. Wilson insists that, given a settled balance of trade between England and India and the exchange rate at par values. the extra shipment of iron and locomotives 'would affect the exchanges with India'. Newmarch cannot accept this, if the rails are sent as capital investment and India does not have to pay for them in one form or another. He also adds: 'I agree with the principle that no one country can have permanently against itself an adverse state of exchange with all the other countries, with which it deals; an adverse exchange with one country necessarily produces a favourable exchange with another.'

Wilson then throws him the following triviality: '1803. But would not a transfer of capital be the same whether it was sent in one form or another? – As regards the obligation it would.' – '1804. The effect therefore of making railways in India, whether you send bullion or whether you send materials, would be the same upon the capital-market here in increasing the value of capital as if the whole was sent out in bullion?'

If iron prices did not rise, this was at least a proof that the 'value' of the 'capital' contained in the rails had not increased. But what is at issue is the value of the money capital, the rate of interest. Wilson is trying to identify money capital and capital in general. The simple fact is, firstly, that £12 million was subscribed in England for Indian railways. This is something that has nothing directly to do with the rate of exchange, and the designation of the £12 million is similarly immaterial as far as the money market is concerned. If the money market is in a favourable condition, it need not have any effect at all, just as the English railway subscriptions of 1844 and 1845 left the money market unaffected. If the money market is already somewhat tight, the rate of interest could be affected, but only in the sense of a rise, and according to Wilson's theory this would necessarily have an effect on the exchange rates that was favourable for England, i.e. it would inhibit the tendency to export precious metal; if not to India, then at least elsewhere. Mr Wilson jumps from one thing to another. In question 1802 it is the exchange rate that is supposedly affected, in question 1804 the 'value of capital' – two very different things. The rate of interest may have an effect on the exchange rates, and the exchange rates may have an effect on the rate of interest. But the rate of interest may also remain constant despite a change in exchange rates, while exchange rates may remain constant despite a change in the rate of interest. Wilson cannot accept that when capital is sent abroad, the mere form in which it is sent can have such a different effect; i.e. that the difference in the form of the capital has this importance, and its money form at that. This is something that contradicts the whole trend of enlightened economics. Newmarch answers Wilson one-sidedly; he gives him not the slightest warning that he has suddenly leapt without reason from the exchange rate to the rate of interest. Newmarch's response to this question 1804 is uncertain and vacillating:

'No doubt, if there is a demand for £12,000,000 to be raised, it is immaterial, as regards the general rate of interest, whether that £12 million is required to be sent in bullion or in materials. I think, however' (a fine transition, this 'however', when he intends to say the exact opposite) 'it is not quite immaterial' (it is immaterial, but, nevertheless, it is not immaterial) 'because in the one case the £6 million would be returned immediately; in the other case it would not be returned so rapidly. Therefore it would make some' (what definiteness!) 'difference, whether the £6 million was expended in this country or sent wholly out of it.'

Is this supposed to mean that the £6 million would return immediately? In so far as this £6 million has been spent in England, it exists in rails, locomotives, etc. that are sent to India, from where they do not return, and it is only by amortization, i.e. very slowly, that their value returns, whereas the £6 million in precious metal might well return very quickly in kind. In so far as the £6 million was spent on wages, it has been consumed; but the money in which it was advanced continues to circulate in the country just as before, or else forms a reserve. The same applies to the profits of the rail producers and to the portion of the £6 million that replaces their constant capital. The ambiguous word 'return' is thus used by Newmarch simply to avoid saying directly that the money remains in the country, and that in so far as it functions as loanable money capital, the difference for the money market (aside from the fact that more metal money might have been absorbed for circulation) is simply that it is spent on A's account rather than B's. Investment of this kind, where the capital is transferred to other countries in commodities rather than in precious metal, can affect the exchange rates (but not the rate with the country in which it is invested) only in so far as the production of these exported commodities requires an additional import of other foreign goods. But then this production cannot balance out the extra import. The same is true with any export on credit, irrespective of whether capital investment or ordinary trade is involved. This extra import, however, can react to produce an extra demand for English goods, e.g. from the colonies or the U.S.A.

*

Newmarch previously said [1786] that English exports to India were greater than imports, as a result of the East India Company's drafts. Sir Charles Wood cross-examines him on this point. This excess of English exports to India over imports from India is in fact brought into being by an import from India for which England does not pay any equivalent: the East India Company's drafts (now the Indian government's) boil down to a tribute extracted from India. In 1855, for example, English imports from India came to £12,660,000; English exports to India were £10,350,000. A balance of £2¼ million in India's favour.

'If that was the whole state of the case, that £2,250,000 would have to be remitted in some form to India. But then come in the advertisements from the India House. The India House advertise to this effect that they are prepared to grant drafts on the various presidencies in India to the extent of £3,250,000.' (This amount was levied for the London expenses of the East India Company and for the dividends to be paid to stockholders.) 'And that not merely liquidates the £2,250,000 which arose out of the course of trade, but it presents £1,000,000 of surplus' (1917).

1922. (Wood:) 'Then the effect of those India House drafts is not to increase the exports to India, but *pro tanto* to diminish them?'

(He should say, to reduce by that amount the need to cover imports from India by exports.) Mr Newmarch explains this by the fact that the English export 'good government' to India for this £3,700,000 (1925). As Minister for India, Wood knew all about the kind of 'good government' that was exported by the English, and he rightly says, not without irony (1926): 'Then the export, which, you state, is caused by the East India drafts, is an export of good government, and not of produce.'

England exports a good deal of 'good government' in this way, and also much capital investment in foreign countries, thus receiving imports that are quite separate from the usual run of business; in part this is a tribute for the 'good government' which has been exported, in part a revenue from capital invested in the colonies and elsewhere, i.e. a tribute for which it does not have to pay any equivalent. It is therefore evident that the rate of exchange is unaffected if England simply consumes this tribute without exporting anything in return. It is also clear that the rate of exchange is still unaffected if it reinvests this tribute not in England but abroad, either productively or unproductively; if for example it uses it to send munitions to the Crimea. Besides, in so far as imports from abroad come into England's revenue – and these must of course either be paid as tribute, in which case no equivalent is needed, or paid for by the exchange of this unpaid tribute, or else in the ordinary run of trade – England can either consume these or alternatively invest them again as capital. Neither the one thing nor the other disturbs the rate of exchange, and this is overlooked by the wise Wilson. Whether it is domestic or foreign products that form a portion of the revenue – the latter case simply presupposing the exchange of domestic products for foreign – the consumption of this revenue, productively or unproductively, in no way affects the rate of exchange, even if it does affect the volume of production. The following extracts should be judged accordingly.

1934. Wood inquires how the sending of war supplies to the

Crimea would affect the exchange rate with Turkey. Newmarch replies: 'I do not see that the mere transmission of warlike stores would necessarily affect the exchange, but certainly the transmission of treasure would affect the exchange.' Here, therefore, he distinguishes between capital in the money form and other capital. But Wilson then asks whether:

'1935. If you make an export of any article to a great extent, for which there is to be no corresponding import' (Mr Wilson forgets that England receives very substantial imports for which there have never been corresponding exports, save in the form of 'good government' or capital previously exported for investment; in any case imports that are not part of the regular movement of trade. But these imports may in turn be exchanged, say, for American products, and if these American products are exported without corresponding imports, this in no way alters the fact that the value of these imports can be consumed without any equivalent outflow abroad; these imports were received without matching exports, and they can therefore also be consumed without entering into the balance of trade), 'you do not discharge the foreign debt you have created by your imports' (but if you have already paid for these imports previously, e.g. by credit given abroad, no debt is created for them, and the question has nothing at all to do with the international balance; it is a simple matter of productive or unproductive expenditure, irrespective of whether the products consumed in this way are domestic products or foreign) 'and therefore you must by that transaction affect the exchanges by not discharging the foreign debt, by reason of your export having no corresponding imports? – That is true as regards countries generally.'

What Wilson's lecture boils down to is that every export without a corresponding import is at the same time an import without a corresponding export; since foreign and thus imported commodities also enter into the production of the article exported. The assumption is that any such export is either based on an unpaid import or gives rise to one – i.e. a debt abroad. This is wrong, even leaving aside the following two circumstances: (1) England gets certain imports gratis and does not pay any equivalent for them, e.g. a part of its Indian imports. It can exchange these for American imports, and export the latter without matching imports; in any case, as far as the value is concerned, it has only exported something that cost it nothing. And (2) it may have paid for imports, e.g. American ones, that form additional capital; if these are consumed unproductively, e.g. in war materials, this does not create a debt to America and does not affect the exchange rate with America. Newmarch contradicts himself in questions 1934 and 1935, and Wood draws his attention to this in question 1938: 'If no portion of the goods which are employed in the manufacture of the articles exported without return' (war materials) 'came from the country to which those articles are sent, how is the exchange with that country affected; supposing the trade with Turkey to be in an ordinary state of equilibrium, how is the exchange between this country and Turkey affected by the export of warlike stores to the Crimea?'

At this point Newmarch loses his calm demeanour; he forgets that he has already answered this simple question correctly under question 1934, and says: 'We seem, I think, to have exhausted the practical question, and to have now attained a very elevated region of metaphysical discussion.'

*

(Wilson has still a further version of his contention that the rate of exchange is affected by every transfer of capital from one country to another, no matter whether this takes place in the form of precious metal or of commodities. Wilson knows of course that the exchange rate is affected by the rate of interest, particularly by the relationship between the interest rates prevailing in the two countries whose reciprocal exchange rate is in question. If he can then prove that an excess of capital in general, and thus first of all in commodities of all kinds, including precious metal, also contributes towards determining the rate of interest, he will already be one step nearer his goal; the transfer of a significant portion of this capital to another country must then alter the rate of interest in both countries, and moreover in contrary directions, thus in the second place also the rate of exchange between the two countries. – F. E.)

Wilson goes on to say in *The Economist*, of which he was at that time the editor (1847, p. 574):

'... No doubt, however, such abundance of capital as is indicated by large stocks of commodities of all kinds, including bullion, would necessarily lead, not only to low prices of commodities in general, but also to a lower rate of interest for the use of capital' (1). 'If we have a stock of commodities on hand, which is sufficient to serve the country for two years to come, a command over those commodities would be obtained for a given period, at a much lower rate than if the stocks were barely sufficient to last us two months' (2). 'All loans of money, in whatever shape they are made, are simply a transfer of a command over commodities from one to another. Whenever, therefore, commodities are abundant, the interest of money must be low, and when they are scarce, the interest of money must be high' (3). 'As commodities become abundant, the number of sellers, in proportion to the number of buyers, increases, and, in proportion as the quantity is more than is required for immediate consumption, so must a larger portion be kept for future use. Under these circumstances, the terms on which a holder becomes willing to sell for a future payment, or on credit, become lower than if he were certain that his whole stock would be required within a few weeks' (4).

With regard to statement (1), we should note that a large *influx* of precious metal can take place at the same time as a *contraction* in production, this being always the case in the period after a crisis. In the following phase, precious metal may flow in from countries where this is mainly produced; the import of other commodities is generally balanced in this period by exports. In both these phases, the rate of interest is low and rises only slowly, for reasons we have already given. This low rate of interest can be explained in all cases without in any way bringing in 'large stocks of commodities of all kinds'. And how are these supposed to have their effect? The low price of cotton, for example, enables the spinner, etc. to make high profits. Why then is the interest rate low? Certainly not because the profit that can be made with borrowed capital is high. But purely and simply because, under the existing conditions, the demand for loan capital does not grow in relation to this profit; i.e. loan capital has a different movement from industrial capital. What *The Economist* is seeking to prove is precisely the opposite: that its movement is identical with the movement of industrial capital.

As for statement (2), if we scale down the absurd assumption of stocks for two years in advance in order to give it some possible sense, this supposes that the commodity market is oversupplied. This would lead to a fall in prices. Less would have to be paid for a bale of cotton. But this in no way means that the money needed to purchase a bale of cotton is cheaper to come by. That depends on the state of the money market. If it is cheaper to come by, this is only because the commercial credit situation is such that it has less need to resort to bank credit than is usual. The commodities that flood the market are means of subsistence or means of production. A low price for either increases the industrial capitalist's profit. How could a low price reduce interest if the abundance of industrial capital and the demand for monetary accommodation were not opposite phenomena instead of being identical? Conditions are such that the merchant and industrialist can give each other easy credit; because of this easing of commercial credit, both industrialist and merchant need less bank credit; hence the rate of interest can be low. This low rate of interest has nothing to do with the influx of precious metal, though the two may coexist, and the same causes that lead to low prices for imported articles may also lead to an excess influx of precious metal. If the import market really was flooded, this would mean a decline in the demand for imported goods, which would be inexplicable given the low prices, unless it were due to a contraction in domestic industrial production; but this would again be inexplicable, given the excess of imports at low prices. A mass of absurdities, in order to show that a fall in prices equals a fall in interest. The two things may simultaneously occur alongside one another. But then they express a movement of industrial capital and loanable money capital in opposite directions, and not in the same direction.

Why, with regard to (3), the interest on money should be low when there is an abundance of commodities is not to be seen even with this further explanation. If commodities are cheap, I need, say, £1,000 to buy a certain quantity, instead of £2,000 as previously. But perhaps I still invest £2,000 and use this to buy double the amount of commodities I did before, expanding my business by advancing the same capital, which I might have to borrow. Now, as before, I spend £2,000. My demand on the money market thus remains the same, even though my demand on the commodity market rises with the fall in commodity prices. But if my demand decreases, i.e. if production does not expand with the fall in commodity prices, which would contradict all *The Economist*'s laws, the demand for loanable money capital would decline, even though profit increased; this increasing profit would however create a demand for loan capital. A low level of commodity prices, moreover, may arise for three reasons. Firstly, from a lack of demand. In that case, the rate of interest is low because production is paralysed, not because commodities are cheap, the cheapness simply being an expression of this paralysis. Or else because the supply is too large in relation to the demand. This may result from an oversupply of markets, etc. that leads to a crisis, and may coincide during the crisis itself with a high rate of interest. Or it may be because the value of commodities has fallen, i.e. the same demand can be satisfied at a lower price. Why should the rate of interest fall in this last case? Because profit grows? If it is because less money capital is needed to obtain the same productive or commodity capital, this simply proves that profit and interest stand in inverse proportion to one another. In any case, *The Economist*'s general thesis is wrong. Low money prices for commodities and a low rate of interest do not necessarily go together. If this were the case, the interest rate would be lowest in the poorest countries, where the money prices of products are lowest, and highest in the richest countries, where the money prices of agricultural products are highest. In general, *The Economist* concedes that, if the value of money falls, this has no influence on the rate of interest. £100 still yields £105; if the £100 is worth less, so too is the £5. The ratio is not affected by a rise or fall in the value of the original sum. Considered as value, a certain quantity of commodities is equal to a certain sum of money. If its value rises, it is equal to a greater sum of money; if it falls, the converse is true. If it is £2,000, then 5 per cent is £100; if it is £1,000, 5 per cent is £50. But this in no way affects the interest rate. The element of truth in all this is simply that more monetary accommodation is required when £2,000 is needed to buy the same quantity of commodities than when only £1,000 is needed. All this shows, however, is that the ratio between profit and interest is an inverse one. For profit grows with the cheapening of the elements of constant and variable capital, while interest falls. However, the converse can also be the case, and frequently is so. Cotton may be cheap, for example, because there is no demand for yarn and cloth; it can be relatively dear because large profits in the cotton industry lead to a great demand for it. On the other hand, the industrialists' profits may be high precisely because the price of cotton is low. Hubbard's list * shows that the interest rate and commodity prices exhibit completely independent movements; while the movements of the

* See above, p. 684.

interest rate are precisely correlated with the movements of the metal reserve and the rate of exchange.

The Economist says: 'Whenever, therefore, commodities are abundant, the interest of money must be low.' Precisely the opposite is the case during crises; commodities are there in excess, not convertible into money, and the rate of interest is therefore high. In another phase of the cycle, there is a great demand for commodities and hence easy returns, but at the same time a rise in commodity prices, and a low rate of interest on account of these easy returns. 'When they' (commodities) 'are scarce, the interest of money must be high.' The opposite is again the case in the slack period following the crisis. Commodities are scarce in absolute terms, but not in relation to demand, and the interest rate is low.

As far as statement (4) goes, it is quite obvious that when the market is flooded, an owner of commodities sells off his stock more cheaply – if he can sell it at all – than when there is a prospect of stocks becoming rapidly exhausted. It is less clear why the interest rate should fall on this account.

If the market is flooded with imported goods, the interest rate may rise as a result of a greater demand for loan capital on the part of the owners of these goods, who hope in this way to avoid having to put them on the market. It may fall, because the ease of commercial credit still keeps the demand for bank credit relatively low.

*

The Economist mentions the rapid effect on the exchange rates in 1847 which resulted from the increase in the interest rate and other pressure on the money market. But it should not be forgotten that despite the turn in the exchange rates, gold continued to flow out until the end of April; the turning-point here only occurred at the beginning of May.

On 1 January 1847, the Bank's metal reserve was £15,066,691; the rate of interest 3½ per cent. The three-month exchange rate on Paris was 25.75, on Hamburg 13.10, on Amsterdam 12.3¼. By 5 March, the metal reserve had fallen to £11,595,535; the Bank rate had risen to 4 per cent; the exchange rate fell to 25.66½ on Paris, 13.9¼ on Hamburg, 12.2½ on Amsterdam. The drain of gold persisted; see the following table:

1847	Bullion reserve of the Bank of England (£)	Money market	Highest three-month rates		
			Paris	Hamburg	Amsterdam
20 March	11,231,630	Bank disc. 4%	25.67½	13.9¾	12.2½
3 April	10,246,410	,, ,, 5%	25.80	13.10	12.3½
10 April	9,867,053	Money very scarce	25.90	13.10⅓	12.4½
17 April	9,329,841	Bank disc. 5.5%	26.02½	13.10¾	12.5½
24 April	9,213,890	Pressure	26.05	13.12	12.6
1 May	9,337,716	Increasing pressure	26.15	13.12¾	12.6½
8 May	9,588,759	Highest pressure	26.27½	13.15½	12.7¾

In 1847, the total export of precious metal from England came to £8,602,597.

Of this there went to the United States	£3,226,411
to France	£2,479,892
to the Hanse towns	£958,781
to Holland	£247,743

Despite the turn in the exchange rates at the end of March, the drain of gold lasted a whole month longer, its probable destination being the United States.

'We thus see' (says *The Economist*, 1847 p. 954) 'how rapid and striking was the effect of a rise in the rate of interest, and the pressure which ensued in correcting an adverse exchange, and in turning the tide of bullion back to this country. This effect was produced entirely independent of the balance of trade. A higher rate of interest caused a lower price of securities, both foreign and English, and induced large purchases to be made on foreign account, which increased the amount of bills to be drawn from this country, while, on the other hand, the high rate of interest and the difficulty of obtaining money was such that the demand of those bills fell off, while their amount increased ... For the same cause orders for imports were countermanded, and investments of English funds abroad were realized and brought home for employment here. Thus, for example, we read in the *Rio de Janeiro Price Current* of the 10th May, "Exchange (on England – F.E.) has experienced a further decline, principally caused by a pressure on the market for remittance of the proceeds of large sales of (Brazilian – F.E.) government stock, on English account." Capital belonging to this country, which has been invested in public and other securities abroad, when the interest was very low here, was thus again brought back when the interest became high.'

England's Balance of Trade

India alone has to pay £5 million in tribute for 'good government', interest and dividends on British capital, etc., and this does not include the sums sent home each year for investment in England, partly by officials as savings from their salaries and partly by merchants as a portion of their profits. The same remittances are constantly made from every British colony, for the same reasons. Most banks in Australia, the West Indies and Canada were founded with British capital, the dividends being paid in England. England also possesses many bonds issued by foreign governments – European, North American and South American – on which it receives interest. On top of this there is its participation in foreign railways, canals, mines, etc., with dividends accordingly. The remittances under all these heads are made almost exclusively in products over and above the total of English exports. Only an infinitesimal sum, on the other hand, goes abroad to the owners of English securities and for the consumption of English residents.

The question as to how this affects the balance of trade and the exchange rates is 'at any particular moment one of time'. 'Practically speaking ... England gives long credits upon her exports, while the imports are paid for in ready money. At particular moments this difference of practice has a considerable effect upon the exchanges. At a time when our exports are very considerably increasing, e.g., 1850, a continual increase of investment of British capital must be going on ... in this way remittances of 1850 may be made against goods exported in 1849. But if the exports of 1850 exceed those of 1849 by more than 6 million, the practical effect must be that more money is sent abroad, to this amount, than returned in the same year. And in this way an effect is produced on the rates of exchange and the rate of interest. When, on the contrary, our trade is depressed after a commercial crisis, and when our exports are much reduced, the remittances due for the past years of larger exports greatly exceed the value of our imports;

the exchanges become correspondingly in our favour, capital rapidly accumulates at home, and the rate of interest becomes less' (*The Economist*, 11 January 1851).

The foreign exchange rates can alter:

(1) As a result of the temporary balance of payments, whatever may be the causes determining this; these may be purely commercial, or may involve capital investment abroad or state expenditures, as in war, etc. – in so far as cash payments are made abroad in this connection.

(2) As the result of a devaluation of money in one country, either of metal money or of paper. This change is purely nominal. If £1 subsequently represented only half as much money as before, it would obviously be reckoned at 12½ French francs instead of at 25.

(3) When the rate of exchange is between countries, one of which uses silver as 'money', the other gold, it is dependent on the relative fluctuations in value of these two metals, since such fluctuations obviously alter the parity between the two. An example of this was in 1850, when the exchange rate was unfavourable to England even though its exports rose enormously. There was still no drain of gold, for all that. This was the effect of the temporary rise in the value of silver as against gold. (See *The Economist*, 30 November 1850.)

Exchange rate parity for £1 is 25 francs 20 centimes in Paris, 13 banco marks 10½ schillings in Hamburg, 11 florins 97 cents in Amsterdam. In proportion as the exchange rate on Paris rises above 25.20, it becomes more favourable for the English debtor to France or for the purchaser of French commodities. In both cases less sterling is needed. In more distant countries, where precious metal is not so easy to come by, if bills of exchange are scarce and insufficient for the remittances to be made to England, the natural effect is to drive up the prices of those products that are customarily shipped to England, since a greater demand for these now arises, with the purpose of sending them to England instead of bills of exchange: this is often the case in India.

An unfavourable rate of exchange, and even a drain of gold, may arise in England if there is a very great surplus in money, a low rate of interest and a high price for securities.

In the course of 1848, England received large quantities of silver from India, since good bills were scarce and mediocre ones not readily accepted as a result of the 1847 crisis and the great lack of credit in trade with India. This silver had scarcely arrived before it all found its way to the Continent, where the revolution led to hoarding on all sides. The same silver largely flowed back to India in 1850, since the exchange rate now made this profitable.

*

The monetary system is essentially Catholic, the credit system essentially Protestant. 'The Scotch hate gold.' As paper, the monetary existence of commodities has a purely social existence. It is *faith* that brings salvation. Faith in money value as the immanent spirit of commodities, faith in the mode of production and its predestined disposition, faith in the individual agents of production as mere personifications of self-valorizing capital. But the credit system is no more emancipated from the monetary system as its basis than Protestantism is from the foundations of Catholicism.

Chapter 36: Pre-Capitalist Relations

Interest-bearing capital, or, to describe it in its archaic form, usurer's capital, belongs together with its twin brother, merchant's capital, to the antediluvian forms of capital which long precede the capitalist mode of production and are to be found in the most diverse socio-economic formations. Usurer's capital requires nothing more for its existence than that at least a portion of the products is transformed into commodities and that money in its various functions develops concurrently with trade in commodities.

The development of usurer's capital is bound up with that of merchant's capital, and particularly with that of money-dealing capital. In ancient Rome, from the latter phases of the Republic onwards, although manufacture stood at a much lower level than the average for the ancient world, merchant's capital, money-dealing capital and usurer's capital – in the ancient form – were developed to their highest point.

We have already seen how hoard formation necessarily arises along with money. But the professional hoarder only becomes important when he transforms himself into a money-lender.

The merchant borrows money to make a profit with it, to use it as capital, i.e. to lay it out. Even in the earlier forms, therefore, the money-lender confronts him in precisely the same way as he does the modern capitalist. This specific relationship was even perceived by the Catholic universities.

'The universities of Alcalá, Salamanca, Ingolstadt, Freiburg im Breisgau, Mainz, Cologne and Trier successively acknowledged the legality of interest on commercial loans. The first five of these approvals are deposited in the consulate archives of the city of Lyons, and are printed in the appendix to the *Traité de l'usure et des intérêts* by Bruyset-Ponthus, Lyons' (M. Augier, *Le Crédit public*, etc., Paris, 1842, p. 206).

In all forms where the slave economy (not patriarchal slavery, but rather that of the later phases of the Greco-Roman era) exists as a means of enrichment, and where money is thus a means for appropriating other people's labour by the purchase of slaves, land, etc , money can be valorized as capital and comes to bear interest precisely because it can be invested in this way.

Two of the forms in which usurer's capital exists in phases prior to the capitalist mode of production are particularly characteristic. I deliberately use the word 'characteristic', for the same forms recur on the basis of capitalist production, though here they are merely subordinate forms. In the latter case they are no longer forms that determine the character of interest-bearing capital. These two forms are, *firstly*, usury by lending money to extravagant magnates, essentially to landed proprietors; *secondly*, usury by lending money to small producers who possess their own conditions of labour, including artisans, but particularly and especially peasants, since, wherever pre-capitalist conditions permit small autonomous individual producers, the peasant class must form their great majority.

Both of these things, the ruining of rich landed proprietors by usury and the impoverishment of the small producers, lead to the formation and concentration of large money capitals. But the extent to which this process abolishes the old mode of production, as was the case in modern Europe, and whether it establishes the capitalist mode of production in its place, depends entirely on the historical level of development and the conditions that this provides.

Usurer's capital, as the characteristic form of interest-bearing capital, corresponds to the predominance of petty production, of peasants and small master craftsmen working for themselves. Where, as in the developed capitalist mode of production, the conditions of production and the product of labour confront the worker as capital, he does not have to borrow any money in his capacity as a producer. When he does borrow, this is for personal necessity, as at the pawnshop. When the worker is, on the other hand, the proprietor of his conditions of labour and his product, in reality or in name, then it is as a producer that he relates to the money-lender's capital, which confronts him as usurer's capital. Newman puts the matter rather inanely when he says that the banker is respected, while the usurer is hated and despised, because the former lends to the rich and the latter to the poor (F. W. Newman, *Lectures on Political Economy*, London, 1851,

p. 44). He overlooks the fact that a difference between two social modes of production and the social arrangements corresponding to them is involved here, and the question cannot just be resolved into the contrast between rich and poor. Rather, the usury that impoverishes the poor petty producer goes hand in hand with the usury that ruins the rich landed proprietor. As soon as the usury of the Roman patricians had completely ruined the Roman plebeians, the small farmers, this form of exploitation came to an end, and the petty-bourgeois economy was replaced by a pure slave economy.

In the form of interest, the usurer can in this case swallow up everything in excess of the producers' most essential means of subsistence, the amount that later becomes wages (the usurer's interest being the part that later appears as profit and ground-rent), and it is therefore quite absurd to compare the level of *this* interest, in which *all* surplus-value save that which accrues to the state is appropriated, with the level of the modern interest rate, where interest, at least the normal interest, forms only one part of this surplus-value. This is to forget that the wage-labourer produces and yields to the capitalist who employs him profit, interest and ground-rent, in short the entire surplus-value. Carey makes this absurd comparison in order to show the great advantage for the worker of the development of capital and the accompanying fall in the interest rate. If the usurer, not content with extracting his victim's surplus labour, gradually obtains the ownership title to his conditions of labour themselves – land, house, etc. – and consistently sets out to expropriate him in this way, it should still not be forgotten that this complete expropriation of the worker from his conditions of labour is not a result towards which the capitalist mode of production tends, but rather the given presupposition from which it proceeds. The wage-slave is just as much excluded by his position as the slave proper from being a debt slave, at least in his capacity as producer; if he can become so at all, it is in his capacity as consumer. Usurer's capital, in this form where it actually appropriates all the surplus labour of the direct producer, without altering the mode of production; where the producers' ownership or possession of their conditions of labour (and the isolated petty production corresponding to this) is an essential precondition; where capital therefore does not directly subordinate labour, and thus does not confront it as industrial capital – this usurer's capital impoverishes the mode of production, cripples the productive forces instead of developing them, and simultaneously perpetuates these lamentable conditions in which the social productivity of labour is not developed even at the cost of the worker himself, as it is in capitalist production.

Usury thus works on the one hand to undermine and destroy ancient and feudal wealth, and ancient and feudal property. On the other hand it undermines and ruins small peasant and petty-bourgeois production, in short all forms in which the producer still appears as the owner of his means of production. In the developed capitalist mode of production, the worker is not the owner of his conditions of production, the farm that he cultivates, the raw material he works up, etc. This alienation of the conditions of production from the producer, however, corresponds here to a real revolution in the mode of production itself. The isolated workers are brought together in the large workshop for specialized and interlocking activity; the tool is replaced by the machine. The mode of production itself no longer permits the fragmentation of the instruments of production that is linked with petty property, any more than it permits the isolation of the workers themselves. In capitalist production, usury can no longer divorce the conditions of production from the producer, since they are already divorced.

Where the means of production are fragmented, usury centralizes monetary wealth. It does not change the mode of production, but clings on to it like a parasite and impoverishes it. It sucks it dry, emasculates it and forces reproduction to proceed under ever more pitiable conditions. Hence the popular hatred of usury, at its peak in the ancient world, where the producer's ownership of his conditions of production was at the same time the basis for political relations, for the independence of the citizen.

As long as slavery prevails, or the surplus product is consumed by the feudal lord and his retinue, the mode of production still remains the same even though slaveowner or feudal lord fall prey to usury; it simply becomes harsher for the workers. The indebted slaveowner or feudal lord takes more out of them, since more is taken from him. Ultimately, he may be completely replaced by the usurer, who himself becomes a landowner or slaveowner as the knights did in ancient Rome. In place of the old exploiter, whose exploitation was more or less patriarchal, since it was largely a means of political power, we have a hard, money-grubbing upstart. But the mode of production itself remains unaltered.

Usury has a revolutionary effect on pre-capitalist modes of production only in so far as it destroys and dissolves the forms of ownership which provide a firm basis for the articulation of political life and whose constant reproduction in the same form is a necessity for that life. In Asiatic forms, usury can persist for a long while without leading to anything more than economic decay and political corruption. It is only where and when the other conditions for the capitalist mode of production are present that usury appears as one of the means of formation of this new mode of production, by ruining the feudal lords and petty production on the one hand, and by centralizing the conditions of labour on the other.

In the Middle Ages, there was no generally prevailing interest rate in any country. The Church prohibited all interest dealings from the start. Laws and courts gave little security for loans. All the higher was the interest rate in particular cases. The low monetary circulation and the need to make most payments in cash compelled people to borrow money, and all the more so, the more undeveloped the system of bills of exchange. There was great variation in both the rate of interest and the concept of usury. In Charlemagne's time, it was considered usurious to take 100 per cent interest. At Lindau am Bodensee in 1344, some local burghers took $216\frac{2}{3}$ per cent. In Zurich the town council fixed $43\frac{1}{3}$ per cent as the legal interest. In Italy, 40 per cent had to be paid on occasion, though from the twelfth century to the fourteenth the rate did not usually exceed 20 per cent. Verona settled on $12\frac{1}{2}$ per cent as the legal interest. Emperor Frederick II fixed 10 per cent, but this was only for the Jews. He would not decree for Christians. 10 per cent was already common in the German Rhineland in the thirteenth century. (Hüllmann, *Geschichte des Städtewesens*, II, pp. 55–7.)

Usurer's capital has capital's mode of exploitation without its mode of production. This relationship also recurs within the bourgeois economy in backward branches of industry, or those that are struggling against the transition to the modern mode of production. In comparing the English rate of interest with the Indian, for example, we must not take the Bank of England's interest rate but rather that charged, for instance, by people lending small machines to petty producers in domestic industry.

Usury is historically important, in contrast to wealth devoted entirely to consumption, as being itself a process giving rise to capital. Usurer's capital and mercantile wealth bring about the formation of a monetary wealth independent of landed property. The less developed is the character of the product as a commodity, the less exchange-value has taken command of production in its whole breadth and depth, the more does money appear as wealth as such, wealth proper, wealth in general, as against its restricted form of appearance in use-values. Hoard formation depends on this. Leaving aside money as world money and as hoard, it is particularly in the form of means of payment that it emerges as the absolute form of the commodity. And it is particularly its function as means of payment that develops interest and with it money capital. What wealth for extravagance and corruption wants is money as money, money as a means to buy everything. (Also for paying debts.) What the petty producer needs money for above all is for payment. (The transformation of services in kind and deliveries to landlords and the state into money rents and money taxes plays a major role here.) In both cases money is needed as money. On the other hand, it is only in usury that hoard formation becomes a reality for the first time and fulfils its dreams. What is sought from the hoard owner is not capital but rather money as money; but through interest he transforms this money hoard, as it is in itself, into capital – into a means by which he takes partial or complete command of surplus labour, and in this way of a portion of the conditions of production themselves, even if these nominally still confront him as someone else's property. Usury seems to live in the pores of production, like the gods in Epicurus's *intermundia*.* It is all the more difficult to get money, the less the commodity form has become the general form of the product. The usurer therefore does not come up against any barrier except the incapacity of those in need of money to pay or their capacity to resist. In small peasant and petty-bourgeois production, money is used principally as means of purchase when the worker loses his conditions of production by accident or some extraordinary dislocation (the worker being generally still their owner in these systems of production), or at least when they are not replaced in the ordinary course of reproduction. Means of subsistence and raw materials form an essential part of these conditions of production. A rise in their price can make it impossible to replace them from the proceeds of the product, just as simple harvest failure can prevent the peasant from replacing his seed

* See above, p. 447.

corn in kind. The same wars through which the Roman patricians ruined the plebeians, forcing them into war services which prevented them from reproducing their conditions of labour, and hence pauperized them (and pauperization, curtailment or loss of the conditions of reproduction, is the prevailing form here), filled the stores and vaults of the former with plundered copper, the money of the time. Instead of providing the plebeians directly with the commodities they needed – corn, horses, cattle, etc. – they lent them this copper, which was of no use to themselves, and made use of the situation to extort enormous and usurious levels of interest, thereby making the plebeians into their debt slaves. The French peasants under Charlemagne were similarly ruined by wars, so that nothing remained for them but to exchange the position of debtor for that of serf. In the Roman Empire it frequently happened, as is well known, that famine led free men to sell their children and themselves as slaves to the rich. So much for general turning-points. When considered in detail, the preservation or loss of the petty producers' conditions of production depends on a thousand accidental circumstances, and each such accident or loss means impoverishment and is a point at which the parasite of usury can seize hold. The peasant only needs one of his cows to die and he is immediately unable to repeat his reproduction on the old scale. He falls prey to usury, and once in that position he never recovers his freedom.

Yet the proper, principal and specific terrain of usury is still the function of money as means of payment. Any monetary obligation – rent, interest, tribute, tax, etc. – that falls due at a certain date brings with it the need for a money payment. This is why usury so generally attaches to tax farmers, *fermiers généraux, receveurs généraux*, from ancient Rome through to modern times. With trade and the generalization of commodity production, purchase and payment become separate in time. Money has to be provided at a particular date. The modern money crises show how even today this can lead to circumstances in which money capitalist and usurer merge into one. This very usury, however, becomes a major means of extending the need for money as means of payment, since it drags the producer deeper and deeper into debt and destroys his customary means of payment in that the interest burden itself makes his regular reproduction impossible. Here usury springs from money as means of payment, and broadens this function of money, its most specific terrain.

The credit system develops as a reaction against usury. But this should not be misconstrued, nor by any means taken in the sense of the ancient writers, the Fathers of the Church, Luther or the early socialists. It means neither more nor less than the subordination of interest-bearing capital to the conditions and requirements of the capitalist mode of production.

In the modern credit system, interest-bearing capital becomes adapted on the whole to the conditions of capitalist production. Usury proper not only continues to exist, but in countries of developed capitalist production it is freed from the barriers that former legislation had always placed to it. Interest-bearing capital retains the form of usurer's capital vis-à-vis persons and classes, or in conditions where borrowing in the sense appropriate to the capitalist mode of production does not and cannot occur; where borrowing results from individual need, as at the pawnshop; where borrowing is for extravagant consumption; or where the producer is a non-capitalist producer, a small peasant, artisan, etc., i.e. is still the possessor of his own conditions of production as a direct producer; finally where the capitalist producer himself operates on so small a scale that his situation approaches that of those producers who work for themselves.

What distinguishes interest-bearing capital. in so far as it forms an essential element of the capitalist mode of production, from usurer's capital is in no way the nature or character of this capital itself. It is simply the changed conditions under which it functions, and hence also the totally transformed figure of the borrower who confronts the money-lender. Even where a man without means obtains credit as an industrialist or merchant, it is given in the expectation that he will function as a capitalist, will use the capital borrowed to appropriate unpaid labour. He is given credit as a potential capitalist. And this fact so very much admired by the economic apologists, that a man without wealth but with energy, determination, ability and business acumen can transform himself into a capitalist in this way – just as the commercial value of each person is always assessed more or less correctly in the capitalist mode of production – much as it constantly drives an unwelcome series of new soldiers of fortune onto the field alongside and against the various individual capitalists already present, actually reinforces the rule of capital itself, widens its basis and enables it to recruit ever new forces from the lower strata of society. The way that the Catholic Church of the Middle Ages built its hierarchy out of the best brains in the nation, without regard to status, birth or wealth, was likewise a major means of reinforcing the rule of the priests and suppressing the laity. The more a dominant class is able to absorb the best people from the dominated classes, the more solid and dangerous is its rule.

Instead of anathema against interest-bearing capital in general, the founders of the modern credit system proceed from its express recognition.

We are not referring here to the reaction against usury which sought to protect the poor from it, such as the *Monts-de-piété* (1350 at Sarlins in Franche-Comté; later at Perugia and Savona in Italy – 1400 and 1479). These are noteworthy only because they display the historical irony which turns pious wishes into their very opposite when they are realized. 100 per cent is a conservative estimate for the interest that the English working class pay to the pawnshops, these off-shoots of the *Monts-de-piété*.[21] Just as little do we have in mind the credit fantasies of such men as Dr Hugh Chamberleyne and John Briscoe, who tried to emancipate the English aristocracy from usury in the last decade of the seventeenth century by way of a land bank with paper money based on landed property.[22]

The credit associations set up in the twelfth and fourteenth centuries in Venice and Genoa arose from the need of the sea trade and the wholesale trade based on it to emancipate themselves from the rule of old-fashioned usury and from the monopolizing

21. 'It is by frequent fluctuations within the month, and by pawning one article to relieve another, where a small sum is obtained, that the premium for money becomes so excessive. There are about 240 licensed pawnbrokers in the metropolis, and nearly 1,450 in the country. The capital employed is supposed somewhat to exceed a million pounds sterling; and this capital is turned round thrice in the course of a year, and yields each time about $33\frac{1}{3}$ per cent on an average; according to which calculation, the inferior orders of society in England pay about one million a year for the use of a temporary loan, exclusive of what they lose by goods being forfeited' (J. D. Tuckett, *A History of the Past and Present State of the Labouring Population*, London, 1846, I, p. 114).

22. Even in the very titles of their works, they gave as their main purpose 'the general good of the landed men, the great increase of the value of land', the exemption of 'the nobility, gentry, etc., from taxes, enlarging their yearly estates, etc.'. Only the usurers would lose from this, these worst enemies of the nation, who had caused the nobility and the yeomanry more damage than an invading army from France could have done.

of money-dealing. If the banks proper that were founded in these urban republics were at the same time institutions for public credit, from which the state received advances against taxes anticipated, it should not be forgotten that the merchants who formed these associations were themselves the most prominent people in those states and were equally interested in emancipating both their government and themselves from usury,[23] while at the same time subordinating the state more securely to themselves. When the Bank of England was to be founded, the Tories objected that banks were republican institutions. Flourishing banks existed in Venice, Genoa, Amsterdam and Hamburg. But who ever heard of a Bank of France or Spain?

The Bank of Amsterdam (1609) was not a milestone in the development of the modern credit system, any more than that of Hamburg (1619). It was simply a bank for deposits. The cheques that the bank issued were in actual fact simply receipts for the coined and uncoined precious metal deposited with it and circulated only with the endorsement of their recipients. But in Holland, commercial credit and dealing in money did develop along with trade and manufacture, and by the course of development itself, interest-bearing capital became subordinate to industrial and commercial capital. This was already evident from the low level of its interest rate. In the seventeenth century, however, Holland served as the model country of economic development, just as England does today. The monopoly of old-fashioned usury, based on poverty, was thrown overboard there automatically.

Right through the eighteenth century we hear the cry for a compulsory reduction in the interest rate, with reference being made to Holland, and legislation proceeds in the same direction; the aim being to subordinate interest-bearing capital to com-

23. The rich goldsmiths, for example (the bankers' forerunners), made Charles II pay interest rates of 20 or 30 per cent on loans. 'This profitable business induced the goldsmiths to become increasingly lenders to the King, to anticipate all the revenue, to take every grant of Parliament into pawn as soon as it was given; also to outvie each other in buying and taking to pawn bills, orders, and tallies, so that, in effect, all the revenue passed through their hands' (John Francis, *History of the Bank of England*, London, 1848, I, p. 31). 'The erection of a bank had been suggested several times before that. It was at last a necessity' (ibid., p. 38). 'The bank was a necessity for the government itself, sucked dry by usurers, in order to obtain money at a reasonable rate, on the security of parliamentary grants' (ibid., pp. 59–60).

mercial and industrial capital, instead of vice versa. The leading spokesman is Sir Josiah Child, the father of normal English private banking. He declaims against the monopoly of the usurers in the same way that the off-the-peg tailors Moses and Son attack the monopoly of the bespoke tailors. This Josiah Child is also the father of English stock-jobbing. As autocrat of the East India Company, he defends its monopoly in the name of free trade. Against Thomas Manley (*Interest of Money Mistaken*) he says: 'As the champion of the timid and trembling band of usurers he erects his main batteries at that point which I have declared to be the weakest . . . he denies point-blank that the low rate of interest is the cause of wealth and vows that it is merely its effect' (*Traités sur le commerce, etc.*, 1669, trs. Amsterdam and Berlin, 1754 [p. 120]). 'If it is commerce that enriches a country, and if a lowering of interest increases commerce, then a lowering of interest or a restriction of usury is doubtless a fruitful primary cause of the wealth of a nation. It is not at all absurd to say that the same thing may be simultaneously a cause under certain circumstances, and an effect under others' (ibid., p. 155). 'The egg is the cause of the hen, and the hen is the cause of the egg. The lowering of interest may cause an increase of wealth, and the increase of wealth may cause a still greater reduction of interest' (ibid., p. 156). 'I am the defender of industry and my opponent defends laziness and sloth' (p. 179).

This violent struggle against usury, the demand for the subjection of interest-bearing capital to industrial capital, is simply the prelude to the organic creations that these conditions of capitalist production produce in the form of the modern banking system, which on the one hand robs usurer's capital of its monopoly, since it concentrates all dormant money reserves together and places them on the money market, while on the other hand restricting the monopoly of the precious metals themselves by creating credit money.

Just as in this case with Child, so opposition to usury can be found in all English writings on banking in the last third of the seventeenth century and the beginning of the eighteenth: the demand for the emancipation of trade and industry from usury, as well as the state. Also colossal illusions about the miraculous effect of credit, of the removal of the monopoly held by precious metals and their replacement by paper, etc. The Scot William

Paterson, founder of the Bank of England and the Bank of Scotland, is in every way Law the First.*

Against the Bank of England, 'all goldsmiths and pawnbrokers set up a howl of rage' (Macaulay, *History of England*, IV [London, 1855], p. 499). 'During the first ten years the Bank had to struggle with great difficulties; great foreign feuds; its notes were only accepted far below their nominal value ... the goldsmiths' (in whose hands the trade in precious metals served as the basis of a primitive banking business) 'were jealous of the Bank, because their business was diminished, their discounts were lowered, their transactions with the government had passed to their opponents' (J. Francis, op. cit., p. 73).

Even before the foundation of the Bank of England, a plan for a National Bank of Credit had already been drawn up in 1683, its purpose being, among other things: 'that tradesmen, when they have a considerable quantity of goods, may, by the help of this bank, deposit their goods, by raising a credit on their own dead stock, employ their servants, and increase their trade, till they get a good market instead of selling them at a loss.'†

After much trouble, this Bank of Credit was established in Devonshire House on Bishopsgate Street. It lent to industrialists and merchants, on security of three-quarters of the value of commodities depoⱬited, in the form of bills of exchange. In order to give these bills currency, a number of people in each branch of business combined together to form a company, from which anyone possessing this bank's bills was supposed to receive commodities for them with the same ease as if he offered cash payment. The bank did not do a flourishing business. The machinery was too complicated, and the risk involved in the depreciation of commodities too great.

If we concentrate on the real content of these writings, which were the theoretical accompaniment to the formation of the modern credit system in England and helped to foster it, we find

---

* The English banker and economist John Law ostensibly believed that the state could increase public wealth simply by inconvertible note issue. In 1716 he founded a bank in Paris, which two years later was made into a state bank based on this principle. Law's operations gave rise to a previously unheard-of degree of speculation, ending in 1720 with the inevitable collapse of his bank.

† John Francis, *History of the Bank of England, Its Times and Traditions*, Vol. 1, London [1848], pp. 39–40.

nothing in them but the demand for the subjugation of interest-bearing capital and loanable means of production in general to the capitalist mode of production, as one of its preconditions. If we just look at the phrases used, the way they coincide with the banking and credit illusions of the Saint-Simonians is often astonishing, right down to the very words.

Just as for the Physiocrats the '*cultivateur*' does not mean the actual worker on the land, but rather the big farmer, so Saint-Simon's '*travailleur*' is not the worker but rather the industrial and commercial capitalist, and this usage is still current with his disciples.

'A *travailleur* [worker] needs helpers, supporters, *ouvriers* [labourers – Marx emphasizes the word in the French quotation]; he looks for intelligent, adept and devoted ones; he puts them to work, and their labour is productive' ([Enfantin,] *Religion saint-simonienne. Économie politique et politique*, Paris, 1831, p. 104).

It should in no way be forgotten that it was only in his last work, *Le Nouveau Christianisme*, that Saint-Simon directly emerged as a spokesman for the working class and declared its emancipation to be the final goal of his endeavours. All his earlier writings are in fact simply a glorification of modern bourgeois society against feudal society, or of the industrialists and bankers against the marshals and law-mongers of the Napoleonic era. How different from the contemporary writings of Owen![24] Even for his followers, as the passage quoted shows, the industrial capitalist remains the *travailleur par excellence*. If one reads his writings critically, it is no surprise that the realization of his credit and banking dreams

24. In working over the manuscript again, Marx would undoubtedly have modified this passage substantially. It was inspired by the role of the former Saint-Simonians under the Second Empire in France, where, by historical irony, the world-shattering credit fantasies of this school were precisely realized, as Marx writes, in a swindle of previously unheard-of dimensions. Marx subsequently spoke only with admiration of the genius and encyclopedic mind of Saint-Simon. If in his earlier writings Saint-Simon ignored the opposition between the bourgeoisie and the proletariat, which in France was only just arising, and if he included the section of the bourgeoisie active in production in the *travailleurs*, this was Fourier's conception also, Fourier who sought to reconcile capital and labour, and it is explained by the economic and political conditions of France at that time. If Owen saw further ahead here, this was because he lived in a different environment, in the midst of the industrial revolution and the class antagonism that was already acutely coming to a head. – F. E.

was the Crédit Mobilier* founded by the ex-Saint-Simonian Émile Péreire, a form that incidentally could come to such prominence only in a country like France, where neither the credit system nor large-scale industry was developed to the modern level. In England and America this kind of thing would have been impossible. In the following passages from the *Doctrine de Saint-Simon. Exposition. Première année, 1828/29*, 3rd edn, Paris, 1831, we already have the Crédit Mobilier in a nutshell. It is easy to understand how the banker can make cheaper advances than the capitalist and private usurer. And so it is also possible for this banker 'to provide the industrialist with his tools more cheaply, i.e. at *lower interest*, than the landlords and capitalists could do, as these could more easily be mistaken in their choice of borrower' (p. 202).

But the author himself adds in a footnote:

'The advantage that was supposed to follow from the intervention of the banker between the idle capitalist and the *travailleurs* is often outweighed and even destroyed by the opportunity that our disorganized society offers for egoism to hold sway, in the various forms of fraud and charlatanry; the bankers often intervene between *travailleurs* and idle capitalists simply to exploit both sides to the detriment of society.'

Travailleur here stands for *capitaliste industriel*. It is wrong, incidentally, to view the resources that the modern banking system has at its disposal simply as the resources of idle capitalists. In the first place, these resources include the portion of capital that industrialists and merchants keep temporarily unoccupied in the money form, as a money reserve or as capital still to be invested, i.e. idle capital, but not the capital of the idle; secondly, that portion of everyone's revenues and savings that is permanently or temporarily set aside for accumulation. And both of these are essential to the character of the banking system.

It must never be forgotten, however, firstly that money in the form of precious metal remains the foundation from which the credit system can *never* break free, by the very nature of the case.

* The Crédit Mobilier's operations, ostensibly in support of industrial projects and protected by the Bonapartist government, were based as Marx points out here on unsound principles and provided the framework for a variety of palpably fraudulent speculations. In 1856 and 1857 Marx wrote several articles for the *New York Daily Tribune* exposing the operations of the Crédit Mobilier, which finally went bankrupt in 1867.

Secondly, that the credit system presupposes the monopoly possession of the social means of production (in the form of capital and landed property) on the part of private individuals, that it is itself on the one hand an immanent form of the capitalist mode of production and on the other hand a driving force of its development into its highest and last possible form.

As was already asserted in 1697, in *Some Thoughts of the Interests of England*, the banking system, by its organization and centralization, is the most artificial and elaborate product brought into existence by the capitalist mode of production. Hence the tremendous power an institution such as the Bank of England has over trade and industry, even though their actual movement remains completely outside its orbit and it behaves quite passively towards them. Such a bank, however, supplies the form of a general book-keeping and distribution of the means of production on a social scale, even if only the form. We have seen that the average profit of the individual capitalist, or of any particular capital, is determined not by the surplus labour that this capital appropriates first-hand, but rather by the total surplus labour that the total capital appropriates, from which each particular capital simply draws its dividends as a proportional part of the total capital. This social character of capital is mediated and completely realized only by the full development of the credit and banking system. On the other hand this also goes further. It places all available and even potential capital that is not already actively committed at the disposal of the industrial and commercial capitalists, so that neither the lender nor the user of this capital are its owners or producers. It thereby abolishes the private character of capital and thus inherently bears within it, though only inherently, the abolition of capital itself. Through the banking system, the distribution of capital is removed from the hands of the private capitalists and usurers and becomes a special business, a social function. Banking and credit, however, thereby also become the most powerful means for driving capitalist production beyond its own barriers and one of the most effective vehicles for crises and swindling.

The banking system further shows, by substituting various forms of circulating credit for money, that the latter is in actual fact nothing but a special expression of the social character of labour and its products, which however, as antithetical to the basis of private production, must always present itself in the last instance as a thing, as a particular commodity alongside other commodities.

Finally, there can be no doubt that the credit system will serve as a powerful lever in the course of transition from the capitalist mode of production to the mode of production of associated labour; however, only as one element in connection with other large-scale organic revolutions in the mode of production itself. On the other hand, illusions about the miraculous power of the credit and banking system, in the socialist sense, arise from complete ignorance about the capitalist mode of production and about the credit system as one of its forms. As soon as the means of production cease to be transformed into capital (which also means the abolition of private property in land), credit as such no longer has any meaning, something incidentally that even the Saint-Simonians have realized. As long as the capitalist mode of production persists, however, interest-bearing capital persists as one of its forms, and in fact forms the basis of its credit system. Only that same sensationalist writer who wanted commodity production to continue while money was abolished (Proudhon) could dream up the enormity of a *crédit gratuit* [interest-free credit], the ostensible realization of the pious wish arising from the petty-bourgeois standpoint.[25]

In the *Religion saint-simonienne. Économie politique et politique*, we may read on p. 45: 'The purpose of credit is that in a society where some people possess tools for industry without the ability or the will to use them, while other industrious people possess no instruments of labour, these instruments can be transferred in the easiest possible manner from the hands of the former, their owners, to others who know how to use them. Let us note that according to this definition credit is a result of the manner and form in which *property* is constituted.'

Thus credit disappears together with this constitution of property. It is further said, on p. 98, that the banks of today 'consider themselves destined to follow the movement initiated by transactions outside their own domain, but not to provide the impulse for these themselves; in other words, the banks play the role of capitalists for the *travailleurs* to whom they advance capital'.

The Crédit Mobilier is latent already in the idea that the banks

25. Karl Marx, *The Poverty of Philosophy*; and *A Contribution to the Critique of Political Economy* [op. cit., p. 86]. [See also above, pp. 446–8.]

should take over this leadership themselves, and should excel 'by the number and usefulness of the firms they control and the works they have promoted' (p. 101).

In the same way, Constantin Pecqueur demands that the banks (called by the Saint-Simonians '*système général des banques*') should 'govern production'. Pecqueur is essentially always a Saint-Simonian, even if far more radical. He wants 'the credit institution ... [to] govern the entire movement of national production'. – 'Just try to create a national credit institution which will advance resources to people of talent and merit, but no property, without binding these borrowers together compulsorily in a close solidarity in production and consumption, but rather, on the contrary, in such a way that they themselves determine what they exchange and produce. In this way you will only achieve what the private banks already do achieve, anarchy, a disproportion between production and consumption, the sudden ruin of some and the sudden enrichment of others; so that your institution will never do more than produce a sum of benefit equally balanced by a sum of misfortune borne by others ... you will simply have provided the wage-labourers whom you assist with the means to compete with one another, just like their capitalist masters do now' (C. Pecqueur, *Théorie nouvelle d'économie social et politique*, Paris, 1842, pp. 433, 434).

We have seen how merchant's capital and interest-bearing capital are the oldest forms of capital. But it lies in the very nature of the matter that interest-bearing capital should appear to the popular mind as the form of capital *par excellence*. In merchant's capital we have a mediating activity, whether this is considered as fraud, labour or whatever. In interest-bearing capital, on the other hand, the self-reproducing character of capital, self-valorizing value, the production of surplus-value, appears as a purely occult quality. Hence it also happens that even a section of political economists, particularly in countries where industrial capital is not yet fully developed, as in France, cling to interest-bearing capital as the basic form and see ground-rent, for example, simply as another form of this, in so far as here too it is the form of a loan that prevails. In this way the internal articulation of the capitalist mode of production is completely misconstrued, and it is quite overlooked that both land and capital are only hired out to capitalists. Instead of money, means of production can of course be loaned in kind, in the shape of machines, business premises, etc. But in this case these represent a certain sum of money, and if, apart from the interest, a portion is paid for wear and tear, this arises from the use-value, the specific natural form, of these capital elements. The distinguishing thing here again is whether they are loaned to the immediate producers, which presupposes the non-existence of the capitalist mode of production, at least in the sphere in which this kind of thing takes place, or whether they are loaned to industrial capitalists, which presupposes precisely that the basis is the capitalist mode of production. It is still more irrelevant and senseless to drag in the renting of houses, etc. for individual consumption. It is plain enough that the working class is swindled in this form too, and to an enormous extent; but it is equally exploited by the petty trader who supplies the workers with means of subsistence. This is a secondary exploitation, which proceeds alongside the original exploitation that takes place directly within the production process itself. The distinction between selling and lending here is completely immaterial and formal, and, as already shown, appears fundamental only for those who are in complete ignorance of the real context.

*

Usury, just like trade, exploits a given mode of production but does not create it; both relate to the mode of production from outside. Usury seeks directly to maintain this mode of production, so as constantly to exploit it anew; it is conservative, and simply makes the mode of production more wretched. The less the elements of production enter as commodities into the production process and emerge from it as commodities, the more does their establishment at a given place by means of money appear as a special act. The less important the role circulation plays in social reproduction, the more usury flourishes.

To say that monetary wealth develops as a special kind of wealth means, as far as usurer's capital is concerned, that this possesses all its claims in the form of monetary claims. It develops in a country all the more, the more the bulk of production is confined to services in kind, etc., i.e. to use-values.

Usury, by its double effect, is a powerful lever in forming the preconditions for industrial capital. Firstly, it always forms an autonomous monetary wealth alongside the class of merchants, while secondly it appropriates the conditions of labour, by ruining the owners of the old conditions of labour.

Interest in the Middle Ages

'In the Middle Ages the population was purely agricultural. Under such a government as was the feudal system there can be but little traffic, and hence but little profit. Hence the laws against usury were justified in the Middle Ages. Besides, in an agricultural country a person seldom wants to borrow money except he be reduced to poverty or distress ... In the reign of Henry VIII, interest was limited to 10 per cent. James I reduced it to 8 per cent ... Charles II reduced it to 6 per cent; in the reign of Queen Anne, it was reduced to 5 per cent ... In those times, the lenders ... had, in fact, though not a legal, yet an actual monopoly, and hence it was necessary that they, like other monopolists, should be placed under restraint. In our times, it is the rate of profit which regulates the rate of interest. In those times, it was the rate of interest which regulated the rate of profit. If the money-lender charged a high rate of interest to the merchant, the merchant must have charged a higher rate of profit on his goods. Hence, a large sum of money would be taken from the pockets of the purchasers to be put into the pockets of the money-lenders' (Gilbart, *History and Principles of Banking*, pp. 163, 164, 165).

'I have heard it said that 10 gulden are now taken at each Leipzig fair in the year, that is 30 gulden on every 100; some add the Neuenburg fair, thus making 40 gulden on every 100. Whether this is true, I do not know. For shame, what the deuce will the end of this be? ... If someone who has 100 florins at Leipzig takes 40 per year, this means he gobbles up a peasant or a burgher. If he has 1,000 florins, he takes 400 each year and gobbles up a knight or a rich nobleman. If he has 10,000 florins, he takes 4,000 per year and gobbles up a rich count. If he has 100,000, as must be the case with the large dealers, he takes 40,000 per year and has gobbled up a great rich prince. If he has 1,000,000, he takes 400,000 and gobbles up a great king. And to do this he does not suffer any danger, either to his body or to his goods, does not work, but sits by his stove and bakes apples; in this way a mean robber could sit at home and gobble up the whole world in ten years.' (This is from *An die Pfarrherrn wider den Wucher zu predigen* of 1540, *Luthers Werke*, Wittenberg, 1589, part 6 [p. 312].)

'Fifteen years ago I wrote against usury, when it had already spread so widely that I could not hope for any improvement. Since that time it has become so arrogant that it is no longer content to be classed as vice, sin, or shame, but has itself praised as a pure virtue and honour. What will deliver us now that shame has become honour, and vice virtue?' (*An die Pfarrherrn wider den Wucher zu predigen*, Wittenberg, 1540).

'Jews, Lombards, usurers and extortioners were our first bankers, our primitive traffickers in money, their character little short of infamous . . . They were joined by London goldsmiths. As a body . . . our primitive bankers . . . were a very bad set, they were gripping usurers, iron-hearted extortioners' (D. Hardcastle, *Banks and Bankers*, 2nd edn, London, 1843, pp. 19, 20).

'The example provided by Venice' (the formation of a bank) 'was thus quickly imitated; all coastal cities, and all cities everywhere which had made a name for themselves by their independence and their trade, founded their first banks. The return of their ships, which was often long delayed, led unavoidably to the custom of giving credit, which was strengthened still further in the wake of the discovery of America and the trade there.' (This is an important point.) 'The chartering of ships made large advances necessary, as was already true in antiquity in the case of Athens and Greece. In 1308 the Hansa city of Bruges possessed an insurance company' (M. Augier, op. cit., pp. 202, 203).

The extent to which lending to landed proprietors, and thus to the wealthy in general for consumption, was still the prevalent form even in England in the final third of the seventeenth century, before the development of the modern credit system, can be seen from the writings of Sir Dudley North, among others. North was not only a leading English merchant, but also one of the most important theoretical economists of his time. 'The moneys employed at interest in this nation, are not near the tenth part, disposed to trading people, wherewith to manage their trades; but are for the most part lent for the supplying of luxury, and to support the expense of persons, who though great owners of lands, yet spend faster than their lands bring in; and being loath to sell, choose rather to mortgage their estates' (*Discourses upon Trade*, London, 1691, pp. 6–7).

In Poland in the eighteenth century: 'Warsaw had a large business in bills of exchange, but one that was principally based on and oriented towards the lending of its bankers. In order to obtain money, which they could lend to the extravagant magnates at 8 per cent and more, these sought and obtained open exchange credit abroad, i.e. a credit that did not have any commodity trade as its basis, but which the foreign drawee would continue to accept as long as the remittances from these exchange dealings continued to return. They paid heavily for this with the bankruptcy of men like Tepper and other respected Warsaw bankers' (J. G. Büsch, *Theoretisch-praktische Darstellung der Handlung, etc.*, 3rd edn, Hamburg, 1808, vol. ii, pp. 232, 233).

The Advantages for the Church in Prohibiting Interest

'Taking interest had been banned by the Church, but not selling property to extricate oneself from need. It was not even forbidden to transfer property to the money-lender for a definite period, until repayment, so that the money-lender not only found his security in this, but could also enjoy compensation for the money he had lent in having the use of this property . . . The Church itself, or the communities and *pia corpora* associated with it, drew great advantage from this, especially in the time of the crusades. This brought a very great part of the national wealth into mortmain, especially since the Jews were barred from practising usury in this way, it being impossible to conceal the possession of such fixed liens . . . Without the ban on interest, the Churches and monasteries could never have got so rich' (ibid., p. 55).

Part Six

The Transformation
of Surplus Profit
into Ground-Rent

Chapter 37: Introduction

The analysis of landed property in its various historical forms lies outside the scope of the present work. We are concerned with it only in so far as a portion of the surplus-value that capital produces falls to the share of the landowner. We assume therefore that agriculture, just like manufacturing, is dominated by the capitalist mode of production, i.e. that rural production is pursued by capitalists, who are distinguished from other capitalists, first of all, simply by the element in which their capital and the wage-labour that it sets in motion are invested. As far as we are concerned, the farmer produces wheat, etc. just as the manufacturer produces yarn or machines. The assumption that the capitalist mode of production has taken control of agriculture implies also that it dominates all spheres of production and bourgeois society, so that its preconditions, such as the free competition of capitals, their transferability from one sphere of production to another, an equal level of average profit, etc. are also present in their full development. The form of landed property with which we are dealing is a specific historical form, a form *transformed* by the intervention of capital and the capitalist mode of production, whether the original form was that of feudal landed property or of small peasant agriculture pursued as a livelihood; in this latter case *possession* of the land and soil appeared as a condition of production for the immediate producer, with his *ownership* of the land being the most advantageous condition, the condition for *his* mode of production to flourish. If the capitalist mode of production always presupposes the expropriation of the workers from the conditions of labour, in agriculture it presupposes the expropriation of the rural workers from the soil and their subjection to a capitalist who pursues agriculture for the sake of profit. It is thus completely immaterial for our presentation if we are reminded that other forms of landed property and agriculture have existed or still exist besides this. This reproach can affect only those economists who treat the capitalist mode of production on the land and the form of landed property corresponding to it not as historical categories but as eternal ones.

Our own reason for considering the modern form of landed property is simply that we need to consider all the specific relationships of production and exchange that arise from the investment of capital on the land. Without this, our analysis of capital would not be complete. We therefore confine ourselves exclusively to the investment of capital in agriculture proper, i.e. in the production of the main plant crops on which a population lives. We can take wheat, since this is the major means of sustenance for modern, capitalistically developed nations. (Instead of agriculture, we might equally well have taken mining, since the laws are the same.)

It is one of Adam Smith's great services that he showed how the ground-rent for capital applied to the production of other agricultural products, e.g. of flax, of dye-stuffs, in independent stock-raising, etc., is determined by the ground-rent yielded by capital invested in the production of the staple crop.* In fact, no further progress has been made in this connection since his time. What we should have to keep in mind as a restriction or addition belongs to the independent treatment of landed property, and not here. We shall therefore deliberately not deal with landed property in so far as this is not related to land set aside for wheat production, but simply refer to this here and there for the purpose of illustration.

For the sake of completeness, it should be noted that what we understand here by land also includes water, etc. in so far as this has an owner and appears as an accessory to the land.

Landed property presupposes that certain persons enjoy the monopoly of disposing of particular portions of the globe as exclusive spheres of their private will to the exclusion of all others.[26] Once this is given, it is a question of developing the

* *The Wealth of Nations*, Book One, Chapter XI, I, Pelican edition, pp. 250–65. See also *Theories of Surplus-Value*, Part II, Chapter XIV, 2, pp. 354–8.

26. Nothing could be more curious than Hegel's development of private property in land. Man as a person must give his will actuality as the soul of external nature, and hence take possession of this nature as his private property. If this is the distinguishing mark of '*the* person', of man as person, it would follow that a man must be a landowner if he is to realize himself as a person. Free private property in land – a very recent product – is for Hegel not a particular social relationship, but rather a relationship of man as a person to 'nature',' the absolute right of appropriation which man has over all "things"'

economic value of this monopoly, i.e. valorizing it, on the basis of capitalist production. Nothing is settled with the legal power of these persons to use and misuse certain portions of the globe. The use of this power depends entirely on economic conditions, which are independent of their wills. The legal conception itself means nothing more than that the landowner can behave in relation to the land just as any commodity owner can with his commodities; and this idea – the legal notion of free private landed property – arises in the ancient world only at the time of the dissolution of the organic social order, and arises in the modern world only with the development of capitalist production. In Asia, it has simply been imported here and there by the Europeans. In the section on 'Primitive Accumulation' (Volume 1, Part 8) we saw how this mode of production presupposes on the one hand that the direct producers are freed from the position of a mere appendage of the soil (in the form of bondsmen, serfs, slaves, etc.) and on the other

---

(*Hegel's Philosophy of Right*, trs. Knox, Oxford, 1967, p. 41; para. 44). The first thing that is clear is that the individual person cannot maintain himself as a proprietor by his 'will' alone, vis-à-vis the will of someone else who similarly wants to give himself corporeal actuality in the same fragment of the globe. Quite other things than a good will are needed for this. Moreover, there is absolutely no way of seeing where 'the person' sets a limit to the realization of his will, whether the existence of his will is realized in an entire country or whether it needs a whole pile of countries in order 'to manifest the pre-eminence of my will over the thing by appropriating it' [p. 236; para. 44, Addition]. Here Hegel comes completely unstuck. 'Taking possession is always piece-meal in type; I take into possession no more than what I touch with my body. But here comes the second point: external objects extend further than I can grasp. Therefore, whatever I have in my grasp is linked with something else. It is with my hand that I manage to take possession of a thing, but its reach can be extended' [p. 238; para. 55, Addition]. But this something else is connected in turn with something else again, so that the limit as to how far my will has to pour out into the soil as soul completely vanishes. 'If I am in possession of something, the intellect immediately draws the inference that it is not only the immediate object in my grasp which is mine but also what is connected with it. At this point positive law must enact its statutes since nothing further on this topic can be deduced from the concept' [p. 238; para. 55, Addition]. This is an extraordinarily naïve confession for 'the concept' to make, and proves that the concept, which makes the great blunder right from the start of taking a quite particular legal notion of landed property which belongs to bourgeois society as absolute, understands 'nothing' of the actual configuration of this landed property. At the same time this involves the admission by Hegel that with the changing needs of social, i.e. economic development, 'positive law' can and must change its provisions.

hand the expropriation of the mass of the people from the land. To that extent, the monopoly of landed property is a historical precondition for the capitalist mode of production and remains its permanent foundation, as with all previous modes of production based on the exploitation of the masses in one form or the other. But the form in which the capitalist mode of production finds landed property at its beginnings does not correspond to this mode. The form that does correspond to it is only created by it itself, with the subjection of agriculture to capital; and in this way feudal landed property, clan property or small peasant property with the mark* community is transformed into the economic form corresponding to this mode of production, however diverse the legal forms of this may be. It is one of the great results of the capitalist mode of production that on the one hand it transforms agriculture from a merely empirical set of procedures, mechanically handed down and practised by the most undeveloped portion of society, into a conscious scientific application of agronomy, in so far as this is at all possible within the conditions of private property;[27] that on the one hand it detaches landed property

---

* See Engels's Addendum to this volume, p. 1038 below; also p. 278, note 27.

27. Quite conservative agricultural chemists, such as Johnston, for example, admit that private property places insuperable barriers on all sides to a genuinely rational agriculture. So too do writers who are professed defenders of the monopoly of private property in the earth, such as M. Charles Comte,* for instance, in a two-volume work which has the defence of private ownership as its special purpose. 'A people,' he says, 'cannot attain the degree of well-being and power that their nature grants them unless each part of the land that sustains them receives the destiny that stands most in harmony with the general interest. In order to give their riches a substantial development, a single will, and above all an enlightened one, if possible, must take in hand the disposal of each individual piece of their territory, and make each portion contribute towards the prosperity of all others. But the existence of such a will . . . would be incompatible with the division of the land into private holdings . . . and with guaranteeing the ability of each proprietor to dispose of his wealth in an almost absolute manner' [*Traité de la propriété*, Vol. I, Paris, 1834, p. 228]. Johnston, Comte, etc., in considering the contradiction between property and a rational agronomy, are simply thinking of the cultivation of the land of a single country as a whole. But the way that the cultivation of particular crops depends on fluctuations in market prices and the constant changes in cultivation with these price fluctuations – the entire spirit of capitalist production, which is oriented towards the most immediate monetary profit – stands in contradiction to agriculture, which has to concern itself with the whole gamut of permanent conditions of life required by the chain of human generations. A striking example of this is provided by forests, which are managed in the

completely from relations of lordship and servitude, while on the other hand it completely separates the land as a condition of labour from landed property and the landlord, for whom more-over this land represents nothing but a certain monetary tax that his monopoly permits him to extract from the industrial capitalist, the farmer. It undoes the connection to such an extent that the landed proprietor can spend his entire life in Constantinople, while his landed property remains in Scotland. Landed property thus receives its purely economic form by the stripping away of all its former political and social embellishments and admixtures, in short all those traditional accoutrements that are denounced as uselessly and absurdly superfluous by the industrial capitalists themselves, and by their theoretical spokesmen, in their passionate struggle with landed property, as we shall see later. The rationaliza-tion of agriculture, which enables this to be pursued for the first time on a social scale, and the reduction of landed property to an absurdity – these are the great services of the capitalist mode of production. Just like its other historical advances, it purchased these too, first of all, by the complete impoverishment of the immediate producers.

Before we come on to our subject itself, a few preliminary observations are still needed, to guard against any misunder-standings.

The presuppositions for the capitalist mode of production are thus as follows: the actual cultivators are wage-labourers, employed by a capitalist, the farmer, who pursues agriculture simply as a particular field of exploitation of capital, as an investment of his capital in a particular sphere of production. At certain specified dates, e.g. annually, this farmer-capitalist pays the landowner, the proprietor of the land he exploits, a contractually fixed sum of money (just like the interest fixed for the borrower of money capital), for the permission to employ his capital in this particular field of production. This sum of money is known as ground-rent, irrespective of whether it is paid for agricultural land, building

---

common interest – and even then only to a limited extent – solely in those rare cases when they are not private property but are subject to state administra-tion.

* This is François-Charles-Louis Comte (1782–1837), a French liberal economist; not to be confused with Isidore-Auguste-François-Marie Comte (1798–1857), the founder of Positivism, whose own defence of private property was altogether more grandiose.

land, mines, fisheries, forests, etc. It is paid for the entire period for which the landowner has contractually rented the land to the farmer. Ground-rent is thus the form in which landed property is economically realized, valorized. We have together here, moreover, and confronting one another, all three classes that make up the framework of modern society – wage-labourer, industrial capitalist, landowner.

Capital may be fixed in the earth, incorporated into it, both in a more transient way, as is the case with improvements of a chemical kind, application of fertilizer, etc., and more permanently, as with drainage ditches, the provision of irrigation, levelling of land, farm buildings, etc. I have elsewhere used the expression '*la terre-capital*' to denote capital incorporated into the earth in this way.[28] This is one of the categories of fixed capital. Interest on the capital incorporated into the earth and the improvements that are thereby made to the soil as an instrument of production may form a portion of the rent that is paid by the farmer to the landowner,[29] but it does not constitute ground-rent proper, which is paid for the use of the soil as such, whether this is in a state of nature or is cultivated. In a systematic treatment of landed property, which lies beyond our present scope, this portion of the landowner's income would be presented in detail. Here a few words on the subject must be sufficient. The more temporary capital investments that are involved in the ordinary production process in agriculture are all made without exception by the farmer himself. These investments, and even simple cultivation if it is conducted in any kind of rational way – i.e. if it cannot just be reduced to brutal exhaustion of the soil, as is the case for instance in the former slave states of North America, against which however the landowning gentlemen insure themselves in the contract – improve the soil,[30] increase its

28. *The Poverty of Philosophy*, London, 1966, p. 143. There I make the distinction between *terre-matière* and *terre-capital*. 'The very fact of applying further outlays of capital to land already transformed into means of production increases land as capital without adding anything to land as matter, that is, to the extent of the land . . . Land as capital is no more eternal than any other capital . . . Land as capital is fixed capital; but fixed capital gets used up just as much as circulating capital.'

29. I say 'may form', because in certain circumstances this interest is governed by the law of ground-rent and may therefore disappear, for instance where there is competition from new lands of great natural fertility.

30. See James Anderson and Carey.*

* James Anderson, *A Calm Investigation of the Circumstances that have Led*

product and transform the earth from a mere raw material into earth-capital. A cultivated field is worth more than an uncultivated one of the same natural quality. Even the more permanent fixed capital incorporated into the earth, which is used up over a longer time, is in large measure the work of the farmer and in certain spheres often exclusively so. But as soon as the lease stipulated in the contract has expired – and this is one of the reasons why the landowner seeks to shorten the term of the lease to a minimum, as capitalist production develops – the improvements made to the land fall to the landowner as his property, as an inseparable accident of the substance, the land. When the new lease contract is concluded, the landowner adds interest on the capital incorporated into the earth to the ground-rent proper, whether he leases the land again to the farmer who made the improvements or to another farmer. His rent thus swells; or, if he plans to sell the land – and we shall go on to see how its price is determined – its value has now risen. He does not sell just the land, but rather the improved land, the capital incorporated into the earth, which has cost him nothing. This is one of the secrets – quite apart from the movement of ground-rent as such – of the increasing enrichment of the land-owners, the constant inflation of their rents and the growing money value of their estates as economic development progresses. Thus they put away in their own private purses the result of a social development achieved without their participation – they are *fruges consumere nati.* * But this is equally one of the greatest obstacles to a rational agriculture, since the farmer avoids all improvements and outlays which are not expected to give their full return during the duration of his lease; and we find this denounced as such an obstacle time and again, both in the last century by James Anderson, the true discoverer of the modern theory of rent,† who was also a practising farmer and for his time a significant agrono-mist, and in our own day by the opponents of the present arrange-ment of landed property in England.

---

to the Present Scarcity of Grain in Britain, London, 1801, pp. 35, 36, 38. (See also *Theories of Surplus-Value*, Part II, Chapter IX, 9, pp. 144–8.)

H. C. Carey, *The Past, the Present, and the Future*, Philadelphia, 1848, pp. 129–31. (See also *Theories of Surplus-Value*, Part II, Addenda, 4, p. 593.)

* 'Those born to consume the fruits'; Horace, *Epistles*, Book I, Epistle 2, l. 27.

† On Anderson's theory of rent, see *Theories of Surplus-Value*, Part II, pp. 114–17, 121–5 and 144–9.

A. A. Walton,* *History of the Landed Tenures of Great Britain and Ireland*, London, 1865, says on this subject (pp. 96–7): 'All the efforts of the numerous agricultural associations throughout the country must fail to produce any very extensive or really appreciable results in the real advancement of agricultural improvement, so long as such improvements mean in a far higher degree increased value to the estate and rent-roll of the landlord, than bettering the condition of the tenant farmer or the labourer. The farmers, generally, are as well aware as either the landlord or his agent, or even the president of the Agricultural Association, that good drainage, plenty of manure, and good management, combined with the increased employment of labour, to thoroughly cleanse and work the land, will produce wonderful results both in improvement and production. To do all this, however, considerable outlay is required, and the farmers are also aware, that however much they may improve the land or enhance its value, the landlords will, in the long run, reap the principal benefit, in higher rents and the increased value of their estates ... They are shrewd enough to observe what those orators' (landowners and their agents speaking at agricultural festivities), 'by some singular inadvertence, omit to tell them – namely, that the lion's share of any improvements they may make is sure to go into the pockets of the landlords in the long run ... However much the former tenant may have improved the farm, his successor will find that the landlord will always increase the rent in proportion to the increased value of the land from former improvements.'

This process still does not appear so clearly in agriculture proper as in the use of land for building. The overwhelming portion of the land used for building in England that is not sold as freehold is leased by the landlords for ninety-nine years, or for a shorter time if possible. When this period has expired, the buildings fall to the landlord, together with the land itself. 'They' (the tenants) 'are bound to deliver up the house at the expiration of the lease, in good tenantable condition, to the great landlord, after having paid an exorbitant ground-rent up to the expiration of the lease. No sooner is the lease expired, than the agent or surveyor will come and examine your house, and see that you put it into good repair, and then take possession of it, and annex it to his lord's domains

* Alfred A. Walton, an architect by profession, was active in support of democratic causes, and a member of the General Council of the First International from 1867 to 1870.

... The fact is, if this system is permitted to be in full operation for any considerable period longer, the whole of the house property in the kingdom will be in the hands of the great landlords, as well as the land. The whole of the West End of London, north and south from Temple Bar, may be said to belong to about half a dozen great landlords, all let at enormous rents, and where the leases have not quite expired they are fast falling due. The same may be said either more or less of every town in the kingdom. Nor does this grasping system of exclusion and monopoly stop even here. Nearly the whole of the dock accommodation in our seaport towns is by the same process of usurpation in the hands of the great leviathans of the land' (ibid., p. 93).

Under these conditions it is clear that, when the 1861 Census for England and Wales gave the number of house-owners as 36,032, out of a population of 20,066,224, the ratio of owners to the number of houses and the population would look quite different if the big proprietors were separated off from the small ones.

The example of property in buildings is important: (1) because it shows clearly the distinction between the ground-rent proper and the interest on the fixed capital incorporated into the land, which can form an addition to ground-rent. The interest on the buildings, as on the capital that the farmer incorporates into the soil in the case of agriculture, accrues to the industrial capitalist, the building speculator or farmer, for the duration of the lease, and has in and of itself nothing to do with the ground-rent that has to be paid each year on specified dates for the use of the land; (2) because it shows how, in the case of land, the capital of others incorporated into it ultimately falls to the share of the landlord, and the interest on this swells his rent.

Some writers, partly as spokesmen for landed property against the attacks of the bourgeois economists and partly in an effort to transform the capitalist system of production into a system of 'harmonies' instead of antitheses, as for example Carey, have sought to present ground-rent, the specific economic expression of landed property, as identical with interest. In this way, the opposition between landowners and capitalists would be abolished. The converse method was applied at the inception of capitalist production. At that time, landed property still passed in the popular mind as the original and respectable form of private property, whereas interest on capital was denounced as usury. Dudley North, Locke, etc. therefore presented interest on capital as a form analogous to ground-rent, just as Turgot* derived a justification of interest from the existence of ground-rent. The more recent writers forget – quite apart from the fact that ground-rent can and does exist without the addition of any interest on the capital incorporated into the soil – that the landowner not only receives interest on other people's capital in this way, without it costing him anything, but gets the capital itself for nothing into the bargain. The justification for landed property, as that for all other forms of property of a particular mode of production, is that the mode of production itself possesses a transitory historical necessity, and so too therefore do the relations of production and exchange that arise from it. As we shall see later on, however, landed property is distinguished from the other forms of property by the fact that at a certain level of development it appears superfluous and harmful even from the standpoint of the capitalist mode of production.

Ground-rent may also be confused with interest in another form, and its specific character thus misconstrued. Ground-rent presents the appearance of a certain sum of money that the landowner draws each year from leasing out a piece of the earth. We have already seen how any particular money income can be capitalized, i.e. can be considered as the interest on an imaginary capital. If the average interest is 5 per cent, for example, an annual ground-rent of £200 may be viewed as the interest on a capital of £4,000. It is the ground-rent as capitalized in this way that forms the purchase price or value of the land, a category that is *prima facie* irrational, in the same way that the price of labour is irrational, since the earth is not the product of labour, and thus does not have a value. On the other hand, however, this irrational form conceals a genuine relation of production. If a capitalist pays £4,000 for land that yields an annual rent of £200, he draws the average annual interest of 5 per cent on the £4,000 in just the same way as if he had invested this capital in interest-bearing securities or had lent it out directly at 5 per cent interest. There is a valorization of a capital of £4,000 at 5 per cent. On this

* Anne-Robert Jacques Turgot, baron de l'Aulne (1727–81), was a pupil of Quesnay and himself a Physiocratic writer, publishing his *Réflexions sur la formation et la distribution des richesses* in 1766. After Quesnay died in 1774, Turgot, as Louis XVI's Controller-General of Finances, sought unsuccessfully to put Physiocratic ideas into practice. See *Theories of Surplus-Value*, Part I, Chapter II, 'The Physiocrats'.

assumption, in twenty years he would have replaced the purchase price of his property by the receipts from it. In England, therefore, the purchase price of landed estates is reckoned at so and so many 'years' purchase', which is simply another expression for the capitalization of the ground-rent. It is in actual fact not the purchase price of the land, but rather of the ground-rent that it yields, reckoned according to the prevailing rate of interest. This capitalization of the rent, however, presupposes the rent itself, whereas the rent cannot be conversely derived and explained from its own capitalization. Its existence, independent of the sale, is rather the presupposition proceeded from.

It follows from this that, taking the ground-rent as a constant magnitude, the price of land will rise or fall in inverse ratio to the rate of interest. If the standard rate of interest should fall from 5 per cent to 4, an annual ground-rent of £200 would represent the annual valorization of a capital of £5,000 instead of one of £4,000 and so the price of the same piece of land would rise from £4,000 to £5,000, or from twenty years' purchase to twenty-five. In the opposite case, vice versa. This movement in the price of land is governed simply by the rate of interest and is independent of the movement of ground-rent itself. But since we have seen that the rate of profit has a tendency to fall as social development proceeds, and so too therefore does the rate of interest, in as much as this is governed by the profit rate; since we have also seen that even leaving aside the rate of profit, the interest rate has a tendency to fall as a result of the growth of money capital for loan, it follows therefore that the price of land has a tendency to rise, even independently of the movement of ground-rent and the price of the products of the soil, of which rent is one part.

The confusion between ground-rent itself and the form of interest that it assumes for the purchaser of the land – a confusion that is based on complete ignorance as to the nature of ground-rent – cannot but lead to the most peculiar and incorrect conclusions. Since landed property is seen in all older countries as a particularly superior form of property, and the purchase of land moreover as a particularly secure capital investment, so the rate of interest at which ground-rent is bought generally stands somewhat lower than is the case with other long-term capital investments, so that the buyer of land may receive, say, only 4 per cent of his purchase price, while he would otherwise receive 5 per cent for the same capital; or, what comes to the same thing, he pays more capital for the ground-rent than he would for the same annual money income in other investments. M. Thiers,* in his generally abysmal book *La Propriété* (it is the printed text of the speech he delivered against Proudhon in the French National Assembly of 1848), concludes from this that ground-rent is low, whereas all that this shows is the high level of its purchase price.

The fact that the capitalized ground-rent presents the appearance of the price or value of land, so that the earth is bought or sold just like any other commodity, provides some apologists with a justification for landed property; the buyer has paid an equivalent for it, as with any other commodity, and the greater part of landed property has changed hands in this way. The same justification would then apply also to slavery, since for the slaveowner who has paid cash for his slaves, the product of their labour simply represents the interest on the capital invested in their purchase. To derive a justification for the existence of ground-rent from its purchase and sale is nothing more than justifying its existence in terms of its existence.

Important as it is for the scientific analysis of ground-rent – i.e. the autonomous, specific economic form of landed property on the basis of the capitalist mode of production – to consider it in pure form and free from all adulterations and blurring admixtures, it is just as important for understanding the practical effects of landed property, and even for theoretical insight into a mass of facts that contradict the concept and nature of ground-rent and yet appear as its modes of existence, to know the elements from which these obscurities in the theory arise.

In practice, everything that the farmer pays the landowner in the form of the lease-price for permission to cultivate the soil appears as ground-rent. Whatever the components out of which this tribute has been put together, and whatever the sources from which it might derive, it has in common with ground-rent proper that the monopoly to a piece of the earth enables the so-called landowner to exact a tribute, to put a price on it. What this has in

* This is Louis-Adolphe Thiers (1797–1877), historian and statesman, Minister of the Interior and Prime Minister under Louis Philippe, and first President of the Third Republic from 1871 to 1873; the butcher of the Paris Commune, 'Thiers, that monstrous gnome', whose scandalous biography Marx traces in 'The Civil War in France', *The First International and After*, pp. 191–5.

common with ground-rent proper is that it determines the price of land, which, as shown above, is nothing but the capitalized revenue from the lease of the land.

We have already seen how interest on capital incorporated into the soil may form a foreign component of the ground-rent of this kind, a component that must form an ever-growing addition to the total rental of a country, as economic development proceeds. But, leaving aside this interest, it is possible for the lease-price to include either partly, or in certain cases entirely (i.e. when ground-rent proper is completely absent and the land thus actually value-less), a deduction from average profit, normal wages, or both together. This part, whether of profit or of wages, appears here in the form of ground-rent because instead of accruing to the industrial capitalist or the wage-labourer, which would be normal, it is paid to the landowner in the form of the lease-price. Economically speaking, neither part forms ground-rent; but in practice it forms income for the landowner, an economic valorization of his monopoly, just as much as genuine ground-rent does, and it has the same effect in determining the price of land.

We are not referring here to the conditions in which ground-rent, the mode of landed property corresponding to the capitalist mode of production, has a formal existence even though the capitalist mode of production itself does not exist, the tenant himself is not an industrial capitalist, and his manner of farming is not a capitalist one. This is how it is in Ireland, for example. Here the tenant is generally a small peasant. What he pays the landowner for his lease often absorbs not only a portion of his profit, i.e. his own surplus labour, which he has a right to as the owner of his own instruments of labour, but also a portion of the normal wage, which he would receive for the same amount of labour under other conditions. The landowner, moreover, who does nothing at all here to improve the soil, expropriates from him the small capital which he incorporates into the soil for the most part by his own labour, just as a usurer would do in similar conditions. Only the usurer would at least risk his own capital in the operation. It is this continuing robbery that forms the object of the dispute over Irish land legislation; what is demanded in this case is essentially that the landowner who gives a farmer notice to quit should be forced to compensate the tenant for the improvements he has made to the land or the capital he has incorporated

—

into it. Palmerston's cynical response to this was: 'The House of Commons is a house of landed proprietors.' *

We say nothing of the exceptional conditions in which, even in countries of capitalist production, the landowner can extort a high rental that bears no relation to the product of the soil, as for example with the leasing of small plots of land to factory workers, in the English industrial districts, either for small gardens or for amateur cultivation in their spare time. (*Reports of the Inspectors of Factories.*)

What we are talking about here is agricultural rent in countries of developed capitalist production. Among English farmers, for example, there are a number of small capitalists who are destined and compelled to apply their capital in agriculture as farmers, by dint of their upbringing, training, tradition, competition and other circumstances. They are forced to be content with a smaller than average profit and to part with a portion of this to the landowner in the form of rent. This is the only condition on which they are permitted to invest their capital on the land, in agriculture. Since landowners everywhere exert a major influence on legislation, and in England even a predominant one, this influence can be exploited to cheat the entire class of farmers. The Corn Laws of 1815, for instance – a tax on bread explicitly imposed on the country in order to ensure the idle landowners the continuance of a rental that had grown abnormally during the Anti-Jacobin War – had the effect, apart from a few exceptionally fruitful years, of keeping the prices of agricultural products above the level to which they would have fallen under a system of free corn import. But they did not have the result of keeping prices at the levels decreed as normal by the legislating landowners, in the sense that these prices formed the legal limit for the import of foreign corn. Leasehold contracts were none the less concluded under the impression that

* The parliamentary session of 1862–3, during which Marx was working on this volume, saw a new round of struggle by the Irish party for the rights of Irish tenant farmers. Palmerston made his notorious remark on 23 June 1863, attacking the modest reforms of the land tenure system that were proposed as 'communist doctrines'. Marx quoted this again the following year when he came to write the *Inaugural Address* of the International Working Men's Association; see *The First International and After*, p. 80. The Irish Tenants' Right Bill, in one form or other, was already ten years old at that time. When it was first put forward, Marx analysed its provisions in an article written for the *New York Daily Tribune*, 11 July 1853, which is reprinted in *Marx and Engels On Ireland*, London, 1971.

these would be the normal prices. As soon as the illusion was destroyed, a new law was passed with new normal prices, which were as much the impotent expression of landed property's greedy fantasies as the old ones had been. The farmers were cheated in this way from 1815 to the 1830s. Hence during this whole era the constant theme of 'agricultural distress'. Hence during this period the expropriation and ruin of an entire generation of farmers and their replacement by a new class of capitalists.[31]

A far more general and important fact, however, is the reduction of wages for agricultural labourers in particular below their normal average, so that a part of the worker's wage is deducted from him, to form a component of the lease-price and thus accrue to the landowner instead of the worker under the guise of ground-rent. This is the general rule in England and Scotland, for example, with the exception of a few favourably situated counties. The proceedings of the Parliamentary committees of inquiry which studied the level of wages paid in England before the introduction of the Corn Laws† – up till now the most valuable contribution to the history of wages in the nineteenth century, and almost unexploited, besides being at the same time a pillory which the English aristocracy and bourgeoisie erected for themselves – proved convincingly and beyond all doubt that the high rents and corresponding rise in land prices during the Anti-Jacobin War were due in part to a deduction from wages and their suppression even below the physical minimum; i.e. to the handing-over to the landowner of a part of the normal wage. Various circumstances had made these operations possible, including the depreciation of money, the manipulation of the Poor Laws in the agricultural districts,‡ etc., while at the same time the incomes of the farmers rose enormously and the landowners fabulously enriched themselves. Indeed, one of the principal arguments for the introduction

31. See the Anti-Corn-Law prize essays.* Mean while the Corn Laws still held prices up to an artificially high level. This favoured the better-off farmers. They profited from the stationary condition in which the protective tariff kept the great mass of farmers, who, with or without good reason, placed their faith in the exceptional average price.

* *The Three Prize Essays on Agriculture and the Corn Law*, Manchester and London, 1842.

† *Report from the Select Committee on Petitions Relating to the Corn Laws* . . ., and *Reports Respecting Grain, and the Corn Laws* . . .; full titles in the Index of Authorities Quoted.

‡ See Volume 1, pp. 829–30.

of the corn duties, from the farmers as well as the landowners, was that it would be physically impossible to lower the wages of the agricultural labourers any further. This situation has not fundamentally altered, and in England, as in all the European countries, a part of the normal wage still goes into ground-rent just as before. When the Earl of Shaftesbury, then Lord Ashley, a philanthropic aristocrat, was so extraordinarily moved by the condition of the English factory workers and threw himself into the Ten Hours agitation as their parliamentary spokesman, the representatives of the industrialists published in revenge some statistics about the wages of agricultural labourers in his own villages (see Volume 1, Chapter 25, 5, e: 'The British Agricultural Proletariat' [pp. 831–2]), which clearly showed how a portion of this philanthropist's ground-rent consisted simply of the plunder that his tenants extracted for him from the wages of the agricultural labourers. These articles are also interesting in as much as the facts they contain may boldly take their place alongside the worst that the committees of 1814 and 1815 revealed. Whenever circumstances compel a temporary rise in the wages of agricultural labourers, the cry resounds from the farmers that the raising of wages to their normal level, such as obtains in other branches of industry, is impossible and would inevitably ruin them without a simultaneous reduction in ground-rent. It is thereby admitted that in the name of ground-rent the farmers make a deduction from wages and hand this over to the landowner. Between 1849 and 1859, for instance, agricultural wages rose in England in consequence of a combination of overwhelming circumstances, such as the exodus from Ireland, which cut off the supply of agricultural labourers from there; the exceptional absorption of the agricultural population by manufacturing industry; the wartime demand for soldiers; an exceptional emigration to Australia and the United States (California); and other reasons that we cannot go into any further here. At the same time, with the exception of the bad harvests of 1854–6, average cereal prices fell by more than 16 per cent during this period. The farmers clamoured for a reduction in rents. In some cases they did obtain this. By and large, however, their demand did not meet with success. They took refuge in a reduction of production costs, including the massive introduction of steam-engines and new machinery, which partly replaced horses and drove these out of economic use, while it also released agricultural labourers and thus brought about an artificial over-population and a fresh fall in wages. And all this happened despite an overall relative decline in the agricultural population during this decade, compared with the growth in the total population, and even an absolute decline in the agricultural population in some purely agricultural districts.[32] Fawcett, at that time Professor of Political Economy at Cambridge (who died in 1884 when Postmaster-General – F.E.), spoke in the same terms to the Social Science Congress on 12 October 1865: 'The labourers were beginning to emigrate, and the farmers were already beginning to complain that they would not be able to pay such high rents as they have been accustomed to pay, because labour was becoming dearer in consequence of emigration.' Here a high rent of land is thus directly identified with low wages. And in so far as the high level of land prices is conditioned by this factor that increases rents, a rise in the value of land is identical with a devaluation of labour, and a high price of land with a low price of labour.

The same holds good for France.

'The lease-price rises because the price of bread, wine, meat, vegetables and fruit rises, while the price of labour remains the same. If elderly people go through their fathers' accounts, which takes us back approximately 100 years, they will find that at that time the price of a working day in rural France was exactly the same as it is today. The price of meat, however, has tripled since then ... Who is the victim of this revolution? Is it the rich man, the owner of the farm, or the poor man who works it? ... The rise in rents is the sign of a public disaster' (*Du mécanisme de la société en France et en Angleterre*, M. Rubichon, 2nd edn, Paris, 1836, p. 101).

Examples of rent as a result of a deduction from average profit on the one hand and from average wages on the other.

The above-quoted Morton,* land agent and agricultural engineer, says it has been noticed in many districts that the rent for large farms is less than for smaller ones, since 'the competition is usually greater for the latter than for the former, and as few small farmers are able to turn their attention to any other business than that of farming, their anxiety to get a suitable occupation leads

32. John C. Morton, *The Forces Used in Agriculture*, a lecture to the London Society of Arts in 1859, based on authentic documents collected from some hundred farmers in twelve Scottish and thirty-five English counties.

* Marx is wrong here. The following quote is from John Lockhart Morton, not John Chalmers Morton (1821–88); both were contemporary agronomists.

them in many instances to give more rent than their judgement can approve of' (John L. Morton, *The Resources of Estates*, London, 1858, p. 116).

This distinction, however, is said to be gradually diminishing in England, and in his opinion emigration, precisely among the class of small farmers, has a lot to do with it. The same Morton gives an example where the ground-rent evidently includes a deduction from the wage of the farmer himself and hence still more certainly of the people he employs. This is the case with farms of under 70–80 acres, which cannot maintain a two-horse plough. 'Unless the tenant works with his own hands as laboriously as any labourer, his farm will not keep him. If he entrusts the performance of his work to workmen while he continues merely to observe them, the chances are, that at no distant period, he will find he is unable to pay his rent' (ibid., p. 118).

Morton concludes from this that unless the farmers in the district are very poor, the farms should not be less than 70 acres, so that the farmer can keep two or three horses.

The extraordinary wisdom of Monsieur Léonce de Lavergne, Membre de l'Institut et de la Société Centrale d'Agriculture: in his *Économie rurale de l'Angleterre* (quoted from the English translation, London, 1855), he makes the following comparison of the annual benefits derived from cattle, which labour in France but not in England, where they are replaced by horses (p. 42):

FRANCE		ENGLAND	
Milk	£ 4 million	Milk	£16 million
Meat	£16 million	Meat	£20 million
Labour	£ 8 million	Labour	—
	£28 million		£36 million

But the higher product in this case is simply because, as he himself points out, milk in England is as dear again as in France, while he assumes the same price for meat in both countries (p. 35); the English milk product would thus be reduced to £8 million, and the total product to £28 million, as in France. It is a bit much for Monsieur Lavergne to take into account at the same time both the quantities produced and the differences in price, so that, if England produces certain articles at greater cost than France, which means at most a bigger profit for farmers and landowners, this appears as a superiority of English agriculture.

M. Lavergne shows on p. 48 that he is not only acquainted with the economic successes of English agriculture, but also shares the prejudices of English farmers and landowners: 'One great drawback attends cereals generally ... they exhaust the soil which bears them.'

M. Lavergne not only believes that other crops do not do this; he believes that fodder and root crops enrich the soil: 'Forage plants derive from the atmosphere the principal elements of their growth, while they give to the soil more than they take from it; thus both directly and by their conversion into animal manure contributing in two ways to repair the mischief done by cereals and exhausting crops generally; one principle, therefore, is that they should at least alternate with these crops; in this consists the Norfolk rotation' (pp. 50, 51).

No wonder then that M. Lavergne, believing these fairy stories about English rural conditions, should also believe that the wages of English rural labourers have lost their former abnormal character since the abolition of the Corn Laws. See what we already said on this subject in Volume 1, Chapter 25, 5, e. We may also listen to what Mr John Bright had to say in his speech in Birmingham on 13 December 1866.* After speaking of the five million families who are not represented at all in Parliament, he continued:

'There is among them one million, or rather more than one million, in the United Kingdom who are classed in the unfortunate list of paupers. There is another million just above pauperism, but always in peril lest they should become paupers. Their condition and prospects are not more favourable than that. Now look at the ignorant and lower strata of this portion of the community. Look to their abject condition, to their poverty, to their suffering, to their utter hopelessness of any good. Why, in the United States – even in the Southern States during the reign of slavery – every Negro had an idea that there was a day of jubilee for him. But to these people – to this class of the lowest strata in this country – I am here to state that there is neither the belief of anything better nor scarcely an aspiration after it. Have you read a paragraph which lately appeared in the newspapers about John Cross, a Dorsetshire labourer? He worked six days in the week, had an excellent character from his employer for whom he had worked

* This is John Bright (1811–89), leader of the Free Trade movement and Anti-Corn-Law League, and later a Liberal minister.

twenty-four years at the rate of eight shillings per week. John Cross had a family of seven children to provide for out of these wages in his hovel – for a feeble wife and an infant child. He took – legally, I believe he stole – a wooden hurdle of the value of sixpence. For this offence he was tried before the magistrates and sentenced to fourteen or twenty days' imprisonment ... I can tell you that many thousands of cases like that of John Cross are to be found throughout the country, and especially in the south, and that their condition is such that hitherto the most anxious investigator has been unable to solve the mystery as to how they keep body and soul together. Now cast your eye over the country and look at these five million of families and the desperate condition of this strata of them. Is it not true that the unenfranchised nation may be said to toil and toil, knowing almost no rest? Compare it with the ruling class – but if I do I shall be charged with communism ... But compare this great toiling and unenfranchised nation with the section who may be considered the governing classes. Look at its wealth; look at its ostentation – look at its luxury. Behold its weariness – for there is weariness amongst them, but it is the weariness of satiety – and see how they rush from place to place, as it were, to discover some new pleasure' (*Morning Star*, 14 December 1865).

We shall go on to show how surplus labour and hence surplus product in general are confused with ground-rent, a portion of the surplus product that is both quantitatively and qualitatively specific, at least on the basis of the capitalist mode of production. The indigenous basis of surplus labour in general, i.e. a natural condition without which this is impossible, is that nature provides the necessary means of subsistence – whether in products of the land, animal or vegetable, or in fisheries, etc. – with the application of an amount of labour-time that does not swallow up the entire working day. This indigenous productivity of agricultural labour (and here we include simple gathering, hunting, fishing, stock-raising) is the basis of all surplus-value; just as all labour is originally first directed towards the appropriation and production of food. (Animals also provide pelts for warmth in cold climates; also cave-dwellings, etc.)

The same confusion between surplus product and ground-rent is expressed in a different way by Mr Dove.* Originally, agri-

* Patrick E. Dove, *The Elements of Political Science*, Edinburgh, 1854, pp. 264 and 273.

cultural labour and industrial labour are not separate; the second is an appendage of the first. The surplus labour and surplus product of the agricultural clan, the common household or the family, comprises both agricultural and industrial labour. The two go hand in hand. Hunting, fishing and agriculture are impossible without appropriate instruments. Weaving, spinning, etc. are first of all conducted as agricultural sidelines.

We have already shown how, just as the labour of the individual worker breaks down into necessary and surplus labour, so the total labour of the working class can be divided in such a way that the part that produces the entire means of subsistence needed by the working class (including the means of production these require) performs the necessary labour for the entire society. The labour performed by the whole remaining part of the working class can be considered as surplus labour. But the necessary labour in no way includes just agricultural labour; it also includes the labour that produces all other products that necessarily enter the worker's average consumption. Some, moreover, perform only necessary labour, from a social point of view, because others perform only surplus labour, and vice versa. This is simply a division of labour between them. It is the same with the division of labour between agricultural and industrial workers in general. The purely industrial character of one section's labour is matched by the purely agricultural character of the other's. This purely agricultural labour is in no way of natural and spontaneous origin but is rather itself a product of social development, and a very recent one at that, which has by no means been everywhere attained; it corresponds to a quite specific stage of production. Just as a part of agricultural labour is objectified in products that either serve simply for luxury or form industrial raw materials but in no way go into foodstuffs, at least not foodstuffs for the masses, so on the other hand a part of industrial labour is objectified in products that serve as necessary means of consumption for agricultural and non-agricultural workers alike. It is. wrong to conceive this industrial labour – from the social standpoint – as surplus labour. It is in part just as much necessary labour as the necessary portion of agricultural work is. It is also simply the autonomized form of a part of the industrial labour which was formerly linked indigenously with agricultural labour, a necessary reciprocal supplement to the purely agricultural labour that has now become separate from this. (Considering just the material aspect, 500 mechanized weavers for example produce a far higher degree of surplus cloth than one, i.e. much more than is required for their own clothing.)

In considering the forms of appearance of ground-rent, i.e. the lease-price that is paid to the landowner under this heading for the use of the soil, whether for productive purposes or those of consumption, we must keep in mind, finally, that the prices of things that have no value in and of themselves – either not being the product of labour, like land, or which at least cannot be reproduced by labour, such as antiques, works of art by certain masters, etc. – may be determined by quite fortuitous combinations of circumstances. For a thing to be sold, it simply has to be capable of being monopolized and alienated.

*

There are three major errors which obscure the analysis of ground-rent and are to be avoided in dealing with it.

(1) The confusion between the various forms of rent that correspond to different levels of development of the social production process.

Whatever the specific form of rent may be, what all its types have in common is the fact that the appropriation of rent is the economic form in which landed property is realized and that ground-rent in turn presupposes landed property, the ownership of particular bits of the globe by certain individuals – whether the owner is a person representing the community, as in Asia, Egypt, etc.; whether this landed property is simply an accidental accompaniment of the property that certain persons have in the persons of the immediate producers, as in the systems of serfdom and slavery; whether it is pure private property that non-producers have in nature, a simple ownership title to land; or finally, whether it is a relationship to the land which, as with colonists and small peasant proprietors, appears as directly implied, given their isolated and not socially developed labour, in the appropriation and production of the products of particular bits of land by the direct producers.

This *common character* of the different forms of rent – as the economic realization of landed property, the legal fiction by virtue of which various individuals have exclusive possession of particular parts of the globe – leads people to overlook the distinctions.

(2) **All ground-rent is surplus-value, the product of surplus**

labour. In its more undeveloped form, rent in kind, it is still a direct surplus product. Hence the error that the rent corresponding to the capitalist mode of production, which is always an excess over and above profit, i.e. over and above a portion of commodity value that itself consists of surplus-value (surplus labour) – that this particular and specific component of surplus-value can be explained simply by explaining the general conditions of existence for surplus-value and profit. These conditions are, first, that the direct producers must work for more time than is required to reproduce their own labour-power, i.e. to reproduce themselves. They must perform some kind of surplus labour. This is the subjective condition. But the objective condition is that they also *can* perform˙surplus labour: that natural conditions are such that a *part* of their available labour-time is sufficient to reproduce and maintain them as producers; that the production of their necessary means of subsistence does not consume their entire labour-time. Natural fertility sets one limit here, as a point of departure or basis. The development of the social productivity of their labour sets the other limit. Looked at more closely, since the production of foodstuffs is the very first condition of their life and of any production at all, the labour employed in this production, i.e. agricultural labour in the broadest economic sense, must be sufficiently fruitful to prevent the entire available labour-time from being absorbed in the production of foodstuffs for the immediate producers, so that agricultural surplus labour and hence an agricultural surplus product is possible. To take this further, the total agricultural labour – necessary and surplus – of one section of society must be sufficient to produce the necessary food-stuffs for the entire society, i.e. also for the non-agricultural workers; this great division of labour between agriculturalists and industrialists must be possible, and similarly that between those agriculturalists who produce foodstuffs and those who produce raw materials. Even though the labour of the direct producers of foodstuffs, taken by itself, breaks down into necessary and surplus labour, in relation to society it thus represents the necessary labour required simply for the production of foodstuffs. The same thing is the case, incidentally, with any division of labour within society as a whole, as distinct from the division of labour within the individual workshop. It is the labour necessary for the pro-duction of particular articles – for the satisfaction of a particular social need for particular articles. If this division is in due proportion, products of various types will be sold at their values (at a further stage of development, at their prices of production), or at least at prices which are modifications of these values or production prices as determined by general laws. This is in fact the law of value as it makes itself felt, not in relation to the individual commodities or articles, but rather to the total products at a given time of particular spheres of social production autonomized by the division of labour; so that not only is no more labour-time devoted to each individual commodity than necessary, but out of the total social labour-time only the proportionate quantity needed is devoted to the various types of commodity. Use-value still remains a condition. But if in the case of the individual commodity this use-value depends on its satisfying in and of itself a social need, in the case of the mass social product it depends on its adequacy to the quantitatively specific social need for each particular kind of product and therefore on the proportional division of the labour between these various spheres of production in accordance with these social needs, which are quantitatively circumscribed. (This point should be introduced in connection with the distribution of capital between the various spheres of production.) The social need, i.e. the use-value on the social scale, here appears decisive for the quota of total social labour-time that falls to the share of the various particular spheres of production. But this is simply the same law that is already exhibited by the individual commodity, i.e. that its use-value is the precondition of its exchange-value and hence of its value. It is a point that bears on the relation between necessary and surplus labour only in as much as an imbalance in this proportion means that the commodity value, and therefore also the surplus-value contained in it, cannot be realized. For example, the proportion of cotton goods produced may be too high even though the labour-time realized in this total product is simply that needed under the given conditions. But too much of society's overall labour has been spent on this particular branch, and so a portion of the product is useless. The total product is therefore sold as if only the necessary proportion had been produced. This quantitative barrier to the quotas of social labour-time devoted to the various particular spheres of production is simply a further developed expression of the law of value in general; even though necessary labour-time takes on a different meaning here. Only such-and-such a quantity of this is required in order to satisfy the social need. The limit in this case emerges through the use-value. Under the given conditions of production, society can spend only so much of its total labour-time on one particular kind of product. But the subjective and objective conditions of surplus labour and surplus-value in general have nothing to do with the particular form, whether this is profit, or whether it is rent. They apply to surplus-value as such, whatever particular form this may assume. They therefore do not explain ground-rent.

(3) A particular peculiarity that arises with the economic valorization of landed property, that is the development of ground-rent, is that its amount is in no way determined by the action of its recipient, but rather by a development of social labour that is independent of him and in which he plays no part. This is why something that is common to all branches of production and their products on the basis of commodity production, and to capitalist production in particular, which is commodity production in its entirety, is easily conceived as a peculiar property of rent (and of the product of agriculture in general).

The level of ground-rent (and with it the value of land) rises in the course of social development, as a result of the overall social labour. Not only does the market and the demand for agricultural products grow, but the demand for the land itself also grows directly, since it is a condition of production competed for by all possible branches of business, including non-agricultural ones. Rent, moreover, and with it the value of land (confining ourselves simply to agricultural rent proper), develops along with the market for the product of land and hence with the growth in the non-agricultural population; it increases with their needs and their demand both for foodstuffs and for raw materials. It lies in the nature of the capitalist mode of production that it constantly reduces the agricultural population in relation to the non-agricultural, because in industry (in the narrow sense) the growth of constant capital in relation to variable is linked with an absolute growth in variable capital (even if a relative decline in relation to constant); while in agriculture the variable capital required for the cultivation of a particular piece of land declines absolutely and can therefore grow only in so far as new land is cultivated, which however presupposes in turn a still greater growth in the non-agricultural population.

In actual fact, what we have here is not a phenomenon peculiar to agriculture and its products. The same applies rather to all other branches of production and products, on the basis of commodity production and its absolute form, capitalist production.

These products are commodities, use-values which possess an exchange-value, and particularly one that can be realized, converted into money, only to the extent to which other commodities form an equivalent for them and other products confront them as commodities and as values; to the extent, therefore, to which they are not produced as direct means of subsistence for their producers themselves, but as commodities, as products which only become use-values by being transformed into exchange-value (money), by being alienated. The market for these commodities develops by way of the social division of labour; the separation between different productive labours transforms their respective products reciprocally into commodities, into equivalents for one another, making them serve one another reciprocally as markets. This is in no way something peculiar to the products of agriculture.

Rent can develop as money-rent only on the basis of commodity production, and particularly of capitalist production, and it develops to the same extent to which agricultural production becomes commodity production, i.e. the extent to which non-agricultural production undergoes an independent development in relation to it; for it is to this extent that the product of agriculture becomes a commodity, an exchange-value and a value. To the same extent that commodity production and hence the production of value develops with capitalist production, so too there develops the production of surplus-value and surplus product. But in the same measure as the latter develops, there develops in landed property the ability to capture a growing portion of this surplus-value by way of its monopoly of the earth and hence to raise the value of its rent and the price of the land itself. It is still the capitalist who has the active function in the development of this surplus-value and surplus product. The landowner has only to seize a portion of surplus product and surplus-value that increases without any effort on his part. This is the peculiarity of his position, not the fact that the value of the agricultural products, and hence of the land itself, is constantly growing as the market for these expands, demand increases and with it the world of commodities that confronts the products of agriculture – in other words the number of non-agricultural commodity producers and the scale of non-agricultural commodity production. Since this happens without his assistance, it appears to the landowner as something unique that the mass of value, the mass of surplus-value, and the transformation of a portion of this surplus-value into ground-rent depends on the social production process, on the development of commodity production in general. That is why Dove, for example, tries to explain rent in general on this basis.* He says that rent does not depend on the size of the agricultural product but rather on its value; this however depends on the size and productivity of the non-agricultural population. But it is also true to say for any other product that it only develops as a commodity with the volume and diversity of the series of other commodities that form equivalents for it. We have already shown this in our general presentation of value. On the one hand, the exchangeability of a product depends entirely on the number of different commodities that exist outside it. On the other hand, the quantity in which it can itself be produced as a commodity depends in particular on this exchangeability.

No producer considered in isolation produces a value or commodity, neither the industrialist nor the agriculturalist. His product becomes a value and a commodity only in a specific social context. Firstly, in so far as it appears as an expression of social labour, and therefore his own labour-time appears as part of the general social labour-time; secondly, where this social character of his labour appears as a social character impressed on his product, in its money character and its general exchangeability as determined by its price.

Thus if on the one hand, instead of explaining rent, it is simply surplus-value or in a still narrower conception only surplus product in general that is explained, on the other hand the mistake is committed of ascribing a character that accrues to all products as commodities and values exclusively to the products of agriculture. This is rendered even more superficial when a withdrawal is made from the general determination of value to the *realization* of a particular commodity value. Any commodity can realize its value only in the process of circulation, and whether and to what extent it does realize this depends on the market conditions of the time.

Thus it is not peculiar to ground-rent that agricultural products develop into values and as values, i.e. that they confront other commodities as commodities themselves and that the non-

* ibid., p. 279.

agricultural products confront them as commodities, nor that they develop as particular expressions of social labour. What is peculiar is that with the conditions in which the agricultural products develop as values (commodities), and with the conditions of realization of their values, landed property also develops the power to appropriate a growing part of these values created without its assistance, and a growing part of the surplus-value is transformed into ground-rent.

Chapter 38: Differential Rent in General

In our analysis of ground-rent we intend to proceed first of all from the assumption that products that pay a rent of this kind – which means that a part of their surplus-value – and therefore also a part of their total price, is reducible to rent – are sold just like all other commodities at their prices of production. For our present purpose we need consider only agricultural products; we could alternatively take the products of mining. Their sale prices are equal therefore to their cost elements (the value of the constant and variable capital consumed) plus a profit determined by the general rate of profit calculated on the total capital advanced, whether used up or not. We assume, therefore, that the average sale prices of these products are equal to their prices of production. The question then arises how a ground-rent can develop on this assumption, i.e. how a portion of profit can be transformed into ground-rent, so that a part of the commodity price thus accrues to the landowner.

To demonstrate the general character of this form of ground-rent, we assume that the factories in a country are powered predominantly by steam-engines, but a certain minority by natural waterfalls instead. We assume the production price in the branches of industry first mentioned to be 115 for a quantity of commodities for which a capital of 100 is consumed. The 15 per cent profit is calculated not just on the consumed capital of 100 but on the total capital that is applied in the production of this commodity value. This production price, as we explained earlier, is determined not by the individual cost price of any one industrialist producing by himself, but rather by the price that the commodity costs on average under the average conditions for capital in that whole sphere of production. It is in fact the market price of production; the average market price as distinct from its oscillations. It is always in the form of the market price, and moreover in the form of the governing market price or the market price of production, that the nature of commodity value presents itself, its character being determined not by the labour-time needed by a certain individual producer to produce a certain quantity of a commodity, or a certain number of individual commodities, but by the socially necessary labour-time; by the labour-time required under the given average social conditions of production to produce the total socially required quantity of the species of commodity available on the market.

Although the particular numerical figures are completely immaterial here, we shall further assume that the cost price in those factories that are driven by water-power comes to only 90, instead of 100. Since the production price of the great mass of goods that governs the market is 115, with a profit of 15 per cent, the factories that drive their machines with water-power will also sell at 115, i.e. at the market price as governed by the average price. Their profit will amount to 25 instead of 15; the governing price of production enables them to make a surplus profit of 10 per cent, not because they sell their commodities above the price of production but because they sell them at this price, because their commodities are produced, or their capital functions, under exceptionally favourable conditions, conditions that stand above the average level prevailing in this sphere.

Two things are immediately evident here.

Firstly, the surplus profit of those producers who use natural water-power as their motive force behaves first of all just like any other surplus profit (this category has already been developed in our presentation of the price of production) which is not the chance result of transactions in the circulation process, of accidental fluctuations in market price. This surplus profit is thus similarly equal to the difference between the individual price of production of these favoured producers and the general social price of production in the sphere of production as a whole, which is what governs the market. This difference is equal to the excess of the general production price of the commodity over its individual production price. The two governing limits of this excess are on the one hand the individual cost price and hence the individual production price, and on the other the general production price. The value of the commodities produced by water-power is lower because a smaller amount of labour is required for their production, i.e. less labour enters in the objectified form, as a portion of the constant capital. The labour applied here is more productive, its individual productivity being greater than that of the labour employed in the majority of factories of the same type. Its greater productivity is expressed in the way that it needs a smaller quantity of constant capital to produce the same amount of commodities, a smaller quantity of objectified labour than the others; and a smaller quantity of living labour as well, since the water-wheel does not need to be heated. This greater individual productivity of the labour applied reduces the value of the commodity, and its cost price and therefore its production price as well. For the industrialist, this presents itself in the following way, that the cost price of the commodity for him is less. He has less objectified labour to pay for, and similarly less wages for less living labour-power applied. Since the cost price of his commodity is less, so too is his individual production price. His cost price is 90 instead of 100. And so his individual production price is also only $103\frac{1}{2}$ instead of 115 ($100:115 = 90:103\frac{1}{2}$). The difference between his individual production price and the general one is determined by the difference between his individual cost price and the general one. This is one of the magnitudes that set limits to his surplus profit. The other is the general price of production, in which the general rate of profit is one of the governing factors. If coal becomes cheaper, the difference between his individual cost price and the general one declines, and so therefore does his surplus profit. If he had to sell the commodity at its individual value, or at the production price determined by this individual value, the difference would disappear. It is the result on the one hand of the fact that the commodity is sold at its general market price, the price at which competition balances the individual prices, and on the other hand of the fact that the greater individual productivity of the labour that he sets in motion does not benefit the workers, but, like the productivity of labour in general, their employer; i.e. it presents itself as the productivity of capital.

Since one limit to this surplus profit is the level of the general price of production, and the general rate of profit is a factor of this, the surplus profit can arise only from the difference between the general and the individual production prices, and hence from the difference between the individual and the general rate of profit. An excess over and above this difference would presuppose the sale of the product above the price of production governed by the market, and not at this price.

Secondly, the surplus profit of the manufacturer who uses natural water-power as his motive force instead of steam has not so far been distinguished in any way from all other surplus profit. All normal surplus profit, i.e. excluding that brought about by accidental business deals or by fluctuations in the market price, is determined by the difference between the individual production price of the commodities produced by this particular capital and the general production price which governs the market prices of commodities for capital right across this sphere of production – the market prices of commodities for the total capital invested in this sphere of production.

But now comes the difference.

To what circumstances does the manufacturer in the present case owe his surplus profit, the excess that the production price governed by the general rate of profit yields him personally?

In the first instance, to a natural force, the motive force of water-power which is provided by nature itself and is not itself the product of labour, unlike the coal that transforms water into steam, which has value and must be paid an equivalent, i.e. costs something. It is a natural agent of production, and no labour goes into creating it.

But this is not all. The manufacturer who operates with the steam-engine also applies natural forces which cost him nothing but which make labour more productive, and, in so far as they cheapen the production of the means of subsistence the workers require, increase surplus-value and hence profit; which are therefore just as much monopolized by capital as are the natural social forces of labour that arise from cooperation, division of labour, etc. The manufacturer pays for the coal, but not for the ability of water to change its aggregate state and transform itself into steam, nor for the elasticity of steam, etc. This monopolization of natural forces, i.e. of the increase in labour-power* that they bring about, is common to all capital that operates with steam-engines. It may increase the part of the product of labour that represents surplus-value as against the part that is transformed into wages. In as much as it does this, it increases the general rate of profit but it does not create any surplus profit, for this consists precisely in the excess of individual profit over and above the average profit. If in our case the application of a natural force, water-power, does

---

* This should presumably read 'productivity of labour'.

create surplus profit, this cannot arise simply from the fact that the increased productivity of labour is due here to the use of a natural force. Further modifying factors must intervene.

Conversely. The simple application of natural forces in industry may affect the level of the general rate of profit, through the amount of labour required to produce the necessary means of subsistence. But it does not in and of itself create any divergence from the general rate of profit, and it is precisely this that we are dealing with now. Moreover, the surplus profit that an individual capital in a particular sphere of production might otherwise realize – for divergences in the rate of profit between particular spheres of production are constantly balanced out to give the average rate – arises, apart from merely accidental divergences, from a reduction in the cost price, i.e. in production costs, which is due either to the fact that capital is applied on a greater than average scale, so that the *faux frais* of production are reduced, while the general causes of a rise in labour productivity (cooperation, division of labour, etc.) can operate to a greater extent and with more intensity, because over a larger field of operation; or else to the fact that, apart from the scale of the capital functioning, better methods of work, new inventions, improved machines, trade secrets in chemistry, etc. are employed – in other words it is due to the application of new, improved and above-average means and methods of production. The reduction in the cost price, and the surplus profit which flows from it, arise here from the manner and form in which the capital functioning is invested. They arise either from its concentration in exceptionally large amounts in a single hand – something that is cancelled out as soon as equally large amounts of capital are employed in the average case – or from the circumstance that capital of a particular size functions in a particularly productive way – and this ceases to operate as soon as the exceptional manner of production becomes universal, or is overtaken by one still more advanced.

The reason for the surplus profit in this case is thus inherent in the capital itself (including the labour that it sets in motion), whether a difference in magnitude of the capital applied or a more efficient application of it; and nothing inherently prevents all capital in the same sphere of production from being invested in the same way. Competition between capitals actually tends to the contrary, it tends to cancel out these distinctions more and more; the determination of value by socially necessary labour-time leads to the cheapening of commodities and the compulsion to produce commodities under the same favourable conditions. Things take a different form with the surplus profit of the manufacturer who makes use of the waterfall. The increased productivity of the labour he applies arises neither from the capital and labour themselves nor from the simple application of a natural force distinct from capital and labour but incorporated into the capital. It arises from the greater natural productivity of a labour linked with the use of a natural force, but a natural force that is not available to all capital in the same sphere of production, as is for example the elasticity of steam; its use therefore does not automatically occur as soon as capital is invested in this sphere. What is used is rather a monopolizable natural force which, like the waterfall, is available only to those who have at their disposal particular pieces of the earth's surface and their appurtenances. It is in no way just up to the capital to call into being this natural condition of greater labour productivity, in the way that any capital can transform water into steam. The condition is to be found in nature only at certain places, and where it is not found it cannot be produced by a particular capital outlay. It is not bound up with products that labour can produce such as machines, coal, etc., but rather with particular natural conditions on particular pieces of land. Those manufacturers who possess waterfalls exclude those who do not possess them from employing this natural force, because land is limited, and still more so land endowed with water-power. It is not ruled out that, although the number of natural waterfalls in a country is limited, the amount of water-power that industry can use may still be increased. A waterfall can be artificially channelled to make its motive power fully usable; a water-wheel can be improved in order to use as much of this water-power as possible; where the ordinary type of wheel is not suited to the supply of water, turbines can be used, etc. Possession of this natural force forms a monopoly in the hands of its owner, a condition of higher productivity for the capital invested, which cannot be produced by capital's own production process;[33] the natural force that can be monopolized in this way is always chained to the earth. A natural force of this kind does not belong to the general con-

33. On the surplus profit, see the *Inquiry* * (against Malthus).

* *An Inquiry into the Principles* . . ., London, 1821. See Index of Authorities Quoted.

ditions of the sphere of production in question nor to those of its conditions that are generally reproducible.

If we now imagine that these waterfalls, together with the land on which they are located, are in the hands of subjects who are accepted as the proprietors of these portions of the globe, as landowners, then these are in a position to prevent the application of capital to the waterfall and its utilization by capital. They can either allow this use or refuse it. But capital cannot create a waterfall from its own resources. The surplus profit that arises from this use of the waterfall thus arises not from the capital but rather from the use by capital of a monopolizable and monopolized natural force. Under these conditions, the surplus profit is transformed into ground-rent, i.e. it accrues to the owner of the waterfall. If the manufacturer pays the latter £10 per year for the waterfall, his profit comes to £15, 15 per cent on the £100 which is now the amount of his production costs. And he is still in a position just as good as, if not better than, the other capitalists in his sphere of production who operate with steam. Nothing is altered if the capitalist owns the waterfall himself. He still draws the surplus profit of £10 not as a capitalist, but as the owner of the waterfall; and for the precise reason that this excess arises not from his capital as such, but rather from his disposal over a natural force that is limited in scope, separable from his capital, and monopolizable, it is transformed into ground-rent.

Firstly, it is clear that this rent is always a differential rent, for it does not contribute to determining the general production price of the commodity, but takes this as given. It always arises from the difference between the individual production price of the particular capital which has the monopolized natural force available to it and the general production price for capital invested in the sphere of production in question.

Secondly, this ground-rent does not derive from any absolute rise in productivity of the capital applied or of the labour it appropriates, which can only ever reduce the value of commodities; it arises from the greater relative returns from certain particular capitals invested in a sphere of production, as compared with those capital investments that are excluded from these exceptional, favourable conditions of productivity which have been created by nature. If for example the use of steam gave an overwhelming advantage which would not occur if water-power was used, even though coal has value and water-power does not, and this advantage more than compensated for that fact, water-power would not be used and could not produce any surplus profit, nor therefore any rent.

Thirdly, the natural force is not the source of the surplus profit, but simply a natural basis for it, because it is the natural basis of the exceptionally increased productivity of labour. Use-value is altogether the bearer of exchange-value but not its cause. If the same use-value could be obtained without labour, it would have no exchange-value. On the other hand, however, a thing cannot have exchange-value without having use-value, i.e. without being such a natural bearer of labour. If the various different values did not balance out into production prices and the various individual production prices into a general production price that governs the market, a rise in labour productivity resulting from the use of a waterfall would simply lower the price of the commodities produced with the waterfall without raising the portion of profit contained in these commodities, just as increased labour productivity in general would not be transformed into surplus-value if capital did not appropriate as its own the productive power, natural and social, of the labour applied.

Fourthly, landed property in the waterfall has in and of itself nothing to do with the creation of the portion of surplus-value (profit) and hence of the price of the commodity that is produced with the aid of the waterfall. This surplus profit exists even if there is no landed property, if for example the land on which the waterfall is located can be used by the manufacturer as unclaimed land. Thus landed property does not create the portion of value that is transformed into surplus profit; rather it simply enables the landowner, the proprietor of the waterfall, to entice this surplus profit out of the manufacturer's pocket and into his own. It is not the cause of this surplus profit's creation, but simply of its transformation into the form of ground-rent, hence of the appropriation of this portion of profit or commodity price by the landowner or waterfall-owner.

Fifthly, it is evident that the price of the waterfall, i.e. the price that the landowner would receive if he sold it to a third party or to the manufacturer himself, does not at first go directly into the production price of the commodities concerned, even though it does go into the individual price for the manufacturer; for rent arises in this case from the production price of those commodities of the same kind that are produced by steam-engines, which is determined independently of the waterfall. The price of the water-fall, besides, is altogether an irrational expression concealing a real economic relationship. The waterfall, like the earth in general and every natural force, has no value, since it represents no objectified labour and hence no price, this being in the normal case nothing but value expressed in money. Where there is no value, there is *eo ipso* nothing to be expressed in money. This price is nothing but capitalized rent. Landed property enables the proprietor to lay hold of the difference between the individual profit and the average profit; the profit captured in this way, which is renewed every year, can be capitalized and then appears as the price of the natural force itself. If the surplus profit that the use of the waterfall yields to the manufacturer is £10 per year and the average interest is 5 per cent, this £10 per year represents the interest on a capital of £200; and this capitalization of the annual £10 that the waterfall empowers its owner to extract from the manufacturer then appears as the capital value of the waterfall itself. The fact that the waterfall does not itself have value but that its price is simply the reflection of the surplus profit extracted, in a capitalist reckoning, is immediately evident in the way that the price of £200 simply expresses the product of the surplus profit of £10 multiplied by twenty years, whereas, if circumstances remain otherwise the same, the same waterfall actually enables its owner to extract this annual £10 for an indefinite time, thirty or a hundred years, while on the other hand, if a new method of production that cannot make use of water-power lowers the cost price of the commodities produced by steam from £100 to £90, the surplus profit would disappear, and the rent and the price of the waterfall along with it.

Now that we have established the general concept of differential rent in this way, we turn to consider this rent in agriculture proper. What will be said of agriculture applies on the whole also to mining.

Chapter 39: The First Form of Differential Rent (Differential Rent I)

The following statement of Ricardo's is completely correct:

'Rent' (i.e. differential rent; he assumes that there is no other rent in existence besides this) 'is always the difference between the produce obtained by the employment of two equal quantities of capital and labour' (*Principles* [Pelican edn, p. 95]).

He should have added 'on equal quantities of land', in as much as he is dealing with ground-rent and not with surplus profit in general.

Surplus profit, in other words, if produced in normal conditions and not as a by-product of fortuitous circumstances in the circulation process, is always produced as the difference between the product of two equal amounts of capital and labour, and this surplus profit is transformed into ground-rent if two equal amounts of capital and labour are employed on equal areas of land with unequal results. It is by no means necessarily required, however, that this surplus profit should arise from the unequal results of equal amounts of capital employed. Capitals of different size could also be employed in the different investments, and this is even the general assumption; but equal proportionate parts, for example £100 of each, give unequal results; i.e. the rate of profit varies. This is the general precondition for the existence of surplus profit in any sphere of capital investment whatsoever. The second thing is the transformation of this surplus profit into the form of ground-rent (of rent in general, as a form distinct from profit); we must always investigate when, how and under what circumstances this transformation takes place.

Ricardo is also correct in this next statement, in so far as his remarks are restricted to differential rent:

'Whatever diminishes the inequality in the produce obtained from successive portions of capital on the same or on new land, tends to lower rent; and whatever increases that inequality, necessarily produces an opposite effect, and tends to raise it' [p. 106].

These causes, however, do not include only the general ones of fertility and location, but also (1) the distribution of taxes, according to whether this is uniform or not; the latter is always the case when, as in England, taxation is not centralized and the tax is levied on the land and not on the rent; (2) the inequalities that result from the differential development of agriculture in different parts of the country, since this branch of industry, on account of its traditional character, is more difficult to equalize than is manufacture; and (3) the uneven way in which capital is divided among the farmers. As the capitalist mode of production's seizure of agriculture, the transformation of the independently operating peasant into a wage-labourer, is in fact the final conquest of this mode of production, these inequalities are greater here than in any other branch of industry.

After these preliminary remarks, I intend to start by summarizing quite briefly the particular features of my development in contrast with that of Ricardo, etc.

*

We start by considering the unequal products of equal amounts of capital applied to different lands of the same area; or, in the case of different-sized lands, the products of equal acreages.

The two general causes of such unequal products, which are independent of capital, are: (1) *fertility* (in dealing with this point, we shall have to discuss what is meant by the natural fertility of land, and the different aspects this involves), and (2) the *location* of land. The latter is decisive in the case of colonies, and decisive everywhere for the sequence in which lands can be successively brought into cultivation. It is also evident that these two different bases for differential rent, fertility and location, can operate in opposite directions. A piece of land may be very well located but of very low fertility, and vice versa. This is an important fact, since it explains to us why, when the land of a particular country is originally cultivated, it is possible to proceed from worse soil to better as well as the other way round. It is finally clear that the progress of social production in general has on the one hand a levelling effect on location as a basis for differential rent, since it creates local markets and improves location by producing means of communication and transport; while on the other hand it increases the differences of geographical location, by separating agriculture from manufacture and forming great centres of production, while also relatively isolating the countryside.

First of all, however, we shall leave aside this point of location and simply consider natural fertility. Apart from climatic and similar aspects, differences in natural fertility are differences in the chemical composition of the soil, i.e. variations in the amount of nutrient elements for plants it contains. However, assuming the same chemical composition and in this sense the same natural fertility of two areas of land, their actual effective fertility will differ according to how far these nutrient elements occur in readily assimilable form, and can be directly used as plant foodstuffs. Thus the extent to which the same natural fertility can be obtained on soils that are naturally equally fertile depends in part on the chemical development of agriculture and in part on its mechanical development. Even though fertility is an objective property of the soil, it thus always involves an economic relation, a relation to the given chemical and mechanical level of agricultural development, and changes with this level of development. By chemical means (e.g. the use of certain liquid fertilizers on stiff clayey soil or calcination of heavy clayey soil) and by mechanical means too (e.g. special ploughs for heavy soil), it is possible to remove obstacles which made soils of equal fertility less equal in practice. (Drainage, too, comes under this heading.) The sequence followed in bringing different types of soil into cultivation may also be changed in this way, as it was for instance between light sandy soil and heavy clayey soil at one period of English agricultural development. This further shows how historically – in the successive course of cultivation – there can be both a transition from more fertile soil to less and vice versa. The same thing can happen as a result of artificially induced improvements in the composition of the soil or of a mere change in the hierarchy of soil types when various subsoil conditions come into play, once the subsoil also begins to be tilled and turned over into top layers. This is brought about partly by the use of new agricultural methods (such as the cultivation of fodder grasses) and partly by mechanical means, which either turn the subsoil into the top layer or mix the two together, or else cultivate the subsoil without turning it up.

All these influences on the differential fertility of different soils boil down to the fact that as far as economic fertility is concerned, the level of labour productivity, in this case the ability of agriculture directly to exploit the natural fertility of the soil – an ability that varies with different stages of development – is just as much a factor in the so-called natural fertility of the soil as its chemical composition and other natural properties.

We thus assume a given level of agricultural development. We further assume that the hierarchy of soil types is calculated in relation to this level of development, as is of course always the case with simultaneous capital investments on different lands. The differential rent can then exhibit an increasing or decreasing series, for although the series is given for the totality of lands actually cultivated, these have always been formed by a successive movement.

Assume four types of soil, A, B, C, D. Assume further that the price of wheat is £3, or 60 shillings per quarter. Since the rent here is simply differential rent, this price of 60 shillings per quarter is equal to the production costs on the worst soil, i.e. equal to capital plus average profit.

Let A be this worst soil, giving 1 quarter = 60 shillings for an outlay of 50 shillings; i.e. a profit of 10 shillings or 20 per cent.

Let B yield 2 quarters = 120 shillings for the same outlay. There is a profit of 70 shillings or a surplus profit of 60 shillings.

Let C yield 3 quarters = 180 shillings for the same outlay. Total profit = 130 shillings. Surplus profit = 120 shillings.

Let D yield 4 quarters = 240 shillings; 180 shillings surplus profit.

We would then have the following sequence:

Table I

Type of soil	Product		Capital advanced	Profit		Rent	
	Quarters	Shillings		Quarters	Shillings	Quarters	Shillings
A	1	60	50	$\frac{1}{6}$	10	—	—
B	2	120	50	$1\frac{1}{6}$	70	1	60
C	3	180	50	$2\frac{1}{6}$	130	2	120
D	4	240	50	$3\frac{1}{6}$	190	3	180
Total	10 qrs	600s.				6 qrs	360s.

The respective rents are, for D, (190 − 10) shillings, or the difference between D and A; for C, (130 − 10) shillings, or the difference between C and A; for B, (70 — 10) shillings, or the difference between B and A; while the total rent for B, C and D = 6 quarters = 360 shillings, the sum of the differences of D and A, C and A, and B and A.

This series, which represents a given product in a given condition, can just as well occur, when considered in the abstract, as a decreasing series (from D down to A, from the more fertile to ever less fertile soil) or as an increasing one (from A to D, from relatively infertile soil to ever more fertile soil), and we have already given the reasons why this may also be the case in actual fact; it may also fluctuate up and down, as for example from D to C, C to A, and A to B.

The process involved in the decreasing series is as follows. The price per quarter gradually rises from, say, 15 shillings to 60 shillings. Once the 4 quarters produced by D (which we may consider as millions) are no longer sufficient, the wheat price rises to the point at which the missing supply can be obtained from C. That is, the price would have to rise to 20 shillings per quarter. When the wheat price rises to 30 shillings per quarter, B can be brought into cultivation, and when it rises to 60 shillings per quarter, so can A, without any need for the capital applied to make do with a rate of profit lower than 20 per cent. The rent for D is thus first 5 shillings per quarter = 20 shillings for the 4 quarters it produces; then 15 shillings per quarter = 60 shillings, then finally 45 shillings per quarter = 180 shillings for 4 quarters.

If the profit rate for D was also 20 per cent to start with, its total profit on the 4 quarters would be only 10 shillings, but this would represent more corn at a price of 15 shillings than at a price of 60 shillings. Since corn goes into the reproduction of labour-power, and one portion of each quarter must replace labour-power and another part constant capital, the surplus-value would therefore be higher under this assumption, and so too, with other factors remaining the same, would the rate of profit. (The question of the profit rate will have to be specially investigated in more detail.)

If the sequence went the opposite way, so that the process began with A, then as soon as new agricultural land had to be taken into cultivation, the price per quarter would rise above 60 shillings; but since the supply needed would come from B, a supply of 2 quarters, it would fall again to 60 shillings; for while B produces at 30 shillings per quarter, it sells at 60 shillings, since its supply is only just sufficient to meet the demand. A rent is thus formed for B which comes initially to 60 shillings, and similarly for C and D; still on the assumption that even though they supply at 20 shillings and 15 shillings per quarter respectively, the market price remains 60 shillings, since the supply of the one quarter that A provides is needed to satisfy the total demand. In this case the rise in demand above the supply that was satisfied first by A, and then by A and B, would not have meant that B, C and D could successively be cultivated, but simply that the overall cultivated area would be expanded, and it might so happen that the more fertile lands came under cultivation only later.

In the first sequence, rents rise with the increase in price and the profit rate declines. This decline could be completely or partially offset by countervailing circumstances, a point which we shall go into in more detail later. It should not be forgotten that the general rate of profit is not uniformly determined by the surplus-value in *all* spheres of production. It is not agricultural profit that determines industrial, but vice versa. But more on this later, too.

In the second sequence, the profit rate on the capital invested remains the same. The mass of profit is represented by less corn, but the relative price of corn compared with other commodities will have risen. It is just that the increase in profit, where there is such an increase, instead of flowing into the pockets of the industrialist farmers as a growing profit, separates off from profit in the form of rent. The price of corn, however, remains stationary under the assumption made here.

The development and growth of differential rent remains the same, both when prices remain the same and when they rise, and both when there is a steady progression from worse soil to better and when there is a steady regression from better soil to worse.

We formerly assumed (1) that the price rises in the one sequence, and remains stationary in the other; and (2) that there is a steady progression from better soil to worse, or conversely from worse soil to better.

But let us assume that the demand for grain rises from the original 10 qrs to 17 qrs; and further that the worst soil, A, is displaced by another soil which yields $1\frac{1}{3}$ qrs for a production cost of 60 shillings (50s. costs plus 10s. representing a profit of 20 per cent), its production price per qr thus being 45s.; or else that the old soil A has been improved as a result of rational cultivation, or has been cultivated more productively at constant costs, e.g. by the introduction of clover, etc., so that its product rises to $1\frac{1}{2}$ qrs for the same advance of capital. Let us further assume that soil types B, C and D supply the same product afterwards as before, but that new types of soil come into cultivation: A' with a fertility between A and B, as well as B' and B" with fertilities between B and C. In this case, the following phenomena are met with.

Firstly, the production price of a quarter of wheat, or its governing market price, would fall from 60s. to 45s., or by 25 per cent.

Secondly, there would be at the same time a progression both from more fertile to less fertile soil and from less fertile soil to more fertile. Soil A' is more fertile than A, but less fertile than B, C and D that were cultivated previously; and B', B" are more fertile than A, A' and B but less fertile than C and D. The sequence would thus take on a criss-cross pattern. The progression would not be towards soil that was absolutely less fertile compared with the formerly most fertile soil types C and D; on the other hand it would not be to absolutely more fertile soil, but simply to soil that was relatively more fertile compared with the previously least fertile A, or A and B.

Thirdly, the rent on B would fall, and similarly the rent on C and D, but the total rental in corn would have risen from 6 qrs to $7\frac{2}{3}$ qrs. The amount of cultivated and rent-bearing land would have increased, and the total product would increase from 10 qrs to 17. Profit, if it remained the same for A, would have risen when expressed in corn; but the profit rate itself might have risen, since

Table II

Type of soil	Product		Capital invested	Profit		Rent		Price of production per quarter
	Quarters	Shillings		Quarters	Shillings	Quarters	Shillings	
A	$1\frac{1}{3}$	60	50	$\frac{2}{9}$	10	—	—	45s.
A'	$1\frac{2}{3}$	75	50	$\frac{5}{9}$	25	$\frac{1}{3}$	15	36s.
B	2	90	50	$\frac{8}{9}$	40	$\frac{2}{3}$	30	30s.
B'	$2\frac{1}{3}$	105	50	$1\frac{2}{9}$	55	1	45	$25\frac{5}{7}$s.
B"	$2\frac{2}{3}$	120	50	$1\frac{5}{9}$	70	$1\frac{1}{3}$	60	$22\frac{1}{2}$s.
C	3	135	50	$1\frac{8}{9}$	85	$1\frac{2}{3}$	75	20s.
D	4	180	50	$2\frac{8}{9}$	130	$2\frac{2}{3}$	120	15s.
Total	17					$7\frac{2}{3}$	345	

relative surplus-value has done so. In this case, wages and thus the outlay on variable capital would have fallen, on account of the cheapening of the means of subsistence, and so too therefore would the total outlay. The total rental in money would have fallen from 360s. to 345s.

We can now draw up the new sequence shown in Table II.

Finally, if only the soil types A, B, C and D are cultivated, as before, but their productivity has risen in such a way that A produces 2 qrs instead of 1; B, 4 qrs instead of 2; C, 7 qrs instead of 3; and D, 10 qrs instead of 4, so that the same causes have operated differently on the different soil types, the total production will have risen from 10 qrs to 23. If we assume that the demand has absorbed these 23 qrs as a result of a rise in population and a fall in price, we arrive at the following result:

Table III

Type of soil	Product		Capital invested	Price of production per quarter	Profit		Rent	
	Quarters	Shillings			Quarters	Shillings	Quarters	Shillings
A	2	60	50	30	$\frac{1}{3}$	10	0	0
B	4	120	50	15	$2\frac{1}{3}$	70	2	60
C	7	210	50	$8\frac{4}{7}$	$5\frac{1}{3}$	160	5	150
D	10	300	50	6	$8\frac{1}{3}$	250	8	240
Total	23						15	450

The numerical ratios are as arbitrary here as in all the other tables, but the assumptions are completely reasonable.

The first and major assumption is that the improvement in agriculture has differing effects on different types of soil and in this case has a greater effect on the better soil types C and D than on A and B. Experience shows that this is the general rule, even if the opposite case is also possible. If the improvement had a greater effect on the worse soils than on the better, the rent on the latter would fall instead of rising. With the absolute growth in fertility of all types of soil, the table also presupposes a growth in the higher relative fertility of the better soil types C and D, hence a growth in the difference in products from the same capital investment and a rise in differential rent.

The second assumption is that total demand keeps pace with the growing total product. *Firstly*, it is not necessary to consider the growth as happening suddenly; series III can be considered as arising gradually. *Secondly*, it is wrong to maintain that the consumption of necessary means of subsistence does not grow when these become cheaper. The abolition of the Corn Laws in England (see Newman)* has proved the opposite, and the contrary conception arose only through the fact that major sudden variations in the harvest, themselves due simply to the weather, produce a sudden disproportionate rise or fall in corn prices. If in this case the sudden and short-lived cheapening does not last long enough to exert its full effect in expanding consumption, the opposite is the case when the fall in price results from a fall in the governing production price itself and is thus of longer duration. *Thirdly*, part of the grain can be consumed in the form of spirits or beer. And the growth in consumption of these two articles is in no way confined within narrow limits. *Fourthly*, the matter depends partly on population growth, while the country may also be a corn-exporting one, as England still was until past the middle of the eighteenth century, so that the demand is not governed by the limits of national consumption alone. *Finally*, the increase and cheapening of wheat production may make wheat into the main staple foodstuff of the mass of the people instead of rye or oats, which already leads to a growth in the market for wheat; the reverse case may arise with a declining product and increasing price. – On these assumptions, therefore, and given the figures we supposed, series III gives the result that the price per quarter falls from 60s. to 30s., i.e. by 50 per cent, while production grows from 10 qrs to 23, compared with sequence I, i.e. by 130 per cent; the rent on soil B remains the same, while on soil C it rises by 25 per cent and on D by 33¼ per cent, the total rental thus rising from £18 to £22½, i.e. by 25 per cent.

The above three tables, in which series I should be taken twice, rising from A to D and falling from D to A, and which may be interpreted either as representing distinctions within a given state of society (e.g. alongside one another in three different countries) or as succeeding one another at various points in the development of the same country, give the following results.

(1) The sequence, when complete, always appears as a decreasing one, whatever the course of its formation might have been;

* F. W. Newman, *Lectures on Political Economy*, London, 1851, p. 158.

for in considering rents, one will always first proceed from the soil that bears the maximum rent and only come last to that which yields no rent.

(2) The production price of the worst soil that yields no rent is always the governing market price, although, considering Table I, where it is taken as an increasing sequence, this production price would remain stationary only if ever better land were cultivated. In this case, the price of the corn produced on the best soil is the governing one, in so far as the extent to which soil A remains the price-governing soil depends on the quantity produced on the best soil. If B, C and D produce more than is demanded, A ceases to govern. Storch has a vague idea of this when he makes the best type of soil the governing type.* In this way, American grain prices govern English ones.

(3) The differential rent arises from the difference in the natural fertility of soil types that is given for the level of agriculture found in existence at the time (leaving aside here the location), i.e. it arises from the limited extent of the best lands and from the fact that the same capital has to be applied to unequal types of soil, which thus yield unequal products for the same capital.

(4) The existence of a differential rent and a graduated differential rent can be based just as well on a declining scale, in a progression from better soil to worse, as on an ascending scale, from worse soil to better; or it can arise in an alternating criss-cross pattern. (The former case may be formed by a progression either from D to A or from A to D. The latter involves both kinds of movement.)

(5) According to its mode of formation, differential rent can develop along with a stationary, rising or falling price of the agricultural product. In the case of a falling price, the total production and the total rental may rise, so that rent is formed on what was previously non-rent-bearing land, even though the worst soil A has been displaced by better, or has itself been improved, and even though the rent on other better types of soil, and even on the best types, falls (Table II); this process can also be linked with a fall in the total rental (in money). Finally, in the case of falling prices which result from a general improvement in cultivation, so that both the product of the worst soil and its price fall, rent on a portion of the better types of soil may remain the same or fall,

* Henri Storch, *Cours d'économie politique* . . ., Vol. 2, St Petersburg, 1815 pp. 78–9. (See also *Theories of Surplus-Value*, Part II, pp. 99 and 293.)

while rising on the best types of soil. The differential rent on any soil, moreover, compared with the worst soil, depends on the price of wheat, per quarter for example, if the difference in the quantity produced is given. But when the price is given, it depends on the difference in the amount produced, and in the case of an increasing absolute fertility of all soil that of the better types of soil rises relatively more than that of the worse soils, so that the size of this difference also grows. Given a price of 60s., therefore (Table I), the rent on D is determined by its differential product vis-à-vis A, i.e. by the excess of 3 qrs; the rent is therefore $3 \times 60 = 180s$. In Table III, however, where the price is 30s., it is determined by the amount of D's excess product over A, $= 8$ qrs; but $8 \times 30 = 240s$.

In this way we can abandon the erroneous conception of differential rent which still prevailed with West, Malthus and Ricardo* and which assumed a necessary progression to ever worse soil, or an ever declining agricultural fertility. As we have seen, differential rent can arise with a progression to ever better soil; it can arise if a better soil takes the lowest place instead of that which was formerly the worst; it can be linked with a steady advance in agriculture. Its only precondition is the inequality of types of soil. In so far as the development of productivity is involved, it assumes that the rise in the absolute fertility of the total acreage does not abolish this inequality, but that it either increases it, leaves it stationary or simply reduces it.

From the beginning to the middle of the eighteenth century, England saw a steady fall in grain prices, despite the falling price of gold and silver, alongside a simultaneous growth in rents (taking the period as a whole), in the total rental, in the extent of land cultivated, in agricultural production and in population. This corresponds to Table I, combined with Table II in an upward direction, but in such a way that the worst soil A is either improved or taken out of cereal cultivation; which however does not mean it is not used for other agricultural or industrial purposes.

From the beginning of the nineteenth century (this date must be indicated more precisely) until 1815, a continuous rise in grain prices, with a steady growth in rent, rental, the extent of land

* Edward West, *Essay on the Application of Capital to Land* . . ., London, 1815; T. R. Malthus, *Principles of Political Economy* . . ., 2nd edn, London, 1836; and *An Inquiry into the Nature and Progress of Rent* . . ., London, 1815; Ricardo, *Principles*, Chapter II.

cultivated, agricultural production and population. This corresponds to Table I in a downward direction. (Reference to be made here to the cultivation of worse lands at that time.)

In the time of Petty and Davenant, complaints of country people and landowners about improvements and ploughing up of commons; fall in rents on better lands, rise in the total rental by extension of rent-bearing land.

(Further references to be given on these three points; similarly on the difference in fertility between different sections of cultivated land in one country.)

In connection with differential rent in general, it should be noted that the market value is always above the total production price for the overall quantity produced. Let us take Table I for instance. The total product of 10 qrs is sold for 600s., since the market price is determined by the production price of A, which comes to 60s. per qr. The actual production price, however, is:

A	1 qr $=$ 60s.	1 qr $=$ 60s.
B	2 qrs $=$ 60s.	1 qr $=$ 30s.
C	3 qrs $=$ 60s.	1 qr $=$ 20s.
D	4 qrs $=$ 60s.	1 qr $=$ 15s.
	10 qrs $=$ 240s.	1 qr $=$ 24s.
		Average

The real production price of the 10 qrs is 240s.; they are sold for 600s., 250 per cent too much. The real average price for 1 qr is 24s.; the market price 60s., similarly 250 per cent too much.

This is determination by a market value brought about by competition on the basis of the capitalist mode of production; it is competition that produces a false social value. This results from the law of market value to which agricultural products are subjected. The determination of the market value of products, i.e. also of products of the soil, is a social act, even if performed by society unconsciously and unintentionally, and it is based necessarily on the exchange-value of the product and not on the soil and the differences in its fertility. If we imagine that the capitalist form of society has been abolished and that society has been organized as a conscious association working according to a plan, the 10 qrs represent a quantity of autonomous labour-time equal to that contained in 240s. Society would therefore not purchase this product at $2\frac{1}{2}$ times the actual labour-time contained in it; the basis for a class of landowners would thereby disappear. This would have the same effect as a cheapening of the product to the same amount by foreign imports. Correct as it is to say that – keeping to the present mode of production, but assuming that differential rent accrued to the state – the prices of agricultural products would remain the same, if other factors did so too, it is still wrong to say that the value of these products would remain the same if capitalist production were replaced by association. The fact that commodities of the same kind have an identical market price is the way in which the social character of value is realized on the basis of the capitalist mode of production, and in general of production depending on commodity exchange between *individuals*. Where society, considered as a consumer, pays too much for agricultural products, this is a minus for the realization of its labour-time in agricultural production, but it forms a plus for one portion of society, the landowners.

A second circumstance, important for what will be presented in the next chapter as differential rent II, is as follows.

It is not only the rent per acre or per hectare that is involved here, or in general the distinction between production price and market price, or between individual and general production price per acre; what is also important is how many acres of each type of soil are under cultivation. Here the importance of this has a direct bearing only on the size of the rental, i.e. the total rent for the whole cultivated area; though it serves for us at the same time as a transition to our discussion of a rise in the *rate of rent*, even when prices do not rise, or the differences in the relative fertility of the soil types do not rise when prices fall. We had earlier:

Table I

Type of soil	Acres	Price of production	Product	Rent in grain	Rent in money
A	1	£3	1 qr	0	0
B	1	£3	2 qrs	1 qr	£3
C	1	£3	3 qrs	2 qrs	£6
D	1	£3	4 qrs	3 qrs	£9
Total	4 acres		10 qrs	6 qrs	£18

If we now assume that the number of acres under cultivation in each class doubles, we get:

Table Ia

Type of soil	Acres	Price of production	Product	Rent in grain	Rent in money
A	2	£6	2 qrs	0	0
B	2	£6	4 qrs	2 qrs	£6
C	2	£6	6 qrs	4 qrs	£12
D	2	£6	8 qrs	6 qrs	£18
Total	8 acres		20 qrs	12 qrs	£36

We shall now take two further cases, the first being one in which production expands on the two inferior soil types, as follows:

Table Ib

Type of soil	Acres	Price of production		Product	Rent in grain	Rent in money
		Per acre	Total			
A	4	£3	£12	4 qrs	0	0
B	4	£3	£12	8 qrs	4 qrs	£12
C	2	£3	£6	6 qrs	4 qrs	£12
D	2	£3	£6	8 qrs	6 qrs	£18
Total	12 acres		£36	26 qrs	14 qrs	£42

and finally an uneven expansion of production and the cultivated area over all four classes of soil:

Table Ic

Type of soil	Acres	Price of production		Product	Rent in grain	Rent in money
		Per acre	Total			
A	1	£3	£3	1 qr	0	0
B	2	£3	£6	4 qrs	2 qrs	£6
C	5	£3	£15	15 qrs	10 qrs	£30
D	4	£3	£12	16 qrs	12 qrs	£36
Total	12 acres		£36	36 qrs	24 qrs	£72

First of all, in all these cases I, Ia, Ib, Ic, the rent per acre remains the same; for the product of the same quantity of capital on each acre of the same type of soil is in fact unchanged. We simply assume what is the case in any country at a particular point in time, i.e. that the various types of soil share the total cultivated area in a definite ratio; and what is always the case in two countries compared together, or in the same country at different points in time, i.e. that the ratio in which the total cultivated area is divided between them changes.

If we compare Ia with Ib, we see that when the cultivation of land in all four classes grows in the same proportion, a doubling of the number of acres in cultivation doubles the total production and similarly the corn and money rent.

If we now compare Ib and Ic successively with I, in both cases we have a tripling of the area under cultivation. In both cases this rises from 4 acres to 12, but in Ib, classes A and B take the major share in the growth, A bearing no rent and B the smallest differential rent; i.e. of the 8 acres newly cultivated, 3 each fall into classes A and B, a total of 6, while only 1 each, a total of 2, fall into C and D. In other words, three-quarters of the increase takes place on A and B and only one-quarter on C and D. On this assumption, the tripling of the expanse under cultivation in Ib compared with I does not involve a tripling of the product, which rises not from 10 to 30, but only to 26. On the other hand, since a substantial part of the growth takes place on A, which does not yield any rent, and of the growth on the better lands the major part is on class B, the corn rent therefore rises only from 6 qrs to 14, and the money rent from £18 to £42.

If we instead compare Ic with I, in which case the non-rent-paying land does not increase its extent at all, while land yielding the minimal rent exhibits only a weak increase, the bulk of the growth accruing to C and D, we find that with the tripling of the cultivated area production has risen from 10 qrs to 36, i.e. by more than three times; the corn rent from 6 qrs to 24, or four times; and the money rent similarly from £18 to £72.

In all these cases, the price of the agricultural product remains stationary, in the nature of things; in each case the total rental grows with the expansion of cultivation, as long as this does not take place exclusively on the worst lands, which pay no rent. But this growth varies. To the extent that the expansion takes place on the better types of soil, so that the quantity produced does not just grow in proportion to the expansion of the land cultivated, but more steeply, the corn and money rent grows. To the extent that the worst soil and the adjacent categories take the principal share of the increase (which assumes that the worst soil is a constant category), the total rental does not rise in proportion to the expansion of cultivation. Thus, given two countries in which land A, which yields no rent, is of the same quality, the rental stands in inverse proportion to the aliquot part of the total cultivated area composed by the worst and the less good soil types, and hence also in inverse proportion to the quantities produced by identical capital investments on equal areas. The proportion between the amount of the worst cultivated soil and that of the better in the total area of a country thus has an effect on the total rental which is opposite to the effect that the relation between the quality of the worst cultivated soil and that of the better and best has on the rent per acre, and hence, with other circumstances remaining the same, also on the rental. The confusion between these two aspects has given rise to all kinds of confused objections against differential rent.

But the most important point is this. Even though, on our assumptions, the ratios between rents on the various types of soil, reckoned on a per acre basis, remain the same, and so too therefore does the rate of rent taken with regard to the capital laid out on each acre, the following phenomenon presents itself. If we compare Ia with I – the case in which the acreage cultivated increases proportionately, along with the capital invested in it – we find that, just as the total production has grown in proportion to the increased land area cultivated, i.e. both have doubled, so the same is the case with the rental. It has risen from £18 to £36, just as the number of acres has risen from 4 to 8.

If we take the total area of 4 acres, the overall rental comes to £18, i.e. an average rent, taking into account also the soil that bears no rent, of £4½. A landowner who owned the entire 4 acres could calculate it in this way, for example, and that is how the average rent for an entire country is statistically reckoned. The total rental of £18 is produced by applying a capital of £10. The ratio between these two figures is what we call the rate of rent: in this case 180 per cent.

The same rate of rent occurs in Ia, where 8 acres are tilled instead of 4, but where all types of soil have shared in the increase in the same proportion. The total rental of £36, with 8 acres and

£20 of invested capital, produces an average rent of £4½ per acre and a rate of rent of 180 per cent.

If we consider Ib, on the other hand, where the increase took place principally on the two inferior soil types, we have a rent of £42 for 12 acres, i.e. an average rent of £3½ per acre. The total capital laid out is £30, i.e. a rate of rent of 140 per cent. The average rent per acre is thus £1 less and the rate of rent has fallen from 180 per cent to 140 per cent. With a growth in the total rental from £18 to £42, there is thus a fall in the average rent, both per acre and reckoned on the capital invested; similarly, production has grown, but not proportionately. This takes place even though the rent on all soil types remains the same, whether reckoned per acre or on the capital invested. It takes place because three-quarters of the increase occurs on soil A, which bears no rent, and soil B, which bears only the minimal rent.

If the total expansion in case Ib had taken place simply on soil A, we would have 9 acres of A, 1 of B, 1 of C and 1 of D. The total rental would still be £18, giving an average rent per acre on these 12 acres of £1½; while £18 rent on a capital of £30 laid out gives a rate of rent of 60 per cent. The average rent would have sharply declined, whether reckoned per acre or on the capital applied, while the total rental would not have grown.

Let us finally compare Ic with I and Ib. Compared with I, the acreage has tripled, and so has the capital laid out. The total rental is £72 for 12 acres, i.e. £6 per acre as against £4½ per acre in case I. The rate of rent on the capital laid out (£72: £30) is 240 per cent instead of 180 per cent. The total product has risen from 10 qrs to 36.

Compared with Ib, where the total acreage under cultivation, the capital applied and the differences between the types of soil tilled all remain the same, though differently distributed, the product is 36 qrs instead of 26 qrs, the average rent per acre £6 instead of £3½, and the rate of rent on an equal total capital advanced is 240 per cent instead of 140 per cent.

Irrespective of whether the different conditions in Tables Ia, Ib and Ic are taken as existing simultaneously alongside one another in different countries, or as successive situations in the same country, and on the following assumptions – a stationary price of grain, because the yield on the worst, non-rent-bearing land remains the same; the same differences in fertility between the various categories of soil cultivated; an equal respective product therefore from equal capital investment on equal aliquot parts (acres) of the area cultivated in each class of soil; and finally a constant ratio between the rent per acre on each type of soil and an equal rate of rent on the capital invested in each piece of land of the same kind – on these assumptions, we get the following results. *Firstly,* the rental always grows with an expansion of the cultivated area and therefore with an increased capital investment, except for the case when the entire growth falls on the non-rent-bearing soil. *Secondly,* both the average rent per acre (total rental divided by total number of acres tilled) and the average rate of rent (total rental divided by the total capital invested) may vary very significantly; and even if both move in the same direction, they may still move in different ratios. If we leave aside the case where the growth takes place simply on the non-rent-bearing soil A, we find that the average rent per acre and the average rate of rent on the capital invested in agriculture depend on the proportionate shares that the various classes of soil make up within the total cultivated area; or, what comes to the same thing, they depend on the way in which the total capital applied is distributed over the soil types of different fertility. Whether much land is tilled or only a little, so that the total rental is larger or smaller (except for the case where the growth is solely on A), the average rent per acre or the average rate of rent on the capital applied remains the same as long as the proportions in which the different types of soil participate in the total acreage remain constant. Despite a rise in the total rental as cultivation extends and more capital is invested, and even a major rise, the average rent per acre and the average rate of rent on capital fall, if the expansion of the rent-free lands, and those that only bear a small differential rent, is steeper than that of the better land, which yields a higher rent. Conversely, therefore, the average rent per acre and the average rate of rent on capital rises to the extent that the better lands constitute a relatively larger share of the total area, and hence relatively more capital investment falls on them.

If we thus consider the average rent per acre or per hectare of the total cultivated land, which is what is generally done in statistical works, since either different countries are compared at the same time or different periods in the history of the same country, we see that the average level of rent per acre, and hence also the total rental, corresponds to a certain extent (without being identical: in fact the proportion tends to increase) not to the relative but to the absolute fertility of agriculture in a country, i.e. to the quantity of products that are supplied on average by a given area. For the greater the share of the total area constituted by the better types of soil, the greater is the volume of products from the same capital investment and the same land area; and the greater, too, is the average rent per acre. And vice versa. Thus rent appears as determined not by the ratio of differential fertility but rather by the absolute fertility, which would refute the law of differential rent. This is why certain phenomena are denied, or else the attempt is made to explain them in terms of non-existent distinctions in average grain prices and the differential fertilities of lands under cultivation, phenomena whose only basis is that the proportion of the total rental, either to the total area of land cultivated or to the total capital invested in the soil – given the same fertility for the non-rent-bearing soil and hence equal production prices, and given the same differences between the various soil types – is not determined only by the rent per acre or by the rate of rent on capital but just as much by the relative proportion of each soil type in the total acreage tilled; or, what comes to the same thing, by the distribution of the total capital applied among the various types of soil. Up till now, this factor has been completely overlooked, in a quite striking fashion. It still shows, and this is important for the further course of our investigation, that the relative level of average rents per acre, and the average rate of rent or the ratio of the total rental to the total capital invested in the soil, may rise or fall even though prices, the difference in fertility of the lands under cultivation and the rent per acre or rate of rent for the capital invested per acre in each actual rent-bearing soil category, or for all actually rent-bearing capital, all remain the same, simply by an expansion of the cultivated area.

*

The following additional points have still to be made, in relation to the first form of differential rent, although they also apply in part to the second form.

Firstly. We have seen how the average rent per acre or the average rate of rent on capital may rise with the extension of cultivation, given stationary prices and an unchanged differential fertility of the lands tilled. As soon as all the land in a country is appropriated, and capital investment on the land, agriculture and population have all reached a certain level – factors that are all taken for granted once the capitalist mode of production becomes dominant and takes control of agriculture too – the price of the untilled land of various qualities (assuming only differential rent) is determined by the price of land of equivalent quality and location that is tilled. The price is the same – after deducting the additional cost of ploughing up new land – even though this land does not bear any rent. The price of land is of course nothing more than capitalized rent. But even in the case of cultivated lands, it is only future rents that are paid for in their price, e.g. twenty years' rent is paid at one stroke if the determining interest rate is 5 per cent. As soon as land is sold, it is sold as rent-bearing, and the prospective character of the rent (which is considered here as the fruit of the soil, something that it is only in surface appearance) does not distinguish the uncultivated land from the cultivated. The price of untilled land, like its rent, which is what this contracted formula represents, is pure illusion as long as this land is not actually used. But it is determined *a priori* in this way, and is realized as soon as buyers are found. Thus if the actual average rent in a country is determined by its actual average annual rental and the ratio of this rental to the total cultivated area, the price of the untilled portion is determined by the price of the tilled and is therefore simply a reflection of the capital investment in the tilled lands, and its results there. Since, with the exception of the worst land, all types of soil bear rent (and this rent, as we shall go on to see in the case of differential rent II, rises with the amount of capital and the corresponding intensity of cultivation), a nominal price is thereby formed for the untilled portions of land, so that these too become a commodity, a source of wealth for their owner. This explains at the same time why the price of land rises for the entire area, even for untilled land. (Opdyke.)* Land speculation, e.g. in the United States, depends on this reflection which capital and labour cast on untilled land.

Secondly. All progress in the extension of cultivation takes place either towards worse soil or on the various given types of soil in different proportions, according to how these are to be found. Progression towards worse soil, of course, is never from free choice; taking the capitalist mode of production as given, it can only be the result of rising prices, and in any mode of production only the result of necessity. But this is not absolutely the case.

* *A Treatise on Political Economy*, New York, 1851.

Bad soil may be relatively preferred to better on account of its location, which is decisive for every extension of cultivation in new countries; but also because even though the soil formation in a certain region may be fertile on the whole, better and worse soil may be closely intermingled in some places, so that the inferior soil has to be cultivated simply because of its proximity to the better. If the worse soil forms enclaves within the better, the better soil gives it the advantage of location as against more fertile land that is not yet part of the cultivated area or about to become so.

The state of Michigan, for example, was one of the first Western states to export corn. Its soil on the whole is poor. But its proximity to the state of New York and its water routes via the Great Lakes and the Erie Canal gave it at first an initial advantage over the states further west, though these were more fertile by nature. The example of this state, in comparison with the state of New York, also shows us the transition from better soil to worse. The soil of New York state, and particularly its western part, is of uneven fertility, particularly for wheat cultivation. Rapacious cultivation made this fertile soil infertile, and then the Michigan soil appeared more fertile.

'In 1838, wheaten flour was shipped at Buffalo for the West; and the wheat-region of New York, with that of Upper Canada, were the main sources of its supply. Now after only twelve years, an enormous supply of wheat and flour is brought from the West, along Lake Erie, and shipped upon the Erie Canal for the East, at Buffalo and the adjoining port of Blackrock . . . The effect of these large arrivals from the Western States – which were unnaturally stimulated during the years of European famine . . . has been to render wheat less valuable in western New York, to make the wheat culture less remunerative, and to turn the attention of the New York farmers more to grazing and dairy husbandry, fruit culture, and other branches of rural economy, in which they think the North-West will be unable so directly to compete with them' (J. W. Johnston, *Notes on North America*, London, 1851, I, pp. 220–23).

Thirdly. It is false to assume that the soil in those colonies and other new countries that can export corn at cheaper prices is therefore necessarily of greater natural fertility. In this case grain is not only sold below its value, but also below its price of production, i.e. below the production price determined by the average rate of profit in the older countries.

If, as Johnston says (p. 223), we 'are accustomed to attach the idea of great natural productiveness and of boundless tracts of rich land, to those new States from which come the large supplies of wheat that are annually poured into the port of Buffalo', this depends first of all on economic conditions. The entire population of a state such as this, e.g. Michigan, begins by being almost exclusively engaged in agriculture, and particularly in the mass crops which alone can be exchanged for industrial goods and tropical products. Their entire surplus product thus takes the shape of corn. This fundamentally distinguishes the colonial states founded on the basis of the modern world market from those of earlier times, and particularly those of antiquity. They receive ready-made, through the world market, products that they would otherwise have to produce themselves, such as clothing, tools, etc. It is only on this basis that the Southern states of the Union could make cotton into their principal product. It is the division of labour on the world market that permits them this. Thus if, considering their newness and their relatively small population, they *appear* to produce a very large surplus product, this is not due to the fertility of their soil or to the productiveness of their labour, but rather to the one-sided form of this labour and thus of the surplus product in which it is expressed.

Besides, relatively less fertile soil which is tilled for the first time and has never been touched by agriculture before has accumulated so much in the way of easily assimilated plant nutrients, at least in its top layers, that it will yield harvests for a quite long period without any fertilizer – as long as the climatic conditions are not completely unfavourable – even on quite superficial tilling. In the Western prairies, a further factor is that scarcely any clearing costs are required, since nature has made them already arable.[33][a] In less fertile regions of this kind the surplus comes not from the high fertility of the soil, i.e. from the yield per acre, but rather

33[a]. It is precisely the recent sudden increase of cultivation of these prairie or steppe regions that has proved so ridiculous the renowned Malthusian thesis that 'population presses on the means of subsistence', producing in contrast to this the agrarian complaint according to which German agriculture and with it everything else in Germany will collapse unless the means of subsistence which are pressing on the population are not forcibly kept away from them. The cultivation of these steppes, prairies, pampas, llanos, etc. is however only in its very beginnings; its revolutionary effect on European agriculture will make itself felt far more strongly in the future than it has done so far. – F. E.

from the great acreage that can be cultivated superficially, since this land costs the tiller nothing, or at least only an infinitesimal amount compared with the older countries. This is true for example where share-cropping is practised, as in parts of New York, Michigan, Canada, etc. A family tills, say, 100 acres superficially, and even though the product per acre is not large, the product of 100 acres provides a sizable surplus for sale. On top of this, cattle, etc. can be grazed almost cost-free on natural pasture, without any need for artificial meadows. The decisive thing here is not the quality of the soil but the quantity. The possibility of this superficial cultivation is of course more or less rapidly exhausted in inverse proportion to the fertility of the new soil and in direct proportion to the export of its product. 'And yet such a country will give excellent crops, even of wheat, and will supply to those who skim the first cream off the country, a large surplus of this grain to send to market' (op. cit., p. 225).

In countries where agriculture is older, any such kind of extensive farming is made impossible by the property relations, the price of uncultivated land as determined by that of cultivated, etc.

We can see from the following example that this does not mean, as Ricardo imagines, that this land is necessarily very fertile, nor that only soil types of the same fertility are cultivated. In the state of Michigan, 465,900 acres were sown to wheat in 1848, to produce 4,739,300 bushels or an average of $10\frac{1}{4}$ bushels per acre; this is less than 9 bushels per acre after deducting the seed-corn. Out of twenty-nine counties in the state, two produced an average of 7 bushels; three an average of 8, two 9, seven 10, six 11, three 12, four 13, a single county 16 bushels, and one 18 bushels per acre (op. cit., p. 225).

As far as practical agriculture is concerned, higher fertility of the soil is the same thing as a greater possibility of immediately exploiting its fertility. Immediate exploitation may be more possible with a naturally poor soil than with a naturally rich one; and this is the kind of soil which a colonist will take up first, and must take up when capital is scarce.

Finally. The extension of cultivation to larger areas (apart from the case just considered, in which resort has to be had to a worse soil than that formerly tilled), on the various soil types from A to D, for example, and therefore the tilling of greater areas of B and C, in no way depends on a previous rise in grain prices, any more than the anticipatory annual expansion of a cotton spinning-mill, for instance, depends on a continuous rise in the price of yarn. Even though a major rise or fall in market price does have an effect on the scale of production, there is still, apart from this – and even given average prices, whose level neither inhibits production nor gives it an exceptional boost – the same perpetual relative overproduction in agriculture which is inherently identical with accumulation and which in the case of other modes of production is directly caused by the increase in population, and in the colonies by a steady immigration. Demand steadily grows, and with this prospect new capital is continuously invested in new land; even though this happens for different crops and according to particular circumstances. The formation of new capitals brings this about automatically. But as far as the individual capitalist is concerned, he measures the scale of his production by the capital he has available, to the extent that he can still control it himself. His intention is to take as big a share of the market as possible. If there is overproduction, he blames it on his competitors, not on himself. The individual capitalist can extend his production just as much by appropriating a greater aliquot share of the given market as by expanding this market itself.

Chapter 40: The Second Form of Differential Rent (Differential Rent II)

Up till now we have considered differential rent only as the result of the varying productivity of equal capital investments on equal land areas of different fertility, so that differential rent was determined by the difference between the yield of capital invested on the worst, non-rent-bearing land, and that of capital invested on better land. In this case we had capital investments in different land areas alongside one another, so that each new investment of capital corresponded to a more extensive cultivation and an expansion of the cultivated area. Ultimately, however, differential rent as such was simply the result of the varying productivity of equal capitals when invested on the land. Can it make a difference, then, whether sums of capital are invested successively in time on the same piece of land with varying productivity, or invested alongside one another on different pieces of land, as long as we assume that the results are the same?

It cannot be denied, first of all, that as far as the formation of surplus profit is concerned, it is all the same whether [i] £3 in production costs spent on an acre of land A yields 1 qr, so that £3 is the production price of 1 qr and its governing market price, while on an acre of land B £3 spent on production costs yields 2 qrs, and therefore a surplus profit of £3, £3 on an acre of land C 3 qrs and a surplus profit of £6, and £3 on an acre of land D 4 qrs and a surplus profit of £9; or whether [ii] the same result is obtained by the application of this £12 in production costs or £10 of capital* in the same sequence to one and the same acre and giving the same results. In each case there is a capital of £10, with successive portions of £2½ being invested, whether these are invested side by side on 4 acres of differing fertility, or successively on one and the same acre, in such a way that, because of the varying product, one

* See above, pp. 800 ff.

of these capitals of £2½ yields no surplus profit, while the other portions give a surplus profit, each in proportion to the difference between its yield and that of the non-rent-bearing investment.

The surplus profits and the varying rates of surplus profit for different portions of capital value are formed in a uniform way in both cases. And rent is nothing but a form of this surplus profit, surplus profit in fact forming its substance. None the less, the second method does give rise to certain difficulties as regards the transformation of surplus profit into rent, this change in form that involves the transfer of surplus profits from the capitalist farmer to the proprietor of the land. Hence the stubborn resistance of the English farmers to any official agricultural statistics. Hence the struggle between them and the landowners when it comes to establishing the actual results of their capital investment. (Morton.) The rent here is fixed when the farms are leased, and the subsequent surplus profits arising from the successive investments of capital accrue to the farmer as long as the tenancy contract lasts. Hence the farmers' battle for long tenancies, and conversely the increase in 'tenancies at will', i.e. at a year's notice, given the superior power of the landlord.

It is clear from the start, therefore, that even if it makes no difference as far as the law of surplus profit formation is concerned whether equal capitals are invested alongside each other on equal-sized tracts of land with unequal results or whether they are invested successively in this way on the same piece of land, it still makes a significant difference for the transformation of surplus profit into ground-rent. In the latter case, the limits of this transformation are both narrower and unstable. Hence in countries where agriculture is intensive (and what this means economically speaking is simply the concentration of capital on the same piece of land instead of its distribution over adjacent tracts) the job of assessor of rents, as Morton explains it in his *Resources of Estates*, comes to be a very important, complicated and difficult profession. In the case of more permanent improvements, the artificially inflated differential fertility of the land is its new natural fertility when the tenancy contract expires, and hence the assessment of rents is the assessment of varying fertility between types of land in general. In so far as the formation of surplus profit is determined on the other hand by the amount of working capital, the level of rent for a working capital of given size is added to the average rent for the land, so as to ensure that the new farmer has sufficient capital to continue cultivation in the same intensive manner.

*

In considering differential rent II, the following points have yet to be stressed:

Firstly. Its basis and point of departure, not only historically but as far as concerns its movement at any given point in time, is differential rent I, i.e. the simultaneous cultivation alongside one another of lands of different fertility and location, the simultaneous application alongside one another of different components of the total agricultural capital to tracts of land of differing quality.

In a historical perspective, this needs no explanation. In colonies, the colonists need only invest a little capital; the main agencies of production are labour and the soil itself. Each individual family head seeks an independent field of employment for himself and his people to work on, separate from those of his fellow colonists. Given agriculture proper, this must always be the case, even in pre-capitalist modes of production. In the case of sheep-farming, and stock-raising in general as an independent branch of production, there is a more or less communal exploitation of the land, and this exploitation is fundamentally extensive from the outset. The capitalist mode of production develops out of earlier modes of production in which the means of production are either in law or in fact the property of the tiller himself, in other words from the pursuit of agriculture as a kind of handicraft. By the nature of the case, it is only gradually from this starting-point that the means of production become concentrated and transformed into capital as against the immediate producers who are transformed into wage-labourers. The capitalist mode of production first takes its characteristic form here particularly in sheep-farming and stock-raising; but this is not the concentration of capital on a relatively small land area, but rather in production on a larger scale; the saving is on the keeping of horses and other production costs, not by the use of more capital on the same land. It follows from the natural laws of farming, moreover, that given a certain level of agriculture and the corresponding exhaustion of the soil, capital, which in this sense is synonymous with means of production already produced, becomes the decisive element in cultivation. As long as the tilled land forms a relatively small portion in relation to the untilled and the soil's natural resources are not exhausted (as is the case when stock-raising and meat-eating predominate, in the period before the preponderance of agriculture proper and vegetable food), the embryonic new mode of production contrasts with peasant production particularly by the amount of land that is tilled for the account of *one* capitalist, and thus also by the extensive use of capital on a greater area. Thus it must always be borne in mind that differential rent I is the historical basis and starting-point from which development takes place. On the other hand, the movement of differential rent II at any given moment occurs only on an area that in turn forms the variegated basis for differential rent I.

Secondly. In the case of differential rent in form II, the variation in fertility is supplemented by differences in the distribution of capital (and creditworthiness) among the farmers. In manufacture proper, a specific minimal scale of business is soon formed in each branch of industry, and accordingly a minimum capital without which a particular business cannot be successfully conducted. Also formed in each branch of industry is a normal average amount of capital above this minimum, which the great bulk of producers must and do dispose of. Anything over and above this can form extra profit; anything below it does not receive even the average profit. The capitalist mode of production takes hold of agriculture only in a slow and uneven manner, as we can see in the case of England, the classical land of the capitalist mode of production in this sector. In so far as there is no free import of corn, or the volume and consequent effect of this is restricted, the market price is determined by those producers who work on inferior soil, i.e. producers whose conditions of production are less favourable than the average. A large part of the total capital applied in agriculture, and generally at its disposal, is to be found in their hands.

It is true that the peasant, for example, devotes a great deal of labour to his small parcel of land. But this labour is isolated, and deprived of the objective social and material conditions of productivity; it is denuded of them.

The effect of this factor is that the genuinely capitalist farmers are in a position to appropriate a portion of surplus profit; this would disappear, at least as far as the present point is concerned, if the capitalist mode of production were as uniformly developed in agriculture as in manufacture.

Let us start by considering simply the formation of surplus profit in the case of differential rent II, without troubling ourselves yet about the conditions under which this surplus profit can be transformed into ground-rent.

It is then clear that differential rent II is simply a different expression of differential rent I, and the same thing as far as its nature is concerned. The differing fertility of different types of land affects differential rent I only in so far as it means that capitals invested on the land give unequal results or products, either for the same size of capital or when taken proportionately. It can make no difference to this differing fertility or its product, and hence to the formation of differential rent for the more fruitfully invested portions of capital, whether this inequality marks different capitals invested successively on the same piece of land or whether the capitals are invested on several pieces of land of different types. In both cases the land shows differing fertility for the same capital investment, but now the same land does for a capital invested successively in different portions what in differential rent I is done by different kinds of land for different capitals of equal size, each forming part of the total capital.

If the same capital of £10, which in Table I* was invested by different farmers in the form of independent capitals of £2½ on one acre each of the four land types A, B, C and D, were instead to be invested successively on one and the same acre of D, so that the first investment yielded 4 qrs, the second 3 qrs, the third 2 qrs and the last 1 qr (or alternatively in the inverse sequence), the price of £3 per qr for the wheat supplied by the least fruitful portion of the capital would not yield any differential rent, though it would determine the production price as long as it is necessary to supply wheat whose production price is £3. And since we assume capitalist production, so that the price of £3 includes the average profit that any capital of £2½ yields, the three other portions of £2½ each will therefore yield surplus profits, according to the difference of their product [from that of the least fertile land], since this product is sold not at its price of production but rather at the price of production of the least fruitful investment of £2½: an investment that yields no rent and in which the price of the product is governed by the general law of production prices. The formation of surplus profits would be the same as in Table I.

Here we may see once again how differential rent II presupposes differential rent I. The minimum product that a capital of £2½ yields, i.e. what it yields on the worst land, is here taken as 1 qr.

* p. 800 above.

Let us assume, therefore, that the farmer of land type D spends, besides the £2½ that yields him 4 qrs and for which he pays 3 qrs in differential rent, a further £2½ on the same land which only yields him 1 qr, just like the same capital on the worst land A. This would then be a non-rent-bearing capital investment, since he would only obtain the average profit. There would be no surplus profit to transform into rent. On the other hand, however, this declining product of the second capital investment on D would not have any effect on the profit rate. It would be the same as if £2½ were newly invested on a further acre of type A, something that could in no way affect the surplus profit or, accordingly, the differential rent for the land types A, B, C and D. For the farmer, this additional investment of £2½ on D would have been just as advantageous as we assumed the investment of the original £2½ on the acre of D to have been, even though that yielded 4 qrs. Let him make two further capital investments of £2½ each, the first giving him an additional product of 3 qrs, the second an additional product of 2 qrs. A further decline would then have occurred, compared with the yield of the first investment of £2½ on D, which gave 4 qrs, hence a surplus profit of 3 qrs. But this would simply be a decline in the level of surplus profit and would affect neither the average profit nor the governing production price. This would be the case only if the extra production which yields these falling surplus profits made the production of A superfluous and thereby threw acre A out of cultivation. In that case the declining yield of the additional capital investment on acre D would be combined with a fall in the production price, e.g. from £3 to £1½, if acre B became the non-rent-bearing land that governs the market price.

The product of D would now be $4 + 1 + 3 + 2 = 10$ qrs, whereas it was formerly 4 qrs. The price per qr, however, as governed by B, would have fallen to £1½. The difference between D and B would be $10 - 2 = 8$ qrs, which at £1½ per qr $= £12$, whereas the money rent on D was formerly £9. This should be borne in mind. On a per acre basis, the rent level would have risen by 33⅓ per cent, despite the declining rate of surplus profit on the two additional capitals of £2½.

From this we can see the very complicated combinations to which differential rent always gives rise, and particularly when form II is taken together with form I, whereas Ricardo for instance deals with it quite one-sidedly and as something straightforward. We can have, for example, as above, a fall in the governing market price and at the same time a rise in rent on the more fertile lands, so that both the absolute product and the absolute surplus product rise. (In the case of differential rent I in a downward series, the relative surplus product can grow, and hence the rent per acre, even though the absolute surplus product per acre remains constant or even declines.) At the same time, however, the yield of successive capital investments on the same soil declines, even though a major part of these falls on the more fertile lands. From one point of view – as far as the product and the production prices are concerned – the productivity of labour has risen. From another point of view, it has declined, since this is what happens to the rate of surplus profit and the surplus product per acre for the various capital investments on the same land.

Given a declining yield for successive capital investments, differential rent II would necessarily involve an increase in the production price and an absolute decline in productivity only if these capital investments could take place only on the worst land A. If an acre of A yielded 1 qr for a capital investment of £2½, assuming a production price of £3, and with a further investment of £2½, i.e. a total of £5, yielded altogether only 1½ qrs, then the production price of these 1½ qrs would be £6, or £4 per qr. In this case every decrease in productivity consequent on a growing capital investment would be a relative decline in the product per acre, while on the better types of land it was only a decline in the excess surplus product.

By the very nature of the case, however, the development of intensive cultivation, i.e. successive capital investments on the same soil, sees these investments predominantly on the better types of land, or at least to a greater extent. (Here we are not referring to the permanent improvements by which formerly unusable land is transformed into usable.) The declining yield of successive capital investments must therefore act principally in the manner described. The better land is selected because it offers the best prospect that the capital applied to it will bring in a profit; i.e. it contains the greater quantity of the natural elements of fertility, and all that is needed is to put these to use.

When English agriculture became still more intensive, after the repeal of the Corn Laws, a large amount of what was formerly wheat-growing land was turned over to other uses, in particular to pasture for cattle, while those fertile tracts most suitable for wheat were drained and otherwise improved. The capital for wheat-growing was thus concentrated in a narrower area.

In this case – and here all possible surplus rates between the highest surplus profit of the best land and the product of the non-rent-bearing land A involve not just a relative but an absolute increase in the surplus product per acre – the newly formed surplus profit (and potential rent) does not represent a portion of the earlier average profit turned into rent (a portion of the product which formerly represented average profit), but rather additional surplus profit, transformed from that form into rent.

It is only in the case where the demand for corn grows in such a way that the market price rises above the production price of A, so that the surplus product on A, B or any other class of land could only be supplied at a higher price than £3 – it is only in this case that a rise in the production price and the governing market price would be combined with a decline in the product of an additional capital investment on any one of the classes A, B, C or D. In as much as this continued for a prolonged period and did not lead to the cultivation of additional land A (of at least A's quality), with other factors also not bringing a cheaper supply, wages would rise as a result of the higher price of bread, other things being equal, and the profit rate would accordingly fall. It would be a matter of indifference in this case whether the increased demand was satisfied by drawing in worse land than A or by additional capital investment, irrespective of which of the four types of land this took place on. The differential rent would rise in combination with a falling rate of profit.

This single case in which the declining yield of capitals subsequently added to the types of land already under cultivation can subsequently lead to a rise in the price of production, a fall in the profit rate and the formation of increased differential rent – for under these circumstances the differential rent will rise on all types of land, just as if worse land than A now governed the market price – was treated by Ricardo as the only case, the normal case, and he reduced the formation of differential rent II simply to this.

This would also be the case if only type A land was tilled and successive capital investments on it did not involve a proportionate growth in the product.

Here, therefore, differential rent I is completely lost sight of in dealing with differential rent II.

With the exception of this case, where the supply from the types of land tilled is insufficient, so that the market price is permanently above the production price either until new and additional worse land is taken into cultivation or until the total product of the additional capital invested on the various types of land can only be supplied at a higher production price than prevailed before – with the exception of this case, the proportionate decline in the productivity of additional capitals leaves the governing production price and the profit rate unaffected.

Three further cases are then possible:

(a) If the additional capital on any of the land types A, B, C or D yields only the profit rate as determined by the production price of A, no surplus profit would be formed, and so no possible rent; no more than if additional land A had been tilled.

(b) If the additional capital yields a higher product, new surplus product (potential rent) is obviously formed, if the governing price remains the same. But this is not necessarily the case, i.e. not if this additional production throws land A out of cultivation and therefore out of the series of competing land types. The profit rate would rise if this was combined with a fall in wages or if the cheaper product was an element of constant capital. If the additional capital displayed its increased productivity on the best land types C and D, the extent to which the formation of increased surplus profit (and therefore increased rent) was combined with the fall in price and the rise in the profit rate would depend completely on the level of this increased productivity, and the amount of capital newly added. The rate of profit can rise even without a fall in wages, through a cheapening of the elements of constant capital.

(c) If the additional capital investment occurs in combination with declining surplus profits, but in such a way that its product leaves a surplus over the product of the same capital on land A, then under all circumstances, if the increased supply does not force land A out of cultivation, there is a new formation of surplus profits, which may take place on D, C, B and A simultaneously. If on the other hand the worst soil A is driven out of cultivation, the governing production price falls, and whether the surplus profit expressed in money, and hence the differential rent, rises or falls depends on the ratio between the reduced price per quarter and the reduced number of quarters forming the surplus profit. In any case, however, we have here the remarkable phenomenon that the production price can fall together with declining surplus profits, instead of having to rise, as it would seem at first sight.

These additional capital investments with decreasing surplus yields correspond completely to the case in which four new independent capitals of £2½ each are invested on types of land whose fertility lies between A and B, B and C, and C and D, respectively yielding 1½ qrs, 2⅓ qrs, 2⅔ qrs and 3 qrs. Surplus profits and potential rents would be formed on all these types of land for all four additional capitals, even though the rate of surplus profit, compared with that for the same capital investment on better land in each case, had fallen. And it would be all one whether these four capitals were invested on D, etc. or were distributed between D and A.

We come now to a basic distinction between the two forms of differential rent.

Given a constant production price and constant differences, the average rent per acre may rise with the total rental in the case of differential rent I, and so may the average rate of rent on capital. But the average is merely an abstraction. The actual level of rent, per acre or reckoned on capital, remains the same here.

On the same assumptions, however, the level of rent measured per acre may rise, even though the rate of rent, measured on the capital laid out, remains the same.

Assume that production doubles by the investment of £5 on each of A, B, C and D instead of £2½, i.e. a total of £20 in capital instead of £10, the relative fertility remaining the same. This would be just the same as if 2 acres of each of these types of land were tilled instead of 1, with costs remaining the same. The profit rate remains the same and so does its proportion to the surplus profit or rent. But if A now bears 2 qrs, B 4 qrs, C 6 qrs and D 8 qrs, the production price still remains £3 per qr, since this increase is due not to a doubled yield on the same capital, but to the same proportionate yield on a doubled capital. The 2 qrs from A would now cost £6, just as formerly 1 qr cost £3. Profit on all the four types of land has doubled, but only because the capital laid out has done so. But the rent has doubled in the same proportion; it would be 2 qrs for B instead of 1 qr, 4 qrs for C instead of 2 qrs, and 6 qrs for D instead of 3 qrs; and the money rents for B, C and D would accordingly be £6, £12 and £18 respectively. The money rent per acre would have doubled just as the product per acre has, and so too would the land price in which this money rent is capitalized. Reckoned in this way, the level of corn and money rent rises, and with it the price of land, because the measure on which it is reckoned, the acre, is a piece of land of constant size. The proportionate level of rents, however, has not undergone any change. Reckoned in relation to the capital invested, i.e. as the rate of rent, the total rental of £36 stands in relation to the capital of £20 laid out as the rental of £18 did to a capital of £10. The same applies to the ratio of the money rent for each kind of land to the capital laid out on it; on C, for example, we have £12 rent to £5 capital, as we formerly had £6 rent to £2½ capital. No new differences arise here between the capitals laid out, but new surplus profits do arise, merely because the additional capital is invested on some rent-bearing types of soil, or on all of them, giving the same proportionate product. If the doubled investment were to be made only on C, for example, the differential rent between C, B and D would remain the same when reckoned on capital; for if the differential rent on C has doubled, so too has the capital invested.

We can see from this that, with the production price remaining the same, a constant rate of profit and unchanged differences (and hence an unchanged rate of surplus profit or rent measured on capital), the level of both product- and money-rent per acre can rise, and with it the price of land.

The same thing can occur in the case of declining rates of surplus profit and hence of rent, i.e. with a declining productivity of additional capital investments which still however bear rent. If the additional capital investments of £2½ each were not to double the product but instead B were to yield only 3½ qrs, C 5 qrs and D 7 qrs, the differential rent on B for the second £2½ capital would only be ½ qr instead of 1 qr, on C 1 qr instead of 2 qrs and on D 2 qrs instead of 3 qrs. The proportions between rent and capital for the two successive investments would be as follows:

	First investment		Second investment	
B:	Rent £3,	Capital £2½	Rent £1½,	Capital £2½
C:	,, £6,	,, £2½	,, £3,	,, £2½
D:	,, £9,	,, £2½	,, £6,	,, £2½

Despite this reduced rate of relative productivity of capital, and hence of surplus profit reckoned on capital, the corn and money rent would have risen for B from 1 qr to 1½ qrs (£3 to £4½), for C from 2 qrs to 3 qrs (from £6 to £9) and for D from 3 qrs to 5 qrs (from £9 to £15). In this case the differences for the additional capitals would have declined, compared with the capital invested on A, the production price would have remained the same, but the rent per acre and hence the price of land per acre would have risen.

We now proceed to show the combinations of differential rent II, which presupposes differential rent I as its basis.

Chapter 41: Differential Rent II – First Case: Price of Production Constant

This assumption implies that the market price continues to be governed by the capital invested on the worst land A.

I. If the additional capital invested on any of the rent-bearing types of land B, C and D is only as productive as the same capital on land A, i.e. if at the governing price of production it yields only the average profit and thus no surplus profit, the effect on rent is nil. Everything remains as it was before. It is the same as if a number of acres of quality A, the worst land, had been added to the area previously cultivated.

II. On each different type of land, additional capitals produce extra products in proportion to their size; i.e. the volume of production grows, according to the specific fertility of each type of land, in proportion to the amount of extra capital. In Chapter 39 we took Table I [p. 825, first table] as our point of departure.

This is now transformed into Table II [p. 825].

It is unnecessary here for the capital investment on all types of land to double, as in the table. The law is the same whenever extra capital is applied on one or more of the rent-bearing types of land, no matter in what proportions. All that it requires is simply that production on each type should increase in the same ratio as capital. Here, rent rises simply as a result of increased capital investment on the land and in proportion to this increase of capital. This increase in the product and rent as a result of and in proportion to increased capital investment is just the same, as far as the amount of product and rent is concerned, as if the cultivated area of the rent-bearing lands of the same quality had increased and these were cultivated with the same capital investment as the same types of land were previously. In the case of Table II, for example, the result would remain the same if the additional capital of £2½ per acre were invested on a second acre each of B, C and D.

Type of land	Acres	Capital (£)	Profit (£)	Price of prod. (£)	Output (qrs)	Selling price (£)	Proceeds (£)	Rent qrs	Rent £	Rate of surplus profit
A	1	2½	½	3	1	3	3	0	0	0
B	1	2½	½	3	2	3	6	1	3	120%
C	1	2½	½	3	3	3	9	2	6	240%
D	1	2½	½	3	4	3	12	3	9	360%
Total	4	10		12	10		30	6	18	

Table II

Type of land	Acres	Capital (£)	Profit (£)	Price of prod. (£)	Output (qrs)	Selling price (£)	Proceeds (£)	Rent qrs	Rent £	Rate of surplus profit
A	1	2½ + 2½ = 5	1	6	2	3	6	0	0	0
B	1	2½ + 2½ = 5	1	6	4	3	12	2	6	120%
C	1	2½ + 2½ = 5	1	6	6	3	18	4	12	240%
D	1	2½ + 2½ = 5	1	6	8	3	24	6	18	360%
	4	20			20		60	12	36	

This assumption also supposes that there is not a more fruitful application of capital, but simply an application of more capital to the same area with the same result as before.

In this case, all proportionate ratios remain the same. However, if we consider not the proportionate differences but the simple arithmetical ones, the differential rent on the various types of land can alter. Let us assume for example that the extra capital has been invested solely on B and D. The difference between D and A is then 7 qrs, as against 3 qrs before; between B and A, 3 qrs instead of 1 qr; between C and B, −1 instead of +1, etc. But this arithmetical difference, which is decisive in the case of differential rent I, in so far as it expresses the difference in productivity for the same capital investment, is here quite immaterial, since it is simply the result of different further investment or non-investment of capital, given the same difference for each equal portion of capital on the various lands.

III. The extra capitals bring forth an extra product, and thus form surplus profits, though at a declining rate and not in proportion to their increase.

Table III

Type of land	Acres	Capital (£)	Profit (£)	Price of prod. (£)	Output (qrs)	Selling price (£)	Proceeds (£)	Rent qrs	Rent £	Rate of surplus profit
A	1	$2\frac{1}{2}$	$\frac{1}{2}$	3	1	3	3	0	0	0
B	1	$2\frac{1}{2} + 2\frac{1}{2} = 5$	1	6	$2 + 1\frac{1}{2} = 3\frac{1}{2}$	3	$10\frac{1}{2}$	$1\frac{1}{2}$	$4\frac{1}{2}$	90%
C	1	$2\frac{1}{2} + 2\frac{1}{2} = 5$	1	6	$3 + 2 = 5$	3	15	3	9	180%
D	1	$2\frac{1}{2} + 2\frac{1}{2} = 5$	1	6	$4 + 3\frac{1}{2} = 7\frac{1}{2}$	3	$22\frac{1}{2}$	$5\frac{1}{2}$	$16\frac{1}{2}$	330%
		$17\frac{1}{2}$	$3\frac{1}{2}$	21	17		51	10	30	

It is once again immaterial, in connection with this third assumption, whether the extra investments of capital put in second time round fall uniformly on the various types of land or not; whether the declining production of surplus profit proceeds in equal or unequal proportions; whether the additional capital investments all fall on the same rent-bearing type of land; or whether they are distributed, uniformly or not, on rent-bearing lands of different quality. All these factors are immaterial for the law to be developed here. The only assumption is that extra capital investments on any of the rent-bearing land types yield surplus profit, but in declining proportion to the increase in capital. In the examples given in the above table, the limits of this decline are 4 qrs = £12, the product of the first capital investment on the best land D, and 1 qr = £3, the product of the same capital investment on the worst land A. Given the same capital investment, the product of the best land on investment of the original capital forms the maximum limit – and the product of the worst land A, which bears no rent and gives no surplus profit, the minimum limit – of the product that the successive capital investments on any of the land types yielding surplus profit actually yield in a situation of a decline in productivity from successive capital investments. While assumption II implies that new plots of land of the same quality as the better types are added to the cultivated area, that the quantity of one or more of the cultivated land types increases, assumption III implies that additional plots of land are tilled whose degree of fertility varies between D and A, between that of the best land and that of the worst. If the successive capital investments take place exclusively on land D, they can encompass the existing differences between D and A, as well as those between D and C and between D and B. If they all take place on land C, they can encompass only the differences between C and A and C and B; if on B, then only the differences between B and A.

But the law is that the rent on all these types of land grows absolutely, even if not in proportion to the additional capital invested.

The rate of surplus profit declines, in relation both to the extra capital and the total capital invested on the land, but the absolute amount of surplus profit increases; just as the falling rate of profit on capital in general is usually combined with an increasing absolute mass of profit. The average surplus profit for the capital investment on B, for example, is now 90 per cent on the capital, while for the first capital investment it was 120 per cent. The total surplus profit, however, increases from 1 qr to $1\frac{1}{2}$ qrs, and from £3 to £$4\frac{1}{2}$. The total rent taken by itself – and not in relation to the doubled sum of capital advanced – has risen absolutely. The differences in the rents from the different types of land and their relationship to one another may change in this case; but this change in these differences is here the result of the wider spread of rents and not its cause.

IV. The case in which the extra capital investments on the better types of land produce a greater product than the original requires no further analysis. It is immediately comprehensible how on this assumption the rents per acre rise, and in a higher ratio than the extra capital, whatever the type of land on which it is invested. In this case, the extra capital investment is combined with an improvement. This includes the case in which a small extra capital produces the same or a greater effect than the previous addition of a larger amount. This case is not quite identical with the former, and this is a distinction that is important for all capital investments. If for instance 100 gives a profit of 10, when applied in a particular form, and 200 a profit of 40, then the profit has risen from 10 per cent to 20 per cent, and in this respect it is the same as if 50, applied in a more effective way, gave a profit of 10 instead of 5. We assume here that the profit is bound up with a proportionate increase in the product. But the difference is that in the one case I have to double the capital, while in the other I produce the doubled effect with the same capital as before. It is certainly not the same whether I produce (1) the same product as before with half as much living and objectified labour, (2) double the previous product with the same labour, or (3) four times the previous product with twice the labour. In the first case labour is set free – in either living or objectified form – and can be applied elsewhere; more labour and capital is available. The release of capital (and labour) is in itself an increase in wealth; it has exactly the same effect as if this extra capital was obtained by accumulation, but it spares the task of accumulation.

Let us assume that a capital of 100 has produced a product of 10 metres [of cloth]. Say that this capital contains as much constant capital as it does living labour and profit. The cost is 10 per metre. If I can then produce 20 metres with the same capital of 100, the cost falls to 5 per metre. If on the other hand I can produce 10 metres with a capital of 50, the cost is still 5 per metre, and a capital of 50 is also released, in so far as the former supply is still sufficient. If I have to invest a capital of 200 to produce 40 metres, the cost is similarly 5 per metre. In this case there is no difference in the determination of value or price, any more than in the quantity produced in proportion to the capital advanced. But in the first case capital is released; in the second case extra capital is spared, given that twice the production is required; in the third case the increased product can be obtained only by a growth in the capital advanced, although not in the same proportion as if the increased product had had to be supplied at the old level of productivity. (This belongs in Part One.)

Considered from the standpoint of capitalist production, then as far as a fall in the cost price is concerned, rather than an increase in surplus-value – and a saving in costs on the surplus-value-forming element, labour, does the capitalist the same service as a rise in surplus-value itself; it similarly forms profit for him, as long as the governing production price remains the same – it is always cheaper to employ constant capital rather than variable. This presupposes in fact the development of credit and the abundance of loan capital that corresponds to the capitalist mode of production. Say I employ on the one hand an additional constant capital of £100, this £100 being the product of five workers over a year; on the other hand, £100 in variable capital. If the rate of surplus-value is 100 per cent, the value that the five workers have created is £200; the value of the £100 constant capital, however, is £100, while as capital it is perhaps £105, if the rate of interest is 5 per cent. The same sums of money express very different values, when their products are considered, according to whether they are advanced to production as sums of constant capital or of variable. Another factor, as far as the cost of commodities from the capitalist's standpoint is concerned, is the further distinction that of the £100 constant capital, in so far as this is invested in fixed capital, only the wear and tear goes into the value of the commodity, whereas the £100 for wages must be completely reproduced in it.

In the case of colonists and independent petty producers in general, who have no access to capital, or only at high interest rates, the portion of the product that represents wages is their revenue, whereas for the capitalist it is a capital advance. They therefore consider this outlay of labour as an indispensable pre-condition for the proceeds of their labour, which is the most important thing for them. As far as their extra labour is concerned, after this necessary labour is deducted, it is always realized in an excess product; and whenever they can sell it or can employ it themselves, they consider it as something that has cost them nothing, as it has not cost any objectified labour. It is only the expenditure of objectified labour which is seen by them as an alienation of wealth. They naturally seek to sell as dear as possible; but even a sale below value and the capitalist price of production still seems to them a profit, as long as this profit is not anticipated by incurring any debt, mortgage, etc. For the capitalist, on the other hand, the outlay of both constant capital and variable is an advance of capital. The relatively greater advance of constant capital reduces the cost price, other things being equal, as it also reduces the value of the commodities. Hence although profit arises simply from the surplus labour, i.e. simply from the employment of variable capital, it can seem to the individual capitalist that living labour is the most expensive element in his production costs, which should be reduced to the smallest possible minimum. This is simply a capitalistically distorted form of the correct statement that the relatively greater application of past labour, compared with living, means an increase in the productivity of social labour and greater social wealth. This is how everything appears from the standpoint of competition: incorrectly, and standing on its head.

Assuming stable production prices, the extra capital investments can be made with constant, increasing or decreasing productivity on the better lands, i.e. on all land from B upwards. On A itself, this would only be possible, on our assumptions, either with productivity unchanged, in which case the land would continue to bear no rent, or if productivity increases; one part of the capital invested on land A would then bear rent, the other not. But it would be impossible on the assumption that A's productivity declines, for in that case the production price would not remain constant, but would rise. Under all these circumstances, however, i.e. whether the surplus product brought in is proportionately above or below this proportion – and thus whether the rate of surplus profit on the capital remains constant, rises, or falls as the capital grows – the surplus product and the surplus profit per acre corresponding to it increase, and so too therefore, potentially, does the rent, in corn and in money. The growth in the simple mass of surplus profit or rent, reckoned per acre, i.e. reckoning the growing mass on a constant unit, and here therefore on some definite quantity of land, an acre or a hectare, is expressed as a growth in the proportion. The level of rent, reckoned per acre, thus grows under these conditions simply as a result of the increase in the capital invested on the land. And this takes place moreover with production prices remaining the same, and irrespective of whether the productivity of the extra capital remains the same, decreases or increases. The latter factors modify the degree to which the level of rent per acre grows, but not the fact that it does grow. This is a phenomenon that is peculiar to differential rent II and distinguishes it from differential rent I. If the additional capital investments were made alongside one another in space on new additional land of the appropriate quality, instead of successively in time on the same land, the mass of the rental would have grown, and so would the average rent of the overall cultivated area, as shown earlier, but not the level of rent per acre. With the result remaining the same, as far as the mass and value of the total production and the surplus product are concerned, the concentration of capital increases the level of rent per acre on a more restricted area, whereas under the same conditions its scattering over a greater area, with other factors remaining the same, could not produce this effect. The more the capitalist mode of production develops, however, the more the concentration of capital on the same area increases, so that the rent per acre rises. Hence in two countries where production prices are the same, the differences between land types the same and the same amount of capital is invested, but in one country more in the form of successive investments on a restricted area and in the other more in the form of coordinated investments on a wider area, the rent per acre and therefore the land price would be higher in the first country and lower in the second, even though the total rental in both countries was the same. This difference in the levels of rent could thus be explained neither in terms of a difference in the natural fertility of the land types nor in the amount of labour applied, but exclusively in terms of the different kind of capital investments.

In speaking of a surplus product here, we mean the aliquot portion of the product in which the surplus profit is expressed. Generally, however, we take surplus product to mean the portion of the product in which the total surplus-value is expressed, or in particular cases the portion that represents the average profit. The specific meaning that this term obtains in the case of rent-bearing capital can give rise to misunderstandings, as we saw previously.

Chapter 42: Differential Rent II – Second Case: Price of Production Falling

The production price may fall while productivity on the additional investments of capital remains constant, falls or rises.

I. WITH THE PRODUCTIVITY OF THE EXTRA CAPITAL INVESTMENT REMAINING CONSTANT

This assumes that the product from the various types of land, corresponding to their respective quality, grows to the same extent as does the capital invested on them. This implies, given that the differences between types of land remain the same, a growth in surplus profit proportionate to the growth in capital investment. In this case, therefore, any surplus investment of capital on land A does not affect the differential rent. On this land, the rate of surplus profit is zero; it therefore remains zero, since it is assumed that the productivity of the extra capital and hence the rate of surplus profit remains constant.

The governing production price can fall under these assumptions only when the governing factor ceases to be the production price of A, the latter's place being taken by the next better land B or some other land better than A; i.e. capital is withdrawn from A – or even from A and B, if the production price of land C becomes the governing one – so that all inferior land drops out of the competition between wheat-bearing lands. The condition for this, under the given assumptions, is that the extra product of the additional capital investments satisfies the demand, and hence the production of the inferior land A, etc. is superfluous for the supply required.

Let us take Table II (p. 825), for example, but assume that instead of 20 qrs, 18 qrs now satisfies the demand. A would drop out; B, with its production price of 30s. per qr, would become the price-governing land. The differential rent then assumes the following form:

Table IV

Type of land	Acres	Capital (£)	Profit (£)	Price of prod. (£)	Output (qrs)	Selling price per qr (£)	Proceeds (£)	Rent		Rate of surplus profit
								in corn (qrs)	in money (£)	
B	1	5	1	6	4	1½	6	0	0	0
C	1	5	1	6	6	1½	9	2	3	60%
D	1	5	1	6	8	1½	12	4	6	120%
Total	3	15	3	18	18		27	6	9	

The total rent, therefore, compared with Table II, would have fallen from £36 to £9, and in corn from 12 qrs to 6 qrs, though the total production has fallen only by 2 qrs, from 20 qrs to 18 qrs. The rate of surplus profit, reckoned on the capital, would have fallen to a third of its former level, from 180 per cent to 60 per cent. Thus a decline in both corn and money rent goes together here with the fall in the production price.

Compared with Table I, there is simply a decline in the money rent; the corn rent in both cases is 6 qrs, but in the one case this amounts to £18, in the other case to £9. For land C, the corn rent has remained the same as in Table I. In fact, the product of A has been displaced in the market by the additional production obtained from the uniformly operating additional capital, and land A thus excluded as a competing agent of production, as a result of which a new differential rent I has been formed in which the better land B plays the same role as the inferior land A did before. B's rent therefore disappears, although nothing has changed in the differences between B, C and D, according to our assumption, because of the investment of additional capital. The part of the product that is transformed into rent falls.

If the above result – the satisfaction of the demand with the exclusion of A – had been brought about by the investment of more than twice the capital on C or D or both of these, things would have taken a different course. Say that a third capital investment was made on C, for example:

Table IVa

Type of land	Acres	Capital (£)	Profit (£)	Price of prod. (£)	Output (qrs)	Selling price (£)	Proceeds (£)	Rent in corn (qrs)	Rent in money (£)	Rate of surplus profit
B	1	5	1	6	4	1½	6	0	0	0
C	1	7½	1½	9	9	1½	13½	3	4½	60%
D	1	5	1	6	8	1½	12	4	6	120%
Total	3	17½	3½	21	21		31½	7	10½	

Here the product on C has risen from 6 qrs in Table IV to 9 qrs, the surplus product from 2 qrs to 3 qrs, the money rent from £3 to £4½. As against Table II, however, where the money rent was £12, and Table I, where it was £6, this rent has now fallen. The total rental in corn, = 7 qrs, has fallen in comparison with Table II, where it was 12 qrs, and risen in comparison with Table I, where it was 6 qrs; in money (£10½) it has fallen against both (£18 and £36).

If a third capital investment of £2½ had been applied to land B, this would certainly have altered the amount of production, but it would have left the rent unaffected, since the successive capital investments are assumed not to produce any difference on the same type of land, and land B does not yield any rent.

If we assume on the other hand that the third capital investment takes place on D instead of on C, we get:

Table IVb

Type of land	Acres	Capital (£)	Profit (£)	Price of prod. (£)	Output (qrs)	Selling price (£)	Proceeds (£)	Rent in corn (qrs)	Rent in money (£)	Rate of surplus profit
B	1	5	1	6	4	1½	6	0	0	0
C	1	5	1	6	6	1½	9	2	3	60%
D	1	7½	1½	9	12	1½	18	6	9	120%
Total	3	17½	3½	21	22		33	8	12	

Here the total product is 22 qrs, more than double that of Table I, even though the capital advanced is only £17½ as against £10, i.e. less than double. The total product is also 2 qrs greater than that in Table III even though in the latter case the capital advanced is greater, i.e. £20.

On land D the corn rent has grown from 3 qrs in Table I to 6 qrs, while the money rent has remained the same at £9. The corn rent for D has remained the same as in Table II, at 6 qrs, but the money has fallen from £18 to £9.

Taking the total rents, the corn rent in IVb is 8 qrs, greater than in Table I, where it is 6 qrs, and in IVa, where it is 7 qrs; it is less however than in Table II, where it is 12 qrs. The money rent in Table IVb = £12 is greater than that in IVa = £10½, and less than that in Table I = £18, and Table II = £36.

In order for the total rental under the conditions of IVb to be the same as in Table I, even though the rent on B disappears, we must have a further £6 surplus profit, i.e. 4 qrs at £1½, which is the new production price. We then again have a total rental of £18, as in Table I. The size of the excess capital required for this will vary according to whether we invest it on C or D, or divide it between the two.

On C, £5 capital yields 2 qrs surplus product, and so £10 additional capital will give 4 qrs additional surplus profit. On D, £5 additional capital will be sufficient to produce the 4 qrs additional corn rent, given the fundamental premise that productivity remains the same for the additional capital investments. We then get the following results.

Table IVc

Type of land	Acres	Capital (£)	Profit (£)	Price of prod. (£)	Output (qrs)	Selling price (£)	Proceeds (£)	Rent		Rate of surplus profit
								qrs	£	
B	1	5	1	6	4	1½	6	0	0	0
C	1	15	3	18	18	1½	27	6	9	60%
D	1	7½	1½	9	12	1½	18	6	9	120%
Total	3	27½	5½	33	34		51	12	18	

Table IVd

Type of land	Acres	Capital (£)	Profit (£)	Price of prod. (£)	Output (qrs)	Selling price (£)	Proceeds (£)	Rent		Rate of surplus profit
								qrs	£	
B	1	5	1	6	4	1½	6	0	0	0
C	1	5	1	6	6	1½	9	2	3	60%
D	1	12½	2½	15	20	1½	30	10	15	120%.
Total	3	22½	4½	27	30		45	12	18	

The total money rental would be exactly half of what it was in Table II, where the excess capital was invested at unchanged prices of production.

The most important thing is to compare the above tables with Table I.

We find that the total money rental remains the same, i.e. £18, despite a fall of a half in the production price, from 60s. per qr to 30s., and the corn rent has accordingly doubled, i.e. from 6 qrs to 12 qrs. The rent on B has disappeared; on C the money rent has risen by a half in IVc, and fallen by a half in IVd; on D it has remained the same, £9, in IVc, and risen from £9 to £15 in IVd. Production has risen in IVc from 10 qrs to 34 qrs, and in IVd to 30 qrs; profit from £2 to £5½ in IVc and £4½ in IVd. The total capital investment has risen in the one case from £10 to £27½, in the other from £10 to £22½, i.e. in both cases to more than double. The rate of rent, the rent reckoned on the capital advanced, is the same throughout in Tables IV to IVd, which already implies that the rate of productivity for the two successive capital investments is taken as remaining the same for each type of land. Compared with Table I, however, it has fallen both for the average of all types of land and for each individual type. In I it was an average of 180 per cent, in IVc it is $\frac{18}{27\frac{1}{4}} \times 100 = 65 \frac{5}{11}$ per cent, and in IVd, $\frac{18}{22\frac{1}{4}} \times 100 = 80$ per cent. The average money rent per acre has risen. Its previous average, in Table I, was £4½ per acre over 4 acres, while in IVc and IVd it is now £6 per acre on 3 acres. Its average on the rent-bearing land was formerly £6 per acre and is now £9. The money value of the rent per acre has thus risen, and represents twice the corn product as before; but the 12 qrs corn rent are now less than half of the total product of 34 or 30 qrs, whereas in Table I the 6 qrs made up three-fifths of the total product of 10 qrs. Thus even though the rent has fallen, taken as an aliquot part of the total product, and similarly if reckoned on the capital laid out, its money value reckoned per acre has risen, and its value in product still more. If we take land D in Table IVd, the production costs here are £15, the capital laid out being £12½. The money rent is £15. In Table I, the production costs on the same land D were £3, the capital laid out £2½, the money rent £9, the latter thus being three times the production costs and almost four times the capital. In Table IVd, the money rent of £15 for D is almost exactly equal to the production costs and only a fifth greater than the capital. Yet the money rent per acre is two-thirds greater, £15 instead of £9. In Table I the corn rent of 3 qrs is three-quarters the total product of 4 qrs; in IVd, at 10 qrs, it is half the total product (20 qrs) of the acre of D. This shows how the money value and corn value of the rent per acre can increase, even though this forms a smaller aliquot part of the total yield and has fallen in relation to the capital advanced.

In Table I, the value of the total product is £30; the rent £18, more than half of this. In IVd the value of the total product is £45, the rent at £18 being less than half.

The reason why despite the fall of £1½ per qr in the price, i.e. a fall of 50 per cent, and despite the contraction of the land in competition from 4 acres to 3, the total money rent remains the same while the corn rent doubles, corn rent and money rent both rising when reckoned per acre, lies in the fact that more quarters of surplus product are produced. The corn price falls by 50 per cent, the surplus product grows by 100 per cent. But in order to bring about this result, the total production must grow by a factor of three, under the conditions we have set, and the capital investment on the better types of land must more than double. The proportion in which the latter must grow depends first and foremost on how the extra capital is divided between the better and the best types of land, always assuming that the productivity of capital on each type of land grows in proportion to its size.

If the fall in the production price was less, less extra capital would be required to produce the same money rent. If a greater supply was needed to drive A out of cultivation – and this depends not only on the product per acre of A but also on the proportionate share that A takes out of the total cultivated area – if therefore a greater mass of extra capital was also required on the better land than A, the money rent and corn rent would have grown still further, other things being equal, even though both disappeared on land B.

If the capital that disappeared from A had been £5, the two tables to be compared in this case would be II and IVd. The total product would have grown from 20 qrs to 30 qrs. The money rent would only be half as large, £18 instead of £36; the corn rent would be the same at 12 qrs.

If a total product of 44 qrs = £66 could be produced on D with a capital of £27½ – corresponding to the old ratio for D, 4 qrs for £2½ capital – the total rental would again reach the level of Table II, and the table would now be as follows:

Type of land	Capital (£)	Output (qrs)	Corn rent (qrs)	Money rent (£)
B	5	4	0	0
C	5	6	2	3
D	27½	44	22	33
Total	37½	54	24	36

The total production would be 54 qrs as against 20 qrs in Table II, while the money rent would be the same, £36. But the total capital would be £37½, whereas in Table II it was £20. The total capital advanced would have almost doubled, while production would have almost tripled; the corn rent would have doubled, the money rent would have remained the same. Thus if the price falls as a result of the investment of excess money capital on the lands yielding higher rent, i.e. all except A, while productivity remains the same, the total capital tends not to grow in the same proportion as production and the corn rent; so that the fall-off in the money rent that results from the falling price may be balanced by a rise in the corn rent. The same law is also apparent in the way that the capital advanced must be greater in the proportion that it is applied more to C than to D, more to the land bearing less rent than to that bearing more rent. This is simply for the following reason. In order for the money rent to remain the same or to rise, a definite additional quantity of surplus product must be produced, and this requires less capital, the greater the fertility of the lands yielding surplus product. If the differences between B and C, and C and D, were still greater, still less extra capital would be needed. The specific proportion depends (1) on the ratio in which the price falls, thus on the difference between B, which is now the non-rent-bearing land, and A, which it has replaced; (2) on the ratio of the differences between the better types of land, from B upwards; (3) on the amount of extra capital newly invested; and (4) on its distribution over the various qualities of land.

We see in fact that this law expresses nothing more than was already developed in the first case: that if the production price is given, whatever its level might be, the rent can rise as a result of extra capital investment. For the result of the exclusion of A from cultivation is a new differential rent I with B now as the worst land and £1½ per qr as the new production price. This is as true for Table IV as for Table II. It is the same law, simply that land B is taken as the starting-point instead of land A and the production price as £1¼ instead of £3.

This is important here only for the following reason. In so far as so and so much extra capital was needed to withdraw capital from land A and make up the supply without it, it is clear that this may be accompanied by a rising, a falling, or a stable rent per acre, if not on all lands, then at least on some, and for the average of the lands tilled. We have seen that corn rent and money rent do not behave in the same way. It is only tradition, however, that still gives corn rent any role in economics. One might just as well prove that a manufacturer could buy far more of his own yarn with a profit of £5 than he formerly could with a profit of £10. This does show however that the landowning gentlemen, if they also happen to own or have a share in manufacturing, sugar refining, spirit distilling, etc., can still draw very considerable profits while money rents are falling, as producers of their own raw materials.[34]

2. A FALLING RATE OF PRODUCTIVITY
FOR THE EXTRA CAPITAL

Nothing new is involved here except that the production price can also fall, as in the case last considered, if the extra capital investments on better types of land than A make A's product superfluous and hence cause capital to be withdrawn from A, or if A is applied to the production of a different crop. This case has already been exhaustively discussed. We have shown how

34. An error in calculation running through the above tables IVa to IVd made it necessary to rework them. This in no way affected the theoretical perspectives developed from the tables, but it did lead in places to quite monstrous numerical ratios for production per acre. Even these are not objectionable in principle. It is quite usual in relief and topographical maps to take a considerably larger scale for the vertical dimension than for the horizontal. Anyone who still feels that his agrarian feelings have been injured is free to multiply the number of acres by any figure he chooses. In Table I, moreover, instead of 1, 2, 3, 4 qrs per acre, we could put 10, 12, 14, 16 bushels (8 bushels = 1 qr), which would keep the figures derived from these in the other tables within the bounds of the possible; the result, the relationship between rise in rent and rise in capital, still comes out just the same. This has been done in the tables added by the editor in the following chapter. – F. E.

the corn and money rents per acre may grow, decline, or remain the same.

For convenience of comparison, we first reproduce:

Table I [a]

Type of land	Acres	Capital (£)	Profit (£)	Price of prod. per qr	Output (qrs)	Corn rent (qrs)	Money rent (£)	Rate of surplus profit
A	1	$2\frac{1}{2}$	$\frac{1}{2}$	3	1	0	0	0
B	1	$2\frac{1}{2}$	$\frac{1}{2}$	$1\frac{1}{2}$	2	1	3	120%
C	1	$2\frac{1}{2}$	$\frac{1}{2}$	1	3	2	6	240%
D	1	$2\frac{1}{2}$	$\frac{1}{2}$	$\frac{3}{4}$	4	3	9	360%
Total	4	10			10	6	18	180% average

If we assume now that a figure of 16 qrs supplied by B, C and D, with a declining rate of productivity, is sufficient to remove A from cultivation, then Table III is now transformed into the following:

Table V

Type of land	Acres	Investment of capital (£)	Profit (£)	Output (qrs)	Selling price (£)	Proceeds (£)	Corn rent (qrs)	Money rent (£)	Rate of surplus profit
B	1	$2\frac{1}{2} + 2\frac{1}{2}$	1	$2 + 1\frac{1}{2} = 3\frac{1}{2}$	$1\frac{5}{7}$	6	0	0	0
C	1	$2\frac{1}{2} + 2\frac{1}{2}$	1	$3 + 2 = 5$	$1\frac{5}{7}$	$8\frac{4}{7}$	$1\frac{1}{2}$	$2\frac{4}{7}$	$51\frac{3}{7}$%
D	1	$2\frac{1}{2} + 2\frac{1}{2}$	1	$4 + 3\frac{1}{2} = 7\frac{1}{2}$	$1\frac{5}{7}$	$12\frac{6}{7}$	4	$6\frac{6}{7}$	$137\frac{1}{7}$%
Total	3	15		16		$27\frac{3}{7}$	$5\frac{1}{2}$	$9\frac{3}{7}$	$94\frac{2}{7}$% average

Here, with a declining rate of productivity on the extra capitals and a varying decline on the different types of land, the governing production price has fallen from £3 to £$1\frac{5}{7}$. The capital investment has risen by half, from £10 to £15. The money rent has fallen by almost half, from £18 to £$9\frac{3}{7}$, but the corn rent by only a twelfth, from 6 qrs to $5\frac{1}{2}$ qrs. The total product has risen from 10 qrs to 16 qrs, or by 60 per cent. The corn rent is somewhat over a third of the total product. The capital advanced stands in a ratio of 15:$9\frac{3}{7}$ to the money rent, whereas the previous ratio was 10:18.

3. A RISING RATE OF PRODUCTIVITY FOR THE EXTRA CAPITAL

This is distinguished from variant I at the beginning of this chapter, where the production price falls while the rate of productivity remains the same, simply by the way that, if a given additional product is needed to remove land A from cultivation, this happens more speedily in the present case.

Both when the productivity of the additional capital investments is falling and when it is rising, the effect of this process can be very uneven, according to how the investments are distributed over the different types of land. Depending on whether this varying effect tends to even out the differences or to intensify them, the differential rent on the better types of land will fall or rise, and so too, therefore, will the total rental, as was already the case with differential rent I. Moreover, everything depends on the size of the land area and capital that is displaced with A, as well as on the relative amount of capital which has to be advanced, given rising productivity, to supply the excess product that is to meet the demand.

The only point worth investigating here, and this takes us directly back to the analysis of how this differential profit is transformed into differential rent, is as follows.

In the first case, where the production price remains the same, the excess capital that might be invested on land A is quite immaterial for the differential rent as such, since now as before land A bears no rent, the price of its product remaining the same and continuing to govern the market.

In the second case, variant I, where the production price falls with the rate of productivity remaining the same, land A necessarily drops out, and still more so in variant II (falling production price with a falling rate of productivity), since otherwise the excess capital on land A would necessarily increase the production price. Here, however, in variant III of the second case, where the production price falls because the productivity of the excess capital rises, this additional capital can under certain circumstances be invested as well on land A as on the better types of land.

We shall assume that an extra capital of £2½ invested on land A produces 1⅓ qrs instead of 1 qr.

Table VI

Type of land	Acres	Capital (£)	Profit (£)	Price of prod. (£)	Output (qrs)	Selling price (£)	Proceeds (£)	Rent qrs	Rent £	Rate of surplus profit
A	1	$2\frac{1}{2} + 2\frac{1}{2} = 5$	1	6	$1 + 1\frac{1}{4} = 2\frac{1}{4}$	$2\frac{8}{11}$	6	0	0	0
B	1	$2\frac{1}{2} + 2\frac{1}{2} = 5$	1	6	$2 + 2\frac{3}{4} = 4\frac{3}{4}$	$2\frac{8}{11}$	12	$2\frac{1}{4}$	6	120%
C	1	$2\frac{1}{2} + 2\frac{1}{2} = 5$	1	6	$3 + 3\frac{3}{4} = 6\frac{3}{4}$	$2\frac{8}{11}$	18	$4\frac{3}{4}$	12	240%
D	1	$2\frac{1}{2} + 2\frac{1}{2} = 5$	1	6	$4 + 4\frac{3}{4} = 8\frac{3}{4}$	$2\frac{8}{11}$	24	$6\frac{3}{4}$	18	360%
	4		20	4	24	22		60	$13\frac{3}{4}$	36	240%

As well as the basic Table I, this table should also be compared with Table II, where the doubled capital investment is combined with constant productivity in proportion to the capital invested.

By our assumption, the governing production price falls. If it were to remain constant, at £3, the worst land, which previously, with a capital investment of only £2½, did not bear any rent, would now yield a rent without the drawing into cultivation of any yet inferior land; the reason for this is that productivity would have increased on the same land, though only for a portion of the capital, and not for the original capital. The first £3 in production costs brings in 1 qr; the second £3 brings in 1¼ qrs; the total product of 2¼ qrs, however, is now sold at its average price. Since the rate of productivity grows with the extra capital investment, this implies an improvement. That may consist in the application of more capital as such to each acre (more fertilizer, more mechanized labour, etc.) or even in the fact that it is only with this extra capital that a qualitatively different and more productive investment of capital can be brought about. In both cases, a product of 2¼ qrs is obtained for an outlay of £5 capital per acre, whereas with half this capital investment, £2½, the product was only 1 qr. Leaving aside transitory market conditions, the product of land A could continue to be sold at a higher production price, instead of at the new average price, only if a significant area of class A land continued to be cultivated with a capital of only £2½ per acre. But as soon as the new proportion of £5 per acre, and hence this improved mode of operation, became universal, the governing production price would have to fall to £2⁸⁄₁₁. The distinction between the two portions of capital would disappear, and then an acre of A which was tilled with a capital of only £2½ per acre would be abnormal and would not be tilled according to the new conditions of production. The distinction would no longer be between the products of different portions of capital on the same acre, but rather between a satisfactory total capital investment per acre and an unsatisfactory one. From this we can see, *firstly*, how when a large number of farmers have insufficient capital (it has to be a large number, for a small number would simply be compelled to sell below their production price), this has just the same effect as the differentiation of types of land themselves in a diminishing series. The poorer type of agriculture on worse soil increases the rent on the better; it can even create a rent on better cultivated land of the same poor quality, which this would not otherwise yield. *Secondly*, we see how differential rent, in so far as it arises from successive investments of capital on the same total area, is actually reduced to an average in which the effects of the different capital investments can no longer be recognized or distinguished. They do not produce rent on the worst lands, but rather, (1) make the average price of the total product, say on an acre of A, into the new governing price, and (2) present themselves as changes in the total amount of capital per acre required under the new conditions for satisfactory cultivation of this land, in which both the individual successive capital investments and their respective effects melt indistinguishably together. The same is true then with the particular differential rents of the better types of land. These are in any case determined by the difference between the average product of the type of land in question and the product of the worst land, in a situation where an increased investment of capital has now become normal.

No land yields any product without a capital investment. This is true even in the case of simple differential rent, differential rent I. When it is said that 1 acre of A, the land that governs the production price, yields such and such a product at this price or that, and that the better types of land, B, C and D, yield so and so much differential product and hence, at the governing price, so and so much ground-rent, this always assumes that a definite capital is applied, i.e. that considered normal under the given conditions of production. Just as in industry a definite minimum of capital is required in each line of business to produce commodities at their price of production.

If this minimum changes as a result of successive investments of capital on the same land, to effect improvements, it happens only gradually. As long as a certain number of acres of A, for example, do not receive this extra working capital, rent on the better cultivated acres of A is generated because the production price has remained constant, while the rent on all the better types of land B, C and D is thereby increased. But as soon as the new type of cultivation has spread sufficiently to become normal, the production price falls; the rent for the better lands falls again, and the portion of land A that does not possess what is now the average working capital must sell below its individual production price, i.e. below the average profit.

With a falling production price, this occurs even when the productivity of the extra capital declines, as soon as increased capital investment brings it about that the total product required is supplied by the better types of land, so that A's working capital, for instance, is withdrawn and A no longer competes in the production of this particular product, wheat for example. The amount of capital that is then applied on average to the better land B, which now governs price, is now established as the normal amount; and in speaking of the varying fertility of land, we assume that this is the new normal quantity of capital applied per acre.

It is clear on the other hand that this average capital investment, e.g. £8 per acre before 1848 in England and £12 per acre afterwards, is what provides the standard when tenancy contracts are drawn up. For the farmer who spends more than this, the surplus profit is not transformed into rent for the duration of the lease. Whether this happens when the contract expires will depend on the competition of those farmers in a position to make the same extra advance. We are not referring here to permanent improvements to the land, which continue to provide an increased product with the same outlay of capital or even a declining one. Although these are the product of capital, they operate just like the natural differential quality of the soil.

We see therefore how differential rent II involves an element that does not develop as such in the case of differential rent I, since this can persist independently of any change in the normal capital investment per acre. On the one hand the results of different capital investments on the price-governing land A are blurred, their product simply appearing as the normal average product per acre. On the other hand there is a change in the normal minimum or average size of the capital outlay per acre, so that this change appears as a property of the soil. Finally there is a distinction in the way the surplus profit is transformed into the form of rent.

Table VI also shows, when compared with Tables I and II, that the corn rent has risen to more than double as against Table I, and by $1\frac{1}{5}$ qrs as against Table II; while the money rent has doubled as against I, but is unchanged from II. It would have grown significantly either if the extra capital had fallen more on the better types of land, or alternatively if the effect of the extra capital had been less on A, so that the governing average price per qr from A was higher (always taking other preconditions as the same).

If the rise in fertility as a result of extra capital had a differing effect on the different types of land, this would give rise to a change in their differential rents.

What has been proved in any case is that when the production price falls as a result of a rising rate of productivity on the extra capital investment – i.e. as soon as this productivity grows in a higher ratio than the capital advance – the rent per acre for a doubled capital investment, say, may not just double, but can more than double. However, it might also fall, if the production price were to fall much lower as a result of a rapid growth in productivity on land A.

Let us assume that the additional investments of capital, on B and C for example, did not increase productivity in the same proportion as on A, so that the proportionate differences for B and C would decline and the growth in the product would not compensate for the falling price. The rent on D would then rise and that on B and C fall, as compared with the case of Table II.

Table VIa

Type of land	Acres	Capital (£)	Profit (£)	Output per acre (qrs)	Selling price (£)	Proceeds (£)	Corn rent (qrs)	Money rent (£)
A	1	$2\frac{1}{2} + 2\frac{1}{2} = 5$	1	$1 + 3 = 4$	$1\frac{1}{2}$	6	0	0
B	1	$2\frac{1}{2} + 2\frac{1}{2} = 5$	1	$2 + 2\frac{1}{2} = 4\frac{1}{2}$	$1\frac{1}{2}$	$6\frac{3}{4}$	$\frac{1}{2}$	$\frac{3}{4}$
C	1	$2\frac{1}{2} + 2\frac{1}{2} = 5$	1	$3 + 5 = 8$	$1\frac{1}{2}$	12	4	6
D	1	$2\frac{1}{2} + 2\frac{1}{2} = 5$	1	$4 + 12 = 16$	$1\frac{1}{2}$	24	12	18
Total	4	20		$32\frac{1}{2}$			$16\frac{1}{2}$	$24\frac{3}{4}$

The money rent, finally, would rise if, given the same proportionate rise in fertility, more additional capital was applied to the better lands than to A, or if the additional capital investments on the better lands acted with an increased rate of productivity. In both cases the differences would grow.

The money rent falls if the improvement resulting from extra capital investment reduces the differences, either all or some, by having more effect on A than on B and C. Whether the corn rent rises, falls or remains stationary depends on the degree of unevenness in this effect.

The money rent rises, and the corn rent with it, either if more capital is added to the rent-bearing than to the non-rent-bearing land, in conditions where the proportionate differences in the additional fertility remain the same, and more capital is added to the lands of higher rent than to those of lower rent, or if, given the same additional capital, the fertility on the better and best lands grows more than on A. Indeed, in the latter case, the rent rises in relation to the degree to which the increase in fertility is greater in the superior categories of land than in the inferior ones.

Under all circumstances, however, the rent experiences a relative rise if the increased productivity is the result of a new addition of capital and not simply of increased fertility for a constant capital investment. This is the absolute point of view, and it shows how, as in all earlier cases, the rent per acre, and now the higher rent per acre (as in the case of differential rent I, the rent over the whole cultivated area – the level of the average rental), is the result of increased capital investment on the land, whether this functions with a constant rate of productivity in a situation of constant or falling prices, with a declining rate of productivity in a situation of constant or falling prices, or with an increasing rate of productivity in a situation of constant or falling prices. For our assumption of a constant price with a constant, falling or rising rate of productivity for the extra capital, and a falling price with a constant, falling or rising rate of productivity, can be reduced to the assumption of a constant rate of productivity for the excess capital in a situation of constant or falling price, a falling rate of productivity in a situation of constant or falling price, a rising rate of productivity with constant and falling price. Even though in all these cases the rent may remain stationary or even fall, it would fall further if the additional application of capital, in otherwise unchanged conditions, were not the condition for higher fertility. The additional capital is then always the cause of the relatively high level of rent, even though this may have fallen in absolute terms.

Chapter 43: Differential Rent II – Third Case: Rising Price of Production. Results

(A rising price of production presupposes a decline in productivity on the lowest quality of land, which pays no rent. The production price we have taken as the governing one can rise above £3 per qr only if the £2½ invested on A produces less than 1 qr, or the £5 less than 2 qrs, or if a still poorer soil than A has to be brought into cultivation.

Given that the productivity of the second capital investment remains the same or even rises, this would only be possible if the productivity of the first capital investment of £2½ had declined. This case is found often enough. For example, if the exhausted top-soil gives declining yields on superficial ploughing, as long as the old method of cultivation is maintained, until the subsoil subsequently supplies higher yields than before when rational techniques lead to its being turned up. Strictly speaking, however, this special case does not belong here. The falling productivity of the *first* capital investment of £2½ leads to a fall in differential rent I for the better types of land, even if conditions there are taken as analogous; here, however, we are concerned only with differential rent II. But since the present special case cannot come about unless we assume that differential rent II is already in existence, for it in fact represents the impact on II of a modification in differential rent I, we shall give an example of it.

Both rent and yield are the same in money terms as in Table II. The increased governing price of production exactly makes up for the deficit in the quantity produced; since the two things vary in inverse proportion, it is evident that their product remains the same.

In the following case we assume the productivity of the second capital investment is higher than the original productivity of the first investment. It is the same if we take the productivity of the

Table VII

Type of land	Acres	Invested capital (£)	Profit (£)	Price of prod. (£)	Output (qrs)	Selling price (£)	Proceeds (£)	Corn rent (qrs)	Money rent (£)	Rate of rent
A	1	2½ + 2½	1	6	½ + 1¼ = 1¾	$3\frac{3}{7}$	6	0	0	0
B	1	2½ + 2½	1	6	1 + 2½ = 3½	$3\frac{3}{7}$	12	1¾	6	120%
C	1	2½ + 2½	1	6	1½ + 3¾ = 5¼	$3\frac{3}{7}$	18	3½	12	240%
D	1	2½ + 2½	1	6	2 + 5 = 7	$3\frac{3}{7}$	24	5¼	18	360%
		20			17½		60	10½	36	240%

second investment as simply the same as the original, as in the following Table VIII:

Table VIII

Type of land	Acres	Invested capital (£)	Profit (£)	Price of prod. (£)	Output (qrs)	Selling price (£)	Proceeds (£)	Rent in corn (qrs)	Rent in money (£)	Rate of surplus profit
A	1	2½ + 2½ = 5	1	6	½ + 1 = 1½	4	6	0	0	0
B	1	2½ + 2½ = 5	1	6	1 + 2 = 3	4	12	1½	6	120%
C	1	2½ + 2½ = 5	1	6	1½ + 3 = 4½	4	18	3	12	240%
D	1	2½ + 2½ = 5	1	6	2 + 4 = 6	4	24	4½	18	360%
		20			15		60	9	36	240%

Here, too, a production price that has risen in the same proportion fully makes up for the decline in productivity, both for product and money rent.

The third case emerges in its pure form only in a situation of falling productivity on the second capital investment, while that on the first investment remains constant, as was assumed throughout in the first and second cases. Here differential rent I is not affected, and the change takes place solely in the proportion arising from differential rent II. We give two examples: in the first the productivity of the second capital investment is reduced to a half and in the second to a quarter.

Table IX

Type of land	Acres	Invested capital (£)	Profit (£)	Price of prod. (£)	Output (qrs)	Selling price (£)	Proceeds (£)	Rent in corn (qrs)	Rent in money (£)	Rate of rent
A	1	2½ + 2½ = 5	1	6	1 + ½ = 1½	4	6	0	0	0
B	1	2½ + 2½ = 5	1	6	2 + 1 = 3	4	12	1½	6	120%
C	1	2½ + 2½ = 5	1	6	3 + 1½ = 4½	4	18	3	12	240%
D	1	2½ + 2½ = 5	1	6	4 + 2 = 6	4	24	4½	18	360%
		20			15		60	9	36	240%

Table IX is the same as Table VIII, except that the decline in productivity in VIII falls on the first capital investment, while that in IX falls on the second.

Table X

Type of land	Acres	Invested capital (£)	Profit (£)	Price of prod. (£)	Output (qrs)	Selling price (£)	Proceeds (£)	Rent in corn (qrs)	Rent in money (£)	Rate of rent
A	1	2½ + 2½ = 5	1	6	1 + ¼ = 1¼	4⅘	6	0	0	0
B	1	2½ + 2½ = 5	1	6	2 + ½ = 2½	4⅘	12	1¼	6	120%
C	1	2½ + 2½ = 5	1	6	3 + ¾ = 3¾	4⅘	18	2½	12	240%
D	1	2½ + 2½ = 5	1	6	4 + 1 = 5	4⅘	24	3¾	18	360%
		20		24	12½		60	7½	36	240%

In this table, too, the total yield, money rental and rate of rent remain the same as in Tables II, VII and VIII, because the product and the sale price again vary in inverse proportion, while the capital investment remains the same.

What is the position, though, in the other possible situation, with a rising price of production, in particular if inferior land which it previously did not pay to cultivate is now taken into cultivation?

Let us assume that this land, which we can call *a*, enters into competition with the others. The formerly non-rent-bearing land A would then yield a rent, and the above Tables VII, VIII and X would take on the following form as Tables VIIa, VIIIa and Xa.

Table VIIa

Type of land	Acres	Capital (£)	Profit (£)	Price of production (£)	Output (qrs)	Selling price (£)	Proceeds (£)	Rent qrs	Rent £	Increase
a	1	5	1	6	1½	4	6	0	0	0
A	1	2½ + 2½	1	6	½ + 1¼ = 1¾	4	7	¼	1	1
B	1	2½ + 2½	1	6	1 + 2½ = 3½	4	14	2	8	1 + 7
C	1	2½ + 2½	1	6	1½ + 3¾ = 5¼	4	21	3¾	15	1 + 2 × 7
D	1	2½ + 2½	1	6	2 + 5 = 7	4	28	5½	22	1 + 3 × 7
				30	19		76	11½	46	

Table VIIIa

Type of land	Acres	Capital (£)	Profit (£)	Price of production (£)	Output (qrs)	Selling price (£)	Proceeds (£)	Rent qrs	Rent £	Increase
a	1	5	1	6	1¼	4⅘	6	0	0	0
A	1	2½ + 2½	1	6	½ + 1 = 1½	4⅘	7⅕	¼	1⅕	1⅕
B	1	2½ + 2½	1	6	1 + 2 = 3	4⅘	14⅖	1¾	8⅖	1⅕ + 7⅕
C	1	2½ + 2½	1	6	1½ + 3 = 4½	4⅘	21⅗	3¼	15⅗	1⅕ + 2 × 7⅕
D	1	2½ + 2½	1	6	2 + 4 = 6	4⅘	28⅘	4¾	22⅘	1⅕ + 3 × 7⅕
	5			30	16¼		78	10	48	

Table Xa

Type of land	Acres	Capital (£)	Profit (£)	Price of production (£)	Output (qrs)	Selling price (£)	Proceeds (£)	Rent qrs	Rent £	Increase
a	1	$2\frac{1}{2} + 2\frac{1}{2}$	1	6			6	0	0	0
A	1	$2\frac{1}{2} + 2\frac{1}{2}$	1	6	$1 + \frac{1}{2} = 1\frac{1}{2}$	$5\frac{1}{3}$	$6\frac{2}{3}$	0	$\frac{2}{3}$	$\frac{2}{3}$
B	1	$2\frac{1}{2} + 2\frac{1}{2}$	1	6	$2 + \frac{1}{2} = 2\frac{1}{2}$	$5\frac{1}{3}$	$13\frac{1}{3}$	$1\frac{1}{3}$	$7\frac{1}{3}$	$\frac{2}{3} + 6\frac{2}{3}$
C	1	$2\frac{1}{2} + 2\frac{1}{2}$	1	6	$3 + \frac{1}{2} = 3\frac{1}{2}$	$5\frac{1}{3}$	20	$2\frac{2}{3}$	14	$\frac{2}{3} + 2 \times 6\frac{2}{3}$
D	1	$2\frac{1}{2} + 2\frac{1}{2}$	1	6	$4 + 1 = 5$	$5\frac{1}{3}$	$26\frac{2}{3}$	$3\frac{2}{3}$	$20\frac{2}{3}$	$\frac{2}{3} + 3 \times 6\frac{2}{3}$
				30	$13\frac{1}{8}$		$72\frac{2}{3}$	8	$42\frac{2}{3}$	

The intervention of land a gives rise to a new differential rent I; on this new basis, differential rent II also develops in a different form. In each of the three above tables, land a has a different fertility; the series of proportionally rising fertilities only begins with A. Accordingly too, therefore, the series of rising rents. The rent of the poorest rent-bearing land, which formerly did not bear rent at all, forms a constant that is simply added on to all higher rents; it is only after this constant is deducted that the series of differences for the higher rents clearly emerges, and so too their parallelism with the series of land types arranged according to fertility. In all these tables, the fertilities from A to D are in the ratios $1 : 2 : 3 : 4$, and the rents are accordingly:

- in VIIa, as $1 : 1 + 7 : 1 + 2 \times 7 : 1 + 3 \times 7$;
- in VIIIa, as $1\frac{1}{3} : 1\frac{1}{3} + 7\frac{1}{3} : 1\frac{1}{3} + 2 \times 7\frac{1}{3} : 1\frac{1}{3} + 3 \times 7\frac{1}{3}$;
- in Xa, as $\frac{2}{3} : \frac{2}{3} + 6\frac{2}{3} : \frac{2}{3} + 2 \times 6\frac{2}{3} : \frac{2}{3} + 3 \times 6\frac{2}{3}$.

In short, if the rent of A $= n$, and the rent of the land of next higher fertility $= n + m$, the series is $n : n + m : n + 2m : n + 3m$ etc. – F. E.)

*

(Since the above third case was not elaborated in the manuscript – there is only the title – it remained the task of the editor to complete this as best he could. Besides this, he also has to draw the resulting general conclusions from the overall investigation of differential rent II in its three major and nine subordinate cases. For this purpose, however, the examples given in the manuscript are of little help. Firstly, they compare lands whose yields, for equal areas, are in the ratios 1: 2: 3: 4, i.e. differences that are sharply exaggerated right from the start and which lead to completely impossible figures when calculations are made on this basis. Secondly, they give a completely false impression. If fertilities in the ratios 1: 2: 3: 4 etc. lead to a series of rents in the ratios 0: 1: 2: 3 etc., we feel able to derive the second series immediately from the first and explain the doubling, trebling, etc. of rents from the doubling, trebling, etc. of the total yields. But this would be completely mistaken. Rents stand in the ratios 0: 1: 2: 3: 4 whenever the scale of fertility is one of $n: n + 1: n + 2: n + 3: n + 4$; it is not the absolute *level* of fertility but rather the *differences* in fertility, reckoned from the non-rent-bearing land as the zero point, that give the ratio of rents.

Marx's original tables had to be given for the sake of understanding the text itself. But in order to give an intuitive basis to the results of the investigation that follow below, I shall now provide a new series of tables in which the yields are given in bushels ($\frac{1}{8}$ qr, or 36.35 litres) and shillings (= marks).

The first table (XI) corresponds to the former Table I. It shows the yields and rents for five qualities of land A–E for a *first* capital investment of 50s., which with 10s. profit makes a total of 60s. in production costs. The yields of corn are given low values: 10, 12, 14, 16, 18 bushels per acre. The governing production price resulting from this is 6s. per bushel.

The subsequent thirteen tables correspond to the three cases of differential rent II dealt with in this chapter and the two previous ones, for an *additional* capital investment on the same land of 50s. per acre, and a price of production that may be constant, falling or rising. Each of these cases is again presented in the shape it assumes (1) with the same productivity for the second capital investment as for the first, (2) with falling productivity and (3) with rising productivity. A few variants arise in this connection which are particularly useful by way of illustration.

In case I, price of production constant, we have:
Variant 1. Productivity remains the same for the second capital investment (Table XII).
Variant 2. Productivity falls. This can happen only if no second investment is made on land A. And, moreover, either:
(a) in such a way that land B likewise yields no rent (Table XIII);

or

(b) in such a way that land B is not completely devoid of rent (Table XIV).

Variant 3. Productivity rises (Table XV). This case, too, excludes a second capital investment on land A.

In case II, where the production price falls, we have:

Variant 1. Productivity remains the same for the second investment (Table XVI).

Variant 2. Productivity falls (Table XVII). These two variants both mean that land A is removed from competition, land B ceasing to bear rent and coming to govern the production price.

Variant 3. Productivity rises (Table XVIII). Here land A remains the governing one.

In case III, where the price of production rises, two modalities are possible. Land A may remain non-rent-bearing and price-governing, or else land inferior to A in quality may come into competition and govern price, which means that A then does yield rent.

First modality. Land A continues to govern price.

Variant 1. Productivity remains the same for the second investment (Table XIX). This is permissible, under our conditions, only if the productivity of the first investment declines.

Variant 2. The productivity of the second investment falls (Table XX). This does not rule out the possibility that the productivity of the first investment may remain the same.

Variant 3. The productivity of the second investment rises (Table XXI). This again reduces the productivity of the first investment.

Second modality. An inferior quality of land (denoted by *a*) comes into competition; land A bears rent.

Variant 1. Productivity on the second investment remains the same (Table XXII).

Variant 2. Productivity falls (Table XXIII).

Variant 3. Productivity rises (Table XXIV).

These three variants conform to the general conditions of the problem, and require no special remarks.

We now append the tables.

Table XI

Type of land	Price of produc-tion (s.)	Output (bushels)	Selling price (s.)	Proceeds (s.)	Rent (s.)	Rent increase
A	60	10	6	60	0	0
B	60	12	6	72	12	12
C	60	14	6	84	24	2 × 12
D	60	16	6	96	36	3 × 12
E	60	18	6	108	48	4 × 12
					120	10 × 12

For the second capital investment on the same land:

First case. The price of production remains constant.

Variant 1. The productivity of the second capital investment remains the same.

Table XII

Type of land	Price of production (s.)	Output (bushels)	Selling price (s.)	Proceeds (s.)	Rent (s.)	Rent increase
A	60 + 60 = 120	10 + 10 = 20	6	120	0	0
B	60 + 60 = 120	12 + 12 = 24	6	144	24	24
C	60 + 60 = 120	14 + 14 = 28	6	168	48	2 × 24
D	60 + 60 = 120	16 + 16 = 32	6	192	72	3 × 24
E	60 + 60 = 120	18 + 18 = 36	6	216	96	4 × 24
					240	10 × 24

Variant 2. The productivity of the second capital investment falls; there is no second investment on A.

(a) Land B ceases to bear rent.

Table XIII

Type of land	Price of production (s.)	Output (bushels)	Selling price (s.)	Proceeds (s.)	Rent (s.)	Rent increase
A	60	10	6	60	0	0
B	60 + 60 = 120	12 + 8 = 20	6	120	0	0
C	60 + 60 = 120	14 + 9½ = 23½	6	140	20	20
D	60 + 60 = 120	16 + 10⅔ = 26⅔	6	160	40	2 × 20
E	60 + 60 = 120	18 + 12 = 30	6	180	60	3 × 20
					120	6 × 20

(b) Land B does not completely cease to bear rent.

Table XIV

Type of land	Price of production (s.)	Output (bushels)	Selling price (s.)	Proceeds (s.)	Rent (s.)	Rent increase
A	60	10	6	60	0	0
B	60 + 60 = 120	12 + 9 = 21	6	126	6	6
C	60 + 60 = 120	14 + 10½ = 24½	6	147	27	6 + 21
D	60 + 60 = 120	16 + 12 = 28	6	168	48	6 + 2 × 21
E	60 + 60 = 120	18 + 13½ = 31½	6	189	69	6 + 3 × 21
					150	4 × 6 + 6 × 21

Variant 3. The productivity of the second capital investment rises; here too, no second investment on land A.

Table XV

Type of land	Price of production (s.)	Output (bushels)	Selling price (s.)	Proceeds (s.)	Rent (s.)	Rent increase
A	60	10	6	60	0	0
B	60 + 60 = 120	12 + 15 = 27	6	162	42	42
C	60 + 60 = 120	14 + 17½ = 31½	6	189	69	42 + 27
D	60 + 60 = 120	16 + 20 = 36	6	216	96	42 + 2 × 27
E	60 + 60 = 120	18 + 22½ = 40½	6	243	123	42 + 3 × 27
					330	4 × 42 + 6 × 27

Second case. Price of production falls.

Variant 1. Productivity of the second capital investment remains the same. Land A is withdrawn from competition, land B ceases to bear rent.

Table XVI

Type of land	Price of production (s.)	Output (bushels)	Selling price (s.)	Proceeds (s.)	Rent (s.)	Rent increase
B	60 + 60 = 120	12 + 12 = 24	5	120	0	0
C	60 + 60 = 120	14 + 14 = 28	5	140	20	20
D	60 + 60 = 120	16 + 16 = 32	5	160	40	2 × 20
E	60 + 60 = 120	18 + 18 = 36	5	180	60	3 × 20
					120	6 × 20

Variant 2. Productivity of the second capital investment falls; Land A is withdrawn from competition, land B ceases to bear rent.

Table XVII

Type of land	Price of production (s.)	Output (bushels)	Selling price (s.)	Proceeds (s.)	Rent (s.)	Rent increase
B	60 + 60 = 120	12 + 9 = 21	$5\frac{5}{7}$	120	0	0
C	60 + 60 = 120	14 + 10½ = 24½	$5\frac{5}{7}$	140	20	20
D	60 + 60 = 120	16 + 12 = 28	$5\frac{5}{7}$	160	40	2 × 20
E	60 + 60 = 120	18 + 13½ = 31½	$5\frac{5}{7}$	180	60	3 × 20
					120	6 × 20

Variant 3. Productivity of the second capital investment rises. Land A remains in competition, land B bears rent.

Table XVIII

Type of land	Price of production (s.)	Output (bushels)	Selling price (s.)	Proceeds (s.)	Rent (s.)	Rent increase
A	60 + 60 = 120	10 + 15 = 25	$4\frac{4}{5}$	120	0	0
B	60 + 60 = 120	12 + 18 = 30	$4\frac{4}{5}$	144	24	24
C	60 + 60 = 120	14 + 21 = 35	$4\frac{4}{5}$	168	48	2 × 24
D	60 + 60 = 120	16 + 24 = 40	$4\frac{4}{5}$	192	72	3 × 24
E	60 + 60 = 120	18 + 27 = 45	$4\frac{4}{5}$	216	96	4 × 24
					240	10 × 24

Third case. The price of production rises.

[First modality.] If land A still bears no rent and governs price.

Variant 1. The productivity on the second capital investment remains the same; which means a declining productivity for the first investment.

Table XIX

Type of land	Price of production (s.)	Output (bushels)	Selling price (s.)	Proceeds (s.)	Rent (s.)	Rent increase
A	60 + 60 = 120	7½ + 10 = 17½	$6\frac{6}{7}$	120	0	0
B	60 + 60 = 120	9 + 12 = 21	$6\frac{6}{7}$	144	24	24
C	60 + 60 = 120	10½ + 14 = 24½	$6\frac{6}{7}$	168	48	2 × 24
D	60 + 60 = 120	12 + 16 = 28	$6\frac{6}{7}$	192	72	3 × 24
E	60 + 60 = 120	13½ + 18 = 31½	$6\frac{6}{7}$	216	96	4 × 24
					240	10 × 24

Variant 2. The productivity of the second capital investment falls; which does not rule out the possibility that the productivity of the first investment may remain the same.

Table XX

Type of land	Price of production (s.)	Output (bushels)	Selling price (s.)	Proceeds (s.)	Rent (s.)	Rent increase
A	60 + 60 = 120	10 + 5 = 15	8	120	0	0
B	60 + 60 = 120	12 + 6 = 18	8	144	24	24
C	60 + 60 = 120	14 + 7 = 21	8	168	48	2 × 24
D	60 + 60 = 120	16 + 8 = 24	8	192	72	3 × 24
E	60 + 60 = 120	18 + 9 = 27	8	216	96	4 × 24
					240	10 × 24

Variant 3. The productivity of the second capital investment rises; which, under the assumptions made, means a fall in productivity on the first investment.

Table XXI

Type of land	Price of production (s.)	Output (bushels)	Selling price (s.)	Proceeds (s.)	Rent (s.)	Rent increase
A	60 + 60 = 120	$5 + 12\frac{1}{2} = 17\frac{1}{2}$	$6\frac{6}{7}$	120	0	0
B	60 + 60 = 120	$6 + 15 = 21$	$6\frac{6}{7}$	144	24	24
C	60 + 60 = 120	$7 + 17\frac{1}{2} = 24\frac{1}{2}$	$6\frac{6}{7}$	168	48	2 × 24
D	60 + 60 = 120	$8 + 20 = 28$	$6\frac{6}{7}$	192	72	3 × 24
E	60 + 60 = 120	$9 + 22\frac{1}{2} = 31\frac{1}{2}$	$6\frac{6}{7}$	216	96	4 × 24
					240	10 × 24

[Second modality.] If an earlier soil (denoted by *a*) comes to govern price, and land A accordingly yields rent. This allows constant productivity for the second investment in all variants.*

Variant 1. The productivity of the second investment remains the same.

Table XXII

Type of land	Price of production (s.)	Output (bushels)	Selling price (s.)	Proceeds (s.)	Rent (s.)	Rent increase
a	120	16	$7\frac{1}{2}$	120	0	0
A	60 + 60 = 120	10 + 10 = 20	$7\frac{1}{2}$	150	30	30
B	60 + 60 = 120	12 + 12 = 24	$7\frac{1}{2}$	180	60	2 × 30
C	60 + 60 = 120	14 + 14 = 28	$7\frac{1}{2}$	210	90	3 × 30
D	60 + 60 = 120	16 + 16 = 32	$7\frac{1}{2}$	240	120	4 × 30
E	60 + 60 = 120	18 + 18 = 36	$7\frac{1}{2}$	270	150	5 × 30
					450	15 × 30

* Later Engels would appear in fact to contradict this assumption

Variant 2. The productivity of the second investment falls.

Table XXIII

Type of land	Price of production (s.)	Output (bushels)	Selling price (s.)	Proceeds (s.)	Rent (s.)	Rent increase
a	120	15	8	120	0	0
A	60 + 60 = 120	10 + 7½ = 17½	8	140	20	20
B	60 + 60 = 120	12 + 9 = 21	8	168	48	20 + 28
C	60 + 60 = 120	14 + 10½ = 24½	8	196	76	20 + 2 × 28
D	60 + 60 = 120	16 + 12 = 28	8	224	104	20 + 3 × 28
E	60 + 60 = 120	18 + 13½ = 31½	8	252	132	20 + 4 × 28
					380	5 × 20 + 10 × 28

Variant 3. The productivity of the second investment rises.

Table XXIV

Type of land	Price of production (s.)	Output (bushels)	Selling price (s.)	Proceeds (s.)	Rent (s.)	Rent increase
a	120	16	7½	120	0	0
A	60 + 60 = 120	10 + 12½ = 22½	7½	168¾	48¾	15 + 33¾
B	60 + 60 = 120	12 + 15 = 27	7½	202½	82½	15 + 2 × 33¾
C	60 + 60 = 120	14 + 17½ = 31½	7½	236¼	116¼	15 + 3 × 33¾
D	60 + 60 = 120	16 + 20 = 36	7½	270	150	15 + 4 × 33¾
E	60 + 60 = 120	18 + 22½ = 40½	7½	303¾	183¾	15 + 5 × 33¾
					581¼	5 × 15 + 15 × 33¾

These tables now give the following results.

First of all, the series of rents is in exactly the same ratio as the series of differences in fertility, taking the non-rent-bearing, price-governing land as the zero point. It is not the absolute yields that determine rent, but simply the differences in yields. Whether the various types of land provide yields of 1, 2, 3, 4, 5 bushels per acre, or 11, 12, 13, 14, 15 bushels, the rents are in both cases successively 0, 1, 2, 3, 4 bushels or their respective monetary equivalents.

What is far more important, however, is the result as regards the total rents yielded in the case of repeated capital investment on the same land.

In five cases out of the thirteen investigated, the total sum of rents also *doubles* with the capital investment; from 10 × 12s., this becomes 10 × 24s. = 240s. These cases are:

Case I, constant price, variant 1: constant rise in production (Table XII).

Case II, falling price, variant 3: increasing rise in production (Table XVIII).

Case III, rising price, first modality, where land A continues to govern price, in all three variants (Tables XIX, XX, XXI).

In four cases, the rent rises to *more than double*, i.e.:

Case I, variant 3, constant price, but increasing rise in production (Table XV). The total rent rises to 330s.

Case III, second modality, where land A yields rent, in all three variants (Table XXII, rent = $15 \times 30 = 450$s.; Table XXIII, rent = $5 \times 20 + 10 \times 28 = 380$s.; Table XXIV, rent = $5 \times 15 + 15 \times 33\frac{3}{4} = 581\frac{1}{4}$ s.).

In one case rent *rises*, but not to twice the rent in the case of the first capital investment:

Case I, price constant, variant 2: falling productivity for the second investment under conditions in which B does not completely cease to bear rent (Table XIV, rent = $4 \times 6 + 6 \times 21 = 150$s.).

Finally, only in three cases does the total rent for the second capital investment remain the same for all kinds of land as with the first investment (Table XI); these are the cases in which land A is withdrawn from competition and land B comes to govern price, thus ceasing to bear rent. Thus not only does the rent for B disappear, it is also deducted from each following member of the rent series, and this is how the result is obtained.

These cases are:

Case I, variant 2, when conditions are such that land A drops out (Table XIII). The sum of rent is 6×20, i.e. $10 \times 12 = 120$s., as in Table XI.

Case II, variants 1 and 2. Here land A necessarily drops out, according to our assumptions (Tables XVI and XVII), and the sum of rents is again $6 \times 20 = 10 \times 12 = 120$s.

This means, therefore, that in the great majority of all possible cases, rents rise, both per acre of the rent-bearing land and particularly in their total sum, as a result of increased capital investment on the land. Only in three cases out of thirteen investigated does the total rent remain unchanged. These are the cases where the most inferior quality of land, which formerly bore no rent and governed price, drops out of competition, and its place is taken by the next higher quality, which thus ceases to bear rent. But in these cases, too, rents rise on the best types of land in comparison with the rents arising from the first capital investment; if the rent for C falls from 24s. to 20s., the rents for D and E rise from 36s. and 48s. to 40s. and 60s.

A case of the total rent being below the level for the first capital investment (Table XI) would be possible only if it was not just land A that dropped out of competition but also land B, so that land C ceased to bear rent and came to govern price.

Thus the more capital is applied to the land and the higher the development of agriculture and civilization in general in a country, the higher are the levels of rent per acre and the total sum of rent and the more gigantic therefore the tribute society pays the great landowners in the form of surplus profits – as long as types of land once taken into cultivation all remain able to compete.

This law explains the amazing vitality of the class of large landowners. No other social class lives in so extravagant a manner; no other class claims such a right as this does to a traditional luxury in keeping with its 'estate', irrespective of where the money for this comes from; no other class piles debts upon debts in such a light-hearted way. And yet time and again they fall on their feet – thanks to the capital of other people that is put into the soil and yields them rent, completely out of all proportion to the profits the capitalist draws from this.

The same law, however, also explains why this vitality of the large landowner is gradually approaching its end.

When the Corn Laws were repealed in 1846, the English manufacturers believed they had thereby made the land-owning aristocracy into paupers. Instead, these aristocrats became richer than before. How did this happen? Very simply. Firstly, they now insisted in their contracts that the farmers should invest £12 a year on each acre instead of £8, while secondly, being represented in large numbers even in the House of Commons, the landlords granted themselves a hefty state subsidy for drainage and other permanent improvements to their estates. Since the worst land was not totally withdrawn from cultivation, but was at most used temporarily for other purposes, rents rose in proportion to the increased capital investment and the landed aristocracy did better than they had before.

But everything comes to an end eventually. The transoceanic steamships, and the railways in North and South America and in India, made some quite singular tracts of land able to compete on the European corn markets. First there were the North American prairies and the Argentine pampas, steppes which nature itself has made arable, virgin soil that offered rich yields for years even on rudimentary tilling and without fertilizer. Then there were the lands of the Russian and Indian communistic communities, which had to sell a portion of their product, and an ever growing one at that, to get money for the taxes exacted by a merciless state despotism – often enough by torture. These products were sold with no regard for their costs of production, sold at the price which the dealer offered, because the peasant absolutely had to have money at the payment date. And faced with this competition – from virgin prairie soil and from Russian and Indian peasants succumbing to the screws of taxation – the European farmer or peasant could not survive at the old rents. One portion of European soil became definitively uncompetitive for corn growing, while everywhere rents fell. Our 'second case, variant 2', falling prices and falling productivity on the additional capital investment, became the rule in Europe, and hence the agrarian complaint from Scotland to Italy, from the south of France to East Prussia. Fortunately, not all prairie land has yet been brought into cultivation by a long chalk; enough is still left to ruin European large-scale landownership completely – and small-scale ownership into the bargain. – F. E.)

*

Rent should be discussed under the following heads:

A. Differential rent.

1. The concept of differential rent. Example of water-power. Transition to agricultural rent proper.

2. Differential rent I, arising from the varying fertility of different portions of land.

3. Differential rent II, arising from successive capital investments on the same land. Differential rent II should be examined

    (a) with price of production constant;

    (b) price of production falling;

    (c) price of production rising.

As well as

    (d) The transformation of surplus profit into rent.

4. Influence of this rent on the rate of profit.

B. Absolute rent.

C. The price of land.

D. Final considerations on ground-rent.

*

We now have the following general result from considering differential rent as a whole.

Firstly, the formation of surplus profits can occur in various ways. On the one hand on the basis of differential rent I, i.e. the investment of the total agricultural capital on an acreage consisting of types of land of differing fertility. Then as differential rent II, on the basis of the varying differential productivity of successive capital investments on the same land, i.e. a greater productivity is obtained, in quarters of wheat, for example, than with the same capital investment on the most inferior land, which bears no rent but governs the production price. No matter how these surplus profits might arise, their transformation into rent, i.e. their transfer from the farmer to the landowner, always presupposes as its initial condition that the various actual individual prices of production (i.e. those independent of the general production price that governs the market) which the partial products of the individual successive capital investments possess are equalized in advance to give an individual average price of production. The excess of this general, governing production price of the product of an acre over the individual average production price, forms and measures the rent per acre. In the case of differential rent I, the differential results can be distinguished in and for themselves, because they take place on different areas of land, outside and alongside one another, given a capital outlay per acre that is taken as normal, and the normal cultivation corresponding to it. In the case of differential rent II, they must first be made distinguishable, they must in fact be transformed back into differential rent I, and this can only be done in the manner indicated.

Let us take Table III, for instance, on p. 826.

For the first capital investment of £2½, land B yields 2 qrs per acre, and for the second capital of equal size, 1½ qrs; a total of 3½ qrs on the same acre. We cannot tell from this 3½ qrs, which grows all on the same land, how much is the product of capital investment (1) and how much of capital investment (2). It is actually the product of the total capital of £5; and the fact of the matter is simply that a capital of £2½ yielded 2 qrs, while one of £5 yields not 4 but 3½ qrs. It would be exactly the same if the £5 were to yield 4 qrs, so that the yields of the two capital investments were equal, or even 5 qrs, so that the second capital investment produced an excess of 1 qr. The production price of the first 2 qrs is £1½ per qr in our example, while that of the second 1½ qrs is £2 per qr. The 3½ qrs together therefore cost £6. This is the individual production price of the total product, and makes an average of £1$\frac{5}{7}$ per qr. For the general production price of £3 as determined by land A, this gives a surplus profit of £1$\frac{2}{7}$ per qr, and thus for the 3$\frac{1}{2}$ qrs a total of £4$\frac{1}{2}$. Given the average production price for B, this is expressed in 1$\frac{1}{2}$ qrs. B's surplus profit is thus expressed in an aliquot part of its product, the 1$\frac{1}{2}$ qrs that forms the rent expressed in corn and is sold at £4$\frac{1}{2}$, given the general production price. But the extra product from an acre of B over that of an acre of A does not directly represent surplus profit and hence surplus product. According to our assumption, the acre of B produces 3$\frac{1}{2}$ qrs, the acre of A only 1 qr. The excess product on B is thus 2$\frac{1}{2}$ qrs, but the surplus product is only 1$\frac{1}{2}$ qrs, for twice as much capital is applied on B as on A, so that the production costs here are double. If there was a similar investment of £5 on A, and the rate of productivity remained the same, its product would be 2 qrs instead of 1 qr; the surplus product would be found by comparing not the 3$\frac{1}{2}$ qrs and the 1 qr but rather the 3$\frac{1}{2}$ qrs and the 2 qrs, so that it would not be 2$\frac{1}{2}$ qrs but only 1$\frac{1}{2}$ qrs. Moreover, if B invested a third portion of capital of £2$\frac{1}{2}$ which yielded only 1 qr, so that this qr cost £3, as on A, its sale price of £3 would cover only the costs of production, yielding only the average profit and no surplus profit, and therefore nothing that could be transformed into rent. The product per acre of any other type of land, compared with the product per acre of land A, indicates neither whether it is the product of the same capital investment or a greater one, nor whether the excess product simply covers the production price or whether it is due to higher productivity of the extra capital.

Secondly. Given a declining rate of productivity on the extra capital investments – and the limiting capital investment, as far as the formation of new surplus profit is concerned, is the one that simply covers the production costs, i.e. that produces a quarter of wheat as expensively as the same capital investment would on an acre of land A, for £5 on our assumption – it results from our previous argument that the limit at which the total capital investment on the acre of B would form no more rent is that at which the individual average production price of the product per acre of B would rise to the production price per acre of A.

If B adds only capital investments that pay the production price, and thus do not form any surplus profit or new rent, then although this increases the individual average production price per quarter, it does not affect the surplus profit formed by the earlier capital investments, which would eventually affect the rent. For the average production price always remains below that of A, and if the extra price per quarter declines, the number of quarters increases in the same proportion, so that the total excess price remains the same.

In the case taken here, the first two capital investments on B, of £5 each, produce a yield of $3\frac{1}{2}$ qrs, i.e. a rent of $1\frac{1}{2}$ qrs, $=$ £$4\frac{1}{2}$, according to our assumption. If a third capital investment of £$2\frac{1}{2}$ is now added, which however only produces one extra quarter, the total production price of the $4\frac{1}{2}$ qrs (including 20 per cent profit) $=$ £9, i.e. the average price per qr $=$ £2. The average production price per qr on B has thus risen from £$1\frac{5}{7}$ to £2, and the surplus profit per qr compared with the governing price of A has fallen from £$1\frac{2}{7}$ to £1. But £1 $\times$ $4\frac{1}{2}$ $=$ £$4\frac{1}{2}$, just as previously £$1\frac{2}{7}$ $\times$ $3\frac{1}{2}$ $=$ £$4\frac{1}{2}$.

If we assume that fourth and fifth additional capital investments of £$2\frac{1}{2}$ are made on B, each producing 1 qr only at its general production price, the total product per acre would now be $6\frac{1}{2}$ qrs, and its cost of production £15. The average production price per qr for B would have risen again from £2 to £$2\frac{4}{13}$, while the surplus profit per qr, compared with the governing production price of A, would have fallen again from £1 to £$\frac{9}{13}$. But this £$\frac{9}{13}$ would now be multiplied by $6\frac{1}{2}$ qrs instead of $4\frac{1}{2}$ qrs, and £$\frac{9}{13}$ $\times$ $6\frac{1}{2}$ $=$ £1 $\times$ $4\frac{1}{2}$ $=$ £$4\frac{1}{2}$.

The first thing that follows from this is that under these conditions no increase in the governing production price is needed to make additional capital investments possible on the rent-bearing types of land, even up to the level at which the additional capital completely ceases to provide surplus profit and simply still yields the average profit. It also follows that the total surplus profit per acre remains the same here, no matter how much the surplus profit per quarter declines; this decline is always offset by a corresponding increase in the quarters produced per acre. In order that the average production price may rise to the general production price (i.e. in this case to £3 for land B), additional capital must be added, the product of which has a higher production price than the governing one of £3. But we shall see that even this is not by itself sufficient to drive up the average price of production per quarter on B to the general production price of £3.

Let us assume that production on land B is as follows:

1. $3\frac{1}{2}$ qrs as before at a production price of £6; i.e. two capital investments of £$2\frac{1}{2}$ each, which both form surplus profits, but of decreasing size.

2. 1 qr at £3; a capital investment in which the individual production price would be equal to the governing production price.

3. 1 qr at £4; a capital investment in which the individual price of production is $33\frac{1}{3}$ per cent higher than the governing price.

We would then have $5\frac{1}{2}$ qrs per acre at £13, for a capital investment of £$10\frac{7}{10}$; four times the original capital investment, but less than three times the product of the first capital investment.

$5\frac{1}{2}$ qrs at £13 gives an average production price of £$2\frac{4}{11}$ per qr, i.e. at the governing production price of £3 there is an excess of £$\frac{7}{11}$ per qr which can be transformed into rent. $5\frac{1}{2}$ qrs for sale at the governing price of £3 gives £$16\frac{1}{2}$. After deducting the production costs of £13, there remains £$3\frac{1}{2}$ surplus profit or rent, which would represent $1\frac{42}{52}$ qrs at the prevailing average production price per qr on B, which is £$2\frac{4}{11}$. The money rent would have fallen by £1, the corn rent by about $\frac{1}{2}$ qr, yet despite the fact that the fourth extra capital investment on B [heading 3 above] produces not only no surplus profit, but rather less than the average profit, there is still surplus profit and rent as before. If we assume that not only this fourth capital investment, but the third, too, produces at over the governing production price in this way, the total production would be $3\frac{1}{2}$ qrs at £6 plus 2 qrs at £8, altogether $5\frac{1}{2}$ qrs for a production cost of £14. The average production price per qr would be £$2\frac{6}{11}$, and would leave a surplus of £$\frac{5}{11}$. The $5\frac{1}{2}$ qrs, sold at £3 per qr, gives £$16\frac{1}{2}$; subtracting £14 for the cost of production, £$2\frac{1}{2}$ is left for rent. This would be $\frac{55}{56}$ qrs at the new average production price. Some rent is still lost, although less than before.

This shows us that the rent on the better lands need not disappear with additional capital investments whose production costs more than the governing production price, at least within the limits of permissible practice, but need only decline, this decline being in proportion on the one hand to the aliquot part that this relatively unproductive capital forms of the total capital outlay, and on the other hand to the decline in its productivity. The average price of its product would still always stand below the governing price and would thus still leave a surplus profit which can be transformed into rent.

Let us now assume that the average price for a quarter on B coincides with the general production price, as a result of four successive capital investments (£2½, £2½, £5 and £5) with declining productivity.

Capital (£)	Profit (£)	Output (qrs)	Price of production		Selling price (£)	Proceeds (£)	Surplus for rent	
			per qr (£)	total (£)			qrs	£
1) 2½	½	2	1½	3	3	6	1	3
2) 2½	½	1½	2	3	3	4½	½	1½
3) 5	1	1½	4	6	3	4½	−½	−1½
4) 5	1	1	6	6	3	3	−1	−3
15	3	6		18		18	0	0

In this case the farmer sells each quarter at its individual price of production, and hence sells the total number of quarters at their average production price per quarter, which coincides with the governing price of £3. Now as before, therefore, he makes a profit of 20 per cent = £3 on his capital of £15. But the rent has disappeared. Where does the surplus go when the individual production price of each quarter is equalized with the general production price in this way?

The surplus profit on the first £2½ was £3; on the second £2½ it was £1½; the total surplus profit on this third of the capital advanced, i.e. on £5, was £4½ = 90 per cent.

The third capital investment of £5 not only yields no surplus profit, but its product of 1½ qrs, sold at the general price of production, brings a loss of £1½. On the fourth capital investment, finally, which is also £5, the product of 1 qr, sold at the general price of production, brings a loss of £3. These two capital investments together thus involve a loss of £4½, equal to the surplus profit of £4½ produced by capital investments (1) and (2).

The surplus profits and the losses of profit cancel out. The rent therefore vanishes. In fact, however, this is possible only because the elements of surplus-value that formed surplus profit or rent now go into the formation of the average profit. The farmer makes this average profit of £3 on £15, or 20 per cent, at the expense of the rent.

The establishment of equality between the individual average production price on B and the general production price on A, which governs the market, presupposes that the amount by which the individual price of the product of the earlier capital investments stands below the governing price is offset more and more, and finally cancelled out by the amount by which the product of the later capital investments comes to stand above the governing price. What appears as surplus profit, as long as the product of the earlier capital investments is sold by itself, gradually becomes part of the average production price and thereby goes into the formation of the average profit, until it is finally absorbed by this entirely.

If, instead of £15 capital, only £5 is laid out on B and the extra $2\frac{1}{2}$ qrs in the last table are produced by $2\frac{1}{2}$ acres of A being freshly cultivated with a capital investment of £$2\frac{1}{2}$ per acre, then the additional capital laid out would amount only to £$6\frac{1}{4}$, i.e. the total outlay on A and B for the production of these 6 qrs would be only £$11\frac{1}{4}$ instead of £15 and their total production costs, including profit, would be £$13\frac{1}{2}$. The 6 qrs would still be sold together for £18, as before, but the capital outlay would have decreased by £$3\frac{3}{4}$, and the rent on B would come to £$4\frac{1}{2}$ per acre, again as before. It would be a different matter if in order to produce the extra $2\frac{1}{2}$ qrs it were necessary to resort to worse land than A, to A_{-1}, A_{-2}, with a resulting production price per qr for $1\frac{1}{2}$ qrs on land A_{-1} of £4, and for the final qr on A_{-2} of £6. In this case, £6 would be the governing production price per qr. The $3\frac{1}{2}$ qrs from B would be sold for £21 instead of for £$10\frac{1}{2}$, which would give a rent of £15 instead of £$4\frac{1}{2}$, and of $2\frac{1}{2}$ qrs in corn instead of $1\frac{1}{2}$ qrs. On A, similarly, the 1 qr would now yield a rent of £3 = $\frac{1}{2}$ qr.

One final remark before we discuss this point further.

The average price of a quarter on B is equalized and coincides with the general production price of £3 per qr governed by A, as soon as the part of the total capital that produces the additional $1\frac{1}{2}$ qrs is offset by the part of the total capital that produces the deficient $1\frac{1}{2}$ qrs. How soon this equalization is reached, or how much capital must be invested on B with deficient productivity for it to be reached, depends, taking the surplus productivity of the first capital investments as given, on the relative underproductivity of the capitals later applied, compared with an equally large capital investment on the poorest, price-governing land A, or on the individual production price of the product of this investment, compared with the governing price.

*

Here is the next point that arises from the foregoing.

Firstly, as long as the additional capitals are invested on the same land with surplus productivity, even if this is decreasing, the absolute corn and money rent per acre rises, even if it declines relatively, in proportion to the capital advanced (i.e. the rate of surplus profit or rent). The limit here is formed by that additional capital which yields only the average profit, or for whose product the individual production price coincides with the general one. The production price remains the same, under these conditions, as long as the increased supply does not make production from the poorer types of land superfluous. Even with a falling price, these additional capitals can still produce a surplus profit within certain limits, even if a smaller one.

Secondly, the investment of additional capital which produces only the average profit, i.e. whose surplus productivity $= 0$, does not alter the amount of surplus profit and hence rent that is formed. The individual average price per quarter therefore rises on the better types of land; the excess per quarter declines, but the number of quarters bearing this reduced excess increases, in such a way that the product of the two remains the same.

Thirdly, additional capital investments for which the individual production price of their products stands above the governing price, so that their surplus productivity is not just nothing but less than nothing, a negative quantity (i.e. a productivity less than that of the same capital investment on the price-governing land A), bring the individual average price of the total product of the better land ever closer to the general production price, and thus more and more reduce the difference between the two, which is what forms the surplus profit or rent. More and more of what would form surplus profit or rent goes into the formation of the average profit. And yet, for all that, the total capital invested on an acre of B continues to yield a surplus profit, even if this declines with the increasing amount of capital of deficient productivity and with the level of this underproductivity. The rent per acre in this case falls in absolute terms as capital grows and production increases, and does not just fall relatively to the growing size of the capital invested, as it does in the second case.

The rent can disappear only if the individual average production price of the total product on the better land B coincides with the governing price, i.e. if the entire surplus profit of the earlier and more productive capital investments has been used to form the average profit.

The minimum limit to the fall in the rent per acre is the point at which this disappears. But this point is not reached as soon as the extra capital investments produce with deficient productivity, but only when the extra investment of deficiently productive portions of capital becomes so great that its effect cancels out the surplus productivity of the first capital investments, so that the productivity of the total capital invested comes to be equal to that of the capital on A and hence the individual average price per quarter on B equal to that on A.

Even in this case, the governing price of production, £3 per qr, remains the same, although the rent has vanished. It is only beyond this point that the production price would have to rise, as the result of an increase either in the degree of deficient productivity of the surplus capital, or in the amount of extra capital of the same deficient productivity. If in the table on p. 865, for example, $2\frac{1}{2}$ qrs were produced at £4 per qr on the same land instead of $1\frac{1}{2}$ qrs, we would have altogether 7 qrs for a production cost of £22; the cost would now be £$3\frac{1}{7}$ per qr; i.e. £$\frac{1}{7}$ higher than the general production price, which would have to rise.

Thus extra capital with deficient productivity, and even capital with increasingly deficient productivity, could still be applied for a long while before the individual average price per quarter on the best lands became equal to the general price of production, i.e. before the excess of the latter over the former, and hence surplus profit and rent, completely disappeared.

Even in this case, moreover, the disappearance of rent on the better types of land would mean only that the individual production price of the product from these better types would coincide with the general price of production; no rise in this general price would yet be required.

In the above example, taking the better land B, which however is lowest in the series of better or rent-bearing land types, $3\frac{1}{2}$ qrs was produced by a capital of £5 with surplus productivity and $2\frac{1}{2}$ qrs by a capital of £10 with deficient productivity, making a total of 6 qrs, i.e. five-twelfths of the total was produced by the latter portions of capital that are invested at deficient productivity. And it is only at this point that the individual average production price of the 6 qrs rises to £3 per qr, coinciding therefore with the general production price.

Under the law of landed property, however, the latter $2\frac{1}{2}$ qrs could not have been produced in this manner at £3 per qr, except in the case where it could be produced on $2\frac{1}{2}$ new acres of type A land. The case in which the extra capital only produces at the general price of production would have imposed a limit. Beyond this, extra capital investment on the same land would have to cease.

If the farmer has to pay, say, £$4\frac{1}{2}$ rent for the first two capital investments, he must continue to pay it, and any capital investment that needs more than £3 to produce a quarter would involve a deduction from his profit. In the case of deficient productivity, therefore, equalization of the individual average price is thereby prevented.

Let us take this case in connection with the previous example, where the production price of £3 per qr on land A governs the price for B.

Capital (£)	Profit (£)	Price of production (£)	Output (qrs)	Price of production per qr (£)	Selling price		Surplus profit (£)	Loss (£)
					per qr (£)	total (£)		
$2\frac{1}{2}$	$\frac{1}{2}$	3	2	$1\frac{1}{2}$	3	6	3	—
$2\frac{1}{2}$	$\frac{1}{2}$	3	$1\frac{1}{2}$	2	3	$4\frac{1}{2}$	$1\frac{1}{2}$	—
5	1	6	$1\frac{1}{2}$	4	3	$4\frac{1}{2}$	—	$1\frac{1}{2}$
5	1	6	1	6	3	3	—	3
15	3	18				18	$4\frac{1}{2}$	$4\frac{1}{2}$

The production costs of the $3\frac{1}{2}$ qrs from the first two capital investments are similarly £3 per qr for the farmer, since he has to pay a rent of £$4\frac{1}{2}$, so that the difference between his individual production price and the general production price does not flow into his pocket. For him, therefore, the surplus in the price of the product of the first two capital investments cannot serve to balance the deficit suffered on the products of the third and fourth capital investments.

The $1\frac{1}{2}$ qrs from capital investment (3) cost the farmer £6, profit included; but he can only sell for £4$\frac{1}{2}$, taking the governing price at £3 per qr. Thus he would lose not only the entire profit, but £$\frac{1}{2}$ or 10 per cent of his invested capital of £5 into the bargain. His loss in profit and capital for the third investment would come to £1$\frac{1}{2}$, and for the fourth investment £3, together making £4$\frac{1}{2}$, exactly as much as the rent for the better capital investments – whose individual production price, however, cannot go into the individual average production price of B's total product as a compensating factor, since this surplus is paid out to a third party as rent.

If it were necessary for the third capital investment to produce its extra $1\frac{1}{2}$ qrs in order to meet the demand, the governing market price would have to rise to £4 per qr. As a result of this increase in the governing market price, the rent on B would rise for the first and second capital investment, and a rent would be formed on A.

Thus even though the differential rent is only a formal transformation of surplus profit into rent, and in this case landed property simply enables the landowner to transfer the farmer's surplus profit to himself, it transpires that the successive investment of capital on the same stretch of land, or, what comes to the same thing, the increase in the capital invested on the same land, tends rather to find its limit in this transference, given a declining rate of productivity on capital and a constant governing price; in fact it comes up against a more or less artificial barrier, a result of the merely formal transformation of surplus profit into ground-rent which is the consequence of landed property. The rise in the general price of production which becomes necessary here, where the limit is narrower than elsewhere, is in this case therefore not only the basis for the rise in the differential rent, but the existence of differential rent as rent is at the same time the basis for the earlier and more rapid rise in the general price of production in order thereby to guarantee the increased supply of the product that has become necessary.

The following should also be noted.

The governing price could not rise to £4, as above, thanks to the extra capital on land B, if land A were to supply the extra product for less than £4, or if newer and poorer land than A came into competition, with a price of production that was above £3 but below £4. We thus see how differential rent I and differential rent II, while the first is the basis of the second, at the same time place limits on one another, leading sometimes to successive investments of capital on the same stretch of land and sometimes to adjacent investments of capital on new additional land. They have a similar effect as limits to one another in other cases, for example where better land is taken up.

Chapter 44: Differential Rent Even
on the Poorest Land Cultivated

Let us assume that the demand for corn is rising and the supply can be satisfied only by successive capital investments with deficient productivity on the rent-bearing lands, by additional capital investment, similarly with declining productivity, on land A, or by capital investment on new lands of inferior quality to A.

Let us take land B as representative of the rent-bearing lands.

The extra capital investment requires a rise in the market price above the former governing production price of £3 per qr, in order to make possible the extra production of 1 qr on B. (This 1 qr may represent 1 million qrs, and each acre 1 million acres.) On C and D, etc., the types of land with the highest rent, there may also be a surplus product, but only with declining surplus productivity; the 1 qr from B, however, is assumed to be necessary in order to meet the demand. If this 1 qr can be produced more cheaply by extra capital on B than by the same extra capital on A, or by descending to land A_{-1} which can only produce at £4 per qr, for example, whereas the extra capital on A could produce at, say, £3¾ per qr, then the extra capital on B would govern the market price.

A would have produced 1 qr at £3 as before. B, also as before, a total of 3½ qrs, at an individual production price of £6 altogether. If an extra £4 in production costs (including profit) was now necessary on B in order to produce a further quarter, while on A this could be produced at £3¾, it would obviously be produced on A and not on B. Let us assume therefore that it could be produced on B for an extra production cost of £3½. In this case, £3½ would be the governing price for the total production. B would sell its product, now 4½ qrs, for £15¾. The production costs of the first 3½ qrs form a deduction of £6 from this and those of the final qr £3½, a total of £9½. The surplus profit remaining for rent is £6¼, against only £4½ before. In this case, the acre of A would also yield a rent of £½; but it would not be the worst land A, but the better land B, that governed the production price of £3½. It is assumed here of course that there is no new accessible land of quality A and as well situated as that already cultivated, but that either a second capital investment would be needed on the stretch of A already cultivated, albeit at a still higher cost of production, or else it would be necessary to bring in still worse land A_{-1}. As soon as differential rent II comes into play, by way of successive capital investments, the limits to the rising production price can be governed by better land, and the worst land, the basis for differential rent I, can then also bear rent. In this case, then, all cultivated land would bear rent in the sense of simple differential rent. We should then have the following two tables, in which price of production refers to the sum of the capital advanced plus 20 per cent profit, i.e. £½ profit on each £2½ capital, making a total of £3.

Type of land	Acres	Price of production (£)	Output (qrs)	Selling price (£)	Proceeds (£)	Corn rent (qrs)	Money rent (£)
A	1	3	1	3	3	0	0
B	1	6	3½	3	10½	1½	4½
C	1	6	5½	3	16½	3½	10½
D	1	6	7½	3	22½	5½	16½
Total	4	21	17½		52½	10½	31½

This is how things stand before the new capital investment of £3½ on B, which only supplies 1 qr. After this capital investment, the situation is as follows.

Type of land	Acres	Price of production (£)	Output (qrs)	Selling price (£)	Proceeds (£)	Corn rent (qrs)	Money rent (£)
A	1	3	1	3½	3½	$\frac{1}{7}$	$\frac{1}{2}$
B	1	9½	4½	3½	15¾	$1\frac{11}{14}$	6¼
C	1	6	5½	3½	19¼	$3\frac{11}{14}$	13¼
D	1	6	7½	3½	26¼	$5\frac{11}{14}$	20¼
Total	4	24½	18½		64¾	11½	40¼

(The calculation here is again not completely correct. For the farmer of land B, the $4\frac{1}{2}$ qrs cost firstly £$9\frac{1}{2}$ in production costs, and secondly £$4\frac{1}{2}$ in rent, altogether £14; an average of £$3\frac{1}{9}$ per qr. This average price of his total production therefore becomes the governing market price. The rent on A would accordingly come to £$\frac{1}{9}$ instead of £$\frac{1}{2}$, while that on B would remain £$4\frac{1}{2}$ as before; $4\frac{1}{2}$ qrs at £$3\frac{1}{9}$ = £14, which, when £$9\frac{1}{2}$ is deducted for production costs, leaves £$4\frac{1}{2}$ for surplus profit. We see that despite the need to alter the figures, the example shows how differential rent II enables the better land that already bears rent to govern the price, and how in this way *all* land, even that which was previously devoid of rent, may be turned into rent-bearing land. – F. E.)

The corn rent must increase once the governing production price of corn rises, i.e. once an increase takes place in the price of a quarter of corn from the price-governing land or in the level of the price-governing capital investment on one of the land types. It is the same as if all types had become less fertile and produced only $\frac{5}{7}$ qr for a £$2\frac{1}{2}$ new capital investment, say, instead of 1 qr. The extra corn that they produce with the same capital investment is transformed into surplus product, representing surplus profit and hence rent. If we assume that the profit rate remains unchanged, the farmer can buy less corn with his profit. The profit rate may remain the same if wages do not rise – either because they are pressed down to the physical minimum, i.e. below the normal value of labour-power; or because the other objects of working-class consumption, those provided by manufacture, become relatively cheaper; or because the working day is prolonged or made more intensive and hence the profit rate in the non-agricultural branches of production, which however is what governs agricultural profit, remains the same, if it does not rise; or because, although the same capital is invested in agriculture, it includes more of the constant and less of the variable variety.

We have now dealt with the first way in which rent can arise on the formerly poorest land A, without the bringing into cultivation of still worse land; namely the way it originates from the difference between its individual price of production, which was formerly the governing one, and the new, higher price of production at which the last bit of extra capital supplies the extra product needed on better soil but with deficient productivity.

If the extra product had to be supplied by land A_{-1}, which can only supply at £4 per qr, the rent of A would rise to £1 per acre. In this case, however, A_{-1} would take the place of A as the worst cultivated land, and A would come into the series of rent-bearing types as its lowest member. Differential rent I would have been affected. This case therefore lies outside a treatment of differential rent II, which arises from the varying productivity of successive capital investments on the same stretch of land.

But differential rent on land A can still arise in two other ways.

With a constant price – any given price, even one lower than previously prevailing – if the additional capital investment leads to surplus productivity, which must *prima facie* always be the case up to a certain point, particularly on the worst land.

Secondly, however, if the productivity of successive capital investments on land A declines.

It is assumed in both cases that the increased production is required by the state of demand.

Here, though, from the standpoint of differential rent, a particular difficulty presents itself on account of the law previously developed, i.e. that it is always the individual average price of production of a quarter for the total production (or the total capital outlay) that is decisive. In the case of land A, however, unlike the better types of land, there is no production price given outside itself, such as would restrict the equalization between the individual production price and the general one. For the individual production price of A is precisely the general production price that governs the market.

Assume:

(1) *The productivity of successive capital investments is rising.* 3 qrs instead of 2 qrs can be produced on 1 acre of A with a capital advance of £5, and at a cost of production therefore of £6. The first capital investment of £2½ supplies 1 qr, the second 2 qrs. In this case, £6 in production costs yields 3 qrs, so that the average cost is £2 per qr; if these 3 qrs are then sold at £2 per qr, A continues to bear no rent, and it is simply the basis of differential rent II that has changed. £2 has become the governing production price instead of £3; a capital of £2½ now produces an average of 1½ qrs on the poorest land instead of 1 qr, and this is now the official yield for all superior types of land when £2½ is invested. A part of their former surplus product goes from now on into forming their necessary product, just as a part of their surplus profit goes into the formation of the average profit.

If we reckon how things stand for the better types of land, however, where the average calculation in no way affects the absolute surplus, since for these soils the general production price is a given barrier to capital investment, then the 1 qr from the first capital investment costs £3 and the 2 qrs from the second investment cost only £1½ each. A corn rent of 1 qr and a money rent of £3 thus arises on A, even though the 3 qrs are still sold at their old price of £9 altogether. If there is then a third capital investment of £2½, with the same yield as the second, a total of 5 qrs would be produced for a production cost of £9. If A's individual average price of production remains the governing one, each quarter must now be sold at £1⅘. The average price would have fallen again, not because of a new rise in the yield of the third capital investment, but rather because of the addition of a new capital investment with the same extra yield as the second. Instead of causing an increase in the rent, as would be the case on the rent-bearing lands, the successive capital investments of higher but constant yield on land A cause a proportionate fall in the price of production, and with it in the differential rent on all other types of land, if other factors remain the same. If however the first capital investment that produces 1 qr at a production cost of £3 is to remain the regulator, these 5 qrs must be sold at £15, and the differential rent for the later capital investments on land A must amount to £6. Additional surplus capital per acre of A, whatever the form in which it is applied, would here be an improvement, while the additional capital would also have made the original capital more productive. It would be nonsense to say that a third of the capital had produced 1 qr, and the remaining two-thirds had produced 4 qrs. £9 per acre would always produce 5 qrs, while £3 would produce only 1 qr. Whether or not a rent arises here – a surplus profit – would depend entirely on the circumstances. Normally, the governing price of production would have to fall. This is the case when this improved but more costly cultivation of land A is undertaken only because it is also on the better types of land – i.e. a general revolution in agriculture; so that now, when we speak of the natural fertility of land A, we assume that it is obtained with £6 or £9 instead of with £3. This would particularly be the case if the majority of acres of land A which are tilled, and which provide the bulk of the country's supply, are transferred to this new method. But if the improvement affected only a small portion of the acreage of A, to start with, this better cultivated part would supply a surplus profit which the landowner would quickly reach out to turn completely or in part into rent, and fix it as such. In this way, if demand kept pace with the growing supply, then to the extent that the whole area of land A was gradually transferred to the new method, rent could gradually form on all land of quality A and the surplus profit would be completely or partially confiscated, according to the market conditions. The establishment of equality between A's production price and the average price of its product in conditions of increased capital outlay might in this way meet an obstacle in the fixation in the form of rent of the surplus profit of this increased capital outlay. In this case, as we saw previously on the better lands in conditions of declining productivity for the additional capital, it would again be the transformation of the surplus profit into ground-rent, i.e. the intervention of landed property, that raised the production price, instead of the differential rent being simply the result of differences between the individual production price and the general one. For land A this would prevent the two prices from coinciding because it would prevent the production price from being governed by A's average production price; a higher production price than necessary would be maintained, and rent created accordingly. Even with the free import of corn from abroad, the same result could be obtained or maintained, if the farmer were compelled to turn to other uses, e.g. pasture, such land as was capable of competing in grain cultivation without yielding rent, at the price of production governed by foreign conditions, with the result that only rent-bearing land – i.e. only land whose individual average price of production per quarter was less than that determined by conditions abroad – would be used for the cultivation of grain. It should generally be assumed that the production price would fall in the given case, though not to the average price. It would stand higher than this, but below the production price of the worst cultivated land A, so that competition from new land would be restricted.

(2) *The productivity of the additional capitals is declining.* Assume that land A_{-1} can only produce each additional quarter at £4, whereas land A can do this at £3¾: less dear, but £¾ dearer than the quarter produced by the first capital investment. In this case the total price of the 2 qrs produced on A would be £6¾; i.e. an average price per qr of £3⅜. The production price would rise, but only by £⅜, whereas if the additional capital was applied to

new land which produced at £3¾, it would rise by a further £⅜ to £3¾ and would thereby cause a proportionate rise in all other differential rents.

The production price of £3⅜ per qr on A would thus be equalized with the average production price with an increased capital investment, and would be the governing one; i.e. it would not yield any surplus profit, and therefore no rent.

But if this quarter produced by the second capital investment was sold at £3¾, land A would now yield a rent of £¾, and moreover this would happen even on acres of A on which no extra capital investment had been made, and which therefore still continued to produce at £3 per qr. As long as there are still untilled stretches of A, the price could rise only temporarily to £3¾. The competition of new stretches of A would keep the price of production down to £3 until all land A able by its favourable situation to produce at less than £3¾ per qr was exhausted. This is what we would assume, even though when one acre of a certain land bears rent, the landowner will not lease out another acre of the same land rent-free.

It depends once more on how far the second capital investment on the available land A has become general, whether the production price is equalized to the average price, or whether the individual production price of the second capital investment, £3¾, becomes the governing one. The latter is the case only when the landowner has the time to fix as rent the surplus profit that was made before the demand was satisfied at a price of £3¾.

*

Liebig* should be consulted on the declining productivity of the soil when successive capital investments are made. We have seen how the successive decline in surplus productivity of capital investments always increases the rent per acre when the price of production is constant, and how it can even do this when the price is falling.

---

* Marx evidently had a high regard for the organic chemist Freiherr Justus von Liebig (1803–73), who was a pioneer in the application of chemistry to agricultural problems. Liebig is referred to several times in both this volume of *Capital* and Volume 1, and it seems that Marx took from Liebig the concept of metabolism (*Stoffwechsel*) that he applied there, suitably transformed, to the analysis of the labour process (Chapter 7). The work that Marx refers to here is Liebig's *Die Chemie in ihrer Anwendung auf Agricultur und Physiologie*, 7th edn, 1862.

The following general point should be noted, however.

From the standpoint of the capitalist mode of production, there is always a relative increase in the price of products if, in order to obtain the same product, an outlay must be made that was previously unnecessary. For the replacement of capital consumed in the course of production does not simply mean the replacement of values expressed in particular means of production. Natural elements which go into production as agents without costing anything, whatever role they might play in production, do not go in as components of capital, but rather as a free natural power of capital; in fact a free natural productive power of labour, but one which on the basis of the capitalist mode of production presents itself as a productive power of capital, like every other productive power. If a natural power of this kind, therefore, which originally cost nothing, goes into production, it does not count in determining prices as long as the product supplied with its aid is sufficient to meet the demand. But if a greater product has to be supplied in the course of development than can be produced with the aid of this natural power, so that this additional product must be produced without the aid of this natural power or with human assistance, human labour, a new and additional element goes into the capital. A relatively greater capital investment is thus needed to obtain the same product. All other circumstances remaining the same, production becomes more expensive.

*

(From a notebook 'Begun mid-February 1876': F. E.)

Differential rent and rent as simply interest on the capital incorporated into the soil

So-called permanent improvements – those which change the physical characteristics of the soil, and in part also its chemical properties, by operations that require a capital outlay and can be considered as an incorporation of capital into the soil – almost all boil down to giving a particular piece of land, the soil in a particular and restricted place, characteristics that other land somewhere else, and often quite close by, possesses by nature. One piece of land is naturally level, the other has to be levelled. One is naturally well drained, the other requires draining artificially. One has a naturally deep top-soil, in the other this has to be artificially deepened. One clay soil is naturally mixed with the requisite amount of sand, in the other this proportion has to be obtained artificially. One meadow is naturally irrigated or covered with layers of silt, the other has to be made so by labour, or, in the language of bourgeois economics, by capital.

Now it is a truly amusing theory which asserts that on the land whose comparative advantages are acquired, rent is interest, while on the other land, which has these advantages by nature, it is not. (In actual fact, this question is confused in practice because rent really does coincide with interest in the one case, so it is also called interest and has to be misnamed as such in the others, where this is positively not the case.) But after the capital investment has been made, the land bears the rent not because capital has been invested in it but rather because the capital investment has made the land a more productive field of investment than before. If we assume that all the land in a country requires this capital investment, each piece of land which has not yet passed through this state has to do so, and the rent borne by the land already provided with this capital investment (the interest that it yields in the given case) is just as much a differential rent as if it possessed this advantage by nature and the other land had to obtain it artificially.

This rent which can be resolved into interest also becomes pure differential rent as soon as the capital laid out is amortized. Otherwise the same capital would have to lead a double existence as capital.

*

It is a most curious phenomenon that all those opponents of Ricardo who struggled against the determination of value exclusively in terms of labour, when faced with the fact that differential rent arose from differences in land, maintained that in this case nature determined value instead of labour, though at the same time they allowed this determination in the case of the land's position, or even, and still more, for interest on capital put into the soil for the purpose of cultivation. The same labour produces the same value for the product created in a given time; but the size or amount of this product, and thus the portion of value which falls to a particular aliquot part, depends for a given quantity of labour solely on the amount of the product, and this in turn on the productivity of the given amount of labour, not on its absolute amount. Whether this productivity is due to nature or society is quite immaterial. But in the case where it itself costs labour, i.e. capital, it increases the costs of production by a new component, which is not the case when nature alone is involved.

Chapter 45: Absolute Ground-Rent

In our analysis of differential rent, we proceeded from the premise that the worst land pays no ground-rent, or, to put it more generally, land pays ground-rent only when the individual production price of its product is below the production price that governs the market, giving rise to a surplus profit that is transformed into rent. The first thing to note here is that the law of differential rent, as differential rent, is completely independent of the truth or falsity of that premise.

If we call the general production price that governs the market P, then, for the product of the worst type of land A, P coincides with its individual production price; i.e. its price pays for the constant and variable capital consumed in the course of production plus the average profit (= profit of enterprise plus interest).

Rent here is zero. The individual production price of the next better type of land B $= P'$ and $P > P'$, i.e. P pays for more than the actual production price of the product of land in class B. Now let $P - P' = d$; d, the excess of P over P', is thus the surplus profit made by the farmer in class B. This is transformed into rent, to be paid to the landowner. For the third class of land C, let the actual production price be P'', so that $P - P'' = 2d$; this $2d$ is now transformed into rent. Similarly for the fourth class D the individual production price is P''', and $P - P''' = 3d$, transformed into rent, and so on. Let us now assume that the premise of zero rent for land in class A, the price of its product being $P + 0$, is false. Instead, say that it pays a rent $= r$. Two things then follow.

Firstly, the price of the product of class A land would not be governed by its price of production, but would contain a surplus over and above this; it would be $P + r$. For assuming the capitalist mode of production in its normal condition, i.e. assuming that the surplus r that the farmer pays to the landowner is neither a deduction from wages nor from the average profit of capital, he can pay it only by selling his product above its price of production, so that it would yield him a surplus profit if he did not have to part with this surplus to the landowner in the form of rent. The governing market price of the total product on the market from all types of land would then not be the price of production that capital generally yields in all spheres of production, i.e. a price equal to the outlays plus the average profit, it would be this production price plus the rent, $P + r$ rather than just P. For the price of the product of class A land always represents the limit of the governing general market price, the price at which the total product can be supplied, and to this extent it governs the price of this total product.

Secondly, however, in this case, even though the general price of the product of the land would be basically modified, the law of differential rent would not in any way be thereby abolished. For if the price of the product of class A, and therefore the general market price, was $P + r$, the price for classes B, C, D etc. would be $P + r$ too. But since for class B, $P - P' = d, (P + r) - (P' + r)$ would also $= d$; and similarly for class C, $P - P'' = (P + r) - (P'' + r) = 2d$; for class D, $P - P''' = (P + r) - (P''' + r) = 3d$, etc. The differential rent would thus be the same as before, and would be governed by the same law even though the rent contained an element independent of this law and underwent a general rise together with the price of the product. It follows from this that whatever the rent on the least fertile types of land might be, not only is the law of differential rent independent of it, but the only way to grasp the true character of differential rent itself is to set the rent for class A land at zero. Whether it really is zero, or something positive, is immaterial as far as the differential rent is concerned, and does not need to be taken into account.

The law of differential rent is thus unaffected by the result of the following analysis.

If we now investigate more closely the basis of the assumption that the product of the poorest land A pays no rent, we get the following result. If the market price of the product, say corn, reaches such a level that an additional advance of capital invested in class A land pays the customary price of production, i.e. yields the customary average profit on the capital, this condition is sufficient for the investment of additional capital on class A land. That is to say, this condition is sufficient for the capitalist to invest new capital at the customary profit and to valorize it in the normal way.

It should be noted here that even in this case the market price must be higher than the production price of A. For as soon as the additional supply is obtained, the relationship of demand and supply is evidently changed. Formerly the supply was not sufficient, whereas now it is sufficient. The price must therefore fall. In order to fall, it must have stood higher than the production price of A. But the less fertile character of the class A land that has been newly cultivated means that the price does not fall again as low as it was when the production price of class B governed the market. The production price of A sets a limit for a relatively permanent rise in the market price, and not just for a temporary one. If on the other hand the land newly brought into cultivation is more fertile than the land A that formerly governed the price, and yet is only sufficient to meet the additional demand, the market price remains unchanged. But the analysis of whether the worst class of land pays a rent coincides in this case too with the question under discussion here, for here too the assumption that class A land does not pay any rent would be explained by the fact that the market price is just sufficient for the capitalist farmer to cover the capital applied plus the average profit; in short, the market price provides him with the price of production of his commodities.

In any case, in so far as he has to act as a capitalist, the capitalist farmer on class A land can cultivate under these conditions. The condition for the normal valorization of capital on class A land is then present. But from the premise that capital could now be invested by the farmer on class A land under the average valorization conditions of capital, it in no way follows that this land in class A is now immediately at the farmer's disposal. The fact that the farmer could valorize his capital at the customary profit if he paid no rent is in no way a reason for the landlord to lease out his land to the farmer for nothing, and be so philanthropic to his client as to extend him a *crédit gratuit*.* This assumption would mean abstracting from landed property, it would mean abolishing landed property, whose very existence is a barrier to the investment of capital and its unrestricted valorization on the land – a

* Interest-free credit. See above, p. 743.

barrier that in no way collapses in face of the farmer's mere reflection that the level of corn prices would enable him to obtain the customary profit on his capital by exploiting land of type A, as long as he did not pay any rent, i.e. if he could actually treat landed property as non-existent. Differential rent presupposes precisely the monopoly of landed property, landed property as a barrier to capital, for otherwise the surplus profit would not be transformed into ground-rent and would not accrue to the land-lord instead of to the farmer. And landed property remains such a barrier even where rent in the form of differential rent disappears, i.e. on type A land. If we consider the cases where capital invest-ment on the land can take place without payment of rent, in a country of capitalist production, we shall find that they all involve a factual – if not a legal – abolition of landed property, an aboli-tion that can occur only under very special conditions of an acci-dental nature.

Firstly. If the landowner is himself a capitalist or the capitalist a landowner. In this case he can *cultivate his land himself* as soon as the market price has risen sufficiently to obtain the price of production from the present land A, i.e. to replace capital plus average profit. And why? Because as far as he is concerned, landed property does not set any barrier to the investment of his capital. He can treat the land as a simple natural element and let his decision be determined exclusively by considering the valorization of his capital, by capitalist considerations. Such cases do exist in practice, but only as exceptions. Just as the capitalist cultivation of the land assumes a separation between functioning capital and landed property, so it generally rules out cultivation by the landed proprietor himself. We can see immediately how this is purely accidental. If an increased demand for corn requires the cultivation of a greater extent of type A land than is to be found in the hands of self-farming proprietors, i.e. if one part of it has to be leased in order to be cultivated at all, this hypothetical abolition of the barrier that landed property places to the investment of capital immediately disappears. It is an absurd contradiction to start from the separation between capital and land, tenant farmer and landowner, which corresponds to the capitalist mode of production, and then to assume the reverse, i.e. that the land-owner is his own farmer, up to the point that, or wherever, capital would draw no rent from cultivating the land if there were no landed property independent of it. (See the passage on rent of mines in Adam Smith, quoted below.)* This abolition of landed property is accidental. It may exist or it may not.

Secondly. A leasehold may include particular pieces of land that pay no rent at the given level of market prices, and are in fact rented free, though they are not viewed in this light by the landowner, since what he pays attention to is the total rental of the land leased and not the particular rent of individual component parts. In this case the rent paid by the farmer for the investment of his capital disappears as far as these non-rent-bearing pieces of his farm are concerned, and with it landed property as a barrier to the application of capital, and this is moreover by contract with the landlord himself. But the only reason why he pays no rent for these pieces of land is that he does pay rent for the land to which they are an accessory. In this case, the combination presupposed is precisely one in which resort does not have to be had to the worse type-A land as an independent and new field of production in order to make up the missing supply. Instead, this worse land simply forms an inseparable filling sandwiched between the better land. But the case that is to be investigated here is precisely that in which tracts of type-A land are farmed independently and have therefore to be independently leased out under the general preconditions of the capitalist mode of production.

Thirdly. A farmer may invest extra capital on his existing leasehold even though at the existing market prices the additional product obtained in this way simply yields him the price of production, the customary profit, and does not enable him to pay an additional rent. Thus for one part of the capital invested on the land he does pay ground-rent, for the other part not. But we can see from the following consideration how little this solves the problem. If the market price (and also the fertility of the soil) enables him to obtain a surplus yield with the additional capital, which, like the old capital, yields him a surplus profit as well as the price of production, then he pockets this profit himself for the duration of the lease. And why? Because as long as the tenancy contract lasts, the barrier that landed property places to the investment of his capital in the land has been removed. Yet the mere fact that in order to secure this surplus profit, he must take on

* p. 910.

additional worse land and lease it separately, shows irrefutably that the investment of additional capital on the old land is not sufficient to produce the increased supply that is needed. The one assumption rules out the other. Now one could say that the rent of the worst type-A land is itself a differential rent compared with the land cultivated by its own proprietor (even though this occurs only as a chance exception), or with additional capital investment on the old leaseholds that do not yield any rent. This however would be (1) a differential rent that did not arise from the differing fertility of types of land and hence did *not* presuppose that type-A land paid no rent and its product was sold at the price of production. While (2) whether additional capital investments on the same leasehold yield rent or not is as completely immaterial for whether the land in class A that is newly taken on pays rent or not, as it is immaterial for example for investment in a new and independent factory, whether another manufacturer in the same branch of production invests a part of his capital in interest-bearing paper because this cannot be completely valorized in his own business; or whether he makes particular extensions that do not yield him the full profit, though they do yield more than the interest. As far as he is concerned, this is a secondary matter. But any new enterprise must yield the average profit, and is set up on this expectation. Additional capital investment on the old leaseholds, moreover, and the additional cultivation of new land in type A, set limits to one another. The limit up to which additional capital can be invested on the same leasehold under less favourable conditions of production is given by the competing new investments on class-A land; on the other hand the rent that this class of land can yield is limited by the competing additional capital investments on the old leaseholds.

But none of these dodges solves the problem, which put simply is as follows. Let us assume that the market price for corn (which in our analysis represents any product of the soil) is sufficient for portions of class-A land to be taken into cultivation and for the capital invested to obtain the production price of the product from these new fields, i.e. replacement of capital plus average profit. Let us assume, in other words, that the conditions for the normal valorization of capital on class-A land are present. Is this enough? Can this capital then really be invested? Or must the market price rise high enough for even the worst land A to yield a rent? In other words, does the monopoly of landed property set a barrier to the investment of capital that would not be present, from a purely capitalist standpoint, without the existence of this monopoly? The very terms of the question itself show how, if for example there are additional capital investments on old leaseholds that yield no rent at the prevailing market price but simply the average profit, this in no way solves the problem of whether capital can now actually be invested on class-A land which would similarly yield the a. erage profit but no rent. This is precisely the question. It is clear from the need to take new land into cultivation that the additional capital investments which yield no rent do not satisfy the demand. If the additional cultivation of land A is undertaken only in so far as this yields rent, i.e. yields more than the price of production, two cases are possible.

Either the market price must rise in such a way that even the final additional capital investments on the old leaseholds yield surplus profit, whether this is pocketed by the farmer or the landlord. This rise in price and the surplus profit from the final additional capital investments would then be the result of the impossibility of cultivating land A unless rent is obtained thereby. For if the price of production, the yield of the average profit pure and simple, was sufficient to induce cultivation, the price would not have risen so high and new lands would already have come into competition as soon as they yielded simply these prices of production. The additional capital investments on the old leaseholds that yielded no rent would then be faced with competition from the capital investments on land A that likewise yield no rent.

Or, alternatively, the final capital investments on the old leaseholds yield no rent, but the market price has still risen high enough for land A to be taken up and to yield rent. In this case, the additional capital investment that yielded no rent was possible only because land A could not be cultivated until the market price allowed it to pay rent. In the absence of this condition, it would already have been cultivated, at a lower price level; and those later investments of capital on the old leaseholds that need the high market price to yield the customary profit without rent could not have taken place. Given the high market price, they yield only the average profit. At a lower price, which would have become the governing one with the cultivation of land A, as its price of production, these investments would not have yielded this profit and so they could not have taken place at all under this condition. The rent of land A would thus form a differential rent compared with these capital investments on the old leaseholds that yield no rent. But if the acreage of A forms such a differential rent, this is simply the result of its not being available for cultivation at all unless it yields a rent; i.e. unless there is a need for this rent which is not determined by any difference in the types of land and which sets a barrier to the possible investment of additional capitals on the old leaseholds. In both cases the rent of land A would not be just the result of a rise in corn prices but the very opposite; the fact that the worst soil has to yield a rent for cultivation to be permitted at all would be the reason why corn prices rise to the point at which this condition can be fulfilled.

Differential rent has the peculiarity that here landed property seizes only the surplus profit that the farmer himself would otherwise pocket, and under certain circumstances does pocket for the duration of his tenancy. Here landed property simply causes the transfer of a portion of the commodity price that arises without any effort on its part (rather as a result of the determination by competition of the production price governing the market), a portion reducible to surplus profit, from one person to the other, from the capitalist to the landowner. Landed property is not in this case a cause that *creates* this component of price or the rise in price that it presupposes. But if the worst type-A land cannot be cultivated – even though its cultivation would yield the price of production – until it yields a surplus over and above this production price, a rent, then landed property is the creative basis of *this* rise in price. *Landed property has produced this rent itself.* Nothing is altered in this if, as in the second case treated here, the rent now paid by land A forms a differential rent compared with the final additional capital investment on old leaseholds that only pays the price of production. For the fact that land A cannot be cultivated until the governing market price has risen high enough to let it yield a rent is the sole basis here for the rise in the market price to a point which, while it pays the final capital investments on the old tenancies only their price of production, still pays a price of production that also yields a rent for land A. The fact that this land must pay rent at all is the cause which works here to create a differential rent between land A and the final capital investments on the old farms.

Whenever we speak of class-A land paying no rent – on the assumption that the corn price is governed by the price of production – we mean rent as a specific category. If the lease-price paid by the farmer involves a deduction from the normal wages of his workers or from his own normal average profit, he does not pay any rent as an independent component of the price of his commodity distinct from wages and profit. We have already noted how this constantly happens in practice. In so far as the wages of agricultural workers in a country are depressed below the normal average level, so that there is a deduction from wages, with a part of wages regularly going into rent, this is no exceptional case for the farmer on the worst land. The same price of production that makes the cultivation of this land possible already includes these low wages as a constituent item, and so the sale of the product at its price of production does not enable the farmer of this land to pay a rent. The landowner can even lease out his land to a worker who is content to pay someone else, in the form of rent, everything, or the greater part of it, that the sale price yields him over and above his wages. In none of these cases is a genuine rent paid, even though a lease-price is. Where relations corresponding to the capitalist mode of production exist, however, rent and lease-price must coincide. This is precisely the normal situation that is under analysis here.

If our problem is not solved by the cases considered above, i.e. those in which capital investments can be made on the land in the capitalist mode of production without yielding rent, still less is it solved by making reference to colonial conditions. What makes a colony a colony – and here we are referring only to agricultural colonies proper – is not just the amount of fertile land to be found in its natural condition. It is rather the situation that this land is not appropriated, is not subsumed under landed property. It is this that makes for the tremendous distinction between the old countries and the colonies as far as land is concerned: the legal or factual non-existence of landed property, as Wakefield[35] correctly notes, a fact already discovered long before him by Mirabeau *père*, the Physiocrat, and other early economists. It is completely immaterial here whether colonists appropriate the land directly or whether they pay the state a simple tax for a valid legal title, under the guise of a nominal land price. It is also immaterial that colonists already settled may be the legal owners of the land.

35. Wakefield, *England and America*, London, 1833. See also *Capital* Volume 1, Chapter 33.

Here, landed property actually forms no barrier to the investment of capital, or of labour without capital; the seizure of part of the land by colonists already established does not prevent later arrivals from making new land into a field of investment for their own capital or labour. Thus if we want to investigate how landed property affects the prices of its products, and rent, in cases where it restricts the land as a field of investment for capital, it is completely absurd to refer to free bourgeois colonies where neither the capitalist mode of production in agriculture nor the form of landed property corresponding to this exists, indeed where landed property does not exist at all. This is what Ricardo does, for example, in his chapter on ground-rent. He starts by saying that he intends to analyse the effect of the appropriation of land on the value of its products, but immediately goes on to take the colonies as his illustration, assuming that land there is in a relatively elementary state and its exploitation not impeded by the monopoly of landed property.

Legal ownership of land, by itself, does not give the proprietor any ground-rent. It certainly does give him the power, however, to withdraw his land from cultivation until economic conditions permit a valorization of it that yields him a surplus, whether the land is used for agriculture proper or for other productive purposes such as building, etc. He can neither increase nor reduce the absolute quantity of this field of occupation, but he can affect the quantity of it on the market. It is a characteristic fact, therefore, and one which Fourier already noted, that in all civilized countries a relatively significant portion of the land always remains uncultivated.

Assuming then that demand requires the taking up of new land which is, say, less fertile than that previously cultivated, will the owner of this land lease it for nothing just because the market price of its product has risen high enough for capital investment to pay the farmer the price of production and thus yield him the customary profit? In no way. The capital investment must yield him a rent. He leases only when a lease-price can be paid. The market price must therefore have risen above the price of production, to $P + r$, so that a rent can be paid to the landowner. Since by our assumption landed property does not bring in anything without being leased, unleased land being economically worthless, a small rise in the market price above the price of production is sufficient to bring new land of the poorest kind onto the market.

The question now arises whether it follows from ground-rent on the poorest land, which cannot be derived from any difference in fertility, that the price of its product is necessarily a monopoly price in the customary sense, or a price that includes rent in the form of a tax, levied in this case by the landowner rather than the state? It is obvious that this tax has its given economic limits. It is limited by additional capital investments on the old lease-holds, by competition from foreign agricultural products (assuming their free import), by competition between landed proprietors and finally by the need of the consumers and their ability to pay. But this is not what is involved here. The question is whether the rent that is paid by the poorest land goes into the price of its product, which by our assumption is what governs the general market price, in the same way as a tax goes into the price of the commodity on which it is levied, i.e. as an element independent of its value.

This in no way necessarily follows, and is maintained only because the distinction between the value of commodities and their price of production has as yet not been understood. We have already seen that the production price of a commodity is not at all identical with its value, even though the production prices of commodities considered in their totality are governed only by their total value, and although the movement of production prices for commodities of different kinds, taking all other circumstances as equal, is determined exclusively by the movement of their values. It has been shown that the production price of a commodity may stand above or below its value and coincides with it only in exceptional cases. But the fact that agricultural products are sold above their price of production in no way proves that they are also sold above their value; just as the fact that industrial products are sold on average at their price of production does not show that they are sold at their value. It is possible for agricultural products to be sold above their price of production yet below their value, just as many industrial products on the other hand yield their price of production only because they are sold above their value.

The relationship of a commodity's price of production to its value is determined exclusively by the proportion between the variable part of the capital with which it is produced and the constant part, i.e. by the organic composition of the capital producing it. If the composition of capital in one sphere of production is lower than that of the average social capital, i.e. if its variable component, that laid out on wages, is greater in relation to the constant component, that laid out on material conditions of labour, than is the case for the average social capital, the value of its product must stand above its price of production. That is to say, such a capital produces more surplus-value given the same exploitation of labour, and therefore more profit, than an equally large aliquot part of the average social capital, because it applies more living labour. The value of its product thus stands above its price of production, because this price of production is equal to the replacement of the capital plus the average profit, and the average profit is less than the profit produced in this commodity. The surplus-value produced by the average social capital is less than the surplus-value produced by a capital of this low composition. The reverse is true if the capital invested in a particular sphere of production is higher in composition than the average social capital. The value of the commodities it produces then stands below their price of production, which is generally the case with the products of the most highly developed industries.

If the capital in a particular sphere of production has a lower composition than the average social capital, this is firstly only a different expression for the fact that the productivity of social labour in this particular sphere of production stands below the average level; for the level of productivity attained is expressed in the relative preponderance of the constant portion of capital over the variable, or in the steady decline of that component of a given capital laid out on wages. If the capital in a particular sphere of production has a higher composition, on the other hand, this expresses a level of development of productivity which is higher than the average.

Leaving aside actual artistic works, which are excluded from our subject by the very nature of the case, it is self-evident that different spheres of production, according to their technical characteristics, require differing proportions of constant and variable capital, and that living labour must play a greater part in some and a smaller part in others. In extractive industry, for example, which should be clearly distinguished from agriculture, raw material completely disappears as an element of the constant capital, and even ancillary materials play a significant role only very occasionally. But the other part of constant capital, fixed capital, does play a major role in mining. Here, too, we can measure the course of development by the relative growth in constant capital compared with variable.

If the composition of capital in agriculture proper is less than the social average, this is *prima facie* an expression of the fact that in countries of developed production, agriculture has not progressed to the same extent as manufacturing industry. Leaving aside all other economic conditions, which have some determining effect, this fact is explicable simply in terms of the earlier and more rapid development of the mechanical sciences, and especially of their application, compared with the later and in part still very recent development of chemistry, geology and physiology, and their application to agriculture in particular. It is also an indubitable and long-known fact[36] that advances in agriculture are themselves always expressed in a relative growth in the constant portion of capital as against the variable. Whether the composition of agricultural capital is less than the social average in a particular country of capitalist production, say England, is a question which can be settled only by statistical investigation and which it would be superfluous for our purpose to go into in detail. In any case, it still holds theoretically that it is only on this premise that the value of agricultural products can rise above their price of production; i.e. that the surplus-value produced in agriculture by a capital of a given size, or, what comes to the same thing, by the surplus labour that it sets in motion and commands (i.e. the total living labour applied), is greater than for an equally large capital of the average social composition.

This assumption is therefore sufficient as far as the form of rent we are examining here is concerned, and it is a necessary assumption for this rent to arise. Where this hypothesis is inapplicable, the form of rent corresponding to it disappears.

This simple fact, however, of a surplus in the value of agricultural products over and above their price of production would in no way be sufficient in itself to explain the existence of a ground-rent independent of the differences in fertility between types of land or successive investments of capital on the same land – in

36. See Dombasle and R. Jones.*

* C. J. A. Mathieu de Dombasle, *Annales agricoles de Roville . . .*, a multipart work published between 1824 and 1837; Richard Jones, *An Essay on the Distribution of Wealth, and on the Sources of Taxation*, London, 1831, p. 227. (See also *Theories of Surplus-Value*, Part III, Chapter XXIV, 1.)

short, of a rent conceptually distinct from differential rent, which we can therefore denote as *absolute rent*. A whole number of manufacturing products are characterized by a value above their price of production, without thereby yielding a surplus over and above the average profit, a surplus profit that could be transformed into rent. It is rather the existence and the concept of the price of production and the general rate of profit it involves which rest on the fact that individual commodities are not sold at their values. The prices of production arise from an adjustment of commodity values under which, after the reimbursement of the respective capital values consumed in the various spheres of production, the total surplus-value is distributed not in the proportion in which it is produced in the individual spheres of production, and hence contained in their product, but rather in proportion to the size of the capitals advanced. It is only in this way that an average profit arises, and a production price for commodities can be arrived at, the characteristic element of which is this average profit. It is the constant tendency of capitals to bring about, by competition, this adjustment in the distribution of the surplus-value that the total capital produces, and to overcome all obstacles towards it. It is therefore their tendency only to tolerate such surplus profits as arise, under whatever circumstances, not from the difference between the values of commodities and their prices of production, but rather from the general price of production governing the market and the individual production prices differing from this; surplus profits which therefore do not arise between two different spheres of production but rather within each sphere of production, so that they do not affect the general production prices of the different spheres, i.e. the general rate of profit, but rather presuppose both the transformation of value into price of production and the general rate of profit. This presupposition, however, depends as already explained on the continuously changing proportionate distribution of the total social capital between the various spheres of production; on a continuous immigration and emigration of capitals; on their transferability from one sphere to another; in short, on their free movement between these various spheres of production as so many available fields of investment for the independent parts of the total social capital. It is assumed in this connection that no barriers, or at least only accidental and temporary ones, prevent the competition of capitals – e.g. in a sphere of production where the value of commodities stands above their price of production or where the surplus-value produced stands above the average profit – from reducing value to price of production and thereby distributing the extra surplus-value of this sphere of production between all spheres exploited by capital in due proportion. If the opposite occurs, i.e. capital comes up against an alien power that it can overcome only partly or not at all, a power which restricts its investment in particular spheres of production, allowing this only under conditions that completely or partially exclude that general equalization of surplus-value to give the average profit, it is clear that in these spheres of production a surplus profit will arise, from the excess of commodity value above its price of production, this being transformed into rent and as such becoming autonomous vis-à-vis profit. And it is as an alien power and a barrier of this kind that landed property confronts capital as regards its investment on the land, or that the landowner confronts the capitalist.

Here landed property is the barrier that does not permit any new capital investment on formerly uncultivated or unleased land without levying a toll, i.e. demanding a rent, even if the land newly brought under cultivation is of a kind that does not yield any differential rent, and which save for landed property could have been cultivated already with a smaller rise in the market price, so that the governing market price would have paid the tiller of this worst land only his price of production. But as a result of the barrier that landed property sets up, the market price must rise to a point at which the land can pay a surplus over the price of production, i.e. a rent. Since however the value of the commodities produced by agricultural capital is above their price of production, by our assumption, this rent forms the excess of the value above the price of production, or a part of this excess (except for a further case that will be examined straight away). Whether the rent is equal to the whole difference between the value and the price of production, or only to a greater or lesser part of this difference, depends entirely on the state of supply in relation to demand and on the scale of the area newly brought under cultivation. As long as the rent is not equal to the excess of the value of the agricultural products over and above their price of production, one part of this surplus always goes into the general equalization and proportionate distribution of all surplus-value between the various individual capitals. As soon as rent was equal to the excess of the value over the price of production, this entire part of the extra surplus-value over and above the average profit would be withdrawn from the equalization process. But whether this absolute rent is equal to the whole extra value over and above the price of production, or only to a part of this, agricultural products are always sold at a monopoly price, not because their price stands above their value but rather because it is equal to their value, or is below their value but above their price of production. Their monopoly consists in this, that their value is not levelled down to their price of production as it is with other industrial products whose values stand above the general price of production. Since one part of the value and the price of production is in fact a given constant, i.e. the cost price, the capital $= k$ consumed in the course of production, the distinction lies in the other, variable part – the surplus-value which in the price of production $= p$ is profit, i.e. the total surplus-value reckoned on the social capital and on each individual capital as an aliquot part of this, but which in the value of the commodity is equal to the actual surplus-value which this particular capital has produced, forming an integral part of the commodity value it has created. If the value of a commodity is above its price of production, the price of production $= k + p$, and its value $= k + p + d$, so that $p + d =$ the surplus-value contained in it. The difference between the value and the price of production is thus d, the excess of the surplus-value produced by this capital over the surplus-value allotted to it by the general rate of profit. It follows from this that the price of agricultural products can stand above their price of production without reaching their value. It also follows that up to a certain point there can be a lasting price rise for agricultural products before their price has reached their value. It equally follows that it is only as a result of the monopoly of landed property that the excess value of agricultural products over their price of production at a particular moment can come to be their general market price. It finally follows that in this case it is not the rise in the product's price that is the cause of the rent but rather the rent that is the cause of the rise in price. If the price of the product from a unit area of the worst land $= P + r$, all the differential rents rise by corresponding multiples of r, since by our assumption $P + r$ becomes the governing market price.

If the average composition of the non-agricultural social capital were $85_c + 15_v$ and the rate of surplus-value 100 per cent, the price of production would be 115. If the composition of the agricultural capital were $75_c + 25_v$, the value of the product and the governing market value would be 125, given the same rate of surplus-value. If the agricultural and non-agricultural products balanced out to give an average price (we assume for the sake of brevity that the total capital is the same in both branches of production), the total surplus-value would be 40, i.e. 20 per cent on a capital of 200. The product of each would be sold at 120. Given an equalization to production prices, therefore, the average market prices of the non-agricultural products would come to stand above their values, and those of the agricultural products below. If the agricultural products were sold at their full value, they would stand 5 higher, and the industrial products 5 lower, than if this equalization took place. If market conditions do not permit agricultural products to be sold at their full value, at the total surplus over their price of production, the effect lies between the two extremes: industrial products would be sold somewhat above their value and agricultural products somewhat above their price of production.

Even though landed property can drive the price of agricultural products above their price of production, it does not depend on this, but rather on the general state of the market, how far the market price rises above the price of production and towards the value, and to what extent, therefore, the surplus-value produced over and above the given average profit in agriculture is either transformed into rent or goes into the general equalization of surplus-value that settles the average profit. In any case, this absolute rent, arising from the excess value over and above the price of production, is simply a part of the agricultural surplus-value, the transformation of this surplus-value into rent, its seizure by the landowner; just as differential rent arises from the transformation of surplus profit into rent, its seizure by landed property, at the general governing price of production. These two forms of rent are the only normal ones. Apart from this, rent can derive only from a genuine monopoly price, which is determined neither by the price of production of the commodities nor by their value, but rather by the demand of the purchasers and their ability to pay, consideration of which therefore belongs to the theory of competition, where the actual movement of market prices is investigated.

If all land available for agriculture in a country were leased out – assuming the capitalist mode of production, and normal conditions everywhere – there would be no land that did not yield rent, but there could be capital investments, particular portions of capital invested on the land, that did not yield rent; for once the land is leased out, landed property ceases to operate as an absolute barrier to the capital investment needed. It continues to operate as a relative barrier even then, in so far as the reversion to the land-owner of the capital incorporated into the soil sets the farmer very definite barriers. In this case, though, all rent would be transformed into a differential rent determined not by the quality of the soil but rather by the difference between the surplus profit arising on a particular class of land after the final capital invest-ments, and the rent that would be paid for the lease of land of the worst class. Landed property operates as an absolute barrier only in as much as any permission to use land, as a field of investment for capital, enables the landowner to extract a tribute. Once this permission has been given, the landowner can no longer place any absolute barrier to the quantitative level of capital investment on a given piece of land. In the case of house-building, a barrier is always imposed by the landed property of a third party in the land on which the house is to be built. But once this land is leased for house-building purposes, it depends on the lessee whether he plans to erect a large house on it or a small one.

If the average composition of agricultural capital were the same as that of the average social capital, or even higher than this, the result would be the disappearance of absolute rent in the sense developed above, namely a rent that is different both from dif-ferential rent and from rent depending on an actual monopoly price. The value of the agricultural product would not stand above its price of production, and agricultural capital would not set more labour in motion, and would thus not realize more sur-plus labour, than did non-agricultural capital. It would be the same thing if the composition of agricultural capital were equalized with that of the average social capital as agriculture advanced.

At first sight it may seem a contradiction to assume that on the one hand the composition of the agricultural capital increases, with its constant part growing vis-à-vis its variable part, while on the other hand the price of agricultural products rises high enough for new and worse land than previously to pay a rent, which in this case could derive only from an excess of the market price over the value and the price of production, in other words only from a monopoly price for the product.

A distinction has to be made here.

When we started to consider the formation of the rate of profit, we saw that capitals of similar technical composition, which set the same amount of labour in motion in proportion to machinery and raw material, may still be composed differently because of the differing values of their constant capital components. The raw material or machinery may be dearer in one case than in the other. In order to set the same amount of labour in motion (and this was necessary, on our assumption, to work up the same amount of raw material), a larger capital had to be advanced in one case than in the other, since with a capital of 100, for example, I cannot set in motion the same amount of labour if the raw material that has to be purchased out of 100 in both cases costs in the one case 40 and in the other case 20. But we immediately see, if the price of the dearer raw material falls down to the level of that of the cheaper one, that these capitals are none the less similar in their technical composition. The value ratio between variable and constant capital would then be the same, although no change had taken place in the technical proportion between the living labour applied and the quantity and nature of the conditions of labour required. A capital of lower organic composition, on the other hand, considered simply in terms of its value composition, could evidently rise to the same level as a capital of higher organic composition, simply by an increase in the value of its constant parts. Let us take a capital of $60_c + 40_v$, which therefore uses a great deal of machinery and raw material in relation to living labour-power, and another capital of $40_c + 60_v$, which uses a lot of living labour (60 per cent), little machinery (say 10 per cent) and little and cheap raw material in relation to its labour-power (say 30 per cent): a simple rise in the value of the latter's raw and ancillary material from 30 to 80 could thus equalize the composition, as the second capital would now need 80 in raw materials and 60 in labour-power for every 10 in machines, i.e. $90_c + 60_v$, which reduced to percentages would also be $60_c + 40_v$, without any kind of technical change in its composition having occurred. Capitals of the same organic composition can thus have a differing value composition, and capitals of the same percentage [value] composition can stand at varying levels of organic composition, displaying various different levels of development of the social productivity of labour. Thus the mere fact that agricultural capital now stood at the same level by value composition would not prove that the social productivity of labour was equally highly developed. All it could show would be that its own product, which again forms part of its conditions of production, is dearer, or that ancillary materials such as fertilizer, which used to be obtained locally, now have to be carted a long way, etc.

Leaving this aside, however, we still have the particular character of agriculture to consider.

Assume that labour-saving machinery, chemical ancillaries, etc. take up a greater share, so that the constant capital grows in relation to the labour-power applied – not just in value but in quantity too. In agriculture, however (as also in mining), we not only have the social productivity of labour to consider but also its natural productivity, which depends on the natural conditions within which labour is carried on. It is possible for the increase in the social productivity of agriculture to simply compensate for the decline in natural productivity, or not even to do this much – and this compensation can only be effective for a certain period – so that despite the technical development, the product does not become cheaper but is simply prevented from becoming dearer. It is also possible, in a situation of rising corn prices, for the absolute amount produced to decline while the relative surplus product grows; i.e. there may be a relative increase in the constant capital, which consists for the most part of machines or livestock, only the depreciation of which has to be replaced, and a corresponding decline in the variable portion of capital, that laid out on wages, which must always be replaced in full out of the product.

But it is also possible that, as agriculture progresses, only a moderate rise in the market price above the average will be needed for poorer land which, given a lower level of technical assistance, would have required a rise in the market price, to be cultivated and also yield a rent.

The fact that in stock-raising, for example, the amount of labour-power applied is on the whole very small compared with the constant capital existing in the livestock themselves, could be taken as refuting the contention that agricultural capital, in percentage terms, sets more labour-power in motion than does non-agricultural capital of the average social composition. It should be noted here, however, that in explaining rent we take as the initial determinant that section of agricultural capital which produces the decisive cereal foodstuffs and thus the major means of subsistence for all civilized peoples. Adam Smith has already shown, and this was one of the services he performed, that in stock-raising and in the general average of all capital invested on the land that does not go into the production of the major staples, such as corn for example, the determination of price is completely different. Price here is determined by the fact that the price of the product of land which is used, say, as an artificial pasture for cattle, but which could equally well be turned into arable land of a certain quality, has to rise high enough to yield the same rent as equally good arable land; in this case, therefore, the rent of the corn-growing land is a determining factor in the price of cattle, so that Ramsay was correct to note that in this way the price of cattle is artificially raised by rent, by the economic expression of landed property, and thus by landed property itself.*

'By the extension besides of cultivation the unimproved wilds become insufficient to supply the demand for butcher's meat. A great part of the cultivated lands must be employed in rearing and fattening cattle, of which the price, therefore, must be sufficient to pay, not only the labour necessary for tending them, but the rent which the landlord and the profit which the farmer could have drawn from such land employed in tillage. The cattle bred upon the most uncultivated moors, when brought to the same market, are, in proportion to their weight or goodness, sold at the same price as those which are reared upon the most improved land. The proprietors of those moors profit by it, and raise the rent of their land in proportion to the price of their cattle' (Adam Smith, Book One, Chapter XI, I [p. 252]).

In this case, too, therefore, the differential rent, as distinct from the corn rent, is in favour of the worst land.

Absolute rent explains certain phenomena which at first sight make rent appear due to a mere monopoly price. Take for instance the owner of a woodland that exists without any human action, i.e. not as the result of afforestation – in Norway, for example – and append this to Adam Smith's example. If he is paid a rent by a capitalist who has timber felled, perhaps to meet English demand, he is paid a greater or lesser rent in timber over and above the

---

* George Ramsay, *An Essay on the Distribution of Wealth*, Edinburgh and London, 1836, pp. 278–9.

profit on the capital advanced. This seems in the case of this purely natural product to be a simple monopoly surcharge. In actual fact, however, the capital here consists almost solely of variable capital laid out on labour, which therefore sets more surplus labour in motion than another capital of the same size. The value of the timber thus contains a greater excess of unpaid labour, or surplus-value, than the product of capitals of higher composition. The average profit can thus be paid from the timber, while a significant excess accrues to the owner of the woodland in the form of rent. We may assume, conversely, that given the ease with which the felling of timber can be extended, and this production thus rapidly increased, the demand would have to rise very steeply to make the price of timber equal to its value, so that the entire excess of unpaid labour (over and above the part that accrues to the capitalist as average profit) would accrue to the proprietor in the form of rent.

We have assumed that land newly drawn into cultivation is of still poorer quality than the worst previously cultivated. If it is better, it bears a differential rent. Here, however, we are precisely investigating the case where rent does not appear as differential rent. There are only two possible alternatives here. Either the land newly taken up is worse, or it is just as good as the last. We have already investigated the position where it is worse. The only case left to investigate is where it is equally good.

Equally good land, and even better, can be newly cultivated as agriculture develops just as much as worse land can, as we have already shown in the case of differential rent.

Firstly, because in the case of differential rent (and rent in general, since even in the case of non-differential rent there is always still the question whether the fertility of the land on the one hand, and its location on the other, permit it to be cultivated at all at the governing price, with profit and rent), two factors operate in opposite directions, sometimes counterbalancing one another and sometimes with one outweighing the other. A rise in market price – assuming that the cost price of cultivation has not fallen, in other words that technical progress has not stimulated additional cultivation – may bring into cultivation more fertile land which was previously excluded from competing by its location. Or else, in the case of less fertile land, it may increase the advantage of location so much that this balances the low yield. Alternatively, even if the market price does not rise, the location can bring better land into competition by way of improved means of communication, as we have seen on a large scale with the prairie states of North America. Even in countries which have long been civilized this is constantly the case, if not on the same scale as in the colonies, where, as Wakefield correctly notes,* location is decisive. Thus firstly the contradictory effects of location and fertility, and the variability of the location factor, which is constantly balanced out, bringing about constant progressive changes which also tend to balance out, alternately bring equally good, better or worse tracts of land into competition with those previously cultivated.

Secondly. With the development of natural science and agronomy, the fertility of the land itself changes, since there is an alteration in the means by which the soil's elements can be made capable of immediate exploitation. In the recent past, for example, light varieties of soil, which were previously considered inferior, have risen to the first rank in France and the eastern counties of England. (See Passy.)† On the other hand, land which was considered poor not on account of its chemical composition but because mechanical and physical obstacles stood in the way of its cultivation was turned into good land as soon as the means for overcoming these obstacles were discovered.

Thirdly. In all countries of old-established civilization, old historical and traditional conditions, in the form of crown lands, common lands, etc. have withheld great stretches of land from agriculture in a purely arbitrary manner. The sequence in which these are brought into cultivation depends neither on their quality nor on their location, but rather on quite external conditions. The history of the English common lands, as these were successively turned into private property by the Enclosure Acts and ploughed up,‡ shows that nothing would be more ridiculous than the fantastic idea that this sequence was worked out by a modern agricultural chemist in the manner of Liebig, and that certain fields were marked off for cultivation on account of their chemical properties while others were excluded. What was decisive here

---

* op. cit., pp. 214–15.

† H.-P. Passy, 'De la rente du sol', in *Dictionnaire de l'économie politique*, Vol. 2, Paris, 1854, p. 515. Hippolyte-Philibert Passy (1793–1880), besides being a 'vulgar economist', also became Finance Minister under the Second Republic of 1848–51.

‡ See *Capital* Volume 1, Chapter 27.

was rather 'the opportunity that makes the thief': the more or less plausible legal pretexts for appropriation which the great landlords found.

Fourthly. Leaving aside the fact that the level of population and capital reached at any given time sets a certain limit to the extension of agriculture, even if an elastic one; leaving aside, too, the effects of accidents which have a temporary influence on market price, such as a series of favourable or unfavourable seasons, the geographical extension of agriculture then depends on the overall condition of the capital market and the state of business in the country in question. In periods when business is poor, the possibility that uncultivated land may yield the farmer an average profit – whether he pays rent or not – will not suffice to divert additional capital to agriculture. In other periods, when capital is abundant, it streams into agriculture even without a rise in market prices, as long as the normal conditions are fulfilled. Better land than that previously cultivated was in fact only excluded from competition by the element of location, or by previous barriers which had not yet been broken through, or else by accident. We have only to deal therefore with kinds of land which are equally good as those last cultivated. Between the new land and that last cultivated, however, there always exists a distinction in the shape of the varying cost of ploughing up, and it depends on the level of market prices and credit conditions whether this is undertaken or not. Once this land actually does come into competition, the market price falls back again to its previous level, other conditions remaining the same, so that the new land will bear the same rent as the corresponding old land. The hypothesis that it bears no rent is demonstrated by its supporters by assuming what should actually be proved, i.e. that the last land did not bear any rent. One could prove in the same way that the last houses to be built yield no rent besides simple interest on the buildings, even if they are rented out. The fact of the matter is that they yield ground-rent even before they bring in house-rent, for they often stand empty a long while. Just as successive capital investments on one piece of land can yield a proportionate surplus product and hence the same rent as the first investments, so can fields of the same quality as those last cultivated yield the same product at the same cost. It would otherwise be incomprehensible how fields of the same quality are ever brought under cultivation successively and not all at once, or indeed why any are at all, since the first would draw after it the competition of all others. The landowner is always ready to draw a rent, i.e. to receive something for nothing, but capital requires certain conditions in order to fulfil its desire. The mutual competition of plots of land depends not on the landowner's intention to have them compete but rather on the availability of capital to compete on new fields with the old.

The extent to which agricultural rent proper is simply a monopoly price can only be a small one, just as absolute rent can only be small in normal conditions, whatever the excess value of the product over its production price may be. The essence of absolute rent consists in this: equally large capitals produce different amounts of surplus-value in different spheres of production according to their differing average composition, given an equal rate of surplus-value or equal exploitation of labour. In industry these different amounts of surplus-value are equalized to give the average profit and are divided uniformly between the individual capitals as aliquot parts of the total capital. Landed property, whenever production needs land, whether for agriculture or for the extraction of raw materials, blocks this equalization for the capitals invested on the land and captures a portion of surplus-value which would otherwise go into the equalization process, giving the general rate of profit. Rent then forms a part of the value of commodities, in particular of their surplus-value, which simply accrues to the landowners who extract it from the capitalists, instead of to the capitalist class who have extracted it from the workers. It is assumed in this connection that agricultural capital sets more labour in motion than an equally large portion of non-agricultural capital. The extent of this gap, or its existence at all, depends on the relative development of agriculture vis-à-vis industry. By the nature of the case, this difference must decline with the progress of agriculture, unless the ratio in which the variable part of the capital declines vis-à-vis the constant part is still greater in industrial capital than in agricultural.

This absolute rent plays a still more important role in extractive industry proper, where one element of constant capital, raw material, completely disappears, and where, with the exception of branches for which the portion consisting of machinery and other fixed capital is very significant, the lowest composition of capital invariably prevails. Precisely here, where rent seems due to a monopoly price alone, extraordinarily favourable market conditions are required for the commodities to be sold at their values or for rent to equal the entire excess of surplus-value in a commodity over and above its price of production. This is the case for example with rent for fishing grounds, quarries, natural forests, etc.[37]

37. Ricardo gives an extraordinarily superficial account of this point. See the passage against Adam Smith over rent of forests in Norway, *Principles*, Chapter II, right at the beginning.

Chapter 46: Rent of Buildings. Rent of Mines. Price of Land

Wherever rent exists, differential rent always appears and always follows the same laws as it does in agriculture. Wherever natural forces can be monopolized and give the industrialist who makes use of them a surplus profit, whether a waterfall, a rich mine, fishing grounds or a well-situated building site, the person indicated as the owner of these natural objects, by virtue of his title to a portion of the earth, seizes this surplus profit from the functioning capital in the form of rent. As far as land for building is concerned, Adam Smith has discussed how the basis of its rent, as with all non-agricultural land, is governed by agricultural rent proper (Book I, Chapter XI, 2 and 3). This rent is characterized first by the preponderant influence that location exerts here on the differential rent (very important, for example, in the case of vineyards, and building land in big towns); secondly, by the palpable and complete passivity displayed by the owner, whose activity consists simply in exploiting advances in social development (particularly in the case of mines), towards which he does not contribute and in which he risks nothing, unlike the industrial capitalist; finally, by the prevalence of a monopoly price in many cases, and particularly the most shameless exploitation of poverty (for poverty is a more fruitful source for house-rent than the mines of Potosí were for Spain);[38] the tremendous power this gives landed property when it is combined together with industrial capital in the same hands enables capital practically to exclude workers engaged in a struggle over wages from the very earth itself as their habitat.[39] One section of society here demands a tribute from the other for the very right to live on the earth, just as landed property

38. Laing, [F. W.] Newman.
39. Crowlington Strike. Engels, *Condition of the Working Classes in England, Collected Works*, Vol. 4, London, 1975, pp. 543–4.

in general involves the right of the proprietors to exploit the earth's surface, the bowels of the earth, the air and thereby the maintenance and development of life. The rise in population, and the consequent growing need for housing, is not the only factor that necessarily increases the rent on buildings. So too does the development of fixed capital, which is either incorporated into the earth or strikes root in it, like all industrial buildings, railways, factories, docks, etc., which rest on it. It is impossible even with Carey's good intentions to confuse house-rent, in as much as this is interest and amortization for the capital invested in the house, with rent of land pure and simple, particularly when, as in England, the landowner and the speculative builder are completely different persons. Two elements come into consideration here: on the one hand the exploitation of the earth for the purpose of reproduction or extraction, on the other the space that is required as an element for any production and any human activity. On both counts landed property demands its tribute. The demand for building land raises the value of land as space and foundation, while at the same time there is a growing demand for those elements of the earth's physical constitution that serve as building material.[40]

We have already given an example of how in cities that are experiencing rapid growth, particularly where building is carried on factory-style, as in London, it is ground-rent and not the houses themselves that forms the real basic object of speculative building; see Volume 2, Chapter 12, pp. 311–12, the evidence of a major London speculative builder, Edward Capps, before the Bank Acts Committee of 1857. He says there, no. 5435: 'I think a man who wishes to rise in the world can hardly expect to rise by following out a fair trade ... it is necessary for him to add speculative building to it, and that must be done not on a small scale; ... for the builder makes very little profit out of the buildings themselves; he makes the principal part of the profit out of the improved ground-rents. Perhaps he takes a piece of ground, and agrees to give £300 a year for it; by laying it out with care, and putting certain descriptions of buildings upon it, he may succeed in making £400 or £450 a year out of it, and his profit would be the increased ground-rent of £100 or £150 a year, rather than the

40. 'The paving of the streets of London has enabled the owners of some barren rocks on the coast of Scotland to draw a rent from what never afforded any before' (Adam Smith [*The Wealth of Nations*], Book I, Chapter XI, II [Pelican edn, p. 268]).

profit of the buildings which . . ., in many instances, he scarcely looks at at all.'

It should not be forgotten in this connection that after the leasehold has expired, and this is ninety-nine years at the most, the land together with all the buildings on it, and with a ground-rent that has in the meantime generally doubled, tripled or more, reverts from the speculative builder or his heir to the original ultimate landowner.

Rent of mines is determined just as is agricultural rent.

'There are some of which the produce is barely sufficient to pay the labour, and replace, together with its ordinary profits, the stock employed in working them. They afford some profit to the undertaker of the work, but no rent to the landlord. They can be wrought advantageously by nobody but the landlord, who, being himself undertaker of the work, gets the ordinary profit of the capital which he employs in it. Many coalmines in Scotland are wrought in this manner, and can be wrought in no other. The landlord will allow nobody else to work them without paying some rent, and nobody can afford to pay any' (Adam Smith, Book I, Chapter XI, II [p. 270]).

It is necessary to distinguish whether the rent flows from an independent monopoly price for the products or the land itself, or whether the products are sold at a monopoly price because there is a rent. By monopoly price here we mean any price determined simply by the desire and ability of the buyer to pay, independently of the price of the product as determined by price of production and value. A vineyard bears a monopoly price if it produces wine which is of quite exceptional quality but can be produced only in a relatively small quantity. By virtue of this monopoly price, the wine-grower whose excess over the value of his product is determined purely and simply by the wealth and the preference of fashionable wine-drinkers can realize a substantial surplus profit. This surplus profit, which in this case flows from a monopoly price, is transformed into rent and accrues in this form to the landowner by virtue of his title to the portion of the earth endowed with these special properties. Here, therefore, the monopoly price creates the rent. Conversely, the rent would create the monopoly price if corn were sold not only above its price of production but also above its value, as a result of the barrier that landed property opposes against the rent-free investment of capital on untilled land. The fact that it is only the title a number of people have to property in the earth that enables them to appropriate a part of society's surplus labour as tribute, and in an ever growing measure as production develops, is concealed by the fact that the capitalized rent, i.e. precisely this capitalized tribute, appears as the price of land, which can be bought and sold just like any other item of trade. For the buyer, therefore, his claim to rent does not appear as something obtained for nothing, without labour, risk or the entrepreneurial spirit of capital, but rather as the return for his equivalent. Rent seems to him, as we have already noted, simply interest on the capital with which he has purchased the land, and with it the claim to rent. In exactly the same way, it appears to the slaveowner who has bought a Negro slave that his property in the Negro is created not by the institution of slavery as such but rather by the purchase and sale of this commodity. But the purchase does not produce the title; it simply transfers it. The title must be there before it can be bought, and neither one sale nor a series of such sales, their constant repetition, can create this title. It was entirely created by the relations of production. Once these have reached the point where they have to be sloughed off, then the material source, the economically and historically justified source of the title that arises from the process of life's social production, disappears, and with it all transactions based on it. From the standpoint of a higher socio-economic formation, the private property of particular individuals in the earth will appear just as absurd as the private property of one man in other men. Even an entire society, a nation, or all simultaneously existing societies taken together, are not the owners of the earth. They are simply its possessors, its beneficiaries, and have to bequeath it in an improved state to succeeding generations, as *boni patres familias*.*

*

In the following analysis of the price of land we disregard all fluctuations due to competition, all speculation in land, and even petty landownership where the earth forms the major instrument of the producers and must therefore be bought by them at some price or other.

I. The price of land may rise without an increase in rent:

(1) merely through a fall in the rate of interest, which means

* Good heads of the household.

that rent is sold more dearly, and so capitalized rent, the price of land, increases;

(2) because of a growth in the interest on the capital incorporated into the land.

II. The price of land may rise because the rent increases.

The rent may increase because the price of the product of the land rises, in which case the rate of differential rent always rises, whether the rent on the worst cultivated land is high, low or non-existent. By the rate of differential rent we mean the ratio between the part of surplus-value that is transformed into rent, and the capital advanced to produce the agricultural product. This is different from the ratio between the surplus product and the total product, for the total product does not include all the capital advanced, i.e. it does not include the fixed capital, which continues to exist alongside the product. It is implied in this, however, that on those types of land that bear a differential rent a growing portion of the product is transformed into excess surplus product. On the worst land, it is the rise in price of the product of the land that creates rent for the first time and hence creates the price of land.

But rent can also grow without any rise in the price of the agricultural product. This can remain constant or even decline.

If it remains constant, rent may grow (leaving aside monopoly prices) because new lands of better quality are cultivated along with equally large capital investments on the older lands, which however are sufficient only to meet the increased demand, so that the governing market price remains unchanged. In this case, the price of the older lands does not rise, but the price of land newly taken up rises above that of the old.

Alternatively, however, rent may rise because with the relative yield remaining the same, and the market price too, the amount of capital exploiting the land grows. Thus even if the rent remains the same in relation to the capital advanced, it might double in amount, say, because the capital itself has doubled. Since there is no fall in the price, the second capital investment yields a surplus profit just as much as the first, which is similarly transformed into rent once the term of the tenancy expires. The amount of rent here rises because the amount of capital producing rent does. The contention that different successive capital investments on the same stretch of land can produce a rent only in so far as their yield is uneven, and hence a differential rent arises, would imply that if two capitals of £1,000 each are invested on two fields of equal productivity only one of them can yield rent, even when these two fields belong to the better class of land which does yield a differential rent. (The sum of the rental, therefore, the total rent of a country, then grows with the amount of capital invested without a necessary rise in the price of the individual unit of land or in its rate or even mass of rent; the rental grows in its total amount in this case in line with the spatial expansion of agriculture. This can even be combined with a fall in the rent on individual holdings.) Were this not so, this contention would mean that capital investments on two different pieces of land alongside one another would obey different laws from successive capital investments on the same piece of land, although we have precisely derived differential rent from an identical law in both cases, from the growth in productivity of capital investment both on the same field and on different fields. The only modification here, which is overlooked, is that when successive capital investments are applied to land in different locations, they come up against the barrier of landed property, which is not the case with successive capital investments on the same land. This is the reason for the opposing tendencies by which these different forms of investment in practice set barriers to one another. There is no difference in the capital involved here. If the composition of capital remains the same, and similarly the rate of surplus-value, the rate of profit remains unaltered, so that with twice the capital there is twice the amount of profit. The rate of rent also remains the same under these conditions. If a capital of £1,000 yields a rent x, then under the conditions assumed here one of £2,000 yields a rent of $2x$. But in relation to the area, it remains unchanged, since by our assumption the doubled capital working in the same field has also risen to its level as a result of the rise in the amount of rent. The same acre that previously brought in £2 rent now brings in £4.[41]

41. It is a service of Rodbertus, whose important text on rent we shall return to in Volume 4,* to have developed this point. The first error he commits, however, in connection with capital, is to see the growth in profit as always expressing a growth in capital, so that the ratio remains the same as the mass of profit rises. But this is wrong, since, even if the exploitation of labour remains the same, the profit rate may still rise as the composition of capital changes, through a fall in the proportionate value of the constant part of capital as compared with the variable. Secondly, he makes the error of treating the proportion of money rent on a piece of land of a definite size, 1 acre for example, as if this had been the general premise of classical economics in its

The proportion of one part of the surplus-value, the money rent (for money is the independent expression of value), to the land is as it stands absurd and irrational; for it is incommensurable quantities that are measured against one another here, a particular use-value on the one hand, a piece of land of so and so many square feet, and value, in particular surplus-value, on the other. All this means in actual fact is that, under the given conditions, the ownership of these square feet of land enables the landowner to seize a certain amount of unpaid labour, which capital has realized by rooting in the soil like a pig in potatoes. *Prima facie*, however, the expression is as if one were to speak of the ratio of a £5 note to the diameter of the earth. But these irrational forms in which certain economic relationships appear and are grasped in practice do not bother the practical bearers of these relationships in their everyday dealings; since they are accustomed to operating within these forms, it does not strike them as anything worth thinking about. A complete contradiction holds nothing at all mysterious for them. In forms of appearance that are estranged from their inner connection and, taken in isolation, are absurd, they feel as much at home as a fish in water. What Hegel says about certain mathematical formulae applies here too, namely that what the common human understanding finds irrational is in fact rational, and what it finds rational is irrational.†

As far as the land area itself is concerned, a rise in the amount of rent is thus expressed in the same way as a rise in the rate of rent, hence the embarrassment when the conditions that would explain the one case are absent in the other.

But the price of land can rise even if the price of its product declines.

In this case, the differential rent may have increased by a further differentiation, and with it the price of the better lands. Or, if this is not the case, increased productivity of labour may have led to a

---

analyses of the rise and fall of rent. This again is incorrect. Classical economics always treated the rate of rent, in as much as it considered rent in its natural form, in relation to the product, and in as much as it considered rent as money rent it treated it in relation to the capital advanced, since these are in fact the rational expressions.

* *Theories of Surplus-Value*, Part II, Chapters VIII and IX, 10.

† *Encyclopaedia*, Part One, para. 231 (cf. *Hegel's Logic*, Oxford, 1975, p. 289).

fall in the price of the product, but with the increased production more than compensating for this. Assume that 1 qr costs 60s. If 2 qrs were produced on the same acre with the same capital instead of 1 qr, and the cost fell to 40s., then 2 qrs would fetch 80s., so that the value of the product of the same capital on the same acre would have risen by a third, even though the price per qr had fallen by a third. The way in which this is possible even though the product is not sold above its price of production or its value was expounded by us in dealing with differential rent. In actual fact, it is possible in only two ways. Either poor land is withdrawn from competition, but the price of the better land rises if the differential rent grows, so that the general improvement has had an uneven effect on the different types of land; or the same price of production on the worst land (and the same value, if absolute rent is paid) is expressed in a larger amount of product, on account of increased labour productivity. The product still represents the same value as before, but the price of its aliquot parts has fallen, while their number has increased. If the same capital is applied, this is impossible; for in that case the same value is always expressed in any portion of the product. It is possible, however, if an extra capital is invested for gypsum, guano, etc., i.e. for improvements whose effects extend over several years. The condition is that the price of the individual quarter, even though it falls, does not fall in the same ratio as the number of quarters grows.

III. These various conditions for a rise in rent, and hence either in the price of land in general or in that of particular types of land, may partly compete with one another, partly exclude one another, and may only take effect in alternation. But it follows from the above discussion that a rise in the price of land does not necessarily mean a rise in rent, and that a rise in rent, which always brings with it a rise in the price of land, does not invariably mean an increase in its products.[42]

*

Instead of returning to the actual natural causes for the exhaustion of land, which incidentally were unknown to any of the economists who wrote about differential rent, on account of the

---

42. For an actual case of a fall in land prices combined with a rise in rent, see Passy.

state of agricultural chemistry in their time, resort is made to the superficial conception that there is a limit to the amount of capital which can be invested in a spatially limited field, e.g. when the *Edinburgh Review* counters Richard Jones by saying that the whole of England cannot be fed by cultivating Soho Square. If this is seen as a particular disadvantage of agriculture, precisely the opposite is the case. Here successive capital investments can be made to bring fruit just because the earth itself functions as an instrument of production, which is not the case with a factory, where it functions only as the foundation, the site, the spatial basis of operations – or at least is only the case to a very small extent. It is certainly possible to concentrate a great productive installation in a small space, compared with fragmented handicraft production, and this is what modern industry does. But once the level of productivity is given, a certain space is always required, and building upwards also has its definite practical limits. Beyond these limits, an expansion of production also requires an expansion outwards. The fixed capital invested in machines, etc. is not improved by use; on the contrary, it depreciates. Here, too, particular improvements are possible as a result of new discoveries, but taking the development of productivity as given, a machine can only deteriorate. When productivity develops rapidly, the whole of the old machinery must be replaced by a more advantageous kind, and it is therefore lost. The earth, on the contrary, continuously improves, as long as it is treated correctly. The advantage of the earth, that successive capital investments can have their benefit without the earlier ones being lost, at the same time implies the possibility of a difference in yield between these successive capital investments.

Chapter 47: The Genesis of Capitalist Ground-Rent

I. INTRODUCTION

It is necessary to clarify the exact nature of the difficulty faced by modern economics, as the theoretical expression of the capitalist mode of production, in its treatment of ground-rent. This has still not been understood even by the large number of more recent writers, as is shown by each new attempt to give ground-rent a 'new' explanation. The novelty in this case consists almost invariably in regression to a standpoint long superseded. The difficulty is not one of explaining the surplus product produced by agricultural capital, and the corresponding surplus-value; this question is solved by analysis of the surplus-value all productive capital produces, whatever the sphere in which it is invested. The difficulty consists rather in showing how, after the equalization of surplus-value between the various capitals to give the average profit, whereby they receive a share in the total surplus-value produced by the social capital in all spheres of production together that is corresponding and proportionate to their relative sizes – in showing how, after this equalization, after the distribution of all the surplus-value that there is to distribute has apparently already taken place, there is still an excess part of this surplus-value left over, a part which capital invested on the land pays to the land-owner in the form of ground-rent. It must derive from somewhere. Quite apart from the practical motives which goaded the modern economist to investigate this question, as spokesman for industrial capital against landed property – motives which we shall indicate in more detail in the chapter on the history of ground-rent*

---

* These motives are in fact indicated in *Theories of Surplus-Value*, Part II, Chapter IX.

– the question was of decisive interest for them as theorists. To concede that the phenomenon of rent for capital invested in agriculture stemmed from a particular effect of the sphere of investment itself, from the earth's crust or certain properties pertaining to it, would be to renounce the very concept of value itself, i.e. to abandon any possibility of scientific understanding in this area. Even the simple perception that rent is paid out of the price of the agricultural product – which is true even when it is paid in kind, if the farmer is to extract his price of production – showed the absurdity of explaining the excess of this price over and above the customary price of production, i.e. the relative expensiveness of agricultural products, in terms of the extra natural productivity of agricultural industry over the productivity of other branches of industry. For on the contrary, the more productive labour is, the cheaper each aliquot part of its product, since the greater the amount of use-value in which the same quantum of labour, i.e. the same value, is represented.

The whole difficulty in analysing rent thus consisted in explaining the excess of agricultural profit over average profit; not surplus-value as such, but rather the extra surplus-value specific to this sphere of production; i.e. not even the 'net product', but rather the extra net product over and above the net product of other branches of industry. The average profit itself is a product, formed by a process of social life proceeding under quite particular historical relations of production, a product which, as we have seen, presupposes very elaborate mediations. If we are to speak of an excess over the average profit, this average profit must first be established as a measure and, as is the case in the capitalist mode of production, as the overall regulator of production. Thus in forms of society where it is not yet capital that performs this function of extracting all surplus labour and appropriating it for itself, at least in the first instance – i.e. where capital has not yet subsumed society's labour or has done so only sporadically – there can be no question at all of rent in the modern sense, of rent as an excess over and above the average profit, i.e. over and above the proportionate share of each individual capital in the total surplus-value that the total capital produces. It shows the naïveté of M. Passy (on which more below) that he speaks of rent in the most primitive conditions as already a surplus over and above profit – over a historically determined social form of surplus-value which, according to M. Passy, however, can exist quite nicely without any society at all.*

For the early economists who were only just beginning to analyse the capitalist mode of production, in their time still undeveloped, the analysis of rent presented either no difficulty at all or else a difficulty of a quite different kind. Petty, Cantillon† and all those other writers who stand closer to the feudal period assume that ground-rent is the normal form of surplus-value, while profit for them is still lumped indiscriminately together with wages or at most appears as a portion of this surplus-value extorted from the landowner by the capitalist. They therefore base themselves on a state of affairs in which, firstly, the agricultural population are still the overwhelming majority of the nation, and, secondly, the landowner still appears as the person who appropriates in the first instance the excess labour of the immediate producers, by way of his monopoly of landed property. Landed property thus still appears as the chief condition of production. They could not yet imagine the problem of investigating, from the standpoint of the capitalist mode of production, how landed property manages to extract again from capital one part of the surplus-value that this has produced (i.e. extorted from the immediate producers) and in the first instance already appropriated.

With the Physiocrats, the difficulty is of quite another kind. As the first systematic interpreters of capital, in fact, they tried to analyse the nature of surplus-value in general. For them this analysis coincided with the analysis of rent, the only form in which surplus-value existed for them. Rent-bearing or agricultural capital, therefore, is for them the only capital that produces surplus-value, and the agricultural labour that it sets in motion is the only labour giving rise to surplus-value, i.e. from the cap-

* op. cit., p. 511.
† Marx regarded Sir William Petty (1623–87) as the founder of that 'classical' political economy which, for all the limitations of its bourgeois standpoint, did 'investigate the real internal framework of bourgeois relations of production', as opposed to the mere apologetics of the 'vulgar economists' (Volume 1, pp. 174–5, note 34). The specific reference here is to Petty's *A Treatise of Taxes and Contributions*, London, 1667, pp. 23–4. (See also *Theories of Surplus-Value*, Part I, pp. 176–7 and 344 ff.)

Richard Cantillon, *Essai sur la nature du commerce en général*, Amsterdam, 1756. Cantillon (1680–1734) was in fact an English economist and merchant, despite his book being published in Holland in French.

italist standpoint the only truly productive labour. For them, the production of surplus-value is, quite correctly, the determinate element. Apart from other services, which we shall discuss in Volume 4,* theirs is the great merit of returning from commercial capital, which operates only in the circulation sphere, to productive capital, in contrast to the mercantilists, who in their crude realism form the true vulgar economists of their day and whose practical self-interest pressed the beginnings of scientific analysis by Petty and his school right into the background. Incidentally, the Physiocrats' criticism of the Mercantile System relates only to its conceptions of capital and surplus-value. We have already noted† how the Monetary System correctly proclaims that production for the world market and the transformation of the product into a commodity, hence into money, is the precondition and requirement for capitalist production. In its continuation as the Mercantile System, it is no longer the transformation of commodity value into money that is decisive, but instead the production of surplus-value – albeit from the irrational standpoint of the circulation sphere, and at the same time in such a way that this surplus-value is expressed in surplus money, in a favourable balance of trade. But it is also the characteristic feature of the self-interested merchants and manufacturers of that time, and belongs to the period of capitalist development that they represent, that the transformation of feudal agricultural societies into industrial societies, and the resulting industrial struggle of nations on the world market, involves an accelerated development of capital which cannot be attained in the so-called natural way but only by compulsion. It makes a substantial difference whether the national capital is transformed into industrial capital gradually and slowly, or whether this transformation is accelerated in time by the taxes they impose via protective duties, principally on the landowners, small and middle peasants and artisans, by the accelerated expropriation of independent direct producers, by the forcibly accelerated accumulation and concentration of capital, in short, by the accelerated production of the conditions of the capitalist mode of production. It also makes an enormous difference in the capitalist and industrial exploitation of the nation's natural productive

* See *Theories of Surplus-Value*, Part I, Chapters II, VI, and Addenda 8–10.

† See *A Contribution to the Critique of Political Economy*, pp. 158–9.

power. The national character of the Mercantile System is therefore not a mere slogan in the mouths of its spokesmen. Under the
pretext of being concerned only with the wealth of the nation and
the sources of assistance for the state, they actually declare that
the interests of the capitalist class, and enrichment in general, are
the final purpose of the state, and proclaim bourgeois society as
against the old supernatural state. At the same time, however,
they show their awareness that the development of the interests of
capital and the capitalist class, of capitalist production, has
become the basis of a nation's power and predominance in modern
society.

The Physiocrats were also correct in seeing all production of
surplus-value, and thus also every development of capital, as
resting on the productivity of agricultural labour as its natural
foundation. If men are not even capable of producing more means
of subsistence in a working day, and thus in the narrowest sense
more agricultural products, than each worker needs for his own
reproduction, if the daily expenditure of the worker's entire labour-
power is only sufficient to produce the means of subsistence
indispensable for his individual needs, there can be no question
of any surplus product or surplus-value at all. A level of productivity of agricultural labour which goes beyond the individual
needs of the worker is the basis of all society, and in particular
the basis of capitalist production, which releases an ever growing
part of society from the direct production of means of subsistence,
transforming them, as Steuart says, into 'free hands'* and making
them available for exploitation in other spheres.

But what should we say of the more recent economic writers
such as Daire, Passy,† etc. who, in the twilight years of classical
economics, when it is actually on its deathbed, repeat the most
primitive ideas about the natural conditions of surplus labour and

* Sir James Steuart, *An Inquiry into the Principles of Political Economy*,
Vol. 1, Dublin, 1770, p. 396. Steuart (1712–80) was the last representative o
the mercantilist school, and his work already represents a transition towards
the classical bourgeois analysis of capitalist production by Adam Smith. It is
with a short chapter on Steuart, therefore, that Marx opens *Theories of
Surplus-Value*.

† Eugène Daire, 'Introduction', in *Physiocrates*, Vol. 1, Paris, 1846;
H.-P. Passy, op. cit., p. 511. Louis-François-Eugène Daire (1798–1847) was
scarcely significant as an original writer. He has the merit, however, of
having edited this collection of Physiocratic writings, which Marx made
frequent use of in *Capital*.

hence surplus-value in general, believing themselves to have said something new and striking about ground-rent, long after this ground-rent has been explained as a particular form and specific portion of surplus-value? It is precisely characteristic of vulgar economics that what in a now superseded stage of development was new, original, profound and justified, it repeats at a time when this is flat, stale and incorrect. It thereby acknowledges that it does not even have an inkling of the problems which classical economics was concerned with. It confuses these with questions that are posed only at a lower standpoint of the development of bourgeois society. It is just the same with its incessant and self-satisfied rumination of the Physiocratic ideas on free trade. These have long since lost any and every theoretical interest, even if they may still be of some practical interest to some state or other.

In a genuine natural economy, where no part of the agricultural product, or only a very small part, is involved in circulation, and this is itself only a relatively insignificant part of that portion of the product that represents the landowner's revenue – as for example in many ancient Roman latifundia, the villas of Charlemagne's time, and more or less throughout the Middle Ages (see Vinçard,* *Histoire du travail*) – the product and surplus product of the great estates by no means consisted simply of the products of agricultural work. It equally included the products of industrial work. The existence of domestic handicrafts and manufacture as an ancillary pursuit to agriculture, which forms the basis, is the condition for the mode of production on which this natural economy is based, in European antiquity and the Middle Ages, as still today in the Indian village communities, where the traditional organization has not yet been destroyed. The capitalist mode of production completely abolishes this connection; a process which can be studied on a large scale particularly during the last third of the eighteenth century in England. People who had grown up in more or less semi-feudal societies, such as Herrenschwand,† for example, still considered this separation of agriculture and manufacture as a foolhardy social venture, an incomprehensibly risky mode of existence, at the end of the eighteenth century. And even

---

* Pierre-Denis Vinçard (1820–82) was a French writer of working-class origin. He took part in the 1848 revolution and was active in the trade-union movement, being also a member of the International Working Men's Association.

† Jean Herrenschwand (1728–1812), a Swiss economist.

in those agricultural economies of ancient times which show most analogy with the capitalist rural economy, Carthage and Rome, the similarity is more with a plantation economy than with the form truly corresponding to the capitalist mode of exploitation.[42a] A formal analogy, though one which proves to be completely deceptive in all essential points as soon as the capitalist mode of production is understood – even if not for Herr Mommsen, who discovers the capitalist mode of production in every monetary economy[43] – such a formal analogy is to be found nowhere in mainland Italy in ancient times, but only perhaps in Sicily, since this served as an agricultural tributary for Rome, its agriculture being essentially designed for export. Here one can find farmers in the modern sense.

An incorrect conception of the nature of rent has been handed down to modern times, a conception based on the fact that rent in kind still survives from the Middle Ages, in complete contradiction to the conditions of the capitalist mode of production, partly in the tithes paid to the Church and partly as a curiosity in old contracts. The impression is thus given that rent arises not from the price of the agricultural product but rather from its quantity, i.e. not from social relations but from the earth itself. We have already shown how, even though surplus-value is expressed in a surplus product, it is not true conversely that any surplus product in the sense of a mere increase in the quantity of the product represents a surplus-value. It can represent a deduction from value. Otherwise the cotton industry would have had to show an enormous surplus-value in 1860, compared with 1840, even though the price of yarn had fallen. Rent may grow enormously as the result of a series of bad harvests, since the price of corn rises, even though this surplus-value is expressed in a smaller amount of

42a. Adam Smith emphasizes how in his time (and this is still true for our own, as far as the plantation economy in tropical and sub-tropical countries is concerned) rent and profit are still not always separate, since the landowner is also the capitalist, as Cato for instance was on his estates.* This separation, however, is precisely the precondition for the capitalist mode of production, the basis of slavery similarly standing in invariable contradiction with the concept of this mode.

* *Wealth of Nations*, Pelican edition, p. 156.

43. In his *Römische Geschichte* Mommsen uses the word 'capitalist' in no way in the sense of modern economics and modern society, but rather in the manner of a popular idea persisting on the Continent – though not in England or America – as an outdated tradition from past conditions.

dearer wheat. Conversely, a series of good years may lead to a fall in rent because the price falls, even though the lower rent is expressed in a greater amount of cheaper wheat. The first thing to note about rent in kind, then, is that it is simply a tradition handed down from a mode of production which has outlived its day, and surviving, as the ruin of its former existence, while its contradiction to the capitalist mode of production is shown by the way that it disappeared automatically from private contracts and, where legislation could intervene, as with the tithes in England, was forcibly dispensed with as an incongruity.* Secondly, however, where it continued to exist on the basis of the capitalist mode of production, it was nothing more, and could be nothing more, than an expression of money rent in medieval guise. Say that wheat stands at 40s. per qr. Out of this 1 qr, one part must replace the wages contained in it and be sold so as to advance these again; another part must be sold in order to pay the part due as taxes. Seed corn and a proportion of fertilizer are themselves involved in reproduction as commodities, wherever the capitalist mode of production and the division of social labour associated with it are developed, and so replacement for these must be bought; a further part of the quarter must be sold to supply money for these. In as much as they do not actually have to be bought as commodities, but are taken from the product in kind, to go once more into its reproduction as conditions of production – which happens not only in agriculture, but also in many branches of production that produce constant capital – they are put down on the books in money of account, and are deducted as components of the cost price. The wear and tear of machinery and fixed capital in general must be replaced in money. Finally there is the profit, which is reckoned on the sum of those expenses that are expressed in real money or in money of account. This profit is represented by a particular part of the gross product, determined by its price. The part that then remains forms the rent. If the contractual product-rent is greater than this residue as determined by the price, it does not form rent but is a deduction from profit. Simply by virtue of this possibility, product-rent is an antiquated and obsolete form, as it does not follow the price of the product

* This is a reference to the Tithe Commutation Acts passed between 1836 and 1860. The Church tithes were accordingly commuted from services in kind into money payments.

and can therefore come to more or less than the actual rent, involving not only a deduction from profit, but also from components required to replace the capital. This product-rent, in fact, as far as it is rent not simply in name but in actual fact, is determined exclusively by the excess of the price of the product over its cost of production. It simply takes this variable magnitude as a constant one. But it is such a homely idea that the product first suffices in kind to feed the workers, then to leave the capitalist farmer more food than he needs, and that the surplus over and above this then forms a natural rent. It would be just the same with a calico producer who manufactures 200,000 yards of cloth. This is not only sufficient to clothe his workers, and to more than clothe his wife, all his offspring and himself, it also leaves him calico to sell and finally to pay a hefty rent in. It is such a simple matter! We deduct the production costs of the 200,000 yards, and a surplus of calico must remain over as rent. But what a naïve idea it is to deduct production costs of, say, £10,000 from the 200,000 yards, without knowing the sale price of calico; to deduct money from calico, an exchange-value from a use-value, and then to determine the surplus yards of calico over pounds sterling. It is worse than squaring the circle, which is at least based on the concept of limits in which line and curve come together. But this is M. Passy's recipe. We deduct money from calico before the calico is transformed into money, either logically or in reality! The surplus is the rent, which however should be treated 'naturally' (see for example Karl Arndt),* and not with diabolical 'sophistries'. It is foolishness such as this, the deduction of the production price from so and so many bushels of wheat, the subtraction of a sum of money from a cubic measure, that this whole restoration of natural rent comes down to.

2. LABOUR RENT

If we consider ground-rent in its simplest form, as *labour rent*, where the direct producer devotes one part of the week, with tools that belong to him either legally or in practice (plough, draught animals, etc.), to land that is in practice his own, and works the other days of the week for the landlord on his estate without reward, then the situation here is still completely clear: rent and

* Karl Arnd, *Die Naturgemässe Volkswirthschaft, gegenüber dem Monopoliengeiste und dem Communismus,* Hanau, 1845, pp. 461–2.

surplus-value are identical. Rent and not profit is the form in which the unpaid surplus labour is expressed. The extent to which the worker (a 'self-sustaining serf') can obtain a surplus over what we would call wages in the capitalist mode of production depends, other things being equal, on the proportion in which his working time is divided between labour-time for himself and statute-labour for the landlord. This surplus over and above the necessary means of subsistence, the nucleus of what appears as profit in the capitalist mode of production, is thus entirely determined by the level of ground-rent, which here not only is, but actually appears as, directly unpaid surplus labour: unpaid surplus labour for the 'proprietor' of the conditions of production, which here coincide with the land itself, or, in as much as they are distinct from it, are still held to be its accessory. That the serf's product must be sufficient in this case to replace his conditions of labour as well as his subsistence is a condition that remains the same in all modes of production, since it is not the result of this specific form but a natural condition of all continuing and reproductive labour in general, of any continuing production, which is always also reproduction, i.e. also reproduction of its own conditions of operation. It is clear, too, that in all forms where the actual worker himself remains the 'possessor' of the means of production and the conditions of labour needed for the production of his own means of subsistence, the property relationship must appear at the same time as a direct relationship of domination and servitude, and the direct producer therefore as an unfree person – an unfreedom which may undergo a progressive attenuation from serfdom with statute-labour down to a mere tribute obligation. The direct producer in this case is by our assumption in possession of his own means of production, the objective conditions of labour needed for the realization of his labour and the production of his means of subsistence; he pursues his agriculture independently, as well as the rural-domestic industry associated with it. This independence is not abolished when, as in India for example, these small peasants form a more or less natural community, since what is at issue here is independence vis-à-vis the nominal landlord. Under these conditions, the surplus labour for the nominal landowner can only be extorted from them by extra-economic compulsion, whatever the form this might assume.[44]

44. When a country was conquered, the first thing for the conqueror was always to take possession of the people. Cf. Linguet. See also Möser.*

This differs from the slave or plantation economy in that the slave works with conditions of production that do not belong to him, and does not work independently. Relations of personal dependence are therefore necessary, in other words personal unfreedom, to whatever degree, and being chained to the land as its accessory – bondage in the true sense. If there are no private landowners but it is the state, as in Asia, which confronts them directly as simultaneously landowner and sovereign, rent and tax coincide, or rather there does not exist any tax distinct from this form of ground-rent. Under these conditions, the relationship of dependence does not need to possess any stronger form, either politically or economically, than that which is common to all subjection to this state. Here the state is the supreme landlord. Sovereignty here is landed property concentrated on a national scale. But for this very reason there is no private landed property, though there is both private and communal possession and usufruct of the land.

The specific economic form in which unpaid surplus labour is pumped out of the direct producers determines the relationship of domination and servitude, as this grows directly out of production itself and reacts back on it in turn as a determinant. On this is based the entire configuration of the economic community arising from the actual relations of production, and hence also its specific political form. It is in each case the direct relationship of the owners of the conditions of production to the immediate producers – a relationship whose particular form naturally corresponds always to a certain level of development of the type and manner of labour, and hence to its social productive power – in which we find the innermost secret, the hidden basis of the entire social edifice, and hence also the political form of the relationship of sovereignty and dependence, in short, the specific form of state in each case. This does not prevent the same economic basis – the same in its major conditions – from displaying endless variations and gradations in its appearance, as the result of innumerable different empirical circumstances, natural conditions, racial relations, historical influences acting from outside, etc., and these

---

* S.-N.-H. Linguet, *Théories des loix civiles, ou principes fondamentaux de la société*, London, 1767. (See also *Theories of Surplus-Value*, Part I, Chapter VII.)

Justus Möser, *Osnabrückische Geschichte*, Berlin and Stettin, 1780.

can only be understood by analysing these empirically given conditions.

As far as labour rent goes, the most simple and primitive form of rent, this much is clear. Here rent is the original form of surplus-value and coincides with it. But it needs no further analysis here that surplus-value coincides with the unpaid labour of others, since this still exists in its visible, palpable form, the labour of the direct producer for himself being still separate both in time and space from his work for the landlord, with the latter appearing directly in the brutal form of forced labour for a third party. Likewise, the 'property' the land has of yielding a rent is reduced here to a palpably open secret, for the same nature that delivers rent also includes the human labour-power that is chained to the land, and the property relationship that forces its owner to exert and activate this labour-power beyond the degree that would be required to satisfy his own indispensable needs. The rent consists in the direct appropriation of this extra expenditure of labour-power by the landowner; for the direct producer does not pay any further rent on top of this. In this case, where surplus-value and rent are not only identical but the surplus-value still palpably takes the form of surplus labour, the natural conditions or limits of rent are immediately evident, because they are the limits of surplus labour in general. The direct producer must (1) have sufficient labour-power, while (2) the natural conditions of his labour, in the first instance the land to be worked, must be fruitful enough, i.e. the natural productivity of his labour must be great enough, to allow him the possibility of surplus labour over and above the labour needed to satisfy his own indispensable needs. It is not this possibility that creates rent; only the compulsion makes the possibility a reality. The possibility itself however is bound up with subjective and objective natural conditions. Here, too, there is nothing at all mysterious. If labour-power is meagre and the natural conditions of labour scarce, surplus labour is also small, but so too then are both the needs of the producers, the relative number of exploiters of surplus labour, and finally the surplus product in which this relatively unproductive surplus labour is realized for this small number of exploiting proprietors.

Finally, it immediately follows from labour rent that, taking all other factors as constant, it depends entirely on the relative scale of the surplus or forced labour whether and how far the direct producer is capable of improving his own condition, enriching himself, producing a surplus over and above his indispensable means of subsistence, or, to anticipate the capitalist mode of expression, whether and how far he can produce some kind of profit for himself, i.e. a surplus over and above the wage that he also himself produces. Rent here is the normal and so to speak legitimate form of surplus labour, which absorbs everything, and far from being an excess over and above profit – i.e. in this case above some other kind of surplus over wages – not only the size of such a profit, but even its very existence, other factors being constant, depends on the size of the rent, i.e. of the surplus labour that has compulsorily to be performed for the proprietor.

Some historians have expressed their amazement that when the direct producer is not a proprietor but only a possessor, all his surplus labour in fact belonging *de jure* to the landowner, it is still possible for this villein or serf to develop independent means of his own and even become quite wealthy. It is evident, however, that in the aboriginal and undeveloped conditions on which this social relation of production and the mode of production corresponding to it are based, tradition must play a predominant role. It is also evident here as always that it is in the interest of the dominant section of society to sanctify the existing situation as a law and to fix the limits given by custom and tradition as legal ones. Even ignoring any other factors, this happens automatically as soon as the constant reproduction of the basis of the existing situation, the relationship underlying it, assumes a regular and ordered form in the course of time; and this regulation and order is itself an indispensable moment of any mode of production that is to become solidly established and free from mere accident or caprice. It is precisely the form in which it is socially established, and hence the form of its relative emancipation from mere caprice and accident. It can attain this form in stagnant conditions of both the production process and the social relations corresponding to it, simply by reproducing itself repeatedly. Once this process has continued for a certain length of time, it is reinforced as usage and tradition and finally sanctified as an explicit law. Now since the form of this surplus labour, statute-labour, depends on the undeveloped condition of all labour's social productive powers, on the crudity of the mode of labour itself, it is natural for only a far smaller aliquot part of the direct producers' total labour to be confiscated from them than in more developed modes of production, and in the capitalist mode of production in particular. Let us assume for example that the statute-labour for the landlord was originally two days per week. These two weekly days of statute-labour thus persist as a constant quantity regulated by customary or written law. But the productivity of the remaining days that the direct producer has at his disposal is a variable quantity, which must develop as he progresses in experience, just as the new needs with which he becomes familiar, the expansion of the market for his product, and the growing security with which he disposes of this portion of his labour-power will spur him to increased exertion of it. It should not be forgotten in this connection that the use of this labour-power is in no way confined to agriculture but also includes rural domestic industry. This gives the possibility of a certain economic development, dependent of course on favourable conditions, innate racial character, etc.

3. RENT IN KIND

The transformation of labour rent into rent in kind in no way changes the nature of ground-rent, economically speaking. This consists, in the forms we are dealing with here, in the fact that ground-rent is the only dominant and normal form of surplus-value or surplus labour; which is expressed in turn in its being the only surplus labour or surplus product which the direct producer who finds himself in *possession* of the conditions of labour needed for his own reproduction has to provide for the *owner* of the one condition of labour that includes everything else at this stage, the land; while on the other hand it is only the land that confronts him as the property of another, a condition of labour that has become independent of him and is personified in the landowner. But when rent in kind is the dominant and furthest developed form of ground-rent, it is always still more or less accompanied by survivals of the earlier form, i.e. rent to be paid directly in labour, statute-labour, and this is irrespective of whether the landlord is a private individual or the state. Rent in kind presupposes a higher cultural level on the part of the immediate producer, i.e. a higher stage of development of his labour and of society in general; and it distinguishes itself from the preceding form by the fact that surplus labour is no longer performed in its natural form, i.e. no longer under the direct supervision and compulsion of the landlord or his representative. Rather, the immediate producer, driven on by force of circumstances instead of direct compulsion and by legal stipulation instead of by the whip, is himself responsible for performing this surplus labour. Surplus production in the sense of production over and above the indispensable needs of the immediate producer has here already become the self-evident rule, and surplus production in a field of production that actually belongs to him, the land he himself exploits, instead of on the lord's estate alongside and outside his own. In this relationship, the immediate producer has the use of more or less his entire labour-time, even if one part of this labour-time, originally it would seem the whole surplus part, still belongs for free to the landowner; it is simply that the latter receives this no longer directly, in its own natural form, but rather in the natural form of the product in which it is realized. When rent in kind is established in its pure form, the burdensome and more or less constant interruption of labour for the landowner which characterizes statute-labour (cf. Volume 1, Chapter 10, 2, 'Manufacturer and Boyar') disappears, or is at least reduced to a few brief intervals in the year in cases where certain statutory obligations persist alongside rent in kind. The work of the producer for himself and his work for the land-owner are no longer palpably separate in time and space. This rent in kind, in its pure form, even though relics of it may be handed down to more developed modes and relations of production, still presupposes a natural economy, i.e. it presupposes that the economic conditions are produced entirely or at least in the main by the economic unit itself, being directly replaced and reproduced out of its gross product. It also presupposes the union of rural domestic industry and agriculture; the surplus product which forms rent is the product of this combined agricultural–industrial family labour, whether the rent in kind includes a greater or lesser amount of industrial products, as was frequently the case in the Middle Ages, or whether it is paid simply in the form of agricultural products proper. In this form of rent, the rent in kind in which surplus labour is expressed need in no way take up the entire excess labour of the rural family. The producer has a greater room to manoeuvre, compared with labour rent, to gain time for excess labour whose product belongs to himself, just like the product of that labour that satisfies his most indispensable needs. In this form, too, greater differences arise in the economic condition of individual immediate producers. There is at least the possibility of this, and the possibility for the immediate producer to obtain the means whereby he may exploit the labour of others. Yet this does not affect our discussion of the pure form of rent in kind, as we cannot embark here on the endlessly varied combinations in which the different forms of rent may be combined, mixed together and amalgamated. The form of rent in kind, bound up with a particular type of product and of production itself; the connection indispensable to it between agriculture and domestic industry; the almost total self-sufficiency that the peasant family thereby obtains, its independence from the market and from the movement of production and of the history of that part of society outside itself; in brief, the character of natural economy in general – makes this form eminently suitable as the basis of those static conditions of society that we can see in Asia for example. Here, as in the earlier form of labour rent, ground-rent is the normal form of surplus-value, and therefore of surplus labour, i.e. of the entire excess labour that the immediate producer must perform for nothing, in actual fact therefore compulsorily, for the owner of his most essential condition of labour, the land – even if this compulsion no longer confronts him in its previous brutal form. Profit, if we incorrectly give this name in anticipation to that fraction of the excess of his labour over and above the necessary labour which he appropriates for himself, so little determines rent in kind that it rather grows up behind its back, meeting a natural limit in the level of the rent in kind. This latter may be such as seriously to endanger the reproduction of the conditions of labour, the means of production themselves, making the expansion of production more or less impossible and reducing the direct producers to the physical minimum of means of subsistence. This is particularly the case when this form is found in existence and exploited by a conquering trading nation, as by the British in India, for example.

4. MONEY RENT

By money rent, in this connection, we mean not the industrial or commercial ground-rent based on the capitalist mode of production, which is simply an excess over the average profit, but the ground-rent that arises simply from a formal transformation of the rent in kind, as this was itself simply transformed labour rent. Instead of the product itself, the immediate producer now has to pay his landowner (whether the state or a private person) the price of this. An excess product in its natural form is no longer sufficient; it has to be transformed from this natural form into the money form. Even though the direct producer still continues to produce at least the greater part of his means of subsistence himself, a portion of his product must now be transformed into a commodity and be produced as such. The character of the entire mode of production is thus more or less changed. It loses its independence, its separation from any social context. What now becomes decisive is the proportion of production costs, which now include greater or lesser expenditures in money; or at least the excess of the part of the gross product to be transformed into money over and above the part that must serve on the one hand again as means of reproduction, on the other hand as immediate means of subsistence. The basis of this type of rent, however, though it is now approaching its dissolution, remains the same as for the rent in kind that forms its starting-point. The direct producer is still the hereditary or otherwise traditional possessor of the land, who has to provide for the landlord, as proprietor of this most essential condition of production, an excess and compulsory labour, i.e. unpaid labour provided without an equivalent in the form of the surplus product transformed into money. Property in those conditions of labour distinct from the land, such as agricultural equipment and other movables, is already transformed in the earlier forms into the property of the direct producers, first of all simply in practice but later also in law, and this is still more of a premise for the form of money rent. The transformation of rent in kind into money rent that takes place at first sporadically, then on a more or less national scale, presupposes an already more significant development of trade, urban industry, commodity production in general and therefore monetary circulation. It also presupposes that products have a market price and are sold more or less approximately at their values, which in the earlier forms need in no way be the case. In Eastern Europe, we can still see something of this transition going on today. How little it can be accomplished without a certain development of labour's social productive power is attested to by various failed attempts under the Roman Empire to make this transformation, followed by regression to rent in kind, after which the attempt was made to transform into money rent at least the part of this rent existing as a state tax. The same difficulty of transition was shown for example in pre-revolutionary France by the amalgamation and adulteration of money rent with residues of its earlier forms.

But money rent as a transformed and contrasting form of rent in kind is the final form of the type of ground-rent we have been considering here, while at the same time the form of its dissolution, i.e. of ground-rent as the normal form of surplus-value and the unpaid surplus labour to be performed for the owner of the conditions of production. In its pure form, this rent, just like labour rent and rent in kind, does not represent any excess over and above profit. In its concept, it includes profit. In as much as profit arises alongside it as a particular part of surplus labour, the money rent, like rent in its earlier forms, is still the normal limit to this embryonic profit, which can develop only in proportion to the possibility of exploiting that labour, whether a person's own excess labour or that of others, which remains after the surplus labour expressed in money rent has been paid. If a profit really does arise alongside the rent, it is not the profit that sets a limit to rent, but inversely rent which sets a limit to profit. As we have already said, however, money rent is at the same time the form of dissolution of the ground-rent we have so far been dealing with here, which coincides *prima facie* with surplus value and surplus labour – ground-rent as the normal and dominant form of surplus-value.

In its further development, money rent must lead – leaving aside all intermediate forms, such as that of the small peasant farmer – either to the transformation of the land into free peasant property or to the form of the capitalist mode of production, rent paid by the capitalist farmer.

With money rent, the traditional relationship fixed by customary law between the landowner and his dependant, who possesses and works one part of the land, is necessarily transformed into a contractual relationship, a purely monetary relationship determined by the firm rules of positive law. The tiller with possession is essentially transformed into a mere tenant. On the one hand this transformation is utilized, where general conditions of production are suitable, for the gradual expropriation of the old peasant possessor and the installation in his place of a capitalist farmer; on the other hand it allows the former possessor to buy himself out of his rent obligation and leads to his transformation into an independent peasant-farmer, with full ownership in the land he tills. The transformation of rent in kind into money rent, moreover, is not only necessarily accompanied, but even anticipated, by the formation of a class of non-possessing day-labourers, who hire themselves out for money. During the period of its rise, when this new class still appears only sporadically, the custom necessarily develops, among the better-off rent-paying peasants, of exploiting agricultural wage-labourers on their own account, just as in the feudal period the wealthier peasant serfs already kept serfs of their own. In this way it gradually becomes possible for them to build up a certain degree of wealth and transform themselves into future capitalists. Among the old possessors of the land, working for themselves, there arises a seed-bed for the nurturing of capitalist farmers, whose development is conditioned by the development of capitalist production, not just in the countryside but in general, and who advance particularly rapidly when, as in England in the sixteenth century, they are aided by such particularly favourable conditions as the progressive devaluation of money at that time, which, given the traditionally long terms of tenancy contracts, enriched them at the landowners' expense.

Moreover, once rent takes the form of money rent and the relation between rent-paying peasant and landowner becomes a contractual relation – a transformation which is only possible given a certain relative level of development of the world market, trade and manufacture – land inevitably starts to be leased to capitalists, who were formerly outside rural limits and who now transfer to the land, and to the rural economy, capital that has been obtained in the town, together with the capitalist mode of operation which has also been developed there: the production of the product as a mere commodity and a mere means of appropriating surplus-value. As a general rule, this form can come about only in those countries that dominate the world market during the transition period from the feudal to the capitalist mode of production. With the intervention of the capitalist farmer between the landowner and the actual working tiller, all relationships that arose from the former rural mode of production are torn asunder. The farmer becomes the real controller of these agricultural workers and the real exploiter of their surplus labour, while the landowner stands in a direct relationship only to this capitalist farmer, and a mere monetary and contractual relationship at that. The nature of rent thereby changes, not only as a matter of fact and accidentally, which happened in places already under the previous forms, but rather normally, in its acknowledged and dominant form. From the normal form of surplus-value and surplus labour, it declines into the excess of this surplus labour over and above the part of it that is appropriated by the exploiting capitalist in the form of profit; the entire surplus labour, both profit and the excess over profit, is now directly extracted by him, received in the form of the total surplus profit and turned into money. It is now only an excess part of this surplus-value which he extracts by virtue of his capital, by the direct exploitation of the agricultural worker, that he hands over to the landowner as rent. How much or how little he parts with in this way is determined on average, as a limit, by the average profit that capital yields in the non-agricultural spheres of production and by the non-agricultural price of production that this governs. Rent has now been transformed from the normal form of surplus-value and surplus labour into an excess over the part of surplus labour that is claimed by capital as a matter of course and normally – an excess peculiar to one particular sphere of production, the agricultural. Instead of rent, the normal form of surplus-value is now profit, and rent now counts as an independent form only under special conditions, not a form of surplus-value in general but of a particular offshoot of this, surplus profit. It is unnecessary to go into any further detail as to how this transformation corresponds to a gradual transformation in the mode of production itself. This already results from the fact that it is now normal for this capitalist farmer to produce the agricultural product as a commodity, and that while formerly only the excess over his means of subsistence was transformed into a commodity, now a relatively minute part of these commodities is directly transformed into his own means of subsistence. It is no longer land, but capital, that has now directly subsumed even agricultural labour under itself and its productivity.

The average profit and the price of production governed by it are formed outside the rural situation, in the orbit of urban trade and manufacture. The profit of the rent-paying peasant does not enter into this equalization process, for his relationship to the landowner is not a capitalist one. In so far as he makes a profit, realizing an excess over and above his necessary means of subsistence, whether by his own labour or by exploiting the labour of others, this happens behind the back of the normal relationship; other factors being equal, it is not the level of this profit that determines the rent, but this profit is conversely determined by the rent as its limit. The high rate of profit in the Middle Ages was not due simply to the low composition of capital, with the variable element laid out on wages being predominant. It was a result of the fraud committed against the countryside, the appropriation of a part of the landowner's rent and the income of his dependants. If the countryside exploited the town politically in the Middle Ages, wherever feudalism was not broken through by exceptional urban development as in Italy, then the town everywhere and without exception exploited the countryside economically through its monopoly prices, its taxation system, its guilds, its direct commercial trickery and its usury.

One might imagine that the very entry of the capitalist farmer into agricultural production would already provide proof that the price of agricultural products, which had always paid a rent in some form or other, would have to stand above the production price of manufactured goods, at least at the time of this entry; either reaching the level of a monopoly price, or having risen to the value of the agricultural products, which actually does stand above the price of production governed by the average profit. For if this were not so, the capitalist farmer, given the prevailing prices for agricultural products, could not possibly first realize the average profit from the price of these products and then pay out of this same price a further excess above this profit in the form of rent. One might conclude from this that the general rate of profit guiding the capitalist farmer in his contract with the landowner was formed without taking rent into account, and that as soon as this general rate comes to govern rural production it thus finds this excess and pays it to the landowner. It is in this traditional manner that Mr Rodbertus explains things, for example.* However:

Firstly. This entry of capital into agriculture as an independent and leading power does not take place everywhere all at once, but rather gradually and in particular branches of production. At first it does not take hold of agriculture proper, but rather branches of production such as stock-raising and particularly sheep-farming, whose main product, wool, offers at first a market price permanently in excess of its price of production, in conditions of the rise of industry; this is not equalized until later on. That was the case in England during the sixteenth century.

Secondly. Since capitalist production sets in only sporadically at first, it can in no way be held against the assumption made here that it first of all takes hold of those farms which generally

* See *Theories of Surplus-Value*, Part II, Chapters VIII and IX, 10.

can pay a differential rent, as a result of their special fertility or particularly favourable location.

Thirdly. Even assuming that the prices of agricultural products do stand above their prices of production when this mode of production gets under way, which in fact presupposes an increasing weight of urban demand, as was undoubtedly the case in England in the latter third of the seventeenth century, it is still the case that once the new mode of production has extended beyond the mere subsumption of agriculture under capital and the improvement in agriculture necessarily bound up with this development, and a reduction in production costs has set in, this will be balanced by a reaction, a fall in the price of agricultural products, as was the case in England in the first half of the eighteenth century.

Thus rent as an excess above the average profit cannot be explained in this traditional way. Whatever the historical conditions under which it may first arise, once it has struck root rent can occur only under the modern conditions previously developed.

We should finally note in connection with the transformation of rent in kind into money rent that the capitalized rent, the price of land, and therefore its alienability and actual alienation, now becomes an important aspect; and that not only can the former rent-payer transform himself in this way into an independent peasant proprietor, but also urban and other holders of money can buy plots of land with a view to leasing them either to peasants or to capitalists, and enjoy the rent on their capital thus invested as a form of interest. This factor, too, helps to promote the transformation of the former mode of exploitation, of the relationship between owner and actual tiller, and of rent itself.

5. SHARE-CROPPING AND SMALL-SCALE PEASANT OWNERSHIP

We have now reached the final point in our development of ground-rent through its different stages.

In all these forms of ground-rent – labour rent, rent in kind and money rent (as simply a transformed form of rent in kind) – the rent-payer is always taken as the actual tiller and possessor of the land, whose unpaid surplus labour goes directly to the landowner. Even in the last form, money rent – in so far as this is pure, i.e.

simply the transformed form of rent in kind – this is not only a possible case, it is so in actual fact.

As a transitional form from the original form of rent to capitalist rent, we can take the system of share-cropping, where the tenant farmer provides, besides his labour (his own or others'), a part of the operating capital, the landowner providing not only the land but also a further portion of capital (e.g. livestock), and the product being divided between share-cropper and landowner in definite proportions, which vary between different countries. The farmer, here, has insufficient capital for full capitalist cultivation. The share that the landowner draws, on the other hand, does not have the pure form of rent. It may include interest on the capital he advances, and a surplus rent on top of this. It may absorb the entire surplus labour of the farmer, or leave him a greater or smaller share of this. The essential thing, however, is that rent here no longer appears as the normal form of surplus-value. On the one hand, the share-cropper, whether he applies his own labour or that of others, has a claim to a share of the product not in his capacity as worker but as owner of a part of his tools, as his own capitalist. On the other hand the landowner claims his share not exclusively on the basis of his ownership of the land but also as the lender of capital.[44a]

In Poland and Romania, for example, a residue from the old system of common property in the land, which has remained after the transition to an independent peasant economy, has served as a pretext for effecting a transition to the lower forms of ground-rent. One part of the land belongs to the individual peasants and is tilled by them independently. Another part is tilled in common and forms a surplus product, serving partly to meet the communal expenses and partly as a reserve in case of harvest failure, etc. The two latter parts of the surplus product, and ultimately the whole surplus product together with the land on which it grows, are gradually usurped by state officials and private individuals, and the originally free peasant proprietor, whose

44a. Cf. Buret, Tocqueville, Sismondi.*

* The works Marx refers to here are Buret's *Cours d'économie politique*, Brussels, 1842; De Tocqueville's *L'Ancien Régime et la révolution*, Paris, 1856; and Sismondi's *Nouveaux Principes d'économie politique*, Paris, 1827. Antoine-Eugène Buret (1810–42) was a follower of Sismondi.

obligation to take part in the common tilling of this land is maintained, is transformed into a statute-labourer or a payer of rent in kind, while those who have usurped the common land transform themselves into landed proprietors, not only of the usurped common land but of the peasant lands as well.

We do not need to go into any further detail here as regards the slave economy (which also passes through a number of gradations from patriarchal slavery predominantly for home use to the plantation system, working for the world market) nor the system in which the landowner cultivates for his own account, possessing all the instruments of production and exploiting labour, whether free or unfree, by deliveries in kind or services paid in money. Here the landowner coincides with the owner of the instruments of production, i.e. with the direct exploiter of workers who are numbered among these elements of production. Rent and profit coincide too – there is no separation of the various forms of surplus-value. The entire surplus labour of the workers, which is expressed here in surplus product, is extracted from them directly by the proprietor of all the instruments of production, which count among them also the land, and in the original form of slavery even the direct producers themselves. Where the capitalist conception prevails, as on the American plantations, this entire surplus-value is conceived as profit; where the capitalist mode of production does not exist itself, and the mode of conception corresponding to it is not transferred from capitalist countries, it appears as rent. In neither case does this form offer any difficulty. The landowner's income, the available surplus product he appropriates, whatever name it might be given, is here the normal and prevailing form in which the entire unpaid surplus labour is directly appropriated, and landed property forms the basis for this appropriation.

Small-scale peasant ownership. Here the peasant is the free proprietor of his land, which appears as his main instrument of production, as the indispensable field of employment for his labour and his capital. No lease-price is paid in this form; thus rent does not appear as a separate form of surplus-value, even if, in countries where the capitalist mode of production is otherwise developed, it does present itself as surplus profit by comparison with other branches of production, though as surplus profit which falls to the peasant, as does the entire product of his labour.

Like the earlier forms, this form of landownership presupposes that the agricultural population has a great numerical preponderance over the urban population, i.e. that even if the capitalist mode of production is dominant it is relatively little developed, so that the concentration of capitals is also confined to narrow limits in the other branches of production, and a fragmentation of capital prevails. By the nature of the case, a predominant part of the agricultural product must be consumed here by its producers, the peasants, as direct means of subsistence, with only the excess over and above this going into trade with the towns as a commodity. No matter how the average market price of agricultural products is governed here, there must evidently be a differential rent, an excess portion of commodity price, for the better or better-located lands, just as there is in the capitalist mode of production. It is simply that the peasant whose labour is realized under more favourable natural conditions pockets this himself. In this form, the land price makes up an element of the peasant's production costs, since, as things develop further, either the price of land is computed at a certain money value in dividing up an inheritance, or, as a holding or its component parts changes hands the land is actually bought by the peasant himself, often by raising the money on mortgage. Where the price of land, which is nothing but capitalized rent, is an element assumed in advance, and the rent seems to exist independently of any differentiation in the land's fertility and location – precisely here, in this form, it is to be assumed in the average case that there is no absolute rent, i.e. that the worst soil does not pay any rent; for absolute rent assumes either a realized excess value of the product above its price of production or an excess monopoly price for the product above its value. But since the rural economy here is largely one of agriculture for immediate subsistence, with the land being an indispensable field of occupation for the labour and capital of the majority of the population, the governing market price of the product only reaches its value under extraordinary conditions; this value, however, will stand as a rule above the price of production, on account of the preponderant element of living labour, even though the excess of the value above the price of production will be limited again by the low composition also of non-agricultural capital in countries where a smallholding economy prevails. The smallholding peasant's exploitation is not limited by the average profit on capital, in as much as he is a small capitalist; nor by the need for a rent, in as much as he is a landowner. The only absolute barrier he faces as a petty capitalist is the wage that he pays himself, after deducting his actual expenses. He cultivates his land as long as the price of the product is sufficient for him to cover this wage; and he often does so down to a physical minimum. In so far as he is a landowner, he does not face any property barrier, since this can present itself only in opposition to a capital (including labour) separate from it, by imposing an obstacle to its application. The interest on the price of land is a barrier, however, as it generally has to be paid over to a third party, the mortgagee. But this interest can precisely be paid out of the part of the surplus labour that under capitalist conditions would form the profit. The rent anticipated in the price of land and the interest paid on it, therefore, can be no more than a part of the capitalized surplus labour of the peasant over and above the labour indispensable for his own subsistence, but this surplus labour does not have to be realized in a portion of commodity value equal to the entire surplus profit, and still less in an excess above the surplus labour realized in the average profit, i.e. a surplus profit. The rent may be a deduction from the average profit or even the only part of this that is realized. In order for the peasant smallholder to cultivate his land or to buy land to cultivate, therefore, it is not necessary, as in the normal capitalist mode of production, for the market price of the agricultural product to rise high enough to yield him the average profit, and still less an excess over and above this average profit that is fixed in the form of rent. Thus it is not necessary for the market price to rise either to the value of his product or to its price of production. This is one of the reasons why the price of corn in countries where small-scale ownership predominates is lower than in countries of the capitalist mode of production. A portion of the surplus labour performed by those peasants working under the least favourable conditions is presented to society for nothing and does not contribute towards governing the price of production or forming value. This lower price of corn in countries of small-scale ownership is a result of the poverty of the producers and in no way of the productivity of their labour.

This form of free smallholding ownership by peasants who farm their land themselves, as the dominant, normal form, constitutes the economic basis of society in the best periods of classical antiquity, while we find it among modern peoples as one of the forms that arise out of the dissolution of feudal landed property. Examples are the yeomanry in England, the peasant estate in Sweden and the peasants of France and western Germany. We are not referring here to the colonies, since there the independent peasant farmer develops under different conditions.

The free ownership of the peasant who farms his land himself is evidently the most normal form of landed property for small-scale cultivation, i.e. for a mode of production in which possession of the land is a condition for the worker's ownership over the product of his own labour, and in which, whether he is free or a dependent proprietor, the tiller always has to produce his means of subsistence himself, independently, as an isolated worker with his family. Ownership of land is just as necessary for the full development of this activity as is ownership of the instrument of labour for the free development of the handicraftsman's trade. It forms here the basis for the development of personal independence. It is a necessary transition point in the development of agriculture itself. The causes of its decline show its limitations. These are: the destruction of rural domestic industry, its normal complement, by the development of large-scale industry; the gradual impoverishment and exhaustion of the soil which has been subjected to this form of cultivation; the usurpation of communal property by large landowners, this communal property always forming a second complement to the smallholding economy and being the only thing which makes possible the upkeep of livestock; the competition of large-scale agriculture, whether in the form of plantations or the capitalist form. Improvements in agriculture also contribute to this, by leading to a fall in the prices of agricultural products, while also requiring greater expenditures and more abundant objective conditions of production, as in England in the first half of the eighteenth century.

The agricultural smallholding, by its very nature, rules out the development of the productive powers of social labour, the social concentration of capitals, stock-raising on a large scale or the progressive application of science.

Usury and taxation must always impoverish it. The outlay of capital in the price of land withdraws this capital from agriculture. Incessant fragmentation of means of production and isolation of the producers themselves. Tremendous wastage of human labour. The progressive deterioration of the conditions of production and the increase in price of the means of production is a necessary law of small-scale landowning. The disastrous effect of good seasons for this mode of production.[45]

One particular evil of small-scale agriculture, where this is combined with the free ownership of land, arises from the way the tiller lays out capital in purchasing land. (The same applies to the transitional form in which the owner of a large estate lays out capital first to buy land and then again to cultivate it himself as his own farmer.) Given the mobile character land acquires as a mere commodity, changes in possession multiply,[46] so that with each new generation, and each division of an inheritance, the land forms a new capital investment, i.e. from the peasant's standpoint it becomes land that he has bought. The price of land here forms a predominant element of overhead costs, or the cost price of the product for the individual producer.

The price of land is nothing but the capitalized and thus anticipated rent. If agriculture is pursued on a capitalist basis, so that the landowner simply receives the annual rent and the farmer pays nothing for the land besides this, it is obvious that the capital which the landowner himself invests in purchasing land, though for him it is an interest-bearing capital investment, has nothing at all to do with the capital invested in agriculture itself. It forms part neither of the fixed capital functioning here nor of the circulating capital;[47] it procures a title for the purchaser to receive the annual rent, but it has absolutely nothing to do with the pro-

45. See the King of France's speech from the throne, in Tooke.*

* Thomas Tooke and William Newmarch, *A History of Prices . . .*, Vol. 6, London, 1857, pp. 29–30.

46. See Mounier and Rubichon.†

† L. Mounier, *De l'agriculture en France d'après les documents officiels. Avec des remarques par Rubichon*, Paris, 1846.

47. Dr H. Maron (*Extensiv oder Intensiv?* [Oppeln, 1859]) bases himself on the false assumption of his opponents. He assumes that the capital invested in the purchase of land is 'investment capital' and simply challenges the respective definitions of the concepts investment capital and operating capital, i.e. fixed capital and circulating capital. His completely jejune ideas about capital in general, even if they are somewhat excusable for a non-economist, given the general condition of German 'national economics', conceal from him that this capital is neither investment capital nor operating capital. In the same way, the capital that someone invests on the stock exchange in the purchase of shares or government paper is by no means actually 'invested' in any branch of production, even if it appears as a capital investment for the investor himself.

duction of this rent. The buyer of the land simply hands the capital over to the person selling it, and the seller thereby renounces his property in the land. Thus this capital no longer exists as the capital of the buyer; he no longer has it; it is in no way part of the capital he can invest in the land itself. Whether he has bought the land dearly or cheap, or even got it for nothing, in no way affects the capital that the farmer invests in his enterprise and in no way affects the rent; the only difference it makes is whether this rent appears to him as interest or not, or as a higher interest or a lower.

Take the case of the slave economy, for example. The price that is paid here for the slave is no more than the anticipated and capitalized surplus-value or profit that is to be extracted from him. But the capital paid in purchasing the slave does not form part of the capital by which profit, surplus labour, is extracted from him. On the contrary. It is capital which the slaveowner has alienated, a deduction from the capital which he has at his disposal in actual production. It has ceased to exist for him, just as the capital invested in the purchase of land has ceased to exist for agriculture. The best proof of this is that it comes into renewed existence for the slaveowner or landowner only when he sells the slave or land again. But then the same relationship is set up for the buyer. The fact that he has bought the slave does not enable him immediately to exploit him. He is only able to do this by putting further capital into the slave economy itself.

The same capital does not exist twice over, first in the hands of the seller of the land and then in the hands of its buyer. It passes from the buyer to the seller, and that is the end of it. The buyer now has no capital, but a piece of land instead. The fact that the rent obtained from the actual investment of capital on this piece of land is now reckoned by the new landowner as interest on capital that he has not invested on the land but has parted with in order to obtain it, does not change the economic nature of the land factor in the slightest, any more than the fact that someone has paid £1,000 for 3 per cent Consols has anything to do with the capital from whose revenue the interest on the national debt is paid.

In actual fact, what is paid over in the purchase of land, just like the money spent on the purchase of government bonds, is only capital *in itself*, just as any sum of value is potential capital on the basis of the capitalist mode of production. What was paid for the land, just as for government bonds or any other bought commodities, is a sum of money. This is potential capital, because it can be transformed into capital. It depends on the use made of it by the seller whether the money he receives really is transformed into capital or not. For the buyer, it can no longer function as such, any more than any other money he has definitively spent. It functions in his accounts as interest-bearing capital, since he reckons the income he receives – as rent from the land or as debt interest from the government – as interest on the money that it cost him to purchase the title to this revenue. He can realize it as capital only by reselling it. But then someone else, the new buyer, steps into the same relationship as the former was in before; no change of hands can transform the money spent in this way into actual capital for the spender.

In the case of the peasant smallholding, the illusion is still more strongly reinforced that land has a value of its own and thus goes into the production price of the product as capital, just like a machine or raw material. But we have seen how there are only two cases in which rent and hence capitalized rent, the price of land, can go into the price of the agricultural product as a determining factor. Firstly, if the value of the agricultural product stands above its price of production, as a result of the composition of agricultural capital – a capital which has nothing in common with capital laid out on the purchase of land – and market conditions enable the landowner to valorize this difference. Secondly, if there is a monopoly price. And these conditions obtain least of all in the case of the smallholding and petty landownership, since it is precisely here that production is designed to a very major extent to satisfy the producer's own needs, and proceeds without being governed by the general rate of profit. Even where smallholding economy is pursued on leased farms, the lease-price includes far more than under any other conditions a part of the profit, and even a deduction from wages; it is then only nominally rent, not rent as an independent category vis-à-vis wages and profit.

Thus the expenditure of money capital on the purchase of land is not an investment of agricultural capital. It proportionately reduces the capital which the small peasants have at their disposal in their actual sphere of production. It proportionately reduces the scale of their means of production and hence narrows the economic basis of reproduction. It subjects the small peasant to usury, since in this sphere there is always less credit proper. It is a constraint on agriculture, even when the purchase of large estates is involved.

It actually contradicts the capitalist mode of production, for which the indebtedness of the landowner, whether his estate is inherited or bought, is on the whole immaterial. Whether he pockets the rent himself or has to pay it over to a mortgagee in no way affects the cultivation of the property leased.

We have seen how, once the ground-rent is given, the price of land is governed by the rate of interest. If this is low, the price of land is high, and vice versa. In normal conditions, therefore, a high price of land and a low rate of interest go together, so that if the peasant has to pay a high price for land when the interest rate is low, the same low rate of interest will also procure him his operating capital at favourable terms of credit. In actual fact, though, things are different when smallholding predominates. Firstly, the general laws of credit do not apply to the peasants, since they presuppose that the producers are capitalists. Secondly, where smallholding predominates (we are not referring here to colonies) and the smallholding peasant forms the backbone of the nation, the formation of capital, and thus social reproduction, is relatively weak, and still weaker is the formation of money capital for loan in the sense previously developed. This assumes the concentration and existence of a class of rich idle capitalists (Massie). * Thirdly, where landownership forms a condition of life for the greater part of the producers, as it does here, and an indispensable field of investment for their capital, the price of land will rise independently of the rate of interest and often in inverse proportion to it, because the demand for landed property will outweigh the supply. Being sold in this case in parcelled lots, the land fetches a far higher price than when sold in large estates, since the number of small buyers is large and the number of large buyers small (*bandes noires*, Rubichon; Newman). † All these reasons lead to a rise in the price of land, even at a relatively high rate of interest. The relatively low interest that the peasant draws from the capital he lays out on the purchase of land (Mounier) contrasts

* Joseph Massie, *An Essay on the Governing Causes of the Natural Rate of Interest*, London, 1750, pp. 23–4.

† These 'black gangs' were groups of speculators in early nineteenth-century France; they dealt particularly in property confiscated from the aristocracy and the Church, buying this land wholesale and selling it in small parcels at a great profit. Marx's reference here is to Maurice Rubichon's *Du mécanisme de la société en France et en Angleterre*, Paris, 1837. Also F. W. Newman, *Lectures on Political Economy*, London, 1851, pp. 180–81.

with the high and usurious rate he himself has to pay to his mortgagee. The Irish system shows the same thing, simply in a different form.

An element that is foreign to production as such, the price of land, can thus rise here to a level which makes production impossible. (Dombasle.)

If the price of land plays such a role, if the purchase and sale of land, the circulation of land as a commodity, develops to this extent, this is the practical result of the development of the capitalist mode of production, in as much as here the commodity becomes the general form of every product and of all instruments of production. On the other hand, this takes place only where the capitalist mode of production is developed only to a limited extent and does not yet display all its characteristic features; because it precisely depends on a situation where agriculture is no longer – or not yet – subjected to the capitalist mode of production, but is rather subjected to a mode of production taken over from forms of society that have disappeared. The disadvantages of the capitalist mode of production, with its dependence of the producer on the money price of his product, are thus combined here with the disadvantages that arise from its incomplete development. The peasant becomes a merchant and industrialist without the conditions in which he is able to produce his product as a commodity.

The conflict between the price of land as an element of the cost price for the producer and as a non-element of the price of production for the product (even when rent is a determining factor in the price of the agricultural product, the capitalized rent which is advanced for twenty years or more never is) is just one of the forms expressing the contradiction between the private ownership of land and a rational agriculture, the normal social use of the land. Yet private ownership of land, and thus the expropriation from the land of the direct producers – private ownership for some, involving non-ownership of the land for others – is the basis of the capitalist mode of production.

Here, in the case of small-scale agriculture, the price of land, as a form and result of private property in land, appears as a barrier to production itself. In the case of large-scale agriculture and large-scale landed property resting on the capitalist mode of operation, property similarly appears as a barrier, since it restricts the farmer in the productive investment of capital, which ultimately benefits not him but the landowner. In both forms, instead of a conscious and rational treatment of the land as permanent communal property, as the inalienable condition for the existence and reproduction of the chain of human generations, we have the exploitation and the squandering of the powers of the earth (not to mention the fact that exploitation is made dependent not on the level of social development reached but rather on the accidental and unequal conditions of the individual producers). In the case of small-scale ownership, this results from a lack of the resources and science needed to apply the social productive powers of labour. In the case of large landed property, it results from the exploitation of these resources for the most rapid possible enrichment of the farmer and proprietor. In both cases, from dependence on the market price.

All criticism of small-scale landownership is ultimately reducible to criticism of private property as a barrier and obstacle to agriculture. So too is all counter-criticism of large landed property. Secondary political considerations are of course left aside here in both cases. It is simply that this barrier and obstacle which all private property in land places to agricultural production and the rational treatment, maintenance and improvement of the land itself, develops in various different forms, and in quarrelling over these specific forms of the evil its ultimate root is forgotten.

Small-scale landownership presupposes that the overwhelming majority of the population is agricultural and that isolated labour predominates over social; wealth and the development of reproduction, therefore, both in its material and its intellectual aspects, is ruled out under these circumstances, and with this also the conditions for a rational agriculture. On the other hand, large landed property reduces the agricultural population to an ever decreasing minimum and confronts it with an ever growing industrial population crammed together in large towns; in this way it produces conditions that provoke an irreparable rift in the interdependent process of social metabolism, a metabolism prescribed by the natural laws of life itself. The result of this is a squandering of the vitality of the soil, which is carried by trade far beyond the bounds of a single country. (Liebig.)

If small-scale landownership creates a class of barbarians standing half outside society, combining all the crudity of primitive social forms with all the torments and misery of civilized countries, large landed property undermines labour-power in the final sphere to which its indigenous energy flees, and where it is stored up as a reserve fund for renewing the vital power of the nation, on the land itself. Large-scale industry and industrially pursued large-scale agriculture have the same effect. If they are originally distinguished by the fact that the former lays waste and ruins labour-power and thus the natural power of man, whereas the latter does the same to the natural power of the soil, they link up in the later course of development, since the industrial system applied to agriculture also enervates the workers there, while industry and trade for their part provide agriculture with the means of exhausting the soil.

Part Seven

The Revenues
and Their Sources

Chapter 48: The Trinity Formula

I[48]

Capital–profit (profit of enterprise plus interest), land–ground-rent, labour–wages, this trinity form holds in itself all the mysteries of the social production process.

Since it is interest that appears as the specific and characteristic product of capital, as we have already seen,* with profit of enterprise appearing in contrast as a wage independent of capital, this first trinity form can be reduced to a second: capital–interest, land–ground-rent, labour–wages, where profit, the form of surplus-value specifically characteristic to the capitalist mode of production, is fortunately set aside.

If we now look more closely at this economic three-in-one, we find, firstly, that the ostensible sources of the wealth annually available belong to completely disparate spheres and have not the slightest analogy with one another. Their mutual relationship is like that of lawyer's fees, beetroot and music.

Capital, land, labour! But capital is not a thing, it is a definite social relation of production pertaining to a particular historical social formation, which simply takes the form of a thing and gives this thing a specific social character. Capital is not the sum of the material and produced means of production. Capital is the means of production as transformed into capital, these being no more capital in themselves than gold or silver are money. It is the means of production monopolized by a particular section of society, the products and conditions of activity of labour-power, which are rendered autonomous vis-à-vis this living labour-power and are personified in capital through this antithesis. It is not only the

48. The following three fragments were found at various points in the manuscript of Part Six. – F. E.

* See Chapter 23 above.

workers' products which are transformed into independent powers, the products as masters and buyers of their producers, but the social powers and interconnecting form of this labour also confront them as properties of their product. Here we therefore have one factor of a historically produced social production process in a definite social form, and at first sight a very mysterious form.

And now to take land, inorganic nature as such, *rudis indigestaque moles** in its primeval wilderness. Value is labour. So surplus-value cannot be earth. The land's absolute fertility does nothing but let a certain quantum of labour give a certain product, conditioned by the natural fertility of the land. The differences in the land's fertility have the effect that the same amounts of labour and capital, i.e. the same value, are expressed in differing quantities of agricultural products; so that these products have different individual values. The equalization of these individual values to give market values means that 'the advantages of fertile over inferior lands are . . . transferred from the cultivator, or consumer, to the landlord' (Ricardo, *Principles*, p. 98 [Pelican edition]).

Lastly, as the third in the league, a mere spectre – labour, which is nothing but an abstraction and taken by itself cannot exist at all, or, if we take what is actually meant here, the entire productive activity of man, through which his metabolic interchange with nature is mediated. But this is not only divested of any social form and specific character; even in its mere natural existence, independent of society, it is lifted right out of society altogether and defined as the externalization and confirmation of life equally for a man who is not yet social and for man as socialized in some way or other.

2

Capital–interest; landed property, private property in the earth, and indeed modern private property, corresponding to the capitalist mode of production – rent; wage-labour – wages of labour. This is the form in which there is supposed to be a connection between the sources of revenue. Wage-labour and landed property, like capital, are historically specific social forms; one of labour, and the other of the monopolized earth, both in fact being forms corresponding to capital and belonging to the same economic formation of society.

* 'A rude and motley mass', from Ovid, *Metamorphoses*, Book I, 7.

The first striking thing about this formula is that alongside capital, this form of an element of production belonging to a specific mode of production, to a specific historical shape of the social production process, alongside an element of production amalgamated with and presented in a specific social form, we have ranked without further ado: the earth, on the one hand, labour on the other, two elements of the actual labour process, which are material elements of any process of production and have nothing to do with its social forms.

Secondly. In the formula capital–interest, earth–ground-rent, labour–wages, capital, earth and labour appear respectively as sources of interest (instead of profit), ground-rent and wages as their products or fruits – one the basis, the other the result; one the cause, the other the effect – and moreover in such a way that each individual source is related to its product as something extruded from it and produced by it. All three forms of income, interest (instead of profit), rent and wages, are so many portions of the product's value, i.e. portions of value in general, or expressed in money, certain portions of money, of price. The formula capital–interest is certainly the most irrational formula for capital, but it is a formula for it. But how is the earth to have a value, how can it create a socially specific quantum of labour, and the particular portion of value of its own products that forms rent at that? The earth, for example, is active as an agent of production in the production of a use-value, a material product, say wheat. But it has nothing to do with producing the *value of the wheat*. In as much as value is expressed in wheat, the wheat is considered simply as a certain quantum of objectified social labour, this labour being quite indifferent to the particular material in which it is expressed or to the particular use-value of this material. It does not contradict this that (1) if other factors remain constant, whether wheat is cheap or dear depends on the earth's productivity. The productivity of agricultural labour is linked to natural conditions, and according to their productivity the same quantum of labour is expressed in more products or fewer, more or fewer use-values. The magnitude of the quantum of labour expressed in one bushel depends on the number of bushels that the same quantum of labour supplies. The quantity of product that the value represents depends here on the earth's productivity; but this value is given, and is independent of this distribution. Value is expressed in use-value, and use-value is a condition for the creation of value; but it is foolish to counterpose a use-value, the earth, on the one hand, and value on the other, and a particular portion of value at that. (2) (Here the manuscript breaks off. – F. E.)

3

Vulgar economics actually does nothing more than interpret, systematize and turn into apologetics the notions of agents trapped within bourgeois relations of production. So it should not surprise us that precisely in the estranged form of appearance of economic relations that involves these *prima facie* absurd and complete contradictions – and all science would be superfluous if the form of appearance of things directly coincided with their essence – that precisely here vulgar economics feels completely at home, these relationships appearing all the more self-evident to it, the more their inner connections remain hidden, even though they are comprehensible to the popular mind. Thus it does not have the slightest suspicion that the trinity from which it proceeds: land–rent, capital–interest, labour–wages or price of labour, consists of a conflation of three things which is *prima facie* illegitimate. First we have the use-value *land*, which has no value, and the exchange-value *rent*; here, then, a social relation, conceived as a thing, is placed in a relationship of proportion with nature; i.e. two incommensurable magnitudes are supposed to have a proportionate ratio. Then *capital–interest*. If capital is conceived as a certain sum of value with its independent expression in money, it is *prima facie* nonsense that a value should have more value than it is worth. This form *capital–interest* is precisely the form in which any mediation disappears, and capital is reduced to its most general formula, but for this reason also it is a form that is absurd and inexplicable in its own terms. This is the very reason why the vulgar economist prefers the formula capital–interest, with its occult quality of a value that is to be unequal to itself, to the formula capital–profit, as here we already get somewhat nearer to the actual capital-relation. Then again, disturbed by the feeling that 4 is not 5 and hence 100 shillings cannot possibly be 110 shillings, he flees from capital as value to the material substance of the capital; to its use-value as one of labour's conditions of production, i.e. machinery, raw material, etc. It is then possible, instead of the incomprehensible first relationship in which $4 = 5$, to construct this time a completely incommensurable relationship between a use-value, a thing, on the one hand, and a specific social relation of production, surplus-value, on the other; as in the case of landed property. As soon as this incommensurability is attained, everything becomes clear to the vulgar economist, and he feels no need for any further reflection. For he has precisely reached what is 'rational' to the bourgeois mind. Finally, *labour–wages*, the price of labour, is an expression, as shown in Volume 1,* which *prima facie* contradicts the concept of value and equally therefore that of price, this being in general only a specific expression of value; and 'price of labour' is just as irrational as a yellow logarithm. The vulgar economist, though, is completely satisfied here, since he has now reached the profound insight of the bourgeois that he pays money for labour, and the very contradiction between this formula and the concept of value relieves him from the obligation of understanding the latter.

*

[49]We have seen how the capitalist process of production is a historically specific form of the social production process in general. This last is both a production process of the material conditions of existence for human life, and a process, proceeding in specific economic and historical relations of production, that produces and reproduces these relations of production themselves, and with them the bearers of this process, their material conditions of existence, and their mutual relationships, i.e. the specific economic form of their society. For the totality of these relationships which the bearers of this production have towards nature and one another, the relationships in which they produce, is precisely society, viewed according to its economic structure. Like all its forerunners, the capitalist production process proceeds under specific material conditions, which are however also the bearers of specific social relations which the individuals enter into in the process of reproducing their life. Those conditions, like these social relations, are on the one hand the presuppositions of the capitalist production process, on the other its results and creations; they are both produced by it and reproduced by it. We also saw that capital, in the social production process appropriate

* Chapter 19, 'The Transformation of the Value (and Respectively the Price) of Labour-Power into Wages'.

[49] This is where Chapter 48 begins in the manuscript. – F. E.

to it – and the capitalist is simply personified capital, functioning in the production process simply as the bearer of capital – pumps out a certain specific quantum of surplus labour from the direct producers or workers, surplus labour that it receives without an equivalent and which by its very nature always remains forced labour, however much it might appear as the result of free contractual agreement. This surplus labour is expressed in a surplus-value, and this surplus-value exists in a surplus product. Surplus labour in some form must always remain, as labour beyond the extent of given needs. It is just that in the capitalist, as in the slave system, etc., it has an antagonistic form and its obverse side is pure idleness on the part of one section of society. A certain quantum of surplus labour is required as insurance against accidents and for the progressive extension of the repro-duction process that is needed to keep pace with the development of needs and the progress of population. It is one of the civilizing aspects of capital that it extorts this surplus labour in a manner and in conditions that are more advantageous to social relations and to the creation of elements for a new and higher formation than was the case under the earlier forms of slavery, serfdom, etc. Thus on the one hand it leads towards a stage at which compulsion and the monopolization of social development (with its material and intellectual advantages) by one section of society at the expense of another disappears; on the other hand it creates the material means and the nucleus for relations that permit this surplus labour to be combined, in a higher form of society, with a greater reduction of the overall time devoted to material labour. For, according to the development of labour productivity, surplus labour can be great when the total working day is short and relatively small when the total working day is long. If the necessary labour-time is 3 hours and surplus labour also 3 hours, the total working day is 6 hours and the rate of surplus labour 100 per cent. If the necessary labour is 9 hours and the surplus labour 3 hours, the total working day is 12 hours and the rate of surplus labour only 33⅓ per cent. It then depends on the productivity of labour how much use-value is produced in a given time, and also therefore in a given surplus labour-time. The real wealth of society and the possibility of a constant expansion of its reproduction process does not depend on the length of surplus labour but rather on its productivity and on the more or less plentiful conditions of production in which it is performed. The realm of freedom really begins only where labour determined by necessity and external expediency ends; it lies by its very nature beyond the sphere of material production proper. Just as the savage must wrestle with nature to satisfy his needs, to maintain and reproduce his life, so must civilized man, and he must do so in all forms of society and under all possible modes of production. This realm of natural necessity expands with his development, because his needs do too; but the productive forces to satisfy these expand at the same time. Freedom, in this sphere, can consist only in this, that socialized man, the associated producers, govern the human metabolism with nature in a rational way, bringing it under their collective control instead of being dominated by it as a blind power; accomplishing it with the least expenditure of energy and in conditions most worthy and appropriate for their human nature. But this always remains a realm of necessity. The true realm of freedom, the development of human powers as an end in itself, begins beyond it, though it can only flourish with this realm of necessity as its basis. The reduction of the working day is the basic prerequisite.

In capitalist society, this surplus-value or surplus product is divided among the capitalists as dividends in proportion to the quota of social capital that belongs to each. (If we ignore accidental fluctuations in the distribution and consider simply the law governing them, their regulating limits.) In this form, surplus-value appears as the average profit that accrues to capital, an average profit that is divided again into profit of enterprise and interest and can accrue under these two categories to different sorts of capitalist. This appropriation and distribution of surplus-value or surplus product by capital, however, meets with a barrier in landed property. Just as the functioning capitalist pumps out surplus labour from the worker, and thus surplus-value and surplus product in the form of profit, so the landowner pumps out a part of this surplus-value or surplus profit in turn from the capitalist in the form of rent, according to the laws developed earlier.

If we speak here therefore of profit as the share of surplus-value accruing to capital, what we mean is an average profit (equal to profit of enterprise plus interest) that is already less than the total profit by the deduction of rent; the deduction of rent is presupposed. Capital-profit (profit of enterprise plus interest) and ground-rent are thus nothing but particular components of the surplus-value; categories in which this surplus-value is distinguished according to whether it accrues to capital or landed property; designations which in no way affect its essence. Added together, they form the total social surplus-value. Capital directly pumps from the workers the surplus labour that is expressed in surplus-value and surplus product. It can be considered in this sense as the producer of surplus-value. Landed property has nothing to do with the actual production process. Its role is limited to transferring a part of the surplus-value produced from capital's pocket into its own. Yet the landowner does play his role in the capitalist production process, not only by the pressure that he exerts on capital and not simply by the fact that large landed property is a premise and condition of capitalist production, but particularly by the way that he appears as the personification of one of the most essential conditions of production.

The worker, finally, as owner and seller of his personal labour-power, receives under the name of wages a part of the product; in this there is expressed the portion of his labour that we call necessary labour, i.e. labour necessary for the maintenance and reproduction of this labour-power, whether the conditions of this maintenance and reproduction are poorer or richer, more favourable or less.

Disparate as these relations may now appear, they have one thing in common: capital yields the capitalist profit, year in year out; land yields the landowner ground-rent; and labour-power – under normal conditions, and as long as it remains a usable labour-power – yields the worker wages. These three components of the total value annually produced, and the portions of the annually produced total product corresponding to them, can be consumed by their respective owners each year, and the sources of their reproduction will not run dry. (We leave accumulation aside here at first.) They appear as fruits of a perennial tree for annual consumption, or rather fruits of three trees; they constitute the annual incomes of three classes, the capitalist, the landowning and the working class, revenues distributed by the functioning capitalist, as the person who directly pumps out surplus labour and makes use of labour in general. Capital to the capitalist, land to the landowner and labour-power to the worker, or rather his labour itself – since he sells labour-power only in its actual externalization, and the price of labour-power, as already shown, is necessarily expressed on the basis of the capitalist mode of production as the price of labour – these appear as the three respective sources of their specific revenues: profit, ground-rent and wages.

And they actually are so in the sense that capital for the capitalist is a perpetual pumping machine for surplus labour, land for the landowner a permanent magnet for attracting a part of the surplus-value pumped out by capital and finally labour the constantly self-renewing condition and means for the worker to obtain a part of the value he has produced and hence a portion of the social product measured by this portion of value, his necessary means of subsistence, under the heading of wages. They are also sources of revenue in the sense that capital fixes one portion of the value of a year's labour and hence of its product in the form of profit, landed property fixes another part in the form of rent and wage-labour a third portion in the form of wages, and that it is precisely by this transformation that these portions are converted into the revenues of the capitalist, the landowner and the worker, without creating the substance itself that is transformed into these various categories. The distribution rather presupposes this substance as already present, i.e. the total value of the annual product, which is nothing more than objectified social labour. But it is not in this form that the matter presents itself to the agents of production, the bearers of the various functions of the production process, but rather in a distorted form. Why this happens we shall see in the further course of our analysis. Capital, landed property and labour appear to those agents of production as three separate and independent sources, and it appears that from these there arise three different components of the annually produced value (and hence of the product in which this exists); from these sources, therefore, there arise not only the different forms of this value as revenues which accrue to particular factors of the social production process, but this value itself arises, and with it the substance of these forms of revenue.

(Here a folio sheet of the manuscript is missing. – F. E.)

... Differential rent is bound up with the relative fertility of different land, i.e. with properties that arise from the land as such. But in as much as it depends firstly on the differing individual values of the products of different types of land, it is simply the characteristic already mentioned; while in as much as it depends, secondly, on the governing general market price, which is different from these individual values, this is a social law brought about by competition which has nothing to do either with the land or with the various degrees of its fertility.

It might appear as if at least in 'labour–wages' a rational

relationship was expressed. But this is just as little the case as with 'land–ground-rent'. In as much as labour is value-forming and is expressed in the value of commodities, it has nothing to do with the distribution of this value among the different categories. And as far as its specific social character as wage-labour goes, it is not this that is value-forming. We have repeatedly shown how wages or the price of labour is simply an irrational expression for the value or price of labour-power; and the particular social conditions in which this labour-power is sold have no bearing on labour as a general agent of production. Labour is objectified also in that value component of the commodity that forms the price of labour-power, as wages; it creates this portion just as much as it does the other portions of the product; but it is objectified in this portion only in precisely the same way as in the portions that form rent or profit. When we have labour as value-forming in mind, we are not considering it in its concrete form as a condition of production, but rather in a social characteristic that is different from that of wage-labour.

Even the expression 'capital–profit' is incorrect here. If capital is conceived in the only connection in which it produces surplus-value, i.e. in its relationship to labour, in which it extorts surplus labour by the compulsion it exerts on labour-power, i.e. on the worker, then this surplus-value comprises not only profit (profit of enterprise plus interest), but also rent, i.e. the entire and undivided surplus-value. Here, on the contrary, as a source of revenue, it is placed in connection only with that part which accrues to the capitalist. This is not the total surplus-value it extracts, but simply the part it extracts for the capitalist. The context disappears even more once the formula is transformed into 'capital–interest'.

If we start by considering the disparity between the three sources, we find secondly that their products or derivatives, the revenues, all belong to the same sphere, that of value. However, this is cancelled out (this relationship not only between incommensurable magnitudes, but also between quite heterogeneous, unconnected and incomparable things) by the fact that capital, like the earth and labour, is considered simply from the standpoint of its material substance, i.e. simply as produced means of production, in which connection abstraction is made both from capital as a relation to the worker and from capital as value.

Thirdly. In this sense, therefore, the formula capital–interest (profit), earth–rent, labour–wages presents a uniform and symmetrical incongruity. In fact, since it is not that wage-labour appears as a socially specific form of labour, but rather that all labour appears as wage-labour by nature (presenting itself like this to those trapped within the capitalist relations of production), the determinate and specific social forms which the objective conditions of labour – the produced means of production and the earth – assume vis-à-vis wage-labour (as they in turn presuppose wage-labour) coincide directly with the material existence of these conditions of labour, or with the shape that they generally possess in the actual labour process, independent of any historically specific social form, even independent of *any* social form of this whatsoever. The form of conditions of labour that are alienated from labour, objectified in relation to it and accordingly transformed, the produced means of production being transformed into capital and the earth into the monopolized earth, into landed property, this form pertaining to a particular period of history is thus taken to coincide with the existence and function of produced means of production and the earth in the production process in general. These means of production are in and for themselves, by nature, capital; capital is nothing but a mere 'economic name' for those means of production; and similarly the earth is in and for itself, by nature, the earth as monopolized by a certain number of landed proprietors. Just as the products become an independent power vis-à-vis the producers in capital and in the capitalist – who in actual fact is nothing but personified capital – so land is personified in the landowner, he is the land similarly standing up on its hind legs and demanding its share, as an independent power, of the products produced with its aid; so that it is not the land that receives the portion of the product needed to replace and increase its productivity, but instead the landowner who receives a share of this product to be sold off and frittered away. It is clear that capital presupposes that labour is wage-labour. It is just as clear, however, that once you proceed from labour as wage-labour, so that the coincidence between wage-labour and labour in general appears self-evident, capital and the monopolized earth must also appear as the natural form of the conditions of labour vis-à-vis labour in general. It now appears as the natural form of the means of labour that they should be capital, as a purely material character which arises from their function in the labour process in general. Capital and produced means of production thus become identical expressions. Likewise land and land monopolized by private property. The means of labour as such, being capital by nature, thus become the source of profit in the same way as the earth as such becomes the source of rent.

Labour as such, in its simple characterization as purposive productive activity, is related to the means of production not in their characteristic social form but rather in their material substance, as the material and means of labour in which they are distinguished from one another only materially, as use-values, the earth as non-produced means of labour, the others as produced. If labour and wage-labour thus coincide, so too do the particular social form in which the conditions of labour confront labour, and their own material existence. The means of labour are then capital as such, while the earth as such is landed property. The formal autonomy these conditions of labour acquire vis-à-vis labour, the particular form of this autonomy they possess, is then a property inseparable from them as things, as material conditions of production, an immanently ingrown character that necessarily falls to them as elements of production. Their social character in the capitalist production process, determined by a particular historical epoch, is an innate material character natural to them, and eternally so, as it were, as elements of the production process. It must then appear that it is the respective share of the earth as the original field of application of labour, the realm of natural forces, the ready-given arsenal of all objects of labour, and the other respective share of the produced means of production (instruments, raw materials, etc.), their shares in the production process in general, that are expressed in the respective shares that fall to them as capital and landed property, or rather to their social representatives in the form of profit (interest) and rent, just as the worker's share appears to him in wages as the share of his labour in the production process. Rent, profit and wages thus appear to grow out of the roles that the earth, the produced means of production and labour play in the simple labour process, considering this labour process simply as proceeding between man and nature and ignoring any historical specificity. It is only the same thing again in a different form to say that the product in which the wage-worker's labour presents itself for him as his proceeds, his revenue, is simply the wage, the portion of value (and hence of the social product measured by this value) that represents his wage. If wage-labour coincides with labour in general, wages must coincide with the product of labour, and the portion of value that wages represents must coincide with the value created by labour in general. But in this way the other portions of value, profit and rent, confront wages just as independently and must arise from sources of their own that are specifically distinct from labour and independent; they must arise from the collaborating elements of production to whose owners they accrue, i.e. profit from the means of production, the material elements of capital, and rent from the earth, or nature, as represented by the landowner. (Roscher.)

Landed property, capital and wage-labour are therefore transformed from sources of revenue in the sense that capital attracts to the capitalist a portion of the surplus-value which it extracts from labour, in the form of profit; monopoly in the earth attracts another part to the landowner in the form of rent; and labour gives the worker the final portion of value that is still available in the form of the wage – from sources by virtue of which one part of the value is transformed into the form of profit, a second into the form of rent and a third into the form of wages – into real sources from which these portions of value themselves arise, together with the portions of the product related to them, in which they exist or against which they are convertible, the value of the product therefore itself arising from these as its ultimate source.[50]

We have already shown in connection with the most simple categories of the capitalist mode of production and commodity production in general, in connection with commodities and money, the mystifying character that transforms the social relations for which the material elements of wealth serve as bearers in the course of production into properties of these things themselves (commodities), still more explicitly transforming the relation of production itself into a thing (money). All forms of society are subject to this distortion, in so far as they involve commodity production and monetary circulation. In the capitalist mode of production, however, where capital is the dominant category and forms the

50. 'Wages, profit and rent are the three original sources of all revenue, as well as of all exchangeable value' (Adam Smith).* 'Thus the causes of material production are at the same time the sources of the original revenues that it yields' (Storch, I, p. 259).

* *The Wealth of Nations*, Pelican edition, p. 155. This view of Adam Smith's is dealt with at greater length by Marx in Volume 2 of *Capital*, Chapter 19, 2, and in *Theories of Surplus-Value*, Part I, Chapter III, sections 4–7.

specific relation of production, this bewitched and distorted world develops much further. If we view capital first in the immediate process of production, as a pumper-out of surplus labour, this relationship is still very simple; the real connection impresses itself on the bearers of this process, the capitalists, themselves, and is still in their consciousness. The fierce struggle over the limits of the working day shows this in a striking way. But even within this immediate sphere, the sphere of the immediate process between labour and capital, the matter does not rest at this simple stage. With the development of relative surplus-value in the specifically capitalist mode of production, involving the growth of the productive forces of social labour, these productive forces and the social context of labour appear in the immediate labour process as shifted from labour to capital. Capital thereby already becomes a very mystical being, since all the productive forces of social labour appear attributable to it, and not to labour as such, as a power springing forth from its own womb. Then the circulation process intervenes, with all sections of capital, even agricultural, participating in it to the same degree. In this sphere, the conditions of the original production of value fall completely into the background. Even in the immediate production process, the capitalist is active also as commodity producer, as manager of commodity production. This production process thus presents itself to him in no way just as the simple production process of surplus-value. Whatever the surplus-value capital has pumped out in the immediate production process and expressed in commodities, the value and surplus-value contained in these commodities must first be realized in the circulation process. Both the restoration of the values advanced in production, and particularly the surplus-value contained in the commodities, seem not just to be realized only in circulation but actually to arise from it. This appearance is reinforced by two circumstances in particular: firstly, profit on alienation, which depends on cheating, cunning, expertise, talent and a thousand and one market conjunctures; then the fact that a second determining element intervenes here besides labour-time, i.e. the circulation time. Even though this functions simply as a negative limit on the formation of value and surplus-value, it gives the appearance of being just as positive a ground as labour itself and of involving a determination independent of labour that arises from the nature of capital. In Volume 2, of course, we had to present this sphere of circulation only in relation to the determinations of form it produces, to demonstrate the further development of the form of capital that takes place in it. In actual fact, however, this sphere is the sphere of competition, which is subject to accident in each individual case; i.e. where the inner law that prevails through the accidents and governs them is visible only when these accidents are combined in large numbers, so that it remains invisible and incomprehensible to the individual agents of production themselves. Further, however, the actual production process, as the unity of the immediate production process and the process of circulation, produces new configurations in which the threads of the inner connection get more and more lost, the relations of production becoming independent of one another and the components of value ossifying into independent forms.

The transformation of surplus-value into profit is, as we saw, just as much determined by the circulation process as by the process of production. Surplus-value in the form of profit is no longer related to the portion of capital laid out on labour, which is where it derives from, but rather to the total capital. The profit rate is governed by its own laws, which permit it to vary while the rate of surplus-value remains the same, and even require this variation. All this conceals the true nature of surplus-value more and more, concealing therefore the real mechanism of capital. This happens still more with the transformation of profit into average profit and of values into prices of production, the governing averages of market price. A complex social process intervenes here, the equalization of capitals, which cuts the relative average prices of commodities loose from their values, and the average profits in the various spheres of production from the actual exploitation of labour by the particular capitals involved (quite apart from the individual capital investments in each particular sphere of production). The average prices of commodities not only seem to differ from their value, i.e. from the labour realized in them, but actually do differ, and the average profit of a particular capital differs from the surplus-value this capital has extracted from the workers employed by it. The value of commodities appears directly only in the influence of the changing productivity of labour on the rise and fall of prices of production; on their movement, not on their final limits. Profit now appears as determined only secondarily by the direct exploitation of labour, in so far as, given market prices that are seemingly independent of this exploitation, it permits the capitalist to realize a profit departing from the average. Normal average profit as such seems immanent in capital independently of exploitation; abnormal exploitation or even average exploitation under exceptionally favourable conditions seems only to determine divergences from average profit, and not this average profit itself. The division of profit into profit of enterprise and interest (not to speak of the intervention of commercial profit and money-dealing profit, which are founded in the circulation sphere and seem to derive entirely from this, and not from the production process itself at all) completes the autonomization of the form of surplus-value, the ossification of its form as against its substance, its essence. One portion of profit, in contrast to the other, separates itself completely from the capital-relation as such and presents itself as deriving not from the function of exploiting wage-labour but rather from the wage-labour of the capitalist himself. As against this, interest then seems independent both of the wage-labour of the worker and of the capitalist's own labour; it seems to derive from capital as its own independent source. If capital originally appeared on the surface of circulation as the capital fetish, value-creating value, so it now presents itself once again in the figure of interest-bearing capital as its most estranged and peculiar form. This is why the form 'capital–interest', as a third in the series to 'earth–rent' and 'labour–wages', is much more consistent than 'capital–profit', since profit still retains a memory of its origin which in interest is not simply obliterated but actually placed in a form diametrically opposed to this origin.

Finally, besides capital as an independent source of surplus-value, there appears landed property, as a limit to the average profit which transfers a portion of the surplus-value to a class that neither works itself nor directly exploits workers, and cannot even, like interest-bearing capital, launch forth in edifying homilies about the risk and sacrifice in lending capital. Since in this case one part of the surplus-value seems directly bound up not with social relations but rather with a natural element, the earth, the form of mutual alienation and ossification of the various portions of surplus-value is complete, the inner connection definitively torn asunder and its source completely buried, precisely through the assertion of their autonomy vis-à-vis each other by the various relations of production which are bound up with the different material elements of the production process.

Capital–profit (or better still capital–interest), land–ground-rent, labour–wages, this economic trinity as the connection between the components of value and wealth in general and its sources, completes the mystification of the capitalist mode of production, the reification of social relations, and the immediate coalescence of the material relations of production with their historical and social specificity: the bewitched, distorted and upside-down world haunted by Monsieur le Capital and Madame la Terre, who are at the same time social characters and mere things. It is the great merit of classical economics to have dissolved this false appearance and deception, this autonomization and ossification of the different social elements of wealth vis-à-vis one another, this personification of things and reification of the relations of production, this religion of everyday life, by reducing interest to a part of profit and rent to the surplus above the average profit, so that they both coincide in surplus-value; by presenting the circulation process as simply a metamorphosis of forms, and finally in the immediate process of production reducing the value and surplus-value of commodities to labour. Yet even its best representatives remained more or less trapped in the world of illusion their criticism had dissolved, and nothing else is possible from the bourgeois standpoint; they all fell therefore more or less into inconsistencies, half-truths and unresolved contradictions. It is also quite natural, on the other hand, that the actual agents of production themselves feel completely at home in these estranged and irrational forms of capital–interest, land–rent, labour–wages, for these are precisely the configurations of appearance in which they move, and with which they are daily involved. It is equally natural, therefore, that vulgar economics, which is nothing more than a didactic and more or less doctrinaire translation of the everyday notions of the actual agents of production, giving them a certain comprehensible arrangement, finds the natural basis of its fatuous self-importance established beyond all doubt precisely in this trinity, in which the entire inner connection is obliterated. This formula also corresponds to the self-interest of the dominant classes, since it preaches the natural necessity and perpetual justification of their sources of income and erects this into a dogma.

In presenting the reification of the relations of production and the autonomy they acquire vis-à-vis the agents of production, we shall not go into the form and manner in which these connections appear to them as overwhelming natural laws, governing them irrespective of their will, in the form that the world market and its conjunctures, the movement of market prices, the cycles of industry and trade and the alternation of prosperity and crisis prevails on them as blind necessity. This is because the actual movement of competition lies outside our plan, and we are only out to present the internal organization of the capitalist mode of production, its ideal average, as it were.

In earlier forms of society, this economic mystification comes in principally in connection with money and interest-bearing capital. It is excluded by the very nature of the case, firstly, where production is predominantly for use-value, for the producers' own needs; secondly, where, as in Antiquity and the Middle Ages, slavery or serfdom forms the broad basis of social production. In the latter case, the dominance of the conditions of production over the producers is concealed by the visible relations of domination and servitude, which appear as direct mainsprings of the production process. In the primitive communities where an indigenous communism prevails, and even in the urban communities of Antiquity, it is the actual community and its conditions that presents itself as the basis of production, the reproduction of this community being production's final purpose. Even in the guild system of the Middle Ages, neither capital nor labour appear unrestrained; their connections are determined by the system of corporations and the relationships this involves, as well as by the corresponding ideas of professional obligation, craftsmanship, etc. Only in the capitalist mode of production . . .*

* Here the manuscript breaks off.

Chapter 49: On the Analysis
of the Production Process

For the analysis now following we can ignore the distinction between value and price of production, since this disappears whenever we are concerned with the value of labour's total annual product, i.e. the value of the product of the total social capital.

Profit (profit of enterprise plus interest) and rent are nothing more than characteristic forms assumed by particular portions of the surplus-value in commodities. The size of the surplus-value sets a quantitative limit for the parts it can be broken down into. Average profit plus rent is therefore equal to surplus-value. It is possible for a part of the surplus labour and hence surplus-value contained in commodities not to go directly into the equalization that gives the average profit, so that a part of the value of the commodities is not expressed at all in their price. But firstly, this is compensated for by a rise in the profit rate, if the commodity sold below its value forms an element of constant capital, or else by the expression of profit and rent in a greater product, if this commodity goes into the part of value consumed as revenue, as an article of individual consumption. Secondly, it is cancelled out in the average movement. In any case, even if a portion of surplus-value not expressed in the price of the commodity is omitted from the price formation process, the sum of average profit plus rent can in its normal form never be greater than the total surplus-value, though it can be less. This normal form assumes a wage corresponding to the value of labour-power. Thus even monopoly rent, in so far as it is not a deduction from wages and does not form a special category, must always indirectly form part of surplus-value. Even if it is not a part of the excess price over and above the production costs of the actual commodity of which it itself forms a component, as in the case of differential rent, or an excess part of the surplus-value in the commodity of which it forms a component over and above its own portion of surplus-value as measured by the average profit (as in the case of absolute rent), it is still a part of the surplus-value of other commodities, i.e. those which are exchanged against this commodity with a monopoly price.

The sum of average profit plus ground-rent can never be greater than the quantity of which these are parts, and this is already given before the division. Whether the entire surplus-value of the commodities, i.e. all the surplus labour they contain, is realized in their price or not is therefore immaterial as far as we are concerned here. In actual fact the surplus-value is not completely realized, for since the amounts of socially necessary labour required for the production of a given commodity are constantly changing owing to the constant changes in productivity of labour, one section of commodities are always produced under abnormal conditions and must therefore be sold below their individual value. At all events profit plus rent equals the entire realized surplus-value (surplus labour), and for our present purpose the realized surplus-value can be equated with the total surplus-value; for profit and rent are realized surplus-value, i.e. the total surplus-value that goes into the prices of commodities, and thus for practical purposes all the surplus-value that forms a component of this price.

Wages, on the other hand, which form the third characteristic form of revenue, are always equal to the variable component of capital, i.e. the component that is laid out not on means of labour but on the purchase of living labour-power, on the payment of workers. (The labour paid in the expenditure of revenue is itself paid for from wages, profit or rent, and thus does not form any portion of the value of those commodities with which it is paid. So it does not come into consideration for the analysis of commodity value and the components into which this breaks down.) It is the objectification of that portion of the workers' total working day in which the value of variable capital and hence the price of labour is reproduced; the portion of commodity value in which the worker reproduces the value of his own labour-power or the price of his labour. The worker's total working day is divisible into two parts. One part is that in which he performs the quantum of labour needed to reproduce the value of his own means of subsistence: the paid part of his total labour, which is the part necessary for his own maintenance and reproduction. The entire remaining part of the working day, the entire excess quantum of labour he performs beyond the labour realized in the value of his wages, is surplus labour, unpaid labour, which is represented in the surplus-value of his total commodity production (and thus in an excess quantity of commodities), surplus-value which is divisible in turn into differently named portions, profit (profit of enterprise plus interest) and rent.

The total portion of commodity value, therefore, in which the total labour that the worker adds during a day or a year is realized, the total value of the annual product that this labour creates, breaks down into the value of wages, profit and rent. For this total labour breaks down into necessary labour, by which the worker creates the portion of the product's value with which he is paid himself, i.e. wages, and unpaid surplus labour, by which he creates the portion of the product's value that represents surplus-value and that subsequently divides into profit and rent. Besides this labour, the worker performs no other, and besides the total value of the product, which assumes the forms of wages, profit and rent, he creates no other value. The value of the annual product in which the labour he has newly added during the year is represented is equal to wages or the value of the variable capital, plus surplus-value, which breaks down again into the forms of profit and rent.

Thus the total portion of the annual product's value which the worker creates in the course of the year is expressed in the annual sum of value of the three revenues; the value of wages, profit and rent. It is evident, therefore, that the value of the constant portion of capital is not reproduced in the annually created product-value, for wages are equal simply to the variable portion of capital advanced in production, while rent and profit are equal to the surplus-value, the excess value produced over and above the total value of the capital advanced, i.e. the value of the constant capital plus the value of the variable capital.

It is completely immaterial for the problem to be solved here that one part of the surplus-value which has been transformed into the form of profit and rent is not consumed as revenue but serves for accumulation. The part of this that is saved as an accumulation fund serves towards forming new, additional capital, but not towards replacing the old capital, whether the component of the old capital laid out on labour-power or that laid out on means of labour. For simplicity's sake, therefore, it can be assumed that the revenues go completely into individual consumption. A double problem arises here. On the one hand, the value of the annual product in which these revenues – wages, profit, rent – are consumed contains in it a portion of value equal to the value of the constant portion of capital that has gone into it. It contains this portion of value on top of the portion of value reducible to wages and the portion reducible to profit and rent. Its value therefore = wages + profit + rent + C, with C standing for the constant portion of its value. How then is the value annually produced, which is simply wages + profit + rent, to buy a product whose value is (wages + profit + rent) + C? How can the value annually produced buy a product that has a higher value than it has itself?

If on the other hand we ignore the portion of constant capital which has not gone into the product and so continues to exist after the annual commodity production, though with a reduced value; if we thus abstract for the time being from the fixed capital that is applied but not consumed, then the constant capital advanced in the form of raw and ancillary materials has gone completely into the new product, while one part of the means of labour has been completely used up, and another partly used up, only part of its value having been consumed in production. The part of the constant capital that has been completely used up in production must be replaced in kind. Taking all other factors as unchanged, and particularly the productivity of labour, the same amount of labour is required to replace it as before, i.e. it must be replaced by an equivalent value. But who is to perform this labour, and who does perform it?

As far as the first problem is concerned – who is to pay for the constant portion of value contained in the product, and with what? – it is assumed that the value of the constant capital that has gone into production reappears as a component of the product's value. This does not contradict the premises of the second problem. For we have already shown in Volume 1, Chapter 7 ('The Labour Process and the Valorization Process') how when new labour is added, even though it does not reproduce the old value but simply makes an addition to it, only creating additional value, the old value is still preserved in the product; and that this happens not by virtue of the value-creating characteristic of labour, i.e. not because it is labour in general, but rather in its function as a specific kind of productive labour. No additional labour was needed, therefore, to perpetuate the value of the constant component in the product on which the revenue, i.e. the total value created during the year, is spent. But additional labour is needed to replace the constant capital consumed during the previous year, in value and in use-value, since without this replacement no reproduction is possible at all.

All newly added labour is expressed in the value newly created in the course of the year, which in turn goes entirely into the three revenues: wages, profit and rent. On the one hand, therefore, there is no excess social labour left over for the replacement of the capital consumed, which has to be reproduced partly both in kind and in value, and partly simply in value (for the mere wear and tear of the fixed capital). On the other hand, the value annually created by labour, which breaks down into the three forms of wages, profit and rent, and is spent in these forms, seems insufficient to pay for or to buy the constant component of capital, which the annual product must contain on top of the value of the revenues.

We can see that the problem posed here was already solved when we dealt with the reproduction of the total social capital, in Volume 2, Part Three. We come back to it here firstly because there surplus-value was not yet developed in its forms of revenue – profit (profit of enterprise plus interest) and rent – and hence could not yet be dealt with in these forms; and secondly because it is precisely in connection with the form of wages, profit and rent that an incredible blunder has run through the analysis of all political economy since Adam Smith.

In Volume 2 we divided all capital into two great classes: department I, which produces means of production, and department II, which produces means of individual consumption. The fact that certain products may serve both for personal satisfaction and as means of production (a horse, corn, etc.) in no way abolishes the absolute validity of this division. It is in no sense a hypothesis, but simply the expression of a fact. Let us take a country's annual product. One part of this product goes into individual consumption, whatever may be its ability to serve as means of production. It is the product on which wages, profit and rent are spent. This is the product of a specific department of the social capital. It is possible that this same capital also produces products belonging to department I. In as much as it does this, it is not the portion of this capital consumed in the products of department II, in products that really do fall to individual consumption, which provides the productively consumed products falling to department I. This entire product II that goes into individual consumption, and on which revenue is spent, is the existence of the capital consumed in it plus the excess produced. It is thus the product of a capital invested simply in the production of means of consumption. In the same way, department I of the annual product, which serves as means of reproduction, raw material and instruments of labour, whatever capacity this product might otherwise have, by its particular nature, to serve as means of consumption, is the product of a capital invested simply in the production of means of production. By far the greater part of the products that form constant capital exist in a material form in which they cannot go into individual consumption. In as much as they might do so, as a peasant for instance could eat his seed-corn or slaughter his draught ox, the economic barrier facing him makes it exactly the same as if this part did exist in a non-consumable form.

As already said, we abstract in both cases from the fixed part of the constant capital which continues to exist both in kind and in value, independently of the annual product of the two departments.

In department II, on whose products wages, profit and rent are spent, i.e. revenues consumed, the product itself, from the point of view of its value, consists of three components. One component is equal in value to the portion of constant capital consumed in production; a second component is equal in value to the variable portion of capital advanced, that spent on wages; finally, a third component is equal to the surplus-value produced, i.e. profit + rent. The first component of department II's product, the value of the constant capital, can be consumed neither by the capitalists or workers in department II, nor by the landowners. It forms no part of their revenues but must be replaced in kind, and for this to be done it must be sold. The two other components of this product, on the other hand, are equal to the value of the revenues produced in this department, wages + profit + rent.

In department I, the product formally consists of the same components. But here the part that forms revenue, wages + profit + rent, in other words the variable capital + the surplus-value, is consumed not in the natural form of the products of this department I but rather in the products of department II. The value of the revenues in department I must therefore be consumed in the part of the product of department II that forms the constant capital of II that is to be replaced. The part of department II's product that has to replace its constant capital is consumed in its natural form by the workers, capitalists and landowners in department I. These spend their revenues on this product II. The product of department I, on the other hand, in so far as it represents the revenue of department II, is productively consumed in its natural form by department II, whose constant capital it replaces in kind. The used-up portion of constant capital in department II, finally, is replaced out of the products of this department itself, which consist precisely of means of labour, raw and ancillary materials, etc., partly by exchange of the capitalists in department I among themselves, and partly by the ability of one section of these capitalists directly to use its own products again as means of production.

Let us take the schema used earlier (Volume 2, Chapter 20, 2) for simple reproduction:

$$\text{I. } 4{,}000_c + 1{,}000_v + 1{,}000_s = 9{,}000.$$
$$\text{II. } 2{,}000_c + \phantom{1{,}}500_v + \phantom{1{,}}500_s$$

In this case, $500_v + 500_s = 1{,}000$ is consumed in revenue in department II by the producers and landowners there; $2{,}000_c$ remains to be replaced. This is consumed by the workers, capitalists and recipients of rent in department I, their income being $1{,}000_v + 1{,}000_s = 2{,}000$. The consumed product of department II is consumed as revenue by department I, and the portion of revenue in department I that is represented in an unconsumed product is consumed as constant capital in department II. Account has still to be given of the $4{,}000_c$ in department I. This is replaced from department I's own product of 6,000, or rather 6,000 — 2,000, for 2,000 has already been converted into constant capital for department II. It should be noted that the figures here are completely arbitrary, so that the correspondence between the value of department I's revenue and department II's constant capital also seems arbitrary. It is important, however, that in so far as the reproduction process proceeds normally and with other factors remaining the same, i.e. abstracting from accumulation, the sum of wages, profit and rent in department I must be equal in value to the constant portion of capital in department II. Otherwise department II cannot replace its constant capital, nor department I convert its revenue from non-consumable into consumable form.

The value of the annual commodity product, therefore, just like the value of the commodity product of a particular capital investment or the value of any individual commodity, can be broken down into two components: component A, which replaces the value of the constant capital advanced, and component B, expressed in the form of revenue as wages, profit and rent. Component B contrasts with component A in so far as, other factors being equal, this (1) never assumes the form of revenue, (2) always returns in the form of capital, and constant capital at that. The other component B, however, has its internal distinctions as well. What profit and rent have in common with wages is that all three are forms of revenue. Yet they are basically distinguished by the fact that profit and rent represent surplus-value, i.e. unpaid labour, and wages represent paid labour. The portion of the product's value that represents wages paid, i.e. replaces wages – and so under our assumptions, in which reproduction proceeds on the same scale and under the same conditions, is transformed back into wages – returns first of all as variable capital, as a component of the capital that has to be advanced once more for reproduction. This component has a double function. It exists firstly in the form of capital, being exchanged as such against labour-power. In the hands of the worker it is transformed into the revenue that the worker draws from the sale of his labour-power; then, as revenue, it is converted into means of subsistence and consumed. This double process is demonstrated by the way it is transacted through monetary circulation. Variable capital is advanced in money, paid out in wages. This is its first function as capital. It is replaced by labour-power and transformed into the externalization of this labour-power, into labour. This is the process as far as the capitalist is concerned. Secondly, however, the workers use this money to buy a portion of their commodity product, which is measured by this money and is consumed by them as revenue. If we imagine the money circulation to be removed, one part of the worker's product is already in the hands of the capitalist in the form of capital. He advances this part as capital, giving it to the worker in exchange for new labour-power, while the worker consumes it as revenue, either directly or by exchanging it for other commodities. Thus the portion of the product's value destined to be transformed in the course of reproduction into wages, into revenue for the worker, returns first of all to the capitalist in the form of capital, variable capital to be precise. It is an essential condition for the repeated reproduction of labour as wage-labour, the means of production as capital, and the production process itself as a capitalist one, that it should return in this form.

So as not to get entangled in useless difficulties, we must distinguish gross output and net output from gross income and net income.

The gross output or the gross product is the entire product reproduced. With the exception of the portion of fixed capital which is applied but not consumed, the value of the gross output or gross product is equal to the value of the capital advanced and consumed in production, constant capital and variable, plus the surplus-value, which breaks down into profit and rent. Or, if we consider not the product of the individual capital but rather the total social capital, the gross output is equal to the material elements forming the constant and variable capital, plus the material elements of the surplus product, in which profit and rent are represented.

The gross income is the portion of value, and the part of the gross product measured by this, which remains over after deducting the portion of value, and the part of the total production measured by it, which the capital advanced and consumed in production replaces. Gross income, therefore, is equal to wages (or the part of the product destined to become the workers' income again) + profit + rent. Net income, on the other hand, is the surplus-value and hence surplus product that remains after wages are deducted, and so it expresses in fact the surplus-value that capital realizes and has to share with the landowners, and the surplus product measured by this.

We have now seen how the value of each individual commodity, and the value of the total commodity product of each individual capital, breaks down into two parts: one which simply replaces constant capital, and another which, although a fraction of it returns as variable capital, i.e. returns in the *form* of capital, is destined nevertheless to be completely transformed into gross income and to assume the form of wages, profit and rent, the sum of these three being what constitutes gross income. We have also seen that the same thing happens with respect to the value of the total annual product of a society. Thus the only distinction between the product of the individual capitalist and that of society is that from the standpoint of the individual capitalist net income is different from gross income, since the latter includes wages while the former excludes them. Considering the income of the society as a whole, national income consists of wages plus profit plus rent, i.e. the gross income. But this too is an abstraction, since the whole society, on the basis of capitalist production, is considered from the capitalist standpoint and hence views as net income only those incomes reducible to profit and rent.

Such fantasies as those of Monsieur Say, on the other hand, to the effect that the entire output, the total gross product of a nation, is reducible to net output, or is not distinct from this, i.e. that this distinction ceases to obtain from the standpoint of the nation as a whole, are simply the necessary final expression of the absurd dogma that has pervaded all political economy since Adam Smith, to the effect that the value of commodities can be ultimately broken down into wages, profit and rent.[51]

It is extremely easy, of course, in the case of the individual capitalist, to see that one part of his product must be transformed back into capital (even ignoring the expansion of reproduction, or accumulation), and moreover not into variable capital but into constant capital, which can never be transformed into income. The simplest perception of the production process makes this obvious. The difficulty begins only when the production process is considered as a whole, on a large scale. On the one hand we have an undeniable practical fact. The value of the entire part of the product that is consumed as revenue, in the form of wages, profit and rent (and it is quite immaterial here whether it is consumed individually or productively), actually disappears completely, on analysis, into the sum of value formed from wages plus profit plus

51. Ricardo makes the following very pertinent observation about the thoughtless Say: 'Of net produce and gross produce, M. Say speaks as follows: "The whole value produced is the gross produce; this value, after deducting from it the cost of production, is the net produce" (Vol. II, p. 491). There can, then, be no net produce, because the cost of production, according to M. Say, consists of rent, wages and profits. In page 508 he says: "The value of a product, the value of a productive service, the value of the cost of production, are all then similar values, whenever things are left to their natural course." Take a whole from a whole, and nothing remains' (Ricardo, *Principles*, Chapter XXXII [pp. 409–10], note). As we shall see later on, however, Ricardo never rejected Smith's erroneous analysis of commodity price, his resolution of this into the value sum of the revenues. He did not bother with it, and assumes its correctness in his analyses by 'abstracting' from the constant portion of commodity value. He thus falls occasionally into the same way of looking at things.

rent, i.e. into the total value of the three revenues, even though the value of this part of the product, just like that which does not go into revenue, contains a portion of value $= C$, equal to the value of the constant capital contained in it, so that it can in no way be limited, *prima facie*, to the value of the revenue. On the other hand, we have an equally undeniable theoretical contradiction – and the easiest though fraudulent solution to this problem is to claim that it is only from the standpoint of the individual capitalist that commodity value appears to contain a further portion of value distinct from that existing in the form of revenue. All further consideration is rendered unnecessary by the maxim that what appears as revenue for one person forms capital for another. How, if the value of the entire product can be consumed in the form of revenues, the old capital can be replaced, and how the value of the product of each individual capital can be equal to the value sum of the three revenues plus C, the constant capital, while the combined value sum of the products of all capitals together equals the value sum of the three revenues plus 0, all this can only appear as an insoluble riddle, and must be explained by alleging that analysis is quite incapable of catching hold of the simple elements of price and must instead satisfy itself with a vicious circle and an infinite regress. So that what appears as constant capital is reducible to wages, profit and rent, but the commodity values in which wages, profit and rent are expressed are determined in turn by wages, profit and rent, and so *ad infinitum*.[52]

The fundamentally false dogma that the value of commodities

52. 'In every society the price of every commodity finally resolves itself into some one or other, or all of those three parts' (viz. wages, profits, rent) . . . 'A fourth part, it may perhaps be thought, is necessary for replacing the stock of the farmer, or for compensating the wear and tear of his labouring cattle, and other instruments of husbandry. But it must be considered that the price of any instrument of husbandry, such as a labouring horse, is itself made up of the same three parts; the rent of the land upon which he is reared, the labour of tending and rearing him, and the profits of the farmer who advances both the rent of this land, and the wages of this labour. Though the price of the corn, therefore, may pay the price as well as the maintenance of the horse, the whole price still resolves itself either immediately or ultimately into the same three parts of rent, labour' (meaning wages) 'and profit.' (Adam Smith [Book One, Chapter VI, p. 153]).

We shall show later on how Adam Smith himself feels the contradiction in this evasion and its unsatisfactory character, for it is nothing more than an evasion for him to send us from pillar to post, even though he never indicates the actual capital investment in which the price of the product is 'ultimately' resolved simply into these three parts without further analysis.

can be ultimately reduced to wages + profit + rent is thus expressed in the contention that the consumer has ultimately to pay the total value of the total product; or that the monetary circulation between producers and consumers must ultimately be equal to the monetary circulation between the producers themselves (Tooke);† contentions that are all as false as the fundamental principle on which they are based.

The problems that lead to this false and *prima facie* absurd analysis can be summarized as follows:

(1) The basic relationship of constant and variable capital is not understood, and so neither is the nature of surplus-value and with it the entire basis of the capitalist mode of production. The value of each partial product of capital, each individual commodity, includes a portion of value = constant capital, a portion of value = variable capital (which is transformed into wages for the worker) and a portion of value = surplus-value (later separated into profit and rent). How then is it possible for the worker with his wages, the capitalist with his profit, and the landowner with his rent, to buy commodities that contain not only one of these components but all three, and how is it possible for the value sum of wages, profit and rent, i.e. the three sources of income taken together, which are to buy the commodities which are to enter into the total consumption of the recipients of these incomes, to contain a further additional value component on top of these three, i.e. constant capital? How can a value of four be bought with a value of three?[53]

† *An Inquiry into the Currency Principle*, London, 1844, p. 36.

53. Proudhon declares his inability to understand this in the narrow-minded formula: *l'ouvrier ne peut pas racheter son propre produit* [the worker cannot buy back his own product], since the interest contained in it is added on to the *prix-de-revient*, the cost price to himself.* But does M. Eugène Forcade teach him any better? 'If Proudhon's charge were true, it would not affect simply the profits of capital, but would destroy the possible existence of industry altogether. If the worker is forced to pay 100 for what he only receives 80 for, if wages can only buy back the value in a product that he has added to it, this means that the worker can buy nothing back, that wages can buy nothing. For the cost price always contains something more than the wages of the worker, and the sale price always something more than the profit of the entrepreneur, e.g. the price of the raw material, which is often paid abroad ... Proudhon has forgotten the perpetual growth in the national capital, he has forgotten that this growth involves all working people, the entrepreneur as well as the worker' (*Revue des Deux Mondes*, vol. 24, 1848, pp. 998–9). Here we have the optimism of bourgeois thoughtlessness in the most appropriate form of its

We have given an analysis of this in Volume 2, Part Three.

(2) It is not understood how and in what way labour, while it adds new value, also preserves old value in a new form, without producing this value afresh.

(3) The interconnection of the reproduction process is not understood, i.e. as this presents itself not from the standpoint of the individual capital, but rather from that of the total capital; the problem of how the product in which wages and surplus-value are realized, i.e. all value newly added in the course of the year, can replace its constant value portion and still be reducible to a value defined simply by revenues; how, moreover, the constant capital consumed in production can be replaced materially and in value by a new capital, even though the total sum of newly added labour is realized only in wages and surplus-value, and is exhaustively expressed in the sum of these two. It is precisely here that the principal difficulty lies, in the analysis of reproduction and the relationship of its various components, both in their material character and in their value.

(4) But there is still a further problem, which becomes yet more difficult once the different components of surplus-value appear in

---

wisdom. First M. Forcade believes that the worker could not survive if he did not receive a higher value than that which he produces, while conversely the capitalist mode of production would be impossible if he really did receive the value he produces. Secondly, he correctly generalizes the problem that Proudhon expressed only from a restricted point of view. The price of a commodity contains an excess not only on top of wages but also on top of profit, i.e. the constant portion. So the capitalist, too, in Proudhon's argument, could not buy the commodity back with his profit. But how does Forcade solve the riddle? By a meaningless phrase – the growth of capital. Thus the steady growth of capital is to mean among other things that while the political economist finds it impossible to analyse commodity price for a capital of 100, it is superfluous to analyse cost price for a capital of 10,000. What would be said of a chemist who, when asked how it is that the soil's product contains more carbon than the soil itself, gave the answer that this came from the steady growth in agricultural production? In vulgar economics, the well-meaning good intention of finding the bourgeois world to be the best of all possible worlds makes any desire for truth and any impulse towards scientific investigation unnecessary.

* *Qu'est-ce que la propriété? ou Recherches sur le principe du droit et du gouvernement*, Paris, 1841, pp. 201–2. This is the celebrated work in which Proudhon comes to the conclusion that 'property is theft'. Proudhon's critic here, Eugène Forcade (1820–69), was simply a 'vulgar economist' whose antipathy to Proudhon's ideas expressed little more than class interest.

the form of mutually independent revenues. This is that the firm determinations of revenue and capital change places and shift, so that they seem to be only relative determinations pertaining to the standpoint of the individual capitalist, and seem to vanish altogether when the total production process is in view. For instance, the revenue of the workers and capitalists in department I, which produces constant capital, replaces the constant capital in department II, which produces means of consumption, both in value and materially. The problem can thus be brushed aside with the notion that what is revenue for one is capital for another, so that these definitions have nothing to do with the actual distinctions in the components of commodity value. Further, commodities that are ultimately destined to form the material elements of revenue expenditure, i.e. means of consumption, pass through various stages in the course of the year, e.g. woollen yarn, cloth. At one stage, they form part of constant capital, at another they are consumed individually and go entirely into revenue. It is possible to imagine, therefore, as Adam Smith did, that constant capital is merely an apparent element of commodity value, which disappears in the overall context. There is also an exchange of variable capital for revenue. With his wage, the worker buys the portion of commodities that forms his revenue. He thereby returns to the capitalist the money form of the variable capital. Some of the products forming constant capital, finally, are replaced in kind or by exchange between the producers of the constant capital itself, a process that seems to have nothing to do with the consumers. When this is overlooked, the illusion arises that the consumers' revenue replaces the entire product, including the constant portion of value.

(5) Apart from the confusion produced by the transformation of values into prices of production, a further confusion derives from the transformation of surplus-value into various separate, mutually independent forms related to the various elements of production, into profit and rent. It is forgotten that the values of commodities are the basis and that the breakdown of this commodity value into particular components, and the further development of these value components into forms of revenue, their transformation into relations that the various owners of the different agents of production have to these particular value components, their distribution among these owners according to particular categories and titles, in no way alter the value deter-

mination and its law. Just as little is the law of value affected by the fact that the equalization of profit, i.e. the distribution of the total surplus-value among the various capitals and the obstacles that landed property partly places in the way of this (in absolute rent), gives rise to governing average prices for commodities that diverge from their individual values. This again affects only the addition of surplus-value to the various commodity prices; it does not abolish surplus-value itself, nor the total value of commodities as the source of these various price components.

This is the *quid pro quo* which we shall discuss in the following chapter, and it is necessarily connected with the illusion that value arises from its own components. Firstly, in other words, the various value components of commodities receive independent forms in the revenues and are related to the particular material elements of production as their sources, instead of to the value of the commodities as their single source. They are indeed related to the elements of production, but not as components of value, rather as revenues, as value components accruing to these particular categories of agents of production, the worker, the capitalist and the landowner. It is possible then to imagine that these components of value, instead of arising from the decomposition of commodity value, actually give rise to it by coming together. This then leads to the neat vicious circle in which the value of commodities arises from the value sum of wages, profit and rent, while the value of wages, profit and rent is determined in turn by the value of commodities, etc.[54]

54. 'The invested circulating capital in materials, raw materials and finished products is itself composed of commodities, whose necessary price is formed from the same elements, in such a way that it would be an unnecessary repetition to count this part of the circulating capital as one of the elements of the necessary price' (Storch, *Cours d'économie politique*, II, p. 140). Among these elements of circulating capital, Storch includes the constant portion. (The fixed is simply circulating in a different form.) 'It is true that the worker's wages as well as the portion of the entrepreneur's profit that consists of wages – if one considers these as a portion of means of subsistence – is similarly composed of commodities sold at their market price, which themselves include wages, capital-rents, ground-rents and profits of enterprise . . . establishment of this fact serves only to prove that it is impossible to resolve the necessary price into its simplest elements' (ibid., note). In a polemic against Say in his *Considérations sur la nature du revenu national* (Paris, 1824), Storch admittedly understands the absurdity of the conclusion which follows from the false analysis of commodity value that resolves it just into revenue, and correctly points out the ridiculous character of this result – from the standpoint of a nation rather than that of the individual capitalist. But he does not himself

If we consider the normal state of reproduction, then only a part of the freshly added labour is applied to the production and hence replacement of constant capital; i.e. precisely that part which replaces the constant capital used up in the production of means of consumption, of the material elements of revenue. This is balanced by the fact that the constant portion of department II costs no additional labour. But the constant capital that is not the product of freshly added labour (taking the reproduction process as a whole, thus including the equalization of departments I and II), even though this product could not be produced without it, is exposed during the reproduction process, in its material aspect, to accidents and dangers that may decimate it. (It may also depreciate in value as the result of a change in the productivity of labour.) One part of the profit accordingly serves as an insurance fund, and thus also a part of the surplus-value and surplus product in which the freshly added labour is expressed. And it in no way affects the nature of the problem whether or not this insurance fund is managed by insurance companies as a separate business. This is the only part of the revenue that is neither consumed as such nor serves necessarily as an accumulation fund. Whether it actually does serve as such a fund, or simply offsets the shortfall in reproduction, is a matter of chance. This is also the only part of surplus-value and the surplus product, and thus of surplus labour, leaving aside the part serving for accumulation, i.e. for expansion of the reproduction process, that would have to continue in existence after the abolition of the capitalist mode of production. In this

---

take a single step further in his analysis of the *prix nécessaire* which, as he explained in his *Cours*, it is impossible to resolve into its actual elements instead of a false infinite regress. 'It is apparent that the value of the annual product can be divided on the one hand into capital, on the other into profit, and that each of these portions of value of the annual product will regularly buy the products that the nation needs, both to maintain its capital and to replace its consumption stock' (pp. 134–5) . . . 'Can they' (the peasant family working for themselves) 'live in their barns or stables, eat up their seed-corn and animal fodder, slaughter their draught cattle for clothes, and satisfy their needs with their agricultural implements? According to M. Say's doctrine, all these questions have to be answered in the affirmative' (pp. 135–6). 'Once it is conceded that the revenue of a nation is equal to its gross product, i.e. that no capital has to be deducted, then it must also be conceded that the nation can consume the entire value of its annual product unproductively, without making the slightest inroad into its future revenue' (p. 147). 'The products that make up a nation's capital are not consumable' (p. 150).

situation, of course, the part regularly consumed by the direct producers would not remain confined to its present minimum level. Apart from surplus labour for those who cannot yet participate in production on grounds of age, or can no longer do so, there would be no other labour for the maintenance of non-workers. If we consider instead the beginnings of society, then no produced means of production are yet in existence, i.e. no constant capital whose value goes into the product and has to be replaced in kind from the product on the same scale, in the course of reproduction, to an extent determined by its value. But in this case nature directly provides means of subsistence that do not first need to be produced. Thus it also gives the savage, who has only few needs to satisfy, the time, if not to use the means of production not yet in existence for new production, then – besides the labour that it takes to appropriate the means of subsistence given by nature – to transform other natural products into means of production, a bow, a stone knife, a boat, etc. This process in the case of the savage completely corresponds, taking simply the material aspect, to the transformation of surplus labour back into new capital. In the process of accumulation, we still have the continued transformation of such a product of excess labour into capital; and the fact that all new capital arises from profit, rent or other forms of revenue, i.e. from surplus labour, gives rise to the false idea that all commodity value arises from a revenue. This transformation of profit into capital rather shows the opposite on closer analysis, i.e. it shows that the additional labour – which always takes the form of revenue – serves not to maintain or reproduce the old capital value but rather to create new and additional capital, in so far as it is not consumed as revenue.

The entire problem arises from the way that all freshly added labour, in so far as the value it creates is not reducible to wages, appears as profit – conceived here as the general form of surplus-value, i.e. a value that costs the capitalist nothing, so that it also certainly does not have to replace anything advanced, any capital. This value exists therefore in the form of additional available wealth, i.e. from the standpoint of the individual capitalist in the form of his revenue. But this newly created value can be consumed productively as well as individually, as capital as well as revenue. Its natural form already dictates that it must in part be consumed productively. It is evident, therefore, that the labour added each year creates both capital and revenue; as is then shown also in the process of accumulation. But the portion of labour-power used for the creation of new capital (i.e. in our analogy the part of the working day that the savage spends not appropriating food but rather preparing the tool with which to appropriate it) then becomes invisible, because the entire product of the surplus labour presents itself first of all in the form of profit, a characteristic which in fact has nothing to do with this surplus product itself, but simply bears on the private relationship between the capitalist and the surplus-value he pockets. In actual fact, the surplus-value that the worker creates breaks down into revenue and capital; i.e. into means of consumption and additional means of production. But the old constant capital handed down from the previous year (apart from the part that is damaged, i.e. proportionately destroyed, i.e. as far as it does not have to be reproduced, and such disturbances of the reproduction process fall under the heading of insurance) is not reproduced in value by the freshly added labour.

We see, moreover, that one part of the freshly added labour is always absorbed in the reproduction and replacement of the constant capital consumed, even if this freshly added labour can be completely resolved into revenues – wages, profit and rent. It is overlooked in this connection, however, (1) that the value component of the product of this labour is *not* the product of the freshly added labour but constant capital that was already in existence and has been used up; hence that the part of the product in which this value component is expressed is not transformed into revenue but replaces the means of production of this constant capital in kind; (2) that the value component in which this freshly added labour is actually expressed is not consumed in kind as revenue but rather replaces the constant capital in another sphere, where it is converted into a natural form in which it can be consumed as revenue, even if this is not exclusively the product of freshly added labour.

As long as reproduction proceeds on the same scale, each element of constant capital used up must be replaced – at least in efficacy if not in quantity and form – by a new item of the appropriate kind. If the productivity of labour remains the same, this replacement in kind involves the replacement of the same value that the constant capital had in its old form. But if the productivity of labour rises, so that the same material elements can be reproduced with less labour, a smaller value component of the product can replace the constant part fully in kind. The surplus can then go towards forming new additional capital, or the surplus labour can be reduced. If the productivity of labour declines, on the other hand, a greater part of the product must go into replacing the old capital; the surplus product declines.

If we abstract from the specific historical form and consider it simply as the formation of new means of production, the transformation of profit or any kind of surplus-value back into capital shows that there is always a situation in which the worker spends additional labour on producing means of production, on top of that spent in obtaining his immediate means of subsistence. The transformation of profit into capital is nothing more than the use of a part of the additional labour in forming new and additional means of production. If this happens in the form of the transformation of profit into capital, it simply means that it is not the worker but the capitalist who has the surplus labour at his disposal. If this surplus labour must first go through a stage in which it appears as revenue (whereas in the case of the savage, for example, it appears as labour immediately directed to the production of means of production), it simply means that this labour, or its product, is appropriated by the non-worker. What is actually transformed into capital is not profit as such. The transformation of surplus-value into capital simply means that the surplus-value and surplus product are not individually consumed by the capitalist as revenue. What really is transformed in this way is value, objectified labour, or the product in which this value is directly expressed, or against which it is exchanged, after prior conversion into money. Even if profit is transformed back into capital, it is not this specific form of surplus-value, profit, that forms the source of the new capital. Surplus-value, in this connection, is simply transformed from one form into the other. But it is not this formal transformation that makes it into capital. It is the commodity and its value that now function as capital. But it is completely immaterial for the objectification of this labour, for value itself, that the value of the commodity is not paid – and it is only in this way that it becomes surplus-value.

The misunderstanding is expressed in various forms. In the form, for instance, that the commodities which constant capital consists of themselves contain elements of wages, profit and rent. Or that what is revenue for one person is capital for another, and that these are therefore simply subjective relationships. Thus the spinner's yarn contains a value component that represents profit for him. If the weaver buys the yarn, he realizes the spinner's profit, but as far as he is concerned this yarn is simply part of his constant capital.

On top of what we said previously about the relationship of revenue and capital, we should note here that what goes into the weaver's capital with the yarn, as a constituent element considered in value terms, is the yarn's value. How the components of this value might be reducible for the spinner into capital and revenue, in other words into paid and unpaid labour, is a matter of complete indifference for determining the value of the commodity itself (apart from the modifications owing to average profit). Always lurking in the background is the idea that profit, and surplus-value in general, is an excess over and above the value of the commodity, which is made only by a surcharge, by mutual cheating, by profit on alienation. But since the production price of the commodity is paid, or even its value, so too are those value components of the commodity that appear to their seller in the form of revenue. Monopoly prices, of course, are not at issue here.

Secondly, it is quite correct that the commodity components which constant capital consists of are reducible like all other commodity value to value components that could be resolved for their producers and the owners of the means of production into wages, profit and rent. This is simply the capitalist way of expressing the fact that commodity value is always just the measure of the socially necessary labour contained in a commodity. But as we have already shown in Volume 1, this in no way prevents the commodity product of a capital from breaking down into separate components, of which one exclusively represents the constant capital component, another the variable capital component and a third simply the surplus-value.

Storch puts forward what is also the opinion of many other people when he says:

'The saleable products that make up the national revenue must be considered by political economy in two different ways: as values, in relation to individuals; and as goods, in relation to the nation; for the revenue of a nation is not assessed like that of an individual, according to its value, but rather according to its utility, or according to the needs which it can satisfy' (*Considérations sur la nature du revenu national*, p. 19).

Firstly, it is a false abstraction to treat a nation whose mode of production is based on value, and organized capitalistically into the bargain, as a unified body simply working for the national needs.

Secondly, even after the capitalist mode of production is abolished, though social production remains, the determination of value still prevails in the sense that the regulation of labour-time and the distribution of social labour among various production groups becomes more essential than ever, as well as the keeping of accounts on this.

Chapter 50: The Illusion Created by Competition

We have shown how the value of commodities, or the price of production governed by their total value, can be resolved into:

(1) A value component that replaces constant capital or represents labour already past, which was spent in the form of means of production for the production of the commodity; in other words, the value or price at which these means of production went into the commodity's production process. We are referring here not to the individual commodity but always to commodity capital, i.e. the form which the product of capital takes over a definite section of time, e.g. annually, and of which the individual commodity simply forms one element, though its value also breaks down into the same analogous components.

(2) The value component of variable capital that measures the income of the worker and is transformed for him into wages, wages therefore which the worker has reproduced in this variable component; in other words the value component which represents the paid portion of the labour freshly added to the first, constant, portion in the production of the commodity.

(3) The surplus-value, i.e. the value component of the commodity product in which the unpaid labour or surplus labour is expressed. This last value component again assumes those independent forms that are at the same time forms of revenue: the forms of profit on capital (interest on capital as such, and profit of enterprise on capital as functioning capital), and ground-rent, which falls to the owner of the land which is playing its part in the production process.

Components (2) and (3), i.e. the value component that always assumes the revenue forms of wages (this only after it has previously passed through the form of variable capital), profit and rent, is distinguished from the constant component (1) by the fact that it contains the whole of the value in which there is objectified the labour freshly added to that constant part, the means of production of the commodity. If we leave aside the constant component of value, it is correct to say that the value of a commodity, in so far as this represents freshly added labour, is always reducible to three elements, wages, profit and rent, which constitute the three forms of revenue,[55] while the respective value magnitudes, i.e. the aliquot parts that these form of the total value, are determined by different, specific laws that have already been developed. It would be wrong however to say that the value of wages, the rate of profit and the rate of rent are independent constituent elements of value, with the value of the commodity, minus its constant component, arising from their combination; in other words, it would be wrong to say that these form constituent components of commodity value or of the price of production.[56]

The distinction can readily be seen.

Assume that the value produced by a capital of 500 is $400_c +$ $100_v + 150_s = 650$; the 150_s breaks down again into 75 profit + 75 rent. We shall further assume, in order to avoid needless difficulties, that this capital is of average composition, so that its production price and its value coincide; which is the case whenever

55. In connection with the division into wages, profit and ground-rent of the value added to the constant capital component, it is self-evident that these are components of value. They can of course be imagined as existing in the immediate product in which this value is expressed, i.e. in the product that the workers and capitalists in a particular sphere of production, e.g. cotton-spinning, have directly produced, say in yarn. In fact, however, they are no more and no less expressed in this product than in any other kind of commodity, any other component of material wealth of the same value. In practice we find that wages are paid in money, i.e. the pure expression of value, and similarly interest and rent. For the capitalist, in fact, the transformation of his product into the pure value expression is very important; this is already assumed in connection with distribution. Whether these values are transformed back into the same product, the same commodity, from whose production they derived, whether the worker buys back a part of the product he directly produced or buys the product of other labour and other types of labour, has nothing to do with the essence of the matter. Rodbertus gets quite needlessly worked up over this subject.

56. 'It will be sufficient to remark, that the same general rule which regulates the value of raw produce and manufactured commodities, is applicable also to the metals; their value depending not on the rate of profits, nor on the rate of wages, nor on the rent paid for mines, but on the total quantity of labour necessary to obtain the metal, and to bring it to market' (Ricardo, *Principles*, Chapter III [pp. 108–9]).

the product of this individual capital can be treated as the product of a part of the total capital corresponding to it in size.

In this case, wages, measured by the variable capital, make up 20 per cent of the capital advanced; the surplus-value, reckoned on the total capital, is 30 per cent, i.e. 15 per cent profit and 15 per cent rent. The total value component of the commodity in which the freshly added labour is objectified is $100_v + 150_s = 250$. Its total amount is independent of its division into wages, profit and rent. The proportionate relationship between these components shows that the labour-power which was paid for with 100 in money, say £100, has supplied a quantum of labour expressed in a sum of money of £250. We can see from this that the worker has performed $1\frac{1}{2}$ times as much surplus labour as he has labour for himself. If the working day were 10 hours, he would be working 4 hours for himself and 6 hours for the capitalist. The labour of the workers who are paid £100 is expressed therefore in a money value of £250. Apart from this value of £250, there is nothing left to be shared between worker and capitalist, or capitalist and landowner. It is the total value freshly added to the value of the means of production, which was £400. The commodity value of £250 thus produced, and determined by the amount of labour objectified in it, sets the limit to the dividends that worker, capitalist and land-lord can draw from this value in the form of revenue – wages, profit and rent.

Let us assume that a capital of the same organic composition, i.e. the same proportion between living labour-power applied and constant capital set in motion, is forced to pay £150 instead of £100 for the same labour-power that sets in motion the constant capital of £400. Let us further assume that profit and rent share the surplus-value in the same proportions. Since it is assumed that this variable capital of £150 sets the same amount of labour in motion as £100 did before, the value newly produced would still be £250 and the value of the total product £650, but we would now have $400_c + 150_v + 100_s$; and this 100_s might break down into 45 profit plus 55 rent. The proportion in which the total value produced is divided into wages, profit and rent would be very different; so too would be the total capital advanced, even though it only sets in motion the same total amount of labour. Wages would make up $27\frac{3}{11}$ per cent of the capital advanced, profit $8\frac{2}{11}$ per cent, and rent 10 per cent on this capital, so that the total surplus-value would be somewhat over 18 per cent.

The increase in wages would affect the unpaid part of the total labour, and with this the surplus-value. The worker would have worked 6 hours of the 10-hour working day for himself and only 4 hours for the capitalist. The proportions of profit and rent would also be different, and the diminished surplus-value would be divided in a changed proportion between capitalist and landowner. Finally, since the value of the constant capital has remained unaltered while the value of the variable capital advanced has risen, the diminished surplus-value would be expressed in a still further reduced gross rate of profit, by which we mean here the ratio of the total surplus-value to the total capital advanced.

These changes in the value of wages, the rate of profit and the rate of rent, whatever the effect of the laws governing the proportions between these parts, could move only within the limits set by the newly created commodity value of 250. The only exception would be if rent were based on a monopoly price. This would in no way affect the law, but simply complicate our treatment of it. For if we are dealing in this case simply with the product itself, it is only the division of the surplus-value that would vary; while if we are considering its relative value vis-à-vis other commodities, the only difference would be that one part of the surplus-value would be transferred from these to our particular commodity.

To recapitulate:

Value of the product		New value	Rate of surplus-value	Gross rate of profit
First case	$400_c + 100_v + 150_s = 650$	250	150%	30%
Second case	$400_c + 150_v + 100_s = 650$	250	$66\frac{2}{3}$%	$18\frac{2}{11}$%

The surplus-value, firstly, falls by a third of its former amount, from 150 to 100. The rate of profit falls by somewhat more than a third, from 30 per cent to around 18 per cent, since the diminished surplus-value has to be reckoned against an increased total capital advanced. But it in no way falls in the same proportion as the rate of surplus-value. This falls from $\frac{150}{100}$ to $\frac{100}{150}$, i.e. from 150 per cent to 66⅔ per cent, whereas the rate of profit falls only from $\frac{150}{500}$ to $\frac{100}{550}$, or from 30 per cent to $18\frac{2}{11}$ per cent. Thus the rate of profit falls proportionately more than the mass of surplus-value, though less than the rate of surplus-value. It is also evident that the values and quantities produced remain the same if the same amount of labour is still applied as before, even though the capital advanced has expanded as a result of the increase in its variable component. This expansion of the capital advanced would also be very significant for the capitalist opening a new business. Taking reproduction as a whole, however, an increase in variable capital means nothing more than that a greater part of the value newly created by the freshly added labour is transformed into wages, and hence first of all into variable capital, instead of into surplus-value and surplus product. The value of the product thus remains the same, since it is defined on the one hand by the constant capital value of 400 and on the other by the figure of 250 which represents the freshly added labour. Both of these have remained unaltered. This product, if it itself went back into constant capital, would still represent the same amount of use-value within the same amount of value; i.e. the same amount of elements of constant capital would keep the same value. The situation would be different if wages rose, not because the worker kept a greater part of his own labour, but rather because the productivity of labour declined and he kept a greater part of his own labour as a result. In this case, the total value in which the same labour was expressed, i.e. paid and unpaid, would remain the same; but this quantity of labour would be expressed in a diminished product, i.e. the price of each aliquot part of the product would rise, since each part represented more labour. The increased wages of 150 would represent a product no greater than 100 did before; the diminished surplus-value of 100 would now represent only two-thirds the former product, $66\frac{2}{3}$ per cent of the mass of use-values that were previously expressed in 100. In this case, the constant capital would also become more expensive, in so far as this product went into it. But this would not be the result of the increase in wages, the wage increase would rather result from the fact that the commodity had become more expensive and that the productivity of the same amount of labour had diminished. The illusion arises that the rise in wages has made the product dearer; but here this is not cause but consequence of a change in the commodity's value, resulting from the diminished productivity of labour.

In otherwise identical circumstances, i.e. where the same amount of labour is applied and still expressed in 250, then if the value of the means of production it applied rises or falls, the value of the same volume of products will rise or fall by the same amount. $450_c + 100_v + 150_s$ gives a product value of 700 for the value of the same amount of products, while $350_c + 100_v + 150_s$ gives only 600, instead of 650 as before. Thus, if the capital advanced for putting the same amount of labour in motion grows or declines, the value of the product rises or falls, conditions being otherwise identical, as long as the increase or decrease in the capital advanced derives from a change in the value magnitude of the constant capital component. It remains unaffected, on the other hand, if the increase or decrease in the capital advanced derives from a change in the value magnitude of the variable capital component, with labour productivity remaining the same. As far as constant capital is concerned, the increase or decrease in its value is not compensated for by any movement in the opposite direction. In the case of variable capital, assuming that the productivity of labour remains the same, the increase or decrease in its value is compensated for by a movement in the opposite direction on the part of surplus-value, so that there is no change in the value of the variable capital plus the surplus-value, i.e. the value freshly added to the means of production by labour and expressed in the product.

If the increase or decrease in the variable capital or wages is the result of a rise or fall in commodity prices, i.e. of a decrease or increase in the productivity of the labour applied in that capital investment, this does affect the value of the product. But in this case the rise or fall in wages is not the cause, but simply the effect.

If in the above example, where we assume that the constant capital remains 400_c, the change from $100_v + 150_s$ to $150_v + 100_s$, i.e. the rise in variable capital, were instead the result of a decline in labour productivity not in this particular branch, e.g. cotton-spinning, but say in agriculture, which provides the workers' sustenance, i.e. if it were the result of an increase in the price of these provisions, the value of the product would remain unchanged. The value of 650 would still be expressed in the same amount of cotton yarn as before.

It also emerges from what has been argued so far that, if the reduction in the outlay on constant capital is the effect of economy, etc. in branches of production whose products go into the workers' consumption, this could lead to a reduction in wages just as could a direct increase in the productivity of the labour applied, because it would cheapen the workers' means of subsistence and hence increase surplus-value. In this case the profit rate would rise for two reasons: on the one hand because the value of the constant capital would have declined and on the other because surplus-value would have increased. In considering the transformation of surplus-value into profit we assumed that wages did not fall but remained constant, since we were concerned there to investigate the fluctuations in the rate of profit independently of changes in the rate of surplus-value. The laws developed there, however, are general ones, and apply also for capital investments where the products do not go into the consumption of the workers, so that changes in the value of the product are without influence on wages.

*

The value freshly added each year by new labour to the means of production or the constant capital component can be separated out and resolved into the different revenue forms of wages, profit and rent; this in no way alters the limits of the value itself, the sum of value that is divided between these different categories. In the same way, a change in the ratio of these individual portions among themselves cannot affect their sum, this given sum of value. The given figure of 100 always remains the same, whether it is broken down into 50 + 50, or 20 + 70 + 10, or 40 + 30 + 30. The value component of the product that is broken down into these revenues is determined, just as the constant value component of the capital is, by the value of the commodities, i.e. by the quantum of labour objectified in them in each case. What is given first, therefore, is the mass of commodity values to be divided into wages, profit and rent; i.e. the absolute limit to the sum of value portions in these commodities. Secondly, as far as the individual categories themselves are concerned, their average and governing limits are similarly given. In this delimitation, wages form the basis. In this respect they are governed by a natural law; their minimum limit is given by the physical minimum of means of subsistence that the worker must receive in order to maintain and reproduce his labour-power; i.e. a definite amount of commodities. The value of these commodities is determined by the labour-time required for their reproduction; i.e. by the portion of labour freshly added to the means of production, or the portion of the working day, that the worker requires to produce and reproduce an equivalent for the value of these necessary means of subsistence. If his average means of subsistence come to 6 hours of average labour per day, he must spend on average some 6 hours of his daily labour working for himself. The actual value of his labour-power diverges from this physical minimum; it differs according to climate and the level of social development; it depends not only on physical needs but also on historically developed social needs, which become second nature. In each country, however, this governing average wage is a given quantity at a given time. The value of all other revenues thus has a limit. This is always equal to the value embodying the total working day (which coincides here with the average working day, since it comprises the total amount of labour set in motion by the total social capital), minus that part of it embodied in wages. Its limit is given therefore by the limit of the value representing unpaid labour, i.e. by the amount of this unpaid labour. If the part of the working day that the worker needs to reproduce the value of his wage has its ultimate barrier in the physical minimum of this wage, then the other part of the working day in which surplus labour is expressed, i.e. the value component that expresses surplus-value, has its barrier in the physical maximum of the working day, i.e. in the total amount of daily labour-time that the worker can provide if he is to maintain and reproduce his labour-power. Since what we are dealing with here is the distribution of the value in which the total labour freshly added each year is expressed, the working day can be taken as a constant quantity, and it is assumed to be so however much or little it may depart from its physical maximum. We thus have an absolute limit for the value component that forms surplus-value and can be broken down into profit and ground-rent; this is determined by the excess of the unpaid portion of the working day over its paid portion, i.e. by the value component of the total product in which this surplus labour is realized. If we call the surplus-value whose limits are thus determined profit, when it is calculated on the total capital advanced, as we have already done, then this profit, considered in its absolute amount, is equal to the surplus-value, i.e. it is just as regularly determined in its limits as this is. It is the ratio between the total surplus-value and the total social capital advanced in production. If this capital is 500 (which can of course be millions) and the surplus-value 100, the absolute limit to the rate of profit is 20 per cent. The division of the social profit as measured by this rate among the capitals applied in the various different spheres of production produces prices of production which diverge from commodity values and which are the actual averages governing market prices. But this divergence from values abolishes neither the determination of prices by values nor the limits imposed on profit by our laws. The value of a commodity is not equal to the capital consumed in it plus the surplus-value it contains; instead, its price of production is now equal to the capital k consumed in it plus the surplus-value that falls to it by virtue of the general rate of profit, say 20 per cent, on the capital advanced for its production, whether this is consumed or simply applied. This surcharge of 20 per cent, however, is itself determined by the surplus-value created by the total social capital, and its proportion to the value of this capital; and this is why it is 20 per cent and not 10 per cent or 100 per cent. The transformation of values into prices of production does not abolish the limits to profit, but simply affects its distribution among the various particular capitals of which the social capital is composed, distributing it across them evenly, in proportion as they form value components of this total capital. Market prices rise above these governing production prices or fall below them, but these fluctuations balance each other out. If one compiles price lists over a prolonged period, and ignores those cases in which the actual value of a commodity alters as a result of a change in labour productivity, as well as cases in which the production process is disturbed by natural or social disasters, it is surprising both how narrow the limits of these divergences are and how regularly they are balanced out. The same rule of governing averages is found here as Quételet demonstrated in connection with social phenomena.* If the adjustment of commodity values to prices of production does not meet with any obstacles, rent is reduced to differential rent, i.e. it is restricted to the cancellation of the surplus profits that the governing prices of production would give to one section of capitalists, these now being appropriated by the landowners. Thus rent has its definite value limits here in the divergences among the individual rates of profit that are produced when production prices are governed by the general rate of profit. If landed property places obstacles in the way of this adjustment of commodity values to prices of

* Adolphe Quételet (1796–1874), a Belgian mathematician whose interests included the application of statistical methods to social phenomena. His work on this subject, *On Man and the Development of his Faculties*, first published in 1835, appeared in an English edition in 1842 and was quite celebrated in its time. Marx's attitude towards Quételet, in so far as it can be inferred from a few brief references, is interesting and characteristic: the regularities Quételet demonstrates in social phenomena are ingenious, but not particularly significant. Cf. 'Parties and Cliques' in *Surveys from Exile*, p. 279.

production, and appropriates an absolute rent, this is limited by the excess value of agricultural products over and above their price of production, i.e. by the excess surplus-value contained in them over and above the profits that capitals receive by virtue of the general rate of profit. This difference then fixes the limit of the rent, which continues to form simply a specific portion of the given surplus-value contained in the commodities.

Finally, if the equalization of surplus-value to average profit in the various spheres of production comes upon obstacles in the form of artificial or natural monopolies, and particularly the monopoly of landed property, so that a monopoly price becomes possible, above both the price of production and value of the commodities this monopoly affects, this does not mean that the limits fixed by commodity value are abolished. A monopoly price for certain commodities simply transfers a portion of the profit made by the other commodity producers to the commodities with the monopoly price. Indirectly, there is a local disturbance in the distribution of surplus-value among the various spheres of production, but this leaves unaffected the limit of the surplus-value itself. If the commodity with the monopoly price is part of the workers' necessary consumption, it increases wages and thereby reduces surplus-value, as long as the workers continue to receive the value of their labour-power. It could press wages down below the value of labour-power, but only if they previously stood above the physical minimum. In this case, the monopoly price is paid by deduction from real wages (i.e. from the amount of use-values that the worker receives for the same amount of labour) and from the profit of other capitalists. The limits within which monopoly price affects the normal regulation of commodity prices are firmly determined and can be precisely calculated.

Just as the division of the commodity value newly added and completely reducible to revenue finds its given and governing limits in the proportion between necessary and surplus labour, wages and surplus-value, so the division of this surplus-value itself into profit and ground-rent finds its limits in the laws governing the equalization of the profit rate. With the division into interest and profit of enterprise, the average profit itself sets the limit for the two together. It supplies the given amount of value they have to share between them, and this is all they have to share. The specific ratio of this division is accidental here, i.e. it is determined exclusively by relations of competition. Whereas in other cases market prices cease to diverge from the average prices which govern them when demand and supply are matching, and the effect of competition is abolished, here this is the only determining factor. And why? Because the same factor of production, capital, has to share the portion of surplus-value accruing to it between two owners of this same production factor. But if the division of average profit has in this case no determining limit as imposed by the laws we have developed, that does not abolish this limit as a portion of commodity value; as little as when two partners in a company share their profit unequally, because of different external circumstances, this in any way affects the limits of this profit.

Thus if the portion of commodity value representing labour freshly added to the value of the means of production breaks down into different portions, which assume mutually independent shapes in the form of revenues, this does not in any way mean that wages, profit and ground-rent are now to be considered as the constituent elements, with the governing price (natural price, *prix nécessaire*) of commodities itself arising from their combination or sum; so that it would not be the commodity value, after deduction of the constant value component, that was the original unity and breaks down into these three components, but the price of each of these three components was rather determined independently, and the commodity's price formed only from the addition of these three independent magnitudes. In actual fact commodity value is the quantitative premise, the sum total value of wages, profit and rent, whatever their relative mutual magnitudes might be. In the false conception considered here, however, wages, profit and rent are three independent value magnitudes, whose total produces, limits and determines the magnitude of commodity value.

It is evident from the start that if wages, profit and rent constituted the price of commodities, this would necessarily hold good both for the constant portion of commodity value and for the other portion in which variable capital and surplus-value are represented. This constant part can therefore be left out of consideration here, since the value of the commodities it consists of would likewise break down into the sum of the values of wages, profit and rent. As already noted, this view also involves a denial of the existence of such a constant value component.

It is also evident that any concept of value would inevitably disappear here. All that was left would be the idea of price, in the sense that a certain amount of money is paid to the owners of labour-power, capital and land. But what is money? Money is not a thing but a particular form of value, so that it again presupposes value. What is said therefore is that a certain amount of gold or silver is paid for those elements of production, or that they are mentally equated with this amount. But gold and silver are themselves commodities like all others (and enlightened economics is proud of this recognition). The price of gold and silver is thus also determined by wages, profit and rent. So we cannot determine wages, profit and rent by equating them with a certain quantity of gold and silver, for the value of this gold and silver, as the equivalent in which they are to be assessed, is precisely supposed to be determined by wages, profit and rent independently of gold and silver, i.e. independently of the value of any commodity, which is precisely the product of those three. To say that the value of wages, profit and rent consists in their being equal to a certain amount of gold and silver is thus simply to say that they are equal to a certain amount of wages, profit and rent.

Let us first take wages. For even in this view, it is necessary to start from labour. How then is the governing price of wages determined, the price around which the market price oscillates?

By the demand for and supply of labour-power, it will be said. But what demand for labour-power are we talking about? Capital's demand. The demand for labour is thus equal to the supply of capital. To speak of the supply of capital, we must first of all know what capital is. What does capital consist of? Let us take its simplest manifestation: money and commodities. Money is simply a form of commodity. So it consists of commodities. The value of commodities, however, is determined in the first instance, on the present assumption, by the price of the labour producing them, wages. Wages are presupposed here, and treated as a constituent element of commodity price. This price must then be determined by the proportion of labour on offer to capital. Capital's demand for labour is equal to the supply of capital. The supply of capital is equal to the supply of a sum of commodities of a given price, and this price is governed in the first instance by the price of labour, the price of labour being equal in turn to the portion of commodity price which constitutes variable capital and is handed to the worker in exchange for his labour; the price of those commodities which make up variable capital is again determined by the prices of wages, profit and rent. The determination of wages cannot start from capital, for wages are themselves a factor entering into the determination of the value of capital.

Moreover, it is no use bringing in competition. Competition makes the market prices of labour rise or fall. But assume that the demand for and supply of labour match one another. How are wages determined then? By competition? But we have precisely assumed that competition ceases to be a determinant, that its effect is abolished by the achievement of equilibrium between its two counteracting forces. And we are precisely out to find the natural price of wages, i.e. a price of labour which is not governed by competition, but on the contrary is what governs competition.

Nothing remains, then, but to determine the necessary price of labour by reference to the worker's necessary means of subsistence. But these means of subsistence are commodities, with a price. The price of labour is thus determined by the price of the necessary means of subsistence, and the price of the means of subsistence, like that of all other commodities, is determined in the first place by the price of labour. So the price of labour is determined by itself. In other words, we do not know how the price of labour is determined. Labour always has a price here, since it is considered as a commodity. Thus in order to speak of the price of labour, we must know what price in general is. But this procedure does not tell us anything about price in general.

Let us assume, however, that the necessary price of labour is determined in this delightful way. What about the average profit, then, the profit of any capital in normal conditions, which forms the second element of commodity price? The average profit must be determined by an average rate of profit; how is this determined? By competition between the capitalists? But this competition already assumes the existence of profit. It assumes different rates of profit and hence different profits, whether in the same branch of production or in different ones. Competition can act on the profit rate only by acting on the price of commodities. Competition can only bring it about that producers within the same sphere of production sell their commodities at the same price, and that in different spheres of production they sell their commodities at prices that give them the same profit, the same proportionate surcharge to the price of the commodity that is already partly determined by wages. Hence competition can only even out inequalities in the rate of profit. In order to even out unequal rates of profit, profit must already exist as an element of commodity price. Competition does not create it from nothing. It makes it higher or lower, but it does not create the level that is present as soon as this equalization has taken place. And in so far as we speak of a necessary rate of profit, we precisely want to know the profit rate independently of the movement of competition, we want to know the rate which actually governs competition. The average rate of profit appears when the forces of the competing capitalists balance one another. Competition can produce this balance, but not the rate of profit which appears when the balance is given. When this balance is brought about, why is the general rate of profit now 10 per cent or 20 per cent or 100 per cent? On account of competition? But on the contrary, competition has abolished the causes that led to departures from the 10 per cent or 20 per cent or 100 per cent. It has brought about commodity prices at which each capital yields the same profit in proportion to its size. But the level of this profit itself is independent of competition. All competition does is persistently reduce all divergences to this level. One person competes with another, and competition forces him to sell his commodity at the same price as the next man. But why is this price 10 or 20 or 100?

There is nothing left for it, then, but to declare that the rate of profit and hence profit itself is a surcharge, determined in an incomprehensible way, on the partial price of a commodity as determined by wages. The only thing competition tells us is that this rate of profit must be a given level. But we already knew that when we brought in the general rate of profit and the 'necessary price'.

It is quite unnecessary to wade through this absurd process again for ground-rent. We can already see that if it is carried through in any consistent way, it makes profit and rent appear as mere surcharges, determined by incomprehensible laws, on top of a commodity price determined in the first place by wages. Competition, in other words, is burdened with explaining all the economists' irrationalities, whereas it is supposed to be the economists who explain competition.

If we ignore the fantastic idea of a profit and rent created by circulation, i.e. price components arising from sale – and the circulation sphere can never yield anything that was not previously put into it – the matter simply comes down to the following.

Say that the price of a commodity as determined by wages is 100, the rate of profit 10 per cent on the wages paid and the rent

15 per cent on wages. The commodity price as determined by the sum of wages, profit and rent is then 125. The surcharge of 25 cannot derive from the sale of the commodity. For if everyone who sells to someone else sells what cost 100 at 125, it is the same thing as if they had all sold at 100. The operation must therefore be considered independently of the circulation process.

If the three elements of the commodity price are divided within the commodity itself, and this commodity now costs 125 – and it makes no difference here if the capitalist first sells at 125 and only later pays the worker 100, himself 10 and the landlord 15 – then the worker receives $\frac{4}{5}$, $= 100$, of the value and the product. The capitalist receives $\frac{2}{25}$ of the value and the product and the landlord $\frac{3}{25}$. Since the capitalist sells at 125 instead of 100, he gives the worker only $\frac{4}{5}$ of the product in which his labour is expressed. It would be the same thing therefore if he gave the worker 80 and kept back 20, with 8 of this accruing to him and 12 to the landlord. He has then sold the commodity at its value, since in actual fact the price surcharges are independent of the commodity's value, which in this assumption is determined by the value of wages. It emerges by way of this detour, therefore, that the term 'wages' in this conception, $= 100$, is equal to the value of the product, i.e. to the sum of money in which this particular amount of labour is expressed; but that this value is different again from real wages, and hence leaves a surplus. It is simply that this is now brought about by a nominal surcharge to the price. Thus if wages were 110 instead of 100, profit would have to be 11 and ground-rent $16\frac{1}{2}$, i.e. the price of the commodity would be $137\frac{1}{2}$. This would leave the proportions quite unaltered. But since the division is always obtained by a nominal surcharge of a certain percentage on wages, the price rises and falls with wages. First wages are posited as equal to the value of the commodity, and then they are again divorced from the value of the commodity. In fact, however, it all comes down, by way of this irrational detour, to the determination of the value of the commodity by the amount of labour contained in it, while the value of wages is determined by the price of the necessary means of subsistence, and the excess of the value over and above wages forms profit and rent.

The dissolution of commodity values after the deduction of the value of the means of production used up in producing them, the dissolution of this given quantum of labour objectified in the commodity product into three component parts, which take the shape of autonomous and mutually independent forms of revenue, namely wages, profit and ground-rent – this dissolution is represented on the immediately visible surface of capitalist production, and hence in the minds of the agents trapped within it, in a distorted way.

Let the total value of some commodity or other be 300, of which 200 is the value of the means of production or elements of constant capital used up to produce it. 100 then remains as the sum of new value added to this commodity in its production process. This new value of 100 is all that is available for division into the three forms of revenue. If we call wages x, profit y and ground-rent z, the sum of $x + y + z$, in our present case, is always $=100$. In the minds of the industrialists, merchants and bankers, and the vulgar economists as well, things proceed quite differently. For them it is not the commodity value that is given as 100, after the deduction of the value of the means of production used up in it, this 100 then being divided up into x, y and z. Instead, the price of the commodity is simply put together out of the value magnitudes of wages, profit and rent, which are determined independently of the commodity's value and of one another; x, y and z are each given and determined independently, and it is only from the sum of these quantities, which may be greater or less than 100, that the magnitude of the commodity's own value results. It results then from the addition of these constituent elements. This *quid pro quo* is necessary:

Firstly, because the commodity's value components confront one another as independent revenues, which are related as such to three completely separate agents of production, labour, capital and the earth, and appear therefore to arise from these. Property in labour-power, capital and the earth is the reason why these different value components of the commodity fall to their respective proprietors, transforming them therefore into their revenues. But value does not arise from a transformation into revenue, it must rather be already in existence before it can be transformed into revenue and assume this form. The opposite appearance is necessarily reinforced all the more in as much as the relative size of these three parts is determined by different kinds of laws, their relationship with the value of the commodities, and limitation by this, being also in no way indicated on the surface.

Secondly, we have seen how a general rise or fall in wages, by causing the general rate of profit to move in the opposite direction, other things being equal, alters the production prices of various commodities, raising some and making others fall, depending on the average composition of capital in the sphere of production in question. In some spheres of production, therefore, experience shows that the average commodity price rises because wages have risen and falls because they have fallen. What is not 'experienced' is the secret regulation of these changes by a commodity value independent of wages. If the rise in wages is local, on the other hand, taking place only in particular spheres of production as a result of specific circumstances, there may then be a corresponding nominal rise in the price of these commodities. This rise in the relative value of one kind of commodity, in relation to others for which wages remain unchanged, is then simply a reaction to the local disturbance of the uniform distribution of surplus-value over the various spheres of production, a means of adjusting the particular rates of profit to the general rate. 'Experience' here again shows the determination of the price by wages. What is experienced in both of these cases is how wages have determined commodity prices. What is not experienced is the hidden basis of this relationship. Moreover, the average price of labour, i.e. the value of labour-power, is determined by the production price of the necessary means of subsistence. If this rises or falls, so does the price of labour. Thus what is experienced here is the existence of a relationship between wages and the price of commodities; but the cause may present itself as effect, and the effect as cause, as is also the case with the movement of market prices, where a rise in wages above their average corresponds to the rise in market prices above prices of production characteristic of periods of prosperity, while the subsequent fall in wages below their average corresponds to the fall in market prices below prices of production. Given the link between production prices and commodity values and leaving aside the oscillating movements of market prices, experience ought always on the face of it to confirm that when wages rise the profit rate falls, and vice versa. But we have seen how the profit rate may be affected independently of wage movements, by movements in the value of constant capital; so that wages and rate of profit may rise or fall in the same direction, instead of in opposite ones. If the rate of surplus-value directly coincided with the rate of profit, this would not be possible. Even if wages rise as a result of the increased price of the means of subsistence, the profit rate can remain the same, or even rise, as a result of greater labour intensity or the prolongation of the working day. All these experiences confirm the illusion produced by the independent, distorted form of the value components, as if the value of commodities was determined either by wages alone, or by wages and profit together. As soon as this seems to be the case for wages, i.e. as soon as the price of labour seems to coincide with the value labour creates, it is self-evidently the case also for profit and rent. Their prices, i.e. their money expressions, must then be governed independently of labour and the value it produces.

Thirdly, let us assume that the values of commodities, or the prices of production that are only apparently independent of these, always coincide directly at the phenomenal level with market prices, instead of simply operating as the governing average prices through continuous compensations for the constant fluctuations in market prices. Let us further assume that reproduction always takes place under the same constant conditions, i.e. that the productivity of labour remains constant for all elements of capital. Let us finally assume that the value component of the commodity product that is formed in each sphere of production by adding a new quantum of labour, i.e. a newly produced value, to the value of the means of production, breaks down always in the same proportions into wages, profit and rent, so that the wages actually paid, the profit actually realized and the actual rent always coincide directly with the value of the labour-power, with the portion of the total surplus-value accruing to each independently functioning portion of the total capital by virtue of the average rate of profit and with the limits to which ground-rent is normally confined on this basis. Let us assume in other words that the distribution of the social value product and the regulation of production prices takes place on the capitalist basis, but in the absence of competition.

Under these assumptions, then, with the values of commodities being and appearing constant, with the value component of the commodity product that is reducible to revenue forming a constant quantity and always presenting itself as such, and finally with this given and constant portion of value always breaking down in the same proportions into wages, profit and rent – even on these assumptions, the real movement would necessarily appear in a distorted form: not as the dissolution of a value magnitude given in advance into three parts which assume the mutually independent forms of revenue, but conversely as the formation of this value magnitude from the sum of the component elements of wages, profit and ground-rent, taken as determined independently and separately. The reason why this illusion would necessarily arise is that in the real movement of individual capitals and their commodity product it is not the value of commodities that appears the premise of its own dissolution but, on the contrary, the components into which it can be dissolved function as the premises for a commodity's value. We saw at the outset that the cost price of a commodity appears to each capitalist as a given quantity and constantly presents itself as such in the actual production process. But the cost price is equal to the value of the constant capital, the means of production advanced, plus the value of labour-power, although this presents itself to the agents of production in the irrational form of the price of labour, so that wages too appear as the worker's revenue. The average price of labour is a given magnitude, since the value of labour-power, like that of any other commodity, is determined by the labour-time necessary for its reproduction. But as far as the component of commodity value that resolves into wages goes, this does not arise from the fact that it assumes the form of wages – that the capitalist advances to the worker his share in his own product in the phenomenal form of wages – but rather from the fact that the worker produces an equivalent corresponding to his wages, i.e. that one part of his daily or yearly labour produces the value contained in the price of his labour-power. Wages, however, are stipulated by contract before the value equivalent corresponding to them is produced. And since they are a price element whose magnitude is given before the commodity and its value are produced, a component of the cost price, wages appear not as a part separated off from the total value of the commodity in an independent form, but rather the reverse, as a given magnitude that determines the total value in advance, i.e. a formative element of price or value. Average profit plays a role in the price of production similar to that played by wages in the commodity's cost price, for the price of production is equal to the cost price plus the average profit on the capital advanced. This average profit has a practical bearing in the mind and accounting of the capitalist himself, as a regulating element, not only in so far as it determines the transfer of capital from one sphere of investment into another, but also for all sales and contracts involved in a reproduction process extending over a prolonged period. But in so far as it has this practical bearing, it is a magnitude fixed in advance, which really is independent of the value and surplus-value produced in any particular sphere of production, and even more independent, accordingly, of each individual capital investment in any of these spheres. Instead of being the result of a division in value, it rather presents the appearance of a magnitude independent of the value of the commodity product, given in advance in the commodity's production process and itself determining the average price of the commodities; it presents the appearance in other words of a formative element of value. Surplus-value, moreover, as a result of the separation of its various parts into forms which are completely independent of one another, appears as a premise of commodity value formation in a far more concrete form. One part of the average profit, in the form of interest, confronts the functioning capitalist from an independent position as an element already presupposed in the production of commodities and their value. Much as the amount of interest may fluctuate, it is at any given moment and for any single capitalist a given magnitude, which for him, the individual capitalist, enters into the cost price of the commodities he produces. The same can be said of ground-rent, in the form of the contractually fixed lease-money paid by the agricultural capitalist, or, in the case of other entrepreneurs, the rent for the space they need for their businesses. These parts into which surplus-value can be resolved, therefore, since as elements of the cost price they are given for the individual capitalist, appear upside-down, as formative elements of surplus-value; forming one portion of commodity price in the way that wages form the other. The secret reason why these products of the dissolution of commodity value constantly appear as the premises of value formation itself is simply that the capitalist mode of production, like every other, constantly reproduces not only the material product but also the socio-economic relations, the formal economic determinants of its formation. Its result thus constantly appears as its premise, and its premises as its results. And it is this constant reproduction of the same relationships which the individual capitalist anticipates as self-evident, as an indubitable fact. As long as capitalist production continues, one part of the labour newly added is constantly resolved into wages, another into profit (interest and profit of enterprise) and the third into rent. This is assumed in the contracts between the proprietors of the various different agents of production, and this assumption is correct, however much the relative quantitative proportions may fluctuate in each individual case. The specific shape in which the value components confront one another is presupposed because it is constantly reproduced, and it is constantly reproduced because it is constantly presupposed.

But experience and appearance also show that market prices – and it is only through their influence that the value determination actually becomes apparent to the capitalist – are in no way dependent on these anticipations as far as their level goes; they are not affected by whether interest or rent is fixed high or low. Market prices are constantly changing, and their average for longer periods is precisely what gives rise to the respective averages of wages, profit and rent, as the constant quantities that therefore ultimately govern market prices.

It seems very simple, on the other hand, to reflect that if wages, profit and rent are formative elements of value, because they appear as presupposed in value production, and are presupposed for the individual capitalist in the cost price and price of production, then the constant capital component, whose value is given in the production of any commodity, is also a value-forming element. But the constant capital component is nothing but a sum of commodities and hence commodity values. We would thus get the absurd tautology that commodity value forms and causes commodity value.

If the capitalist had any interest at all in considering this – and what he considers as a capitalist is determined exclusively by his own self-interest and the resulting motives – he is taught by experience that the product he himself produces goes into other spheres of production as a constant capital component, while products from these other spheres go into his own product as constant capital components. Since for him, therefore, as far as his new production goes, additional value seems to be formed by the magnitudes of wages, profit and rent, this must also apply to the constant component that consists of the products of other capitalists, and hence the price of the constant capital component, and with it the total commodity, can be reduced in the last instance, even if in a way that cannot be entirely fathomed, to the sum of value that results from the addition of independent value elements governed by different laws and formed from different sources: wages, profit and rent.

Fourthly, it is completely immaterial for the individual capitalist

whether commodities are sold at their values or not, and so therefore is the whole determination of value. Right from the start, this
is something that goes on behind his back, by virtue of relations
independent of him, since it is not values but rather prices of
production differing from them that form the governing average
prices in each sphere of production. The value determination as
such interests and affects the individual capitalist, and capital in
any particular sphere of production, only in so far as the diminished or increased amount of labour that is required with the rise or
fall in the productivity of the labour producing the commodities
in question enables him in the one case to make an extra profit at
the existing market prices, while in the other case it compels him
to increase the price of his commodities, since more wages, more
constant capital, and hence also more interest, falls to the share
of each unit product or individual commodity. This interests him
only in so far as it raises or lowers his own production costs for the
commodity, i.e. in so far as it places him in an exceptional position.

Wages, interest and rent, on the other hand, appear to him as
governing limits not only to the price at which he can realize the
portion of profit that accrues to him as functioning capitalist, the
profit of enterprise, but also to the price at which he has to sell
the commodity if continuing reproduction is to be possible. It is a
matter of complete indifference to him whether he realizes the
value and surplus-value contained in the commodity on its sale or
not, as long as he extracts from the price the customary profit of
enterprise, or a greater profit, above the cost price as individually
given for him by wages, interest and rent. Apart from the constant
capital component, therefore, wages, interest and rent appear to
him as the limiting elements to commodity price, and hence as
creative and determining elements. If he manages to drive wages
down below the value of labour-power, for example, i.e. below
their normal level, or to obtain capital at a lower rate of interest
and pay a lease-price below the normal level of rent, he does not at
all mind selling his product below its value, or even below the
general price of production, i.e. parting with a portion of the
surplus labour contained in the commodity for nothing. The same
applies to the constant capital component. If an industrialist can
purchase raw material, for instance, below its price of production,
this protects him from loss even if he resells it below the price of
production in the finished commodity. His profit of enterprise can

remain the same, and even grow, as long as the excess of the commodity price above the elements of it that must be paid for, replaced by an equivalent, remains the same or grows. But on top of the value of the means of production going into the production of his commodities, it is precisely wages, interest and rent that go into this production as limiting and governing amounts of price. These therefore appear to him as the elements determining the price of his commodities. Profit of enterprise, from this standpoint, appears either as determined by an excess of market price, resulting from chance relations of competition, over the immanent value of commodities as determined by the above-mentioned elements of price; or, in so far as it is itself included in the market price as a determinant element, it appears as dependent in turn on competition among buyers and sellers.

Both in competition between the individual capitalists and in competition on the world market, given and presupposed amounts for wages, interest and rent go into the account as constant and governing quantities; constant not in the sense that they do not change, but rather in that they are given in any one particular case and constantly set the limit for the ever fluctuating market price. In competition on the world market, for example, it is exclusively a question of whether, with the given levels of wages, interest and rent, the commodity can profitably be sold at or below the given general market price, i.e. whether it can be sold to realize an appropriate profit of enterprise. If wages and the price of land are low in one country but interest on capital is high, because the capitalist mode of production is not fully developed, while in another country wages and the price of land are nominally high whereas the interest on capital is low, a capitalist in the first country will use more land and labour and a capitalist in the other relatively more capital. In calculating how far competition between the two is possible, these factors are determining elements. Experience shows here in theory, and the self-interested calculation of the capitalist shows in practice, that commodity prices are determined by wages, interest and rent, by the prices of labour, capital and land, and that these price elements are in fact the governing elements of price formation.

There still of course remains one element that is not assumed in advance but results from the market price of commodities, namely the excess over the cost price formed from the addition of these elements, wages, interest and rent. This fourth element appears in each individual case as determined by competition, and in the average case by the average profit, which is again governed by the same competition, simply over a longer period.

Fifthly, on the basis of the capitalist mode of production, it is so completely obvious a step to split up the value in which the freshly added labour is expressed into the revenue forms of wages, profit and ground-rent that this method is used even where the conditions of existence for these forms of revenue are completely lacking. (Not to speak of past historical periods, which we have given examples of in connection with ground-rent.) That is to say, everything is subsumed under them, by way of analogy.

If an independent worker labours for himself and sells his own product – we may take a small peasant, since in this case all three forms of revenue can be used – he is first of all considered as his own employer (capitalist), employing himself as a worker, and as his own landowner, using himself as his own farmer. He pays himself wages as a worker, lays claim to profit as a capitalist and pays himself rent as a landowner. Once the capitalist mode of production and the relationships corresponding to it are assumed as the general social basis, this subsumption is correct in as much as he does not have his labour to thank but rather his possession of means of production – which in this case are always taken to have the form of capital – that he is in a position to appropriate his own surplus labour. Furthermore, in as much as he produces his product as a commodity and is therefore dependent on its price (and even if he is not, this price can be estimated), the amount of surplus labour he can valorize is not dependent on its own magnitude but rather on the general rate of profit; and likewise the possible excess above the quota of surplus-value determined by the general rate of profit is again not determined by the amount of labour he performs, but can be appropriated by him because only he is the owner of the land. Because a form of production that does not correspond to the capitalist mode of production can be subsumed under its forms of revenue (and up to a certain point this is not incorrect), the illusion that capitalist relationships are the natural condition of any mode of production is further reinforced.

If however wages are reduced to their general basis, i.e. that portion of the product of his labour which goes into the worker's own individual consumption; if this share is freed from its capitalist limit and expanded to the scale of consumption that is both permitted by the existing social productivity (i.e. the social productivity of his own labour as genuinely social labour) and required for the full development of individuality; if surplus labour and surplus product are also reduced, to the degree needed under the given conditions of production, on the one hand to form an insurance and reserve fund, on the other hand for the constant expansion of reproduction in the degree determined by social need; if, finally, both (1) the necessary labour and (2) the surplus labour are taken to include the amount of labour that those capable of work must always perform for those members of society not yet capable, or no longer capable of working – i.e. if both wages and surplus-value are stripped of their specifically capitalist character – then nothing of these forms remains, but simply those foundations of the forms that are common to all social modes of production.

This kind of subsumption, incidentally, is also characteristic of modes of production previously dominant, e.g. the feudal. Relations of production that in no way corresponded to it, standing completely outside it, were subsumed under feudal relationships; e.g. 'tenures in common socage' in England (as opposed to 'tenures on knight's service'), which simply involved monetary obligations and were feudal only in name.

Chapter 51: Relations of Distribution and Relations of Production

The value freshly added in a year by freshly added labour – and so also the part of the annual product in which this value is expressed, and which can be extracted and separated from the total product – can therefore be divided into three parts which take on three different forms of revenue, forms that express one part of this value as belonging or accruing to the owner of labour-power, one part to the owner of capital and a third part to the owner of landed property. These are thus relations or forms of distribution, for they express the relationships in which the total value newly produced is distributed among the owners of the various agents of production.

In the customary view, these relations of distribution appear to be natural relations, relations arising from the nature of all social production, from the laws of human production pure and simple. It cannot be denied, of course, that pre-capitalist societies display other modes of distribution, but these are then explained as undeveloped, incomplete and disguised, not reduced to their purest expression and highest form, modalities of these natural relations of distribution with a different hue.

The only bit of truth in this conception is this: once any kind of social production is assumed (e.g. that of the indigenous Indian communities or the more artificially developed communism of the Peruvians), it is always possible to distinguish between the portion of labour whose product is directly consumed individually by the producers and their dependants, and – leaving aside the portion for productive consumption – a further portion of labour that is always surplus labour, whose product serves to satisfy general social needs, no matter how this surplus product is distributed and who functions as the representative of these social needs. The identity of the different modes of distribution thus comes down to the fact that they are identical if we abstract from their distinctions and specific forms and cling on just to their unity in contrast to what distinguishes them.

A more developed and critical awareness concedes the historically developed character of these relations of distribution,[56a] but holds all the more firmly to the supposedly constant character of the relations of production themselves, as arising from human nature and hence independent of all historical development.

The scientific analysis of the capitalist mode of production proves the contrary, i.e. that this is a mode of production of a particular kind and a specific historical determinacy; that like any other particular mode of production it assumes a given level of social productive forces and of their forms of development as its historical precondition, a condition that is itself the historical result and product of a previous process and from which the new mode of production proceeds as its given foundation; that the relations of production corresponding to this specific and historically determined mode of production – relations into which men enter in their social life-process, in the production of their social life – have a specific, historical and transitory character; and that finally the relations of distribution are essentially identical with these relations of production, the reverse side of the same coin, so that the two things share the same historically transitory character.

In dealing with the relations of distribution, it is usual to start from the ostensible fact that the annual product is divided into wages, profit and ground-rent. But expressed in this way, that is wrong. The product is divided into capital on the one hand and revenues on the other. One of these revenues, wages, only ever assumes the form of a revenue, the revenue of the worker, after it has previously confronted the same worker in the *form of capital*. The confrontation between the produced conditions of labour and the products of labour all together as capital, and the immediate producers, gives the material conditions of labour right from the start a specific social character vis-à-vis the workers, and hence sets up a specific relationship which the workers enter into, in production itself, to the owners of these conditions of labour and to one another. The transformation of these conditions of labour into capital also involves the expropriation of the immediate producers from the land, and hence a specific form of landed property.

56a. John Stuart Mill, *Some Unsettled Questions of Political Economy*, London, 1844.

If one part of the product were not transformed into capital, the other would not assume the forms of wages, profit and rent.

On the other hand, if the capitalist mode of production pre-supposes this specific social form of the conditions of production, it constantly reproduces it as well. It not only produces the material products, but constantly reproduces the relations of production in which these are produced, and with them also the corresponding relations of distribution.

It may be said, incidentally, that capital (and landed property, which this includes as its antithesis) itself already presupposes a distribution: it presupposes the expropriation of the workers from the conditions of labour, the concentration of these conditions in the hands of a minority of individuals, the exclusive ownership of the land by other individuals, in short, all the relations that were developed in the section on primitive accumulation (Volume 1, Part Eight). But this is a completely different distribution from what is understood by relations of distribution when a historical character is claimed for these, in contrast to the relations of production. What is meant under this rubric are the different titles to the part of the product that falls to individual consumption. The former relations of distribution, on the other hand, are the foundation of particular social functions which are ascribed to specific agents of production within the relation of production itself, as distinct from the immediate producers. They give the actual conditions of production, and their representatives, a specific social quality. They determine the whole character and movement of production.

Two characteristic traits mark the capitalist mode of production right from the start.

Firstly. It produces its products as commodities. The fact that it produces commodities does not in itself distinguish it from other modes of production; but that the dominant and determining character of its product is that it is a commodity certainly does so. This means, first of all, that the worker himself appears only as a seller of commodities, and hence as a free wage-labourer – i.e. labour generally appears as wage-labour. It is unnecessary after the argument already developed to demonstrate once again how the relationship of capital and wage-labour determines the whole character of the mode of production. The principal agents of this mode of production itself, the capitalist and the wage-labourer, are as such simply embodiments and personifications of capital and wage-labour – specific social characters that the social production process stamps on individuals, products of these specific social relations of production.

The character (1) of the product as a commodity, and (2) of the commodity as the product of capital, already involves all the relations of circulation, i.e. a specific social process which products must pass through and in which they assume specific social characters; it involves equally specific relationships between the agents of production, determining the valorization of their product and its transformation back into either means of subsistence or means of production. But even leaving this aside, the two above characters of the product as commodity and the commodity as capitalistically produced commodity give rise to the entire determination of value and the regulation of the total production by value. In this quite specific form of value, labour is valid only as social labour; on the other hand the division of this social labour and the reciprocal complementarity or metabolism of its products, subjugation to and insertion into the social mechanism, is left to the accidental and reciprocally countervailing motives of the individual capitalist producers. Since these confront one another only as commodity owners, each trying to sell his commodity as dear as possible (and seeming to be governed only by caprice even in the regulation of production), the inner law operates only by way of their competition, their reciprocal pressure on one another, which is how divergences are mutually counterbalanced. It is only as an inner law, a blind natural force vis-à-vis the individual agents, that the law of value operates here and that the social balance of production is asserted in the midst of accidental fluctuations.

What is also implied already in the commodity, and still more so in the commodity as the product of capital, is the reification of the social determinations of production and the subjectification [*Versubjektifierung*] of the material bases of production which characterize the entire capitalist mode of production.

The *second* thing that particularly marks the capitalist mode of production is the production of surplus-value as the direct object and decisive motive of production. Capital essentially produces capital, and it does this only as long as it produces surplus-value. In dealing with relative surplus-value and then with the transformation of surplus-value into profit, we have seen how a mode of production peculiar to the capitalist period is based on this – a particular form of development of the social productive powers of labour, but as powers of capital that have asserted their autonomy vis-à-vis the worker, thus directly opposing his own development. Production for value and surplus-value involves a constantly operating tendency, as we went on to show, to reduce the labour-time needed to produce a commodity, i.e. to reduce the commodity's value, below the existing social average at any given time. The pressure to reduce the cost price to its minimum becomes the strongest lever for raising the social productivity of labour, though this appears here simply as a constant increase in the productivity of capital.

The authority that the capitalist assumes in the immediate production process, as personification of capital, the social function he dons as manager and ruler of production, is essentially different from authority on the basis of production with slaves or serfs, etc.

Although on the basis of capitalist production the social character of their production confronts the mass of immediate producers in the form of a strict governing authority, and the social mechanism of the labour process has received here a completely hierarchical articulation – though this authority accrues to its bearers only as the personification of the conditions of labour vis-à-vis labour itself, not to them as political or theocratic rulers as in earlier forms of production – the most complete anarchy reigns among the bearers of this authority, the capitalists themselves, who confront one another simply as owners of commodities, and within this anarchy the social interconnection of production prevails over individual caprice only as an overwhelming natural law.

It is only because labour is presupposed in the form of wage-labour, and the means of production in the form of capital (i.e. only as a result of this specific form of these two essential agents of production), that one part of the value (product) presents itself as surplus-value and this surplus-value presents itself as profit (rent), the gains of the capitalist, as additional available wealth belonging to him. And it is only because it presents itself as *his profit* that the new additional means of production, designed for the expansion of reproduction and forming a portion of the product, present themselves as new additional capital, and the expansion of the reproduction process in general presents itself as a process of capitalist accumulation.

Even though the form of labour as wage-labour is decisive for the shape of the entire process and for the specific mode of production itself, it is not wage-labour that is value-determining. What matters in the determination of value is the overall social labour-time, the total amount of labour which society has at its disposal and whose relative absorption by the different products determines, as it were, their respective social weight. But the particular form in which social labour-time plays its determinant role in the value of commodities coincides with the form of labour as wage-labour, and the corresponding form of the means of production as capital, in so far as it is on this basis alone that commodity production becomes the general form of production.

Let us consider, moreover, the so-called relations of distribution themselves. The wage assumes wage-labour, profit assumes capital. These specific forms of distribution thus assume specific social characters for the conditions of production and specific social relations for the agents of production. The specific relation of distribution thus simply expresses the historically determined relation of production.

To take profit, for example. This specific form of surplus-value is the presupposition for the fresh formation of means of production in the form of capitalist production; i.e. it is a relationship governing reproduction, even if it appears to the individual capitalist that he could consume the whole profit as revenue. There are limits to this, however, which he encounters already in the form of the insurance and reserve fund, the law of competition, etc., and which prove to him in a practical way that profit is not simply a category appertaining to the distribution of the product for individual consumption. The entire capitalist production process, moreover, is governed by the prices of products. But the governing prices of production are themselves governed in turn by the equalization of the rate of profit and the distribution of capital among the various spheres of social production which is appropriate to that equalization. Thus profit appears in this case as the principal factor not just of the products' distribution but also of their actual production, part of the distribution of capitals and labour itself among the various spheres of production. The division of profit into profit of enterprise and interest appears simply as a distribution of the same revenue. But it arises first of all from the development of capital as self-valorizing, surplus-value-producing value, this specific social form of the dominant production process. It develops from within itself credit and the credit institutions, and with this the whole configuration of production. In interest, etc., the ostensible forms of distribution go into the price as determining elements of production.

It might appear for ground-rent that this is a form of distribution pure and simple, since landed property as such performs no function in the production process, at least not in the normal case. But the fact that (1) rent is limited to the excess above the average profit, while (2) the landowner is reduced from guide and master of the production process and the entire process of social life to a mere leaser of land, usurer in land and simple recipient of rent, is a specific historical result of the capitalist mode of production. It is a historical precondition for this mode of production that the earth has to receive the form of landed property. And it is a product of the specific character of this mode of production that landed property obtains forms which permit the capitalist mode of operation in agriculture. It is possible to give the name of rent to the landowner's income in other forms of society. But this is essentially different from rent as it appears in the present mode.

The so-called relations of distribution, therefore, correspond to and arise from historically particular and specific social forms of the production process and of the relationships which men enter into among themselves in the process of reproducing their human life. The historical character of these relations of distribution is the historical character of the relations of production, and they simply express one side of these. The capitalist distribution is different from those forms of distribution that arise from other modes of production, and every form of distribution vanishes along with the particular form of production that it arises from and corresponds to.

The view that considers only the relations of distribution to be historical, and not the relations of production, is simply the perspective of a criticism of bourgeois economics that is incipient but still timid and restrained. It is also based, however, on a confusion and identification of the social production process with the simple labour process, as this would have to be performed by an abnormally isolated person without any social aids. In so far as the labour process is a simple process between man and nature, its simple elements remain common to all social forms of its development. But each particular historical form of this process further develops the material foundations and social forms. Once a certain level of maturity is attained, the particular historical form is shed and makes way for a higher form. The sign that the moment of such a crisis has arrived is that the contradiction and antithesis between, on the one hand, the relations of distribution, hence also the specific historical form of relations of production corresponding to them, and, on the other hand, the productive forces, productivity, and the development of its agents, gains in breadth and depth. A conflict then sets in between the material development of production and its social form.[57]

57. See the essay on competition and cooperation (1832?).*

* Apparently *A Prize Essay on the Comparative Merits of Competition and Cooperation*, London, 1834.

Chapter 52: Classes

The owners of mere labour-power, the owners of capital and the landowners, whose respective sources of income are wages, profit and ground-rent – in other words wage-labourers, capitalists and landowners – form the three great classes of modern society based on the capitalist mode of production.

It is undeniably in England that this modern society and its economic articulation is most widely and most classically developed. Even here, though, this class articulation does not emerge in pure form. Here, too, middle and transitional levels always conceal the boundaries (although incomparably less so in the countryside than in the towns). We have seen how it is the constant tendency and law of development of the capitalist mode of production to divorce the means of production ever more from labour and to concentrate the fragmented means of production more and more into large groups, i.e. to transform labour into wage-labour and the means of production into capital. And this tendency also corresponds to the independent divorce of all landed property from capital and labour,[58] or the transformation of all landed property into the form of landed property corresponding to the capitalist mode of production.

The question to be answered next is: 'What makes a class?', and

58. F. List observes correctly: 'The predominance of owner-management on large estates simply indicates inadequate civilization, means of communication, local industry and wealthy cities. This is why we find it all over Russia, Poland, Hungary and Mecklenburg. It was formerly predominant in England too, but with the arrival of trade and industry these estates were broken up into middle-sized farms and leased out' (*Die Ackerverfassung, die Zwergwirthschaft und die Auswanderung*, 1842, p. 10).*

* Friedrich List (1789–1846), the most important German economist of the first half of the nineteenth century, closely represented the demands of the embryonic industrial bourgeoisie in Germany and is particularly remembered for his forceful arguments for protective tariffs.

this arises automatically from answering another question: 'What makes wage-labourers, capitalists and landowners the formative elements of the three great social classes?'

At first sight, the identity of revenues and revenue sources. For these are three great social groups whose components, the individuals forming them, live respectively from wages, profit and ground-rent, from the valorization of their labour-power, capital and landed property.

From this point of view, however, doctors and government officials would also form two classes, as they belong to two distinct social groups, the revenue of each group's members flowing from its own source. The same would hold true for the infinite fragmentation of interests and positions into which the division of social labour splits not only workers but also capitalists and landowners – the latter, for instance, into vineyard-owners, field-owners, forest-owners, mine-owners, fishery-owners, etc.

(At this point the manuscript breaks off. – F. E.)

Frederick Engels: Supplement and Addendum
to Volume 3 of Capital*

The third volume of *Capital* has already experienced several interpretations of different kinds since it has been open to the judgement of the public. This was only to be expected. In my editing I was concerned above all to produce a text which was as authentic as possible, to present the new results Marx had obtained as far as possible in Marx's own words, and to intervene myself only where this was absolutely unavoidable, even there leaving the reader in no doubt as to who was addressing him. For this, however, I have been reproached, and it has been said that I should have reworked the material at hand into a systematically elaborated book, *en faire un livre*, as the French say. I should in other words have sacrificed the authenticity of the text to the reader's convenience. But this was not how I conceived my task. I had no authority for any such reworking; a man like Marx has the right to be heard himself, to convey his scientific discoveries to posterity in his own full and genuine presentation. Nor did I have any desire to do so; to interfere in such a way with the legacy of a man so superior to myself would have seemed to me an act of disloyalty. Thirdly, it would have been simply pointless. For people who either cannot read or do not want to, who have already taken more trouble to misunderstand the first volume than was necessary to understand it correctly – for people such as these, any expense is wasted. But for those who are set on a genuine understanding, it was precisely the original text that was most important; for these, any reworking on my part would have had at most the

---

* Engels's Addendum to *Capital* Volume 3 was the last piece he wrote, apart from a few final letters. It dates from May 1895, only two months before his death. The Addendum is compiled from two articles which Engels planned to write for *Neue Zeit*, though only the first of these, 'Law of Value and Rate of Profit', was completed. For the second article, 'The Stock Exchange', there is simply a brief outline.

value of a commentary, and a commentary on something that was unpublished and inaccessible. The original text would have still had to be referred to as soon as the first controversy arose, and at the second or third its full publication would have been indispensable.

Controversies of this kind are a matter of course for a work that brings with it so much that is new, and does so only in a hurriedly drafted first elaboration, partly incomplete. Here, however, my intervention can be of use, in removing difficulties of understanding, bringing more to the fore important perspectives whose significance does not emerge strongly enough in the text, and appending certain particularly needed supplements to a text written in 1865, to bring it up to the state of things in 1895. There are in fact already two points where I feel a short discussion is required.

I. LAW OF VALUE AND RATE OF PROFIT

It was only to be expected that the solution of the apparent contradiction between these two factors would lead to debates after Marx's text was published, as it already had before. Many indeed had expected a complete miracle and were disappointed to be faced with a simple, rational, prosaic and cautious treatment of the antithesis, instead of the anticipated hocus-pocus. The most joyously disappointed, of course, was the illustrious Loria, with whom we are already acquainted. He has finally found the Archimedian point from which even a little pixie of his calibre can lift the firm edifice of Marx's gigantic construction into the air and shatter it. What, he cries out in indignation, is this supposed to be a solution? This is pure mystification! When economists speak of value, they mean value that is actually confirmed in exchange.

'But to concern oneself with a value at which commodities are neither sold *nor ever could be sold* (*nè possono vendersi mai*) is something that no economist with a trace of understanding has ever done, nor could he do so ... When Marx maintains that the value at which commodities are *never* sold is determined in proportion to the labour contained in them, what is he doing but putting forward the principle of orthodox economics in reverse: i.e. that the value at which commodities are sold does *not* stand in relation to the labour applied to them? ... It does not help at all for Marx to say that, despite the divergence of individual prices from individual values, the total price of all commodities taken together coincides with their total value, or with the quantity of labour contained in the total amount of commodities. For since value is nothing but the ratio in which one commodity is exchanged for another, the very idea of a total value is already an absurdity and a nonsense . . . a contradiction in terms.'

Marx says right at the beginning of his work that exchange can equate two commodities only by virtue of a uniform and equally large element contained in them, i.e. the equal amounts of labour they contain. And now he refutes himself most solemnly by assuring us that commodities exchange in a completely different ratio from the amounts of labour they contain.

'When was there ever so complete a *reductio ad absurdum*, a greater theoretical bankruptcy? When was a scientific suicide ever committed with greater pomp and solemnity?' (*Nuova Antologia*, 1 February 1895, pp. 477–9).

We can see our Loria is overjoyed. Was he not right to treat Marx as his equal, as an ordinary charlatan? Look now! Marx is having his readers on in the same way as Loria, he is living on mystifications just like that most insignificant Italian Professor of Economics. But while Dulcamara might permit himself this, since he knows his job well, Marx the clumsy northerner ties himself up in knots and gives out nonsense and absurdity until nothing remains for him but ritual suicide.

We shall save for later the contention that commodities are never sold at the values determined by labour, nor ever can be. For the moment, let us examine Mr Loria's assurance that 'since value is nothing but the ratio in which one commodity is exchanged for another, the very idea of a total value is already absurdity and nonsense'.

The ratio in which two commodities exchange for one another, their value, is thus something completely accidental, alighting on commodities from outside, which can be one thing today and something else tomorrow. Whether a hundredweight of wheat exchanges for a gram of gold or a kilo does not depend in the least on conditions inherent in this wheat or gold, but rather on circumstances totally foreign to them both. For otherwise these conditions would also have to prevail in exchange, to govern it generally and have an independent existence even aside from exchange, if one were to be able to speak of a total value for commodities. This is nonsense, says the illustrious Loria. Whatever ratio two commodities might exchange in, that is their value, and there's an end. Value is thus identical with price, and each commodity has as much value as it can fetch in its price. Price is then determined by supply and demand, and anyone who asks further is a fool if he expects an answer.

But there is one small drawback. In the normal situation, demand and supply match one another. Let us then divide all the commodities in the world into two halves, a group of demand and an equal group of supply. We assume that each represents a price of one billion marks, francs, pounds sterling, etc. According to the book, this should make a total price or value of two billion. Nonsense, absurdity, says Mr Loria. The two groups together might represent a price of two billion. But as far as value goes, things are quite different. If we take price, then $1 + 1 = 2$. But if we take value, then $1 + 1 = 0$, at least in this case, where the totality of commodities is at issue. For here one side's commodities are only worth one billion because each side is willing and able to pay this sum for the commodities on the other side. Once we combine the totality of commodities on each side in the hands of a third, not only do neither the first nor the second any longer have any value in hand, but the third does not either. At the end of the day, no one has anything. We may admire once again the superior quality of our southern Cagliostro's concept of value, not even the slightest trace of it being left. This is the very pinnacle of vulgar economics![1]

1. The same gentleman, 'known by his fame' (to use Heine's words), later took the trouble to answer my Preface to Volume 3 – i.e. after this had been translated into Italian in the first issue of *Rassegna*. His answer can be found in *Riforma Sociale* of 25 February 1895. After first showering me with the deluge of flattery that is unavoidable with him and therefore doubly repulsive, he declares that he would never have dreamed of plagiarizing Marx's contribution to the materialist conception of history. He had acknowledged this as far back as 1885, in passing, in the context of a review article. That is why he kept so stubbornly silent where it really mattered, i.e. in his book on the subject, where Marx is not mentioned until p. 129 and even then merely in connection with small-scale landownership in France. And now he boldly declares that Marx was not the original proponent of this theory; if Aristotle had not already indicated it, then Harrington undoubtedly put it forward in 1656,* and it was developed long before Marx by a galaxy of historians, politicians, jurists and economists. All this can be read in the French edition of Loria's work. A complete plagiarist, in other words. After I had made it impossible for him to go on bragging with his plagiarisms from Marx, he had the cheek to maintain that Marx had also decked himself out with other people's quills, just as he does himself.

In Braun's *Archiv für soziale Gesetzgebung*, VII, no. 4, Werner Sombart gives an outline presentation of Marx's system which is quite excellent on the whole. This is the first time that a German university professor has managed to see by and large in Marx's writings what Marx actually said, and he further declares that criticism of the Marxian system should consist not in a refutation ('that can be left to someone with political ambition'), but rather in a further development. Sombart, too, is understandably pre-occupied with our present subject. He discusses the significance of value in Marx's system and arrives at the following result. Value is not present at the phenomenal level, in the exchange relationship of capitalistically produced commodities; it does not dwell in the consciousness of the agents of capitalist production; it is not an empirical fact but an ideal or logical one; Marx's concept of value, in its material specificity, is nothing more than the economic expression of the fact that the social productivity of labour is the

---

Replying to my other charges, he again insists that Marx never intended to write a second volume of *Capital*, let alone a third. 'And now Engels triumphantly replies that he has precisely refuted me with the second and third volumes! But I am most pleased with these volumes, to which I owe such great intellectual stimulation that no victory was ever so dear to me as this present defeat, if in fact it is a defeat. For is it really so? Is it actually true that Marx wrote this mass of disjointed notes, which Engels has put together in a pious spirit of friendship, with the intention of publication? Can it actually be assumed that Marx entrusted the culmination of his work and his system . . . to these pages of writings? Is it really sure that Marx would have published this chapter on the average rate of profit, in which the solution promised for so many years is reduced to the most disconsolate mystification, the most vulgar playing with words? It is at least permissible to doubt this . . . This proves, it seems to me, that Marx did not intend, after publishing his splendid book, to give it a successor, let alone planned to leave the completion of this gigantic work to his heirs, and outside his own responsibility.'

This is what is written, on p. 267. Heine showed his utter contempt for his philistine German public by saying that the author eventually gets into the habit of treating his readership as a rational being. What then must our illustrious Loria take his readers for?

In conclusion, a new load of praise which I am unfortunate enough to bear. Here our Sganarell compares himself with Balaam, who came to curse but whose lips burbled 'words of blessing and love' against his will. What distinguished the worthy Balaam was that the ass he rode was more intelligent than its master. This Balaam, however, evidently left his ass at home.

* This is a reference to the publication in 1656 by James Harrington (1611–77) of *Oceana*, which sets out the model for a utopian communist society; Harrington also made several attempts to put his scheme into practice.

basis of economic existence; the law of value is what ultimately governs economic processes in a capitalist economic order, and its general content for such an economic order is that the value of commodities is the specific-historical form in which the productivity of labour which ultimately governs all economic processes has its determining effect. This is what Sombart says. Now it cannot be said that this conception of the significance of the law of value for the capitalist form of production is incorrect. Yet to me it does seem too generalized, and capable of a closer and more precise formulation; in my view, it in no way exhausts the whole significance that the law of value has for those stages of society's economic development that are governed by this law.

In Braun's *Sozialpolitisches Zentralblatt*, no. 22, of 25 February 1895, there is a similarly excellent article on the third volume of *Capital* by Conrad Schmidt. Particularly worthy of note in this is the demonstration of the way in which Marx's derivation of average profit from surplus-value provides an answer, for the first time, to the question never even raised by previous economists as to how the level of this average profit rate is determined, and how it comes to be, say, 10 per cent or 15 per cent and not 50 per cent or 100 per cent. Since we know that the surplus-value appropriated in the first place by the industrial capitalist is the sole and exclusive source from which profit and ground-rent flow, this question is solved automatically. This part of Schmidt's essay might have been directly written for economists of Loria's ilk, if it were not such a waste of time to try opening the eyes of people who will not see.

Schmidt, too, has his formal reservations about the law of value. He calls it a scientific *hypothesis* put forward to explain the actual exchange process, which proves the necessary theoretical point of departure, illuminating and indispensable even for the phenomena of prices under competition, which appear completely to contradict it. Without the law of value, in his opinion too, any theoretical insight into the economic mechanism of capitalist reality is impossible. In a personal letter which he has allowed me to mention, Schmidt declares that the law of value in the capitalist form of production is a fiction, though a theoretically necessary one.* In my opinion, however, this conception is completely inapposite. The law of value has a far greater and more definite

* Schmidt wrote to Engels on 1 March 1895. Engels's reply is dated 12 March, and the salient part of this can be found in *Selected Correspondence*, London, 1965, pp. 451–5.

importance for capitalist production than that of a mere hypothesis, let alone a necessary fiction.

With both Sombart and Schmidt – I bring in the illustrious Loria here simply as a humorous vulgar-economic foil – insufficient regard is paid to the fact that what is involved is not just a logical process but a historical one, and its explanatory reflection in thought, the logical following-up of its internal connections.

The decisive passage is to be found on p. 275 of Volume 3:

'The whole difficulty arises from the fact that commodities are not exchanged simply as *commodities*, but as the *products of capitals*, which claim shares in the total mass of surplus-value according to their size, equal shares for equal size.'

To illustrate this distinction, we might suppose that the workers were in possession of their means of production, working on the average for the same hours at the same intensity and exchanging their commodities directly with one another. Two workers would then have added an equal new value to their products in a day, but the products of each would still differ in value according to the labour previously embodied in the means of production used up. This latter portion of value would correspond to the constant capital of the capitalist economy, the portion of value newly added that was applied to the workers' means of subsistence would correspond to the variable capital, and the remaining portion of new value to the surplus-value, which would in this case belong to the worker himself. Both workers would thus receive equal values, after deducting the replacement for the 'constant' portion of value that they had simply advanced; but the ratio between the portion of surplus-value and the value of the means of production would be different in each case, corresponding to the rate of profit under capitalism. Since however each of them receives in exchange the replacement for the value of his means of production, this would be a matter of complete indifference.

'The exchange of commodities at their values, or at approximately these values, thus corresponds to a much lower stage of development than the exchange at prices of production, for which a definite degree of capitalist development is needed ...

'Apart from the way in which the law of value governs prices and their movement, it is also quite apposite to view the values of commodities not only as theoretically prior to the prices of production but also as historically prior to them. This applies to those conditions in which the means of production belong to the worker, and this condition is to be found, in both the ancient and the modern world, among peasant proprietors and handicraftsmen who work for themselves. This agrees, moreover, with the opinion we expressed previously, viz. that the development of products into commodities arises from exchange between different communities and not between the members of one and the same community. This is true not only for the original condition but also for later social conditions based on slavery and serfdom, and for the guild organization of handicraft production, as long as the means of production involved in each branch of production can be transferred from one sphere to another only with difficulty, and the different spheres of production therefore relate to one another, within certain limits, like foreign countries or communistic communities' [above, pp. 277–8].

If Marx had been able to go through the third volume again, he would undoubtedly have elaborated this passage significantly. As it stands, it gives only an outline sketch of what needs to be said on the point in question. Let us therefore go into the matter somewhat more closely.

We all know that at the beginnings of society products are used by the producers themselves, these producers living in indigenous communities that are organized more or less on a communist basis; that the exchange of their surplus products with foreigners, which introduces the transformation of products into commodities, is of later date. It takes place first of all simply between individual communities of different tribes and only later does it come to prevail within the community, where it makes a decisive contribution to the dissolution of this community into larger or smaller family groups. Even after this dissolution, however, the family heads who exchange with one another remain working peasant farmers, who produce almost all their requirements on their own holdings, with the aid of their families, and obtain only a small portion of the items they need from outside, in exchange for their own surplus product. Not only does the family pursue agriculture and stock-raising, it also works up the products of these activities into finished articles of use, still doing its own milling in places with the hand mill, baking bread, spinning, dyeing, weaving flax and wool, curing leather, erecting and repairing wooden buildings, producing tools and equipment, and often doing its own carpentry and metalwork too; so that the family or family group is basically self-sufficient.

Now the little that such a family has to obtain from others by exchange, or buy, consisted right up to the early nineteenth century, in Germany, predominantly of objects of handicraft production, i.e. things whose mode of production was in no way strange to the peasant and which he himself failed to produce only because either the raw material was unavailable or the purchased article was much better or very much cheaper. For the peasant of the Middle Ages, therefore, the labour-time needed to reproduce the objects he obtained in exchange was quite accurately known. The village smith and cartwright were at work under his very eyes; similarly the tailor and shoemaker, who in my own youth still travelled round to our Rhineland peasants in turn, working up materials provided into clothes and shoes. Both the peasant and the people from whom he bought were workers themselves, and the articles exchanged were their own products. What had they applied in the production of these articles? Labour, and labour alone: to replace tools, to produce raw material and work it up, all they spent was their own labour-power; how else then could they exchange these products of theirs with those of other working producers than in proportion to the labour applied to them? The labour-time applied to these products, then, was more than just the most suitable measure for the quantitative determination of the magnitudes to be exchanged; no other measure was possible. Or are we to believe that peasant and village artisan were so stupid that one of them would part with the product of ten hours' labour for that of a single hour? For the entire period of natural peasant economy, no other exchange is possible except that in which the amounts of commodities exchanged tend more and more to be measured according to the amounts of labour embodied in them. From the moment money penetrates into this economic mode, the tendency of adaptation to the law of value (Marx's formulation, *nota bene!*) becomes more explicit, though it is already infringed by the interventions of usurer's capital and fiscal extortion, so that the periods over which prices approximate on average to values, down to a negligible difference in magnitude, already become more drawn out.

The same applies to exchange between the products of peasants and those of urban artisans. At the beginning, this takes place directly, without the mediation of the merchant, on the town market-days when the peasant sells and makes his purchases. Here, too, the artisan's conditions of labour are known to the peasant, and the peasant's to the artisan. He is himself still one part peasant, and not only has his kitchen-garden and orchard but also very often a bit of a field, one or two cows, pigs, fowl, etc. People in the Middle Ages were thus in a position to reckon up each other's production costs in raw and ancillary materials, and in labour-time, with a fair degree of accuracy – at least as far as articles of general daily use were concerned.

But how could the amount of labour be reckoned, even indirectly and relatively, when this served as the measure of exchange for products that required more prolonged labour, interrupted and at irregular intervals, and uncertain in its results, products like corn or cattle, for instance? And, moreover, with people who were unable to count? Evidently, only by a lengthy process of zig-zag approximation, often groping back and forth in the dark, in which, as in other things, wisdom was attained only by painful accident. But the need for each person to have a rough idea of his own costs helped time and again in the correct direction, and the small number of types of article coming into exchange, as well as the stable mode of their production, often over centuries, made the goal more easily attainable. That it in no way took so long until the relative values of these products were established with a fair degree of accuracy is shown by the simple fact that the commodity in which this seems most difficult on account of the long production time of the individual item, i.e. cattle, was the first fairly generally recognized money commodity. In order to arrive at the value of cattle, its exchange ratio with a whole series of other commodities must already have won established recognition to a relatively unusual degree, it must be unchallenged over an area of several tribes. And the people of that time were certainly clever enough – the cattle-breeders as well as their customers – not to part with the labour-time they had spent without an equivalent in exchange. On the contrary, the closer people stand to the original state of commodity production – e.g. Russians and Orientals – the more time they still spend today in extracting full compensation for the labour-time spent on a product by long and stubborn haggling.

Proceeding from this determination of value by labour-time, commodity production as a whole, and with it the manifold relationships in which the different aspects of the law of value make themselves felt, now develops as presented in Part One of *Capital* Volume 1; therefore, in particular, the conditions become established under which labour is value-forming. These conditions, moreover, prevail although those involved do not become aware of them, so that they can be abstracted from everyday practice only by tedious theoretical analysis; they operate in the form of a natural law, which as Marx showed followed necessarily from the nature of commodity production. The most important and incisive progress was the transition to metal money, but this had the consequence that the determination of value by labour-time was no longer visibly apparent on the surface of commodity exchange. Money became the decisive measure of value for practical purposes, and all the more so, the more diverse were the commodities coming into trade, the more they originated from distant countries, and the less therefore the labour-time needed for their production could be checked. Even the money itself came mostly from abroad at first; and when it was obtained in a particular country as precious metal, the peasant and artisan were in no position to assess even approximately the labour applied to it, while their own awareness of the value-measuring property of labour was also pretty well obscured by the custom of reckoning in money; money came to represent absolute value in the popular conception.

To sum up, Marx's law of value applies universally, as much as any economic laws do apply, for the entire period of simple commodity production, i.e. up to the time at which this undergoes a modification by the onset of the capitalist form of production. Up till then, prices gravitate to the values determined by Marx's law and oscillate around these values, so that the more completely simple commodity production develops, the more do average prices coincide with values for longer periods when not interrupted by external violent disturbances, and with the insignificant variations we mentioned earlier. Thus the Marxian law of value has a universal economic validity for an era lasting from the beginning of the exchange that transforms products into commodities down to the fifteenth century of our epoch. But commodity exchange dates from a time before any written history, going back to at least 3500 B.C. in Egypt, and 4000 B.C. or maybe even 6000 B.C. in Babylon; thus the law of value prevailed for a period of some five to seven millennia. We may now admire the profundity of Mr Loria in calling the value that was generally and directly prevalent throughout this time a value at which commodities never were sold nor could be sold, and which no economist will ever bother himself with if he has a glimmer of healthy common sense!

We have not so far mentioned the merchant. We could refrain from referring to his intervention up to this point, where we now proceed to the transformation of simple commodity production into capitalist production. The merchant was the revolutionary element in this society, in which everything else was stable as if by heredity; where the peasant received not only his hide of land by inheritance, and almost inalienably, but also his position as a free proprietor, free or dependent copy-holder or serf, the urban artisan receiving his trade and his guild privileges in the same way, and each of them his clientele into the bargain, his market outlet, not to mention a talent cultivated from youth upwards for his inherited calling. Into this world now steps the merchant, and he is the starting-point of its transformation. Not, however, as a conscious revolutionary; on the contrary, as its own flesh and blood. The medieval merchant was no individualist, he was essentially a guildsman like all his contemporaries. On the land, there prevailed the mark community that sprang from primitive communism. Each peasant originally had an equally large hide of land, the same size and quality, and a correspondingly equal share in the rights on the common mark land. After the mark community became a closed one, and new hides were no longer distributed, partitions of the hides occurred through inheritance, etc., and corresponding partitions also of mark rights; but the full hide remained the unit, so that a half, quarter or eighth of a hide gave a half, quarter or eighth right in the common mark. All subsequent trading companies modelled themselves after the mark community, and particularly so the guilds of the towns, their organization being nothing but the application of the mark constitution to a handicraft privilege instead of to a particular area of land. The focal point of the entire organization was the equal participation of each associate in the rights and customs enjoyed by the group as a whole, as strikingly expressed in the licence for the Elberfeld and Barmen 'yarn association' of 1527 (Thun, *Industrie am Niederrhein*, II, 164 ff.). The same holds good for mining operations where each '*kux*' had an equal share, its rights and duties being divisible in the same way as with the hide in the mark community. Nor is this less true of the merchant companies that brought overseas trade into being. The Venetians and Genoans in the ports of Alexandria and Constantinople, each 'nation' in its own *'fondaco'* – a dwelling house, inn, warehouse, exhibition and sales room as well as a central office – formed complete trading partnerships closed off against competitors and customers, which sold at prices agreed among themselves, with commodities of a definite quality, guaranteed by official inspection and often hall-marked, and combined together to decide the prices the local people should pay for their products, etc. The Hanse proceeded in the same way on the German 'bridge' (*Tydske Bryggen*) at Bergen in Norway, and so did their Dutch and English competitors. Woe to anyone who sold below price, or bought above it! The boycott he encountered meant unmitigated ruin, leaving aside the direct penalties the society would impose on the guilty party. But still closer associations were formed for particular purposes, like the Maona of Genoa in the fourteenth and fifteenth centuries, which for many years dominated the alum mines of Phocaea in Asia Minor and the island of Chios; the great Ravensberg trading company which did business in Italy and Spain from the end of the fourteenth century, founding settlements there; and the German company of the Augsburg Fuggers, Welsers, Vöhlins, Höchstetters, etc., along with the Nuremberg Hirschvogels and others, who together took part in the Portuguese expedition to India of 1505–6 with a capital of 66,000 ducats and three ships, extracting a net profit of 150 per cent, or even 175 per cent according to some (Heyd, *Levantehandel*, II, p. 524), and a whole series of other 'company *monopolia*' which made Luther so enraged.

Here for the first time we encounter profit, and rate of profit. And the efforts of the merchants are in fact deliberately and consciously bent towards equalizing this profit rate for all parties involved. With both the Venetians in the Levant and the Hanse league in the North, each merchant paid the same prices for his product as did his neighbour, they cost him the same in transport, he received the same prices for them, and similarly bought return cargo at the same price as every other merchant in his 'nation'. The rate of profit was therefore the same for each. With the big trading companies, the distribution of profit in proportion to the share of capital put in is as automatic as the participation in the mark rights in proportion to the authorized share of the hide or the share of the *kux* in mining profits. The equal rate of profit, which is one of the end results of capitalist production in its full development, thus emerges in this case in its most simple form as one of the points from which capital has historically proceeded, in fact as a direct offshoot of the mark community, which is in turn a direct offshoot of primitive communism.

This original rate of profit was necessarily very high. Business was very risky, not just on account of the widespread practice of piracy, but also because the competing nations often indulged in all kinds of violent action when the opportunity presented itself; finally, the market outlet and conditions depended on privileges granted by foreign rulers, which were frequently enough broken or revoked. Profit had therefore to include a high insurance premium. On top of this, the turnover was slow, the conclusion of deals tedious, though in the best periods, which seldom lasted very long, commerce was a monopoly trade with monopoly profit. The high level of the average rate of profit is also shown by the equally high levels of interest that prevailed, which still had always to be less on the whole than the customary percentage profit on trade.

But the high if equal level of the profit rate associated with this form of cooperation, a rate that was the same for all parties, held good only within the company, i.e. in this case the 'nation'. Venetians, Genoans, Hanseatics, Dutch, each nation had a particular rate of profit, and one that was also to begin with more or less specific to each individual market area. The equalization of these various company rates of profit was brought about in the opposite way, by competition. First of all, equalization between the profit rates in different markets for one and the same nation. If Alexandria offered higher profit for Venetian goods than did Cyprus, Constantinople or Trebizond, then the Venetians directed more capital to Alexandria and withdrew this from their trade with the other markets. Next came the gradual equalization of profit rates between the individual nations exporting the same or similar commodities to the same markets, which very often meant that certain of these nations were displaced and vanished from the scene. This process was constantly interrupted, however, by political events, as when the entire Levantine trade went into decline as a result of the Mongol and Turkish invasions, the great geographical and commercial discoveries from 1492 onwards only accelerating this decline and making it permanent.

The sudden extension of the market area that now followed, and the associated revolution in trade routes, did not at first bring any essential change in the mode of conducting trade. The trade with India and America was also pursued, as before, predominantly by trading companies. But firstly, greater nations stood behind these trading companies. In place of the Catalonians who traded with the Levant, it was the whole of a vast and united Spain that traded with America; next to it two countries as important as England and France; even Holland and Portugal, the smallest, were at least as big and powerful as Venice, the largest and strongest trading nation of the previous period. This gave the travelling merchant, the 'merchant adventurer' of the sixteenth and seventeenth centuries, a backing that made the company which offered its members armed protection more and more superfluous, thereby making its expenses directly burdensome. Then, too, wealth in individual hands was now developing far more rapidly, so that soon individual merchants could deploy the same funds on an undertaking as a whole company could before. The trading companies, where they still continued to exist, were mostly transformed into armed corporations which conquered entire newly discovered countries, under the protection and ultimate sovereignty of the mother country, and exploited them monopolistically. But the more that colonies in the new zones were founded principally for the sake of the state, the more company trade retreated in the face of the individual merchant, so that the equalization of the rate of profit became ever more the exclusive result of competition.

So far we have dealt only with the profit rate for trading capital. For so far there was only trading and usurer's capital, industrial capital having still to develop. Production was still predominantly in the hands of workers in possession of their own means of production, and their labour therefore did not yield a surplus value to any capital. If they did have to part with a portion of their product to a third party without compensation, this would be in the form of tribute to feudal lords. Thus merchant capital could extract its profit, at least in the beginning, only from the foreign buyers of domestic products or the domestic buyers of foreign products; only towards the end of this period – i.e. for Italy with the decline of the Levantine trade – could foreign competition and the greater difficulty in finding an outlet compel handicraft producers of export commodities to part with their commodities to the export merchant at less than their value.

We find here therefore the phenomenon that, in retail domestic trade between individual producers, commodities are sold on average at their values, while in international trade as a rule they are not, for the reasons given. This is in complete contrast to the present-day world, where prices of production prevail in international and wholesale trade, while in urban retail trade price formation is governed by quite different rates of profit. Beef, for example, undergoes a greater price increase en route from the London wholesaler to the London consumer than from the wholesaler in Chicago to the London wholesaler, transport included.

The instrument that brought about this gradual revolution in price formation was industrial capital. The Middle Ages already saw the beginnings of this, in three particular areas: shipping, mining and textiles. Shipping on the scale pursued by the Italian and Hanseatic maritime republics was impossible without sailors, i.e. wage-labourers (whose wage relationship might be concealed under the cooperative form of a share in the profit), or, for the galleys of that time, without oarsmen who were either wage-labourers or slaves. The mining companies, which originally consisted of workers cooperating with each other, had already been transformed in almost all cases into joint-stock companies for exploiting the mines by wage-labour. And in the textile industry, the merchant began to take the small master-weavers directly into his service, supplying them with yarn and having this transformed into cloth on his own account against a fixed wage, becoming instead of a simple merchant a so-called 'putter-out'.

Here we can see the very beginnings of capitalist surplus-value formation. We can ignore the mining companies, as closed monopoly corporations. As far as shipping goes, it is self-evident that profits had at least to be equal to those customary on land, with an extra addition for insurance, wear and tear of boats, etc. What then was the situation with the textile putters-out, who were the first to bring to market commodities that had been produced directly for the account of a capitalist, and came into competition with commodities of the same kind produced for the account of the artisan?

The profit rate on trading capital was already in existence, as a given fact. It was even equalized already to an approximate average, at least for each particular locality. What then could move the merchant to take on the extra task of the putter-out himself? Only one thing: the prospect of greater profit at the same sale price as the others. And he did have such a prospect. By taking the small master into his service, he broke through the traditional barriers to production, in which the producer simply sold his own finished product and nothing more. The merchant capitalist bought labour-power which continued to possess for some time its instrument of production but had already ceased to possess its raw material. Since he could in this way ensure regular employment for the weaver, he could on the other hand depress his wages so that one portion of the labour-time performed remained unpaid. The putter-out thus came to appropriate surplus-value on top of his previous trading profit. For this, however, he had also to apply an additional capital, in order to buy yarn, etc., and leave it in the hands of the weaver until the product was finished, having already had to pay the full price for the yarn when he bought it. Firstly, in most cases he already needed extra capital to advance to the weaver, who was as a rule brought to subject himself to the new conditions of production only by debt servitude. Secondly, and even apart from this, the calculation takes the following form.

Assume that our merchant conducts his export business with a capital of 30,000 ducats, sequins, pounds sterling or what have you. Out of this, 10,000 might be involved in buying domestic commodities, while 20,000 is applied in overseas outlets. Say that the capital turns over once in two years, an annual turnover of 15,000. Our merchant now wants to have weaving done on his own account, to become a putter-out. Let us assume that the production time for each piece of cloth of the kind he sells is an average of two months, which is of course very high. Let us further assume that he has to pay everything in cash. He must then advance enough capital to supply his weavers with yarn for two months. Since his annual turnover is 15,000, he buys cloth to the tune of 2,500 every two months. Let us say that 2,000 of this is the value of yarn, and 500 is weavers' wages; our merchant then needs an additional capital of 2,000. We shall assume that the surplus-value he appropriates from the weaver by way of this new method comes to only 5 per cent of the value of the cloth, which gives a surplus-value rate of 25 per cent, certainly very modest ($2,000_c +$ $500_v + 125_s$; $s' = \frac{125}{500} = 25$ per cent, $p' = \frac{125}{2,500} = 5$ per cent). Our man then makes an extra profit of 750 on his annual turnover of 15,000, so that he gets his additional capital out again in $2\frac{2}{3}$ years.

But in order to accelerate his sales and therefore his turnover, and in this way make the same profit with the same capital in a shorter time, or a greater profit in the same time as before, he will hand over a small portion of his surplus-value to the buyer and sell more cheaply than his competitors. These will gradually also convert themselves into putters-out, and the extra profit is then reduced for all to the average profit, or even a lower one, for a capital that has increased on all sides. An equal rate of profit is reestablished, even if possibly at a different level, by the abandonment of a portion of the surplus-value made at home to the foreign buyers.

The next step in capital's subjugation of industry occurred with the introduction of manufacture. This too enables the manufacturer, who in the seventeenth and eighteenth century was generally still his own export merchant (as was almost universally the case in Germany up till 1850, and still is in places today), to produce more cheaply than his old-fashioned competitor, the hand-worker. The same process is repeated; the surplus-value appropriated by the manufacturing capitalist permits him or the export merchant who shares it with him to sell more cheaply than his competitors, until the new mode of production has become universal, when there is once again an equalization. The rate of profit in trade already prevailing, even if it is equalized only locally, remains the Procrustean bed on which excess industrial surplus-value is remorselessly chopped off.

If manufacture already owed its rise to the cheapening of its products, so much the more so did large-scale industry, which cuts the production costs of commodities lower and lower with its incessant revolutions in production, mercilessly displacing all earlier modes of production. It is large-scale industry, too, that finally conquers the home market decisively for capital, puts an end to petty production and the natural economy of the self-sufficient peasant family, displaces direct exchange between the petty producers and puts the entire nation in the service of capital. It similarly equalizes the rates of profit in the various branches of commercial and industrial business, to give *one* general rate of profit, and with this equalization finally secures for industry the position of power due to it, by removing the greater part of the obstacles that previously stood in the way of the transfer of capital between one branch and another. In this way the transformation of values into prices of production is largely completed, for the whole of exchange. This transformation thus proceeds according to objective laws, although those involved are not aware of this nor do they intend it. If competition reduces excess profits above the general rate to this general level, and thus removes any above-average surplus-value from the first industrial appropriator, this offers no theoretical difficulty at all. In practice it does so all the more in as much as those spheres of production with excess surplus-value, i.e. with a high variable capital and low constant capital, a low capital composition, are by their very nature those subjugated last and least completely to capitalist operations; agriculture above all. As far as the increase of production prices above commodity values is concerned, an increase required in order to raise the deficient surplus-value in the products of spheres of higher capital composition up to the level of the average profit rate, this looks extremely difficult from a theoretical point of view, but as we have seen it happens most easily and rapidly in practice. For commodities in this category, if they are first of all produced capitalistically and come into capitalist trade, enter into competition with commodities of the same kind which are manufactured by pre-capitalist methods and are thus dearer. The capitalist producer, for his part, can still extract the rate of profit prevailing in his locality even if he renounces a portion of the surplus-value, this rate of profit having at first had no direct relationship to surplus-value, since it arose already from trading capital long before there was any capitalist production at all and so long before any industrial profit rate was possible.

2. THE STOCK EXCHANGE

(1) From Volume 3, Part Five, and especially Chapter [27], we may see the position the stock exchange holds in capitalist production in general. But since 1865, when this book was written, a change has occurred that gives the stock exchange of today a significantly increased role, and a constantly growing one at that, which, as it develops further, has the tendency to concentrate the whole of production, industrial as well as agricultural, together with the whole of commerce – means of communication as well as the exchange function – in the hands of stock-exchange speculators, so that the stock exchange becomes the most pre-eminent representative of capitalist production as such.

(2) In 1865 the stock exchange was still a *secondary* element in the capitalist system. Government papers made up the major part of stock-exchange values, and even these were still relatively small in amount. The joint-stock banks, on the other hand, which were

already predominant on the Continent and in America, were in England just beginning to swallow up the aristocratic private banks. Quantitatively, they were still relatively unimportant. Even railway shares were relatively weak compared with their present position. Directly productive establishments in the joint-stock form were rare – at that time, 'the master's eye' was still an unconquered superstition – and, like the banks, they operated mostly in the *poorer* countries, in Germany, Austria, America, etc.

At that time, then, the stock exchange was still just a place where the capitalists plundered one another of their accumulated capitals, and it concerned the workers only as a new piece of evidence of the demoralizing general effect of the capitalist economy, confirming the Calvinist principle that divine election, alias accident, is already decisive in this life as far as bliss and damnation, wealth (pleasure and power) and poverty (renunciation and servitude) are concerned.

(3) Now it is different. Since the crisis of 1866, accumulation has proceeded at an ever growing pace, and in such a way moreover that in no industrial country, least of all England, can the extension of production keep step with that of accumulation, or the accumulation of the individual capitalist be fully employed in the expansion of his own business: the English cotton industry in 1845; the railway bubble. With this accumulation, there is also a growth in the number of rentiers, people who have tired of routine exertion in business and who simply want to amuse themselves or pursue only a light occupation as directors of companies. And thirdly, in order to aid the investment of the mass of money capital thus afloat, new legal forms of company with limited liability were devised wherever they did not yet exist, the obligation of the shareholders, which was formerly unrestricted, being also more or less reduced. (For joint-stock companies in Germany in 1890, to 40 per cent of the subscription!)

(4) Accordingly, a gradual transformation of industry to joint-stock undertakings. One branch after the other experiences this fate. First of all iron, where gigantic investments are now needed (this was already true of mining before, where this was not already organized in shares). Then the chemical industry, ditto. Engineering. On the Continent the textile industry, though in England still only in a few districts of Lancashire (spinning, Oldham; weaving, Burnley, etc.; cooperation in tailoring, but only as a preliminary step, and to fall back again to the 'master' in the next crisis),

breweries (a few years ago the American breweries sold off to English capitalists, then Guinness, Bass, Allsop). Then the trusts, which set up giant enterprises with a common management (e.g. United Alkali). The ordinary individual firm more and more simply a preliminary step, in order to bring the business into a position where it is big enough to be 'promoted'.

The same goes for trade. Leafs, Parsons, Morleys, Morrison, Dillon, all promoted. Similarly now already with retailers, and moreover not only in the guise of cooperation à la C.W.S.

The same for banks and other credit institutions, even in England. Immense numbers of new institutions, all limited liability. Even old banks such as Glyns, etc. transformed into limited companies with seven private shareholders.

(5) The same thing in the realm of agriculture. The enormous extension of the banks, which particularly in Germany (under all kinds of bureaucratic names) are more and more the holders of mortgages, ultimate ownership of the land falling into the hands of the stock exchange, and this still more so when estates fall to their creditors. Here the agricultural revolution in prairie cultivation is impressive in its effect; if this continues, we can look forward to the time when land in England and France too will be in the hands of the stock exchange.

(6) Then there are foreign investments, all in joint-stock form. Just to take England: American railways, North and South (look up the stock list), gold mines, etc.

(7) Then colonization. Today this is a pure appendage of the stock exchange, in whose interest the European powers divided up Africa a few years ago, and the French conquered Tunis and Tonkin. Africa directly leased out to companies (Niger, South Africa, German South-West and East Africa), and Mashonaland and Natal taken possession of for the stock exchange by Rhodes.

Quotations in Languages other than English and German

pp. 433–4, n. 43 'De Wisselbank heeft haren naam niet ... van den wissel, wisselbrief, maar van wisselen van geldspeciën. Lang vóór het oprigten der Amsterdamsche wisselbank in 1609 had men in de Nederlandsche koopsteden reeds wisselaars en wisselhuizen, zelfs wisselbanken ... Het bedrijf dezer wisselaars bestond daarin, dat zie de talrijke verscheidene muntspeciën, die door vreemde handelaren in het land gebragt worden, tegen wettelijk gangbare munt inwisselden. Langzamerhand breidde hun werkkring zich uit ... zij werden de kassiers en bankiers van hunne tijd. Maar in die vereeniging van de kassierderij met het wisselambt zach de regering van Amsterdam gevaar, en om dit gevaar te keeren, werd besloten tot het stichten eener groote inrigting, die zoo wel het wisselen als de kassierderij op openbaar gezag zou verrigten. Die inrigting was de beroemde Amsterdamsche Wisselbank van 1609. Evenzoo hebben de wisselbanken van Venetië, Genua, Stockholm, Hamburg haar ontstaan aan de gedurige noodzakelijkheid der verwisseling van geldspeciën te danken gehad. Van deze allen is de Hamburgsche de eenige die nog heden bestaat, om dat de behoefte aan zulk eene inrigting zich in deze koopstad, die geen eigen muntstelsel heeft, nog altijd doet gevoelen etc.'

p. 756, n. 28 'Rien qu'à appliqueur à des terres déjà transformées en moyen de production de secondes mises de capital on augmente la terre-capital sans rien ajouter à la terre-matière, c'est-à-dire à l'étendue de la terre ... La terre-capital n'est pas plus éternelle que tout autre capital ... La terre-capital est un capital fixe, mais le capital fixe s'use aussi bien que les capitaux circulants.'

p. 965, n. 50 'C'est ainsi que les causes de la production matérielle sont en même temps les sources des revenus primitifs qui existent.'

p. 982, n. 53 '... profits du capital, ... anéantirait la possibilité même de l'industrie. Si le travailleur est forcé de payer 100 la chose pour laquelle il n'a reçu que 80, si le salaire ne peut racheter dans un produit que la valeur qu'il y a mise, autant vaudrait dire que le travailleur ne peut rien racheter, que le salaire ne peut rien payer. En effet, dans le prix-de-revient il y a toujours quelque chose de plus que le salaire de l'ouvrier, et dans le prix-de-vente, quelque chose de plus que le profit de l'entrepreneur par exemple, le prix de la matière première, souvent payé à l'étranger ... Proudhon a oublié l'accroissement continuel du capital national; il a oublié que cet accroissement se constate pour tous les travailleurs, ceux de l'entreprise comme ceux de la main-d'œuvre.'

pp. 985–6, n. 54 'Le capital circulant employé en matériaux, matières premières et ouvrage fait, se compose lui-même de marchandises dont le prix .écessaire est formé des mêmes éléments; de sorte qu'en considérant la totalité des marchandises dans un pays, il y aurait double emploi de ranger cette portion du capital circulant parmi les éléments du prix nécessaire.'

'Il est vrai que le salaire de l'ouvrier, de même que cette partie du profit de l'entrepreneur qui consiste en salaires, si on les considère comme une portion des subsistances, se composent également de marchandises achetées au prix courant, et qui comprennent de même salaires, rentes des capitaux, rentes foncières et profits d'entrepreneurs, ... cette observation ne sert qu'à prouver qu'il est impossible de résoudre le prix nécessaire dans ses éléments les plus simples.'

'Il est clair que la valeur du produit annuel se distribue partie en capitaux et partie en profits, et que chacune de ces portions de la valeur du produit annuel va régulièrement acheter les produits dont la nation a besoin, tant pour entretenir son capital que pour renouveler son fonds consommable.'

... 'Peut-elle' (...) 'habiter ses granges ou ses étables, manger ses semailles et fourrages, s'habiller de ses bestiaux de labour, se divistir de ses instruments aratoires? D'après la thèse de M. Say il faudrait affirmer toutes ces questions.'

... 'Si l'on admet que le revenu d'une nation est égal à son produit brut, c. à d. qu'il n'y a point de capital à en déduire, il faut aussi admettre qu'elle peut dépenser improductivement la valeur entière de son produit annuel sans faire le moindre tort à son revenu futur.'

'Les produits qui constituent le capital d'une nation ne sont point consommables.'

Index of Authorities Quoted

[Titles as given here may differ in detail from those in the text, since the latter may follow Marx's own versions.]

I. BOOKS BY NAMED OR ANONYMOUS AUTHORS

Anderson, Adam, *An Historical and Chronological Deduction of the Origin of Commerce, From the Earliest Accounts to the Present Time. Containing, an History of the Great Commercial Interests of the British Empire*, with an appendix, Vol. 2, London, 1764, 451

Anderson, James, *A Calm Investigation of the Circumstances that have Led to the Present Scarcity of Grain in Britain: Suggesting the Means of Alleviating that Evil, and of Preventing the Recurrence of Such a Calamity in Future* (written December 1800), 2nd edn, London, 1801, 756

Anti-Corn-Law Prize Essays, see *The Three Prize Essays on Agriculture and the Corn Law*

Aristotle, *De Republica Libri VIII*, in *Opera ex Recensione Immanuelis Bekkeri*, Vol. 10, Oxford, 1837, 509

Arnd, Karl, *Die naturgemässe Volkswirtschaft, gegenüber dem Monopoliengeiste und dem Communismus, mit einem Rückblicke auf die enschlagende Literatur*, Hanau, 1845, 485, 925

Augier, Marie, *Du crédit public et de son histoire depuis les temps anciens jusqu'à nos jours*, Paris, 1842, 728, 747

Babbage, Charles, *On the Economy of Machinery and Manufactures*, London, 1832, 199, 209

Balzac, Honoré de, *Les paysans*, 130

Bastiat, Frédéric, see *Gratuité du crédit. Discussion entre M. Fr. Bastiat et M. Proudhon*, Paris, 1850

Bell, G. M., *The Philosophy of Joint-Stock Banking*, London, 1840, 679

Bellers, John, *Essays about the Poor, Manufactures, Trade, Plantations, and Immorality*, London, 1699, 400

Bosanquet, James Whatman, *Metallic, Paper, and Credit Currency, and the Means of Regulating their Quantity and Value*, London, 1842, 494, 526

Briscoe, John, *A Discourse on the Late Funds of the Million-Act, Lottery-Act, and Bank of England. Shewing, That They are Injurious to the Nobility and Gentry, and Ruinous to the Trade of the Nation. Together with Proposals for the Supplying their Majesties with Money on Easy Terms, Exempting the Nobility, Gentry, &c. from Taxes, Enlarging their Yearly Estates, and Enriching the Subjects in the Kingdom, by a National Land-Bank. Humbly Offered and Submitted to the Consideration of the Lords Spiritual and Temporal, and Commons in Parliament Assembled*, 3rd edn, with an appendix, London, 1696, 736

Buret, Antoine-Eugène, *Cours d'économie politique*, Bruxelles, 1842, 939

Büsch, Johann Georg, *Theoretisch-praktische Darstellung der Handlung in ihren mannichfaltigen Geschäften*, 3rd edn, Vol. 2, Hamburg, 1808, 748

Cairnes, John Elliot, *The Slave Power: Its Character, Career, and Probable Designs: Being an Attempt to Explain the Real Issues Involved in the American Contest*, London, 1862, 507–8

Cantillon, Richard, *Essai sur la nature du commerce en général. Trad. de l'anglois*, in *Discours politiques*, Vol. 3, Amsterdam, 1756, 919

Carey, Henry Charles, *The Past, The Present, and the Future*, Philadelphia, 1848, 757

Principles of Social Science (in 3 vols), Vol. 3, Philadelphia, London, Paris, 1859, 523

Chalmers, Thomas, *On Political Economy in Connexion with the Moral State and Moral Prospects of Society*, 2nd edn, Glasgow, 1832, 354, 572

Chamberlayne, Hugh, *A Proposal for a Bank of Secure Current Credit to be Founded upon Land, In Order to the General Good of Landed Men, to the Great Increase of the Value of Land, and the No Less Benefit of Trade and Commerce*, London, 1695, 736

Chamberlen, Hugh, *A Few Proposals, Humbly Recommending, to the Serious Consideration of His Majesty's High Commissioner, and the Right Honourable, the Estates of Parliament, the Establishing a Land-Credit in this Kingdom; With several Explanations of, and Arguments for, the Same; Together with Full Answers to All Such Objections, As Have Hitherto Appeared Against It*, Edinburgh, 1700, 736

Cherbuliez, Antoine, *Richesse ou pauvreté. Exposition des causes et des effets de la distribution actuelle des richesses sociales*, Paris, 1841, 258

Child, Josias, *Traités sur le commerce et sur les avantages qui résultent de la reduction de l'interest de l'argent, avec un petit traité contre l'usure; par Thomas Culpepper. Trad. de l'Anglois*, Amsterdam, Berlin, 1754, 521, 738

The City; or, The Physiology of London Business; With Sketches on 'Change, and at the Coffee Houses, London, 1845, 514

Forcade, Eugène, 'La guerre du socialisme. II. L'économie politique révolutionnaire et sociale', in *Revue des deux Mondes*, new series, Vol. 24, Paris, 1848, 982–3

Francis, John, *History of the Bank of England, Its Times and Traditions*, Vol. 1 (3rd edn), London, 1848, 737, 739

Fullarton, John, *On the Regulation of Currencies; Being an Examination of the Principles, on Which it is Proposed to Restrict, Within Certain Fixed Limits, the Future Issues on Credit of the Bank of England, and of the Other Banking Establishments Throughout the Country*, 2nd edn, London, 1845, 530, 580–88, 591–2

Gilbart, James William, *The History and Principles of Banking*, London, 1834, 460, 530–33, 746

An Inquiry into the Causes of the Pressure on the Money Market During the Year 1839, London, 1840, 673, 667–8

A Practical Treatise on Banking, 5th edn (in 2 vols), Vol. 1, London, 1849, 482–3

Gratuité du crédit. Discussion entre M. Fr. Bastiat et M. Proudhon, Paris, 1850, 466

Greg, Robert Hyde, *The Factory Question, Considered in Relation to Its Effects on the Health and Morals of those Employed in Factories. And the ' Ten Hours Bill', In Relation to its Effects upon the Manufactures of England, and Those of Foreign Countries*, London, 1837, 202

Hamilton, Robert, *An Inquiry Concerning the Rise and Progress, the Redemption and Present State, and the Management, of the National Debt of Great Britain*, 2nd edn, Edinburgh, 1814, 519

Hardcastle, Daniel, *Banks and Bankers, 2nd edn, with an appendix, Comprising a Review of the Failures Among Private and Joint-Stock Banks*, London, 1843, 678, 747

Hegel, Georg Wilhelm Friedrich, *Encyclopädie der philosophischen Wissenschaften im Grundrisse*, Part 1, *Die Logik* (ed. Leopold von Hennig), in *Werke*, Vol. 6, Berlin, 1840, 914

Grundlinien der Philosophie des Rechts, oder Naturrecht und Staatswissenschaft im Grundrisse (ed. E. Gans), *Werke*, Vol. 8, Berlin, 1840, 752–3

Heine, Heinrich, *Disputation*, 673

Afterword to 'Romancero', 1031

Heyd, Wilhelm, *Geschichte des Levantehandels im Mittelalter*, Vol. 2, Stuttgart, 1879, 1039

Hodgskin, Thomas, *Labour Defended Against the Claims of Capital; or, The Unproductiveness of Capital Proved, With Reference to the Present Combinations Amongst Journeymen. By a Labourer*, London, 1825, 513, 523

MacCulloch, 2nd edn, London, 1852, 157, 331, 344–5

Rodbertus-Jagetzow, Johann Karl, *Social Briefe an von Kirchmann. Dritter Brief: Widerlegung der Ricardo'schen Lehre von der Grundrente und Begründung einer neuen Rententheorie*, Berlin, 1851, 236, 913

Roscher, Wilhelm, *Die Grundlagen der Nationalökonomie. Ein Hand- und Lesebuch für Geschäftsmänner und Studierende*, 3rd edn, Stuttgart, Augsburg, 1858, 332, 422, 441, 522, 965

Roy, Henry, *The Theory of the Exchanges. The Bank Charter Act of 1844. The Abuse of the Metallic Principle to Depreciation. Parliament Mirrored in Debate, Supplemental to 'The Stock Exchange and the Repeal of Sir J. Barnard's Act'*, London, 1866, 483, 486

Rubichon, Maurice, *Du mécanisme de la société en France et en Angleterre*, new edn, Paris, 1837, 767, 944, 947

Saint-Simon, Claude-Henri de Rouvroy, comte de, *Nouveau christianisme. Dialogues entre un conservateur et un novateur. 1er dialogue*, Paris, 1825, 740–41

Say, Jean-Baptiste, *Traité d'économie politique, ou simple exposition de la manière dont se forment, se distribuent et se consomment les richesses*, 3rd edn, Vol. 1, Paris, 1817, 392

Traité d'économie politique, ou simple exposition de la manière dont se forment, se distribuent et se consomment les richesses, 4th edn, Vol. 2, Paris, 1819, 980

Schmidt, Conrad, 'Der dritte Band des *Kapital*', in *Sozialpolitisches Centralblatt*, Berlin, 25 February 1895, 1032–3

Die Durchschnittsprofitrate auf Grundlage des Marx'schen Werthgesetzes, Stuttgart, 1889, 28

'Die Durchschnittsprofitrate und das Marx'sche Werthgesetz', in *Neue Zeit*, 11th year, 3–4, Stuttgart, 1893, 28

Sismondi, Jean-Charles-Léonard Simonde de, *Nouveaux principes d'économie politique, ou de la richesse dans ses rapports avec la population*, 2nd edn, Vols 1–2, Paris, 1827, 608, 939

Smith, Adam, *An Inquiry into the Nature and Causes of the Wealth of Nations. With a Memoir of the Author's Life*, Aberdeen, London, 1848, 241, 446, 601–2, 752, 902, 907–10, 923, 965, 980–81

Sombart, Werner, 'Zur Kritik des ökonomischen Systems von Karl Marx', in *Archiv für soziale Gesetzgebung und Statistik . . .*, Vol. 7, Berlin, 1894, 1031

Some Thoughts of the Interest of England. By a Lover of Commerce, London, 1697, 742

Steuart, Jacques, *Recherche des principes de l'économie politique; ou essai sur la science de la policie intérieure des nations libres . . .*, Vol. 4, Paris, 1789, 487

On the Operation of the Bank Charter Act of 1844, as It Affects Commercial Credit, 2nd edn, London, 1847, 475–6

Tuckett, John Debell, *A History of the Past and Present State of the Labouring Population Including the Progress of Agriculture, Manufactures, and Commerce* (in 2 vols), Vol. 1, London, 1846, 736

Ure, Andrew, *The Philosophy of Manufactures: or, An Exposition of the Scientific, Moral and Commercial Economy of the Factory System of Great Britain*, London, 1835, 199
Philosophie des manufactures ou économie industrielle de la fabrication du coton, de la laine, du lin et de la soie, avec la description des diverses machines employées dans les ateliers anglais. Trad. sous les yeux de l'auteur et augmenté d'un chapitre inédit sur l'industrie cotonnière française, Vol. 1, Paris, 1836, 510

Verri, Pietro, *Meditazioni sulla economia politica*, in *Scritti classici italiani di economia politica. Parte moderna*, Vol. 15, Milan, 1804, 329

Vinçard, Pierre-Denis, *Histoire du travail et des travailleurs en France*, Vols 1–2, Paris, 1845, 922

Vissering, Simon, *Handboek van praktische staathuishoudkunde*, Vol. 1, Amsterdam, 1860–61, 434, 436

Wakefield, Alfred A., *History of the Landed Tenures of Great Britain and Ireland, from the Norman Conquest to the Present Time, Dedicated to the People of the United Kingdom*, London, 1865, 758

West, Edward, *Essay on the Application of Capital to Land, with Observations Shewing the Impolicy of Any Great Restriction of the Importation of Corn, and that the Bounty of 1688 Did Not Lower the Price of It*. By a Fellow of University College Oxford, London, 1815, 350, 798

Wolf, Julius, 'Das Rätsel der Durchschnittsprofitrate bei Marx', in *Jahrbücher für Nationalökonomie und Statistik*, ed. J. Conrad, 3rd series, Vol. 2, Jena, 1891, 104–5
Sozialismus und Kapitalistische Gesellschaftsordnung. Kritische Würdigung beider als Grundlegung einer Sozialpolitik, Stuttgart, 1892, 108

2. PARLIAMENTARY REPORTS AND OTHER OFFICIAL PUBLICATIONS

An Act for vesting certain sums in commissioners, at the end of every quarter of a year, to be by them applied to the reduction of the National Debt. (Anno vicesimo sexto Georgii III regis), 520

General Index

Abstinence, 570
Accumulation, rate of, 349
Accumulation fund, 973, 987–8
Accumulation of capital, 373, 607,
   633–5, 1021, 1045–6; and falling
   rate of profit, 329–31, 349, 357–8,
   365, 375, 523; and foreign trade,
   344; and labour productivity, 176,
   325–30, 523; and relative surplus
   population, 324–5, 364–5; general
   laws, 328, 331; limits, 523
Accumulation of money capital,
   599, 607–52
Africa, 1047
Agriculture, 754, 809–15; and
   cottage industry, 931–2; and
   manufacture, 454, 922; capitalist
   751–2, 810–16, 901–2, 906;
   composition of capital in, 149,
   894, 899–902; contradictions
   in capitalist, 755–7; decline of
   living labour in, 372, 767, 775;
   development of capitalism in,
   754–5, 789–90, 859–60, 936–7,
   1023; in colonies, 808–10, 890,
   904; labour productivity in, 212–
   13, 790–91, 847, 901, 955;
   natural conditions for, 212–13;
   pre-capitalist, 298, 751, 814–15,
   921–2, 942–4; products of,
   776–8; rationalization of, 215,
   754–6, 813–15, 818, 847, 948–50;
   under communism, 216, 799–
   800; use of waste products in,
   195–6; workers in, 755–6, 764–8,
   890
Agronomy, 754, 790, 904
Alexander, Nathaniel, 542, 685

Alienation, 177–8, 373, 731, 956,
   964, 968–9
America, U.S. of, 164, 623–4, 1046
Amortization, 174, 203–4, 213, 465,
   716, 745, 924–5
Anarchy of capitalist production,
   288–9, 295–6, 365–6, 708, 969–70,
   1020–21
Ancillaries, 176, 197, 213
Anderson, Adam, 451
Anderson, James, 756–7
Anderson, James Andrew, 658–9,
   697
Anne, Queen of England, 746
Annuities, 465
Antiquity, 444–50, 728–9, 731, 922–
   3, 970
Apologetics, 513, 762
Arbuthnot, John, 683
Archimedes, 1028
Argentina, 859
Aristotle, 509, 1030
Arnd, Karl, 485, 925
Ashley, Lord, see Shaftesbury
Asia, 650, 686, 699–700, 732,
   753
Attwood, Thomas, 671, 694
Augier, Marie, 728, 747
Australia, 634, 699, 725, 766
Authority, 1021

Babbage, Charles, 199, 209
Babylon, 1037
Baker, Robert, 182, 184, 218, 220,
   222
Balance of payments, 622–4, 649–50,
   702–4, 725–7
Balzac, Honoré de, 130

j

Note on Previous Editions of the Works of Marx and Engels

Until recently there existed no complete edition of the works of Marx and Engels in any language. The Marx–Engels Institute, under its director, D. Riazanov, began to produce such an edition in the late 1920s. For reasons never since made clear, the project did not survive the mid-1930s. However, eleven indispensable volumes did emerge between 1927 and 1935, under the title *Karl Marx – Friedrich Engels: Historisch-Kritische Gesamtausgabe*, commonly referred to as the *MEGA* edition. The *MEGA* contains the works of both men down to 1848, and their correspondence, but nothing more. For the next thirty years, the field was held by the almost inaccessible Russian edition, the Marx–Engels *Sochineniya* (twenty-nine volumes, 1928–46).

Only in 1968 did the East Germans complete the first definitive edition in the German language, the forty-one volume *Marx–Engels Werke* (*MEW*). Until then, the works of Marx and Engels existed only in separate editions and smaller collections on specific themes. For this reason, the translations into English have followed the same pattern – the only general selection being the *Marx–Engels Selected Works* (*MESW*), now expanded to a three-volume edition. Recently, however, the major gaps in the English translations have begun to be filled up, Lawrence and Wishart have produced a complete translation of *Theories of Surplus-Value*, as well as the first adequate translation of *A Contribution to the Critique of Political Economy* and Marx's book on *The Cologne Communist Trial*. They plan to issue a complete English-language edition of even greater scope than the *MEW*, though this will inevitably take many years to complete. The Penguin Classics editions, previously published as the Pelican Marx Library, occupy an intermediate position between the *MESW* and the complete edition. The most important of Marx's larger works, the three volumes of *Capital* and the *Grundrisse*, as well as three volumes of political writings and a volume of early writings are published in Penguins.

Chronology of Works
by Marx and Engels

1. Date of composition, except for *Capital*, where the date of first publication is given.

2. M = Mars, E = Engels.

3. The following abbreviations are used:

P. Engels: Engels, *Selected Writings*, Harmondsworth, 1967.

LW: Lawrence and Wishart.

MECW: Karl Marx and Frederick Engels, *Collected Works*, Lawrence and Wishart, 1975

MESW: Karl Marx and Frederick Engels, *Selected Works in Three Volumes*, Progress Publishers, 1969.

P: Penguin Classics.

P *EW*: *Early Writings* (Penguin Classics).

P *FI*: *The First International and After* (Penguin Classics).

P *RI848*: *The Revolution of 1848* (Penguin Classics).

P *SE*: *Surveys from Exile* (Penguin Classics).

Date	Author	Title	English edition
1844–5	E	*Condition of the Working Class in England*	Blackwell 1958
1845	M	*Theses on Feuerbach*	P *EW*
1845–6	M & E	*The German Ideology*	*MECW5*
1846–7	M	*The Poverty of Philosophy*	*MECW6*
1847	M & E	*Speeches on Poland*	P *R1848*
1847	M	*Wage Labour and Capital*	*MESWI*
1847–8	M & E	*Manifesto of the Communist Party*	P *R1848*
1848	M & E	*Speeches on Poland*	P *R1848*
1848	M & E	*Demands of the Communist Party in Germany*	P *R1848*
1848–9	M & E	*Articles in the* Neue Rheinische Zeitung	P *R1848* (selection)
1850 (March)	M & E	*Address of the Central Committee to the Communist League*	P *R1848*
1850 (June)	M & E	*Address of the Central Committee to the Communist League*	P *R1848*
1850	M & E	*Reviews from the* Neue Rheinische Zeitung Revue	P *R1848*
1850	M	*The Class Struggles in France: 1848 to 1850*	P *SE*
1850	E	*The Peasant War in Germany*	LW 1956
1851–2	E	*Revolution and Counter-Revolution in Germany*	*MESW I*
1852	M	*The Eighteenth Brumaire of Louis Bonaparte*	P *SE*
1852	M	*Revelations of the Cologne Communist Trial*	LW 1970
1856	M	*Speech at the Anniversary of the People's Paper*	P *SE*
1857–8	M	*Grundrisse*	P
1859	M	*A Contribution to the Critique of Political Economy*	LW 1971
1852–61	M & E	*Articles in the* New York Daily Tribune	P *SE* (selections)
1861	M	*Articles in* Die Presse *on the Civil War in the United States*	P *SE* (selections)
1861–3	M	*Theories of Surplus Value*, Vol. 1 Vol. 2 Vol. 3	LW 1969 LW 1970 LW 1972
1863	M	*Proclamation on Poland*	P *SE*
1864	M	*Inaugural Address of the International Working Men's Association*	P *FI*

Date	Author	Title	English edition
1864	M	*Provisional Rules of the International Working Men's Association*	P *FI*
1865	E	*The Prussian Military Questions and the German Workers' Party*	P *FI* (extract)
1865	M	*Wages, Price, and Profit*	*MESW II*
1866	E	*What Have the Working Classes to Do with Poland?*	P *FI*
1867	M	*Capital*, Vol. 1	P
1867	M	*Instructions for Delegates to the Geneva Congress*	P *FI*
1868	M	*Report to the Brussels Congress*	P *FI*
1869	M	*Reports to the Basel Congress*	P *FI*
1870	M	*The General Council to the Federal Council of French Switzerland* (a circular letter)	P *FI*
1870	M	*First Address of the General Council on the Franco-Prussian War*	P *FI*
1870	M	*Second Address of the General Council on the Franco-Prussian War*	P *FI*
1871	M	First draft of *The Civil War in France*	P *FI*
1871	M & E	*On the Paris Commune*	LW 1971
1971	M	*The Civil War in France*	P *FI*
1871	M & E	*Resolution of the London Conference on Working-Class Political Action*	P *FI*
1872	M & E	*The Alleged Splits in the International*	P *FI*
1872	M	*Report to the Hague Congress*	P *FI*
1872–3	E	*The Housing Question*	*MESW II*
1874	M	*Political Indifferentism*	P *FI*
1874	E	*On Authority*	*MESW II*
1874–5	M	*Conspectus of Bakunin's Book* Statism and Anarchy	P *FI* (extract)
1875	M & E	*For Poland*	P *FI*
1875	M	*Critique of the Gotha Programme*	P *FI*
1876–8	E	*Anti-Dühring*	Progress, 1972
1879	M & E	*Circular Letter to Bebel, Liebknecht, Bracke,* et al.	P *FI*
1880	E	*Socialism: Utopian and Scientific*	*MESW III*
1880	M	*Introduction to the Programme of the French Workers' Party*	P *FI*
1873–83	E	*Dialectics of Nature*	Progress, 1972
1884	E	*The Origin of the Family, Private Property, and the State*	*MESW III*

Date	Author	Title	English edition
1885	M	*Capital*, Vol. 2	P
1886	E	*Ludwig Feuerbach and the End of Classical German Philosophy*	*MESW III*
1894	M	*Capital*, Vol. 3	P